Business

Advanced Level
GNVQ3

Editor

Paul Callaghan

Contributors:

Tom Harrison John Ellison Jeff Hindmarch
Tony Gough Bernard Callaghan Albert Toal
Nigel Hill Geoffrey Knott Nick Waites

Second Edition

 Business Education Publishers
1994

© PAUL CALLAGHAN, TOM HARRISON, JOHN ELLISON, JEFF HIND-MARCH, TONY GOUGH, BERNARD CALLAGHAN, ALBERT TOAL, NIGEL HILL, GEOFFREY KNOTT and NICK WAITES 1993

ISBN 0 907679 66 8

First published in 1993
Second Edition 1994
   Reprinted 1994

Cover design by Caroline White

Graphic Design and illustrations by Gerard Callaghan

Published in Great Britain by Business Education Publishers Limited
Leighton House 10 Grange Crescent Stockton Road
Sunderland Tyne and Wear SR2 7BN

Tel. 091 567 4963 Fax. 091 514 3277

British Cataloguing-in-Publications Data
A catalogue record for this book is available from the British Library

Printed in Great Britain by Bath Press, Avon

Preface

This book has been written as a major learning resource for GNVQ courses. It covers the mandatory units for Business Advanced Level GNVQ3 courses offered by Business and Technology Education Council, City and Guilds and RSA Examinations Board. The mandatory units are:

- Business in the Economy
- Business Systems
- Marketing
- Human Resources
- Employment in the Market Economy
- Financial Transactions and Monitoring
- Financial Resources
- Business Planning

Each of its eight units is examined on an element by element basis and the range statements for each element are comprehensively analysed. The book has been designed as the principal resource base for students of GNVQ Business in schools and colleges.

It uses contemporary issues and examples to explore the modern business environment and is fully supported by assignments to help the learning process.

It provides students with a broad integrated examination of the wide range of human, financial, economic, managerial and legal aspects which are essential to the study of modern organisations. The book has been written in a way which makes it simple for students to obtain a thorough understanding of the concepts, language and practice of modern organisations. The book adopts an integrated and interdisciplinary approach and is written in a lively and accessible style. As a single, substantial information source it provides an essential learning resource for all Business Advanced Level GNVQ3 students.

The book should be used in association with *Core Skills for GNVQ* and *Assignments for GNVQ Business* which are also published by Business Education Publishers Ltd. A range of books specifically written for the GNVQ options is also available.

A tutor's manual containing suggested solutions to the assignments is available from the publisher for centres which adopt the book. This manual can also be supplied on computer disk in a format readable by PCs running Windows©.

Acknowledgements

The production of this book has involved the contributions of many people who deserve our thanks. These include Caroline White, Moira Page, Julie, Sonya, Lilias Smith and Sheila Callaghan. Many thanks also to Gerard Callaghan who produced most of the excellent diagrams and charts with skill and good humour.

We would like to thank the National Council for Vocational Education for permission to publish details of the specifications on which this book is based. We would also like to thank EFL Brech for some quotations from his book *The Practice of Management*, published by Longman.

Thanks are due to David Symons, Andrew Adams and David Hind for permission to adapt some material which had previously been published by Business Education Publishers Ltd.

Our greatest thanks most go to our families who have once again been shamefully neglected during the writing and publishing process.

Any errors or omissions are the responsibility of the authors.

PC
TH
JE
JH
AG
BC
AT
NH
GK
NW
Durham
June1994

Table of Contents

Unit 1 Business in the Economy

Element 1.3 The Supply of Goods and Services by Business

Unit 2 Business Systems

Element 2.1 Administration Systems

Element 2.2 Communication Systems

Unit 3   Marketing

Unit 5   Employment in the Market Economy

Element 5.1   Employment in Business Sectors

Element 5.2   The External Relationships Relating to Employment

Unit 1

Business in the Economy

This unit has been written to cover the following specifications of the General National Vocational Qualification Business Level 3:

UNIT 1   BUSINESS IN THE ECONOMY LEVEL 3

Element 1.1:   Explain the purposes and products of business

Performance criteria:

1   demand for goods and services is identified and described
2   demand in relation to particular product is identified
3   industrial sectors are identified and described
4   the product of businesses in different industrial sectors is identified and described
5   purposes of selected business organisations are explained

Element 1.2:   Explain government influences on business

Performance criteria:

1   government approaches to economic management are explained
2   governmental interventions in national and international markets are described
3   reasons for governmental intervention are explained
4   effects of government and EC policy on business decisions and actions are explained using relevant examples taken from business

Element 1.3:   Investigate the supply of goods and services by business

Performance criteria:

1   the supply of goods or services by business sectors is investigated using economic relationships
2   different ways of evaluating the supply of goods and services are illustrated by the use of relevant information drawn from various sources
3   information and relationships as tools for investigation are evaluated

(extract from General National Vocational Qualifications Mandatory Units for Business GNVQ3 offered by Business Education and Technology Council, City and Guilds and RSA Examinations Board - published by the National Council for Vocational Qualifications April 1993 - reproduced by kind permission of the National Council for Vocational Qualifications)

GNVQ3 Business - Unit Number U1016174

Element 1.1 The Purpose and Products of Business

Running a business can at first sight be deceptively simple. All that you have to do is to produce something that people are willing to buy at a price which is higher than the cost involved in making it. You provide a product or service which satisfies your customers. You organise the resources which are required to produce it and you sell it at a profit. Nothing could be easier – or could it? If it were that simple we would all be running our own businesses, making lots of money and the economy would be booming. Of course if you look around you in your local area or at the UK economy as a whole, you can see many successful businesses. Some are long established and have grown slowly over many years. Others have been started more recently and have expanded rapidly. The UK has many examples of organisations, both large and small, which are well managed and successful.

In examining the economy, however, you will also encounter many businesses that are floundering. You will see that some failures are the result of mismanagement. Other businesses are the victims of the harsh economic climate in which we live. Others fail simply because the ideas on which they were based were wrong. The founders of the business believed that there was a opportunity when in reality none existed. In this book we will attempt to provide you with some of the skills and knowledge which are necessary to work in business as an employee, to recognise business opportunities and possibly to run your own business at some time in the future. We hope to show you that the simple description of running a business which we gave at the start of this section is, in practice, much more complex. To do it successfully you will need intelligence, education and training, experience, business acumen and a degree of luck. We hope to be able to help you in developing much of this, but the luck you will have to make for yourself!

What is a Business?

The purpose of business is to provide people with the things they need. What people need varies from person to person, country to country and economy to economy. In an undeveloped or subsistence economy, needs are likely to be for the necessities of existence: for food, water and shelter. In a more sophisticated economy, needs are likely to be more complex. A middle-class European might regard a CD player as an essential need. This is a relatively expensive need and will also require the person to spend money on compact disks if it is to provide any enjoyment. In undeveloped economies, such as Albania or Ethiopia, a person's needs will reflect their subsistence or primitive economies: food, water and shelter are the main priorities and would, not surprisingly, take precedence over a CD player.

Faster growing economies are characterised by their increasing material wealth and needs. As an economy grows, the desire for more goods and services creates demand. This demand is met by producers who seek to satisfy the consumers' wants. Such producers employ people to make the goods and of course, pay them wages. The employees now have more money to enable them to demand more goods – and so it goes on. Growth feeds off itself to create wealth which, in turn, creates more sophisticated needs that in their turn create even greater wealth. To satisfy the growing needs for greater numbers of people, more and more business opportunities arise.

So, a business is simply an organisation that is formed to produce and supply goods or services to satisfy the needs of people (or *consumers* as they are more specifically known). Sometimes a need is *latent*: that is, it exists but the consumer is unaware of it. The latent need can be awakened and turned into a *sale* by using effective *marketing*. A business sets out to achieve the satisfaction of needs at a profit which is ultimately returned to the owners of the business.

The Demand for Goods and Services in a Complex Society

The society in which we live is both complex and refined. As a consumer, you demand a variety of goods and services which allow you to maintain the quality of your life. In order to satisfy your demands, suppliers must produce the goods and services which you want. Producers achieve this by combining factors of production (land, labour and capital) in the most efficient manner.

Producers hire workers, rent or buy premises, invest in plant and machinery and purchase raw materials, and then organise the manufacture of the final product in such a way that they will make a profit. Society also gains: its scarce resources are being used in the way consumers wish, rather than being wasted in producing things people do not need. Suppliers (or producers) who work this way, under such a system, are known as commercial organisations or *businesses*.

There are many state organisations that also provide goods and services to society. Like commercial organisations, they, too, must employ staff, occupy premises and raise capital. The fundamental difference between these two types of organisation is that each tries to meet a different objective: the commercial organisation, part of the private sector, will seek to make a profit; the public sector organisation will wish to provide for the public good and improve the state of society.

As an individual you lack the knowledge, skills and physical resources to manufacture products that fulfil all your needs, whether they are simple or sophisticated. It would be as difficult for you to make a biro or a floppy disk on your own as it would be for you to make a television set or a computer.

Of course, with even very limited skills, and working alone, you might be able to supply yourself with some of the goods and services that you need. You might farm and be sufficiently capable of growing food to feed yourself without any help from other people. But what if you require other goods and services? It is unlikely that you will also have the ability and resources to produce your own combine harvester or tractor. Without such products, which are manufactured by others, your life would be not only unsophisticated but also much more difficult.

A similar situation exists in the supply of services. If you feel you are strong and resourceful, you may try to protect yourself and your property from the dangers threatened by thieves or vandals. If you are not sufficiently strong, however, then you may turn to the state and demand its protection.

How, then, are these goods and services produced? It is clear that individuals, working independently, are unable to meet the complex physical and social needs that they have. To meet that complexity of need, society has developed for itself a system whereby people join together to form *organisations* – and they are extraordinarily diverse. They manufacture products, which they distribute and sell. They also provide all the services that are needed. Such organisations include both the BBC and ICI: both make 'products': the BBC's product is a 'service', ICI's is a 'good'.

Clearly, then, if the individuals within society are to have all of their various needs satisfied, there must be co-operation between them. Each worker must specialise in a certain aspect of the supply process. Workers must be organised and be allocated a specific role in which to perform co-ordinated tasks. These tasks are normally organised with the aim of producing a given product or service, although there are some organisations that do not specialise and that make an extremely diverse range of products. In the private sector of the economy, such businesses will usually have the objective of making a *profit* for their owners.

Activity

Consider the following list of organisations and decide which provides a 'good' and which provides a 'service'.

British Rail	*Ford Motor Company*	*British School of Motoring*
Tarmac	*Abbey National*	*Mirror Group Newspapers*
Forte	*Marks and Spencer*	*The A A*

Now prepare a list of those characteristics which distinguish a 'good' from a 'service'.

How supply and demand meet in the market

In this country the production of most of the goods and services we need are produced through the market. By this we mean that private producers recognise consumer needs and supply what people want. They respond to demand. We shall see later that the state also has a role in providing some goods and services that the market is unable or unwilling to provide. However in this first section we shall concentrate on examining the private sector market system.

The basis of the market system is the interaction of the forces of demand and supply. *Demand* is the willingness and ability of consumers to purchase the goods and services they want: this implies that consumers not only desire the product, but also that they have the money to be able to buy it.

Supply is the willingness and ability of producers to meet these demands. Again, this implies that suppliers not only want to produce the goods and services, but also have the necessary combination of raw materials and finance, and an appropriately skilled workforce, to ensure that production is feasible. When suppliers and consumers transact they do so by entering into legally enforceable agreements, called *contracts*.

The market is based on the belief that individuals will seek to maximise their personal satisfaction by demanding that combination of products and services which will give them the greatest level of satisfaction for the money they have.

The market system is based on the following ideas:

- it gives freedom to the individual consumer to spend money as he or she wishes;
- it indicates consumers' demands and needs to producers and so ensures production of what consumers actually want;
- it encourages competition between producers and so leads to a greater level of efficiency in the production of goods and services;
- it adequately rewards the most efficient organisations, through high profits, and the best workers through high wages.

The market mechanism is not only relevant to the private sector of the economy: it has also become an increasingly important concept for the public sector. The market mechanism has assumed a more important role throughout the public sector as public authorities (such as hospitals and local councils) have been made to act as both suppliers and consumers.

What is Demand?

The *demand* for any product means the amount of a product that consumers are willing to buy at a range of different prices. The market demand for a product means simply *the total amount that will be bought in a specific market over a stipulated period.*

What determines demand?

1. *The* price of the product. *Usually, the higher the price set by the producers, the less of the product will be demanded by consumers; conversely, as price falls, more of that product will be bought, as existing buyers now demand more of it, or new consumers are attracted to it, or both. However, demand is not infinite, even for 'free' products or services. For example, a visit to your doctor would not cost you anything directly, yet you would not visit your doctor every week.*

2. *Consumer needs, tastes and preferences.* Demand is determined not only by price, but also by need. If cigarettes were free, the majority of people would still not smoke, because they believe that smoking is harmful. Therefore, the need and, consequently, the demand, for a product is influenced by each individual's tastes or preferences.

3. *Consumer income.* Different individuals desire different products and services and, obviously, have varying abilities to pay for them. As income increases, more and more products are demanded. However we need to qualify this statement somewhat. Some goods are said to be *superior goods* and so as consumer income rises they will buy more of them. Perhaps we could use restaurant meals as an example. Other goods can be described as *inferior goods*. By this we mean that as consumers' incomes rise they chose to buy less of the goods and switch their purchases to more desirable 'superior' products. If we use restaurant meals as an example of a superior good perhaps we can use cheap convenience foods as an example of an 'inferior' good.

4. *The 'pool' of consumers.* The number of consumers in a market will influence demand. If the number of consumers rises, demand increases. For instance, in this country we have a ageing population. This means that the proportion of older people in the population is increasing. As this happens the demand for certain goods and services, such as health care and retirement homes will increase.

5. *The price of other goods and services.* The level of demand for a product can be influenced by the price of other products and services. For instance, if the price of a Vauxhall Cavalier rose, you might choose to buy a Ford Mondeo because it is a *substitute*. The demand for Mondeos would increase, even though they have remained at the same price. Alternatively, if the price of petrol rose, this might affect the demand for both Cavaliers and Mondeos as people would travel less and would demand fewer cars. Petrol is a *complementary* product to cars. If the price of the complement (in this case, petrol) rises, demand for the first product (cars) is likely to decrease.

   Finally, the price of other purchases in a consumer's budget will influence demand. If a person's rent rises, that person will have less money to spend on other things. If the price of a necessity goes up, the consumer will switch spending from less necessary purchases to pay the higher price for the necessity.

Factors which determine the level of demand for a product or service are as follows:

1. the price of the product or service;

2. the tastes or preferences of consumers (Is the product enjoyable? Fashionable? etc.);

3. the level of income of consumers;

4. the number (or 'pool') of consumers of the product;

5. the price of other goods/services which are:
   - substitutes
   - complementary products
   - also bought by the consumer.

One fact, however, is certain: a consumer will not buy a product unless it gives some level of *satisfaction* (or *utility*) when it is bought.

Expressing demand graphically

Sometimes it is easier to show ideas graphically. The *demand curve* is one such idea. Let us use the Ford Motor Company's demand for Mondeos as an example. If Ford found that it could sell varying amounts of its Mondeos in a certain period (say, one month), this could be tabulated:

Price £	Quantity of Mondeos Demanded
12,500	4,000
11,500	10,000
10,000	15,000
9,500	20,000
9,000	25,000
8,500	35,000

Demand schedule for Ford Mondeos

Alternatively, this information could be presented in graphical form as we show in the next figure.

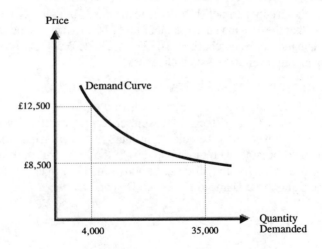

Demand curve for Ford Mondeos

As you can see, the demand curve in this example is typical of that for most products in that it slopes from top left to bottom right. It graphically expresses the relationship between the *quantity of a product* that consumers are willing to purchase and a *range of prices*.

Activity

Which factors do you think are most important in determining the demand for a car such as the Ford Mondeo? Of the factors which are listed above which are within the supplier's control and which are outside the supplier's control?

Changes in price

If Ford decided to set a price of £8,500, it would find that it could sell 35,000 cars. If it increased the price to £12,500, it would sell fewer – only 4,000 Mondeos. Changes in the price of the product cause movements up and down the demand curve – or more precisely *along* the demand curve. This is known as an *extension* or *contraction* in demand. A change in price does *not* move the demand curve itself, but merely changes the quantity bought because the price has changed. This is important to note.

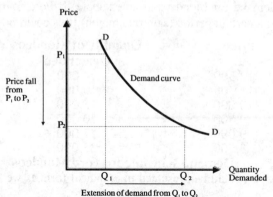

Change in price moving demand along a demand curve

Changes in the price of the product do not shift the demand curve but merely move quantity demanded along it. Does this mean that the demand curve cannot move? No. In fact, the other factors we mentioned earlier as influencing demand (those numbering (2), (3), (4) and (5)) will shift the demand curve if they change. The following examples illustrate such changes.

Changes in consumer needs, tastes and preferences

The next figure shows the *demand curve* for the records of a top band which is currently fashionable. People like them and buy their CDs. If their CDs were cheaper, perhaps more would be sold. If the CDs were more expensive, fewer might be sold. Consider, however, what would happen if people's tastes changed and the band became even more popular. If the price had been higher, proportionately more CDs would have been bought, and so on at various possible prices. In fact, the whole demand curve has shifted to the right, from Demand Curve1 to Demand Curve2.

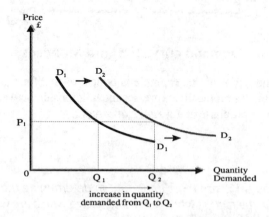

Shift in demand curve to the right as a result of a change in preference

Obviously, the reverse would be the case if the band became less popular and fewer people bought their CDs (in other words, there would be a shift in demand to the left).

A change in the income of consumers

Now consider the result an decrease in consumers' income would have on a product's demand curve. In the south east of England, during the late 1980s, there was a general decrease in the income of consumers. This was caused by the recession in the economy and increasing unemployment. Many people lost their jobs and had less money to spend. Even those who were still in work felt the pinch as many business were doing less well and so could not pay their staff as well as they had paid them during the mid-1980s boom. This decreased the demand for products generally, but had a particularly strong impact on the price of housing. How did this affect the demand for housing in the south east? As you can see, the demand curve for housing shifted to the left because of the fall in consumer incomes. Conversely, as incomes rise this will mean there will be higher demand for housing and the demand curve for housing will shift to the right.

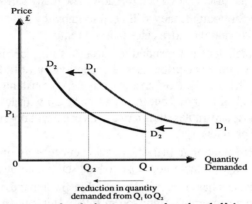

Shift in demand curve to the left as a result of a fall in consumer income

A change in the price of other goods

A fall in the price of a substitute shifts the demand curve for a product to the left, and *vice versa*. So a fall in the price of Levi's jeans moves Wrangler's demand curve to the left, as Wrangler's are *substitutes* for Levis.

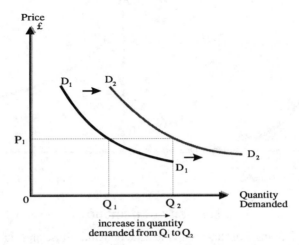

Shifts in demand as a result of changes in the price of other goods

A fall in the price of a complement shifts the demand curve to the right and vice versa: for example, a fall in the price of gas shifts the demand curve for gas central heating to the right.

An increase in the price of other goods purchased could shift the demand curve to the left and vice versa: for instance, an increase in the price of food moves the demand curve for cinema visits to the left. An *increase in the price of a substitute* or a *fall in the price of a complement* will move demand to the right as shown in the figure at the bottom of the previous page.

Elasticity of Demand

Elasticity of demand is the term that describes the responsiveness of demand to a change in price. In effect, how far will the demanded quantity stretch or shrink if its price is lowered or raised? Producer will find this information useful in two respects:

- if they wish to raise the price, they need to know how many sales might be lost;
- if they decide to increase output, they will need to know by how much the price should be lowered in order to gain the extra sales that are required.

If a product has a demand which does not respond to variations in price, it is said to have an *inelastic demand*. This situation can be seen when price rises or reductions have little effect on the quantity of a product that is sold. This is a characteristic of most necessities. A substantial price increase in the price of bread means that people will still buy it, but they will make do with less of the other things. When a product does not have any close substitutes, then a rise in its price will not result in consumers switching their purchases to alternative products.

Suppliers often have the achievement of an inelastic demand curve as an objective, since this will mean that they will be able to raise their price without losing a substantial amount of custom.

The converse is true when a product has an *elastic demand*. Elastic demand occurs when even a relatively small price increase results in a substantial reduction in sales. This happens either because consumers no longer buy the product at all (this is known as the *income effect*), or because they shift their purchasing to an alternative product (this is called the *substitution effect*).

The slope of the demand curve can graphically illustrate this. (See the figures below.)

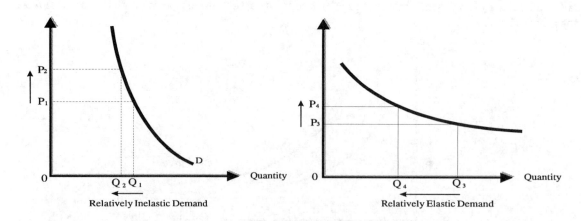

Relatively Inelastic Demand   Relatively Elastic Demand

Elasticity of demand

The diagram on the left, showing a product with inelastic demand, illustrates that a relatively large price increase (from P_1 to P_2) will have only a limited effect on the quantity purchased (a fall in quantity from

Q_1 to Q_2). The diagram on the right, showing a product with elastic demand, illustrates a much smaller increase in price (a rise from P_3 to P_4) but a much more dramatic reduction in demand (the quantity purchased falls from Q_3 to Q_4). Expressing this as a formula we can determine price elasticity of demand as follows:

$$\frac{\%\ \text{Change in Quantity Demanded}}{\%\ \text{Change in Price}} = \text{Price Elasticity of Demand}$$

A percentage change is used both for 'quantity demanded' and for 'change in price'. If you do not use a percentage, then the scale of the change in 'quantity demanded' or the price change may be deceiving. A simple example will illustrate this:

Price £	Quantity Demanded
5	100
6	75

In this case, an increase in price of 20% (from 5 to 6) results in a 25% fall in demand (from 100 to 75 units). This is a more than proportionate fall in demand. (Expressed simply, demand shrinks more than price stretches.) Thus demand is said to be *elastic*. The equation would show:

$$\text{Elasticity of Demand} \quad = \quad \frac{25\%}{20\%} \quad = \quad 1.25$$

If elasticity is greater than 1 (that is, demand changes in a greater proportion than price), then it is said to be elastic. A less than proportionate change would result in a figure less than 1. For example: if price rose 20% and demand fell by only 5%. This would indicate inelastic demand. The example below illustrates this.

$$\text{Elasticity of Demand} \quad = \quad \frac{5\%\ \text{fall in quantity demanded}}{20\%\ \text{price rise}} \quad = \quad 0.25$$

Percentages are used to avoid confusion, for example:

Price £	Quantity Demanded Units
40	100
60	75

The rise in price from £40 to £60 may *look* substantially less than the fall in demand from 100 units to 75 units. In fact, there is a 50% rise in price (from £40 to £60) and a 25% fall in demand (from 100 units to 75 units). Demand, in this case, is *inelastic*, having a value of .5.

$$\text{Elasticity of Demand} \quad = \quad \frac{25\%}{50\%} \quad = \quad .5$$

Products will not necessarily have the same elasticity of demand throughout a range of prices. As the price rises, the demand for a product usually becomes more elastic, because consumers tend to switch demand to cheaper substitutes. This switch in demand from one product to another can also be calculated by using what is called 'cross elasticity'. This simply illustrates how a change in the price of one product affects the demand for another product. So:

$$\text{Cross Elasticity of Demand} \quad = \quad \frac{\%\ \text{Change in Quantity Demanded of product A}}{\%\ \text{Change in Price of product B}}$$

This can occur when consumers switch to cheaper substitutes, but it is also important when considering the effect of the price change of one product upon its complement. (Remember these are products which tend to be purchased together, such as cars and petrol, electricity and electric central heating.) Here a rise in the price of one product will result in the fall in demand for the other. For example, as petrol goes up in price, so demand for large petrol-hungry cars will fall.

A further variant of elasticity is that which relates to a rise or fall in income and its effect on demand for a product or service. Thus, an increase in a person's income will usually result in an increase in the demand for a product. This is more pronounced for what we described earlier as 'superior goods', such as holidays and consumer durables.

Alternatively, an individual whose income rises may well demand less of an 'inferior good', such as poor quality food. This is because they are now able to purchase better quality products since they now have a higher income to spend. So, for instance, as income rises a person may buy fewer sausages but more steak.

Income elasticity can be defined as follows:

$$\text{Income Elasticity} \quad = \quad \frac{\% \text{ Change in Quantity Demanded of a Product}}{\% \text{ Change in Income}}$$

When the quantity demanded of a product *increases* positively in response to a rise in income, this is the normal expected response and indicates that the product is acceptable or superior. If the quantity demanded of a product actually *falls* when income rises, this indicates a negative income elasticity and the product is likely to be an inferior good.

It is not only the producer who benefits from knowing how to anticipate the elasticity of demand. Clearly, the government, through its taxation policy, is extremely influential in the raising and lowering of prices. The Chancellor of the Exchequer must be aware of the likely effect, either of a change in the general level of taxation (such as increases or decreases in VAT or income tax), or of specific tax (for example, a change in the duty on petrol, alcohol or tobacco). If it is the government's objective to increase its tax yield from petrol duty, then it must be confident that the tax increase – and the consequent price increase – will not result in such a reduction in the demand for petrol that the overall tax revenue from it falls. The most appropriate goods to tax specifically, therefore, are those with inelastic demand since increasing the tax on them will not deter consumption. These products are mostly those which have no close substitutes: inevitably the Exchequer taxes products like petrol, alcohol and tobacco.

Activity

Consider the following items and try to categorise them according to their price elasticity of demand. Rank them as having 'very inelastic demand', 'moderately inelastic demand', moderately elastic demand' or 'very elastic demand'.

Bread	*Meals in restaurants*	*Tobacco*
Cinema visits	*The Sun newspaper*	*Cadbury's cream eggs*
Floppy disks	*Short break holidays*	*Shoe polish*
Petrol	*Alcohol*	*Shoes*
Furniture	*Persil*	*Electricity*

You will have noted that in the above list we have some items which are 'brands', for instance the Sun newspaper, Cadbury's cream eggs and Persil, and some which are the name of a type of good or service, such as Shoe polish or Bread. This second category is sometimes described as the 'generic' product. Do you think in general that brands or generic products have a greater price elasticity?

The Different Sectors of the Economy

Classifying organisations by the goods and services they produce

In the first part of this section we looked at consumer demand – what people want. Now let us see how the British economy tries to meet this demand. We can classify the different parts of the British economy by the type of goods and services each organisation produces. Traditionally, this country has been regarded as a highly developed manufacturing nation with an economy which ranks in productive output in the top ten in the world. However, one of the most significant factors we shall recognise in this part of the book is that the UK has declined as a manufacturing economy and that both manufacturing output and employment has fallen as a percentage of the total economy. We shall see that in the post-war period, Britain's traditional industrial base has been eroded and, to some extent, been replaced by service industries which have developed as a result of changes in our society, in technology and in the manufacturing output of other countries in the world.

When we use the phrase the 'UK economy' we are describing all the activities which produce goods and services in Britain. We can categorise these activities by the type of output produced. We can divide these categories into three sectors.

- *Primary sector* This sector of the economy comprises agriculture, fishing, and mining and mineral extraction.
- Secondary sector. *This sector covers the production of all other goods. It includes manufacturing, construction and the public utilities including gas, electricity and water.*
- *Tertiary or Service sector*. This includes all services such as distribution and retailing, financial services, travel and tourism and the public services such as education and health.

In recent years, the contributions to the UK economy of the primary and secondary levels of activity have declined. The tertiary or service sector has grown greatly in significance as the next table shows.

		1980	1990
AFF	**Agriculture, forestry and fishing**	2.0%	1.4%
EWS	**Energy and water supply** (including mining, and North Sea oil and gas production)	9.3%	4.8%
C	**Construction**	5.9%	7.2%
M	**Manufacturing**	25.7%	21.2%
S	**Services**	57.1%	63.4%
	Total	100%	100%

Source: Annual Abstract of Statistics 1992

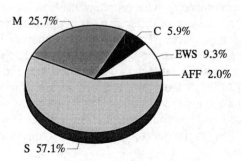

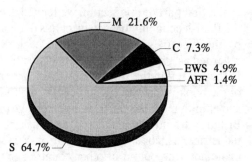

% Contribution to UK Gross Domestic Product by sector

At one time in the past, it might have been reasonably easy to use the level of activity as a criterion by which to classify a business: each business tended to stick to what it knew how to do: the brewer brewed beer; the car manufacturer made cars; the furniture store sold furniture.

Some businesses can still be categorised in this way: a farmer with no other business interests is clearly operating in the primary sector. However, in recent years, the size of businesses has tended to become bigger as they have diversified and spread their interests beyond their original level of activity.

Example 1

Scottish and Newcastle plc operates at all three levels of activity. It has subsidiaries which produce malt (one of the raw materials of beer); retail outlets (i.e. Waverley Vintners Ltd.) and leisure companies (Center Parcs and Pontins), as well as continuing to brew beers, its original business base. Scottish and Newcastle has diversified its interests because it wishes to be less vulnerable to certain aspects of the business environment that might threaten its growth. If beer and lager sales are declining, leisure interests might be enjoying a boom time; what Scottish and Newcastle has lost on the alcohol swings, it has made up for on the leisure roundabout.

Example 2

Nissan Manufacturing (UK) Ltd. used to sell its cars on to an independent dealer network over which it could exert little control. In January 1992, it set up its own dealer network; the new dealerships were still independent garages, but now they had to conform to a quality of service standards specified by Nissan Manufacturing (UK) Ltd..

Example 3

MFI is a well-known retailer of furniture and kitchen units. Much of what it sells is manufactured by a company called Hygena, a subsidiary of the MFI group.

So, unless a business is small, it is unlikely that it will be restricted to one level of activity, although a broad reference to its level of activity will usually relate back to the origins of the business.

The output of the UK economy

The total of all economic activity which takes place in the UK in all its various sectors is known as the UK gross domestic product (GDP). This includes not only physical products such as chemicals or manufactured goods but also less obvious economic activity such as insurance or banking. From the above categorisation you can see that the service sector of the economy accounted for almost three times the output of manufacturing and that both agriculture and energy and water supply account for only a very small share of GDP. These shares have changed quite dramatically over the 1980s and 90s. In 1979 when the Conservative government took power, manufacturing accounted for almost 30% of GDP while the service sector made up about 55%. This shift from manufacturing to services has been a notable characteristic of the UK over this period. What is somewhat worrying is that many of our major competitors have not seen such rapid decline in their manufacturing sector. Apart from the United States, which demonstrates many of the characteristics of UK industrial decline, other countries such as Germany and Japan have continued to develop and expand their manufacturing sectors.

We can break down the categories still further. In manufacturing, mechanical engineering, chemicals, motor vehicles, and food, drink and tobacco each account for about one tenth of manufacturing output while metals and minerals, and electrical engineering each make up about 15% of manufacturing output. The major sector of manufacturing is wood, paper, rubber and plastic which has a 20% share of manufacturing output.

The service industry covers a wide range of activities including retailing, distribution (including hotels and catering) and financial services in the private sector, and defence, education, health and public administration (including both central and local government) in the public sector of the economy.

The regional balance

The pattern of industry in the UK is not evenly spread. You will see from the map that the distribution of manufacturing varies considerably from region to region with manufacturing playing a more important role in the regional economies of the Midlands than in other parts of the country. The West Midlands has seen a particularly traumatic change over the last twenty years. Its traditional concentration on heavy engineering and motor manufacture has been hit particularly hard and it has gone from being a region of low unemployment in the 1950s and 60s to one in which unemployment is above the national average by the 1990s.

As you would expect, much of the financial services sector is concentrated in the South East of the country with more than 25% located in London alone. This tended to benefit the South East in the 1980s as the service sector flourished but has tended to have a disproportionately hard impact in the recession as the service sector has begun to shed jobs.

Activity

Look at the region in which you live or the city or town in which you study and make a list of the major industries which exist there. Try to rank the industries in order of importance and estimate the workforce in each of these industries. Classify each of the industries as primary, secondary or tertiary sector and produce a pie chart for your area which is similar to that shown on the previous page. Compare the makeup of your chart with that for the country as a whole.

Manufacturing as a percentage share of regional GDP (1992)

The changing pattern of industrial activity

In common with most industrialised economies, the UK has seen a significant decline in the share of agriculture and manufacturing as a proportion of GDP. In the early 1960s, manufacturing had a share of about 35% of GDP and as we have already noted, this has fallen to less than 23% by the end of the 1990s. This decline has been particularly felt in mechanical engineering and textiles which had been two of the bedrock industries of the UK economy until the second half of this century.

Similarly the energy sector's share has reduced quite dramatically in the post-war period. The coal industry in particular has seen a rapid decline. From its position as a major industry and significant employer at the end of the war, it has gradually been run-down so that by 1993 it will employ less than 30,000 people.

The decline in manufacturing and energy has been counter-balanced, to some extent, by the growth in the service sector. In fact some economists in the 1980s believed that the UK could survive without a significant manufacturing sector as long as services continued to grow. This process is known as de-industrialisation and many commentators now recognise that the decline in manufacturing in the 1980s may have significantly weakened the UK economy and left it in a position where it is finding it difficult to compete with the rest of the world. Certainly the deterioration in the UK's balance of payments in the late 1980s and 90s has been to a large extent due to the inability of UK manufacturers to compete with foreign suppliers.

The hope that the service industry would fill the gap has also come into question. The decline in financial services in the recent recession has been quite severe and this sector is anticipating substantial job losses in the 1990s as the industry becomes more streamlined and automated.

The reasons for structural change

There are a number of reasons why the structure of the UK economy has changed so significantly over the last fifty years.

Changes in demand

Clearly over time consumers' demands and tastes change. As the population becomes richer we tend to spend a smaller proportion of our income on basic necessities such as food and clothing and a greater proportion on services such as education, tourism and leisure. Even within such categories the nature of our spending will change over time. So in the 1990s we will spend a smaller share of our income on newspapers and magazines that we did ten years ago and a greater proportion on electronic entertainment such as televisions, videos and computers.

Changes in technology

The inevitable development of new technology has a number of effects on the structure of the economy. New products are developed. So for instance twenty years ago no one would have had a computer in their home, while today they are much more common place. We have already mentioned the rise of electronic entertainment and we see the growth of the video industry as a prime example of this.

Technology also effects the way we produce things. Car manufacture is a good example of the introduction of robotics into the workplace. Many of the tasks which we carried out by man twenty years ago are now undertaken by machines. Even in the service industry the introduction of information technology is having a major effect on the way tasks are carried out and the number of people required to run the business. The introduction of electronic cash dispensers (hole in the wall cash machines) on the outside of banks has meant that far fewer branches and cashiers are needed by the banks even though their volume of business has increased substantially.

Changes in the pattern of international production

When we hear people say that the world is becoming a smaller place they do not mean this literally but rather that transport, technology and economic development has increased the ability of goods and services to be produced in one part of the world and consumed in another. Many relatively low cost goods such as textiles or coal were traditionally produced in the industrial heartlands of the UK. These are now produced in low cost economies elsewhere in the world with, for example, textiles coming from Thailand or Egypt and coal coming from Poland or Columbia. Even our more technically advanced industries are feeling the impact of overseas competition. We no longer produce black and white television sets in this country for even though there may still be a market for such goods it is cheaper to produced them in the far east and ship them to this country. Many of our stable industries have fallen to foreign competition. The great British motor cycle industry has now collapsed as consumers choose to buy Japanese bikes. Such changes are not necessarily bad. As we shall discuss in the section on international trade in Element 1.2, there is much to be gained from countries concentrating their productive efforts on those products they can produce most cheaply. Our membership of the European Community has meant that our domestic market is now open to imports from our European partners. Conversely, of course, our manufacturers now have access to the largest consumer market in the world.

Maturity of the economy

The UK was the birthplace of the industrial revolution. It was here that many of the industrial process we know today were invented and developed. In the nineteenth century we went through a process of *industrialisation* as we saw workers leave the land and move to the urban areas to find better paid work in factories and this was seen as a natural part of progress. Some economists argue that the UK is undergoing a similar process in the latter part of the twentieth century but this time of *de-industrialisation*. As the manufacturing sector declines, workers switch to jobs in the service sector. Such a transformation cannot take place over night. People have to be retrained or relocated. For some this may be impossible because they are unable or unwilling to learn new skills or to move home. Thus this structural change brings with it unemployment which may take decades or even generations to eradicate. (We discuss this process of *structural unemployment* in more depth on in Element 1.2 when we consider the economy's problems.)

Other economists are more pessimistic. They argue that the process of de-industrialisation is more profound and long-lasting. It is not simply a case of short term readjustment. They believe that the service industries can never replace manufacturing in terms of jobs and that the UK economy must live with growing unemployment for the foreseeable future. If this is the case, it will have a major impact on how we live in the twenty-first century. Not only will we have an ageing population, so that the percentage of the population who have retired will increase and will have to be supported by the working population, we will also have a growing proportion of unemployed whom the state will have to support or ignore and allow them to fend for themselves as best they can. The effects on society of either choice will clearly be great.

Activity

1.   Identify an occupation which is less in demand than it was when you were born and suggest reasons for the decline.
2.   Identify an occupation which did not exist when you were born and explain the reasons why it has come into existence.

The Purposes of Different Business Organisations

We have examined how the British economy has developed over the second part of the twentieth century and we have identified the different types of organisation which exist today. Now we shall look at why these business have come into existence – what their purposes are.

The specific purposes for which different business organisations are formed are many and varied, and may not, of course, always be clearly defined. Some are formed with a precise economic objective in mind, such as the desire to make a profit for the person who has established the business. Some, such as the organisations which make up the state and government, evolve as a result of the emergence of particular needs in society which require government intervention. Such organisations usually have a definite public service objective. For example, the government established the National Health Service in 1946 to meet the needs of society for a high standard of free health care, available to all.

Other organisations are formed for charitable reasons. A group of concerned people recognise that there is a need which is not being met by the state and so take it upon themselves to establish an organisation which seeks to help in some way. An organisation such as Oxfam was established with the clear objective of providing famine relief in the poorest parts of the world.

While all of these formal organisations differ in the original purposes for which they were established, they nevertheless, have some common characteristics. These may be simply stated as follows.

The establishment of an organisation is usually for a specific purpose

For example, the Automobile Association was founded with the precise objective of promoting the interests of motorists within this country. Other organisations may be launched with one prime aim, but may later diversify in order to follow alternative causes or objectives. For instance, Guinness, the brewery company, was established to produce alcoholic drinks, but now has subsidiaries making a variety of products such as fishing tackle boxes and cassette cases. This illustrates how a business may try to evolve as the commercial environment changes and new commercial opportunities emerge.

Organisations usually have a distinct identity

People belonging to a specific organisation can identify themselves as being part of a group either as a result of where they work or of what they do. A Manchester United footballer wears a red shirt to show he is part of the particular organisation. A member of a trade union is given a membership card to signify he belongs to that union. Manufacturing companies promote their brand names through advertising. This sense of identity can produce extreme loyalty to the organisation.

Most organisations require some form of leadership

We have seen that organisations are normally formed for a specific purpose. In order to achieve this purpose, it is necessary to co-ordinate the efforts of the members of the organisation. This requires management, or leadership. Formal organisations such as companies have a specified management hierarchy which may be appointed by the owners of the organisation. For instance, the shareholders of a company appoint the directors. Alternatively, the leadership may be elected, as in the case of a club or society where the members vote to have a chairman, secretary and committee. However, once appointed, this management team has the responsibility for ensuring that he organisation achieves its objectives.

Organisations are accountable

By accountability we mean that the organisation as a whole and those people who are part of the organisation cannot do as they please. A private sector organisation will be accountable to its owners or shareholders. A government organisation will be accountable to Parliament or the local authority and through these bodies to the electors. Charitable organisations are accountable to their members and to those who have contributed to the charity's funds.

The purposes of private sector organisations

For business organisations it is possible to distinguish between a number of differing purposes or objectives.

Primary objectives

The prime objective of any business organisation is to survive. In order to achieve this it must make a profit. Some people believe that all businesses are seeking to make the maximum profit possible. This, however, is not always the main goal of an organisation. Many businesses are happy to achieve a satisfactory level of profit. By that we mean sufficient profit to keep them in business and provide the owners and the workers with a reasonable standard of living. Most people in business could work longer hours and take less holidays, but in the end most of us are seeking to balance the demands of work and the rewards that work provides with other aspects of our lives such as family, friends and leisure activities.

Secondary objectives

The organisation may also make a profit through the achievement of what we may refer to as secondary objectives. These can be classified as:

- economic;
- social.

Examples of economic objectives are increased productivity, reduced costs and increased sales. Social objectives may include promotion of a public image, the improvement of industrial relations, or the provision of better working conditions for employees.

When these secondary objectives are considered in detail, an underlying theme connects them all. This is to increase profit. So be wary when you consider the motives behind the actions of business organisations, as there is usually profit involved!

As an organisation may have a variety of objectives, and not only one solitary aim, it is often necessary to rank these objectives in order of importance. So, for example, an organisation may be faced with two problems: the need to increase revenue from sales, and the legal requirement to improve the safety conditions in the production area. It might see little improvement in profitability from tightening the safety procedures or spending money on fencing in machines. Extra revenue from sales would help the organisation's profit levels far more. However, when it is faced with possible sanctions from the Health and Safety Executive, such as the closure of dangerous production lines, safety becomes the prime objective. It is somewhat cynical to say that were it not for the law, business organisations would put profit before safety. However, the Health and Safety Executive has itself noted an increase in industrial accidents during periods of recession, which it has attributed to employers spending less on safety and employing more outside contractors. This may have short-term advantages for the employer, but in the longer run such cost cutting can prove more expensive, through loss of production occurring when vital staff are off sick, claims for compensation being made following accidents, and higher insurance premiums resulting.

Non-profit maximising objectives

In the previous section we assumed that a business organisation would have profit as its main objective. However, this is not so in all organisations. As we have already noted, an individual trader is not always seeking the greatest level of profit, but simply enough profit to satisfy his or her particular wants or needs.

We can also identify objectives other than profit in large organisations as well as small ones. Consider a large company and how different groups involved in its running will hold different objectives.

An important factor to recognise is that in the large organisations of today's business world there is a distinction between *ownership* and *management and control*. The owners are the shareholders who have bought a part of the company, and their degree of ownership is in proportion to the percentage of the shares they hold. In many organisations, the major shareholders are often large financial institutions such as insurance companies, pension funds and unit trust investment companies. Their objective is to earn the maximum return on their investment, and to do this the investment managers of these institutions will buy and sell shares in companies according to their assessment of the potential profitability of each organisation. This means that a company must be sufficiently profitable to satisfy such institutional shareholders.

A second group who are involved in the company are the managers and executives. In small companies the managers are the owners. In the larger corporate bodies, in which there is a substantial share capital, ownership and management will invariably be in different hands, with the shareholders electing a board of directors as salaried, professional managers of the business. While the owners have ultimate control over the managers, with the power to dismiss them, the business could not be effectively carried on without permitting managers a broad degree of commercial freedom. Having this freedom they may pursue policies which are more personal than organisational. Some examples may illustrate this point.

A manager's power or salary is sometimes linked to the company's sales, and so he may prefer sales maximisation to profit maximisation. Executives may also regard the size of the business as a reflection of their power and so might encourage the growth of the company, even if this means a lower profit per share to the shareholders. Furthermore, the executive may wish to see any profit that the company does make reinvested in the company to encourage further growth and new developments. This may be at odds with the aims of the shareholders, who would rather see profits distributed to them in the form of dividends on their shares, so giving them an immediate return on their investment.

Such conflicts are rarely seen in public. Instead, the shareholders will put pressure on the managers in more discreet ways, such as by threatening to vote them out of control if they do not follow the shareholders' line. The success of such action depends on whether or not the directors can command the confidence of a majority, fifty one percent, of all shareholders, and can therefore choose to ignore the wishes of blocks of shareholders who remain in the minority when it comes to the vote.

Final points to consider when looking at the objectives of managers are what are known as behavioural objectives. These are distinct from economic objectives and refer to a manager's desire to increase his or her power, status or work-force.

Behavioural objectives

As long as they are increasing the number of people working under them, many managers are happy. They feel that this increases their power. Conversely, managers may simply seek an 'easy life', resisting attempts to increase the size of their part of the company as this may bring with it extra stress or strain. Clearly, behavioural objectives depend upon the individual managers concerned. You can probably identify within your own experience the type of person who is a 'go-getter', and others who are perhaps more casual in their attitudes. It is therefore not an easy task for the shareholders to select management who are both competent and efficient and who will steer the fortunes of the business in a way which is compatible with the shareholders' objectives.

The purposes of public sector organisations

If we are to examine the purposes of public sector organisations, it is first necessary to distinguish between organisations which are established to provide a service such as health care or education and those which have been established to produce a product for sale to the general public. Whilst it is not always easy to categorise public sector organisations in this way, the distinction illustrates the importance of organisational type upon objectives.

Public sector service organisations

One of the objectives of the state which has evolved over the last century has been that of improving the welfare of its citizens. Collectively, the organisations which seek to achieve this are known as the 'welfare state'. They include:

- National Health Service;
- Social Security system;
- Education system;
- Housing and Social Services departments of local authorities.

Each of these is given the responsibility by government for ensuring that there is an acceptable level of provision of the services which they administer. When the National Health Service was established in 1946, its objective was to "secure improvement in the physical and mental health of the people of England and Wales and the prevention, diagnosis and treatment of illness". As you will realise, this is a very broad objective. The Act of Parliament which established the National Health Service did not go into specific detail. It did not say that all people who require a kidney transplant should be given one, or that all children should be inoculated against polio. The objective was phrased in such wide terms as to allow the administrators of the Health Service to determine where priorities and needs lay. It is therefore the responsibility of the Department of Health and Social Security, the Regional Health Authorities and, ultimately, individual hospitals and general practitioners to determine how best the health care of the nation should be provided. However, this does not mean that such decisions can be made only with needs of the patient in mind.

Unfortunately, the State has limited resources and the extent of the resources made available to the Health Service is determined by the overall evaluation of the competing demands of all aspects of the State by the central government. This involves a political judgement as to the amounts of taxation we as taxpayers are willing to pay and, also, judgement concerning the areas of expenditure to which this taxpayers' money will be allocated. No doubt we would all welcome substantial improvements in the standards of health care, education and social services, but we might not be willing to vote into power a government who proposed doubling taxation to finance such improvements. Obviously there are those who would accept higher taxation if this was accompanied by improved services, but politics do not operate in a way which presents the electorate with such straightforward choices. The political parties will advocate only that combination of taxes and services which they believe will gain them a parliamentary majority. Raising taxation is regarded by all of them as essentially unpopular. In fact, the Thatcher governments have made the cutting of taxes a major plank in its policy. Such cuts must inevitably be accompanied by cuts in public services. Nevertheless, such a policy has found support from the electorate in the last three elections.

In this context, there is a yearly battle in cabinet, where the Chancellor of the Exchequer sets out the amount of revenue he thinks he can safely raise, and then the competing government departments each argue their case for a large share of the resulting expenditure.

These considerations give us some guidance as to the objectives of the public sector services. It is possible to define the objectives of those departments which provide a service as being twofold:

- the provision of as wide-ranging a service as possible in meeting the needs of the population;
- the efficient and cost-effective use of the budget which they have managed to receive.

Public sector producer organisations

This group of organisations is sometimes referred to collectively as 'public enterprise', and it is a rapidly dwindling group. Included would be organisations such as British Coal and British Rail. These organisations all produce a product or service which is directly marketable to the general public. In other words, they sell what they make. Their objectives have certainly not remained constant over the period of their existence. Successive governments have used these Nationalised Industries to further various political aims. Many were taken into public ownership in the late 1940s by the post-war Labour government. Initially they had two main objectives:

- to provide as wide a range of services as possible;
- to break even, taking one year with another.

These two objectives were not necessarily compatible, and for many years the major industries incurred substantial losses, safe in the knowledge that the government would cover any financial shortfall. The 1960s witnessed a change in government attitude towards public enterprise. The government encouraged these organisations to operate along 'commercial lines' as the main objective. Most of the industries underwent a process of 'rationalisation', resulting in the closure of many loss-making coal mines and non-viable branch lines. Nevertheless, the government maintained as an objective, the need to provide an acceptable level of output of these products to the public.

The coming to power of the Conservative government in 1979 saw a further change of attitude to these organisations. Objectives were much more closely related to those of the private sector, with maximum profit becoming the main aim. The government, with its philosophy of non-intervention into the economy, set about a radical programme of privatisation - the sale of the nationalised industries to the private sector. Examples include British Telecom, British Gas and British Airways. The political justification behind the policy of privatisation is a complex argument, but the effect upon the objectives of public sector producer organisations certainly cannot be ignored.

Charitable organisations

As we have already noted, most charitable organisations were established by a group of like-minded people who saw some need in UK society or in the world which was not being met by private or public-sector organisations. Charities fall some way between the public and private sector, for while they are non-profit making organisations, they are not part of the government or the state. They are regulated by the state in that they must be registered with the Registrar of Charities who will decide whether they have a truly charitable purpose and are being operated in a satisfactory way. This should prevent unscrupulous people setting up money-making businesses and pretending they are charitable. For a genuine charitable organisation, once it is recognised as having charitable status, it can gain tax benefits both for the organisation itself and for those who donate to the organisation. For example under the 1986 Finance Act, those who are part of a pay-as-you-earn scheme can donate to charities as a tax free deduction from pay. There are also tax benefits for higher rate taxpayers and for companies which donate to charities.

Some charitable organisations are established to achieve a single particular objective and once this is accomplished they are disbanded. Others have a wider purpose and will continue for as long as is necessary. For example the National Society for the Prevention of Cruelty to Children (NSPCC) was founded at a time when there appeared to be widespread cruelty to children in our society. While society as a whole no longer condones such cruelty, the NSPCC still sees itself as having an important role to play in individual cases of cruelty.

Activity

Choose any organisation that you wish and try to find out its objectives. You could choose your college or school and see if it has a stated 'mission statement' or list of aims or objectives. Alternatively you could examine an organisation of which you are a member such as the St John's Ambulance Brigade, the Scouts or Guides. If you wish you could approach a large organisation and ask them for their annual report. This will usually contain a statement of the organisation's aims and objectives.

Assignment *The Mondeo deal*

Parry and Lewis Ltd., a car dealer in Blackburn, has an exclusive dealership agreement with the Ford Motor Company, for whom it is their main dealer in the area. In the spring of 1993, Ford, in an attempt to boost sales during what is a generally a quiet time of the year decided to introduce a limited number of its 'Mondeo' saloon cars at 5% below the standard list price for a limited period. Parry and Lewis Ltd. were allocated 100 of the new models which were to be delivered to them on 1st March 1993. Ford informed the garage that advance publicity for the deal would be in the press and form part of a TV advertising campaign from late January.

John Hall, a local builder, saw the TV adverts and decided to buy one of the special deal Mondeos and went to the Parry and Lewis showroom and agreed to buy one of the cars for delivery in March. He put down a ten per cent deposit on the deal. On 25th February, however, Ford notified Parry and Lewis Ltd. that, because of an industrial dispute at one of its factories, the delivery of the 100 special edition Mondeos would be delayed until late May. Parry and Lewis then wrote to all those who had placed deposits on the new Mondeos advising them that delivery would be delayed until late May or early June.

At the beginning of March, Fiat announced a special offer on one of their models of a similar specification to the Mondeo. They also offered a very attractive trade in deal and and low interest rates on borrowing for new car purchases. John Hall was tempted by this offer, especially as his wife had recently been made redundant from her job. The Fiat was £573 cheaper than the Mondeo and substantially lower on fuel consumption. This was particularly attractive as the government had recently increased the price of petrol by 10p a gallon in the budget. Mr. Hall decided to cancel his order for the Mondeo and buy a Fiat instead. He therefore rang Parry and Lewis and asked for a refund of his deposit.

Tasks

Imagine that you are working as a commercial trainee for Parry and Lewis and you have become aware of what has happened. As you now know something of the factors that influence demand try and use some simple economic analysis (and perhaps illustrate your answer with some demand curves) to explain the following points.

1. Why do you think Ford introduced the special cut price offer on the Mondeo in the first place?;

2. What would be the effect of the price cut on the demand for Mondeos?;

3. What were the main economic factors that first encouraged Mr Hall to put a deposit on the Mondeo and then decided him to switch his purchase to a Fiat?;

4. What is the effect on the supply of Mondeos as a result of the industrial action?

Development Task

Try and find out the prices of new cars that are on sale in your area. Attempt to identify which models are in direct competition (in other words are substitutes) and whether there is any major difference in the price of each.

Element 1.2 Government Influences on Business

The Nature of the UK Economy

If we could all have everything that we wanted, then there would be no such thing as an economic problem. If we could simply pluck food from the trees, and there were sufficient trees to provide as much as we all needed, then nobody would go hungry. If cars and televisions, houses and clothes, also grew on trees then we would all be able to travel and be entertained, housed and clothed. Life would be one long round of enjoyment. Enough of the fairy tale and back to reality. In the real world there are not enough resources to meet everyone's needs. There is in fact a scarcity of resources. You might not believe it when you hear about food mountains or offices standing empty. But these are simply examples of where our economy has got it wrong. It has used scarce resources to produce something that people do not want and has not used those same resources to supply things that people do want. Offices are built and left empty while schools, colleges and hospitals could be maintained or new ones constructed. There are many reasons for such misallocation of resources, some are economic and some are political. Nevertheless this need to allocate scarce resources in the most effective and efficient way is the fundamental problem facing all economies today.

Consumers, business organisations and the state all demand resources to meet their varying needs. Consumers want food, drink, houses and a decent standard of living. Business organisations want more investment in plant and machinery, skilled workers and raw materials to allow them to produce more goods for sale and so allow them to make profits and prosper. The government needs additional resources so that it can provide the goods and services which a modern society must have to survive.

These problems do not solve themselves! We need to understand how we should best spend our money and we should be able to understand and discriminate between the arguments of those who seek to spend the wealth of the nation. To be able to act as rational decision makers, we must be able to understand how wealth is created and the most appropriate means of allocating it between a succession of competing demands.

The problems caused by the scarcity of resources means that economies have to address three main questions. These are:

- What to produce?;
- How to produce it?;
- How to allocate the goods and services that are produced to consumers with competing demands?

1. *What to produce?*
   This question involves a decision over what goods and services the economy should produce. Should society concentrate its resources on goods for private consumption or should it regard the needs of the State as a whole as being more important.

2. *How to produce it?*
   This involves technical problems such as, should we have labour intensive industries which employ many workers or should we have capital intensive industry which although employing fewer people is able to use high technology and produce goods and services at lower cost. The question, however, is wider than simply technical deci-

sions. Should the productive capacity of the economy be left in the hands of private enterprise or should the State itself take responsibility for production either by owning the manufacturing capacity itself or by regulating and controlling the actions of private industry?

3. *How to allocate the goods and services that are produced to consumers with competing demands?*

   This often depends on the spread of income and wealth throughout a society. If all consumers had equal wealth and income then it would be a relatively simple process of allowing individuals to choose how to spend their money on whatever they wished. Society, however, does not have such an equal distribution of income and wealth. All societies have rich and poor. Those with less income and wealth still have legitimate needs and demands. They want to be clothed, housed and have their children educated. If society wishes to meet these needs then it may not be possible to allow all goods and services to be distributed by individual purchasing power. The State may decide that some goods should be provided free or with some degree of subsidy. The State may decide that it is important to redistribute income and wealth through a system of taxes and benefits. As we discuss these questions you will realise that there are no simple and easy answers.

It is important that you should recognise the limitations which exist because of scarcity. We must value the differing claims on these resources and understand that the State, through the actions of the Government, has established a framework in which these demands are met – or not. We shall see that in this country the way that most of our daily needs are met is through a *free market*. Manufacturers produce goods and services which we, as consumers, decide whether or not to buy. Of course all our needs are not met in this way. You may have been educated at state schools, treated in a NHS hospital or live in a council house. All of these services have been provided by the State either free of charge or with some degree of subsidy. Thus in the UK we have an economy which has both private and state provision of goods and services. We describe it as a *mixed economy* or as a *social market*.

The economy we have in the UK is not the only model adopted in the world. Other countries organise and manage their economies in many different ways. In some, the government plays a very minor role merely acting as the provider of the underlying political and economic framework in which individuals and organisations are free to act as they see best to meet their own interests. In such an economy freedom of the individual consumer and producer is seen as of paramount importance and the interests of the state are seen as best being served by little government intervention. This is described as a *market economy*.

At the other extreme of the economic spectrum are those economies which regard the interests of the State as being the overriding objective. If the State prospers, individuals prosper. If the State tries to pursue policies of fairness and equity then its citizens should accept this and act fairly and equitably. In this case the role of the State and the government is centre-stage. The State not only acts as a regulator, it may also be the main producer and also decide how the goods and services it supplies are distributed. This type of economy is described as a *command economy*. Let us now examine the operation of these different types of economies.

Activity

In the previous section we noted that society is faced with three fundemenatl problems: 'What to produce', 'How to produce it' and 'How to allocate the goods and services between competing consumers'. Consider each of the following situations and explain which of the three questions is being addressed:

1.   *The government's decision to increase the level of policing in a particular area.*

2.   *The privatisation of the Post Office.*

3.   *Virgin Airlines decision to begin flying the London to Hong Kong route.*

4.   *A local authority deciding to provide free home helps for the elderly.*

The Different Types of Economy

Command economy

Command or planned economies, which are often synonymous with a *communist* political system, existed in the USSR and Eastern Europe for over forty years until the communist system was overthrown in the late 1980s. While they still exist in China, North Korea, Vietnam, Cuba and a few other countries the demand for democracy and the free market has been a powerful force in the last decade and increasingly, even in these countries, we are beginning to see some economic reforms.

The economic theory which underpins these command economies is based on *Marxism* or *socialism*. In theory at least, the State decides how to allocate resources by assessing the benefit (and the costs) to specific users and consumers without considering the consumer's wealth. The government through a central body identifies what to produce and how much of it to produce. It assesses the country's resources, its productive capacity and how these goods and services should be distributed. It decides on the most appropriate distribution, basing its judgement on the needs of the State and its citizens, rather than allowing the wealth or purchasing power of individual consumers to determine how scarce goods and services are shared out.

The State is the main producer and the main employer. It controls the factories and the farms, the railways and the shops. The question of who gets such goods is determined by a rigorously enforced incomes policy which gives higher incomes to those workers which the government regards as most important. Individual consumers then have the freedom to spend their income as they wish – if they can afford the product and find it in the shops. Prices tend to be fixed by the government and products are rationed according to what the government believes should be produced. Most resources are commonly owned by the State and private property tends to be limited to items such as clothing, cars and furniture.

There are several difficulties apparent in command economies including:

- the lack of a profit incentive which often leads producers and workers to be less efficient;
- the inability of central planners to judge the 'real' needs of consumers;
- the need for an expensive and often inefficient bureaucracy in order to manage and administer the central planning process;
- the fact that people like to own their possessions whether it is land or shares and so often resent common ownership.

These economic failings as well as the autocratic and repressive political system which tends to exist in command or planned economies have led to the fall of the Communist bloc in Eastern Europe and other parts of the world to be replaced in many of the former socialist states with a chaotic introduction of a free market with massive inflation as government price controls are abandoned and growing unemployment as their traditionally overstaffed industries have to compete with the more efficient western democracies.

Free market economies

In contrast to the command economies of the old communist bloc, the western world tends to allocate resources through the *market mechanism*. This is a deceptively simple system of resource allocation. It works within the existing distribution of income and wealth by accepting that there are rich and there are poor and it is not the responsibility of the market to change that. It has as its basis the understanding that individual consumers will seek to maximise their personal satisfaction by demanding that combination of products and services which will give them the greatest level of satisfaction for the money they have. The market system is based on the following ideas.

- Each consumer is free to spend as he or she wishes, and, if the consumer is rational, the products bought should give him or her the maximum satisfaction possible within the budget available.

- The movement of prices will indicate to the producers what they should supply in the future. If a product or service is in demand and not enough is being produced, consumers will compete between themselves for this scarce commodity and will bid the price up. The higher price will then encourage producers to make more, which in turn will solve the problem of the shortage and reduce the excess demand. The reverse is true if demand is lower than supply. Producers will find themselves with stocks left on their hands. They will lower the price to get rid of them and produce less in the future. This reduces supply until it equals demand.

- Competition for customers between producers means that the producers must keep their prices as low as possible. To keep prices low and still make a profit the producers must reduce their costs of production. In fact, they must be as efficient as possible. If they are efficient and can produce and sell their products, they will make a profit. This will allow the most efficient producers to pay the highest wages to attract the best labour, pay the highest rents in order to have their business located in the prime sites, and pay high prices in order to get the best machinery and best quality raw materials available These things should help enable them to produce the best product.

- Alternatively, an inefficient organisation will have high costs, and so will either have to charge a higher price and sell less, or else will have to keep prices down in order to sell more but make little profit. This will mean that the least efficient producers will not make a profit, and consequently will go out of business.

The market mechanism, then, if it works efficiently, will:

- provide freedom to individual consumers to spend their money as they wish;

- indicate the consumers' demands and needs to producers and so ensure production of what consumers actually want;

- encourage competition between producers and so lead to a greater level of efficiency in the production of goods and services;

- adequately reward the most efficient organisations through high profits, and the best workers through high wages.

The basis of the market system is the interaction of the forces of demand and supply. By demand is meant the willingness and ability of consumers to purchase the goods and services they want. It is important to recognise that this implies that the consumer not only desires the product but also has the money to be able to buy it. Supply is the willingness and ability of producers to meet these demands. Again this implies that the supplier not only wants to produce the goods and services but also has the necessary combination of raw materials and finance, and an appropriately skilled work-force to ensure that production is feasible.

Mixed economies

The UK economy and those of most of Western Europe incorporate some features of both the free market and command economies. Most goods and services are produced and distributed through the market mechanism and consumers have the freedom, more or less, to buy what they wish. As we explain in the next section, however, the State has decided to intervene in the market because it fails in some aspects of its operation. In the UK we have a large public sector which incorporates central and local government and the nationalised industries such as the Post Office and British Rail which employs, either directly or indirectly, a substantial proportion of the workforce. Teachers, doctors, nurses and policemen are all employed in the public sector. The State provides us with many services which we regard as essential such as defence and law and order. Furthermore the State acts as a regulator and controller of private sector activity. In fact for much of this century the State increased both in size and in influence. It is only in the 1980s and 1990s that we have seen the government decide that many of the activities of the State are better undertaken by the private sector. Privatisation has moved many of the nationalised industries out of the public sector and away from planned and command elements of government control into the world of the free market and the market mechanism.

The market mechanism is not only relevant to the private sector of the economy: it is also becoming an increasingly important concept for the public sector. While central and local government have always worked within the broad parameters of the market, especially in respect of their dealings with outside business organisations, they have tended to avoid the realities of the system by not having their activities governed by the profit motive. The conservative governments of Margaret Thatcher and John Major, however, firmly believe in the interaction of the forces of demand and supply in all sectors of the economy, and as such the market mechanism is assuming a more important role throughout the public sector as public authorities act as both suppliers and consumers.

Activity

Since the late 1980s most of the countries of Eastern Europe have changed from being command economies and have begun to introduce reforms which bring some degree of freedom to their economies. Study the media for a few days and you may well see stories describing the difficulties these countries are having in achieving such reforms. These may include stories about industries being run down, growing unemployment and rising prices. Identify one such story and analyse the reasons why it is proving so difficult to change the nature of that country's economy.

Government Intervention in the Market

As we saw earlier the market system is, at least in theory, a very efficient mechanism for allowing individual consumers the freedom of choice to spend their income and wealth as they wish. It also acts as a means of indicating to producers which goods and services are in demand, and benefits society in general by ensuring that scarce resources are not wasted. The problem of how products are allocated to competing consumers is solved through the power of the purse: those that have sufficient income can purchase what they desire, those with less money are left wanting. There are, however, several major deficiencies in this system, and these have, over the years, prompted governments into a policy of market intervention. These deficiencies in the market system are known as market failures or market imperfections. As a simple means of classification, market failures can be divided into the following three categories:

1. failings caused by the type of good or service demanded;
2. failings resulting from the development of the economy;
3. failings which are inherent in the market system.

The type of goods and services provided

The market system is perfectly capable of providing private goods such as clothes or televisions. These are goods which are produced by the private sector and consumed by private consumers. Neither the State or other consumers are affected either to their advantage or detriment by the production and consumption of private goods. Private goods alone, however, cannot meet all the demands and needs of society. Society needs to be supplied with two further types of goods or service.

These are:

*   public goods;
*   merit goods.

Public goods

Public goods are goods or services which benefit or harm the State as whole. Their consumption is not just a matter of a private company producing a private good and selling it to a private consumer without others being effected. The benefits (or costs) gained from the consumption of such goods either directly or indirectly effect others. If fact we describe this benefit (or cost) as being indiscriminate or diffuse.

For example, the provision of a police service will help society as a whole. If you are protected by a police service, criminals who are likely to commit offences against you are deterred or arrested. This public service, however, not only protects you, but also the rest of society. To charge a single individual for the benefit gained would be to ignore the fact that the rest of society is also gaining a benefit. Therefore it is fairer to charge society as a whole for the provision of the service rather than charge individuals. If this type of goods was to be provided through the market system it would be necessary for individual consumers to hire personal body guards or security systems. While this may be feasible for those in society who have sufficient money to pay for such protection, there are many who have not and who would consequently find themselves without protection.

The two factors which distinguish public goods from private goods are:

*   are non-rival in consumption;
*   are non-exclusive.

Non-rival in consumption

To describe public goods as *non rival in consumption* means that, should a given level of service be provided, the fact that one individual consumes and benefits from it will not preclude others from similarly consuming and benefiting. Thus a number of people can consume the service simultaneously. The example we used of the police service illustrates the point. The protection of one person does not prevent others from being protected. Of course, this does not mean that all individuals will benefit to the same extent. An old lady may benefit more from the protection of the police than will a young person trained in the martial arts. It simply means that all can consume the goods simultaneously to some degree.

Now contrast the consumption of public goods with that of most private goods. Private goods are rival in consumption. If you were to eat a Mars Bar the one certain fact is that no one else will now be able to eat it! The consumption of such products by one individual means that less of the commodity will now be available to others, and therefore some means of rationing allocation of the products to rival consumers must be found. This is where the price mechanism comes in. Those willing to pay the price demanded will be able to consume the product while those unwilling to pay the price will not. With public goods, however, the question is not one of rationing but of the State deciding what level of provision to make so that all can benefit. In other words, the state attempts to quantify the overall benefit to society from the provision of the service and tries to ensure that the cost of providing it does not exceed this benefit.

Non-exclusive

The second characteristic of public goods is that they are *non-exclusive*. This means that it is either impossible or simply too expensive to exclude certain individuals from gaining the benefits of public goods. With private goods, if a consumer is not willing to pay the price asked, he or she can be excluded from consumption, simply by the supplier not selling the product to him or her. With public goods, if individuals refuse to pay it is difficult to prevent them gaining the benefits from it. For example, if you decided not to pay that portion of your taxes which finances the police force, would the police then be able to distinguish between muggers who may attack you from those who may attack others whose tax has gone to pay for the service? It would be an almost impossible task. As individuals who elect not to pay for the service cannot be excluded from its benefits, the State resolves that society as a whole must be forced to pay through taxation.

The figure below shows how the distinction between the two categories produces a combination of four possible types of goods ranging from the totally private to the totally public.

The distinction between private and public goods

	Excludable	Non-Excludable
Rival Consumption	*Private goods.* An additional consumer will reduce the amount available to others. Products or services can be sold through the market system. Example would include most products we buy such as clothing and food.	*Common property resource.* In this case an additional consumer will mean less for others but there is no means of preventing or rationing consumption. Few examples of this except perhaps common grazing land or a crowded seaside beach.
Non-Rival Consumption	Goods where an extra consumer does not restrict others but where it is possible to sell the product through the market mechanism. Examples include a football match, cinema or theatre performance, which is not full and so an extra spectator does not prevent others from gaining their enjoyment. If it is a full house it becomes a private good.	*Public goods.* Supplied by the State but which cannot be sold because their benefits are diffuse or indiscriminate. Examples such as national defence, law and order, roads and street lighting.

We can see that once a public good is provided, individuals may benefit from it whether or not they have paid for it. This would make provision through the price system very difficult as private producers would understandably be unwilling to supply it because they may be unable to cover their costs. They are faced with a serious problem known as the *free rider phenomenon*. This occurs when some individuals, despite wishing to gain the benefit of the public good, refuse to pay for it as they believe others will provide the finance thereby allowing those who do not pay to enjoy a *free ride*. When offered the choice, if you want the provision of this service you must be prepared to pay for it; if you do not want the service you will have nothing to pay, the meaner members of society (although some would refer to them as the shrewder members) will decide not to pay for the service in the hope that the rest of society will choose to do so, whereupon they will then gain the benefits free of charge. The larger the group who are to benefit from the public good provision, the greater is the potential for the free rider and the less feasible it becomes to provide the service through voluntary contributions.

For example, if a fence dividing the gardens of two neighbours is blown down, they may be able to reach an agreement to pay jointly for its repair as they are the only two people who will benefit from this action. There are no 'free riders' (unless of course we count those other neighbours who considered the broken fence to be something of an eyesore). If, on the other hand, we look at the larger issue of national defence, there would certainly be a number of 'free riders' if we were offered the choice of whether to pay or not. These would be the people refusing to pay simply because they know that others would finance the system anyway and they would still benefit. (Of course others may refuse to contribute to defence because they are opposed on principle to spending on weapons of any kind).

There are two problems to be faced by the State when raising finance for public goods:

- the consideration of equity;
- externalities.

Equity

One method of charging for public goods is by levying taxes individually so that at the chosen level of provision each citizen pays an amount of tax equal to the level of benefit they receive. This approach is known as the *benefit approach to taxation* in that it tries to equate an individual's tax bill with the level of benefit he or she receive from publicly provided services. One major disadvantage of this method of taxation is that it may be regarded as inequitable, since it disregards the distribution of income and wealth within society. In fact, it could turn out that the poorer members of society pay the most for the services.

For instance, the police may have to protect those living in very rough parts of town more than those living in the leafy suburbs. Consequently, the poorer inhabitants would be asked to pay more under a benefit approach. An alternative means of taxation to this is one based not on the benefits gained by an individual but on their wealth, income and personal circumstances. This is referred to as the *ability to pay approach* and is essentially the tax system which is currently followed in the United Kingdom. While the financing of public good provision through general taxation does overcome the free rider problem, it still leaves the difficulty of assessing correctly the most appropriate level of provision of public services.

Externalities

A second problem is that of externalities. The decentralisation of the provision of certain public services such as policing and roads means that they are partly financed from local authority rates. Thus the citizens of Derbyshire will be asked to pay through their local taxes for the Derbyshire Constabulary. This is fine, in that it is the inhabitants of Derbyshire who will gain the benefit of the law and order provided. However, there may also be some spillover or external effects, in that the Derbyshire police may also arrest criminals who, although living in that county, commit their crimes in neighbouring counties. In this way the citizens of adjoining areas are benefiting from a service financed by Derbyshire taxpayers. It may be the case that there is a reciprocal externality, in that neighbouring constabularies arrest criminals contemplating deadly deeds in Derbyshire. But nevertheless the fact remains that one county's taxpayers are providing a service which benefits other consumers who are not contributing to its cost. There are a number of ways of avoiding the problem of externalities. Consider the following solutions:

- public goods could be provided on a central basis financed through central government taxation. In this way the externalities do not matter as citizens are faced with a tax bill according to their ability to pay;

- the area benefiting from the service provided by its neighbour can be made to compensate the provider for the benefit gained. The difficulty here is in accurately assessing the extent of the benefit. For instance, can the Derbyshire Constabulary quantify the number of criminals they catch who intend to commit crimes elsewhere?;

- the level of service provided in adjoining communities could be standardised. In this way the taxpayers of one county enjoy the same level of provision as their neighbours. This, however, does not take into account the different levels of need in communities. For example, Derbyshire may be caught in a crime wave while the next county is relatively trouble-free.

All of these solutions inevitably involve some element of central government intervention. The most commonly adopted method of dealing with externalities is for the central Exchequer to provide part of the financing of those public goods. Thus the financing of the police force is on a fifty-fifty basis, with half coming from the local rates and half from the Home Office. Similarly, the cost of roads is divided so that main trunk roads are paid for by the Department of the Environment, while the costs of minor roads comes from the local authority budget. Ultimately the provision of public goods is a matter of social choice expressed through the ballot box. The extent of provision is thus a reflection of how far an elected government fulfils the demands of its citizens.

Merit goods

The second category of products and services which are provided by the State in this country is made up of those which are regarded as providing some element of benefit to society as a whole but which could be produced by private enterprise and sold through the market mechanism. These are referred to as *merit goods*. Examples of such goods include education, the Health Service, parks and museums.

The characteristic which differentiates merit goods (such as education) from private goods (such as clothing) is that the benefit gained does not fall solely on the individual but on society as a whole. If you were to wear well-tailored clothing the rest of society would gain no benefit whatsoever. Yet with a trained and educated population, society can enjoy more production, research and innovation, all of which lead to a better standard of living for everyone.

The State's provision of merit goods

As with public goods, there are two reasons why the State should intervene to provide merit goods, and again the reasons are:

- the consideration of equity;
- externalities.

Equity

Let us concentrate our analysis on the provision of education. It is certainly feasible to have an education system which is solely provided by private suppliers. Individuals would have the freedom to choose the type and standard of education they regarded as being most appropriate to their children's needs and abilities. The private schools, colleges and universities would offer a wide range of educational methods and parents would be able to decide either to put their children through progressive schooling or to opt for a more traditional approach. Institutions would in effect compete for pupils and students, and those providing the most successful and popular modes of education would attract the biggest intake and of course make the most profit. Parents would have to pay for the services provided, and the better-off sections of society would naturally have a wider choice in the education of their children. You may regard this as inequitable because the poorer sections of society would be faced with a lower standard of education than their more affluent contemporaries. You may even argue that education is a right and a necessity for life. Yet many more pressing necessities are provided through the market system and not by the State: food and clothing for instance.

Externalities

The concept of externalities was introduced when considering the financing of public goods. Externalities are the social benefits or costs gained or borne by society in general or by those who do not directly consume the service provided. If we stay with our example of education, an educated electorate should, in theory at least, return a government whose policies are in accord with the perceived wishes of society as a whole. Thus an education does not simply benefit you in enhancing your chances of obtaining a good job and enjoying the finer things of life; it will also be to the advantage of the rest of us in society. The argument is, therefore, that if society as a whole benefits from a service provided to an individual, then it should bear all, or at least some, of the costs of that provision. If the state did not subsidise, perhaps some individuals would choose not to consume as much. Thus, without free education some parents might choose not to send their children to school either because they believe that the benefit to be gained is not worth the price they are asked to pay or simply because they have insufficient income and choose to spend it on other things of more immediate benefit such as food or clothing. Whatever the reason, if some choose not to educate their children to their full capability then society in general will be the worse off. The State, therefore, intervenes in the market and provides certain services free or at a subsidised rate.

These social benefits (or social costs) are often ignored by individual decision-makers,who are not directly affected. This is somewhat understandable in that individuals seek to maximise their own personal satisfaction even to the detriment of others. What is perhaps more worrying is when decision-makers in the public sector choose to ignore health or education. The difficulty is that externalities are often unquantifiable in that it is not possible to put an exact valuation on them. It is often simpler to ignore them. If the external effects of health care or education are undervalued or disregarded entirely, one of the main justifications for State provision or subsidy is removed. It is then much easier to argue for the privatisation of these services. Some goods or services will also result in an external cost to society even though they are individually consumed. Perhaps one of the clearest examples of this is pollution. Factories can belch out smoke and in so doing ruin the environment of others. Chemical effluent can pollute rivers and endanger wildlife. These external costs are not borne by the producers of the goods but by society as a whole. If the individual private producer was faced with bearing this social cost himself, then total costs of production would rise and, as a consequence, there would be a reduction in the level of output. As a producer does not bear the cost, the government must intervene to protect other members of society, or at least to compensate them. Legislation could be passed to prohibit or limit these harmful-side effects. In the case of pollution this had been done under the Control of Pollution Act 1974.

Alternatively, some form of taxation could be levied on the producer, such as a hefty rate bill. The community could then use the revenue raised to provide social benefit, for instance a lower rate bill for domestic ratepayers or a new sports centre, which in some way would act as compensation for the social cost caused by the pollution. The producer now faced with higher costs, which more accurately reflect the true cost of production (as they would include the social cost), would be faced with the choice of either reducing production (and with it pollution) or passing on the higher costs in the form of price rises to the ultimate consumers of the product. In this way the consumer would be compensating those members of society harmed by the production of the product he wishes to buy.

The extent of State provision

The extent to which the State should intervene in this manner is something of a political debate involving the exercise of value judgements. It may be argued that education and health care should be the right of everyone regardless of their status or income. This is part of the rationale for the establishment of the State education system and the National Health Service. Others would argue that people with money should be allowed to spend it as they like and not have it taken from them in taxation to finance the schooling and health care of others. They should be allowed to send their children to private schools or enrol on private health schemes. The Conservative Government has taken this view to some extent in its policy of encouraging the development of private education and health schemes. The full scope of this debate is somewhat beyond the limits of this course and we shall satisfy ourselves in noting that where merit goods exist and society does benefit there is a justification for State finance and provision.

Activity

Classify the following goods and services as either 'public goods', 'merit goods' or 'private goods'

Smarties	*Local authority housing*	*The Royal Navy*
BBC	*Thorpe Park*	*The Natural History Museum*
Harrods	*Wembley Stadium*	*British Airways*

The development of the economy

Over the last hundred years the economy of the United Kingdom has developed in such a way that government intervention has become necessary in certain other areas:

- to promote competition;
- to protect consumers;
- to encourage large-scale projects.

Government policy to promote competition

We have noted that there are considerable disadvantages to the consumer resulting from the growth of oligopoly markets. For this reason the government will sometimes attempt to prevent the growth of dominant firms by restricting merger and take-over activity through its competition policy. The State is usually reluctant to interfere in the free workings of the economy and the evolution of a particular market. It will normally only intervene if it can see clear disadvantages arising out of the increased concentration in a market or the behaviour of market suppliers. The government steps in to protect the individual (or the State itself) if the behaviour of such dominant organisations are seen to be detrimental to the public interest. However, the definition of 'public interest' varies a great deal! There are many recent examples of the government allowing companies to take over competitors and so achieve market dominance. A very good recent example is the British Airways take-over of British Caledonian. The merger gives BA 93% of the UK domestic flight market and yet the government was happy to allow the take-over to go ahead. Such government intervention in the market (or in some cases the lack of government action) is but one example of the ways in which the State influences the economy. This next section will consider in some detail how and why the State intervenes in the operation of the free market.

As we saw earlier, one of the most noticeable characteristics of the UK's changing industrial structure has been the increasing pre-dominance in most markets of a few very large organisations. This development has resulted in an increasing concentration of output and resources in the hands of these organisations.

As was noted earlier, the market structure which has evolved has tended to be either monopolistic, in which there is only one major supplier or oligopolistic, where a few large companies share the market between them.

A high degree of concentration in an industry is often used as a measure of the lack of competition in a market. Such a degree of concentration can result in:

- excessive prices;
- a lack of efficiency;
- a lack of innovation;

In this way it can be detrimental both to the consumer and to the public interest. Economists would refer to this as a welfare loss to society.

While practically all organisations in private enterprise seek to maximise their profits, it is the monopolist or oligopolist who has the power to push up prices without fear of competition. You might assume that in an oligopolistic market, in which there are few suppliers, there would be fierce competition as each sought to extend output. However, this is not always the case, as in many markets the few large-scale producers are satisfied with their market share and would refrain from initiating a mutually damaging price war caused by one supplier dropping his price and the others being forced to follow suit. It is difficult to be precise about the extent of the welfare loss to society which is attributable to market concentration. Various attempts at quantifying this welfare loss have suggested that it may be in excess of 10% of the Gross National Product (GNP). If this is correct, as some governments believe, then there is considerable justification for State intervention.

Government policy to protect consumers

The growth and development of technology has meant that long-term planning and production processes are now essential for many products. For example, the launch of a new car requires:

- a research and development programme;
- considerable time and effort spent on design;
- massive investment in capital and machinery;

All of this must take place before the new model can be unveiled. If a manufacturer has invested considerable time and money in the production of a new product, he is very reluctant to allow consumers to have the final decision on whether it will or will not be a commercial success. Large-scale producers, therefore, attempt to control the demand for their products by influencing consumers through advertising. If such advertising is found to be sufficiently persuasive, producers are able to develop products over the long term and at considerable cost, confident in the knowledge that consumers will ultimately purchase whatever they, the suppliers, determine. This reduction of uncertainty in the future level of demand may be deemed necessary because of the money spent in production, but it nevertheless can be regarded as an attempt at reducing the freedom of choice of individual consumers, one of the key features of the market system.

One might say that the potential of advertising significantly to influence consumer demand is debatable, and yet, when we consider that total expenditure on marketing in the UK is in excess of 10% of GNP, it is obvious that producers, at least, are convinced of its power positively to influence the demand for their products. The argument about the powerful influence of advertising is one for debate between economists and psychologists alike. As yet, no conclusive agreement has been reached on its effects. The government does, however, regard it as necessary to regulate and control advertising to a certain extent. While not seeking to manacle the entrepreneur, some advertising is still deemed to be undesirable.

With the establishment of the Advertising Standards Authority, the government has attempted to keep all advertisements 'legal, decent and honest'. The advertising of some products which are regarded as being harmful are restricted in their advertising. Thus cigarette advertising is prohibited on television. Yet tobacco companies are allowed to sponsor sporting events, with the result that television viewers are regularly exposed to the names of different cigarette brands, thus possibly negating the effect of the ban on 'direct' advertising.

Government policy to promote large-scale projects

During the last hundred years, one of the most marked changes in the nature of industry has been the rapid growth in the scale of projects. The investment needed for large-scale projects is immense. Often the risk involved is so great, or the length of time before the realisation of any return on the investment so long, that private enterprise is unable or unwilling to provide the initial investment.

If there is considerable social benefit to be gained from the project, the State may then deem it necessary to provide the finance. Often the criteria upon which the government bases its decisions are difficult to ascertain. Projects where the government is going to be the main consumer of the product are prime areas for State aid. Increasingly, though, the Conservative Government has indicated that such projects should be financed by private enterprise or not provided at all. The Channel tunnel is an excellent example. Clearly, in less economically stringent times the opportunity for State finance of large-scale projects increases considerably.

Failures inherent in the system

The final category of market failures is related to characteristics which are intrinsic to the system. We shall examine these under two headings:
- The unequal distribution of income and wealth;
- The effects of the business cycle.

The unequal distribution of income and wealth

One of the foundations of the market system is that each individual has the freedom to dispose of his income in any way he may choose. However, this freedom is not unlimited. Each individual has a budget restraint, that is, he is restricted by his level of income and wealth. The market system simply assumes a given distribution of income and capital and makes no attempt to rectify any inequality in the economy. Within the UK, however, there is a very unequal distribution of wealth. Approximately 80% of the wealth of the nation is concentrated in the hands of 50% of the population, leaving the other 50% with only 20% of the wealth. The price system, by ignoring this problem in its basic assumptions, allows poverty to co-exist side by side with affluence.

The decision as to whether such a situation should be changed is very much a value judgement. Since the nineteenth century all governments have to a greater or lesser extent pursued a policy of redistribution through taxation and social benefits. Redistribution is more likely to tax those in a higher wage bracket in order to provide more social benefits for those on lower income levels. A Conservative government is more inclined to lower personal taxation, justifying it on the grounds that individuals should have as much freedom as possible to spend their money in whatever way they choose. Of course the redistribution effect of taxation is not solely limited to income tax. Indirect wealth taxes in the shape of Inheritance Tax and Capital Gains Tax also usually penalise the richer sections of society more than the less affluent.

The effects of the business cycle

When left to operate freely, the market tends to develop into a pattern which can be described as a business cycle. This means that it is subject to successive booms and slumps over a regular cyclical period. This pattern can be observed quite clearly if we examine economic activity in the UK over a long period. It has, in fact, been apparent since the industrial revolution.

In the nineteenth century the peaks (booms) appeared every seven to ten years. At these times the level of employment was usually fairly high relative to surrounding years. In between the booms were periods of lower economic activity, which usually fell to its lowest level roughly midway between the peaks. After the First World War the pattern altered somewhat, and the country was faced with nearly two decades of high unemployment, with the slump reaching its trough in the depression of the mid-nineteen thirties. From the end of the Second World War until the start of the 1970s, the economy was running at a relatively high level of activity, with little unemployment (it never exceeded 2.5% of the work-force and often ran as low as 1%). Concurrently with this period of high and stable employment levels, the economy experienced a much lower inflation rate than that which the country was to face in the 1970s. With the 1970s came a return to the slump/boom pattern of the pre-war years. It must be emphasised, however, that the cycle in these later years was characterised by ever-deepening troughs in the slump years and much more modest recoveries in the booms. What was also apparent in the last decade was that the timespan for each cycle had fallen from a seven to ten year period to one of only three to four years.

In this period, 1970 and 1972 were slight recession years. 1974 saw the peak of a mild boom, followed in 1976 by a further period of growing unemployment. By 1978 the economy had started to pick up slightly, but this was to be followed by the worst period of recession since the 1930s. The slump which started in 1979 was not restricted to the United Kingdom, but in this country it was been particularly far-reaching, and the decline in output and growth in unemployment was as dramatic as that of the early 1930s.

From 1985 until 1988 there was an upturn in the economy. Unemployment continued to fall so that by 1988 it was below two million. Production and economic activity was increasing and the pound had strengthened considerably against foreign currencies. The effect of this recovery was most clearly felt in the south of the country. From 1989 until early 1993, however, there was one of the worst recessions in the post-war period. Business confidence collapsed and unemployment rose to almost three million. Only in the early summer of 1993 did it seem that the recession was beginning to end and confidence was slowly recovering. We shall discuss the government's policy to solve these problems later in this element.

The breakdown of the market mechanism is most harshly illustrated from a social viewpoint by the case of unemployment. The general level of employment, it can be argued, is dependent on the overall demand for goods and services in the country as a whole. If there is a high level of demand, more jobs are available, as producers seek to increase their level of output. Conversely, if producers fear a fall in demand for their products they will invest less and in so doing create unemployment. The fall in employment will reduce demand and their worst fears will have been realised. They will then lay off or make redundant production staff and in so doing add to the level of unemployment and precipitate further consequent falls in demand. And so it goes on, until some producers anticipate a potential increase in demand, invest more, and increase job vacancies.

The social horrors of the depression in the 1930s impressed on economists and governments alike the unacceptability of large-scale unemployment. In response to these problems economists, and particularly the Cambridge economist John Maynard Keynes, argued that the State must intervene in the economy to maintain and stabilise a certain level of aggregate demand and so reduce the risk of continued unemployment. Development of these theories led to the proposition that, when the economy is prone to inflation, governments should also intervene to curb rising prices. This theory as a whole was the beginning of macro-economics (control of the economy by the government) and the policies which have been a consistent feature of post-war governments. As with the other market failures, the extent of government intervention is often a political value judgement and the relative costs to society of unemployment or inflation are regarded differently by the opposing political parties.

Forms of State Intervention

In the preceding section we concentrated on an analysis of the market failures that have encouraged successive governments to intervene in the market economy. In this section we shall look at the ways in which the government intervenes. These can be divided into three basic areas:

- Finance;
- Legislation; or
- Provision.

Finance

The state can intervene in the market through finance in two ways:

- positively, through grants, benefits and subsidies;
- negatively, by taxation.

Positive finance

The government may seek to redistribute the wealth and income of the country in favour of those it regards as being most in need. It can do this through a system of grants, benefits and subsidies. Let us look at some examples.

Pensions

One of the earliest forms of government financial help, the retirement pension, is provided to those who have contributed to the State scheme throughout their working life. The state, in effect, manages part of the income of individuals so that they will be provided for after their working days have ended.

Social Security

A similar contribution system to that of the State Pension scheme operates for unemployment benefit, in that those in work are statutorily obliged to insure themselves through the State while they are in work against the eventuality of being unemployed. Since the Second World War, the Welfare State has expanded to look after those who, although they have not contributed to a State scheme, find themselves in difficult financial circumstances. This system of social security was initially envisaged to provide a safety net for those relatively few members of society who would not be working, the assumption being that most people could and should find paid employment.

Circumstances have changed dramatically as the period of continuous full employment enjoyed in the 1950s and 1960s has come to an end. The social security system now finds itself having to cope with millions of people, many of whom have never worked and so have never accumulated sufficient entitlements to allow them to enjoy the benefit of unemployment pay. Many, it now seems likely, will never find paid employment and may be faced with the prospect of living off the social security system for the rest of their lives. The pressure that this extra number of unemployed has placed on the system has led to severe strains on its administrative and legal framework and has drawn forth considerable criticism and calls for reform. Social Security has now become the largest single component of central government expenditure, and there is little to suggest that this will cease to be the case in the near future.

Education grants

The State education system has developed a range of grants for students seeking to enter further and higher education. The student grant system is administered through local authorities, and while many grants are mandatory there is also a considerable area of discretion in the offering of some grants. Clearly, in these times of financial stringency for local authorities there is an increased reluctance to be generous in such discretionary awards. Indeed, the introduction of student loans and of charges in some institutions for higher education courses (which now seems to be be imminent) would further reduce this area of positive finance.

Grants and loans to industry

The Department of Trade and Industry is empowered to give grants and loans to some new businesses and, also to those locating in the Development Areas. In so doing, the State is directly intervening in the operation of the business market and choosing to subsidise the running of some categories of business in an effort to counteract the disadvantages they have in respect of other more established organisations or organisations operating in the more prosperous regions of the country. Other forms of grants, benefits and subsidies would include such things as rent and rate rebates, home improvement grants and grants to community or cultural organisations. Collectively this area of government expenditure is called transfer payments.

Negative finance

Negative finance involves withdrawing money from the economy in the form of taxation. The taxation system in the United Kingdom has evolved so as to fulfil four major aims. These aims have developed as the State has increased its intervention into the economy.

Taxation is used:

- as the means by which the government raises revenue to finance the provision of goods and services. The earliest taxes were raised to allow the State to fight wars, both domestically and abroad. As the State's services expanded it needed to impose a wide variety of taxes on property and commodities. The Napoleonic Wars saw the introduction of the first tax on income, and, significantly, it is often during periods of national crisis that the State is able to impose new or heavier taxes, as the populace is willing to bear a heavier burden at such times;

- by the State as the most important method of redistributing income and wealth. By the last quarter of the nineteenth century the extension of the voting franchise increased the pressure on the government to redistribute income and wealth by taxing the more affluent sectors of society in order to finance the provision of education and other welfare services and benefits;

- to regulate the consumption of particular goods which are regarded by the State as being harmful to its citizens or which the State wishes to conserve. It was also during the nineteenth century that the government began to use taxation to deter the consumption of certain goods, particularly alcohol, which it regarded as being harmful;

- as an effective means of controlling the economy. This final use of taxation as a means of implementing macro-economic policy stems from the introduction of Keynesian demand management since the Second World War.

The complex requirements of these aims mean that the government must attempt to impose a system of taxation which is both acceptable to the taxpayer and also achieves its own objectives. In this country, tax is levied on three different categories of tax base:

- Income;
- Expenditure;
- Wealth.

Income

This is the most important in terms of revenue raised. The single most significant tax is personal income tax. Also included in this category should be National Insurance contributions (which are, in effect, a form of taxation). Corporation Tax levied on company profit also falls into this category.

Expenditure

The second category is tax levied on expenditure, and this includes Value Added Tax and Stamp Duty on the purchase of more expensive houses.

Wealth

Finally, the government also levies taxes on accumulated capital in the form of Capital Gains Tax and Inheritance Tax.

Activity

Identify all the taxes that your family has to pay. Which of these taxes is obvious (or to use the proper term 'evident') and which are less evident. Categorise each of the taxes into either a tax on income, expenditure or wealth.

Legislation

Control over the working of the market system has been exercised by successive UK governments through the passage of legislation in Parliament. The two main fields of intervention are the control of ant-competitive practices and consumer protection law. In both these fields UK law has been supplemented radically over recent years by EC law. Competition law is concerned with imposing restrictions on the power of the producer while consumer protection law has as its object the protection of the interests of the consumer. It is proposed to consider legislative intervention in both these areas of activity.

Restrictions on the power of the producer

One of the largest areas for State concern has been the concentration of industry. This has already been mentioned as the shift of economic power into the hands of a relatively few larger companies and the resultant fall in the level of competition. Monopolies and oligopolies can lead to a suppression of innovation and investment, and higher prices for the consumer. Since the Second World War, successive governments have embarked on a series of measures collectively known as Competition Policy.

Legislation has been passed to curb market practices which are considered to be anti-competitive and therefore contrary to the public interest. In a sense this gives rise to a curious situation in which the government attempts to limit trading freedom to make agreements which reduce competition, whilst at the same time encouraging a free market in which the stronger organisations inevitably seek to eliminate their competitors. Legislation in this field seeks to find a balance between these conflicting forces.

Legal control of monopolies and mergers

The first piece of modern legislation was the *Monopolies and Trade Practices Act* 1948, which created the body now known as the Monopolies and Mergers Commission. legislative powers were strengthened by the Monopolies and Mergers Act 1965. The Commission's main responsibility is to act as a watch-dog enquiring into possible monopoly or oligopoly situations, reporting its findings to the government for possible further action. The Fair Trading Act 1973 repealed and re-enacted the 1948 and 1965 Acts and established the Office of the Director-General of Fair Trading. The Director-General was given authority to refer to the Commission possible areas where market concentration could be detrimental to the public interest, and was also given authority to assist the Commission in its investigation of such situations. The 1973 Act:

- defines both a monopoly situation and a merger situation;
- grants investigatory powers to the Secretary of State for Trade and Industry to issue orders to deal with monopolies and mergers.

Under the 1973 Act a monopoly/merger situation exists if the following circumstances arise:

- either a single enterprise has (or through a merger, is likely to have) control of 25% of an individual market (a monopoly share);
- or if the total assets of the organisation exceed £30m.

The Monopolies and Mergers Commission is technically independent of the government. It has the duty to *"investigate and report on any question … with respect to the existence of a monopoly situation … or with respect to the creation of a merger situation.."* Both the Secretary of State and the Director-General of Fair Trading can report matters to the Commission for investigation.

In its report the Commission will decide if either of the above circumstances exist and, if so, whether or not there are any factors which could justify the government in allowing them to continue. There are many instances of industries in which there is one company with more than twenty five percent of the market and the fact that they have not been referred to the Commission reflects the belief of successive governments that competition is nonetheless adequate in these industries. If a referral is made, the Commission will consider whether or not the merger or the level of concentration operates in the public interest. To decide this, the Commission must bear in mind factors such as:

- the need to promote effective competition within the UK;
- the need to protect consumers' interests regarding the price and variety of goods;
- the need to minimise the costs of production;
- the need to develop new techniques and products;
- the need to ensure unrestricted entry for new competitors into existing markets; and
- the need to ensure a balanced distribution of industry and employment within the UK.

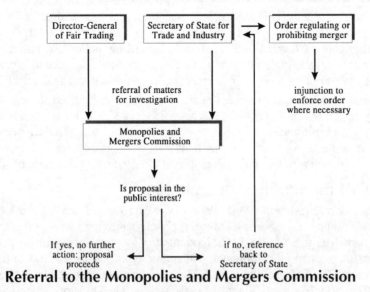

Referral to the Monopolies and Mergers Commission

If the Commission's report indicates areas of concern, the Secretary of State for Trade and Industry on behalf of the government has the following options open to him. He may by order:

- require the transfer of property from one organisation to another;
- require the adjustment of contracts;
- require the reallocation of shares in an organisation;
- prohibit a merger taking place.

The above orders are enforceable by court action through an injunction, that is a court order prohibiting or requiring specified action.

Legal control of anti-competitive practices

In order to make sense of the legislation designed to control trading practices regarded as anti-competitive, it is useful both to identify the parties involved in operating them, and the nature of the restraints imposed.

Restraints in the form of restrictive trade practices are commonly operated within agreements made between suppliers, and in agreements between suppliers and their distributors and retailers.

Agreements between suppliers

Suppliers often from agreements or associations with other suppliers in the same industry with the aim of either:

- limiting the supply of goods or services;
- fixing a standard price;
- standardising contractual terms of sale;
- purchasing raw materials through a 'common pool' at an agreed price.

Agreements between suppliers and distributors or retailers

Suppliers who are dominant in a market may enter into agreements with distributors or retailers under which a minimum price is set for the resale of the supplier's products. These agreements may also restrict the distributor who may be required to exclusively stock the supplier's products. In return the retailer may be granted sole dealership over the product in a particular area and substantial discounts on the supplier's standard price.

Examples of other restrictive practices include:

- *Full line Forcing*. This involves a supplier requiring a distributor or retailer who wishes to stock the supplier's major product, to carry the full range of his products. For example, a shopkeeper wishing to sell a major brand of baked beans may be required to carry the full range of the supplier's tinned products;
- *Tie-in sales*. This is a less extreme form of the same arrangement, whereby the sale of one product is tied to the sale of others. Thus, a purchaser of a certain type of photocopier may also have to enter into a service agreement with the supplier to purchase all photocopying paper from him;
- *Reciprocal trading*. This involves organisations agreeing to purchase each other's products exclusively. Thus other competitor's products cannot be purchased where such an agreement is in force;
- *Long term contracts*. Here a distributor agrees to carry the supplier's products exclusively for a long period and therefore effectively restricts competitors from entering the market.

The individual practices mentioned above are all examples of the means by which dominant suppliers may exert pressure on distributors or retailers. The ultimate sanction which may be used against distributors or retailers who fail to agree to such practices is a withdrawal of supplies.

The use of anti-competitive trading practices is not confined to the United Kingdom. Such practices operate within the other member states of the European Community. In consequence legislative control of such practices is found in domestic legislation and under Community law.

EC competition law

The main competition provisions are found in Articles 85 and 86 of the Treaty of Rome. They prohibit trade agreements that endanger freedom of trade between member states by preventing, restricting or distorting competition within the European Community. Examples of such agreements are those which:

- fix prices or trading conditions;
- limit production, markets, technical developments or investment;
- share markets or sources of supply;
- apply dissimilar conditions to equivalent transactions with other trading parties;
- make the conclusion of a contract subject to the acceptance of unconnected supplementary obligations.

Fines can be imposed by the EC Commission on the parties to such an agreement. However, an agreement that otherwise infringes the Articles may be allowed to continue in certain circumstances, for example where the agreement exists in order to promote technical or economic progress which will also benefit consumers.

All companies within the European Community who find themselves in a dominant market position are nevertheless subject to the constraints of European Community Competitive law. In particular Article 86 of the Treaty of Rome charges the European Commission with the responsibility of ensuring that such companies do not abuse their dominant position within the market place. Such abuses could occur where a company

- directly or indirectly imposes unfair trading conditions, such as purchase or selling prices;
- contracts on different terms in equivalent transactions with trading parties, placing them at a competitive disadvantage;
- limits production markets or technical developments to the prejudice of consumers;
- makes trading contracts subject to unconnected conditions which impose unreasonable obligations on trading partners.

While it is understandable to associate a dominant position with large companies enjoying a high market share of around 40% or more, it is possible for a relatively small organisation to control a particularly narrow market through, for instance, the ownership of important intellectual property rights. A company is in a dominant position when it can operate in a market without having to consider the activities of its competitors, so creating a non competitive market.

Tetra Pak investigation

The following decision, Tetra Pak II 1992, serves as an illustration of the wide power of the European Commission to enforce competition law and the sorts of abuses of power which may occur. Tetra Pak is a world leader in the field of packaging liquid food in cartons, and enjoys a 80-90% market share. Following an investigation into its activities, the European Commission decided that the organisation was in breach of competition law, and imposed a fine of 75m Ecu (which is about £52m).

Sale contracts governing Tetra Pak equipment and cartons were found to contain onerous conditions which prevented the purchaser from adding accessory equipment to machines, modifying them or renewing parts, and restricting the freedom to repair and maintain. Such tying conditions were held to be abuses of power, particularly when goods were purchased outright and even where maintenance services were provided free of charge, they were still found to be unlawful. The requirement that only Tetra Pak Cartons should be used on machines purchased from Tetra Pak was clearly designed to ensure that the sale of a machine was tied to the purchaser of cartons and a serious infringement of Article 86. To justify this restrictive practice Tetra Pak argued that such an integrated distribution systems brought with it economies of scale and a cost saving for customers, but this was not accepted by the Commission. It was a further abuse to allow Tetra Pak to inspect all the wording used on cartons by their purchasers and to make the resale of machines subject to their consent. Leasing contracts for machines were also found to contain restrictive conditions in relation to accessories and modification and while they would be acceptable in a genuine contract of hire, here the lease arrangements were equivalent to a sale of the machines, and such claims were consequently abuses of power. It was also unlawful to operate a discriminatory policy between Member States so that in some countries only excessively priced and lengthy leasing arrangements were available rather than outright purchase. In addition draconian penalty clauses for breach of contract and exclusive long term supply agreements were found to be abuses of power and in breach of competition law. Previously in 1991 Tetra Pak had been found guilty of an abuse of their dominant position when the Commission held that the take-over of another organisation, Liquipak, which was an exclusive licensee of certain technology was unlawful. The Commission ordered that all the present abuses including the buying up off competitor's machines, warning customers off using competitor's machines and pressurising suppliers to cut of supplies to competitors, should be brought to an end. While this decision and the record fine imposed by the Commission are the subject of an appeal, the case nevertheless provides a useful example of the need for business organisations to operate within the rules laid down by European competitive law.

UK competition legislation

The Competition Act 1980 echoes the language of EC competition legislation. Under the Act, trade practices, other than those registrable under the Restrictive Trade Practices Act 1976, (see below) which *"involve a course of conduct which has, and is intended to have the effects of restricting, distorting or preventing competition in connection with the production, supply and acquisition of goods and the securing of services in the UK"* are treated as *"anti-competitive practices"*. Whereas EC legislation deals with competition within the broad geographical area of the Community, the 1980 Act is obviously restricted to UK markets.

A detailed investigation procedure is set out under the 1980 Act. Essentially all the alleged anti-competitive practices are subject to preliminary investigation by the Director General of Fair Trading. If the practice is proven to be anti-competitive, action can be taken by the Secretary of State for Trade and Industry.

Particular practices by individual organisations may now be investigated and if necessary prevented without the need to investigate the industry as a whole. However, only large organisations are brought under scrutiny, that is companies with a turnover of more than £5m or more than a 25 percent share of their particular market.

Unlike the Restrictive Trade Practices Act 1976 there is no presumption under the 1980 Act that an agreement referred to the Commission operates against the public interest. In determining this question of public interest, the Commission simply takes into account all matters which appear to it to be relevant in the particular circumstances. For example, a manufacturer may offer his product to a supermarket at much bigger discounts than he offers to corner shops. The practice of offering such discounts could be referred to the Commission as being 'anti-competitive' in that the number of corner shops is likely to be reduced because of his practice. The Commission in deciding the question of public interest, would have to balance the advantage to the consumer of obtaining lower-priced products against the convenience of the consumer of local shopping.

Having reached a conclusion on a reference, the Commission must then report to the Secretary of State for Trade who has the power, by order, to declare an anti-competitive practice unlawful if the offender refuses to refrain from that type of conduct. The Act expressly excludes restrictive practices already registrable under the Restrictive Trade Practices Act 1976 to prevent an overlap of proceedings.

The types of practice which may be investigated by the Director-General of Fair Trading under the 1980 Act include the giving of specific discounts, rebates and allowances, full-line forcing, tie-in sales, reciprocal trading and long-term contracts.

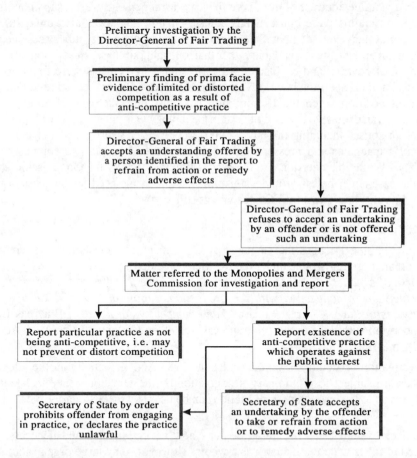

Investigation procedure under the Competition Act 1980

The Restrictive Trade Practices Act 1976

It was mentioned above that the Competition Act 1980 does not apply to agreements registered under the Restrictive Trade Practices Act 1976. Under this Act, duties are imposed on the Director General of Fair Trading. He is required to compile and maintain a register of restrictive agreements, and also to bring such agreements before the Restrictive Practices Court, which has the function of deciding whether they are contrary to the public interest. The types of agreement registrable under the Act are those made by suppliers of goods which leads to a restriction relating to:

- the price charged for goods;
- the terms and conditions of supply of goods;
- the quantities or description of goods to be supplied;
- the process of manufacture to be applied to any goods;
- those who may obtain the goods;
- the area in which the goods may be obtained.

A registrable agreement is presumed to be contrary to public policy and it is for this reason the Director General of Fair Trading must bring such agreements before the Restrictive Practices Court. If the parties can satisfy the court that the agreement does not harm the public interest then it may be declared valid. To assist the parties there are eight grounds, called the *eight gateways*, set out in the Act. If they can establish any one of the gateways then the agreement will be treated as a valid one.

The gateways seek to:

- protect the public against injury;
- counteract restrictive measures taken by anyone not a party to the agreement;
- enable the parties to negotiate fair terms with a monopolistic supplier or customer.

In fact, relatively few agreements have been approved by the court, indicating the tough line that it has taken with regard to restrictive practices.

> In *Re Net Book Agreement* 1957 the court considered an agreement by book publishers not to permit the retailing of books below published prices. The agreement was justified on the grounds that its removal could lead to unfair competition from large supermarkets and department stores only carrying a limited number of best-sellers, which could mean that the specialist book sellers were forced out of business.

> In *Chemist Federation Agreement* 1958 an agreement by the Federation to limit the sale of patent medicines to the public, by qualified pharmacists only, was declared void. The court was unimpressed by the argument that the restriction was necessary to protect the public against injury in view of the potentially dangerous nature of the goods being sold.

> The agreement itself does not need to be legally enforceable. In one case an arrangement between a group of contractors to delay submitting their individual tenders until they had met to discuss each other's tenders was held to constitute a restrictive trading agreement (Re: *Installations at Exeter Hospital Agreement* 1970).

The Resale Prices Act 1976

One of the most fundamental aspects of competition between retailers is that they should have the ability to charge whatever price they wish. Yet one of the most widely used restrictive agreements was the practice by dominant suppliers of imposing standard prices for their goods on all their retail outlets. These *resale price maintenance* agreements were forced on distributors and retailers by suppliers, who could always threaten to withhold supplies to ensure compliance. Such agreements were originally controlled by legislation in 1964, their regulation now being contained in the Resale Prices Act 1976. Under this Act it is unlawful for suppliers to make agreements to withhold supplies from, or supply on less favourable terms to, distributors who do not observe resale price conditions. As with other restrictive practices, the Restrictive Practices Court has power to grant exemption on one or other of the grounds specified in the Act upon an application made by the Director-General of Fair Trading.

So far, only three exemptions have been made, relating to books, drugs and maps. Apart from these exemptions it is *prima facie* unlawful for a manufacturer to withhold supplies in an attempt to enforce a minimum resale price. Such a refusal to supply goods could, however, be justified if the producer shows that the dealer in question has, within the preceding twelve months, been selling the same or similar goods as a *loss leader*, that is selling at a retail price below wholesale cost in order to attract custom for that and other products.

> In *Oxford Printing Ltd. v. Letraset Ltd.* 1970 the defendants withheld supplies from the plaintiffs, who had cut the price of the defendant's products and also used them to promote the sales of a competitor's product. Such withholding of supplies was held to be lawful in the circumstances.

Consumer Protection

Consumer Protection legislation provides a further example of how the state attempts to regulate the workings of the market system.

All commercial activity involves transacting for goods or services which are ultimately supplied to customers, clients or consumers. Whether buying food, clothes, household goods, holidays, shoes, renting a flat or opening a bank account, individuals are engaged in business relationships within a legal framework which confers rights and imposes responsibilities. Organisations involved in the supply of goods and services are subjected to numerous legal constraints designed to protect the customer/consumer. The principle of caveat emptor (let the buyer beware) still applies so that it is left to the parties to a contract to negotiate its terms and a consumer will remain legally bound by a contract despite the fact that it subsequently proves to be less than beneficial. The law recognises however the unequal bargaining power of the parties and consumer protection law has developed dramatically over recent years in an attempt to redress this imbalance both at National and European Community level.

In civil law the parties to a transaction are protected by the law of contract under which the innocent party is provided with legal redress in the event of a breach by the other. The object of legal remedy in these circumstances would be to put the innocent party in the position they would have been had the contract been performed as it should have been. Contracts for the sale of goods and the supply of services are also regulated by statute, for instance the Sale of Goods Act 1982 and the Unfair Contract Terms Act 1977.

The criminal law also has an important role to play in consumer protection. Criminal offences relating to the supply of goods and services have been created by numerous statues including the Consumer Credit Act 1974, The Trade Descriptions Act 1968 and 1972, the Consumer Protection Act 1987, the Unsolicited Goods and Services Act 1971, the Food Safety Act 1990 and many others. Both local authorities and the Office of Fair Trading have a role to play in enforcing the law and investigating unfair trading practices.

Activity

Study the business media for a few days and see if you can find examples of

1. *a monopoly/merger situation which could be the subject of an investigation.*
2. *a trading agreement which it is alleged may break EC competition law.*
3. *a prosecution for an alleged breach of consumer protection law.*

	Civil Law	Criminal Law
Enforcement	Rescission of contract Sue for damages (or defence to an action for damages) in the County or High Court Arbitration	Local Authority: Trading Standards Department Prosecution in the Magistrates and Crown Courts Compensations orders under the Power of Criminal Courts Act 1973 Director General of Fair Trading
Defective Products	Sale of Goods Act 1979 Supply of Goods and Services Act 1982 Tort of Negligence Consumer Protection Act 1987 Codes of Practice	Consumer Protection Act 1987 Food Safety Act 1990 Road Traffic Act 1988 and other specific legislation Health and Safety at Work Act 1974
Defective Services	Supply of Goods and Services Act 1982 Professional Negligence Regulation by trade or professional associations	Trade Descriptions Act 1968 Consumer Credit Act 1974 Health and Safety at Work Act 1974
False Statements	Misrepresentation Breach of Contract Negligent mis-statement Tort of Deceit	Trade Descriptions Act 1968 Consumer Protection Act 1987 Property Misdescription Act 1991 Weights and Measures Act 1985 Fair Trading Act 1973
Exclusion of Liability	Common Law rules of incorporation and interpretation Unfair Contract Terms Act 1977	Consumer Transactions (Restrictions on Statements) Order 1976 and (Amendment) Order 1978

Contracts for the Sale of Goods

Contracts for the sale of goods are perhaps the most significant category of business agreement because they are the type which are most commonly encountered in the commercial world. A sale of goods contract is basically one in which goods are exchanged for money. Examples of this type of contract range from the sale of a loaf of bread for seventy pence to the purchase of an aircraft for tens of millions of pounds.

The law relating to contracts for the sale of goods is contained in the Sale of Goods Act 1979. As a general rule the principle of freedom of contract applies to them. Essentially therefore the buyer and seller are free to negotiate the terms of the contract and make whatever bargain suits their own purposes. Many of the rules contained in the 1979 Act apply only where the parties have not expressly made their intentions clear on the matter in the contract. Some of the provisions in the Act, however, cannot be overridden by agreement between the parties. A contract for the sale of goods is defined in as a *"contract by which the seller transfers or agrees to transfer the property in goods to the buyer for a money consideration, called the price"*.

Contracts of Hire

The essence of a contract of hire is that the hirer, in return for some consideration, usually an agreed fee or the periodical payment of a sum of money, enjoys the possession and the use of goods belonging to someone else, the owner. It is never intended that the hirer shall become the owner of the goods himself under the terms of the contract. Contracts of hire are fairly common in the business world and the period of use by the hirer may range from hours to years. Examples of such contracts include the hire of a mobile crane for a specific task lasting two days; the rental of a household television set over a number of years; the hire of a car for a week whilst on holiday; and the hire of sports equipment at a sports centre. In recent times there has been a growth in the commercial leasing of plant and equipment, particularly motor vehicles, to businesses. Commercial leasing, which is a form of hiring, can be a tax efficient method of acquiring plant and equipment for use in a business.

Contracts of hire are governed partly by the *Supply of Goods and Services Act* 1982 and may also be regulated partly by the *Consumer Credit Act* 1974. In order to come within the 1974 Act the contract must be a 'consumer hire agreement'. This is defined in the 1974 Act as *"an agreement made by a person (the owner) with an individual (the hirer) for the bailment of goods, which: is not a hire purchase agreement, is capable of subsisting for more than three months, and does not require the hirer to make payments exceeding £15,000"*.

The expression bailment describes a situation in which one person has possession of goods belonging to another. A contract of hire is one of several possible types of contract of bailment. Another example would be a contract under which goods are stored in a warehouse on behalf of a business.

Consumer hire agreements are regulated by the Consumer Credit Act 1974 which lays down strict rules as to their form and content. The agreement must be in writing and signed personally by the hirer. If either of these conditions are not fulfilled the owner has no right to sue the hirer under the agreement. The hirer must be given a copy of the agreement containing full information about his rights and duties and about the protection given to him by the 1974 Act. If any of these formalities are not complied with then no legal action can be taken against the hirer without the permission of the court.

Contracts for the Supply of Services

A contract for the supply of services (or contract for services) usually involves the exchange of an individual's time skill or effort in return for money. A person providing a service could do so by engaging in such diverse activities as surveying a house, tuning a car engine, transporting commodities, or providing legal advice. The contract for services is distinct from the contract of employment (or contract of service) which is considered in Unit 5, *Employment in the Market Economy*. The basic obligations owed by those who provide services in the course of a business are outlined in Part II of the Supply of Goods and Services Act 1982.

Contracts for the Sale or Supply of Goods on Credit Terms

There are various forms of credit transaction which provide ways of getting goods on credit, ranging from contracts of hire purchase, credit sale and conditional sale agreements, to the use of 'plastic money'. A contract of hire purchase, as its name suggests, combines elements of two types of contract. It is in effect a contract of hire which gives one party (the hirer or debtor) an option to purchase goods from the other (the owner or creditor) at the end of a period of hire. During the period of the agreement the debtor pays the creditor by instalments (usually monthly) and the ownership of the goods remains with the creditor. The agreement will contain a term giving the debtor an optional right to purchase the goods at a nominal price once all the instalments have been paid. Ownership of the goods will be transferred to the debtor if and when he exercises the option to purchase. He will invariably do this as soon as he has paid all of the instalments because the real point of the agreement, in practice, is to enable him to acquire ownership.

Many hire purchase agreements come within the definition of consumer credit agreements and these are regulated by the Consumer Credit Act 1974.

At first sight a hire purchase transaction appears to involve only two parties. In practice, however, the vast majority of hire purchase transactions involve a third party, a finance company. The person who supplies the goods may not be able to wait for his money and may require instant payment, while his

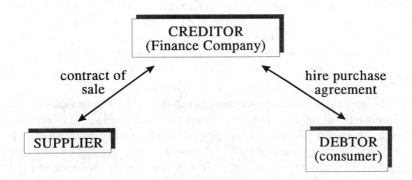

Hire purchase transaction

customer wishes to have time for payment. The supplier will therefore sell the goods to a finance company, which will supply them to the customer on hire purchase terms under a separate contract.

Credit sale and conditional sale agreements are credit transactions under which the price of the goods is payable by instalments. They will often be financed by a finance company in exactly the same way as hire purchase agreements. The rights of a customer and the degree of customer protection available to him will vary considerably depending on whether one or both of the parties are entering into the contract in the course of a business. A greater degree of legal protection is available to a private individual than to a business. Anyone to whom goods or services are supplied can be regarded as a consumer and, as we shall see later, the law gives protection to all consumers. However, the protection available is greater in the case of the private consumer. The Fair Trading Act 1973 defines a private consumer in as: *"the person to or for whom goods or services are, or are sought to be, supplied in the course of a business carried on by the supplier, and who does not receive or seek to receive the goods or services in the course of a business carried on by him"*.

Many of the legal rules which govern consumer protection apply only where goods or services are supplied in the course of a trade or business. There is no generally applicable precise definition of the expression 'business', although there are a number of decided cases which give some guidance.

> In *Havering London Borough v. Stevenson* 1970 a car hire firm regularly sold its cars after a period of use in the business. A sale in these circumstances was held to be in the course of its trade or business as a car hire firm.

> On the other hand, in *Davies v. Sumner* 1984 the defendant was a self employed courier, who had a contract with a TV company to transport films and video tapes. He purchased a new car in June 1980, and travelled 118,000 miles in it before trading it in for another in July 1981. The mileometer had gone around the clock, and showed only 18,000 miles. The defendant did not disclose the true mileage, and was later charged with having applied a false trade description "in the course of a trade or business". The House of Lords held that he was not guilty, as this was a one-off sale which could not be regarded as an integral part of his business.

> In *Blakemore v. Bellamy* 1983 the defendant's spare time activity of buying, refurbishing and selling cars was held to be a hobby rather than a business. This was so even though he had sold eight different cars over a period of fifteen months and he had not driven them all himself or had them insured.

Business sellers may sometimes masquerade as private sellers for example by advertising in the small ads in a newspaper. The purchaser may be misled by this and think that his legal remedies are limited because he has purchased from a private seller. In order to prevent such disguised business sales the Business Advertisements (Disclosure) Order 1977 was made under the Fair Trading Act 1973. Under this regulation it is a criminal offence for a trader or a businessman to advertise goods for sale without making it reasonably clear that the goods are being sold in the course of a business.

Contractual terms

Contractual terms will be expressly agreed by the parties but in relations to the sale of goods and the supply of services it is those terms implied into the contract by Statute which are of most significance. In a contract for the sale or supply of goods the law imposes obligations on the supplier by the legal mechanism of implied terms in the contract of supply. These statutory implied terms operate as if the seller had said to the buyer "I promise you that...". Most of these terms are classified as contractual conditions, which, if broken, will give rise to the right to accept the breach and repudiate the contract, reject the goods and sue for damages.

The implied terms contained in the Sale of Goods Act 1979 automatically become part of any contract for the sale of goods. These terms have been used as a model for incorporation by statute into all other contracts involving the supply of goods. The Supply of Goods (Implied Terms) Act 1973 imply virtually identical terms in contracts of hire purchase. The Supply of Goods and Services Act 1982 imply equivalent provisions into contracts for the transfer of goods, a term which includes contracts of barter and the supply of goods element of contracts for work done and materials supplied. The 1982 Act also implies equivalent provisions into contracts for the hire of goods.

Implied terms in sale of goods contracts

There is an implied condition that the seller has the right to sell the goods. If this is broken, for example because the goods belong to someone else, the buyer will be able to repudiate the contract and recover in full the price he paid.

> In *Rowland v. Divall* 1923 three months after buying a motor car the purchaser discovered that it had been stolen before it came into the seller's possession. The seller therefore had no right to sell it. The purchaser returned the car to its original owner and sued the seller. It was held that he was entitled to the return of the price. The fact that the buyer had used the car for over three months did not affect his right to recover the full purchase price.

Where there is a contract for the sale of goods by description there is an implied condition that the goods will correspond with the description. Whenever the buyer has not seen the goods before the contract is made the sale is obviously a sale by description. Also, if goods are packaged, for example food inside a tin or cardboard box, there is a sale by description.

> In *Beale v. Taylor* 1967 the buyer purchased a car advertised as a 1961 Herald Convertible having had a trial run in it as a passenger. The buyer soon found the car to be unsatisfactory. On an examination by a garage it was discovered that the car had been made up of halves of two different cars. The rear portion was part of a 1961 Triumph Herald 1200 model while the front was part of a earlier 948 model. The two portions had been welded together unsatisfactorily into one structure, and the vehicle was unroadworthy and unsafe. The Court of Appeal held that the seller had broken the promise implied into the contract relating to description and was liable in damages to the buyer.

One of the most important implied conditions relates to the quality and fitness for purpose of the goods supplied.

> *"Where the seller sells goods in the course of a business there is an implied condition that the goods supplied under the contract are of merchantable quality."*

The Sale of Goods Act provides however that there is no such condition:

- *"as regards defects specifically drawn to the buyer's attention before the contract is made; or*
- *if the buyer examines the goods before the contract is made, as regards defects which that examination ought to reveal".*

For the condition to apply therefore the seller must be a business seller. The implied condition does not apply to private sales; the seller may be anyone in the chain of distribution, such as a manufacturer, wholesaler or retailer; the condition does not apply where a defect has been drawn to the buyer's attention prior to the sale, or where the buyer has examined the goods before buying them and ought to have discovered the defect.

> In *Frost v. Aylesbury Dairies Ltd.* 1905 the dairy supplied milk contaminated with typhoid germs and was held liable despite establishing that it had used all reasonable care to prevent such contamination.

The expression merchantable quality is defined so that goods are merchantable if they are as fit for the purpose or purposes for which goods of that kind are commonly bought as it is reasonable to expect having regard to any description applied to them, the price (if relevant) and all other relevant circumstances".

Under this definition the standard of quality will vary according to the circumstances of the case. Goods must be reasonably fit for their ordinary uses, although account may be taken of any description applied to them and, where relevant, the price. Clearly if goods are described as 'seconds' or 'manufacturer's rejects' they will not be expected to be of perfect quality. Similarly, the standard of quality and durability expected of shoes priced at £18 will be lower than that expected of those priced £58. However if the £58 shoes had been reduced in a sale to a price of £18, the sale price would probably not be relevant in determining the standard of quality expected.

> In *Crowther v. Shannon Motor Company* 1975 it was held that a second-hand car which needed a replacement engine after three weeks was not of merchantable quality. The car had been described as being in excellent condition.

The requirement of merchantable quality extends not only to the goods themselves but also to their packaging and any instructions supplied with them.

> In *Wormell v. RHM Agriculture (East) Ltd.* 1987 the plaintiff was a farmer who purchased a chemical spray from the defendant in order to kill wild oats. The instructions provided with the spray indicated that its use outside a certain period carried the risk of injury to the crop. The plaintiff was aware of the warning and decided to take that risk. In fact, because of the late application, the spray was totally ineffective. The plaintiff claimed damages for the costs of the spray and the wasted labour in applying it. The Court of Appeal accepted that, as a matter of principle, any instructions supplied with goods would be treated as part of the goods themselves in assessing merchantability or fitness for purpose. On the facts, however, it was held that the seller was not liable as the instructions had clearly stated that spraying after a certain period of growth was not recommended. The seller was not bound to give full and exhaustive reasons for the instructions given.

Goods may be unmerchantable even if they can easily be put right.

> In *Grant v. Australian Knitting Mills Ltd.* 1936 the buyer purchased underpants which contained a chemical. This caused dermatitis, a skin disease, when the buyer wore them. The chemical would have been removed if the buyer had washed them before he wore them. It was held that the goods were not of merchantable quality, and the seller was liable.

In *Rogers v. Parish (Scarborough) Ltd.* 1987 the plaintiff bought a new Range Rover from the defendant's garage. Although it was driveable and roadworthy the car had a number of defects in its engine, gearbox, oil seals and bodywork. The defendant argued that the car was of merchantable quality within the definition as it could be driven in safety on a road and therefore was "fit for the purpose for which goods of that kind are commonly bought". The Court of Appeal rejected the defendant's argument on the grounds that it was based upon too narrow an interpretation of the definition. The judge said that:

> *"the purpose for which goods of that kind are commonly bought would include not merely the purpose of driving the vehicle from one place to another but of doing so with the appropriate degree of comfort, ease of handling, reliability and pride in the vehicle's outward and interior appearance".*

Where the buyer requires the goods for a special or unusual purpose, the seller may be liable for a breach of condition if the goods are not fit for that purpose. There is an implied condition that:

> *"Where the seller sells goods in the course of a business and the buyer, expressly or by implication, makes known ... to the seller ... any particular purpose for which the goods are being bought, there is an implied condition that the goods supplied under the contract are reasonably fit for that purpose".*

Consumers sometimes place reliance on the expertise of the seller. For example when a customer goes into a shop and asks whether the shop has something that will perform a particular task, say fixing a broken ornament or removing stains from a carpet.

In *Cammell Laird & Co. Ltd. v. Manganese Bronze & Brass Co. Ltd..* 1934 the buyers supplied the sellers with a specification for ships' propellers which they were to manufacture for the buyers. Reliance was placed upon the sellers regarding matters outside the specification, including the thickness of metal to be used. The propellers were found on delivery to be too thin. The buyer's action was successful on the ground that the unfitness concerned a matter on which the buyers had relied upon the seller's skill.

In *Teheran-Europe Co. Ltd. v. ST Belton Tractors Ltd.* 1968 industrial equipment was sold to the plaintiff buyer for the purpose of exporting and resale in Persia. The seller knew this but was not familiar with the Persian market, unlike the buyer who carried on a business there. The equipment infringed Persian regulations and the plaintiff sued the seller for breach of this condition. The Court of Appeal held that the seller was not liable as the buyer had relied on his own skill and judgement as to whether the equipment was suitable for resale in Persia. There was no reliance on the skill or judgement of the seller.

Implied terms in contracts for the supply of services

The Supply of Goods and Services Act 1982 sets out terms which will be implied both into contracts for the supply of services and into contracts for work done and materials supplied. These terms will apply, for example, to contracts for dry cleaning, entertainment and professional services, home improvements and motor vehicle maintenance. The most important implied term states that:

> *"In a contract for the supply of a service where the supplier is acting in the course of a business, the supplier will carry out the service with reasonable care and skill".*

This requirement has wide ranging application embracing most situations where a client or customer is paying for services. It applies to builders, hairdressers, dry cleaners, surveyors, auctioneers, tour operators, bankers, car repairers and many others who provide services in the course of their business. The following cases illustrate the scope of the duty:

In *Curtis v. Chemical Cleaning and Dyeing Company* 1951 the plaintiff took a wedding dress to the defendant dry cleaners for cleaning. When she came to collect the dress she found that it had been stained. It was held that the company were liable for the damage to the dress which had been caused by their failure to take care of it.

In *Davey v. Cosmos Air Holidays* 1989 the plaintiff booked a two week package holiday in the Algarve for himself and his family. During the holiday the whole family suffered diarrhoea and the plaintiff's wife and son both contracted dysentery. The evidence showed that the illness was caused by a general lack of hygiene at the resort, and the fact that raw sewage was being pumped into the sea just fifty yards from the beach. The defendant tour operators had resident representatives at the resort who knew of the dangers. It was held that the defendants were liable for breach of the implied duty in the contract to take reasonable care to avoid exposing their clients to a significant risk of injury to their health.

In *Lawson and Lawson v. Supasink Ltd.* 1984 the plaintiffs employed the company to design, supply and install a fitted kitchen at a price of £1,200. Plans were drawn up and agreed but the company did not follow them when installing the units. The plaintiffs complained about the standard of work before the installation was complete. After taking independent expert advice the plaintiffs demanded the return of their deposit and asked the defendants to remove the kitchen units. The defendants refused and the plaintiffs sued. The judge found that the kitchen was installed in 'a shocking and shoddy manner' and that the work was 'beyond redemption'. He awarded damages of £500 for inconvenience and loss of the use of the kitchen; damages of the difference between the cost of equivalent units and the contract price; and the return of the deposit. On appeal the defendants argued that they had substantially performed the contract and were therefore entitled to the contract price less the cost of remedying any defects. This was rejected by the Court of Appeal on the grounds that the standard of workmanship and design was so poor that the doctrine of substantial performance could not be applied, having regard to the large sums which would have to be spent to remedy the defects.

The nature of product liability

Generally the goods we use, for example a washing machine, or that we consume, such as a meal, are items we have actually bought. But we can act as consumers in other ways. A person whose washing machine has broken down may use a friend's as a temporary measure, and maybe the meal that you have eaten has been bought for you in a restaurant. The fact that you do not own the goods does not prevent you from using or consuming them, but it may have an effect upon the nature of your legal rights. The reason for this can be explained quite simply.

If you buy goods from a commercial seller we have already established that the contract automatically includes a number of promises, that the seller has to fulfil. Such promises would include those which relate to product standards. If the goods do not match up to these standards the consumer has the contractual right to reject the goods and sue the seller for damages. In fact there has been a breach of contract. The undertakings in question are imposed upon the seller under the Sale of Goods Act 1979, and the seller remains liable even if he has taken all reasonable care to try and ensure that the products he is selling meet the standards required by the Act, and therefore is not at fault if they fail to do so. An illustration of this principle would be where a shop sells a catapult to a child, who is injured when the catapult snaps, the shopkeeper is liable under the contract even though he carried out sample inspections of the catapults before buying them himself.

This actually happened in a case called *Godley v. Perry* 1960. Lawyers call liability that arises without fault or blameworthiness 'strict liability'.

It follows that a buyer who suffers physical harm from a purchased product can recover compensation for the harm by alleging a breach of contract. However what if the catapult had not injured the little boy who bought it, but his friend who was standing beside him? Earlier we mentioned the washing machine a friend had let you use, and the meal bought for you in the restaurant. Would you have any rights if you received a serious electric shock from the washing machine because the manufacturer had not properly earthed it, or if the meal caused you food poisoning because it was not properly cooked? In all three cases the problem seems to be that as the injured parties have no contract with anyone, they cannot therefore pin liability on anyone. Even the buyer who finds that the seller is now out of business seems to be in the same predicament.

In fact in each case it is possible to seek compensation for the harm that they have suffered. The law recognises the existence of a duty, which manufacturers and producers owe to anyone they might reasonably expect to be harmed as a result of negligently manufacturing the goods or providing the service. This is not 'contractual liability', but 'tortious liability', and it arises under the tort of negligence.

A tort is a civil wrong, and torts are imposed as a part of the general law. We are all subject to them, whether we like it or not.

> The principle that a consumer, whether or not he is an actual buyer, who suffers harm as a result of a manufacturer's negligence can sue the manufacturer for damages, was established by the House of Lords in *Donoghue v. Stevenson* 1932. In this case a woman suffered physical illness and shock after discovering that the contents of a bottle of ginger beer she was in the process of drinking included the decomposed remains of two snails. The bottle had been bought for her by a friend. The court decided that the manufacturer owed her a duty of care, therefore putting him under an obligation to use reasonable care in the manufacture of the product.

This duty of care is sometimes said to be a duty owed towards the 'ultimate consumer'. It is a very important aspect of the law regarding product liability. It is especially important to note however, that it is liability based upon fault. If a manufacturer can demonstrate that the manufacturing process, the design of the product and other production aspects have been performed with proper care he will not be liable. A manufacturer must therefore ensure that he acts as a reasonable manufacturer would have acted in the circumstances, to fulfil the duty of care which he owes to the ultimate consumer of his products.

> In *Vacwell Engineering Ltd. v. BDH Chemicals Ltd.* 1971 the defendants, who were chemical manufacturers, were held liable under the tort of negligence when one of their products caused an explosion. Their liability arose through a failure to warn prospective users that if the product came in contact with water it could lead to an explosion.

Sometimes it may be very difficult for a person to prove that a manufacturer was in fact negligent, because it will not be possible to precisely identify how the breach occurred. How, for example, did the snails come to be in the bottle of ginger beer? It may be possible for the consumer in such cases to rely upon a rule of evidence known as *'res ipsa loquitur'*. This means 'let the facts speak for themselves'. Under this rule the courts will infer negligence of the defendant where there is no reasonable explanation for the damage caused, for example a new car with faulty brakes, or a television that explodes. However the activity causing the damage must be something totally within the control of the defendant, which would not be expected to occur if reasonable care had been exercised. The rule has the effect of shifting the burden of proof to the manufacturer to prove the absence of negligence.

> In *Hill v. James Crowe (Cases) Ltd.* 1978 the plaintiff, a lorry driver, was injured when he fell off a badly nailed wooden packing case on which he was standing in order to load his lorry. The manufacturer of the packing case gave evidence that the standards of workman-

ship and supervision in his factory were high and argued that he had not failed to fulfil his duty to the plaintiff to take reasonable care in producing the case. The Court held that the defendant was liable for the bad workmanship of one of his employees even though, in general terms, he had a good production system. He had not proved that the plaintiff's injuries were not due to the negligence of one of his employees.

The *Donoghue v. Stevenson* principle extends to a wide range of subject matter, from hair dye in the case of *Watson v. Buckley* 1940, to lifts in *Haseldine v. Daw* 1941, and in even in the case of a tombstone in *Brown v. Cotterill* 1934!

In 1985 the EC issued a directive requiring the United Kingdom Parliament to introduce legislation imposing strict liability on producers and to fulfil that obligation the Consumer Protection Act 1987 was passed.

Activity

Carry out a simple consumer survey into what people buy and their level of satisfaction with their purchases. The target group for the survey could be friends, family members, or members of the local public. Conduct some basic questions to find out:

- *how frequently consumers make purchases of goods and services.*
- *how satisfied they are with the purchases they make.*
- *how aware they are of their legal rights.*
- *how they would go about making a complaint.*

As an alternative, or complementary activity, try to arrange a meeting with someone involved in managing a local retailing business that supplies domestic consumers. Seek to establish how the business regards the legal framework which provides for consumer protection, how it seeks to comply with the legal rules in its dealings with consumers, and how it handles complaints.

Legal change and the EC directive

It has already been noted that one consequence of our membership of the EC is that we are obliged to implement changes agreed in principle within the Community. One method of achieving legal change is through the use of the directive. A directive is binding as to the result to be achieved but allows the member state to choose the precise content of the rules.

The preamble to this Directive tells us that it has a two-fold purpose:

- to establish a uniform system of product liability within the EC in order to remove distortions of trade and competition which arise because of the differences between the laws of member states in this field; and
- to solve the problem of a fair apportionment of the risks inherent in modern technological production.

There were lengthy negotiations between the EC member states on the terms of the Directive. This gave rise to a number of optional provisions in final text of the Directive and means that full harmonisation of some aspects of product liability law throughout the EC will not have been achieved. The Directive provides for a review of the working of the optional provisions in 1995 in order to reconsider the question of full harmonisation after that review.

The UK response to the three options which were available under the Directive has been:

- to incorporate the development risks defence;

- to exclude unprocessed agricultural produce and game; and
- to reject an overall financial limit (£41m) for damage caused by identical products with the same defect.

The Consumer Protection Act 1987

Liability under the Act arises *"where any damage is caused wholly or partly by a defect in a product"*. In order to succeed in a claim, the plaintiff must prove two things:

- that the product was defective; and
- that the defect caused the injury or damage.

If the plaintiff can prove these things, the defendant will be liable even though he took all possible care in relation to the product. This is the crucial difference between strict liability under the Act and liability based upon negligence which, as we have seen, depends upon proof of fault by the defendant.

Liability falls upon all or any of the following persons:

- the *producer* – this term is defined and includes the manufacturer of the product, the producer of any raw material or the manufacturer of a component part;
- the *'own brander'* – any person who, by putting his name on the product or using a trade mark or other distinguishing marks in relation to it, has held himself out to be the producer of the product;
- the *importer into the EC* – a person importing the product into the Community from a non Community state for the purpose of supplying it in the course of his business;
- any *supplier who cannot identify the person who produced the product, or supplied it to him*. In such circumstances that person will be liable, regardless of whether he was a business supplier, provided he supplied the product to someone else and the following conditions are met:
  - *he is requested by a person suffering any damage to identify any producer, own brander or importer into the EC;*
  - *the request is made within a reasonable time after the damage occurs;*
  - *at the time of the request it is not reasonably practicable for the injured party to identify all of the potential defendants; and*
  - *he fails, within a reasonable time, to comply with the request or to identify the person who supplied the product to him.*

Thus it will be imperative, where litigation is threatened, for businesses to be able to identify the supplier of the products or component parts used in any goods sold by the business. It will be particularly important to differentiate, by product coding for example, between the products of two or more suppliers who are supplying identical components for incorporation into the same type of finished product. This will apply to all component parts ranging from electric motors to nuts and bolts.

Where two or more persons are liable for the injury each can be sued for the full amount of the damage. The party who is sued may be entitled to a contribution or indemnity from anyone else who is liable, under the Civil Liability (Contribution) Act 1978. Of course the injured person can recover compensation only once, regardless of the number of possible defendants or the legal basis of his claim. The injured person will usually choose to sue the defendant against whom liability can most easily be established and who is most likely to be able to afford to pay the damages or to have insurance cover.

In order to succeed in a claim, the plaintiff will have to prove that his injury was caused by a defect in the product. A product will be regarded as defective when *"the safety of the product is not such as persons generally are entitled to expect"*. The Act gives us some guidance as to the factors which will be relevant in deciding whether a product is defective. It provides that:

"In determining what persons generally are entitled to expect in relation to a product all the circumstances shall be taken into account, including:

- the manners in which, and purposes for which, the product has been marketed, its get-up, the use of any mark in relation to the product and any instructions for, or warnings with respect to, doing or refraining from doing anything with or in relation to the product;
- what might reasonably be expected to be done with or in relation to the product; and
- the time when the product was supplied by its producer to another person;

and nothing in this section shall require a defect to be inferred from the fact alone that the safety of a product which is supplied after that time is greater than the safety of the product in question".

Clearly it is very important for any business to ensure that the packaging of their products is such that it does not suggest or imply that the product can be used in a manner or for a purpose which is unsafe. Appropriate warnings of the dangers associated with the use of foreseeable misuse of the product must be amply displayed on the packaging and, where necessary, on the goods themselves. A further precaution which may be taken by the producer of goods is the date coding of products. Thus if a safer product is subsequently developed and put onto the market, the level of safety provided by the original product cannot be judged solely by reference to improved safety features in the new product.

Defences

A number of specific defences are provided for by the Act. These are in addition to the obvious defences that the product was not defective or that it was not the cause of the plaintiff's loss. Thus it is a defence to show:

- that the defect was attributable to the defendant's compliance with a legal requirement; or
- that the defendant did not supply the goods to anyone.
  Where a finished product incorporates component products or raw materials, the supplier of the finished product will not be treated as a supplier of the component products or raw materials by reason only of his supply of the finished product. Thus, for example, a builder using high alumina cement could argue that he was not a supplier of that cement for the purposes of the Act. He could invoke this defence if the building subsequently deteriorated due to defects in the cement.
  The defendant can also escape liability if he can show that he had not supplied the goods in the course of his business and that he had not own branded, imported into the EEL, or produced the goods with a view to profit.
  This defence could be invoked, for example, in relation to the sale of home made jam at a coffee morning in aid of charity.
- the nature of the fourth defence depends upon whether the defendant is a producer, own brander or importer into the EC. If he is, he can escape liability by proving that the defect was not present in the product at the time he supplied it. If he is not, he must show that the defect was not present in the product at the time it was supplied by any person of that description.
- finally there is the 'development risks defence' that, given the state of scientific and technical knowledge at the time the product was put into circulation, no producer of a product of that kind could have been expected to have discovered the defect if it had existed in his products while they are under his control.

The development risks defence has provoked much discussion. Its adoption was optional under the terms of the directive. It is argued that the defence reduces the strictness of liability by introducing considerations which are more relevant to negligence. Its main impact will be seen in those areas which are at the forefront of scientific and technical development. The pharmaceutical industry, for example, could benefit from it in relation to the development of new drugs. It may seem ironic that if an event like the Thalidomide tragedy were to re-occur the victims could be prevented from recovering compensation because of the operation of this defence. The tragedy was in fact a major cause of pressure for the introduction of strict product liability laws throughout Europe.

- Where the defendant is a producer of a component product, he will have a defence if he can show that the defect in the finished product is wholly attributable to its design or to compliance with instructions given by the producer of the finished product.

Damage

Assuming the plaintiff succeeds in his claim, the question arises as to the types of loss he will be compensated for. Damages are recoverable for death or for personal injury. This includes any disease or other impairment of a person's physical or mental condition. The plaintiff will also be able to claim compensation for damage to his property.

However, exceptions to this provide significant limitations on liability under the Act. There is no liability for loss of or damage to:

- the product itself;
- any property in respect of which the amount of the claim would be below £275; or
- any commercial property – property of a type which is not ordinarily intended for private use, occupation or consumption and which is not actually intended by the plaintiff for his own private use, occupation or consumption.

Any of these excluded losses could be the subject of a claim in contract or negligence.

Administrative machinery of consumer protection

Both central and local government have important roles to play in the field of consumer protection. The major role of central government is the promotion and implementation of legislation, whilst the enforcement of this legislation is mainly the responsibility of local government.

The Role of Central Government in Consumer Protection

The consumer protection responsibilities of central government are spread across a number of departments, many of which have a junior minister with responsibility for consumer affairs.

The Home Office *has responsibility for liquor licensing, dangerous drugs and poisons; as well as explosives and firearms.* The Department of Trade's *responsibilities in the field of consumer protection include weights and measures, consumer credit, fair trading, consumer safety, trading standards, and monopolies, mergers and restrictive practices. The Department is also responsible for a number of national consumer protection bodies, including:*

- the Office of Fair Trading;
- the Monopolies and Mergers Commission;
- the British Hallmarking Council;
- the National Consumer Council;
- the Consumer Protection Advisory Committee;

- the Nationalised Industry Consumer Councils; and
- the British Standards Institution.

The Ministry of Agriculture looks after food and drugs, food additives, pesticides, and public health standards in slaughterhouses. The Food Safety Directorate created in 1989, has specific responsibility for food safety matters.

The Office of Fair Trading

The Office of Fair Trading, created by the Fair Trading Act 1973, has a significant national role in relation to the broad task of protecting the interests of the consumer. The 1973 Act created the post of Director General of Fair Trading. The Director has wide powers under the 1973 Act and other legislation, notably the Consumer Credit Act 1974 and the Estate Agents Act 1979.

The duties of the Director are:

- to review commercial activities and report to the Secretary of State;
- to refer adverse trade practices to the Consumer Protection Advisory Committee;
- to take action against traders who are persistently unfair to consumers;
- to supervise the enforcement of the Consumer Credit Act 1974 and the administration of the licensing system under that Act;
- to arrange for information and advice to be published for the benefit of consumers in relation to the supply of goods and services and consumer credit;
- to encourage trade associations to produce voluntary Codes of Practice; and
- to superintend the working and enforcement of the Estate Agents Act 1979.

Review of commercial practices

Under this general heading the Director has three functions:

- to keep under review commercial activities in the UK relating to the supply of goods and services to consumers; and to collect information about these activities in order to become aware of practices which may adversely affect the *economic interests* of consumers;
- to receive and collect evidence of commercial activities which he thinks are adversely affecting the *general interests* of consumers, for example on economic, health or safety grounds;
- to supply information relating to adverse trade practices to the Secretary of State and make recommendations as to any action which the Director considers necessary to combat them.

Referral of adverse trade practices to the Consumer Protection Advisory Committee

The Director has power to refer to the Consumer Protection Advisory Committee any consumer trade practice which in his opinion adversely affects the economic interests of consumers. The type of activity which can give rise to such a reference include trade practices relating to:

- the terms or conditions on which goods or services are supplied;
- the manner in which those terms or conditions are communicated to the consumer;
- promotion of goods or services by advertising, labelling or marking of goods, or canvassing;
- methods of salesmanship employed in dealing with consumers;

- the way in which goods are packed; or
- methods of demanding or securing payments for goods or services supplied.

A reference by the Director may include proposals for the creation of delegated legislation by the Secretary of State. The Director has power to make such proposals where he considers that a consumer trade practice is likely to have any one of the following effects:

- misleading consumers as to their rights and obligations under the transactions; or
- withholding adequate information on the rights and obligations of consumers; or
- subjecting consumers to undue pressure to enter into transactions; or
- causing the terms of the consumer transactions in question to be so adverse as to be oppressive.

The Consumer Protection Advisory Committee must report to the Secretary of State, usually within three months, indicating whether it agrees with the Director's proposals as they stand, or in a modified form. If so the Secretary of State may make regulations giving effect to the proposals. It is a criminal offence to contravene any such regulations.

An examples of such a regulation is the Mail Order Transactions (Information) Order 1976, which applies to goods sold by mail order which have to be paid for in advance. Under the regulations, any advertisement for such goods must state the true name or company name of the person carrying on the mail order business, as well as the true address of the business. Thus, for example, an advertiser giving only a P.O. Box number would be committing an offence if he required payment in advance.

The Director has power to bring proceedings in the Restrictive Practices Court against any person who persistently maintains a course of conduct which is unfair to consumers. Before making a reference to the Court, the Director must first attempt to obtain a written assurance from the trader that he will refrain from the unfair trade practice. If the trader refuses to give an assurance, or breaks an assurance once it has been given, the Director must apply for an order restraining the continuance of the unfair conduct. If the trader does not comply with the order, he will be in contempt of court and liable to imprisonment.

A course of conduct will be regarded as being unfair to consumers if it involves a breach of any legal obligations, either criminal or civil, by the trader. Examples of unfair conduct include persistently giving short measure or applying false trade descriptions, or repeatedly delivering unmerchantable goods.

The Director has a duty to encourage trade associations and other organisations to prepare Codes of Practice and circulate them to their members. The codes should be designed to give guidance to traders relating to the safeguarding and protection of the interests of consumers.

A code of practice is a statement by a trade association which aims to establish and define the standards of trading which it expects from its members. Voluntary codes of this type have been introduced, following consultation with the Office of Fair Trading, to cover many areas of business. Such codes often provide a mechanism for the arbitration of consumer complaints as an alternative to legal proceedings in the courts.

Codes of practice provide a means whereby, in effect, a sector of industry or commerce can regulate itself.

The role of local authorities in consumer protection

Responsibility for the enforcement of most consumer protection legislation, other than that which gives the consumer a right to sue for damages, rests with local authorities. It is carried out by trading standards or consumer protection departments. In practice, these departments see their major role as one of giving guidance to traders. This is done by a combination of education and persuasion. Prosecution for criminal offences is seen as a last resort when other measures fail.

Another important aspect of the work of these departments is the verification of weights and measuring apparatus, and the analysis of samples. They also act as a channel of information from members of the public to the Office of Fair Trading about unfair trade practices.

Trading standards officers have wide investigatory powers to enable them to carry out their enforcement functions effectively. They can make sample purchases of goods or services; enter premises; require suppliers to produce documents; carry out tests on equipment; and seize and detain property. A person who obstructs a trading standards officer, or makes a false statements to him commits a criminal offence.

Many Acts of Parliament and regulations made under them are enforced by trading standards officers. They include the *Consumer Credit Act* 1974, the *Food Safety Act* 1990, parts of the *Road Traffic Act* 1988, the *Trade Descriptions Act* 1968, the *Weights and Measures Act* 1985, the *Unsolicited Goods and Services Act* 1971, and the *Consumer Protection Act* 1987.

Most, but not all, of the criminal offences designed to protect the consumer apply only to persons supplying goods or services in the course of a trade or business. Enforcement of the criminal law in this area is, as we have seen, primarily the function of trading standards departments. Traders who are charged with criminal offences will be prosecuted in the Magistrates or the Crown Court. If convicted, they will be liable to a fine or, in some cases, imprisonment. Following a conviction the criminal courts also have power to make a 'compensation order' to the victim of the crime. In this context the victim will be the consumer who has suffered loss as a result of the offence.

The power to make a compensation order is contained in s.35 of the Powers of Criminal Courts Act 1973. This provides that any court convicting a person of an offence may, in addition to its sentencing power, make an order requiring the offender to pay compensation for any personal injury, loss or damage resulting from the offence or any other offence taken into consideration.

In deciding whether to make an order the court must take account of the ability of the defendant to pay. There is a limit of £1,000 compensation for each offence of which the accused is convicted. Under the Criminal Justice Act 1982 the power to make compensation orders was extended. They may now be made "instead of or in addition to" a fine.

The power to make compensation orders is particularly useful from the point of view of the consumer. It saves him the trouble and expense of bringing proceedings in the civil courts. It will be used only in relatively straightforward cases, however. It is not designed to deal for example with complicated claims.

The Food Safety Act 1990

The Food Safety Act 1990 is designed to strengthen consumer protection in relation to food safety, an area of increasing concern in recent years. The Act consolidates existing provision in this areas, adds a number of new regulatory powers and substantially increases the penalties for offences relating to the quality and safety of foods.

It is an offence to process or treat food intended for sale for human consumption in any way which makes it injurious to health. Food is injurious to health if it causes any permanent or temporary impairment of health. The offence can be committed by food manufacturers, food handlers, retailers or restaurants. The offence may be committed, for example, by adding a harmful ingredient, or subjecting food to harmful treatment such as storing it at an incorrect temperature or storing cooked meat alongside uncooked meat.

Under the Act, food intended for human consumption must satisfy the *food safety requirement*. It is an offence to sell, offer or have in one's possession for sale, prepare or deposit with another for sale any food which fails to meet this requirement. Food which is injurious to health, unfit for human consumption, or so contaminated that it is not reasonable to expect it to be eaten, will fail to satisfy the food safety requirement.

In *David Greig Ltd. v. Goldfinch* 1961 a trader was convicted of selling food which was unfit for human consumption (under an equivalent provision in the *Food and Drugs Act* 1955). He sold a pork pie which had small patches of mould under the crust. The fact that the mould was of a type which was not harmful to human beings was held to be no defence to the charge.

It is also an offence to sell any food which is not of the nature, substance or quality demanded.

In *Smedleys Ltd. v. Breed* 1974 a customer was supplied with a tin of peas which contained a small green caterpillar. The caterpillar had been sterilised in the defendants' processes and did not constitute a danger to health. The defendants had an extremely efficient system for eliminating foreign bodies from their products. They were found to have taken all reasonable care to avoid the presence of the caterpillar in the tin. Nevertheless, their conviction for supplying food which was not of the substance demanded was upheld by the House of Lords.

The Weights and Measures Act 1985

The 1985 Act provides for the inspection and testing of weighing and measuring equipment for use in trade. Under the Act it is an offence to use for trade, or to have in one's possession for use in trade, any weighing or measuring equipment which is false or unjust. It is also an offence to give short weight or short measure.

The Act restricts the units of measurement which can lawfully be used by a trader. It lays down detailed requirements as to the packing, marking and making up of certain types of goods; and provides that, in relation to pre-packed or containerised goods, a written statement must be marked on the container giving information about the net quantity of its contents.

Consumer Credit Act 1974

The Consumer Credit Act 1974 contains a list of over thirty five criminal offences associated with contravention of the Act. These include, for example, trading without a licence; failure to supply copies of consumer credit agreements; refusal of a trader to give the name of a credit reference agency which he has consulted; failure by a credit reference agency to correct information on its files; and obstruction of enforcement authority officers.

Road Traffic Act 1988

The Road Traffic Acts, and regulations made under them, contain a large number of criminal offences relating to the construction and use of motor vehicles and the safe loading of vehicles. Under the 1988 Act it is an offence for any person, whether or not he is a trader, to sell or supply a motor vehicle which is unroadworthy. This offence will be committed where, for example, a vehicle is sold with defects in its braking or steering system or in its tyres. It is also an offence to fit defective or unsuitable parts to a motor vehicle; and to sell a motor cycle crash helmet which does not comply with safety regulations.

The Unsolicited Goods and Services Act 1971

This Act was passed to impose criminal and civil liability on traders carrying on the practice of *inertia selling*. This involves sending goods or providing services which have not been ordered and demanding payment or threatening legal action if payment is not made. The Act provides that unsolicited goods or services need not to be paid for, and unordered goods may be retained by the recipient if they are not collected by the sender within six months of delivery. It is an offence for the sender to demand payment for unsolicited goods or services.

Trade descriptions legislation

We have previously examined the circumstances in which a person would be regarded as transacting in the course of a trade or business. An important application of this question arises in relation to criminal liability under the Trade Descriptions Act 1968 for false statements made in business transactions. There can be no liability under the 1968 Act unless the person applying the false description does so within the course of a trade or business rather than a private sale. This is one reason why the Business Advertisements (Disclosure) Order 1977 requires a trader to identify himself as such when he advertises in the classified advertisements in newspapers. The fact that a business organisation is the vendor or purchaser does not automatically mean that a sale is in the course of a trade. The transaction must be of a type that is a regular occurrence in that particular business, so that a sale of business assets would not normally qualify as a sale in the course of a trade or business.

Where there is a genuine private sale and, for example, the seller falsely describes the goods, the buyer's remedy will be rescission. He may also claim damages in a civil law action for misrepresentation or breach of the term implied into the contract by the Sale of Goods Act 1979. A buyer from a business seller can also exercise these remedies, but in addition may report the trader to the trading standards department with a view to a prosecution for a breach of the criminal law under the 1968 Act. In all trade descriptions cases there is potentially liability under the civil law which illustrates the fact that here consumer protection law is founded upon the interrelationship between civil and criminal activities. Prosecutions for trade description offences are brought in the Magistrates Court and exceptionally in the Crown Court with the possibility of an appeal to the Divisional Court of the Queen's Bench Division of the High Court by way of case-stated on a point of law. There is no requirement for a re-hearing of the evidence, rather the appeal court is concerned with determining the validity of the legal reasoning upon which the decision to convict or acquit is based.

Two principal offences under the *Trade Descriptions Act* 1968 relate to false description of goods, and making misleading statements about services. A number of defences are also provided for. Further offences of giving misleading price indications are contained in Part III of the Consumer Protection Act 1987.

False description of goods

The 1968 Act provides that *"any person who, in the course of a trade or business:*

- *applies a false trade description to any goods; or*
- *supplies or offers to supply any goods to which a false trade description is applied;*

shall be guilty of an offence".

Two different types of conduct will amount to offences under this section. The first is where the trader himself applies the false trade description. This offence could be committed, for example, by a trader who turns back the mileometer of a car to make it appear that the car has not travelled as many miles as it actually has. The second involves supplying or offering to supply goods to which a false trade description has been applied by another person, for example where a retailer sells a garment to which the label "pure new wool" has been attached by the manufacturer, where the garment is partly composed of man-made fibres. There is a strict duty therefore not to pass on false trade descriptions applied by another subject to a defence which we will consider later.

A false trade description may be applied verbally or in writing, for example in a label on goods or in an advertisement, communicated by pictorial representation or even by conduct.

> In *Yugotours Ltd. v. Wadsley* 1988 a photograph of a three-masted schooner and the words
> "the excitement of being under full sail on board this majestic schooner" in a tour operator's

brochure was held to constitute a statement for the purpose of the Act. By providing customers who had booked a holiday relying on the brochure with only a two masted schooner without sails the tour operator was guilty of recklessly making a false statement contrary to the Trade Descriptions Act.

The meaning of the term "trade description" extends to statements relating to quantity, size, composition, method of manufacture, fitness for purpose, place or date of manufacture, approval by any person or other history including previous ownership of goods.

In *Sherratt v. Geralds The American Jewellers Ltd.* 1970 the defendant sold a watch described by the maker as a diver's watch and inscribed with the word "waterproof". The watch filled with water and stopped after it had been immersed in water. It was held that the defendant was guilty of an offence.

To constitute an offence under the Act the trade description must be false or misleading to a material degree.

In *Robertson v. Dicicco* 1972 a second-hand motor vehicle was advertised for sale by a dealer and described as "a beautiful car". The car, although having a visually pleasing exterior was unroadworthy and not fit for use. The defendant was charged with an offence but he argued that his statement was true as he had intended it to refer only to the visual appearance of the vehicle. It was held that he was guilty because the description was false to a material degree. A reasonable person would have taken the statement to refer to the mechanics of the car as well as its external appearance.

A trade description applied to goods for sale can be false even when it is scientifically correct if it is likely to mislead a customer without specialist knowledge.

In *Dixon Ltd. v. Barnett* 1989 a customer was supplied with an Astral 500 telescope which was described as being capable of up to "455 x magnification". The evidence showed that the maximum useful magnification was only 120 times, although scientifically 455 times magnification could be achieved. The Divisional Court held that the store was nevertheless guilty of an offence despite the fact that the statement was scientifically sound. An ordinary customer would have been misled by the statement because he would be interested in the maximum useful magnification rather than a blurred image produced at 455 times magnification.

The Divisional Court in *Denard v. Smith and another* 1990 considered whether it is a false trade description to advertise goods in a shop at the point of sale as items offered for sale when they are temporarily out of stock and are not immediately available. The court held that unless customers are informed of the non-availability of the goods at the time of purchase the advertisement constituted a false trade description of offering to supply goods.

An offence under s.1 may be committed by *"any person"*. This is not limited to the seller, but may include the buyer, particularly where he is an expert in relation to the subject matter of the contract.

In *Fletcher v. Budgen* 1974 a car dealer bought an old car from a customer for £2 saying that it was only fit to be scrapped. In fact the dealer repaired the car and advertised it for a resale for £135. It was held that he was guilty of an offence because he applied a false trade description to the car when he bought it in the course of his business.

False statements relating to the provision of services, accommodation or facilities

Suppliers of services, such as holiday tour operators, hairdressers and dry-cleaners will be liable to prosecution under the *Trade Descriptions Act* 1968 if they make false statements knowingly or recklessly in the course of their business:

"It shall be an offence for any person in the course of any trade or business:

- *to make a statements which he knows to be false; or*
- *recklessly to make a statement which is false;as to any of the following matters:*
  - *the provision ... of any services, accommodation or facilities;*
  - *the nature of any services, accommodation or facilities*
  - *the time at which, the manner in which or persons by whom any services, accommodation or facilities are provided;*
  - *the examination, approval or evaluation by any person of any services, accommodation or facilities; or*
  - *the location or amenities of any accommodation."*

In order to obtain a conviction the prosecution must show mens rea, (guilty mind) either that the trader knew that the statement was false, or that he was reckless as to its truth or falsity. A statement is made recklessly if it is made regardless of whether it is true or false. It need not necessarily be dishonest. The knowledge or recklessness must be present at the time the statement is made.

In *Sunair Holidays Ltd. v. Dodd* 1970 the defendant's travel brochure described a package holiday in a hotel with "all twin bedded rooms with bath, shower and terrace". The defendant had a contract with the hotel owners under which they were obliged to provide accommodation of that description. A customer who booked the package was given a room without a terrace. The defendant had not checked with the hotel to make sure that its customers were given the correct accommodation of that description. It was held that the statement was not false when it was made, and therefore the defendant was not guilty of an offence.

It must be shown that the trader, at the time the statement is made, either knows that it is false or is reckless as to its truth or falsity; and that the statement actually *is* false. Subsequent developments are irrelevant if these elements are present at the time the statement is made.

In *Cowburn v. Focus Television Rentals Ltd.* 1983 the defendant's advertisement stated: "Hire twenty feature films absolutely free when you rent a video recorder". In response to the advertisement a customer rented a video recorder. The documentation supplied with it indicated that he was entitled only to six films, and that they were not absolutely free because he had to pay postage and packing. When he complained, the defendant refunded his postage and packing and supplied twenty free films to him. It was held that the defendant was guilty of an offence because the statement in his advertisement was false and recklessly made. The fact that he subsequently honoured the advertisement provided no defence, as this was done after the offence had been committed.

Conduct of the defendant subsequent to the false statement is relevant however to determine whether an inference of recklessness can be maintained.

In *Yugotours Ltd. v. Wadsley* 1988 (mentioned previously) the fact that statements in a holiday brochure and accompanying letter were clearly false and known to be so by the company meant that when the company failed to correct the statement. The court stated that there was sufficient material before the court to infer recklessness on the part of the maker of the statement. *"If a statement is false and known to be false, and nothing whatever is done to correct it, then the company making the statement can properly be found guilty of recklessness notwithstanding the absence of specific evidence of recklessness".*

In *Wings Ltd. v. Ellis* 1984 the false nature of a statement in their travel brochure was not known by a tour operator when its brochure was published. Some 250,000 copies of the brochure contained an inaccurate statement that rooms in a hotel in Sri Lanka were air conditioned. The brochure also contained a photograph purporting to be a room in the same hotel which was of a room in a different hotel. When the mistake was discovered, reasonable steps were taken to remedy it by informing agents and customers who had already booked by letter. Despite this, a holiday was booked by a customer on the basis of the false information. It was held by the House of Lords that the tour operator was guilty of an offence under s.14 because the statement was made when the brochure was read by the customer, and at the time the defendant knew that it was false. The fact that the tour operator was unaware that the uncorrected statement was being made to the customer did not prevent the offence being committed.

For corporate liability the prosecution must establish that a high ranking official of the company had the necessary mens rea. The Chairman of a company would certainly suffice but not the "Contracts Manager" in *Wings Ltd. v. Ellis* who had approved the photograph of the hotel which gave a wrong impression.

Defences Under the Trade Descriptions Act 1968

It is a defence to any charge under the 1968 Act that the defendant innocently published a misleading advertisement received by him for publication in the ordinary course of his business.

A number of separate defences are contained in the Act. These are available to a defendant who can prove:

1. *"That the commission of the offence was due to a mistake or to reliance on information supplied to him or to the act or default of another person, an accident, or some other cause beyond his control; and*

2. *that he took all reasonable precautions and exercised all due diligence to avoid the commission of such an offence by himself or any person under his control".*

In order to have an effective defence, the onus is on the defendant to prove any one of the reasons listed in paragraph (1) above and all of the elements in (2). He must also supply to the prosecution, at least 7 days before the hearing, a written notice giving such information as he has to enable the other person to be identified.

In *Baxters (Butchers) v. Manley* 1985 the defendant was accused of offences under the 1968 Act in relation to the pricing and weight of meat exposed for sale in his butcher's shop. He claimed that the offences were due to the act or default of the shop manager. This claim was accepted by the court, but the defence failed because he was unable to prove that he had taken reasonable precautions to avoid the commission of the offence by his manager. In particular he had failed to give the manager any detailed instructions or guidelines on the requirements of the Act; there was no staff training; and the standard of supervision by a district manager was inadequate.

To establish that he took all reasonable precautions and exercised all due diligence the defendant needs to show that he has an effective system of operation. A court should also bear in mind the size and resources of the organisation in determining the steps you would expect a reasonable business to take.

In relation to enforcement of the 1968 Act, as we have seen, wide investigatory powers are conferred on local authority trading standards officers. Before a prosecution is brought, however, the local authority is required to inform the Department of Trade. This is to prevent numerous unnecessary prosecutions for the same false trade description.

The legality of bringing a second prosecution where there are a number of complaints in relation to the same false statement was at issue in *R. v. Thomson Holidays Limited* 1973. In this case a misleading statement in a travel brochure constituted an offence. The Court of Appeal held that a separate offence was committed every time someone read the brochure, and that it was not necessarily improper to bring more than one prosecution in these circumstances.

Misleading price indications

The offence of giving a misleading price indication is contained in the 1987 Act, which provides:

"A person shall be guilty of an offence if, in the course of any business of his, he gives (by any means whatever) to any consumers an indication which is misleading as to the price at which any goods, services, accommodation or facilities are available".

The types of statements which would be caught by s.20 include:

- false comparisons with recommended prices, for example a false claim that goods are £20 less than the recommended price; or

- indications that the price is less than the real price, for example where hidden extras are added to an advertised price; or

- false comparisons with a previous price, for example a false statement that goods were £50 and are now £30; or

- where the stated method of determining the price is different to the method actually used.

In *Richards v. Westminster Motors Ltd..* 1975 the defendant advertised a commercial vehicle for sale at a price of £1,350. When the buyer purchased the vehicle he was required to pay the asking price plus VAT, which made a total price of £1,534. It was held that the defendant was guilty of giving a misleading indication as to the price at which he was prepared to sell goods.

In *Read Bros. Cycles (Leyton) v. Waltham Forest London Borough* 1978 the defendant advertised a motor cycle for sale at a reduced price of £540, £40 below the list price. A customer agreed to purchase the motor cycle and negotiated a £90 part exchange allowance on his old vehicle. The defendant charged him the full list price for the new cycle, and stated that the reduced price did not apply where goods were given in part exchange. It was held that the defendant was guilty of giving a misleading price indication.

Consumer Safety

Part II of the *Consumer Protection Act* 1987 consolidates, with amendments, previous legislation on consumer safety including the Consumer Safety Act 1978 and the Consumer Safety (Amendment) Act 1986.

The 1987 Act creates a new offence, of supplying consumer goods which are not reasonably safe. An offence is also committed by offering or agreeing to supply unsafe goods or exposing or possessing them for supply.

In deciding whether goods are reasonably safe, the court must examine all the circumstances, including:

- the way in which the goods are marketed;

- the use of any mark, for example indicating compliance with safety standards;
- instructions or warnings as to the use of the goods;
- whether the goods comply with relevant published safety standards;
- whether there is a way in which the goods could reasonably have been made safer.

The offence can be committed only in relation to consumer goods. Consumer goods are goods which are ordinarily intended for private use or consumption, with the exception of food, water, gas, motor vehicles, medical products and tobacco.

The Secretary of State has power to make regulations for the purpose of ensuring that goods of any particular type are safe. Safety regulations can cover the design, composition or finish of goods; and ensure that appropriate information is given in relation to them. They may also restrict the distribution of particular types of goods or prohibit their supply or exposure for supply.

A considerable number of regulations, made under previous legislation, are still in force. These relate for example to aerosols, babies' dummies, balloons, cosmetics, electrical goods, night-dresses, toys and many other types of product. Breach of safety regulations is an offence under the 1987 Act.

Under the Act any person who suffers injury or loss as a result of a breach of safety regulations has the right to sue the trader for damages for breach of statutory duty. This right cannot be restricted or excluded by any term or notice in any contract.

The Secretary of State also has a number of other powers under the 1987 Act. He may, for example, serve a 'prohibition notice' on a trader requiring him to stop trading in unsafe goods of a particular description. Alternatively, where a trader has distributed goods which are unsafe, the Secretary of State may serve on him a 'notice to warn'. This requires the trader, at his own expense, to publish warnings about the unsafe goods to persons to whom they have been supplied.

Power is also given to local authorities under the Act, to serve a 'suspension notice' on any trader. This in effect freezes the goods in the hands of the trader for up to six months. The power to serve a suspension notice arises if the authority has reasonable grounds for suspecting that goods are not reasonably safe, or are in breach of safety regulations. A trader who fails to comply with a suspension notice is guilty of a criminal offence.

A Magistrates Court has power to order the forfeiture of goods where there has been a contravention of the safety provisions of the 1987 Act. Where goods are forfeit they must either be destroyed, or released for the purposes of being repaired, reconditioned or scrapped.

Activity

Monitor the use of local and national advertising of products and services on radio, television and in newspapers and similar publications. Fix a period to carry out this task of say, 2 weeks. Concentrate particularly on special offers and special deals which are available. Watch how far the advertising you have examined satisfies the requirements of trade descriptions legislation. See if you can obtain from your local authority's consumer protection department any information it makes available to the public on consumer protection, and the details it publishers on its role in the enforcement of consumer protection laws.

Activity

Obtain a copy of a standard form contract used by a business locally or nationally. A useful source of such a contract is the booking form found at the back of tour operators brochures.

Analyse the contract in the light of the consumer legislation you have been examining to see if you can identify terms in the contact which are designed to meet the obligations used in law by the business and the consumer. Is the contract a fair one to both sides, or is it too one-sided?

Provision

The government provides many services and products which it believes the market system cannot adequately supply. We have already discussed the necessity for the State to provide public goods such as law enforcement and defence. Earlier we also examined the more controversial area of merit goods where the government provides a health and education system which could be market supplied but which the government believes would be in such cases inadequately or insufficiently provided. In this country we also have State provision of some goods and services which are produced by state-owned organisations and sold to the general public through the market mechanism. This is sometimes referred to as *public enterprise* and we shall now briefly examine the sector of the State's operation which falls under this heading.

The scope of public enterprise

There is considerable debate as to which aspects of the State's activities should be included under the heading 'public enterprise'. The relevant organisations are often referred to as public corporations or nationalised industries, but using such titles can be somewhat misleading. Even the Government itself has found difficulty in defining what it regards as a nationalised industry. For instance, one official definition used in a National Economic Development Office Report (NEDO) in 1976 included under this heading only those public corporations operating in the market economy. It therefore omitted public corporations such as the BBC, which does not charge for its service but gains revenue from the government who in turn raise it indirectly through the licence fee system. Earlier, in 1968, a House of Commons Select Committee had defined nationalised industries as having three characteristics which set them apart from other aspects of the government's activities. These were:

- that the industries were wholly owned by the State or sufficiently owned by the State to be controlled by it;
- that the industries operated in such a way that the majority of revenue came from sources other than from direct Parliamentary or Treasury subsidy;
- that they are run by Boards of Directors appointed by the appropriate Minister of State

By this definition, the major industries included in such a category would be such organisations as British Coal, British Rail and the Post Office. Some of these industries, either in their entirety or in part, are regarded by a Conservative government as strong candidates for denationalisation.

There are also a number of other miscellaneous public corporations which do not fall under the definition of a nationalised industry previously cited. Among the most important of these is the Bank of England, which reports directly to the Treasury. The British Broadcasting Corporation and the Scottish and Welsh Development Agencies are also government-controlled bodies but are financed directly from the central Exchequer.

Activity

You have been in the education system at least since the age of five. Identify the different ways in which the State has used finance, legislation/regulation and provision to influence your education.

Government Economic Control

As we have seen in the previous section the UK economy is made up of hundreds of thousands of business organisations producing goods and services for millions of consumers both at home and abroad. Each of these business seeks to prosper and make profits. They make their own decisions about what to produce, how to produce it and how much to sell it for. If the people managing these businesses are shrewd and are able to recognise their consumers needs and are able to meet these needs efficiently then in theory, at least, they should be successful. However, economies do not work as simply as this. Consider these two alternative sets of circumstances.

- in the first, imagine that many of these businesses simultaneously decide that demand for their products is likely to fall. They begin to lose confidence that they can increase or even maintain their current level of sales. As individual businesses they must take what appears to be the most appropriate steps to secure their survival in the future. They may cut back on production, lay off workers and defer investment plans. Of course if many businesses do this at the same time they actually create the fall in demand that they had all feared. Their decision to make workers redundant will cut consumer purchasing power and their lack of investment will feed through into other industries such as construction or machine tool engineering which will consequently also make workers redundant, further adding to the fall in demand;

- in the second situation imagine that many businesses anticipate an upturn in demand for their products. They try to hire more workers, buy new plant or build new factories. This is fine except if this increased demand for labour, plant or land is widespread it could lead to increases in the cost of these resources which the businesses may then pass onto consumers in the form of higher retail prices.

What we have just described are two extremes in a totally free market economy. In the first, a lack of confidence among producers has resulted in an increase in unemployment, a decline in investment and a fall in demand for goods and services. This has led to a *recession*, or even worse to a *slump*.

In the second, collective over-confidence in the business community has resulted in increased competition for resources, so pushing up their cost which then feeds through into higher retail prices. This has led the economy to become 'over-heated' and the *boom* has led to inflation.

These are two extremes of what can be described as the *business cycle* in which the economy lurches from slump to boom and back again, triggered by changes in business confidence. If it is allowed to happen it can produce tremendous fluctuations in employment and price levels causing considerable economic and social upheaval.

In fact what we have just described does happen and has happened ever since the industrial revolution (before that booms and slumps were more likely to be the result of good or bad harvests rather than business confidence). The most dramatic example of a boom-slump cycle occurred in the 1920s and 1930s when the world's economy expanded dramatically for a number of years in the 1920s only to collapse into a terrible depression in the 1930s.

It became clear to many economists that left to its own devices the economy would continue to swing through this cycle and so from the 1930s, first in America and later in this country, we saw governments taking a much more positive role in controlling and influencing the economy. They began to try and create a business environment conducive to steady economic growth. They attempted to boost both business confidence and the economy as a whole when the economy was in the downside of the cycle and conversely to dampen economic activity and take the heat out of the economy when it was likely to over-inflate. Such government action is known as *counter-cyclical policy*. It means that the government must judge the economic activity of the economy and the stage in the business cycle at which it is at and stimulate it when it is in a slump and deflate it when it is in a boom.

When you consider the progress of the UK economy in the last thirty years with its 1970s boom, early 80s recession, middle 80s boom and late 80s and early 90s slump you may say that the government has not done much of a job. Nevertheless it has been trying. What we will consider in this section is what the government has been attempting to achieve, the problems it has been facing and the methods it has used to solve these problems.

The Economic Objectives of British Governments

As we have already noted the depression of the 1930s plunged this country into an unparalleled economic crisis. Mass unemployment, social deprivation, bankruptcy and economic decline faced the British people while the government sat back and allowed market forces to take their course. Policies were haphazard and piecemeal with little attempt at overall management of the economy because:

- the causes of the depression were not fully understood; and
- the government did not have the policy instruments capable of rectifying them.

The setting of objectives

A major step forward in the understanding of the macro economic workings of the country came from the work of John Maynard Keynes, a Cambridge economist, who in 1936 published his famous book entitled "The General Theory of Employment, Interest and Money". From the beginning of the depression Keynes had been severely critical of the lack of government intervention to reduce the problem. In fact the governments of the time in this country made matters worse by reducing public expenditure on transfer payments and capital spending alike. Keynes made this point in 1931 when he argued:

> *"The Government's programme is as foolish as it is wrong ... Not only is purchasing power*
> *to be curtailed, but road building, housing and the like are to be retrenched. Local authorities are to follow suit. If the theory which underlines all this is to be accepted, the end will be that no one can be employed, except those happy few who grow their own potatoes, as a result of refusing, for reason of economy, to buy the services and anyone else.."*

By 1944 the Government was willing to publish the economic objectives which would be pursued by post-war governments. It committed itself to the role of managing the economy and ensuring that certain basic objectives were sought. It stated:

> *"The Government believe that, once the war has been won, we can make a fresh approach, with better chances of success than ever before, to the task of maintaining a high and stable level of employment without sacrificing the essential liberties of a free society."*
> *(Government White Paper on Employment Policy, 1944)*

This was to set the pattern of government economic objectives for the next thirty years. In essence successive governments adopted the following four major economic objectives from the mid-1940s until 1979:

- a high and stable level of employment;
- price stability;
- economic growth;
- a balance of payments equilibrium.

The conflict of objectives: the economic problems of the UK

A major problem facing successive governments was whether all four objectives could be met at the same time. For example, high levels of employment can increase the level of demand in the economy. It can also lead to rising wage rates as employers compete for staff by offering higher rates. Both higher levels of demand and higher wage rates can lead to rising inflation which may cause a fall in business confidence as business people are deterred by increasing costs. As their confidence in their future is weakened they are less likely to invest in new projects or re-invest in existing ones. This decline in investment results in consequent job losses. Similarly if the economy is growing it will usually mean a more prosperous population. In such circumstances this will often lead to a greater consumption of imported products causing a deficit in the balance of payments. Therefore it has been very difficult for governments to pursue all of these policies simultaneously. It was necessary, therefore, for governments to choose a combination of policy objectives which would be politically acceptable and economically viable.

In reality the conflict between these objectives proved to be less problematic than had been anticipated, at least in the relatively stable and prosperous 1950s and 1960s. It is true that, while these decades did not produce for the UK the spectacular economic growth experienced by Germany and Japan, production gradually increased and the effects of inflation and unemployment were not felt. The Balance of Payments did prove to be more of a recurrent problem but in a period of relatively low-priced energy and raw materials, the comparatively small trade deficits which occurred were but minor ripples on an otherwise tranquil economic sea.

The full impact of these problems was not felt until the late 1970s, when the objectives became much more difficult to attain and we will concentrate our analysis of the economic policy of the government on the period from 1979. What were the major problems facing the economy and what were their underlying causes?

Objective 1: A high and stable level of employment

The first objective was to create high and stable levels of employment. Since 1979, however, the UK has faced rapidly increasing unemployment. By the early 1980s levels of unemployment, unknown since the depression of the 1930s, were being experienced. More disturbing was the increase in long-term unemployment.

The late 1980s saw a decline in the number of unemployed, but numbers began to rise again in 1990. By 1993 unemployment had risen to almost 3 million and the rate of male unemployment was at a level higher than at any time since the great depression.

Let us now examine the causes of the unemployment which has hit the UK particularly hard. An examination of the unemployment figures for the last thirty years offers an opportunity to pin-point just when the dramatic rise began; it allows us also to isolate some of its causes. The figures below show this change:

Unemployment is shown as a percentage of the workforce: between 1955 and 1970 it remained between 1% and 2%. It would be wrong, however, to assume that recent governments have attempted to achieve a situation where 100% of the workforce is in employment: when the government states that it 'seeks to achieve full employment', it is describing a situation where there are more vacancies than there are people actively looking for work.

Of course, some of those who seek work will not always be able to find the exact job they want, at the wage they require, or in the area where they live. Thus, in the 1950s and 1960s, when this country was described as having full employment, there were areas in the country, such as Scotland, the North East of England and South Wales, where unemployment rates were above the national average. This is described as *regional unemployment*.

Unemployment is, in fact, often categorised according to its causes. There are six main categories:

- frictional or transitional unemployment;
- casual or seasonal unemployment;
- structural unemployment;
- technological unemployment;
- cyclical or demand-deficient unemployment;
- real-wage or classical unemployment.

Frictional unemployment

Temporary breaks from employment, lasting a comparatively short time, are known as *frictional unemployment* or *transitional unemployment*. It does not usually lead to the social problems associated with long-term unemployment. This assumes that there is an unfilled vacancy which the temporarily unemployed person will eventually fill. As long as the frictionally unemployed form only a small proportion of the workforce, the effects on overall productive output are minimal. In fact, the movement of workers to more efficient and rewarding jobs is often encouraged by government. Frictional unemployment is usually caused by some degree of immobility of labour. This means that people may find it difficult to move to another area for a job or may have to retrain following the loss of a job. The number of unfilled vacancies in the economy is a good guide to the level of frictional unemployment.

Seasonal unemployment

Some industries tend to operate seasonally and so those who work in such employment will find themselves temporarily unemployed in the 'off season'. Examples of seasonal unemployment are found in agriculture and the building industry. Some of the workers in these industries are sometimes referred to as casual workers. While seasonal unemployment is not a major problem in the UK, it does cause hardship for those whose jobs are seasonal or casual and in those areas of the country where industries are predominantly seasonal. The government has made some attempts to attract year-round industries to these areas and pays state benefits to workers who face seasonal layoffs. These policies have been

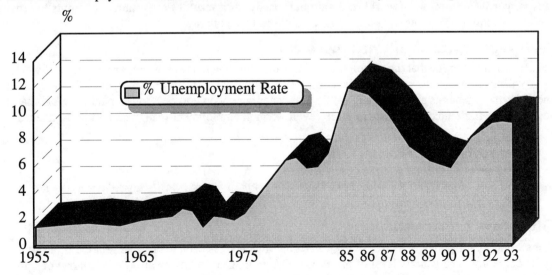

UK unemployment rate 1955 - 93

only partially successful. It should be noted that for these workers it is often not a case of 'this job instead of another job', but more 'this job instead of the dole'.

Structural unemployment

This is a long-term version of frictional unemployment: it exists mainly because of immobility in the labour market. This results from basic changes in the demand and supply for goods and services in the economy. For example, the textile industry has suffered widespread unemployment as a result of foreign competition from South East Asia.

Much regional unemployment can be explained by the decline in demand for the products of the basic industries which predominated in those areas, In areas such as Scotland, South Wales and the North East of England the decline of coal, steel and shipbuilding has been particularly marked. Such unemployment, resulting in deep structural changes in demand patterns, is often difficult to solve in the short-term, given the existing immobility of labour.

Technological Unemployment

Structural unemployment may result from supply changes; for instance, a reduction in the demand for a particular type of labour created by the introduction of robot machines. This is known as *technological unemployment*. Similarly, technological advances in the printing industry have meant that computer typesetting and compositing of newspapers is now perfectly feasible, a process which was bitterly resisted by the Fleet Street print and graphics unions. Technological unemployment will always occur in a dynamic economy but, often, attitudes to change are deeply influenced by the general level of unemployment in the economy.

Cyclical unemployment

The economy has always followed a cyclical pattern, alternating from boom to slump, with levels of unemployment reflecting this cyclical trend. This cyclical pattern in the post-1945 period has been less well defined.

Cyclical unemployment is the result of an overall lack of aggregate demand for goods and services in the economy. The business cycle has tended in the past to follow this fairly regular pattern. However, since the middle 1970s, the UK has been faced with continuous and growing large-scale unemployment. This is, partly, as a result of world recession but, partly, as a result of government attempts to reduce the level of inflation by lowering aggregate demand in the economy.

Real-wage or 'classical' unemployment

Some economists argue that the reason why there is unemployment is that wages are too high. If workers were willing to accept lower wages then employers would take on more employees. They argue that unemployment benefits should be cut as this will encourage people to take lower paid jobs and that the power of the trade unions to keep up wages even when unemployment is high should be weakened.

Activity

Find out what the unemployment rate is in your own area and suggest what are the main causes of this unemployment.

Objective 2: Price stability

The second major policy objective of post-war governments has been to achieve relative price stability in the economy. The general level of prices can change in either a downward (*deflationary*) or upward (*inflationary*) direction. Deflationary trends occurred in recent UK history when prices fell for much of the pre-war period, rising only after 1935. The post-war period, however, has been one of continuous inflation, as the table below shows.

UK Inflation Rates 1960-1992

Year	% Increase	Year	% Increase	Year	% Increase	Year	% Increase
1961	2.7	1969	5.2	1977	15.8	1985	6.1
1962	3.2	1970	6.4	1978	8.3	1986	3.4
1963	1.7	1971	9.4	1979	13.4	1987	4.2
1964	3.9	1972	7.1	1980	18.0	1988	4.9
1965	4.7	1973	9.2	1981	11.9	1989	7.5
1966	3.7	1974	16.1	1982	8.6	1990	7.7
1967	2.4	1975	24.2	1983	4.6	1991	9.0
1968	4.8	1976	16.5	1984	5.0	1992	3.6

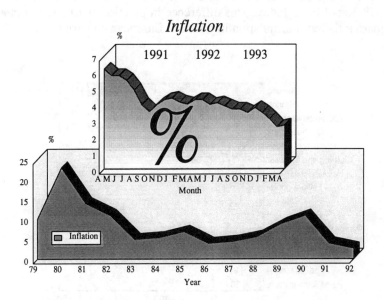

UK inflation rate 1979 - 93

What is inflation?

A simple definition of inflation is *'a rise in the level of prices that is sustained over a period of time'*. The definition tells us nothing about why inflation is regarded by business, government and nation as undesirable or even evil: it is because inflation makes goods and services more expensive for the business to provide, thereby making the business less competitive. Similarly, on a national scale, if the goods of 'UK plc' become more expensive in comparison to those of 'Japan Inc.' or 'Germany Ltd.', then UK exports become less attractive to consumers whatever country those consumers are in.

Inflation can also be seen as a fall in the value of money. A pound will buy less this year than it would last. This discourages people from holding money as the value is falling. Particularly hard hit are those on fixed incomes such as pensioners living on private or occupational pensions. As prices rises their pension stays the same and so they are able to buy less with the same pension.

How is it measured?

The rate of inflation in the UK is measured using the Retail Price Index (RPI) which is a monthly index that shows the annual percentage change in consumer prices. The index is made up of a 'basket' of goods and services, the prices of which are monitored on a monthly basis. The individual items which make up the 'basket' do not, however, have an equal weighting in the index: in the UK food has a weighting of 13% whilst fuel and light has a weighting of 4.7%. (The weightings of each category of goods and services is shown in the figure below Each item has a figure after it and these are weights in parts of 1,000, so Housing has a weighting of 170 out of 1,000 - or 17%.) This results in an increase in food prices exerting a greater effect on the RPI than the same percentage increase in the price of recreation and education. The weightings signify the importance of each of the items in the average monthly family budget. The following diagram shows how the retail price index is made up.

Our partners in the EC have different life-styles and preferences, and so use different weightings to those used in the UK Retail Price Index. This difference in practice gives rise to potential difficulties in accurately comparing the rates of inflation in different European countries.

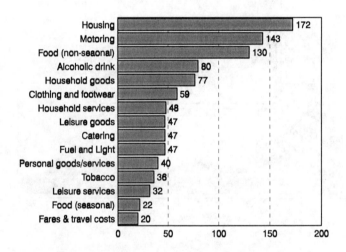

The make-up of the Retail Price Index

Why it's not wanted ...

Inflation is unwelcome for the following reasons:

- people on fixed incomes (e.g. pensioners) suffer: the amount of money they have is fixed, whilst prices are rising continuously;
- lenders lose; borrowers gain;
- speculative investment in property and commodities becomes more attractive than investment in industry;
- international trade competitiveness is reduced, unless there is a devaluation in the currency, since exports become relatively more expensive and imports become relatively cheaper.

How high is it?

The rate of inflation can vary enormously, from zero (which is rare), to a small part of a percentage point ('creeping inflation'), to rises in tens or hundreds of percent ('hyperinflation', as in Germany in the 1930s or some Eastern European and South American countries today). An indication of inflation can be gained by looking at *The United Kingdom in Figures*, a collection of statistics published by the Government Statistical Office. A glance at the table, 'Internal Purchasing Power of the Pound', will show you that what you would pay £1 to buy in 1990, could have been bought for 2p in 1914, 10p in 1960, 53p in 1980 and 91p in 1989. The highest measured rate of inflation that has occurred in the UK was 26.9% in 1974-5 which, though unacceptably high, compares very favourably with the world's highest recorded rate of (hyper)inflation: in Germany in 1923 inflation reached 755%.

The 1960s were successful years in achieving relative price stability. Only from the late 1960s did the pace of inflation quicken, reaching a peak of nearly 27% in August 1975. Since then, the trend has varied upwards and then downwards again to its present level of around 4.0%. Currently, the trend is downward: inflation fell from 9% in January 1991 to 4.1% by the following January. Inflation has been a world-wide problem in the post-war period and its causes are difficult to identify. Currently, the UK is improving its inflationary tendency relative to some of its major competitors, like Germany, though it must improve its performance even further to match low-inflation competitors like Japan.

UK Inflation compared to its trading rivals: 1991
Year on Year Increase %

Italy	6.0
EC average	4.9
UK	4.5
Germany	4.2
US	3.1
France	3.1
Japan	2.9

What causes it?

There are three basic theories relating to the causes of inflation:

- demand-pull inflation;
- cost-push inflation;
- monetary causes of inflation.

There are other explanations, including that of the monetarists who place the cause of inflation in a much wider social and economic context.

Demand-pull inflation

One view of inflation is that changes in the price level are linked to changes in aggregate demand and supply. By *aggregate demand* is meant the total demand for goods and services. *Aggregate supply* is simply the total supply of such goods and services.

Keynes was concerned with situations where a very low level of aggregate demand resulted in massive cyclical unemployment. As aggregate demand expanded, producers responded by increasing their production of goods and services, thereby increasing aggregate supply and reducing the level of unemployment. The general level of prices remained unchanged as output increased. However, as the economy approaches its full employment level it becomes increasingly difficult for output (*aggregate supply*) to continue to expand smoothly in response to increases in aggregate demand. As demand begins to outstrip supply producers have two options. They can increase the amount they produce by hiring new staff and investing in new plant or they can take advantage of the increasing demand by putting up their prices and earning higher profits.

The mechanism by which excess demand results in prices being increased can be briefly illustrated as follows:

If overall aggregate demand exceeds aggregate supply in the economy, this may be seen in a number of ways for instance unemployment is low; numerous job vacancies exist; overtime is offered and worked by employees; shortages of goods exist.

These conditions will affect producers in two ways:

- some raise their prices as high as the market will bear;
- there will be a vigorous demand for labour which enables the trade unions to press for, and obtain, higher wages for their members. Employers concede these increases, which are then passed on to consumers in higher prices.

Prices then begin to increase in the overall economy and, as the inflationary process begins, something else starts to happen: expectations reinforce price rises. This effect is created by both the worker and by the consumer. In wage negotiations, unions will, naturally, demand a higher settlement if they anticipate a rise in the level of prices in the coming year. This reinforces the increase in wages and, once again, prices rise. Workers will either spend the cash they have or borrow; in either case, it will simply add to overall aggregate demand in the economy. If consumers expect an increase in price levels they will buy soon rather than later when the prices would be higher. As this will increase current purchasing it will push up prices.

Cost-push inflation

An alternative explanation for increases in inflation is that the inflationary stimulus does not come from the demand side of the economy but from the supply side. Inflation is caused by increases in the costs of the factors of production which, in turn, leads to producers passing on their cost increases to consumers as higher prices. The original increases in costs may be caused by:

- increases in the costs of raw materials or other factors of production;
- trade unions pushing up wages ahead of what is justified by productivity.

Successive governments of differing political persuasions have tried to lay the blame for inflation on trade unions. Recent evidence indicates that, for most of the 1980s, the objective of trade unions was one of simply trying to maintain wage levels in line with inflation, rather than trying to outstrip inflation with excessive pay demands.

Monetary causes of inflation

'Monetarist' economists, such as Milton Friedman, see the cause of inflation as an excessive increase in the money supply. Put simply, any increase in the quantity of money in circulation leads, after a time lag, (during which real output may change), to increases in the level of prices, and *vice versa*.

If money supply increases by a greater proportion than the increase in the output of goods and services, then inflation will result. To say this another way, the value of money has fallen. To maintain stable prices the growth of the money supply must keep pace with the expansion of output. If output (measured in terms of the country's economic growth) only increases by say, 2% then the money supply must be controlled so that it too only increases by 2%.

To support this analysis, monetarists have produced empirical evidence, over a long historical period and from many countries to show a cause and effect link between an increase in the money supply and a resultant increase in the level of prices.

This section began by noting that this was an area of considerable debate among economists. To a non-monetarist economist very little of the previous explanation is valid. The areas of conflict are numerous. To these economists changes in the money supply do not always result in inflation. Even the empirical evidence, which seems so conclusive to the monetarists, is not entirely accepted as providing practical evidence of the theory. The monetarist explanation of inflation is one example of an area where economists disagree fundamentally on the causes of the inflationary disease which results inevitably in widely different prescriptions for its cure. The debate still rages quite fiercely amongst economists. The UK, as we shall consider soon, experimented with 'monetarist' policies early in the 1980s. However, by 1985/86, hard-line monetary policy had largely been superseded.

Causes of recent inflation in the UK

Several factors can be suggested as the possible cause(s) of inflation in the UK in the 1970s and 80s. First, examine the evidence for demand-pull inflation, using the statistical indicators of excess demand. You will see that unemployment levels have been extremely high and rising in the 1970s and 80s, compared with earlier decades. Yet consumer demand increased dramatically in the middle 80s as income tax cuts, easy credit and general feeling of economic growth spurred consumers into increasing their purchasing. Much of this increased expenditure was financed through borrowing. Many people saw their houses increase in value over a very short period. This gave them extra 'equity' in their property. (Equity used in this context means the difference between the value of their house and the mortgage they owe.) Many people were able to increase their borrowing either by using this equity as security for personal loans or by increasing their mortgages and so spreading the cost of borrowing over a number of years. This increased demand both pushed up domestic prices and led to a massive increase in imports. Of course as house prices plummeted in the late 80s and 90s these same people were then caught in a 'negative equity trap' as the value of their houses fell below the value of their mortgages so leaving them owing more money than their houses were worth. This led to a rapid decline in demand leading to the recession.

An alternative explanation of the 80s inflation centres on the cost-push theory. Here there are two possible explanations:

- wage-push inflation;
- a rise in import prices.

Wage-push

The 1970s and 80s certainly saw an increase in wage levels. These are illustrated in the table below:

Percentage changes in wage rates

Year	% Change	Year	% Change	Year	% Change	Year	% Change
1961	4.2	1969	5.3	1977	6.6	1985	8.5
1962	3.6	1970	9.9	1978	14.1	1986	7.9
1963	4.8	1971	12.9	1979	14.9	1987	7.8
1964	4.8	1972	13.8	1980	11.4	1988	8.7
1965	4.3	1973	13.7	1981	12.9	1989	9.1
1966	4.6	1974	19.8	1982	9.4	1990	9.7
1967	3.9	1975	29.5	1983	8.4	1991	8.0
1968	6.6	1976	19.3	1984	6.0	1992	4.9

At first sight, the statistics seem to suggest evidence of a wages explosion (from 1970 onwards) which resulted in higher prices after an appropriate time lag. Other statistics, such as those detailing industrial disputes, seem to suggest a more militant attitude on the part of the unions. There is no doubt that, superficially at least, the evidence for wage-push is inviting. But, on closer inspection, the argument is less compelling. For example, once inflation gets under way, it becomes difficult to clearly distinguish cause and effect. It may have been that wages were merely responding to anticipated inflation, rather than causing it. Furthermore, monetarist economists conclude that monetary expansion is essential to permit wage-push inflation to continue. But, even if this is true in principle, in practice governments may find that even when they allow unemployment to rise to very high levels this may only cut down wage settlements by a certain amount.

Rise in import prices

An alternative, or complementary, cost-push cause, is seen in the rise in import prices which occurred after the early 1970s. One major element in inflation was the rise in oil prices, which led to increased production costs, which in turn resulted in higher prices, which led to a stimulation for wage increases – which thereby fuelled wage-push inflation. Also if the value of the pound falls against other currencies this will result in higher import prices. As we shall explain later when we consider the UK's trading relationships we shall see that much of what we buy is in the form of food and raw materials. As import prices rise we still need to buy these products and so instead of demand for imports declining we simply have to pay more, thus fuelling inflation. Economists describe imports as having an 'inelastic' demand. So as prices rise we still buy more at a higher price rather than reducing our consumption of imports.

The truth is that inflation is probably caused by many factors which interact with each other. This complexity makes identifying the cause extremely difficult and gives rise to governments looking for easy, obvious targets – whether they be irresponsible trade unions, too much government spending or excessive growth in the money supply. It is this difficulty in determining the underlying cause of inflation which results in conflicting approaches to the solution of inflation.

Activity

1.   *Try and find out the price of a range of goods and services in the year that you were born. For instance how much did a newspaper, a pint of beer or a visit to the cinema cost?*

2.   *Calculate the rate of inflation of these goods over the period since then and try to identify which products have risen in price faster than the overall rate of inflation and which have risen slower.*

Objective 3: Economic growth

Only by achieving growth in production can the UK economy provide people with an increase in their wealth and standard of living. UK post-war growth has been relatively low: 2 to 3% in good years and 0% (or even a negative figure) in poor years. Even in the late 1980s, when growth figures were reasonably impressive, much of its benefit was lost to foreign suppliers. A survey in 1992 suggested that during the period from 1979 to 1992 UK manufacturing output (excluding oil production) had only increased by 7%, a aggregate growth of only 0.5% per year for the period.

The next table illustrates the varying growth rates between different selected economies.

Average % annual growth in Gross Domestic Product
1983-1987 (Selected Countries)

USA	4.1
Japan	3.9
UK 3.1	
Italy	2.5
Germany	2.1
France	1.6

(Source: The British Economy 1988 (Lloyds Bank))

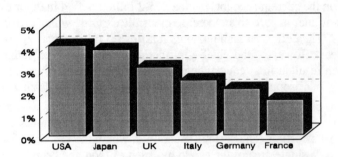

Comparison of UK growth rate with other major economies

The reasons for the UK's poor performance are tied in with the reasons for economic growth itself. Long-term growth represents an increase in potential aggregate supply and so, initially, it is determined by the economic resources available to the economy, together with their efficient and full utilisation. Capital, and how it is used, is probably the most decisive factor of production in determining growth rates.

It has often been suggested that the United Kingdom's poor performance has been due, in part, to a failure to re-invest and modernise its capital stock. The use of machinery which is older and less efficient than our rivals has produced slower rates of growth. Why this reluctance to invest has happened is another difficult question and the search for an answer produces a very wide range of hypotheses. There are those who suggest that the United Kingdom's investment spending has been wrongly directed and that we should have been putting more money into factories and machines rather than houses and welfare. Left-wingers argue that it is the basic capitalistic structure of the economy which is to blame or that the lack of investment policy and lack of lending by the banks which is the root cause of the problem. Others argue that it is the variations in the political and policy targets inherent in the Labour/Conservative political pendulum in the post war period which has led to a discontinuity in business planning and confidence which is essential to industry and commerce.

The recession of the late 80s and 90s has seen growth pushed to the fore as an economic objective. In the 1992 Autumn Statement the government promised that growth would be a key objective and yet the policies which it introduced still, on its own figures, promised growth rates of only 0.5% to 2% for the mid 1990s.

Objective 4: Balance of payments equilibrium

The UK has also experienced fluctuating fortunes in trying to achieve a balance of payments equilibrium. In the early 1960s, the balance of trade deteriorated into increasing deficit, resulting in the devaluation of the pound in 1967. Thereafter, a trade surplus resulted, but this did not last beyond the early 1970s.

In the early 1970s the current account moved in to massive deficit, reaching almost £3.55 billion in 1974. This was the result of many factors, most important of which were the price rises in primary products (especially oil) and the decline in the growth of world trade. To some extent, these deficits were alleviated by surpluses on 'invisibles', but that still left an unfavourable overall deficit. This was resolved by relying on both overseas borrowing and drawing on official reserves of foreign currency.

The years after 1977 showed a considerable improvement, reaching a current account surplus of over £2.5 billion in 1980. An important element in this improvement has been the effect of North Sea oil in reducing the petroleum trade deficit.

More recently, the balance of payments has plunged into deficit again: in 1991 the deficit had decreased to £4.4 billion on the current account, from a £15.2 billion deficit in the previous year. This substantial improvement was due, in part, to an increase in visible exports, which drove the volume of sales abroad to record levels. The deficit on manufactures fell to £3.5 billion in 1991, from a peak of £11.4 billion the previous year. However, the chief contributor to this improved situation was the UK economic recession, which resulted in a reduced demand for visible goods, especially manufacturing inputs: the deficit in these goods dropped sharply from a 1990 deficit of £18.7 billion to a 1991 figure of £10 billion.

The government claimed in the 1980s that the international market would sort itself out and that the situation was not one to cause any grievous concern. Many economists in the 1990s would strongly disagree with that assertion. The parlous situation in which the UK finds itself is exemplified when the focus is placed on a single area of the economy, such as food and drink. We shall examine the position of the balance of payments in more detail later when we consider the UK's trading relationship with the rest of the world.

The Management of the Economy

The most distinctive feature of government economic management in the post-1945 period is that it can be divided into two distinct eras:

- the Era of Keynesianism and Demand Side Economics from 1945 to the late 1970s;
- the Era of Monetarism and Supply Side Economics from the late 1970s.

In the thirty five years or so, following the White Paper of 1944 on economic objectives, both Labour and Conservative governments pursued policies that owed much to the ideas of Keynes and the economists who followed in his footsteps.

Monetarists believe that this should be the single paramount target of economic policy and that in achieving it the other problems will subsequently be solved. This switch has been accompanied by the re-appraisal of the basic causes of inflation and the appropriate methods of economic control. We shall begin with an analysis of the Keynesian approach and its means of application.

Keynesian demand management

As has already been noted, the basis of Keynesian economics is that the problems of unemployment and inflation are the result of disequilibrium in the economy's demand for goods and services and its ability to supply them. A series of simple diagrams may illustrate these concepts. Firstly, consider a state of equilibrium. This is shown by the diagram at the top of the next page.

Here we have a situation where aggregate (or total) demand for goods and services equals the supply. In such circumstances it is argued that there are no upward or downward pressures on the level of prices. There is an equilibrium. Prices remain stable and as such there is no inflation. What the diagram does not illustrate, however, is whether or not there is unemployment in the economy. We do not know the number of workers (or other resources) required to produce the level of supply shown.

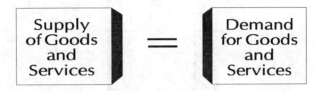

The economy in balance

What if there is unemployment?

In a situation where there is unemployment, Keynesian economics would:

- prescribe an increase in demand, and thereby;
- precipitate a corresponding increase in the supply of goods and services, and thereby;
- require employers to hire more workers, and so reduce the level of unemployment.

Let us follow these stages through in the form of diagrams. Firstly, we have the economy in equilibrium but with an unacceptable level of unemployment:

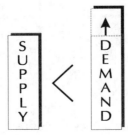

Economy in equilibrium but with high unemployment

The government therefore stimulates demand so that it is now greater than supply:

Government policies stimulate demand

Producers then respond to the higher demand by increasing output to achieve a new equilibrium but at a higher level of employment. Once again, supply equals demand:

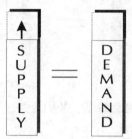

Suppliers respond to higher demand by increasing output

What if there is inflation?

If the country is facing the problem of inflation but without unemployment, Keynesian economics diagnoses this is an excess of demand over supply. Again this can be illustrated with the aid of diagrams. We begin where demand exceeds supply. Producers are unable to increase output as there is no spare capacity within the economy. Instead they respond by increasing prices:

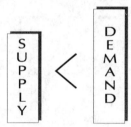

Demand in the economy exceeds supply

To counter this inflationary tendency the government must depress the level of demand in the economy until it again matches the ability of suppliers to produce and so equilibrium is regained with stable prices.

Government takes measures to reduce aggregate demand

Is demand management really so simple?

The relative simplicity of this analysis made it attractive and easy to understand. Governments would first identify the problem they wished to rectify and then adjust the level of demand accordingly. Critics noted, however, that in practice the mechanics of supply and demand in the economy often did not work as smoothly as the theory would predict. For instance, let us return to our first example in which the government sought to reduce unemployment by increasing demand and so encouraging a rise in output. What if the increased demand is for products made by those sectors of the economy which are already over stretched? Here no amount of demand pull could induce an increase in employment in those industries. The result is that producers simply respond to the excess demand by raising their prices. And then you've got inflation!

What if the increased demand is not channelled towards domestically produced goods and services? Then you will have a situation where consumers demand more imports, and instead of the United Kingdom's unemployed finding work, it will be the workers of other countries who benefit. Obviously the art of demand management lies in being able to influence those elements of demand which can be directed towards domestically produced goods in industries which are capable of expansion. This leads us to the problem of defining and evaluating the components which collectively comprise aggregate demand.

The constituents of aggregate demand

Aggregate demand may be described as the total effective demand or expenditure of all buyers of capital or consumer goods within the economy as a whole. Put simply this means that it comprises all the money that is spent on goods and services by all the individuals and organisations within the country within a specified period (such as a year). Clearly this includes:

- individuals;
- businesses; and
- the government;

and so we sub-divide aggregate demand into these three sectors then distinguish the type of spending made in each sector. The following figure illustrates one way of making this division. The process of division allows the government to identify more clearly the areas within which its policies may be applied. The two most significant elements of aggregate demand in terms of the amount spending they represent are:

- personal consumption; and
- government consumption.

Relatively small changes in either of these have a substantial influence on overall demand, and so it is these two areas that together form the main focus of Keynesian demand management. (As we shall see in the next section this revolves around the use of fiscal policy which involves changes in taxation and government spending.)

The government faces clear policy alternatives in order to solve either unemployment or inflation.

The important factor to note is that the two problems require alternative and contradictory courses of action. Keynesian economics held that it was unlikely that the economy would face both problems simultaneously. For a Keynesian economist inflation was consequence of excess aggregate demand while unemployment was caused by insufficient demand. However, the governments of the post-war years recognised that there could be circumstances in which there existed substantial unemployment with a small level of inflation, and vice versa. In fact both in the late 1970s and again in the late 1980s the UK faced both high levels of inflation and growing unemployment.

The Constituents of Aggregate Demand

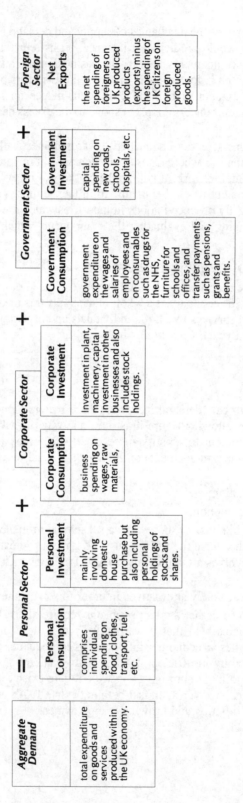

Aggregate Demand	=	Personal Sector		+	Corporate Sector		+	Government Sector		+	Foreign Sector
		Personal Consumption	Personal Investment		Corporate Consumption	Corporate Investment		Government Consumption	Government Investment		Net Exports
total expenditure on goods and services produced within the UK economy.		comprises individual spending on food, clothes, transport, fuel, etc.	mainly involving domestic house purchase but also including personal holdings of stocks and shares.		business spending on wages, raw materials,	Investment in plant, machinery, capital investment in other businesses and also includes stock holdings.		government expenditure on the wages and salaries of employees and on consumables such as drugs for the NHS, furniture for schools and offices, and transfer payments such as pensions, grants and benefits.	capital spending on new roads, schools, hospitals, etc.		the net spending of foreigners on UK produced products (exports) minus the spending of UK citizens on foreign produced goods.

Activity

Undertake a simple survey of about 10 people. You could choose members of your family or friends or other students. If you wish you could sample members of the general public. Ask them to answer a few simple questions. Such as:

1.   *What do you regard as the most pressing economic problem facing the United Kingdom today:*
     (a) Unemployment   *(b) Rising prices*
     (c) Low economic growth   *(d) Balance of payments deficit?*

2.   *Would you be willing to accept higher prices to reduce the level of unemployment?*

3.   *Would you be willing to pay higher taxes if this reduced the level of unemployment?*

Analyse your results and produce a summary in the manner in which opinion polls are reported.

The Era of Monetarism and Supply Side Economics

In the late 1970s there emerged a strong challenge to Keynesian thinking, described as the *monetarist revolution,* in which the four basic economic objectives stated in 1944 were reduced to a single aim: the elimination of inflation. Monetarists believed that stable prices were a pre-requisite for economic growth. Only with a stable pound would investors feel confident to put their money in Britain. As investment rose this would both create jobs and so reduce unemployment and stimulate economic growth. The regenerated British economy would also be more capable of competing in world markets and so exports would rise and imports would fall so the balance of payments problem would also be solved.

The Conservative Government of 1979 proclaimed that inflation was the number one economic 'evil'. Tackle price rises, they claimed, and everything else would fall into place. Mrs. Thatcher was keen to embark upon what became known as the 'Monetarist Experiment'. The basis of monetarism is that inflation is caused by too much money circulating in the economy. Any expected rise in inflation was likely to be self-fulfilling, due to several factors:

- *Consumers*. If consumers expect prices to rise in the future, they will be tempted to 'buy now', prior to any increase. The resultant increase in demand will inevitably lead to pressure upon prices, thus creating inflation;

- *Trade Unions*. Similarly, if unions foresee rising prices, then they will invariably make pay claims higher than this anticipated rate of inflation, in an attempt to achieve a rise in the actual standard of living of their members. Should these pay claims be met, then this again causes inflationary pressure;

- *Borrowers*. Anyone who believes inflation is rising is well advised to borrow money now, as the inflation rate will erode the real value of the repayments. Thus, increased borrowing may occur, with a knock-on effect on spending and, consequently, prices;

- *Lenders*. People who are lending money, and who anticipate price rises, will obviously attempt to increase their rates of interest to guarantee a decent real rate of return. The consequence of this is to put further pressure on the inflation rate.

These four factors mean that controlling inflation is much more difficult if there is an expectation that prices will rise.

The monetarist experiment – the early years

The Labour Government, which lost to Mrs. Thatcher's Conservatives in the 1979 General Election, had already begun to face one unpleasant fact of economic life: it had to curb public spending (or, as Chancellor Denis Healey preferred to phrase it, to 'cut the fiscal deficit'). The only real alternative that a government has is to raise taxes, but this, of course, is unpopular with voters at all times – and especially so when real income is already being reduced by slow growth.

The government has two options open to it:

- either to reduce its state benefits (child benefit, old age, sickness, unemployment benefit etc.); or
- reduce its public investment programmes.

The first option is rarely the one taken, since reducing benefits seems to make the government politically and morally vulnerable to its opponents and to invite criticism that it is taking an inequitable approach to its electorate. Instead, a government will wield its axe over public investment programmes which, in practice, may simply mean the cancellation of a few dozen large contracts with companies in the private sector. (This is the current approach that Germany has been forced to take as a result of re-unification, rising inflation and workers who insist on maintaining their living standards.) As Sir Humphrey Appleby might justify it, by the time the crumbling sewers and potholed roads have become the focus of public attention, the government responsible for their dilapidated condition will have long gone.

Alternatively it can see to hold down public sector wages. This policy means that many of the poorest paid workers in the country will be hit hard. Nurses, hospital auxiliaries, teachers and civil servants will have to have their wages held down. Such a policy may prove to be difficult to implement and politically unpopular.

The situation which Thatcher inherited consisted of an inflation rate which was 13.4%, and an unemployment rate of 5.4% or, some 1.5 million people. In order to tackle inflation, there would inevitably be a cost: higher unemployment.

The Government believed that a reduction of inflation to single figures by 1981 would result in the loss of some 700,000 jobs, or an increase in the unemployment rate to 7.5%. This, they felt, was politically acceptable as a short-term measure. The political implications of this policy are interesting. The 1979 Conservative election campaign had featured a large drive against Labour's failure to curb unemployment. Posters proclaiming 'Labour isn't working', accompanied by pictures of lengthy 'dole' queues, helped Mrs. Thatcher into power. To embark upon policies which would inevitably cause an increase in unemployment would appear to have been a politically dangerous move. However, the Thatcher strategists were convinced that, by 1982, the unemployment rate would start to fall again since, by that time, inflation would have been eliminated.

However, events did not turn out as expected. By 1981 it was clear that the actual unemployment rate in 1981 was 10%, whilst inflation was still running at 11%. The optimistic predictions of 1979 seemed to be ill-founded.

The Conservatives continued their policies of severe fiscal and monetary contraction. Public spending was drastically reduced ('The Cuts'), whilst monetary policy saw the development of the Medium-Term Financial Strategy.

The Medium-Term Financial Strategy

This policy was based upon the theory that, if people were told that inflation would be low, they would reduce spending and borrowing by acting in a rational manner. The aim of the Medium-Term Financial Strategy was to publish a variety of economic indicators to convince the nation that inflation was about to fall. The Chancellor used his Autumn Statement in 1981 to signal the Government's monetary targets, such as the level of increase in the money supply and the PSBR (the Public Sector Borrowing Requirement), for the next three to five years. It was hoped that these would dampen expectations of rising prices, and thus bring about a fall in the rate of inflation itself.

Problems with the Medium-Term Financial Strategy

The Government ran into problems on two fronts:

- *Lack of understanding*. Much of the Government's target audience simply did not understand these figures and its implications, so they remained sceptical that inflation would fall; consequently, they did little to moderate spending and modify pay claims;
- *Credibility*. If a government fails to meet a target, its whole credibility is challenged. The Government invariably overshot their monetary targets and so lost credibility. This worsened the problem. Finding themselves with little immediate success, in terms of either inflation or unemployment, the Government tightened its policies further, with the result that the country was thrown into a severe recession in 1981-82. Some Conservatives – the 'Wets' – began to call for a reversal of policies – for a return to Keynesian expansionist policies.

'TINA': 'There Is No Alternative'

The 'Wets' received scant encouragement from Mrs. Thatcher, who openly claimed that things would get worse before they got better, but that things would only improve if the government continued to pursue its policies fully. The phrases, *'There is no alternative'* and *'The lady's not for turning'* became popular amongst Government supporters.

In March 1982, Government popularity was at rock bottom. However, by June 1983, when the next election was held, the Conservatives were re-elected with a massive majority. The economy had begun to recover, at least in respect of falling inflation, although the reasons for the improvement were not universally agreed upon.

Explanations fell broadly into two categories:

- *Government supporters* claimed that the strict monetary and fiscal policies which had been implemented had resulted in the reduction in inflation, but at a huge cost in unemployment.
- *Government critics* argued that it was the rise in unemployment which had actually led to falling inflation. The shock to the economy had been so severe that inflation had been forced to fall. Three million unemployed was far too high a price to pay for the control of inflation.

The middle 1980s saw a gradual dropping of the hard-line monetarism of the early Thatcher years. By 1985 the policy began to look as though it had worked. Inflation had fallen, economic growth was beginning to pick up, unemployment appeared to have reached its peak and the balance of payments had moved into surplus. Nigel Lawson as Chancellor of the Exchequer wanted to cap the Conservative economic miracle and vigorously argued that the British economy was now strong enough for the pound to enter the European Exchange Rate Mechanism. (We discuss this in some detail in the section on Europe.) He introduced policies designed to encourage enterprise by cutting interest rates to allow businesses to borrow more cheaply and cut taxes to stimulate consumer demand. The overall policy was labelled 'Supply Side Economics'.

The importance of supply side economics

As we have already noted, before 1979, governments had adopted Keynesian policies which saw government intervene in the running of the economy in order to correct market failures and thereby influence the level of aggregate demand. The dual problems of high inflation and high unemployment in the mid 1970s led to the development of a new school of thought.

Monetarism was one part of the supply side 'revolution'. Believers in monetarism held that economic growth and prosperity flow from enterprise and entrepreneurial activity, which are fostered and promoted by free markets. They claim that government intervention is not necessarily the way to solve market failures. What is needed is to create a structure and culture under which markets can operate more effectively and efficiently. Therefore government policies should be designed in order to nurture the entrepreneurial spirit.

Supply side economic policies are, therefore, aimed at freeing the 'wealth makers' from the constraints of market distortions, on the basis that this will then create a 'knock on effect', whereby markets will expand, thus solving problems of unemployment.

Supply side policies

Various policies have been adopted as 'supply side economics'. Monetarist policies have already been considered.

The range of other policies includes the following:

- privatisation;
- deregulation of the financial sector;
- the move towards the Single European Market;
- deregulation of other areas such as transport, the broadcasting industry and the legal system;
- income tax reforms;
- labour market policies.

Privatisation and the Single European Market are considered at length later in this unit.

Deregulation

The deregulation of the bus and broadcasting industries were primarily designed to increase the competition within these sectors. The intended effects were to increase efficiency, with an increase in choice to the consumer. In theory at least, more competition should lead to lower prices, and possibly more innovation and an improvement in the standards of the service. In practice, the true effects remain to be seen.

The government would point to the substantial reduction in the prices of long distance coach travel following the deregulation, and the increase in choice in urban areas, with the development of many more 'link' services, using smaller vehicles. However, the question remains to be answered whether the long run effects, particularly on unprofitable rural areas, will be so encouraging. Bus operators are tempted to concentrate resources on the more profitable urban routes, to the possible detriment of the outlying districts. The continued existence of subsidised public transport provision in such areas has therefore had to continue to some extent.

The deregulation of the broadcasting industry has occurred in two main ways. We have seen the introduction of satellite and cable TV and new independent radio stations and we have allowed the franchises to ITV regions to be sold with the revenue being paid to the government.

This deregulation has led mainly to fears over quality. Choice will no doubt increase over the coming years, with the increasing popularity of satellite and cable TV networks. The quality of the programming for the new stations has raised many questions. There could also be the effect that the increase in channels leads inevitably to a reduction in the revenues of the established organisations, as their viewing figures fall. The consequence would again be a drop in quality. Programmers would concentrate on the 'big draw' programmes – 'soap operas', 'game shows' and the like. The removal of limited interest programmes would be virtually assured. The desirability of such a move is questioned by many critics of the deregulation.

The legal profession is the latest to come under scrutiny in terms of removal of barriers to competition. The archaic rules which govern the legal system, in terms of who can do what, and where, have long been criticised. The government has proposed a widespread change in the practices of both solicitors and barristers, designed to encourage more competition. However, the opposition from within the profession has been considerable, and the future of such radical changes is somewhat clouded.

Income tax reforms

When the Conservatives came to power in 1979, they inherited a basic income tax rate of 33%, rising in stages to a maximum rate of 83%. There was also an 'unearned income surcharge' of 15%, with the result that the top marginal tax rate could be 98%. This, the Conservatives claimed, was a disincentive to work at all levels of pay.

The first step towards the reduction of the personal income tax burden was to lower the top tax rate to 60%, remove completely the unearned income surcharge, and to lower the basic rate to 30%. Subsequent budgets have seen the standard rate lowered to 25% with a base rate of 20% and the 'top rate' now standardised at 40%. Targets for top rates vary, although some extreme economists claim that the most effective system would be one which consisted of only one tax rate for all – preferably as low as possible.

The results of these tax reforms have been widely disputed. Initially receipts to the Inland Revenue actually increased in real terms, suggesting a significant positive result in terms of the incentive work. Supporters of the reforms suggested that people were now willing to work longer and harder, as they could see more tangible benefits with an increased take home pay.

However, there is considerable disagreement about where this actual increase in work came from. It is argued that the vast majority of workers do not have a choice over their working hours. They are fixed, regardless of tax rates. Some workers, who seek to achieve a given level of net take home pay, may actually work less, as they can now gain this aspiration level by working fewer hours. It is generally accepted that the largest incentive to work more is felt by those at the top of the pay scale. They benefit most from the tax reforms, and are often in a position to determine their own working hours, and therefore their level of pay. Supporters of the tax reforms claim that it is exactly these entrepreneurs who are the wealth makers, and increased efforts on their behalf will lead to spin off benefits for everyone else.

It was also suggested that the increase in the receipts to the Inland Revenue may have come from an increased willingness to declare earnings, without the fear of punitive taxation. This may be true, but suggests not a weakness in the previous tax rates, but problems with regard to its enforcement, if tax evasion and tax avoidance were so rife.

However since the start of the recession Inland Revenue tax receipts have fallen dramatically. As unemployment has risen the numbers paying income tax has fallen. Corporate tax receipts have also tumbled as the recession has made it more difficult for businesses to make a profit.

Finally it is worth considering the change in the method of taxation. Whilst the direct burden of income tax has gradually declined, there has been an increase in indirect taxation. Value Added Tax, for example, has been increased from 8% to 17.5% since 1979, a move which was seen by many critics as very regressive. Indirect taxes are often regarded as hitting the lower paid more than the well paid, as poorer people spend a greater proportion and save a lower proportion of their income than rich people. As indirect taxes such as VAT are levied on spending then the poor have a proportionately higher tax bill than the rich. The introduction of VAT on domestic fuel in the 1993 spring budget is seen as hitting the poor particularly hard. It is important to concentrate on the overall tax burden that people face rather than simply considering how much income tax they are asked to pay. Statistics show that a person on average wages will now pay a larger proportion of his income in total tax, when both income tax and VAT are included than in 1979. This would suggest that the tax reforms have benefited some, whilst leaving others worse off.

Labour market policies

The 1980s and 90s have seen considerable reforms introduced by the government to influence the operation of the labour market. The Thatcher administration claimed that it was the failure of the labour market to operate freely which contributed to the high levels of unemployment which the UK has experienced. In particular, the Trade Unions have attracted particularly severe criticism as a barrier to freedom of trade.

The Conservatives claim that it is unions who keep wages artificially high, and therefore create unemployment. Were wages allowed to settle at an appropriate lower level, then many of the unemployment problems would be solved. Employers would be keen to take on more staff, as their wages would no longer be prohibitive. As a result, various pieces of legislation have been aimed at reducing the powers of unions, in areas such as secondary picketing, political funds and the election of the leadership. Perhaps the greatest single factor in the decline of the power of Trade Unions has been the problem of unemployment itself. A union is unlikely to be strong when employers can point to vast pools of unemployed workers who are willing to take on jobs.

The abolition of the Wages Councils was another move designed to improve the workings of the labour market. These councils were set up to protect the pay levels of workers in what were generally non-unionised industries. The removal of the councils has, its critics would claim, led to lower wage rates in these industries, as employers have exploited the lack of organisation of the labour force. Supporters would point to increased employment in these essentially serviced-based industries as sufficient justification for the move.

One final area of controversy relating to the labour market is the differential between wages and benefits. It has long been claimed by right-wing economists that if the gap between wages and benefits is not sufficiently wide, then there will be little incentive for people to work. People will take the view that it is 'not worth their while' to work, when they can get nearly as much through various state benefits.

Opinions on this vary. As we saw in the section on unemployment some economists claim that the vast majority of the jobless of this country are 'voluntarily unemployed' – they choose not to work. Such economists take the 'classical' view of unemployment. They argue that it is the disincentive effect of benefits which is the main reason for voluntary unemployment.

Other economists oppose this view, although it is generally accepted that there is a need for the existence of some degree of pay/benefit gap. It has been argued that rather than reduce the level of benefits, as proposed by many right wing economists, the state should encourage a rise in the level of earning through minimum wage legislation.

Government Methods of Controlling the Economy

Fiscal Policy

Fiscal policy involves controlling the economy using taxation and government spending. It has been applied by governments since the 1940s in their attempts to control the economy. While it is based on Keynesian principles, it is still used today. Keynesians argue that unemployment and inflation are the result of disequilibrium in the economy's aggregate supply and demand. The economy experiences a series of booms and slumps with the fluctuations of the business cycle. Thus fiscal policy is essentially counter-cyclical; that is, when the economy is in recession the government pursues *expansionary* measures and, conversely, when the economy becomes 'over-heated' the government follows a *contractionary* policy.

Fiscal Policy to Expand the Economy

If unemployment exists, there are two ways in which a government can stimulate aggregate demand:

- by reducing taxation (tax cuts);
- by increasing its own expenditure.

Now look at how each of these policies work.

Tax cuts

What is taxation?

Government, both local (such as a county council) and central, raise money (revenue) to spend on public services (expenditure) by taxing individuals, households and businesses:

- through *direct* taxation such as income tax, corporation tax, unified business rate and the council tax;
- through *indirect* taxation such as value added tax and customs and excise duty.

While taxation is primarily used as a means of raising revenue to pay for public expenditure, Central government sometimes decides to use taxation as a *fiscal* instrument by reducing or increasing the amount of money in the economy: for instance reducing income tax by 1p in the pound gives the population another one billion pounds a year of disposable income.

Simply altering the level of taxation, however, can be a crude fiscal instrument, that is often criticised for being 'non-discriminatory' or 'non-selective'; that is, it affects every taxpayer in the same way. So a cut in the basic rate of tax puts money into the pockets of the rich as well as the poor.

Chancellors of the Exchequer can be more subtle in cutting taxes, adjusting thresholds and allowances as well as its overall rate and so helping certain sections of society such as those on low pay.

How do income tax changes affect business?

If the percentage rate of income tax increases, then some individuals will regard this as a disincentive to work harder; they will see that the more they earn, the higher the proportion of their income will be deducted in the form of income tax. This is likely to have two major effects on business:

- the motivation to work may diminish unless an employer can find alternative ways of motivating the worker;
- individuals will have less disposable income to spend on goods and services which business produces.

If the percentage rate of income tax falls, then some politicians would argue that people are motivated to work harder and spend more. An income tax reduction will mean:

- an increase in personal disposable income, which will mean more to save or spend on goods on services;
- a greater motivation to work;
- a consequent increase in business output.

If, instead of a rise in income tax, there is a rise in VAT and excise duty, then prices will rise, demand will fall and the result is a tendency towards inflation (accompanied by a consequent loss of revenue to the government, perhaps). If those duties are decreased, however, prices should fall and there will be an increase in demand, but the tendency will still be inflationary.

If a government raises corporation tax, then businesses will probably wish to maintain the level of dividend they pay. So they will retain less profit, which will mean a lower level of investment in the business. In the long term, either lower dividends or lower investment will show through in a lowering of personal or organisational demand.

Decreasing corporation tax will lead to a higher level of retained profit, which leads to higher levels of investment or higher dividends. Theoretically, these will feed through the economy and show themselves in increased demand, which may be consumer demand or organisational demand.

The government may choose to undertake all or some of these policy measures. The effectiveness of the measures depends on the willingness of individuals and businesses to raise their level of spending. The effect on demand in the UK economy could be reduced if the extra spending is on imported goods or if savings are chosen in preference to more spending. One worrying aspect of the current recession is that a cut in tax may simply lead people to pay of debts they have accumulated in the 1980s boom rather than encouraging them to increase consumer spending.

Increase in government expenditure

Additionally, the government may also increase its own spending. It can do this by:

- *greater expenditure on goods and services or by employing more people in the public sector*. This will create an immediate and direct increase in the level of demand;

- *increased expenditure on what are called 'transfer payments'* (these include benefits, grants etc.) which will result in positive changes in consumer spending;

- *a higher level of capital investment* by building more schools, hospitals, roads, etc. While this type of spending may provide tangible benefits to society, it does take longer to bear fruit as projects must be planned, designed, and approved before implementation. There may, therefore, be a time lag in the period between electing to proceed with such expansion and the positive effect being felt in the economy.

The overall impact of such changes is that the government should face a budget deficit. Revenue falls while expenditure rises. This is known as budget deficit financing and will lead to increases in borrowing by the government (the Public Sector Borrowing Requirement). The estimated PSBR for 1992-93 is £37 billion, with the Treasury estimating that it will rise to £44 billion in 1993-94. Because of the high level of government borrowing the government chose in the 1992 Autumn Statement to protect capital spending but only at the cost of imposing a 1-1.5% pay limit on public sector employees.

Fiscal policy that contracts the economy

If the policy objective is reduction in inflation, the government must pursue methods which are the reverse of those already outlined.

Tax increases

Taxes should be raised to discourage spending. Here the most effective means of reducing expenditure is to tax more heavily those people who spend the greatest proportion of their income (for to tax those who save heavily may simply result in a reduction in savings rather than in expenditure).

Reduction in government expenditure

Reductions in spending may be undertaken and this may mean a fall in public sector employment and a fall in the government's investment programme. The overall outcome should be a budget surplus (or at least a fall in the budget deficit). This would withdraw income from the economy and so reduce aggregate demand.

One of the major difficulties with fiscal policy designed to influence demand is that it may contradict the other aims of taxation and government spending. One of the primary objectives of taxation is to act as a means of redistributing income and wealth. Yet as we have noted the most effective method of reducing spending is to tax the poor sections of society more heavily as they are the people more likely to cut spending rather than cutting savings.

Similarly government spending is the process by which a wide range of public and merit goods provision is financed. Thus to cut spending in order to reduce demand will also be detrimental to the level of supply of such services. The basic difficulty with fiscal policy is not that it is ineffective in countering inflation or unemployment. Rather, it is its inherent inability to reduce both at the same time. This flaw led to the development of the government's alternative means of control, monetary policy.

Monetary Policy

The emergence of monetary policy has perhaps been the most significant change in the economic management in the post-war period. It became the corner-stone of British economic policy for most of the 1980s and still plays an important part in macro economic control in the 1990s. However we shall see that over this period the way that monetary policy has been applied has changed and from being the sole means of economic control for much of the Thatcher period it is now seen as being one of the three means of control together with fiscal policy and supply side measures.

What is Monetary Policy?

The crux of monetary control is the need for the government to regulate the growth of the money supply so that it grows in line with the country's productive capacity. If money supply grows at a faster rate than the country's productive output it will lead to inflation as money becomes worth less in relation to goods and services. If on the other hand the money supply grows at a slower rate than the output of goods and services there will deflation as the growth of the economy is held back through a shortage of money. To understand how monetary policy works you must first be clear about what the government is trying to control.

The money supply

The money supply or stock of money in its widest sense is the amount of notes and coins and bank and other financial deposits in the economy. While it is obvious that notes and coins (currency) can be regarded as 'money' it is less easy to recognise that bank or building society deposits, often in the form of figures in accounts, are also money. Most transactions involving large amounts of money undertaken in the economy rely on cheques as the means of transfer. This will result in the commercial banks readjusting their accounts as money is drawn from an account in one bank and moved into an account in another bank. In most cases there is no need for a physical movement of notes and coins to accompany this as there will be similar transfers occurring in the opposite direction. Thus banks do not need to hold currency to cover all of the deposits they hold, only sufficient to allow them to meet their customer's demands for notes and coins.

Therefore, depending on the measure of the money supply we use, bank and building society deposits account for between two-thirds and three-quarters of the money supply.

The creation of money

The government, through the Bank of England, is responsible for the printing and minting of notes and coins and so it has direct control over this part of the money supply. But in addition the commercial banks through their activities of accepting deposits and making loans, also pay an active role in creating money. A simple example will illustrate this:

- if an individual deposits £100 into his or her bank account the commercial bank will have an increase in it liabilities (the money it owes) of £100;
- the bank will then hold a percentage of this as a reserve;
- the bank will lend the rest out to a borrower;
- the borrower will then spend the money (it is unlikely that someone will borrow simply to save). In most cases this will result in a seller receiving cash for the sale of some goods or services to the borrower;
- the seller then deposits the money received into his or her bank account. This has the same effect as the initial deposit because the bank will gain hold some of the deposit in reserve and lend out the rest.

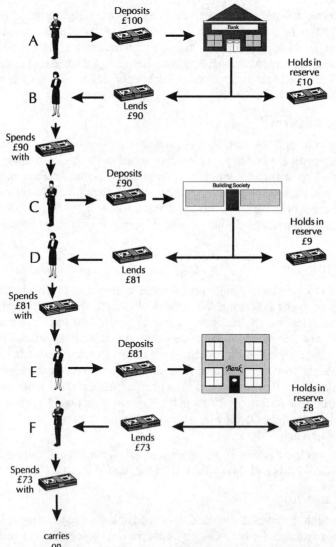

The creation of money - the money multiplier

This process of deposit, reserve, lend, spend and deposit will continue with the original £100 in notes circulating through the economy. After each cycle in the process, the deposits of the commercial banks have risen by the amount of the deposit made. The depositors rightly regard their deposits as money and as such the money supply is increased. This process is called the money or bank multiplier.

The figure on the next page shows a simplified version of this process.

Even in this simple example the original £100 in notes has been multiplied so that:

A has deposits of £100

C has deposits of £90

E has deposits of £81

This process will continue until either the entire £100 is held in the commercial banks' reserves, or remains in circulation, or is partly in both. The money supply is growing as each depositor increases his or her holding of money. This gets us back to the original problem. If the supply of money grows faster than the growth in the output of goods and services then the result will be inflation. How then does the government attempt to control the growth in the money supply?

Means of monetary control

In order to control the growth in the money supply the government uses three methods:

- *control of the demand for money* so that the borrowers seek fewer or smaller loans from the banks or other sources of credit;
- *control of the supply of money* so that the commercial banks and other lenders make fewer or smaller loans;
- *base control*, this involves the control of the production of the original notes and coins.

We shall now consider the method and effectiveness of each of these options.

Control of the demand for money

If we examine the demand relationship of any product we can see that as prices rise the demand for the goods or services normally falls. Relate this idea to a particular product, money, and you will realise that its price (the interest rate you pay to borrow it or the deposit rate you must forgo to hold money in the form of cash) will influence its demand. Thus, in theory at least, if interest rates are high, people will borrow less and if interest rates fall they will borrow more. Thus the government will seek to raise and lower interest rates as a means of controlling the demand for money. This is achieved by a complex inter-reaction between:

- the government;
- the money markets; and
- the commercial banks.

To understand this, it is necessary to recognise that while the commercial banks wish to keep a part of their deposits in a relatively liquid form (i.e. not tied up in long term loans) they also wish to earn some interest on them, which of course they will not do by merely keeping it as cash in their tills. The commercial banks therefore lend money on a short term basis. They lend money to institutions to the Money Market. This is made up of institutions called Discount House because they are always willing to purchase certain types of securities (i.e. certified loans) at a discount.

Thus discount houses will lend money to the government by guaranteeing to take up any of its weekly loan demands, known as Treasury Bills, which are not wanted by the general public. In order to finance the purchase of these Treasury Bills (in effect to lend money to the government) the discount houses borrow from the commercial banks at what is known as 'call and short notice'. This simply means that the banks can recall their loans to the discount houses very quickly if they need to.

This process allows the government to influence interest rates throughout the economy. If the Bank of England offers a high rate of interest on its loans from the discount houses this attracts money. To finance these loans to the government, the discount houses offer high rates to the banks for 'call' money. The bank transfer funds to the money market leaving less to lend out to ordinary borrowers and so the price (interest rate) to borrowers goes up. Conversely, to lower the interest rates, the Bank of England makes its rates lower, attracting less money to the government and so allowing more to be borrowed elsewhere in the economy.

The Bank of England also acts as 'lender of the last resort' to the discount houses so that if they are short of funds, should the banks require an immediate payment of a loan or to discount a treasury bill, the discount houses borrow from the Bank of England. It will set its lending rate according to the level of interest rates it seeks to achieve in the economy. In this way the discount houses know what rate they should charge to commercial banks seeking immediate cash.

The effects and effectiveness of interest rate policy will be considered after we have examined the other means of monetary control.

Control of the supply of money

The supply of money is controlled by the Bank of England monitoring and regulating the amount of money the commercial banks can, and are willing to, lend out. Until 1981 the Bank of England specified a certain percentage of the commercial bank's deposits which the banks had to hold in reserve and so could not lend out to the general public. Now, however, no specified reserve ratio is required. Instead the banks are required to be 'prudent'. This means that they should take into account of the type of deposits they hold and when they could be withdrawn (i.e. with long-term deposits accounts there is no risk of an immediate withdrawal). The reserves they hold should reflect the imminence of likely withdrawals of deposits. For example, a current account can be withdrawn 'on sight' (i.e. at once) and the banks must, therefore, hold a higher percentage of this type of account in reserve in readiness than they would deposit accounts.

How then, can the government influence the amount the banks choose to lend out?

The method employed is called *Open Market Operations*. This involves the government borrowing money from the general public (by sale of Treasury Bills or Gilt Edged Securities). The lender (the public) pays the money to the government in the form of a cheque. The Bank of England acts as a banker for all the banks who are required to keep ½% of their deposits there, and at this stage, the Bank withdraws the amount it is owed from these deposits. Because the commercial banks' deposits at the Bank of England are now reduced, they must transfer funds from elsewhere to maintain the ½% balance at the Bank. This means that they have less money to lend out. In this way the Bank of England can influence the ability of the commercial banks to create loans.

Another way that the government can influence the supply of credit is by imposing credit controls. This can involve the introduction of restrictions on hire purchase or other credit transactions. So for instance if the government specified that if consumers wished to buy a stereo system on credit they had to put down an initial deposit of one third of the retail price, this would discourage some consumers as they are unable to raise this initial deposit in the form of cash.

Base control

This, the final method of control was introduced in the mid-1980s and involves the government controlling the 'monetary base'.

The monetary base comprises:

- the notes and coins in circulations; and

- the commercial banks' deposits at the Bank of England.

The concept behind the means of control is that we, as individuals in the economy, need to hold a certain amount of cash to conduct our everyday affairs. We will not choose to carry less cash around simply because the government asks us to do so, and the Bank of England uses this demand for cash to influence the bank lending. Clearly the banks also need cash to be able to meet the possible withdrawal demand to their customers. If the Bank of England reduced the amount of notes and coins in circulation in the economy this would not influence an individual's money holding and so the banks feel the squeeze. They must 'top up' their cash reserves by reducing the amount of money they lend out and in so doing, the expansion of credit and the growth of the money supply is reduced.

The explanation above has been purposely simplified to allow you to grasp the concepts behind monetary control and some of the finer detail has been omitted because of the lack of space. The important point to understand is that the government reduces the growth of the money supply by holding down borrowing from the commercial banks and other lenders and so limits the process of credit creation.

Activity

Visit a local bank and a local building society. List the rates of interest which are on display. Consider the deposit rates first. What factors will get you a higher rate of interest on your deposits with a bank or building society? Now consider the lending rates. What factors will allow you to get a cheaper loan and what will mean that you have to pay more? (Here are some clues. For deposits think about length of time and amount deposited. For the loans and overdrafts think about the level of security and degree of risk.)

Assessment of the effectiveness of monetary policies

Control of the demand for money

Policies for control of the borrowing demand have been aimed at two potential 'target areas'.

Domestic consumers

Early evidence suggested that the interest rate was not the sole determinant of domestic borrowing. 'Weekly payments' are often seen by consumers as being more important, as they illustrate how much people can afford. As a result, credit companies have been guilty of extending the terms of loans as rates have gone up, thus giving the impression that repayments are staying the same or even going down. In fact people are paying more in total and simply repaying this over a longer period. Indeed, as credit companies are faced with increased rates, they tend to launch 'hard sell' promotional campaigns, which can actually lead to an increase in borrowing.

Commercial borrowers

Demand for borrowing from businesses is far more 'interest rate conscious'.

Large businesses, faced with higher interest charges, often adopt the following policies:

- *Reduction in investment* – leading to job losses and further problems for the development of the economy;
- *Slower payment to smaller suppliers* – forcing the smaller organisation to borrow short-term. Invariably, this will involve the use of expensive overdrafts to cover costs, such as wages, which cannot be deferred. Not only does this negate the effect of government policy, but it also leads to increased bankruptcies and liquidations. (The Chancellor of the Exchequer attempted to rectify this in the 1992 budget, when he promised that government contractors would honour their bills within thirty days.)

From the late 1980s until it was forced to leave the Exchange Rate Mechanism (ERM) in 1992 the government centred much of its economic policy on the use of interest rates. It was described as a 'one club armoury', since its opponents regard it as a blunt and primitive weapon or as inappropriate as a golfer's bag which contains just one 'stick'. As a result, the UK saw a period of spiralling interest rates, much higher than any of our economic rivals. The aim of this policy was to dampen consumer credit spending. Mortgage rates rose and this, rather than high credit rates, led to a reduction in borrowing. When people could no longer afford their mortgage repayments, they tended not to seek further credit.

However, the need to hold the value of the pound at its over-valued rate in the ERM meant that interest rates had to be kept too high for too long, for if the government lowered interest rates it feared that foreign speculators would not hold as much of their money in sterling and so sell pounds and force down the value of sterling.

These high rates of interest dampened consumer spending so much that it helped to cause and to deepen the recession. Once the pound left the ERM the government was able to make substantial interest rate cuts as its policy objective shifted to trying to stimulate economic growth. At the time of writing it is as yet too early to say whether this change of policy will prove successful.

Control of the supply of money

Control of the supply of money has proved difficult as the government is reluctant to impose direct controls on the banks and other lenders. They are difficult to impose and regulate as lenders want to lend money as it is their means of making a profit. A reduction in one element of the money supply can lead to an increase in another. For example, if the government reduces the amount the commercial banks can lend, borrowers turn to Building Societies or Finance Houses as means of credit. To effectively control credit, the government would have to regulate every credit transaction that takes place in the economy. This would involve policing thousands of lenders and millions of credit transactions.

The government's ability to control the supply of money in this way is now in considerable doubt. Indeed, many government advisors have virtually abandoned reference to the control of the supply of money.

Control of the monetary base

One difficulty in controlling the money supply simply by using the amount of notes and coins in circulation is that consumers are increasingly holding less cash. In fact it has been suggested that we are moving towards a 'cash-less' society. Consumers now use cheques and credit cards as a way of making large transactions and the increased availability of bank cash machines means that people carry less cash as it is relatively easy to make a withdrawal as and when we need cash. Thus base control is now playing a less important role in monetary policy. The monetary base is monitored using a measurement called MO and is seen by the Treasury as just one means of judging changes in the money supply rather than the definitive means of controlling it.

The impact of government borrowing on monetary control

As we outlined earlier, one of the means by which the government can influence commercial bank borrowing is by attracting money to itself by offering higher interest rates. This leaves less in circulation in the economy to be loaned and borrowed. However, this process assumes that when the government does borrow it holds the money and so keeps it out of circulation. If instead of holding the money, as it were 'in limbo', the government simply spends the money it borrows, then it goes back out into the economy to be loaned and borrowed as before and in so doing increases the money supply. The answer to this problem of monetary control then is, on the surface, quite simple - the government should not spend the money it borrows. Unfortunately, the problem is not that easy to solve. Increasingly governments have been facing budget deficits (i.e. their revenue is less than their expenditure). They must borrow to spend and pay their way. As we have already noted the difference between government revenue and expenditure is called the Public Sector Borrowing Requirement (PSBR) and its size will play a large part in determining the effectiveness of monetary policy.

Advocates of monetarism argue that the larger the PSBR is, the less powerful the policy can be. Thus the suggestion is that public expenditure must be cut to reduce the PSBR. This to some extent explains the government's determination to trim the size of the public sector.

Those who advocate a short-term increase in government spending, even at the cost of a greatly enlarged PSBR, suggest that as expenditure on jobs, services and government investment rises this will reduce unemployment and so lower the government's spending on benefits. It is almost a case of swings and roundabouts. The government should pay out now (to create jobs) to avoid having to pay out in the future (in the form of social security and unemployment benefits). This approach has generally not been favoured by the government in the 1980s and 90s and instead it has followed a policy of reducing the public sector and of privatisation.

Central government control over the local authorities

One area of the public sector which has felt the effects most severely of the policy aimed at reducing expenditure has been local government.

As local authorities are dependent on central government funds in the form of grant aid as a major proportion of their income, it is here that the central administration has chosen to implement its policy of retrenchment. Each authority receives an annual grant depending on its ability to raise income from local taxes and the predicted level of its spending needs. Its income from local taxes is determined by the quantity and quality of both domestic and commercial property it has in its area, and its spending needs reflect the number of people who live in its area and their age structure and the geographical make-up of the area. Since 1979, local authorities have seen a continued cut in the central government's estimates of their spending needs and a consequent fall in grant aid. Some councils have responded to this by maintaining the level of their services and transferring the cost from grant income to higher local taxes.

The government countered this continued higher spending by introducing a policy of cash limits on higher expenditure tied to a system of penalties by which, as council spending increased, their grant was proportionately reduced. This had the required effect in some areas – some councils did introduce spending cuts. Other authorities chose to bear the penalty burden rather than slash services.

The ultimate step on the part of central government is to 'cap' those authorities it regards as overspending. By this, central government will actually specify the local council tax rate an authority is able to levy and, if that authority then chooses to set a higher rate, ratepayers will be entitled by law to refuse to pay any tax bill in excess of the government's 'cap' limit. Councillors who vote through council tax increases above the government limit are personally liable to be penalised. Government critics see capping as the sacrifice of local autonomy as central government in effect controls local authorities' revenue and expenditure. Supporters of the government's policy argue that this is a necessary price to pay for overall monetary control of the public sector.

Privatisation

A further policy to reduce government borrowing and increase its short-term revenue has been privatisation. Since 1979 roughly £40 billion has been collected from the sale of about fifty privatised businesses. The present Conservative Government is committed to selling off parts or all of the remainder of the public corporations in an attempt to reduce State involvement in industry. These include: the

British Technology Group; British Coal; British Rail; the Civil Aviation Authority and London Transport.

The arguments against privatisation

There are three major arguments put forward against privatisation.

Financial

The industries which are currently being sold off, or have been sold off, are necessarily the more profitable areas of the public sector, for it is unlikely that private investors would wish to take over a loss-making concern. The possible result of such a policy might be that the government will be left with only the major loss-making nationalised industries (such as Nuclear Electric?) and with no possibility of cross subsidy.

Private monopoly

Government is in danger of merely transferring a State monopoly to a private monopoly, with no attempt made to introduce competition to improve efficiency.

Job losses

Trade unions claim that privatisation will be accompanied by large job losses – hardly desirable in times when unemployment is already high, but this has certainly been the case in even the most profitable privatised companies, such as British Telecom.

The Conservatives' Nationalised Inheritance

In 1979 the Conservatives inherited a network of nationalised industries, yet they believed that the State provision of goods and services should be kept to a minimum. Public goods, such as defence and policing, would still be provided by the State. Merit goods, such as education and health care, would be opened up more and more to market competition. The nationalised industries themselves, it was envisaged, would be 'streamlined' and then sold off as soon as they came in to profit.

The network of nationalised industries was large. The scope of the corporations was considerable, the number of employees vast. The industries took up a significant portion of UK investment, squeezing out private sector investment. For several years the Conservative government felt that they had been a drain on the PSBR. There was also considerable criticism that many of them were 'cosy monopolies', which were not exposed to the rigours of market forces and, as such, showed a tendency to be inefficient and lacking in innovation. The state, it was claimed, had proved itself to be no better, and at times far worse, than the private sector in running such industries.

The privatisation programme

The programme of privatisation in the 1980s and 90s started relatively quietly. The initial moves were not heralded as a major policy departure, but the 'sell-offs' soon gathered pace.

Council house sales

The initial step in the programme was the introduction of the sale of council houses. This particular move had many strong critics in its initial phases, but as the number of properties sold rose, the criticism began to waver. The major drawbacks of this programme, it was suggested, were the fact that only the 'good' houses were being sold off. As there was very little public sector house building at the time, due to monetary constraints, the result was a diminishing stock of council houses, both in number and in quality. However, since its inception in 1980, some 800,000 tenants have taken advantage of the scheme. As a result of the size of the operation, the opposition parties would find it extremely difficult, both practically and politically, to buy back the properties.

Phase 1 (1981/83) 'Testing the water'

In this first period the government was 'testing the water' to see what the public's reaction to privatisations would be. It also wanted to try a number of different methods of privatisation including asset sales to an individual private company, share sales by tender and fixed price share sales. A number of small or relatively unknown organisations were sold off, including Cable and Wireless and Amersham International. Other sales in this phase included Sealink and British Rail Hotels, which were already operating in a fairly commercial environment, and as such did not raise too many outcries. The government also sold off some of its share in British Petroleum during this period, although they did retain a controlling interest.

Phase 2 (1984/87) 'Selling off the family silver'

The second period of the Thatcher administration witnessed the most ambitious sales. Shares were sold in companies such as British Telecom, British Gas, British Airways, British Petroleum and the TSB. All of these moves were greeted with varying degrees of opposition, but all provided substantial boosts to the government's short term revenue. The opposition came from within the conservative party as well as from outside it. In a famous speech Harold Macmillian, a conservative prime minister in the 1950s and 1960s accused the Thatcher government of 'selling off the family silver'. As a direct result of these sales, the government was able to substantially relax its fiscal policies, moving considerably towards the reduction of the tax burden on individuals. The opposition to the privatisation of British Telecom is considered as an example below.

Phase 3 (1988 to date) 'Getting rid of the problem children'

The third phase of privatisations involved selling off some of the major utilities such as Electricity and Water and major industries such as Rover and British Steel. The latter in particular were seen as inefficient and a drain on the government's finances. The government is planning to privatise some of its other 'problem children' including British Coal and British Rail. Between 1979 and 1992 the following were privatised:

Nationalised Industry	Year	Price £m
British Petroleum	1979/87	6090
British Aerospace	1981	390
Cable & Wireless	1981	1021
Amersham International	1982	64
National Freight Corporation	1982	354
Britoil	1982	1053
Associated British Ports	1983	97
Enterprise Oil	1984	384
Jaguar	1984	297
British Telecom	1984	4793
British Gas	1986	6533
British Airways	1987	854
Royal Ordnance	1987	186
British Airports Authority	1987	1223
Rover	1988	48
British Steel	1988	2427
The Water Authorities	1989	5240
Electricity Boards (distributors)	1990	5200
CEGB (Electricity Generators)	1991	3600
Scottish Electricity Generators	1991	2880

In addition, the following were sold: Ferranti; The Forestry Commission; Sealink; Unipart; Short Bros; The Plant Breeding Institute; British Rail Hotels.

The Proceeds from Privatisation

The increased pace of the sale of public assets, resulting in increased revenues to the Treasury, is well illustrated in the table below (assets are in £billions):

Year	Assets (£bn)
1979 - 80	0.4
1980 - 81	0.2
1981 - 82	0.5
1982- 83	0.5
1983 - 84	1.1
1984 - 85	2.1
1985 - 86	2.7
1986 - 87	4.5
1987 - 88	5.1
1988 - 89	7.1
1989 - 90	4.2
1990 - 91	5.3
1991 - 92	8.0
1992 - 93	8.0
1993 - 94	5.5(estimated)
1994 - 95	5.5(estimated)

Whilst most people equate the word 'privatisation' with the sales of public assets, such as state industries, remember that it has happened at local level, too. Local authorities have privatised services, such as refuse disposal and leisure centres, and health authorities have contracted out cleaning and laundering to private companies.

British Telecom – an example of privatisation

British Telecom was privatised in 1984, with no major restructuring. This meant, effectively, that a public monopoly was transferred directly into private hands.

The policy dilemma

In order to guarantee a good sale price, and thereby substantial revenue for the Treasury, there was a need to keep any legislation which applied to BT fairly light. Private investors would not be attracted to an organisation which was still operating within a political strait-jacket. However, the transfer of a complete monopoly could lead to inefficiency in terms of costs, prices, innovation and so on. The government's strategy was to privatise first and then regulate later, if at all. Some constraints were placed upon BT in its initial phases within the private sector:

OFTEL was established to act as a regulator or 'watch-dog' over the telephone industry. Consumers were to pass any complaints on service or prices to OFTEL, who would investigate and then make recommendations for action. As with most watch-dog organisations, OFTEL had no power to implement its own recommendations, and had to rely on the good business sense of BT's managers who wished to avoid bad publicity. This seems to have worked to a degree, although critics would still claim OFTEL is a 'toothless watch-dog'. (Similar concerns were voiced about OFWAT, the 'watch-dog' responsible for the ten regional water companies which were privatised in 1989; in 1992 they returned a collective profit of £1.5 billion at a time when its inefficiency meant that thirty percent of mains water was lost to 'seepage', resulting from old pipes, and a quarter of the country's households were faced with rationing and restrictions on the use of water.)

Price restrictions

Until 1989, BT was limited as to the size of its price rises. The formula of Retail Price Index minus 3% was applied, meaning that BT could raise prices by no more than 3% less than the prevailing rate of inflation. Despite this restriction, BT has still managed to accrue vast profits in its early years in the private sector - upwards of £2 billion p.a. Critics suggest that this is potential revenue lost to the government. Supporters argue that the tax on these profits still boosts Treasury funds and, had BT been left in the public sector, it would not have performed so well anyway. The original RPI minus 3% formula was imposed only until 1989. From then until 1993 the current pricing formula has restricted BT from increasing prices by RPI minus 6.25%. In 1991 BT announced a half-yearly profit of £1.61 billion, a 5.1% increase on 1990. The *Financial Times* analysed BT's accounts and concluded that it could safely cut its prices by £1 billion per annum and still be earning for itself profits as high as the rest of UK industry and higher than any other European telecommunications carrier.

The price structure was reviewed in 1992. BT, which claims that recession and increased competition have adversely affected their profits, are prepared to accept a new formula of RPI minus 7.25 for the first part of the five year pricing regime, but will then want a reduction in the formula below that level. (BT returned a reduced profit of £3.07 billion in 1991-92).

There is no guarantee that such constraints will be reimposed by the government, nor is there any indication of what BT's policy would be, should such constraints not be enforced. Perhaps, in the longer term, competition will emerge that may curb BT's prices and profits, but as long as it remains a virtual monopoly, a tough regulatory body is needed. Perhaps OFGAS, who won a reduction in gas prices for domestic consumers by threatening to take British Gas to court, might stand as an example. The Telephone Users' Association, in their submission to OFTEL's current review of BT's prices, suggested that an open audit of BT's business would be good for competition. It also wants made clear where BT 'cross subsidises' one service at the expense of another (e.g. where domestic consumers subsidise business consumers).

Competition

Competition for BT's market is negligible. Mercury Telecommunications (owned by Cable & Wireless) is licensed to compete over a limited range of services, but its operations do not really affect BT's market share to any great extent. (Independent estimates put Mercury's share of the UK telecommunications market at only 5%.) The idea of constructing a second telecommunications network is inefficient (BT is a natural monopoly), and as such direct competition is difficult to foresee. A glimmer of hope that increased competition might materialise, lies in the applications made by the National Grid (owned by the twelve regional electricity operating companies) for a telephone licence to compete with BT and Mercury for customers in the business market. British Waterways, British Aerospace and British Rail have applied for similar licences.

Wider share ownership

One final point about privatisation. A major objective in the 1980s was to bring about a 'share owning democracy', an ideal which was inherent in much government thinking. Initially, the 'people's shares' (or 'popular capitalism', or 'share holding democracy') certainly attracted a large number of new shareholders. However, a large number of people also used the initial phase of privatisation to 'make a killing'. Very large profits were made because shares were heavily over-subscribed. Many realised a fast profit as they quickly sold out to large financial institutions. The 'Crash of 1987' also saw many small investors frightened off share buying as their prices tumbled; many people were exposed to the harsh realities of the stock market for the first time. The long-term effects of this event have still to be assessed, but doubtless some people have adopted the philosophy of 'once bitten, twice shy'.

By March 1992 there were again fewer than ten million shareholders in the UK (*Source: National Opinion Polls, March 1992*), though a Treasury survey, conducted in 1991, showed that since 1981 individual share ownership had risen from 7% to 25% of the adult population. 54% of individual shareholders have shares in only one company, usually one that has been privatised. Only 17% of shareholders have holdings in four or more companies. (A comparison of these figures with those for 1990 – respectively 60% and 17% – suggests a slight broadening and deepening of the ownership pattern.) Evidence suggests that a majority of share holding 'Investors' have tended to take a quick profit on those shares by selling their stake to institutional shareholders, such as pension funds and insurance companies. Whether successive governments since 1979 have been successful in widening the base of share ownership is therefore somewhat doubtful.

Nationalised industries

The few remaining large businesses in this category are British Rail, British Coal, the Post Office and London Transport. They are controlled by management boards, appointed by government ministers, who give them the responsibility for day-to-day decision-making. General policy is guided by the government, which believes that national corporations should conduct themselves as commercial enterprises. Their efficiency is scrutinised by the Monopolies and Mergers Commission and they are expected to conduct themselves in accordance with the following 'guidelines'. They are expected:

- to follow clear government objectives which have been set out for them;
- to achieve a required rate of return of 8% or greater;
- to have financial targets and performance aims;
- to have a corporate plan;
- to hold performance reviews;
- to have, and stick to, principles relating to investment appraisal and pricing;
- to have external financing limits;
- to have a systematic monitoring of their performance.

Regional policy

The policies previously mentioned have been aimed at solving problems in the country as a whole by seeking to reduce the aggregate level of inflation or unemployment. A glance at the map on the next page, which shows each region's share of manufacturing output, reveals that the UK is not homogeneous, but is diverse and uneven in what it produces and how much is produced. For example, only 14% of the output of Greater London is accounted for by manufacturing, whilst in the West Midlands manufacturing accounts for one third of that region's Gross Domestic Production. In Greater London, the banking and financial sectors account for 25% of regional GDP, a figure far higher than that for the West Midlands. However, in the UK there are some regions which have specific problems of unemployment above the national average, low growth rates and many associated social problems such as crime, poor housing and so on.

Successive governments have made various attempts to alleviate these particular problems through Regional Policy. They have attempted this by two different types of policies which:

- encourage unemployed workers to move to more prosperous regions;
- induce companies and firms to move to the regions of high unemployment.

Encouragement of the mobility of labour

Some workers are less able to move from one area to another in search of work because they are highly immobile. The government has tried to help by giving financial incentives (travelling and re-settlement grants), encouraging re-training (through Skills Centres and Government Training Schemes) and improving workers' knowledge of opportunities in other regions (through Job Centres and Department of Employment). Such policy may well alleviate unemployment in the short-term, but it tends to have the longer term effect of moving workers away from their traditional home areas, leaving these regions to decline and to some extent reinforcing regional inequality in the UK.

Encouraging business to re-locate in the regions

The government has previously sought to give financial assistance to businesses willing to locate in the regions. Certain regions, such as the North East and West Cumbria, have in the past been designated Development Areas. In these areas, Regional Development Grants are available which help businesses purchase new capital assets and also provide a grant for each new job created. Additionally, other areas were designated as Intermediate Areas. These included the West Midlands, Humberside and parts of Yorkshire, Lancashire, South Wales and the South West. In these regions, lesser grants were available for businesses which created new jobs.

At present the UK appears to lack a strong regional policy. Industrial policy is designed to encourage enterprise and economic growth in all areas of the country In those areas where extra help is needed, this is presently provided by the Department of Trade and Industry's Enterprise Initiative. Aid is concentrated on Assisted Areas (Development Areas and Intermediate Areas), which account for over 35% of the working population. The two main instruments for rendering regional aid are:

- *regional selective assistance*, which is available through the Assisted Areas, for investment projects carried out by businesses that meet certain criteria;
- *Regional Enterprise Grants; these are available in Development Areas and other areas covered by EC schemes to support investment and innovation in business that employ fewer than twenty five people.*

In the 1980s the government was of the view that its supply side policies would prevail, and that it should serve as a catalyst to the creation of business, rather than directly intervening to ensure its creation. Assistance which is currently provided for businesses is no longer in the form of grants or subsidies for factories, but is given or lent as money to carry out market research, financial planning or export drives. That help is available regardless of area. Part of the aversion to regional aid that could be seen in successive governments in the 1980s is suggested by a phrase that Mrs. Thatcher used before she was deposed: people in areas of high unemployment, she asserted, should stop being 'moaning minnies' and look after themselves. This complemented an earlier opinion, by one of her senior colleagues, that the unemployed should 'get on their bikes and look for work'. Such opinions together scarcely formed a coherent regional policy.

Instead, the EC has become an increasingly important source of funds, particularly in view of the reduction in the UK government direct support, through its Regional Fund. This provides money to finance specific projects in the poorer areas of Europe. Unfortunately, several of the UK's regions now fall within the category occupied by the likes of Sicily, Estremadura and Calabria.

Regional policy - success or failure?

This type of policy has been used in some ways for fifty years and yet there are still considerable inequalities between the regions. Does this mean that the policy has failed? Certainly the policy has not achieved its objective of a fair distribution of industry throughout the country. Nevertheless, it has created and maintained many hundreds of thousands of jobs in the regions. The policy itself has been very costly to promote and it is estimated that the costs of each job created is well in excess of £10,000. Clearly the problem of regional unemployment grew in the period when national unemployment also rose. Whether the current trend for a fall in unemployment will be felt equally throughout them UK will be interesting. Many critics of the government now believe that an overall policy of reducing mass unemployment together with a reinforced regional policy is necessary if the growing inequality in the regions is to be reduced.

How successful has government economic policy been since 1979?

Any answer must be subjective. Certainly, some measure of success can be claimed in the control of inflation. Having inherited a rate of over 13%, this was reduced to below 4% by 1992. However, critics would argue that the cost in terms of lost jobs was socially unacceptable. At the current time, inflation has fallen from a rate of over 8% in 1989, to about 4% and for the first time in half a century it has fallen below the rate for Germany, if only marginally. By the end of 1992 unemployment had almost reached 3 million and was predicted to keep rising throughout 1993 (this accounts for about 10% of the workforce), using the current method of calculation. This is a slight improvement on the 3.26 million which the country experienced in 1986, but is nowhere near as low as the figure inherited by the Conservatives in 1979. It has been pointed out that many of the new jobs which have been created are either part-time, or in the growth leisure and service industries. The UK's manufacturing base is dangerously narrow, and economic growth without manufacturing growth can only be short-lived.

There has been a long-term decline in the share of UK output accounted for by agricultural and manufacturing sectors as the economy has become more service-oriented. The contribution that manufacturing has made to the Gross Domestic Product has declined markedly since the beginning of the 1960s, when it was 35%, to today's 20%. This reduction in the level of manufacturing means that British citizens are consistently relying on imports to satisfy their needs, as no UK substitute exists.

This lack of UK manufactured goods not only exists in the high-tech consumer market, but also in what could be referred to as 'low-tech' markets, or even the 'no-tech' markets. The UK construction industry is currently importing materials, such as bricks and putty, because of the limited supply from domestic producers. Thus much of the benefit of the mid-1980s boom in house construction has been lost abroad.

The balance of payments appears to be a problem which is resistant to control. The figure for 1988 was some £15 billion in deficit; in 1989 it was nearly £20 billion, and in 1990 it was £16 billion. The main explanation of this lies in the boom in consumer spending mentioned above. However, criticism also exists of the problems of British companies' export levels. While these were hit by a strong pound while sterling was in the ERM there still remains a general lack of competitiveness. The government is attempting to alter the negative attitude of UK firms towards world trade and, in particular, trade within the Single European Market. Whether the situation improves or worsens as a result of these developments remains to be seen. The government claims that the balance of payments deficit is an irrelevance, and that market forces will rectify the situation in the near future. Economic growth has fluctuated a great deal during the 1980s and early 1990s. The recession of the early 1980s, when growth was negligible, gave way to a boom during the mid-1980s (Between 1983 and 1987 the *Financial Times* index of stockmarket shares multiplied by a factor of five). The UK experienced growth rates which were comparable with its rivals. However, the manufacturing base was not growing and, as such, growth has slowed down considerably. High interest rates for most of the late 1980s and early 1990s have deterred recent investment. Imports remain attractive to UK consumers; as such, much of the benefit of the growth years of the mid-1980s has disappeared. With regard to overall economic policies, the government would appear to have invented a new alternative. After Keynesianism and Monetarism, demand side and supply side economics, there is now a policy called 'suck it and see', a combination of a number of alternative approaches whose chance of long-term success is a matter for considerable and continuing debate.

The United Kingdom's Relations with the Rest of the World

International Trade

Trading between nations is almost as old as humankind itself and few nations are, or can be, independent of others. In the same way as a business trades or carries out transactions with other businesses, so do nations. The global economy, according to the World Resources Institute, was valued in 1992 at US$20 trillion and approximately $195 billion of this amount is in world trade. Such enormous figures give some indication of the extent of world trade. The United Kingdom has traditionally been a trading nation. In fact one of the reasons for the establishment of its empire was the need to find new markets for its goods and sources of supply of raw materials. Britain is still heavily dependent on international trade. Without imports of raw materials our industries would not be able to produce. Without imports we, as consumers, would not have the range and variety of foodstuffs we have come to expect. What is more without export markets our industries could not sell as much as they do and so would employ fewer people, make less profit and consequently the economy as a whole would be poorer.

The possibility for trade arises where one country has a surplus of a product or service that another country needs. If it were not for surpluses there would be no trade of any sort. However as we shall see later in this section the reasons why world trade has developed as it has are partly historical, partly economic and partly political.

The first part of this section attempts to answer the question, why is there international trade? It then examines the mechanisms by which trade takes place and how it is measured before going on to examine the performance of the UK economy and the arrangement of trading 'blocs' in which it operates.

Why should the UK trade?

Every economy has a certain combination of resources which may be combined to produce goods and services and, of course, each country has a different mix of resources. The UK has a workforce capable of producing highly sophisticated technological products, but has a shortage of many of the raw materials required to manufacture them. If every country in the world were to attempt to produce all its needs domestically and no international trade took place, then the world and its population would be much poorer, for each country would have to divert some of its resources from producing those products which it is most capable of making, towards less productive but necessary goods and services. The problem is: which goods and services should each country produce?

Countries tend to try and produce some of the basic necessities they need domestically so as not to be totally dependent on others. So the UK decides to produce some food in this country which could be produced more cheaply abroad. However, a country should specialise in the production of those goods or services *for which it has a comparative advantage over others*. Trade encourages specialisation and also makes it feasible.

Comparative advantage in trade

Some countries can produce many goods more cheaply and effectively than the rest of the world. Does this mean that the less efficient countries should produce nothing and buy from the cheaper country? No, it simply means that they should produce those products in which they have the *least comparative disadvantage* and the country which can produce most cheaply should specialise in those goods and services in which it has the greatest *comparative advantage*.

For example, assume that there are two countries: one has an agricultural economy while the second has a highly trained manufacturing workforce. If both specialise in the production of those goods which they can make most efficiently, then the overall output of both agriculture and manufactures will be *maximised*. They can then trade between each other. The agricultural economy sells food to the manufacturing economy and vice versa. In this way both end up with sufficient food and manufactures to meet their needs.

Least comparative disadvantage in trade

What if one of the countries is more efficient in the production of *both* types of output? Clearly, it would be unrealistic for the less productive one to produce nothing. If it did, it would have nothing to trade and would not survive. Therefore it is most sensible for the less efficient country to produce those things in which it has the least comparative disadvantage.

Reality of world trade

Of course, the situation outlined is a simplification of what actually happens in international trade. In many countries, industries have grown and developed prior to the establishment of an effective system of international trade and transport. The capital investment which has already been made has created an industrial structure which cannot easily be changed. A country's labour force may well have developed certain specific trades or skills. To change them would cause considerable social and economic upheaval. Overall, there is a gross imbalance in the terms of world trade, with developed nations (the 'Western' countries or 'the North') benefiting from a net inflow of US$50 billion each year.

One of the major fears facing the world, particularly in times of recession, is that countries begin to look inwards. They mistakenly believe that their domestic economies would be better off if imports were controlled and restricted. In so doing they fail to recognise that other countries will react in the same way by restricting imports into their countries. It may be obvious but it is nevertheless worth saying that one country's imports are another country's exports. So by putting up trade barriers and restrictions which reduce world trade, all will eventually suffer. This type of policy, in which a country seeks to defend its domestic industries against competition from abroad, is called *protectionism*. During the great recession of the 1930s many countries turned to protectionism in a misguided attempt to stimulate their own flagging economies. The result was to dramatically reduce world trade and so harm many exporting industries. This deepened the world recession as exporting industries closed and laid off workers which further depressed domestic demand.

Since the Second World War most countries, and the UK in particular, have recognised that they must export to survive. Most developed countries came together in an organisation called the General Agreement on Tariffs and Trade (GATT). This aims to reduce trade barriers and encourage international trade. A little later in this section we shall consider the role of the General Agreement on Tariffs and Trade in more detail and examine how it tries to reduce barriers to world trade.

The Balance of Payments

How does the UK assess the value of its trade? How important is the balance of payments to the economy as a whole?

Nations, like businesses, need to keep a record of their income and expenditure. The national 'balance sheet' is known as the *balance of payments* and, at the end of a trading period, it will show either a profit (*surplus*) or a loss (*deficit*). A country's balance of payments statement is simply a comprehensive summary of all of the individual trading activities in which both the private and the public sector of the economy take part.

The balance of payments statement covers a specific period and the most important time period over which it is measured is one year. At this time, the government uses the figures to determine how much the country has bought or sold in the previous twelve months and whether this trade has resulted in a surplus or a deficit. The balance of payments is made up of two parts. The first is known as the *Current Account* which includes trade in goods and services. The second part of the balance of payments is sometimes called the *Capital Account,* but is more correctly called its *transactions in external assets and liabilities*.

The mechanics of the balance of payments

The system used to analyse the balance of payments is known as *double entry book-keeping*. All that this means is that every international trading transaction is entered into the account twice. For instance, if ICI sells £1m worth of chemicals to France, the value of the chemicals (£1m) is entered into a trade account as a credit. The French company buying the chemicals must also pay for the goods, either in francs or by transferring the payment into £ sterling. This is entered into a second account as an increase in the UK's currency holdings. This increase, whether in francs or pounds, is shown in sterling. If the payment has been made in francs, this entry is made by converting the value of the francs at the prevailing exchange rate.

The current account of the balance of payments

Let us begin by examining the current account of the balance of payments. The current account has two elements, visible trade and invisible trade. Visible trade (or as it is called trade in *visibles*) excludes trade in services, or *invisibles*: It includes raw materials, semi-processed or intermediate products and finished manufactured goods which can be seen and recorded as they cross national frontiers.

- *Visible trade.* Most of us tend to visualise imports and exports as tangible products being taken in and out of the country – Japanese cars shipped into the UK or British machinery sold abroad. This is called 'visible' trade, for the obvious reason that the goods are tangible and can be seen. This trade is vital for the survival of the UK, because this country is not self-sufficient in many of the products that it needs. About half of the food eaten in the UK is produced in other countries; in fact the UK imports much more food than we export and has what is called a £5 billion *food trade gap*. It also has a scarcity of raw materials and so must import such commodities as copper, zinc, iron ore, and rubber. Fortunately, the rest of the world buys many of our products to compensate for our visible imports and, also, the UK often acts as a middleman for the rest of the world's trade. So many of the imports seen on the debit side of the account as visible imports are then re-exported, following manufacture into some finished product or simply after being re-packaged.

The UK spends about one third of its national income on imports, a proportion that has increased as the UK has grown richer. It can only continue to purchase goods from abroad by earning foreign currency through selling its own products and services to foreigners and this has meant that it has, to a greater or lesser extent, been able to pay its way in the world.

Activity

Make a list of everything that you buy in a week. Include in this food, entertainment, transport and all the other purchases that you make. Then try to decide which products have been imported or at least have part of their ingredients or components imported. We think you will be somewhat amazed when you add it all up. Much of the food and drink you consume will have been imported. Even if you buy a Bruce Springstein CD, the CD itself may have been made in this country but Bruce's royalties will go back to the USA.

We illustrate the breakdown of the UK's visible trade in the table below.

Visible Trade of the UK

Exports	%	Imports	%
Food, beverages and tobacco	7.8	Food beverages and tobacco	10.3
Basic materials	2.0	Basic materials	4.2
Fuels	6.0	Fuels	5.0
Manufactures	82.2	Manufactures	79.0
Others	2.0	Others	1.5
Total	**100.00**	**Total**	**100.00**

Source: Monthly Digest of Statistics April 1992 (HMSO)

The UK still accounts for about 10% of world trade, but this is a declining percentage. In most years since 1945, the UK has imported more goods than it exported, which left a deficit in the balance of visible trade. However, since the exploitation of North Sea oil in the late 1970s, the country has not found it necessary to import as much oil and, in fact, has become a net exporter of oil. This has meant that exports have improved relative to imports, leading to a visible trade surplus in the early 1980s. Unfortunately, the rest of our visible exports have not fared as well: the improvement in the oil trade has been offset by a decline in the import/export balance for other goods, especially in manufactured products.

The late 1980s saw an increase in imports but this was not accompanied by any similar increase in the level of exports. Therefore a rapid deterioration of the visible trade balance resulted.

The surplus or deficit in visibles is often referred to as the *balance of trade*.

You can see how this situation has changed over the years from to the table below.

Visible Trade Balance — £ Million

	1980	1981	1982	1983	1984	1985
Visible Exports	47149	50668	5331	60700	70265	77991
Visible Imports	45792	47416	53421	62237	75601	–81336
Visible Balance	1357	3252	1910	–1537	–5336	–3345

	1986	1987	1988	1989	1990	1991
Visible Exports	72627	79153	80346	92389	102038	103704
Visible Imports	–82186	90735	101970	116987	120713	113823
Visible Balance	–9559	–11582	–21624	–24598	–18675	–10119

Source: United Kingdom Balance of Payments (HMSO)

- *Invisible trade*. As the table shows, the UK has had a massive *visible* trade deficit for some years. If this was the only type of trade in which countries were involved, then the UK would have gone deeper and deeper into debt. However, another important aspect of international trade is the import and export of services. As these are not physical products and cannot be seen, this is known as *invisible trade*. The UK is second only to the US with regard to invisible trade. The City of London is the major financial centre in the world; its provision of banking, insurance and shipping services is a major foreign currency earner for the UK. For these services, the UK receives payments from abroad and although it may, at times, have to pay out large sums, for instance on claims for the Los Angeles riots, the Piper Alpha oil rig explosion or the Exxon Valdez spillage, its receipts for these services outweigh the costs which it might have to bear.

Another important form of invisible trade is tourism. The position of tourism in the balance of payments might confuse you. For example, an American tourist coming on holiday to London is, in fact, part of our *invisible exports*. Although the tourist is coming into this country, he or she is bringing in money to spend in the UK, which is the equivalent of selling a British product abroad. Conversely, when a British tourist goes on holiday to Spain, that is part of our *invisible imports,* since sterling spent abroad is the equivalent of staying in the UK and importing a foreign product.

The invisible trade balance is normally in surplus and this helps to offset any visible trade deficit, helped by earnings from tourism. Also included in the invisible balance of the current account of the balance of payments are two other categories:

- property income from abroad and paid abroad;

- current transfers from abroad and paid abroad.

- *Property income from abroad and paid abroad.* Property income means all payments of interest, profits and dividends. UK individuals and companies invest money abroad in the hope of earning profits. Prior to 1979, this type of transaction was controlled by the government, who sought to restrict the outflow of funds from the UK. However, these capital transfer controls were lifted and this freedom, combined with the low potential earning from UK domestic investment, has resulted in a substantial increase in UK investment abroad. This investment has come from large British companies and financial bodies such as insurance companies, pension funds and unit trust investment companies. Of course foreign companies and individuals also invest in Britain. A recent example would be the purchase of Rowntree Mackintosh by the Swiss company, Nestlé. Part of the profits made from sales of Kit-Kats or Smarties is transferred back to Switzerland and forms a negative outflow on the current account. For both our investments abroad and foreigners investment in the UK we shall see later that the initial investment is counted as part of the second half of the balance of payments but the income from it forms part of the current account.

- *Current transfers from abroad and paid abroad.* Current transfers includes gifts between individuals in different countries. So if you send your cousin in Australia a £10 note for her birthday this would technically form a negative outflow from the balance of payments current account. The major element of current transfers, however, is not personal gifts. It is the payments made by the government in aid or as part of a relief programme or transfers between the government and other international organisations such as the EC. So for example when the government donates millions to help the Kurds in Iraq this would be included in the current transfers category as would our regular payments to the EC as part of our membership commitments. Conversely when the EC gives aid to Britain as part of its regional development programme this will show as a positive figure in the current transfers category.

Activity

Go to the library and find a copy of the Monthly Digest of Statistics or the United Kingdom Balance of Payments report. These will give details of the UK's trade statistics. Try and identify a trend in these figures over the last five years to help you decide whether this country's trade position is improving or deteriorating.

The following table shows the balance in invisible trade for the UK for recent years. Property income and current transfers are included in this figure.

Invisible Trade Balance   **£ Million**

	1980	1981	1982	1983	1984	1985
Invisible Balance	1487	3496	2741	5302	7146	6222

	1986	1987	1988	1989	1990	1991
Invisible Balance	9747	7423	6103	4195	4292	5719

Source: United Kingdom Balance of Payments (HMSO)

When we combine the UK's trade in visibles with its trade in invisibles we produce the *current account of the balance of payments*. This gives us an idea of how the country is performing as a trading nation. If it is in surplus then we are doing well and will build up extra foreign currency which we can use to pay off debts accumulated in poorer years or we can save the money as foreign reserves which we can use in the future.

The import and export of goods forms the major item on the current account with property income also playing a major part. Trade in services is a much lower contributor and current transfers is the least significant item.

If we are running a deficit on the current account, however, this shows that our trading performance is poor and that we are not generating enough from exports to pay for our imports. It means that we are not paying our way in the world and we will most probably have to borrow from other countries, institutions or individuals. The next table shows the UK's current account for the 1980s and early 1990s. From it you can see that our good overall trading performance in the early 1980s, to a large extent the result of the oil bonanza, has steadily deteriorated over the late 80s and early 90s. During the middle 80s the country experienced a short lived boom when credit was cheap and easy to obtain. Many consumers reacted by buying foreign goods such as cars and stereos and taking holidays abroad. The recession of the late 1980s and early 90s has curbed this credit boom and should have meant that the current account would return to surplus. It is of considerable concern to the government that despite the recession the current account continues to run at a hefty deficit.

Current Account of the Balance of Payments 1980/90
£ Million

	1980	1981	1982	1983	1984	1985
Visible Balance	1357	3252	1910	−1537	−5336	−3345
Invisible Balance	1487	3496	2741	5302	7146	6222
Current Account Total	2844	6748	4649	3765	1810	2877

	1986	1987	1988	1989	1990
Visible Balance	−9559	−11582	−21624	−24598	−18675
Invisible Balance	9747	7423	6103	4195	4292
Current Account Total	−188	−4159	−15521	−20403	−14383

Source: United Kingdom Balance of Payments 1991 (HMSO)

A little help on interpretation: If the figures shown have a minus sign (–) in front, this means that more money has left the country than has come into it, in other words a deficit. If there is no sign, or a positive sign (+), then this means that more money has come into the country than has gone out and so there is a surplus. Thus, on its current account the UK has had a deficit for each year since 1986.

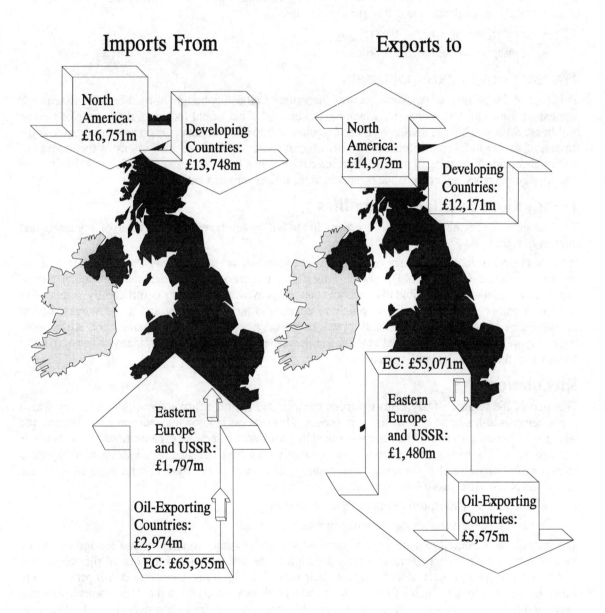

Imports From

North America: £16,751m

Developing Countries: £13,748m

Eastern Europe and USSR: £1,797m

Oil-Exporting Countries: £2,974m

EC: £65,955m

Exports to

North America: £14,973m

Developing Countries: £12,171m

EC: £55,071m

Eastern Europe and USSR: £1,480m

Oil-Exporting Countries: £5,575m

UK trade - based on 1992 figures

Transactions in external assets and liabilities

The second part of the balance of payments is sometimes called the *Capital Account,* but is more correctly called transactions in external assets and liabilities. This covers all transfers of capital into and out of the country. These occur as a result of investments, government lending or borrowing and the transfer of money through bank accounts. It is sub-divided into :

- transactions in external assets;
- transactions in external liabilities.

Transactions in external assets

This part of the balance of payments records the value of all assets bought abroad by UK citizens and companies minus the value of assets which have been sold. This would include the purchase of land or buildings. So if you bought a villa in Spain it would fall into this category. Of greater importance is the buying of shares in foreign companies by British companies or financial institutions or the lending of money abroad or the placing of money in foreign banks. When British companies or financial institutions buy foreign currency either for trade or speculation, it falls into this category.

Transactions in external liabilities

This category covers the value of assets bought in the UK by foreigners less the value of any assets that they have sold.

It would clearly be to the advantage of the UK if investment in this country was always greater than UK investment abroad as this would improve domestic employment and the demand for capital goods. However it is not always possible to create an economic environment which is sufficiently attractive to foreign investors. This problem is obviously of concern to the government and it encourages foreign investment by offering grants and incentives to foreign companies who establish plants here. An example is the way in which central and local government persuaded the Japanese car company, Nissan, to build a factory in the North East of England.

Speculation

This part of the balance of payments is further complicated by the influx and outflow of money which is not being used for trade or investment purposes. This process is known as *currency speculation* and takes the form of the transfer of bank deposits held by governments, private organisations and individuals into and out of UK banks. These deposits can be easily transferred abroad. Such speculative capital is known as *hot money* and it is moved from country to country by its owners who hope to make the maximum profit. This profit level depends on two factors:-

- the rate of interest offered in different countries;
- the changing value of the currency in which it is held.

The interest rates offered to depositors of capital vary from country to country and are influenced by each country's government. If interest rates are high in the UK relative to the rest of the world, this will encourage foreign speculators to deposit their money in this country because it will provide them with a high rate of return. Such inflows of money will be shown as a credit in the transactions in external assets and liabilities account. If these speculators then chose to withdraw their deposits and move them to another country which has now increased its interest rates above those offered in the UK, this will then be shown as a debit in the account.

A further factor influencing foreign currency speculation is the relative strength of specific currencies. For instance if a speculator decides to deposit money in a UK bank because of the high rate of interest offered here, his money will be converted into pounds. Therefore if the pound were to fall in value he could lose out when he exchanges his money out of sterling again, despite having a high rate of interest paid. This can be illustrated using a simple example.

A German speculator deposits 2.5m deutschmarks in a London bank. At the time of the original deposit the exchange rate stands at 2.5Dm = £1. Thus, his account is credited with £1m. If the London interest rate is 10% and he keeps the money in the London bank on deposit for 1 year his account now shows a value of £1.1m. But let us suppose that during the year in which the money is held in London the value of the pound has fallen to 2Dm = £1. Now when he transfers his assets back to Germany and back into deutschmarks, he will only receive the prevailing exchange rate. At the new prevailing exchange rate his £1.1m is now only worth 2.2m Dm. (£1.1 × 2Dm), and so his assets (in German currency) have fallen from 2.5m Dm to 2.2m Dm. Therefore despite getting a high rate of interest on his deposit he has lost money (at least in terms of his holding in D-marks) because of the fall in the value of the pound relative to the D-mark.

Thus as well as a good interest rate speculators also seek a stable – or better still an appreciating currency. If the pound is depreciating, that is falling in value, the government will have to offer higher interest rates to compensate for any potential fall if it is still to attract foreigners to put their money in Britain. The importance of this hot money speculation on the value of the pound will be explained later when we consider floating exchange rates.

The balancing item

A final item must be included in the balance of payments to allow for any errors or omissions which can quite easily result as the statistics are collected and collated. These can be caused either by mistakes on the part of the traders who may incorrectly record prices or exchange rates for their transactions or as a result of a statistical error on the part of the government statistical office which collates the figures.

To counteract this discrepancy an extra entry is included into the accounts and this is called *the balancing item*. When this adjustment is added the accounts should give a reasonable indication of the state of the country's position with regard to trade, capital movements and currency transactions.

Official financing

If the overall balance of payments is in deficit, the country has spent more abroad than it has received and this has to be financed in some way. It can do this either by borrowing from abroad or by drawing from the foreign currency reserves which it has accumulated as a result of previous trade surpluses.

The government will borrow foreign currency, either from the International Monetary Fund (IMF) or from foreign banks, foreign financial institutions or from individuals. If the overall balance is a surplus, then the government can use the surplus currency to add to its reserves or to repay debts it has already incurred. These transactions form part of the external assets item in the balance of payments.

The reserves

The government is reluctant to deplete its reserves since it must also use these foreign currency assets to maintain the value of its currency when it comes under speculative pressure. We shall discuss the way in which the government must use its foreign reserves to hold up the value of the pound in some detail a little later in this section.

The Value of the Pound

Sterling as a reserve currency

Much of the world's trade is carried on in the US dollar and, to a lesser extent, in other major currencies, such as the £ sterling and the deutschmark. These are *reserve currencies* because most countries in the world tend to hold these three currencies or gold. This means that the value of these currencies can be influenced, not only by the actions of their own countries' governments and by trade transactions, but also by that of other countries, organisations or individuals. This has placed a strain on the pound in recent years.

This problem is heightened by speculation in sterling which influences its value. The events of so called 'Black Wednesday' in September 1992 provide a vivid illustration of this. Speculators in both Britain and abroad decided that the pound was not worth the value at which it was being held in the Exchange Rate Mechanism (ERM). They sold pounds which forced its value down. Despite attempts by the Bank of England to maintain its value by using foreign reserves and borrowing foreign currency to buy sterling and so hold up its value, the sheer size of the speculation and the amount of pounds that were being sold was sufficient to force the government to take the pound out of the ERM and allow it to fall in value. This meant an effective devaluation of the pound. We shall look at Britain's membership of the ERM and the manner in which it was forced to leave the mechanism and devalue in more detail later in this section.

Fixed and floating exchange rates

Before 1971 the pound's value in relation to other currencies was fixed; after that date a system of floating exchange rates was introduced. In theory, this was based on the value of a currency being determined by its supply and demand. We can explain this simply in this way.

Suppose that the exchange rate between the American dollar and pound sterling is $2 to £1. This rate means that a British company selling a product costing £10 would ask $20 from an American consumer and an American company selling a product for $20 would ask £10 from a British consumer. Suppose also that the UK has a balance of trade deficit with the United States. This means that the UK does not sell as much to the USA as it imports from that country.

Because of our demand for US imports British consumers have a high demand for dollars to pay for them. As American consumers do not buy as many British imports they have a lower demand for pounds. The British consumers are trying to exchange a lot of pounds for dollars while the Americans do not wish to exchange as many dollars for pounds. Thus the supply of pounds onto the foreign exchange markets is high while demand for pounds is low and vice versa for the dollar.

Just as the supply and demand for any freely traded commodity determines its price then our high demand for dollars and the Americans' relatively low supply pushes up the value of the dollar and their low demand for pounds and our relatively high supply forces down the value of sterling. As the value of each currency is measured against each other this means that the value of sterling falls against the dollar. Because of this the pound falls in value to, say, $1.50 to £1.

As the exchange rate of the pound falls, UK exports to America become relatively cheaper as American buyers do not have to pay as much in their own currency to purchase British goods. Now the British company selling its product for £10 is willing to accept $15 in the USA. On the other hand the American company still wants $20 for its product but now asks £13.33p in Britain. UK exports therefore become more attractive to Americans and so they buy more British goods. Conversely we find American imports more expensive and so buy less.

In buying more of our goods the Americans now need more pounds to pay for them. We, of course, need fewer dollars as our imports fall. Demand for pounds goes up and its supply falls and the demand for dollars falls while its supply rises. Again the forces of supply and demand effect the relative values of the two currencies. The pound begins to rise against the dollar. Eventually the value of the pound against the dollar should stabilise at a point where we demand the same amount of American imports as they demand British exports. To put it another way the currency should stabilise when the balance of trade between the two countries is in equilibrium.

If we extend the explanation to our trade with the world as a whole - if we have a trade deficit, the value of the pound falls against other currencies until our exports become cheap enough to attract more foreign buyers and their imports become more expensive putting off British consumers. The pound stops falling when trade is in balance. Of course if we have a trade surplus, the value of the pound rises, making our exports less attractive and imports cheaper to British buyers. The pound rises until we again get a trade balance.

In theory, therefore, the price of the pound (its exchange rate) will rise or fall according to the demand for it and the supply of it, until demand equals supply at the point where imports match exports and the balance of payments actually balances.

This appears a wonderfully simple mechanism which should mean that we have self-adjusting trade balances. We should never have a massive deficit as the pound will fall to compensate nor should we have a massive surplus as this will lead the pound to rise. However, as we shall explain, there are a number of reasons why such a theory has not worked in practice.

Complications for floating the pound

There are two main problems when the pound is allowed to float freely.

- *The influence of speculation.* The idea behind floating the pound was that the demand for currency for use for trade purposes would be the main determining factor in setting the exchange rate. However, there is considerable speculation in world currencies, with people using them not as a means of financing trade, but as commodities which can be traded in to make profit.

  A recent estimate suggests that 95% of all currency transactions in foreign exchange markets are undertaken for speculation rather than for financing foreign trade. If speculators decide that sterling is about to fall in value, they will transfer all their money from sterling to dollars, deutschmarks or some other stronger currency. This will cause a massive growth in demand for foreign currency and a similar drop in demand (and an increase in supply) of pounds. The result will be that the pound falls in value against the dollar. Such currency transactions for profit rather than trade are known as speculation. We have already mentioned the power of the speculators on 'Black Wednesday' in September 1992 when selling of pounds led to its suspension from the ERM and its subsequent devaluation. Speculators consider two main factors when deciding in which currency to leave their money. The seek a high interest rate in return for depositing their money and they do not leave their money in a currency which is going to depreciate or fall in value.

- *The effect of the exchange rate on domestic inflation.* The exchange rate also has a significant effect on the rate of domestic inflation, since the UK is dependent on imported food, raw materials and much else. These have to be bought even if their price goes up.

A fall in the value of the pound – which causes import prices to rise – will not result in a significant fall in imports, but merely an increase in their price. If the exchange rate falls 5%, this will cause a 1% increase in domestic inflation.

If a government is trying to minimise inflation, it must keep the value of the pound as high as possible. However, if it does this, it can result in fewer exports (since they will be more expensive abroad) and more imports (because they will be cheaper in the UK), thus worsening the balance of payments. The government must decide what is its more urgent priority: keeping down inflation or eradicating a balance of payments deficit.

Activity

Over the period of a week plot the changing value of the pound against the dollar and the Dmark. Try and identify the reasons for any fluctuation in the exchange rate.

Future prospects for the UK balance of payments

The UK has been in balance of payments deficit for most of the last thirty years. However, North Sea oil has meant the UK has become a net exporter of oil, thus adding to the credit side of the balance of payments. It should be noted that this favourable addition to the credit side of the balance is somewhat misleading, since UK exports in products or commodities, other than oil, have actually fallen relative to imports over the same period. Deficits greater than £10 billion are treated now as commonplace. In the first two months of 1992 the current account deficit stood at £1558 million. The trade gap continues to widen: since the 1987 election, which returned a Conservative government to office for the third successive time, only one month has seen the current account in the black.

Means of Controlling the Balance of Payments

If this situation continues what are the possible solutions for the UK government?

Many people believe that the UK should try and protect some of its infant industries. 'Infant industries' are those industries which are only just establishing themselves. For example, the French government places import restrictions on certain electrical products. This is to allow the domestic French economy to develop their production. Traditional industries also may require protection from foreign competition. Imports can be restricted by the use of:

- tariffs;
- quotas.

Tariffs are taxes which can be levied on all imports or on specific commodities. The effect of a tariff will depend on the demand for the product. If there is relatively inelastic demand and the domestic industry is unable to produce the product at a price which is less than the import price plus the tariff then the tax will be relatively ineffective. If demand for the import continues then it is in effect a tax on the domestic consumer. It will be a successful means of curbing imports only if the product has an elastic demand or home producers can step in to meet the demand for imports which has been diverted to domestic products because of the import tariff.

Quotas are restrictions placed on the *quantity* of a commodity which is allowed in to the country. Quotas may be statutory (imposed by the government) or voluntary.

There are several problems associated with in the introduction of tariffs and quotas.

- *The UK is party to a general world agreement which discourages tariffs.*. This is called GATT (The General Agreement on Tariffs and Trade). This agreement is signed by 170 countries and has led to a general reduction in tariffs and quotas throughout the world. It is based on four principles:

- that there should be no 'favoured nation status'. In other words, all GATT member nations should receive the same treatment in respect of import controls;

- when import controls are imposed these should be in the form of tariffs and not statutory quotas;

- that there should be consultation between members wherever possible on matters relating to trade restrictions.

- GATT members should work to reduce tariffs between members. GATT has proved very successful in reducing the imposition of tariffs and quotas and doing this has led to a significant increase in world trade. GATT has worked hard to reduce the $500 billion that unequal or restricted access to world trade and their financial and labour markets is estimated to cost the poor countries of the world each year. The workings of the GATT are considered in greater detail later in this element.

- *The UK is a member of the European Economic Community (EC)* This restricts our freedom to influence trade both within the EC – to and from fellow member countries – as well as outside the EC. The EC has two functions:

  - it is a customs union and as such does not, at least in theory, allow the imposition of any trade restrictions such as tariffs and quotas between its member states; the implications of the Single European Market are considered later;

  - it imposes a common external tariff. This means that imports to any country in the EC are subject to the same level of tariff taxation. In this way the EC increases the import price of those goods which are also produced within the EC and so allows Community producers to compete on equal terms with imports which are produced more cheaply abroad. The structure and functions of the EC are discussed more fully later in the element.

- *There is the possibility that such trade restrictions could actually be disadvantageous if levied on specific countries*. It is suggested that these countries could retaliate in turn and impose similar restrictions on our exports to their countries. However, it has been pointed out that Japan, whose imports are often suggested as a possible target for such *import controls*, does not import on any major scale from the UK and so any retaliation on their part would be relatively ineffective.

Import controls have been suggested as a possible short-term solution to any future balance of payments problem as they would allow a gradual realignment of the UK's industries without the shock of rapid upheaval in our industrial base caused by massive unemployment. Those who hold the opposite view have argued that such measures are merely 'featherbedding' inefficient British industry. In other words, tariffs and quotas would not allow such industries to face the harsh realities of economic life in the world today. If industries are inefficient, then they should be allowed to 'go under', and their resources used in more cost-effective and competitive industries.

Perhaps the reality of the world economic situation is such that if you look at declining industries in most of the Western nations, you will find that they are being subsidised to a much greater extent than those in the UK. Therefore, the UK government could recognise that it must try and combine a realistic economic approach to international trade with the need for an understanding and compassionate approach to those workers faced with long-term unemployment. Such job losses are partly a consequence of the decline in our traditional industries, like coal, steel and shipbuilding, and so the imposition of trade controls should not always been seen as the abandonment of free market ideals but, instead, a recognition that UK governments are prepared to protect the jobs of its workers.

The Government can stimulate investment by UK exporters

A further alternative, which has been suggested and tried in the past, is the encouragement of UK industry to invest and, in so doing, to become more internationally competitive. Such a policy may involve the government in persuading the banks to give loans at cheaper rates to exporters. The government can also give exporters specific tax relief on investment or guarantee that exporters will be paid for their products sold in certain countries.

This can prove difficult in practice, as was found in the early 1970s by the Heath Government. It sought to encourage British industry to re-invest, prior to the UK's entry into the EC. The cheap loans which were given were often not used for investment in exporting industry but instead were used for property speculation and domestic consumption, helping in the process to fuel inflation.

The main policy at the current time is not to directly subsidise exports, but more to encourage businesses to attempt to break into foreign markets. Aid is given in the form of grants to facilitate research into foreign markets and to prepare detailed financial analyses of such export projects. Subsidies for actual products or services are now virtually non-existent.

Deflation of the economy

Finally, if the balance of payments deficit is sufficiently large, as it was in 1974, 1975 and 1976, the government may be faced with the need to *deflate* the overall economy and in so doing reduce the demand for imports. Unfortunately, this will have the side effect of also making it more difficult for exporters to produce, as interest rates may increase and this can also lead to higher domestic unemployment.

The UK has been extremely lucky to have the cushion of North Sea oil which has protected the country from even greater balance of payments problems in recent years. However, when the oil runs out, the UK could well be faced with a disastrous situation. Therefore, policies designed to revitalise export industries – and ensure that the products the UK makes can compete with those of the rest of the world – are even more imperative.

The European Community and the European Union

The *European Community* (EC) or as it will now be called the *European Union* was first conceived in the aftermath of the Second World War. That war had torn Europe apart causing millions of deaths and destroying the social and economic infrastructure of the continent. It had been the final episode in the centuries of warfare which had plagued Europe and placed France and Germany as bitter rivals. Clearly it was time for a change and it was obvious to a group of far-seeing statesmen in both countries that it was imperative that a structure was established that would guarantee peace in Europe and provide a framework for democracy and social and economic collaboration. The two architects of the new order were the Frenchmen, Jean Monet and Robert Schumann. The former was a senior civil servant and the latter was the country's Foreign Minister and they argued that what was needed was a plan for co-operation which was innovative in approach yet achievable in scale. They suggested that the coal and steel industries of France and Germany be placed under the joint control of a single authority and in so doing go some way to removing the possibility of future wars between the two.

In 1950 Germany and France agreed to this proposal, which was known as the '*Schumann Plan*'. Other European countries were invited to participate and from the start, Italy, Belgium, Luxemburg and the Netherlands decided to do so.

This agreement was formalised in 1951 with the formation of the *European Coal and Steel Community* (ECSC). This historic move was to lay the foundations of the present European Community.

The next major landmark in European integration came in 1957 when the original six members of the ECSC took their collaboration one stage further and signed two treaties. The first was to establish the *European Atomic Energy Community* (Euroatom) in which they agreed to harmonise their development of atomic power. The second, and by far the more significant, was the Treaty of Rome which created the *European Economic Community* (EEC) or the '*Common Market*' as it became known. This treaty laid down the principle that, over time, the six would seek to move towards closer economic co-operation and co-ordination. Initially this would take the form of a 'customs union'. This would allow producers in one state in the community to sell their goods in another without government restrictions or import duties. Formerly it had been a common practice for a government to protect its domestic economy with such import controls or by subsidising its own industries.

Throughout this early period of European integration, Britain chose to stay on the side-lines. It still regarded itself as a major world power which tended to distance itself from the rest of Europe. A famous headline which read 'Fog in the Channel, Europe cut-off' summed up the view of our unique position in the world. Britain had only recently transformed its Empire into the Commonwealth and it felt that its strong political and trade links both with its former colonies and with the United States would be prejudiced if it were to side with the Europeans.

This view changed somewhat in the late 1950s and by the early 1960s the British government had decided to apply for membership of the EEC. If it had assumed that it would be welcomed with open arms it was to be proved wrong. The British had not reckoned with the French President, General Charles de Gaulle. He wished to preserve the position of France and Germany as the main political forces in Europe and did not welcome the entry of another major player. Under the conditions of the Treaty of Rome any new member would have to be unanimously accepted by all existing members and so de Gaulle was able to prevent Britain's entry by using the French veto. It was only after he had left the Presidency that Britain was able to resume negotiations on entry.

In 1973 following a period of negotiation and preparation the United Kingdom, Ireland and Denmark joined the EEC and 'the Six' became 'the Nine'. Norway had intended to join at the same time but a national referendum had voted against it. Doubts too still existed in the UK and Edward Heath, the Conservative Prime Minister who had led Britain into Europe with such enthusiasm, faced strong opposition from within the ranks of the Tory Party. (It is clear to see that today's euroscepticism among the Conservative party is long-standing and deep-seated.) Heath lost the 1974 election and in 1975 the new Labour Prime Minister, Harold Wilson, chose to call a referendum on Britain's continued membership of the Community. Despite intense opposition from across the political spectrum, both the Labour government and the Conservative opposition favoured staying in and a majority in the referendum confirmed this.

The Community has continued to grow and in 1981 Greece became the tenth state to join and in 1986 Spain and Portugal brought the membership to twelve. With the unification of Germany in 1990 the 18 million citizens of former East Germany became part of the Community.

Austria, Sweden, Finland and Norway are joining in 1994 and others including Cyprus, Malta, Turkey and Switzerland have either made an application to join or are considering applying. Several Eastern European countries including Poland and the Czech republic would like to move towards economic union in the future.

The growth of the European Community

1952

Belgium, France,
Italy, Luxemborg,
West Germany and
the Netherlands-
join together to
regulate their
coal and steel
industries.

1958

The six sign the treaty
of Rome to form the
EEC. Communist
Eastern bloc
countries were
disbarred from
membership

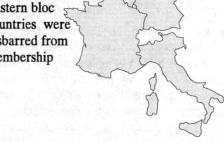

1973

Britain, Denmark and the
Irish Republic join
the EEC to form The
Nine. Norway had
planned to enter, but its
citizens rejected this in a
referendum

1981

Greece joined

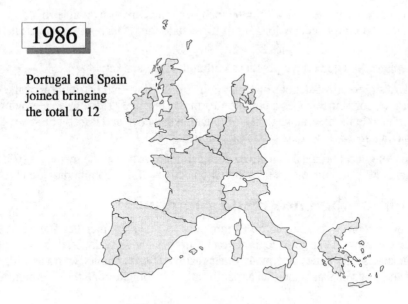

1986

Portugal and Spain
joined bringing
the total to 12

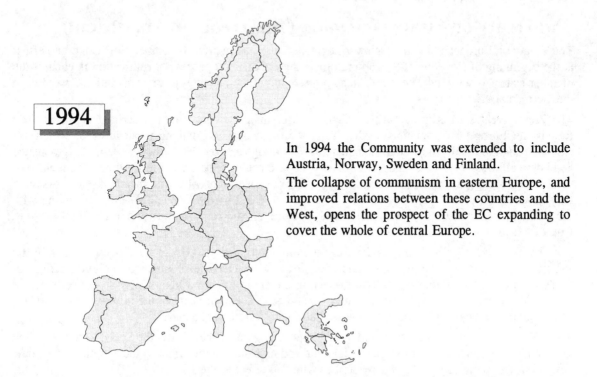

1994

In 1994 the Community was extended to include
Austria, Norway, Sweden and Finland.

The collapse of communism in eastern Europe, and
improved relations between these countries and the
West, opens the prospect of the EC expanding to
cover the whole of central Europe.

The aims and objectives of the EC

As suggested by its title, the EC had economic aims and objectives. These include:

- the creation of a single market within the member states that is available to all manufacturers and producers belonging to these states and which is free from tariff barriers;

- the maintenance of competitive practices within the free market;

- the standardisation of regulations governing the production and distribution of the goods; and the use of euro-currency as a common form of currency. The aim of removing controls to enable the free movement of EC nationals between the member states can be seen as having social as well as economic implications.

The EC also has its long term political objective, political union between the members. Clearly, as for each of the member states, the economic and political objectives of the Community are closely related.

The operation of the European Community

Through the Treaties which have brought the Community together the member states have given the Community institutions powers to act and legislate on a European wide scale. Such powers affect trade, economic development, social policy and many other matters. For example EC trade with the outside world is regulated and controlled as is internal agricultural production through the Common Agricultural Policy.

The Single European Act of 1986 widened the Community's powers and paved the way for the removal of trade barriers and the establishment of the Single Market. It also gave the Community authority to act in new spheres such as the environment.

The Treaty on European Union (The Treaty of Maastricht)

The Treaty on European Union which was negotiated in Maastricht in November 1991 came into effect at the beginning of November 1993, after completing the difficult process of ratification in each of the member states. It survived a second Danish referendum and challenges to its constitutional validity in the German and UK courts.

The Treaty creates a European Union which has three main elements, often described as *pillars*. The first is the European Community itself, the powers and decision making procedures of which are extended and modified. The second element relates to foreign and security policy, and the third to justice and home affairs. The second and third pillars operate outside of the formal institutional framework of the EC and are based on new inter-governmental arrangements between the member states. As such they do not form part of the body of the EC which is created by the Council of Ministers acting with the Commission and European Parliament and they are not subject to the jurisdiction of the European Court of Justice.

The first part of the Treaty expands the areas of community activity. Under the Treaty the task of the European Community will be to promote a harmonious and balanced development of economic activities, sustainable and non-inflationary growth respecting the environment, a high degree of convergence of economic performance, a high level of employment and of social protection, the raising of the standard of living and quality of life, and economic and social cohesion and solidarity.

The UK, however, negotiated to opt out of two important parts of the Treaty, the Social Chapter (which we examine later) and the third stage of economic and monetary union which is the adoption of a single currency. The remainder of the Treaty applies with full effect to the UK.

The Treaty formally extends the legal competence of the EC in a number of areas. In some respects this is simply a confirmation of competence in areas where the community already takes action, for example its long standing practice of bringing forward consumer protection proposals as single market measures or under broader powers to eliminate distortions in competition. In other respects the EC's competence has genuinely been extended. The Treaty on European Union gives or extends EC competence in the following areas:

- Citizenship of the EC
- Transport policy
- Research and technological development
- Culture
- Public health
- Consumer protection
- Trans-European networks in the areas of transport, telecommunications and energy
- Industry
- Education
- Civil protection
- Development co-operation with third world countries
- Environment
- Economic and monetary policy

The Treaty operates, like the Single European Act, by inserting amendments into the Treaty of Rome.

The Maastricht Treaty makes express provision for the principle of *subsidiarity*. Under this principle the community will act within the limits of the powers conferred upon it and of the objectives assigned to it. In areas which do not fall within its exclusive competence the community can take action only if and in so far as the objectives of the proposed action cannot be sufficiently achieved by the member states and can be better achieved by the community. Thus action should only be taken at EC level where such action if taken at the national or regional level would be inadequate or inappropriate. Any action by the community must not go beyond what is necessary to achieve the common objectives of the treaties. The principle of subsidiarity is designed to safeguard the residual powers and competences of the member states.

The Institutions of the European Community

The Community has five main institutions:

- the Council of Ministers;
- the European Council;
- the European Parliament;
- the European Commission;
- the European Court of Justice.

The Council of Ministers

This is the Community's major decision-making body. It consists of one minister, usually the Foreign Minister, from each of the twelve member states. When specific topics, such as finance or agriculture are under discussion, the states are represented by the minister with those specific responsibilities. Thus over a transport issue, the membership will comprise the transport ministers from the government of each member state, and over agricultural matters, the agricultural ministers.

The Council meets each month and its Presidency rotates every six months between the members in alphabetical order. For example Britain held the Presidency for the last six months of 1992. Its meetings are held in private usually in the country which currently holds the Presidency although the headquarters of its secretariat is in Brussels.

Decisions in the Council are taken on the basis of unanimity in some cases, and by qualified majority in others. A qualified majority is secured when 54 out of 76 votes are cast in favour of a measure. France, Germany, Italy and the UK have ten votes each, Spain has eight, Belgium, Greece, the Netherlands and Portugal five each, Denmark and Ireland three each and Luxemburg two.

As might be expected the Council of Ministers has not worked in total harmony over the years, with individual ministers seeking to protect their own national interests at the expense of broader European interests.

The council can make major policy statements to the European Parliament, for debate there. Its strength lies in the fact that it has the final say over Community legislation.

The European Council

In 1974 the heads of member states agreed to meet regularly with the President of the Commission as the 'European Council'. This now meets twice a year. The Council acts both as the Council of the Community, in discussing Community matters, and as a forum for political co-operation.

The significance of the European Council in the workings of the Community has grown substantially. Its twice yearly meetings, which tend to take the form of 'European summits', often provide the setting for major initiatives or policy proposals and the country which holds the Presidency for a six month period is in a strong position to promote its own ideas. However one major drawback of this system is that while agreements can be reached at this level, each member state's head of government then has to take the decision back to his or her domestic parliament for ratification, a process which is often far from easy.

The European Parliament

The European Parliament is made up of Members (MEPs) from each member state. The number of members from each state is broadly determined by its population size with Germany, Italy, France and the United Kingdom each having the largest number of seats. Each member country uses its own national electoral system and while the other 11 use some form of proportional representation, the UK still continues with its 'first past the post' approach.

It sits for a five year term with elections in 1989, 1994 and 1999 and so on. It holds its meetings mainly in Strasbourg although some of its meetings are held in Brussels and its secretariat is largely based in Luxemburg. Its main sessions are open to the general public. MEPs do not sit in national groups but rather in political groupings. There are six official political groups to which members can belong: Communists and Allies; Socialists; Christian Democrats; European Progressive Democrats; and Liberals and Democrats.

A considerable amount of the Parliament's work is carried out by committees, and the largest political group is able to exert its influence by choosing the chairperson for these committees, and through being the largest single voting block in the Parliament. The work of the committees reflects the various responsibilities of the Community generally. They range from the committees for Political Affairs, Legal Affairs and Economic and Monetary Affairs, to Regional Policy, Planning and Transport, Social Affairs, Employment and Education and Development and Co-operation. There is also, of course, a Budget Committee.

As under our own Parliamentary system, individual members can raise matters which are of concern to their own constituents before the European Parliament, as well as debating issues of general European interest. Discussion is by means of public debate.

The Powers of the Parliament

These are closely controlled. However, the Parliament can:

- *dismiss the commissioners who control the Commission* (i.e. the executive arm of the Community, which is considered below). To do so however a censure motion must be passed by a two thirds majority. The Parliament oversees the work of the Commission ensuring that it acts in the best interests of the Community. This is achieved by MEPs tabling questions to the Commission and to the Council.

- *exercise certain powers in respect of the Community's budget*, having a final say regarding some items of expenditure, and having the ultimate power to reject the entire budget, a power it has used on some occasions. In such circumstances a conciliation procedure operates between the Parliament and the Council of Ministers. The passing of revenue for the budget depends upon each member state contributing its agreed contribution of EC funds. Wealthier member States contribute more than the poorer ones. The overall effect this will have on an individual member state can be that it contributes far more than it receives in grants and subsidies. Mrs. Thatcher caused considerable political controversy over the United Kingdom's contribution to the budget when she sought to reduce the amount the United Kingdom was obliged to provide, on the grounds that it imposed an inequitable burden on the UK as a substantial net contributor.

- *present its views on proposals submitted by the Commission to the Council of Ministers.* The Parliament and the Commission work closely together on legislative proposals. It should be pointed out that although the Commission is an administrative body, the Commissioners can and do present policy proposals to both the Parliament and the Council of Ministers.

The European Commission

The Commission is situated in Brussels and is in effect the Community's administrative arm and to some extent can be compared to our own civil service, although as we shall see its powers are wider. Its responsibilities include the drafting of Community legislation and managing of the Community's budget. The Commission is run by seventeen Commissioners, who although nominated by individual member states are bound to act independently of their national governments and to promote the interests of the Community as a whole. The Commission operates under the direction of the Commissioners, with each member state being represented by at least one Commissioner. Some countries, including the UK, have two. The commissioners can present policy proposals to the legislative bodies of the Community, however their main responsibility is the control of the enormous bureaucracy, numbering many thousands to staff, who administer the policies of the Community. Like the Council of Ministers, the Commission has as its head a President. Jacques Delors has been a particularly active President of the Commission. It is said of the Commission that it acts as a counter-balance to the Council of Ministers, taking a European view rather than a national one.

The European Court of Justice

This is Europe's supreme judicial body. It sits is Luxemburg and comprises thirteen judges, one from each member state plus one more. Its judgments are final on matters of European law and take precedence over national law. The work of the judges is assisted by three Advocates-General, whose function is to present before the court impartial arguments on matters which are at issue. Unlike British courts, the function of the European court involves the discovery of facts using its own initiative, as well as reaching decisions through issuing judgements.

The jurisdiction of the court is wide. It can:

- hear actions brought against a member state by either the Commission (which enforces Community law) or another member state alleging non-compliance with Treaty obligations;
- hear actions brought against the Institutions of the Community by member states, organisations and individuals; and
- give a ruling on the interpretation of any of the Treaties. Such a ruling, which is a preliminary one, will follow a request to the court from a court or tribunal of one of the member states. After the ruling has been given it is left to the court or tribunal in question to apply the ruling to the facts of the case before it.

Under Article 177 of the Treaty of Rome the preliminary ruling of the European Court must be sought where a court in a member state from which there is no right of appeal is hearing a case which turns upon the meaning of one of the treaties.

European Community Law

The United Kingdom has been a member of the European Communities since 1972 following the *European Communities Act* of that year. As a Member State the United Kingdom is bound by EC law. The most significant feature of EC law is that it overrides any conflicting provisions in the national laws of Member States. This was acknowledged by the European Court of Justice in the case of *Costa v. ENEL* 1964 where it was stated:

> *"The law stemming from the treaty, an independent source of law, would not, because of its special and original nature, be overridden by domestic legal provisions, however framed, without being deprived of its character as community law and without the legal basis of the community itself being called into question".*

The European Communities Act gives legal force in the UK to EC law and provides for the supremacy of EC law so that it is the highest form of UK law.

> In 1974 Ld Denning MR in the case of *Bulmer Ltd. v. Bollinger* said in relation to EC law *"when we come to matters with a European element the treaty is like an incoming tide. It flows into the estuaries and up the rivers. It cannot be held back. Parliament has decreed that the treaty is henceforward to be part of our law. It is equal in force to any statute".*

The main driving force has been the determination to complete the internal market by the end of 1992.

EC legislation is concerned with numerous matters in particular:

- revising physical, technical and fiscal barriers to trade between Member States;
- opening up of public procurement to community wide tendering;
- encouraging the free movement of goods, services and capital within the community;
- harmonisation of laws relating to business;
- enabling the free movement of individuals including rights of establishment and the mutual recognition of qualifications;
- consumer protection; and
- employment and social policy.

Following the Single European Act 1986, community law has also had a major impact on the environment, competition, agriculture and fisheries, transport and energy.

Types of EC Law

The channels through which community law flows are many and various. In fact there are three main sources, the treaties, secondary legislation of the community and unwritten general principles. All Member States who have joined the EC since its inception are required to adopt the community measures in force when they acceded.

Primary legislation

The primary legislation of the EC consists of the European Treaties and associated documents which have been agreed by the Member States. These include:

- the Treaty of Paris 1951;
- the Treaty of Rome 1957;
- the Euratom Treaty 1957;
- the Merger Treaty 1965;
- various Treaties of Accession on the admission of new members to the community;
- a number of Association Agreements with non members; and
- the Single European Act 1986 which extended the areas of competence of the EC, introduced the co-operation procedure and a programme for the completion of the single market by the end of 1992.
- the Treaty on European Union 1993.

The treaties set out the framework of EC law to create the institutions which operate the community and lay down procedures for making secondary legislation on an ongoing basis.

Member States must adapt their law in order to comply with the provisions of the treaties. The Equal Pay (Amendment) Regulations 1983 amended the Equal Pay Act 1970 to bring it into line with Article 199 of the Treaty of Rome and the Equal Pay Directive 1975.

The provisions (articles) of Treaties may be directly enforceable in national courts if they create rights and obligations as between individuals, and individuals and the state.

To be directly applicable the provision must be clear and unconditional and must require no further legislative intervention either on the part of the Member States or the Community Institutions to implement it or give it effect. Examples include:

- Article 30 which prohibits restrictions on imports;
- Article 48 which prohibits discrimination in employment based on nationality;
- Articles 85/86 which prohibit anti-competitive practices;
- Article 119 on equal treatment of men and women in employment.

  In *Bourgoin v. Ministry of Agriculture* 1986 the UK government wrongfully prohibited the import of French turkeys during the Christmas season contrary to Article 30. The prohibition was eventually lifted by the Court of Appeal which ordered the UK government to pay the French turkey producer £3.5m compensation.

Secondary legislation

The European Treaties confer significant law making powers on the Institutions of the Community although these powers only extend to areas where the Community has competence to legislate. There are some areas that remain within the exclusive domain of the national sovereignty of the member state.

Under Article 189 *"in order to carry out their task the Council of Ministers and the Commission shall in accordance with the provisions of the Treaty, make Regulations, issue Directives, take Decisions, make Recommendations or deliver Opinions."*

Regulations are generally applicable and are binding in their entirety. They are directly applicable in all Member States. These is no requirement at national level to take any action to bring them into effect. They take effect on the date specified or the 20th day following their publication in the Official Journal.

Directives are binding on Member States and set out general principles that have to be observed. Article 189 states that "A Directive shall be binding as to the result to be achieved upon each Member State to which it is addressed, but shall leave to the national authorities the choice of form and methods."

Directives are the major instrument for achieving the harmonisation of national laws between Member States. They operate by setting out the objective which the proposed new laws must achieve, giving a time limit within which Member States must achieve them. A directive could be described as an instruction to Member States to amend their laws to achieve a particular result within a particular time. States can decide for themselves how this is to be achieved but in the UK directives are implemented by a new statute or by delegated legislation. There is however no need to implement a directive if the directives objective is already achieved by current domestic law.

If a national court believes that a directive has not been implemented correctly then it is required to limit or extend the national provisions in a manner consistent with the directive. In Consumer Protection law a good example of where the UK Government failed to achieve the object of a directive is the Product Liability Directive (see Element 1). Its aim was to impose strict liability on procedures of defective products for damage caused. By redrafting the development risk defence the UK Government conferred on manufacturers a defence to product liability which was more extensive than the legislation envisaged.

It was generally thought that directives where not enforceable until implemented by the Member State. The European Court has ruled however that in certain exceptional cases a directive or at least some of its provisions may be directly enforceable before the implementation. Those circumstances are that:

- the date of implementation has expired;
- the terms of the directive are clear, precise and unconditional;
- the person against whom the directive is pleaded is the State.

The main reason behind this exception is that a Member State should not be allowed to rely on its own failure to implement a directive in an action brought by an individual against the state. For this purpose the state has been given a wide definition and would cover a public authority.

> In *Foster v. British Gas* 1990 the court held that a provision in a directive which has direct effect *"may be relied upon in a claim for damages against a body, whatever its legal form, which has been made responsible for providing a public service under the control of the state"*.

> In *Francovitch v. Italian Republic* 1992 the European Court of Justice reaffirmed the principle of community law that a Member State is liable to make good damage to individuals caused by a breach of community law for which it is responsible. Here the Italian Government had failed to legislate to implement an EC directive on the protection of employees on the employers insolvency. This was despite the fact that the European Commission had already brought proceedings against the Italian Government for this very infringement. The court confirmed that an individual can sue the State directly for damages under community law for failure by the State to take the necessary steps to achieve the result required by the directive. Three conditions must be satisfied:
>
> - the result required by the directive must involve conferring individual rights;

- the content of these rights may be determined by reference to the directive;
- there must be a causal link between the breach of the obligation of the State and the damage suffered by the person affected.

The importance of this decision is that it provides employees in the private sector as well as the public sector with a remedy if they suffer damage as a result of the failure of a Member State to implement a directive or implement it incorrectly.

Decisions are legally binding on those Member States to whom they are addressed. They may also be addressed to individuals, business organisations or public sector bodies for example a decision could be made to grant a particular organisation exemption from the rules relating to competition policy.

One of the principal roles of the European Court of Justice is to consider the validity of the acts done or measures adopted by Member States or the European Institutions when challenged on the grounds of incompatibility with the Treaties. Also under Article 177 the court has jurisdiction to give a preliminary ruling on the meaning or interpretation of any aspect of community law. Every national court or tribunal is entitled to request a ruling if either party requests or on its own motion.

The European Commission is the guardian of the Treaties and as the executive arm of the EC it is responsible for the implementation of agreed policies. The Commission must ensure compliance with Community obligations and for this purpose it has power to impose fines and bring individuals, organisations or even Member States before the European Court of Justice. Between 1982 and 1989 the Commission instituted 3,902 proceedings against Member States of which 266 related to the UK. An example is the Product Liability Directive of which the Commission has complained that the UK Government has failed to implement in six respects. The power of the Commission to impose fines is illustrated by the decision in Tetra Pak 1992 (see Element 1).

Activity

Establish the name of the Euro-Constituency you live in. What is the name of the M.E.P (Member of the European Parliament) who is at present your elected representative, which political party does he or she represent, and where is his or her office in your constituency? See if you can find out what the size of your Euro-Constituency electorate is, and how many Parliamentary Constituencies are included within its boundary.

Write to your M.E.P's office to ask for literature describing and explaining how the European Community and its institutions work.

The Community Budget

The EC has its own budget which is financed by revenue which the member states are obliged to provide. Its budget differs from those of its member states in that the EC's budget must balance. It is agreed annually by the Council of Ministers and the European Parliament on the basis of a draft budget prepared by the Commission. The Community has a very large budget. In 1991 it was 56,000 billion ecu which is about £39 billion. (To put this figure in perspective the UK government's budget for 1991 was about £205 billion). This accounts for about 1% of the combined GNP of the Community's member states.

The UK contributes approximately 20% of the EC's budget. For many years this has been a source of dispute as our GNP is only about 16% of the total of all EC member states and our share of EC spending is only about 7% of the total. Thus the UK is a net contributor to the Community while other countries with higher GNP per head such as Denmark and the Netherlands receive a net benefit. Nevertheless other major economies as Germany and France are, like the UK, net contributors.

One of the main reasons why the UK is a net loser from the EC in terms of financial contribution and benefit is that we are major importers of food, much of which is from outside the EC. We therefore receive comparatively small amounts from the Agricultural Fund while having to make major contributions. This imbalance was tackled to some degree in the 1980s when Mrs Thatcher negotiated a reduction in UK contributions but is still nonetheless a bone of contention.

EC expenditure

The EC spends its resources in a number of ways:

- By far the largest element of the Community's expenditure is on agricultural support and this currently accounts for over 50% of the EC's total spending.

- The second largest area of expenditure is on the European Regional Development Fund. The Fund provides cash to support the development of the poorer regions of the Community. It finances projects such as transport infrastructure improvements and telecommunications. This element of spending accounts for approximately 10% of the EC's budget.

- The third major element is spending through the Social Fund. This accounts for about 7% of spending and is used for projects providing training and employment, particularly for the long term unemployed and for the young. A breakdown of the EC's spending is shown in the diagram below.

EC revenue

The EC raises its revenue from four sources:

- the Community raises this money by levying customs duties on goods entering the Community. These are collected by the individual member states and then forwarded to Brussels;

- additionally each member contributes part (about 1.5%) of its VAT revenue to the Community budget;

- all member states also makes a contribution to Community funds based on its gross national product;

- finally the EC raises revenue from levies imposed on imported agricultural produce. These levies are intended to raise the price of imported food stuff to a level at which EC produced goods can compete within the Community market.

Activity

Try to identify any aspect of European Funding in your area. If you live in a development area then you will no doubt see infrastructure projects such as roads which have signs that indicate that they have received funding from the European Regional Development Fund. If you live in other areas you may have to look a little harder but we are sure you can find examples of European funding for projects or for people.

The Single Market

Since the inception of the Community in 1957 the establishment of a single market has been a primary objective. It has come about in stages over the last thirty five years and is complete, at least in principle, by the end of 1992.

In forming the Single Market Europe as a whole has recognised the need to combine to form a cohesive unit in the face of considerable competition from its major economic rivals. As we have already noted the market itself now has over 344 million consumers which is almost as large as the United States and Japan combined and has the potential with the forming of the European Economic Area and increased membership of the Community to become even larger. This area will be responsible for almost 50% of world trade, much of it now within the Community itself. For instance more than half of Britain's trade is now with other EC members.

The historical background

The idea of establishing a Single European Market is not a new one. Indeed, the concept dates back to the Treaty of Rome which established the original European Economic Community in 1957. The growth of the EC is shown on the map opposite. The original plans for the establishment of the Single European Market were based on political and economic motives. Europe had just come through a terrible war, and a common desire existed for peace and unity. The EC was perceived as an outstanding opportunity for nations to rebuild after the War and to give to each other mutual support. It was hoped that the possibility of any future conflict in Europe would also be minimised by the 'economic marriage' of various states.

In 1985, the EC heads of government committed their states to the formation of a *Single European Market* by 1992. Their proposals were formalised in the package of Treaty reforms known as the Single European Act, which came into operation on 1 July 1987. The difference between these new proposals and those of 1951 is that the motive behind them is now primarily economic. Europe as a whole has recognised the need to combine to form a cohesive unit in the face of considerable competition from their major economic rivals.

In 1991 the EC and EFTA (the European Free Trade Association) agreed to form a single European Economic Area, to come in to existence on 1 January, 1993, the same day as the Single Market. This enlarged nineteen nation Economic Area would hold a market of 380 million consumers, stretching from the Mediterranean Sea to the Arctic Ocean. It will be responsible for almost 50% of world trade. Recent years have seen a considerable rise in the importance of trade between member states: in 1990, 68% of total trade was conducted within the European Economic Area. Almost 50% of UK exports are now destined for EC states, whilst over 50% of our imports come from these same eleven nations.

In 1993 there are four more applications to join the market from Austria, Cyprus, Malta and Turkey. Finland, Norway, Iceland, Sweden and Switzerland are also thinking of applying. Improving relations between East and West, and the establishment of 'market economies' in countries such as Poland, and the old Baltic and Soviet states, makes it likely that there will be a flood of applicants from the old Eastern bloc countries.

Economic pressures behind the need for a Single European Market

Various economic factors have played an important part in convincing the member states that the time is right for them to come together. These can be summarised under the following headings:

- *the evolution of the world economy.* The emergence of Japan as the strongest economy in the world and the growth of the Pacific Basin as an area of rapid growth has highlighted the need for Europe to united in a combined market;

- *the increased mobility of capital.* The world financial markets are now so structured as to facilitate easy transfer of funds between countries. However, the problem of this freedom undermining domestic economic policy has encouraged many EC member states to seek 'safety in numbers';

- *the UK Government's domestic economic policies.* Traditional economic thinking in post-war Europe was based on Keynesian demand management policies. Recent years have seen a movement towards 'supply-side' policies involving the government in creating an environment suitable for economic growth. In fact the UK Treasury's Economic Progress Report in October 1988, describes the move a Single Market as being designed to:

  '...improve economic performance by removing unnecessary regulation and exposing economies to market forces. Just as the Government has vigorously pioneered this approach in the UK, so they have vigorously promoted it within the EC.'

The Single European Act 1986 set down a timetable committing the member states to finalising an internal market without frontiers within which the free movement of goods, persons, services and capital is ensured. In practice this has many consequences including:

- *Removal of barriers which increase costs.* This includes the removal of customs posts, passport controls and other physical barriers preventing the free movement of goods and people. Whilst customs posts do not technically prevent competition, controls increase the cost of the incoming (or, indeed, outgoing) product and, as such, will deter competition.

- *Removal of barriers which prevent movement and market entry.* Examples include the removal of technical and legal barriers which prevent free movement of goods and the provision of services throughout the Community; the removal of policies for public sector purchasing and supply which are discriminatory or protective (thus for example the National Health Service will have to ask for tenders from throughout the Community when it seeks to place major purchasing contracts). These have been policies which have been frequently adopted, whereby a government will only buy goods or services from within its own country; freedom of movement for people allowing them to live and work where they wish within the Community and entailing mutual recognition of qualifications; free movement of capital within the Community.

- *Barriers which distort the market.* Specific taxes or subsidies and price controls will distort the level of competition which is possible. This type of policy will invariable favour the 'native nation'. Therefore there will be a reduction in differences in taxes on goods and services between member states.

The task of removing these numerous barriers to trade is not easy. However, in order to facilitate the move towards the Single European Market, a significant change was made to the way in which EC decisions are made. Previously, proposals of this kind would need unanimous support before being accepted as EC policy. Now, the proposals need only to obtain 'qualified majority voting' between ministers, so, in theory, allowing much more flexibility for change.

Potential gains from the Single European Market

To quote the DTI, the single market means a *process of liberalisation which allows market forces to work ... All new proposals will be assessed for their impact on business..* The aim is therefore to reduce costs to business, in order that these benefits may be passed on to the final consumer in the form of reduced prices and wider choice.

Economists are optimistic in their predictions of the benefits the Single Market will bring. In order to turn the concept into a reality there are many obstacles that must be overcome.

Possible problems in the establishment of the Single European Market

Various problems have been identified which could lead to severe problems in the practicalities of the Single European Market. They include:

- *Taxation*. A truly united Europe will necessitate some form of *standardisation of indirect taxation*. This will inevitably reduce the power of member countries to set their own tax rates; as such it will remove some of their sovereignty. VAT, or its equivalent, varies substantially throughout Europe, both in terms of the level and also the range of goods and services on which it is charged. Duties on items, such as drink and tobacco, vary considerably. Should the UK be required to reduce these tax levels on the basis of standardisation, then this might lead to a number of problems; for example, successive British governments have long cited health issues as a major motive for punitive taxes, and will be reticent to alter this policy;

- *Trade with the rest of the world*. A Single European Market would necessitate a *common policy towards trade* with other nations within the world. Traditional markets would therefore be affected as some countries are made to fall into line with other member states;

- *Mutual recognition*. Whilst the theory of mutual *recognition of qualifications* is admirable, the practical problems could prove to be insurmountable. Standards of qualifications vary considerably, as do standards of workmanship. The language barrier is also a major hurdle to the establishment of a freely mobile European workforce;

- *Financial markets*. Again, in theory, banks and other financial institutions will be able to establish themselves freely in all member countries. However, the availability of credit in certain states, such as Germany, could be particularly problematic. Institutions keen to lend money to the German public will find severe opposition from a State government committed to a strict monetary control policy;

- *Public procurement policies*. The expenditure of public authorities throughout the EC amounts to a significant proportion of total spending. Traditionally, many member states have confined this spending to domestic producers/suppliers. The Single Market will mean freedom of competition in all markets and, as such, public authorities will be expected to open themselves up to competition from other member nations. In practice, this may prove politically difficult to implement. If a government or local authority is concerned solely with cost, then the cheapest product or service may well come from another EC state. However, whether spending outside the domestic market will be *politically* acceptable is more uncertain. Many public authorities have spending criteria other than simple cost; for example, the preservation of local industries and employment. An authority which actively imports, to the detriment of its own domestic workforce might face a potentially disastrous political backlash.

European Monetary Union

In 1991 the present twelve states of the EC signed the Treaty of Maastricht. As well as dealing with the subjects of political union, the Treaty contained a timetable for the establishment of Economic and Monetary Union (EMU). The timetable contained procedures to ensure that, after 1996, each member moves to a single European currency once finance ministers have decided which of the EC currencies comply with the 'convergence' criteria. The five 'convergence' criteria are that each country should:

- have an inflation rate no higher than 1.5% above the average of the three EC countries with the lowest price rises;
- have interest rates that are within 2% of the average of the three members with the lowest rate;
- have a budget deficit no greater than 3% of its Gross Domestic Product (GDP);
- have a Public Sector Borrowing Requirement (PSBR) no greater than 6% of GDP;
- have a currency that has not been devalued in the previous two years and one that remains within the normal 2.25% fluctuation margin of ERM.

Those countries which fulfil all five of the criteria will adopt the ecu as their single currency by 1999; the UK has reserved the right to opt out.

The advantage of a single currency

It is calculated that, since each EC country has its own currency, a traveller who started a journey with £100, and changed it into the local currency of each member country, would have only £28 remaining at the end of the journey, yet would have spent nothing. This is due to the cost of converting currency as one moves from country to country: a single European currency, such as the ecu, would avoid these charges.

Under EMU a single central bank in Europe would set interest rates and regulate exchange rates for all EC member states. If all the member states agreed to implement full monetary union, the pound might become a thing of the past. The present twelve currencies would be merged into a strong, single European currency, the ecu (European Currency Unit). This would allow Europe to compete effectively against the US and Japan – after all, the Americans have the dollar, the Japanese the yen, so why not Europe the ecu? There are two main arguments against EMU:

- *A single currency can only be created at a punitive cost to some of the poorer members.* There are significant differences in the economies of the twelve countries; these differences would benefit the richer parts of Europe while causing unemployment in the poorer areas. Poorer countries would be unable to adjust the value of their currency in order to help them to compete with their richer partners. They would have to face up to a period of slow or zero economic growth while they (painfully) lowered their costs;
- *The loss of control over the currency by national parliaments.* Since control would pass to a non-elected committee of bankers, they might well take decisions that are against the interests of individual countries.

European Monetary System (EMS)

The European Monetary System is designed to eliminate the problems caused by fluctuating exchange rates. Those countries which are 'full' members of the EMS set agreed ranges of exchange rates for all of their currencies, based on a weighted average of a basket of currencies. When a member state's currency reaches the extremes of its given range, the Central Banks of the other member states buy or sell as appropriate in order to avoid the currency moving outside of its limits.

A three-stage process has been proposed, aimed at achieving full monetary union within the EC. The stages are:

- All member states to become full participants of the EMS;
- A central decision making body to be established, consisting of the representatives from member states, with the role of centralising financial decision-making. This would lead to a standardisation of all financial variables, such as interest rates, throughout the EC;

- The implementation of a common currency, the (ecu), and thus the total harmonisation of all financial decision-making within the EC.

The UK Conservative Government was not fully supportive of these moves. Various arguments have been advanced against full monetary union, such as the fact that it is a distortion on the free operation of market forces, but more particularly that it will remove the sovereignty of the government to conduct the UK economy in the manner which they see fit. As such, the UK has so far resisted any temptation to become a full member of the EMS. However, the Prime Minister has agreed, in principle, to stage one of the process outlined above. This was to be at a time when the UK inflation rate was lower, and therefore more comparable to the rest of the EC. No date was fixed, and stages 2 and 3 still appear to be very distant targets.

Activity

The European Union already has a currency, the ecu. It is made up of a 'basket' of European currencies. Try to find out the relative proportions of each European currency in the ecu and what its value is against the pound.

The Exchange Rate Mechanism (ERM)

The ERM is the Exchange Rate Mechanism. It keeps most European currencies, although since September 1992, not the pound sterling, linked to each other within fixed rates or bands. Thus the European currencies move as a block or raft against the yen, dollar and other world currencies. Each EC government is obliged to set its currency at a level that will keep it at its ERM rate; thus, if a currency is falling in the money markets, the government must make it more attractive by raising domestic interest rates. When it is rising, the government will cut its interest rates in an attempt to encourage currency traders to divest themselves of their currency.

The ERM is a mechanism for linking the currencies of participating European countries within specified limits; its purpose is to bring about relative currency stability between member countries. If the ERM brings about a stabilisation of currencies, this halts those fluctuations which brings uncertainty to business people who need to be certain of the costs of its imports and its receipts from exports. The ERM keeps currencies within a fixed band, thus giving greater certainty over prices and costs.

Doubts on the future of the Single European Market

The predictions of the benefits of the Single European Market were all based on the 'medium term', following what the EC describe as 'adjustments'. The actual nature of these 'adjustments' will necessarily vary from member state to member state. Inevitably, there will be winners and losers. Some domestic markets will find themselves 'overthrown' by fierce foreign competition, with resultant costs in terms of industrial closures and job losses. Other industries will find the opportunity to expand into a much larger market decidedly to their advantage.

Some nations were more prepared than others for 1992, and there is considerable variance between industries within those nations. The government in the UK has been involved in an 'awareness raising' campaign aimed at consumers, but more specifically at industry. The message is that 1992 is not the 'end of the process', but the beginning. The UK lagged behind the rest of Europe in its planning for 1992, partly because of a lack of awareness of the opportunity which 1992 onwards will afford to business. The signs are that business is now accepting the need for change and preparation, although this is by no means a universal view.

Many critics claim that the problems of the Single Market are far from being ironed out. The government commitment to the policy will be tested should its own sovereignty be challenged. Mrs. Thatcher is quoted as saying:

> "*we have not successfully rolled back the frontiers of the state in Britain to see them reimposed* (in Brussels)."

The Director-General of the Britain's Institute of Directors, Sir John Hoskyns, said that 1992:

> "... *will fail to open frontiers, but cripple Europe with regulatory overheads so that a still fragmented Community will have gone down with the old British disease.*"

Such pessimism does not augur well for the future of the Single European Market. Talk of a staggered introduction of the measures may lead to what a leading economic commentator has described as:

> "... *the inner core of countries moving on to economic and monetary union on their own, as the more peripheral countries carry on making noises about sovereignty and imagined freedom of action.*"

Supporters of the Single Market argue that the largest economic benefit of a 'borderless' market will be seen in a reduction in costs to producers and prices to consumers. In addition, economies of scale will eventually reduce costs (and thus prices) even further. In the longer term, the Single Market will bring about a climate where industries of a size that can compete with those of the US and Japan will flourish. The figures below show the relative sizes of these three markets in 1988.

	EC	US	Japan
Population	324million	246million	123million
Gross Domestic Product	£2.54billion	£2.63billion	£1.45billion

Whether the programme is a roaring success or an utter disaster remains to be seen.

The Treaty of Maastricht is a significant step in the road towards European unity. This union is based on the existing European Community established by the Treaty of Rome but this structure is supplemented by new common policies on foreign affairs, security, interior affairs and justice.

The treaty has the aim of promoting balanced and sustained economic and social progress throughout the community. It seeks to achieve this by removing internal frontiers within the community and moving towards economic and monetary union.

The Social Chapter

Whilst most people are by now aware of the Single Market, few will know of the Social Charter – other than the Conservative Government's opposition to it. The Charter is intended to standardise working conditions throughout the Community so that workers in each member state enjoy improved working conditions and worker consultation. The UK government argued that the adoption of the chapter would make the EC uncompetitive. Member states, except for the UK, gave a commitment to the social chapter and reached a compromise whereby they 'opted in' to the agreement.(We consider the Social Chapter in more detail in Unit 5, *Employment in the Market Economy*.

The European Economic Area

The establishment of the European Economic Area (EEA) in 1994 further extends the scope of the Community's influence. This development sees the joining together of the European Community states and a number of members of the European Free Trade Association (EFTA) to form the world's biggest integrated market. Five of the EFTA states, Austria, Sweden, Finland, Norway and Iceland, while not as yet being granted full membership of the EC are allowed to enjoy the benefits of the Community's single market. They do not gain membership of the European Parliament, are not tied by European Community Law but must implement a number of directives of the Commission. In essence EEA is again a 'customs union' without the political and monetary ties of the Community.

In return the EFTA members have agreed to permit the free movement of goods, services, people and capital. As such it is seen as the first step towards full membership of the Community by several of the EFTA states. Jacques Delors has described it as trial run for those seeking to join the EC.

The EFTA countries were keen to establish this new relationship because they had been fearful that they would be disadvantaged by the introduction of the EC's single market. Over 50% of EFTA's trade is with EC members and they were clearly worried that the Community's Single Market arrangements would reduce this. With the new EEA agreement the market now extends from the Mediterranean to the Arctic and has 380 million consumers.

This will create a market with the following characteristics:

- free movement of goods as barriers to trade are removed (although there will still be border controls between the EFTA states and the EC as free movement only applies to goods produced within the EEA and not those imported from abroad);
- control of monopolies and competition which will cover the entire EEA area;
- the abolition of restrictions on capital movements which will encourage investment throughout the EEA;
- free movement of people which will allow workers to move throughout the EEA where their qualifications and diplomas will be mutually recognised.

GATT

The General Agreement on Tariffs and Trade is an international agreement between 103 governments which together account for around 90% of world trade. It was established in 1947 with the objective of providing a secure and predictable international trading environment and helping to reduce barriers to trade in order to promote free trading between nations. This, it was believed, would contribute to economic growth and development throughout the world. It hoped to reduce the damaging trade wars and protectionist measures which characterised the depression of the 1930s.

Its members include all of the countries of the Organisation for Economic Co-operation and Development (OECD), many of the developing countries and most of the Eastern and Central European countries which are currently in the process of moving from planned to market economies. Among these countries are Poland, Hungary and Romania.

GATT is committed to ending *protectionist* practices:

- whereby one nation safeguards its domestic industries by imposing a limit on the amount of goods that can be imported (the *quota* system);
- whereby imported goods are made to pay a surcharge (or tariff) before they can enter the country, thus making them less competitive.

GATT operates in three ways:

- it establishes a set of rules which are agreed by all parties. These could be said to be the basic 'ground rules' for international trade;
- it acts as a forum for trade negotiations which can seek to liberalise world trade and break down trade barriers;

- it is also a form of 'international court' where governments can resolve trade disputes with other GATT members.

The bulk of GATT's work is to dismantle tariffs and eliminate quotas, subsidies and other obstacles to free, international trade. It tries to achieve this through 'rounds' of talks. From 1948, early GATT rounds focused on dismantling the barriers to trade in manufactured goods and ignored agricultural products. In 1994, GATT concluded the so-called 'Uruguay Round' of trade talks, involving 103 nations, which began in 1986. It was the biggest trade negotiation the world has ever seen.

The central concern has been the trade in agricultural produce, with the EC bloc of countries resisting American demands to reduce their agricultural subsidies. Some Europeans and Americans wanted to stem the flood of Japanese imports, especially expensive, technological imports such as cars and consumer goods. The US also believed that the EC was restricting its imports into Europe.

Agreement on agriculture proved difficult to find. Ranged on one side of the argument were the US and its allies in the Cairns Group of farm exporters (Australia, Argentina, New Zealand etc.). They maintained that the Common Agricultural Policy (CAP) disadvantaged them in two ways:

- it stopped the entry of cheaper, foreign meat and cereals entering EC countries because of a system of levies and tariffs which made these goods more expensive than the already expensive EC farm products;

- the CAP awards export subsidies that allow EC farmers to dump their surplus products on the world market at the expense of cheaper and more efficient producers. Although EC produce is expensive within the EC, it can be sold cheaply on the open world market because the EC (that is, the European taxpayer) pays the difference between the price it fetches on that open market and the internal EC price.

The IMF

The International Monetary Fund was set up, like GATT, in 1947 to promote increased international trade. The IMF was established to supervise the operation of a new international monetary order where orderly currency arrangements between member countries could be negotiated.

The IMF has two main areas of responsibility:

- exchange rates;
- international liquidity.

The IMF acts as banker to 143 countries, including most western nations as well as China, Hungary, Romania and Yugoslavia. It accepts annual deposits from each country in a combination of its own currency, foreign currencies and gold. This is referred to as the country's *quota*. The member countries then have the right to draw on these deposits. They are also allowed to borrow in excess of their deposits to help finance a temporary balance of payments deficit. The loan is then repaid in better years. If a country wishes to borrow very substantial sums, the IMF will ask that certain conditions are met by the borrowing country. As the size of the loan increases the stringency of the conditions which the debtor country has to meet also increase. The UK has used these facilities in the past, particularly in 1976 when the restrictions imposed by the IMF at this time were a strong influence on domestic economic freedom forcing the then Labour government to implement very tight monetary control and substantially reduce public spending.

The policies of the IMF are determined by an executive board of governors made up of twenty two member nations. These include seven permanent members (the USA, West Germany, France, the UK, Japan, Saudi Arabia and China) and fifteen other members elected on a regular basis from each of the geographical areas in which the other members are located. While the traditional policy of the IMF has been to finance only short-term loans to help solve temporary balance of payments problems, it has in recent years been increasing its longer-term loans to the developing nations to help them develop their economies.

G7

The Group of Seven are the seven advanced leading industrial nations – USA, Japan, Germany, Italy, UK, France and Canada. Between them they account for two-thirds of the world's output of goods and services. The main forum of debate is the World Economic Summit meetings, which have taken place annually since 1975. Since 1986, talks have been going on to create a new framework for global trade; these have been organised by the General Agreement on Tariffs and Trade (GATT).

A major fear of the G7 nations is that the current round of GATT negotiations (the 'Uruguay round) will end in deadlock or disagreement, precipitating the world into a new period of protectionism, such as that which worsened the already deep Great Depression of the 1930s. Such a bleak scenario includes the world dividing itself up into three rival trade blocs: Europe; North America (the US, Canada and Mexico) and the Pacific Rim, dominated by Japan.

The G7 agenda, unlike the GATT agenda, includes 'non economic' as well as economic topics:

* looking for growth in the world economy;
* endorsing any GATT agreement that may be reached;
* relieving debt to the poorer nations;
* global environmental concerns;
* co-operation to prevent drug trafficking;
* aid for Eastern Europe and the CIS.

Those of a sceptical nature who look at the G7 nations, note that they are all what Third World countries would call 'northern': that is, they are all geographically located above the equator that divides the affluent north from the under-developed and undeveloped south. Sceptics would also note that Third World debt to the 'First World' is now almost US$1.5 trillion, a sum that is equivalent to 44% of the Third World's gross national product. Each year the poor countries pay US$77 billion in interest alone. In 1989 the World Bank lent US$28 billion.

Challenges to the EC

The 'Japanese Miracle'

In the early 1980s a Japanese economist was attending a symposium on the world in the twenty-first century. He predicted that Japan would be the research laboratory of the world and the rest of Asia the factory, while the USA would be the granary. "And what about Europe?" asked one of the Europeans present. "Ah yes," the Japanese speaker said, "Europe will be Japan's boutique."

In the period between 1945, the end of the Second World War, and 1960, the UK failed to seize the opportunity and advantage over the war-damaged economies of Germany and Japan, to re-tool and invest for the future.

In 1945 Japan had been defeated by the US and its allies and had surrendered unconditionally; its people were almost at starvation point and its industries had collapsed. In an over-populated island, with little cultivable land and even fewer resources, the country seemed to face only a bleak future. Yet Japan rebounded from its predicament to become the world's wealthiest nation and a 'superpower' of the 1990s.

1945 saw the American General MacArthur force a democratic constitution and radical reforms upon the occupied nation in an historic clash of cultures. Whilst some of these changes have survived, the Japanese clung to many of their traditions. In the post-war years, an alliance of paternalistic politicians, big business and elite bureaucrats assumed the running of the country: 'Japan Inc.' used military efficiency to create world-beating industries, from cars to computing: so much so that by 1991 it was running a trade surplus of $104 billion and the first six months of 1992 saw the country export $163 billion worth of goods.

A specific instance of this failure by UK manufacturers to exploit their advantage is seen in the way that Japan was allowed to capitalise upon what its researchers found post-austerity consumers wanted: goods like motor-bikes, televisions, electronics etc. These were markets which Japan built up aggressively and swiftly, through a determined policy of market penetration.

The emergence of Japan as an 'economic superpower' is a result of several factors:

- the failure of European (especially British) and American businesses to be as aggressive, competitive and innovative: for example, in 1980 the number of UK patent applications was 19,710 and in 1990 it was 19,932; in Japan in the equivalent years the respective numbers of patent applications were 165,730 and 317,353;

- the high levels of investment and re-investment in equipment and machinery;

- the drive to secure a larger share of the market rather than being contented with short-term profits;

- a workforce which was prepared to be flexible, to accept change, new practices and new technologies and which reacted positively to training in order to secure continuous improvement;

- more methodical planning and the patience to implement long-term strategies;

- a banking system that had the foresight and patience to wait for returns over the long-term and which made risk-capital available to businesses;

- its culture: workers have a lifetime commitment to their company and show more uniformity of purpose – pressure to conform in Japanese society is felt far more keenly by Japanese workers than by their Western counterparts.

The emergence of Japan to a position to where it now occupies second place in the world economic league table with a gross domestic product of $3.4 billion has been hailed as a 'miracle'. However much Japan's emergence as a world economy is due to its willingness to sacrifice short-term objectives in order to gain long-term strategic goals, it has been due also to the West's inability to respond to, and exploit, changing markets. As Japan continues to pose a trading threat to countries, like the West and the UK, they find themselves seeking protection form partner countries who find themselves similarly threatened: the EC is as much a 'ring fence' against aggressive competition as it is a political and philosophical ideal.

The 'Tiger Economies'

A new threat is also beginning to emerge from the Far East. The smaller nations of South East Asia, the 'tiger economies' of Malaysia, Hong Kong, Singapore, Taiwan and South Korea are all blessed with sizeable pools of cheap labour; already they are flexing their muscles and giving signs that they are, collectively, the 'new Japan'. Indigenous industries, of car manufacturing, shipbuilding and electronics are growing rapidly and posing a 'second front' on which the UK and EC might well have to fight.

Eastern Europe – the New Market?

The years 1989 to 1992 witnessed a startling transformation in the geopolitics of Europe. What was known, up till 1991, as the 'Eastern bloc' – those countries of Eastern Europe which were Marxist-Leninist (Socialist) states, many of which belonged to the military alliance, commonly known as the Warsaw Pact – rapidly disintegrated. A timetable of that disintegration reads as follows:

June 1989	Poland
October 1989	Hungary
November 1989	East Germany
November 1989	Bulgaria
November 1989	Czechoslovakia
December 1989	Romania
July 1990	Yugoslavia
June 1991	Albania
August 1991	USSR

That disintegration was completed when the USSR began the process of 'defederalising' itself into its constituent republics and allowing each state to have the autonomy to decide how to govern itself and run its economy. All of the republics (now known collectively as CIS or the Commonwealth of Independent States) increasingly came to accept the 'Western model' of a free market economy and a more liberal, democratic order.

One of the principal reasons for the disintegration of the Eastern Bloc was not philosophical or a love of freedom, as many right-wing politicians like Bush and Thatcher claimed. Rather, it was a gradual decline in living standards in countries like the USSR. Since the early 1980s, countries like the USSR began to spend more on imports than they earned in exports, principally because the price of raw materials they produced had fallen below the cost of manufactured Western goods. Additionally, they suffered badly from prohibitions that banned the export of technology, especially computer technology, to them. These factors, considered alongside their huge spending on armaments, saw prices of food and consumer goods rising faster than wages, leading to a deterioration in the living standards of the Eastern bloc citizen. The transformation of Eastern Europe, from socialist satellites of the USSR into a collection of autonomous states who can decide with whom they trade, has opened up countless opportunities for business. Together with the CIS, Eastern Europe is one of the largest underdeveloped markets in the world. Political and economic reforms will create new customers as the distribution and transport infrastructure is improved. As local businesses begin to address the unfulfilled demands of domestic consumers, UK suppliers will need to place themselves in order to take advantage of the new opportunities.

Activity

One of the fastest growing economies in the world which we have not mentioned is China. If you have bought a toy for a friend or relative lately check the packaging and there is a strong chance that it was made in China. Try and find out a little about the Chinese economy, for instance how many people live there, the rate of growth and predictions for future development.

Assignment *The Trade Deals*

Mills and Casson International is an import/export company based in the East End of London. In 1989 the company negotiated two important trading contracts. The first was for the import of cotton shirts from Singapore. The initial contract agreement was made in January and a price of S$6.60 per shirt was agreed. (The currency for Singapore is the Singapore dollar, represented by S$). The contract was for 20,000 shirts which were to be delivered in July. Payment was to be made on delivery and in Singapore dollars. In January the exchange rate was £1 = S$3.30 but by July it had changed to £1 = S$3.20.

The second contract involved the export of £100,000 worth of Harris Tweed Cloth to the USA. The initial agreement was reached in May and the American buyer promised to pay US$150,000 for the goods on delivery. (The exchange rate in May was £1 = US$1.50). Delivery was not made until late August. The US$150,000 were paid although by then the exchange rate had changed to £1 = US$1.45.

Tasks

You are employed as a trainee in the finance department of Mills and Casson International. Your section head, Gerard Dominic, has asked you to examine the financial implications of each of the contracts

1. Prepare a memorandum to Mr. Dominic in which you explain the cost of the shirts in sterling to the company in the light of the change in the exchange rate.

2. Prepare a second memorandum relating to the American deal. Explain whether Mills and Casson have benefited or not from the change in the exchange rate between the pound and the dollar.

3. Write a report to Mr. Dominic in which you examine the advantages and disadvantages of the company negotiating its import and export deals in sterling or in some other currency.

Development Task

4. From the financial pages of a quality newspaper obtain the value of sterling against the US dollar, the French franc, the West German Deutchmark, the Swiss franc and the Italian lira. Plot the changes of the pound against each of these currencies for a month on a chart, and produce an explanation of any major fluctuations.

Element 1.3 The Supply of Goods and Services by Business

The Supply of Goods and Services by Business

We have already examined the nature of the UK economy and noted that it is extremely diverse. Like other highly developed western economies it has businesses in both the private and public sectors which provide a range of goods and services to meet the needs of consumers. In this section we shall look at the economic relationships which govern supply. We have already seen that in the private sector business need to make a profit in order to survive. In order to make a profit they must sell their products at prices which are higher than the cost of producing them. As demand for a product increases this means that more consumers want to buy the product at the prevailing price – and some are willing to pay more than the prevailing price. In Element 7.3, *The Costs of Goods and Services* we shall examine the costs of producing goods and services in more detail and so in this section we will concentrate on the economic relationships which determine the price and quantity supplied by producers.

The economic relationships determining supply

The supply of a product or service is determined by the willingness and ability of producers and suppliers to meet the demands of consumers at a variety of prices. If the price offered by consumers is relatively high, producers are willing to supply more – if they can. Of course, this is not always possible: for example, if an English tennis player reached the singles final at Wimbledon there would be a dramatic increase in the demand for seats for the centre court on finals day. Why, then, do the Wimbledon authorities not respond to these higher prices by substantially increasing the number of seats available for that day to meet this increase in demand? They would like to have more seats available but the centre court has a limited capacity and they are unable to increase that capacity overnight. However if we looked at another product, for instance, computer games, we see that as demand rises, the manufacturers of such games *increase* their production to meet this increase in demand.

The reasons for this are as follows:

- efficient producers will make more profit for each unit they supply;
- less efficient suppliers will now be able to make profit as the price they can sell their goods for exceeds their costs of production;
- alternative products become less attractive to producers as they can earn a higher price for the goods which are increasing in demand. Consequently, suppliers transfer their productive resources to the manufacture and supply of those goods in demand.

Conversely, as the price of a product falls, the tendency is for suppliers to *reduce* production. There are three main reasons for this:

- efficient producers will make less profit per unit supplied;
- inefficient suppliers will not be able to make any profit at all, and so will go out of business;

- alternative products become more attractive to producers as they can earn a higher price for them. Consequently, suppliers transfer their productive resources to the manufacture and supply of these goods.

The pattern of the supply curve is shown in the next figure.

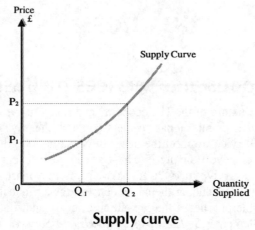

Supply curve

There are many reasons why a producer is able to supply a certain quantity of a product at a certain price, but the main reason relates to the costs of production. Consider what will happen as a producer increases the level of output. Initially, the costs of production for each unit (referred to as the *average cost of the product*) will fall as the producer is able to take advantage of economies of scale (the more that is produced, the less in costs per unit). Such *economies of scale* include bulk buying, specialisation, mechanisation and an increased ability to raise finance. Eventually, as production increases past a certain level (known as the *optimum level of production* or the most efficient level of production), these savings may decrease; it is said that the producer begins to suffer from *diseconomies of scale*. Examples of diseconomies of scale include: more problematic labour relations; the need to employ people who perhaps do not have the requisite skills for the job and an increased reliance on outside suppliers.

As in the case of demand, the supply of a product can be illustrated using either a schedule or a graph. Using the same example we used when looking at demand, Ford is willing and able to supply more Mondeos as their price increases:

Price £	Quantity Supplied per Month
11,000	45,000
10,500	35,000
10,000	28,000
9,500	20,000
9,000	13,000
8,500	5,000

Supply Schedule for Ford Mondeos

As you will notice from the figure, the supply curve usually slopes from top right to bottom left, in the opposite direction to the demand curve. The higher the price the supplier is able to achieve by selling the product, the more of it that will be produced. Now consider the factors that will influence the *supply* of goods and services.

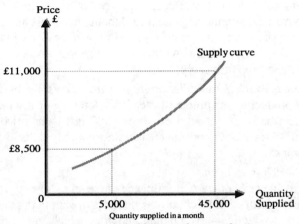

Supply curve for Ford Mondeos

What determines supply?

1. *The price of the product. The* price that consumers are willing to pay is, obviously, the most important factor affecting the level of supply, and changes in the price that the producer can get for his products will move supply along an existing supply curve. As in the case of demand, this is technically referred to as *extensions* and *contractions of supply.* This is shown in the next figure.

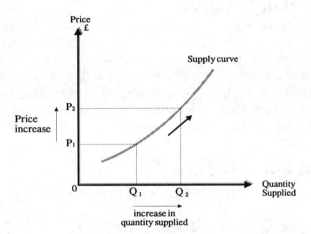

A change in price moves supply along the Supply Curve

However, there are other important determinants of supply:

2. *The objectives of the producing business.* Many producers are not, surprisingly enough, interested in making the maximum profit. They may prefer instead to make a *satisfactory profit.* This simply may be sufficient profit to give a reasonable return on the money invested and provide the producer with a decent living, without incurring the risks associated with expanding the business. In such a case, even a price rise might not be sufficient to encourage the business to expand its production.

3. *The cost of production. One* factor affecting all types of production is the cost of the inputs required to manufacture the product; e.g. labour, materials and power. If these inputs increase in price, then the business's level of profitability will change, and the amount of the goods or services it is willing to provide may reduce, if the price of the product does not rise proportionately.

4. *Alternative products which the supplier might produce. For* some businesses, the choice is one of producing one product instead of another. For instance, a company producing plastic ashtrays might produce plastic dustbins. If the price of dustbins rises, and that of ashtrays does not, the business may simply transfer production from ashtrays to dustbins.

5. *The technology which is available*
   The level of available technology will influence the level of supply. If a new process is introduced, or new production machinery is developed, suppliers may be willing to increase the level of production – even though the price which can be charged remains the same. The introduction into the manufacturing process of new materials which are cheaper will have the same effect. For instance, the availability of man-made fibre has increased the willingness of shirt manufacturers to produce at a relatively low price.

6. *The influence of government.* The government may be influential in promoting or discouraging the production of certain goods or services. An increase in the tax on cigarettes will result in a reduction in demand for the product and a consequent reduction in supply. Exporters may benefit from government help through tax concessions or subsidies.

Changes in the Supply Curve

One of the crucial factors determining the level of supply of a product is the ease with which producers can increase or decrease output in response to a rise or fall in demand and price. The supply of certain products cannot be increased quickly, even though the price has risen. If the price of apples rises in October, farmers must wait until the following harvest to raise their level of supply.

The supply of other products can be changed relatively easily. If the demand for a pop group's records increased substantially, their record company would be able to increase supply of records to the shops almost immediately. This relationship, between price and the responsiveness of supply to change, is called the *elasticity of supply*.

Movement of the supply curve

Just as the demand curve moves to the left or right when the factors influencing demand change, so the same is true for supply.

The following statement, then generally holds true:

- *changes in the price of a product cause a movement along an existing supply curve* (an extension or contraction of supply).

The other factors which can cause a shift in the supply curve are:

- changes in the objectives of the supplier;
- changes in the cost of inputs;
- changes in the price of other products that the supplier can produce;
- changes in technology or the production process;
- changes in government policy.

Let us consider a few possible shifts in the supply curve:

- if the supply process is revolutionised (e.g. by the introduction of robot welding machines in the production of cars), this will mean that producers are willing to produce more cars at the existing price. This would result in a shift of the *supply curve* to the right;

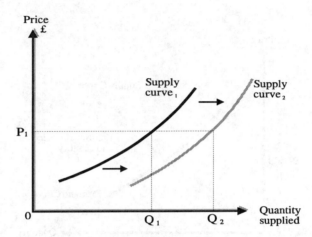

Improved production techniques shift supply to the right

- conversely, an increase in the selling price of another product, which the supplier is also capable of making, may encourage manufacturers to switch production, and so result in a shift in supply to the left. (For instance, an increase in the profit to be made from bingo encouraged many cinema owners to stop showing films and switch to bingo, which resulted in a reduction in the supply of cinemas).

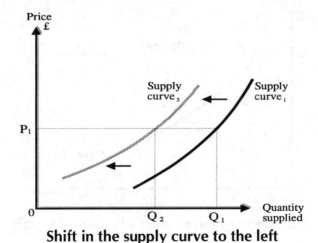

Shift in the supply curve to the left

The Interaction of Demand and Supply

The market is made by the combination of supply and demand for a product or service. All that the market does, is that it fixes a price at which consumers are willing to buy; this price is equal to the amount that suppliers are willing to produce. As you can see in the figure below, there is a point at which the price (£9,500) attracts 20,000 buyers, and this is also the price at which Ford is willing to supply 20,000 cars. The level of supply equals the level of demand: the market is said to be in *equilibrium*. Both consumers and suppliers are satisfied. There are no consumers willing to pay £9,500 for a Mondeos who cannot get one. In other words, there is no shortage of supply. Similarly, Ford does not have any excess stock which it cannot sell at that price, so there is no surplus production.

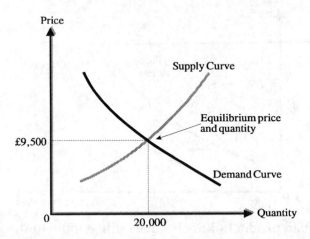

Demand and Supply curves for Mondeos shows equilibrium

This situation is fine in theory, but in practice what often happens is that there is an excess of demand over supply or vice versa. This is because the price which is set (usually by the producer) is not the equilibrium price. The following figures illustrate this more clearly.

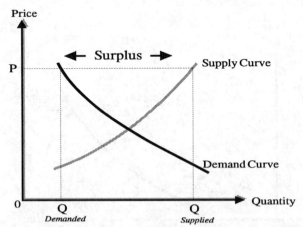

Price set too high causing a surplus of supply

In the two diagrams, the producer has misjudged demand when setting the price of the product. The first figure illustrates a situation in which the producer has set a price which is too high: it will not, therefore, attract sufficient buyers to meet the level of supply which the manufacturer wishes to create. The result is a *surplus* of products and the producer is left with unsold goods.

In the second figure, the producer has underestimated demand and the result is a shortage. The producer has more customers than the business is willing to supply at that price; the result is a shortage of products and a line of disappointed customers.

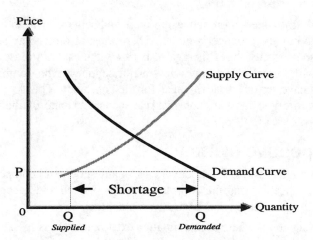

Price set too low causing a shortage of supply

In situations such as this, what usually happens is that the supplier responds quickly and readjusts the price:

- *upwards* if there is an evident shortage of the product;
- *downwards* if it is necessary to eliminate a *surplus*.

In either case, this moves the price closer to the equilibrium position.

An alternative course of action is to change the *level of supply*. If there is a surplus, the manufacturer reduces the level of supply and so shifts the supply curve to the left and finds a new equilibrium.

In the case of a shortage, the manufacturer responds by increasing output, if this is possible, and the new equilibrium is established.

The demand curve can also shift because of changes in the factors that are influencing demand, and the equilibrium position can change because of this.

In theory, the market should, eventually, reach an equilibrium position, where supply meets demand at a price which satisfies both consumer and producer. At the point of equilibrium, there are no sellers who do not find a buyer and no buyers who cannot find a seller. However, in the real world, most markets are not in equilibrium. You constantly see 'cut price offers' (indicating excess supply), queues (indicating excess demand), or stockpiling.

Activity

Which of the following would cause a increase in the price of cars?

(a)   the closure of the Nissan car factory in the North East of England

(b)   an increase in the price of petrol

(c)   a boom in the demand for cars

Different Forms of Market

The process of supply and demand, and the interaction between the two, determines a market price for a product. However, to say this is to assume that there is always a perfectly free market in operation, something that in real life, exists only rarely.

To achieve this perfectly free interaction between buyers and sellers, there must be many buyers who are all in competition to buy the producer's goods. There must also be many sellers, all of whom are competing for the consumer's custom. This, again, is rarely the case. In most of the product markets in the UK today, you will normally find only a few major suppliers who dominate the market - a lack of competition that can have serious disadvantages for the consumer. This type of market is described as an *oligopoly* but, before you look at such markets, consider some of the other different market structures which exist – at least in theory.

Perfectly competitive markets

If a situation existed where there were many buyers and many sellers, all competing against each other for products of a similar quality, and the contractual terms offered and accepted were all relatively similar, you could say that the market was perfectly competitive.

In reality, there are few situations where such a situation exists and there is so-called *perfect competition*. However, this model can be useful in measuring the competitiveness of other markets. For a perfectly competitive market to exist, seven conditions would have to be fulfilled. These would be:

- many sellers;
- many buyers;
- no seller or buyer who is either supplying or buying a significantly large share of the market, so that no individual is influencing the price of the product or the market as a whole;
- an awareness, on the part of all buyers and sellers involved, of the contractual terms (including the price) that is being offered throughout the market;
- freedom for suppliers to enter the market and produce goods – if there is sufficient profit incentive to encourage them to do this;
- similar freedom for existing suppliers to leave the market if they believe there is insufficient profit to be made;
- relatively similar products, offered by all producers, which are comparable in terms of price, quality, delivery, etc. so that no supplier enjoys a competitive advantage through offering a better product.

If these conditions were met, in theory there would be competition between suppliers for potential customers and, as a result, the price would be kept as low as possible. The most efficient suppliers, those who can keep their production costs down, will make the most profit and so be able to pay the highest wages; high wages will, in turn, attract the best labour; higher profits mean higher rents can be afforded – so the business will secure the prime locations, produce the best products and make the most profit. Other, less efficient producers, will be less cost-effective and so will make less profit. The least efficient will make no profit and will, consequently, be driven out of business.

Perfect competition will therefore:

- encourage efficiency in production;
- keep prices down for consumers.

Perfect competition rarely exists in the real world. It is, however, a useful concept for explaining the behaviour of markets. When a market does not have the characteristics of perfect competition, there will be a tendency for one side of the market to gain significant advantages – and such advantages are usually to the benefit of the producer.

Imperfectly competitive markets

The concept of the optimum, or most efficient, production level is important in determining how many producers will be able effectively to compete in a market and, by implication, how competitive it is. If the optimum level of production in an industry is such that one producer can meet total market demand, it is likely that only one producer will exist. In such a situation a *monopoly* will evolve. If one supplier's optimum production is such that only a proportion of market demand can be supplied, a few suppliers may end up sharing the market, and what is termed an *oligopoly* will evolve.

In the UK economy, most markets for manufactured products are oligopolies. Here a relatively few dominant suppliers are in a powerful position and can, therefore, dictate contractual terms to the buyer. The consumer has little influence on the selling price of the product, and in many cases the manufacturer determines the product range which will be offered to the consumer.

A perfect example of this practice can be seen in the market for washing powders and detergents. The market is a two-company oligopoly dominated by Procter and Gamble and Unilever. There appears to be considerable competition between these two giants, but this competition rarely involves the price of the product. Both companies see it as being in their mutual best interest to keep washing powder prices high and to compete through advertising rather than through price. Such behaviour is common in many markets and, because of this, both the government, through agencies such as the Office of Fair Trading and the Monopolies and Mergers Commission, and the courts have occasionally sought to redress the balance between the unequal bargaining position of consumers and suppliers.

In the following diagram we show the different types of market that exist, and their respective structures.

Theoretically, all of these market forms can exist, and all are to some extent found in the UK. However, the most important form of market structure in this country is the oligopoly. It has been estimated that about twenty of the twenty two main industrial and service sectors of the UK economy are oligopolies. Thus, in the case of most of the goods and services you purchase, choice is limited to those supplied by a few major companies. This may not always appear to be true, because oligopolists often produce a range of brands of the same type of product. They try to create *brand differentiation*. Consumers see a wide variety of brands on the supermarket shelf and believe, when they choose a 'rival' product, that they are purchasing from a different manufacturer. In fact, both brands are made by the same company. The washing powder market is a prime example of oligopoly.

This does not always not always mean that consumers do not have a choice. They are able to choose between a number of retail outlets. At this stage (that is, prior to entering into a contract for goods or services), the consumer may be able to buy from numerous shops or supermarkets. It is at the production stage, however, that the oligopoly market form is most evident. Most consumer durables, such as fridges, TVs, cookers, etc., are produced by a relatively small number of companies. Most of the processed food you eat is canned, if not actually grown, by big companies such as Heinz.

The formation of oligopoly markets

Oligopoly markets have evolved as massive companies have grown up. These businesses dominate most markets. Their growth is the result of economies of scale gained from large-scale production. As output increases, the average cost of production falls as businesses are able to use more specialist methods of manufacture, mass production or increased mechanisation.

Essentially, such investment in new plant, machinery and methods means that a producer may be much more efficient, in terms of cost per individual item made, if it produces on a very large scale, rather than if it only makes a few units of production. The cost of the factory rent, rates, etc., must be paid whatever the level of production, so if more is produced, the initial (or fixed) cost is shared out over more products. To a great extent, it is the size at which the plant or factory is most efficient – its *optimum size* – which determines how large it will become and how much of the market it can supply.

The level of market concentration

The growth of oligopolies is very pronounced in the UK economy. This growth is measured by the *level of concentration* in individual markets. This indicates how many producers supply a large percentage of the total market demand. A high degree of concentration, with only a few producers supplying most of the market, indicates an oligopoly. A low level of concentration suggests production is shared among many suppliers and, therefore, competition is, presumably, greater.

Does an oligopoly market always mean that there is a lack of competition? Obviously, from the examples already given, you will realise that there is some competition between oligopolists.

Competition can be seen in the continuous advertising campaigns by which the market leaders attempt to maintain or extend their market share. Their aim is to try to tie consumers to the producer's particular brand. Often, such brand names are considerably more expensive than those products which are not extensively marketed. Branded products in supermarkets are normally about 10% more expensive than the supermarket's own label, which is usually not heavily marketed. In the washing powder market, it is estimated that 40% of the total selling price is accounted for by advertising costs. This also means that Procter and Gamble, and its main rival Unilever, are always among the top twenty largest spenders on advertising in the UK.

Manufacturers use sales gimmicks, such as competitions and free gifts, to attract and hold customers. However, does the consumer really benefit from this type of competition? The main advantage to the consumer of fierce competition is that prices will tend to be kept as low as possible. Suppliers will be forced to reduce profit margins in order to attract new custom through low prices. If this were true in oligopoly markets, there would be little cause for concern. However, as you have seen, the oligopolist's main concern is with maintaining a market share which allows the business to produce at an optimum level. If it has reached this level, an oligopolist will have no incentive to lower the price. Competition through advertising is an attempt to maintain market share (and maintain output at optimum size), rather that to increase it. It is only when a new competitor tries to enter the market and tries to become established, that a price war develops from which the consumer just might benefit.

Supplier dominance

It is the consumer who generally loses out in an oligopoly situation and dominant suppliers who will be able to demonstrate market power. The consumer is in an unequal bargaining position for two reasons:

- lack of choice – the consumer is restricted to a limited number of suppliers
- lack of competition – there is no effective competitive drive between the dominant suppliers.

The continued growth of oligopoly markets

The UK has the highest degree of market concentration (that is, the greatest number of oligopolistic industries) in the world. This trend is continuing and will not be reversed unless either:

- new producers enter the market, thereby reducing concentration; or
- the government takes steps to prevent the extension of oligopolies.

In 1991 the Monopolies and Mergers Commission carried out its biggest ever investigation, into the supply of cars. Its report largely absolved car manufacturers of profiteering and keeping the price of their products artificially high- a conclusion that was fiercely condemned by the Consumers' Association as a 'sell out'. The Consumers' Association agreed with those aspects of the MMC report which criticised the manufacturers' policy that restricted dealers to their own product only as well as the informal arrangement that limited the import of Japanese cars to 11% of the UK market. The Consumers' Association wishes to see the system of exclusive franchises abandoned and a completely free market develop.

New suppliers entering the market

New suppliers find it difficult to enter an existing market. Eddie Shah's attempt, in 1986, to enter the capital-intensive newspaper market with *Today*, required him to make large-scale investment in the new technology which would allow him to print the paper cheaply; Shah had also to institute a major (and costly) advertising campaign on TV in order to attract readers away from their existing newspapers. Initially, *Today* was commercially unsuccessful, but Shah lacked the resources to run it at a loss for a long enough period of time that would allow the paper to properly establish itself. This forced him to sell control to Rupert Murdoch. Now that the paper is making a profit, this is earned by Murdoch's International News group, which publishes the *Sun, News of the World, Times* and *Sunday Times*. One of the main forms of new competition is entry into the market by a foreign competitor. An example of this has been in the car industry, where the market dominance of Ford, Rover Group and Vauxhall has been challenged by the *market penetration* of Japanese car manufacturers. The effects upon UK oligopolies of entry in to the Single Market looks likely to be interesting, as domestic oligopolists and their European competitors already jockey for position under the watchful eyes of the European Commissioner for Competition.

Activity

Examine the markets for the following products:

>   *Chocolate*
>   *Cola*
>   *Petrol*
>   *Beer*

For each try to identify the main brands and the producers of those brands. Estimate the degree of competition in these markets and decide if there is a substantial degree of price competition or if competition is, in the main, confined to advertising.

Assignment *Business Books*

Business Books Ltd. is a book publisher with a relatively small list of titles. Book-publishing involves the company in the following forms of commercial activity:- negotiating with and commissioning authors to write books; appraising and editing draft manuscripts; arranging the typesetting; printing and binding of books with outside printers; marketing and distributing books to wholesalers and retailers and acquiring and managing finance and staff. The book-publishing trade is highly competitive particularly in the market for student textbooks for business studies courses. Financial returns on successful titles are high but such profits can often be offset by the losses incurred with poor sellers. Businesses which make up the industry tend to be secretive about their activities for fear of attracting competitors into profitable areas. The company has recognised that a potential gap exists in the market for a business problems textbook for students. Currently there is only one textbook available which the company believes to be overpriced, poorly written and printed on inferior paper. However, being the only book available it enjoys massive sales and makes substantial profits for its publisher, Hammond Ltd. In an attempt to break into this lucrative market, Business Books have commissioned a new business problems text book. Now the company must decide on the quantity of books to print and the appropriate price to sell the book and it has undertaken a small scale survey of schools and colleges teaching courses in Business Studies. The first schedule shows potential demand for the book at a range of prices. The second shows the printing costs at different print runs The third schedule shows the potential book sales resulting from different levels of advertising spending.

From the results of a questionnaire these are estimated likely sales at a range of possible prices

Possible Price (£)	Sales (Est)
15	300
14	500
13	1,000
12	1,500
11	2,000
10	2,500
9	3,000
8	4,000
7	5,000
6	6,000
5	7,000
4	8,000
3	9,000
2	10,000
1	12,000

Printing costs vary with the number of the print run and are as follows:

Print run (books)	Costs (£)
2,000	5,800
3,000	6,600
4,000	8,200
5,000	8,600
6,000	8,800
7,000	9,000

To sell the books, advertising will be necessary. Below is an estimate of the advertising budget required to achieve certain sales:

Potential Book Sales (£)	Advertising Costs (£)
2,000	1,500
3,000	2,200
4,000	3,000
5,000	4,500
6,000	10,500
7,000	16,500

There are additional costs of typing (£150) and typesetting (£4,800). These costs must be paid before any books can be printed. The company will also have to pay author's royalties of 10% of the price of each book sold.

Tasks

You are a publications assistant employed by Business Books and have been assigned the task of overseeing the books publication. The managing director of Business Books Ltd. has asked you to prepare an informal report in which you advise on the number of 'Business Problems' textbooks to print and the price to charge to ensure the maximum revenue.

Unit 2

Business Systems

This unit has been written to cover the following specifications of the General National Vocational Qualification Business Level 3

Unit 2   Business Systems Level 3

Element 2.1:   Investigate administration systems

Performance criteria:

1   purposes of administration systems in business organisations are explained
2   administration systems to support legal and statutory requirements are described
3   a business organisation's administration systems are investigated and described
4   effectiveness of systems in supporting the functions of the business organisations is evaluated
5   users' opinions of investigated administration systems are described

Element 2.2:   Investigate communication systems

Performance criteria:

1   purposes of communication systems used by business organisations are explained
2   a business organisation's communications systems are investigated and described
3   effectiveness of systems in supporting the functions of the business organisation is evaluated
4   users' opinions of investigated communication systems are described
5   electronic technology changing communication systems is identified

Element 2.3:   Investigate information processing systems

Performance criteria:

1   purposes of information processing systems used by business organisations are explained
2   a business organisation's information processing systems are investigated and described
3   effectiveness of systems in supporting the function of the business organisation is evaluated
4   effects of the Data Protection Act on users and operators of information processing systems are identified and explained
5   effects of computer technology on users and operators is identified

(extract from General National Vocational Qualifications Mandatory Units for Business GNVQ3 offered by Business Education and Technology Council, City and Guilds and RSA Examinations Board - published by the National Council for Vocational Qualifications April 1993 - reproduced with the kind permission of the National Council for Vocational Qualifications)

GNVQ3 Business - Unit Number U1016175

Element 2.1 Administration Systems

Introduction

The way businesses meet the organisational objectives they have set for themselves is by their management of their resources. How well such resources are managed determines how efficiently and effectively the business is running and hence how successful it is. The tools used to manage business resources are the structures and systems in place in the organisation which regulate its operations. In this Unit we shall be investigating particular aspects of resource management by examining three of the most important systems found in any business. These are:

- administration systems;
- communication systems; and
- information processing systems

Before looking in detail at these specific systems however, we need to establish what the expressions '*systems*' and '*structures*' mean, what the relationship is between them, and how systems and structures emerge in organisations.

Organisational Structures

A structure is the framework an organisation uses to enable it to carry out its decision making. Basically this means the network of relationships between people within an organisation, both as individuals and as members of groups. The larger the organisation the more complex the network is likely to be. Examining an organisational structure will reveal the interrelationships between the members of the workforce and show us the ways in which they communicate with each other, how their work for the organisation is co-ordinated, what their roles and responsibilities are and how authority, responsibility and powers are distributed amongst them. These are all issues which we will be looking at more closely in Unit 4, *Human Resources*, but it is important for us to consider briefly the use of organisational structures as a means of achieving organisational objectives because it helps to explain the place of systems in business operations. Three main theories are seen as providing the basis upon which organisational structures should be determined:

- the classical theory;
- the behaviourist theory; and
- the systems theory.

The classical/traditional theory

This theory emphasises the need to structure the organisation according to the *tasks* it has to perform. The theory sees organisational effectiveness in terms of activities being grouped within *functional areas*, probably on a departmental basis, with groups of staff within functional areas working in an environment in which:

- the tasks associated with the function are clearly established;
- authority is delegated;
- lines of command are kept short;
- individual staff should be answerable only to one boss;
- the responsibilities of employees for managing activities should be kept at realistic levels.

The behaviourist theory

This theory, sometimes called the *human relations theory*, focuses upon the way people in groups work with each other. It is derived from the work of the American researcher, Elton Mayo, and recognises that structures should reflect the needs that workers have in carrying out their tasks. Mayo found that members of the workforce operated more effectively if they were happy in their jobs and felt they were making a worthwhile contribution which the organisation acknowledged. This indicates the value to an organisation of a structure which allows for *consultation* to take place between workers and managers and enables the workers to contribute to decision making. Attention should also be paid to the working environment, recognising as Mayo found, that the psychological and social rewards and benefits of working are important to workers even though their ultimate reward may remain an economic one.

The systems theory

Systems theory sees organisations as part of a system involving the acquisition of resources from the external environment, their conversion into products or services, and the supply of these products or services to the market which demands them – in other words, back into the environment again. The resources coming in to the business are its *inputs*, and what it supplies to the market using these inputs are its *outputs*. This theory sees the organisation as an *open system*.

The organisation is not a self contained entity, whose efficiency and effectiveness can be determined by analysing it through examination of its internal structures and systems alone. It is not a closed system as the other theories see it, but one which interacts with its environment and which is in a dynamic relationship with this environment. The figure below illustrates this input/output model.

Systems theory and the business organisation

Looking at a business organisation as an open system implies the need for a structure which is responsive to the external environment of the organisation, which produces what the system requires, and can adapt to the changes in these wants. The external environment is, of course, made up of many factors, of which customers' wants is but one. Businesses are influenced and affected by all these factors in one way or another. How well they respond to them is a product of how they are structured, and the internal systems in operation within the organisation – the '*transformer*' in the figure above.

Organisations are complex systems in their own right and their ability to convert inputs into outputs depends not only upon the structures they use, but also what their objectives are, the quality of the workforce they employ in terms of skills and attitudes, and the nature of the technology operated by the organisation. These are the *sub-systems* of the organisation. Work carried out by E.L.Trist and others at the Tavistock Institute of Human Relations recognised the significance of the social and technological sub-systems, stressing the relationship between them and the importance of looking at changes in technologies in the context of the people who will be required to use them. The social system in an organisation needs to be in harmony with its technical/technological system.

Organisational Systems

A system describes the interaction and interrelationship between a set of separate parts which combine together to form a complex unified whole. A system is influenced by the environment in which it operates. In a business the way in which it is structured tells us about its basic shape, the way it has been designed. Its systems show us how it actually works. For example, the position of every employee in a business can be plotted diagrammatically to show who wields power over whom. This will show us the *power/authority structure*. What it does not do is to show us how the workforce communicates one member with another in practice. For this we would need to dig deeper within the organisation to look at its *communications system*.

In a business there will be many systems in operation. Indeed the organisation itself can be described as a system since its component parts are being managed in ways which seek to integrate them in the most effective way possible to achieve its objectives. This overall system is made up of a variety of *sub-systems*, which may themselves consist of further sub-systems.

This is not as difficult to understand as it may seem. A helpful analogy in understanding organisations and how they work is the human body. It is a system based upon a design, or structure, with many sub-systems in it which enables it to work properly; the nervous system, respiratory system and so on. These sub-systems in turn rely upon other systems in order to operate effectively – thus the nervous system can be affected by deficiencies in the body's chemical system. A healthy body is one in which all systems are working properly and in harmony with each other. There is one obvious and important difference between the human body and the organisation when we compare their systems and structures. In the human body both are designed for us. In the organisation we have to design them for ourselves. To do so we therefore need to understand organisations, basing our understanding upon what evidence we have of what works and what does not work. We need also to be clear about the kinds of measurements we can make about organisations. In particular we should be clear about two expressions which we have already referred to in this unit and which you will encounter throughout the book, organisational *efficiency* and *effectiveness*.

Efficiency and effectiveness

The twin concepts of efficiency and effectiveness have become increasingly important as measures used in the assessment of organisational performance.

- *Efficiency*. This describes the relationship between an organisation's use of its resources and its productive output. Efficiency emphasises the optimum use of its resources, and an efficient business is therefore one which achieves the maximum level of production possible through the use of its resources.
- *Effectiveness*. This is concerned with the achievement of organisational objectives or goals. The closer the organisation comes to achieving its objectives, the more effective it can be said to be.

Ideally businesses should always aim to combine these qualities in their operations. It does not follow however that achievement of one necessarily involves achievement of the other. An organisation may for example achieve the overall sales target it has set for itself, yet have done so in ways which have been excessively demanding on its resources. The Hoover promotion in 1992 which offered customers spending over £100 on a product two free flights to Europe or the USA dramatically increased the company's sales and caused its factory to go on to seven days a week production and take on extra staff. The company did not, however, anticipate how many customers would comply with the conditions it set out, and the excessive demand for flights, together with adverse publicity resulting from problems in meeting its promises, resulted in the parent company in the United States bailing out its European subsidiary, transferring a figure in the region of £20m to provide flights and save the company's good name - an interesting illustration of a conflict between organisational efficiency and effectiveness.

For any organisation to operate efficiently and effectively, every individual employee and every department must work together as a co-ordinated whole. Each part of the organisation must seek to attain similar high standards. If there is one weak element in the system, it will tend to undermine the rest. For example, even the best planned organisation using the latest technology will prove ineffective if the workforce is badly trained or unmotivated. Conversely, as one often sees with successful football clubs, when all the elements work together in harmony the end result can be greater than just the sum of the individual parts. *'Synergy'* is the name given to this beneficial outcome. For example, a well motivated worker in a good group can spark off ideas or suggestions for improvements that can be developed and refined by fellow group members. The workers in the group are not simply carrying out their tasks, they are in fact improving the organisation's chances of success by inspiring change through innovation.

Activity

Try to obtain any information you can about your own local authority which is available to the public. You might try writing to the authority, or alternatively going along in person to the local council offices. Using any information you obtain, for example information about the finances of the authority which it sends out each year to council tax payers, see if you can identify what the authority has to say about its own efficiency and how it tries to achieve efficiency. You may also try to establish from the data you have collected what the objectives of the authority are. If you are able to establish any of its objectives how do you think their achievement might be measured.

Systems – designed or evolved?

Systems hold the organisation together. They are the means by which the separate parts are able to interact, to work as a unified whole. Efficient and effective organisations will be a reflection of many features of good business practice, but certainly these objectives cannot be realised by a business whose vital systems, like administrative and communications systems, are not appropriate for the tasks required of them. This of course suggests that systems should result from a process of analysing the systems needs of an organisation, a task which could be carried out by senior managers or by outside specialists. An example of the latter would be the employment of consultants specialising in *organisation and methods analysis* (O and M), who could be brought in to study how to improve the efficiency of employees engaged in office work and administrative and financial procedures.

Clearly a system which is designed to meet the particular requirements of the organisation in question, perhaps as in our O and M example as the result of scientific analysis, is preferable to a system which is a product of evolution rather than design. Yet in many organisations systems are often in operation whose characteristics are attributable not to any plan or design laid down by managers, but rather the custom and practice of the workplaces and where if anyone were to challenge the appropriateness of the system the likely response would be: "This is the way we have always done it, so it must be alright". There is no reason to suppose that a kind of trial and error approach from which such systems are generated is necessarily bad for a business. In smaller organisations particularly this kind of approach may work well. However the question for businesses operating in competitive markets is not, does the system work for if it does not it will have to be modified; it is how well it works that must be addressed. Systems, as we shall see, are often used as a method of measuring organisations' performance but it must be remembered that systems themselves need to be assessed to gauge how well they are meeting their objectives. Where systems result from evolution rather than design it is less likely that their efficiency and effectiveness will be questioned.

Administrative Systems

Administration is used in two different senses in an organisational setting.

- It is frequently used as a reference to the activities carried out by the senior managers in determining aims and policies.
- It is also used to describe the control of the day to day running of a business. It is this latter meaning of the term that we are using here.

EFL Brech, in his book *The Practice of Management*, sees administration as:

"That part of the management process concerned with the institution and carrying out of procedures by which the programme is laid down and communicated, and the progress of activities is regulated and checked against targets and plans."

This definition may be a useful one to bear in mind when we look both at administration and communication systems of organisations.

The purposes of administration systems

Administration systems are concerned with the day to day management of a business. In a registered company it will be the principal role of the company secretary and the staff in his or her department to operate and apply the administrative systems the company uses. Smaller organisations are less likely to co-ordinate administration in this way, by using specialist staff located in their own specific department. However even the smallest businesses will be likely to employ someone with a title like office manager or administrator whose job is to handle the administration necessary for the business to function.

Whilst the company secretary's department will have primary responsibility for administrative systems throughout the organisation, exercising what is called a *staff function*, other departments are likely to have limited responsibilities themselves, and in some organisations the structures used will be designed to enable individual departments to exercise considerable autonomy. For instance, each department may be responsible for its own recruitment and training rather than this area being handled centrally by personnel staff, or it may have the authority to order its own supplies. Whatever arrangement is made for handling administrative activities, the basic purposes of administration systems remain the same. These are:

- providing support systems for the resources of the organisation;
- keeping records relevant to the activities of the organisation;
- monitoring the performance of the organisation.

Let us consider each of these purposes in turn.

Support systems for the resources of the organisation

The main resources of any business are people, money and property. The people are the workforce it employs, its most important resource. Its money is the capital it has raised and the income it receives from its trading activities. Its property is made up of its land and premises, its plant and equipment, and such items as its intellectual property rights, for instance copyrights and patents.

In a manufacturing organisation in which a *departmentalised structure* is used, where each department is handling its own functional area, purchasing, production, sales and marketing and so on, there must be systems in place which aid the functional activity. Some of these systems may be organisation wide where the support required is common across all areas. An example would be the general system of communications used by the business as every department is likely to have similar needs. Thus the communications system, at a very simple level, would expect to transfer incoming mail and incoming calls received by the business, to the relevant staff or departments concerned and do so with speed and accuracy.

Other systems however will be unique to the particular department concerned. For instance, in a production department there must be a suitable system of materials control, which ensures that the right quantity and quality of material is available when and where required. A *materials control system* is unique to the particular requirement of a production department.

We shall be looking at specific examples of support systems of this kind a little later.

Keeping records

The maintenance of a record keeping system is essential to all organisations. The reasons for keeping records are:

- *To help guide the organisation in the future.* Comprehensive data on the way an organisation has operated in the past may assist it in providing a basis for future action. Data on costs, markets, products, research findings and such items may assist managers in future decision making, by providing them with evidence of past experience;

- *To fulfil statutory obligations.* Legislation requires that organisations maintain detailed records of specific areas of operation. This tends to focus upon financial activities and the employment of staff. In both these areas there is a range of specific recording obligations which have to be met, for instance recording all business transactions for the purposes of VAT calculations, and maintaining recording systems to handle the taxable income of staff and their national insurance contributions.
  Company legislation imposes further detailed recording obligations in respect of registered companies, often for the purpose of providing publicity information of value to customers, potential investors, and the members of the company itself. Thus a register of shareholders must be maintained by a company which has to be amended when new shareholders join the company or existing members leave;

  - *To provide evidence of transactions.* Detailed records are needed to establish a permanent record of the inputs and outputs of the organisation:

  - what it purchases;

  - what it sells;

  - the parties it deals with;

  - when transactions have been made;

  - whether payment has been made or is still due.
    These are all matters which need careful and accurate logging.
    Similarly records are needed of purely internal matters;

  - personnel details;

  - staff training;

  - minutes of meetings and so on.

- *To track the way in which the organisation is performing by monitoring its activities.*
  This is considered below.

Monitoring business performance

It is crucial for any business that it should have systems in place which provide managers with the *information* they need in order to *monitor* the operations of the business. Through the monitoring role they are able to identify not only problems and deficiencies but also the extent to which the business is functioning as it should.

One of the most important resource areas requiring monitoring is that of finance. By obtaining financial information from across the organisation, business managers can exercise control over departments by examining and regulating their expenditure, and can analyse the information they obtain to assist them in their future planning. They may, for example, wish to compare last year's figures with this year's figures,(called an *intra-firm* comparison), or examine their figures with those of their competitors,(an *inter-firm* comparison).

Increasingly organisations use *management information systems* (MIS) based upon computer software packages to handle the data required for the monitoring role. An MIS is in fact an integrated manual and computerised system, which provides information to managers not only for monitoring and controlling resources but also to aid decision making functions. Whilst an MIS can be used for information of all kinds, the evidence is that it is financial applications which dominate. We shall consider further the use and application of MIS later in the Unit.

Routine and non-routine functions

If we look at the kinds of activities which take place within a business organisation, one observation we might make is that the activities it carries out, whatever the nature of the function involved, can be categorised into those which are of a *routine* type and those which are *non-routine*. By routine we mean activities of the same kind which are carried out on a regular basis. Business organisations are not alone in experiencing both routine and non-routine activities. We are all aware of how our individual lives mirror this division. We talk about the daily routine, which implies a predictable and orderly way of doing things. The routine is the known. It is getting up at the same time each day, eating the same breakfast, arriving for work or at school or college by nine, carrying out the same kinds of activities there you performed yesterday and the day before. We are also aware that sometimes the routine is broken. Today is different because you are going to a meeting or an event that starts at a different time and in a different place and the activities are not so easy to predict with accuracy. To handle non-routine activities requires more thought and care: you need to be *adaptable*.

The working environment embraces both routine and non-routine events. Those which are routine are generally easy to manage through a systems approach. If you operate an office and you know or can reasonably anticipate on the basis of previous experience what kinds of events and activities will occur or be required on a daily basis, it is possible to design a system which can adequately manage the processes involved. Suppose the work of the staff in the office is to process application forms. The system needed is simply one which supplies the forms to the staff, instructs them how to process the forms and then collects them when they have been completed. But if a form has been wrongly completed, and the instructions given to the staff have not anticipated such a situation, the routine suddenly becomes non-routine. The member of staff must now by-pass the system to handle the problem for the system has not accommodated it. This is obviously a very simple illustration, but it makes the point that systems in organisations evolve or are designed without too much difficulty around functions which are routinely carried out. They need to be somewhat more sophisticated to accommodate the non-routine.

At a more significant level in organisational activity, a business may find that it engages in project work which involves the various functional areas of its operations in activities of a kind unfamiliar to them. The project is a "one off". The successful completion of the project will be hindered if inappropriate, non adaptable standard systems are used to support it. The systems support must be specifically tailored to the particular need.

Activity

Using as a model an organisation you are familiar with, such as your school or college, or a business you have worked for perhaps as part of a holiday job, conduct a simple audit into the administrative systems operating within your chosen organisation.

First of all try to identify how the organisation manages administrative matters. To aid you note down which staff are involved in administration and what administrative functions they perform. Then, using the three general headings at the bottom of page 167 which identify the basic purposes of administrative systems, go on to describe the administrative support systems your chosen organisation uses. Is there any evidence to show how well these systems work? Discussions with staff who use them may be a way of obtaining helpful information. Finally see if you can establish how the organisation handles non-routine matters.

The Influence of the Law on Business Systems

As we have previously noted, businesses are subject to legal regulation in certain spheres of their activity. Where this is the case both civil and criminal consequences may follow the failure of the organisation to comply with its obligations. It could be fined, have property confiscated, have all or some of its operations suspended, or be liable to compensate by the payment of damages those who have been affected. We shall now look in more detail at the administrative systems needed to fulfil the legal requirements imposed upon business. We can do so by reference to two main resource areas, the workforce and the financing of the business.

The Workforce, the Law, and Systems

The law as it applies to the relationship between an organisation as employer and the staff it takes on as employees is detailed and comprehensive. The legal nature of this relationship is examined in Unit 5, *Employment in the Market Economy*, and here we shall be looking simply at specific aspects of the law as it applies to workers, to discover how employers need to operate systems to satisfy their legal obligations. Overwhelmingly these obligations are *statutory* (in other words they have been created by Acts of Parliament – statutes), and a useful starting point is to consider the impact of health and safety legislation upon businesses and how they need to respond to meet statutory health and safety obligations.

Health and safety legislation

The law concerning the health and safety of workers comes from a number of different sources. The principal statute is the *Health and Safety at Work Act* 1974. The Act specifies various duties to be observed by both employers and employees in order to encourage a higher level of safety consciousness in the workplace. The aims of the Act are to minimise the risk of harm and to enhance the welfare of employees, whilst providing a means for those suffering injury in the workplace to obtain compensation.

The Act is supported by hundreds of statutory regulations dealing with specific aspects of health and safety, ranging from the display of notices, to the control of substances hazardous to health (COSHH).

In addition, there are numerous EC Directives dealing with health and safety matters, from protective equipment to carcinogens, that is cancer inducing substances.

There is also a number of codes of practice approved by the *Health and Safety Executive* (HSE) which whilst not a part of the statutory framework, can be considered when criminal proceedings are commenced against an employer, where failure by the employer to observe a relevant code will be taken into account.

The 1974 Act introduced health and safety requirements for the protection of workers which are either *absolute* ("an employer shall") or *qualified*: the Act frequently uses the wording "as far as reasonably practicable". You will find a detailed account of health and safety law in Unit 4, *Human Resources*. The task faced by a business as an employer of labour is to translate legal duties and obligations into a practical workable framework so that a system is in place which fulfils all the statutory responsibilities that are owed. To introduce such a system requires:

(a) a clear awareness and appreciation of the scope of the legislation on health and safety – in short what is required of the employer to keep within the law;

(b) someone in the organisation who has sufficient authority to take overall responsibility for health and safety matters. Preferably such a person should receive some training if they are unfamiliar with health and safety law. Since however, such staff are likely to be senior managers, they are unlikely to need training for the purpose of converting legal obligations into appropriate organisational action – structures, systems, policies and procedures.

A health and safety system

The system introduced will seek to co-ordinate the various requirements of the legislative framework. The most important requirements that must be attended to are listed below. The organisation will need to:

- publish a general policy on health and safety;
- provide adequate instruction and training for staff;
- establish a safety committee;
- appoint safety representatives;
- provide first aid training and facilities;
- display notices;
- notify regarding injuries and dangerous occurrences;
- keep records;
- manage health and safety;

We shall now examine each of these in some detail.

Publish a general policy on health and safety

This is required by section 2 of the 1974 Act. It does not apply to employers with less than five employees. The policy should be revised as necessary, and must be brought to the notice of employees. A copy could be given to new starters; a revised policy could be posted on a staff notice board, but it would be more satisfactory to give each member of staff an individual copy.

The statement should seek genuinely to identify problems and issues of health and safety applicable to the organisation and the arrangements and procedures devised to handle them. The statement is likely to include:

- inspection procedures (how, when, by whom);

- emergency arrangements (for example, evacuation procedures, assembly points);
- safety precautions (the wearing of protective clothing, the guarding of dangerous machinery);
- consultative arrangements and training.

It should also name the person ultimately responsible for the policy - ideally a senior manager, and the names of other relevant staff with details of their duties such as the name of the safety officer responsible for the physical monitoring of the workplace. An example of a general health and safety policy statement is provided below. It does not provide the kind of detail that has been suggested should ideally be included. However it does make reference to additional safety documents which the company publishes and which would be likely to accompany the general statement.

BLUE PRINT GRAPHIC DESIGN
Policy on Health and Safety at Work
Health and Safety at Work Act 1974

It is the company's policy to ensure the health and safety at work of all employees. To implement this policy the company requires that accident prevention is just as much an aspect of efficient operation as is any other management function. However accident prevention requires the active co-operation of all employees who must accept a joint responsibility for health and safety at work, to pre   vent injury to themselves and others. The co-ordination and monitoring of the safety at work policy and   effective safety communication with Blue Print Graphic Design will be the responsibility of the company's safety representative. The Management will ensure that every effort is made to meet statutory requirements and codes of practice relating to the company's activities and any relevant recommendations from bodies dealing with industrial health and safety.

To achieve this, the company will:

(a) provide safety training;

(b) appoint a safety representative;

(c) give information about specific hazards to anyone concerned;

(d) issue personal protective equipment where necessary;

(e) check and continually improve safety arrangements.

Since employees are now under a legal obligation to co-operate in matters of health, safety and welfare, all must accept personal responsibility for the prevention of accidents. As and when the law requires, employees will be informed of any revision of this policy statement.

A Charles
Managing Director.

Provide adequate instruction and training for staff

Ensuring *"as far as reasonably practicable"* that the workforce can operate safely inevitably involves the organisation in identifying activities and operations it carries out which have a potential for harm. Most of us have at some time or other experienced the testing of evacuation procedures involving the sounding of fire alarms, with staff leaving the building and gathering at predetermined assembly points where a check can be made that they are all present whilst the empty building is examined. These rehearsals are intended to familiarise staff with the relevant procedures and alert management to any areas of potential difficulty. How frequently such procedures should be used, and whether staff should be warned in advance, are matters of professional judgement for those with responsibility for safety matters. What is clear is that they are a basic and essential feature of a good safety system.

Workers engaged in specific activities which are potentially dangerous or harmful obviously require special attention. Their training must draw their attention to health and safety hazards inherent in their work so that they may become aware of them, and must receive proper instruction to demonstrate to them how to minimise or eliminate the risks involved. These risks may be risks they face themselves, for example where they involve the placing of the hands or face close to dangerous equipment and where safety equipment (for instance protective clothing of a suitable kind) should be used. Equally the risks may be those faced by fellow workers, for instance where the job involves driving a fork-lift truck, with restricted visibility for the driver, through parts of the premises where other workers are carrying out activities in a noisy environment which may prevent them from hearing the vehicle approach.

To summarise, a system is needed which:

   (i) identifies the kinds of health and safety risks and hazards mentioned above, looking across the activities of the workforce as a whole;

   (ii) exposes people to appropriate instruction and training;

   (iii) provides them with appropriate equipment;

   (iv) monitors whether the instruction/training needs updating or needs to be reapplied and whether equipment is being used properly.

As with most aspects of health and safety detailed records should be kept to show what has been done, and when, and information should be provided to senior management so that they can assess the operation of the safety policy as it is applied in practice.

Establish a safety committee

This committee will have as its remit the requirement to review the measures taken to ensure health and safety obligations are fulfilled.

Appoint safety representatives

Safety representatives may be appointed by recognised trade unions. Their function is:

- to represent employees in consultations with the employer and the safety committee and, where appropriate, officers of the Health and Safety Executive (HSE);

- to make representations on matters affecting their members and those employed at the workplace;

- carry out inspections;

- receive information from HSE inspectors;

- attend meetings of safety committees (safety representatives can require the establishment of such committees);

- investigate potential hazards and dangerous occurrences at work.

Staff representatives are allowed paid time off work to undergo any necessary training and are entitled to facilities and assistance, as "reasonably required", from the employer.

They should be permitted to make workplace inspections every three months if written notice has been given, or in any case where there has been a substantial change in conditions of work at a location and it is the scene of a notifiable accident. The representative is also entitled to inspect documents required by law to be kept by the employer. Thus management must ensure the system provides the opportunities for the safety representative to carry out his/her relevant functions, in particular to carry out inspections and be able to report back to management where the situation demands action at a senior level, for instance to modify a production process, carry out repairs, provide new safety equipment and so on.

Provide first aid training and facilities

Detailed first aid regulations apply to almost all UK organisations, and the requirements of the regulations (the *Health and Safety (First-Aid) Regulations* 1981) will need to be satisfied as part of the system of general health and safety applying to the organisation. The regulations require:

(i) the provision of a suitable number of trained first-aiders;

(ii) the appointment of a person whose job is to take charge of any situation relating to an injured/ill employee needing help from a medical practitioner or nurse and who is to be responsible for first-aid equipment provided by the organisation.

In determining the number of first-aiders required and the nature of the facilities and equipment provided at the workplace a range of factors is to be considered, including:

- the number of employees;
- the nature of the business;
- where the staff are located on or around the establishment;
- the proximity of outside medical services;
- whether there is shift working.

The provision of facilities in organisations employing more than 400 staff usually involves making available a suitably equipped and staffed first-aid room, as well as first-aid boxes and kits (a code of practice actually suggests the contents of such boxes!).

Employers must inform staff of the first-aid arrangements in operation. This information would usually include identifying the location of equipment and facilities and the personnel involved in administering it. A supporting code of practice suggests that a notice providing this information should be put in a conspicuous position at all work places within the establishment.

Display notices

In addition to the requirements for notices under the first-aid regulations, a number of other notices must be displayed. These include:

- a copy of the insurance certificate covering the risks for which an employer is obliged to insure under the *Employers Liability (Compulsory Insurance) Act* 1969;
- in factories, printed copies of regulations in force, and details giving the addresses of the inspector for the district and superintending HSE inspector for the division and the name and address of the employment medical officer for the area;
- in offices, shops and railway premises, a copy of the *Offices, Shops and Railway Premises Act* 1963. A thermometer on each floor of the building which can be easily read must also be displayed;
- in all workplaces, a poster detailing the responsibilities under general legislation relating to health and safety (Alternatively a leaflet can be given to all members of the workforce detailing this information).

Notify regarding injuries and dangerous occurrences

Under regulations employers must notify the HSE by the quickest practical means:

(i) if any person, as a result of an accident arising out of or in connection with work, dies or sustains a reportable injury or condition, or

(ii) there is a dangerous occurrence. Reportable injuries and conditions include fractures of any bone, an injury requiring immediate medical treatment resulting from contact with electricity, and acute illness requiring medical treatment resulting from absorption of any substance by inhalation, ingestion or through the skin. Dangerous occurrences include the collapse of scaffolding and a range of events such as explosions and the escape of flammable substances.

Within seven days of any of these events the enforcing authority must be notified in writing by way of a report using an approved HSE form.

Keep records

These must cover any incident which must be reported (as described above) and show:

- the date and time of the incident;
- the full name and occupation of the person(s) involved and the nature of the incident;
- the place where the incident occurred;
- a brief description of the circumstances;
- in the case of a disease, the date it was diagnosed and the name or nature of it.

Manage health and safety

Obviously organisations may well introduce within their health and safety systems reporting procedures which go beyond what legislation requires. It may for example be appropriate to keep a written record of all health and safety incidents, however minor they are.

Under the *Management of Health and Safety at Work Regulations* 1992, more onerous duties are placed upon employers in relation to the management of health and safety at work. These regulations are considered in Unit 4, *Human Resources*, in the section on health and safety at work.

We have looked at the legislative requirements employers must satisfy in dealing with health and safety issues as they affect the workforce in some detail. The level of detail may give you some idea of the implications for an employer in designing and operating an administrative system, bringing together in a coherent and co-ordinated way, the various strands of the legislative framework. As we mentioned previously, the employer has no choice in the matter, for the employer who is in breach of these obligations can be prosecuted, and may also be sued. A conscientious and concerned employer will presumably however welcome the opportunity to protect and provide for the workforce which is after all the most valuable asset of the business.

Activity

Assume that you have obtained a job with a newly established engineering company which employs 180 staff, and have been asked by the managing director to design a system for the company which meets the requirements of the Health and Safety at Work Act 1974. Identify on a step by step basis how you might go about setting up a suitable system and indicate how the system would operate. Your first step might be: "Arrange a meeting with heads of department to discuss and establish general and specific health and safety considerations applicable to this business."

Other Systems for Employment Requirements

Taxation – the PAYE system

We noted earlier that one of the reasons why a business must keep financial records is to meet its obligations regarding tax liability. A company has a direct tax levied against it on the profits it makes, called *corporation tax*. It is also responsible in law as a *tax collector* for the *Inland Revenue*, under the PAYE system.

PAYE, which stands for Pay As You Earn, is a statutory scheme under which an employer is responsible for deducting from employees' salaries, where these are paid on a weekly or monthly basis, the amount of their liability for income tax. This is then paid over to the Inland Revenue. If you are an employee you will be familiar with the system. Similar arrangements operate regarding national insurance contributions, which the employer is also responsible for deducting from salary at source (and adding to by way of an employer's contribution).

The effect of this system on an employer is the imposition of a significant administrative burden involving the calculation and collection of employees' tax (and N.I. contributions). Even a small employer with only a handful of staff on the payroll will find it necessary to appoint someone to handle the task, perhaps on a part-time basis, and of course from an internal administrative point of view a system will need to be used to ensure that the calculations used to assess the tax and insurance contributions of each worker are accurately arrived at, and paid over on time (payments are made monthly).

Pensions

In the United Kingdom there are two sources from which an employee may receive a pension. These are:

1. *From the State.* Under the state scheme the employer acts as the agent of the state by sharing the administrative responsibility for the scheme until the employee retires, when the state assumes responsibility for administration and payment of pensions. The current scheme is made up of two components:
    (i)   a basic flat rate pension payable to women on reaching the age of 60 and men 65;
    (ii)   an additional earnings related pension – *SERPS* – the State Earnings Related Pension Scheme, under which the basic pension is topped up in accordance with the actual earnings of the employee (since April 1978).

2. *Under a contract.* Employers, either through choice or as a result of discussions with the workforce, may enhance the state scheme by means of an *occupational pension scheme* under which the employer will pay a separate, work related pension to the employee. Such schemes are clearly beneficial to employees, and often provide the employer with a valuable means of selling the job to the prospective employee. In addition, normally the annual contributions made by an employer to the scheme should be wholly allowable for tax purposes in a company's financial year of payment (that is, tax relief is granted).

The administration of pension arrangements, particularly where a business operates its own occupational scheme, is time consuming and detailed. Larger organisations actually have pension departments as part of their administrative machinery to handle this work.

Information processing

One further area of business operations where the law has an impact on the administrative systems of organisations is in the field of information processing. In Element 2.3 we shall be looking in detail at information processing systems. Here we shall consider briefly how information processing is legally controlled and how, in consequence, this requires a systems response by the organisation.

When computers first began to appear in organisations as a means of sorting, storing and transmitting information it was recognised that here was a potential threat to the privacy and rights of individuals. Personal information, such as employment records, marital status, disciplinary action and so on, held on computer by a personnel department, could be used in ways which would damage the rights of the individual employee. It could for instance be released to other organisations without the knowledge of the employee. In order to control the use of personal data the *Data Protection Act* 1984 was introduced. Personal data is essentially information about identifiable living people, held in a form which enables it to be processed automatically. Usually this means information held on computer, but it can also include other types of equipment having the capability of automatic processing, such as microfiche sorters, some telephone logging systems, punch card sorters and manual flexitime recording systems.

The data protection system

The scheme introduced by the Act is to grant rights to individuals (*data subjects*) – that is living people, but not companies – regarding someone who holds personal data about them (*the data user*). There are eight principles which the data user must observe. These are that:

- personal data should be obtained and processed fairly and lawfully;
- personal data can be held for registered purposes only;
- personal data must not be used or disclosed except as described in the registration granted to the data user;
- personal data held for any purpose should be adequate, relevant and not excessive in relation to that purpose;
- personal data should be accurate and, as appropriate, kept up to date;
- personal data should not be kept for longer than necessary for the purpose concerned;
- the data subject should be given access to personal data in accordance with the Act (which lays down an appropriate procedure); and
- appropriate security measures should be taken in relation to the data to avoid unauthorised access, alteration, disclosure, loss or destruction.

A data user to whom the Act applies must apply for and be granted registration by the *Data Protection Registrar*, must pay the appropriate fees, and observe the eight principles.

Fulfilling the requirements of the system

To ensure that a business is meeting its statutory obligations under the Act it should:

- obtain a copy of the set of guidelines issued by the Registrar;
- if it has not registered under the Act check at regular intervals to make sure it remains so entitled;
- if it is registered, check that where necessary the registration has been renewed and is wide enough to cover everything the business is doing or is considering doing. In addition if the business is a registered data user it must satisfy itself that it is operating procedures to ensure it is satisfying the data protection principles, for example by taking appropriate measures to prevent unauthorised personnel from accessing the data base, and by having arrangements in place for dealing with any subject access requests which are made to it (a data subject has the statutory right to be told if a data user holds

personal data about him/her and to be supplied with a copy of that information. A fee, currently £10 per request, is payable to the data user for such information).

The Registrar has produced guidelines for data users, and guidance notes covering a range of subject areas. Further information is available from the office of the Data Protection Registrar, Springfield House, Water Lane, Wilmslow, Cheshire, SK9 5AX.

Statutory Financial Information Requirements

Businesses are also obliged by law to satisfy a range of recording and reporting requirements dealing with financial information. Below we consider some of the main examples, but before doing so we need to identify why businesses should be concerned with financial information.

Reasons for recording and reporting financial information

Registered companies, that is to say all public and private companies with a share capital, are subject to detailed statutory regulation. This is especially apparent in relation to their financial affairs. Registered companies must establish and maintain financial systems that enable them to meet their statutory reporting obligations. We are not concerned here at looking in detail at financial procedures used by companies to satisfy statutory requirements, but simply at identifying the main statutory demands placed upon companies regarding financial information.

There are four reasons why businesses need systems in place to record financial transactions:

1. because of statutory demands arising under the *Companies Act* 1985. We shall be looking at the nature of these demands below;

2. because of the liability of a company for *corporation tax* on profits made through trading, and for *VAT* (value added tax) on sales. Obviously it is essential that proper books of accounts and records of purchasing and sales transactions be maintained as an accurate statement of trading activities, so that the Inland Revenue can be provided with them when it is considering the liability of the corporation for tax purposes;

3. because publication of financial information which presents a fair and accurate statement of its trading record and its financial health is, in the case of a public company, an essential feature of its operations, since it will be looking to investors to provide it with long term finance. Investors who are unable to assess the financial condition of the company will clearly be unwilling to risk putting their capital into it; and

4. because business managers need financial information about their companies in order to control them internally and analyse their performance. They need to regulate expenditure, monitor how departments are spending their budget, and periodically produce statements which value the company by assessing its assets, liabilities and capital. Essentially then the manager is looking for a system which enables him or her to record, analyse and control the business financially. Again this brings us back to reasons for ensuring efficiency in an organisation. Financial records give the best indication of organisational efficiency. Using this information to analyse performance by means of particular techniques such as *break even analysis* enables the manager to obtain a picture of organisational efficiency, or lack of it, and then to take steps to overcome any problems which have emerged.

Specific statutory recording and reporting requirements

- The *Companies Act* 1985 requires every company to ensure that adequate accounting records are kept which are sufficient to show and explain its transactions. They must be capable of showing with reasonable accuracy at any time the financial position of the company, and enable a balance sheet and profit and loss account to be prepared so as to provide a true and fair view of the company's financial position and profit or loss.

- Accounting records must contain entries on a daily basis of all monies received and expended with details of transactions, and a record of assets and liabilities. In addition, if a company deals in goods it must keep statements of stock held at the end of each financial year and keep records of all (non-retail) sales and purchases of goods indicating the goods themselves and the sellers/buyers.

- The balance sheet, profit and loss account and notes to the financial statements, and the auditors and directors reports must be presented to a general meeting of the company and thereafter to the Registrar of Companies (small and medium sized companies can provide the Registrar with "modified" financial statements giving less information). The form and contents of these annual accounts must be in accordance with the fourth Schedule to the 1985 Act, which was itself adopted to meet the requirements of the EC's Fourth Directive on Company Law.

In order to produce financial statements various systems will be used by a business, and all businesses, not just registered companies (which are required by law to keep records of transactions) find it necessary to keep books of accounts. The system of bookkeeping that businesses use for this aspect of their financial affairs is the *double entry system* of bookkeeping. In brief, the main features of this system are:

- *The maintenance of ledgers*. Ledgers are books which are used as a running record of financial transactions of various kinds entered into by a business. In most businesses they will include books recording personal accounts which provide details of transactions with suppliers (*purchase* or *credit ledgers*) and customers (*sales* or *debtors ledgers*), and books covering all other transactions, called nominal ledgers. These cover the payment of wages, and accounts covering such items as capital and property;

- *The maintenance of cash books*. The basic principle of double entry bookkeeping is that every business transaction is entered twice in its books of account, once on the debit side of an account and once on the credit side.

We shall look in more detail at business financial controls and records in Unit 6, *Financial Transactions and Monitoring* and Unit 7, *Financial Resources*.

Administration Systems in Operation – some examples

In every aspect of business operations you will find administration systems at work, sometimes operating successfully and sometimes perhaps not so successfully. Sometimes you may even come across activities that seem to be largely uncoordinated and where it is apparent that there is an absence of any planned control, and with the inevitable consequences in terms of organisational efficiency and effectiveness. Consider for example the kind of chaos that would result within any kind of organisation that did not operate a filing system for its records, or where each department operated different filing systems and which staff from other departments sought regular access to. The result would be messy, complicated, time wasting and a recipe for errors.

In this final section of our examination of administration systems we shall look at specific examples of systems drawn from various functional areas of business activity.

Accounting systems

We have already made reference to accounting procedures and practices, and here we shall simply select one further example to illustrate the ways in which managers exercise their functions as financial administrators. The example we have chosen is budgetary control.

Budgeting

Budgeting is an essential aspect of financial control in an organisation. A budget is simply a plan based upon estimates of future spending and future revenue. The budget seeks to allocate costs and expenses in relation to a set objective for a defined period of time. This may be for the whole organisation or on a department by department basis. The system by which budgetary control is exercised involves the following steps:

- defining objectives (usually on a departmental basis) and allocating expenditure to particular programmes;
- establishing the standards of operation which these programmes should meet;
- systematically collecting data on actual spending;
- comparing actual performance (that is the spending that has occurred) with the set standard (or target). These comparisons may be made at different intervals, for example to match with seasonal variations in demand for a product or service;
- taking appropriate action when the discrepancy between actual and planned spending is unacceptable, for instance questioning the validity of the original objectives or re-examining operating methods. In this way objectives may be redefined and the process above be repeated.

There are many advantages in operating a budgetary control system. As well as assisting the process of clarifying aims and policies, and assisting the organisation to develop its corporate strategies, central control is improved, since it is possible to monitor actual performance against what has been budgeted for. It also helps to improve efficiency by showing how well resources are being used in relation to specific activities.

Sales administration

Sales involves organising and controlling the selling and distribution of the products of a business. Whilst there may be a separate sales department, many businesses choose to locate sales within a marketing department which will have a wider remit extending to related matters such as market research and advertising.

Sales will be the responsibility of a sales manager, supported by administrative staff and a team of sales representatives. The manager's job will involve him or her ensuring the smooth operation of the systems used to handle the sales function, and where appropriate, devising new systems or revising existing ones to meet the overall objectives of the sales function. We look in some detail at the kinds of documentation used in sales in Unit 6, *Financial Transactions and Monitoring*.

Amongst the administrative systems found in a sales department are those designed to handle communications with business customers, those dealing with records and reports generated by the sales team, and those which control the use of credit supplied by the business to its customers

Systems for dealing with customers

General and specific enquiries must be routed to appropriate staff to be dealt with promptly. Records of such enquiries should be kept and appropriate follow up action taken. Standardised forms for handling quotations and orders are required, and a suitable customer recording system used so that accurate up to date data is maintained enabling staff to identify quickly the stage at which a customer's transaction has reached e.g. whether the goods have been dispatched.

Systems for handling data generated by sales staff

Commonly sales staff will be expected to report to the sales manager, providing details of each customer visited, the position the customer contact holds in the business, matters which were discussed, issues requiring further action, at what stage negotiations stand and so on. Such reporting may, instead of reporting each call made, gather together all the relevant data such as the orders that have been taken on a daily basis, presenting what is sometimes called an *omnibus report*. Data of this kind will in turn provide the basis for compiling statistical records for the sales office detailing customers past, present and prospective. The information for each customer can include such details as the name of the chief buyer, what discounts are available to the customer, its credit rating, and special details such as the particular needs of the customer, as well as the size and frequency of the customers' orders.

Credit arrangements

The provision of credit facilities for customers is initially something to be determined as a matter of policy at senior management level. Large organisations with many customers will often employ a credit manager. Administrative systems to deal with the credit arrangements will involve:

- the checks needed to ensure the creditworthiness of the customer, for example bank and trade references, and information obtained from trade protection organisations;
- how much credit should be allowed, and on what terms;
- when and how to respond to breaches of credit facility arrangements, for instance, at what stage a letter advising that payment is overdue should be issued, and the tone and style that such a letter should adopt.

Often a credit rating will be identified for each customer based upon experience gained in handling the customer's account, or upon information obtained in advance regarding the customer's financial standing. The rating will indicate how much credit the particular customer is permitted.

Distribution administration

Distribution involves the transfer of goods from the producer to the consumer. This may involve a distribution chain, where the manufacturer sells to a wholesaler, the wholesaler sells to a retailer, and the retailer sells to the ultimate consumers, such as you and me.

Distribution, like sales, will normally be the responsibility of the marketing department, which will seek to keep distribution costs as competitive as possible whilst evaluating the effectiveness of alternative distribution outlets. For instance in choosing whether to deal with wholesalers, or deal directly with retailers, the marketing department will take into account the benefits of bulk sales to wholesalers, reduced administrative costs in dealing with larger but fewer accounts, and the opportunities for avoiding seasonal variations in output. It will also recognise that dealing direct with retailers reduces the overall time the goods are passing through the distributive network, and brings the manufacturer closer to the market and thus to market trends.

There are two main aspects to distribution:

- transportation of goods; and
- storage of goods.

For a manufacturer, warehousing will almost always be required to store finished products because of the difficulty of accurately matching demand to the level of production. Various administrative systems are necessary in order to manage the stock held in the warehouse. These will include arrangements for:

- checking goods in and goods out;
- determining the sequence by which the goods for distribution are selected. For example, the system may be that the first goods to be received at the warehouse are the first to be distributed (for instance FiFo – first in, first out) or some variant of this system, such as last in first out (LiFo);
- the physical movement of goods within the warehouse – manual and automated, and the monitoring of the most suitable place(s) for the goods to be stored;
- keeping stock records.

Automated warehouses use computer controlled equipment to physically shift goods. This equipment will be linked to a data processing computer which maintains accurate stock records, and can generate advice notes, invoices and can calculate stock being stored at any time in the warehouse. The use of bar codes on products, which can be read by computer linked equipment, has significantly improved stock control in recent years.

Personnel administration

The function of a personnel department (which we discuss further in Unit 4, *Human Resources*) is to manage the human relationships within the organisation and ensure the physical well-being of the workforce so as to achieve its maximum contribution to the efficiency of the organisation. This general functional responsibility is usually divided up into sections which manage specific aspects of personnel; staff welfare, education and training, industrial relations, and the hiring and firing of staff. All this demands a considerable degree of administrative back-up. One simple example will illustrate the kinds of administrative work involved, the keeping of personnel records. These are records of all members of the workforce, full-time and part-time, which the personnel department will hold either using manual systems or on disk. Such records will be designed to provide the business with all the information it needs about its employees. This might extend to:

- name, address, date of birth;
- marital status, children, next of kin;
- nationality;
- national insurance number;
- educational record and qualifications;
- employment record;
- present post indicating roles and responsibilities and salary;
- details of appraisal interviews;
- details of disciplinary action taken;
- details of assessments, and of potential;
- statements of staff development undertaken.

Obviously this material may need updating from time to time, and so all staff need to be circulated with documents enabling them to provide new relevant information for inclusion on their personal files at appropriate intervals. A data base of this kind can be used for many purposes, for instance as evidence of misconduct resulting in disciplinary action for an industrial tribunal hearing, or to calculate the gender balance or the age pattern of the workforce.

Services administration

Services operated within a business include catering services and the arrangements used for the maintenance of plant and equipment. Let us use maintenance services to illustrate the kinds of administrative support systems a maintenance section will use. These will normally include:

(i)   regular periodic inspection carried out to plant and equipment;

(ii) the recording of the findings of inspections;

(iii) mechanisms for instructing maintenance staff to remedy any problems identified by inspections and the completion by such staff of schedules detailing the work carried out;

(iv) in the case of preventive maintenance, the compilation of an inventory of plant, identifying the most vulnerable areas of likely breakdown/wear, supported by an inspection schedule indicating the frequency of inspection of these areas.

Inspection cards will be required in the maintenance department, and it is likely that administration staff will carry out measurement of the standard times allowed for inspections.

Assignment *Southern Engineering Ltd.*

You work in the personnel department of a manufacturing company, Southern Engineering Ltd., which employs 400 staff in total. The personnel director has asked you to review existing health and safety arrangements within the company with the intention of revising these arrangements if necessary.

Tasks

1. Produce a document for the personnel director which sets out the administration arrangements necessary to satisfy the company's legal responsibilities under health and safety legislation. Your document may use any format appropriate but it should seek to address all the aspects that an efficient and effective health and safety system in an organisation requires.

2. Design a standard report form which Southern Engineering Limited can use for maintaining records regarding injuries and dangerous occurrences arising within the workplace. The report form should be accompanied by a single set of instructions for anyone likely to be involved in completing it.

Development Task

Using an organisation you are familiar with, select one of its departments or areas of functional responsibility and carry out an audit of the various administration systems the department operates, indicating what the system is for, how it works, who is responsible for it, and whether there is any way in which its efficiency can be measured.

Element 2.2 Communication Systems

Introduction

In the previous element we looked at the administration systems of business organisations. We examined the meaning of the expression *'system'* when used in an organisational context, and saw that in a business each functional area will have its own specialised administrative systems which enable managers to run the enterprise smoothly, and work towards the goals of efficiency and effectiveness. Organisations cannot work properly without the necessary administration systems in place. They are fundamental to organisational operation. They do however depend upon an even more fundamental system within the organisation, one upon which all forms of organisational activity depend, its communications system.

If we were to look upon organisational systems of every kind and assess them in terms of their importance to the enterprise we would find that whatever the type of business being conducted it is always the systems in place for facilitating and supporting communication processes which are ultimately the most important to the organisation. Its achievements of goals and objectives principally depend on its capacity to communicate both internally and externally. Communication is the bedrock upon which all other systems sit.

In this element we shall explore the place of communications and communications systems in organisations.

People and Organisations

This Unit takes as its focus organisations – what they are, how they work, and what influences them. This really makes our true starting point *people*, for it is they who create organisations and populate them. Understanding how people think and act helps us to understand organisations, since it is people who make organisations what they are. Studying people enables us to learn why some organisations work well and others work badly.

There are of course many characteristics of human behaviour and activity which would emerge from a detailed study of people. For our purposes we need mention just two of these characteristics:

- the capacity and need to communicate; and
- the capacity and desire to organise.

Communicating and organising

The concept of human beings as communicators is one which is readily apparent. If you are in any doubt try spending a day in isolation from all forms of communication, avoiding the radio, TV, newspapers and above all other people! The idea of people as organisers is perhaps not so immediately obvious, yet a moment's reflection reveals that the human race has an innate capacity for organising and creating organisations. We are surrounded by organisations which maintain our civilised existence. Social organisations hold societies together. Political organisations control them and business organisations manage the use of their resources.

Organisations as groups

Organisations, whatever their purpose, are made up of people who have formed themselves into groups. There are certain characteristics of group membership that are useful for us to record.

We can say of people in groups that:

(a) generally the larger the number of individuals that make up the group the less will be each individual's influence and control over it;

(b) membership of a group inevitably involves identifying the nature of an individual's role within it, that is the rights and responsibilities that go with membership;

(c) the group will usually have a purpose for its existence. A business organisation, whether it comprises two people operating as a partnership, or a multi-national public limited company with thousands of employees, will always have a set of objectives. Whilst the purpose or rationale of groups will vary from one to the other, there must always be some kind of objective or the group will not survive;

(d) the group will have a structure, in other words it will have an organised framework which holds it together. In the case of a business organisation, the form this structure takes is of particular importance for as we have previously seen, if it is not suitable, the organisation cannot operate efficiently or effectively.

(e) the structure within which the group operates will require systems to enable it to function as a coherent whole. We noted in the element that the use of systems is particularly important in organisations. This is most apparent where communications are concerned. In a business the staff it employs are collectively working towards common objectives. These objectives, whatever they may happen to be, can only be worked towards if all the staff, whatever their roles and responsibilities within the overall structure, are able to communicate with each other so as to enable the business to come together as a coherent whole. Effective communications systems in businesses are a pre-requisite of successful continued achievement of objectives. The human resources of the organisation should make up a team, but teams only work properly when each member can communicate whenever necessary with the other team members.

The Purpose of Communications Systems in Businesses

We can identify certain specific purposes associated with the activity of communicating within an organisation, as well as between the organisation and those people and organisations it deals with as part of its external affairs. These purposes are:

(a) handling information;

(b) informing actions; and

(c) taking decisions.

We need to consider each of these purposes in turn, but it is probably artificial to regard each of them as entirely separate from the others. For instance the board of directors of a company who are holding a business meeting to decide whether to amalgamate with another company can only make a proper decision by obtaining the necessary data relevant to the proposal, analysing it and then acting upon it. All three purposes above are associated with the decision making mechanism and processes the board is involved in. Thus whilst the expression communications systems refers collectively to all the systems within the business designed broadly to aid the general communications processes, within the overall system are sub-systems which have more specific roles.

Handling Information

If you consider the organisation you work for or the school or college you are studying at, you will notice how, as part of a constant process, information is being generated, transferred, stored and retrieved. The task of handling this activity involves the establishment and maintenance of an information system within the organisation. Before looking at information systems, however, we need to consider what information is and how and why it is transferred.

Information transfer

Any organisation, whether it is a small business with only a few employees or a multi-national company with a staff of thousands, is involved in a continuous process of information transfer. This will include communication with outside individuals and organisations. Orders will be received, demands for payment made or letters of complaint received. There may be mail-shotting of customers, and so on. These are all examples of *external* information transfer.

Internally, information is passed from superiors to subordinates and vice versa. Instructions are given, advice sought, tasks are allocated and worked on individually and in teams and praise and criticism handed out. In fact everywhere we look in an organisation we see information transferred in a wide variety of forms: orally; in writing; electronically or even in the non verbal message conveyed by the shake of the head as the boss informs the worker that he or she cannot leave work early. If this activity were to stop, the organisation would be unable to function, for information is as essential a resource as its workforce or its capital equipment. Denying it this information would be like restricting the flow of oxygen to the human brain: at first it works distortedly but finally it stops working altogether. For many organisations it is the information system itself which may produce this distorting effect. This is because the system does not function efficiently and thus creates a blurred picture to the 'brain' of the organisation. In other words, the individuals who manage it are not receiving the right information or are receiving the information they need at the wrong time. A common complaint made by managers is "I wish you had told me this sooner, so that I could have done something about it." Obviously it is of vital importance to the organisation that such a situation is avoided at all costs. Later in this element we will be examining some of the symptoms which ineffective or inappropriate information systems reveal, and then considering how the causes can be dealt with. Our immediate task however is to examine the nature and scope of 'information transfer', in order to gain some idea of why this information transfer process is so vitally important. The first observation that can be made concerns the nature of the process, and involves us in looking at the functions of communications.

Why do we communicate?

If you reflect for a moment on the major aspects of your communications with others and examine what your reasons or motives are for communicating, you are likely to come up with a list more comprehensive than to simply to seek or to give information. For example it may be that you are merely being sociable, making an enquiry after someone's family, or it may be that you are providing psychological support to a friend or colleague who has a particular problem. Your communications could also have a more mercenary or commercial motive such as trying to persuade someone to buy your car. These then are only some of the purposes underlying our communications with others.

In a sense all of the examples given above have relevance to organisations. We can recognise that a workforce will be well motivated if its members enjoy satisfactory social relationships with each other. Furthermore if individual workers, in need of personal psychological support, are given it by the organisation's personnel department to enable them to overcome their problems, then they may be able to achieve their full work potential once again. In the same way that you might try to sell your car, all commercial organisations are trying to sell their products or services and are thus in the business of persuading customers to buy. Furthermore within an organisation managers may spend time trying to persuade staff to improve their timekeeping, change their working practices or increase their output.

When the underlying purpose of a communication is social, psychological or persuasive it is not always easy to measure how successful it has been, for it does not necessarily have a tangible end product. Your friend may be pleased that you asked about her family, your colleague consoled by your words of help or the buyer persuaded to part with his money. But other factors may have played a part. The purchaser may have bought the car irrespective of your persuasion. In the case of transferring information, however, the success of the transfer process can be gauged by assessing whether the recipient has acquired the knowledge or information and if it was expressed in such a way as to ensure it was understood. Thus the handbook for a personal computer will fail if the user cannot follow the instructions to run a program, and an insurance salesperson will not be achieving potential sales targets where the 'sales pitch' he is exposing prospective customers to goes completely above their heads.

Next we need to consider why it is necessary to transfer the information in the first place. It is only by considering who is passing on the information, to whom it is directed and its nature, that it is possible to decide whether the information transfer is necessary at all. For this purpose a distinction may be drawn between the internal and external communications of the organisation.

The scope of information transfer

Internal communications

The structure of an organisation refers not only to the physical environment in which the staff work but also to its social and psychological environment. By this is meant such factors as the respective positions and the authority and status of staff. It is the organisation's structure which will influence the flow of information within it. For instance, in a small organisation with only one boss who likes to know everything that is going on, all the important information will be directed from or to that individual. In a large organisation its functions will almost certainly be separated and dispersed. The managing director or chief executive will wish to be made aware only of information relating to major issues and will not normally be bothered to deal with every message of a trivial nature or to sign every letter that leaves the organisation.

To determine the effectiveness of the process it is necessary to ascertain whether the right information gets to the right person at the right time or if there is some structural barrier to communication which needs to be identified and overcome. Appropriate organisational structures are those which recognise that information flows are necessary for the smooth running of the enterprise. Furthermore the processes used for satisfying the informational needs of the organisation must be appropriate. For instance, when an accident occurs in the production process at work, there should be an existing procedure of which all staff are aware to cope with the situation. The procedure will involve not only the completion of an accident report form which is designed to enable all the information relevant to the incident to be recorded, but also to identify the departments of the organisation which should receive a copy of the report. There is little point in circulating the report to all departments; the sales department would have little use for such information. And for those departments that do require it, the report will have failed to do its job if the information it contains is ambiguous, unclear, or positively misleading.

External communications

It is important that the organisation is alert to the character and quality of the communications it has with outsiders. The organisation must be able to respond appropriately to information it receives and also be aware that the information it gives out will affect the value of its reputation with the outside world. Therefore such information needs to be transmitted intelligibly and in an appropriate format. Two examples may help to illustrate the significance of these aspects of the organisation's external communications.

- Most organisations keep detailed computer records. They include lists of customers and their addresses, staffing records with previous employment histories, disciplinary action taken – perhaps even convictions. To cope with the danger that misuse of this information can cause to individuals, the *Data Protection Act* 1984 was introduced. We came across this Act in the last element. It obliges data users to register with the Data Protection Registrar if the data files they keep fall within the Act. Failure to do so can result in fines up to £2000. When an organisation receives advance notification of important changes in the law of this kind, which have a direct affect upon its operations, it must have a system developed for passing the information in an appropriate form to the relevant personnel, so that they become aware of the changes, and can meet them. Similarly information which has organisation wide implications may come from other sources, such as Head Office, the Inland Revenue, or the main trade union representing the workforce and will require distribution through a suitable system.

- Our second example relates to the output of information. Imagine the chaos and the damage to the reputation of a bus company whose published timetables contain inaccuracies about times, routes and destinations. Again there is a vital need to ensure that the organisation communicates accurately and intelligibly to its recipients, using a suitable format.

An information process in practice

It is useful at this stage briefly to sketch an information process in practice. Let us take two familiar organisations, firstly your own local authority, and secondly the college or school at which you study, and examine how their information needs can be interlinked.

Your local authority will employ a workforce of many hundreds. It administers and performs the various duties and functions which by law the council must carry out. These operations are financed by grants provided from central government and income derived locally from the Council Tax, as well as from other sources such as council house rents. For this financial relationship to work there must be detailed flows of information between the local authority and central government to establish revenue needs. Thus it must provide central government with details of the number of children of school age, retired people and disabled citizens in its area. Furthermore there needs to be communication between the authority and its council tax payers to establish how much they will be required to contribute in charges for the coming financial year. This takes the form of a demand from the authority, containing information that tells the householder how much income the authority needs, where it is coming from, how it is calculated and how it is to be spent. The introduction of the Council Tax in April 1993 has altered the basis upon which local charges are raised, but has not eliminated the need for local authorities to obtain information about the inhabitants in their areas.

Let us suppose that the authority is one obliged to provide education services. The education department will consist of administrators responsible for ensuring that school buildings are physically maintained and that staff are employed and paid for their teaching. The education department must therefore compile and maintain detailed records of the physical and human resources that it controls. It must ensure that it regularly updates any changes to these resources and feeds back information to schools through head teachers. This takes the form of education budgets. At the same time, the schools themselves will be disseminating information in a variety of ways. They will be publishing prospectuses, listing the courses and subjects they offer, detailing examination results, and advertising extra mural activities. They will be informing new students and pupils of their timetables and gathering data about them using a variety of formats, such as enrolment forms and record cards. Your school or college will have a committee structure designed to enable it to operate efficiently and effectively. Committee members require notice of meetings and agendas; records will need to be kept of the meetings that are held and important decisions communicated to those who are affected by them. Information will be passed down from the school or college management to the teaching staff detailing changes in employment conditions, training opportunities and internal promotions. Information will be passed up through the committee structure from the staff to the management, identifying examination performance, reports of meetings and conferences attended.

Thus if you stop for a moment to consider the organisation in which you work, the local authority in whose area you live or the school or college at which you are studying, and examine the work it does, you may begin to appreciate the enormous amount of time and effort that is devoted to the business of giving and receiving information. It is very much like a production process. An organisation can only function satisfactorily if its members operate together as a team, working together to meet the aims and objectives of that enterprise. It is inevitable that there must be information systems to assist the workforce in obtaining a clear view of what they need to know to do the job, whether it is in respect of the nature of their role, or simply whom to contact to obtain a particular file. If the system is deficient, the members of the organisation are starved of the knowledge they require to perform their work. Like a computer controlled production process that has been incorrectly programmed there can be little hope that the end product will be what was originally intended. Data given or received which is inaccurate or incomplete, which arrives too late, is not actually needed, or is incomprehensible, hinders rather than assists the achievement of overall business objectives.

An information system

Much of the business of managing an organisation is directed towards ensuring that its policies are effectively implemented. The term 'policy' is very wide. In its broadest sense it refers to the general aims of the organisation and is often framed in terms of organisational and individual objectives. Organisational objectives can be drawn in both economic and social terms. For example, a business may establish a corporate policy to span the next five years, which indicates planned areas of expansion and anticipated levels of growth. Equally the policy may include more specific individual objectives set for personnel within the organisation. These objectives may emerge out of a job description, or be a target or task set by a superior, such as a monthly sales target. Furthermore because of its underlying importance, a general policy statement on communications is likely to emerge in any examination of the objectives of the organisation. Such a statement will not be an end in itself, but simply the means by which the other objectives can be satisfactorily met. In arriving at this statement it is necessary to examine two related but nevertheless distinct aspects of the communications process:

- who communicates with whom; and
- what is being communicated.

Who communicates with whom?

The larger an organisation is, the more functionally sectionalised and departmentalised it becomes. In such circumstances there may be neither the time nor the need for individual employees to be aware of those activities of the organisation which fall outside their own work responsibilities. However people in more senior posts acting in a controlling capacity need to take a much broader view. This is necessary to enable them to co-ordinate the work of the staff they are responsible for, and so achieve a satisfactory integration of this work with the activities of the rest of the organisation in order that it operates as an integrated whole. Thus in larger organisations there will be lines of communication, paths along which information passes backwards and forwards. These lines of communication may be:

- *downwards* (communications from a superior to a subordinate);
- *upwards* (subordinate to superior); or
- *horizontal* (communications between people of a similar status).

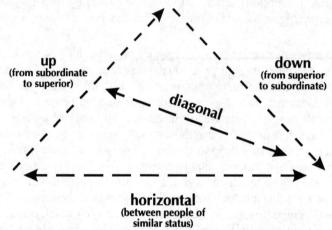

Even an organisation employing a small number of staff, such as a small retailer, is likely to have identifiable lines of communication which follows this pattern. How formal or informal these lines of communication are often depends upon the size and type of the organisation. In a local authority for example, the range and complexity of work being carried out, together with the large number of employees performing it, leads to an essentially formal and clearly defined organisational and communications structure. It is unlikely that a junior clerical assistant will have direct access to the chief executive. Such formal arrangements would be less likely in the case of a building site where a much more informal structure is appropriate to the type of team work the jobs involve.

What is being communicated?

The information content of an organisation's internal communications is wide ranging and will vary according to the type of work being carried out. Nevertheless, all organisations require basic systems dealing with such matters as financial records. The following list includes some common examples:

- work rules;
- orders and instructions;
- grievance and disciplinary procedures;
- contracts of employment;
- accident reports;
- sales records;
- financial statements;
- statistical data;
- stock control records; and so on.

These examples are essentially related to the internal aspects of communications and fall within the expression 'control'; they are all control mechanisms in the hands of managers. Additionally there are the external communications of the organisation, involving relationships with the outside world. This includes those it supplies or buys from, and those to whom it is responsible legally and economically. We have already seen that one of the aims of communications is to persuade. In practice the dissemination of information by an organisation may often involve an attempt to convince the recipients that the company's product is worth buying or that the local authority is providing a valuable service to its residents. In other words the information process often forms part of a marketing strategy. This is true not only for external communications but internal communications as well. When management inform the shop-floor workers that a fall in demand prevents the payment of a wage increase this year they will doubtless try to convince the workforce that there is no alternative. If the management's powers of persuasion are poor they may well face industrial unrest.

As one aspect of its external information processes, an organisation will issue or receive communications that are purely informative, with no hidden persuasive component. These will include invoices, rates demands, general correspondence, and a wide range of other documentation.

Having identified both the extent of the lines of communication and examples of the nature and content of the information being transferred it is finally possible to describe the information system or systems of an organisation. However, whether or not the system operates as an effective and coherent whole can really be answered only by returning to our earlier discussion of objectives and determining how successfully these are being met. In practical terms the way to ensure that the organisation's information transfer is satisfactory is by adopting appropriate formats. Thus it is important to bear in mind who the recipient is, what the information consists of and the purpose of the communication. But like any other system, regular monitoring is essential to prevent the existing system from losing its capacity to cope with demands that steadily change. If your organisation is unaware that competitors are processing data ten times more quickly, it will soon find itself becoming uncompetitive through its lack of cost effectiveness. The reason why the competitors are able to process information more quickly may be that they have invested in an appropriate computer system while your organisation has retained its traditional manual systems. Monitoring therefore is a way of recognising needs, by identifying operational problems or issues, and is vital in assessing how well or how poorly the information system is performing.

Elements in the Design of an Information System

A communications policy

We have already noted that larger organisations will often acknowledge the major role played by communications, by adopting a communications policy. Such a policy is likely to describe the purpose of the communications activity and the importance management attaches to it, but it will not usually be a detailed statement describing the system. It is more likely to be a statement of the organisation's philosophy than a practical guide on how to implement and operate a communications network.

But this is not to suggest that communications policies are cosmetic shams and of no real value. On the contrary, they can be instrumental in creating the ethos or atmosphere of the workplace. Most of us quickly gain a sense of the social climate of an organisation when we enter its premises. Sometimes we will be aware of a cold impersonal attitude of its staff to us or perhaps just a feeling of indifference. Alternatively a warm, friendly and helpful approach will be immediately apparent. This social climate is also a reflection of the measure of staff contentment with their working environment, both in physical terms such as pay, accommodation, equipment, canteen facilities etc., and in psychological terms - for example, their job satisfaction, the quality of their relationships with fellow employees, and their perception of their role.

A major contributor to the quality of the working environment is the communications system operating within it. Since such systems are pervasive, infiltrating every aspect of work, it is essential that they are effective. Breakdowns in communications damage not only business efficiency but staff morale.

Consequently a policy that both emphasises the overall importance of good communication, and states how this objective is to be realised is beneficial in the following ways:

(a) the mere existence of such a policy suggests that management is aware of and receptive to the role of communications in the organisation, and that planning and decision making throughout the undertaking should take place mindful of the communications issues involved;

(b) it lays a foundation upon which to build a more detailed communications network specifically related to information flows;

(c) as a consequence of (a) and (b) the organisation's internal operations run effectively because relevant data is available when and where it is needed and staff consultation procedures are improved; and

(d) attention is paid to developing good public relations and thus enhancing the image of the organisation in its external relations.

The factors that a communications policy might identify to deal specifically with communications as they affect employees personally include:

(i) the importance of good employer/employee relations. In a large organisation this is achieved by a personnel or welfare officer taking responsibility for the handling of:
(a) disciplinary measures;
(b) employees' grievances;
(c) the monitoring of career development;
(d) personal problems, such as illness, or the death of a member of the employee's family.

(ii) the need for machinery to enable consultation to take place between management and workforce; and

(iii) the importance of providing induction for new starters, and of keeping staff generally informed about the organisation and what is happening within it.

Putting such a policy into practice goes a long way towards ensuring that good industrial relations can develop and, more broadly, that employees are happy in their jobs. Thus an information system will often emerge out of a general statement of organisational policy. In smaller organisations, however, it will invariably be considered without reference to broader communications policy. In fact many information systems, whether the enterprise is large or small, are not actually the product of an overall design at all, but simply the outcome of piecemeal developments as the organisation has evolved. In consequence the system may be ill-suited to the enterprise it serves, containing unseen barriers to communications. In the design of an information system it is vital to be aware of the ways in which barriers to communications occur.

The cost of an information system

Clearly the process of communication costs money. A large part of an organisation's man hours are devoted to it, and thus it needs to be as cost effective as possible. In large organisations experts are sometimes brought in to examine the needs of the system and suggest ways of improving it and making it more effective. Costs may be viewed in absolute terms, that is the operating costs to the organisation of both its internal and external communications systems. This can be done by assessing the man hours involved, the equipment which has to be bought and specific costs such as computer time for data processing or telephone or telex charges. It may also be looked at in relative terms by comparing one approach with another, for instance by evaluating the operating costs of a telex system as opposed to telephone usage.

Absolute costs are essentially policy considerations to be determined by senior managers, making budget allowances and identifying areas in which savings can be made. In both public and private sector organisations, restrictions are often placed upon outgoing telephone calls requiring that all but urgent calls be made during the cheaper periods of the day. Determining relative costs involves careful costing exercises. It may be that replacing typewriters with word processors will increase efficiency, but there may be training costs and a larger initial outlay. There may also be the job of convincing older staff of the benefits of the new methods. A comparison is often made between the cost of a telephone call as against a letter. To arrive at a proper conclusion not only must one consider the time factor involved, but hidden costs such as maintenance of the typewriter, the salary of the typist and so on.

Informing Actions

We have looked in some detail at the issues associated with the transfer of information and the need for effective business systems to satisfy an organisation's internal and external information demands. We need to be clear however that providing the necessary data to the appropriate personnel at the right time is only one element of effective communication. If the employee does not know what to do with the information or data received, or does not understand it, then the overall communications system has failed. Information, as we have already seen, is needed for a purpose. It is something upon which an employee must decide to act, or decide that no action is required, as the case may be. At the lower end of an organisational hierarchy there will be less likelihood of staff having to exercise judgements over the information they receive than for more senior staff, and certainly managers. The routine receipt by a clerical assistant of information about staff absences, where the assistant's role is simply to collate this information on a weekly basis and complete an absence return form, passing it on to the personnel director, requires no more than that the system ensures the data about absences from across all departments is channelled to the clerical assistant, who in turn has been instructed how to process it and to whom to pass it to. The personnel director, as recipient of this information is handling it in a very different way, which may involve difficult professional judgements and actions. For example the data may reveal that employee X, who has a poor absence record and has previously been interviewed and warned by the personnel director, is a conscientious member of staff whilst at work but has personal problems at home which appear to be the cause of the absenteeism, has now been absent again without permission. The director must now assess how to handle the situation in the light of this new information.

Information then can provide the raw material upon which decisions as to action are based. At a simple level, information received by staff may involve no more action than the mere mechanical processing of it. All they require is the instruction or training to show them how to handle this purely clerical role. But at a more sophisticated level, information received by senior managers will be the trigger by which they take particular forms of action – in other words, manage. The communications sub-systems used for the purposes of aiding the taking of action, by informing the decision maker of relevant information, may like other systems, be both formal and informal.

- *Formal systems*
  Formal systems range from those specific or precise aspects of organisational operations, such as the system for reporting absences previously mentioned, to those of a more general kind like Management Information Systems (MIS) which aim to provide managers with a variety of data of various kinds so that, for instance, a financial picture of the business can be examined for the purpose of making budget allocations, or altering borrowing arrangements and so on.

- *Informal systems*
  Informal systems can include the arrangements that might be made by the manager with

certain of his or her more amenable staff, who are encouraged to report back on their colleagues so the manager knows what is actually being said and done behind his back. It is often said that knowledge is power, and knowledge comes from acquiring the right kinds of information.

Thus organisation systems which:(a) provide instructions and training; (b) provide data on business performance; and (c) disseminate information of a more general kind – such as vacancies in other parts of the business or changes in organisational procedures, provide us with examples of information being communicated which assist staff at all levels in taking different forms of action.

To Aid Decision-making

Effective decision-making is founded upon obtaining and interpreting all appropriate information. Without such information, decisions are likely to be the product of guesswork or speculation. Managers require accurate, relevant and up-to-date information to act rationally and competently. Imagine a large manufacturing company deciding to invest in expensive new manufacturing equipment without first identifying whether it can afford the equipment and physically accommodate it within the existing plant. The person taking the decision will need to know how much loss of production will result whilst it is installed, which personnel if any, have the skills to operate it and whether the market can absorb the higher output of goods produced using the new machinery. It would be foolish to contemplate such a course of action without first obtaining information to provide the answers to these questions. A local authority would not attempt to carry out a road improvement scheme, close a school, or increase charges for its leisure facilities without its officers first seeking all the data necessary to advise the members of the alternative courses of action available, and the consequences of pursuing them.

Whether the decision-making takes place in a commercial company or a public body, the decision-makers ultimately have to account to the people they represent, be they shareholders or tax payers. It is essential that managers have access to all the information appropriate to their responsibilities. Nothing is as damaging to a manager's reputation as a public recognition that he was unaware of important information. You may have noticed how often in Parliament, Members try to embarrass their political opponents by revealing information that the opponent was unaware of.

Most organisations have well established systems in place for facilitating decision making processes. These systems will not only ensure which kinds of information are required, but will pre-determine how particular kinds of decision making are to be handled – by whom, and by what means. Such arrangements can be seen in the following example.

Suppose a production manager, after a visit to an exhibition of robotic equipment, feels that there are certain items of equipment available on the market which would considerably improve the cost effectiveness of the production department. For a decision to purchase the equipment to be made, the business in question has a system in place which requires various procedures to be followed:

(i) the manager must produce a full report on the proposal, giving costs, alternative methods of acquisition, data on the anticipated cost savings, the impact on the staff, the likely disruption involved to production, health and safety implications and so on;

(ii) the report must be submitted to the production director, who is also required to produce a brief report commenting on the main report and possibly recommend actions;

(iii) an additional copy of the main report has to be passed to the finance director, who must also provide a briefing paper on the cost implications of the proposal;

(iv) consideration of these reports and the paper is placed on the agenda of the next meeting of the full board, with copies of each document going to each member of the board;

(v) the board meets and discusses the reports. It can accept or reject the proposal or accept it subject to conditions. In the event of disagreement there must be a vote. If equal numbers of votes are cast for and against, the managing director can exercise a casting vote. The discussion, decision and voting are formally minuted.

Activity

Taking the GNVQ Business Course you are studying on, see if you can identify within the course itself any of the communications characteristics discussed so far in this element. To help you do so try answering the following questions:

- *how is the course formally organised to handle communications within it?*
- *how do communications within the course occur informally?*
- *what are the primary purposes of the different types of communications you have recognised?*
- *how far do you think the communications model operating within a course like yours reflects the kind of model that a commercial business would use?*

Further implications of communications systems

Because communications are so fundamental to organisational activity they impinge upon every aspect of operations. So far we have recognised three purposes which are met by the use of communications systems: handling information;informing actions; and making decisions.

Communicating is also imperative in other aspects of business operations notably in its external relationships, where the approach it takes towards its clients and suppliers, and indeed the public at large, may enhance or damage its reputation.

Effective external communications enhance the reputation and image of the organisation and result in good customer relations. When a customer contacts a business wanting to know whether the order has been processed yet, or a prospective buyer asks if the business can supply a specific product, at what price, and how soon, reputations can be made and lost depending upon the efficiency of the response. An organisation which unduly delays in responding to customers' enquiries or complaints, or where the telephone is never answered, will develop a poor standing in the eyes of its existing and potential customers.

By now it will be clear to you that taking an overview of organisations from the standpoint of communications activity reveals two distinct fields of operation. There is the internal dimension of communication systems, which concentrates on efficiency and effectiveness, and the external dimension of its work, which should certainly strive for efficiency and effectiveness, but it is also concerned with less obviously measurable yardsticks, such as keeping the customer satisfied. We now need to look at the internal and external dimensions, and consider the differing communications formats used by businesses in handling their communications systems.

Internal and External Communication Methods and Formats

As we have seen, it is important to recognise that business communication has two different aspects to it. On the one hand there are the communications within an organisation – its internal communications – and on the other there are its external communications. In a sense it is artificial to split up the communication activity of an organisation in this way. The skills of communication are essentially the same whether a person is dealing with his fellow employees or his organisation's customers and clients. However, different needs are met by the use of different methods and the internal information demands of an organisation do not necessarily coincide with the external demands. For example, most external dealings tend to be formal, whereas internal information transfers, especially verbal exchanges, are often of a less formal kind. In addition, the formats used for the purpose of giving, receiving and exchanging information vary widely according to the nature and content of the information, who is providing it and who is receiving it. Thus the means used to arrange an interdepartmental football competition are unlikely to have much in common with those used in designing and implementing a feasibility study on company relocation. This is particularly so if the study has to be presented to the entire board in the form of a fully documented formal report, accompanied by an oral presentation. Similarly, the way in which an organisation communicates its response to a letter of complaint from a customer, is unlikely to be the same as the treatment given to a grievance raised by an employee concerning conditions of service.

Methods of internal communication

Conveying information involves making a number of decisions. It is of course necessary to know what the content of the information is. This may not always be as simple as it seems. If the communicator is part of the information chain, it is possible that such a person may be confused about the message to be transferred, having failed to receive it clearly. If a senior issues you with a vague instruction to, "Tell the staff about the safety arrangements", you will need to ascertain the following points:

(i)   which safety arrangements?;

(ii) which staff – all of them?;

(iii) where are the safety arrangements described?;

(iv) why is this communication necessary – perhaps a legal obligation or a policy decision?

Whatever the reason, it is difficult to place communication of information in context if there is no apparent purpose in transferring it; what precisely is it that the staff need to be told? When you are the initiator of the communication it will be easier to obtain answers to most of these questions; you will presumably know why you need to transfer the information, for instance!

Having ascertained what the information is, why it needs to be transmitted and who needs it, a choice must then be made as to how it should be transmitted, that is the method of delivery. In its simplest form this involves asking:

(i)   should the method be formal or informal?; and

(ii) should the method be verbal or non-verbal?

Most of the physical means available to transmit information are capable of being used either formally or informally. Letters, reports, speeches and instructions can all be delivered in a style and tone which reflects strict conventions or alternatively a relaxed and more individual approach. However, many communications have to be fitted into prescribed formats allowing for no choice. All organisations rely on the use of forms to simplify and standardise information flows. A company may, for instance, use standard form contracts to trade under, accident report forms to detail accidents occurring at work, and invoice forms for billing customers. Sometimes such forms must comply with statutory requirements. For instance, information regarding the insurance of premises and the ownership of a business must be displayed publicly in a standard form. Thus a distinction needs to be drawn between circumstances where an organisation:

- chooses to use a form as part of its internal communications system. An example is the use of forms to obtain and record employees' personal details;

- is obliged by law to provide information, without a particular format being prescribed, for instance the requirement that employers provide employees with written details of the contract of employment that exists between them; and
- is obliged by law to provide information using a prescribed format, for instance, to register with the Data Protection Registrar to store personal records on computer.

Among the most common means used to transmit information internally are: memoranda, notes, notices, reports, accounting statements, files, agendas, minutes, telephone conversations, meetings, public address systems and face to face contact. Evidence suggests that for the average employee involved in administrative or clerical duties, a breakdown of the working hours he or she spends using different methods of communication will reveal around three quarters of that time spent in oral communications (that is speaking and listening).

Forms of Internal Communication

The memorandum

The memorandum is a very common means of transferring information in written form within the organisation. Memoranda may be handwritten, although usually they are typed, and their main purpose is to convey a brief message. The layout of the memorandum is standardised, and most organisations will use memoranda that have pre-printed headings and carry their business name. The memorandum will indicate:

- from whom it has come;
- to whom it is addressed;
- the date;
- a reference or heading; and
- who, if anyone, has received copies.

The originator should keep a copy of the memorandum. If several copies are being sent, a tick is placed against the names of each individual receiving one, to indicate that this is his/her copy. In addition to the addressee, copies should be sent to individuals who need to know the message being sent. It may, for example, be courteous to keep a superior informed of a matter which is being dealt with by a member of his or her staff. It also gives the superior an opportunity to intervene if he or she is concerned about the way the matter is being dealt with.

Clearly it is important for an employee who uses a memorandum to be familiar with the organisation's structure and so be aware of whom within it ought to be given a sight of the communication. Whilst it is necessary to circulate all communications between staff, it should be recognised that key personnel within a section or department may be unable to perform their jobs satisfactorily if they are not provided with essential information, and 'kept in the picture'.

A memorandum does not need to be signed, although the originator may initial it. Nor does it needs compliments such as 'Dear Sir', or 'Yours sincerely'.

The main uses of memoranda are:

(i) to issue an instruction, for instance, "please attend the meeting to be held at...";

(ii) to record a fact or series of facts that the recipient should be aware of, thus, "I attended the meeting as you instructed";

(iii) to put forward suggestions. An example might be, "I would suggest that in future you deal with the clients in a more tolerant way," or, "I feel it would help the department if extra time were made available at the staff meetings";

BLUE PRINT GRAPHIC DESIGN

Memorandum

To: Mr. G. Baker

From: Mrs. J. Bruce   Reference: JB/AC

Copies to: J. Adams   Date: 23rd May 1993
            P. Hudson (for information)

Subject: **Staff Briefing**

Confirmation has been received from head office that the Briefing
meeting will take place on 6th June. Please attend.

(iv) to express a point of view, thus, "In response to your comments at the meeting last
week, I take the view that the major priority of the department is cost cutting."

It has already been noted that the initiator should keep and file a copy of each memorandum. Like any written communication its great value is that it provides a permanent record for the initiator and it is valuable evidence of any action taken if a dispute arises. Indeed it is useful to follow up important oral exchanges by means of a confirmatory memorandum whenever possible.

Usually a memorandum form is small in size and this physically prevents messages from becoming too wordy.

Instructions

Whilst a memorandum may be used to pass on instructions, there are also other commonly used written methods. For instance, staff may receive an instruction manual. This might contain information on the operation of equipment used in the place work. It could also describe the action to be taken in the event of an accident at work, or the procedure to be adopted by a member of staff who is unable to report in for work.

Simple instructions may appear on equipment or in the office or plant to identify what action should be taken in the event of a fire. The method which is used is obviously largely determined by the specific context. For example, it would be appropriate to give to all new starters a plant diagram indicating the location of fire exits with general instructions on the action that should be taken in the event of a fire breaking out.

Instructions are used to:

- tell the recipient to act in a certain way, for example, "In the event of a generator failure you should report the matter to the plant manager immediately";

- tell the recipient they are restrained from acting in a certain way, for example, "Under no circumstances should unauthorised staff enter the research and development unit";

- simply tell a potential user how to use an item of equipment, for example, "To operate, press button A, select the appropriate file and type your message".

In expressing instructions, style is very important. The imperative form should be used when the instruction must be complied with, for instance, "Enter all new client details on Form 5A" or "You must enter..." Since failure to observe an instruction may have serious consequences it is essential to use such expressions as "must", "ought" and "should". Such language will make the recipient fully aware of the nature of the obligation that is imposed when a written instruction is personal rather than directed towards the workforce generally. The use of imperative language may appear to be authoritarian. "Telephone the Sales Director and pass on my congratulations", as an instruction to an assistant, is likely to result in the Sales Director receiving a less enthusiastic message than if the assistant received the instruction prefixed with "please", although even with the addition "please" the instruction is still clearly a command.

As with all forms of communication, the method and the delivery should always reflect the context, and in the case of instructions it is essential that they be expressed both clearly and logically. This may involve sequencing the instructions as a list of numbered points, rather than combining them all, in no particular order, as a general statement. For instance, a set of instructions to a market researcher engaged in field work might read:

- greet the interviewee with the time of day – "good morning" etc.;

- introduce yourself and the name of your company;

- show evidence of your identity;

- briefly explain the nature and purpose of the survey;

- explain that the survey will last only ten minutes, and the information obtained will be of great value.

Presented in this way the interviewer can learn the instruction sequence and consequently relate to the interviewee as an efficient professional, whereas a muddled set of instructions could result in a messy presentation and a refusal by the potential interviewee to be interviewed.

Internal publications

Large organisations find it helpful to regularly publish a bulletin or magazine for distribution to all members of the workforce. Bulletins are usually cheaply produced, whilst magazines are often glossy and attractive, reinforcing the reputation and status of the organisation. Such magazines are usually produced by very large companies, such as Shell and ICI but, whether it is a magazine or a mere bulletin that is used, such a publication is a useful way of passing on information that is:

- purely personal – weddings, retirements, deaths of staff etc.; or

- organisational – changes in personnel, company trading activity, new systems being introduced, and so on.

Notice boards

Notice boards are one way of communicating generally within an organisation. They are invariably split into sections dealing with a range of topics from sport to Union meetings.

Some organisations make use of a display board. This may be restricted to information on one topic, but may be placed strategically so as to gain maximum impact. For instance, a display board concentrating on health and safety matters might be located at the entrance to the staff canteen where employees queue up for meals.

The advantages of a notice board are in its:

- cheapness;
- ability to be kept up to date easily; and
- accessibility.

They do, however, suffer from certain drawbacks including:

- the possibility that some staff ignore them altogether;
- the likelihood that staff may be selective and examine only those sections of the board which are of interest to them;
- the fact that notices inevitably lack detail because of the physical limitations of the board;
- the tendency for the board to become overcrowded which can cause people to ignore it because of the poor visual presentation of material.

Suggestion boxes

Suggestion boxes are used very successfully by some organisations as a method of encouraging employees to put forward their own ideas on all aspects of the organisation's business such as improvements to the company's products, or its systems. They have the advantage of improving employee involvement in the company affairs, and in the case of the best ideas, may produce savings for the company. It is common to offer cash payments for ideas which are accepted. Despite appearing to be a relatively modern way of communicating within a large organisation where the individual's voice might not otherwise be heard, suggestion schemes have in fact been in use for at least one hundred years.

Meetings

The experience of most employees, irrespective of whether they work in the public or the private sector, is that the further up the organisational ladder they climb the more meetings they are required to attend. They may have to prepare documents for meetings, attend and speak at meetings, and take notes at meetings. The fact is that 'the meeting' is generally regarded as one of the most appropriate ways of enabling views to be aired, shared and discussed and in this way provide a suitable forum for arriving at decisions. Those who have experienced meetings soon become aware that the efficient and effective use of a person's time is not always realised by attending a meeting.

A recent training film for business managers conveys this message humorously. The entire working day is spent attending meetings, which leaves no time to prepare for them, so this work has to be carried out at home. As a consequence most of the staff attending the meetings are so tired that they fall asleep.

Agendas

The success of a meeting often depends upon the way in which the chairperson conducts it, but it is more likely to be successful if every member knows in advance when and where the meeting is to be held, and the nature and order of the business. If reports or other written documents are to be considered at the meeting these should be issued in advance, rather than 'tabled' (that is, first presented at the meeting itself). The document used to inform staff of a meeting is called an agenda.

Meeting of the Policy and Resources Committee to be held on Thursday 24 May 1993 Commencing at 10.30a.m., in the Board Room

Agenda

1. **Apologies for absence**

2. **Minutes of the last meeting**
   To approve the Minutes of the last meeting held on Thursday 22 April 1993 (copy enclosed)

3. **Matters arising**

4. **Report of the Resources Sub-Commitee**
   To consider the report of the Resources Sub-Committee on Office Equipment required (copy enclosed)

5. **Any other business**

15 May 1993

Minutes

It will be noticed that the second item on the specimen agenda refers to the minutes of the last meeting. Minutes are records kept of the business of meetings. They include not only decisions made by the meeting, but also the discussions which lead to any decision. Minutes are in fact a type of report. It is usually the responsibility of a secretary appointed by the members of the meeting to keep a record of the proceedings as members discuss issues and reach decisions. It is then the Secretary's responsibility to prepare formal minutes from this record. The minutes will be typed and distributed to members of the meeting, usually accompanied by the next agenda. Minutes are of particular value when the meetings which they record are held regularly as, for example, in the case of a local authority committee which meets each month. Under such an arrangement the first proper business of the meeting is the approval of the minutes of the last meeting.

Highways Committee

20 February 1993 (7.15 - 8.00 p.m.)

217 Members present - Councillor Blake (Chairperson), Councillor Askew (Ms.), Coleman, Clarke (Mrs), Lawes, Smith, Smythe (Mrs), Williamson and Young.

218 Apologies for absence - Apologies for absence were received from Councillor Martin

219 Minutes - The minutes of the meeting of the committee held on 26 January 1993 were approved as a correct record and signed by the Chairperson.

220 Report of the Chief Highways Officer - The report of the Chief Highways Officer dated 14 January 1993 (ref.no.CHD/1/93) was received and approved. The report examined the use of high intensity lighting for major road junctions.

221 Ashford Road Roundabout Improvements - The committee considered the planned improvements to the Ashford Road Roundabout and the recommendation of the Chief Highways Officer's report.

Recommended - That provision be made for the installation of high intensity lighting in the layout of the Ashford Road Roundabout Improvements Scheme.

This process has the effect of reminding members what was previously discussed and decided, enabling them to check whether agreed action has been taken, and allowing them the opportunity to accept (or reject) the minutes as an accurate record of the previous meeting. As with other written records, minutes should be clear, precise, and as concise as possible, but without losing essential accuracy, if they are to be approved as a true account of the previous meeting. The style of writing appropriate to minutes is to keep sentences short. It is not necessary to link one point with another. Where reference is made to the statements of individuals speaking in the meeting indirect speech should be used. Finally, for reference purposes, a system of numerical recording is commonly used against each minuted item.

It should be noted that there is a statutory obligation for local authorities to keep minutes of their proceedings, and that these minutes are made available for public inspection. Consequently, local authority minutes are formally framed, sometimes providing full details of motions and amendments which were put to council meetings.

Abstracts or summaries

Anyone who has administrative and clerical responsibilities deals with written material constantly. In a managerial post, in order to cope efficiently, a person will find it necessary to reduce or condense much of the written material they are faced with. Letter, reports, memoranda and other communications are being generated on a daily basis and if every word has to be read the manager is likely to develop a steadily increasing backlog of incomplete or untouched work that fills the in-tray. Two ways in which this difficulty can be overcome are by improving personal reading techniques and by requiring subordinates to summarise material.

Using techniques to improve reading skill

To do this it is necessary to become aware of the different levels of reading. These are skimming (or scanning), 'normal' reading and in-depth reading. Which level a person uses firstly depends upon having a proficiency in all three. Having acquired this it becomes possible to adopt whichever technique is best suited to the time available for reading the material, and the nature of the material itself. Most people read at the normal level without difficulty, for normal reading is reading for pleasure - reading a newspaper, a magazine or a novel. The rate at which material is understood at this level will generally not matter. If, however, the material being read is hard to understand because the ideas it expresses are difficult to grasp or the vocabulary used is largely unfamiliar, there is a tendency to read it superficially. In-depth reading involves spending time in working towards an understanding of difficult material. It is a valuable skill for the student! In the working environment constant change means that even experienced staff face reading challenges from time to time. A clear example of this is the effort made by people experiencing for the first time the language of computing. Thus in-depth reading is very much a part of working life. By its nature it is a slower process than normal reading and can consume large quantities of the manager's limited time.

Certainly there is a loss of efficiency when, after ploughing through a body of complex written material, it is realised that none of it was really relevant after all. To help avoid this problem, and to generally improve reading speeds, the technique of skimming is used. It is a technique with which most people are familiar, although success in using it does not automatically follow from knowing it. It involves glancing through material, paragraph by paragraph, to gain a feel for the content. Then the reader may return and re-read the material thoroughly if the content is relevant and time permits, or simply rely upon the general impression obtained. In the latter case this may be enough to enable the reader to participate effectively at a meeting, or telephone a customer, or perhaps interview applicants for new jobs.

Preparing an abstract or summary

These two expressions are essentially the same. Summarising involves the process of writing a shorter version of a communication, whether the original is oral (for example the discussions of a meeting which are converted into minutes) or written (such as a lengthy report).

The task of summarising may become necessary at any time. A superior may call a member of staff into the office with the instruction, "Can you provide me with a written summary of the developments in our negotiations with the council over the planning application for the new factory?" Or perhaps an internal telephone call may be received for the employee's superior from a senior member of the organisation who simply instructs, "Will you pass on the following details concerning the Bridgewater Contract?", and then narrates a sequence of events.

Three skills are vital for effective summarising:

(a) *A thorough understanding of the material*
This is essential in order to produce an effective summary. You may recall having your ability to understand unfamiliar material assessed through comprehension exercises at school.

(b) *Selecting the essential points from the material*
There must be no alteration to the factual content and no additions to the material made. The main theme and major factual components should emerge from the information selected and arguments that have been used.

(c) *Writing the summary clearly and, of course, concisely*
If this is not achieved the whole purpose of the summary is defeated. Textual material can often be condensed by using a single word to replace a group of words, and by reducing sentence (and hence paragraph) length.

A summary should read as a whole, rather than as a collection of disconnected sentences. To achieve such unity involves maintaining a logical sequence to the ideas being expressed in the passage, and exercising care in linking sentences. A wide vocabulary will clearly help.

Papers

Though given different names, papers, documents or briefs are all contributions to debate, discussion and decision making. Their function is to assist someone to perform another task. The format of these 'papers' is usually looser than a report and subject to the licence of a writer. They will, however, usually have some of the features of a report: title, sub-headings, indications or policy options, etc.

A briefing paper/document, usually referred to as a brief, provides the essential background information on a topic that is necessary to guide another person charged with further development of that topic. Its function is not to offer conclusions, but to describe a situation and its boundaries, and indicate areas of decision.

A discussion paper/document, like a brief, provides the necessary background information but goes further either in indicating the areas to be resolved by further discussion and decision, or offering for further discussion or decision, conclusions offered tentatively, with arguments organised for and against with an identified preference.

Notes

Notes are short pieces of writing intended to identify only key points or issues, in which discussion or contextual information is omitted. Notes for a talk, or speaker's notes, are a listing of the major points or issues identified without more information or argument than is necessary. In this it is akin to a summary report, but the intention is oral delivery and not written presentation. Notes can be seen as pieces of writing preceding either papers or reports.

One special sort of note that is sometimes used is to keep a record of a meeting or a set of decisions, akin to minutes, but recording much more fully the reasoning and arguments that were used than a 'minute' might do.

Activity

Try applying some of the communication methods referred to above to your course. Begin by preparing a memorandum for distribution to all course members, staff, and anyone else you consider should be involved, inviting them to a meeting you have called. The purpose of the meeting is to discuss a proposal that a monthly course news and views bulletin should be published. Prepare an agenda for the meeting, and support it by producing a paper for discussion at the meeting which sets out your views on why you feel such a bulletin would be a worthwhile venture. If you wish to complete the process go on to hold the meeting. Identify someone who will take minutes at it, and after the meeting is concluded copy and distribute the minutes to everyone who was present at the meeting.

How effective do you feel these various communications methods were in achieving their objectives?

Reports

Reports may be made verbally, but are usually written. A report is a document which examines a specific topic or topics in order to:

- convey information;
- report findings;
- put forward ideas and suggestions.

In addition, a report will usually make recommendations upon which action can be taken.

There are many ways of classifying reports. This is a reflection of the variety of activities that they are used for and the differing contexts in which they are used. The most common distinctions are between formal and informal, and between routine and special reports.

Formal and informal reports

Formal reports are detailed and require structure and subdivision. Informal reports are usually shorter, less structured and more generally used. The more structured nature of a formal report reflects the greater detail of the information contained in it, and it is likely to consist of:

- a title page;
- a contents page;
- a summary of the recommendations;
- an introduction (containing the terms of reference);
- the information on which the report is based;
- conclusions;
- recommendations;
- appendices;

- references to information sources relied upon, for example the use of books, papers and other reports which are listed in the reference section of the report with their titles, their author and where they can be located.

It should be stressed that even the so called 'informal report' is essentially a formal document for it must observe certain conventions of layout. Representing a work of research, argument and recommendation, a report provides its author with a significant test of his or her communication skills. It is certainly possible that an individual's reputation may be enhanced or seriously damaged by the quality of the report they produce. The report may circulate amongst a range of senior staff throughout the organisation, be discussed at meetings, and be filed for public reference. Whatever its progress it will carry the author's name.

Routine and special reports

Routine reports are a common feature of most industrial, commercial and public organisations. As their name suggests, they are produced as a matter of internal routine as part of the information system of the organisation. For example, a routine report would be a report on sales figures produced by the sales department, or an annual report dealing with trading activity for each fiscal year. Routine reports are generally standardised. A special report is a 'one-off', dealing with a non-routine matter. This could be an evaluation of the performance of a group of employees, a report of a conference attended, or an enquiry into the restructuring of the entire organisation. Because a special report is not concerned with a routine issue its structure will not be standardised. It will, however, be based upon terms of reference. These are simply the set of instructions given to its author(s). Furthermore, the format of the report is likely to follow the sequence identified below:

(a) a statement of the terms of reference of the report. These will specify its objective or objectives;

(b) a statement of facts or arguments, set out logically, regarding the subject being investigated;

(c) the identification of viable solutions to the problem, giving the respective strengths and weaknesses of each course of action. This stage is usually referred to as the 'findings';

(d) the recommendation, supported by appropriate reasons.

In addition, detailed information may be contained in appendices included at the back of the report. The body of the report will contain references to the appendices, but the text will be prevented from becoming too detailed by including the appendix material separately.

Different stages of reports

Before a full report is given, a variety of reports which fall short of a full report may be requested. Thus:

(a) an interim report is either a review of general progress and indication of future lines of enquiry or a report concerned with one topic of particular urgency which cannot await the full report;

(b) a field report indicates the evidence on which a full report may be used; it is thus raw material for the conclusion and thus rarely indicates the nature of the conclusion;and

(c) a summary report is entirely dominated by its conclusions, giving only such argument and evidence as is necessary to give a context to these conclusions.

The qualifying verbs customarily used in requests for reports (and other forms of communication) indicate the stage at which the communication is being made:

(a) to 'draft' is to produce a report in a form with a certain roughness of presentation and tentativeness of conclusion, but as a preliminary to a final, more polished version;

(b) to 'prepare' is a slightly more advanced stage of drafting but still subject to a final revision and reassessment;

(c) to 'write' or 'provide' is to produce the final version or one in which only minor textual amendment will be necessary.

External Written Communications

Since organisations exist to meet the needs of customers and clients they spend a significant proportion of their time communicating with them. But external communications do not stop there. Whether an organisation likes it or not, it has to deal with outside bodies and individuals who impose demands upon it. For instance, it must deal with the Inland Revenue when its corporation tax is assessed, the Department of Social Security in making national insurance contributions and the local authority when paying its business rates. It also enters into relationships with: its suppliers, from the local electricity board for its power supplies to printers for its stationery; its advisers, including accountants and lawyers; its bank; the landlord from whom it may rent its property; and the trade union, whose members it employs.

Obviously communication between the organisation and this diverse range of outsiders takes place in many different ways. Often communications will be oral. These take place over the phone or by meeting face to face. For the moment, however, we are concerned with the methods used to communicate in writing, whether the organisation is the initiator or at the receiving end of the process. The major form of external written communication is the official letter.

Official/Business Letters

There are a number of reasons why it is essential for such official letters to meet high standards of communication. For instance:

(i) outsiders invariably judge an organisation by the letters it writes, especially if they have not dealt with it in any other way, thus a business letter performs a public relations role;

(ii) the letter may be designed to convey an instruction, for instance to a bank, and it could be financially harmful if it is misinterpreted;

(iii) a letter may give rise to legal liability, for instance if it is defamatory or where it constitutes an offer or an acceptance in contractual negotiations.

It should also be borne in mind that the contents of a letter may be widely circulated, for example, if it is a letter to a newspaper editor explaining a company's reasons for closing a local plant or perhaps responding to a specific public criticism. In such circumstances the construction of the letter is particularly important. Not only are there public relations to be maintained (or perhaps restored) but also the tort of defamation to be considered, for unjustifiable statements that harm the reputation of an individual or an organisation may be actionable and result in the writer paying substantial damages as compensation.

The purpose of the official letter

In commerce and industry business letters are used for many different purposes. The writer needs to be quite clear about the purpose of the letters he or she is writing, for what it says and how it says it reflects who the recipient is and why the communication is being made. It is not difficult to appreciate that the letter a company writes to another company apologising for a delay in supplying goods will be in a very different tone from one that it writes to its bank complaining that the bank has wrongfully dishonoured a cheque drawn by the company. Similarly, a local authority housing department might be expected to respond by letter to a request for information about the availability of a council house somewhat differently than it would to a council tenant's statement that unless a different rent collector is appointed the tenant will assault the existing rent collector the next time he appears.

The type of letter that an organisation writes in terms of its *content*, *style* (formal or informal) and *tone* (friendly or restrained) reflects the purpose of the communication. Whatever the purpose is, however, it should always be borne in mind that the use of business correspondence is a means of avoiding a time-consuming and unnecessary face to face meeting. It also provides both parties with a permanent record of the arguments that they have made, and matters they have agreed.

Writing official letters

The layout

The general layout of a business letter says something of the organisation which has written it. If the layout is pleasing to the eye and contains at a glance the major information the recipient requires – who the sender is, when it was sent, and what it is concerned with – the recipient is encouraged to regard the organisation sending it as efficiently run. Thus, it is not just a case of satisfying standard conventions when writing an official letter. It also has to do with providing a communication in a form which advertises a chosen image for the organisation. The point has already been made that the content of a letter should always be presented courteously.

Regarding content, it is sometimes said that the 'ABC' of efficient and effective official letters is:

- *Accuracy;*
- *Brevity;*
- *Clarity.*

But looking beyond content, there are other features of a letter which make an impact on the reader:

(i) the design of the printed letter head;

(ii) the quality of the paper;

(iii) the style and quality of the typewriter or printer head used;

(iv) the positioning of the text within the space available; and

(v) the use of margins.

A well written letter that meets the requirements of accuracy, brevity and clarity may nevertheless be let down if the letterhead is out of date and has to have typed amendments made to it, the paper is thin, and the text is cramped on to a page that is too small, or located at the top of the page leaving a large gap below it.

Having made the observation that a business letter should be regarded in its totality, covering content, style and layout, we can now go on to identify the conventions that a business letter should observe. These include:

The sender's address

If the letter does not contain a printed letter head, the sender's address should be included in the top right hand corner of the first page.

The date

This appears after the sender's address, and is usually inserted on the right hand of the page. The month should be written in full to distinguish clearly the date from the reference included in the letter.

The salutation or greeting

It is usual now to use the recipient's name whenever possible, for example, 'Dear Mr. Green'. When the recipient is named in this way the letter should be ended, 'Yours sincerely'. If the greeting, 'Dear Sir' or, 'Dear Madam' is used the letter should close 'Yours faithfully'. If the letter is written to someone the writer knows well it will begin, 'Dear Paul' and may end, 'With best wishes'. Letters to a newspaper editor begin simply, 'Sir'.

Title or subject line

This is an underlined heading which briefly indicates the subject of the letter. Although not essential it can be very helpful for the addressee. For example, it allows the appropriate file to be found quickly. It is a particularly useful device, therefore, when dealing with accounts and policies, when the number or reference can be inserted as a heading.

The sender's name

This appears after the close, and usually in the form of a signature. It is common practice to print the name beneath the signature, and to indicate the status of the writer, for example, 'Senior Housing Officer', or, 'Company Secretary'. Sometimes the letters 'p.p.' are used against the signature. This carries a specific legal meaning and indicates that the signatory is empowered to sign on behalf of another person or the organisation itself.

It is common for less senior staff to be allowed to sign letters, and in this case the indication of the signatory's status will include who he or she is acting on behalf of, thus 'Assistant Marketing Manager, for Marketing Manager'. Sometimes a personal assistant may sign a letter under specific authority. If so, the following forms of words would appear, 'Dictated by Mrs. Pearce and signed in her absence'. It is sometimes the practice to send all letters in the name of a senior manager, leaving the writer to add the manager's signature on items of routine correspondence.

References

The purpose of using references in business letters is to link subsequent correspondence on the same subject matter with the file, and also to ensure that a reply can be directed to the right department or individual. It is therefore a means of ensuring that correspondence is dealt with promptly, and that the author of the letter can, if necessary be traced. This is obviously more important in larger organisations than smaller ones. Usually two references are provided. They appear as 'Your Ref:' and 'Our Ref:' enabling both the sender and the recipient to link the letter to their respective filing systems. The normal practice is for the initials of the person signing the letter to appear first, followed by an oblique and then the initials of the secretary/typist. Longer references may refer to the file number or the department.

Enclosures

Very often the enclosure is of more value than the covering letter which accompanies it. It is vital to indicate that a letter includes enclosures, as a reminder to whoever prepares the letter for posting. Common devices are asterisks and stickers, but the most common method is to type 'Enclosure', 'Encl' or 'Enc.' at the bottom left hand side of the letter.

The recipient's name and address

This may appear either at the top left hand side of the letter beside the date, or alternatively at the bottom left hand side, below the sender's signature.

Types of official letter

The main types of letters are:

(a) letters requesting and providing information;

(b) letters of complaint;

(c) circulars and standard letters;

(d) references and testimonials.

Letters requesting or providing information

For many organisations these types of letters make up a substantial proportion of their business correspondence. This is perhaps even more the case for public sector organisations, such as local authorities, than for private sector ones. Local authorities receive many requests for information relating to the services they provide. If the letter is requesting information it is essential that the writer has first clearly established in his or her mind precisely what he or she wants to know. For example, suppose a company was to write to a local authority in the following way: 'Please let us know of the grants that you offer.' Such a request is most unhelpful. The council needs to know what specific need the enquiry is related to. The company may be interested in grants for setting up a new business, or for taking on additional staff, and so on. Presumably the company is clear about the purpose for which the grant is being sought, so this should be clearly expressed in the letter.

When a letter supplies information, the writer should seek to ensure that it is written in a form which is understandable to the recipient. This may seem a very obvious requirement, but often staff who have worked in a particular department for a long time are so familiar with procedures and technical expressions that they forget that outsiders do not share this knowledge. Equally, it may be obvious from the content of the letter of request that the writer faces particular difficulties which should be recognised when responding to it. Many examples can be given. The letter may indicate that the writer has great difficulty in communicating and so very simple language should be used in writing a reply. It may be evident that the writer is distressed, for instance, a pensioner worried about his inability to meet the rates demand, or a single parent anxious about the housing conditions for his or her family. In such circumstances whatever information is provided should be accompanied by some general words of support, although of course one should beware of making promises that it may not be possible to keep.

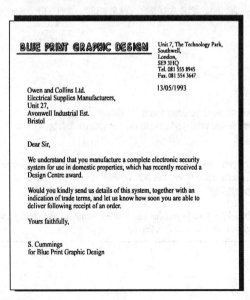

In business situations perhaps the most common type of written enquiry is that from one of the parties in the chain of distribution to another (for example retailer to wholesale, or wholesaler to manufacturer) requesting information on prices, specifications of goods, availability, trade discounts and so on. The reply to such an enquiry will usually be a letter of quotation. As with any letter of enquiry the writer should be courteous, set out questions clearly and in sufficient detail, and include any information that is relevant to the enquiry, for instance, that the matter is urgent.

The reply should deal with each question raised accurately and completely and should reflect a tone and style which indicates a genuine desire to be of service. This may, for instance, involve providing additional information which was not requested but which will clearly be helpful to the enquirer. Finally, it is in the interests of the organisation sending the reply to do so as soon as possible. In the case of a commercial organisation this can only enhance its reputation, and it may well result in an order being placed. An example of a letter of enquiry is shown on the foot of the previous page.

Letters of complaint

A letter of complaint will invariably be based upon a grievance held by the complainant. An organisation may receive such letters; it may also need to write them itself. Often when the complaint comes from an individual, the letter will reflect strong emotions. These may be quite justified yet be most unhelpful in constructing a letter which is appropriate to its purpose. Thus, such a letter should not be abusive, threatening (if it is the first letter that has been written) or contain allegations which it may not be possible to substantiate. Rather it should set out the facts as the writer understands them, avoid irrelevances, and be polite. For instance, it is good practice to make it clear in the letter that the writer anticipates a favourable response to the complaint if it is found to be established after enquiry. These observations are of particular importance when an organisation is making the complaint. Compare the following examples of letters of complaint sent by an organisation to a customer:

BLUE PRINT GRAPHIC DESIGN   Unit 7, The Technology Park,
Southwell,
London,
SE9 3HQ
Tel. 081 555 8945
Fax. 081 554 3647

13/05/1993

Dear Sir,

We refer to the as yet unpaid sum of £378 owed to us by you. We find it intolerable that we should have to write to you demanding payment of your bill.

It is our policy to vigorously pursue claims against our debtors, and since you have chosen to ignore this debt we shall have no alternative but to commence legal proceedings unless payment is made forthwith.

We should point out to you that this company is not run as a charity, even though you obviously believe that it is.

BLUE PRINT GRAPHIC DESIGN

Unit 7, The Technology Park,
Southwell,
London,
SE9 3HQ
Tel. 081 555 8945
Fax. 081 554 3647

13/05/1993

Dear Mr. Smith,

We are sure that there must be some good cause for your delay in settling payment of your account Number 876413. If we can assist in any way in overcoming any difficulties you may have we should be glad to do so. If so, would you either call in, or give us a ring as soon as possible.

It may be that you have already made payment, in which case we apologise for inconveniencing you.

Yours sincerely,

BLUE PRINT GRAPHIC DESIGN

Unit 7, The Technology Park,
Southwell,
London,
SE9 3HQ.
Tel. 081 555 8945
Fax. 081 554 3647

13/10/1993

Dear Mr. Smith,

We have received no reply to our reminder of the non-payment of your account. We must now regretfully point out to you that unless we hear from you as to the position within the next seven days, we shall have to consider taking steps to recover the amount.

Yours sincerely,

If it is discovered that the complaints made in the letter received from as customer or client are justified, it will be necessary to write a letter of apology, offering to make amends. This may involve financial compensation or adjustment, the replacement of goods, or an indication that an employee in the organisation has been disciplined.

Of course, the examination of the complaint may reveal that it is totally without foundation, or there is some real doubt about its justification. In this case it will not be appropriate to make an offer of amends, unless in circumstances of genuine doubt, the organisation chooses to maintain goodwill, by making perhaps a token gesture.

Whatever the circumstances, letters responding to criticisms must be very carefully constructed. If the criticism is well founded the response should admit the error using restrained language, thus, "upon immediate enquiry it became clear that an administrative error resulted in your goods being misdirected. Please accept the company's apologies for the inconvenience you have been caused". It would be excessive for example, to add, "You may be assured that this will never happen again", for even in the most efficient organisations errors can and do occur and there can be no guarantee that a similar problem might not arise in the future.

Even if the organisation does not believe the complaint to have any foundation, it is still necessary to provide a response, and the question arises as to how this should be framed. Since the organisation will doubtless wish to maintain goodwill, as future orders may depend upon maintaining a sound relationship with the customer, it is vital that the customer is not made to feel foolish. It may help if the response is sent out under the signature of a senior member of staff, to signify the importance the organisation attaches to the criticism. This is especially true where the organisation is a service provider, particularly in the public sector, where because of the size of organisations it is easy to fall into the trap of responding to correspondence of all kinds by means of standardised letters which appear as cold, bureaucratic and impersonal.

An example of a reply to an unfounded complaint is shown below.

BLUE PRINT GRAPHIC DESIGN

Unit 7, The Technology Park,
Southwell,
London,
SE9 3HQ.
Tel. 081 555 8945
Fax. 081 554 3647

13/10/1993

Dear Mrs. Taylor,

Thank you for your letter of 20 April 1993. I am sorry that you felt you received discourteous treatment when our accounts department contacted you by telephone regarding your bill. I have spoken to the member of staff you dealt with and put your complaint to him.

I am satisfied that he dealt with the matter correctly. However, I am glad you drew my attention to your concern, since we value good customer relations, and are always prepared to investigate customers' criticisms or complaints.

I hope the matter is now satisfactorily cleared up, and that we can remain of service to you in future.

Yours sincerely

When there is doubt about the substance of the complaint there is clearly no need to provide an admission of responsibility or an apology. Nevertheless, in the interests of goodwill, which in turn reflects upon the reputation and good name of the organisation, it is important that the response reflects the concern of the organisation and recognises that the writer of the letter of complaint is genuinely upset or annoyed.

The reply might read as follows:

```
BLUE PRINT GRAPHIC DESIGN          Unit 7, The Technology Park,
                                   Southwell,
                                   London,
                                   SE9 3HQ.
                                   Tel. 081 555 8945
                                   Fax. 081 554 3647

                                   13/10/1993

Dear Mr. Jones,

I am sorry to learn of your annoyance at the refusal of the department's collectors
to remove your kitchen units that are in your rear yard. The refuse collection
teams are under instruction to collect all refuse on their weekly visit which in
their opinion can be physically lifted and safely carried on their vehicles.

It is, however, sometimes necessary to arrange for a larger refuse vehicle to
collect specific items. Such an arrangement will need to be made in this case.

If you would kindly contact this office (extension 225) letting us know when it
would be convenient to remove your kitchen units, immediate arrangements will
be made to do so.

Yours sincerely,
```

Finally it should be noted that letters of complaint should be dealt with promptly. This, of course, is true of all business correspondence but in the case of complaints it may take time to carry out an enquiry. Thus it is essential to notify the complainant as soon as the letter of complaint is received that the matter is being dealt with, for example:

> Thank you for your letter indicating that your account has been overcharged by £874. We are investigating and hope to give you a explanation within five days

To summarise, complaints are an inevitable outcome of administrative, commercial and industrial activity. Complaints may or may not be justified, but the manner in which organisations respond in writing (and indeed orally) to them may, in the view of the customer or rate-payer, be as important as the product or service itself.

Circulars and standard letters

Circulars are used more commonly for advertising purposes, whereas standard letters may fulfil a variety of purposes, for example, inviting job applicants to attend for interviews or inviting customers to a company presentation. In the case of a standard letter, whilst the bulk of the information it conveys is standard, some provision will need to be made for the non-standard aspects of it.

Thus a standard letter inviting applicants to attend for interview might read:

> You are invited to attend an interview for the post of
> Marketing Assistant
> The interview will be held on ... 1993, at Crown
> House,
> High Row, Carlington,
> commencing at ...am/pm.
>
> If you are unable to attend would you please contact
> the Personnel Department as soon as possible.

Such letters can be stored on a word processor and the blanks completed as appropriate for each separate occasion.

Circulars are addressed, 'Dear Sir or Madam', 'Dear Elector' and so on, whereas most standard letters will contain the salutation, 'Dear Mr. Jones', 'Dear Ms. Peters', etc. Referring to the recipient's name creates a more personal impression than using 'Sir' or 'Madam' but it will not usually be possible to personalise a circular because of the large number of copies involved. Since a circular is aimed at selling a product, a service or, as in the case of an election, a person and party, it should be designed to:

(i) *create an instant impact*
   perhaps through the use of a headline, or photograph, or the dramatic use of colour;

(ii) *encourage the recipient to read it*
   a 'lightweight' text using simple language and a style appropriate to the message
   should achieve this. A prospective local government candidate, for example, will not
   try to sell him or herself in the same way as a double glazing business will in marketing new windows;

(iii) *be memorable*
   very often achievable by using a slogan or some striking advertising 'copy', for
   instance "can you afford not to read this?".

References and testimonials

All organisations are called upon from time to time to write references and, to a lesser extent, testimonials.

- A *reference* is a statement, commonly given on a standard form provided by the
  prospective employer but sometimes produced as a letter, which is provided for a future

employer (company, college etc.), by someone who has knowledge of the applicant; and contains a statement of the applicant's qualities and abilities. These may be qualities of character, or abilities related to work performance.

- A *testimonial* is a letter of commendation, written either by the employer or by some other person or body with whom the applicant has had dealings.

A major distinction between a testimonial and reference is that a reference is sent direct from the person providing it to the person requiring it, whereas a testimonial is held in the possession of the applicant who sends a copy of it in support of a job application. Not surprisingly, prospective employers value references more highly than testimonials, for a testimonial can be easily forged and tends to highlight the strengths of the applicant and ignore his or her weaknesses.

When an organisation, or indeed an individual, is required to provide a reference it may recognise a moral obligation to be as open and honest in its assessment as possible. In consequence, it may quite genuinely make statements which it believes to be true, but which in fact are not true. The law recognises that a person has a right to protect his or her reputation, and an action can be brought for damages under the tort of defamation where such reputation has been harmed by an untrue statement of a defamatory kind. The defence of privilege exists to strike a balance between the need to protect reputations and allow freedom of expression in a communication made between a person acting under a moral obligation to provide a reference and a person having a professional interest in receiving it. If an organisation writes a letter of reference containing untrue statements about the applicant, providing the reference was issued without malice, the existence of privilege will provide a complete defence to the organisation.

A letter of reference usually follows a traditional layout, and an example is included next:

Anne Clark: 6 South Green, Stainmore, Essex.

I have known the above for over five years, and I am very happy to write in support of her application for the position of clerical officer.

Anne joined this company as a sales clerk, and after three years was promoted to her present position as sales assistant.

She has shown a conscientious and mature attitude to her job and can work well with others, although recently she has found difficulty in working with one of her colleagues with whom she has had a number of disagreements. She is an ambitious young woman whose career prospects are limited in this organisation by the lack of promotional posts available.

I have every confidence that if her application is successful you will find Anne to be a valuable addition to your staff. I will certainly be sorry to lose her. Please contact me if you require any further details.

Yours faithfully,

A final note on references. Firstly there is no legal obligation upon an organisation to provide a reference. Secondly the permission of the referee should be sought before his or her name and address are included on the application form. In cases where an appointment needs to be made rapidly, it is possible that the referee will be telephoned to provide an oral reference, and it does not assist the applicant if the referee is not prepared. In any case there may be reasons why a referee will decline the invitation to act in this capacity.

Activity

Suppose the business you work for, an employment agency, is anxious to update its client files. Construct a suitable letter to be sent out to all its clients who have been on its books for the last two years, designed to obtain from them up-to-date information on their employment needs. At the same time produce a letter which can be distributed to the main businesses in your area which is designed to inform them of the services your agency is able to offer. Finally write a reply to a client who alleges he was unprofessionally treated when, during a telephone conversation with your agency last week, he was kept waiting for a long time, was passed to three different members of staff, and was finally told by a new secretary that she had no idea how to deal with his request for an appointment, following which she put the phone down.

Influences of Technology on Communications

The combination of computer and telecommunications technologies has profoundly affected the ways in which communications systems are designed and the facilities they provide. The main features of these technologies are described in Element 3.3 and this section concentrates on their influence on communication systems in general.

A number of systems can be identified as being particularly significant and are described in the following paragraphs:

- telex;
- facsimile transmission (FAX);
- local area network (LAN);
- wide area network (WAN);
- electronic mail;
- electronic data interchange (EDI);
- electronic diary and calendar;
- electronic noticeboard;
- viewdata and teletext;
- enhanced telephone systems.

Telex

Telex is a system of written communication used primarily by industry and commerce. A telex directory is also provided. Telex facilities are operated by British Telecom. It is a communications system which, rather like the public telephone network, allows subscribers to communicate with one another. Each subscriber is given a telex number or code (you will often see it at the top of business letter headings next to the telephone number) and must have a teleprinter which is a combination of keyboard and printer. There is no screen, so all messages sent or received are printed onto hard copy. The transmission rate of approximately six characters per second is slow compared with more modern telecommunications systems, but the limitations of keyboard entry and printer speed on the teleprinter, make any faster speed unnecessary.

The advantages of using telex are that:

    (a) the message can be transferred virtually instantaneously;

    (b) a written record is kept of the communication;

    (c) messages can be sent at any time so, provided the recipient's teleprinter has been left on, it is possible, for example, to pass a message from the United Kingdom during working hours to New Zealand while the staff of the organisation are at home because of the different time zone.

    (d) errors typed out on the teleprinter can be easily identified by inserting the word "error" and then retyping the correct message.

Its main disadvantage is that there is no storage facility for messages. Any transmission has to be printed as soon as it is transmitted so that if the receiver is faulty, the system comes to a halt. However, systems now exist to allow telex to be accessed through Prestel, using a microcomputer system or LAN workstation (see later section) with full word processing facilities.

Because the use of telex facilities is costly (charges are based upon time rather than the number of words) the message should be terse but understandable. Normally, grammatical rules are dispensed with. An example of a telex message would be:

"MANAGING DIRECTOR VANDOR P.L.C. ARRIVING 17:30 FRIDAY 31ST OCTOBER. PLEASE MEET. ARRANGE BOARD MEETING FOR 20:00 SAME DAY. MAIN AGENDA ITEM JORDANIAN CONTRACT. CIRCULATE FINANCIAL REPORT 89/S/2 IN ADVANCE. BOOK HOTEL ACCOMMODATION ONE NIGHT"

Facsimile Transmission (FAX)

Fax is an electronic system which uses telephone lines to transfer documents from a sender to a recipient. The document is printed out on the recipient's Fax machine, saving the time that would otherwise be taken up in sending material through the post. This system can use either the telephone or telex networks to allow users to transmit an accurate copy of a document. The information (text or picture) is digitised by a facsimile machine which scans the page automatically to produce the required signals. Computer storage is used within the network so that signals can be queued if there is a hold-up in the system. Modern systems can transmit an A4 page in less than a minute. Fax machines differ quite widely in their transmission speeds and it is worth remembering that the speed of a transmission between two machines is dictated by the slowest; it is no good, therefore, having a high speed Fax if the machines you are communicating with are comparatively slow.

Local Area Networks (LAN)

A LAN comprises a number of microcomputers connected for the purpose of resource sharing (including disk storage and printing facilities) and communication. Each user's terminal is called a workstation. A LAN allows:

    • the sharing of centrally stored information;

    • electronic communication between individual users.

Sharing information

Information can be regarded as a resource, so sharing it brings similar benefits to those available from sharing hardware. For example, a common information store supports the use of a database system, which itself reduces the need to duplicate information for different users in a business. Traditional computer processing methods require that each application has its own files and this results in duplication of many data items and the process of updating them. For example, stock control and purchasing functions both make use of commodity details, such as Stock Codes, Descriptions and Prices, so a change in the Price of a commodity requires more than one input. Even if database methods are not used, the various application files can be held in a common disk store and be available to all users on the LAN.

Network security

Although LANs facilitate sharing of information it is not always desirable to share all of it with everyone and security mechanisms must be available to exclude unauthorised users from the system and to restrict authorised users to the particular files and processes with which they are properly concerned. Security is also concerned with preventing data loss, so provision must exist for the backing up of files. The separation of users' files and access control is effected through a network's multi-user operating system. The operating system's facilities provide for the creation and control of directories (equivalent to manual filing cabinets) to separate users and their files, as well as password controls to limit access.

Wide Area Networks (WAN)

WANs are used to connect computers on different sites or even in different parts of the world. They make use of telecommunications systems (in this country the principal provider is British Telecom) including terrestrial and satellite radio links. These networks extend beyond the idea of the office as a single room or group of rooms. A user can be 'at the office' at home (teleworking) if he or she has the necessary terminal link. Organisations with offices abroad can benefit from the immediate communication facility normally available to people in the same room. They can also provide connections between LANs. For example, a business may install a LAN at each of its branches and use a WAN to allow communications between them. This gives each branch of the business some local control over its processing and at the same time allows information needed for strategic or corporate decision-making to be gathered electronically and then processed centrally using the Head Office mainframe or minicomputer.

Electronic mail

Unlike telex and facsimile transmissions, which require paper for input and output, electronic mail systems based on computer networks are paper-less (except when a user requires hard copy). A major advantage is the facility for message storage if a destination terminal is busy, or has a temporary fault. When it is free, the message can be transmitted.

Certain basic features can be identified as being common to all electronic mail systems:

- a terminal for preparing, entering and storing messages. The terminal will be intelligent, possibly a microcomputer, mainframe terminal or dedicated word processor. In any event, it should have some word processing or text editing facilities to allow messages to be changed on screen before transmission. A printer may also be available for printing out messages received over the system;

- an electronic communication link with other workstations in the network and with the central computer controlling the system;

- a directory containing the electronic addresses of all network users;

- a central mailbox facility (usually the controlling computer) for the storage of messages in transit or waiting to be retrieved.

Ideally, the following facilities are available to electronic mail users:

- messages are automatically dated upon transmission;
- messages are automatically acknowledged as being received when the recipient first accesses it from the terminal;
- multiple addressing; that is the facility to address a message to an identified group, without addressing each member of the group individually;
- priority rating to allow messages to be allocated different priorities according to their importance.

Networks require two particular features to support electronic mail:

- a message storage facility to allow messages to be forwarded when the recipient is available. This means that the recipient does not have to be using the system at the time the message is sent;
- compatibility with a wide range of manufacturers' equipment. Devices attached to a network have to be able to talk to the communications network using protocols or standards of communication.

Benefits of electronic mail

The following major benefits are generally claimed for electronic mail systems:

- savings in stationery and telephone costs;
- more rapid transmission than is possible with conventional mail;
- electronic mail can be integrated with other computer-based systems used in an organisation;
- all transmissions are recorded, so costs can be carefully controlled;
- electronic mail allows staff to telework, that is, to work from home or another location via a terminal;
- the recipient does not have to be present when a message is sent. Messages can be retrieved from the central mailbox when convenient.

Electronic mail refers to communication over long, as well as short distances by way of WANs, but internal office communication through a LAN is referred to as electronic messaging.

Electronic Data Interchange (EDI)

Similar to electronic mail, EDI allows users to exchange business documents, such as invoices and orders, over the telephone network.

Electronic diaries and calendars

An ordinary desk diary is generally used by managerial or executive staff to keep a check on important meetings and much of the time it is quite adequate for the purpose. A conventional calendar is usually pinned to a wall for staff to check the date. Electronic diaries and calendars do not attempt to replace these traditional facilities. To begin with, it would be extremely tedious if it were necessary to sit at a computer terminal simply to discover the date.

An electronic diary and calendar system may provide the following facilities:

- *diary entries*
  Entries are made under a particular date and can be retrieved using the relevant date. Used in this way, the system 'apes' the conventional diary by producing a list of entries for any date entered. At this level, it could be argued that a desk diary does the job just as well;

- *search and retrieval on event*
  Instead of entering the date, the user requests a list of entries conforming to particular criteria. For example, a request for a list of Board Meetings over the next six months would produce a list with the relevant dates. Similarly, for example, a request for a list of those supposed to be attending a Board Meeting on a particular date would produce a list of attendees' names;

- *flexible search and retrieval*
  This facility can be used to produce a number of alternative strategies based on specified criteria. Suppose, for example, that a Board
  eeting has been called, but the exact date has not been set. The problem is to set a date which falls within the next three weeks and is convenient for all Board
  members. The search and retrieval facility allows the searching of each member's electronic diary for dates when all of them are available. The system may produce a number of possible dates. Such tasks can be extremely time consuming to carry out manually.

At this point, it is important to note that the above examples assume a comprehensive diary system that is kept up to date. The system fails if, for example, one director's diary entries are incomplete.

Electronic notice boards

Electronic notice boards are essentially a localised version of the viewdata systems described later. The system may be used by an organisation to advertise staff promotions, training courses, new staff appointments and retirements.

Viewdata and teletext systems

The combination of the telecommunications and computer technologies has produced an 'information explosion' and there are now many services providing specialist information, which organisations can use either independently or in conjunction with their own computerised information systems.

Viewdata or videotex

The principle of a central database and frames of information forms the basis of viewdata systems. The major public viewdata system in the UK is Prestel. Each user requires a telephone, TV monitor or television set, electronic interface, a modem (for modifying computer signals for transmission over the telephone network), an autodialler (for contacting the database and identifying the terminal user) and an electronic device to generate the picture from the received data.

Its major benefit is that it provides an interactive system (communication is two way). A user can transmit messages to the database.

Teletext

Teletext systems, such as Ceefax provide a public service based on a central computer database, which users can access by way of an ordinary television set with special adapter and keypad. The database consists of thousands of 'pages' or frames of information which are kept up to date by Information Providers. Pages can be accessed and displayed on the television screen through the use of the keypad, directly via page number or through a series of hierarchical indexes. Major subject areas include Sport, News, Business, Leisure and Entertainment, Finance and Travel. Pages are transmitted using spare bandwidth unused by television pictures, in 'carousels' or groups. The user may have to wait some time while the carousel containing the required page is transmitted. Its major drawback is that communication is one way. The user cannot send messages to the database, only receive.

Enhanced telephone systems

Modern telephones can be equipped with a variety of extra facilities that make the process of telephoning more efficient:

- visual display of the number you are dialling helps to prevent mis-dialling;
- automatic redial button for the last number;
- secrecy button to prevent the person you are calling from hearing any disparaging comment you may make!
- call timer to provide immediate feedback on the cost of a call;
- memory bank allowing single key dialling of regularly used numbers;
- current date and time;
- conference facilities allowing several users on different extensions to talk to each other.

Switchboards

Many businesses need more than one line if they are to handle all their incoming and outgoing calls efficiently and switchboards vary widely in the range of sophisticated features they provide, including, for example:

- status indicators to show whether a line is busy, free or on hold;
- the facility to link incoming calls to particular extensions.

Call logging

As the term suggests, this facility allows a business to automatically record call details, including the source extension, destination and time taken. The system can result in huge savings for a large business, in that employees know that their calls are logged and are discouraged from making unauthorised personal calls. In addition, the telephone costs for individual departments can be monitored and budgeting plans can be tailored accordingly.

Cellular phones

These phones use radio transmission via local transmitters linked to a large national network. Computers are used to allow links to be maintained even while the caller is moving from one transmission area to another. Typical facilities include last number redialling and a hands-free facility, which is important for safety if the user is driving.

Radio paging

Radio pagers are small, portable devices that allow the carrier to be contacted by radio transmissions; normally, the recipient will then go to the nearest telephone or use a cellular phone to call the sender of the signal. A number of facilities may be provided:

- bleeping of the pager from any extension on a Private Automatic Branch Exchange (PABX);
- multiple paging allows several people to be contacted by one transmission;
- visual display to provide a simple message to indicate, for example, the urgency of the call;
- voice contact which combines the facilities of a cellular phone and a radio pager;
- automatic paging linked to a security system; this can warn a guard of intruders.

Answering machines

Although most people don't like talking to machines, they can be extremely useful for a business where the proprietor has to be out of the office on various occasions; without an answering machine, valuable business may be lost.

Forms

The nature and scope of forms

We live in an environment of forms. (We even have a Unit in this book, Unit 6, *Financial Documents and Monitoring* which looks in detail at forms). The major social events of our existence such as births, marriages and deaths are recorded on them. We complete them for licences, insurance policies, job applications, property purchases, credit transactions, membership of organisations, and so on. They encroach on most aspects of our lives and, if we work in an administrative job, the likelihood is that processing of forms will be a main aspect of our jobs.

What is a form and why is it necessary? A form is simply:

- a document of a standardised type;
- prepared in advance; and
- used as a means of eliciting information from the person completing it. This is achieved by including instructions indicating the nature of the information being required and leaving spaces or blocks where it can be inserted.

As with any type of information gathering mechanism, the skill in obtaining an accurate and comprehensive response lies in designing appropriate questions and presenting them in a suitable layout. Nevertheless, it should be remembered that there may be considerable skill involved in effectively completing a form as well.

Individuals and organisations alike are constantly exposed to a bombardment of forms to be completed. Nevertheless, many organisations find it useful and necessary to produce their own forms. They may be used as part of an internal system of communication, such as stock records and computer input forms, or as an aspect of external communications, for instance application forms, market research surveys, and questionnaires used to test consumer satisfaction with products and services. A local authority will use many types of forms to obtain relevant information ranging from grant applications for loft insulation to planning applications and forms dealing with council house applications. You may have had to complete a form to apply for assistance with this course from your employer, you certainly had to complete a registration form to commence the course, and later on you may have to complete an examination entry form. In addition you have to complete a form to: tax a car; obtain insurance; join a trade union; obtain credit; apply for a passport; take out a mortgage; record your income for tax purposes, to name but a few examples.

The advantages of using forms to obtain and record information are:

(a) the information obtained can be precisely tailored to the needs of the organisation by the use of suitable questions;

(b) the information is provided in a standard order which assists the processing of it;

(c) unnecessary correspondence can be avoided; and

(d) detailed information can be rapidly accessed.

It might also be added that the effective use of forms in an organisation can save time and money. However, these benefits can be offset by the over enthusiastic use of forms generating irrelevant and unnecessary information. Thus the first question to be asked before designing a form is whether it is really necessary. Perhaps there is a simpler way of obtaining the information. Even if this is so the fact remains that the form is a major tool of communication for all types of organisations. It is an indispensable mechanism for obtaining information, and monitoring processes and activities.

The design and layout of forms

The design and layout of forms is a skilled task, often carried out by specialists. Essentially it involves constructing questions appropriate to the information being sought and ordering them in a suitable way.

The following should be considered in designing a form:

(i) *Instructions to the recipient*
It helps to remember that a form involves two-way communication. The recipient should be clear how the form should be completed, to whom it should be returned, when it should be returned by and, perhaps, what purpose it serves the organisation seeking to obtain the data. A valuable general instruction is to indicate that no part of the form should be left unanswered, and that questions that do not apply to the recipient should be answered, "Not applicable".

(ii) *The questions*
Questions can be framed in different ways, but as long as they are clear and precise it is simply a matter of design preference as to the method used. An example of different approaches is the use of direct and indirect questions, thus "What is your reason for seeking the job?" (direct), "Is there anything you are dissatisfied about in your present post" (indirect) and open and closed questions thus " Have you ever bought one of our products? Please answer yes or no" (closed); "if you have ever bought one of our products what did you like about it?" (open). The language of each question should be kept as simple as accuracy permits, and it should never be necessary for the recipient to spend time working out what a question means. If a question inevitably involves the use of technical expressions, a note of explanation should be provided, preferably as close to the question as possible. The designer should be aware of the types of reader who will complete the form, to ensure that its language reflects the most basic level of literacy that any reader may possess. A questionnaire for completion by accountants would probably use a wider range of vocabulary than would be desirable in a form to be completed by nine year old school children!

(iii) *The responses*
It should be absolutely clear how the recipient is required to respond to the questions. Common methods of response include: "Please place a tick in the appropriate box", "Please answer 'yes' or 'no'", and "Please state briefly your reasons". If the recipient is confused it is possible for the answer given to be the opposite of the correct one. When a written or typed response is asked for, sufficient space should be made available.

(iv) *Question sequence*
This should be logical. An application form for a job might commence with a section dealing with the applicant's personal details: name; age; marital status; number of dependants. It would then require information on qualifications and work experience. This would be followed by a section identifying the applicant's interests and hobbies, a section specifying referees, and finally a section enabling the applicant to identify the qualities which make him or her suitable for the post.

(v) *Processing considerations*

Sometimes the information obtained needs to be collated for the preparation of statistical or survey reports. It may be that the organisation is seeking to identify trends and general patterns rather than use information obtained on an individual basis. If this is so it is vital that the information is presented in a way which is as easy as possible to process. If the information is to be processed electronically then the capacities of the data processing equipment will need to be considered. In such cases instructions may be of vital importance: the machine may be unable to pick up and 'read' anything other than black ink or print.

(vi) *Legal implications*

Many forms are the direct product of statutory provisions. Applications to renew business leases, to provide information for the Registrar of Companies, to register as an elector, to complete an income tax return, and to tax and insure a motor vehicle all involve the completion of forms that are required by statute. Often criminal penalties can be imposed if the information provided is known to be false. In the case of insurance proposals, the proposer (the applicant) is under a positive legal obligation to provide information materially relevant to the risk to be insured, even if this is not asked for on the form. An organisation insuring its premises against fire is likely to find the insurance company avoiding the policy if it discovers that the organisation is knowingly employing a convicted arsonist. It will be no defence for the organisation to say that the policy did not ask "Do you have in your employment any convicted arsonists? If so please give details."!

Specific types of forms

The variety of forms in common use is so vast that it is impossible to give anything other than a very general description of what they include. It may, however, help to identify the broad categories into which they fall. These categories relate to the purpose of the form and, clearly, the content of the form will usually reflect the purpose or objective the organisation has in using it. Thus the forms are used:

(i)   to keep records – financial, personnel, statistical, and so on;

(ii) for applications – for jobs, grants, hearings before an industrial tribunal;

(iii) for making orders or bookings – goods from a supplier, a package holiday, a credit transaction, internal requisitions;

(iv) to monitor processes and make assessments – stock records, the evaluation of product quality, work sheets, income tax returns;

(v)   for carrying out surveys (usually by means of questionnaires) – consumer reaction to a new product, the voting intentions of the public, the Census.

Oral Communication

Having examined in some detail the written methods used by organisations in the communication process, we must conclude by looking at the methods of oral communication that organisations use. These include:

- the use of the telephone;
- dictation;
- verbal presentation of reports;
- interviewing; and meetings.

It should be recalled that oral communication involves not only the skills of speaking but of listening as well. A communication system is ineffective if its staff are poor listeners; poor listening can result in letters having to be redrafted and/or retyped, orders being misdirected and meetings needing to be rearranged.

The larger and more complex an organisation becomes the more important it is for those operating the communications system to guard against it becoming too unwieldy. When oral messages are being transferred, the larger the number of employees involved in the chain of communication, the greater the danger of the message becoming distorted. The story is told of the message being sent along the trenches during the First World War which began its life as "3000 Germans advancing on the West flank. Send reinforcements" but ended up as "3000 Germans dancing on a wet plank. Send three and four pence"! Doubtless this is just a humorous observation, but it illustrates an important principle. Most of us have experienced how messages passed from one person to another are embroided and elaborated on. A good listener then is someone who:

(i) concentrates on the speaker's delivery without being distracted by external or internal factors (noise and day-dreaming, for example, or the speaker's mannerisms);

(ii) is not emotionally affected by the statements the speaker makes;

(iii) listens to everything that is being said, rather than concentrating on main points, or homing in only when the speaker sounds more interesting;

(iv) recognises that people are able to take in words much faster than they can be spoken, and develops a strategy for overcoming the spare time this disparity provides. Note taking is a useful device for doing so. Obviously, the nature of the subject matter is a significant factor. If the speaker is using complex language and sophisticated concepts the spare time for thoughts the listener may have is likely to be very limited.

Styles of oral communication

As a general proposition oral communications are either formal or informal. Informal speech is used largely in our social and domestic relationships. The language used is abbreviated for we know each other well, and lengthy explanations are not called for. Compare a chat you might have with a close friend with the casual conversation you might have with a stranger at a business function, and assess how much the language you use varies according to the recipient. Formal speech is appropriate to the work environment where the speaker represents the organisation and should, therefore, deliver his or her words with more care and precision, in a carefully structured way. Clearly, a telephone conversation with a business customer does not warrant a style or tone which is over familiar or excessively casual. A personal telephone call to a friend, however, is quite a different matter. The nature of oral communication is affected not only by the purpose of the statements being made, the formal/informal distinction, but also by the physical proximity of the parties. Face to face communication enables much closer awareness to develop through the uses of forms of non-verbal communication such as facial expressions and other forms of body language, whereas more distant communication, for example the use of the telephone, effectively eliminates the use of non-verbal signs and emphasises the importance of the language being used.

The significance of these elements of formality/informality, and physical distance lies in the different social rules which govern oral communications. For instance, in face to face communication we tend to respond in different ways to the people we are dealing with, according to our perceptions of what they expect of us. You might feel it quite out of order to crack a joke with your Head of Department, whereas you do this all the time with colleagues of the same grade as yourself. Status then is an important factor in the determination of what we say to others. If the Head of Department leads the conversation by telling a joke we may feel this is a suitable opening for a humorous anecdote that it would not otherwise have seemed appropriate to tell. Thus, it is not true to say that being physically close necessarily produces a less formal approach to oral communication, nor that it is impossible to communicate informally over a distance (for instance phoning a friend).

Methods of oral communication

The telephone

Within most organisations the telephone is a vital tool in the business of communicating. It is important not just as a link with customers and clients, but also as a means of communicating internally throughout the organisation if it is equipped with a PABX (Private Automated Branch Exchange) system. It is often necessary to think out what needs to be said before making a telephone call. If information to be imparted over the phone is complex it is especially important to make sure it has been understood and correctly recorded by the person at the receiving end. Asking for imparted information to be repeated may be useful in identifying any confusion that may arise. You should use the following guidelines when using the telephone:

- when making or receiving a call identify yourself and establish the identity of the person you are talking to at the outset;
- keep a pad and pen or pencil immediately to hand in order to avoid keeping the other person waiting;
- speak as clearly as possible; often telephone conversations are conducted in very noisy environments which makes it difficult to distinguish the voice on the telephone from other extraneous sounds;
- avoid keeping a caller waiting for long periods while searching out information : it is far better to arrange to call back;
- when the call is completed make a note of the details of the conversation and take appropriate action (pass the message on, or place the note in the relevant file).

Dictation

Dictation is used as a means of conveying a message orally which is to be transposed into writing – usually into a letter. If the dictation is face to face it provides the secretary taking down the message with an opportunity to clarify any problems straightaway. If, however a tape is made, the person dictating the message should ensure that it is delivered clearly, that punctuation is identified and that difficult words or expressions such as unusual surnames are spelt out.

Interviews

Probably the most important factor in conducting an interview is to be properly prepared. The interview room should be laid out so that the interviewer and the interviewee are close enough to be able to hear each other properly. The interviewer (or the panel) should have examined the application prior to the interview and have identified a systematic approach to the questioning of the applicant. Of course, not all interviews are concerned with appointing new staff; they may be disciplinary or involve dealing with a complaint from a customer. Whatever the case, the interviewer should have examined the background details carefully before the interview is conducted. The following points should be observed during an interview:

(i) the interviewee should be welcomed and the chairperson of the interview panel should introduce him or herself and other members;

(ii) the purpose of the interview should be explained and the interviewee encouraged to feel at ease;

(iii) the responses of the interviewee to questions should be carefully listened to. It is important not to disturb the interviewee's train of thought or to monopolise the conversation;

(iv) the questions themselves should be pertinent, and a note should be kept of the points that need to be remembered as the interview proceeds;

(v) the interview should be concluded when the interviewers have received the information they need.

The situation should be summarised. If it is possible to do so any decision which has been reached should be communicated immediately. Alternatively, it should be explained that a decision will be communicated at a later stage, and an indication given as to when this is likely to be. It is courteous to thank the interviewee for attending and, in the case of a job application for which a decision can be made after the interviews have been completed, it may be thought appropriate to provide the unsuccessful applicants with some brief words of reassurance. We will be considering the interview process in much more detail later in the book in Unit 4, *Human Resources*, when we look at issues of staff recruitment.

Activity

Monitor the use of oral communications with the people you come into contact with over the next week. See if you can identify and describe the different styles and approaches that you encounter. You might find it useful to expand this activity by telephoning a selection of different organisations in your area to find out how well they deal with queries. Try phoning a bank, a supermarket, a car dealership and the finance department of thhe local authority and a put standard question to each of them, for instance what are their opening hours throughout the week. How effectively do you feel they have handled your simple request?

Assignment *The Organisation*

Choose an organisation with which you are familiar. This could be an organisation you have worked in, or your local authority, or the school or college you are studying at.

Tasks

1. Collect any available information that describes the structure of your chosen organisation, and from this produce an organisation chart displaying either the line authority within the organisation or its committee structure. (You can find examples of these structures in Element 4.2.)

2. Investigate the operation of the communications system within your chosen organisation, to enable you to produce an information sheet for distribution to all the staff of the organisation, which describes:

    *   the method used by the organisation for receiving and storing data;
    *   the system of administration and clerical support it operates; and
    *   the method it uses for distributing information.

Development Tasks

3. Prepare some outline notes on the material you have produced under Task 2 that you could use to present a short talk. The talk would be given to other members of your group, and would:

    *   describe the communication system operated by your organisation; and
    *   introduce your ideas on how the system might be improved.

Element 2.3 Information Processing Systems

Computer-based Information Processing Systems

The word *system* may be defined as "a set of connected parts which together perform a particular function or achieve particular aims". Telephone systems, railway systems and the human nervous system provide familiar examples. Although a car is not generally referred to as such, it may be viewed as a personal transport system comprising, amongst other things, four wheels, a body, an engine and gearbox; the system will only operate successfully as a form of transport if all these components are present and connected in the right way. An essential additional element is the driver, without whom the car is simply a motionless piece of metal.

Similarly, a *computer system* comprises a number of connected parts or components that, together, allow the *electronic processing* of *data* to produce *information* which is meaningful to its users. It is helpful, at this point, to differentiate between the terms data and information. Generally, raw data, such as the number of hours a person has worked, is not useful in itself but requires processing to produce useful information; continuing with the example, processing will involve the multiplication of the 'hours worked' figure by an 'hourly rate of pay', before a 'gross pay' amount is obtained. Further processing of similar items of data is necessary to produce all the information needed for the payslip.

A computer system comprises both *hardware* and *software*, each being useless without the other. The term *hardware* describes the physical electronic and mechanical components, whilst the various sets of instructions or *programs* which control the hardware and permit it to perform a multitude of functions, including general control of the hardware and user tasks such as graphic design, word processing and payroll calculation, are collectively known as *software*.

Administrative systems in commercial and governmental organisations make extensive use of computer processing and can be described as *computer-based information processing systems*. This broader term assumes the inclusion of any associated clerical or operational procedures, as well as the staff who are involved in operating the system.

The following section examines some of the terms used to identify the various components that form a *computer system*.

Hardware

The hardware components of a computer system can be categorised by function as follows:

Input

To allow the computer to process data it must be in a form that the machine can handle. Before processing, data is normally in a 'human readable' form, for example, as it appears on an employee's time sheet or a customer's order form. Such alphabetic and numeric (decimal) data cannot be handled directly by the internal circuitry of the computer, so it has to be translated into the *binary* (a number system which uses only two symbols, 0 and 1) representations of the data to make it 'machine-sensible'. There is a wide variety of input devices that carry out this function but the keyboard and *mouse* are most commonly used. Data entering the system as input is transmitted directly to *main memory* or *RAM* (Random Access Memory).

Main memory or RAM

This component has two main functions:

- to temporarily store *programs* currently in use for processing data;
- to temporarily store *data*:
    - entered through an input device and awaiting processing;
    - currently being processed;
    - which results from processing and is waiting to be output.

Processor or central processing unit (CPU)

The processor is the 'brain' of the computer and amongst other things, monitors the operation of all the other components, ensures that they perform according to the requirements of the software currently in use and carries out any program instructions requiring the arithmetic or logical processing of data.

Output

Output devices perform the opposite function of input devices by translating machine-sensible data into a human-readable form, for example, onto a printer or the screen of a visual display unit (VDU). Sometimes, the results of computer processing may be needed for another stage of the same application or for a different application, in which case they are output to *backing store*. They can be retrieved from here as often as necessary. For further clarification of this kind of activity, refer to the example which follows the section on backing store.

Backing store

Backing store performs a *filing* (see later in the Unit,) function and the importance of its role can be established by reference to two features of a computer system, one relating to the main memory or RAM component and the other to an aspect of the system's operation. These features can be described as follows.

- *Memory Volatility*
  It is not practical to store data files and programs in main memory because of its
  volatility. This means that the contents of main memory can be destroyed, either by
  being overwritten as new data is entered for processing and new programs used, or when
  the machine is switched off.
- *Retrievable Data*
  Backing storage media (usually magnetic tape or disk) provide a more permanent store
  for *programs*, which may be used many times on different occasions, and *data files*,
  which are used for future reference or processing.

When the results of processing are output to a printer or VDU screen, the user is provided with visual information which is not normally retrievable by the computer unless it is also recorded on a backing storage medium. The following example illustrates some aspects of filing operations.

Example

In a payroll operation, data on hours worked by employees, together with other relevant data for the current pay period, needs to be processed against the payroll details held on the payroll *master file* (which we discuss later in this section) to produce the necessary payslips. The payroll master file is held on backing store and is placed 'on-line' (under the control of the computer system's processor) when needed for processing. Any such files can be stored indefinitely, but because magnetic disk and magnetic tape are re-usable, obsolete files can be erased to allow the recording of new or updated information.

Peripherals

Those hardware devices which are external to the CPU and main memory, namely those used for input, output and backing storage are called *peripherals*. The following diagram illustrates how data passes between the various hardware elements during the processing cycle. It illustrates what is often referred to as the *logical structure* of the computer system.

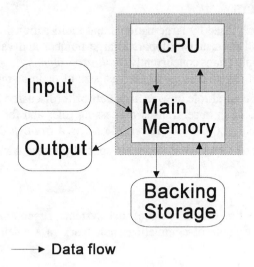

Data flow

Computer Systems Classified

Computer systems can be broadly classified according to their:

- purpose;
- size and complexity.

Purpose

There are two categories under this heading:

- *General-purpose Computers*
  As the term suggests, general-purpose machines can carry out processing tasks for a wide variety of applications and because most organisations will make use of them, the reader may assume that any reference to the term *computer* refers to this type, unless otherwise indicated.

- *Dedicated or Special-Purpose Computers*
  In their logical structure, these machines are fundamentally the same as the general-purpose type except that they have been programmed for a single, specific application. Dedicated word processors provide one example, although these relatively expensive machines have been made virtually obsolete by the development of sophisticated word processing packages for implementation on general-purpose systems. The dedicated computer 'on a chip' or *microprocessor* is used for a huge variety of specialist functions including, for example, the control of washing machines, traffic lights and car fuelling systems.

Size and complexity

It should be emphasised that the following categories are broad guidelines only and that changes in technology are continually blurring the differences between them. For example, there are now powerful microcomputer systems (often referred to as super-micros) which far exceed the power and flexibility of earlier generation minicomputer systems. However, the generally accepted categories are as follows.

Mainframe computers

Such computers are commonly used by large national and multi-national organisations such as banks, airlines and oil companies. They usually support a large number and variety of peripherals and can process a number of large applications concurrently (*multiprogramming*). The mainframe's power stems from the very high speeds of the processor and the vast size of main memory.

Mainframes may also play a central role in *wide area networks* (discussed later in the unit). Their huge capital cost invariably places them in centralised processing roles and for the same reason, about fifty per cent of the mainframes currently in use are rented or leased from specialist companies.

Mainframe computers are generally accommodated in special-purpose, air-conditioned rooms to ensure trouble free operation.

Supercomputers

With processing speeds many times those of mainframe systems, supercomputers are used for scientific and statistical work, being capable of completing such work in a small fraction of the time that a mainframe would require.

Minicomputers

Minicomputers are scaled-down versions of mainframe systems. Costing less and being robust enough to operate without a special environment, they can be used in *real-time* (see later in the unit) applications such as the control of manufacturing processes in an engineering factory. They are also used by medium-sized organisations for all their processing needs or by larger organisations as part of a networked system of computers. The minicomputer is technically very similar to the mainframe, except that it usually only has magnetic disk storage and the main input/output peripherals tend to be visual display units (VDUs).

Minicomputers can also support a number of applications, apparently at the same time, and are often used in *time-sharing* systems where many applications such as word processing, invoicing and customer enquiry can be carried out by way of terminals located in the various departments of an organisation.

Microcomputers

The microcomputer is the smallest in the range and was first developed when the Intel Corporation succeeded in incorporating the main functional parts of a computer on a single *chip* using *integrated circuits* (IC) on silicon. Subsequently, the techniques referred to as *large scale integration* (LSI) and *very large scale integration* (VLSI) have continued to pack more and more circuitry onto a single chip, thus further increasing the power and storage capacity of microcomputers and computers generally.

Originally, microcomputers were only capable of supporting a single user and a single application at any one time. The vast increases in processor speed and memory capacity now permit their use for *multi-tasking*. This means that with appropriate software such as Microsoft Windows, a user can, for example, word process a document while a complex spreadsheet calculation is being executed in the *background*. Such concurrent running of tasks also facilitates the exchange of data between tasks, for example, the transfer of a diagram from a design package into a document on screen.

Multi-user operation is made possible through networking and it is now common practice to link microcomputers into a *local area network* (LAN), to allow resource sharing (disk, printer, programs and data files), as well as electronic communication between users (this known as *electronic mail* and is discussed in element 2.2, Communication Systems). Microcomputers can now support applications previously restricted to mini and mainframe systems, including, for example, *computer-aided design* (CAD) and *database* work (discussed later in the unit).

The range of microcomputer software is now extremely wide and the quality generally very high. There are *software packages*, which can be bought ready to install for most business applications. One recent area of growth has been in the development of graphic-based applications and most popular applications software can now be operated through a *graphical user interface* or GUI (discussed later in the unit) and a *mouse*.

The low cost of microcomputers and the increase in the range of software available, makes their use feasible in almost any size and type of organisation. In the small firm, a microcomputer may be used for word processing, stock control, costing and general accounting. In the larger organisation they may be used as *intelligent terminals*; such systems provide the user with the processing facilities of the mainframe or minicomputer to which they are attached, and at the same time, the independent processing power provided by the microcomputer's own processor, main memory and backing storage.

Activity

Much of the staff training programme at Pilcon Electrics plc relates to computing and information technology. You are employed as an assistant to the Information Technology (IT) Training Manager. The IT training programme includes a seminar on recent developments in computer technology. This activity requires the gathering of relevant information and its organisation into a suitable form, for use in the seminar. Using the information in this text as a guide, consult a variety of sources, including magazines and newspapers. You should find the following headings useful for classifying the information.

- *Major manufacturers of mainframe and minicomputer systems;*
- *Major manufacturers in the microcomputer field;*
- *Major features of several computer systems supplied by identified manufacturers;*
- *Major users of mainframe and minicomputer systems (for example, airlines and insurance companies) and summary of applications for which they are used;*

The main aim of the seminar is to help staff to understand the major technological divisions, which can be used to categorise computer systems. This may be achieved by reference to the main features of each category and the use of illustrative examples. You can choose to present the information in whatever way you feel is appropriate. You may, for example, prepare the information for presentation on an overhead projector. Alternatively, it may be better to provide the information as a handout, for use in discussion groups. Diagrams and illustrations from advertisements or magazine articles will be helpful.

Information Processing Equipment and Methods

Input and output devices

This section is concerned with equipment designed for input, output or both. The most common methods of input involve the use of *display* devices such as the Visual Display Unit (VDU) and the first part of this section deals with such equipment. Printers are the next devices to be considered in that they provide 'hard copy' output of the results of computer processing, sometimes at incredible speeds. The next part examines equipment which automates input and removes the need for keyboard data entry. Equipment in this category includes, for example, OCR (Optical Character Recognition) devices and Bar Code Readers. Finally, an examination is made of some special-purpose output devices involving output onto microfilm and speech synthesis.

Display devices

Visual Display Unit

The most commonly used device for communicating with a computer is the Visual Display Unit (VDU). Input of text is through a full alphanumeric keyboard and output is displayed on a viewing screen similar to a television. The term VDU terminal is normally used to describe the screen and keyboard as a combined facility for input and output. On its own, the screen is called a *monitor*. So that an operator can see what is being typed in through the keyboard, input is also displayed on the screen. A square of light called a *cursor* indicates where the next character to be typed by the operator will be placed.

- *Text and Graphics* - Most display screens provide both a text and graphics facility. Text consists of letters (upper and lower case), numbers and special characters such as punctuation marks. Most applications require textual input and output. Graphics output includes picture images, such as maps, charts and drawings.

- *Screen Resolution* - A screen's resolution dictates the clarity or sharpness of the displayed text or graphics characters. The achievement of high quality graphics generally requires a higher resolution or sharper image than is required for textual display. Images are formed on the screen through the use of *pixels* (picture elements). A pixel is a tiny dot of light on the screen and the resolution is determined by the number of pixels on the screen. The greater the density of pixels, the better is the resolution.

- *Dot Matrix Characters* - Textual characters are usually formed using a matrix of pixels as is shown in the following example, and as with screen resolution, the clarity of individual characters is determined by the number of pixels used. Selected dots within the matrix are illuminated to display particular characters.

A Dot Matrix Letter P

Colour or monochrome display

Many applications make use of colour, not only in graphic design where it is essential, but also to improve the *user interface*. Thus, for example, a word processing package may use two or three different colours to separately highlight the text entry, menu and status bar areas. Packages which make use of colour can be used on either monochrome (black and white, amber and black or green and black) or colour screens, because not every prospective purchaser will have a colour monitor.

Dumb and intelligent terminals

A *dumb* terminal is one that has no processing power of its own, possibly no storage, and is entirely dependent on a controlling computer. Where a terminal is connected by way of a telecommunications link, each character is transmitted to the central computer as soon as it is entered by the operator. This makes editing extremely difficult and slow and for this reason, they are not generally used for remote (the terminal is geographically distant from the computer and connected to it by telecommunications link) data entry.

An *intelligent* terminal has some memory and processing power and as such, allows the operator to store, edit and manipulate data without the support of the computer to which it is connected. The processing facility is provided by an internal processor, usually a microprocessor. Storage is normally in the form of 'buffer' memory in which several lines of text can be held and manipulated before transmission. The facility may also include local backing storage on floppy disk and a printer. Microcomputer systems are often used as intelligent terminals.

Keyboards

In specialist applications, the standard keyboard is not always the most convenient method of input and a *concept* keyboard may be used. In a factory, for example, a limited number of functions may be necessary for the operations of a computerised lathe. These functions can be set out on a touch-sensitive pad and clearly marked. This is possible because all inputs are anticipated and the range is small. The operator is saved the trouble of typing in the individual characters which form instructions. Concept keyboards also have applications in education, particularly for the mentally and physically handicapped. Instead of specific functions, interchangeable overlays, which indicate the function of each area of the keyboard allow the teacher to design the keyboard to particular specifications.

Alternatives to keyboards

Two methods of input make use of the screen display itself.

Touch screen

Touch screen devices allow a screen to be activated by the user touching the screen with a finger. This is particularly useful where a menu of processing options is available on the screen for selection.

Light pen

A light pen is shaped like a pen and contains a photo-electric or light sensitive cell in its tip. When the pen is pointed at the screen the light from the screen is detected by the cell and the computer can identify the position of the pen. By 'mapping' the screen to allocate particular functions to particular locations on the screen, the position of the pen indicates a particular function. The light pen enables specific parts of a picture on display to be selected or altered in some way, making it particularly useful for applications such as computer aided design (CAD).

Devices to control cursor movement include the *joystick*, the *mouse* and the *crosshair* cursor.

Joystick

The joystick is similar to a car's gear lever, except that fine variations in the angle of movement can be achieved. The cursor movement is a reflection of the movement of the joystick in terms of direction and speed and it is commonly used for computer games and for CAD.

Mouse

The mouse is a hand held device that allows the user to move the cursor by moving the mouse across a flat surface. It is very popular with 'user friendly' software designed for a WIMP user environment (which we discuss later in this unit). Two or three select buttons are fitted on the mouse to enable the user to choose a particular screen position or to execute particular functions.

Crosshair cursor

The crosshair cursor has a perspex 'window' with 'cross hairs' rather like a telescopic rifle's sighting mechanism. It can be moved over hardcopy images of maps, or survey photographs and allows precise selection of positions through the crosshair 'window'. The images are digitised into the computer's memory and can then be displayed on the screen for modification. The keyboard or a keypad built into the device can be used to enter additional information, for example to identify rivers or roads on a digitised map.

Printers

Printers can be categorised according to their speed of operation and the quality of print. They are also identifiable as *impact* or *non-impact* and as *character*, *line* or *page* printers.

Impact printers

Impact printing uses a print head to strike an inked ribbon which is located between the print head and the paper. Individual characters can be printed by either a dot matrix mechanism or by print heads which contain each character as a separate font. The solid font types, such as the *daisy wheel* have been made virtually obsolete by the dot-matrix type, so are not dealt with in this text.

Impact dot matrix printers

These are *character* printers, forming each character as printing proceeds from a matrix of dots produced by columns of pins in the print head. The number of pins in the matrix is one factor determining printing quality. An 18 pin head offers reasonable quality (Near Letter Quality or NLQ) at high speed and the 24 pin (arranged in two columns of 12) provides both high print quality and high speed.

Line printers

A line printer prints a complete line of characters, rather than in the serial fashion used by character printers. Two types of line printer are described here, the *barrel* or *drum* printer and the *chain* printer.

- *Barrel Printer*

  This type has a band with a complete set of characters at each print position. Each print position has a hammer to impact the print ribbon against the paper. There are usually 132 print positions on the barrel. One complete revolution of the barrel exposes all the characters to each print position. Therefore a complete line can be printed in one revolution. The barrel revolves continuously during printing, the paper being fed through and the process repeated for each line of print. Typical printing speeds are 100 to 400 lines per minute. The mechanism is illustrated below.

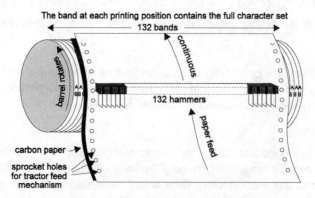

Barrel Printer Mechanism

- *Chain Printer*
  Several complete sets of characters are held on a continuous chain that moves
  horizontally across the paper. The ribbon is situated between the chain and the paper and
  an individual hammer is located at each of the 132 print positions. A complete line can
  be printed as one complete set of characters passes across the paper. Thus, in one pass as
  many lines can be printed as there are sets of characters in the chain. Printing speeds are
  higher than is possible for barrel printers. The chain printer mechanism is illustrated in
  the following diagram.

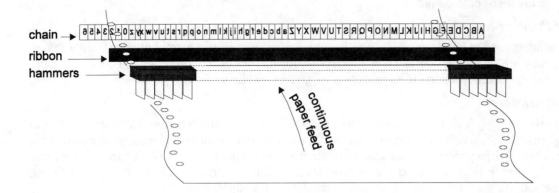

Exploded view of chain printer mechanism

Line printers are expensive compared with character printers but may well be necessary where large
volume output is required. Printing speeds of up to 3000 lines per minute are achieved with impact line
printers. Even higher speeds are possible with non-impact printers.

Non-impact printers

Most non-impact printers use dot matrix heads. They do not require mechanical hammers and print
heads do not strike the paper. A variety of printers is available using a wide range of technologies. The
most popular are as follow.

Thermal printers

Characters are burned onto heat-sensitive thermographic paper. The paper is white and develops colour
when heated above a particular temperature. The heat is generated by rods in the dot matrix print head.
By selective heating of rods, individual characters can be formed from the matrix. Printing can be carried
out serially, one character at a time or, through the use of several heads, on a line printer basis. Serial
thermal printing is slow but speeds in excess of 1000 lines per minute are possible with line thermal
printing.

Electrosensitive printers

This type produces characters in a similar fashion to the thermal printer except that the paper used has
a thin coating of aluminium which covers a layer of black, blue or red dye. Low voltage electrical
discharges in the matrix rods produce sparks which selectively remove the aluminium coating to reveal

the layer of dye underneath. Operated as line printers with heads at each print position, printing speeds in excess of 3000 lines per minute are achieved.

Laser printers

They use a combination of two technologies, electro-photographic printing used in photo-copying and high intensity lasers. A photo conductive drum is initially charged and then a high intensity laser beam selectively discharges areas on the drum. As with photocopiers, toner material is spread over the surface to form an ink image. This is then transferred to the paper and made permanent through heating. Effectively, complete pages are printed at one time so they come under the heading of *page* printers. Because of its cost the laser printer was until recently only found in very large systems requiring exceptionally high speed output.

Laser Printers and Microcomputers

Laser printers used to be too costly for use in a microcomputer environment, but with rapidly falling prices, they are providing considerable competition for the dot matrix printers. Although still more costly than dot matrix printers, laser printers offer greater speed and quality.

Ink jet printers

Ink jet printers spray high-speed streams of electrically charged ink droplets from individual nozzles in the matrix head onto the paper to form characters. Many will hold colour cartridges to produce excellent colour output. Ink jet printers provide a possible alternative to the laser printer. The ink jet printer cannot match the laser printer for speed but it provides a possible alternative for users whose printing requirements are not satisfied by any printer in the dot matrix impact range.

Summary of printers

Generally speaking, the smaller, low speed, character printers are of use with microcomputer systems, but their increasing popularity has produced increased sophistication in small printers. Features which have improved printing speeds include *bi-directional* printing (in two directions) and *logic-seeking* which allows the printer to cut short a traverse across the paper if only a few characters are required on a line. The most popular printers for microcomputers are, impact dot matrix, electrosensitive, ink jet and laser.

Other data capture devices

Source data is normally collected in human-readable form. For example, customer orders are recorded on order forms and weekly pay details may be recorded on time sheets. Prior to processing, such data has to be translated into machine-sensible form and this usually involves a keying operation. There are a number of devices available which allow data to be collected in a printed or handwritten form directly readable by a computer input device.

Optical character readers (OCR)

OCRs are designed to read stylised characters which are also readable by humans. There are a number of designs for such characters but any individual design is known as the character *font*. There are a number of industry standard fonts. The OCR reflects light off the characters and converts them into digital patterns for comparison with the stored character set. Originally, a highly stylised appearance was preferred to aid machine recognition but some OCRs can read the character sets of popular makes of office typewriter. Ideally, OCRs should be able to read any characters but the wider the range of styles that need to be read, the more difficult becomes the recognition process. In some applications, a restricted character set of, perhaps numerals and certain alphabetic characters may suffice and the reading process becomes quicker and more accurate. Nevertheless, large OCRs are capable of reading several character sets comprising more than 300 characters.

The reading of hand printed characters presents particular problems because of the almost infinite variation of printing styles. Recognition is possible provided that the person preparing the data has a visual guide of the preferred style. The character set will usually be limited to numerals and a few alphabetic characters. Artificial intelligence techniques are being applied to OCRs to allow the 'learning' of new character sets. A microcomputer with a *scanner* attached can be used to capture text from printed documents; character recognition software then converts the text image to a form which can then be edited with a word processor.

Applications of OCR

OCR is often used to capture sales data at the point-of-sale (POS). A POS terminal is essentially an electronic cash register linked to a computer or with storage of its own. Data captured at the terminal can, for example, be sent to update computer files. Sometimes POS registers have direct-access memory to hold product prices and descriptions, so that the details can be printed on the customer receipt. An OCR-character coded, price label, attached to each product, can be scanned with a wand (light pen) or laser 'gun'.

Optical mark readers (OMR)

An OMR is designed to read marks placed in pre-set positions on a document. The document is pre-printed and the values which can be entered are limited as each value is represented by, for example, a box in a certain position. Thus, a suitable application for OMR is a multi-choice exam paper, where the answer to each question has to be indicated by a pencil mark in one of several boxes after the question. The figure below illustrates such a form. The OMR scans the document for boxes containing pencil marks and thus identifies the values selected. Optical mark readers can read up to 10,000 A4 documents per hour.

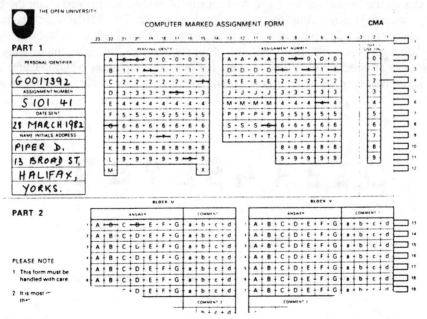

Bar code readers

Bar code is also an optical code which is normally read by a light pen or laser scanner. The code makes use of a series of black bars of varying thickness. The gaps between each bar also vary. These bars and gaps are used to represent numeric data. The values represented are often printed underneath in decimal form.

Bar codes are commonly used to store a variety of data such as price and stock code concerning products in shops and supermarkets. A sticker with the relevant bar code (itself produced by computer) is attached to each product. Sometimes, the check-out will have a built-in scanner station over which the goods pass. By using the data from the code, the cash register can identify the item, look up its latest price and print the information on the customer's receipt.

Another useful application is for the recording of library issues. A bar code sticker is placed inside the book cover and at the time of issue or return it can be scanned and the library stock record updated. By providing each library user with a bar coded library card, the information regarding an individual who is borrowing a book can be linked with the book's details at the time of borrowing.

Magnetic ink character reader (MICR)

This particular device is employed almost exclusively by the banking industry, where it is used for sorting and processing cheques in large volumes. The millions of cheques which pass through the London Clearing System could not possibly be sorted and processed without the use of MICRs.

Highly stylised characters, usually of the E13B font illustrated below, are printed along the bottom of the cheques by a special printer, using ink containing iron oxide. The MICR first magnetises the characters as the cheque passes through and then decodes them by induced voltage signals. A high degree of reliability and accuracy is possible, partly because of the stylised font, but more importantly, because the characters are not affected by dirty marks. This is obviously important when cheques may pass through several hands before reaching their destination. Such marks may cause problems for an optical character reader.

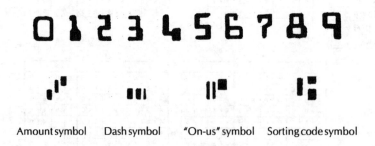

Amount symbol   Dash symbol   "On-us" symbol   Sorting code symbol

Digitisers

Examples of digitisers in use are provided by the light pen, the mouse and the joystick, described earlier. A particularly useful device for collecting pictorial data is the *graphics tablet*. A pen-like stylus enables the user to 'draw' on the tablet and reflect the results on the computer screen or store the results for future manipulation. The tablet is addressable by the computer through a matrix of thousands of tiny 'dots', each of which reflect a binary 1 or 0. When a line is drawn on the tablet, the stylus passes over these dot locations, causing the binary values in memory to change. Thus a particular drawing has a particular binary format which can be stored, manipulated or displayed. Digitisers are used in other applications, for example, in the capturing of photographic images, via a 'digitising' camera and the subsequent production of a digitised image.

Voice recognition devices

Human speech varies in accent, personal style of speech and pitch and the interpretation of the spoken word makes the development of voice recognition devices a difficult process. In normal conversation, humans make assumptions about the listener, often cutting sentences short or emphasising a point with a facial expression. Voice recognition devices to deal with complete human language are unlikely to be developed for some time to come. There are however, devices which can be 'trained' to recognise a limited number of words spoken by the individual doing the training. Devices can be used to give commands for machinery control, for example, 'up', 'down', 'left', 'right', 'fast', 'slow' etc. Paralysed persons can control a wheelchair or lighting and heating through a voice recognition device controlled by a microprocessor.

Special-purpose output devices

Computer output microform (COM) recorders

COM recorders record information from computer storage onto microfilm or microfiche. Microfilm is a continuous reel, whereas, microfiche is a sheet of film with a matrix of squares or pages. Either form can be viewed with a magnifying viewer. COM can result in large savings in paper costs, storage space and handling. For example, a 4 inch × 6 inch microfiche sheet can store the equivalent of 270 printed pages. COM is particularly useful for the storage of large amounts of information which do not need to be updated frequently.

Graph plotters

A plotter is a device designed to produce charts, drawings, maps and other forms of graphical information on paper.

Voice output devices

Voice synthesis is still in its infancy, in that the complexities of human speech have yet to be mastered satisfactorily. There is a tendency for such devices to become confused between the pronunciation of words such as 'though' and 'plough'. Speech ROM 'chips' are available for many microcomputer systems. Educational applications include 'speak and spell' and arithmetic. Large scale application is possible where the range of output can be anticipated, for example, stocks and share prices, railway timetables, speaking clock etc. Such services may be provided via an answer phone service.

Filing and file storage devices

This section deals with the ways in which information is stored, organised and processed by computer.

Files, records and fields

In data processing, it is necessary to store information on particular subjects, for example, customers, suppliers or personnel and such information needs to be structured so that it is readily controllable and accessible to the user.

In traditional data processing systems, each of these 'topics' of information is allocated a *file*.

The following figure illustrates the structure of a typical Personnel File.

Works Number	Surname	Initial	Department	Grade	D.O.B.	Salary
357638	Watkins	P.	Sales	3	100755	10500
367462	Groves	L.	Marketing	4	170748	16800
388864	Harrison	F.	Sales	2	121066	9500
344772	Williams	J.L.	Production	4	010847	18000

A file consists of a collection of related *records*. The Personnel file which is shown above has a record for each employee. For example, the row containing information on P. Watkins is one individual record. The complete file would be made up of a number of such records, each one relating to a different employee. Each record contains specific items of information relating to each employee and each item occupies a *field*. In the preceding example, there are seven such fields, *Works Number, Surname, Initial, Department, Grade, DOB*, and *Salary*, each field containing values for a given category of information, Thus, the field value of record 388864 for *Department* is 'Sales'.

Types of file

Files can be categorised by the ways in which they are used and there are four generally recognised categories.

Master files

These are used for the storage of *permanent* data which is used in applications such as stock, sales and payroll. Some of the fields tend to contain data which is fairly static, for example, customer name and address, whilst data in some fields is continually changing, for example, customer balance, as *transactions* are applied to the file. Such *updating* is carried out, either through the direct entry (on-line) of individual transactions, or from an accumulated set of entries stored on a *transaction file*.

Transaction files

These are temporary and only exist to allow the updating of master files. Each transaction record contains the *key field value* of the master record it is to update (to allow correct matching with its relevant master record), together with data gathered from *source documents*, for example, invoice amounts which update the balance-owing field in customer accounts.

Reference files

As the name suggests, they are used for reference or look-up purposes and common examples are price catalogues and customer name and address files.

Archive or historical files

These contain data which, for legal or organisational reasons, must be kept and tend to be used on an occasional basis only.

The identification of records – primary and secondary keys

In most organisations, when an information system is operational it will be necessary to identify each record uniquely. In the Personnel File example provided earlier, it might be thought that it is possible to identify each individual record simply by the employee's Surname. This would be satisfactory as long as no two employees had the same surname. In reality most organisations will of course have several employees with the same surnames, so to ensure uniqueness, each employee is assigned a unique number, for example, a Works Number. The Works Number field is then used as the *primary key* in the filing system, each individual having his or her unique Works Number and so a unique primary key. Uniqueness is not always necessary. For example, if it is required to retrieve records which satisfy a criterion, or several criteria, *secondary keys* may be used. Thus, for example, in an information retrieval system on Personnel, the secondary key *Department* may be used to retrieve the records of all employees who work in, say, the Sales Department.

File storage media

File storage media may be classified according to the kind of access to records they provide:

- serial access;
- direct access.

Serial access media

Serial access means that in order to identify and retrieve a particular record it is necessary to 'read' all the records which precede it in the relevant file. Magnetic tape is a serial access medium because there are no readily identifiable physical areas on the medium which can be *addressed* . In other words, it is not possible to give a name or code and refer this to a particular location. It is said to be *non-addressable* and to look for an individual record stored on such a medium requires the software to examine each record's *key field* in sequence from the beginning of the file until the required record is found.

Direct access media

Storage media such as floppy or hard disks allow *direct access* to individual records, without reference to the rest of the relevant file. They have physical divisions which can be identified by computer software (and sometimes hardware) and are *addressable*, so that particular locations can be referred to by a name or code to retrieve a record which is stored at that location. Retrieval of an individual record stored on such a medium is possible (depending on the way the file is organised) by specifying the relevant *primary key field value*, thus providing the software with a means of finding and retrieving the specific individual record directly.

File organisation methods

Another function of the *primary key* is to provide a value which can be used by computer software to assign a record to a particular position within a file. The file organisation method chosen will dictate how individual records are assigned to particular *logical* positions within a file. The physical nature of magnetic tape means that the only sensible way of organising records is in a particular order, according to a primary key, whereas the addressing facilities provided by magnetic disk permit the organisation of files in a variety of ways. There are three commonly-used methods:

- sequential;
- indexed sequential;
- random.

Sequential

This method is the same as that used on magnetic tape and because the addressing facilities of magnetic disk are not used, records must be stored in sequence according to the primary key and be accessed in the same order.

Indexed sequential

Records are again stored in sequence using the primary key and an index is produced when the file is created. If *direct access* to individual records is required, the index is used; otherwise, the file may be processed in the same way as a purely sequential file. This method is ideal where an application sometimes requires sequential access to records and direct access at other times.

Random

This is a method which is impractical in any non-computerised situation, but is commonly used for computer file storage where direct access to records is the primary requirement. The procedure for placing a specific record in a particular position on disk uses a mathematical formula called a *hashing algorithm*, which generates a disk *address* from the record's primary key. The same algorithm is used subsequently whenever a record needs to be retrieved. Random files can be accessed sequentially, but with less efficiency than sequentially organised files.

File storage media and file organisation methods

Serial access media are limited in the file organisation methods they permit because they are *non-addressable*. Direct access media are more versatile in that they allow a variety of file organisation methods in addition to those allowed by serial access media.

Choice of storage medium and file organisation method

Choice should be based on the type and purpose of the system to be used. For example, an on-line enquiry system or stock control system needing frequent, rapid, direct access to individual records within large files can only be implemented using a direct access medium and a file organisation method which permits such access. Very large *archive* files are probably best held off-line on magnetic tape as the medium's lack of an addressing facility would necessitate such files being maintained *sequentially*. It may be reasonable to hold sections of such archival information, those which are most in demand, as sequential indexed files on magnetic disk. An illustration of this is provided by the Police National Computer system, which holds more recent information on magnetic disk, with older files held on magnetic tape. Systems which do not require direct access, for example, monthly payroll files, can be efficiently stored and processed on magnetic tape and even if the computer system only has disk storage, which is the case with all microcomputer and most minicomputer systems, sequential organisation is likely to be the chosen method. Applications which require both sequential and direct access are generally best served by indexed sequential files.

Activity

Much of the staff training programme at Pilcon Electrics relates to computing and information technology related issues. You are employed as an assistant to the Information Technology (IT) Training Manager. The IT training programme includes a seminar on recent developments in input and output devices. This activity is concerned with the gathering of relevant information and its organisation into a suitable form, for use in the seminar. Using the information in this text as a guide, consult a variety of sources, including magazines and newspapers.

Present the information in table form, identifying the function of each input and output device, its features and the applications for which it is particularly suitable. You can use cuttings from magazines to illustrate your document.

Computer Software

Software is the generic term which is used to describe the complete range of computer programs which will convert a general-purpose digital computer system into one capable of performing a multitude of specific functions. The term "software" implies its flexible, changeable nature, in contrast to the more permanent characteristics of the hardware or equipment which it controls.

The particular type, or types, of software controlling the computer system at any particular moment will determine the manner in which the system functions. For example, a certain type of software might cause the computer to behave like a word processor; another might turn it into an accounting machine; another may allow it to perform a stock control function. In other words, the behaviour of the computer is entirely determined by the item of software currently controlling it.

Computer programs

The terms software and program tend to be used synonymously, so what precisely is meant by the term computer program? At the level at which the computer operates, a program is simply a sequence of numeric codes. Each of these codes can be directly converted by the hardware into some simple operation. Built into the central processing unit (CPU – the heart of the computer) is a set of these simple operations, combinations of which are capable of directing the computer to perform complex tasks. Computer programs, in this fundamental form, are termed machine code, that is code which is directly "understandable" by the machine.

The numeric codes of the program are stored electronically in the main memory of the computer. Because this memory is volatile (its contents can be changed), it is possible to exchange the program currently held in the memory for another when the computer is required to perform a different function. For this reason the term stored program is often used to describe this fundamental characteristic of the modern digital computer.

Programming languages

When it is considered that a typical program might contain tens of thousands of machine code instructions it might seem that programming is a formidable task, well beyond the capabilities of all but the most determined and meticulous of computer professionals. Indeed, if machine code were the only computer language in use, it is extremely unlikely that society would today be experiencing such a widespread presence of computers in almost every aspect of industrial, commercial, domestic and social life.

Fortunately for the computer industry, programming techniques have evolved along with advances in hardware. There is now a proliferation of programming languages designed to allow the programmer to concentrate most of his attention on solving the problem, rather than on the tedious task of converting the solution to machine code form. Such computer languages are termed high-level languages. High-level languages provide a method of specifying complex processing tasks in a form relatively easy to use and understand by programmers, but not immediately "understandable" by a computer; the computer itself, using another program called a language processor or translator, performs the task of converting the high-level instructions into a usable form.

Examples of commonly used computer languages are COBOL, Pascal, BASIC and C.

Categories of software

The tree diagram in the figure below illustrates the different categories of software and, to some extent, their relationships to each other. This section begins by examining the distinction between systems software and applications software.

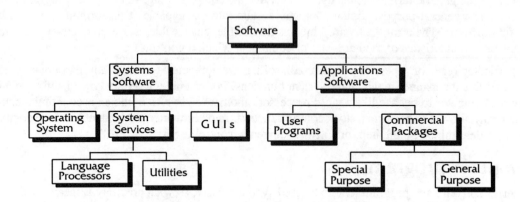

The term *systems software* covers the collection of programs usually supplied by the manufacturer of the computer. These programs protect the user from the enormous complexity of the computer system, and enable the computer to be used to maximum effect by a wide variety of people, many of whom will know very little about the inner workings of computers. Without systems software a modern digital computer would be virtually impossible to use; as computer hardware has evolved, so systems software has been forced to become more and more complex in order to make effective use of it.

Broadly speaking, systems software consists of three elements:

- those programs concerned with the internal control and co-ordination of all aspects of the computer system, namely the Operating System;
- a number of other programs providing various services to users. These services include translators for any languages supported by the system and utility programs such as program editors and other aids to programming;
- graphical user interfaces (GUIs) providing intuitive, easily learned methods for using microcomputer systems.

Applications software refers to programs which have some direct value to the organisation, and will normally include those programs for which the computer system was specifically purchased. For example, a mail order company might acquire a computer system initially for stock control and accounting purposes, when its volume of business begins to make these functions too difficult to cope with by manual means.

Applications programs would be required to record and process customers' orders, update the stock file according to goods sent or received, make appropriate entries in the various accounts ledgers, etc.

Commercially produced applications software falls into two main categories:

- special-purpose packages, such as a company payroll program used to store employee details and generate details of pay for each individual employee.
- general-purpose packages which may be used for a wide variety of purposes. An example of a general-purpose package is a word processor, a program which allows the

computer to be used somewhat like an electronic typewriter and is therefore appropriate to numerous processing tasks.

User programs are those written by people within the organisation for specific needs which cannot be satisfied by other sources of software. These program writers may be professional programmers employed by the organisation, or other casual users with programming expertise.

Systems software

First generation computers are normally defined in hardware terms, in that they were constructed using valve technology, but another important characteristic of this generation of computers was the equally primitive software support provided for programmers and other users. Modern computers perform automatically many of the tasks that programmers in those days had to handle themselves; writing routines to control peripheral devices, allocating programs to main store, executing programs, checking peripheral devices for availability, as well as many other routine tasks.

In subsequent generations of computers, manufacturers started addressing themselves to the problem of improving the programming environment by providing standard programs for many routine tasks. Many of these routines became linked together under the control of a single program called the executive, supervisor, or monitor, whose function was to supervise the running of user programs and, in general, to control and co-ordinate the functioning of the whole computer system, both hardware and software. Early programs of this type have evolved into the sophisticated programs collectively known as Operating Systems.

Systems software has four important functions:

- to facilitate the running of user programs;
- to optimise the performance of the computer system;
- to provide assistance with program development.
- to simplify the use of the computer system for users other than computer specialists;

The operating system takes care of the first two requirements, system services provide assistance with program development and graphical user interfaces(GUIs) simplify the use of the computer system.

Operating systems

If a computer system is viewed as a set of resources, comprising elements of both hardware and software, then it is the job of the collection of programs known as the operating system to manage these resources as efficiently as possible. In so doing , the operating system acts as a buffer between the user and the complexities of the computer itself. One way of regarding the operating system is to think of it as a program which allows the user to deal with a simplified computer, but without losing any of the computational power of the machine. In this way the computer system becomes a virtual system, its enormous complexity hidden and controlled by the operating system and through which the user communicates with the real system.

The main functions of operating systems

Earlier it was stated that the function of an operating system is to manage the resources of the computer system. These resources generally fall into the following categories:

Central Processing Unit (CPU)

Since only one program can be executed at any one time, if the computer system is such that several users are allowed access to the system simultaneously, in other words a multi-user system, then access to the CPU must be carefully controlled and monitored. In a time-sharing multi-user system each user is given a small time-slice of processor time before passing on to the next user in a continuously repeating sequence. Another common scheme is to assign priorities to users so that the system is able to determine which user should have control of the CPU next.

Memory

Programs (or parts of programs) must be loaded into the memory before they can be executed, and moved out of the memory when no longer required there. Storage space must be provided for data generated by programs, and provision must be made for the temporary storage of data, caused by data transfer operations involving devices such as printers and disk drives.

Input/Output (I/O) Devices

Programs will request the use of these devices during the course of their execution and in a multi-user system conflicts are bound to arise, when a device being utilised by one program is requested by another. The operating system will control allocation of I/O devices and attempt to resolve any conflicts which arise. It will also monitor the state of each I/O device and signal any faults detected.

Backing Store

Programs and data files will usually be held on mass storage devices such as magnetic disk and tape drives. The operating system will supervise data transfers to and from these devices and memory and deal with requests from programs for space on them.

Files

These may be regarded as a limited resource in the sense that several users may wish to share the same data file at the same time in multi-user systems. The operating system facilitates access to files and ensures restricted access to one program at any one time for those files which are to be written to. Resource allocation is closely linked to one part of the operating system called the *scheduler*. The term scheduling refers to the question of when, in a multi-user system, should a new process be introduced into the system and in which order the processes should be run.

The above is by no means an exhaustive list of the functions of an operating system. Other functions include:

- interpretation of the command language by which operators can communicate with it;
- error handling. For example, detecting and reporting inoperative or malfunctioning peripherals;
- protection of data files and programs from corruption by other users;
- protection of data files and programs from unauthorised use;
- accounting and logging of the use of the computer resources.

System services

Often a manufacturer will provide a number of programs designed specifically for program or application development. Three such aids are:

Language processors

These are computer programs designed to convert high-level language programs into machine code, that is, into a form directly usable by a computer. Common types of language processors are compilers and interpreters.

Utility programs

As part of the systems software provided with a computer system there are a number of utility programs specifically designed to aid program development and testing. These include:

Editors

These permit the creation and modification of source programs and data files. The facilities offered by these programs usually include such things as character, word and line insertion and deletion, automatic line numbering, line tabulation for languages which require program instructions to be spaced in a specific manner, the storage and retrieval of files from backing storage, and the printing of programs or other files.

Debugging aids

Programs in which the appropriate translator can find no fault will often contain errors in logic, known as *bugs*, which only become apparent when the program is run, producing results which are contrary to expectations, or even causing the computer to cease functioning. These bugs are often very difficult to detect and may lead to long delays in the implementation of the program. Debugging aids help programmers to isolate and identify the cause of bugs.

File Managers

These simplify and facilitate a number of operations connected with program development and maintenance such as:

- keeping backup copies of important files;
- deleting files and creating space for new ones;
- merging files;
- providing details of current files held on backing storage;
- sorting file names into specified orders.

Without the help of such dedicated programs, operations such as these could be extremely time-consuming and consequently expensive.

Graphical user interfaces(GUIs)

The vast majority of microcomputer users are interested merely in using a computer as a tool, without any real interest in the technical details of its operation. A typical user will probably want to run one or more common general-purpose applications, organise files into directories, delete files and format disks. Though the operating system will provide these services, the user needs to have a certain amount of technical knowledge to perform these tasks. Graphical user interfaces provide a more intuitive means of performing common tasks. They usually make use of a pointing device, typically a mouse, by means of which a pointer is moved around the monitor screen on which small pictures (or icons) are displayed. These icons represent, among other things, programs which can be run by moving the mouse pointer over the icon and then clicking one of the buttons on the mouse. Applications run in their own self-contained areas called windows. In addition, it is usually possible to activate pull-down menus which provide access to standard functions. When a GUI uses Windows, Icons, Mouse, Pointers and Pull-down menus, it is referred to as a WIMP environment. The figure on the following page shows an example of a GUI produced by Microsoft, namely, Microsoft Windows.

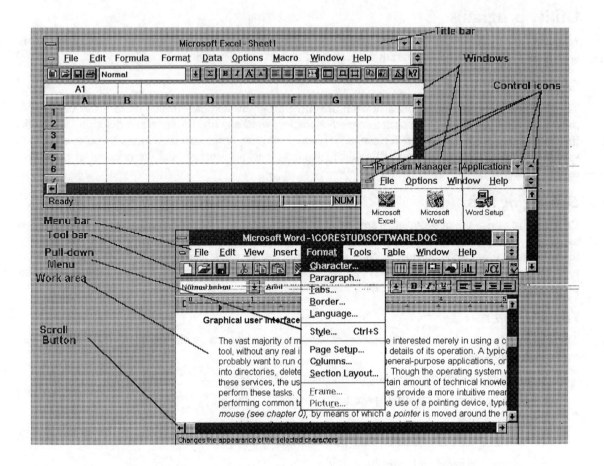

Three windows are shown in the figure:

1. A window running a Program Manager containing icons representing available applications programs. An application is run by positioning the pointer over the application's icon and clicking one of the mouse buttons, a very simple, easily remembered operation. This is really a utility window rather than an application.

2. A window running "Excel", a spreadsheet program (see later in this unit).

3. A window running the word processor, "Microsoft Word for Windows".

Only Microsoft Word, in the window with the black title bar, is active, that is, currently in use. Either of the other two can be made the active window by merely positioning the pointer in the window and clicking the mouse. Thus it is possible to be working on several applications at the same time, switching from one to the other very quickly and with minimum effort.

All such windows, no matter what the application, have a number of common features, including:

- a title bar with the name of the particular application and the name of the document being edited or created by that application;

- a menu bar containing the names of a number of pull-down menus;

- horizontal and vertical scroll bars providing access to parts of the document not shown in the window;
- a number of control icons for sizing, maximising, minimising and closing the window;
- a tool bar containing icons which, when selected, perform frequently required tasks, such as saving documents to disk or printing documents.
- a help facility providing detailed information on the operation of all aspects of the application on the screen while the application is running.

The major advantage of applications having these common features is that, having learned how one application operates, it is possible to use much of the same knowledge with other windows applications, thus significantly reducing the time required to become proficient in the use of unfamiliar applications.

Applications software

An analysis of the uses to which companies and individuals put computers would reveal that the same types of tasks appear time and time again. Many organisations use computers for payroll calculations, others to perform stock control functions, accounting procedures, management information tasks and numerous other common functions. These types of programs are classed as applications software, software which is applied to practical tasks in order to make them more efficient or useful in other ways. Systems software is merely there to support the running, development and maintenance of applications software.

An organisation wishing to implement one of these tasks (or any other vital to its efficient operation) on a computer has several alternatives:

- ask a software house, that is, a company specialising in the production of software, to take on the task of writing a specific program for the organisation's needs.
- use its own programming staff to produce the software "in house".
- buy a commercially available program "off the shelf" and hope that it already fulfils, or can be modified to fulfil, the organisation's requirements.
- buy a general purpose program, such as a database or spreadsheet package, that has the potential to perform the required functions.

The final choice will depend on such factors as the urgency of the requirements, financial constraints, size of the company and the equipment available. It is beyond the scope of this book to enter into a discussion regarding either the strategy for making such a decision or to investigate specific items of software available for specific applications; but, with the immense and growing, popularity of general-purpose packages, particularly for personal microcomputer systems, it is worth looking in more detail at this category of software.

General purpose packages for microcomputers

Discussion of this class of software will be restricted here to the following headings, though they are not intended to represent an exhaustive of all the categories of general purpose packages which are available:

- word processors
- spreadsheets
- databases
- graphics packages, including desktop publishing(DTP), business graphics, graphic design and computer aided drawing(CAD).

What characterises these software types as belonging to the category of general-purpose packages is that they have been designed to be very flexible and applicable to a wide range of different tasks. For instance, a spreadsheet can be used as easily for simple accountancy procedures as for stock control; a database can be used with equal facility to store information on technical papers from journals, stock item details and personnel details for payroll purposes. In fact, particularly in respect of modern personal computer software, the trend is for general-purpose packages to do more and more. For example, recent word processors, such as Microsoft's "Word for Windows" and "Wordperfect", include facilities once only found in desktop publishing packages, facilities for drawing diagrams and for producing graphs, in addition to the normal functions associated with a word processor; the graphic design package "Corel Draw", includes some word processing functions and graph drawing functions; the spreadsheet "Excel" has a number of facilities normally associated with database packages. Fierce market competition has resulted in the major software houses continually improving on their last version of a piece of software, attempting to outdo their competitors.

The suitability of a particular general-purpose package for a specific application will be largely dependent on the particular characteristics of the package. Though the general facilities afforded, for instance, by different database packages may be roughly equivalent, each manufacturer will adopt its own style of presentation and will provide certain services not offered by its competitors. A prospective buyer should have a clear idea of the main uses for which the package is to be purchased right at the outset, because some packages may be much more suitable than others.

Some advantages of general-purpose software compared to other forms of applications software are as follows:

- because large numbers of the package are sold, prices are relatively low;
- they are appropriate to a wide variety of applications;
- as they already have been thoroughly tested, they provide a great reduction in the time and costs necessary for development and testing;
- they are suitable for people with little or no computing experience;
- they are very easy to use;
- most packages of this type are provided with extensive documentation.

Some of the disadvantages are as follows:

- sometimes the package will allow only a clumsy solution to the task in question;
- the user must still develop the application in the case of a spreadsheet or database for example. This requires a thorough knowledge of the capabilities of the package, and how to make the best use of them;
- the user will need to provide his own documentation for the particular application for which the package has been tailored;
- unless the software is used regularly, it is easy to forget the correct command sequences to operate the package, particularly for people inexperienced in the use of computer software of this type;
- the user must take responsibility for his own security measures to ensure that vital data is not lost, or to prevent unauthorised personnel gaining access to the data.

Word processors

The word processor performs much the same function as a typewriter, but it offers a large number of very useful additional features. Basically, a word processor is a computer with a keyboard for entering text, a monitor for display purposes, one or more disk drives for storage of files produced by applications and a printer to provide the permanent output on paper. A word processor is really nothing more than a computer system with a special piece of software to make it perform the required word processing functions; some such systems have hardware configurations specifically for the purpose (such as special keyboards and letter-quality printers) but the majority are merely the result of obtaining an appropriate word processor application package.

Word processors are used for such purposes as producing:

- letters
- legal documents
- books
- articles
- mailing lists
- and in fact any type of textual material.

Some of the advantages they have over ordinary typewriters are as follows:

- typing errors can be corrected before printing the final version;
- the availability of such automatic features as page numbering, the placing of page headers and footers and word/line counting;
- whole document editing, such as replacing every incidence of a certain combination of characters with another set of characters. For instance, replacing each occurrence of the name "Mr. Smith" by "Mrs. Jones";
- printing multiple copies all to the same high quality;
- documents can be saved and printed out at some later date without any additional effort.

However, word processors do have some drawbacks. For instance, prolonged viewing of display monitors can produce eyestrain. They are generally considerably more expensive than good typewriters, and to be used properly, a certain amount of special training is required.

On the whole, word processors are now firmly established in the so-called "electronic office" and there is no reason to suppose that their use will not continue to expand.

Typical word processor facilities

A typical word processing package will provide most of the following facilities:

Word wrap

As text is typed, words move automatically to the start of a new line if there is insufficient room for them at the right-hand margin. With this facility, the only time that the Enter key needs to be pressed, to move the cursor to the beginning of a new line, is at the end of paragraphs or when a blank line is required.

Scrolling

Once the bottom of the screen is reached during text entry, the top of the text moves, line by line, up out of view as each new line of text is entered. This ensures that the line being entered is always visible on screen. The directional arrow keys on a standard keyboard allow scrolling to be carried out at will to view various parts of the document.

Deletion

This facility allows the deletion of characters, words, lines or complete blocks of text.

Insertion

This is concerned with the insertion of single letters or a block of text.

Block marking

Usually, a special function key allows the marking or highlighting of text to be dealt with separately from the rest of the document. The marked text may be moved, deleted, copied or displayed in a different style, for example, in italics or bold print.

Text movement or copying

The user may need to move or copy a marked block of text to a different part of the document;

Tabulation

Tabulation markers can be set to allow the cursor to be moved directly to column positions with the use of the TAB key. This is useful when text or figures are to be presented in columns;

Formatting

Text can be aligned left, with a straight left margin and a ragged right margin:

```
XXXX XXX XXXXX X XXXX XXXXXXXXXX XXX XXXXXXX XXXX XXXXXXX XXX
XXXXXX XX XXXXXXX X XXXXX XXXXXXX XX XXXX X XXX XXXX X XX
XXXXXXXXX XXXX XXXXX XXX X XXXXXXXXXX XXXXXX XXX XXXXXXXXX XX
XXXXXXXXXXXXXX XXXX X.
```

or it can be justified so that it has a straight left and right margin:

```
XXXX XXX XXXXX X XXXX XXXXXXXXXX XXX XXXXXXX XXXX XXXXXXX XXX
XXXXXX XX XXXXXXX X XXXXX XXXXXXX XX XXXX X XXX XXXXXXXXXXXX XXX
XXXXXXXXXXXXXX XXX XXXXXXX XX XXXXXX XXX XXXXXX XXXX XXXXXXXXX
XXXX XXXXX XXX X XXXXXXXXXX XXXXXX XXX XXXXXXXXX XX XXXXXXXXXXXXXX
XXXX X.
```

or it can be right aligned with a straight right margin only:

```
   XXXX XXX XXXXX X XXXX XXXXXXXXXX XXX XXXXXXX XXXX XXXXXXX XXX
   XXXXXX XX XXXX X XXXX X XX XXXXXX X XXXXXXXXXXXXXX XXX XXXXXXX
XX XXXXXX XXX XXXXXX XXXX XXXXXXXXXX XXXX XXXXX XXX X XXXXXXXXXX
                 XXXXXX XXX XXXXXXXXX XX XXXXXXXXXXXXXX XXXX X.
```

or it can be centred:

```
       XXXX XXX XXXXX X XXXX XXXXXXXXXX XXX XXXXXXX XXXX
    XXXXXXX XXX XXXXXX XX XXXXXXX X XXXXX XXXXXXX XX XXXX X
    XXXX XXXXXXXXX XXXX XXXXX XXX X XXXXXXXXXX XXXXXX XXX
           XXXXXXXXX XX XXXXXXXXXXXXXX XXXX X.
```

Printing Styles and character fonts

Text can be printed in a variety of styles, including bold, italic or underlined. Most word processors allow these styles to be displayed on the screen as well as on the printer and are known as WYSIWYG (What You See Is What You Get) packages;

Different character fonts, that is variations in the shapes of characters, and sizes of characters can be mixed in the same document:

This is Bauhaus 12 point

```
This is Courier 10 point
```

This is Times New Roman 14 point

THIS IS UMBRA 18 POINT

This is Franklin Gothic 24 point

Mailing

This allows a user to personalise standard letters. The mailing list is, in effect, a file of names and addresses, details from which can be inserted into marked points in a standard letter. The word processor prints multiple copies of the standard letter selected by the user and personalises each with data extracted from the mailing list.

Additional features

These include facilities for the checking of spelling in a document by reference to a dictionary held on disk, the import of text and figures from other packages such as spreadsheets, the incorporation of graphics, the export of text to other packages and the electronic transmission of text to other computers.

Spreadsheets

Just as word processors are designed to manipulate text, spreadsheets are designed to do the equivalent with numerical information. A spreadsheet program presents the user with a blank grid of "cells" each of which is capable of containing one of three types of information:

- a label consisting of alphanumeric characters;
- a number;
- a formula, which usually will make reference to other cells.

These are sufficient to allow a wide range of applications to be implemented in a very convenient and easily understandable way. For example, suppose that a small business dealing in the sale of personal computer systems wishes to use such a program to record on a monthly basis, the sales attributed to each of its four salespersons. The spreadsheet might be set up as follows:

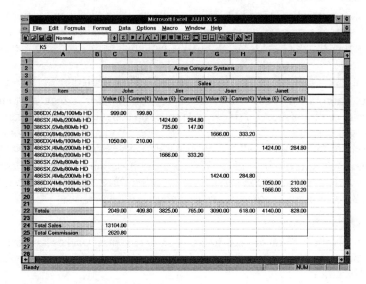

Column A contains labels describing the systems purchased. Columns C and D, E and F, G and H and I and J show respectively, the sales and commissions for each of the four salespersons. The commission is calculated automatically by means of a formula stored in the commission columns D, F, H and J. The next figure shows the formulas used for calculating John's commissions.

	Microsoft Excel - JJJJ1.XLS			
File Edit Formula Format Data Options Macro Window Help				
Normal				
K5				
	A	**B**	**C**	**D**
1				
2			Acme Computer Systems	
3				
4			Sales	
5	Item		John	
6			Value (£)	Comm(£)
7				
8	386DX /2Mb/100Mb HD		999	=C8*20/100
9	486SX /4Mb/200Mb HD			=C9*20/100
10	386SX /2Mb/80Mb HD			=C10*20/100
11	486DX/8Mb/200Mb HD			=C11*20/100
12	386DX/4Mb/100Mb HD		1050	=C12*20/100
13	486SX /4Mb/200Mb HD			=C13*20/100
14	486DX/8Mb/200Mb HD			=C14*20/100
15	386SX /2Mb/80Mb HD			=C15*20/100
16	386SX /2Mb/80Mb HD			=C16*20/100
17	486SX /4Mb/200Mb HD			=C17*20/100
18	386DX/4Mb/100Mb HD			=C18*20/100
19	486DX/8Mb/200Mb HD			=C19*20/100
20				=C20*20/100
21				
22	Totals		=SUM(C8:C20)	=SUM(D8:D20)
23				
24	Total Sales		=C22+E22+G22+I22	
25	Total Commission		=D22+F22+H22+J22	
26				
27				
28				
Ready			NUM	

Thus his sale of the 386DX costing £999 is entered in cell C8 and the commission is calculated using the formula "=C8*20/100". This calculates 20% of the retail price. The actual value of the commission is displayed in cell D8.

The column totals, shown in cells C22 to J22, were calculated using a built-in function "=SUM(range)" which calculates the sum of a range of cells. For example, John's total commission, shown in cell D22, was calculated using the formula "=SUM(D8:D20)". Note that empty cells are treated by formulas as having a value of zero.

Any changes in the data on the spreadsheet would cause all the calculations to be repeated.

This automatic calculation facility gave rise to the expression 'what if' which is often used to describe an important capability of spreadsheets. It is possible to set up complex combinations of inter-dependent factors and see 'what' happens to the final result 'if' one or more of the factors is changed. The spreadsheet, once set up, takes care of all the recalculations necessary for this type of exercise.

The earliest program of this form was called 'Visicalc' and it ran on an Apple Microcomputer. Many such programs now exist, having capabilities far exceeding those of Visicalc, but they still closely resemble the original concept in appearance and operation.

Typical spreadsheet facilities

Apart from the entry of labels, numbers and formulae, a spreadsheet package normally allows the user to use various facilities from a menu to handle the data stored on the worksheet. Typically, spreadsheets offer the following facilities.

Copying

This allows the copying of fixed values or labels, or formulae which are logically the same in another part of the worksheet. Thus, for example, in the earlier worksheet sample, the formula "=SUM(C8:C20)", which totalled a group of values for John, could be copied to succeeding columns to the right as "=SUM(D8:D20)", "=SUM(E8:E20)" and for "=SUM(F8:F20)", and so on. The formula is logically the same but the column references change, according to the position of the formula.

Formatting

A cell entry can be centred, or left or right justified within a cell. Numeric values can be displayed in a variety of formats including fixed decimal, integer, percent and scientific or as money values prefixed by a $ or £ sign to 2 decimal places. Individual formats can be selected "globally", that is throughout a worksheet or for selected ranges of cells.

Functions

These include "=SUM(range)", which adds the contents of a specified range of cells, "=AVERAGE(range)", which calculates the average value in a specified range of cells, "=MIN(range)", which extracts the minimum value held in a specified range of cells, and "=SQRT(cell)", which returns the square root of a value in a specified cell. The full range of functions usually include those used in mathematics, trigonometry, finance and statistics. These are examples of functions found in "Excel".

Macros

Groups of regularly used key sequences can be stored and then executed by one key press in combination with the Alt key, for example, Alt C. These can be useful when the spreadsheet has been tailored for a particular application which may be used by inexperienced users. Without macros, each user would have to be completely familiar with the spreadsheet commands needed. With macros, one experienced user can tailor the spreadsheet so that training time for other staff is minimised.

Graphs

Numerical data can be displayed in a variety of graphical forms, including bar charts, line graphs, scatter diagrams and pie charts. Lotus 123 provides graphical output directly but others allow numerical data to be exported to another package for graph production. The range and quality of graphs vary greatly from one package to another. With the use of a colour printer, very attractive and presentable graphs can be produced to illustrate business reports;

Consolidation

This feature allows the merging of several worksheets into a summary sheet, whilst keeping the original worksheets intact. Consolidation adds together cells with the same co-ordinates in the various worksheets.

Other facilities

These include, amongst others, cell protection facilities to prevent alteration of certain entries, the alteration of individual column widths and the display of cell contents as formulae instead of the results of their calculation. Spreadsheets have a number of attractive features compared to traditional programming solutions to processing needs:

- designed for laymen;
- easy to learn and use;
- wide range of uses;
- relatively cheap;

- easily modified;
- well tried and tested;
- provide quick development time.

On the debit side, they tend to be:

- too general purpose and therefore they tend to provide satisfactory rather than ideal solutions;
- the problem must still be analysed and a solution method identified.

Databases

At one time database programs, or Database Management Systems (DBMS) as they are often called, were restricted to mainframe computers because of the large memory requirements demanded of such applications. Currently, however, even personal business microcomputers have sufficient internal memory (4 megabytes – roughly 4 million characters of storage – is quite common) to make such applications not only feasible but also extremely powerful.

These programs allow files, comprising collections of records, to be created, modified, searched and printed.

Here are just a few examples of database applications:

- names and addresses of possible customers for a mail order firm;
- details of the books in a library giving author, title and subject covered by each book, to aid with locating books of a certain type;
- details of the items stored in a warehouse, giving location, cost, number currently in stock and supplier;
- lists of people on the electoral register for a certain region;
- details of the employees of a large firm.

Typical database facilities

A typical database program will offer, as a minimum, the following facilities:

- user-definable record format allowing the user to specify the fields within the record;
- user-definable input format to allow the user to define the way the data is to be entered into the computer;
- file searching capabilities for extracting records satisfying certain criteria from a file;
- file sorting capabilities so that records can be ordered according to the contents of a certain field;
- calculations on fields within records for inclusion in reports;
- user-definable report formats, so that different types of reports containing different combinations of record fields may be produced.

Database packages for microcomputers

These packages fall broadly into two groups, *Card Index* and *Relational*. Generally, card index systems are simpler to set up and operate but they provide less sophisticated data manipulation and search facilities than do the relational type. Further, the relational type provide a programming language which allows the development of *user friendly*, tailored applications. Thus, a user can be protected from the complexities of package operation by being presented with, for example, a menu driven system with options for record insertion, modification, deletion and retrieval and perhaps the production of summary reports. The card index type cannot be programmed in this way, so the user must have a more detailed knowledge of package operation. On the other hand, card index packages tend to be easier to use. The superior data management facilities provided by the relational type tend to be under-used unless professional database designers and programmers are involved in the development of the database application. The business executive who plans to use the database as a personal tool without such professional help, will probably be well advised to purchase a card index package rather than a relational database package.

Another factor to be considered when choosing a database, is disk space and access speed. In contrast with spreadsheet packages, database packages require frequent disk accesses when carrying out sorting and retrieval operations. Floppy disk access times tend to be too slow and their storage capacity inadequate for anything but the simplest application. A package should also allow sorting with the use of indexes, so that files do not have to be physically sorted. Indexed sorts are much quicker and a number of different indexes can be set up so that the database can be displayed in a variety of logical orders without re-organising the data on disk.

Graphics packages

Common types of graphics packages provide facilities for:

- business graphics;
- graphic design;
- desktop publishing;
- computer aided design.

Some graphics packages will to a greater or lesser degree cater for all of these applications, but many are designed specifically for one of them.

Business graphics packages allow the production of such things as Bar Charts, Line Graphs and Pie Diagrams; diagrams of a statistical nature likely to be included in business reports.

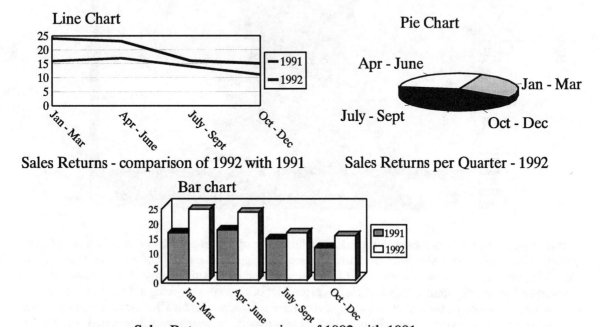

Sales Returns - comparison of 1992 with 1991

Sales Returns per Quarter - 1992

Sales Returns - comparison of 1992 with 1991

Packages for graphic design consist of a collection of special functions aimed at aiding the graphic designer. The artist uses the screen as his canvas and a light-pen, mouse or equivalent device as his brush. They generally allow work of professional quality to be produced in a relatively short amount of time, and include such facilities as

- large colour palette;
- geometric figure drawing, e.g. lines, rectangles, circles;
- filling areas with colour or patterns;
- undoing mistakes;
- moving/copying/deleting/saving areas of the screen display;
- choice of a variety of character fonts;
- printing the finished design;
- provide a large number of pre-drawn pictures for inclusion in designs. This is called *clip-art*.

The following figure shows a typical graphic design program with the user in the process of editing a picture;

Desktop publishing programs are designed to facilitate the production of documents such as posters, illustrated articles, books and other documents which combine large amounts of text with illustrations. As such they tend to contain a number of facilities in common with graphic design packages, but emphasise layout and printing. These packages place a lot of emphasis on being able to experiment with arranging sections of the document and seeing its overall appearance. Text is also given more importance; a rudimentary word processor may be provided, or text may be imported from a prepared file, and the user is generally able to experiment with different type fonts on text already displayed on the screen.

Typically, a DTP package will have facilities for:

- modifying text by means of using different fonts and type styles;
- importing text from word processors;
- displaying text in columns;
- importing pictures/diagrams from graphic design packages;
- resizing pictures;
- producing simple geometrical shapes such as lines, rectangles and circles;
- mixing text and graphics.

Here is an example of a poster produced with a DTP program:

A I K I D O
The Way of Harmony

Learn How To :

- ◆ Defend yourself effectively

- ◆ Relax under pressure

- ◆ Become fitter and healthier

- ◆ Increase your self-awareness

- ◆ Improve physical and mental co-ordination

Beginners always welcome

British Aikido Federation

Computer-aided design constitutes perhaps one of the most widely used commercial applications of computer graphics. Here the user simulates real-world geometrical objects using various software drawing tools. Often these tools are selected and used in a WIMP style environment. Sometimes a graphics tablet is used in conjunction with a pressure-operated stylus, or a light-pen might be used to draw electronically on the VDU screen. Whatever the physical method of using the system, the types of software tools and facilities available are fairly standard, providing tools for operations such as:

- drawing common objects (lines, curves, circles, ellipses, rectangles, polygons etc.);
- editing objects (modifying or deleting objects);
- filling shapes with patterns or colours;
- generating three-dimensional objects;
- rotating two-dimensional and three-dimensional objects;
- viewing three-dimensional objects from different direction;
- displaying three-dimensional objects in wireframe or solid form;
- applying different texturing effects to solid objects.

Some examples are shown below:

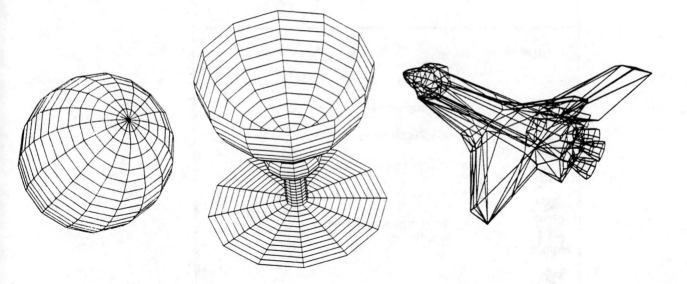

Applications of CAD programs include:

- engineering drawing;
- architectural design;
- interior design;
- printed-circuit and integrated circuit design;
- advertising material;
- computer animation for TV advertising;
- special effects in films.

Information Processing Applications

This section examines some of the *applications* of computer-based information processing systems commonly found in major organisations, although as explained in the previous section, they also apply, albeit on a reduced scale, to smaller organisations as well. The following systems are described:

- Accounting;
- Marketing;
- Computer-aided Design and Manufacture (CAD/CAM).

Following the descriptions of the above-mentioned systems, attention is given to two types of computer-based system which may play various roles in the management of particular business functions, but what is more important, can improve the *quality* and *quantity* of *management information*. The systems described are:

- Management Information Systems (MIS);
- Decision Support Systems;

Electronic mail is designed to improve both the internal communications of an organisation and its links with external bodies.

Accounting

Payroll

Payroll systems are concerned with the production of payslips for employees and the maintenance of records required for taxation and other deductions. In a manual system, the preparation of payroll figures and the maintenance of payroll records is a labour intensive task. Although tedious and repetitive, it is a vitally important task. Most employees naturally regard pay as being the main reason for work and resent delays in payment or incorrect payments, unless of course it is in their favour! The weekly or monthly payroll run affects almost all employee records in the payroll master file, so batch processing (see later in this Unit) is normally used. This processing method allows numerous opportunities to maintain the accuracy of the information. The repetitive nature of the task makes it a popular candidate for computerisation, especially with organisations which employ large numbers of people.

The automatic production of reports for taxation purposes also provides a valuable benefit. Smaller organisations with only several employees probably do not regard payroll as a high priority application for computerisation. The benefits are not as great if the payroll can be carried out by one or two employees who also carry out a number of other tasks.

Sales accounting

When credit sales are made to customers, a record needs to be kept of amounts owing and paid. Payment is normally requested with an invoice, which gives details of goods supplied, quantities, prices and VAT. Credit sales are usually made on for example, a 14, 21 or 28 day basis, which means that the customer has to pay within the specified period to obtain any discounts offered. Overdue payments need to be chased, so sales accounting systems normally produce reports analysing the indebtedness of different customers. Debt control is vital to business profitability and computerised systems can produce prompt and up-to-date reports as a by-product of the main application.

Purchase accounting

These systems control amounts owed and payments made to suppliers of services, goods or materials used in the main business of the company. For example, a car manufacturer will need to keep records of amounts owing to suppliers of car components and sheet steel manufacturers. Delayed payments to suppliers may help cash flow, but can harm an organisation's image, or even cut off a source of supply when a supplier refuses to deliver any more goods until payment is made. A computerised system will not ensure payment, but it can provide the information that payment is due.

General ledger

The general ledger keeps control of financial summaries, including those originating from payroll, sales and purchase accounting and acts as a balance in a double entry system. Computerised systems can automatically produce reports at the end of financial periods, including a trial balance, trading and profit and loss account and balance sheet.

Apart from the basic ledgers described in the preceding section a computerised accounting system will normally provide *stock control*, *sales order processing* and *invoicing* modules.

Other finance-related applications

Stock control

Any organisation which keeps stocks of raw materials or finished goods needs to operate a stock control system. Although stock constitutes an asset, it ties up cash resources that could be invested in other aspects of the business. Equally, a company must keep sufficient quantities of items to satisfy customer demand or manufacturing requirements. To maintain this balance a stock control system should provide up-to-date information on quantities, prices, minimum stock levels, and re-order quantities. It should also give warning of excessively high, or dangerously low levels of stock. In the latter case, orders may be produced automatically. A stock control system can also generate valuable management reports on, for example, sales patterns, slow-moving items, and overdue orders.

Sales order processing

This system will normally deal with:

- the validation of orders, checking, for example, that the goods ordered are supplied by the business or that the customer's credit status warrants the order's completion;
- the identification of individual items ordered. A customer may request several different items on the same order form and any particular item will probably appear on many different order forms, so the quantities for each are automatically totalled to produce *picking lists* to enable warehouse staff to retrieve the goods for dispatch;
- the monitoring of back orders. If an order cannot be fulfilled, it may be held in abeyance until new stocks arrive, so the system is able to report all outstanding back orders on request.

Invoicing

This system uses information stored in the customer files and stock files to produce invoices automatically, usually on pre-printed continuous stationery. For the sales order processing system to be fully effective, it needs access to the customer file (sales ledger) for customer details and to the stock file, so that prices can be extracted according to stock item codes entered with the order. This latter facility means that the sales order processing system may often be integrated with invoicing.

Marketing

Marketing information systems, often using a database (see later section on Processing Methods) approach, are widely used by many large national and international businesses to generate information, from a wide range of data sources, to support marketing decisions. Three marketing decision areas which make use of such information systems are:

- *strategic* and relating to, for example, expansion of the company's existing market share and the identification of new marketable products;
- *tactical*, for example, planning the marketing mix;
- *operational*, for example, day-to-day planning of sales calls and ad hoc promotions.

At the operational level, for example, data gathered from sales invoices, sales force staff and accounting information can be used to establish customer types. Thus, customers can be classified as 'low', 'medium' or 'high' volume users according to the frequency and volume of their orders. This information can help sales staff to target particular categories of customer and to plan the timing of sales calls.

At the tactical level, an invoice-based database can provide information on sales variance between different market segments over time or sales projections based on current patterns.

A *spreadsheet* package (as described earlier in this unit) can be used to develop marketing *models* concerning, for example, the projection of future product sales performance using past and current performance figures. Such models could be also be used to perform 'what-if' analysis on the financial viability of a product at various sales levels.

Activity

Everest is a manufacturer of specialist mountaineering clothing and equipment. There are 120 employees. The company designs and produces, in its own small factory, all the products it sells. Everest's main customers are the specialist climbing shops which are common in mountainous areas of this country and western Europe. It also has three retail outlets of its own. This activity is concerned with the identification of systems which may benefit from the use of computers. You are to adopt the role of a section leader in one of the following functional areas of the business: marketing; accounts; stock control; sales; product design; production control; manufacturing; distribution; personnel; salaries and wages. As part of a consultation exercise, you have been asked to help with the analysis of the information systems used in your area of work.

- *Identify one suitable application and detail:*
- *the contributions it makes to the overall operation of the company, at the operational, tactical or strategic level. Provide examples of such contributions;*
- *the information outputs it can provide;*
- *the most appropriate type of software; give examples of commercial products.*

Computer-aided design and manufacture (CAD/CAM)

Computer-aided design (CAD)

CAD is used in the design of ships, cars, buildings, microprocessor circuits, clothing and many other products. With the use of CAD a manufacturer has a distinct advantage over non-computerised competitors, in terms of speed and flexibility of design.

Computer-aided manufacture (CAM)

As the term suggests, the production line and its associated machinery are computer-controlled and in integrated systems, the manufacturing process may be controlled directly from the outputs of the CAD system. Further details of CAD/CAM are given later in this unit.

Management information systems (MIS)

Although computers can perform routine processing tasks very efficiently, it is generally recognised that, for a business to make use of a computer solely for the processing of operational information, constitutes a waste of computer power. A MIS is designed to make use of the computer's power of selection and analysis to produce useful *management* information.

A MIS has a number of key features:

- it produces information beyond that required for the routine operational needs of an organisation;
- timing of information production is critical;
- the information it produces is an aid to decision-making;
- it is usually based on the database concept.

The information provided tends to relate to the different levels of management. The claims for MIS are sometimes excessive and it is rarely the complete answer to all the information needs of a business, but when successfully implemented, it provides a valuable information advantage over competitors.

Decision support systems (DSS)

A DSS aims to provide a more flexible decision tool than that supplied by a MIS which tends to produce information in an anticipated, pre-defined form and as such, does not allow managers to make unplanned requests for information. DSS tend to be narrower in scope than MIS, often making use of microcomputer systems and software packages. Examples of DSS include, *electronic spreadsheets* (explained earlier in this unit), for example, Lotus 123 and Excel and *relational database management systems* such as dBase IV. In addition, *financial modelling* and *statistical packages* are considered to be DSS tools. A major benefit is the independence they allow for information control by individual managers and executives. When, for example, a sales manager requires a report on sales figures for the last three months, a microcomputer with database package may provide the report more quickly than the centralised mainframe computer facility.

The Information Processing Cycle

Computer-based information processing systems employed at the operational level of an organisation, for example, in the areas of payroll calculation or sales order processing, frequently involve a repeated cycle of events, which can be identified as follows:

- data collection and input or data capture;
- processing of the data, including reference to and the updating of relevant files;
- reporting of output.

This section examines this cycle, by outlining the broad procedures that may be followed at each stage and the methods commonly used in computer-based systems for *capturing* input data, *storing* and *retrieving* information in the form of computer files and *reporting* results of processing according to the requirements of users.

Data capture

Depending on the application, this stage in the cycle may include one or more of the following procedures.

Source document preparation

To ensure standardisation of practice and to facilitate checking, data collected for input (for example, customer orders) are transcribed onto source documents specially designed for the purpose.

Data transmission

If the computer centre is geographically remote from the data collection point, the source documents may be physically transported there, or be keyed and transmitted via a terminal and *telecommunications network* (explained later in this unit) to the computer.

Data encoding and verification

This involves the transcription, usually through a keyboard device, of the data onto a storage medium such as magnetic tape or disk; a process of machine verification, accompanied by a repeated keying operation assists the checking of keying accuracy. *Key-to disk* and *key-to-tape* systems are used for encoding, commonly making use of diskette and cassette tape storage, from which media the data is then merged onto a large reel of magnetic tape or onto magnetic disk for rapid subsequent input.

Data input and validation

Data validation is a computer-controlled process that checks the data for its validity according to certain pre-defined standards. For example, an account number may have to comprise 6 digits and be within the range 500000 to 900000.

Sorting

To improve the efficiency of processing sequentially organised files, input data is sorted into a sequence determined by the *primary key* of each record in the relevant master file.

Processing, storage and retrieval

This stage is entirely computer controlled and involves the processing of input data according to the requirements of the program currently in use. Thus, for example, in payroll processing, data on hours worked for each employee may be input and processed against information regarding rates of pay and tax codes held on the payroll master file, to produce the necessary payslips. In addition, the payroll information regarding, for example, pay to date and tax paid to date is updated on the master file.

Reporting of output

The destination of the results of processing also depends on the application and the requirements of the users. Output may be in the form of thousands of printed payslips or invoices or it may be simply a screen display of information in response to a user enquiry.

Activity

Everest is a manufacturer of specialist mountaineering clothing and equipment. There are 120 employees. The company designs and produces, in its own small factory, all the products it sells. Everest's main customers are the specialist climbing shops which are common in mountainous areas of this country and western Europe. It also has three retail outlets of its own. This activity is concerned with the identification of systems which may benefit from the use of computers. You are to adopt the role of a section leader in one of the following functional areas of the business: marketing; accounts; stock control; sales; product design; production control; manufacturing; distribution; personnel; salaries and wages. As part of a consultation exercise, you have been asked to help with the analysis of the information systems used in your area of work.

- *Identify one suitable application and describe its information processing cycle.*

Methods of Information Processing

There are a number of types of information processing system, categorised according to the ways in which data is controlled, stored and passed through the system; the major categories are identified here:

- batch processing;
- on-line processing, which includes real-time and time-share processing;
- distributed processing;
- database systems.

To allow particular methods of processing a computer must have the necessary *operating system* software; thus any particular computer system is equipped with, for example, a batch processing or real-time operating system, or even a combination of types, depending on the needs of the user organisation. It should be noted that the software used to control a database system is known as a *database management system* (DBMS) and that the computer on which it is installed still needs appropriate operating system software. The role of operating systems is briefly explained earlier in this unit.

Batch processing systems

Such systems process *batches* of data at regular intervals. The data is usually in large volumes and of identical type. Examples of such data are customer orders, current weekly payroll details and stock issues or receipts. Although associated with large organisations using mainframe or minicomputer systems, the technique can be used by a small business using a microcomputer.

The procedure can be illustrated with the example of payroll, which is a typical application for batch processing. Each pay date, whether weekly or monthly, the payroll details (such as hours worked, overtime earned or sickness days claimed) are gathered for each employee (these details are referred to as *transactions*) and processed in batches against the payroll *master file*. The computer then produces payslips for all employees in the company. A major feature of this and similar applications is that a large percentage of the payroll records in the master file are processed during the payroll 'run'. This percentage is known as the *hit rate*. Generally, high hit rate processing is suitable for batch processing and if, as is usual, the master file is organised sequentially, then the *transaction file* will be sorted into the same sequence as the master file. In the case of magnetic tape, transactions must be sorted because the medium only allows *serial* (one record after another in their physical order) access.

Batch processing methods closely resemble manual methods of information processing, in that data on transactions is collected together into batches, sent to the computer centre, sorted into the order of the master file and processed. Such systems are known as 'traditional' data processing systems. There is normally an intermediate stage in the process when the data must be encoded using a *key-to-tape* or *key-to-disk* system.

A disadvantage of batch processing is the delay, often of hours or days, between collecting the transactions and receiving the results of processing and this has to be remembered when an organisation is considering whether batch processing is suitable for a particular application.

Conversely, batch processing has the advantage of providing many opportunities for controlling the accuracy of data and thus is commonly used when the immediate updating of files is not crucial.

On-line processing systems

If a peripheral, such as a Visual Display Unit or keyboard, is *on-line*, it is under the control of the computer's processor or Central Processing Unit (CPU). On-line processing systems therefore, are those where all peripherals in use are connected to the CPU of the main computer. Transactions can be keyed in directly. The main advantage of an on-line system is the reduction in time between the collection and processing of data.

There are two main methods of on-line processing:

- real-time processing;
- time-share processing.

Real-time processing

Process control in real-time

Real-time processing originally referred only to process control systems where, for example, the temperature of a gas furnace is monitored and controlled by a computer. The computer, through an appropriate sensing device, responds immediately to the boiler's variations outside preset temperature limits, by switching the boiler on and off to keep the temperature within those limits.

Real-time processing is now used in everyday consumer goods, such as video cameras, because of the development of the 'computer on a chip', more properly called the *microprocessor* (identified earlier in this unit). The important feature common to all real-time applications is that the speed of the computer allows almost immediate response to external changes.

Information processing in real-time

To be acceptable as a real-time information processing system, the *response-time* (that is the time between the entry of a transaction or enquiry at a VDU terminal, the processing of the data and the computer's response) must meet the needs of the user. The delay or response time may vary from a fraction of a second to 2 or 3 seconds depending on the nature of the transaction and the size of the computer. Any delay beyond these times would generally be unacceptable and would indicate the need for the system to be updated.

There are two types of information processing systems which can be operated in real-time. These are:

- transaction processing;
- information storage and retrieval.

Transaction Processing. This type of system handles clearly defined transactions one at a time, each transaction being processed completely, including the updating of files, before the next transaction is dealt with. The amount of data input for each transaction is small and is usually entered on an *interactive* basis through a VDU. In this way, the user can enter queries through the keyboard and receive a response, or the computer can display a prompt on the screen to which the user responds. Such 'conversations' are usually heavily structured and in a fixed format and so do not allow users to ask any question they wish.

A typical example of transaction processing is provided by an *airline booking system* and the following procedures describe a client's enquiry for a seat reservation:

1. A prospective passenger provides the booking clerk with information regarding his/her flight requirements;
2. Following prompts on the screen, the clerk keys the details into the system so that a check can be made on the availability of seats;
3. Vacancies appear on the screen and the client can confirm the booking;

4. Confirmation of the reservation is keyed into the system, usually by a single key press and the flight seating records are immediately updated;

5. Passenger details (such as name, address, etc.) can now be entered.

Such a system needs to be real-time to avoid the possibility of two clients booking the same seat, on the same flight at the same time, at different booking offices.

Information Storage and Retrieval. This type of system differs from transaction processing in that, although the information is updated in real-time, the number of updates and the number of sources of updating is relatively small.

Consider, for example, the medical records system in a hospital. A record is maintained for each patient currently undergoing treatment in the hospital. Medical staff require the patient's medical history to be available at any time and the system must also have a facility for entering new information as the patient undergoes treatment in hospital. Sources of information are likely to include a doctor, nurses and perhaps a surgeon, and new entries probably do not number more than one or two per day.

This is an entirely different situation from an airline booking system where the number of entries for one flight record may be 200-300 and they could be made from many different booking offices throughout the world.

Time-share processing

The term *time-sharing* refers to the activity of the computer's processor in allocating *time-slices* to a number of users who are given access through terminals to centralised computer resources. The aim of the system is to give each user a good *response time*. These systems are commonly used where a number of users require computer time for different information processing tasks. The processor time-slices are allocated and controlled by a time-share operating system. The CPU is able to operate at such speed that, provided the system is not overloaded by too many users, each user has the impression that he or she is the sole user of the system. A particular computer system will be designed to support a maximum number of user terminals. If the number is exceeded or the applications being run on the system are 'heavy' on CPU time the response time will become lengthy and unacceptable.

Time-share systems are possible because of the extreme speed of the CPU in comparison with peripheral devices such as keyboards, VDU screens and printers. Most information processing tasks consist largely of input and output operations which do not occupy the CPU, leaving it free to do any processing required on other users' tasks.

Distributed processing

As the term suggests, a distributed processing system is one which spreads the processing tasks of an organisation across several computer systems. Frequently, these systems are connected and *share resources* (this may relate to common access to files or programs, or even the processing of a single complex task) through a data communications system (explained later in this unit). Each computer system in the network must be able to process independently, so a central computer with a number of remote intelligent terminals cannot be classified as distributed, even though some limited validation of data may be carried out separately from the main computer. Examples of distributed systems include mini or mainframe computers interconnected by way of *wide area networks* (we discuss this later in the unit), or a number of *local area networks* similarly linked.

Distributed systems provide a number of benefits:

Economy. The transmission of data over telecommunications systems can be costly and local database storage and processing facilities can reduce costs. The radical reduction in computer hardware costs has favoured the expansion of distributed systems against centralised systems;

Minicomputers and microcomputers. The availability of minicomputer and microcomputer systems with data transmission facilities has made distributed processing economically viable. An increasingly popular option, in large multi-sited organisations, is to set up local area networks of microcomputers at each site and connect them through communications networks to each other and/or to a central mainframe computer at the Head Office. This provides each site with the advantages of local processing power, local and inter-site communications through *electronic mail* (explained later in this unit) and access to a central mainframe for the main filing and database systems;

Local management control. It is not always convenient, particularly where an organisation controls diverse activities, to have all information processing centralised. Local management control means that the information systems will be developed by people with direct knowledge of their own information needs. Responsibility for the success or otherwise of their division of the organisation may be placed with local management, so it is desirable that they have control over the accuracy and reliability of the data they use.

Database systems

Databases are based on the idea that a common 'pool' of data, with a minimum of duplicated data items, can be organised in such a way that all user requirements can be satisfied. Therefore, instead of each department or functional area within an organisation keeping and maintaining its own files, where there are subjects of common interest, they are grouped to form a 'subject' database. Database systems are available for mainframe, mini and microcomputer systems.

A number of different types of database are available, but the differences between them relate to the way the information is organised and the general features described above are common to all. A particular type that is available for all types of computer system, but is particularly popular on microcomputer and minicomputer systems, is known as a *relational* database. dBase IV provides an example.

Card index systems

Computerised card indexes, such as Cardbox, are not databases according to the definition provided at the beginning of this section, but they do provide a simple alternative for information storage and retrieval and are equivalent to, though more effective than, manual card index systems.

Activity

An earlier activity placed you in the role of assistant to the IT Manager, at Pilcon Electrics plc. In this role, you are to prepare materials to illustrate the different types of information processing system which exist. The activity requires identification of a range of applications, sufficient to illustrate all the processing categories outlined in the preceding text. For each application, briefly describe:

- *its general function;*
- *the way it operates, from input through to output;*
- *the method(s) of processing it uses;*
- *the reasons for the selected processing method(s).*

Operating Computer Systems Effectively

It is vitally important for the effectiveness of a computerised information processing system, that its daily operation is controlled by a disciplined set of standards. Such *operating standards* will vary in detail from one organisation to another but all are concerned with the maintenance of a reliable and effective system. Even the temporary loss of computer facilities, perhaps owing to hardware failure, can prevent a business from continuing its normal trading activities. For example, an Estate Agency which uses computer storage for all its property records (which may run into thousands) will be unable to carry out automatic property searches according to clients' requests. Although printed property details may be available, a manual search process may be impractical because of the time involved.

Computerisation is often undertaken because of business expansion, which would otherwise involve extra staff recruitment. Once a business comes to rely on computer-based systems, it cannot simply revert to manual procedures. The staffing levels necessary for a computerised system and a particular volume of business are generally much lower than would be necessary for a manual system coping with a similar volume of business. In short, a business which loses its computer facility and access to its data for a 'significant' period will cease to function effectively. What counts as a significant period will depend on the nature of the business and degree of dependence on computer-based systems. For example, a theatre's seat reservation system is fundamental to its business operation and loss of the facility for a few evenings could lead to considerable loss of business. On the other hand, a small retail business which loses access to its accounting records for a day is unlikely to suffer any loss of business. Permanent loss of important data, caused perhaps by damage to storage media, may well lead to complete business failure.

In recognition of the fact that large mini and mainframe installations are staffed by specialist computer operators, this unit concentrates on the operation of stand-alone and networked microcomputer systems which may well come within the direct experience of many business users. It must be emphasised that the operating standards in larger, more complex installations servicing the processing needs of numerous administrative departments need to be more comprehensive and rigorous than those described here.

Stand-alone systems

System start-up

If the computer system is to be used throughout business hours, then the start-up and shut-down procedures should, ordinarily, be necessary only at the beginning and the end of the working day. Switching off the equipment for short periods does not increase its working life. On the contrary, the process of switching on again is more likely to result in system damage, particularly if the process is repeated several times each day. The procedures for system start-up are fairly straightforward, but the fact that manufacturers' operation manuals describe them in detail signifies the importance of carrying them out correctly. Network start-up procedures are slightly more complex than those for stand-alone systems. The procedures for stand-alone systems are invariably as follow:

- ensure that all components are properly connected (this should only be necessary the first time that the equipment is used);
- switch on the power sockets serving the computer system components. If there is a master switch for the complete power supply, switch this on first. It is important that mains power is not initiated after the computer system is turned on, as the resulting power surge may damage the equipment;
- turn on the monitor and printer; and then the system unit; if the system has a hard disk drive, the operating system should have been installed onto the hard disk during the installation process and will be loaded into main memory automatically. In the case of systems without a hard disk insert a system diskette (a diskette containing an operating system) into the disk drive designated in the instruction manual before switching on. The system carries out an initial self-test procedure, to determine that all components are connected and functioning correctly.

System shut-down

The shut down of the computer system should reverse the procedures for system start-up. Thus, the system unit is switched off, followed by the peripherals and then the power supply. It is important that proper exit procedures from packages in use at the time are followed. Some packages use the procedure to close files which, if left open, may prevent access to them the next time the package is used. In addition, diskettes should be removed from drives before the system unit is switched off.

Staff training

It is important that at least one and preferably two or three staff members are trained in the identification and, if possible, correction of routine faults which do not warrant dealer attention. This may involve, for example, the recovery of corrupted files or the replacement of printer ribbons. 'In house' attention to simple problems may well shorten the 'down time' (the time when the computer system is not available for operational use). Of course, it is essential that remedial action by staff is restricted to that for which they are properly trained. In addition, no action should be taken which may invalidate the manufacturer's warranty or the dealer's maintenance agreement. Such actions will include, for example, tampering with or removing electronic components or electro-mechanical devices such as disk drives.

Fault logging and reporting

Even if proper hardware maintenance is carried out and components are serviced according to manufacturers' recommendations, faults will occur. A written log should be maintained for the recording of all faults or breakdowns and the times at which they occurred. A pattern of faults may help a service engineer to identify possible causes, in which case, remedial action can be taken to avoid them in future. If faults are not the result of normal wear and tear or user mishandling, then a fault history may be crucial in convincing the supplier that faulty goods were supplied.

If a fault appears to correct itself immediately and does not result in inconvenience or loss of data, it should still be recorded, because it may occur again with more serious consequences. For example, during a file processing operation, an error message may indicate that an attempt to read a particular file has failed. Assuming that the error is reported by the applications package rather than the operating system, an exact diagnosis is unlikely to be provided. Assume further, that the user repeats various operations and at the second attempt no error is indicated. The user decides that it is not worth reporting and the following day, the error recurs and a complete file is apparently lost. Hopefully, operational procedures for taking regular back-up copies would prevent serious loss in such circumstances but the inconvenience could be avoided by prompt error reporting. If the error in this example was caused by a damaged diskette, immediate copying of the data onto a fresh diskette may have solved the problem. If the disk drive was at fault an engineer could have been called to repair it before the system was used again. Fault recording should be a matter of routine, not a matter for individual judgement.

Damage and loss prevention measures

- *protection against fire*
  As a first step, smoking in and around computer rooms can be banned. Scrap paper, including obsolete print-outs, should not be allowed to accumulate in waste paper bins but should be properly organised. Backup copies of all master files should be taken at regular intervals (frequency will depend on level of file activity) and kept with master copies of applications and systems software in a fireproof safe at a different location. Copies of current data files and software, together with procedure manuals and user guides, should be kept in a fireproof, lockable cabinet on the premises.

- *disk handling and storage*
  Disks should be kept in their protective sleeves and stored in disk boxes away from direct sunlight, radiators, magnetic fields and other hazards which may physically distort them or corrupt the stored data.

- *disk identification*
  Proper labelling of disks giving details of their contents, should help prevent accidental use of the wrong files. The details should include version numbers, dates and titles of contents.

- *computer access control*
  Access to equipment can be controlled through physical measures such as locked doors. Limiting access to files can be effected through both physical and software controls. Physical control may be exerted by the locking away of storage media and procedural controls such as the maintenance of a log which users have to sign, giving the date, time and purpose of access.
  Software controls include the use of passwords which may limit access to certain files or the processing which can be carried out on them. For example, a personnel manager may have authorisation to alter salary values in personnel records, whilst a clerk in the personnel section may have authority only to read them.

- *operating procedures*
  The risk of accidental damage to equipment or files may be minimised by ensuring that all users are properly trained in the operation of the computer system and that only staff trained in a particular application are authorised to use it for that purpose.

Recovery procedures

Although most users would prefer not to consider the possibilities of major hardware or software loss, it is extremely foolish not to provide for them. Of course, there may be circumstances when, because of a combination of disasters, no recovery is possible, but in most cases, sensible preparation can prevent catastrophe.

- *Hardware failure*
  If hardware damage or failure is too serious to prevent immediate repair, the business should be ready to make use of alternative facilities for their data processing needs. For example, the supplier may loan computer hardware to the business while repairs are carried out or use may be made of bureau facilities. The business can prevent serious financial loss by ensuring that insurable risks such as fire are covered.

- *Software failure*
  Procedures for taking regular security copies of data files and the logging of transactions should allow the reconstruction of any damaged files. A file may be inaccessible because of the corruption of the file directory (which keeps track of the location of files on disk) or part of the file itself. Operating system utilities are usually provided which allow the user to re-create the directory and thus gain access to the file or to recover the undamaged sections of the file. Where a file has been deleted accidentally, data recovery software such as Norton Utilities can retrieve it. For security purposes, the Norton package provides a facility for erasing files permanently.

Job scheduling, logging and control

A computer facility constitutes a limited resource so its use has to be planned and controlled in order to achieve a number of objectives:

- to ensure that jobs with high priority are dealt with before jobs of relatively lower priority;
- to ensure that all necessary work is identified and processed promptly;
- to maximise use of the computer system;
- to provide feedback on the level of use and the possible need for system expansion or modification;
- to limit its use to authorised users and for authorised work;
- to ensure that procedures for security copying of files and reconciliation of control totals are carried out as planned;
- to minimise the chances of file and hardware damage which is more likely to occur with undisciplined use.

The logging procedure involves the recording of details such as user, job, file version, date and time. The use of the system should have been planned during the process of systems design so job priorities should be known.

Activity

You are assistant to the IT Training Manager at Pilcon Electrics. A number of stand-alone microcomputers are being used by several executive staff who require some guidance on the basic management of a computer system.

- *Design and produce a small booklet which highlights the main features of good operational practice. Use the previous headings and your experience to determine its content. The booklet will only be useful if the information it provides is concise and clear.*

Local area networks

Local area networks are formed by connecting microcomputer systems together for the purposes of *resource sharing* and *communication*. These resources relate, in the main, to the storage of files and the production of printed output. One microcomputer workstation, usually more powerful than the user workstations, is normally dedicated to the function of *file server* and apart from handling access by workstations to the files held centrally on its large capacity hard disk, is used by a *network manager* (a specially trained member of staff) to control use of the network by allocating *user passwords* and file storage space to individual users or user groups.

Each user is allocated a *login code* and password which are keyed by the user in response to the operating system prompts on the screen. The network manager has a *super-user* password which gives him or her access to network facilities unavailable to ordinary users. Thus, for example, the network manager can change user passwords, re-allocate file storage space and allocate priorities for printer access to individual workstations.

When a user has finished using the network, the signing-off procedure will include the automatic recording of the user identification and the date and time the workstation has been in use.

Production Systems and Technology

Computer-aided design and manufacture (CAD/CAM)

CAD/CAM is revolutionising the manufacturing process in terms of massively improved productivity and quality control. The principles of these computer-based technologies and the features of the equipment are described in the following paragraphs. Although they represent massive capital invest-ment, it is now obvious that for some manufacturers, there is no alternative system. For example, it would be impossible for any major car manufacturer to survive without almost fully automated production lines.

Computer-aided design

With the use of a graphics terminal and crosshair cursor (described earlier in this unit), or similar device, a designer can produce and modify designs more rapidly than is possible with a conventional drawing board. Ideas can be sketched on the screen, stored, recalled and modified. The computer can also be instructed to analyse a design for comparison with some specified criteria. Drawings can be rotated and tilted on the screen to reveal different three-dimensional views.

The complex calculations needed to produce such drawings and the huge amount of memory they occupy has meant, until recently, that CAD software could only be used satisfactorily on powerful mainframe or minicomputer systems. The massive increases in speed and capacity of microcomputer systems permits their use for some CAD work. A CAD system must also be based on the use of very high resolution screens to allow designers to work in fine detail with the same degree of accuracy that is required in the manufacturing process.

Computer-aided manufacture

A number of areas of computer use can be identified in the manufacturing process:

- industrial robots;
- computer numerical control (CNC) of machine tools;
- integrated CAD/CAM;
- automated materials handling;
- flexible manufacturing systems (FMS);
- process control.

Industrial robots

Basically, a robot replaces the actions of a human arm and consists of three main elements, a mechanical arm with 'wrist' joint, power unit and microprocessor or central controlling computer. To be called a robot, it must be able to react, albeit in a limited way, to external events and alter its course of action according to a stored program. Such sensitivity to the environment is provided by *sensors*, for example, to recognise stylised characters and differentiate between shapes.

The main areas of use are in spot welding, paint spraying, die casting and to a lesser extent, assembly. Use of robots can provide significant benefits for industry, its employees and the population in general, namely:

- operation in environments unsuitable for the health of workers;
- performance of tasks, particularly those which are repetitive, at a consistent level of quality, which is generally high, and without fatigue;
- lack of human weaknesses generally allows robots to be many times more productive;
- labour costs are drastically reduced and the capital costs of robots are recoverable through increased production and a consequent fall in the unit costs of production (the cost of producing a single unit of a particular product).

Computer numerical control (CNC)

CNC operation of machine tools has been widespread for some years because the repetitive nature of machining tasks lends itself to simple programming. However, as is the case with robots, the use of microprocessors allows the machine tool to vary its actions according to external information. The actions of the machine can be compared with a design pattern held by the computer.

Any significant variations from the pattern are signalled to the machine tool which, through the microprocessor, reacts appropriately (known as *Computer Aided Quality Assessment* – CAQ). Other information regarding tool wear or damage can be picked up by sensors and communicated to the human supervisor who takes remedial action.

Integrated CAD-CAM

In fully integrated CAD-CAM systems, the designs produced using CAD are fed straight through to the software which controls the CNC machine tools, which can then produce the design piece. The CAD software checks the compatibility of the design with a component specification already stored in the computer.

Automated materials handling

A fully automated materials handling system consists of a number of sub-systems:

- stock control;
- part or pallet co-ordination;
- storage and retrieval;
- conveyor control.

Installation generally proceeds one sub-system at a time, each being fully tested before proceeding with the next sub-system. A materials handling system, controlled by a central computer, allocates storage locations in the warehouse, automatically re-orders when a predetermined minimum level is reached, retrieves parts as required by the factory and delivers them by conveyor belt to the waiting robots or CNC machines.

Flexible manufacturing systems (FMS)

Such systems are beneficial where production batches are small and necessitate frequent changes in the sequence and types of processes. The aim of FMS is to remove, as far as possible, the need for human intervention (other than a supervisor or 'machine minder') in the production process. The main elements of FMS are, CNC machine tools (with diagnostic facilities), robots, conveyor belt and central computer and controlling software. In simple terms, the computer has information on parts, machine tools and operations required. The robots serve the CNC machines by presenting them with parts to be machined and loading the correct machine tools from racks.

Process control

Industrial processes, such as iron smelting and chemical manufacture, can be controlled by computers in a *real-time* (the system responds immediately to changes in conditions) environment, so that, for example, conditions of temperature, speed or pressure can be kept within prescribed limits.

Communications Systems and Technology

Computer-based communications systems include, amongst others, electronic mail, electronic data interchange (EDI), Telex, facsimile transmission (FAX), remote job entry (RJE) and electronic funds transfer at point-of-sale (EFTPOS), their general aim being to enhance the speed and efficiency with which information can be transmitted between geographically remote users.

Communications systems

Electronic mail

Electronic mail requires the use of computer terminals, generally equipped with word processing software, for the preparation of messages prior to transmission via the telecommunications network. Each user has an address or unique identification code which is used by other users in the same way that telephone numbers are used to make contact with particular people, although electronic mail systems allow several or many users to be sent the same message at the same time. An electronic mail system also makes use of computer systems at various points in the network to allow the storage of messages when the intended recipient is not available to take them or their terminal is not switched on. At no time is there any requirement for messages to be printed, although users are free to do so if they do require hard copy.

Facsimile transmission

This service allows the transmission of facsimiles or exact copies of documents or pictures through a data communications network. Using a fax machine connected to a telephone line, the user simply dials the fax number of the intended recipient, waits for the correct signal and the document is fed through the fax machine and transmitted. The fax machine sends picture elements or *pixels* obtained by scanning the document in a series of parallel lines; a synchronised fax machine at the other end prints a facsimile (we also consider how to use a fax later in this Unit) from those pixels.

Telex

Conventionally, the Telex system requires the use of dedicated terminals (teletypes), which only allow the use of upper case characters and do not provide any editing facility. Messages can only be printed and there is no message storage facility if the destination terminal is not working. However, Telex can now be accessed, from a microcomputer with word processing software, through the Prestel viewdata system. Prestel is a public *viewdata* system, with which subscribers can communicate, either via a microcomputer with a *modem* (see later in this Unit) and appropriate software, or from a dedicated Prestel terminal.

Electronic data interchange

Similar to electronic mail, EDI allows users to exchange business documents, such as invoices and orders over the telecommunications network.

Remote job entry (RJE)

RJE systems make the simplest use of data communications to transmit bulk data rapidly to a central computer; transmission is one-way, from an RJE terminal located at the remote site to central computer, which is probably situated at the Head Office of the organisation. In a wholesaling business, for example, each distribution warehouse could transmit details of stock changes and requirements via an RJE terminal at the end of each day via a simple dial-up link. In the 1960s, RJE terminals commonly consisted of a card or paper tape reader and printer; currently transmission is direct from key-to-disk or key-to-tape systems.

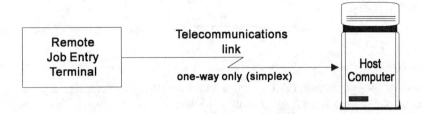

Remote Job Entry

Communications technology

Local area network (LAN)

A network confined to, say, one building and comprising interlinked microcomputers distributed in different rooms, is known as a Local Area Network or LAN. They do not need to make use of the telecommunications network and their extent is limited to a maximum of two or three miles.

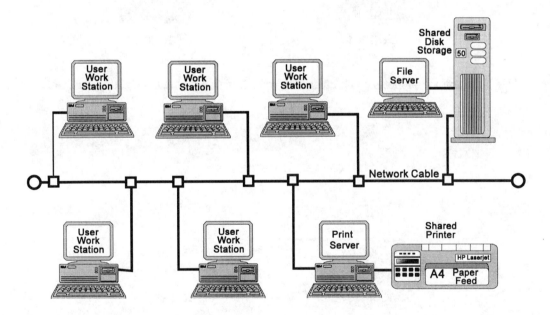

Wide area network (WAN)

A computer network distributed nationally or even internationally makes use of telephone and sometimes, satellite links, and is referred to as a Wide Area Network or WAN. In large organisations with several branches, it is becoming popular to maintain a LAN at each branch for localised processing and to link each LAN into a WAN covering the whole organisation. In this way, branches of an organisation can have control over their own processing and yet have access to the main database at head office. Equally importantly, inter-branch communication is possible.

Data communications

Data communications networks allow different *transmission modes* and carry *signals* which represent the information being transmitted.

Transmission modes

- simplex mode allows communication in one direction only and as such, is only appropriate for tasks such as remote job entry or RJE;

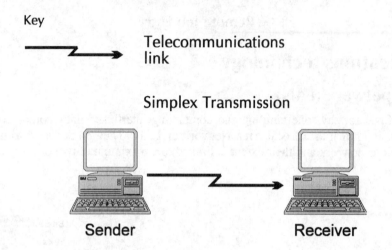

Key

Telecommunications link

Simplex Transmission

Sender   Receiver

- half duplex mode supports communications in both directions, but not at the same time;

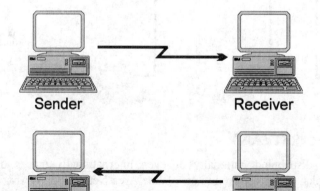

Half-duplex Transmission

Sender   Receiver

Receiver   Sender

- duplex mode allows communications in both directions at the same time and is appropriate for interactive systems, such as airline booking systems, when on-demand enquiries are needed.

Duplex Transmission

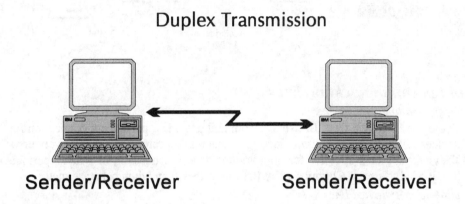

Sender/Receiver   Sender/Receiver

Types of signal

There are two types of signal which can be transmitted along a communications medium (cable or satellite link, for example), *analogue* and *digital*.

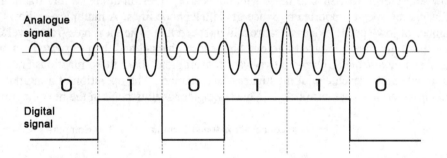

The telephone network was originally designed to carry the human voice and carries signals in continuous sine wave form, whereas computers handle data in digital form. The telephone network is being modernised with digital exchanges which permit the transmission of digital signals directly and in many areas of the country it already transmits the human voice in this form. Where computers need to communicate over analogue links, a device called a *modem* (*mo*dulation *dem*odulation) is required to appropriately modify the signals. A modem modulates the signal from the transmitting computer into the appropriate analogue form for transmission along the telephone line and a modem at the receiver device fulfils the opposite function; modems normally have facilities for both sending and receiving, so that two-way communications are supported.

Modems in Telecommunications link

Terminal

Telecommunications
link

Modem

Modem

Host
Computer

Digital
signal

Analogue
signal

Digital
signal

Types of telecommunication lines

- *Dedicated lines*
  These can be leased from British Telecom and provide a permanent connection for
  devices in a network. They provide high transmission rates and are relatively error-free.
  They are only cost-effective for high-volume data transmission, or when a permanent
  link is vital to users. Charging is by flat rate rather than when calls are made.

- *Dial-up or switched lines*
  These are cheaper, but support lower transmission rates than leased lines. They are more
  cost-effective for low volume work and allow the operator to choose the destination of
  transmissions.

Special communications equipment

A number of different machines and devices exist to improve the efficiency of telecommunications
networks. The most notable are *multiplexers* (MUX)and *front-end processors* (FEP).

- *Multiplexers*
  Low speed terminals, such as those with keyboards, transmit at only a tiny fraction of the
  transmission speed supported by voice-grade telephone lines. A multiplexer allows a
  number of low-speed devices to share a high-speed line. The messages from several
  low-speed lines are combined into one high-speed channel and then separated out at the
  other end by a *demultiplexer*. In two-way transmissions, both these functions are carried
  out in one unit at each end of the higher speed channel. The operation of a multiplexer
  linking several remote terminals to a host computer is illustrated in the next diagram.

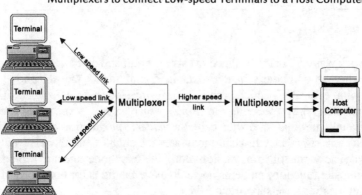

Multiplexers to connect Low-speed Terminals to a Host Computer

- *Front-End-Processors (FEP)*
  This is the most sophisticated type of device for communications control and is usually a minicomputer held at the site of a mainframe host computer. Its main task is to handle all the communications traffic, leaving the mainframe free to concentrate on processing tasks.

Evaluating Information Processing Systems

The effectiveness of an information processing system for any particular business can be measured by comparison with various criteria, in particular:

- the degree to which the system provides *security of information* for the business and according to the requirements of the Data Protection Act 1984;
- the *efficiency* of the system (including any clerical or administrative procedures) for the collection, storage, processing and distribution of information it was designed to handle;
- its *cost-effectiveness*.

Security of information

An information processing system should provide controls serving the following functions:

- the prevention of information loss caused by software or procedural errors, or by physical hazards;
- the protection of information from accidental or deliberate disclosure to unauthorised individuals or groups;
- the protection of information from accidental or deliberate corruption or modification. This is known as maintaining information *integrity*;
- the protection of the rights of individuals and organisations to restrict access to information which relates to them and is of a private nature, to those entitled or authorised to receive it. This is known as *data privacy*.

Security against data loss

The loss of *master files* can be an extremely serious occurrence for any business, so properly organised security procedures need to be employed. Among commercial organisations that have lost the major part of their information store, a large percentage subsequently go out of business.

The main causes of information loss are as follows:

- environmental hazards – such as fire, flood and other natural accidents;
- mechanical problems; for example, the danger of disk or tape damage caused by a drive unit malfunction;
- software errors – resulting from programming error;
- human error. A wrong file may be loaded, the wrong program version used, a tape or disk mislaid, or physical damage caused to tape or disk;
- malicious damage. It is not unknown for staff to intentionally damage storage media or misuse a program at a terminal.

The standard solution to such problems is to take regular *backup copies* of master files held on magnetic disk or tape and to store the copies in a separate secure location. It is also necessary to maintain a record of *transactions* affecting a file since the last copy was taken, so that if necessary they can be used to reconstruct the latest version of the file. The method used to achieve this is referred to as the *grandfather*, *father* and *son* (or *generation*) system.

Security against unauthorised access

Unauthorised access to an information system may:

- provide information vital to competitors;
- result in the deliberate or accidental corruption of information;
- allow fraudulent changes to be made to information;
- result in loss of privacy for individuals or organisations; this is particularly important when a business is holding personal information which is subject to the rules laid down by the Data Protection Act 1984 (see next section).

Protection methods may be *physical* and include the use of security guards, locks, electronic alarms and identity cards and fingerprint or voice recognition; the effectiveness of such protection depends on the maintenance of appropriate administrative procedures. Software methods generally make use of password controls; a user must key in a password in response to a prompt on screen. Series of passwords may also be used to maintain different levels of security; for example, a clerk in a Personnel Department may be given authority to display information regarding an employee's career record, but only the Personnel Manager is authorised to change information held in the file. A range of security controls can be used to prevent unauthorised access by employees and by those attempting to *hack* or break into an information system.

Data *encryption* can be used to scramble information being transmitted along telecommunication links to ensure that hackers who tap into them cannot make sense of the information.

Data Protection Act 1984

The Act sets boundaries for the gathering and use of personal data. It requires all holders of *computerised* personal files to register with a Registrar appointed by the Home Secretary. The holder of personal data is required to keep to both the general terms of the Act, and to the specific purposes declared in the application for registration.

Terminology

The Act uses a number of terms that require some explanation:

- *data*. Information held in a form which can be processed automatically. By this definition, manual information systems are not covered by the Act;
- *personal data*. That which relates to a living individual who is identifiable from the information, including any which is based on fact or opinion;
- *data subject*. The living individual who is the subject of the data;
- *data user*. A person who processes or intends to process the data concerning a data subject.

These requirements may result in a business having to pay more attention to the question of security against unauthorised access than would otherwise be the case; appropriate education and training of employees are also needed to ensure that they are aware of their responsibilities and fully conversant with their roles in the security systems. The Act also provides the right of a data subject (with some exceptions) to obtain access to information concerning him or her; normally, a data user must provide such information free or for a nominal charge of around £10.

Efficiency and cost-effectiveness of information processing systems

The efficiency of an information processing system will depend on:

- the *quality of its design*. This will depend on the components chosen to construct it, their fitness for the purpose and the ways in which they are connected to form the complete system. The components will include the hardware of the computer system, supporting software and documentation, operational staff and users. The ways in which they are connected will be determined by the various clerical and administrative procedures used to operate the system. In respect of the hardware, an application may operate efficiently on a powerful minicomputer but a network of microcomputers may lack sufficient power to provide acceptable response times (the time taken to output results following a user request for information);

- its *suitability* for the selected *purpose*. A payroll system designed for an organisation with 100 employees may be wholly inadequate to the task of handling 500 payroll records;

- how *effectively* the system is *implemented*. For example, a system may be perfectly designed in terms of the hardware and software, but the users may be inadequately trained and unable to operate it efficiently.

To be *cost-effective*, the value of information produced by an information system must exceed its cost. The cost of a computerised information system must take account of, amongst other things, hardware and software purchase and maintenance, the employment of specialist staff, training of users, insurance and security systems. Most costs are on-going, because, even if a computer system is bought outright, financial provision must be made for its replacement, probably within a maximum of five years. These costs can be offset by the possible benefits of reduced labour costs, or increased business using the same number of staff. Other benefits and costs are described in the next section.

Activity

Use the previous list of criteria to assess the effectiveness of the computer facilities at your college or place of work. You need to be objective, use your experiences and talk to technical and academic staff. You should monitor the levels and types of use, over a period of time. You may find, for example, that some applications operate effectively, whilst others involve considerable delay. You also need to monitor the frequency and duration of 'down time' (when the facilities are not available, either because of maintenance, or breakdown). Analyse and summarise your findings, using whatever software you think is appropriate.

Effects of Computer-based Systems

A number of effects, grouped as costs and benefits, are described in the following paragraphs; some can be measured *quantitatively* or in financial terms and some are less tangible and involve *qualitative* judgements on, for example, working conditions and levels of job satisfaction. Whether one views a particular effect to be a cost or a benefit will often depend on personal circumstances. So, for example, feelings of insecurity on the part of some older members of staff, who may feel that they are too old to learn new skills, can probably be contrasted by the career opportunities that are presented to younger people with up-to-date Information Technology skills.

Financial costs

- Hardware purchase;
- Software development or purchase costs;

- Opportunities for fraud; may be increased by the hidden nature of much computer processing;

- Hardware and software installation;

- Training in the use of new hardware, software and modified clerical systems;

- Re-deployment; as an alternative to redundancy this will usually involve re-training costs;

- Insurance against fire or natural disasters which may destroy equipment and data;

- Changes in working practices; health and safety regulations on the use of VDUs, for example, may require the provision of regular breaks from such work, although with proper planning, other tasks may be allocated during some of those periods;

- Hardware and software maintenance; a hardware maintenance contract will normally be negotiated with the supplier and as the information needs of the organisation change, modifications to software may be necessary; hardware normally has a maximum life of about five years and breakdowns will be more frequent as time passes unless equipment is properly maintained;

- Provision for depreciation; equipment will become obsolete within three to five years and provision must be made for its replacement;

- Specialist accommodation; for VDU operators, this may involve the purchase of appropriate, computer workstation furniture, changes to lighting and the installation of window blinds. In the case of mainframe systems an air-conditioned and secure room large enough to accommodate the hardware and any specialist operating staff is needed; this may even require a change of premises;

- Redundancy; depending on the length of service involved redundant staff are normally entitled to financial payment;

- Conforming with health and safety regulations;

- Security systems to secure the hardware, and software mechanisms such as password systems to secure the data;

- Conforming with the requirements of the Data Protection Act; in respect of personal information held on computer files, organisations must take measures to keep it secure and confidential;

- Running costs, including salaries of specialist computing staff and consumables such as disks and tapes for storage.

- Other costs

- Feelings of insecurity amongst older staff; lack of appropriate skills and apprehension about radical change in working conditions, as well as the threat of redundancy are likely to produce such feelings;

- Redundancy; apart from the financial cost to the organisation, there are social costs which affect the people being made redundant;

- De-skilling of some tasks; although word processing may be regarded as requiring higher level skills than typing, an accounts clerk maintaining a manual system probably feels that the change to a computer-based system will remove the need for certain aspects of their skills.

Financial benefits

- Improved operational efficiency; this is not automatic as the computer-based system may be badly designed and the staff may be ill-trained, but given proper design and implementation administrative systems will normally be more efficient;

- Better control of resources; administrative systems such as those for financial control and the control of resources such as staff and raw materials benefit particularly from the rapid production of up-to-date information by computer;

- Improved productivity; redundancy does not always follow from computerisation, particularly if the organisation is an expanding business. Computer-based systems should permit large increases in the volumes of business which can be handled, without the need for extra staff;

- Improved security of information; with proper physical security, clear operational procedures to restrict access to computer facilities to those properly authorised, and sophisticated use of software control mechanisms (such as passwords), computer-based information systems can be made more secure than equivalent manual systems;

- Opportunities to share data; this is most likely where database systems (see earlier in this Unit) are employed;

- Improved quality of information for decision-making at the operational, strategic and corporate levels in an organisation.

Other benefits

- Increased job satisfaction; this is highly subjective and depends entirely on the individual concerned and the nature of their job before and after computerisation;

- Removal of some tedious filing and calculation work; for some the change to data entry work may be considered an improvement, but, for example, a wages clerk may have gained more satisfaction from operating a manual system;

- Improved external image; an organisation can improve its external image by the improved presentation of correspondence and by an improved service to its customers or clients, but badly designed procedures can also make life more difficult for them;

- Improved working conditions; this is highly debatable in respect of an office environment, but computer-based manufacturing systems usually provide a less dirty and dangerous environment for employees as much of the work is done by robots and other computer-controlled machinery.

Activity

The commercial banks are continuing to increase the level of automation and Automatic Teller Machines (ATMs) are commonplace. In addition, voice processing techniques are being used to allow people to carry out banking transactions by telephone. Research these topics and write a short magazine article dealing with the communications and computer technologies which support the use of ATMs and telephone banking, the employment and social effects which may arise from widespread use of these systems; your discussion should deal with those who work in the banking industry and its customers. Illustrate the article with examples and be as objective as you can.

Assignment *The Personal Touch*

Hailes Bookshop in Cambridge is internationally reputed to be one of the finest and largest bookshops in the world. The shop occupies a complete block of terraced Victorian buildings. There are three floors and each floor has several sections, divided according to subject. If a book is in print, Hailes will have a copy. Despite its volume of business, its only concession to automation to date, has been to use electronic tills. All other tasks are carried out manually and communications between staff are generally face-to-face. There is a family atmosphere amongst the staff and management and the firm even employs a tea lady who wheels her trolley of tea and biscuits from department to department at break times. However, there is increasing competition from bookshops which adopt a supermarket approach. These 'book supermarkets' are highly automated and make extensive use of computers for almost all their data processing applications. Their staff have little or no knowledge of the products they sell and customers are left to sort out their own needs. In contrast, Hailes employs staff with specialist knowledge of books in a number of subject areas, but not in popular fiction. It is in this area that Hailes is experiencing severe competition.

The directors of Hailes are willing to accept the idea that some applications and particularly stock control, could benefit from computerisation. A software consultancy, DataSoft, has been approached by the Hailes directors for advice on the best approach to computerisation. DataSoft have recommended the use of a Local Area Network, which they point out, will allow automation of a range of routine office tasks, apart from the standard data processing tasks envisaged by the Hailes directors. DataSoft have also emphasised the potential benefits of electronic messaging between the various departments of the shop and the provision of access to external electronic mail systems. The Hailes directors are proud of the friendly atmosphere amongst staff and the frequent personal contacts. They are unwilling to sacrifice the 'personal touch' to the objective of automated efficiency, but are very conscious of the need to improve their competitiveness.

Task

Assume the role of sales representative for DataSoft and prepare a report for presentation to the directors of Hailes Bookshop, concerning the potential for computerisation of various aspects of the business. Your report should make reference to applications including:

- general accounting and administration;
- specialist applications, which may make use of general purpose software such as: spreadsheets and databases;
- electronic mail; and bar code reading;

and outline with the use of examples the benefits each application may provide for this particular business.

Unit 3

Marketing

This unit has been written to cover the following specifications of the General National Vocational Qualification Business Level 3

Unit 3   Marketing Level 3

Element 3.1:   Analyse market research

Performance criteria:

1   relevant sources of information are identified which establish potential market need
2   appropriate research methods are identified and the criteria for selection explained
3   research instruments to collect data are described
4   data is analysed and conclusions are drawn
5   a report on the findings of market research is prepared

Element 3.2:   Use consumer trends to forecast sales

Performance criteria:

1   characteristics of consumers are investigated
2   economic information is analysed to identify effects on consumption
3   economic information and consumer trends are used to predict demand for products and services
4   consumer information is used to forecast sales for a business organisation

Element 3.3:   Investigate marketing activities

Performance criteria:

1   objectives of marketing activities are explained
2   marketing activities for competing products are compared for effectiveness in achieving objectives
3   new product developments and product life cycles are identified
4   marketing mixes used by organisations are identified and explained
5   ethical considerations of sales and marketing activities are explained and authorities to ensure ethical standards of are identified

(extract from General National Vocational Qualifications Mandatory Units for Business GNVQ3 offered by Business Education and Technology Council, City and Guilds and RSA Examinations Board - published by the National Council for Vocational Qualifications April 1993 - reproduced with the kind permission of the National Council for Vocational Qualifications)

GNVQ3 Business - Unit Number U1016176

Element 3.1 Analyse Market Research

Introduction

The study of marketing as a key area of business is a relatively recent development. Indeed, many people argue that in this country the study of the subject is still not taken seriously enough. In this section of the book we intend to demonstrate exactly why marketing should be regarded as being of prime importance to organisations of all descriptions. With the current popularity of topics such as Total Quality Management and the general acceptance of the importance of the consumer to the survival and prosperity of businesses, marketing is at last beginning to take on a much more prominent role in the running of organisations. It is interesting to note that surveys suggest that the majority of chief executives and managing directors in the United Kingdom tend to be from an accountancy background, whilst their American counterparts are more likely to have a background in marketing. In Germany, a greater proportion of engineers predominate in the higher executive positions. In this section of the book we will argue that it is not the discipline from which a business leader comes that is important, more the philosophy which he or she adopts in managing the strategic development of the organisation.

A Definition of Marketing

Marketing is a subject which draws upon a wide range of other disciplines. Key elements in the study of marketing include an understanding of concepts from areas such as economics, psychology, sociology and statistics. As such, a simple definition of the subject is somewhat difficult to arrive at. If the general public were asked to define marketing, many would respond with answers such as 'selling' or 'advertising'. Some would cite market research, whilst there would also doubtless be several other less complimentary definitions arising from individual experiences with rather dubious organisations. In a sense, marketing encompasses all of these areas and many more. The British Chartered Institute of Marketing (CIM) uses the following comprehensive definition:

> *"Marketing is the management process responsible for identifying, anticipating and satisfying customer needs profitably."*

This single sentence demonstrates quite clearly but succinctly the breadth of the subject.

- Firstly, marketing is seen as a management process. As such, all levels of management must take responsibility for the marketing effort, and be involved at all stages. Indeed, it can be argued that the principles of marketing apply all the way down any organisational hierarchy. With many organisations, it is the lowest paid members of the organisational structure who actually deal with the general public or the clients. If they do not share the marketing ideas or the company, the impression presented to the customers will inevitably be unfavourable. We will examine this idea more in the next section on marketing as a philosophy.

- The second element of the CIM definition suggests that marketing is concerned with the identification and anticipation of customer needs. This is area of the subject referred to as market research. Without research, no organisation can hope to correctly define the needs, wants and desires of its consumers, and as such will have little prospect of survival. Business history is littered with disaster stories of supposedly brilliant inventions which, when launched onto an unsuspecting public, sank without trace. The fundamental failure in the vast majority of these instances was the lack of perception of market needs. We will look at the principles and techniques involved in market research later in this Unit.

- The notion of satisfying the needs of consumers is the next part of the definition. Based upon the findings of the previously undertaken research, organisations must design products and services which will satisfy the highlighted demands. Products and services must then be; priced correctly, promoted efficiently and effectively, and distributed in such a manner so that they reach the consumers in the right place; and at the right time. These four variables – product. price, promotion and place – are known as the 'Four P's' of marketing and collectively form the organisation's marketing mix. Place, in this instance, stands for distribution, which unfortunately does not begin with the letter P! The vast majority of tactical work carried out by marketing departments is involved with these four areas, and as such we devote much of this section of the book to the study of these factors.

- The final element of the definition suggests that marketing should be carried out profitably. Without doubt, most commercial enterprises use the various marketing tools in order to ensure that their operations are carried out profitably. However, it is worth pointing out that many other organisations do not actually operate solely on a profit maximising basis.

  The growth in the marketing activities of bodies such as charities and central and local government suggests that the profit motive is not always the only driving force behind the carrying out of marketing tasks.

Marketing, therefore, is all about making the company outward-looking or customer oriented. To do this you have to be able to put yourself in the customers' shoes, (or, even better, inside their minds) in order to really understand what they want and what they feel about things. Only in this way can a business organise itself successfully to meet the needs of its present and potential customers.

Marketing is a philosophy

As we mentioned above, marketing should really be seen as a philosophy rather than as a functional part of the organisation. The way in which an organisation thinks throughout its structure is vital to its success. By reading the definition of the term, it should be apparent to you that most areas of an organisation's operation are somehow touched by the presence of marketing. For example:

- any new product developments will inevitably involve the Research and Development arm of an organisation;
- the actual design and production of the product may involve the design team, engineers and the whole manufacturing aspect of the business;
- finance will inevitably be involved throughout the process, from the initial costings through to the final pricing decisions;
- the distribution aspects may involve anything from warehousemen to drivers to shop assistants.

It is clear that the influence of marketing is spread to all corners of all organisations, and it is therefore imperative that all members involved in whatever capacity within the organisation think with like minds. Obviously any of the so-called 'customer-facing staff' need to be acutely aware that their clients are their livelihood, but this thinking should run throughout the whole organisation. Many companies now operate on a system of 'internal customers', whereby different departments and sections within the organisation must treat each other as if they were external clients. This internal marketing enables organisations to instil the idea within all of their staff to be customer oriented, that is they should be always looking to see what the customer wants, and to try their best to satisfy their needs.

There are other philosophies which have existed in business organisations throughout history. Indeed, some organisations still do not fully embrace marketing as a way of thinking, merely using it as a functional tool to help sell products. Other philosophies which have or still do exist include the following:

- the Product Approach;
- the Production Approach;
- the Selling Approach;
- the Societal Marketing Approach.

The product approach

This type of philosophy is still common with 'inventors' who start from their own product, and then attempt to find a market for it, instead of the other way round. An idea is hatched and developed, with little or no thought given to what the eventual consumer may actually be looking for. A classic example of this approach in recent times was the development of the Sinclair C5, the brainchild of the inventor, Sir Clive Sinclair. It was he who had developed and sold the highly successful Spectrum range of computers and the C5 was another product which he believed would take the world by storm. The product was an electrically powered vehicle, which was not quite a fully-blown motor-cycle. The idea was that this would provide ideal transport around the congested towns and cities in the world, whilst also being very friendly to the environment. However, the end product was the subject of almost total ridicule when it was launched, not least because its design was less than flattering. The product flopped, and Sir Clive lost a substantial part of his financial fortune. Had sufficient thought been given to the potential market, the product could have been developed and marketed in a substantially different, and probably more successful way. It is interesting to note that the C5 has apparently found favour among the golfers in certain countries as an electronic caddy, so perhaps every cloud has a silver lining!

The production approach

With this type of philosophy, an organisation devotes the majority of its thought and effort to looking at ways to improve the way in which the product is produced. Whilst all competitive businesses must always be conscious of the needs to improve their efficiency and effectiveness in terms of production, an obsession with this type of philosophy can lead to the company ignoring its customers in the outside world and becoming obsessed with its own internal operations.

The selling approach

This approach is associated with products which people do not essentially need, and involves the use of high-pressure sales techniques designed to convince people that they actually do want the particular product or service. It tends to be the approach adopted by the poorer quality financial services companies, some double glazing manufacturers and some suppliers of rather expensive vacuum cleaners! Anyone who has been subjected to the five hour sales pitch of a desperate sales representative will understand the tactics which can be employed.

Again, all products will need some aspect of selling. However, an organisation which gives little attention to the true needs of its potential market, and insists on the high-pressure approach, will tend to be one which does not generally possess a product which provides good value for money. Any organisation which has designed its product following research of consumer needs and wants should help itself in the sales effort and should not have to rely on such tactics. Indeed, there is a large body of consumer protection legislation, developed over a number of years, which prevents such organisations exploiting potential customers.

The societal marketing approach

This type of approach is actually very different from the three mentioned above. It is in reality an extension of the basic marketing philosophy discussed earlier, and includes not only the needs and wants of the individual consumer but also of the collective society in which we all live. Many organisations are now producing 'environmentally friendly' products and services, although it could be suggested cynically that this is a result of necessity in terms of sales as opposed to any true belief in the commonalty of the society. A trip around the local supermarket will reveal hundreds of products which claim to be friendly to the environment, although research suggests that not all claims are as true as they could be!

In order to be successful in these very competitive times, all organisations need to adopt an outward looking stance. They need to constantly be seeking information as to the needs and wants of both internal and external customers and be striving to deliver the best quality, given whatever resource constraints exist. Product or sales driven organisations still exist, some would say in too large numbers. However, many organisations are now realising that the only way to be successful in the current climate is to firstly discover what the customer wants, and then try to provide it. The marketing philosophy is beginning to gain in influence!

Activity

Consider the above approaches to marketing, and look for two products which fall into each category. Discuss the approach which the manufacturers of these products or services have adopted, and list the good and bad aspects of each approach. You do not need to go into too much detail in order to assess the marketing activities, merely to provide an overview. Present your information in the form of a table, showing each product and each category.

Marketing Research

The overall purpose of carrying out marketing research is to reduce the risks associated with business decisions. Good decisions are more likely to be made when the most accurate and relevant information becomes available for consideration by decision makers at the appropriate time, and in a manageable format. Research should be the first step taken by any venture, prior to even embarking upon any business.

It is worthwhile reconsidering the CIM definition of marketing stated earlier, which reflected upon the need to 'identify and anticipate' customer requirements. It is through the process of market research that this aspect of the marketing role is fulfilled.

As marketing is a philosophy as well as an organisational function, the provision of good information is important to all sections of an organisation to help in the adoption of the marketing concept. Marketing research is partly an information tool but also a management tool which has two basic uses:

* to reduce the level of uncertainty and therefore risk which is associated with any planning process;
* to monitor performance once those plans have been implemented.

In this section we go on to consider the various approaches which are available to marketers in respect of the gathering of information. The majority of the first section is devoted to the consideration of primary data, whilst the next section deals in more detail with the gathering of information on external environmental factors.

Scope of marketing research

Marketing research is a term which refers to a whole range of research activities which are described below and are seen as crucial to helping provide solutions to marketing problems. Market research and consumer research are major elements of marketing research and concentrate on specific problems relating to individual markets on the one hand, and actual or potential customers on the other.

There is a wide range of types of research which exist, and each has its own merits. The type of research which is carried out by an organisation will depend upon the organisation, the product, the industry and many other variables. The following list highlights the broad scope of marketing research.

Market research

This is research which is carried out into the size and nature of market. It will cover various aspects including:

- geographical location;
- the market shares of major competitors;
- how the product is distributed through the various channels; and
- the general nature of environmental and economic trends.

Sales research

Much data may already be available internally within the organisation on this subject, but much other information may have to be obtained from external sources. Data usually considered under this heading would include:

- an analysis of the variations in the sales levels of each geographical territory;
- the nature, length, timing and so on of territorial sales visits; and
- the effectiveness of the sales force, in relation to the methods employed and the incentives provided.

Some form of retail auditing may also be included in this type of research, whereby the level of sales, measured either in volume or monetary value, is analysed to determine the relative effectiveness of different outlets. The major producers of Fast Moving Consumer Goods (FMCG's) such as food, electrical goods, washing powder and CDs, spend much time and effort on this type of research, in order to determine exactly how best to target their marketing efforts.

Product research

Each product or service which an organisation offers or is considering offering should be very thoroughly researched. Topics covered would normally include:

- an analysis of competitive products in terms of relative strengths and weaknesses;
- an investigation of any potential new uses for existing products;
- the testing of new product concepts and the actual new products themselves;
- research into areas such as packaging and the provision of more or less variety.

Advertising research

In the same way that a product may well fail if it is not appropriately researched, so may any promotional or advertising strategy. All promotional campaigns should begin by defining the target audience and the objectives of the campaign, and then subsequent research should be carried out to assess variables such as:

- the appropriateness of the copy (that is the words and images used to advertise the product);

- the media which is to be used (such as newspaper or television advertising); and
- the overall effectiveness of the campaign.

All research into advertising and promotion should be a continuous process, with sufficient effort spent evaluating the success (or failure) of campaigns in order to learn from them.

Export marketing research

Many more organisations are now looking to overseas markets as ways of expansion. This area of research is very specialised and can be very complex, but should incorporate all of the above mentioned types of approach.

The points just made are merely guidelines for research, and are not meant to form a comprehensive checklist. The type of research undertaken and the data collected will inevitably differ from organisation to organisation. For example, public sector organisations and private sector organisations will usually adopt very different approaches to their market research.

As the scope of marketing research is so wide, it is imperative from the outset to consider exactly what information is required and to seek only the appropriate data. This prevents a lot of wasted time and money. Therefore the first step should be to clearly state the objectives of the research, and then to actually consider what information is needed and how it may be collected.

Many organisations have now moved towards the development of comprehensive Marketing Information Systems as part of their marketing research effort and this has helped to make sure that the process of research, and in particular the assessment of research needs, is a continual process.

Research in relation to planning and control

The whole purpose of planning is to make decisions on the future use of resources in order to achieve certain pre-determined results over a certain period of time. The organisation can obviously control the inputs to the process, which are essentially the Four P's of the marketing mix which we discussed earlier, but the organisation may have little control over the market reaction, as the outputs are to an extent uncontrollable. The more dynamic or turbulent the market is, the less controllable the reactions will be to the marketing effort.

The more turbulent the environment in which an organisation is operating becomes, the greater is the need for it to have an effective marketing information system. The more information which an organisation has available, the more likely it will be to cope with change.

As a rule, it is likely that a wise organisation will carry out some research on a continual basis as a means of enhancing its control of the process. For example, most organisations will constantly monitor aspects such as:

- quality;
- delivery times; and
- costs.

It is also probable, however, that there will be a need to carry out 'ad hoc' research, as and when necessary, concerning specific elements of the marketing effort.

Experimentation may be crucial to new product development, and may be carried out on either an ad hoc or continuous basis. In some instances it may prove impossible to experiment, for example where construction work would need to be carried out at great expense. Here, demand forecasting will assist in predicting future demand, for example the provision of a new leisure facility such as a swimming pool.

'Continuous' and 'Ad Hoc' research

As mentioned above, research as a total process must be continuous in order to provide the correct information for the purposes of planning and control. It should be recognised that research is a fundamental focus for the marketing department in providing the data on which management decisions will be based.

Strategic planning research

When an organisation is planning its future, it will need to undertake research into new market opportunities. In fact if the organisation wants to have a clear view of its future then it needs to broaden its research into the whole macro-environment to include consideration of political, economic, social and technological factors affecting the marketing effort.

The second element of planning research involves identification and selection of target markets. The organisation needs to research market size, growth and profitability to determine the market potential This can be achieved through segmentation analysis. This breaks down the market into its constituent parts so that sets of buyers can be differentiated.

Future marketing plans can be devised to target:

- a small number of segments (niche marketing);
- several segments (selective marketing); or
- the total market made up of all current and potential consumers (intensive marketing).

Researchers must determine the most appropriate criteria to be used in segmenting the market for the analysis to offer accurate consumer data. The organisation can then develop marketing strategies to target specific markets and segments. The organisation must then decide on its tactics on how to apply its strategies and will develop a marketing mix for to use within a specified time scale.

It has already been noted that for most organisations this type of research will be carried out on an almost continuous basis. Remember the more turbulent the marketing environment, the more important continuous research will be.

Monitoring and control research

The second major field of marketing research concerns monitoring and control of the marketing plans which the organisation has implemented. This will include research into areas such as:

- profitability;
- efficiency; and
- the general effectiveness of various strategies and tactics.

This is the type of research which tends to be more ad hoc, and will be carried out as and when required.

The research process

In any organisation the research process should be systematic, and should clearly evolve from the problems which the organisation faces. The success of any marketing research campaign depends just as much on a clear definition of the problem and the approaches as it does on the quality of the information obtained and the way in which it is presented.

Various stages are usually followed when carrying out research. These include the following:

- problem definition;
- deciding the value of the information;
- selection of the data collection methods;

- selection of measurement techniques;
- selection of the sample;
- selection of the method of analysis;
- specification of time and cost;
- preparation of the research proposal;
- evaluation and implementation of the proposal.

Problem definition

The first stage for an organisation in any research must be to determine the exact nature of the problem and what information is likely to be of use when attempting to solve that problem.

Deciding the value of the information

There is always a danger that the organisation may spend time and money finding out the wrong type of information, or that too much data is collected. It is therefore essential to establish from the outset what the 'downside' risks are which are involved in the research process. The organisation needs to assess each type of information in terms of costs of collecting it and the benefits which it will gain from having the information, in order to determine whether that information is actually needed. It is vital to remember that research takes time, and that time means money.

Selection of the data collection methods

As will be discussed later in this Unit, there is a variety of research methods which are available to all organisations. Choices must be made as to whether the organisation seeks primary data or secondary data, whether it will use experiments or surveys, and so on.

Selection of measurement techniques

The organisation must decide which questionnaires, attitude scales, observation and/or projective techniques are required (These are all discussed in more detail later in this Unit).

Selection of the sample

The organisation must decide whom to use as a sample for its research, and how many people it should seek to involve in order to provide a realistic sample which will truly reflect the total population.

Selection of the method of analysis

In these days of information technology, many highly sophisticated computer packages are available to analyse market research information. These are, however, almost exclusively 'number-crunching' programmes designed to analyse quantitative information such as how many respondents answered in a specific way. Research is much more than this, and as such, the analysis of more qualitative information, for example detailed individual opinions, requires much more of a personal approach rather than a mechanical one when it comes to the analysis stage. The method of analysis which the organisation selects will largely depend upon the questions which it has asked and the size and nature of the sample it has chosen.

Specification of time and cost

The cost of research is similar to the length of a piece of string - it is as long as you want it to be. A wise manager will make a sensible assessment of the cost before beginning the research and the cost must obviously reflect the value of the information which is being sought. It is no good spending £100,000 to find out information which will increase sales by £5,000. The timescale of the research is also important and will similarly reflect both the value of the information to the organisation and how urgent it is to find out the information.

Preparation of the research proposal

At this stage, and only after the previous factors have been considered, it should be possible to prepare a detailed proposal for the overall research task to be undertaken.

Evaluation and implementation of the proposal.

Once the proposal has been agreed and accepted by all of the parties concerned in the effort, the research can finally commence. This whole process may sound lengthy and expensive, but as was mentioned earlier it is essential that research is carried out in a systematic manner in order to provide the relevant information for the decision making process. There are many pitfalls involved in marketing research, so the better planned the research campaign is, the less likely it is to provide invalid or inaccurate information.

Activity

You are asked to draw up a plan for some research. You do not have to carry out the actual research. Take a particular problem in which you are interested. It may be the appropriateness of the college library opening times, the effectiveness of a company's telephone answering/reception service, the price of activities in your local Leisure Centre or any other situation. Draw up an outline plan, using the guidelines you have just read, which describes how you would carry out research into this problem.

Problems involved in marketing research

Whether the research is of a continuous or ad hoc nature, or whether it concerns planning or control decisions, there are numerous problems which can occur which act as limitations to the marketing research process.

The major limitations which are likely to arise are as follows:

- sampling errors;
- non response errors;
- data collection errors;
- analytical and reporting errors;
- experimental errors.

Sampling errors

If a non-representative sample is selected then inaccurate results which are supposed to approximate to the total population are likely to occur. For example, if a college is assessing the reasons why its students attend courses, it would receive widely differing responses from full-time students to those on part-time day release courses. A truly representative sample would include elements of all types of student in an appropriate proportion, in order to reflect the overall population. As will be seen later, it is also likely that the possibility of error will increase where non-probability based samples are used.

Non response errors

If some of the selected sample do not respond to the researcher, or are perhaps not even contacted, this will introduce a bias. For example, a street-based questionnaire may only attract the people who have the time to spare to answer the questions, or those who simply like to fill in questionnaires (watch in your local high street for the type of person!). Either way, this may introduce non-response errors, as the sample will become biased with the inclusion of a large proportion of non-respondents.

Data collection errors

There are several possible errors which can be the result of the way the data is collected. For instance:

- it is fairly common for respondents to simply give the first answer to any questionnaire in order to get away from the interviewer. It has also been found that people will respond in a way they think they should, simply in order to impress the interviewer;
- bias may exist within a questionnaire which leads respondents to a particular answer, for example a particular emphasis placed on a phrase by the interviewer may lead to a particular response;
- the questionnaire itself may be badly designed, and may not help in the process of data collection;
- simple clerical errors should be include in this category, as they do occur. Even the introduction of Optical Character Readers to scan computer based questionnaires is not infallible;
- finally, it is always possible that certain respondents will deliberately set out to offer false replies to questions, for whatever motives. This can be avoided to an extent by the insertion of series of 'control' or 'check' questions which may be helpful in identifying 'rogue' responses, but anyone who is deliberately attempting to cause problems will often be successful!

Analytical and reporting errors

These type of errors may occur in interpreting the collated data and perhaps in setting the report within the relevant context of the research aims and objectives set out at the beginning of the process. It is essential when analysing the data and preparing the report to always refer back to the initial problem definition and setting of objectives in order to satisfy the prime goals of the project.

Experimental errors

These may occur if uncontrollable events occur during the test period. For example, if a competitor launches a rival product when an organisation is carrying out research into the test launch of a product, this may cause problems. Often these outside occurrences are unpreventable, but they can cause the whole process to be invalidated.

An example of an external event disrupting a campaign was that of the Newcastle Journal, a local daily morning newspaper based in Newcastle upon Tyne. The Journal decided to launch a promotional campaign in nearby Sunderland, providing complimentary copies of their newspaper to households which already had a paper delivered from a newsagent. The problem was the timing – and football. During the campaign Newcastle United were winning promotion to the Premier League while Sunderland were only just surviving in the first division. The resultant response of readers in Sunderland to the praise heaped upon their local rivals on the sports pages of the Journal seriously damaged the validity of the research, if not resulting in undermining sales of the Journal in Sunderland!

Types of research

The problems and limitations of research described above tend to apply mostly to areas of primary or field research. This type of research involves collecting data which is original and usually applicable to a specific marketing context. It is worth noting that in planning the research process, it is normally essential that researchers begin with secondary or desk research. This involves the use of both internal and external sources of information.

Secondary research

Internal sources

Internal sources of secondary research are often the first starting point in any research project. It is surprising how many organisations do not realise just how much information they already possess which will be of use to their research. The following are cited as examples of potential sources, and are not meant to be an exhaustive list.

- previous research studies;
- past sales figures;
- competitor information;
- competitor information;
- delivery data;
- the sales force.

Previous research studies

All too often, organisations have research carried out which is then simply filed away. This information will often provide a valuable guide as to the basis of current research projects, and should always be available and considered.

Past sales figures

Most organisations keep detailed records of their previous sales. These can be analysed in a number of ways to provide useful new data. For example, sales could be considered according to:

- company size;
- market segment;
- geographical location; or
- timing of purchase.

From this data, certain trends may well emerge. It is not uncommon for the unwritten '80/20' rule to emerge, namely that 80% of the organisation's sales are to 20% of its customers. This allows the company to focus its marketing efforts more efficiently, avoiding the costly chasing of customers who perhaps may never repay the investment put into the effort by buying its products.

Competitor information

All market-led organisations should keep a constantly updated file on their competitors. Information which is freely available, such as brochures, company reports, annual accounts and product information should all be kept on file to provide an insight into the means of operation of rivals. Many organisations now use a 'debriefing session' if they employ new staff from their competitors, using the opportunity to gain further information about their commercial adversaries. Obviously, there are limits, enforced legally, as to the amount of information which people can disclose, and industrial espionage is by no means recommended, but there are still many ways in which information on opponents can be discovered and used profitably.

Delivery data

This can be supplemental to the sales records discussed above. Details on the distribution of a product or service can again serve as a useful platform for further research projects.

The sales force

It is the sales force who are the eyes and ears of any organisation. It is they who are dealing on the front-line with the customers, and they should be trained to feed back all relevant information into the system for future reference. This information will include not only data on the customers themselves but also intelligence on the operations of the competition. This kind of information may be anecdotal in some cases, but use of any data from customer-facing staff can prove invaluable in the quest for competitive advantage.

External sources

There is a wealth of information from secondary sources available to the marketer. Information is big business and many companies make very handsome profits by gathering information about markets, compiling it into reports and selling them to anyone who wants to buy them. Various government departments and other governmental bodies produce statistics and information on a wide range of markets as well as on the economy and changing social trends. Information can come from freely available sources such as trade directories or the Yellow Pages, or from much more specialised sources. As a general rule, the more specialised the information, the more expensive it is to obtain.

We now look at some of the more common sources of market information including:.

- Mintel Reports;
- Key Note Reports;
- government statistics;
- audits;
- panels.

Mintel reports

Mintel produce a monthly journal containing about six reports on markets of interest and these are almost always consumer markets. Monthly Mintel reports are about ten to twenty pages long and give the kind of basic information that marketers need for a preliminary scan of the market, such as:

- market size;
- projected growth;
- main competitors;
- market share of main products;
- advertising spend of main brands;
- significant trends.

In addition, Mintel publish specialised reports which provide more detailed information on certain markets. For example, Mintel publish reports on the retailing and leisure markets, which provide a much more in-depth analysis of certain aspects of the operation of those particular industries.

Key Note reports

Key Note reports differ in that they produce reports for business to business markets. They do not have a regular monthly edition but cover a range of business markets and update the reports on a regular basis. Around seventy five pages long, they provide a fairly detailed introduction to marketers. Like Mintel Reports, Key Note reports are available commercially, and do not come cheap, although many good business libraries stock a wide range of this type of information.

Government statistics

There is an almost equally large and bewildering range of government statistics available to the marketer. The best place to start is the free guide from the CSO (Central Statistical Office) entitled, Government Statistics: A Brief Guide to Sources. Vast amounts of data can be discovered from these sources, although as it has been stated throughout this section, it is imperative to know from the outset exactly what information is being sought, in order to avoid the possibility of wasting effort wading through mountains of irrelevant statistical data.

Audits

Retail audits record sales to consumers through a sample of retail outlets, usually at two monthly intervals. Though retail audits have existed for many years, the spread of EPOS (electronic point of sale) tills has greatly facilitated the task of data collection. Two companies, A C Nielsen and Retail Audits, are the most well-known in this field. They collect data of retail sales, typically goods sold through supermarkets or major retail chains, and sell the figures to anyone who wants to buy them. Both retailers and manufacturers find such detailed, up-to-date tracking of sales useful since it enables them to work out matters such as market shares, the performance of new products, the effect of a price change, a sales promotion or a new advertising campaign. It offers continuous monitoring of their performance in the market place.

Panels

Panels are groups of consumers who record their purchases, their media habits and/or attitudes in a regularly kept diary. The diary will be very easy to keep; usually it is simply a matter of ticking boxes. Companies such as Audits of Great Britain (AGB) have massive databases of panellists who complete such diaries. These are monitored in a similar way to the television viewing figures, with each purchase and so on meticulously logged. Once again, the growth in the use of information technology has assisted in the capture of such data, especially with the use of bar code readers which reduce the need to physically write down the full extent of a panel member's weekly purchases.

Activity

Select a product of your choice, preferably one which you yourself consume. Your task is to discover as many sources of information about this product as possible. You may find it useful to consult the staff at your local and/or college library to help you in this task. There may well be information immediately available in the form of the Industry Reports outlined above, but you should also seek out ways of contacting suppliers, distributors and consumers. Your do not need to list down names and addresses, but simply to discover the sources of this type of information.

Primary research

Once a researcher has obtained as much information as possible from secondary research, he or she should be aware of what information is still needed to satisfy the research brief. This is called the information gap. Any remaining information will be found, as far as possible (since the collected data can never be perfect), by primary research.

It has already been noted that it is not just the quantity of information which has been collected which is important, but also the quality of the information. It is always important to assess the relevance, accuracy, origin and purpose, format and age of the data sources used in providing the final report.

It is inevitable, given the problems involved in research have already been outlined, that the information will not be totally accurate. All necessary efforts, however, should be made to make sure that the data gathered is of an appropriate standard to the type of problem which is faced. Numerous methods of collecting primary data exist, and the following section considers a number of these.

There are two basic approaches which can be adopted when considering primary research. These are:

- observation;
- surveyi/Interrogation.

Observation

This method involves watching the way in which consumers perform, usually in response to some pre-arranged stimulus. This may be carried out by the use of hidden cameras or by a trained observer. This method is commonly used in the retailing industry for instance to monitor such things as:

- the manner in which customers move through a store;
- the way in which they respond to certain displays;
- the way in which they scan the shelf space. It is acknowledged that shelf space and shelf location are two of the most important selling points for in-store products, so it important to understand just exactly what catches the consumer's eye and where this occurs.

Survey/interrogation

As opposed to simply watching the behaviour of consumers, it is often preferable to ask them what they feel about certain aspects of the marketing mix. To do this, extensive surveys of buyer behaviour are carried out. To many people, this type of survey approach is what is thought of as being traditional research. Images of an interviewer with a clip-board standing in a shopping mall spring to most people's minds when asked to define the subject of research. Obviously there is a lot more to it than straightforward street surveys, and the following sections will consider a number of different approaches which can be adopted to surveying.

Survey methods

Surveys can be conducted either as:

- a census survey, gaining responses from all possible respondents in a population; or
- a sample survey, where a proportion of the overall population is selected to represent as accurately as possible the views of the total population.

In most marketing research situations, a census survey is virtually impossible to administer for reasons of cost or because of the geographical dispersion of the population. A sample would therefore be selected to represent the views of the total population. The various sampling techniques will be discussed later in this section. Once a sampling frame (or the number and type of people to be sampled) has been constructed, an appropriate survey method is selected to allow the data collection. Many survey methods are available to the researcher, and the following is a selection of the most widely used.

Personal interviews

Personal interviews may be highly structured, with the interviewer reading through a list of questions, often with a limited choice of set answers. This would lead to the collection of 'quantitative data'. These are data to which statistical techniques can be applied and from which specific conclusions can be drawn. For example, 20% of the target market finds new 'Washing Powder X' makes their whites whiter, or 47% of working women between the ages of twenty and thirty five and from social classes A, B and C1 do not believe that any brand of washing powder has significantly superior whitening capabilities than any other. On the other hand, personal interviews can be far less structured, with the interviewer working through the list of topics but allowing the respondents to develop their views as they wish. This kind of interviewing produces 'qualitative' information. The emphasis is on insight, attitudes, explanation and depth of understanding. Although of great value in helping the marketer to get closer to his customers, conclusions from such interviews are difficult to justify statistically and projections made from such information are less reliable.

There are a number of advantages of using personal interviews, including the following:

- much information can be obtained in great depth;
- the interviewer can explain exactly what is required – it is a two-way communication process;
- products, photographs or other stimuli can be used;
- the interviewer can also record observations;
- the interviewer can persuade people to agree to be questioned and relatively high response rates can usually be achieved.

There are, however, some disadvantages:

- they are usually expensive to administer;
- there is a danger of interviewer bias;
- some types of respondent may distort answers to please the interviewer or to avoid appearing foolish;
- some types of respondent, e.g. busy executives, are reluctant to agree to lengthy personal interviews.

Telephone interviews

Often used in business to business research and increasingly in consumer research, telephone interviews are quick and often very cost-effective. Telephone interviews must be short and to the point or the respondent may become irritated and discontinue the interview. In the USA, this type of approach for consumer research is very common, but many people in this country still resent the intrusion on their Sunday morning lie-in by a researcher seeking their views on a variety of kitchen or bathroom designs!

The main advantages of telephone interviews are as follows:

- two way communication, enabling explanations to be made where necessary;
- they are quick and cost-effective;
- national and international samples are possible;
- as it is easy to identify respondents they can be called again later if necessary;
- lack of eye contact reduces respondent embarrassment;
- the interviewer can key responses directly into a computer;
- response rates are quite high.

The main disadvantages of telephone surveys are:

- questions must be simple and total interview time short;
- they are restricted to respondents with telephones;
- they are suitable only for target markets where the vast majority of buyers are telephone subscribers;
- some people regard telephone surveys as an invasion of their privacy and refuse to participate.

Postal surveys

This involves mailing, or distributing door-to-door, a written questionnaire to a sample of buyers for their completion at home or at work. Questionnaires must then be collected or the respondent left to post it back. Two methods are being increasingly used in an effort to boost responses:

- firstly, an incentive may be offered to all respondents who complete and return the questionnaire. This may be a small incentive for which all respondents qualify, for instance a book token. This kind of incentive is popular in business to business research and is almost seen as recompense for the considerable amount of time that may be involved in the completion of some written questionnaires;
- alternatively, an attractive prize (such as a colour TV and video recorder) may be offered to the first completed questionnaire drawn out. This is popular for surveys requiring a large number of responses, usually in consumer markets.

The advantages of postal questionnaires are:

- they cost little;
- they lack any interviewer bias;
- total anonymity for respondents whose answers should thus be accurate;
- long, thought-provoking or complex questions can be asked to a suitable target audience;
- respondents, who are reluctant to agree to personal or telephone interviews, may be prepared to co-operate;
- diverse audiences can be reached.

The disadvantages of postal surveys are:

- questionnaires must be short unless sufficient incentive is offered;
- for many types of respondent the questions must be simple;
- without incentives, response rates are low;
- questions may be misinterpreted or missed;
- the meaning of questions cannot be explained;
- those who respond may not be typical of the whole sample.

The panel

This survey method involves the selection of a panel of customers and potential customers for the purpose of identifying their perceptions, attitudes and motivation towards a product or range of products. The panel usually numbers between eight and twelve and is recognised as an excellent technique of collecting qualitative data. Difficulties do arise with panels in formulating a group which truly represents the population. Group dynamics can also undermine the effectiveness of individual members and lead to an unrepresentative sample. The panel, however, remains a useful tool for recording attitudes towards products and examining closely the motivational forces behind them. It is essential, of course, that any such discussions – they are often referred to as focus groups – are chaired by a trained professional, otherwise the findings may be of a somewhat dubious nature.

Activity

You are required to design and implement a simple observation method of research. For example, you may decide to monitor the 'traffic' through a bank over a period of one hour, or to assess how many people purchase a particular brand of baked beans at your local supermarket over a given period. You will need to ask permission to carry out this task, and you should be as unobtrusive as possible. Collate the information which you gather, and write a very brief report outlining the findings.

Questionnaire design

Questionnaires are used to record and collate responses from the chosen population sample. Their careful design is crucial to the effectiveness of the research. A pilot study should always be carried out to ensure research objectives will be met. Any poorly structured questions or inappropriate questions can then be rewritten or removed from the questionnaire before the research is undertaken on a larger scale. Misleading questions or questions which influence responses should be avoided to help remove bias from the research.

Question types

There are four main types of question:

- open;
- closed;
- direct; and
- indirect.

Open questions

These allow respondents to express views openly and in their own words, for instance "Why do you visit this museum?" In the case of a postal or written questionnaire, the question may be phrased as "Write in the space provided below your reasons for visiting this museum."

Closed questions

This type of question seeks to elicit controlled responses through presenting optional answers to questions. For example, the question may read

"Have you visited this museum before ?   (please tick box)   ❏ *Yes*   ❏   *No.*"

Closed questions offering more than two alternative answers are termed multi-choice, for example:

How did you hear about this hotel ?(please tick whichever boxes are appropriate)

Through a travel agent	❏
Through a Tourist Board	❏
Personal recommendation	❏
Through television advertising	❏
Through press advertising	❏
Other (please specify)	_____

Direct questions

These seek to gain an exact, specific response. All of the examples given so far are direct questions.

Indirect questions

This type of question can be used in a personal interview to establish attitude and behaviour patterns from respondents. They use a series of seemingly general statements to establish a rationale for attitudes towards a specific subject. Indirect questions require great skill in their use and are often administered in conjunction with an unstructured questionnaire, that is a questionnaire with no particular order to the questions.

Most questionnaires employ direct open and closed questions for reasons of simplicity and efficiency of interviewer time.

Recording attitudes and opinions

Some tabular formats exist to help in the recording of attitudes and opinions. The best known of these are the Likert scale and the Semantic differential.

Likert scales

Respondents are asked to indicate the extent to which they agree or disagree with a series of statements. Usually, respondents are given a choice from five or six options on a scale ranging from "strongly agree" to "strongly disagree". The total of the responses are then correlated.

For example :

The Maxim Motor Company provides:	Value for money cars	A high level of customer care	A welcoming showroom
Strongly agree	☐	☐	☐
Tend to agree	☐	☐	☐
Neither agree or disagree	☐	☐	☐
Tend to disagree	☐	☐	☐
Strongly disagree	☐	☐	☐

Semantic differential scales

Respondents are asked to rate variables under consideration on a relative basis, usually using a seven point scale.

For example, tourists may see a table like this in a hotel questionnaire:

Please rate our hotel by circling the number which best reflects your experience under the following headings:

comfortable bedrooms	7	6	5	4	3	2	1	uncomfortable bedrooms
hygienic conditions	7	6	5	4	3	2	1	unhygienic and dirty
excellent food	7	6	5	4	3	2	1	poor food
hospitable staff	7	6	5	4	3	2	1	rude staff
good facilities	7	6	5	4	3	2	1	poor facilities
appropriate for families	7	6	5	4	3	2	1	inappropriate for families

This technique offers a simple way of collecting data as well as a flexible technique of analysing results since the data can be treated in a number of ways. For instance, each heading can be taken separately and compared with results from other hotels, or the total scores can be compared either with past performance or with other hotels. This would also provide management with a clear identification of the hotel's strengths and weaknesses.

Sampling techniques

As mentioned earlier, it is very rare that a true census survey can be undertaken due to the number of constraints placed upon researchers. It is therefore normal to select an appropriate sample which will reflect the parent population. Various methods of selecting a sample can be chosen, and the following section considers the more popular methods employed by researchers:

- simple random sampling;
- stratified random sampling;
- cluster sampling;
- quota samples.

Simple random sampling

Sometimes called probability sampling, the researcher starts with a complete list (the population or sample frame) of the market or group to be surveyed. He or she then determines the size of sample required and chooses the sample from the complete list on a random basis, which means that each individual in the sample frame has the same likelihood of ending up in the sample.

Stratified random sampling

Random sampling can sometimes distort results in markets where some customers are more important than others. In this case, stratified random sampling would be used. This involves the weighting of the sample on the basis of the importance of the various segments making up the market. Imagine that a company has 10,000 customers segmented as follows:

5000 light users accounting for £5m turnover;

3,000 medium users accounting for £20m turnover;

2,000 heavy users, accounting for £25m turnover.

A randomly chosen sample of 200 would not be fully representative of the company's business.

Heavy users account for half the turnover and they should also make up half the sample;

Medium users representing 40% of turnover should be 40% of the sample;

Light users, although half the population, make up only 10% of sales and should, therefore, form no more than 10% of the sample.

Thus the 'strata' of the stratified sample would be:

100 heavy users randomly chosen from the heavy user population of 2,000

80 medium users randomly chosen from the medium user population of 3,000

20 light users randomly chosen from the light user population of 5,000.

Cluster sampling

There is also third, less costly and very commonly used, way of producing random sample. Cluster sampling reduces the cost of the marketing research by concentrating the sampling in one or several representative areas.

Random samples are therefore often drawn from a small number of tightly defined locations (clusters) which are typical of the target market. This method is considered to be statistically accurate enough for most commercial market research.

Quota samples

Quota controlled samples are frequently used by commercial marketing research agencies to minimise the cost of fieldwork. The research agency initially uses secondary sources to divide the population into groups. In the case of the consumer research, these groups will often be social and/or age. The research agency then decides, on the basis of published statistics, on controlled quotas (or groups) of respondents for each interviewer in the field. For example, the interviewer might be told to question:

20 housewives aged 20 – 35;

15 housewives aged 36 – 50; and

25 housewives aged 51 and over.

Using this method the agency can be certain that the quotas are an accurate reflection of the total population.

There is no guarantee, however that the individuals within those age bands will represent an accurate sample of all housewives within that age band. The interviewer will simply question the first twenty housewives who agree to be interviewed in the twenty to thirty five year old age band. This method is very commonly employed in commercial research, simply because it is often considered to be the most cost-effective way of producing data of sufficient accuracy.

Sample size, as we have already mentioned, is determined according to the degree of accuracy required. The larger the sample, the more accurate will be the resulting data. However, it is useful to note that very few samples of a national nature exceed 20,000 respondents. Only a few exceed 15,000, while 2,000 is an average sample size for national research such as political opinion polls – although their recent records do not stand too close scrutiny! For small scale research perhaps 200 – 300 would be a satisfactory sample size, depending on the size of the total population and the purpose of the research.

Quantitative and qualitative data

As we mentioned earlier, data which has been collected can either be quantitative or qualitative in nature. As the two names suggest:

- quantitative data concerns statistical data or facts concerning, for example market share, demand forecasts, number of repeat customers;
- qualitative data concerns information which cannot be statistically analysed, for example attitudes, opinions and lifestyle data.

The former is far easier to analyse, particularly with the growth of high powered computer analysis packages. It should be obvious that when designing a questionnaire, you must pay attention to the need to analyse the final data, and because of this, questions will usually be designed in a particular way. More open questions, which we discussed above, which allow the respondent to provide his or her opinions and feelings in a more unstructured manner, are considerably more difficult to analyse but can provide invaluable information. Most organisations will therefore employ a combination of qualitative and quantitative research in carrying out their research projects.

Many organisations are still relying on instinct and poor data in looking to solve the complex marketing problems they face. The move to more globalised markets and the prediction of greater competition has increased the need for effective research and management of the collated information. As buyers become ever more sophisticated in their buying habits and in their changing demands, organisations must be in tune with the market place. The establishment of long term relationships with customers – the key to continued success – requires a strong and ongoing research commitment.

Activity

An important element of market research is, as has been described, Primary Research. This involves the researcher seeking information which is not available in any secondary or previously published format. As part of this activity, you should carry out a survey of the travel to and from either your college, school or workplace. Construct a very short questionnaire, containing no more than five questions, and ask a sample of about twenty people to complete it. The information should provide you with data which you can analyse to get a picture of the mode of travel, the distance people travel, and any other information you feel would be of interest.

When you have collected the data, analyse the information and produce a short report on your findings, including some conclusions. You should also analyse the problems you had when designing the questionnaire, obtaining the required sample and their responses, and any difficulties you had at the analysis stage.

Activity

When information is collected in numerical form, it is important to be able to both analyse it and present it in a manner which will be useful to the user of the data. This analysis will involve some calculations and also the presentation of the information in a graphical form.

A survey was recently carried out to discover what full time students studying on a GNVQ course spent their money on. The findings, for a month, were as follows:

Food	*£77.21*
Entertainment	*£72.12*
Travel	*£37.25*
Records/CD's	*£30.07*
Clothes	*£28.97*
Books	*£18.20*
Stationary	*£12.05*
Other items	*£4.13*

You are asked to analyse this data and to draw some valid conclusions about student lifestyle. You should also present the information in a graphical format which is easy to understand, using, if possible, an IT Spreadsheet/Graphics package.

Assignment *Boogaloo Cafe*

Andy Fitzpatrick recently graduated from Northlands University with a degree in Business Studies. Always an enterprising soul, Andy had supplemented his income during his time as a student by acting as a DJ in a local nightclub, Rossi's, and became so hooked on the entertainment business that he turned down a place on the IBM Management Trainee Programme to go into business himself.

His original idea was to create a 'continental style cafe' located within the Northlands City Centre, designed to appeal to both students and some of the more 'upmarket' locals. He wanted to provide something slightly different to the norm, something about which people would talk. Having become very friendly with the owner of the nightclub, Alesandro Meazzini, he broached the idea about a joint venture, with Alesandro providing the majority of the finance whilst Andy would take a share in the business in return for providing ideas and management skills.

Between the two of them, they managed to raise sufficient capital to secure a five-year lease on a property in the centre of the City. The Local Authority had granted outline planning permission to change the premises into an entertainment/dining venue, and an application for a drinks license had been lodged with confidence. The bank were impressed by their initial plans, and promised they would back the venture provided that more detailed research was carried out into the market potential. Andy and Alesandro were then left staring at a blank sheet of paper. They had the property secured, they had the money to fit out the building to whatever style they chose, but they were not sure exactly what that style should be.

Andy's initial dream had evolved from summer vacations abroad, travelling round many of the major capital cities of Europe. He had been impressed by the relatively small and intimate, but very lively venues where jazz music was played to diners who passed away the night. He liked the idea of featuring 'Continental newspapers' through which people could browse whilst drinking cappuchino and listening to live music. The aim was to create an atmosphere that would change with the time of day, open from breakfast until midnight, attracting a wide range of people. However, the detail was still to be finalised. What kind of decor should their be? What about food? Should it be the 'traditional pub grub' or something different? Should it be cheap and filling or expensive and elite? What about drinks? A 'normal' pub would attract the wrong type of clientele, but would students be willing to pay for expensive imported bottled lagers? What about the name? Andy had initially thought of the 'Boogaloo Cafe', but even this was open to suggestions.

Andy had been well taught, and knew the value of discovering consumer wants and needs prior to developing the final product. Being keen to repay his debt to the education system - and also spotting some cheap research - Andy approached the local College of Further Education and asked the Marketing Lecturer if her students would be interested in carrying out some research for him, as part of an assignment. The brief was simple - find out what people want from a venue like this.

Tasks

You have been asked by your lecturer to carry out this assignment. Initially, you are required to complete four different tasks:

1. Prepare a brief report on the various ways in which Andy could obtain the primary information which he is seeking, given the nature of the product and the target market.

2. Design a questionnaire which could be used as part of the research project to elicit what you believe is the appropriate information.

3. Describe and justify how you would select an appropriate sample of the target population for the questionnaire.

4. Prepare a brief paper which justifies the design of the questionnaire.

Element 3.2 Use consumer trends to forecast sales

Market Analysis

All markets are influenced by a wide range of variables. The phrase 'no man is an island' applies equally to the operations of all organisations. The success or failure of organisations is to some extent determined not by their own efforts but by the interaction of innumerable forces, some of which are completely beyond their control. The whole process of marketing planning is driven by information obtained on the environments within which an organisation operates.

Marketing Planning

Situation overview

All successful organisations make *plans*. The planning process is vital to ensure a measured and consistent approach to the development of any organisation. It allows the business to develop in a managed way, in an appropriate direction. Organisations who undertake any form of planning are more likely to be able to respond to changes in the future, and less likely to be taken by surprise when environmental factors alter. Just as all organisations which adopt the marketing philosophy should always be outward looking towards the consumer, so should they also be forward looking, in order to anticipate and manage changes in any of the multitude of variables which impact upon the successful running of a business.

Any successful and useful *marketing plan* must devolve from an overall *corporate plan*. Most large organisations, and many smaller ones, now adopt a strategic viewpoint, with a considered opinion being formed about future developments and the best manner in which to handle them. When looking to the future, it is vital to also consider the present. One method of assessing both the current and future situations is to use SWOT analysis. This is an analytical tool which allows organisations to consider its internal capabilities and also the external environment. The principle of a SWOT analysis is shown in the figure below.

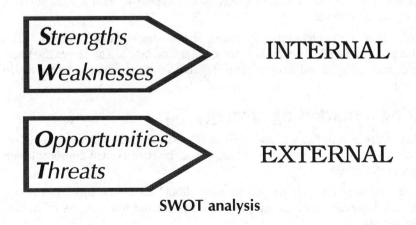

SWOT analysis

Strengths and weaknesses

An organisation can use *internal* analysis for numerous purposes. An *internal audit* will enable the organisation to identify its own particular strengths and weaknesses. For example, the organisation may have a particularly good reputation in a certain product area, built up over a number of years. Alternatively, it may have a particularly talented design team with a proven track record of success. Or, a business may find that its plans to expand are limited by financial resourcing problems, or perhaps regards its distribution system as being outdated and inefficient. All of these strengths and weaknesses should be carefully analysed to consider the impact they will have upon the future development of the organisation.

Opportunities and threats

This section of the SWOT analysis focuses upon the factors which are *external* to the organisation. For example, a competitor analysis may be undertaken to consider what their likely strategies may be. The identification of competitive advantage in competing organisations will offer a threat to an organisation, while any perceived competitor weaknesses will offer opportunities. Again all aspects of the external environment should be carefully analysed.

Essentially, the SWOT analysis is one way of providing the basic background for the setting of future marketing objectives. If an organisation discovers that a particular weakness is exposed to a strong threat – for example a poor design team faced by a competitor who is about to launch a revolutionary new product – then defensive action must be taken to protect the organisation against this threat. Alternatively, if a strength is matched to an opportunity – for example, a very strong personal sales team faced with an increase in the number of potential clients within an industry – then this will provide an opportunity ripe for exploitation.

Setting marketing objectives

The matching process should lead logically to a statement of *company objectives*. The objectives should be stated as precisely and in as much detail as possible, otherwise it will prove impossible for the business to monitor its progress towards achieving them.

For example, a publisher of diaries might decide to enter the growing personal organiser market. The objective might be to secure a firm foothold in that market, but it would be impossible to know when the objective had been achieved if it was stated in such a vague way. A better way of stating the objective would be to quantify it – for the business to say that it intends to gain a 20% share of the personal organiser market within two years.

Objectives can be quantified in *monetary or volume* terms. Interim targets might be set, against which progress can be monitored and, if necessary, remedial action taken. The larger the business, the more important it is to have detailed and unambiguous targets so that the whole workforce strives to achieve that common goal.

Formulating a marketing strategy

Having decided where it wants to go, and defined it accurately, the business has to decide how it is going to get there. Of course, a marketing strategy must be realistic and consistent with the strengths and weaknesses of the business.

As the figure on the next page shows, its strategy should cover the medium to long-term. It will concentrate on developments, such as the planned dates for the introduction of new products or the opening of new outlets.

1. STRATEGIC ASPECTS

   ..up to 10 years
   - Broad objectives
   - New products
   - New markets
   - New initiatives

2. TACTICAL ASPECTS

   ..less than 1 year
   - Short term activities
   - Doing it better than the competition
   - Adding value
   - Effective promotion
   - Marketing strategy and tactics

As the figure illustrates, tactical plans are to do with competing in the market-place, or 'doing it better than the competition'. Tactics are often focused on getting the customer to perceive the '*added value*' of their particular product and are often ways of effectively promoting the company's products in the market-place.

What makes companies successful?

Peters and Waterman in their book, *In Search of Excellence*, summarise this as '*being close to the customer*'. By this they mean that organisations must be willing and able to listen to the desires and wants of customers. They must have an effective market intelligence system which will allow them to provide the products which the market wants.

In order to survive in this kind of situation, all organisations need to carefully analyse their markets in order to fully understand and appreciate the kind of environment in which they are competing. They need to comprehend the internal environment, the external environment and, possibly most importantly, they need to understand their customers. Without this type of knowledge and appreciation, most organisations will be doomed from the outset. This section of the book will consider the whole area of environmental analysis, and will pay special attention to the role of consumer behaviour and segmentation in the marketing process.

Macro-environmental Analysis

The macro environment is that which is beyond the control of the organisation. It is probably the most difficult to predict, as the variables are many, varied and complex. However, all successful organisations must attempt to get as clear an understanding as possible of the factors which are likely to have an effect upon their future activities. It is wise to take a logical and ordered approach to considering the overall external environment, and one of the most common approaches is to use what is known as '*PEST*' or '*STEP*' analysis. The four types of environmental factor which are considered in this type of analysis are:

- social factors;
- technological factors;
- economic factors;
- political factors.

There are other factors which are important, but these four are generally believed to be of prime interest. The following sections will discuss ways in which these factors can be analysed.

The social environment

The social environment – demographic aspects

Demography is the study of populations, a subject of great interest to the marketer since people are the end result of most of his or her activities. Ultimately, marketers are interested in people buying their product or service in sufficient volumes to make business profitable. The demographic make-up of the population will help them to work out whether they are likely to achieve this objective.

There are five main demographic factors of interest to the marketer:

- population size;
- population growth;
- geographical distribution;
- age distribution;
- changing family patterns.

Organisations who are alert to the national demographic trends can respond accordingly in determining what steps to take. However we need to consider many other factors in shaping a marketing strategy.

Population size

The sheer size of the population may be more relevant to some products than to others. For luxury goods consumed only by a wealthy elite, total population size will be of little relevance, but will be much more important for basic goods which may be bought by a high percentage of the population.

Population growth

For basic products, strong population growth means an increasing potential market.

Geographical distribution

The marketer needs to know where the people are and whether the market is densely or sparsely populated. A densely populated market, such as Singapore, is easier and less costly to penetrate than a more sparsely populated market, such as exists in neighbouring Malaysia. In the United Kingdom, there has been a slow but continued migration of younger citizens from rural communities into urban areas. One impact on rural communities has been an increase in the average age of residents. This in turn has a major influence on the nature of the services offered in these areas. The trend of the 1980s was very much one of migration towards the South East of the country, although in recent years there has been a tendency for this trend to be somewhat reversed as many organisations relocated their headquarters away from the costly areas. All of these moves have an impact upon the successful operation of an organisation which is perhaps targeting a specific geographical location or region.

Age distribution

Since different age groups often buy various goods and services, the age distribution of the population is highly relevant to marketing planning. In the UK, a number of demographic trends are currently apparent. Since the birth rate fell from the mid-1960s, the youth market is declining. This will have adverse repercussions for companies which rely heavily on that market, for example, record companies selling pop records, publishers of teenage magazines and fashion shops. The next generation, the twenty five to forty five year olds, often known as the *baby boomers* (as they were born during the population boom of the 1950s and 60s) will be a large market. The other demographic group showing strong growth is retired people. In particular a new, younger, more affluent retired group is emerging, keen to spend money, especially on leisure. Activities, from gardening to foreign holidays, represent significant market opportunities here.

Advances in medical science have led to increased life expectancy and thus a declining death rate. The General Household survey forecast that the over fifty fives section of the population will be the only age group to grow in numbers by the year 2020. In responding to this demographic change, marketers must tune in to the needs and wants of what is fast becoming the biggest market opportunity for many organisations. Generally speaking, over fifty fives will be "empty nesters", in that their children will have left home to begin their own family. This has major implications for the marketer, as many new needs become apparent. Over one third of over fifty fives are dubbed *WOOPIES*, that is 'Well Off Older Persons'. These people have more discretionary income (money left over after tax, national insurance deductions and basic living expenses) available to spend on leisure activities. It should be noted that special care must be taken when targeting this group. Research into this market has shown that the emphasis on service must be increased, with courtesy and congeniality even more important in securing repeat custom. Above all, this group of people do not want to be labelled as 'old'!

Changing family patterns

The typical family is no more. Mr. and Mrs. Average, both in their first marriage with two kids, the husband at work and the wife at home, now represents less than 4% of all families. Divorces are increasingly common, as are single-parent families. Such trends mean that the number of households is increasing at a faster rate than the population. Thus, items such as fridges which are purchased by households rather than individuals have more potential sales growth than is apparent from the bare population statistics. The huge growth in the working women population has revolutionised many markets, the growth in convenience food and labour saving appliances being two of the more obvious examples.

It is also worth considering the changes in the ethnic population of the UK. There has been a major change in the ethnic population in post war times, with growing Asian and black communities. This has been an additional factor in the already rapid increase in the sophistication of customer needs. Markets are becoming more fragmented as a result of the many demographic changes described above. Mass markets have been broken down into micro-markets which have their own strong identities and characteristics. The media has become more differentiated in order to serve the needs of these micro-markets, which enables marketers to position products through careful media advertising campaigns. One only needs to browse through the magazine racks in a newsagent to see evidence of the existence of micro-markets.

The social environment - behavioural aspects

Marketing is a behavioural discipline. It is about people and the way people behave when purchasing goods and services.

Social trends

Any community will have a large variety of secondary cultural or social values. These may be attitudes, beliefs or trends which are less firmly adhered to than the core cultural values; indeed, they may be accepted only by certain sections of the community. Current examples in the UK would be physical fitness and healthy eating, both clear national trends, both followed more determinedly by some sections of society than by others, but both affording considerable marketing opportunities.

Aesthetic values

A marketer needs to know what a society rates as attractive and unattractive in terms of design, styling, fashion and colour. Early Japanese cars, for example, suffered in European markets because their styling was geared to American tastes. This resulted in a brash, chromy image from which they struggled to recover.

The technological environment

Technology is changing continuously and at an ever increasing rate. Think of just a few of the major inventions which have occurred in the twentieth century: electric lighting; radio; television; photocopying; X-rays; life support machines; synthetic fibres; plastics; electronic circuits; the computer. A business that does not keep up with technological advances will fail, sooner or later. As far as the technological environment is concerned, the marketer should be concerned with three main factors in his planning:

- new processes;
- new materials;
- generic replacements.

New processes

New ways of doing things are being constantly fuelled by technological innovation. One has only to think of cash dispensers outside banks, EPOS tills in supermarkets (the tills which record the price of each item simply by reading its bar code), flexible manufacturing systems which enable many of the operations involved in building a car to be performed automatically by robots. A business has to keep up with these changes. If it does not, and its competitors adopt them, it will soon become uncompetitive.

New materials

Carbon fibres, graphite, and kevlar are just three of the new high performance materials which have come to prominence in recent years. They are now widely used in the manufacture of sporting equipment from squash rackets to racing cars, from fishing rods to catamarans. Any manufacturer of high performance sporting goods who had not adapted to these new materials would find sales falling dramatically.

Generic replacements

A generic product is a product class. Coffee is a generic product, Nescafe is not: it is a particular brand of coffee. From time to time, a technological innovation will make a generic product (and obviously all the specific products within that class) obsolete. Cassette recorders took over from reel-to-reel tape recorders. Calculators made slide-rules obsolete. Drawing office equipment is gradually being replaced by computer aided design (CAD).

The American marketing professor, Theodore Levitt, has explained why this happens. Nobody, says Levitt, buys drills. Customers buy holes. It is not the drill itself which they value, but its hole making capabilities because it is the holes for which they have a need. If a new, more cost-effective method of making holes was developed (lasers, perhaps), customers would soon abandon traditional steel twist drills and turn to the new hole making method. If drill manufacturers could not supply the new hole makers, they would soon find themselves without a business. As Levitt says, *customers do not buy products, they buy the service which that product performs for them.*

The economic environment

The economic environment within a country will often be directly influenced by the political attitude of its government. However, national economies are becoming increasingly dependent upon world economic trends and marketers need to be alert to all economic factors which might influence their business.

In analysing investment potential in any particular country, the marketer will need to be aware of the following economic factors:

- income levels;

- inflation;
- purchasing power;
- distribution of Income.

Income levels

The most accurate measure of a country's wealth is its 'per capita income': that is, its national income divided by its population. This ratio gives a rough indication of that country's standard of living. A typical Gulf State might have a per capita income of around $20,000 per annum, whereas some African countries would struggle to exceed $100 per annum. Most western economies have per capita incomes of around $10,000 per annum, with the US in the lead and the UK lagging some way behind wealthier European countries, such as Switzerland, Germany, Sweden and Austria.

Inflation

Inflation erodes the purchasing power of the consumer. It causes severe problems for marketers who have to set prices accurately and estimate demand. At times of high inflation, people feel worse off. They may spend less or they may '*trade down*'. For example, it is possible that high UK inflation in the 1970s contributed to the move away from branded groceries towards cheaper '*own label*' products.

Purchasing power

There are two kinds of purchasing power in which marketers are interested:

1. *Disposable income*: This is the amount of money that people have left after deductions, such as tax and National Insurance contributions, have been made. This is more useful measure than per capita income, but may still not describe the amount of money people actually have to spend.

2. *Discretionary income* is a better indicator of spending power. It describes the amount of money people have left over to spend as they choose once they have made their essential expenditure on housing, food, basic clothing, etc.

Distribution of income

Marketers want to know how a country's wealth is distributed. For example, not only has Sweden a higher per capita income than the UK, but this income is much more evenly distributed. There are few very poor or very rich people and there is a very large, comfortable middle-income bracket. The UK's (lower) national income is distributed much less evenly, with a much larger population of poor people, a smaller middle class and a much larger percentage of rich people. Although there are several countries with a higher per capita income than the UK, the British market is, after the US and Germany, the third best market for BMW cars. Some very poor countries can be surprisingly good markets for luxury products because although the large majority of the population is very poor, the ruling elite is extremely wealthy. Some African countries, for example, are very good markets for Mercedes cars and malt whisky.

Political environment

There are three aspects of the political environment which can affect a company's ability to carry out its business:

- the attitude of the government towards business activity;
- legal controls on business activity;
- the influence of pressure groups.

Government's attitude towards business activity

Some countries are accused of 'economic nationalism', of over-protecting their own industries against foreign competition. In such countries the government's objective often appears to outsiders to be one of making life as difficult as possible for foreign business. This can lead to the kind of administrative harassment which makes it very difficult for a business to trade in that country.

An example is the Japanese insistence that Trebor Sherbet Lemons must be made in a more subdued yellow, not because the colouring poses a health hazard to consumers, but because of the colouring has a 'potentially harmful effect on the eyesight'. Trebor's sales to Japan run at only 250,000 per year and, given such problems, Trebor questions whether it is worth the effort - which is, perhaps, the effect the Japanese wish to achieve.

Legal controls on business activity

Legislation can affect business life. In the UK, the Sunday trading laws have made it difficult for many retailers who would like to open for business on Sundays to do so. Cigarette manufacturers have found their freedom to advertise progressively curtailed. Brewers and pubs have had to adjust to the effects of 'drink drive' legislation.

Alternatively, opportunities can arise from legislation. When the income tax regulations on company cars were changed, Ford saw the opportunity to introduce a new 1.4 litre engine to offer motorists the largest permissible engine size in the bottom tax band and a 1.8 litre engine to do the same in the middle tax band. New health and safety regulations present opportunities to makers of safety equipment which many businesses are obliged to use under the new laws.

Legal constraints do not have to be formal regulations. They may be unwritten 'gentlemen's agreements', such as the informal arrangement between the UK and Japan that imports of Japanese cars into the UK will be kept to 10% of new vehicle registrations. The opening of the Nissan factory in Sunderland and the manufacture of Honda cars in the UK, are two examples of Japanese companies reacting to their political environment and finding new ways to sell more cars in this country.

The influence of pressure groups

The influence of pressure groups can often lead to the introduction of the kind of legal constraints mentioned in the previous section. As mentioned previously ASH and other anti-smoking pressure groups were instrumental in bringing about the tightening of restrictions on TV advertising of cigarettes.

Many pressure groups are currently seeking to persuade governments to impose further legal constraints on business activities of various kinds. Ecological pressure groups, such as Greenpeace and Friends of the Earth, are trying to curb business activities that have adverse effects on our natural environment. Such groups favour the introduction of a 'carbon tax' on the use of all fuels that come from non-renewable sources.

Ecological pressure groups favour further regulations to reduce the lead content in petrol; the government has already responded by introducing tax advantages on lead free petrol, but the pressure groups see this as only a start since most petrol sold still contains lead. They would like to see the complete banning of CFCs and similar gases that are harmful to the ozone layer. Some companies, such as Johnsons, have already responded by investing in more expensive aerosol manufacturing plant to produce propellant gases that do not have this harmful effect.

Activity

When involved in any kind of predictions of future behaviour, it is important to consider the wider environmental variables which may affect that behaviour. One of the most important variables to be studied is that of government policy.

Over a period of two weeks, you are asked to study the 'quality' newspapers to monitor the actions of the Government. Select one particular action which the Government takes during that time period, and assess what impact it might have on the marketing plans for an organisation. The type of organisation which you select is not important. What is important is to choose a Government action which will have implications.

Micro-environmental Analysis

Whilst the influencing factors of the external macro environment may be beyond the control of the organisation, it is sometimes more easy to exert influence over the actors within the micro environment. This is particularly true of the internal organisation and operations of a business, but the micro-environment consists of many other variables of equal importance. These factors concern the organisational philosophy and capability, the organisation's suppliers, the customers, the competitors and the publics.

Organisational Factors

The initial factor which determines a market orientation is how the functions of marketing are adopted and used by an organisation. Many organisations have a classically organised marketing department with a marketing manager at its head and with staff alongside to carry responsibility for promotion, research, sales and new product development. The figure below illustrates the organisational situation which may exist in a manufacturing company.

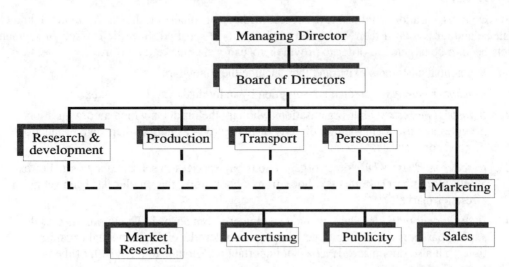

However, it should be pointed out that this type of organisational structure is not ideal. It was mentioned earlier that marketing is as much a philosophy as a functional area of an organisation's operation. As such, the marketing personnel need to play a pivotal co-ordinating role throughout the whole organisation, attempting to ensure that the operational plans of each functional department are in tune with the marketing strategy. The dotted lines show some of the lines of communication which will exist where the marketing department is fully co-ordinated with the other departments.

In the public sector, marketing is rarely represented by a classical marketing department, although the functional elements of marketing may be located somewhere within the departmental and committee structures. It is only recently that many public sector organisations are discovering the need to adopt a marketing orientation, and as such are attempting to allow the marketing philosophy to pervade throughout their organisations.

Research is often carried out by consultants who are employed by local authorities to offer advice and information covering a host of aspects of the service provision. Officers are often given the responsibility of liaising with consultants, reporting the findings to the relevant committee along with recommendations. Political factors as well as planning policy and financial considerations can play a big part in formulating the marketing strategy for the leisure department. Along with consultants, officers can utilise attendants and computerised information systems to collect useful research data on which marketing decisions can be based. Many local authorities now have a publicity department which deals with the more important newsworthy occurrences which crop up on a regular basis.

Suppliers

Any companies or individuals who supply resources needed by another can have a direct influence on the organisation's operation. The marketer must be aware of price changes for fuel, labour, equipment, building costs, raw materials and so on to enable future plans to remain relevant to the organisation's objectives. The marketing department itself is a purchaser of advertising, consultancy expertise, market research and perhaps staff training and must optimise its budget. In many organisations the Purchasing function is divorced from the Marketing function, but the communication links between the two must be strong – both formally and informally – if the marketing philosophy is to prevail and contribute towards the successful operation of the organisation.

Customers

Obviously no organisation will be able to succeed without customers or clients. An in-depth knowledge of their behaviour is vital if their wants and needs are to be satisfied. Specific markets or segments of markets need to be targeted in order to provide a focus for the marketing effort.

Numerous potential customers exist, and they include the following:

1. *Consumer markets*. Personal consumption by individuals and households;

2. *Industrial markets*. Other organisations who buy the products which an organisation provides and use them – either directly or indirectly – as part of their own production of goods or services;

3. *Reseller markets. Where* other organisations buy services to sell on at a profit. For example, if you purchase this text book from a book store, the retailer has been acting in a reseller market;

4. *International markets*. These include any buyers from abroad. The importance of the export market is considerable, not simply on a micro level for individual organisations, but also on a macro level as an important contributor to the health of the national economy.

Each customer market has particular features which can be identified through careful analysis. This marketing activity is known as *market segmentation*, and involves grouping target customers into manageable groups with some common strand, for example age, sex, geographical location and so on. This allows the marketing effort to be much more manageable and focused. The nature of customers and their behaviour is considered at length later in this section.

Competitors

The vast majority of organisations face competition of some kind. It is important when considering what the competition may be to carefully define the market in which the organisation is operating. A myopic approach to market definition – that is defining the market too narrowly – may result in the organisation being unaware of potential competition. For example, it could be argued that British Rail has no competition in its market – if that market is defined as rail transport of passengers and freight. This is clearly a mistaken view to take, as BR faces competition from all other providers of any type of transportation, and its marketing policies must reflect this in terms of their product development, pricing strategies, promotional policies and the like. Competitors have to be identified, monitored and bettered to maintain and develop a customer base.

To understand the nature of the competition, marketers must identify the different desires which customers will need to satisfy. If an individual needs to improve his health, he has a number of options, for example, exercise, diet, move home to a rural location, change job and so on. If the individual wishes to exercise, there is a whole range of activities to choose from, either formal such as squash, fitness training, and tennis, or informal such as jogging, walking and cycling. If the individual chooses fitness training, he or she then has to choose between a private club or a local sports centre. In seeking to compete strongly for this individual's business, a local authority run sports centre can offer a high standard of service in giving expert advice to customers on a training program, providing good facilities and equipment, and projecting an attractive image through the promotional campaign to that specific user group. Operating at the right price and providing the facilities in an accessible location will ensure effective positioning of the fitness training service in relation to the competition.

Publics

Any organisation must realise that a large number of *publics* take an interest in its activities. A *public* is defined as any identifiable group which has an interest in or an influence on the activities undertaken by a business organisation to achieve its objectives.

The term '*public relations*' should be seen as referring to a broad interface with such groups which seeks to gain some kind of favourable response from their members. The needs of identified publics must be analysed and specific packages offered to them to elicit responses of goodwill, donations of time or money, or positive mentions to friends and associates.

Examples of publics include :

- banks, insurance companies, building societies;
- newspapers, magazines, broadcast media companies;
- local publics such as clubs, local residents, schools and colleges - customers and non-customers;
- government departments, Councillors and Members of Parliament, development agencies such as Department of Trade and Industry, Department of Employment;
- internal publics such as shareholders, workforce, contractors.

The micro-environment produces pressures and influences on the relationships with customers, suppliers, and the competition, but an organisation must direct its effort into monitoring publics and understanding their needs and opinions to ensure overall success.

The following section will take one of the actors in this micro-environment – customers – and consider their behaviour in more detail.

Customer Behaviour

The previous two sections have described the environment within which marketing is carried out. The focus now will be more specifically on the *customer*. Much time and money is spent analysing customer behaviour through the application of complex market research techniques. The need to understand what makes a customer or potential customer 'tick' is fundamental to the success of any organisation.

There is a number of basic questions which are generally asked when consumer or customer behaviour is studied. The organisation wants to know the answers to:

- who?
- what?
- how? and
- when?

The following sections explore these fundamental questions, and reinforce the notion that knowledge of the consumer is vital.

Who are our customers?

Marketers want to know *who* their customers are and as much as possible about them as possible. A profile of customers can be built up with such facts as:

- age;
- sex;
- family circumstances;
- income;
- occupation;
- activities;
- interests and opinions;
- where they live;
- what sort of house they live in; and
- other factors concerning their lifestyle.

Marketers seek to divide the total buying population into *segments* so that sets of buyers can be differentiated according to their characteristics.

What do they buy ?

The reasons *why* people buy a product might come from any part of the marketing mix. Market share figures tell marketers which customers are attracted to which products and give some indication as to what it is that the customers are seeking to buy. Careful identification of customer needs helps an organisation to produce the closest possible match between what the customer wants to buy and what the company is selling to ensure a good chance of success.

How do they buy ?

This is particularly important as it seeks to identify trends and habits in *how* people buy products. For instance, customers may use an agent to purchase the product such as a ticket booking agent for the theatre or a travel agent for a foreign holiday. The growth in mail order selling enables some buyers to consider their purchase in the comfort of their own home before entering into an exchange through the postal service or by telephone.

When do they buy ?

Trends concerning *when* and how often people buy are of great importance to marketers and assist in planning the marketing effort to ensure products are available in the right quantities at the right time. The time of day or week is helpful and assists in deciding on perhaps opening times for retail outlets or leisure facilities. Many banks now open until 5pm and some open on Saturdays, as the banks' own research demonstrated that many customers were unable to use the facilities during limited daytime opening. The whole debate on Sunday Trading is considering this question, as the supporters of the movement argue that many people simply do not have the time during a busy working week to use retail facilities.

Seasonality factors affect many organisations and so longer term planning can account for predictable changes in the level of demand for services during, for example, the summer season or Christmas time.

Another aspect of this question concerns repeat business or customer loyalty. It is often said that long term relationships with customers are the marketers' goal. For this reason, knowing the proportion of repeat customers to new ones offers the organisation an insight into the successful positioning of a product.

The Buying Process

The basic stages involved in the buying decision making process are as follows:

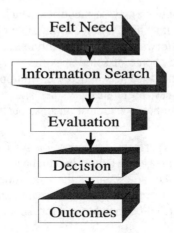

The purchase decision-making process

Felt need

Making a purchase is almost like solving a problem when it comes to the stages involved in deciding on which product to buy. Initially, the customer will experience a felt need which requires satisfaction. The need itself may arise out of internal stimuli or external stimuli. For example, you personally may decide that you need a new hairstyle, whilst an external stimulus may be the need to purchase a new suit to attend an important job interview. The nature of the felt need can range from basic needs such as food, heat or water to complex needs such as self esteem. People involved in marketing communications use these motivating factors in designing a more attractive message which will play on these needs and hopefully develop a need or a want into a purchase.

Information search

Having identified with a felt need, an individual has identified a problem. The next step in solving the problem is to carry out some research to identify the possible solutions. The individual may have encountered the problem before and may have stored an appropriate answer in his or her memory. If this is not the case, then other sources of information must be used. The search for information can take many forms, and may be as simple as asking a friend or reading some holiday brochures. Many organisations now attempt to provide as much information as possible to help in this search for information. For example, insurance brokers have computer databases which will provide a series of quotes for a particular circumstance from a range of companies. The role of information technology in improving the data available is continually increasing.

A further example of almost perfect information is the purchase of equities or shares. The Stock Exchange Automated Quotation computer (SEAQ) provides a continually updated list of all people and organisations wishing to sell shares. An individual wishing to purchase shares in, for example, ICI, would simply ask a Stock Broker to call up the information on a terminal, and would be able to see at a glance where the best price was available. This is perhaps an untypical example, as price would be the sole determining factor in this purchase, and the computer does not provide any assistance in the decision to actually purchase those type of shares. However, as communications technology improves at an ever increasing rate, the era of improved information for decision making is arriving.

Evaluation

In general, a number of possible solutions may be identified which would satisfy the felt need if they were selected – in fact the consumer may have a range of possible options. The evaluation process can be complex or it can be very straightforward, and will be influenced by a number of factors. The most important determining factor for the choice of solution is the person's culture. Human behaviour is mostly learned from family surroundings, society and key institutions such as schools and government. Children learn a basic set of prejudices, preferences, values and behaviour in this way. Much of the evaluation of product alternatives will be done almost unconsciously and some buyers will choose the same product for different reasons.

In many instances, the whole process is performed subconsciously. The decision to purchase a newspaper on the way to college in the morning may be an almost habitual act. A person may always read the same newspaper, always purchase it from the same shop, at the same time and so on. This can be contrasted with the decision to purchase a house. Here the information search and evaluation stages are much more lengthy and involved, and will be carried out much more formally.

Decision

The end result of evaluation is a decision to either purchase or not. If a purchase is made, there is inevitably some form of further evaluation which takes place. Most people have at some time in their lives bought things which they have regretted. This is called *post-purchase evaluation*, and will be a vital contributing factor to the decision whether or not to repurchase. This is the reason why so many organisations spend a lot of time and effort on after-sales service, as they realise that the marketing effort is not concluded at the point of purchase, but should be continuous. The growth in the belief in relationship marketing – where organisations attempt to establish long term relationships with their customers in order to encourage loyalty and repeat purchases – is testament to the continuity of the process.

Activity

You should have learned that consumer buying behaviour is influenced by a wide range of factors. Basic economic principles play a part in the buying process, insofar as price will inevitably influence any purchasing decision. However, there are many other factors which form part of the consumer judgement on actually making the purchase. One of the factors which retail outlets place great importance upon is the location of the products within the store.

All large supermarket chains take the science of positioning of products within a store very seriously. For this activity you are should visit two large supermarkets, such as ASDA, Sainsbury's or Tesco, and note which products are located near to the checkouts. Make a note of the products which are located in this area, and assess why the organisation has decided to place them there. Your answer should make a comparison between the two separate supermarkets you have visited, making reference to the differences and similarities in the organisation's placement decisions. You should try to relate your answer to the consumer buying process, and analyse exactly what influence the retail outlet believes that placing those products in that particular part of the store will have on buyers' decisions.

Segmentation

Market segments are groups of customers in a market who have something in common. The criteria by which marketers distinguish between segments is all important. A market can be segmented in a number of ways, but it is a useless exercise for the marketer to use an irrelevant criterion. For example, a college which segments its potential target market on the basis of hair colour would not be able to derive a particularly effective targeting strategy. The chosen criteria must be relevant to the behaviour of customers in markets so that the differing needs and wants of the market segments can be identified and targeted.

Criteria for segmentation

There are many different criteria available to the marketer for segmenting a market. More than one criteria can be used to identify segments more clearly. Obviously, the more variables which are used, the smaller will become the segments. It is possible for example to segment on sufficient criteria to allow each individual consumer to be a segment of one. This, however, would not be the wisest of decisions, as segments need to be both manageable and viable enough to justify the marketing expenditure and effort. The following are the types of segmentation which are commonly used in consumer goods industries:

- demographic segmentation;
- geographic segmentation;
- benefit segmentation;
- behaviour segmentation;
- geo-Demographic segmentation;
- lifestyle segmentation.

Demographic segmentation

Age, sex and income are three widely used criteria. The appropriateness of these criteria should be fairly self evident. For example, the location of a new night-club may be influenced by the age distribution of the local population. The attractions which are staged may be influenced by the sex breakdown, and the product itself, pricing and promotional efforts will perhaps reflect the distribution of income.

Social class is also commonly used as a demographic segmentation variable, in particular the method used by the National Readership Survey which breaks the UK population into the following six bands:

A: *Upper middle class*. Forming 3% of the population and consisting mainly of wealthy business or professional persons.

B: *Middle class*. Covering 10% of the population and defined as intermediate managerial and professional occupations.

C1: *Lower middle class*. 24% of the population represented by workers from supervisory, clerical and junior management jobs.

C2: *Skilled working class*. Often can be high wage earners but tend to be lower educational achievers, representing the largest percentage (30%) of the population and covering jobs such as printers, plumbers, electricians.

D: *Manual workers, semi-skilled and unskilled workers*.

E: *Members of the population at the lowest level of subsistence including OAP's, the unemployed*.

The NRS method is much criticised as being out of date in a fast changing society where many purchases are made outside of the bands described above. It is said that we are moving towards a classless society, and that this type of segmentation is no longer appropriate. For example, the classifications only account for female workers in a household where the male is out of work. However, in spite of these criticisms, this method is still very widely used. Any attempt to purchase advertising space from television stations or other media will be greeted by large amounts of detail on the socio-economic classifications of viewers, readers or listeners, and organisations still avidly consume such information.

Family life cycle is another demographic technique. Some versions of this method identify nine different life cycle stages which serve as market segments. At each stage, lifestyle is dictated by the level of family development which gives a clear insight into the behaviour patterns of members of each group.

The nine groups can be described as follows:

I.   *Bachelor stage* young single people not living at home;

II.   *Newly married couples* young, no children;

III. *Full nest I* youngest child under six;

IV.   *Full nest II* youngest child over six;

V.   *Full nest III* older married couples with dependent children;

VI.   *Empty nest I* older married couples, no children living with them, head of household still working;

VII. *Empty nest II* as VI but head of family retired;

VIII *Solitary survivor in the labour force*;

IX.   *Solitary survivor retired*.

Organisations such as mail order companies use family life cycle segmentation to track the purchases made by their clients over their lifetimes. At specific points through their lives, the mail order customers will be targeted with special promotions appropriate to the life cycle position. All of the information on purchases is stored in massive consumer databases, allowing a very accurate assessment to be made of each consumers life cycle stage.

Geographic segmentation

The analysis of consumption patterns on a regional or local basis can often help to target marketing communications and product offerings very successfully. The analysis of a *catchment area* and the *spatial distribution* of customers can assist the marketer in formulating future marketing plans. For example, large producers of Fast Moving Consumer Goods (FMCG's) such as Procter and Gamble use sophisticated computerised geographic segmentation techniques to decide on the centres of population. Large retailers will obviously seek to locate where the optimum catchment areas exist.

Benefit segmentation

Some markets can be segmented on the basis of the *benefit* sought by customers. For example, the range of courses provided by colleges may be segmented according to the benefits which they offer. Some potential students are seeking qualifications for future employment, others a route into higher education, whilst others may simply be fulfilling an interest in a particular subject. The way in which a GNVQ course in business and a recreational course in flower arranging are marketed are significantly different, as the potential customers view the benefits of the course from very different perspectives.

Behaviour segmentation

Frequency of purchase is another common method of segmentation. The way in which regular customers are treated by organisations may differ from that of irregular customers. There is an obvious debate as to who should receive 'more attention', but it is sufficient to state at this point that their treatment can differ substantially.

Geo-Demographic segmentation

One of the most successful and relatively new methods of segmentation combines the principles of demographic and geographic techniques. The most well known of these techniques is ACORN which stands for "*A Classification Of Residential Neighbourhoods*". ACORN is based on detailed census data (originally from the 1971 census) and classifies households according to the neighbourhood in which they are found. Residents from similar types of neighbourhood are found to have similar demographic characteristics such as age, social class, race and purchasing behaviour. Over forty different variables are contained in the ACORN analysis. More recently ACORN has been linked with over one million post codes to provide an extremely detailed classification for each of the small residential units covered by individual postcodes. Thirty eight neighbourhood types were identified which have since been consolidated into eleven ACORN types now in common use.

Computer systems are now able to link ACORN with postcodes and mailing lists or customer data bases, to provide the marketer with an extremely powerful targeting tool. ACORN is criticised along with other geo-demographic techniques as a predictive tool since the variables for determining consumer behaviour are vast. However geo-demographic techniques are developing as technological innovations, particularly in telecommunications, open up new opportunities for application. The rapid growth in targeted direct mail promotions in this country is largely a result of the improvement of these segmentation techniques. The Post Office offers – at a price – its own *Consumer Location System* (CLS). This combines the ACORN information with a number of other databases, and is argued by the Post Office to provide the most accurate segmentation and targeting information available.

Lifestyle segmentation

This technique covers people's day to day habits, values and attitudes, leisure interests and work patterns. Often referred to as '*psychographics*' the lifestyle concept is best used when applied to a specific brand marketed by a company. While lifestyle models have been extensively used, they remain limited when used in a general context.

The market research company, Taylor Nelson, has been operating continuous research in this field since the early 1970s. The company's applied futures unit identified three broad social value groups ;

- the *outer directed* groups;
- the *inner directed* groups; and
- the *sustenance driven* groups.

From these groups, a further seven social value segments have been identified :

1. *Self explorers*. Motivated by self expression and self realisation – 16% of the population;
2. *Social resistors*. The caring group concerned with fairness and social values, often appearing intolerant and moralistic – 11%;
3. *Experimentalists*. Highly individualistic, motivated by fast moving enjoyment, materialistic and pro-technology – 14%;
4. *Conspicuous consumers*. Materialistic and pushy, motivated by acquisition, competition and getting ahead. Pro-authority and law and order – 19% of the population;
5. *Belongers*. Seek a quiet family life are conservative and rule followers – 18%;
6. *Survivors*. Strongly class-conscious and community spirited – 16% of the population;
7. *Aimless*. Live from day to day and comprising young unemployed and the old – 5% of the population;

The growth during the 1980s of the use of acronyms for lifestyles was started by the YUPPYs with their characteristic filofaxes, red braces and Porsches. Other categories which are still used: DINK's (Double income/no kids) OIK's (one income/kids) and the WOOPies mentioned earlier in this section. The collapse of the affluent lifestyles of the 1980s did lead to certain acronyms being attached to those who were suffering the effects of the recession, such as BOBO's (burnt out but opulent) and LOMBARD's – the description of which you will have to discover yourselves!

Each of the segmentation methods described above have their good and bad points, but none are individually powerful enough as marketing tools. The segmentation criteria chosen by marketers must be relevant to the context within which they are working. Quite often we find that demographic segmentation is used alongside geographic criteria as a simple but powerful form of segmentation analysis. The National Garden Festival series has been seen to adopt this approach in helping to design and plan each festival and then monitor visitor profiles and target promotion. For example, the Gateshead Garden Festival marketing team identified the need for over one hundred different advertisements to be targeted through different media to different market segments, such as female visitors between the ages of thirty five and forty five, with young children, travelling from within a seventy mile radius. Each segment was carefully picked off with a promotional campaign aimed specifically at those specific consumers.

This section has considered a range of issues in terms of the environment in which organisations operate and the behaviour of the consumers within markets. The final section will bring together the theory of the marketing mix and demonstrate how all of the information which has been gained can be used to provide a successful marketing campaign.

Assignment *Lightning Trainers*

In 1977, Lightning Trainers was established with the help of various Central Government and Local Authority grants in the depressed area of South West England. The brainchild of two former tin miners - Derek Watson and Steve Storey - the company had grown from very humble beginnings to have a turnover of almost £10m per annum. The company were contesting in a very competitive market of sports and leisure footwear which was essentially dominated by the massive brands such as Nike, Reebok and Adidas. The company positioned themselves at the lower end of the price and quality ranges, as they believed that they did not have the financial presence to compete with the multinationals. However, it was becoming more and more evident that in order to survive, let alone expand, the company would have to move more and more into the 'fashion' market of leisure shoes. They will need to produce a more expensive, probably a 'branded product', which will appeal to a certain type of consumer.

Having had no formal business education, and employing only three people in the Marketing Department, the pair decided to call in some consultants to advise them as to their future. You are acting in the role of a Marketing Consultant employed by Maximillian's Marketing Company (MMC), and have been asked to advise Derek and Steve on certain aspects of their future development. Your own particular expertise is in considering the segmentation of markets and the external factors which can affect the demand for products.

Tasks

Your brief is very wide, and will serve not only to provide relevant information for Derek and Steve but also to assist in their marketing education. They have asked for advice in two specific areas:

1. The segmentation process involved in marketing
2. The role of external factors in the industry.

Your task is to provide a report which satisfactorily covers these two areas. Your aim should be to attempt to explain the basic principles behind the two concepts, and then to illustrate their applications by using the Leisure Footwear industry as an example. As such, you will need to consider the variables which might be used when segmenting this particular market and the macroenvironmental factors likely to influence demand. You are asked to pay particular attention to any likely changes in these variables and factors, as the information is to be used as the basis for an estimation of future levels of demand.

Element 3.3 Investigate Marketing Activities

The Nature and Purpose of Marketing

This Unit has so far concentrated mainly on exploring the issues connected with the background research which goes into preparing an organisation for its commercial activities. This final element will develop these themes and introduce the specific marketing activities themselves. It will demonstrate why such activities may be undertaken, how they can be undertaken in a variety of situations, and also examine some of the moral and ethical issues which can arise when considering the overall nature and role of marketing.

It is useful to commence this element with a reconsideration of the nature of the functions of marketing and then to consider the objectives behind such functions.

The functions of marketing

It is generally accepted that, in terms of organisations, marketing involves five main functions, namely:

1. market research into needs/wants, the environment and so on;
2. producing the correct product;
3. promoting the product;
4. distributing the product;
5. pricing the product.

The first of these functions has been covered in the opening two Elements of this chapter. The latter four are usually grouped together as the *'Four 4 P's'* of marketing, or 'the Marketing Mix'. The marketing mix is the set of controllable variables which is selected by a marketer in order to achieve certain predetermined objectives. These specific objectives will be discussed below.

Each element of the Marketing Mix contains a wide range of decisions. For example:

- *Product.* This would include decisions on areas such as quality, options of colour or size, packaging, and guarantees.
- *Place.* Decisions in this area would include geographical coverage, location, inventory and transport.
- *Price.* Topics to be considered under this heading would include the overall price level, discounts, range, seasonality, and credit terms.
- *Promotion.* This area of decision making would include discussion on matters such as advertising, personal selling, publicity, sales promotion and direct marketing.

The above is by no means an exhaustive list, and each of the elements of the marketing mix will be explored in more detail later in this element.

It should be remembered that the marketer has at his or her disposal a vast range of marketing tools, some or all of which can be used to achieve an efficient allocation of resources and a maximum satisfaction of customer needs. The art of marketing is to achieve the optimum balance when allocating resources between each of the competing needs of the mix elements.

The Objectives of Marketing Activities

The balance of the mix of marketing elements will be determined by a whole range of factors, but overall by the objective which the organisation is seeking to fulfil. The overall objective is obviously to identify a group of potential customers with an unsatisfied need which will be met by the business. These needs are identified by the research process we discussed earlier, considering the broad factors of the environment in which the organisation is operating and moving on to a narrow analysis of the needs of individual consumers. This process will involve the segmentation of markets into smaller, more manageable pieces, and the targeting of the marketing effort towards one or more of these specified segments. Once an unsatisfied or poorly satisfied need is identified, the organisation is in a position to implement its main marketing activities.

This is the stage at which the marketer moves away from the planning phase into the implementation of *marketing strategies* and *tactics*. To compete successfully in the market segment, a business must meet customers' needs more closely than they are being met by any other supplier. Meeting customers' needs involves more than just selling them a suitable product. It involves 'giving them what they want', in the broadest sense of the phrase. Sir John Egan, past Chairman of Jaguar, expressed it in this way:

> *"Business is about making money from satisfied customers. Without satisfied customers there can be no future for any commercial organisation."*

Customers usually want to satisfy a number of needs when they purchase a product. Very often these needs are fairly clear and relate almost entirely to the product itself. For example, when people buy table salt, they want it to be dry, fine, white, free-flowing and salty. But is that all they want? Surely, they want also to buy it in a suitable container which will keep it dry and free-flowing and with a hole of the right size in the top? In other words, customers are also interested in the packaging. Is that it? Not really, because as with most buyers of most products, they certainly do not want to pay more than a reasonable price for it. Anything else? Yes, because, ideally, they do not want to be put to too much inconvenience when they have to buy salt. Having to travel to a specialist salt shop on the edge of town, or to send away to the Salt Mail Order Co. Ltd., would be rather inconvenient. Most people would much prefer to be able to buy salt at no extra inconvenience at the same time and in the same place as they buy their other groceries. In other words, customers are interested in the *availability* and *accessibility of the product*.

The specific objectives of the marketing mix activities are, as already mentioned, many and varied. They will be influenced by a range of factors, including the product itself, the state of competition within the market, the nature, type and numbers of consumers, and the whole operating environment of the organisation. The next section considers some of the main objectives which organisations seek to fulfil.

Increase sales

This may appear to be the most obvious of the objectives for all commercial organisations. No organisation can survive without ensuring an adequate level of sales in order to cover its costs and provide an element if profit for the stakeholders of the business. Most organisations will constantly seek to increase their overall level of sales in order to boost profitability. It can be seen, however, from other sections of this book that not all organisations are driven by the 'profit maximisation' motive, and as such not all organisations are constantly seeking to increase their level of sales. Indeed, organisations which grow too rapidly can often end up in as much financial trouble as those which do not grow at all, due to problems of managing the rapid expansion and overtrading without sufficient working capital. For the vast majority of organisations, however, the objective of increasing sales would still appear to be a prime consideration when implementing marketing activities.

Increase market share

The level of market share held is an important driving force for many organisations. Some academic and business research suggests that organisations can only compete successfully in markets in which they are dominant, that is they are the market leaders. While this may be true in some instances, it is certainly not the case in all markets, otherwise all market structures would rapidly become monopolies. Indeed, some companies actually take some advantage from not being the market leader. For example, Avis is regarded as being the second largest car hire company in the world, behind Hertz. Part of its promotional message, however, is a claim that 'when you are second, you have to try a little bit harder', implying that their level of service is better than that of their main rival, who they suggest may actually be somewhat complacent. Whether this attitude would change should they become market leader is a matter of some conjecture!

Quite often, in a fiercely competitive market, the objective may be a variation on this theme, namely to simply maintain the level of market share currently held by the organisation. This is sometimes referred to as *maintenance marketing*, and involves the company attempting to ensure loyalty within its own customer base, whilst attempting to poach other custom from rivals to counterbalance any outflow from its own ranks of customers.

One illustration of this type of practice in action is under conditions of competitive oligopoly. The competitors may all be reasonably satisfied with their level of market share, until one undertakes an aggressive marketing campaign to boost penetration, for example by a reduction in prices. Almost inevitably, this will result in retaliatory action by the rest of the market, and market share levels will generally return to their pre-competitive state, but all organisations will be left with lower profit levels.

Enhancement of product or corporate image

On many occasions, marketing activities are undertaken not simply to increase immediate level of sales but in order to put across some other type of message to the market. One such example is where an organisation attempts to enhance the image of either its product or the organisation as a whole in the eyes of the consumer. This is frequently done using various promotional tools, for example product endorsement or sponsorship. Beamish Stout sponsored some of the series of the successful TV detective series, *Inspector Morse*, and as a result the level of awareness and consumer perception of its product rose substantially. Morse was perceived as being a reasonably high quality TV programme, and this quality rubbed off on consumers' perceptions of Beamish Stout.

Of course the reverse can also be true. An often cited example is National Power's sponsorship of the World Cup coverage in Italy in 1990, when following a defeat for one of the British teams, a commentator made the quote, "this night of disaster was brought to you by National Power". Similarly, the Grand National was sponsored for the first time in 1993 by Martell Cognac. Most people who watched the 'race' will be aware of the problems which arose and subsequent declaration of the race as being void. Such external events are obviously beyond the control of the sponsor, but they do serve to highlight just one of the risks associated with the objective of image enhancement.

Many of the large companies run campaigns aimed solely at raising their company profile or image. BP ran a very successful promotional campaign which featured a young man in the middle of Africa studying to become a doctor, who appeared to be having difficulty when the sun went down. However, the 'hook' to the advertising campaign was that electricity had been provided to the village by a BP-funded project, and so the young man was able to continue his studies. The aim of this high profile campaign was not to directly sell more petrol through BP filling stations in the UK, but to raise the image of the company as a whole. Obviously, the company hoped that this would ultimately result in an increase in sales, but this was not the immediate short term objective.

Activity

A major part of any marketing mix decision is the way in which an organisation communicates its message to the potential consumer. One of the most important ways in which this is done is by using visual media, such as TV or Magazine adverts, company logos or corporate brochures. Each visual image which is issued by an establishment should attempt to say something about the organisation or the products or services which it provides.

For this activity you are asked to take six visual images which have been issued by an organisation. These can be advertisements, company literature, or any other type of image which you may consider appropriate. When you have collected these images, you should consider exactly what message the organisation is attempting to convey to the consumer. For example, the image may be one of quality or of fun. When you have decided what the message is meant to be, you should assess whether or not the image performs its function, or whether there are any barriers to communication which exist, for example a confusing image which might convey the wrong message, or the location of a particular advertisement in a magazine which does not suit the product or the organisation.

Quality assurance

A further objective of marketing activities which is not directly related to immediate increases in sales is the aim of reassuring consumers about the quality of a particular product. This can be done in a variety of ways, including the use of pricing and distribution policies. The area of pricing, as will be seen later in this section, involves a great deal of psychology. Consumers generally perceive more expensive products to have higher quality, and as such the setting of a higher price should be part of the marketing mix to ensure a quality position. Similarly, products which are distributed only through exclusive outlets will also attract a perceived quality which is not available to those which are intensively distributed. This serves to illustrate the golden rule that all elements of the marketing mix need to be consistent with each other in order to achieve the required position for the product within a given target market segment.

The above section on objectives is meant to provide only a flavour of the types of goals which organisations set when determining their allocation of resources between the various marketing mix elements. The following sections discuss each of the 'Four P's' individually in more detail, but it is important to remember that each cannot be dealt with separately in practice. Coherence and consistency of approach are vital to the success of all marketing activities.

Product

Providing that the market research has been carried out professionally and successfully, the organisation should be in good position to clearly identify the needs and wants of current and potential consumers. It can be argued that the first element of the marketing mix – product – is the most important. A high quality, well designed product may sell well even with poor marketing communication or distribution networks to support it. With the wrong product, all of the other marketing activities become totally useless. It may be possible to convince consumers in the short terms to purchase the wrong product, perhaps by very persuasive advertising or hard sales techniques, but no business is going to survive without being able to 'deliver the goods'.

Analysing products

A product is basically anything which an organisation sells. The product does not have to be physical, it can also be service. The most important point to remember is that people buy to satisfy needs. A person who buys a drill does not buy the drill for its own intrinsic value, but for the holes it will produce. IBM claim not to sell computers but solutions to business problems. One make-up supplier states that they do not sell 'cosmetics', but 'hope'!

Philip Kotler has developed an all-embracing definition of a product. According to him a product is:

> *Anything that can be offered to a market for attention, acquisition or consumption that might satisfy a want or a need. It includes physical objects, services, persons, places, or-ganisations and ideas.*

Theodore Levitt provided a four stage model for analysing products, referred to as the "total product concept".

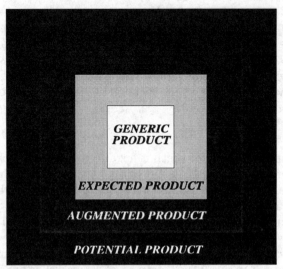

The total product concept

The generic product

The starting point for analysing products is in identifying the *'generic'* product or the *'type'* of product with which we are dealing. Generic products were traditionally available in grocers' stores, without any packaging or branding attached. Products such as tea, butter, flour and sugar were all available as generic products. These days most products are branded, and as such cannot be treated as 'commodities', although there has been a definite comeback in recent years in the popularity of generic products with unbranded products in supermarkets and the growth in popularity of health food stores.

This first level is concerned with identifying the *core benefit* sought by customers. For example, if the need which is to be satisfied is travel from home to college, then there is a range of ways of satisfying that core need. For example, one could walk, cycle, ride a horse, drive, take a bus and so on. Each of these generic products would satisfy the core need of transport. A further example would be the purchase of a portable radio/cassette. The core benefit in this instance is the ability to receive radio transmissions and listen to music.

The expected product

When people buy a radio/cassette, however, they don't just want any old box which will pick up broadcasts and produce a sound vaguely reminiscent of music. They expect additional things from a radio/cassette player. They expect a certain quality of sound; they expect stereo; they expect an FM wave band; they expect the controls to look sophisticated; they expect the choice of battery or mains operation and they expect it to be very, very loud!

These requirements are the *expected* product, and very quickly become the norm or the generic product. As such, any organisation wishing to compete at even the lowest levels of markets must conform with these minimum expectation levels. An example of environmental pressure leading to changes in the expected product is that of aerosol sprays. As a result of the much publicised damage to the environment caused by the use of CFC's in such sprays, virtually all manufacturers now proudly proclaim their products to be 'CFC Free' or 'Ozone Friendly'. A new entrant to the market who did not confirm to this expected product level would have no chance whatsoever of success.

Technology is the other major reason for changes in expectation levels. If one considers what is regarded as basic on a car of the 1990s compared to what was offered as standard a decade ago, the evidence of technological development and its influence on consumer expectations is plain to see. What were once regarded as optional extras are now regarded as essential requirements to even the most basic models.

The augmented product

In order to gain an advantage over their competitors, suppliers always try to offer something over and above the expected product, since it may be that something extra which clinches the sale over a rival product. This is the concept of gaining competitive advantage via product design. Occasionally, the *augmentation* may be physical, for instance by the addition of a new feature or use. Often, however, the process is more subtle, and involves adding a range of benefits, over and beyond the core benefit. Examples would include the level of quality or the packaging of the product, or any after sales service which was provided. An illustration of such augmentations is shown in the diagram. In conclusion. it should be noted that today's augmented product becomes tomorrow's expected product. To overcome this problem, and to keep ahead of the competition, the marketer has to move to the potential product.

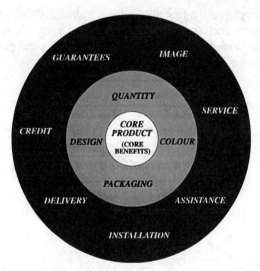

The Concept of the Augmented Product

The potential product

According to Levitt, the potential product includes 'everything that might be done to attract and hold customers'. Even for the most basic and mature of products, alert marketers can discover new ways of making their product more attractive to buyers. A good example is steel, a very mature product which one would expect to be very difficult to distinguish from its competitors. This, however, is not the case. In the 1980s, suppliers of steel used the concept of the *potential product* to offer new and valuable benefits to buyers. For example, Swedish steel maker Avesta AB developed an 'improved machinability steel', which is actually easier to drill than normal stainless steel, so causing less wear and tear to very expensive tools – a significant benefit to buyers. BSC Stainless in Sheffield now offers stainless steel sheet with a range of patterned finishes, which is opening up new uses for the material, such as exterior cladding for buildings. They have added real value to their product in the eyes of suppliers. It is the role of marketing management to identify the best ways to add value, and, according to Levitt, the most successful companies in many markets are the ones whose marketing departments are most thorough in their identification of the potential product. If you sell soap, beer, banking services, fast food or any competitive product, you have constantly to look forward towards the potential product.

The product range

Products are continuously evolving to meet ever-changing market needs. The potential product becomes the augmented product, which in turn becomes the expected product. Companies dependent on one product, or a very restricted range of products, are always in a vulnerable position in today's rapidly changing environment. For example, it is likely that a leisure provider is offering the market place *a range of products*. For example, a large city centre hotel will offer not only accommodation but also leisure facilities, catering, banqueting, restaurant and bar facilities. A swimming pool will offer club membership and coaching, public swimming sessions, school use, saunas, sunbeds and perhaps beauty therapy. As most industries are still growing and experiencing rapid change and turbulence, the products within a range must be monitored and managed carefully to ensure that dying products are replaced with new ones at the appropriate times.

The product life cycle

It is thought by most marketing theorists that all products eventually die, although some such as Heinz baked beans show little sign of decline. The vast majority of products experience a period of rapid growth shortly after their launch, followed by a levelling off in sales and eventual decline. The diagram below shows the life cycle curve for a typical product.

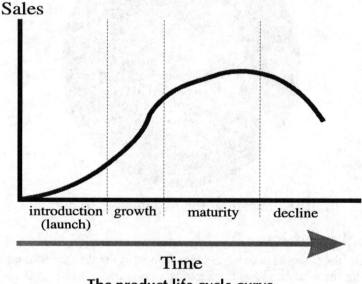

The product life cycle curve

It is also widely accepted that all products follow a different life cycle pattern and that it is difficult to predict the arrival of the next stage for some products. Although it is widely accepted that all products do follow a life cycle, the exact pattern and duration of the life cycle will differ for each product. The generic product, bread, is at the mature stage of an extremely long life cycle, but if you look at specific bread products you will see that the branded white sliced loaf, which underwent rapid growth after the Second World War and was at its mature stage in the 1960s and most of the 1970s, has now been in decline for several years. It has suffered from the move away from highly processed food towards more healthy, traditional, high-fibre diets. Many of these high-fibre, unsliced, bread products are currently at the growth stage of their life cycle.

Thus the *time horizon*, represented by the horizontal axis on the graph is of indeterminate length, as are the sales figures represented by the vertical axis. The shape of the curve will also vary. Some products may have a longer, flatter curve if their peak in sales follows very gradual growth over a long period of time. Other products typically exhibit much more rapid growth, and some an equally rapid decline. Examples of such product life cycle curves are shown in the following two graphs. The first graph shows a typical 'fashion' product life cycle. Most items of clothing now come into this category with two buying seasons per annum. Sales rise quickly each autumn for the winter fashions, followed by a short mature stage and an equally quick decline. By the end of the January sales very little additional business is done with the winter fashions, which is why summer clothes can appear in the shops whilst there is still snow on the ground. Although their life lasts longer (about five years on average), most individual car models show a similar life cycle pattern, with a strong rise in sales for their first year, a two to three year mature period and declining sales for their last year to eighteen months as buyers become rather tired of the model.

A 'Fashion' product life cycle

Fashion products may give their manufacturers the problem of having to produce a continuous stream of new designs, but the problem is predictable: it is in the nature of their business, so they have to plan accordingly. Life cycles of some products, however, are much less predicable: they are known as 'fads'. Their sales can escalate dramatically, there can be shortages of the product as everyone clamours to buy

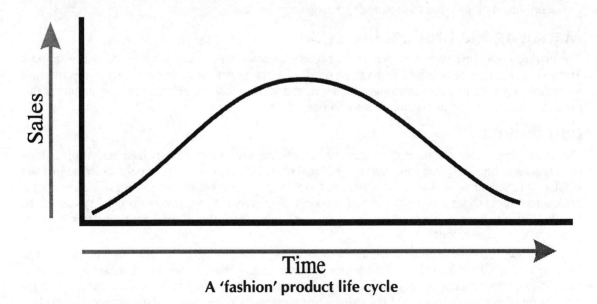

A 'fashion' product life cycle

but, for some reason, the trend can subside as quickly as it grew, often leaving manufacturers and retailers with excessively high stocks. Skateboards are the most well-known example of the 1980s. An even better example from thirty years ago was the 'hoola-hoop', a fad which, unlike skateboards, gripped everyone. Every household had to have its hoola hoop but the sales explosion lasted for only one summer. The next figure shows a typical 'fad' life cycle with its steeply rising growth curve, the short or non-existent mature phase followed by an equally sudden decline.

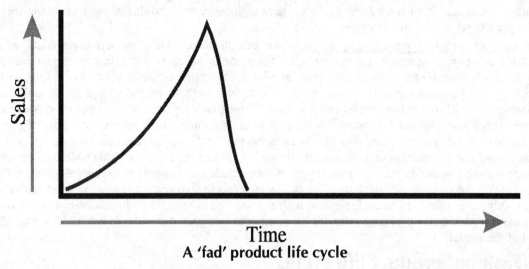

A 'fad' product life cycle

The record industry is one which shows examples of both fashion products and fads. Over the years, hundreds of acts have enjoyed short term success only to be rapidly consigned to the bargain bins of the record shop. Music obviously runs hand in hand with fashion, and as such the longer the fashion trend stays in place, the longer the popularity will be of the artist or group. Those acts which can adapt their image to suit the current fashion trend and as such remain popular with continually new segments of the record buying public are those who enjoy long term success.

Managing the product life cycle

The marketer will have two objectives in the management of the product life cycle and will want both axes to extend as far as possible. To be more specific, at the growth stage the marketer will want sales to continue growing to their highest possible level, and at the mature stage will want to continue at this plateau level for as long as possible before decline sets in.

Introduction

This stage begins when the product is launched onto the market. It may already have undergone a long development stage, including *'test marketing'*, but the product life cycle begins only when the product is fully launched on to the market. At first, sales growth can be very slow, mainly because most people are hesitant about trying new ideas and new products. They prefer to watch other people try them first. In 1962 Everett Rogers produced his famous *'adoption of innovations'* model which describes how people react to innovations.

As can be seen from the diagram at the top of the next page, Rogers states that genuine innovators, who are prepared to take risks and like having new products simply because they are new, are a very small proportion of the population, only 2.5%. Manufacturers, therefore, have to work very hard to push the sales of most new products beyond this group during the introductory stage of the product life cycle.

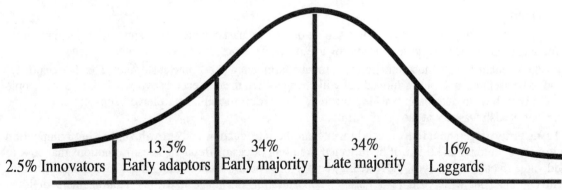

| 2.5% Innovators | 13.5% Early adaptors | 34% Early majority | 34% Late majority | 16% Laggards |

Everett Roger's Innovation Adoption Model

Moreover, the manufacturer will almost certainly be losing money at this stage. Development costs may have been considerable, and the marketing costs at this introductory stage will also be high. Advertising, direct mail, exhibitions and sales promotions are all communications techniques which may need to be used at this stage in order to generate awareness of the new product and to give consumers an incentive to try it. Distributors may have to be offered financial incentives to stock the product or to give it favourable shelf space and special display material may have to be produced for them. With low production volumes, costs will also be high, so it is most unlikely that the product will manage to reach break-even point. Some genuine innovative new products can be profitable at this stage because marketers are able to charge a very high price for them. They can afford to go for the top end of the market where the small group of 'innovators' will be prepared to pay handsomely for the status value of such a conspicuous purchase. The first CD players and the discs themselves would be good examples.

Growth

The growth stage is the *'take-off'* phase when the 'early adopters' begin to purchase the product. They are typically fashionable, successful and keen to be associated with new ideas and products once it is clear that they are socially acceptable. They will be joined later in the growth stage by the 'early majority' who do want to be fashionable but are followers rather than leaders.

Sales will now be climbing rapidly. This will attract attention in the business world and new competitors will be attracted to the market. Their products may even have new features or be offered at a lower price. The Japanese company, Brother, is the world leader in portable electronic typewriters. When they launched the first electronic typewriter they had an eighteen month opportunity to exploit the market and build their position before they faced highly aggressive competition. As the market has matured this period has shortened. Now, when they introduce a new model, they expect to have a *'window of opportunity'* of only four weeks before a competitor comes out with a product which does the same things at a lower price, or offers more benefits at the same price.

At the growth stage, whether it is four weeks or four years, prices are likely to remain quite high although, as competition begins to intensify, the first pressures on prices will be seen. Thus price competition affects growth products, such as fax machines, car phones and, to a lesser extent so far, compact discs. Manufacturers will continue to push hard with promotional activities at this stage, especially advertising designed to increase interest and build brand loyalty. Although marketing costs are still high, they are now a much smaller proportion of the growing sales which help to move the product into profitability.

Maturity

Sales growth for all products slows down sooner or later as market penetration approaches its maximum. Products such as video recorders or microwave ovens have now reached their *mature* stage.

During the mature stage most remaining potential consumers will become customers. The 'late majority' tend to be sceptical and old-fashioned but will change when the evidence is overwhelming. Such people would now buy an automatic washing machine, but are most unlikely to have been converted to the concept of dish washers at the present time.

The maturity stage should last much longer than the introduction and growth stages, but competition will now be intense and this will be reflected in falling prices or frequent sales promotions that seek to add value in customers' eyes. Advertising, and perhaps public relations activities, such as sponsorship, will continue but will be more defensive, concentrating on image and the encouragement of loyal customers.

By now, however, marketers may have to consider more tangible ways of supporting the stagnating sales of their brand. Their objective will be to prolong the mature stage and stave off the decline stage for as long as possible. Product modifications may have be made in the hope of giving the brand a new lease of life.

Extending the product life cycle

This is a tactic particularly favoured by car manufacturers. During the early part of the mature stage, product modifications can be purely cosmetic. Often called 'concept cars', a special model will be introduced with a number of extra features, such as superior upholstery, sun roof, and perhaps an improved stereo as standard. Often they will have a special exterior appearance to increase their distinctiveness. As the mature stage proceeds, such modifications may need to become more fundamental, a completely updated model may need to be introduced, probably retaining most of the mechanical parts of its predecessor, but with a new external appearance. Fords have been masters of *extending the product life cycle* in this way, giving models a timely face-lift before their sales began to decline. Extending the product life cycle in this way can be much cheaper and less risky than launching a completely new product. Ford discovered this to its cost when it replaced the very successful Cortina with the Sierra. The Sierra was initially unpopular, largely because of its different exterior appearance. Loyal Cortina buyers deserted in droves, mainly to the Cavalier, a more conventional looking car which offered the option of a boot, and it was five years before the Sierra regained market leadership of a segment which the Cortina had previously dominated for a decade. It will be interesting to see whether the company have learned from this experience with the launch of the Ford Mondeo, the recent replacement to the Sierra range.

One of the most successful attempts in recent years to extend a product's life cycle is that of Lucozade. For years the product was perceived as being something drank only by ill people – a tonic. Its market share was constantly decreasing, until the producers relaunched the product with the aid of Daley Thompson, the athlete. Combined with a range of sponsorship deals for athletic and sporting events, and repackaging in plastic bottles, the product was successfully repositioned as a sports drink. This campaign was taken a step further with the introduction of 'isotonic lucozade' – a classic example of marketing something which means nothing to the consumer! Further repackaging and promotional campaigns have firmly established the brand as one of the market leaders on this particular segment of the soft drinks market.

Decline

All products eventually enter a stage of *declining sales*, perhaps because they have become obsolete or because the competition has a rival product which offers much better value. Declining sales result in over-capacity and a consequent temptation to cut prices, simply to keep production lines going and employees in jobs. The remaining Ford Capris in the car showrooms in 1987 could be bought for very low prices. Small black and white televisions cost no more now than they did fifteen years ago, which means that in real terms they cost considerably less.

Fierce price competition hits profits, with the result that manufacturers' first reaction is to make marketing economies elsewhere. Product modifications and development come to an end, advertising is cut or curtailed. Despite such economies, the declining products may still be unprofitable as sales and prices continue to fall. As a result, many suppliers will withdraw from the market. Some products simply disappear: slide rules, for example, have been replaced by calculators. Similarly, in the Music Industry, when groups become unpopular or no longer fashionable, record companies are very quick to drop them from their labels. It is interesting to note, however, that many groups extend their own product life cycle as performing artists by switching their audience. For example, many bands who were famous in the 1970s such as The Bay City Rollers, Sweet, Slade and Gary Glitter (ask your parents!) now perform successfully on the college circuit, whilst those famous in the 1960s such as the Searchers and Gerry and the Pacemakers (ask your grandparents!!) still earn a living by playing the 'club' circuit.

Product portfolio analysis

The point made earlier about organisations avoiding placing all of their resources into one or a limited range of products should be remembered. A company relying on only one product, which suddenly goes into decline, will find its future rather less than rosy. It is important therefore to spread the risks associated with all business ventures over a range or basket of products. This allows for those which are less successful to be subsidised by those which make large profits. Ideally, an organisation should strive to have a range of products at different stages in their product life cycles, as each stage generates differing levels of profit in return for differing levels of investment.

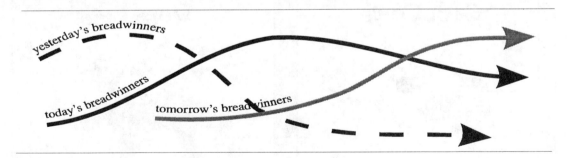

Peter Drucker's Breadwinners

Peter Drucker has suggested that a business needs a range of products, each at a different stage of its life cycle, so that a succession of profitable products will always be on stream. Drucker labels this stream of products as 'today's breadwinners', 'tomorrow's breadwinners' and 'yesterday's breadwinners'. The profits from today's breadwinners must be used to finance the development of tomorrow's breadwinners, which will be able to replace yesterday's breadwinners.

The major problem with this concept is the difficulty involved in actually determining where exactly in their life cycle your products lie. Various analytical tools have been developed to help overcome this. The Boston Consulting Group from the USA devised a theory which allows organisations to assess their *product portfolio* in terms of the market growth rate and the organisation's level of market share. The principle is that organisations should aim to have a broad range of products across a series of markets in order to spread the risk.

The model used a four segment diagram to illustrate the position of the various products according to the pre-determined criteria.

BCG Portfolio Approach

Certain elements of the BCG Matrix can be related to the theory of the product life cycle. For example, those products which have recently been introduced into the market will quite often be regarded as *'Problem Children'*. Those which have successfully reached the 'growth stage' will be regarded as *'Stars'*, whilst the maturity of the market will lead to products becoming *'Cash Cows'*. Finally, when the market enters the 'decline stage', the products will generally be *'Dogs'*.

There are ways, however, in which the analogy with the product life cycle falls down. Take for example problem children, or as they are sometimes known, *'Question Marks'*. It is assumed that few businesses would launch new products into markets which are not growing, and also that new products will take

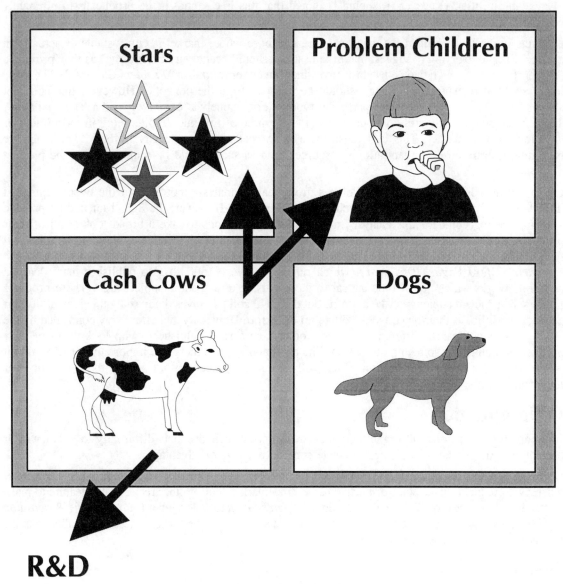

BCG Analysis - the internal flow of funds

time and investment to become established. Therefore the majority of new products will fall into this category. There can be products, however, which have been on the market for lengthy periods of time which are also '*Problem Children*'. These are the products which have never really taken off in the market, and the organisation must make decisions as to whether or not to keep investing in these products. If successful, the continued or increased investment may result in the product becoming a '*Star*', but failure to move the product will simply lead to a waste of a lot of investment money. In some instances, the decision will be made to withdraw from that market completely.

Products in the '*Star*' category will require considerable investment to keep them in the position of market leader. In many instances, this investment may be so large as to considerably reduce the level of available profits. However, it should be noted that this is essential if the product is to ultimately become a '*Cash Cow*'.

Products in the lower half of the diagram represent those whose market is either stable or actually in decline. Simple logic might suggest that organisations should keep their '*Cash Cows*' as they provide a source of revenue which can be used for investment in either '*Stars*' or '*Problem Children*'. The same logic would also suggest that 'Dogs' should be dropped from the portfolio. However, this need not always be the case, as there are two particular types of dog, namely a '*Cash Dog*' and a '*Genuine Dog*'. The former will actually still continue to provide a source of revenue despite being in a declining or very low growth market. This is because there is no need to invest heavily in them. The latter are becoming a drain on the organisation's resources, and as such should be removed from the product portfolio.

Obviously decisions such as these involve a great deal of analysis, not least of the overall financial implications of retaining or dropping each individual product. However, the BCG Matrix does provide a useful starting point for this analysis, and allows organisations to take a broad look at all of their products in relation to each other as opposed to in isolation. Certain products within a portfolio will never make money, but will still be retained. For example, the Oxford University Press publishes the *Complete Oxford English Dictionary*, which retails for over £1500. It also publishes many learned academic works which are of little appeal to those outside of a specific subject area. These products rarely sell sufficient copies to make a profit, but the OUP still perceives them as a vital element of their product portfolio, as their objectives – being part of Oxford University and effectively controlled by the Dons – are significantly different from most other commercial publishers, who look to all of their products to contribute something to bottom line profitability. It is therefore important to realise that it is the objectives of the organisation which will govern their actions, not simply the drive for ever increasing profits.

Differentiation

In competitive situations, all organisations need to present their products differently to either win or protect custom. Marketers will seek to create competitive edge or advantage.

Branding is widely used in FMCG (Fast Moving Consumer Goods) markets to make products distinctive, whereby a product is given some distinctive name, trademark colour or other recognisable feature to make it 'stand out from the crowd'. The ultimate aim of *differentiation* is to develop a *Unique Selling Proposition* or USP. This is generally done by adding value to product, either in the form of increased quality or in the provision of excellent customer service.

Quality

It is generally recognised that *quality* is an important factor in success in the market place. Research carried out for books like *In Search of Excellence and The Winning Streak* showed that successful companies, like Marks and Spencer, Sainsbury, Clark's Shoes, MacDonalds and IBM all place great emphasis on maintaining quality standards throughout the business.

Quality should be seen as 'fitness for purpose'. MacDonalds do not serve the most *cordon bleu* dishes in town, but that is not the point. For what the consumer expects from a fast-food hamburger restaurant, MacDonald's can rarely be faulted. Sainsburys are so keen on quality that they have an objective that all their own-label products should be of higher quality than their branded equivalents – even though they usually sell for a lower price.

Customer service

Branding can also add value in customers' eyes by establishing an association with high levels of *customer service*. IBM have always maintained that not only is their product quality the highest, but so is the service they offer to customers. Theodore Levitt has pointed out that the more technologically sophisticated the product, the more customers are dependent upon the service back-up offered by the supplier. The buyer of a new computer system may need installation, may need help in the choice of software, may need training for staff in how to use the computer and may also require maintenance support in the future.

Services can also use branding to great effect in this respect. There is no doubt that some companies do build a reputation for offering unusually high levels of customer service. The best example is Marks and Spencer, where the customer knows he or she is always right. This is particularly true with the growth in importance of relationship marketing, whereby long term relationships are seen as the goal to continued commercial success.

New Product Development

The process of *New Product Development* is inherent in all organisations who are seeking continued success. It must be a continuous process, as products, markets and consumers are all constantly changing. Any organisation which achieves success and then rests on its laurels will not be around for much longer. There are various stages through which all new products must go, and these are as follows;

- idea generation;
- screening;
- market analysis;
- product development;
- product testing;
- commercialisation/launch.

Idea generation

Numerous methods exist for the generation of new product ideas. Ideas are the basis of all new products. Some products are more innovative than others. Some, such as penicillin, nylon, kevlar or the jet engine represent a totally new breakthrough, often the result of many years of slow and expensive research and development. Other new products are *'adaptive'*, which means that they are improved versions of an existing product. The degree of innovation in an adaptive product can vary enormously, but they are not classified as inventions, just modifications. Some new products do not appear to offer any kind of improvements or modification compared to existing products in the market place. Such products are often referred to as *'me too'* products.

The first task of a business intent on an effective new product development programme is to create an atmosphere in which the communication of new ideas flourishes. The most successful organisations in the world encourage their employees to experiment, to share ideas, to make mistakes. This is all designed to develop the correct culture of forward thinking required for any innovative organisation. In addition to sustaining the kind of corporate culture in which ideas can flourish, a number of specific techniques may be used to stimulate the generation of ideas.

Brainstorming

Brainstorming might involve a number of people, (usually around eight to twelve), placed in fairly comfortable, relaxed surroundings with a leader to guide the session. The leader will have already prepared certain key words or concepts thought to be appropriate for stimulating the thoughts of the participants. The leader introduces one of these words and the other participants shout out the first word or idea that comes into their head. It does not matter how ridiculous the idea appears, the participant should shout it out because the whole session relies for its effectiveness on group dynamics. One person's banal suggestion might spark off another idea from a second participant, which in turn prompts a really good idea from a third member of the group. Most ideas will be voiced spontaneously, so it is often chaotic and might at times degenerate into farce. A record is kept of all points (ideally, on tape) and if two or three good ideas emerge from a session, it is time well spent.

The Suggestion Box

Internal idea generation can be maximised by involving the entire workforce of the business in the process. Many businesses have suggestion boxes, with financial incentives to contribute. Employees, whose suggestions are taken up, are paid for their suggestion according to how much money it makes or saves the company. Suggestions may not be exclusively concerned with new product developments. They can include ideas for cost saving in the workplace or for a new way of promoting a product, but new product ideas will often be a significant proportion of all suggestions. Many of these are successfully implemented. Smith's, for example successfully introduced square crisps on to the market, an idea originally suggested by a shopfloor employee.

Research and Development

Larger companies, like ICI, employ very large numbers of staff in their research and development (R&D) departments. Being at the forefront of new technological development is important for many businesses, but in some industries, such as pharmaceuticals or computers, it is essential. It is one of the problems of many UK companies in recent history that they have tended to neglect R&D, whilst their competitors throughout the world have rapidly caught up and in many instances overtaken their position. However, recent trends would suggest a realisation that their is a definite need to invest in research and development, even if only to remain in the same position.

The sales force

It is often said that the sales force is the company's eyes and ears in the market place. This information-gathering role should always be fully exploited by companies, because the close relationships which sales people often have with customers can be a very fruitful source of new product ideas.

Marketing research

We have already discussed the role of market research extensively earlier in this Unit. For many companies, especially those in consumer markets, marketing research will be the most fruitful source of ideas for new product development.

Competitors

It is fairly common for firms to use competitors as sources of new product ideas. Most companies gather and file all their competitors' literature, and some take the process a stage further by buying, using and dismantling their competitors' new products. The Japanese company, Yamaha, established themselves in the guitar market by this process of 'reverse engineering'. They would take the state of the art US and UK guitars, strip them down, and rebuild them in an improved and cheaper manner. Although it is essential to maintain extensive and up-to-date knowledge of competitors' activities, to make sure your own company is not slipping behind, using competitors' products as sources of new ideas is of much more dubious value. At best, the copying of a competitor's product results in a 'me too' product. At worst, the firm may find itself copying a product for which there is no demand, particularly if the competitor has not based the product on a thorough analysis of customers' needs.

Screening

The purpose of idea generation is to develop as many new ideas as possible. From the start of the screening stage, the new product development process concentrates on reducing the number of ideas down to the tiny number which are worthy of launching on to the market. In order to do so, the ideas generated will be assessed according to a series of criteria, which are likely to initially include the following.

Compatibility with company strengths

Many ideas can be eliminated quickly and easily on the grounds that they are not really appropriate to the company's strengths and resources. If the firm believes that other businesses would be better at developing a particular idea, they should abandon it (or possibly sell it to another business). At the screening stage most ideas can be eliminated if the company makes a ruthless assessment of its own ability to exploit them.

Compatibility with existing products

The company must also ask itself how well a prospective new product would fit in with its existing range of products. If the new product is complementary to its existing products, it will impose less strain on the company's resources because it will build upon existing customer relationships, sales visits, and distribution channels.

Value engineering

Once it is decided that the new idea is compatible with the company's strengths, financial resources and existing product range, it may still need to satisfy itself that the manufacture of the product is feasible.

Market demand

The final screening step would involve a quick assessment of the likely demand for the new product. The aim at this stage would be to identify those ideas for which the likely demand would be too small to generate sufficient sales to enable the company to recover the anticipated development costs of the new product.

The whole point of the screening stage is that it should be performed quickly and inexpensively in order to identify early those products which are unlikely to make it through the remainder of the process – before too much money has been invested in their development.

Marketing analysis

Most of the original ideas have been eliminated by this stage, but the cost incurred in the development of those which remain begins to escalate, especially from the product development stage. The objective is still to eliminate potential losers at the earliest possible stage in order to minimise the potential loss. It is now that a comprehensive marketing analysis and forecast is made, before the very costly product development stage is entered, since the business wishes to satisfy itself that the new product is a potential winner. The issues considered in such a market analysis will include the following:

- volume or value;

- assumptions;
- market potential.

Volume or value

Some estimate or forecasts will be prepared both in volume terms and in value terms. Initially it is wiser to prepare forecasts in volume terms, as this removes the danger of external factors such as inflation making the predictions appear useless. When forecasts need to have monetary values attached to them, the conversion should be reasonably straightforward.

Assumptions

All forecasts are difficult to make, especially those dealing with the future! There are many variables within the business and marketing environments over which organisations have little or no control, but which can fundamentally effect business operations. As it is impossible to accurately predict all of these outcomes, certain assumptions must be made. These assumptions should obviously be as realistic as possible, and may need to be constantly updated, but it is upon these assumptions of future trends that all predictions are based.

Market potential

Many models and methods exist which are designed to estimate the future market potential for specific products or industries. The technicalities behind these methods are beyond the realm of this book, but most are based on research carried out by methods discussed earlier combined with some form of statistical analysis, such as time series analysis or linear regression. The aim of all of these models is to predict the likely future demand for products, and to calculate the difference between the organisation's present level of sales, the present market size, and the future market size.

Business analysis

The successful marketing of a product or service entails not only the achievement of a certain level of sales, but also achieving this at a profit. All marketers should be reasonably familiar with the basic concepts of financial and management accounting, which are covered elsewhere in this book. This will allow them to realise the link between costs, sales and profitability. Without an appreciation of the financial side of the organisation, it is very easy for the marketing department to make unreal assumptions which can be just as damaging given successful sales as they can if no sales are achieved at all.

Product development

Any product idea which has successfully completed the previous phases of the product development process may now be in a position to be physically produced. Once again, several differing stages will be involved, and the costs of the project now begin to accelerate appreciably. The stages are:

- manufacture;
- packaging;
- branding.

Manufacture

The actual physical production of a product will usually commence with a prototype, which should be as close to finished product as possible, although there are inevitably further changes to be made to most products following further research and testing. If the company is following the true marketing philosophy, then the product should not only be manufactured efficiently, but should also deliver the required benefits which were first highlighted by the initial research.

Packaging

For many products, especially those in the FMCG markets, the packaging can be almost as important as the product itself. Innovation in packaging methods is as creative and active as in new products themselves. Some recent examples of success stories would include the development of pump action toothpaste dispensers and the 'draughtflow' cans now favoured by many beer producers. The role of the environment upon packaging should also not be ignored, as can be evidenced by the development of new ring pull systems for soft drink cans and the alterations in packaging of items such as washing powders and detergents.

Branding

The brand of the product should be developed at this stage in order that it can be tested along with the product itself. This may involve the development of a brand name, an appropriate design or logo, but should always remain consistent with the overall position which is sought by the product within the target market segment.

Product testing

Most professional organisations will test their products extensively before they are launched onto the market. This will usually involve laboratory tests, which may or may not involve customers, but will ultimately involve test marketing the product itself, perhaps in a specific region, in order to assess the market reaction. At all stages of testing, the results should be fed back to the design team who may make minor (or major) alterations to the product in order to arrive at what should hopefully be the 'finished article'.

Launch/commercialisation

The final stage – and one at which many products still fail – is the launch or commercialisation of the product. Many organisations underestimate the costs involved in launching products onto unsuspecting markets, and even though the product itself may be 'right', it can still fail.

The next diagram shows the fall out rate of new products at the different stages identified. It can be seen that a vast number of ideas fall by the wayside early in their lives, and that the number of ideas which actually come to commercial fruition is very small. However, successful organisations are those which accept that this will be the case, and encourage a culture to be developed whereby their staff are encouraged to try - and not criticised for honest failure - in order to achieve the benefits conferred by the elusive successful launch of a product which may become a market leader.

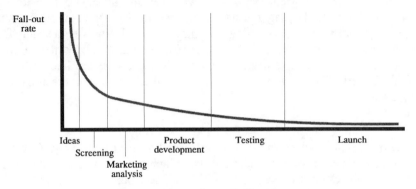

The new product fall-out rate

Price

A price is a value or sum of money at which two parties agree to carry out an exchange transaction. The price offered to a customer in many markets within this country is fixed. In this situation, a customer simply accepts the price, and enters into a transaction. Alternatively, the customer can refuse the price, and opt for another purchase. The alternative scenario is where the price is negotiable, and the buyer and seller will indulge in discussions of some form until an acceptable agreement is reached, Obviously, with negotiable prices, there are many situations when a mutually accepted price cannot be reached, and as such no transaction will take place.

Pricing is the element of the marketing mix which students often least associate with the marketing function. It is easy to see why the pricing function could be regarded as merely an accountancy task, but this view is mistaken. Price is just as fundamental to the overall marketing effort as any of the other marketing mix elements, and as such should be treated as part of the coherent and combined marketing effort.

There are four reasons why price is such an important element of the marketing mix:

- quality;
- image;
- a fair price;
- price bands.

Quality

One message which has been constantly stressed throughout this Unit is the need to adopt a consistent approach to the whole marketing effort. Once a target market segment has been defined, and an overall approach selected, the whole message put out by all elements of the marketing mix must be the same. If the approach to be adopted for the product is one of quality, then the price must reflect this. It is a fact of life that consumers tend to view items of high price as having some kind of intrinsic value, whilst those priced lower reflect something 'cheap and nasty'. When consumers lack full knowledge of a product they will often make assumptions based upon the information which they do possess. Frequently this is information on price, and as such price can be an instant indicator of quality – or lack of it – to the uninformed consumer.

Image

Some products have *'pose value'*. They are the car, the jeans, the pub or the wellies to be seen in. In some pubs, the tables are covered by empty lager bottles. They are shapely bottles with attractive labels and gold foil around the neck. The lager inside costs around twice as much as the humble draught variety, although it costs no more to make and its taste may be virtually indistinguishable. The consumers are buying the image of the bottles more than the lager inside, which is why they go to the trouble of bringing the bottle as well as the glass back to the table. Those bottles are like badges. They make a statement about the buyers. They have pose value. A relatively high price is essential if a product is to have this prestige value.

A fair price

There is evidence of a *'plateau effect'* in price. People resist a very expensive price which seems to be a 'rip off' but are also suspicious of a very cheap price, which tends to be associated with poor quality. Most people are price conscious, seeking good value for money, but this does not usually result in their buying the cheapest available product. The concept of a 'fair price' suggests that many purchasers may seek products which lie somewhere in the middle of the extremes.

Price bands

Although the price plateau principle almost certainly applies, it may exist at different levels for different groups of buyers. When buying groceries an affluent middle-class family will have a different notion of 'good value for money' than an 'unemployed' family. Therefore, marketers will often try to offer a range of products priced within certain bands, roughly in line with what the customers expect to pay, for instance, £9.99, £14.99 and £19.99. This price banding is particularly popular in the clothing market.

Pricing of New Products and Price Changes

Organisations usually alter their prices due to one of three events:

- the product changes;
- the market changes;
- the consumer changes.

It is this important area of strategic price setting where many organisations go wrong. Short term alterations in price are usually as much to do with promotion as pricing, but when the long term price structure is wrong, an organisation could be heading for trouble. It is essential, therefore, for any organisation to consider a number of factors when setting prices in such situations.

Costs

It has already been mentioned that most organisations wish to trade profitably. As such, they must take account of the costs involved in the whole of the business effort when deciding a price for which to sell the finished article. While organisations which embrace the marketing philosophy will by definition be outward looking, they must also keep a firm eye on the internal effects of costs. For most organisations, this involves some element of *cost-plus approach*, whereby the organisation studies its own cost structures and then adds-on an element for profit. This is a fairly simplified approach, commonly referred to as *'mark-up'*, and can obviously not be employed in isolation from the other factors to be considered.

One specific costing approach sometimes adopted by organisations is that of *target pricing*. With this approach the organisation will set itself a specific target, usually based on some kind of break-even analysis. The company will aim to achieve a set level of sales or profits above the previously calculated break-even point.

Company objectives

We have already mentioned that not all organisations, whether in the short term or the long term, are seeking to maximise profits. Other objectives do exist, and these objectives may override the desire to set prices where they will gain the maximum short term profit. Examples of such objectives include the use of *marginal cost pricing*, whereby an organisation decides to allocate only costs incurred by the production of a marginal unit to the product in terms of its price. The 'overhead' element of the cost is therefore absorbed by other parts of the organisation's portfolio. The immediate result of this approach is that the unit price can often be kept very low, with a resultant competitive advantage. The danger of this method is that a product's price does not reflect its true cost of production. The worst scenario is when the product or products which are effectively subsidising the marginally costed product fail. The full cost must then be transferred, and this can result in significant rises in price, and a resultant dramatic reduction in demand.

Another corporate objective which may be important is that of *buying market share*. Here an organisation attempts to compete on price even though little or no profit is made. This can be combined with the marginal costing approach discussed above, but the aim is to dislodge competitors, and to gradually raise prices to a level where profits will become respectable.

Demand

It should be obvious from the unit on *Business in the Economy* where we discuss the factors that influence the supply and demand for products that demand is generally responsive to price. Whilst marketers would argue that there is much more which influences the level of demand, the influence of 'the market' cannot be ignored. Basic economic theory would suggest an inverse relationship between price and the level of demand, and marketers should attempt to research the price level which different market sectors will bear. As the market itself is affected by so many external factors, so the organisation's pricing decision must take account of these variables. For example, should the country be in a recession, then the marketer must be aware of this and avoid setting prices at an unacceptable level.

The concept of *price discrimination* should also be considered, as it may be possible to set prices at different levels for different market segments. For example, entry into many leisure facilities is priced at a number of different levels according to age, group size, time of year and so on.

Perceived quality

Consumers tend to associate a high price with high quality. This quality may be perceived in the mind of the customer, rather than being inherent in the product, but if it is there, sellers can charge for it. Leading brands of perfume can command a much higher price than less established brands. It is debatable whether the core product is significantly superior, but the augmented product, enhanced by stylish packaging and years of successful advertising, has attained a very high value market position, and is priced accordingly. This is known as *'perceived value pricing'*;

A variation of this pricing strategy can be adopted for the luxury versions of standard products. Known as *'product line pricing'*, it involves charging significantly higher prices for 'top of the range' products due to their higher perceived value. Cars are a good example. The top of the range Cosworth Sierra costs almost three times as much to buy as the cheapest two door 1.3 litre version. It does not cost three times as much to produce. The profit margin is much higher, but the pricing is in accordance with the relative values perceived by customers.

The competition

Some companies base their prices largely on those charged by the competition. This *'competition oriented pricing'* is very common in extremely price sensitive markets and is more likely to be practised by the weaker companies. Petrol companies often respond to competitors' price changes within hours. Supermarkets and retailers of electrical goods in the same town will keep a eye on prices charged by their competitors. It is now common for retailers to offer to refund customers the difference if they can find the same product sold cheaper elsewhere.

Competition oriented pricing can be very dangerous, leading to rash price cutting and a downward spiral in prices which only leaves the industry as a whole much less profitable. Many of the most successful companies are those which have refused to cut prices, relying instead on their higher quality, better service or some other benefit which offers value for money. Kelloggs does not try to be as cheap as its own-label competitors. Rover refused to respond to competitors' heavy discounting when it introduced its new 800 model because of the adverse effect such price cutting could have on perceived quality.

In today's highly competitive markets, however, virtually all companies must take some account of the prices charged by competitors. However good the rest of their marketing mix, few companies can afford to be too far out of line with the rest of the industry.

Distributors

In some industries distributors exert a powerful influence over the pricing strategies of manufacturers. Today, the large retail chains in the UK often dominate their smaller suppliers and can, should they choose, more or less dictate prices to them. Even where manufacturers are stronger and in full control of their pricing strategy, if they sell through distributors they must take account of their distributors' needs.

Legal constraints

In some countries there is extensive legal constraints on pricing. There are no longer statutory controls on pricing in the UK, but there are certain rules designed to ensure that consumers are not misled by pricing. Under the *Consumer Protection Act* 1987, for example, the once common practice of buying in special cheap goods for sales and advertising them at apparently massively reduced prices is no longer permitted. Only genuine price reductions can be marked up or advertised. Goods displaying a price reduction (such as 'Now only £19.95 – was £35') must have been previously stocked and offered for sale at that higher price.

Tactical pricing

A company's pricing strategy will probably result not in a single fixed price but a *price range*, a minimum and a maximum price at which the company will sell. Tactical pricing refers to the task of setting specific prices within that range and altering them if necessary as conditions change or to secure a short term tactical advantage over the competition. There are many examples of pricing tactics, for example:

- Promotional discounts
- Loss leaders
- Psychological pricing
- Customary pricing

Promotional discounts

They are a very popular form of price cutting. To be effective, they must offer the customer sufficient incentive to buy extra, or to change brands, and they must have a time limit in order to induce action now. It is also believed that price discounts, which are clearly of a short-term nature, do not have detrimental effect on the product's perceived quality, because consumers see them as a promotion and not as the 'real price'.

Loss leaders

This is occurs when an organisation uses a small number of products as loss leaders. They are offered at an incredibly cheap price (to be precise, a loss-making price). They are designed to attract customers into the store in the hope that, once there, they will also buy many normally priced items. Very popular with retailers, especially supermarkets at one time, this price tactic has become less common in recent years.

Psychological pricing

How many prices in the shops end in 99p? Probably, the overwhelming majority. There are sound psychological reasons for charging £9.99 rather than £10. Research has shown that although many customers will mentally round up the price, many will round it down, particularly if, subconsciously, they want to give themselves a reason for buying.

Customary pricing

Sometimes customers become accustomed to seeing a certain price for a product or product type. It becomes difficult to raise the price without having a major adverse effect on demand (for instance chocolate bars). Rather than increase the price, a supplier might be tempted to reduce the amount of product, aided perhaps by a creative re-design of the packaging. These tactics led to the phenomenon of shrinking bars of chocolate in the inflationary 1970s, which in turn created the conditions for the success of Yorkie, as Rowntree recognised the demand for a decent-sized, chunky, chocolate bar.

Activity

When seeking to make a purchase of any kind, quite often price is a major influencing factor in the buying decision. Often we do not have perfect information on the prices of products, and as such we can make 'mistakes' by purchasing a product at a higher price than it is available elsewhere. The increasing use of Information Technology is helping to provide wider knowledge of prices, but the data is often incomplete or even influenced by the supplier of that information, such as an Insurance Broker or a Travel Agent, who will have their own agenda in terms of the products which they sell.

For this activity, you are asked to look at the holiday market. As an exercise, select a particular popular holiday destination, such as Majorca or Benidorm, and find out as much information as possible about the various packages which are available. You should select a two week period, on a self-catering basis, and obtain as many different packages as possible. The deals which are offered will all differ slightly, in terms of location and the actual specifications, but most importantly they will probably differ in price. When you have collected the information, analyse it all and make comparisons of the similarities and differences between the different offers from the various Tour Operators and Travel Agents. Finally, you should make an informed decision as to which is the best deal - and start saving!

Place/Distribution

Products must be made available to customers and potential customers through a system of distribution. This is the third 'P' in the marketing mix and is all about *place*. In fact, distribution is about places – places where the product will be made, stored, bought and used. Two words accurately describe the concept of distribution, *'availability'* and *'accessibility'*. A company needs to make sure that its products are available, that it is in fact possible for customers to buy them. This sounds obvious, but in the 1960s lack of availability was one of the big failings of British industry.

As competition increases, however, being widely available may still not be enough to ensure success in the market place. Consumers can be notoriously fickle and very lazy. They will often opt for the product which is easiest to buy, rather than the ideal product. It will always be an important objective of any marketer to make his product or service more accessible (easier to buy) than those of his competitors (although the exclusivity associated with some 'difficult to buy' products can be highly valued by some customers).

Basic definitions

At this point we would like to give you some basic definitions which you should find useful in understanding the 'place' aspect of the marketing mix.

Place. As an element of the marketing mix, place or distribution involves those management tasks concerned with making the product available and accessible to buyers and potential buyers.

Availability. Availability describes the fact that a product or service is capable of being acquired and used by buyers and potential buyers.

Accessibility. A product is accessible if potential buyers find it easy and convenient to acquire and use.

Physical distribution. The management tasks concerned with efficient movement of goods and services both into the company and outwards to the customer.

Channels of Distribution. The system of organisations through which goods or services are transferred from the original producer to end users.

Middlemen. Middlemen, or distributors, are those businesses which handle goods or services in the channel of distribution between the producer and the end users.

The Economics of Middlemen

There is a cost attached to using middlemen. They have to be given their cut of the profits. So why do manufacturers use middlemen, and not keep all the profits for themselves? There are two main reasons why manufacturers feel it is beneficial to use middlemen. They are:

- lower costs; and
- higher sales.

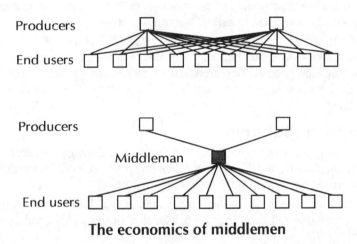

The economics of middlemen

Lower costs

Fewer lines of contact

The basic economic reason for the use of middlemen is that they reduce the lines of contact between producers and end users, as shown in the next diagram.

Without the middleman there are 24 lines of contact. With the middleman, there are fourteen lines of contact. The cost of delivering goods to one middleman, rather than twelve end users, will be much lower. Clearly, it is more efficient to use middlemen. Imagine how much more efficient it becomes when there are millions of customers rather than twelve.

Lower stockholding costs

Using middlemen saves the producer money because the producer now needs to hold lower stocks. The middlemen assume the responsibility of holding sufficient stocks to meet end user demand.

Lower sales administration costs

If the manufacturer is dealing with thousands of customers, sales administration costs will be enormous. The manufacturer will need to employ a small army in tele-sales for incoming orders and the associated paperwork with confirmation of order slips, delivery notes, invoices and statements, will be very costly.

Dealing with a relatively small number of distributors relieves the manufacturer of a large proportion of these costs.

Lower sales force costs

With distributors a much smaller sales force can be employed. The distributors' sales people perform that task in their local area, leaving the manufacturer's sales force to sell to the distributors themselves and possibly to a small number of very important customers.

Higher sales

The second broad reason for using distributors is that it should enable a manufacturer to increase sales. There are three main reasons for this:

Accessibility. Being placed in the area, normally in a good location, distributors make it much easier for customers to buy;

Knowledge of the local market. The locally based distributor is also much closer to customers in other ways, understanding their needs and priorities much better than a remote manufacturer. This would be especially true when referring to export sales;

Specialisation. Manufacturers specialise in manufacturing. That's what they are good at. Retailers specialise in displaying large numbers of goods and making it easy for customers to buy them. That's what they are good at. Research into successful companies has shown that an important factor in their success is that they concentrate on what they're good at, but do not try to be good at everything.

The functions of middlemen

The basic role of middlemen, therefore, is to make the product more available and accessible to customers and potential customers in a more cost-effective way than might be achieved by the manufacturer alone. They do this by performing some or all of the following functions:

- *Breaking bulk*. They take goods in the large quantities which the manufacturers want to sell but are prepared to sell them in the much smaller quantities that end users usually wish to buy;
- *Storage*. This relieves manufacturers' storage problems and costs and increases availability to customers.
- *Stockholding*. The buffer stocks held by distributors reduce delivery times to end users and reduce the risk of stock-outs;
- *Delivery*. Whereas manufacturers typically deliver to distributors with 38 tonne articulated lorries, the distributor probably delivers to many small customers with a small van, thus increasing accessibility;
- *After sales service*. Dealers often provide a valuable local point for after sales service, as in the case of cars or electrical goods;
- *Price setting*. Distributors may have the authority to decide their own pricing or may be required to sell at prices laid down by the manufacturer;
- *Promotion*. Local distributors often perform a valuable role promoting manufacturers' products on a local basis. Sometimes manufacturers will recognise this and reach co-operative advertising agreements with their middlemen, with both parties sharing the cost;
- *Personal selling*. This can take two forms. A local retail outlet provides an obvious sales advantage to a manufacturer. For industrial products, a similar cash and carry type sales

desk may exist but the distributor may also have its own sales force calling on local companies. This is a valuable extension to a manufacturer's selling capabilities.

Activity

Select three different products which you purchase regularly. For each of these products, you are required to trace the chain of distribution, from the initial manufacturer to you, the final consumer. You may not be able to find out all of the information immediately, but you should persevere! For each of the products, write a paragraph which explains the reasons for the type of distribution which as been implemented, and describe what, in your opinion, is the specific value which each level of the distribution chain adds.

Channels of Distribution

The marketer has a number of decisions to make as far as channels of distribution are concerned. The marketer must decide how many middlemen (if any) are required between the manufacturer and the consumer, what kind of distribution network would be most suitable for the product, how to select individual distributors and how to manage the system once it is in place.

Channel levels

The number and type of middlemen in a channel of distribution can vary as shown in the next diagram

The number of levels or tiers between a manufacturer and end user can be as few as none (a zero level channel) or as many as three (a three level channel). It can be more, but that is unusual. One level or two level channels are by far the most common.

- *Zero level channel.* A zero level channel is more correctly termed direct marketing and is growing in popularity. Mill shops attached to large textile factories are becoming more common and many small companies concentrate on selling their products direct to the end user;

- *One level channel.* In consumer markets, the one level channel is becoming the most common because of the growth of the large retail chains who buy directly from the manufacturer, rather than from wholesalers. In business to business markets, many transactions are made without middlemen but, where channels are used, the most normal arrangement will be one agent or wholesaler between manufacturer and end user;

- *Two level channel.* Two level channels are still common in consumer markets, since many small retailers do not have the buying power to purchase directly from the manufacturer and therefore have to buy their stock through wholesalers. Sometimes small retailers band together into a buying syndicate (e.g. Spar, or Mace) to increase their buying power. An organisation, like Spar, in reality acts as a wholesaler, but since it is owned by its customers (the retailers) its margins are lower than those of an independent wholesaler;

- *Three level channel.* Agents differ from distributors in that they do not normally hold stock or own it. They concentrate on promoting and selling manufacturers' products and receive a commission on all sales from the manufacturer, who delivers the product straight to the customer. Such practices are common with items such as machinery, which is often purpose-built or would be very expensive to hold in stock for long periods of time.

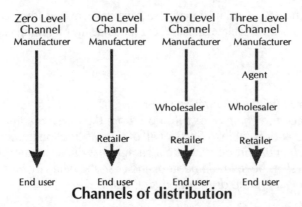

Channels of distribution

Most manufacturers will not choose between these different channel levels. They will adopt some combinations of all four. A computer manufacturer, for example, will deal directly with its largest customers who are spending very large sums of money. Medium-sized computer systems, typically bought by smaller businesses, will be sold through professional local dealers, fully-qualified and competent to provide advice, training, installation, servicing etc. Their cheapest products, perhaps a small home computer, may be available from many high street shops and small computer dealers. If the manufacturer has a minimum order size, the small dealers will have to buy through wholesalers. The manufacturer may also use agents, especially abroad, where the company may not be well known, which makes distributors reluctant to carry stocks.

Channel Networks

Not all one level or two level channels are the same. Distribution networks can vary and a manufacturer needs to decide on the type of network which best suits his product. There are three broad choices:

Intensive distribution. The aim of intensive distribution strategy is to secure as many outlets as possible in order to maximise availability and accessibility to potential buyers. This type of distribution is most suited to products where convenience of purchase and impulse buying are important factors influencing sales. Examples of products requiring intensive distribution would be petrol, cigarettes, ice cream and crisps. The manufacturer of such products wants his brands on sale in every conceivable outlet. A regional manufacturer of soft drinks for example will want his products on sale in supermarkets, small grocery shops, fish and chip shops, newsagents, confectioners, pubs, cafes, fast food outlets, vending machines, and any other outlet which will stock the product.

Exclusive distribution. At the other end of the spectrum, availability and accessibility are deliberately restricted. Prestige products which need to protect their image of up-market exclusivity will grant sole dealerships to distributors in each area. The dealers will be chosen very carefully because their image and competence must match up to the high standards demanded by the manufacturer. You would not expect to find Porsche cars sold by a back street garage. A dealer of IBM business computers has to meet a number of very stringent requirements.

Selective distribution. Selective distribution involves the use of more than one, but less than all, of the distributors who are willing to stock the product in a particular area. The manufacturer may want the distribution of the product to be as intensive as possible but may also want to protect the image of the company and its brands by exercising some control over the type of retailers selling it. An example is that of white goods (such as washing machines), brown goods (for instance televisions) and other domestic appliances.

Competition is fierce and manufacturers will want their brand on show in as many retail outlets as possible, but there will still be some criteria that retailers are required to meet, such as minimum stockholding levels and standard premises.

Vertical integration

In addition to the three broad classes of channel network, other variations are possible.

Vertical integration. This describes a co-ordinated channel of distribution, where all the members work together for the common good with the aim of achieving greater efficiency and, thereby, a competitive advantage. Vertically integrated channels may or may not be under common ownership.

In the past Burton's was the ideal of a vertically integrated channel. Burton's motto used to be 'From sheep to shop' and Burton's did, indeed, control all activities involved in transforming the wool from the sheep's back into a made-to-measure suit bought at its store. Nowadays, Burton's is a retailer, sourcing much of its merchandise from other manufacturers.

Forward integration. Thornton's is a good example of forward integration. The Derbyshire manufacturer of quality confectionery has gradually developed a network of its own high street shops.

C & J Clark the shoe manufacturers, practise both forward and backward integration, acquiring retail outlets at one end of the chain of demand and building up a substantial shoe machinery business at the other. Channel members in vertically integrated channels do not have to be under common ownership. Many large retail chains practise backward integration by exercising very tight control over their suppliers.

Franchising is a very popular method of forward integration. Benetton shops for example are all franchises. A Benetton shop is an independent business started by its owner under a franchise arrangement with Benetton. Under a franchising agreement the franchiser (Benetton) agrees to supply the shop with merchandise, and to provide management and promotional help. In return the franchisee (the individual store) agrees to buy exclusively from Benetton and to pay the franchiser a royalty on all sales. Franchising is an increasingly popular form of business ownership.

Selecting Channel Members

For all but the most intensive of distribution networks the manufacturer will need to exercise some control over the recruitment of channel members. A number of criteria may be used:

- *Image of the product.* The more exclusive and expensive the product, the more up-market the image of the distributor will have to be;
- *The standing of the company.* Distributors buy a large volume of goods on credit from manufacturers. The manufacturer will want to be satisfied that all distributors are of sound financial standing and able to meet their debts;
- *Complexity of the product.* Technical products such as business computers demand a high level of knowledge on the part of dealers. The ability to train buyer's staff and to service products may also be required;
- *Perishability of the product.* Products requiring special equipment, such as freezers, obviously can be sold only through outlets with the correct equipment. Manufacturers requiring intensive distribution (such as ice cream companies) will often supply the middleman with suitable equipment;

- *Location of customers*. Manufacturers will obviously want more middlemen in areas where they have the greatest concentration of customers.

Promotion and Marketing Communication

In planning the mix elements, the final component, that of promotion or marketing communications, must be carefully constructed to ensure the successful launch and subsequent development of new products, and the effective communication with existing and potential customers about existing products. There exists within all industries a wide range of approaches to promotion, varying from the intensive, multi-million pound television based campaigns of the major organisations to the small advertisement in the local free newspaper which may be favoured by a plumber. As with all elements of the marketing mix, it is vital to select the appropriate way in which to effectively and efficiently spend limited resources. As such, the first step in the promotion decision process is to consider the various ways in which such budgets can be spent.

The Communications Mix

The communications mix consists of several key elements :

Advertising

Advertising can be defined as follows:

> *"Any paid form of non-personal presentation and promotion of ideas, goods, or services by an identified sponsor."*.

Organisations can use any of the following media in communicating messages in the form of advertising:

Broadcast media. This would include media such as commercial television and radio, and is frequently the most expensive media available;

Printed media. The timing of the publication of printed media can be anything from daily to annually or even less frequently. Media contained in this category would include newspapers, magazines, periodicals, journals and so on;

Outdoor media. This segment would include any media which is generally located outdoors and in a fixed position. Items would comprise billboards, posters, neon signs and hoardings, among others;

Cinema advertising. A media which is self-explanatory, although not overly popular due to the low and infrequent attendance levels.

Sales promotion

This can be defined as

> *"Short term incentives to encourage purchase or sale of a product or service."*

Items which would be included as sales promotion would include instruments such as on-pack offers, coupons, tokens, free gifts, price promotions and competitions.

Publicity

A rather more complex definition for the area of publicity. It can defined as

> *"Non personal stimulation of demand for a product, service, or business unit by planting commercially significant news about it in a published medium or obtaining favourable presentation of it upon radio, television, or stage, that is not paid for by the sponsor."*

Publicity would include the activities of providing press releases, seminars, exhibitions, and the whole area of public relations, which covers projects such as sponsorship, open days and charitable donations.

Personal selling

The difference between personal selling and most other forms of communication is that it is a two-way process. It is possible for the consumer to answer back or to ask questions when confronted by a personal sales representative. When confronted by an advert on the television or in a newspaper, the communication is all one way. This area of marketing communication is often seen to focus on selling techniques and sales force management, as well as telemarketing, fairs and trade shows. For many organisations, personal selling is too expensive to consider if the target segment of a market is a mass audience. Consider the problems and costs involved if Coca Cola attempted to ensure a personal sales representative visited each of its customers on a regular basis. Therefore it is much more commonly found in business to business marketing, where the customer base is generally smaller and the costs of the individual transactions larger.

Direct marketing

It is possible to add other media to this list, such as direct marketing. This is a popular derivative of advertising which is aimed at achieving an immediate decision to buy from the product offering communicated to the receiver. Catalogue selling and direct mail are just two of the direct marketing activities available, and this area of promotion is certainly growing in this country. Party Plan activities and Telesales are often placed within the field of promotion with obvious justification.

While there is a certain logic to the categories stated above, there is inevitably an area of overlap for some promotional vehicles, and as such too strict classification is generally unnecessary.

A list of 'other advertising media' exists, which covers one-off media which seem difficult to attribute to the media categories already listed above. These include the following : Television and films in hotels, electronic advertising displays, Prestel, litter bins, parking meters, sound advertising on buses, van posters, video in clubs/pubs and many more. In the 1990s it is possible to advertise through just about any medium available, and as we become more and more used to advertising messages being pushed our way, this trend is likely to continue to increase.

Customer care

It can be argued that another important element of any communications mix should include customer care. Many industries focus on such care as not only a necessary approach to marketing services, but as a key marketing communication tool. Customer care refers to the manner with which all customers (and potential customers) are handled by the staff of an organisation. It will often require a staff training programme to ensure that all staff adopt the required manner and approach. Activities such as telephone manner and the handling of complaints would also fall under this category. Many organisations now realise that the development of a good reputation – one of the keys to success – involves all aspects of communicating with the consumer. All of the good work done by an expensive advertising campaign can be undone by one surly uncooperative retail assistant.

The role of promotion within the marketing mix

It should be obvious that much of the activity undertaken as part of the 'promotion' element of the mix impacts upon or is impacted by other mix elements. For example, a sales promotion offer which offers a '20% off' coupon is also partly a pricing issue. It is vital therefore not to look at promotion in isolation from other aspects of the mix, as they are all interrelated. Much of the work carried out by the promotional team is often predetermined by other mix ingredients and the overall marketing strategy.

As mentioned in the section on pricing, a product which adopts a 'quality' stance in the market will require a promotional campaign of an appropriate nature. A niche strategy will obviously involve the use of appropriate promotional tools and media to reach the targeted market segment.

Target audience

The first stage when devising any promotional campaign is to define the target audience. It is crucial that the message has a high impact with as little wastage as possible. Detailed information on likely audiences is identified through an organisation's research effort, and is often in the form of *customer profiling*. The information derived from even the most basic profiling work will help to determine the age range, socio-economic group, geographical location, sex, family life-cycle stage or benefit sought. This will permit the promotional mix to target specific market segments in specific locations to make the maximum possible use of the promotional budget. In terms of segmentation strategies, it would be necessary to target either a few segments (niche marketing), several segments (selective marketing), or the entire market (mass marketing).

Promotion and the product life cycle

The promotional mix must be devised with the product life cycle firmly in mind. Different products will require differing emphasis on the mix elements from the introductory stage through to the growth, maturity and decline stages. Generally, a new product will need to be "pushed" to the marketplace in the early stages through awareness building media advertising.

If the product is in the embryonic or introductory stage of its life cycle, the segmentation strategy adopted may move from niche through to mass marketing to allow the product to become established. The approach adopted will depend not only on the product life cycle but also on the state of buyer awareness of the potential consumers. Certain strategies and tactics are deigned to simply create awareness, others to develop interest, arouse desire or provoke action. It is vital to select the appropriate promotional means.

The promotional budget

There are numerous methods available for allocating a promotional budget. Each has its own merits, and are adopted to a greater or lesser extent by organisations.

Percentage of sales

With this method, a percentage of the total sales of an organisation is allocated towards the promotional budget. This can be done either on a historical basis or on a projected basis. Each has its own drawbacks. If the budget is set on the basis of previous years sales, and it is accepted that there is some kind of direct relationship between promotion and sales levels, then the organisation is actually attempting to predetermine the sales levels for the coming year. Should the budget be set as a percentage of future sales, the problem arises if sales do not come up to expectations. This would necessarily limit the budget at a time when increased promotional spending may be the cure which is required.

Competitive parity

This is a very reactive approach. Organisations simply assess or ascertain the levels of spending of their rivals, and allocate their own budgets as a reaction to this. This effectively removes control of the budget, and therefore the overall strategy, from the hands of the organisation itself. A more proactive approach is generally agreed to be more appropriate.

The investment approach

With this technique, promotion is viewed as an investment for the future, and its future benefits are regarded as more important than any immediate or short term gains. This method has the benefit of taking the longer term view which fits in with the whole philosophy of planning. Future benefits can be discounted by using the appropriate financial techniques to provide a present value for any expenditure. The major problem, however, is that future benefits may be extremely difficult to identify, and as such the discounted present value may under or overestimate the true worth of the expenditure.

The objective and task method

This is very much the approach favoured by academic marketers. Objectives are set, and the appropriate budget allocated in order to achieve them. Unfortunately, the nature of promotional activity is such that even if strict quantifiable targets are set, it is often impossible to determine how much spending will be required in order to reach them, as promotional activity does not exist within a vacuum, removed from all other environmental factors.

The affordable approach

The most commonly adopted method is to simply decide how much an organisation can afford to 'spare' and to see what can be bought for this money. In terms of marketing theory, this method is completely incorrect, as it regards promotion as a bolt-on extra to all other activities, as opposed to an integral business venture. It is often, however, the procedure which many organisations use.

In reality, most organisations will use a combination of some or all of the methods to determine their budgets, combining good business and academic practice with gut feeling and financial necessity.

Ethical Considerations

One of the major problems faced by many students and practitioners of marketing is the moral stance which they should adopt. Cynics would suggest that far from being a way of satisfying established needs, marketing is concerned with giving the public what the organisation believes it should want. The adage 'the public gets what the public wants' can be easily adapted to read 'the public wants what the public gets' (with acknowledgements to Paul Weller and the Jam!). Numerous moral and ethical issues are raised within the whole area of marketing, including the following:

- Inflation
- Social Problems
- Selling False Dreams

Inflation

It can be argued that the customer pays indirectly for all expenditure on marketing of a product, which merely serves to push up prices artificially with all of the attendant problems. Expensive packaging and promotional campaigns are blamed for inflating the end price of many products. The move towards 'basics' and unbranded products which was discussed earlier shows a reaction to this criticism, although even more cynical people would suggest that this is the result of astute marketers spotting an opportunity and exploiting it.

Social problems

In recent years, people have been killed in the USA simply so that the murderer can steal the particular brand of training shoes they were wearing. People with branded clothing have been robbed, whilst crime is often blamed on the 'wannabee' mentality of individuals influenced by seeing the high standard of living of others, and being convinced by marketing techniques that they are somehow missing out. The society in which we live is one which condemns us to an extent if we do not conform to media created norms, and it is said that it is marketing which helps create these norms. A recent trend has seen the growth in sales of computer game systems. Heavy promotional spending by the market leaders has led to a generation who are more interested in Sonic the Hedgehog than any other activity. Whether this is a problem caused by, influenced by or not affected at all by marketing is an area of considerable debate.

Selling false dreams

Most people will have at some time bought a product or service which did not turn out to be what they had hoped. Mail order companies claim to have more returns and problems from their cheaper items than for the more expensive ones, as they are marketed in such a way as to create a false image. To take this argument one step further, it can be claimed as discussed above that marketing itself creates the needs, wants or dreams of consumers.

Consumer Protection

There are many other examples of ethical problems which may or may not have been caused by marketing activities. Included in this would be all of the above practices, plus areas such as pollution and health and safety. In order to mitigate against such problems, considerable legislation has been passed which is aimed at protecting the consumer from such excesses of the industry. Many organisations exist to assist in the battle against the unscrupulous business. Publications and television programmes such as *'That's Life'*, *'Watchdog'*, *'Checkpoint'* and *'Which?'* all contribute greatly in this arena.

The Trading Standards Authority is established as a reference point for investigations of complaints as to various malpractices of business, and is not afraid to use the power of the media to put across its own message. The Advertising Standards Authority is effectively the trade association for the Advertising Industry. Its aim is to ensure that all advertisements are *'legal, decent and honest'*. Both of these organisations have the whole myriad of legal courses of action available to support their actions. It is reassuring to know that the battle against unethical organisations is not being waged alone.

Activity

Find a recent copy of 'Which' magazine, and select one of the products (preferably a consumer good or service) which is reviewed in that publication. For each of the brands which is reviewed, try to obtain examples of their promotional media, for example newspaper advertisements or direct mail leaflets. Study this media, and assess whether, in light of the reviews which have been carried out, they comply fully with the 'legal decent and honest' rules which are imposed by the Advertising Standards Authority.

Assignment *The Cockcroft Art Centre*

The Cockcroft Arts Centre is located in the City of Coventry. It was established in 1969 as a Centre for Visual and Performing Arts, in a small building near to the City Centre. Through a succession of generous funding arrangements it has been able to move to its current premises, which consist of a row of three Victorian terraced houses, each three storeys high plus basements. Initially, the Centre was established as a centre where local students could display or perform their work. On moving to the new premises, the Centre decided to concentrate solely upon the Visual Arts, and this has been the case since 1981. During an average year, the Centre features about 12 themed exhibitions, mainly of Contemporary Art by local artists. Attendance has been gradually increasing, but the Centre is beginning to feel the financial strain. Total income is approximately £150,000 per year, whilst fixed expenditure on staff alone totals almost £90,000. Other variable costs soon erode any potential profit margin. All exhibitions are free to enter, but visitors are asked to make a donation to the running costs in a small box marked 'donations' as they enter the building. A recent survey carried out by students showed that the main visitors to the Centre were students and staff of the local University, school parties, plus a few repeat visitors. The Centre was competing for visitors with a range of other leisure pursuits, as well as five other arts venues within a 30 mile radius. The other venues were not regarded as competition by the Cockcroft Management Team, as they each either specialised in a different form of visual art or were very broad in their appeal. Attendance figures totalled over 65,000 during the previous year, but almost one third of that figure had been to see an exhibition of 'Thunderbird Models - as seen on TV'. In addition to the actual galleries, the Centre also has a successful Bistro in the Basement, which accounts for nearly 25% of the Centre's revenue - the majority of the rest coming from public funding. Small income is also received from a gift shop, sponsorship and an 'art-for-hire' scheme. The entrance to the Bistro is quite separate to the Centre, and no references to the Centre are currently made within the Bistro. The outside of the building is rather unprepossessing, and signposts are virtually non-existent. As such, many people do not even know the Centre exists. Due to lack of funds, the Centre currently promotes itself in only one way. For each exhibition, the Centre prints 5,000 leaflets and distributes these randomly around libraries, colleges, schools and other public buildings.

Partly as a result of the success of the 'Thunderbirds' exhibition, and partly because the tolerance of the funding bodies is beginning to run out, the Centre Management Team have decided that it is right to consider a new approach. They have approached the local college and asked for a team of students to come up with suggestions as to how they can improve their whole marketing performance.

Task

As part of this Marketing Team, you have been asked to prepare a report for Brian Patterson, the Director of the Cockcroft Arts Centre, which outlines some of the ways in which the Cockcroft Centre is currently not performing its marketing activities to the full potential. You are also asked to make reasoned suggestions as to ways in which the Centre could improve its performance. You must remember, however, that the Centre is basically a non-profit making organisation, has a very limited budget, and must never become involved in any practices which might be regarded in any way as unethical.

Unit 4

Human Resources

This unit has been written to cover the following specifications of the General National Vocational Qualification Business Level 3

Unit 4   Human Resources Level 3

Element 4.1:   Investigate human resourcing

Performance criteria:
1   responsibilities in human resourcing are explained
2   systems for employee relations are described
3   training and development opportunities are identified
4   legal requirements regulating employment practices are explained
5   types of redress available to employees when legislation is not upheld are described
6   human resource management which improves business performance is identified

Element 4.2:   Investigate job roles in organisational structures

Performance criteria:
1   organisational structures in different types of business organisations are described
2   job roles within structures are described
3   purposes of job descriptions are explained and examples are produced
4   purposes of person specifications are explained and examples are produced

Element 4.3:   Evaluate job applications and interviews
Performance criteria:

1   recruitment procedures are identified
2   letters of application are evaluated for clarity and quality of presentation
3   curriculum vitae are evaluated for clarity and quality of presentation.
4   interviewer techniques are practised and appraised
5   interviewee techniques are practised and appraised
6   legal and ethical obligations in recruitment are explained

(extract from General National Vocational Qualifications Mandatory Units for Business GNVQ3 offered by Business Education and Technology Council, City and Guilds and RSA Examinations Board - published by the National Council for Vocational Qualifications April 1993 - reproduced by kind permission of the National Council for Vocational Qualifications)

GNVQ3 Business - Unit Number U1016177

Element 4.1 Human Resourcing

In this element we shall examine how organisations manage their human resources. Let us begin by considering the responsibilities which the 'Personnel' or 'Human Resource' department has. A good starting point is to look at the definition of personnel management used by the Institute of Personnel Management. It states that the personnel function is:

> *"that part of management which is concerned with people at work and with their relation-*
> *ships within an enterprise. Its aim is to bring together and develop into an effective*
> *organisation, the men and women who make up the enterprise. Also, having regard for*
> *the well-being of the individuals and of working groups, to enable them to make their best*
> *contributions to the organisation's success."*

Many organisations have departments which have the function of personnel or human resources management. This does not mean that other managers do not manage people, they certainly do. There is a need, however, for specialism in this area to guide the organisations on policies and planning and control of human resources. A personnel department can take an unbiased overall view of other departments and can provide practical assistance in dealing with staff on matters such as recruitment and selection. The Personnel department is a *functional* department and can provide, to anyone within the organisation, advice and help on the function of human resource management.

Personnel/Human Resource Activities

The activities vary depending on the organisation needs and development. Many of the tasks are carried out solely within the personnel department. These may include short-listing of potential recruits, updating a personnel database and others. Nevertheless, many of the important activities are carried out in partnership with others in the organisation, at all levels of management. These may include manpower planning, training, discipline, performance evaluation and others.

Some organisations see the personnel department as another service to the internal workings of the organisation. As such, they may be grouped together with other functional departments including finance, works study, administration, planning and others. The overall grouping may be called Management Services or Business Services departments.

The following are some of the activities that may form the duties of the Personnel Department:

- manpower planning
- recruitment and selection
- training and development and training needs analysis
- job satisfaction, motivation and morale
- job analysis and job evaluation
- performance appraisal
- employee welfare, benefits and compensation
- payment systems
- health and safety
- industrial relations
- employment legislation

- discipline
- equal opportunities and equality of treatment

Some organisations may add other activities to this list, such as counselling in the case of personal problems or trauma caused by attending scenes of horrific accidents. We explain and discuss these individual functions later in this unit.

Some organisations expect the line managers to manage some or all of the above without any specialist assistance. This is especially true in small organisations which cannot afford specialist functional managers. It is also true of some larger organisations, where the top management may fear that any interference with the line managers right to manage their own personnel may break traditional bonds of command. Without a specialist personnel department working closely with line managers, the activities which are given attention may well depend on the priorities of the manager at any given time and some may be left undone by default. As the organisation depends upon the quality and motivation of its personnel, then the long term prospects may suffer, especially as the strength of competition increases. An important, though difficult, area within personnel is manpower planning and we shall consider this first.

Manpower planning

It is a function of the organisation's senior management to decide overall policy and objectives. An important aspect of this is the establishment of a personnel policy and personnel objectives for the organisation as a whole. This is often referred to as the *manpower plan*. A long term strategy is needed for the organisation and the manpower plan is an integrated part of this overall corporate strategy. Manpower planning may be defined as the means by which an organisation may plan its future employee requirements. This will involve determining the number and quality of employees that will be required in the future. Obviously the organisation's requirement for manpower will be set by the anticipated future demand for its product or service and as such is part of the long term development of the organisation. Clearly it is important to ascertain whether or not this future demand is capable of being met by the present workforce and if it cannot there is then the need to establish plans to ensure that the present staff can be trained or developed or that new employees can be recruited to fill the gap.

The aims of manpower planning

In order to survive every organisation must meet its own needs and demands for employees This may be expressed under the following headings:

- *recruitment*. The organisation must ensure that the right kind of employee is attracted. Thus its recruitment policy is determined by its specific manning needs.
- *experience*. Well trained and experienced employees must be encouraged to stay with the organisation. This is achieved by creating an appropriate working environment, career structure and adequate rewards.
- *task performance*. All employees must carry out their duties and responsibilities in an efficient and effective way and the employer must be able to monitor this and rectify any deficiencies in its employee's performance.
- *motivation*. Employees must be motivated so that they will do more than just carry out instructions. For the organisation to grow and survive it must have employees who are willing to seek improvements in their work tasks and use their ingenuity in achieving this.

The use of manpower planning in guiding management

Manpower plans can guide management decision making in a number of respects. These include: recruitment; staff development, including management development; training, involving the number and categories of staff who require training; anticipating the need for redundancies; productivity bargaining; improving industrial relations; estimating labour costs; health, safety and welfare; accommodation requirements; and disciplinary procedures.

The need to update the organisation's manpower plan

The manpower plan will need updating at various intervals as a result of changes in:

- *new technology*. To maintain a competitive position the organisation must adapt to changes in new technology. This may mean updating the skills of existing employees or hiring new employees with new skills. New technology may require changes in the methods of work as well as the equipment which is used. This may also involve a corresponding change in the attitude of the workforce to new technology.

- *government intervention*. The government from time to time introduces legislation which requires a modification of an organisation's manpower plans. A contemporary example is the change in female compulsory retirement age contained in the Sex Discrimination Act 1986.

- *new organisational goals*. Changes in market conditions often force an organisation to rethink its business strategy. This can mean a major revision of its manpower requirements.

- *the changing needs of society*. The public's ideas, tastes and needs all tend to change. Such change may cause an organisation to grow or decline. For example tobacco firms have been forced to diversify into the manufacture of other products as smoking has become less socially acceptable. This has obviously meant a reduction in the number of workers in the tobacco industry.

The time scale of manpower planning

Planning by its very nature involves the anticipation of future events. The further we project into the future the less certain is our plan. Therefore we can divide manpower planning into different time scales.

Short term manpower planning

Planning up to 1-2 years ahead provides for the personnel needs of the organisation in its present form. Examples are the replacement of people who retire or training programmes for new starters. There should be adequate data available to use in forecasting such short term changes. The organisation should have job descriptions of all existing staff and personnel records will indicate the age of individuals to anticipate retirements. Often a computer system is used to hold a data base for personnel information. This enables information such as the identification of workers within a given age range to be obtained very quickly.

Long term manpower planning

If an organisation looks further ahead such as over the next 5 years there will obviously be a greater degree of uncertainty. However, the training of certain employees such as accountants or engineers may require a considerable amount of such forward planning. Also if the organisation is involved in long term projects it will have to anticipate its manpower needs in advance and allow sufficient time to recruit or train appropriate staff.

Long term manpower planning attempts to provide for the personnel needs of the organisation as they may develop in the future. This has to take into account any new objectives the organisation may wish to pursue. To achieve this the needs of both direct and indirect workers may be taken into account. If for instance, a hospital decided to provide a new service such as bone marrow transplants, not only would doctors and nurses (regarded as direct staff) be required but also vital ancillary staff (regarded as indirect staff) such as laboratory scientific officers, administrators, porters, and others. New technological advances are always difficult to predict with any degree of accuracy. However, there are three factors which are usually associated with new advances:

- an increase in productivity;
- the opportunity to gain an increase in quality; and
- a change in skills required by the personnel involved.

Predictions of the current developments in new technology suggest that staff in the future may have to change their work skills three times in their working careers. Technological advances which demonstrate the three factors previously mentioned can be found in almost every manufacturing and service industry. Many advances can be identified in the field of health care. For example the chemical balance found in a sample of a patient's blood may well give a vital clue as to the person's state of health and the possible treatment. At one time a hospital laboratory worker had to perform individual tests which were lengthy and depended heavily on the skills of the laboratory analyst. Now machines are used which run many different tests on a small sample and handle large numbers of samples from different patients. The tests are printed out as results which can be compared with the normal range found in people or compared with previous results from a patient undergoing treatment. The tests are carried out by machinery which can give similar good quality results continually and can be monitored by checking its analysis of test or control samples with known chemical balances.

Laboratories throughout the country can co-operate by checking the quality and accuracy of each others machines and agree new high standards. This means that there is much higher productivity, expressed as tests completed per laboratory scientific officer. There is also the opportunity to improve the quality of the results at the same time. The skills needed in the pathology laboratory have thus changed from the ability to carry out individual tests, to the ability to correctly programme and maintain complex machinery and both to spot and correct machine based errors. There is also the need to be able to understand the science involved and to discuss the results with interested staff. To the older staff this may represent the loss of hard won skills, but to the newer staff it may mean a removal of the drudgery of repetitive procedures. Naturally the greatest benefit will be to the patient, with the medical staff armed with knowledge on which to base their diagnosis and treatment for better health care.

Personal selection

When an economy grows, more jobs are generated and more movement between jobs becomes likely. Organisations must therefore seek to be efficient and effective in recruitment and selection of the personnel needed for the future of the organisation. Recruitment can be seen as the first step in filling a vacancy. It involves examining the job to be done, where the best candidates are likely to be found and how best to make contact and attract them. Selection is the next process where various means are employed to choose the most suitable candidate, in particular the selection interview, which should be prepared for by both the employer and the candidate! These processes can be expensive in terms of advertising, expenses of candidates and above all the administrative time taken up. Subsequent expense will emerge in the form of induction and other training costs. Recruitment campaigns are needed to attract suitably skilled staff. Relocation and other allowances are offered to make the jobs seem more attractive. Before any job is advertised, even if it is for replacement staff, it will be necessary to establish a justification for the post or position. It may be possible to rearrange the work patterns to tackle the work in a different way so saving staff costs, or, if there is a limit on the total number of staff employed, allowing another department to have the new employees. For example, by using more standardised documents, two typists using word-processors could replace three typists using the old system and outdated typewriters. The 'saved post' could be transferred to an area which is seeking to build up new business for the future, without additional expense to the company. Assuming that the post was justified, then the department concerned may carry out some form of task analysis producing a job description for the future candidate. The Work-study, Organisation and Methods or Personnel department may be called in to give expert help and assistance. This assistance is likely to cover the following aspects:

- drafting a job description or specification;
- advertising the post;
- short-listing candidates;
- planning the selection interview;
- conducting the interview.

We shall consider the processes involved in recruitment and selection in more detail in Element 4.3.

Industrial relations and manpower planning

By industrial relations we mean the relationships which exist between the organisation and its workforce. Every organisation should attempt to develop good industrial relations as the effects of industrial action can be severely damaging. As organisations increase in size individual bargaining between a manager and an individual worker becomes no longer practical. In such circumstances the trade unions will undertake this role on behalf of individual workers. This is referred to as '*collective bargaining*'. With the development of 'white collar' or staff unions managers and workers will sometimes find themselves in the same union and clearly this may tend to complicate the roles each play. A climate where good communications and morale are present is usually conducive to good industrial relations. The effect of poor industrial relations may damage industrial output and confidence in British industry both domestically and internationally and so government agencies have been established to assist in the promotion of industrial relations. The most important of these is ACAS (the Advisory, Conciliation and Arbitration Service). Codes of Practices designed by ACAS are intended to assist the promotion of good industrial relations. We examine industrial relations and the role of the trade unions in Unit 5, *Employment in the Market Economy*.

Training and Development

The need for training and development

Human resource needs are dynamic not static. We live in times of increasing rate of change and it is estimated that the average worker will need at least three new sets of skills during a working life. For example, a trained typist may be trained to operate a computing system involving word-processing, desk-top publishing, spreadsheets and databases. At a later stage this person may be promoted to a management post requiring not technical skills but managerial skills, requiring essential extra training and development.

Training and development need the active support of management. Training should reduce profitable results both for the organisation and the individual. Its purpose is to help individuals and organisations improve on quality competitiveness and productivity, test ideas, encourage change and seek out tomorrow's ideas. Many organisations have excellent training policies and facilities for employees. However, when sales are down, organisations may carry out cost-cutting exercises and some may see training as a luxury when profits are low. The training programme could be halted until business resumes former high levels. Unfortunately this short term measure has an adverse effect in the longer term. In a few years time, due to natural wastage of staff, there will be a shortage of skilled labour. The organisation may not be able to seize new opportunities because of skill shortages and lose business to their competitors. Unfortunately, attracting skilled workers from other organisations may not be the answer to this problem. The organisation may have to pay higher salaries as an incentive to recruitment. This adds to the overall cost of the product or service, resulting in lower profits.

The words training, education and development are sometimes used interchangeably. However, there are generally recognised differences as explained below:

- *Training*. *Training* is often focused on attaining knowledge, skills and competences for a particular job. It is narrower in focus than education but has direct application to the workplace. For example, training may be given to pass a driving test and become a licensed car driver.

- *Education*. *Education* is usually used in the context of general learning and providing the basic knowledge and skills for many experiences in life. For example, reading writing and numeracy skills are needed to at least a basic levels for most occupations.

- *Development*. *Development* suggests not just training for a job. It also relates to seeking a broadening of experience and capability and focused on career advancement. Thus knowledge and skills are important. However, there may be a need for experience in a broad category of situations to enhance an individuals development. Becoming a Manager may mean more than just having technical skills related to the product or service given by a department. An overall, broad experience in achieving effective and efficient use of all resources, will be needed. Development may be a lifetime experience. Even passing a driving test does not produce a skilled driver. Years of experience under all road conditions may be needed.

Systematic training

There are circumstances where unplanned or "ad-hoc" training may take place to meet an unsuspected need, for example, when a new technique would be beneficial to the organisation. However, in the majority of cases, there must be a system that plans and monitors the training within the organisation. We can trace this system by first examining the Corporate Policies and Plan of an organisation. This should include a Manpower (Human Resources) Plan which describes the strategy for ensuring planning and monitoring of the improved quality of human resource within the organisation.

This strategy could provide for the setting up of Training department or section within a Personnel or Human Resource Management Department. The training that follows may be completed within the organisation or by outside personnel. A training policy will guide the actions of people within the organisation in a more effective way.

Training needs analysis

Often training within an organisation can be haphazard. The initiative for training may come solely from individual members of staff when they feel they have a need for extra skills. However, although it is important to meet these

individual needs, it is equally important that the organisation should satisfy the training needs that will help meet organisational objectives. Training needs analysis is a technique for identifying both organisational and individual training needs.

Performance gap

A training need is the gap between actual performance of an individual in a job and the standard of performance required. The first step in training needs analysis may be to survey the whole organisation and find the strengths and weaknesses where improved training may help. For example, customer complaints may point to a need for better quality of products and service throughout the organisation. This training would then have to be discussed with department heads and individuals and a timetable set for training by various means.

The first stage is to identify the causes for this gap for correction later. However, management must decide if the gap can be closed by extra training. This is not always the case, not everyone can be helicopter pilots, especially with vertigo! Gaps can be due to a number of reasons including inadequate initial training or tasks not clearly defined.

The second stage is to examine the standard set for the job or task and determine if it is up-to-date, clearly expressed and feasible.

The final stage is to examine the tasks or overall job. A persons job can be split into a number of individual tasks for study. Each task is then seen as a major element of work leading to a specific result. Jobs of different personnel may be examined as to how they are similar, linked or diverse before group training will be effective. Each task should be defined in terms of the responsibilities, duties, knowledge, skills and competences that are required.

Job related training

Job related training is the most common form of training employed over the full range of occupations. The increasing number of workers who participate in job related training demonstrates the fact that employers are more aware of the benefits that can be gained from having a highly trained and fully skilled workforce. Such training includes work experience or 'on the job learning' as well as participation in more structured courses. It is still the case that training is more likely to be provided away from the employer's premises at a learning institution but increasingly employers are providing their own training facilities or relying upon open learning opportunities. The main advantage of internal training is that the trainers should have accurate, up to date knowledge and understanding of the real problems of the business and so are better placed to offer realistic solutions. External training enjoys the benefit of trainers with specialists knowledge who are able to offer an objective view of problems.

Generally full-time staff are more likely to benefit from job related training than part-time staff and the longer that employees have served with their employers the more likely they are to receive it. It is ironic that despite the high level of unemployment in Britain research has shown that five percent of large businesses and six percent of small ones were having difficulty in filling certain vacancies. This indicates that there is still a significant skill shortage in the UK, meaning that there are not enough people available with the skills needed to do the jobs that need to be done.

Training for employment

One of the most significant changes in the structure of the workforce over the last ten years has been the increase in the number of young people who are being trained for employment, either on full-time courses at colleges or other educational and training institutions or on a part-time basis as part of their employment. This has partly been the result of government measures to reduce youth unemployment and increase the skills of the workforce and partly the result of organisations recognising that it is in their own best interest to train and develop their workforce.

The government has taken a number of measures to increase the level of training for young people. These include the following:

- *Training and Enterprise Councils* (TECs). The establishment of a network of Training and Enterprise Councils in England and Wales and Local Enterprise Companies (LECs) in Scotland. These bodies bring together business people, industrialists, educationalists and the local authorities in an attempt to set up training and development programmes which will enhance the skill base in each region. There are now 82 TECs and 22 TECs. They try to respond to the needs of local business and industry by providing training programmes which meet employers actual needs and so increase the possibility of employment for trainees on completion of the programme. They are now responsible for Youth Training, Employment Training and the Enterprise Allowance Scheme

- *Employment Training* (ET). Employment Training is a government programme operated by the TECs which has the objective of providing training for the longer-term unemployed. It is hoped that such programmes will help them get back into employment. The type of programme on offer are very varied ranging from basic literacy to more high level and specialist skill training. The programmes often involve the trainee in working with an employer as well as undertaking off-the-job training.

- *Youth Training* (YT). This was originally introduced in the mid 1980s as the Youth Training Scheme (YTS). This was a one year programme of training and work experience for school leavers. It was later extended into a two year programme in a range of occupations. In 1990 it was replaced by Youth Training (YT) which is administered by the TECs and has a greater emphasis on the need to gain vocational qualifications. It has about one third of million people on different schemes throughout the country.

Management Style

Now we can move from what is involved in the management of human resources , to how it is done. Because human beings are unique it follows that managers will manage differently in the sense of having different styles or approaches to the way in which they carry out their functions. The style that management adopts is extremely important. Most problems have no easy answer and usually no single answer, since problems require answers or solutions which best suit the particular situation, specific task and the people carrying out the work. Another way of expressing this is to say that just as people are unique – so too are problems. An example of a specific problem is a proposal to reduce the number of hours in the working week. Suppose management is faced with implementing this change. The final solution should take into account the needs of the employees and their problems such as unsociable hours and bus timetables. Management may solve the problem by exerting its authority and deciding the shift times and work patterns without consulting the workforce. This *'autocratic'* management style is demonstrated when a manager simply 'tells' people what to do. A variation could be a 'sells' style where the management have made their plans but explain them to the workforce in a way that may convince them that the chosen solution is the best option for the work force. This is referred to as a *'paternalistic'* style since it may be viewed as treating the employees rather like children. Alternatively management may decide to adopt a *'consultative'* style and discuss the problems with the employees before making a decision. The most *'democratic'* style may be to allow full participation by all employees in the decision-making process. They are given time to discuss the various possibilities and come to an agreed decision to suit all parties. The following figure summarises the different management styles which can be used:

The use of the most appropriate management style

To decide which management style to use it is necessary to consider:

- the personality, skill, experience and ability of the manager;
- the situation;
- the need for the workforce to participate in decision making.

Personality

Every manager differs in his or her ability to adopt a particular style successfully. Clearly a manager should evaluate his or her own personality and talents before adopting a particular management style. Often a very inexperienced manager can find that democratic management is difficult to handle.

The situation

Sometimes the situation itself may dictate the style to use. For example in a crisis or an emergency the workforce may look to management for a strong lead in decision making. In fact the workers may come to expect and feel the need for a largely autocratic style. If there was a fire on the fifth floor you would not expect a debate and a show of hands to decide on which exit route to use but someone who can get you out quickly and safely. Rules and procedures which have been laid down by management are expected to be followed implicitly in such circumstances.

Participation

The workforce may not feel the need to participate in certain decisions. If the decision involves a problem that is not directly related to a person's task, then there may little interest in active involvement. However, keeping people informed of decisions on changes may still be important and could be considered to be a lesser form of participation. Some organisations make an effort to keep all employees informed of top level decisions through the use of briefing meetings and in-house magazines and newspapers designed to give news, views and interests for dissemination throughout organisation as a whole.

Participation in decision making has the advantage of using more fully the untapped potential of all employees of the organisation. There is also the advantage that employees become more interested in the organisation and so want it to succeed and consequently work harder to achieve this. New processes are more likely to succeed where the people who have to make them work have a part to play in deciding the changes to be made.

Participative methods

Group methods

Many methods have been tried to gain the participation of employees as part of the management process. Group methods include:

- staff committees which may be both formal and informal;
- quality circles where groups meet to consider particular problems;
- autonomous work groups in which some work decisions are made by the group rather than their supervisor;
- project teams where a group meets on a regular basis representing different departments in the organisation to tackle specific problems.

Individual approach

Apart from these group methods many organisations try to stimulate individual approaches. Some people prefer to think and work on their own and are inhibited by performing within a group. Suggestion schemes, often with financial or non-financial rewards, are used in a variety of forms to stimulate the employee to put forward ideas for change. The best schemes also force management to vet the ideas thoroughly and put the useful ones into action as soon as possible.

Types of problems

It would be wrong to think that all management's problems can best be resolved by committees or some other method of wider consultation. By its very nature participation is a relatively slow process and if time is short it may be better for a single individual to make the decision. Naturally if more participation is needed then management must try to plan further ahead to allow time for it to take place. Generally the problems best tackled by participative means are those which do not have 'one best answer' but a variety of alternatives to choose from and the best in any particular situation is the one which best suits the organisation and its structure, the situation, the customer and the staff needs. There are of course many problems whose nature demands a technical answer. These should be made by experts. Suppose that you are lying in a hospital bed and the doctor about to give you an injection held a debate and asks for a show of hands among nurses, porters, administration and catering staff as to what quantity of the drug should be injected. You would lose all confidence in the quality of the expertise of the hospital in such circumstances! Technical problems need technical decisions by experts and should not be confused with the many general and human problems faced by management. That said, all managers usually possess some particular expertise; they may have become managers from a base of accountancy, personnel or the law. They nevertheless need to be able to make use of other technical and professional experts in order to make decisions and get things done, when the problem falls outside their own field of knowledge and experience.

Interpersonal skills

The interpersonal skills needed by a manager must include the ability to be a good listener as well as a good communicator. At meetings the manager will often act as a leader in proposing new ideas, or in counselling certain courses of action. However, the manager should 'take a back seat' and have a chairman's role in encouraging debate and decision making by others. Everyone should be given the chance to contribute at the appropriate time and the meeting should not be dominated by a few strong personalities. Often a consensus decision is to be preferred. This is one where all agree to the decision without a vote. The process of voting may leave those who are against a motion which has been passed with a feeling of defeat, certainly something which should not be encouraged if the organisation is to work in harmony.

Consultation

Consultation between management and workers requires skills of 'listening and asking' but may also involve management taking the initiative to 'inform' workers by using various techniques. Consultative committees are set up in many organisations with representatives of management and elected representatives of staff.

Consultative committees allow management to listen to the ideas and problems of staff through their representatives. Management should also be encouraged to include items of the agenda which enable them to establish employees views. The downward communication process should be carried out by each team or group leader. The consultation process is shown in the diagram on the next page.

Face to face communication is effective if questions and discussion are also possible. It is far less effective where the manager is not interested in the views or concerns of the employees.

Items for consultation

Policy and prime objectives are decisions made by the most senior management and being fundamental to the enterprise are not normally open to consultation, however how best such policies may be put into practice is often the matter for detailed discussion. While technical and urgent decisions are best made by the individual manager, consultation should be used where it does not slow decision making down

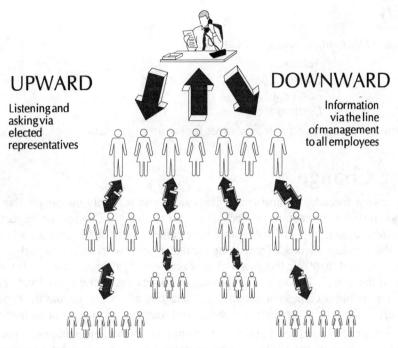

UPWARD

Listening and
asking via
elected
representatives

DOWNWARD

Information
via the line
of management
to all employees

Consultation

or limit its flexibility. Long term decisions or those which will affect a large number of employees, their work practices or working conditions, are likely to be better discussed in advance of planning and action. Good consultation is a practice which should help to reap long term advantages, if it is used at the right times and is effectively operated.

Conclusion

In discussing management styles we have emphasised two factors:

- *the manager's ability to adopt a particular style in the light of the particular situation*. It is probably accurate to say that most managers have a 'natural' or 'preferred' style which fits the individual's personality or which the manager learned from other managers, in other words the style in which they are 'being themselves';

- *subordinates have views on the style of manager they prefer*. Although it varies depending upon the problem involved there is considerable evidence to indicate that the 'consultative' style is commonly preferred. This style demonstrates the essential importance of communication systems within the organisation and the need for managers to be highly skilled communicators. Consultation can be a difficult and demanding process to handle, especially in the face of a hostile workforce. Participative methods and styles do not of course remove the responsibility of management ultimately to manage the organisation. They do however help to improve the organisational 'climate' if they are used effectively, and can be a useful tool to the imaginative manager.

The management task has never been easy and if anything it has grown more difficult and will continue to increase in difficulty as organisations become more complex, workers expectations become more sophisticated and technological change accelerates.

Activity

Consider the following management styles:

- Autocratic
- Consultative
- Participative
- Democratic

Identify the advantages and disadvantages facing an organisation which adopts each of these styles

Managing Change

One common constant faced by all business organisations and certainly the people that they employ is that at some point they will be required to accept or react to change. Change has impact on all facets of society creating new dimensions and increasing uncertainty. Individuals have an inbuilt reluctance to accept change which makes the task of managing change within an organisation such a demanding one. In 1991 Colin Carnal said that "We live in a period of accelerating change. Great political event changes our perception of the world. Fundamental changes in society restructure our lives. New technology means that the impossible becomes commonplace. Change is all around us and the capacity to manage change effectively is the crucial attribute of a successful manager in today's organisation".

Change causes stress and resistance, it creates uncertainty and inevitability imposes new demands upon employees. For these reasons the ability to manage change is the single most important characteristic that any leader in an organisation can demonstrate. Managers should always adopt a planned, proactive but flexible attitude to change to try to lessen the impact. A good manager should be fully prepared for change and anticipate its occurrence.

In order to minimise resistance to change in an organisation and enable employees to cope with the pressures it is important to develop procedures which enable those affected by the change to participate in its implementation. This will involve establishing support systems such as networks and ensuring the free flow of information. The overriding view of the numerous theorists on change management is that change is more likely to be successfully implemented adopting a democratic style of management rather than a bureaucratic or dictatorial approach. Resistance to change can be reduced through involvement, communication, training and staff development and by creating an environment that understands and is conducive to change.

While it is the purpose of this section to identify and address some of the problems associated with the management of any change process you should appreciate that within any organisation change will also occur naturally as the organisation develops and expands.

Successful management of the change process involves

- Understanding change
- Anticipating change
- Identifying change triggers
- Understanding resistance
- Planning the change process

An example of a change that has been introduced into many work organisations is the adoption of a performance related appraisal scheme. Resistance from employees to the introduction of such a scheme would normally be related to:

- a lack of understanding of the main goals and objectives of the scheme;

- a lack of efficient promotion of the scheme;
- a lack of training;
- a lack of information;
- a lack of employee or Trade Union involvement;
- a lack of time to develop the scheme.

Any or all of the above could result in a lack of acceptance and understanding, frustration and confusion, leading to a lack of commitment and increased pressure on the staff affected. To reduce the negative impact of such a change therefore it is important to manage the change process and so contribute towards organisational effectiveness and efficiency.

Understanding change

Before embarking on a change process it is crucial that management fully understands what is meant by change. There must be an appreciation of the nature and causes of change at both the individual and organisational level. It is by coming to terms with the inevitability of change that management will be equipped to face up to the needs of the organisation and react positively to it. If at an early stage in the change process managers are made aware of the reasons for change, the time scales involved, the impact on employees and the planning requirements then they will be in a better position to manage the change effectively. The ability to identify common issues and objectives relating to change such as maintaining motivation and commitment and carry out effective communications is a management skill that is normally only acquired through effective training.

Any effective training programme for those involved in managing the change process should cover

- the identification of change
- the identification of feelings and responses to change
- factors influencing change
- why people react differently to change
- understanding the barriers to change
- the role of the leader during change
- change mechanisms
- understanding and overcoming resistance
- communicating change

Anticipating change

In any organisation change is inevitable so that management needs to be proactive in creating an open culture for change management. The culture of a company defines how people should behave in a given set of circumstances. It prescribes behaviour in line with organisational attitudes and beliefs. To create a climate conducive to change necessarily involves change. Such a climate is characterised by a participative style of management where those affected by the change are invited to participate in planning the change and there is genuine teamwork and open communications. This has been referred to as "bottom up" change management and helps to reduce resistance to change by encouraging a feeling of ownership.

Resistance to change

Fear of change is understandable. Those individuals affected by it will be concerned as to whether they can cope with the new demands that are placed upon them. They are also aware that if they are unable to acquire new skills that this could lead to a termination of their employment. A further concern is that a restructuring or reorganisation of the workplace may result in a reduction in requirements for staff and ultimately lead to a redundancy situation. In such an atmosphere it is understandable that individuals focus on their own best interests rather than those of the organisation. It should be stressed that this resistance to change is not confined to staff and will normally include management of an organisation. Adopting a planned approach to change will help to decrease resistance.

There is a tendency in organisations for management to underestimate the impact of change on employees and to simply expect them to go along with it without any resistance. Because managers often feel under pressure themselves by the change their reaction is often to isolate themselves from the staff. If there is a lack of communication between management and staff then it is likely that this will cause frustration and anger and a misunderstanding of the reasons for implementing the change. It is a natural reaction for individuals to feel that changes in work methods are being introduced because they are inefficient rather than inefficient processes. This leads to anger resistance and a sense of betrayal.

Planning for change

It makes sense that if a change process is going to involve a high financial commitment and meet resistance from staff that is should be made the subject of explicit planning.

This involves:

- identifying foreseeable resistance to change and removing the restraining factors;
- determining the general abilities of management to lead the change. If there are obvious deficiencies in communication or counselling skills then they should be remedied through training before the change is introduced;
- setting clear goals and objectives is a prerequisite to change. Where possible employees should be involved in the decision making process as they generally have the most detailed knowledge of the possible problems. Involvement also helps the creation of the ownership of ideas and helps to reduce the resistance;
- the costs of the change both in terms of time and resources should be calculated;
- a realistic timetable should be agreed from planning the change to full implementation. Pushing the change through too quickly will result in a lack of understanding and inevitably resistance;
- obtaining a firm commitment to the change from all levels of management so that they present a united front is crucial to the success of the change process;
- change can only be implemented smoothly if there is a two way communication flow so that individuals know when, how and why change will affect them. Information should be provided as early as possible by management through official memos presentations or internal company media. Those on the receiving end of the change should be given the opportunity to give their views;
- one valuable exercise is to identify those individuals or departments in an organisation who are proactive to change and these change agents can then be encouraged to lead their colleagues through the process;
- introducing steps to overcome resistance to change such as the introduction of incentives is an obvious step to take in the change process;
- networks will occur naturally in any work organisation and they can be very effective in conveying information. Networks should be encouraged therefore to increase interpersonal relationships so that individuals can draw on each others experience and gain moral support.

- introducing a process of evaluation so that responses and feedback can be measured is a valuable exercise bearing in mind that new methods or systems will always require modification.

Activity

"Change causes stress and resistance, it creates uncertainty and inevitably imposes new demands on employees." Make a list of the issues you would expect to be included in an effective training programme for those involved in managing a process of change.

Legal Requirements Regulating Employment Practices

In this section we shall examine the range of legal requirements which face an organisation when it is employing staff. Since the mid 1960s there has been a dramatic increase in intervention by both national governments, and more recently by European Community institutions in individual employment relationships. Generally this intervention, in the form of employment legislation has as its primary purpose the objective of regulating employment contracts. While it is generally acknowledged by European and national governments and the majority of employers that certain rights such as security in employment, severance payment, health and safety, equal opportunities and trade union membership should be embodied within statutes, a number of proposed rights such as minimum wage and a maximum number of contractual hours for employees are more controversial and do not have universal acceptance.

The main source of individual employment rights, particularly in relation to unfair dismissal and redundancy payments, remains the Employment Protection (Consolidation) Act 1978 as amended. In the table on the following page an attempt has been made to identify the main statutory employment rights, their source and the means of enforcement. As a number of rights arise only after a period of continuous employment, this has also been included where appropriate. Rights are only exercisable within strict time limits and these are shown, along with the various types of redress available if the right has been infringed.

In this section it is proposed to examine legal requirements relating to equal opportunities in particular equal pay and maternity rights, individual rights relating to security of employment contained in unfair dismissal and redundancy legislation and health and safety at work. Terms and conditions of employment are dealt with in Element 4.3, *Job Applications and Interviews*, where we examine the contract of employment.

Statutory employment rights

For each of the following rights under statute there is reference to the person qualified to benefit, the statutory source and the time period and means by which the right is legally enforceable.

Statutory right	Statutory source	Means of Enforcement	Time limits	Redress
To be given an itemised pay statement in writing containing specified particulars	EPCA 78 s.8	Complaint by an employee to an Industrial Tribunal	Within three months of cessation of employment (where appropriate)	A declaration and/or compensation
To a guarantee payment for an employee with continuous employment of one month	EPCA 78 s.12	Complaint by an employee to an Industrial Tribunal	Within three months of the day to which the payment relates	An award of the payment
To be paid during suspension from work on medical grounds for an employee with continuous employment of three months	EPCA s.19	Complaint by an employee to an Industrial Tribunal	Within three months of the day to which the payment relates	An award of the remuneration
Termination of employment for an employee with continuous employment of not less than one month	EPCA 78 s.49	Complaint by an employee to the Court	Within six years of the breach of contract	An award of damages
To a written statement of the reasons for dismissal for employees with two years continuous employment	EPCA 78 s.53(1)	Complaint by an employee to an Industrial Tribunal	Within three months of the effective date of termination	An award of two weeks pay
Not to be unfairly dismissed for an employee with two years continuous employment	EPCA 78 s.54	Complaint by an employee to an Industrial Tribunal	Within three months of the effective date of termination	An award of compensation, reinstatement or re-engagement
Not to be dismissed for trade union membership and activities	EPCA 78 s.58	Complaint by an employee to an Industrial Tribunal	Within three months of the effective date of termination	An award of compensation, reinstatement or re-engagement
Not to have action short of dismissal taken because of trade union membership or activities	EPCA 78 s.23	Complaint by an employee to an Industrial Tribunal	Within three months of the effective date of termination	An award of compensation
Not to be unreasonably excluded or expelled from membership of a trade union where a closed shop is in operation	Employment Act 1980 s.4	Complaint by an employee to an Industrial Tribunal	Within six months of the act complained of	A declaration and/or compensation
Not to be unjustifiably disciplined by a trade union for refusing to participate in industrial action	Employment Act 1988 s.3	Complaint by a trade union member to an Industrial Tribunal	Within three months of the allegation that the right has been infringed	A declaration

Statutory right	Statutory source	Means of Enforcement	Time limits	Redress
Not to be called to participate in industrial action without the approval of a secret ballot	Employment Act 1988 s.1(1)	Complaint by a trade union member to a Court	After the internal grievance procedure or six months after invoking the procedure and it is not complete	A court order that is 'appropriate'
Not to be refused employment because of membership or non membership of a trade union	TULR(C)A 1992 s.137	Complaint to an Industrial Tribunal	Within three months of the conduct complained of	A declaration or compensation/re commendation
To prevent a trade union indemnifying an individual in respect of penalties for relevant offences or contempts	TULR(C)A 1992 s.15	Complaint to the court	Within three months of the conduct complained of	A court order that is appropriate
To be paid maternity pay and be entitled to return to work in the event of pregnancy or confinement for an employee who has been continuously employed for not less than two years and for all employees from Oct 1994	EPCA 78 s.33 and The Trade Union Reform & Employment Rights Act 1993	Complaint to an Industrial Tribunal	Within three months of the last day of the payment period	An award of compensation
To take paid time off to carry out trade union duties for an employee who is an official of a recognised trade union	TULR(C)A 1992 s.168	Complaint to an Industrial Tribunal	Within three months of the failure	A declaration or compensation
To take time off to carry out the public duties	EPCA 78 s.29	Complaint to an Industrial Tribunal	Within three months of the failure	A declaration or compensation
To take paid time off for trade union activities for an employee who is a member of a recognised independent trade union	TULR(C)A 1992 s.170	Complaint to an Industrial Tribunal	Within three months of the failure	A declaration or compensation
To take reasonable time off to look for work or make arrangements for training following notice of redundancy	EPCA 78 s.31	Complaint to an Industrial Tribunal	Within three months of the failure	A declaration or compensation
To a redundancy payment for an employee who has been continuously employed for two years	EPCA 78 s.81	Complaint to an Industrial Tribunal	Within six months of relevant date	A declaration or compensation
Not to be discriminated against because of race, gender or marital status in securing work, at work or in the case of dismissal	Sex Discrimination Act 1975 (amended); Race Relations Act 1976	Complaint to an Industrial Tribunal	Within three months of act of discrimination	A declaration or compensation
To equal pay when engaged on like work or equivalent work	Equal Pay Act 1970 (as amended)	Complaint to an Industrial Tribunal	Within six months of termination of employment	A declaration or compensation

Equal pay and maternity rights

Equal opportunity legislation relating to the sexes was originally contained in the *Sex Discrimination Act* 1975 and the Equal Pay Act 1970 and while both Acts have been considerably amended, not least because of the UK's membership of the European Community, they still remain the corner stones of Equal Opportunity law. While the Equal Pay Act is concerned with pay and related matters arising from the contract of employment, the sex discrimination legislation covers non financial matters from the contract or any other matter not dealt with in the contract of employment. In cases of doubt a decision as to jurisdiction must be left to the Industrial Tribunal.

At present there is still widespread inequality in the way men and women are financially rewarded for the work that they do and general agreement that the status of women must be improved. A conservative interpretation of the equal pay legislation in the courts and a tendency to employ women exclusively in low paid jobs so that comparisons are difficult to make, have meant that the law has provided little assistance in redressing the balance. By restricting the right to equal pay under the *Equal Pay Act* 1970 to cases where *'like work'* or *'work rated as equivalent'* can be shown, many women in low paid jobs were effectively excluded from a remedy. Despite the introduction of the *Equal Pay Amendment Regulations* 1983 applicants have still found it necessary to turn to European Community law to maintain a successful claim. Certainly the Treaty of Rome and various European Community Directives have had considerable impact in the field of equal pay.

EC Law

Article 119 of the Treaty of Rome imposes a requirement of equal pay for equal work and by virtue of the *European Communities Act* 1972 this Article is directly applicable to the UK. Following *McCarthy v. Smith* 1981 it was confirmed that Article 119 is directly enforceable in domestic courts who in theory should apply the law of the national state first. In *Pickstone v. Freemans plc* 1988 the House of Lords held that a complainant could rely on domestic or European law in attempting to secure a remedy. There is no doubt that a wide interpretation of equal pay rights is achievable by applying Article 119.

In addition to the Treaty of Rome each member state of the European Community is required to bring its domestic law into line with Community law. This is achieved mainly by Directives from the European Community outlining the law which member states should then adopt. An example is the Equal Pay Directive which expands the principle of equal pay in Article 119. A failure to incorporate a Directive into domestic law could be pointed out by the Court of Justice of the European Community.

> In *Commission for the European Communities v. The United Kingdom* 1982 the Commission successfully argued that UK law had not adopted "the necessary measures" to adopt the Equal Pay Directive. Under existing British law a worker's claim that work is of equal value would have to be dropped if the employer refused to cooperate by not introducing a job classification system. This decision led to an amendment in UK Equal Pay law by the 1983 Equal Pay Amendment Regulations.

This whole process of effecting change on a reluctant member state by means of EC Directives laying down the law and the state being left with the form and method of implementation can be very drawn out. Attempts have been made therefore to enforce European Directives directly in national courts. The European Court of Justice has ruled that a Directive may be relied on by an individual before a national court where the Directive is *"sufficiently precise and unconditional"*. Such actions however are limited to where the respondent is a government authority acting "as an employer". The rationale for restricting the direct enforcement of European law to government authorities is that it is the member states' responsibility to bring its own domestic law into line and private employers should not be made responsible for that failure.

A Member State of the European Community may not take advantage of its own failure to comply with Community law.

> So held the European Court of Justice when asked by the House of Lords to give a preliminary ruling in *Foster and Others v. British Gas plc* 1990. British Gas, a statutory corporation governed by the *Gas Act* 1972, was privatised by the *Gas Act* 1986 and its rights and liabilities were transferred to British Gas plc with effect from August 1986. British Gas followed a policy of requiring its employees to retire at an age when under UK law they were entitled to a state pension, 60 for women and 65 for men. The complainants were female employees of British Gas who were required to retire at the earlier age when they wished to continue working. They claimed that their compulsory retirement was contrary to the Equal Treatment Directive on the implementation of the principle of equal treatment without discrimination on the grounds of sex in employment, vocational training and promotion and working conditions. While the dismissals contravened the directive they did not offend UK law, so the issue was whether the Directive could be relied on directly against British Gas. The European Court held that while it had jurisdiction to give a ruling determining the categories of persons against whom the Directive could be relied on it was for the national court to decide whether a party to the proceedings fell within one of those categories. Relying on *Marshall v. Southampton and South-West Area Health Authority* 1986 where it was held that a person could rely on a Directive against the state, the court ruled that *"whenever the provisions of a Directive appeared to be unconditional and sufficiently precise about their subject matter, but implementing measures were not adopted within the prescribed period, the provisions of the Directive could be relied upon as against national provisions which are incompatible with the Directive provisions, or insofar as they defined rights which individuals could assert against the state ... It followed that a body, whatever its legal form, which had been made responsible pursuant to a measure adopted by the state, for providing a public service under the state's control and for that purpose had special powers beyond those which resulted from the normal rules applicable in relations between individuals, was included among the bodies against which the provisions of a Directive having direct effect might be relied upon."*

This directive has been held to be unconditional and sufficiently precise to be relied upon by an individual and applied by the national courts against such a body.

The Equal Pay Act 1970

The main objective of the *Equal Pay Act* 1970 is to secure equal treatment for men and women in the same employment in relation to terms and conditions of employment. Originally certain terms were excluded from the operation of the Act including those affected by laws relating to the employment of women. In fact such laws are gradually being removed for example by the *Sex Discrimination Act* 1986 and the *Employment Act* 1989. Terms *"affording special treatment to women in connection with pregnancy or childbirth"* are still outside the province of the Act and so a man has no right to paternity leave in circumstances where a woman is entitled to maternity leave. Also, terms *"related to death or retirement, or to any provision made in connection with death or retirement"* are also excluded. This would not cover terms related to the *"membership of an occupational pension scheme"*.

> In *Worringham v. Lloyds Bank* 1982 the European Court of Justice ruled that a contribution to a retirement benefits scheme paid by the employer in the name of the employee by addition to his gross salary is pay under Article 119 of the Treaty. This meant that women were to be treated the same as men in relation to the repayment of pension contributions on the termination of employment.

In an extremely important decision the European Court of Justice in *Barber v. Guardian Royal Exchange Assurance Group* 1990 held that pensions are pay within the meaning of the directly enforceable provisions of Article 119 of the Treaty of Rome. This means that an occupational pensions scheme that discriminates on the grounds of sex and offends Article 119 may be declared unlawful.

The dramatic impact of the above ruling therefore is that pension benefits cannot discriminate on the grounds of sex, and any condition differing according to sex contravenes Article 119. Pensions must now be equated with pay and if rates are determined by gender criteria they are now unlawful. People must be treated as individuals rather than members of gender groupings so that in determining pay and pensions the fact that statistically women live longer, or take more sick leave than men, should be disregarded in determining levels of sick pay or pension benefits. Also despite the present difference in the State pension age, as a result of this case, pension ages under occupational schemes must be equalised. The court further confirmed that the Treaty takes precedence over Directives so that Social Security Directives which permitted the implementation of equal treatment in occupational pension schemes to be deferred, are consequently overridden by the decision. Finally the court has decided that the principle of equal pay applies to each element of remuneration and is not satisfied by a comprehensive assessment of overall pay. This means that differences in contractual terms between men and women employed on equal work cannot be offset against each other. Applying the equality clause therefore, each aspect of the contract of employment must be equalised.

The mechanism by which the Equal Pay Act attempts to achieve its objectives is the *'equality clause'*. The Equal Pay Act is one of the few employment law statutes that actually implies a term into a contract of employment. Under the Act *if the terms of a contract under which a woman is employed at an establishment in Great Britain do not include (directly or by reference to a collective agreement or otherwise) an equality clause they shall be deemed to include one.*

Under the equality clause a woman has the right to equal pay with a man if either:

- *she is employed on 'like work' with a man in the same employment;*
- *she is employed doing 'work rated as equivalent' with a man following a job evaluation study; or*
- *she is employed to do work of 'equal value' with a man in the same employment in terms of the demand placed upon her.*

There are therefore three avenues upon which a claim could be based, *'like work'*, *'work related or equivalent'* or *'equal value'*. Equal value was introduced by the *Equal Pay Amendment Regulations* 1983. A claim based on equal value can only be considered where there is no basis for a claim on *'like work'* or *'work rated as equivalent'*.

Like work

The problem of using the concept 'like work' as a criterion for achieving fair treatment for women at the workplace, is that in fact large numbers of women workers are often at establishments where there are no male employees upon which to draw comparisons. Accordingly, the definition of 'like work' has been given a *'broad brush approach'* interpretation by courts and tribunals.

The Act provides that a *"woman is to be regarded as employed in like work with men if, but only if, her work and theirs is of the same or a broadly similar nature and the differences (if any) between the things she does and the things they do are not of practical importance in relation to terms and conditions of employment: and accordingly in comparing her work and theirs regard shall be had to the frequency or otherwise with which any such differences occur in practice as well as to the nature and extent of the differences".*

Insignificant differences in work and vague or unrealistic responsibilities are to be ignored therefore, in deciding whether individuals are engaged in like work.

> In *Electrolux v. Hutchinson* 1977 female workers engaged in broadly similar work to their male counterparts were held to be entitled to equal pay, despite that the men alone would be required to work overtime, at weekends or at night. The fact that the men were rarely called on to do extra work was a major consideration.

The decision as to whether similar work is being carried on demands not a comparison between the contractual obligations of the parties, but rather a consideration of the things actually done and the frequency with which they are done.

> In *Coomes (Holdings) Ltd. v. Shields* 1978 the female counter clerks in bookmakers shops were paid a lesser rate of pay than their male counterparts. The employers sought to justify the differences on the grounds that the male employees had extra duties, including acting as a deterrent to unruly customers and transporting cash between branches. The Court of Appeal held that, in deciding the question as to *'like work'*, it was necessary to consider the differences between the things the men and women were required to do. Furthermore, it was necessary to consider the frequency with which such differences occur in practice. Finally, the court must consider whether the differences are of any practical importance. This approach should enable the court to place a value on each job in terms of demands placed upon the worker, and if the value of the man's job is higher he should be paid an increased rate for the job. In the present case the differences were not of sufficient importance to justify a different rate of pay.

> In *Thomas v. National Coal Board* 1987 the EAT held that for the purposes of determining *'like work'* there was no implicit requirement that a selected male comparator should be representative of a group. It was possible therefore to compare the terms and conditions of female canteen assistants with the only male canteen attendant. The EAT also held however that the Tribunal was entitled to find that the additional responsibility of the male attendant in working permanently at night alone, and without supervision, was a *"difference of practical importance in relation to terms and conditions of employment"* and so not *'like work'* for the purposes of the Act.

Work rated as equivalent

The second means by which an equality clause will operate is if the employer has carried out a job evaluation study or work rating exercise and the women's work is rated as equivalent to that of a man employed at the same establishment. The study must be carried out in accordance with the Act which provides that *"a woman is to be regarded as employed on work rated as equivalent with that of any men, if but only if, her job and their job have been given an equal value in terms of the demands made on a worker under various headings (effort, skill, decision making etc.) on a study undertaken with a view to evaluating in those terms the jobs to be done by all or any of the employees in an undertaking or group of undertakings"*.

To maintain an equal pay claim based upon job evaluation therefore it is necessary that a valid study has been carried out adopting one of the principal job evaluation methods laid down by ACAS. The fact that both trade unions generally and a number of employers are wary of job evaluation studies and there is still doubt as to whether an employer is bound to implement a scheme which has been carried out, means that equal pay claims based on work rated as equivalent are relatively rare.

The comparison

For both *'like work'* and *'work rated as equivalent'* it is left to the woman rather than her employer, to choose the male comparator but such a person must be typical and cannot be a hypothetical person. The comparison could even be with the man whom the woman replaced provided there was only a short break between this occurring. Both the applicant and the comparator must be employed which includes employees and contractors providing personal services.

A further requirement is that the comparison must be between the applicant and another in the *'same employment'* which would include the same establishment. Comparison with an individual employed by the same or associated employer at a different establishment is also permissible provided common terms and conditions of employment are observed at both establishments.

> In *Leverton v. Clwyd County Council* 1988 the complainant, a nursery nurse, sought to compare herself with higher paid clerical staff employed at different establishments by the council. To prevent a comparison the employers argued that common terms and conditions of employment were not observed for the relevant employees despite the fact that they were covered by the same collective agreement. In particular the nurses worked a 32.5 hour week and had 70 days annual holiday compared with the comparators 37 hour week and 20 days basic holiday. Both the Tribunal and the EAT felt that these differences were sufficient to defeat the contention that there were common terms of employment observed at the different establishments and so the claim failed. By a majority the Court of Appeal agreed. *"Although common terms and conditions of employment does not mean 'identical' terms and conditions, as that would defeat the whole purpose of the legislation, there must be a sufficient element of common identity to enable a proper comparison to be made"*.

The above case gives considerable support to the notion of cross establishment comparison where the applicant and the comparator are covered by the same collective agreement. This is particularly significant in the public sector where national agreements prevail and even in the private sector where employers have multi-site operations and employees with standard terms and conditions of employment.

Equal value

In cases where the provisions of *'like work'* and *'work rated as equivalent'* do not apply, a further option is to rely on an equality clause based on work of equal value added by the Equal Pay (Amendment) Regulations 1983. Under the regulations a woman is employed on work, which is, in terms of the demands made on her (for instance under such headings as effort, skill and decision making), of equal value to that of a man in the same employment. In such circumstances the equality clause has the effect of modifying less favourable terms in the woman's contract to bring them in line with the man's contract and inserting any beneficial terms in a man's contract into the woman's contract of employment. If a complaint is presented, the Tribunal has no jurisdiction to hear the case unless it is satisfied either that there are no reasonable grounds for determining that the work is of equal value or it has required a member of the panel of independent experts to prepare a report with respect to that question and has received that report. The panel is designated by the Advisory, Conciliation and Arbitration Service (ACAS) but must not comprise officers or members of that body.

There would be no reasonable grounds for determining that the work is of equal value if different values have been given to the work and that of the male comparator following a study and there is no evidence that the evaluation was made on a system which discriminated on the grounds of sex.

> In *Bromley v. H J Quick Ltd.* 1987 the employer had commissioned an independent job evaluation study under which grading boundaries were decided. Despite a different ranking under the study, a number of female clerical workers brought an equal value complaint com-

paring their work to male managers. The Tribunal decided that because of the job evaluation study there were no reasonable grounds for determining that the work was of equal value. On appeal on behalf of the women it was argued that the job evaluation did not fall within the requirement of the regulations because the study in question was non analytical and the regulation demanded an analysis of the characteristics of each job. It was also argued that if there was any ground for alleging discrimination which cannot be dismissed, the Tribunal must refer the case to an independent expert. Both arguments were rejected by the EAT. Stressing that it was necessary for a Tribunal to examine carefully the job evaluation scheme upon which the employer relies, the EAT felt that the study in question, although having blemishes, was valid. *"Although systems which are not analytical and which are based on a 'felt fair' hierarchy or a paired comparison on a 'whole job' basis are much more vulnerable to sex discrimination, the proposition that any job evaluation study which is not analytical is thereby invalid , could not be accepted".*

An important equal value claim considered by the House of Lords was the decision in *Hayward v. Cammell Laird Shipbuilders Ltd.* 1988. Here a female canteen assistant, employed at a shipyard, claimed that she was doing work of equal value to male comparators, who were shipyard workers paid at the higher rate for skilled tradesmen in the yard. An independent evaluation convinced the Tribunal that the women's work was of equal value. However when comparing all her terms and conditions of employment with the male comparator which revealed a free canteen lunches and two additional days holiday, the Tribunal found that she was not entitled to a higher rate of pay. The approach was upheld by the EAT and the Court of Appeal but on final appeal to the House of Lords, the decision was reversed. The Lords suggested that individual contractual terms should be compared with similar provisions in the comparator's contract and a decision reached as to their respective merits. One such term related to pay, and a comparison could be drawn between the complainant's basic pay and the male comparator's. Despite the fact that when looked at as a whole, the complainant's contract was no less favourable. The ruling suggests therefore that if a woman can point to a term of her contract which is less favourable than a term of a similar one in the man's contract she is entitled to have that term made not less favourable irrespective of whether she is less favourably treated as a whole.

Defence

At this point it is convenient to consider the main defence to an equal pay claim. An equality clause shall not operate in relation to a variation between the woman's contract if the employer proves that the variation is genuinely due to a material factor which is not the difference of sex. If the claim is based on an equality clause relying on *'like work'* or *'work rated as equivalent'* then there must be a material difference between the woman's case and the man's for the defence to operate. For claims based on equal value however, it is slightly different and the factor may be a material difference.

In *Snoxell and Davies v. Vauxhall Motors* 1977 the EAT held that an employer cannot establish a defence, that the variation between the woman's contract and the man's contract was genuinely due to a material difference between her case and his, when it can be seen that past discrimination has contributed to the variation. Even if the original discrimination occurred before the effective date of the Act *"it cannot have been the intention of the legislation to permit the perpetuation of the effect of the earlier discrimination".*

Genuine material differences would include a consideration of factors such as the place of employment or academic qualifications of the individual involved.

In *Rainey v. Greater Glasgow Health Board* 1987 the House of Lords held that the word 'material' means 'significant and relevant' and the difference had to be between the woman's case and the man's. The decision involves a consideration of all the relevant circumstances and they might go beyond personal qualifications, skill, experience or training. It could be that the difference was reasonably necessary to achieve some result such as economic necessity or administrative efficiency and was not directly related to the personal characteristics of the individual involved.

In *R. v. Secretary of State for Social Services and Others ex parte Clarke and Others* 1988 speech therapists sought to compare their work to that of clinical psychologists and pharmacists. The response of their employer, the Health Authority was to point to the National Health Service (Remuneration and Conditions of Service) Regulations 1974 which provide that officers' remuneration which has been negotiated and approved by the appropriate body is the sum payable and the employer was bound to pay the salary in accordance with the Regulations. Even if their work was of equal value, the pay variation was *"genuinely due to a material factor which is not the difference of sex"*, the material factor being the requirement that the employers comply with the Regulations. On a judicial review of the Tribunal's decision, the Divisional Court of the Queen's Bench Division held that the mere fact that the applicants' pay had been approved under Regulation did not provide a defence to an equal pay claim. Whether an employer had satisfied the defence required evidence and the simple assertion that the employers were bound by law to pay the salaries was not enough.

A complaint in relation to equal pay may be presented to a Tribunal by an individual, an employer and in certain circumstances, by the Secretary of State for Employment. If the Tribunal finds that a claim has been established, it can make a declaration to that effect and award up to two years' back pay to the successful applicant. The burden of proof rests with the complainant and it is for the employer to an establish a defence.

Maternity rights

The right to maternity leave and pay was first introduced in the *Employment Protection Act* 1975 and the law is now contained in the *Employment Protection (Consolidation) Act* 1978 as amended by the *Employment Act* 1980. Despite the very basic nature of the right to maternity pay and leave, legislative provisions governing the right are difficult to interpret and were described by Browne-Wilkinson J as of *"inordinate complexity, exceeding the worst excesses of a taxing statute"*. He further observed that this was especially regrettable bearing in mind that they are regulating the rights of ordinary employers and employees.

To qualify for maternity pay and leave with the right to return to work, the employee must have been continuously employed for two years as at the beginning of the eleventh week before the date of her expected confinement. It is important for the claimant to show that the contract of employment subsisted until the eleventh week, even if by that time the employee had finished work. In the case of maternity pay, it is also necessary for the woman to notify the employer, in writing if requested, at least twenty one days before the absence begins or as soon as is reasonably practicable that she will be absent from work because of the pregnancy. The same notice could be used to inform the employer that she intends to return to work after the birth of the child. A further requirement for the woman is that if requested by her employer she must produce a certificate from a registered medical practitioner or a certified midwife indicating the expected number of weeks of her confinement.

A qualified applicant is entitled to statutory maternity pay for a period not exceeding in aggregate six weeks, during which the applicant is absent from work wholly or partly because of the pregnancy or confinement. The amount of pay is nine tenths of a week's pay minus the amount of any maternity allowance payable. Any wages to which the claimant is entitled are set off against the statutory payment. If an employer fails to meet his obligation to make the payment, then an employee can present a complaint to a Tribunal within three months and they can order that the payment is made. An employer who fulfils the statutory obligation in relation to maternity pay is entitled to recover the full amount paid as a rebate from the Maternity Fund financed by National Insurance Contributions.

The right to maternity leave includes the right to return to work with your original employer or successor at any time before the end of the period of twenty nine weeks beginning with the week in which the date of confinement falls. The right is to return to the original job on terms and conditions which are not less favourable than those which would have been applicable to the applicant had she not been absent. If the employer can show that it is not practicable by reason of redundancy to permit the applicant to return to work, she is entitled, where there is a suitable available vacancy, to be offered alternative employment. This alternative employment must be suitable and appropriate with provisions which are not substantially less favourable than the original contract.

This then is a significant limitation on the right to return to work, for if there is a redundancy situation and no suitable available employment or suitable alternative work which is unreasonably rejected, then the right to return is lost. Some protection is provided however where the employer fails to make an offer of suitable alternative work.

> In *Community Task Force v. Rimmer* 1986 the EAT held that the test of availability of employment is not qualified by considerations of what is economic or reasonable, so that despite the difficulties involved in offering an employee alternative employment in these circumstances, failure to do so made her dismissal automatically unfair.

The right to return to work was also amended to accommodate small employers so that the Act now provides that if immediately before the absence, the employer had five or less employees, and it is not reasonably practicable for the employer to permit a return to work, the right to return does not apply.

Failure to comply strictly with the notice requirements may also prejudice the right to return. Having served the original notice, the employer is entitled to confirm the position by sending the employee an intermediate enquiry in writing at any time later than forty nine days from the expected date of confinement with the purpose of asking whether the employee still intends to return to work. The letter of enquiry must notify the employee of her obligation to reply within fourteen days. To exercise the right to return, the employee must notify her original employer (or his successor) in writing at least twenty one days before the date on which she proposes to return. The employer may postpone the return for not more than four weeks from the notified date provided he informs the employee before that notified date and gives specified reasons for the postponement. The employee may also postpone the return to work by four weeks if she notifies the employer of her ill health supported by a medical certificate before the notified day of return. Such a postponement can only be exercised once. If there has been an interruption of work (due to industrial action or some other reason) which would make it unreasonable to expect the employee to return to work on the notified day, she may return when work resumes after the interruption or as soon as is reasonably practicable.

It should be noted that there may also be a contractual right to return to work following maternity leave which an employee could rely on in preference to the statutory right. Whether relying on the statutory or contractual right to return, if an employer refuses to allow the employee to return in breach of this right, then this is deemed to be a dismissal and the employee is entitled to present a claim for unfair dismissal. It should be noted that the period of maternity leave will count towards continuous employment for the purpose of qualifying to present an unfair dismissal claim.

> In *Kelly v. Liverpool Maritime Terminal Ltd.* 1988 the Court of Appeal explored the legal position when an employee who is on maternity leave becomes ill and does not return to

work on the agreed date. The case concerned the exercise of a contractual right to return but it had been agreed that her leave would be on terms which mirrored the statutory scheme. While on leave, the applicant aggravated an old back injury and sent her employers a letter stating that she would be unable to return to work on the agreed date (approximately twenty nine weeks after the birth) and enclosing a doctor's certificate covering her absence for four weeks. Receiving no response, the applicant sent in three more doctor's certificates to her employer covering further periods of absence. Finally the employer responded as follows, "in view of your continued absence and the company's obligation to offer you employment at the termination of your maternity leave having ceased, I must regretfully inform you that you will not be able to resume your employment with us". On behalf of the employee it was argued that her contract of employment had subsisted during the period of sick leave following maternity leave, and the employer's letter constituted a dismissal, which in the circumstances was unfair. The employer argued that the maternity leave had in fact been extended by a further four weeks on the ground of the employee's ill health by virtue of her letter, but after that period the entitlement ceased and the employment had terminated. The Court of Appeal agreed with the employer that the maternity leave had been extended by four weeks but that it terminated on the expiration of that period along with the contract of employment. Failure to respond to the employee's sick notes could not be construed as passive acceptance that the employment contract continued.

Under a provision of the *Employment Protection (Consolidation) Act* 1978 (inserted by the *Employment Act* 1980) an employee who is pregnant and on medical advice who makes an appointment to attend at a place for ante-natal care has the right not to be unreasonably refused paid time off to enable her to keep the appointment. If challenged, the employee should be prepared to verify that she is pregnant by producing a medical certificate to that effect and producing an appointment card. This does not apply when the employee's appointment is the first during her pregnancy. Once again, an employee who feels that the employer is infringing her right, may complain to an Industrial Tribunal within three months and the Tribunal has power to make a declaration and award compensation.

Reference has been made elsewhere to the significance of the Charter of Fundamental Social Rights of Workers (the Social Charter) solemnly declared by the member states of the European Community other than the United Kingdom. As a response to the Social Charter, the European Commission's Action Programme proposed a directive on the protection pregnant women at work. The directive was produced under Article 118A which authorises directives on health and safety and permits the council to act by means of a qualified majority voting. While the directive may still be the subject of a challenge to its legal validity it completed the legislative process on 19th October 1992. Despite the fact that the UK government disapproves of its content it has two years to implement its provisions. In addition member states must report to the Commission every five years on its practical implementation.

The directive states that its purpose is to improve the safety and the health of pregnant workers and workers who have recently given birth or who are breast feeding. It goes on to identify and deal with the possible hazards to pregnant women at the workplace and to those who have recently given birth. The right to maternity leave of at least 14 weeks is extended to all pregnant workers which would benefit approximately 150,000 women a year in the UK. The requirement of two years continuous employment for full-time employees and five years for part-time workers to qualify for maternity leave will no longer apply. Finally the directive confirms and extends a decision of the European Court which forbids discrimination against women on the grounds of pregnancy. The provisions of the directives have been included in the Trade Union Reform and Employment Rights Act 1993.

Dismissal and Redundancy

A contract of employment must inevitably terminate at some time, either by the death or retirement of the employee, or by the death of the employer or the dissolution or winding up of the business. Also, as a general rule, contracts of employment for a fixed term will terminate when the contractual period expires, and contracts to do a specific job are automatically terminated on the completion of the project. Otherwise, under the common law, either side to a contract of employment may lawfully terminate it, either by giving reasonable notice or summarily (without notice) in some cases where the other party had committed a serious breach of contract. Since the *Industrial Relations Act* 1971, employees are given statutory protection against arbitrary dismissal by an employer, the provisions relating to which are included in the *Employment Protection (Consolidation) Act* 1978 as amended (see later under Unfair Dismissal).

Dismissal or otherwise

The meaning of dismissal is defined in the *Employment Protection (Consolidation) Act* 1978. It occurs in three different ways

- *the contract under which he is employed is terminated by the employer, whether it is so terminated by notice or without notice, or*

- *where under the contract he is employed for a fixed term, that term expires without being renewed under the same contract, or*

- *the employer terminates the contract, with or without notice, in circumstances such that he is entitled to terminate it without notice by reason of the employer's contract.*

The Act envisages a dismissal arising expressly, by the employer terminating the contract, impliedly by the employee terminating the contract in response to the employer's conduct and finally a termination on the expiration of a fixed term contract of employment.

Express dismissal

This occurs when an employer expressly terminates a contract of employment with or without notice. We have already said that an employer is normally required to give the employee notice in accordance with the terms of the contract or least the statutory or common law minimum period. For a dismissal with notice, therefore, there is normally no room for any misunderstanding in relation to the employer's intentions. In cases of alleged summary dismissal, however, where there is no notice, there have been claims by the employer that it was not his intention to dismiss but rather merely to discipline. While the words, "you're dismissed, fired, sacked", etc. leave little doubt as to the employer's intentions, if he uses more ambiguous language, perhaps to register his discontent with the employee, the argument that there has been no express dismissal could have some merit.

In *Tanner v. D T Kean* 1978 the complainant had been told that he could not use the company van outside working hours. When the employer discovered that he was doing so, after abusing the employee, he said to him, "that's it, you're finished with me". The EAT held that in deciding whether the words or actions of the employer amounted to a dismissal, all the circumstances should be considered. *"A relevant and perhaps the most important question is how would a reasonable employee in all the circumstances have understood what the employer intended by what he said and did?"* Here the words spoken in the heat of the moment indicated a reprimand rather than a dismissal.

Implied dismissal

In a large number of cases it may seem superficially that the contract of employment has been terminated by the employee's conduct in 'walking out' and treating the contract as at an end. Where however, the reason for leaving was due to the conduct of the employer or those under his control, it may be that the employee could show that the employer is responsible for the contractual termination. In such circumstances an employee could argue that he has been impliedly dismissed, commonly referred to as a constructive dismissal.

Originally the test for determining whether a constructive dismissal had taken place was to judge the reasonableness of the employer's conduct. Since *Western Excavating (ECC) Ltd. v. Sharp* 1978 however, the Courts have rejected that approach as being too vague and now the so called 'conduct test' is to be applied based upon strict contractual principles. The aim of the new test is to bring some degree of certainty to the law by requiring the employee to justify his leaving as a response to the employer's repudiatory conduct. *"If the employer is guilty of conduct which is a significant breach going to the root of the contract of employment, or which shows that the employer no longer intends to be bound by one or more of the essential terms of the contract then the employee is entitled to treat himself as discharged from any further performance."*

A breach by the employer of the express terms of the contract of employment covering such matters as wages, job location, contractual duties and job description, normally comes about when the employer unilaterally attempts to impose a change on the employee without his consent.

> In *Hill Ltd. v. Mooney* 1981 the EAT held that an attempt by an employer to unilaterally alter his obligation to pay the agreed remuneration was a breach which went to the root of the contract and consequently constituted a repudiation of it. The complainant was entitled therefore to regard himself as constructively dismissed when he resigned following the employer's decision to unilaterally change the basis upon which sales commission was payable to him. *"Although a mere alteration in the contractual provisions does not necessarily amount to a fundamental breach constituting repudiation, if an employer seeks to alter that contractual obligation in a fundamental way such attempt is a breach going to the very root of the contract and is necessarily a repudiation. The obligation on the employer is to pay the contractual wages, and he is not entitled to alter the formula whereby those wages are calculated."*

The need to look for a clear breach of contractual term in applying the conduct test has encouraged both Tribunals and courts in the absence of relevant express terms to imply terms into a contract of employment. An excellent example is provided by the need to maintain trust and confidence in the employment relationship.

> In *Courtaulds Northern Textiles Ltd. v. Andrew* 1979 the EAT stated that *"there is an implied term in a contract of employment that the employers will not, without reasonable and proper cause, conduct themselves in a manner calculated or likely to destroy or seriously damage the relationship of confidence and trust between the parties"*. Here a comment made to the complainant by his assistant manager that "you can't do the bloody job anyway" which was not a true expression of his opinion was held to justify the complainant in resigning and treating himself as constructively dismissed. While criticism of a worker's performance would not necessarily amount to repudiatory conduct so as to lead to constructive dismissal, here telling the employee that he could not do his job, when that was not a true expression of opinion, was conduct which was *"likely to destroy the trust relationship which was a necessary element in the relationship between the supervisory employee and his employers"*.

In many cases the employee resigns in response to an act which is the 'last straw' and the culmination of a long period of events which have caused the employee distress. In such circumstances it would be perfectly valid for a tribunal to consider whether the events, taken together, constitute a breach of the implied term of trust and confidence, and so justify a finding of constructive dismissal.

It is a breach of the implied obligation of mutual trust and confidence for an employer to fail to treat an allegation of sexual harassment with due seriousness and gravity, and in such a case an employee is entitled to resign and treat herself as constructively dismissed. This was the situation in *Bracebridge Engineering Ltd. v. Dorby* 1990.

> In *British Aircraft Corporation v. Austin* 1978 the EAT re-stated the well known common law obligation that employers are under an implied duty to take reasonable care for the safety of their employees. *"As part and parcel of that general obligation employers are also under an obligation under the terms of the contract of employment to act reasonably in dealing with matters of safety or complaints of lack of safety which are drawn to their attention by employees."* Here the employer's conduct in failing to investigate the employee's complaint about supplying her with appropriate eye protectors amounted to a fundamental breach of her contract of employment. *"It was a serious breach which put the complainant in an unfair dilemma, either she carried on with a risk to her eyesight or she would be obliged to give up her job."* This conduct was held to be sufficient to entitle the employee to leave, regard herself as constructively dismissed and seek a remedy for unfair dismissal.

It should be recognised of course that all contracts of employment require interpretation, and the fact that an employer interprets a contract in a way which subsequently proves to be incorrect, does not constitute a serious breach entitling an employee to regard himself as constructively dismissed.

> In *Brigden v. Lancashire CC* 1987 the employee, a college lecturer, claimed constructive dismissal when he resigned following the failure of her employer to upgrade her when her workload reached a certain level. Such a failure the Court of Appeal held, while incorrect, did not of itself constitute a repudiatory breach for the purposes of constructive dismissal.

> Also in *Murco Petroleum Ltd., v. Forge* 1987 it was held that an employee has no implied contractual right to receive a pay rise every year even though this was the employers normal practice. The failure to provide a rise therefore did not constitute a repudiatory breach of the contract entitling the employee to resign and claim constructive dismissal.

Quite often, of course, the employee who walks out is aggrieved not at the employer's conduct but at the conduct of a fellow employee for whom the employer is responsible.

> In *Isle of Wight Tourist Board v. Coombes, 1976,* the applicant secretary walked out following a remark by her superior "She is an intolerable bitch on a Monday morning." This was held to be a fundamental breach of the contract of employment, and so a constructive dismissal was held to have occurred when the secretary walked out.

An employer is of course vicariously responsible for the actions of his employees within the scope of their employment so that if a supervisor in reprimanding an employee does so in a reprehensible manner this can be taken to be the "employers' conduct" for the purpose of constructive dismissal.

> In *Hilton International Hotels (UK) Ltd. v. Protopona 1990 an employee resigned when she was subjected to an officious and insensitive reprimand not justified by her conduct. The Industrial Tribunal held that she was "humiliated intimidated and degraded to such an extent that there was breach of trust and confidence which went to the root of the contract".* The employer nevertheless appealed against the finding of constructive dismissal arguing that the person who had carried out the reprimand, while a supervisor, had no authority to effect a dismissal. This the EAT found was an irrelevant consideration and restated the general prin-

ciple that an employer is bound by acts done in the course of a supervisory employee's employment. *"Therefore, if the supervisor is doing what he or she is employed to do and in the course of doing it behaves in a way which if done by the employer would constitute a fundamental breach of the contract between the employer and employee, the employer is bound by the supervisor's misdeeds."*

Resignation

There is not dismissal if the employee expressly terminates the contract of employment by resigning.

In *Kwik-Fit v. Lineham* 1992 as a direct consequence of issuing a written warning to a depot manager in accordance with the company's disciplinary procedure, he walked out in protest. While the employer took the view that the manager had resigned he nevertheless presents a complaint of unfair dismissal. The EAT held that where words or action of resignation are unambiguous an employer can accept them as such unless there are 'special circumstances'. *"Words spoken or action expressed in temper or in the heat of the moment or under extreme pressure, or the intellectual make-up of an employee may be such special circumstances"*. In a case such as this, where there are special circumstances, an employer is required to allow a reasonable period to elapse, perhaps a matter of days, before accepting a resignation to determine an employee's true intention.

There will normally be a contractual provision as to the length of notice to be given and, in addition, there is a statutory minimum period of one week where the employee has at least one month of continuous employment. Failure to comply with notice requirements is a breach of contract for which the employee could be made liable in damages. Employers rarely sue in these cases due mainly to the problem of quantifying their loss which would include the additional cost of advertising for and hiring a replacement during the notice period.

The unilateral act of resigning must be distinguished from the consensual termination of employment which normally involves an exchange of consideration, e.g. a lump sum in return for the loss of the job.

Such was the case in *Logan Salton v. Durham County Council* 1989. Here the complainant was a social worker who, as a result of disciplinary hearings, had been redeployed by his employer. In a statement to be considered at a further disciplinary hearing the complainant was given notice of a number of complaints against him and a recommendation that he be summarily dismissed. Prior to that meeting his union representative negotiated on his behalf a mutual agreement to terminate his employment with the Council. By that agreement the employment contract was to terminate in seven weeks' time and an outstanding car loan of £2,750 wiped out as a debt. Despite the fact that the agreement was signed by both parties, the complainant subsequently complained to an Industrial Tribunal that he had been unfairly dismissed. It was argued that a dismissal had occurred in law, for the mutual agreement to terminate was either void as an agreement entered into under duress, or void because it offended the EPCA 78 by attempting to remove statutory protection. Both these arguments were rejected by the Industrial Tribunal and on appeal by the EAT. The EAT found that here there was a separate contract to terminate and the termination did not depend upon the happening of some future event. Furthermore, the fact that the appellant was aware of the employer's recommendation of dismissal did not constitute duress, bearing in mind the financial inducement. *"In the resolution of industrial disputes, it is in the best interests of all concerned that a contract made without duress, for good consideration, preferably after proper and sufficient advice and which has the effect of terminating a contract of employ-*

*ment by mutual agreement (whether at once or at some future date) should be effective be-
tween the contracting parties, in which case there probably will not have been a dismissal."*

Frustration

There is no dismissal if it can be shown that the contract of employment has been brought to an end
through the operation of the common law doctrine of frustration. Frustration occurs where, due to a
change in circumstances, performance of the contract becomes impossible or radically different than
the performance envisaged by the parties when they made the contract. The specified events upon which
a claim of frustration could be based are limited generally to long illness, and imprisonment. Certainly
the distinction between the termination of a contract of employment by dismissal and termination by
frustration is of critical importance.

> In *F C Shepherd & Company Ltd. v. Jerrom* 1986 the Court of Appeal considered the posi-
> tion of an apprentice plumber who was sentenced to Borstal training for a minimum period
> of six months. Failure to dismiss him in accordance with standard procedures for appren-
> tices led the tribunal and the EAT to find that he had been constructively dismissed unfairly
> and so entitled to compensation. The Court of Appeal disagreed however and held that the
> four year apprenticeship contract had been frustrated by the six month sentence.

It is difficult in any given case to say whether the circumstances of an illness are such that it is no longer
practical to regard the contract of employment as surviving. Obviously the seriousness and length of
the illness are crucial factors but generally all the circumstances are relevant, including the nature of
the job, the length of employment, the needs of the employer and obligations in relation to replacement,
and the conduct of the employer.

> In *Notcutt v. Universal Equipment Company* 1986 the Court of Appeal considered the posi-
> tion of a worker who, two years from retirement and with 27 years' service, suffered an
> incapacitating heart attack with a medical prognosis that he would never work again. A find-
> ing that the contract was terminated by frustration meant that the employee was not entitled
> to sick pay during his statutory period of notice. The court held that *"there is no reason in
> principle why a periodic contract of employment determinable by short or relatively short no-
> tice should not in appropriate circumstances be held to have been terminated without notice
> by frustration, according to the accepted and long established doctrine of frustration in the
> law of contract. The coronary which left the complainant unable to work again was an unex-
> pected occurrence which made his performance of his contractual obligation to work
> impossible and brought about such a change in the significance of the mutual obligations
> that the contract if performed would be a different thing from that contracted for."*

Unfair Dismissal

The introduction of the right not to be dismissed without good reason in the *Industrial Relations Act*
1971 was a recognition that an employee has a stake in his job which cannot be extinguished simply by
serving contractual notice. In the same way that a tenant may acquire security of tenure in his home and
resist the enforcement of a notice to quit unless it is reasonable in the circumstances, an employee,
through continuous employment, can acquire security in his job. The right not to be unfairly dismissed
is intended to act as a constraint on employers who feel they have the authority to hire and fire as they
please. The extent to which the law of unfair dismissal achieves the objective of constraining management
prerogative is arguable. Over the last twenty years unfair dismissal has developed into a highly complex
area of law recognised as such as early as 1977 by Philips J in *Devis & Sons Ltd. v. Atkins* 1977, when
he said, *"the expression 'unfair dismissal' is in no sense a common-sense expression capable of being
understood by the man in the street"*. The present unfair dismissal law is contained in the *Employment*

Protection (Consolidation) Act 1978, (as amended) (EPCA 78) and which, despite the vast number of reported cases on unfair dismissal, remains the primary source of the law.

Under the Act in every employment to which the section applies, every employee shall have the right not to be unfairly dismissed by his employer. Having established that a prospective applicant is classified as an employee, it is then necessary to determine whether the employee is qualified to present a claim for unfair dismissal.

Qualifications

To fall within the provisions of the Act an employee must be able to show continuous employment in a job which is not an excluded category of work. The minimum period of continuous employment for full-time employees is not less than two years ending with the effective date of termination. A part-time employee is also protected after five years employment for at least eight hours per week.

A further requirement is that if on, or before, the effective date of termination, the employee has reached the 'normal retiring age' or, if more than the age of 65 (whether male or female), then there is no right to present a claim. The House of Lords in *Waite v. Government Communication Headquarters* 1983 felt that normal retiring age refers to the age that employees can normally be compelled to retire, unless there is some special reason to apply a different age in a particular case.

Certain reasons for dismissal are classified by statute as automatically unfair, such as dismissal for a reason connected with trade union activities. Here a claim may be presented despite the fact that the employee has insufficient continuous employment or is over age.

> In *Discount Tobacco and Confectionery Ltd. v. Armitage* 1990 the complainant was employed as a shop manageress from February 1 1988. In May 1988, having failed to acquire a written statement of her terms and conditions of employment, she enlisted the help of her union official. A written contract of employment was then supplied to her but when it proved to contain a number of discrepancies which the complainant intended to raise, she was promptly dismissed. The reason for dismissal put forward by the employer was capability and because of her short period of employment she was not qualified to present a claim for unfair dismissal. The employee alleged however that the true reason for dismissal was for membership of a trade union and the Tribunal agreed, awarding her compensation for unfair dismissal. The EAT affirmed the decision stating that for the purposes of the Act there is *"no genuine distinction between membership of a union on the one hand and making use of the essential services of a union officer on the other"*. Turning to a union official for help in elucidating terms and conditions of employment is an important incident of union membership and a dismissal for that reason is automatically unfair.

In addition to qualifying through service, an employee must not fall within one of the excluded categories of employment.

- Persons employed in the police force.
- Share fishermen e.g. members and crew paid by a share of the profits.
- Employees who work ordinarily outside Great Britain.
- Employees who are employed on fixed term contracts of one year or more and have agreed in writing to exclude their rights.
- Employees covered by a designated dismissal procedure agreement.
- Certain registered dock-workers.
- Members of the armed forces.

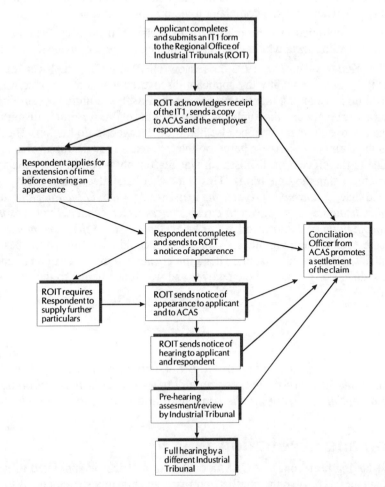

Steps in application brought before an Industrial Tribunal

The procedure involved in presenting a complaint of unfair dismissal is shown on the next page. An employee must initiate proceedings by submitting an IT1 form to the Central Office of Industrial Tribunals or Regional Office of Industrial Tribunals within three months of the effective date of termination of employment.

The effective date of termination is when the notice period given expires and the three month period runs from that date. In cases of summary dismissal, with wages paid in lieu of notice, the effective date is the date of dismissal.

If a complaint of unfair dismissal is presented outside the three month time period from the effective date of termination then the Industrial Tribunal has jurisdiction to hear the complaint if it decides that it was not reasonably practicable to present the complaint with the three month time limit.

In *St. Basils Centre v. McCrossan* 1991 the complainant presented his application by first class ordinary post in Birmingham on a Friday but it did not arrive at the Central Office of Industrial Tribunals in London until the following Tuesday, one day out of time. Here the Industrial Tribunal was entitled to conclude that the complaint should be heard and that it was not reasonably practicable for the complaint to be presented in time.

In some cases it could be argued that the reason for the delay in presenting the claim was due to the time involved in investigating facts which give rise to the belief that the dismissal is unfair.

In *Churchill v. Yeates & Son Ltd.* 1983 the reason relied on by the employer for dismissal was redundancy, but subsequently the applicant discovered that someone else was doing his old job. In addition to alleging that the process of dismissal was unfair because of lack of consultation or warning, etc., the applicant presented his claim for unfair dismissal out of time when he discovered that someone else had been engaged to do his job. The Tribunal ruled that as the claim of unfairness based on the true reason for dismissal was not related to unfairness due to the process of dismissal, it was reasonably practicable for the applicant to present his claim within the time limits. This somewhat harsh decision was reversed by the EAT who held that *"ignorance of a fact, the existence of which is fundamental to the right to claim unfair dismissal, can amount to circumstances which render it not reasonably practicable for a complaint of unfair dismissal to be presented within the three month limit"*. This is the case even if there are other grounds which could have formed the basis of a timely complaint. Here the new factual allegation challenged the honesty and genuineness of the reason for dismissal given by the employer and was fundamental to the success or failure of the claim.

Activity

Visit or write to your regional office of Industrial Tribunals. Make a request for information and guidance relating to presenting a complaint before an Industrial Tribunal. Prepare a brief guide for a potential applicant on the procedure and formalities in making a complaint of unfair dismissal.

Consultation and negotiation

A copy of the IT1 having been sent to ACAS, a conciliation officer is appointed to get in touch with both parties in an attempt to resolve the conflict and reach an amicable settlement. It should be stressed that in many cases an agreement is reached because of the intervention of the conciliation officer. While he is under a statutory duty to endeavour to promote a voluntary settlement of the complaint by encouraging an agreement to reinstate the employee, or make a payment of compensation, there is no requirement for the parties to cooperate or even communicate with him.

It is the function of the conciliation officer to consult with the parties and act as a channel of communication through which the parties do their bargaining. It is up to the parties themselves to negotiate a settlement rather than the conciliation officer. A negotiated settlement can only normally be achieved if the parties to the conflict are willing to compromise their positions to some extent so that an agreement can be reached without the need for further proceedings. If a private settlement is reached, and this is often to the benefit of both parties given the saving in time, expense, and adverse publicity, then it must still be approved by an ACAS Conciliation Officer.

If the employee is resolved to proceed with the complaint, however, then prior to a full hearing by the Tribunal, there is a pre-trial assessment at which the details of the claim are presented. At this stage any party to the proceedings could be warned by the Tribunal that full costs may be payable if he proceeds to a full hearing. Under the *Employment Act* 1989 the Secretary of State has power to require that at a pre-trial review a deposit of £150 will have to be paid by a party wishing to continue with the proceedings.

If the complaint proceeds to a full hearing the burden of proof is on the complainant to show that he has been dismissed unless that is conceded. After hearing the evidence then it is up to the Tribunal to decide whether the dismissal is unfair or otherwise, there is no formal burden of proof.

Reason for dismissal

To assist the complainant in a claim for unfair dismissal, the Act provides that an employee is on request entitled to be provided within fourteen days with a written statement giving the reasons for dismissal. The period of continuous employment to qualify for this right has been increased from six months to two years by of the Employment Act 1989. The aim of the amendment was to bring the qualifying period for the right in line with the qualifying period for bringing a complaint of unfair dismissal. The right to a statement of the reason or reasons applies where the dismissal is express or the non-renewal of a fixed term contract, but not if the complaint is based on a constructive dismissal. If an employer unreasonably refuses to comply with a request the employee may present a complaint to the tribunal who may declare what it finds the reasons for dismissal are and also compensate the employee with an award of two weeks' wages.

The purpose of the statutory right to compel the employer to supply the employee with the reason or reasons relied on for dismissal is to enable the employee to scrutinise them in advance of the proceedings and also to tie the employer down to that reason in any subsequent proceedings. The Act requires an employer to state truthfully the reason that he was relying on in dismissing the employee so that the employee does not start with the disadvantage of not knowing the reason for dismissal if he wishes to pursue a claim for unfair dismissal.

The Act states that it is the employer who must show the reason or principal reason for the dismissal, and that the reason falls within one of the four categories of reasons identified or is a substantial reason of a kind such as to justify the dismissal of an employee holding the position which that employee held. If the employee establishes the true reason for dismissal, and that it falls within one of the five statutory reasons then the dismissal is prima facie fair. The final determination of fairness is achieved by applying the test of reasonableness. Guidance was provided by Lord Bridge in *West Midlands Co-operatives Society v. Tipton* 1986, who said that there are three questions which must be asked in determining whether a dismissal is fair or unfair.

- What was the reason (or principal reason) for the dismissal.

- Was that a reason falling within the Act or some other substantial reason of a kind such as to justify the dismissal of an employee holding the position which that employee held ?

- Did the employer act reasonably or unreasonably in treating that reason as a sufficient reason for dismissing the employees.

The burden of proving, on the balance of probabilities, the real reason for dismissal, and that it is a statutory reason, is upon the employer. Failure to establish this true reason will make the decision to dismiss automatically unfair.

> In *Timex Corporation v. Thomson* 1981, the complainant, a long serving manager, was selected for redundancy following a re-organisation of managerial posts. The reasons for his selection were lack of engineering qualifications and unsatisfactory job performance. The Tribunal concluded that the true reason for his dismissal was not redundancy but incompetence and held the dismissal to be unfair. The EAT confirmed that the Tribunal was entitled to find that they were not satisfied that the employer had put forward the true reason for dismissal. *"Even where there is a redundancy situation it is possible for an employer to use such a situation as a pretext for getting rid of an employee he wishes to dismiss. In such cir-*

cumstances the reason for dismissal will not be redundancy." Here the employer had not satisfied the burden cast by the Act and so the dismissal was consequently unfair.

In practice the employer will normally be able to show that the reason for dismissal relied upon, will fall within one of the broad heads contained in the Act.

Capability or qualifications

A reason related to the employee's capabilities or qualifications for performing the work he is employed to do

The Act defines 'capability' as meaning skill, aptitude, health, physical or mental quality of the job, and 'qualification' as meaning any degree, diploma or other academic, technical or professional qualification relevant to the job.

> In *Blackman v. The Post Office* 1974 the employee was recruited for a particular job on a unestablished basis. A collective agreement provided that such an employee's employment should only be continued if he passed a written aptitude test. Despite showing aptitude for the job, the employee failed the test three times. The Tribunal held that the employer might rely on either 'capability' or 'qualifications' as grounds relied on for dismissal.

> In *Taylor v. Alidair Ltd.* 1978 the applicant pilot was dismissed when as a result of an error judgement, the passenger plane he was flying landed so hard that serious damage was caused to the plane. The Court of Appeal held that "the company has reasonable grounds for honestly believing that the applicant was not competent". As a result of this serious act of incompetence the belief was reasonably held, and the dismissal was consequently a fair one.

Misconduct

A reason which relates to the employee's conduct

Misconduct on the part of an employee may take numerous forms and may cover such matters as lateness, absenteeism, incompetence, insubordination, breach of safety rules, immorality, etc. Of course, the gravity of the misconduct and its regularity are key factors in determining whether the employer has acted reasonably in treating it as a ground for dismissal.

> In *Trust House Forte Hotels Ltd., v. Murphy* 1977 a night porter who admitted stealing liquor from his employer was held to be justifiably dismissed for misconduct at work.

Examples of misconduct at work sufficient to justify dismissal include the following.

> In *Boychuk v. Symons Holdings Ltd.* 1977 the applicant was carrying on sexual relations during working hours. Also, in *Wilcox v. Humphries and Glasgow Ltd.* 1975 the applicant was in breach of safety instructions. Finally, in *Atkin v. Enfield Group Hospital Management Committee* 1975, the applicant was justifiably dismissed for wearing provocative badges after having failed to heed repeated warnings.

In addition, misconduct of various kinds outside of work may be held to justify dismissal.

> In *Cassidy v. H.C. Goodman* 1975 the Tribunal held that for an employee to be justifiably dismissed on the grounds of misconduct outside of work, the misconduct had to be of exceptional gravity, and also of a kind likely to damage the employer's business. Here this was not the case: the employer had merely been unhappy about the applicant's private life, and had requested him to settle down.

> Alternatively, in *Singh v. London County Bus Services Ltd.* 1976 the applicant, who drove a one-man operated bus, was convicted of dishonesty committed outside his employment. The

EAT held that misconduct does not have to occur in the course of employment to justify dismissal so long as it could affect the employee when he is doing his work. Here the employee's conduct justified dismissal.

Redundancy

The redundancy of the employee

A redundancy situation will exist if the employer closes down his business or part of his business, and no longer requires the services of the particular employee. It does not follow, however, that a redundancy situation will automatically produce a fair dismissal . The employer must have consulted with his workforce, observed proper selection procedures and considered possible alternatives. He must have acted in good faith and consistently.

Also, it may be that a redundancy situation could be dealt with otherwise than by dismissing employees, such as by reducing overtime, introducing short-time working or restricting recruitment.

> This point was argued in *Attwood v. William Hill Ltd.* 1974 where the employer closed down betting shops and declared the managers redundant without giving warning or offering alternative employment. The Tribunal held that a redundancy situation existed, but the employees did not have to be made redundant, and more effort should have been taken to find them alternative work.

Statutory contravention

Because the employee could not continue to work in the position which he held without contravention of a restriction or a duty imposed by Statute

This means simply that an employer could not be expected to employ a worker if the employment was in contravention of a legal provision. An example would be the case of a bus driver who was disqualified from driving.

> In *Gill v. Walls Meat Co. Ltd.* 1971 for the employer to have continued to employ the applicant, who worked on an open meat counter would have infringed food regulations, for he had grown a beard. Since he had refused alternative employment his dismissal was held to be fair.

Some other substantial reason

Some other substantial reason such as to justify the dismissal of someone holding the employee's position

This reason provides a ground upon which an employer might rely if he cannot rely on one of the previous categories.

> In *Saunders v. Scottish National Camps* 1987 the reason relied on by the employer was that the employee in question was a homosexual. This was held to be some other substantial reason and within the final category.

The onus on the employer, then, is to establish as a fact that the reason for dismissal was within the Act. He must also show that he believed in the existence of the reason, and that the belief was supported by reasonable grounds such as might have arisen from a thorough investigation. If the employer has carried out a reasonable inquiry to establish the facts, it will be easier for him to show that at the time of the dismissal there existed in his mind a genuine belief in the reason relied on. If, then, an employer alleges misconduct and the facts show misconduct is not the true reason why the employee might have been at fault obviously misconduct will not be a sufficient reason.

In *Price v. Gourley* 1973 the applicant worked in a cake shop for 7 years and received top wages for her grade. She was dismissed, and when she asked for a reason was told by the manager that it was "just one of those things." At the Tribunal the employer alleged incompetence, but as he did not prove that any deterioration in her conduct had occurred, it seemed unreasonable that it had been 7 years before he had taken action. The true reason for the dismissal, the Tribunal held, was simply that the employer was attempting to reduce overheads by dismissing a highly paid employee and replacing her with an employee receiving lower pay.

Fairness

Having fulfilled the requirements of the Act and shown a valid reason for dismissal, the Act further provides that the determination of the question whether the dismissal was fair or unfair, shall depend upon whether the employer acted reasonably in treating it as a sufficient reason for dismissal. This question must be determined in accordance with equity and the merits of the case, in particular the size and administrative resources of the employer.

A certain amount of guidance has been given in relation to the question of fairness. The tribunal must determine the reasonableness of the employer's conduct, not whether they believe the conduct to be fair. They must ignore the temptation to substitute their own views as to the right course for the employer to adopt, and recognise that there is a 'band', of reasonable responses to an employee's conduct.

Within this 'band', there are a number of views reasonable employers could take different views. The role of the Tribunal is to decide whether the decision of the employer in the case before it comes within the band of reasonable responses, which the employer might have adopted. If the dismissal is within the band of reasonable responses, it is fair, otherwise it is unfair.

The determination of reasonableness, then, is a matter for the Industrial Tribunal acting as an Industrial Jury, and provided the correct approach is adopted the conclusion reached cannot be interfered with. The process involves a consideration of the reason for dismissal relied upon, and also of the procedure adopted. In considering the reason relied on, the Tribunal is entitled to take account of good industrial practice.

It should be stressed, however, as previously stated, that, given the reason relied on, the decision to dismiss need only fall within the band of reasonable responses you would expect from a reasonable employer.

> In *Saunders v. Scottish National Camps* 1987 the complainant, a handyman employed at a children's' holiday camp, was dismissed when the employer discovered that he was a homosexual. The reason for dismissal was that the employee indulged in homosexuality and it was unsuitable to employ someone of that sexual orientation in children's' camps. Both the Industrial Tribunal and the E.A.T. found the dismissal to be fair. They decided that a large proportion of employers in that situation would perceive that employment of homosexuals should be restricted where there is close contact with children. This is despite the fact that such a view may not be rational or capable of being supported by evidence which is scientifically sound.

As part of the social and legal recognition of the equal status of women in the work place the EPCA 78 provides that an employee shall be treated as unfairly dismissed if the reason for the dismissal is that she is pregnant or a reason connected with pregnancy.

> In *Brown v. Stockton on Tees BC* 1988 the employer in deciding which of a number of care supervisors to make redundant took account of the fact that one of them was pregnant and if retained he would subsequently have the inconvenience of coping with her maternity leave.

The House of Lords confirmed that as the employees requirement of maternity leave was the reason she was selected for redundancy, that was a reason connected with her pregnancy and therefore unfair dismissal.

In *Whitbread v. Thomas* 1988 the tribunal considered the situation where all three employees in an off-licence had been dismissed following serious stock losses from the shop over a number of years. The employer had resorted to this blanket dismissal when, after extensive investigations involving warnings and short-term transfers to other shops, he had been unable to discover the culprit. The decision of the Industrial Tribunal was that a blanket dismissal for what could have been incompetence was unjustifiable and consequently unfair. On appeal however the EAT held that an employer who cannot identify the culprit is entitled to dismiss all the members of the group when three conditions are satisfied. Firstly the act complained of must be sufficient to justify dismissal if committed by an individual. Secondly the tribunal must be satisfied that the act was committed by one of the group. Thirdly there must have been a proper investigation to identify the person responsible. Here the conditions were satisfied and the employer was entitled to dismiss as the decision was within the band of reasonable responses open to a reasonable employer and consequently a fair one.

Disciplinary procedures

In addition to examining the reason relied on, the process of determining reasonableness also involves a consideration of the procedure adopted by the employer. There exists a Code of Practice on Disciplinary Practice and Procedures drawn up by the ACAS. This provides, amongst other things, that employees should be given fair warning before dismissal. For minor infringements, an informal oral warning should be given first, then possibly a formal oral warning followed if necessary by a final oral warning, and if necessary a final written warning. If the misconduct continues, a final step could be disciplinary suspension without pay before dismissal. Of course the graver the conduct the less need there would be for a long drawn out procedure. Whether an employer has adopted the Code, or something similar, and has also complied with it is of assistance in assessing whether he has acted reasonably.

The present judicial opinion was expressed however by the House of Lords in *Polkey v. AE Dayton Services Ltd.* 1987. The case involved a van driver who was dismissed by reason of redundancy without consultation. It was argued that the dismissal was nevertheless fair because, even if the proper procedural steps had been taken the decision would still have been to dismiss. This argument was rejected by the House of Lords who held that it is an approach which is no longer to be adopted. If an employer fails to take the proper procedural steps laid down before dismissing an employee, that is normally sufficient to amount to unreasonableness constituting unfair dismissal. While there may be cases where procedural steps may be futile and can be dispensed with, these will be extremely exceptional.

It is now established that in assessing the fairness of the employers decision to dismiss or otherwise it is necessary to consider whether the disciplinary code was fully adhered to.

In *Stoker v. Lancashire County Council* 1992 the complainant was employed by the County Council as a laboratory technician at a Polytechnic. His contract of employment incorporated the college's two stage disciplinary procedure involving a hearing and then a possible appeal but in addition he was also entitled to have any decision reached confirmed by a committee of the Council with the possibility of further appeal. A decision to dismiss the complainant because of misconduct was taken following a disciplinary hearing and appeal and this decision was subsequently ratified by the Council disciplinary sub-committee and appeals sub-committee. Rather than allowing a full rehearing of the case as provided for in the disciplinary procedure the Council sub-committee confined itself to a renew of the 'sentence' after hearing from both sides. Both the Tribunal and Appeal Tribunal felt that this short-cut was permissible in the circumstances given the fact that the complainant *"had been afforded every reasonable opportunity, and indeed much more than that, both to state his own case and challenge that of the respondents"*. The Court of Appeal disagreed however and felt that the Industrial Tribunal had *"misinterpreted the contractual disciplinary procedures"*. As the disciplinary procedure required a full rehearing at the two external stages this should have been complied with. *" A reasonable employer can be expected to comply with the full requirements of the appeal procedure in its own disciplinary code"*.

Even if the employer invokes the appropriate disciplinary procedure leading to a dismissal it must be implemented fairly and in accordance with the rules of natural justice.

In *Spink v. Express Foods Group Ltd.* 1990 prior to the dismissal of the complainant sales representative the employer had taken disciplinary proceedings against him which involved holding a disciplinary inquiry. The fact that the employer deliberately decided not to reveal the purpose of the inquiry to the complainant and the allegations against him made the proceedings and the decision to dismiss unfair. The EAT held that *"it is a fundamental part of a fair disciplinary procedure that an employee knows the case against him. Fairness requires that someone accused should know the case to be met; should hear or be told the important parts of the evidence in support of the case; should have an opportunity to criticise or dispute that evidence and adduce his own evidence and argue his case."*

Furthermore in *Louies v. Coventry Hood and Sealing Co. Ltd.* 1990 the complainants dismissal for alleged theft was found by the EAT to be unfair on the grounds that employer's belief in his guilt was based largely on the statement of two witnesses and the complainant was denied access to those documents throughout the disciplinary proceedings. *Where the essence of the case against an employee is contained in written statement by witnesses, it is contrary to the rules of natural justice and prima facie unfair for an employer to refuse to let the employee see these statements"*.

The effect of an unjustifiable delay in carrying out disciplinary proceedings could make a decision to dismiss unfair which would otherwise have been held to be fair. This would be the case even where it is shown that the complainant suffered no prejudice as a result of the delay.

This was the decision of the EAT in *The Royal Society for the Prevent of Cruelty to Animals v. Cruden* 1986. Despite the gravity of the complainant's gross misjudgement and idleness, in this case the protracted delay in implementing disciplinary proceedings against him rendered the decision to dismiss unfair. *"The EPCA 78 is concerned with whether the employer had acted fairly and not whether the employee had suffered an injustice."* In an attempt to do justice in the case however the EAT reduced both the basic award and the compensatory award to nil to reflect the complainant's grave neglect and the fact that the employer would be failing in his duty if he failed to dismiss in these circumstances.

In *Slater v. Leicestershire Health Authority* 1989 the Court of Appeal held that the fact that a manager had carried out a preliminary investigation of the applicant's misconduct and had then conducted a disciplinary hearing leading to a decision to dismiss did not of itself render the dismissal unfair. While a breach of the rules of natural justice is clearly a matter to take account in determining reasonableness, it is possible for the same person to conduct an investigation and still carry out a fair inquiry.

Activity

Write to your local office of the Advisory Conciliation and Arbitration Service and request a copy of the Code of Practice on Disciplinary Practice and Procedures. Make use of the Code to prepare a brief guide as to the stages involved in a well drafted disciplinary procedure.

Unfair selection for redundancy

In cases where the reason for dismissal is redundancy the dismissal will be prima facie (On the face of it) fair. If however the circumstances of the dismissal show that the employer failed to act reasonably then a redundancy dismissal would be found to be unfair and a remedy awarded.

Consequently if in a redundancy selection the employer failed to observe agreed industrial practice, this could render a decision to dismiss on grounds of redundancy unfair.

Guidance in relation to the approach to be adopted by Industrial Tribunals in determining the fairness of redundancy selections was provided by the Employment Appeal Tribunal in *Williams v. Compair Maxim Ltd.* 1982. Here the complainants had been dismissed for redundancy, the employer having failed to consult with the recognised trade union. Selection had been left to departmental managers, one of whom gave evidence that he had retained those employees whom he considered would be best to retain in the interests of the company in the long run. Length of service was not a factor taken into account. The Industrial Tribunal's finding of fair dismissal was reversed by the EAT which held the decision to be perverse. Measuring the conduct of the employer in question with that of a reasonable employer, a Tribunal taken to be aware of good industrial practice, could not have reached the decision that the dismissals were fair. The employer's decision to dismiss was not within the range of conduct which a reasonable employer could have adopted in these circumstances. While accepting that it was impossible to lay down detailed procedures for a selection process, the EAT felt that reasonable employers would attempt to act in accordance with five basic principles and should depart from them only with good reason.

- As much warning as possible should be given of impending redundancies to enable the union and employees to inform themselves of the facts, seek alternative solutions and find alternative employment.

- The employer will consult with the union as to the best means of achieving the objective as fairly and with as little hardship as possible. Criteria should be agreed to be applied in selection and the selection monitored.

- The criteria agreed should not depend upon subjective opinion of the person selecting but it must be capable of objective scrutiny and include such matters as attendance record, job efficiency, experience or length of service.

- The employer must seek to ensure that the selection is made fairly in accordance with these criteria and consider union representations.

- The employer should examine the possibility of finding suitable alternative employment.

The above principles, the court held, are also reflected in the *Trade Union and Labour Relations (Consolidation) Act* 1992 which applies where there is a recognised Trade Union. In addition the code of practice on redundancy as an integral part of employment law should also be taken account of by an employer wishing to act fairly. Here the dismissals were carried out 'in blatant contravention of the standards of fair treatment generally accepted by fair *employers'* and were consequently unfair.

The approach adopted in Compair Maxim was applied approvingly by the Northern Ireland Court of Appeal in *Robinson v. Carrickfergus Borough Council* 1983. Here a technical offi-

cer of the council had been dismissed by reason of redundancy without warning or consultation, but because there was no agreed redundancy procedure which applied to him the
tribunal had decided by a majority that his dismissal was fair. This decision was reversed by
the Court of Appeal who held that by applying the Compair Maxim principles the decision
to dismiss was *"outside the range of conduct which a reasonable employer could have
adopted".*

Certainly the need for consultation in a redundancy situation is one of the fundamentals of fairness and
it is only in exceptional cases that a failure to consult can be overlooked.

So said the EAT in *Holden v. Bradville* 1985. Here the employer had argued that both the
need for secrecy in a company takeover and the practical difficulties involved in interviewing and consulting up to thirty three employees selected for redundancy meant that the
employer could ignore the need for consultation prior to dismissal. This argument was rejected by the EAT who held that in a redundancy situation you should presume that
consultation is a prerequisite to fair selection but it was up to an Industrial Tribunal to decide whether in the particular circumstances of the case before it, even without consultation,
the selection is nevertheless fair. This case was not one where consultation was impracticable and nor was there evidence to support the view that consultation would have made no
difference to the result. *"There was at least a chance that an employee could have pointed
to her good performance record, her experience and her age and seniority as factors in favour of her retention, with sufficient eloquence and force to persuade the management to
take her name off the redundancy list and replace it with that of one of her colleagues".*

Redundancy Payments

Redundancy occurs when an employee is dismissed because an employer has closed his business or the
business is closed in the place the employee works. Alternatively there is redundancy if the employer
no longer requires or has a reduced requirement for employees to carry out work of a particular kind.
In both cases there must be no suitable alternative employment. As far as unfair dismissal is concerned
a dismissal by reason of redundancy is a statutory reason for dismissal and provided the employer
consults when he need to and adopts rational criterion for selection, such a dismissal may be classified
as fair.

The right to a redundancy payment for workers dismissed because there is no longer a demand for their
services was first introduced in 1965 under the *Redundancy Payment Act.* The 1965 Act represented a
major statutory intervention in the individual employment relationship, for while redundancy/severance
payments have always been contractually agreed, the Act made the State redundancy payment a statutory
requirement for qualifying employees. It was the first example of any State provision for compensation
for workers who lost their jobs through no fault of their own. The complex provisions of the Act are
now found in the *Employment Protection (Consolidation) Act* 1978.

The object of redundancy provision is to compensate a worker for the loss of a long term stake he has
in his job. In the mid 1960s it was thought that the provision of lump sum severance payments to
redundant employees would encourage a shake out of underemployed labour in industry generally, with
less risk of industrial action. It was also thought that such payments would encourage mobility of labour
to accommodate technological advances. Under the original scheme every employer made contributions
to the Redundancy Fund and until October 1986 received a rebate of 35% for every payment made. As
from October 31 1986 however, the rebate was abolished except for those employers who employ less
than ten employees. Industrial Tribunals have jurisdiction over disputes relating to entitlement and the
amount of any redundancy payment and also where the complaint is one of unfair dismissal due to unfair

selection for redundancy. It should be recognised that between 1965 and 1971 disputes in relation to redundancy provided the main work of Industrial Tribunals in industrial conflict. When the right not to be unfairly dismissed was introduced in 1971 however, employees were more likely to argue that they had been dismissed unfairly rather than redundant and so entitled to increased compensation. For both the right to a redundancy payment and the right to claim unfair dismissal an employee must qualify by establishing a minimum of two years continuous employment.

Certain categories of employees are also excluded from making a claim:

- Persons who have attained retirement age which under the Employment Act 1989 is 65 for both men and women.
- Persons employed under a fixed term contract of two years or more who agree in writing to exclude their rights to a payment provided they do so before the expiration of the term.
- Share fishermen, i.e. paid by a share of the profits.
- Crown employees.
- Persons ordinarily employed outside Great Britain unless on the date of dismissal for redundancy they are in Great Britain following the employer's instructions.
- Persons who are covered by a redundancy agreement approved by the Secretary of State.
- Certain registered dockworkers.
- Certain National Health Service employees.
- "Office holders" who are not employees.
- Domestic servants in a private household who are close relatives of the employer.

To qualify to make a claim for a redundancy payment, an employee must have been dismissed by reason of redundancy, laid off or kept on short time.

In *Brown v. Knowsley BC* 1986 the applicant having been employed in a college of further education under a number of fixed term contracts was offered a one year temporary contract from 1 September 1983, stipulated to last as long as funds from the Manpower Services Commission were provided for the course she taught. On 3 August 1984 she was given written notice that as the MSC funding had ceased, her employment terminated on 31 August 1984. The applicant's claim for a redundancy payment was rejected by the tribunal who found there to be no dismissal but rather a discharge of the contract by performance. The EAT agreed that there had been no dismissal, and held that the contract was terminable on the happening or non-happening of a future event, in this case the withdrawal of funding by the MSC.

If an employee leaves prematurely in a redundancy situation without waiting to be dismissed, then this will prejudice the success of a claim.

In *Morton Sundour Fabrics v. Shaw* 1966 the employee in question, having been warned of the possibility of redundancy, left to take other employment. The court held that as he had not been dismissed, he was therefore not entitled to a redundancy payment.

Even when notice of dismissal by reason of redundancy has been served, if employees subsequently accept an offer of voluntary early retirement, as an alternative to redundancy, they would not be entitled to a redundancy payment.

This was the controversial decision of the EAT in *Scott v. Coalite Fuels and Chemicals Ltd.* 1988. By reaching an agreement as to a voluntary termination of employment, the nature of an earlier notice of dismissal was consequently changed so that the tribunal was entitled to find that there had been no dismissal for the purpose of redundancy.

If an employee succumbs to pressure to resign in a redundancy situation, the resignation could still be treated as a dismissal for the purposes of redundancy.

> In *Caledonian Mining Co Ltd. v. Bassett* 1987 a sympathetic approach was taken by the EAT to employees who in a redundancy situation had written to their employer terminating their employment. The men had originally been told that manpower on their site would be reduced, and asked whether they would be interested in alternative employment. Despite an expression of interest by the men, the employer did not respond and failed to offer alternative work. The men did receive an offer from the National Coal Board which they accepted. This led to the letter of termination which the employer argued constituted a resignation, and as there had been no dismissal in law there was no right to a redundancy payment. The EAT agreed with the tribunal however and held that the men had been encouraged to resign and take another job with the intention of avoiding redundancy payments. The true position here was that the employer had caused the men to resign, and in reality the employer was terminating the contract. Accordingly the employees were dismissed in law and entitled to a redundancy payment.

Redundancy dismissal

The right to a redundancy payment arises when a qualifying employee has been dismissed by reason of redundancy. The reason for dismissal must therefore be redundancy, a presumption of which arises in favour of the applicant unless the contrary is proved. It is for the employer to rebut the presumption of redundancy on the balance of probabilities by showing that the dismissal was for some reason other than redundancy.

Redundancy could occur because the business is closed or it is intended that it will be. Such a closure could relate to the whole business or just a part of it and be permanent or temporary. In addition redundancy could arise if the business is closed in the place where the employee works. If, however, the employee's contract provides that he could be required to move to a new work location, and the employer attempts to trigger the clause, then there is no redundancy. Even without an express clause there is an implied term in the contract of employment that the employee may be moved to a new work location within reasonable commuting distance from home.

Redundancy will also occur if the requirements of the business for employees of a particular kind have ceased or diminished. To replace an employee with a self-employed person will be a dismissal by reason of redundancy and the dismissed employee will be entitled to a payment. This will also be the case where it is the employee himself who is being reinstated on self-employed status. Liability to make redundancy payments could be one of the costs of an employer transferring work from employees to independent contractors. Benefits would include the loss of future rights to redundancy payments and possible unfair dismissal rights and lower National Insurance contributions.

The fact that the dismissed employee has been replaced by another employee will not normally lead to a finding of redundancy for it cannot be said that the requirements of the business for an employee have ceased or diminished. There would be a redundancy, however, if it could be shown that the replacement employee was moved because of a reduction in requirements. Here an employee is being dismissed to make way for an employee who would otherwise be surplus to requirements and so the dismissed employee is entitled to a redundancy payment.

In situations where the employee's skills have become outdated because of changes in working methods to which he cannot or is not prepared to adapt, there have been conflicting views as to whether, if he is dismissed, it is by reason of redundancy or incapability.

In the history of the law of redundancy there are early examples of the courts being called upon to draw a distinction between diminishing requirements for an employee because of a reduction in a particular kind of work carried on, and diminishing requirements for an employee due to his failure to adapt to new working methods.

> In *North Riding Garages Ltd. v. Butterwick* 1967 a workshop manager with thirty years experience was dismissed following a takeover and reorganisation of the business. The manager found it difficult to adapt to new methods which had been introduced, in particular coping with costs estimates. The repair side of the workshop for which he had been responsible was deliberately run down and the sales side increased. Following his dismissal a new workshop manager was engaged. The Tribunal upheld the employee's claim for a redundancy payment deciding that the presumption of redundancy had not been rebutted. On appeal, however, it was held that there had been no change in the requirements of the business to carry out a particular kind of work, for there was still a need for a workshop manager. It was the employee's personal deficiencies which caused the dismissal rather than redundancy. *"An employee remaining in the same kind of work was expected to adapt to new methods and higher standards of efficiency, unless the nature of the work he was required to do was thereby altered so that no requirement remained for employees to do work of the particular kind which was superseded."*

> "Personal deficiencies" was again the reason put forward by the employer for dismissal in *Hindle v. Percival Boats* 1969. The claimant, a highly skilled woodworker with twenty years boat-building experience was dismissed for being "too good and too slow" when fibreglass became the main material for boat-building rather than wood. He claimed a redundancy payment on the grounds that his dismissal was attributable wholly or mainly to a reduction in the employer's requirements for woodworkers. A majority of the Court of Appeal held that there was no dismissal by reason of redundancy, for the true reason for dismissal was that the claimant was too slow and his continued employment uneconomical. In the dissenting judgement, however, Lord Denning, MR., placed great emphasis on the statutory presumption of redundancy. *"Redundancy payment is compensation to a man for the loss of the job; and a man should not be deprived of it merely because the employer thinks or believes that he is being dismissed for a reason other than redundancy."*

The contemporary approach to change seems to be that so long as the job function remains, there is no redundancy. If an employee is given a very wide job function, that is likely to mean where there are technological or social changes in the way that a job is performed, that does not make it a different kind of work for the purposes of redundancy.

In cases where the reason for dismissal is redundancy, but the employer was entitled to terminate the contract by reason of the employee's misconduct, the right to a redundancy payment will be lost.

Suitable alternative employment

If, before employment terminates, the employer makes the employee an offer either to renew the contract of employment or re-engage the employee under a new contract which constitutes suitable alternative employment, then provided the new contract is to commence within four weeks of the previous one terminating, an unreasonable refusal to accept such an offer will mean that the employee will not be entitled to make a claim for a redundancy payment. Failure to take up an offer of a new contract on identical terms and conditions of employment therefore would normally constitute an unreasonable refusal to accept re-engagement and, as a consequence, an employer will lose the right to make a claim for payment. If the offer is of alternative employment, it is necessary to determine its suitability in relation to the previous employment. For the new employment to be "suitable" it must be substantially similar to the previous job and not employment of an entirely different nature at the same salary. The question is one of fact and degree and one which the Tribunal must examine in the light of the particular circumstances of the case including such matters as the nature of the work, the rates of pay, the place of work, the new status, and fringe benefits. Personal factors affecting the employee may also be considered such as social and family links, accommodation, and the children's education.

> In *Devonald v. J D Insulating Company Ltd.* 1972 the applicant was required to move from a factory in Bootle to another in Blackburn. He refused, and on his claim for redundancy the tribunal held that suitable alternative employment had been offered as he was already required under his present employment to do outside contract work.

In practice the question as to whether the alternative employment is suitable or not will be considered at the same time as the issue as to whether it is reasonable to refuse it or not. While it is reasonable to refuse unsuitable work, it is unreasonable to refuse suitable alternative employment.

> In *Fuller v. Stephanie Bowman Ltd.* 1977 the applicant typist refused to move from Mayfair to a new office in Soho. She found the move distasteful, particularly as the new office was above a sex shop. The tribunal found that the refusal to move was unreasonable in the circumstances, as it was based on undue sensitivity and the claim for redundancy consequently failed.

> The decision of the EAT in *Gloucestershire County Council v. Spencer* 1985 supports the view that it is for management to set the appropriate standard of work to be achieved. Here the number of cleaners at a school had been reduced from five to four and the hours of work of the remaining employees cut by forty five minutes. The employer recognised that standards would drop, but maintained nevertheless, that the new terms constituted an offer of suitable alternative employment. This offer was rejected by the remaining cleaners on the grounds that they felt they could not continue to do a satisfactory job. The Industrial Tribunal agreed and found that while the alternative jobs were 'suitable' within the meaning of the section, the employees' refusal to accept the new terms was not unreasonable as they could not do the new jobs adequately in the time allotted. The EAT held that the Tribunal was in error, for the standard of work set by the management, cannot be reasonably objected to by employees as a ground for refusing to work. Accordingly the offer of suitable alternative employment had been unreasonably rejected and the applicants were not entitled to redundancy payments.

If an employee accepts an offer of alternative employment on different terms and conditions, he is entitled to a trial period. The length of the period is four weeks, but if the new job requires retraining, the parties can specify a longer trial period in writing. If, for any reason, during the trial period the employee gives notice to terminate his employment, or the employer terminates for a reason connected with the change to the new job, then the employee is treated as dismissed from the date that the previous contract terminated. To determine his rights to a redundancy payment it is then necessary to examine the original reason for dismissal, whether the offer of alternative work was suitable, and whether the termination by the employer reasonable. In cases where the offer of new employment involves changes in employment terms, which would otherwise constitute a repudiatory breach, then under the common law, an employee who nevertheless accepts the new job for a period could still change his mind and resign claiming constructive dismissal.

Redundancy procedure

The *Trade Union and Labour Relations (Consolidation) Act* 1992 contains a number of rules relating to the procedure to be invoked in a redundancy situation where an independent trade union is recognised in relation to the class of employees involved. The primary duty imposed on the employer is to consult with trade union representatives. If an employer proposes to dismiss 100 or more employees as redundant within 90 days or less or 10 or more employees within 30 days then he must consult within the 90 or 30 day periods respectively. In other cases the employer must consult at the earliest opportunity. For the purposes of the consultation the employer is required to disclose to the trade union representative:

- the reasons for the disposals;
- the numbers and descriptions of employees whom it is proposed to dismiss as redundant;
- the total number of employees of any such description employed by the employer at the establishment in question;
- the proposed method of selecting the employees who may be dismissed; and
- the proposed method of carrying out the dismissals with due regard to any agreed procedure including the period over which the dismissals are to take effect.

The employer is further obliged to consider any representations made by the trade union representatives, respond to them, and give reasons if they are rejected.

If an employer fails to comply with the consultation requirements then the trade union could seek a remedy by presenting a complaint to an Industrial Tribunal. The Tribunal can make a declaration as to non-compliance and also make a protective award requiring the employer to pay the specified employees their wages for the "protected period", specified not to exceed the consultation period to which they were entitled, 90, 30 or 28 days. An employer who fails to comply with a protective award can be required to do so on an individual complaint to a Tribunal by an employee.

The ACAS Code stresses the need for the fullest consultation between employers and employees or trade unions in advance of a redundancy situation. They should produce agreed selection and appeal procedures. Failure to warn and consult may of course render a redundancy dismissal unfair. To make a selection based on 'attitude of work' without any warning or consultation was held to be unfair in *Graham v. ABF Ltd.*. 1986. This was despite the fact that a full consultation may well have produced the same result. For the purpose of selection, the Code advocates objective criteria including skill, age, length of service, standard of performance and future requirements for employees.

Finally, mention should also be made of the fact that an employee with two years' service who is given notice of dismissal by reason of redundancy has the right, during the notice period, to be given reasonable time off during working hours, to look for new employment or make arrangements for future training. The employee is also entitled to be paid at the appropriate rate during the period of absence and can present a claim to a tribunal if his rights are denied.

Redundancy calculation

If an employee believes that as a qualifying worker he has been dismissed by reason of redundancy, the onus is upon him to make a claim to his employer for a redundancy payment. If the employer denies the claim or simply refuses to make a payment, the remedy of the employee is by way of complaint to an Industrial Tribunal. If a redundancy payment is made (otherwise than in compliance with an order of the Tribunal specifying the amount), then an employer is guilty of an offence if he fails without reasonable excuse to give the employee a written statement indicating how the payment was calculated. The sum is calculated in the same way as a basic award by reference to the age of the claimant, the length of continuous employment and the weekly pay of the claimant.

Amount of the payment

Age (inclusive)	Amount of week's pay for each year of employment
18 – 21	½
22 – 40	1
41 – 65	1½

Given that the aim of the payment is to provide a lump sum for the employee while he is seeking new employment, the fact that he will soon qualify for state retirement pension is also a factor in calculating the amount. Accordingly, for each month that the claimant is over sixty-four at the relevant date, the amount is reduced by one twelfth.

The *Employment Act* 1989 (EA 89) equalises the age at which men and women cease to be entitled to a statutory redundancy payment and in so doing brings the age limits on entitlement to redundancy payment into line with those on the right to claim unfair dismissal. The tapering provision which previously started at 64 for men and 59 for women and which had the effect of reducing the redundancy payment by one twelfth for each month of employment beyond those ages, will in future apply to both men and to women. An employee will be excluded from the redundancy payment scheme where there is a normal retiring age of below 65 for employees holding the position which he held, applicable to both men and women alike, and the employee has reached that age. If the normal retiring age is over 65, or is different for men and women, or there is no normal retiring age, the age limit for entitlement will be 65.

Another feature of the calculation is the fact that each year the maximum week's pay is adjusted to reflect the current average wage which is presently £205. Consequently the maximum redundancy payment is 20 years × 1½ (for employment between the ages of 41-65) × £205 = £6,150. For employees on a weekly fixed rate then the contractual rate is the current average wage. In cases where the wage does vary, however, a week's pay is calculated by reference to the average hourly rate of remuneration over the last twelve weeks of employment.

In a complex decision relating to the calculation of an average week's wage for the purpose of redundancy entitlement, the House of Lords held in *British Coal Corporation v. Cheesbrough* 1990 that in calculating an employee's average rate of remuneration, work in overtime hours must be treated as if they had been done in normal working hours and the remuneration reduced accordingly. Where however an employee's contract provides for bonus payment only for work done during normal working hours, the overtime hours worked should not be treated as if they would attract bonus payments.

While the payment is made by the employer, originally he was entitled to claim a rebate from the Redundancy Fund financed by weekly levies from employers. Under the *Employment Act* 1988 the Redundancy Fund was abolished.

Health and Safety at Work

While it is the fundamental aim of business activity to produce goods and services there is an increasing awareness that in achieving this aim the workforce must not be subjected to unacceptable risks to their health or safety. The catalogue of major disasters in the 1980s has been mirrored by a steady rise in the number of accidents at the workplace.

In the United Kingdom legal intervention in the field of health and safety has a long history and the earliest examples of employment legislation, the nineteenth century Factories Acts, were designed to ensure that a slender cushion of legislative protection was provided for those categories of workers at particular risk. The criminal codes in relation to health and safety law were contained in numerous statutes and statutory instruments e.g. the *Factories Act* 1961, the *Office Shops and Railway Premises Act* 1963. Eventually in 1972 the Robens Committee on Safety and Health at work criticised this fragmented state of the law. As a result of the Robens Committee recommendations the *Health and Safety at Work Act* 1974 was passed.

The aims of the Act were to:

- lay down general duties applicable across the industrial spectrum;
- provide a unified system of enforcement under the control of the Health and Safety Executive and local authorities;
- create the Health and Safety Commission to assist in the process of changing attitudes and producing detailed regulations applicable to each industrial sector backed up by codes of practice designed to give guidance as to how general duties and specific regulations could be satisfied.

By imposing legal duties on employers, employees, contractors, manufacturers and others backed up by criminal sanctions, the 1974 Act is designed to achieve minimum standards of conduct and so minimising the risk of injury and enhancing the welfare of those at the workplace. In addition to criminal sanctions however the possibility of civil redress must also be considered so that those injured at the workplace have a further avenue of redress to secure compensation by relying on common law principles.

As previously stated UK businesses also operate in a European legal framework and health and safety issues are an established part of European Community social policy. Since the adoption of the Single European Act 1986 the regulation of Health and Safety at work in the UK as been refined by European Community law initiatives. In 1990 the Chairman of the Health and Safety Commission said that "the European Community has now to be regarded as the principal engine of health and safety law affecting the UK not just in worker safety but also major hazards and most environmental hazards". Article 22 of the *Single European Act* 1986 added a new Article 118A to the Treaty of Rome and so introduced a new concept "the working environment".

Article 118A provides that "Member States shall pay particular attention to encouraging improvements especially in the working environment, as regards the health and safety of workers and shall set as their objective the harmonisation of conditions in this area, while maintaining the improvements made".

The significance of Article 118A is that it incorporates the qualified majority procedure rather than unanimity for the adoption of health and safety provisions by the Council of Ministers. This means that despite the objection of individual member states the majority view as to setting health and safety standards throughout the European Community will prevail. Furthermore the European Parliament has suggested that the expression "working environment" in Article 118A should be given a wide definition so that it could embrace matters such as the arrangement of a workplace as well as physical and psychological conditions at work. The working environment provisions were also acknowledged by the acceptance of the Charter of Fundamental Rights of Workers in December 1989 as an integral part of the development of the internal market.

There is no doubt that recently there has been a dramatic acceleration in the pace of the community legislation on health and safety compared with the minimal achievement of the previous two decades. Between 1970 and 1986 only six Directives aimed specifically at promoting health and safety at work were proposed by the Commission and adopted by the Council.

1. Council Directive for the provision of safety signs at place of work 1977.
2. Council Directive on the protection of workers from the risks related to exposure to chemical, physical and biological agents at work 1980.

3. Council Directive on the protection of workers from the risks related to exposure to chloride monomer 1978.

4. Council Directive on the protection of workers from the risks of exposure at work to metallic lead and its toxic compounds 1982.

5. Council Directive on the protection of workers from the risks related to exposure to asbestos at work 1983.

6. Council Directive on the major accident hazards of certain industrial activities 1986.

Despite the worthy aims of the Commission's Action Plans of 1978 and 1984 to promote a programme of health and safety measures, only moderate progress was made. Following the Single European Act, however, there is now a new emphasis in relation to health and safety. In 1987 a third action programme for health and safety was published by the European Commission and subsequently approved by resolution of the Council of Ministers. The programme contemplates a legislative package and a large number of Directives are proposed on a number of topics such as: the organisation of safety; selection and use of plant and machinery; selection and use of personal protective equipment; revision of the safety signs directives; medical assistance on ships; protection of agricultural workers using pesticides; safety in construction; carcinogenic agents; pesticides; amendments to the asbestos directive; and amendments to the lead directive.

In December 1988 further Directives were recommended by the Commission to deal with: temporary and mobile work sites; health and safety for fishing vessels; agriculture; modes of transport; extractive industries; and nuclear plants.

Other health and safety Directives promised in the Commission's Action Programme relating to the implementation of the Community Charter of Fundamental Social Rights of Workers are:

- the establishment of a safety, hygiene and health agency;
- information for workers exposed to dangerous agents;
- the protection of workers exposed to physical agents;
- the protection of pregnant women at work; and
- the protection of young people.

In addition to these numerous Directives the Commission propose to issue recommendations on economic factors in process control systems, prevention of back injuries, safety in agricultural building and electricity, safety in sea fishing, prescribed occupational diseases, assessment of exposure to dangerous agents and provision and organisation of occupational health services.

The third action programme resulted in the production of a Framework Directive for the Introduction of Measures to Encourage Improvement in Safety and Health of Workers, in March 1989 which was approved by the Council for implementation by member states by January 1 1993. A number of daughter Directives were also proposed to:

- require employers to evaluate health and safety risks;
- introduce preventive measures and develop a preventive policy;
- designate competent personnel or use outside agencies;
- make arrangements for first aid, fire precautions and emergency procedures;
- maintain records and report accidents and diseases;
- provide information to workers;
- consult workers or their representatives on health and safety measures;
- provide health and safety training for workers;

- allow workers' representatives time off with pay; and
- allow them to receive appropriate training.

Three of the above daughter Directives have since been adopted by the Council of Ministers.

(a) *Minimum health and safety requirements for the workplace*
The Directive relates to new workplaces and provides for specified requirements relating to structural stability, fire precautions, ventilation room temperature, lighting, electrical safety etc.

(b) *Minimum health and safety requirements for use by workers of machines and equipment*
This involves providing information and consulting with employees about safety equipment and bringing the existing equipment up to minimum standards within four years.

(c) *Minimum health and safety requirements for the use by workers of personal protective equipment*
Personal protection equipment is equipment designed to be worn or held by the worker to provide protection against one or more hazards.

Further daughter Directives on the use of visual display units working time and the provision of minimum health and safety requirements for handling heavy loads where there is a risk of back injury have been formally adopted by the Council for implementation in member states by January 1 1993.

In order to implement the directives a number of regulations have been produced clarifying the new law and repealing out of date law. In addition practical guidance in the form of codes of practice have also been produced to ensure compliance with the regulations which are in force from the beginning of 1993.

The new regulations apply to virtually all work activities and place duties on employers in relation to their employees and in some circumstances to the public and self employed contractors in relation to themselves and others who may be affected by their acts or omissions. The regulations cover:

- Health and Safety Management – Management of Health and Safety Regulations
- Work Equipment Safety – Provision and use of Work Equipment Regulations
- Manual Handling of Loads – Manual Handling Operators Regulations
- Workplace Conditions – Workplace (Health Safety and Welfare) Regulations
- Personal Protective Equipment – Personal Protective Equipment at Work Regulations
- Display Screen Equipment – Health and Safety (Display Screen Equipment) Regulations

In the next section the formal enforcement of health and safety law is considered however it should be stressed that in relation to the above regulations the main focus is initially to promote awareness and enforcement is not likely unless:

- the risks to health and safety are immediate and evident, or
- employers appear deliberately unwilling to recognise their responsibilities to ensure the long term health, safety and welfare of employees and others affected by their activities.

Management of Health and Safety at Work Regulations 1992

These regulations are aimed at improving health and safety management and apply to almost all work activities in Great Britain and offshore. Under them employers are required to adopt a well organised and systematic approach to comply with their statutory duties in relation to health and safety. In pursuing this objective employers are required to:

- carry out a risk assessment of health and safety so that preventive and protective measures can be identified. While there is an existing obligation in the Health and Safety at Work Act for employers of five or more employees to prepare a written health and safety policy there is now an additional obligation on them to record the findings of the risk assessment.

- make arrangements for putting into practice the health and safety measures that follow from the risk assessment. These arrangements will include planning, organisation, control, monitoring and review and must be recorded by employers with five or more employees.

- appoint competent people to help devise and implement the appropriate measures and ensure that employees including temporary workers are given appropriate health and safety training and understandable information.

- provide appropriate health surveillance for employees and set up emergency procedures where the risk assessment shows it to be necessary.

- consult employees safety representatives, provide facilities for them and co-operate with other employers sharing the same working environment.

In relation to employees the regulations require them to follow health and safety instructions and report dangers. Finally as far as the management of health and safety is concerned it should be recognised that there is an overlap between the new regulation and some existing requirements contained in duties and regulations. A specific regulation will replace a general duty but there is no requirement to for instance carry out two risk assessments for the purposes of different regulations.

Provision and use of Work Equipment Regulations 1992

Under the regulations general duties are placed upon employers in relation to equipment used at work and minimum requirements are identified to apply to all industries.

The expression "work equipment" is given a very wide definition and covers machinery of all kinds ranging from a hand tool to a complete plant. The 'use' of such equipment includes all activities ranging from installing and repairing to transporting and dismantling.

It should be stressed that employers who already use 'good practice' in the use of work equipment will find themselves in compliance with the new regulations.

The general duties will require an employer to:

- assess working conditions in particular risks and hazards when selecting work equipment.

- ensure that equipment is suitable for its use and that it conforms with EC product safety directives.

- give staff adequate information, instruction and training and maintaining equipment in efficient working order and a good state of repair.

In addition to the general duties the regulations also contain specific requirements in relation to equipment which will replace existing regulations. They include:

- guarding of the dangerous parts of machines.

- protection against specific hazards such as articles or substances, fire risks and explosion.

- ensuring adequate lighting, maintenance, warnings, stability, control systems and control devices.

The regulations apply to existing work equipment in use and further regulations will be made to implement EC directives requiring that new work equipment sold in member states should satisfy specific requirements.

Manual Handling Operations Regulations 1992

These regulations are aimed at preventing injuries which occur at the workplace due to the mishandling of loads by incorrect lifting, lowering, pushing, pulling, carrying or simply moving them about. Such operations should have been identified in the risk assessment. The regulations require an employer to ensure that:

- there is a genuine need to move a load and that manual handling is necessary rather than mechanical means
- the weight size and shape of the load is assessed along with the working environment and the handler's capabilities
- in so far as is reasonably practicable the risk of injury is reduced by for example reducing the load, employing mechanical means or training the handler.

Workplace (Health Safety and Welfare) Regulations 1992

The aim of these regulations is to replace numerous parts of existing legislation including the Factories Act 1961 and the Office Shops and Railway Premises Act 1963. They cover many aspects of health safety and welfare at the workplace in particular the working environment which includes temperature, ventilation, lighting, room size, work stations and seating. Facilities at the workplace are covered which includes toilets, washing, eating and changing facilities, drinking water, clothing storage, rest areas and facilities along with the need for cleanliness and effective removal of waste. Specific aspects of safety are included in particular relating to safe passage of pedestrians and vehicles, windows and skylights, doors, gates and escalators and floors.

Personal Protective Equipment at Work Regulations 1992 (PPE)

By these regulations some old law relating to PPE is replaced but more recent legal rules, in particular the Control of Substances Hazardous to Health or Noise at Work Regulations, remain in force. Personal protective equipment includes protective clothing, eye foot and head protection, harnesses, life jackets and high visibility clothing. Where risks are not adequately controlled by other means there is a duty to provide PPE free of charge for employees exposed to risks. The PPE provided must provide effective protection as appropriate to the risks and working conditions, take account of the worker's needs and fit properly. Further regulations are necessary to comply with a separate EC directive on the design certification and testing of PPE. The present regulations require an assessment of risks to determine the suitability of PPE; the provision of storage facilities; adequate training information and instruction; appropriate methods of cleansing maintenance and replacement and effective supervision to ensure its proper use.

Heath and Safety (Display Screen Equipment) Regulations 1992

These regulations apply where an individual habitually uses display screen equipment as a significant part of normal work. Duties are imposed on employers if equipment is used for the display of text, numbers and graphics but some systems are excluded including transport systems for public use, cash registers, window typewriters and portable systems not in prolonged use. The duties require employers to:

- assess display screen work stations and reduce risks revealed.
- ensure that minimum requirements are satisfied in relation to the display screen, keyboard, desk and chair, working environments and task design and software

- plan the work so that there are changes of activity and appropriate breaks and

- provide information and training for display screen users, eye testing and special spectacles if needed.

Enforcement of health and safety law

Enforcement of the safety legislation is in the hands of the Health and Safety Executive and local authorities which have a number of powers at their disposal. The main power is to appoint inspectors who have authority to enter premises, take samples and require information to be given. The breach of a general duty or a specific regulation under the Health and Safety legislation is a criminal offence. This can lead to a prosecution in the criminal courts. Less serious offences are dealt with summarily in the Magistrates Court and those of a more serious nature are tried on indictment in the Crown Court. Conviction in summary proceedings carries a fine of up to £5000, or for an indictable offence, an unlimited fine and/or up to two years imprisonment. The fundamental aim of those enforcing the law is to encourage a positive attitude to health and safety at the workplace rather than to take numerous employers through the criminal courts. There is no doubt however that some employers resent the economic cost of health and safety and it may only be the threat of criminal prosecution, that will cause the more recalcitrant employers to respond.

One of the major innovations of the Health and Safety at Work Act was the introduction of constructive sanctions. A Health and Safety Inspector who believes that an employer is contravening one of the statutory provisions may serve on that person an improvement notice requiring that the contravention be remedied within a specific period of not less than twenty one days. The notice will specify the provision which is contravened and state how it is being broken. In cases where the contravention involves an immediate risk of serious injury, the inspector may serve a prohibition notice which will direct that the particular activity is terminated until the contravention is rectified. Such a notice may take immediate effect or be deferred for a specified time. Failure to comply with a prohibition notice, for example by using a machine which has been identified as a serious source of danger, is an offence triable on indictment in the Crown Court.

While liability is generally associated with fault the courts have recently confirmed that even where there was little evidence of personal blame, an occupier of factory premises may still be held liable under the Factories Act 1961 if he fails to make his premises as safe as is reasonably practicable for all persons who may work there, even if they are not employees.

> In *Dexter v. Tenby Electrical Accessories Ltd.* 1991 contractors were employed by the defendants to install fresh air fans at their factory premises and for this purpose an employee of the contractor was required to work for a period on the factory roof despite the fact that the defendants were unaware that the employee was working on the roof they were nevertheless liable as occupiers of the factory when he suffered injuries after falling through it. The Health and Safety Executive charged the defendant with a contravention of s29(1) of the *Factories Act* 1961 which provides "there shall, so far as is reasonably practicable, be provided and maintained safe means of access to every place which any person has at anytime to work, and every such place shall, so far as is reasonably practicable, be made and kept safe for any person working there". While the Magistrates accepted the argument that the defendants had no control over the employee's place of work and so there was no case to answer, this was rejected in an appeal by the prosecution to the Queen's Bench Divisional Court. The appeal court held that lack of knowledge was no defence and if a person is ordered by his employer, a contractor, to work on a factory roof, the occupier of the factory is liable under the Act if the roof is in an unsafe condition.

General duties

Most of the general duties contained in the 1974 Act impose on a number of different categories of person, a standard of care based on the idea of reasonable practicability. The most important general duty is that contained in s.2(1) and imposes on employers a duty to ensure, so far as is reasonably practicable, the health, safety and welfare of their workers. More specifically this duty involves under s.2(2) in so far as is reasonably practicable:

- providing and maintaining safe plant and safe work systems
- making arrangements for the use, handling, storage and transport of articles and substances;
- providing any necessary information, instruction, training and supervision;
- maintaining a safe place of work and a safe access to and exit from it;
- maintaining a safe working environment.

The scope of the general duty, contained in s.2, qualified by the words "reasonably practicable" is difficult to determine and little guidance has been provided by the courts. However the meaning of this phrase is obviously crucial in determining the scope of an employer's duty. It would be wrong to assume that it imposes a standard of care comparable with the duty to take reasonable care at common law. The statutory duty requires the employer to take action to ensure health and safety unless, on the facts, it is impracticable in the circumstances.

In *Associated Dairies v. Hartley* 1979 the employer supplied his workers with safety shoes which they could pay for at £1 per week. An employee who had not purchased the shoes suffered a fractured toe when the wheel of a roller truck ran over it. There was an obvious risk to workers from roller trucks in the employer's warehouse. Accordingly an improvement notice was served on the employer requiring him to provide his employers with safety shoes free of charge (estimated cost £20,000 in the first year and £10,000 per annum thereafter). The Court of Appeal held that while such a requirement was practicable in all the circumstances of the case, it was not reasonably so, bearing in mind the cost in relation to the risk of injury. The improvement notice was therefore cancelled, the court confirming that in relation to the general duty, practicability alone is not the test, for it is qualified by the term "reasonable".

The issue of 'practicability' under s.2 and its scope in relation to an employer with a large workforce working with contractors was raised in *R. v. Swan Hunter Shipbuilders Ltd., and Telemeter Installation Ltd.* 1981. Here eight men had been tragically killed by a fire which broke out on a ship under construction on the River Tyne. The fire had been fuelled by an oxygen enriched atmosphere caused by the failure of an employee of a sub-contractor (Telemeter) to turn off the oxygen supply over night. Both the employer and the sub-contractor were convicted of offences under the Act in the Crown Court and subsequently appealed to the Court of Appeal. The employer argued that the duty to provide a safe system of work to persons other than their own employees imposed an intolerable burden where there was a large workforce with many different direct employers. The Court however having examined the wording of s.2(1) and s.2(2), decided that providing employees with a safe system of work may involve a duty to an employer to provide instruction and information to persons other than their own employees about potential dangers. Such instructions need not be given if the employer can show on the balance of probabilities that it was not reasonably practicable in the circumstances. Here the employer was aware of the dangers and by sub-contracting the work, they were under a duty to 'inform and instruct'. In the words of

Dunn L J *"If the provision of a safe system of work for the benefit of his own employees involves information and instruction as to potential dangers being given to persons other than the employer's own employees, then the employer is under a duty to provide such information and instruction. His protection is contained in the words 'so far as is reasonably practicable' which appear in all the relevant provisions. The onus is on the defendants to prove on the balance of probabilities that it was not reasonably practicable in the particular circumstances of the case".*

The fact that a working practice adopted by employers is universal within the industry is not conclusive evidence that the general duty under s.2(1) has been discharged. The High Court in *Martin v. Boulton and Paul (Steel Construction) Ltd.* 1982 held that a universal practice whilst of great weight, is not conclusive evidence that it was not reasonably practicable to use some other and safer method.

Activity

Locate a written statement on general policy on health and safety in the text book. Prepare a brief guide as to the content of the statement. To what extent does the statement comply with the Management of Health and Safety at Work Regulations 1992 in relation to the obligation to carry out a risk assessment and make arrangements to deal with its findings.

Safety representatives

A further requirement of s.2 for employers other than those with less than five employees is the obligation to prepare and revise a written statement of their general policy on health and safety and bring this statement to the notice of their employees (see Element 2.1). The statement should be more than a bland statement of responsibilities but rather a genuine attempt to identify specific health and safety problems of the employer in question and the arrangements that have been made to deal with them. Matters to be included would cover inspection procedures, emergency arrangements, safety precautions, consultative arrangements and training. Safety representatives may be appointed by recognised trade unions in which case s.2 further provides that it is the duty of an employer to consult with such representatives in order to promote health and safety at the workplace. In many cases this will involve consultations with safety committees which have the function of reviewing measures taken to ensure health and safety at work. Safety representatives have a number of powers, including the right to inspect the workplace and require the establishment of a safety committee. By regulation, a safety representative is entitled to paid time off work to undergo such training as is reasonable in the circumstances. It is worth noting that the general duties owed under s.2 apply to employees only and this would not include those training under a Youth Training Scheme as they are not treated as persons working under a contract of service. Following the *Health and Safety (Youth Training Scheme) Regulations* 1983 however, trainees on YTS are included under the umbrella of the Act.

Both employers and those who are self employed are required, in the words of s.3, to *"conduct their undertakings in such a way, in so far as is reasonably practicable, to protect persons other than their own employees from risks to their health and safety."* This would require an employer to give anyone who may be affected, information relating to health and safety risks arising from the way in which the business is run.

In *Carmichael v. Rosehall Engineering Works Ltd.* 1983 an employer was found to be in breach of his duty under s.3 when he failed to provide two youths on a work experience programme with suitable clothing for carrying out a cleaning operation using flammable liquid. The failure to give proper instruction and information, as to the possible risks to their health and safety, was a factor which led to the death of one of the boys when his paraffin soaked overalls burst into flames.

Further guidance as to the interpretation of s.3 was provided by the Court of Appeal in *R. v. Mara* 1987. Here the defendant, Mr. Mara, a director of a cleaning company called CMS Ltd., was convicted of an offence in that he had permitted a breach of his company's duty under s.3. The company had failed to conduct its undertaking in such a way as to ensure that persons not in its employment were exposed to health and safety risks. The facts were that the cleaning company had contracted to clean premises owned by International Stores plc on weekdays. This involved using electrical cleaning machines. As the loading bay could not be cleaned because it was in constant use, it was agreed that employees of International Stores should do the work using CMS equipment. One Saturday morning whilst using a CMS cleaning machine, a Store's employee was electrocuted due to the defective condition of the machine's cable. Mr. Mara was convicted and fined for an offence under s.3. On appeal however it was submitted that as the incident occurred on a Saturday morning, when the cleaning company did not work, it was not 'conducting its undertaking' at all, and so could not be in breach of its duty. The Court of Appeal rejected the submission however, holding that s.3 could not be limited to situations where a company's undertaking is in the process of actively being carried on. The way in which CMS Ltd. conducted its undertaking was to clean during weekdays and leave their equipment for use by their client's employees, at weekends. By failing to ensure that its equipment was safely wired the company was in breach of its s.3 duty to its client's employees. Consequently the director had rightly been convicted of an offence.

This case provides an example of a rare prosecution brought against an industrial director of a company rather than the company itself. Under the Act proceedings may be taken against a director of a company which, with his consent or due to his negligence committed an offence. In a prosecution brought against Mr Chapman in 1992 whose company had contravened a prohibition notice, the Crown Court used its powers under the *Company Directors Disqualification Act* 1986 to ban him from being a company director for two years in addition to a £5,000 fine and a £5,000 fine on the company.

By virtue of s.4 a general duty is imposed on those who control work premises to ensure *so far as is reasonably practicable the safety of the premises, any means of access and exit from the place of work, and of any plant or substance provided for use on the premises.*

The duty extends to persons in control of non-domestic premises which are made available as a place of work and is owed to those who are not their employees. Under s.4(2) *"It shall be the duty of each person who has control of non-domestic premises or of the means of access thereto or therefrom or any plant or equipment in such premises, to take such measures as is reasonable for a person in his position to take to ensure, so far as is reasonably practicable, that the premises, all means of access available for use by persons using the premises and any plant or equipment in such premises is safe and without risk to health."*

In *H M Inspector of Factories v. Austin Rover Group Ltd.* 1989 the defendants were prosecuted for a breach of s.4(2) when the employee of a contractor working on the defendants' premises was killed following a sudden flash fire where he was working. A combination of breaches of safety instructions had contributed to the cause of the fire and at the original trial the defendants were convicted of a s.4(2) offence for failing to take precautions which would have constituted "reasonable measures" and been "reasonably practicable" for a person in the position of Austin Rover. On appeal and then further appeal to the House of Lords however, it was held that in determining the reasonableness of the measures to be taken under s.4(2) account must be taken of the extent of control and knowledge of the occupier in relation to the actual use to which the premises are put. *"If the premises are not a reasonably foreseeable cause of danger, to anyone acting in a way which a person reasonably may be expected to act, in circumstances which reasonably may be expected to occur during the carrying out of the work, or the use of the plant or substance for the purpose of which the premises were made available, it would not be reasonable to require an individual to take further measures against unknown and unexpected risks."*

A successful prosecution under s.4(2) requires the proof of:

- unsafe premises and a risk to health;

- the identity of the individual having control of the premises; and

- the fact that the person in control ought reasonably to have taken measures to ensure safety.

On proof of these three matters the onus then shifts to the accused to show that it was not reasonably practicable to take such measures. As in the present case, the defendant could not have reasonably foreseen the unknown and unexpected events which made the premises unsafe, they would not be held to be in breach of s.4(2). Lord Jauncey made the important point that the *"safety of premises was not an abstract concept. It must be related to the purpose for which the premises were being used at any one time. Some premises might be unsafe for any normal use, for instance because of large unguarded holes in the floor or unstable walls. Other premises might be completely safe for the purposes for which they were designed but completely unsafe for other purposes, for example, an upper floor warehouse designed to a loading capacity of x lbs might become unsafe if loaded to a capacity of 2xlbs. If A made the warehouse available to B who used it within the designed loading capacity, it could not be said that the warehouse was unsafe and a risk to health under s.4(2) because B at some future date exceeds that capacity contrary to A's instructions".*

A further general duty imposed on those who control work premises is to *use the best practicable means to prevent the emission of offensive substances and to render harmless and inoffensive those substances emitted.*

Those who design, manufacture, import or supply any article for use at work are required in so far as is reasonably practicable to ensure the article's safety, to carry out necessary testing and examining and provide sufficient information about the use of the article at work to render it safe and without risks to health.

Finally there is a general duty on every employee while at work to take reasonable care for the health and safety of himself and of other persons who may be affected by his acts or omissions at work and to cooperate with employers in the discharge of their health and safety duties. Those employees who act in disregard of health and safety should be counselled but in the end dismissed if they are a danger to themselves or others. Wilful breaches of a safety rule, for instance a no smoking policy was held to be a justifiable reason for dismissal in *Roger v. Wicks and Wilson* 1988.

Certainly there is no room to be complacent about compliance with health and safety law for of the 5000 or so deaths at the workplace over the last ten years in the UK, the Health and Safety Executive estimated that over 70% are due to the failure of companies to provide workers with adequate safety equipment, training, supervision and instruction as they are bound to do under the legislation. Lack of enforcement, particularly against individual directors or managers is a particular cause for concern and the small number of prosecutions that are brought against companies only result in a limited fine in the Magistrates Court.

Civil redress

A further major objective of the law relating to health and safety at the workplace is to provide a means by which those who have suffered injury may recover compensation. Since the mid 1960s, state benefit has been available for employees who suffer injury from accidents arising out of and in the course of employment or contract prescribed industrial diseases. If injury is caused through fault however, whether of the employer or a fellow worker, an injured person can bring a claim for damages through the courts. If it can be shown that injury has occurred as a result of a failure to comply with a regulation under the *Health and Safety at Work Act* 1974 or some other statutory obligation, for instance under the *Factories Act* 1961, then a claim could be brought for damages under a civil action for breach of statutory duty. This action has the status of a separate tort and can provide a means of redress for persons who suffer harm as a result of a breach of a duty imposed by statute.

The tort of breach of statutory duty

To succeed in an action based upon breach of statutory duty it is necessary to prove:

- that the statute in question imposes a statutory duty on the defendant which is owed to the plaintiff;
- that the defendant is in breach of the statutory duty; and
- that the plaintiff suffered injury as a result and the harm caused was of a kind contemplated by the statute.

In cases where the duty imposed by statute is a strict one, then the burden on the plaintiff is to prove that it has been broken without the need to show any fault on the part of the defendant. In applying s.14(1) of the *Factories Act* 1961 therefore, *"Every dangerous part of any machinery ... shall be securely fenced unless it is in such a position or of such construction as to be as safe to every person employed or working on the premises as it would be if securely fenced"* , it is necessary to show:

- that the Factories Act applies to the premises in question and that the s.14(1) duty is imposed on the employer and is owed to the employee;
- that the machine in question is a source of danger and that it was not securely fenced;
- that the employee suffered injury as a result of the failure to securely fence and the harm was a type contemplated by the section.

In *H Wearing v. Pirelli Ltd.* 1977 the plaintiff suffered a broken wrist when his hand came into contact with a rubber coating around a revolving metal drum which had not been securely fenced. The House of Lords held that the employers were liable for breach of their statutory duty under s.14(1) to fence securely dangerous parts of machinery despite the fact that the employee's hand had come in contact with the rubber coating only, rather than the machinery itself.

Common law negligence

An alternative course of action for an employee who has suffered harm due to the fault of his employer or a fellow employee is to base a claim on common law negligence. Under the common law, an employer owes a legal duty of care to ensure the health and safety of his employees and this duty takes effect on an implied term of the contract of employment. An employer is required to take reasonable care with regard to the safety of his employees by providing a safe system of work. The provision of a safe system of work involves an obligation to provide safe fellow employees, safe plant and equipment, safe working premises and safe working methods. If an employer is in breach of his common law duty to take reasonable care, and damage in the form of injury is caused as a result, he will be liable.

It should be stressed that in civil proceedings it is often the case that a claim is based upon both the breach of a common law duty and for breach of statutory duty if relevant.

In *Smith v. Vange Scaffolding & Engineering Company Ltd. and Another* 1970 the plaintiff scaffolder suffered injury when he fell over a welding cable when walking back from his place of work. The High Court held that the employee's immediate employers were liable for breach of their common law duty of care because they were aware of the dangerous state of the site where their employees worked. In addition the employers were in breach of their statutory duty imposed, by regulation 6 of the Construction (working places) Regulations 1966, to provide a suitable and sufficient access to an egress from the plaintiff's place of work.

Certainly there is no intention that statutory regulation is designed to supersede the common law so that even if an employer has complied with a regulation, for instance to supply his workers with safety equipment, an employee is still entitled to pursue a claim under the common law if he is injured due to a failure to wear it.

In *Bux v. Slough Metals* 1973 the plaintiff lost the sight of one eye as a result of a splash from molten metal when he was pouring it into a die. While safety goggles had been supplied, the plaintiff refused to wear them because they misted up, and no attempt was made to persuade him otherwise. The Court of Appeal held that while the employer had provided suitable goggles for the purpose of safety regulations, they were nevertheless negligent under the common law. The evidence suggested that the plaintiff would have followed clear instructions to wear the goggles, and that the question whether or not an employer's common law duty of care extended to instructing, persuading or insisting on the use of protective equipment depended on the facts. By failing to make use of the goggles the plaintiff was guilty of contributory fault and damages were reduced by forty percent.

As far as safety equipment is concerned, the contemporary view seems to be that the common law duty to make it available and ensure that employees are aware of it does not necessarily carry with it any further obligation to inspect it or insist that it is worn. Obviously there is some obligation on the employee to take some responsibility for his own safety by ensuring that safety equipment is renewed when necessary.

In *Smith v. Scott Bowyers Ltd.* 1986 the plaintiff, who was just twenty years of age, and employed by the company for nineteen months, suffered injury when he slipped on the greasy factory floor. To help minimise the risk the employer provided the workers with wellington boots with diamond ridge soles and they were renewed on request. Having already replaced one pair of boots the accident was due to the plaintiff's failure to renew the replacement pair which had also worn out and were a danger. In an action for damages for breach of the employer's duty of care, the High Court found that the failure of the employers to emphasise the danger and carry out checks of the safety equipment made them in breach of the legal duty of care they owed to the plaintiff. Damages were to be reduced by one third however, due to the plaintiff's contributory fault. On appeal however, the Court of Appeal reversed the decision and held that there was no breach of the employer's duty to take reasonable care. The failure of the employee to renew the boots was due to his own lack of care and could not be taken as the fault of the employer. *"The employer's duty to provide employees with properly designed Wellington boots would not be filled out with any further obligation to instruct them to wear them or to inspect the condition of the soles from time to time."*

The common law duty encompasses an obligation to provide safe plant and appliances. If an employer was aware that machinery or tools are not reasonably safe, and an employee is injured as a result, the employer will be in breach of his duty under the common law.

In *Bradford v. Robinson Rentals* 1967 the employer provided an unheated van for the employee, a 57 year old, to make a 400 mile journey during the winter, which would involve him in at least 20 hours driving. The court held that the employer was liable for the employee's frost bite, which was the type of injury that was reasonably foreseeable from prolonged exposure to severe cold and fatigue. The court also confirmed that even if the plaintiff had been abnormally susceptible to frost bite he would still be entitled to succeed under the rule that the defendant must take his victim as he finds him.

In the past an employer could satisfy his duty to provide safe equipment by showing that he purchased the equipment from a reputable supplier and that he had no knowledge of any defect. Now however, following the *Employers Liability (Defective Equipment) Act* 1969, injury occurring to an employee under those circumstances may be attributed to the deemed negligence of the employer. If damages are awarded against the employer then it is up to him to seek a remedy from the supplier of the defective equipment.

The obligation to provide a safe system of work also encompasses a requirement to provide safe fellow employees. If there are untrained or unskilled people employed at the workplace then a higher standard of care is owed by the employer to ensure their safety and the safety of those who work with them.

In *Hawkins v. Ross Castings Ltd.* 1970 the plaintiff was injured following a spillage of molten metal, due partly to the employer's failure to comply with safety regulations in relation to the maintenance of a safe pouring systems. An additional contributing factor was the fact that the plaintiff was working closely with a seventeen year old untrained Indian who spoke little English and yet was required to carry and pour molten metal with the plaintiff. This factor contributed to the employer's liability.

The duty to provide safe fellow employees exits irrespective of any issue of the employer's vicarious liability for the actions of his employees. Vicarious or substituted liability is considered later in the chapter.

The employer's common law duty also imposes an obligation to provide safe working methods and safe working premises. To determine whether an employer is providing safe working methods, it is necessary to consider a number of factors including:

- the layout of the work place;
- training and supervision;
- warnings; and
- whether protective equipment is provided.

It should be stressed that the common law duty on an employer is to take reasonable care, and if he gives proper instructions which the employee fails to observe then the employer will not be liable if the employee is then injured.

In *Charlton v. Forrest Printing Ink Company Ltd.* 1980 the employer gave proper instructions to an employee who was given the job of collecting the firm's wages. The instructions required the employee to vary his collecting arrangements to prevent robbery. The employee failed to do this and suffered severe injury when he was robbed. The Court of Appeal held that the employer was not liable as he had taken reasonable steps to cut down the risk. The normal industrial practice of firms of that size in that area was to make their own payroll collection rather than employ a security firm. The employers *"did what was reasonable in the circumstances to eliminate the risk and no more could have been expected of them. They could not be held liable for the injuries incurred by the employee".*

It should be stressed that the common law duty is not one of strict liability but rather a duty to take reasonable care in the circumstances.

> In *Latimer v. AEC* 1953 after a factory was flooded, the employer asked his workforce to return, warning them of the dangerous state of the factory floor. Sawdust had been used to cover most of the damp areas but not enough was available, and the plaintiff slipped, and was injured. To determine whether the employer had broken the common law duty of care he owed his employees the court weighed the cost of avoiding the injury against the risk of injury and held that the employer had acted reasonably in the circumstances.

In addition, the standard of care owed by an employer will vary with regard to each individual employee. A young apprentice should be provided with effective supervision while this may not be required for an experienced employee.

> In *Paris v. Stepney BC* 1951 the plaintiff, a one-eyed motor mechanic, lost the sight of his good eye while working at chipping rust from under a bus. Despite there being no usual practice to provide mechanics with safety goggles, the court decided that they should have been provided to the plaintiff. The defendants were liable as they could foresee serious consequences for the plaintiff if he suffered eye injury. *"The special risk of injury is a relevant consideration in determining the precautions which the employer should take in the fulfilment of the duty of care which he owes to the workman."*

Defences available to the employer

Finally it should be mentioned that in very exceptional cases the plaintiff may be taken to have consented to the risk of injury and the defence of "volenti non fit injuria" (no wrong is done to one who consents) established.

> In *Imperial Chemical Industries v. Shatwell* 1965 two employees, both experienced shot firers, in contravention of specific safety instructions, fired a shot causing injury to both of them. The House of Lords held that the employer could rely on volenti as an absolute defence, due to the act of gross disobedience.

It is more likely that the employer will be able to rely on the Law Reform (Contributory Negligence) Act 1945 which provides a partial defence. If the employer can show that the injured employee contributed to his injury by his own fault then damages may be reduced to *"such extent as the court thinks just and equitable having regard to the claimants share in the responsibility for the damage".* You will remember that in the case of *Bux v. Slough Metals* 1973 mentioned previously; the damages awarded were reduced by forty per cent to reflect the plaintiff employee's contributory fault.

As we mentioned earlier, part of the common law duty is that an employer must take reasonable care to ensure that he provides his workers with safe fellow workers. To engage an employee who has a past record of dangerous behaviour could put the employees at risk and constitute a negligent act on the part of the employer for which he could be made directly liable. Certainly if an employer is aware of an employee who by incompetence or practical jokes is creating a dangerous situation at work he should take steps to discipline him and if necessary dismiss him. Moreover the legal responsibility of an employer covers the situation when an employee under his control causes harm to a fellow employee or a third party by some wrongful act. This is by virtue of the doctrine of vicarious (substituted) liability.

Vicarious liability

There are some situations where the law is prepared to impose vicarious (substituted) liability on an individual who is not at fault for the commission of the wrongful (tortious) act of another. The best known example of this situation is the common law rule which imposes vicarious liability on employers in respect of torts committed by their employees during the course of their employment. Accordingly, if one employee (Jones) by his negligent act causes harm to a fellow employee (Smith) then in addition to the possibility of (Smith) pursuing a legal action against (Jones) he may have the further option of suing his employer who will have become vicariously liable if the negligent act occurred during the course of Jones's employment. The same principle applies equally where the injuries are caused by an employee to some third party. However, while employers have a choice as to whether they insure against the risk of injury to third parties, under the *Employer's Liability (Compulsory Insurance) Act* 1969, an employer is required to insure himself in respect of injuries caused by his employees to their colleagues.

The imposition of vicarious liability does not require proof of any fault on the employer's part, or any express or implied authorisation to commit the wrongful act. All that must be proved for the purpose of vicarious liability is:

- an actionable wrong committed by the worker;
- that the worker is an employee;
- that the wrongful act occurred during the course of his employment.

What then is the theoretical basis for imposing liability in these circumstances? A number of reasons have emerged, such as he who creates and benefits from a situation should assume the risk of liability arising from it. There is also the idea that if an organisation embarks on an enterprise and as a result harm is caused by one member of the organisation, it should be the responsibility of the organisation to compensate for the harm. It is after all the employer who selects and controls the employees who work for him. The employer has the responsibility of training staff and can of course dismiss those whose work is performed incompetently. The practical reason for vicarious liability is of course that if the employee were solely liable he would have to insure himself, and the cost of this would be indirectly borne by the employer in the form of higher wages. Under the present system insurance costs are borne directly by the employer who, as a principle of sound business practice, will normally carry adequate insurance.

To determine an employer's liability it is first necessary to establish the employment status of the worker who is alleged to have committed the wrongful act. This is because the legal position differs dramatically depending on whether the worker is employed as an employee under a contract of service rather than as a self employed contractor under a contract for services. Usually this issue may be settled without argument but in the small proportion of cases where there is doubt the courts are left with the task of identifying the true contractual status of the worker. It is convenient to deal with the legal position of employees and independent contractors separately.

Employees

As a general principle an employer is vicariously liable for the tortious acts of his employees committed during the course of their employment. The phrase 'course of employment' has produced numerous interpretations in the courts, but essentially it concerns the question of whether the employee was doing his job at the time of the tortious act. It should be emphasised that an employee will have both express and implied authority to perform work for his employer and while he will normally have no authority to commit torts, he may nevertheless be guilty of a tortious act in the performance of his authorised duties.

In *Century Insurance Ltd. v. Northern Ireland Road Transport Board* 1942 a tanker driver while delivering petrol at a garage, lit a cigarette and carelessly threw away the lighted match which caused an explosion and considerable damage. His employer was held to be vicariously liable for his negligence as the employee had acted within the course of his employment. By supervising the unloading, the employee was doing his job, but by smoking he was doing it in a grossly negligent manner.

Even if an employee is carrying out an act outside the basic obligation of his contract of employment, his employer may nevertheless be made vicariously liable if the act is carried out for the benefit of the employer.

In *Kay v. ITW* 1968 the employee injured a colleague when he negligently drove a five ton diesel lorry which was blocking his way. Despite the fact that he was contractually authorised to drive only small vans and trucks, his employer was held to be vicariously liable for his action.

If an employee is doing something of purely personal benefit at the time of the negligent act then he may be regarded, to quote from the colourful language of the Victorian era as "off on a frolic of his own", and his employer will not be responsible.

In *Hilton v. Thomas Burton (Rhodes) Ltd.* 1961 the plaintiff's husband was a demolition worker who was killed through the negligent driving of one of his colleagues. The defendant employer denied vicarious liability as, at the time of the accident, the van was being driven from a cafe on an unauthorised break. The court held that although the van had been driven with the permission of the employer, at the time of the incident the driver was not doing that which he was employed to do. Accordingly the employer was not liable for the negligent driving.

Guidance in relation to the possiblity of vicarious liability being imposed when industrial action causes damage to property was recently provided by the Judicial Committee of the Privy Council in *General Engineering Services Ltd. v. Kingston and St. Andrews Corporation* 1989. The claim was based upon the notion that the corporation, having a statutory duty to extinguish fires, were vicariously liable for the negligence of the members of their fire brigade who had failed to respond promptly to an emergency call. The reason for the delay was that the fire brigade, in dispute with their employer, were operating a go slow. As a consequence of taking seventeen rather than three minutes to respond to a fire, a building and its contents were burned to the ground. Both the court of first instance and the Jamaica Court of Appeal held that in operating the go slow the brigade were not acting in the course of their employment, so that the employers could not be made vicariously liable. This was confirmed on final appeal to the Judicial Committee of the Privy Council. Here it was held that an act is deemed to have been done in the course of employment if it is either a wrongful act and authorised by the employer, or a wrongful and unauthorised mode of doing some authorised act. If however the employee's unauthorised and unlawful act could be regarded as independent and not connected with the authorised act so as to constitute a mode of doing it, the employer is not responsible. Here by operating a go slow the fire brigade were not carrying on a wrongful or authorised mode of doing an otherwise authorised act. By stopping and starting on their way to a fire this manner of driving had no connection with the authorised activity of driving to the scene of a fire as quickly as possible.

Taking industrial action therefore in furtherance of an industrial dispute, may have the effect of repudiating an essential obligation of the contract of employment, and if so unconnected with the employee's job, take him outside the course of his employment for the purpose of vicarious liability.

The extent to which an express prohibition by the employer will prevent vicarious liability will depend upon the nature of the prohibition. If it merely attempts to instruct the employee how he is to do his job, the employee may still be within the course of his employment for the purposes of vicarious liability.

> In *Rose v. Plenty* 1976 a milkman, contrary to an express prohibition, engaged a thirteen year old boy to help him deliver the milk. The boy was subsequently injured by the milkman's negligent driving and sued both the milkman and his employer. The Court of Appeal held that despite the prohibition of the employer, he remained vicariously liable as the milkman had acted within the course of his employment. Scarman L J having considered the prohibition stated that *"There was nothing in the prohibition which defined or limited the sphere of his employment, the sphere of his employment remained precisely the same as before the prohibition was brought to his notice. The sphere was as a roundsman to go the rounds delivering milk, collecting empties and obtaining payment. Contrary to instructions the roundsman chose to do what he was employed to do in an improper way. But the sphere of his employment was in no way affected by his express instructions"*.

It seems therefore that only an express prohibition which effectively cuts down the 'sphere of employment' will prevent the establishment of vicarious liability. The fact that contemporary courts seem to favour the idea of a very wide sphere of employment in individual cases, severely limits the opportunity of employers to restrict liability by express instruction. It is only by deciding the authorised parameters of an individual's job, and deciding that the act complained of fell outside these parameters that vicarious liability can be successfully denied.

If the act is done on the employer's premises with the employer's interest in mind, the employer may be made liable provided the act has a close connection with the employee's job.

> In *Compton v. McClure* 1975 the employer was held to be vicariously liable for the negligence of an employee who, when late for work, caused an accident when driving negligently on the factory road.

> Even the manager in a public house in *Stone v. Taffe* 1974 was held to be within the course of his employment when he negligently failed to ensure that a stairway was properly lighted for a customer, despite the fact that the injury occurred two and a half hours after licensed closing time.

> The question as to whether an employee is acting within the course of his employment while required to travel from home to a workplace other than his regular one was recently addressed by the House of Lords in *Smith v. Stages and Another* 1989. Here an action was brought on behalf of an employee, who as a passenger in the defendant's car, suffered personal injuries as a result of the negligent driving of the defendant, a fellow employee. Despite the fact that the employers neither required nor authorised the journey by car to and from their particular workplace they were joined as second defendants on a claim that they were vicariously liable for the driver's negligence. The House of Lords held that employees who are required to travel to and from non regular workplaces, and in receipt of wages for doing so, remain within the course of their employment, even if they have a choice as to the mode and time of travel. Here the employee chose to travel in his own vehicle with the employer's knowledge and so the employers were vicariously liable for his negligent driving. Employees are in the course of their employment when going about their employer's business, and this will be the case if an employee is 'on duty' on his way to and from the workplace. This would not be so in relation to an employee travelling from home to and from his regular workplace whatever the mode of transport, unless obliged by his contract of service to use the employer's transport. A number of prima facie propositions were sug-

gested by the House of Lords in relation to the question as to whether an employee is acting in the course of his employment during travelling time. The receipt of wages would indicate that an employee was travelling in his employer's time, and acting in the course of his employment. Equally so would an employee travelling in the employer's time between different workplaces. An employee travelling in his employer's time from his ordinary residence to a workplace, other than his regular workplace, to the scene of an emergency such as a fire accident or mechanical breakdown of plant, would also be acting in the course of his employment. Deviations or interruptions of a journey undertaken in the course of employment unless merely incidental would normally take an employee outside the course of his employment.

While it may be reasonable for an employee to use a degree of force in protection of his employer's property, or to keep order, an employee who commits an assault which has no connection with his work will be solely liable for his conduct.

So in *Warren v. Henleys Ltd. 1948* the employer was held not to be vicariously liable for a physical attack by a petrol pump attendant on one of his customers. The claim that the attendant was acting within the scope of his employment was rejected, for while the attack developed out of an argument over payment for petrol, it was in reality motivated by an act of private vengeance.

It is important to draw a distinction between vicarious liability and the direct or primary liability of an employer.

In *Carmarthenshire County Council v. Lewis* 1955 a child at a local authority nursery school wandered from the school yard onto the highway and caused the death of a lorry driver who had swerved to avoid the child. An action was brought against the council in negligence on the grounds that the child's teacher left her unattended for a short time. In fact at the relevant time the teacher was attending to the needs of another child. The court held that the teacher had in fact fulfilled the common law duty of care required of her by acting as a prudent parent would in the circumstances. Consequently there could be no vicarious liability imposed on her employer. However, the fact that the child could reach the street so easily, indicated that the council were failing in their legal duty to operate a safe system at the school, and so were held to be directly liable for their primary negligence.

A further example of the distinction between the direct and vicarious liability of an employer is provided by the decision in *Nahhas v. Pier House (Cheyne Walk) Management* 1984. Here the tenant of a luxury flat deposited the key with a porter during a stay in hospital. This was the normal system operated by the owners, but unfortunately a porter, one of their employees, used the key to steal jewellery from the plaintiff's flat. In fact the porter had a long criminal record involving eleven prison terms of which his employer, the owners, were unaware. The court held that while the system of depositing keys was not negligent, the failure by the employer to thoroughly check the porter's background constituted a breach of the legal duty of care owed to the tenants which resulted in damage. Consequently the employers were liable for their primary negligence and also responsible vicariously for the criminal act of the porter carried out during the course of his employment.

Certainly to impose liability on an employer for the tortious or criminal acts of an employee under his control, there must be a connection between the act complained of and the circumstances of employment. The fact that employment gives the employee an opportunity to commit the wrongful act is insufficient to impose vicarious liability on the employer.

In *Heasmans v. Clarity Cleaning Company* 1987 the Court of Appeal found it possible to absolve the defendant cleaning company from liability for the acts of one of their cleaners who, while employed on the plaintiff's premises, used the plaintiff's telephone to make international telephone calls to the value of £1411. The mere fact that the cleaner's employment provided the opportunity to fraudulently use the plaintiff's telephone was not itself sufficient to impose liability on the defendant.

The increasing practice of employees contracting out areas of work to contractors and sub contractors has important implications when determining liability for injuries caused due to negligence at the workplace.

In a recent Scottish case, *Sime v. Sutcliffe Catering Scotland Ltd.* 1990 an employee brought a claim alleging negligence by the above catering company when, carrying out her work as a canteen assistant she slipped on some food dropped by a fellow worker and suffered injury. The case was complicated by the fact that the employee was not directly employed by the catering company but by a paper manufacturer, Tullis Russell and Company. Previously the paper manufacturer had contracted out the management of the canteen to the above company, but following pressure from the trade union, had agreed to retain existing canteen staff, including the employee. It was never established whether the worker who had dropped the food was an employee of the catering company or not. The issue therefore was whether the catering company could be held liable vicariously to a worker for the possible negligent act of a worker who they did not employ. The Scottish Court of Session held that responsibility should be with the employer in control. Although not directly employed by the catering company, whether the employer relationship is *"such as to render the company liable for the negligence depends upon whether the substitute employer has sufficient power of control and supervision purely to be regarded as the effective employer at the critical time".* As the *"whole day to day management of the catering operation and staff was undertaken by the catering company and the canteen manager had complete control over the way in which all the canteen workers did their job"*…and *"since one of the employed persons caused the accident by being negligent in dropping food stuff onto the floor and failing to clean it up the company had to accept responsibility for that negligence".* The fault of the injured employee was also recognised and damages were reduced by twenty five percent to reflect her contributory negligence. *"Where a person is working in or near a kitchen where a number of people are working with food or dirty dishes and where it is quite predictable that food might be spilt it is reasonably necessary that a look out be kept for any wet or slippery patches on the floor."*

Independent contractors

Generally vicarious liability has been confined to the employer/employee relationship and where contractors are employed, responsibility for their wrongful acts is solely their own. The justification for not extending vicarious liability to employers of contractors, other than in exceptional cases, stems from the fact that the contractor is not subjected to his employer's control in the same way as an employee. One important exception, which in recent times has assumed significance, is the situation where the contractor has been employed to carry out a statutory duty imposed on the employer. This is because of the recent move towards requiring public bodies to put out many of their statutory functions for competitive tender among contractors and so the possibility of imposing liability on employers for the tortious acts of a contractor have increased significantly. The law in this area is not new.

The case of *Hardaker v. Idle District Council* 1896 remains the leading authority in relation to the delegation of statutory duties. The council acting under a statutory power to construct a sewer, employed a contractor to carry out the work. The contractor negligently pierced a gas main and the plaintiff's property was damaged by the resultant explosion. In an action by the plaintiffs against the contractor and the council employer, the court held that in exercising their statutory power the council owed an overriding duty to the public. This duty was to construct a sewer so as not to damage the gas main and put the public at risk. The council could not discharge this duty by simply employing a contractor to carry out the work, and accordingly they remained responsible to the plaintiff for its breach.

There are then certain legal duties that cannot be delegated, and if the wrongful act of a contractor constitutes a breach of such a duty, owed by an employer to a third party, then the contractor's employer may be made vicariously liable for the default.

In *Rogers v. Nightriders* 1983 a mini cab firm undertook to provide a hire car to the plaintiff for a journey and did so by engaging a contractor driver. The plaintiff was injured in an accident caused by the negligent maintenance of the mini cab by the contractor. In an action against the mini cab firm the court held that they were not liable as an employer could not be made vicariously liable for their contractor's default. On appeal however, it was held that as the employer had undertaken to provide a vehicle to carry the plaintiff, and since they ought to have foreseen harm to the plaintiff if the vehicle was defective, they owed a duty of care to the plaintiff to ensure that the vehicle was reasonably fit. Such a duty could not be delegated to a contractor and accordingly the employers were liable for breach of the primary duty that they owed to her.

This case is a further example of the distinction that must be drawn between vicarious and direct or primary liability previously considered. By providing a negligent contractor, the employer in *Rogers v. Nightriders* had failed to fulfil a direct duty of care he owed to those he could reasonably foresee being affected.

Types of Redress

An employee who alleges that contractual or statutory employment rights have been infringed has the opportunity of seeking redress through the courts or tribunals and seeking a remedy. As a general rule all contractual matters are dealt with in the ordinary courts at either the county court or high court level, whereas statutory rights such as an unfair dismissal are enforceable by presenting a complaint before an industrial tribunal. To illustrate the role of courts and tribunals in this section we will consider redress for wrongful dismissal enforceable in the ordinary courts and the remedies for unfair dismissal enforceable before an industrial tribunal.

Dismissal and notice

If an employee wishes to terminate a contract of employment he is required to comply with the employee's contractual requirement in relation to notice. Generally the length of the notice period will depend upon the nature of the employment and may increase in relation to the number of years' service. In addition, there are statutory minimum periods of notice that apply where the contract is silent or provides for less favourable periods. The statutory statement of the main terms and conditions of employment supplied under s.1 of the Employment Protection (Consolidation) Act 1978 (EPCA 78) will stipulate the notice period to which the employee is entitled. The present statutory minimum periods to which an employee is entitled are as follows.

After continuous employment for:	Minimum notice required:
4 weeks up to 2 years	I week
2 years up to 12 years	I week for each year
12 years or more	12 weeks

There is nothing to prevent an employee from waiving his right to notice or, in fact, accepting a lump sum payment in lieu of the notice period to which he is entitled. Failure by the employer to comply with notice requirements would entitle the employee to bring an action for damages in the ordinary courts based on breach of contract. Such a claim is known as 'wrongful dismissal' referring to the wrongful manner in which the contract of employment has been terminated.

Wrongful dismissal

Summary dismissal occurs when the contract of employment is terminated instantly without notice and it is prima facie (on the face of it) wrongful. Such a dismissal is justifiable under the common law, however, if it can be shown that the employee is in repudiatory breach of the contract of employment because of his 'gross misconduct'. By summarily dismissing, the employer is accepting the repudiatory breach of the employee and treating the contract as discharged. Whether the alleged misconduct may be classified as gross is a question of fact and degree, but it would normally include conduct such as disobedience, neglect, dishonesty, or misbehaviour.

A fundamental question that is often asked is whether the employment relationship can survive the nature of the misconduct.

In *Pepper v. Webb* 1969 the action of the head gardener in wilfully disobeying a reasonable order was sufficient to amount to gross misconduct and provide grounds for summary dismissal, despite the contract of employment providing for three months' notice. It should be stressed, however, that the reaction of the gardener in this case represented the culmination of a long period of insolence, and the isolated use of choice obscenities by an employee to an employer may not amount to gross misconduct if there is provocation.

Also, in *Laws v. London Chronicle* 1959 an employee who disobeyed an express order of her managing director was nevertheless held to be wrongfully dismissed in the circumstances. The employee had acted out of loyalty to her immediate superior when she walked out of an editorial conference despite the express instruction of her managing director to remain.

The action of a betting shop manager in *Sinclair v. Neighbour* 1967 in borrowing 15 from the till and leaving a IOU, contrary to express instructions, was regarded as sufficient grounds to justify summary dismissal.

The remedy for a successful claim of wrongful dismissal is an action for damages amounting to the loss of wages payable during the notice period.

In *Addis v. Gramophone Company Ltd.* 1909 the House of Lords ruled that when a servant is wrongfully dismissed from his employment, the damages for the dismissal cannot include compensation for the manner of the dismissal, for his injured feelings, or for the loss he may sustain from the fact that the dismissal in itself makes it more difficult for him to obtain fresh employment.

In *Stapp v. Shaftesbury Society* 1982 the court held that if there is no adequate reason which would justify summary dismissal, and if by the summary dismissal the employee as a consequence is deprived of his right to bring a claim for unfair dismissal by shortening the relevant period of continuous employment, the employee could have a remedy at common law for unfair dismissal. The measure of damages payable *"might include the loss of the right to complain of unfair dismissal which the employee would have had, had he not been summarily dismissed"*.

Of course since 1971 an aggrieved employee who is qualified has the further option of complaining to a Tribunal that the instant dismissal is unfair.

In relation to breaches of discipline it is often the practice that express agreement will be reached between the employer and a trade union to identify types of conduct and classify it as 'gross misconduct' which will warrant instant dismissal.

This was the position in *W Brooks & Son v. Skinner* 1984 where the employer had agreed with the trade union that anyone who became drunk at the firm's Christmas party, so that he was absent from the next shift, would be instantly dismissed. In accordance with the agreement the complainant was instantly dismissed and brought a claim of unfair dismissal. Agreeing with the Tribunal the EAT held that failure to communicate to the employees the consequences of absence from work after the party, made the decision to dismiss summarily an unfair one. *"Whether or not an employer is justified in treating a particular matter of conduct as sufficient to justify dismissal must include in the particular case, that the employee knew that his conduct would merit summary dismissal. Though there is much conduct which any employee will know will result in instant dismissal, there are also instances of conduct, particularly those which have been dealt with in other ways at other times by the employer, which the employee may well consider will not merit summary dismissal."*

Remedies for unfair dismissal

If a complaint of unfair dismissal is successful, the Tribunal has authority to make an order for reinstatement or re-engagement or make an award of compensation. Irrespective of whether he has requested the remedies on his IT1, the Tribunal is obliged to explain the remedies of reinstatement and re-engagement to a successful complainant and discover whether he wishes to apply for such an order.

An order for reinstatement requires the employer to treat the complainant in all respects as if he had not been dismissed. By such an order, the employer would be required to make good any arrears of pay or any rights or privileges which would have accrued but for the dismissal. If the employee would have benefited from improvements in terms and conditions but for the dismissal, then the order must reflect the improvement from the date it was agreed. In exercising its discretion to make an order of reinstatement the Tribunal must take account of:

- the wishes of the complainant;
- whether it is practicable for an employer to comply with such an order; and
- whether the complainant contributed to the dismissal and whether it would be just to make such an order.

If the Tribunal decides not to make an order for reinstatement it must then consider the possibility of re-engagement. An order of re-engagement requires the employer, his successor, or an associate to employ the complainant in comparable work, or other suitable employment, and on making such an order the Tribunal must specify the terms upon which the re-engagement is to take place. Such terms include the identity of the parties, the nature of the employment, remuneration, an amount payable for arrears of pay, rights and privileges restored, and the date the order must be complied with.

For re-engagement the Tribunal must take account of the following considerations:

- the wishes of the employee;
- whether it is practicable for the employer to comply with an order for re-engagement; and

- where the employee contributed to some extent to the dismissal and whether it would be just to order re-engagement and if so, on what terms;

and except where the Tribunal takes account of contributory fault, re-engagement should be ordered on terms as far as reasonably practicable as favourable as an order for reinstatement.

In *Nairne v. Highland & Islands Fire Brigade* 1989 the complainant was found to be unfairly dismissed because of a procedural irregularity, in that the purpose of a disciplinary interview had not been made clear to him, and he was never warned that he could be dismissed. This was despite the fact that the reason for dismissal was justifiable. The employee in question was a fire officer, who for the second time had been found guilty of a drink/driving offence and as a result had been disqualified from driving for three years. It was a contractual requirement of his job that he was able to drive and it was unreasonable to employ a substitute driver for a three year period. The finding of unfair dismissal was affirmed on appeal and the extent of the employee's contributory fault increased from 25% to 75%. Such a high degree of contributory fault and the fact that there was no suitable alternative job available made this an unsuitable case to order re-engagement.

If a Tribunal decides not to make either order it must make an award of compensation. But even if either order is made, a Tribunal has no power to ensure that it is complied with. Failure to comply or fully comply with an order of reinstatement or re-engagement can only lead to an award of compensation subject to the maximum limit.

In *Artisan Press v. Strawley and Parker* 1986 after finding that the complainants had been unfairly dismissed from their jobs on security staff because of membership of an independent trade union, the Tribunal ordered that they should be reinstated. The employer purported to re-employ them, but in fact their job duties differed significantly and rather than security, the new jobs involved cleaning with minor security functions. A further complaint of non-compliance with the reinstated order was upheld, the Tribunal awarding sums of £18,367 and £20,080 respectively. On an appeal against the amount of the additional awards, the EAT refused to accept the employer's argument that a distinction should be drawn between non-compliance with an order of reinstatement and failing to comply fully with such an order. *"Under the Act 'reinstatement' means treating the employee as if he had not been dismissed. If the employee is reinstated, but on less favourable terms, then he has not been reinstated. "* Here the amount of the awards would not be interfered with.

Regardless of the loss therefore, which could include substantial arrears of wages, if the employer refuses to re-employ, the complainant's compensation is limited to the statutory compensation in force at the time, the basic compensatory and additional awards. In practice few orders for reinstatement or re-engagement are made and fewer still are not complied with. The main redress for unfair dismissal remains to secure an award of compensation.

Compensation

An order for compensation as redress for unfair dismissal may consist of a basic award, a compensatory award, an additional award and where the dismissal related to the membership or non-membership of a trade union, a special award.

Basic award

The basic award is payable in all cases of unfair dismissal irrespective of loss and is based upon the complainant's continuous employment and average week's wage. It should be noted however that if it can be shown that the complainant contributed to the dismissal through his own fault, or has unreasonably refused an offer of reinstatement, the amount of the basic award can be reduced by a just and equitable proportion. The computation of the basic award is the same as for a redundancy payment, so the present maximum is £6,150.

The amount of the basic award is calculated by reference to the period the employee has been continuously employed, ending with the effective date of termination. By reckoning backwards from the effective date of termination the number of years employment can be determined allowing:

- one and a half weeks' pay for each year of employment in which the employee was not below 41 years of age;
- one week's pay for each year the employee was not below 22 years of age;
- a half week's pay for each year of employment between 18 and 21 years of age.

To calculate the basic award therefore it is necessary to determine the employee's gross pay up to a maximum of £205, his length of service up to a maximum of 20 years and his age. The maximum award payable therefore is for an employee who is dismissed after 20 years' service, over the age of 41, with a gross wage in excess of £205. He will be entitled to a basic award of $20 \times 11/2 \times £205 = £6150$.

In many cases the employee's period of continuous service will cover more than one age rate barrier. In such circumstances it is necessary to calculate the entitlement at the relevant rate, e.g. for an employee who is made redundant at the age of 44 who, after 15 years' service has a gross wage of £160, is entitled to:

$$
\begin{array}{ll}
3 \text{ years} \times 11/2 \times £160 & £620 \\
\text{plus} & \\
12 \text{ years} \times 1 \times £160 & \underline{£1,920} \\
& \overline{£2,540}
\end{array}
$$

A disturbing rule for employees close to retirement is that on the effective date of termination, for each month that an employee is over the age of sixty four, the amount of the basic award is reduced by one-twelfth for each complete month worked. The justification for this is that the point of the basic award is to compensate the employee for the loss of accrued redundancy rights which, of course, are not payable on retirement.

If the employee is entitled to a redundancy payment because of an unfair dismissal by reason of redundancy, the basic award is reduced by the amount of the redundancy payment. Since both awards are calculated in the same way, in most cases the redundancy payment will reduce the basic award to nil.

Finally there is one case where there is a minimum basic award payable regardless of the calculation and that is where the dismissal is connected with trade union membership. The minimum payment is £2,650 but even that sum could be reduced because of contributory fault.

Compensatory award

In assessing the amount of the compensatory award, up to the present maximum of £11,000 under the Unfair Dismissal (Increase of Compensation Limit) Order 1991, a Tribunal must have regard to the loss sustained by the complainant in consequence of the dismissal. If there is no loss, then no compensatory award is payable.

> Such was the position in *Isleworth Studios Ltd. v. Richard* 1988 where the complainant was unfairly dismissed when his fixed term contract was prematurely brought to an end. The fact that during the unexpired term of the contract the complainant went on to earn £10,000 in excess of what he would have earned in his former employment meant that he had suffered no loss.

The amount of a compensatory award should take account of any failure by the employee to mitigate his loss, for instance by refusing an offer of suitable alternative employment. The Court of Appeal held in *Babcock Fata v. Addison* 1987 that any money paid in lieu of notice should be deducted from a compensatory award as should any ex gratia payment made. Heads of compensation that are assessable include the loss of fringe benefits attached to the job, expense incurred in seeking alternative work, net wages lost up to the hearing, estimated future earnings, the termination of continuous employment which necessarily limits future rights and the loss of pension rights. The compensatory award, like the basic award, may be reduced because of the complainant's contributory fault.

Under the Industrial Tribunals (Interest) Order 1990 provision is made for interest to be payable on any sums *"payable by virtue of a relevant decision of a Tribunal"* with effect from *"a calculation day"* which is defined as *"the day immediately following the expiry of the period of forty two days beginning with the relevant decision day"*.

Additional award

If the Tribunal makes a reinstatement or re-engagement order with which the employer fails to comply, the Tribunal will make an additional award unless it was not practicable to comply with the order. The additional award has now no limit following the Trade Union Reform and Employment Rights Act 1993.

Special award

The special award may be payable if the dismissal is in connection with membership or non-membership of a trade union. The amount of a special award is one week's pay multiplied by 104 or £13,400 whichever is greater, up to a maximum of £26,800.

Interim relief

If the dismissal is in connection with trade union membership or participating in trade union activities, an application may be made for interim relief within seven days of the dismissal, supported by a signed certificate from a trade union official that there are reasonable grounds to believe that this is the true reason for dismissal. A Tribunal satisfied that there are reasonable grounds can order that the employment should continue until the final hearing.

All compensation is of course payable by the employer but either the complainant or the employer can join as a party to the proceedings, a specified person who could be made to contribute the whole or a portion of the compensation payable. This would be the case where it could be shown that the employer was induced to dismiss the employee by pressure being placed by a trade union, for instance the threat of industrial action, and the reason for the pressure was that the complainant was not a member of a trade union.

The statutory remedies of reinstatement, re-engagement and compensation are the intended redress for a victim of unfair dismissal. Certainly the possibility of obtaining an injunction to restrain a dismissal in breach of a contract of employment is now extremely unlikely.

> In *Alexander v. Standard Telephones and Cables Ltd. and Wall* 1990 the common law rule that the courts will not grant an injunction which will have the effect of compelling specific performance was re-emphasised, the High Court indicating a solitary exception where it can be shown that the employer has not lost confidence in the employee in question. Since this will rarely be the case in a dismissal situation, the prospect of an injunction to restrain a dismissal must now be highly unlikely.

Assignment *Unfair Dismissal*

For the purpose of this assignment you are to assume the role of Sarah Maxwell, a newly appointed legal advisor employed at the regional office of ACAS in the North East of England. One of the main functions of your job is to assess the legal position and advise conciliation officers when complaints of unfair treatment are presented to the Industrial Tribunal. Complaints of unfair dismissal have been presented in relation to the following areas of conflict.

1. The first dispute involves a Mr. Simmonds who was employed by Hennessy, a transport company from 1978 to May 1991 as a HGV driver at their Gateshead depot. All drivers at the Gateshead depot are members of the Transport and General Workers Union. Mr. Simmonds, unhappy at the attitude of the TGWU shop steward of the depot, left the union in March 1991. Although there is no closed shop at the depot the other drivers threatened to strike if Mr. Simmonds was not sacked or moved elsewhere. In April 1991 the Transport Manager at the company's head office in Newcastle upon Tyne instructed Mr. Simmonds by letter that he must either rejoin the TGWU or work under similar conditions from the Middlesbrough depot where union membership is not an issue. Mr. Simmonds replied by letter in late April stating that the company had no right to move his place of work, particularly to pacify militant trade unionists, and that he was left with no option but to tender his resignation. Mr. Simmonds employment terminated at the end of May. In early June Mr. Simmonds started proceedings alleging unfair dismissal.

2. Tom, Bill and Harry have been employed for many years as store keepers by Brightsides plc, a large central heating company with a national reputation. The men work at the company's Darlington depot and between them man the store on a shift system eighteen hours a day, six days a week. For some time the store at its Darlington depot has been plagued by serious stock losses and despite extensive efforts to identify the cause of the culprit or culprits the management have been unable to do so. All three storekeepers have received both oral and written warnings and earlier in the year were temporarily transferred to other depots in the North East for a six week period. There was no evidence during that period of losses at any depot including Darlington. Now that Tom, Bill and Harry have returned however, following a stock check last week the stock losses at Darlington are more serious than ever. The three men have been dismissed with wages paid in lieu of notice and were told that the reason for dismissal was their failure to prevent the stock losses. All three have presented individual complaints alleging unfair dismissal.

Task

1. In the role of Sarah Maxwell your task is to prepare reports on the above scenarios in which you (a) assess the legal position and (b) bearing in mind the likely outcome of an unfair dismissal claim, make constructive suggestions as to how to resolve the conflict.

2. Arrange to visit an industrial tribunal with the aim of acquiring material to enact a role play exercise of the unfair dismissal claim brought by Mr. Simmonds or Tom, Bill, and Harry.

Element 4.2 Job Roles in Organisational Structures

Types of Business Enterprises

The meaning of the expression business enterprise

Businesses are organisations specialising in commercial activities. They are often referred to as business enterprises, and the expression 'enterprise' gives some indication of the nature of their operations and the objectives that they pursue. It suggests organisations involved in adventurous or risk bearing operations which aim to achieve some financial gain. Such gains will be the reward for those who have invested in the business and taken the risk of losing their investment if the enterprise or undertaking fails. People involved in setting up and managing such activities are sometimes referred to as entrepreneurs, and expressions such as entrepreneurialism and the 'enterprise culture' have become part of the language of British business during the 1980s and 1990s.

There are characteristics which appear to be shared by all kinds of business organisations, whatever their size, shape or location. For example all businesses:

(a) establish objectives or goals which guide their business activities;

(b) have as their prime beneficiaries those who have put capital into the enterprise; and

(c) produce and supply goods and services of one sort or another to meet the demands of consumers.

But these general characteristics provide only a limited insight into practical business operations. Business organisations are remarkably diverse. What they do, how they do it and why they do it varies widely from organisation to organisation. There are various explanations for this diversity. Some of them are relatively superficial: business organisations differ by reference to their products, some producing goods, others, services. Other explanations however touch upon the more subtle aspects of organisational activity, for instance by considering the objectives the owners of the business are pursuing. Are they perhaps profit maximisers, aiming to achieve the highest possible level of financial return for the business, or are they content to trade at a level of profit which simply enables the business to survive?

By examining the range of organisations which function in the business sphere and looking at such features as the activities they undertake, whom they seek to benefit, and how they are structured, it becomes possible to understand more about the nature of business organisations.

Business Activity

All businesses are necessarily engaged in business activity, and business activity is simply a description of human commercial activity, involving the interactions of buyers and sellers. Business activity is trade. It involves:

(a) demands being made for goods and services from consumers; and

(b) the meeting of those demands by producers, and by suppliers who distribute them to consumers.

The history of business is history of organisations being set up to produce and to distribute. In the course of carrying on these activities they also become consumers themselves. Thus two distinct groups of consumers emerge, commercial consumers and private, or as they are sometimes called, ultimate consumers, that is you and I.

A practical starting point in any study of business organisations is an examination of the classifications which can be applied to them. Businesses may be classified by the nature or level of their activity, by the ownership sectors to which they belong, and by their legal form.

The Classification of Businesses

By level of activity

This classification identifies an organisation according to its place within broadly defined bands of economic activity. These are the primary, secondary and tertiary bands.

Primary

This covers organisations engaged in the initial stages of the production process. It includes activities such as agriculture, mining and quarrying, and other related operations involving extraction such as oil and gas drilling.

Secondary

This extends to the second stage in the production process. It covers all organisations engaged in manufacturing goods – everything from aircraft to adhesives. Because the term goods is such a broad one a sub-division is sometimes made which separates them into those treated as capital or investment goods (e.g. buildings, plant and equipment) and those treated as consumer goods. Consumer goods may in turn be categorised as either durables (motor vehicles, fridges etc.) or non durables (food, clothing).

Tertiary

This covers organisations providing services. The term services, like goods, is a very wide one. It extends from private sector service industries such as finance, insurance, travel and tourism and catering, to public services such as health, education and policing.

By ownership sector

This method of classification groups organisations according to who has ownership and, therefore, control over them. It places organisations into either the private or the public sector. Public sector organisations are state controlled, private sector organisations are owned and controlled by their members. The private sector includes organisations like Lloyds Bank plc, Marks & Spencer plc, ICI and National Power. Public sector organisations involved in business activity include British Coal, British Rail and the BBC. They are run as public corporations, the traditional form of organisation used by the state to run public businesses. In practice, the public sector is considerably more complex because as well as operating businesses it also provides what are called "public goods", that is goods supplied to the whole community. Public goods include social goods such as defence and law and order, and merit goods like education and health. Public goods are considered in detail in Unit 1, *Business in the Economy*. For present purposes we may simply note that public sector provision of these goods to the community does not involve business activities in the commercial sense that we have discussed so far.

Some business organisations are hybrids. The term is used when the owners include both private sector investors and the state. They are usually referred to as mixed enterprises, or sometimes 'government companies'.

As well as limited state involvement in business, local authorities also have business interests. Many of them operate local authority companies through which they trade. For example municipal airports are run by local authorities usually on the basis of a joint venture involving a number of neighbouring councils.

By legal form

The other major classification applied to business organisations is that provided by the law. Legally all organisations must be either corporations or non corporate bodies. In the case of the private sector most of its corporations are registered companies with limited liability, whilst sole traders and partnerships make up the non-corporate sector.

Diagrammatically the main features of the classifications described so far can be seen in the following figure:

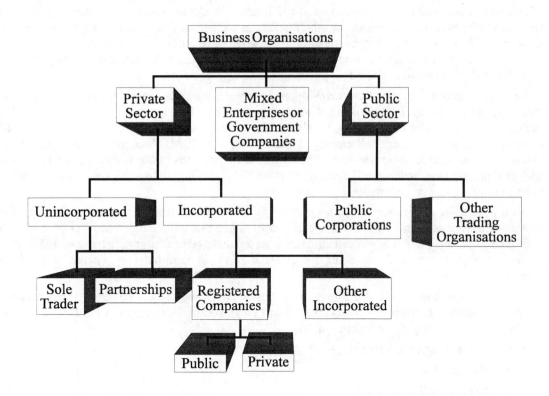

Classification of business by sector and legal status

Sole traders (or sole proprietors)

The term 'sole trader' is used to describe an individual who is self-employed and operates a business taking sole responsibility for its management and finances. In practice, a sole trader rarely works alone, and will usually employ staff to assist in operating the business. There are no legal formalities governing the creation of such a business.

A sole trader's business will normally be financed entirely by its owner, which means that any opportunities for raising further capital are limited. This can severely restrict the growth of the business. Also, whilst the sole owner is entitled to all of the profits of the business, he or she also has personal unlimited liability for any losses which the business incurs. The sole trader form of business is most suitable for an individual who wishes to retain absolute control of a business enterprise that only requires a modest amount of financial investment. Examples of such enterprises include: a retail shop; the service trade, such as plumbing or hairdressing; farms.

Responsibility for decision-making in a sole trader business rests directly with its owner; there is no individual or group to whom the owner is directly accountable, except him or herself. Such a position is attractive to someone who wants to 'be their own boss'. Sole traders provide a valuable service to the community by offering a wide range of goods and services and making them available in a convenient way.

Over recent years there has been an increase in the number of one-person businesses. There are often grants and tax incentives available to encourage people to set up this kind of enterprise. When the climate of business is one where unemployment and redundancies are commonplace, or rising, the result can be a flood of new small businesses into the market. In the period from 1981 to 1988, the number of self-employed people in the UK grew steadily from two to three million; a significant proportion of this growth was due to the number of one-person businesses being set up. In one year alone – 1988 – over 10,000 new businesses were started.

Lump-sum redundancy payments, which workers in larger organisations who are made redundant may receive, often provide the initial funding of such enterprises; with little alternative employment available, such people may well be tempted to 'go it alone'. On the other hand, a large number of people make a conscious decision to become self-employed and in total over 200,000 employees each year take the step towards self-employment. Interestingly, the incentive that leads to this is their perception that they will gain greater independence and freedom to make their own decisions; financial rewards are found to be of only secondary importance.

As well as needing a marketable idea for a business, any aspiring business person needs to prepare a sound business plan, in order to raise any additional funding that will be required from the bank. Even with such a business plan, it is still essential that a person undertakes appropriate training and learns the ground rules of running and organising a business if he or she is to have any chance of becoming a success.

Probably the most important factor for small business survival and success however is the character of the person running it. A profile of a successful self employed business person would include most, if not all, of the following characteristics:

- high motivation to succeed;
- self-discipline;
- organisational ability;
- self-belief;
- the ability to relate to other people;
- 'self-starting' and initiative;
- leadership;
- adaptability.

Nationally, new business start-ups were running at about 1,700 per week in 1989 compared with 1,250 per week in 1988. Although the recession of the early 1990s has affected business confidence, many individuals are still prepared to take the risk of creating their own business, as the previous figure indicates.

The Department of Employment recently published a report which showed that there was a 29% growth in the number of small businesses between 1979 and 1989, from 1.3 million to 1.6 million. Whilst the Department of Employment claims that small businesses create jobs more quickly than large companies, whether national wealth is created on the same scale is debatable. Businesses employing fewer than ten people were responsible for creating half a million jobs between 1987 and 1989, a figure that represents half of the total net growth of jobs – despite the fact that they employ less than 20% of all people. Interestingly, the very smallest businesses – those employing fewer than four people – created most jobs.

Partnerships

There are no legal formalities required when individuals agree to run a joint business and, in so doing, establish a partnership. The agreement to form the partnership will be a contract, but there is no legal requirement as to the form this must take. Indeed the *Partnership Act* 1890, which regulates partnership law, simply says that a partnership arises out of a business enterprise operated by two or more people working in common with the aim of making a profit. All partners in such a business (the legal maximum is 20) will usually agree to put their capital into a business, work on its behalf and receive in return a share of the profits, usually in proportion to the amount of capital each has contributed.

Professional people providing business services collectively are only permitted to do so by law as partnerships; for instance, partnerships of solicitors, chartered accountants and architects. Because of this legal restriction such firms are not subject to the usual maximum permitted membership of twenty. Indeed, in the largest firms of accountants and solicitors the number of partners maybe numbered in hundreds.

The major risk in operating as a partnership is that, if the business should get into financial difficulties, then the individuals who make up the partnership are personally liable for any debts that the business may incur. The partners' personal wealth – for instance his or her house and car, – will then be used to pay off the debts of the business.

One advantage of operating a business as a partnership is the increased amount of capital which it makes available to the business. This, in turn, means that the business is able to raise more loan finance from other institutions, such as the banks. The more capital that a business can raise from within itself, the more it is likely to be able to raise from external sources.

An additional advantage that partnership offers is the opportunity for shared management responsibilities and access to a wider range of experience and expertise. For example, in a partnership of solicitors it would be usual to have individuals who specialise in different areas of law: criminal law; civil law; company law; family law etc.

Perhaps the principal disadvantage of a partnership is the likelihood that partners will disagree, so that reaching a joint decision can sometimes be difficult. Since in law every partner is an agent of the other partners and of the firm as a whole, it follows that each partner is ultimately responsible for the action of any or all of the partners. If one partner acts irresponsibly, then all other partners are individually and jointly liable.

It is crucial, therefore, that each partner has trust and confidence in their co-partners and that the relationship is based on the utmost good faith.

Ideally the relationship of the partners in the partnership should be regulated by a partnership agreement. This agreement may vary the provisions of the Partnership Act which, broadly, are as follows:

- all partners are entitled to take part in the management of the business;

- differences arising from the ordinary business operations of the partnership are decided by majority vote;

- no change can be made to the nature of the partnership without the consent of all partners;

- no person may be introduced as a new partner without the consent of all existing partners;

- all partners are entitled to an equal share of the business and profits arising from its operation, irrespective of the amount of time they have given to it; each must contribute equally towards any losses.

If no partnership agreement exists, then any dispute which occurs will be resolved according to the terms of the Partnership Act.

Limited companies

The most common form of business enterprise is the registered company limited by shares. In the UK there are about one million registered limited companies and between them they employ the majority of the workforce in the UK, generating about two-thirds of the income made by the private sector.

A company may have as few as two members (in a company, members are referred to as shareholders), but may grow to become a huge multi-national, such as ICI and BP, with tens of thousands of shareholders.

There are two forms of limited liability company:

- *private limited companies*
  which have certain restrictions placed on the trading in their shares, preventing them from the sale or disposal of shares on the open market;

- *public limited companies*
  which trade their shares and other securities, such as debentures, on the open market through the Stock Exchange, and through intermediate securities markets.

Approximately ninety nine per cent of all companies are private. Public limited companies, although fewer in number, are usually much larger organisations in terms of turnover, assets employed and number of employees.

Perhaps the most significant feature of the registered company in a legal sense is its status as a corporation. Corporations are organisations which have their own legal identity, making them persons in their own right, with the capacity to make contracts, commit civil wrongs (called torts) and exceptionally commit crimes. A corporation conducts its business through human agents it employs for this purpose. In a registered company the most senior agents are its directors. In a limited liability company it is not the company whose liability is restricted, but that of its members. An outsider claiming payment from the company for goods or services supplied, may use all the assets of the company to meet the claim. If the debt is not fully discharged however, it is not possible to recover the amount outstanding from the members. Their liability is to the company itself, and is met as soon as they have paid for their shares in full. Compare this arrangement with the financial position of partners in a partnership. The partnership is not a corporate body, but an unincorporated association. As we have seen, the members have personal, unlimited liability. Shareholders in a company however are financially safe once their shares are paid for.

To form a limited company, a registration procedure contained in the *Companies Act* 1985 must be followed. Those wishing to set up the company, (called promoters) must prepare and send to the Registrar of Companies in Cardiff certain constitutional documents, together with the appropriate registration fees. If the documents are in order, the Registrar grants the company a certificate of incorporation. In the case of a private company it can commence trading straight away.

The main constitutional documents which must be submitted to the Registrar of Companies are:

- The Memorandum of Association
- The Articles of Association.

The Memorandum of Association

The *Companies Act* 1985 specifies that this document must include:

- *the name of the company*
  in the case of a private company the name must have 'limited' as the last word; in the case of a public company it will be 'public limited company'
- *the location of its registered office*
  identifying whether the company is situated in England or Scotland
- *the liability of the members*
  the amount of capital they are responsible for providing
- *the capital of the company*
  this sets a limit on the amount of capital the company is allowed to raise. It is referred to as the 'Authorised Share Capital'.
- *the objects*
  for which the company has been established.

The Articles of Association

The articles are concerned with the internal administration of the company, and it is for those concerned in setting up the company to decide on the rules they wish included in their Articles. The *Companies Act* 1985 does, however, provide a set of model Articles which a company may fully or partly adopt.

The matters which are normally dealt with in the Articles are:

- the appointment and powers of the directors;
- the rules in relation to shareholders' meetings and voting;
- the types of shares and the shareholders' rights attached to each type;
- the rules and procedures of transferring shares.

Once a company has been incorporated, its Articles may be altered if seventy five per cent of its members vote in favour of the alteration.

Both the Memorandum and Articles are open to public scrutiny, subject to the payment of a fee, at Companies House in Cardiff.

A company has two main sources of control over its affairs. These are the shareholders in a general meeting, and the directors. The most important matters, such as changes in its constitution and the appointment of directors, rest with its shareholders in a general meeting. Most decisions require a simple majority vote, although some matters may require a seventy five per cent majority. (It is worth noting that the majority and seventy five per cent votes relate to the numbers in attendance or voting by proxy and not to the total membership.)

Since voting power plays such an important role in company matters, the types of shares which the company issues are of considerable significance. Some shares, such as *ordinary* shares, usually carry full voting rights whilst other shares, such as *preference* shares, may carry no voting rights at all.

The Articles provide for the directors to be responsible for the daily running of the company, to make decisions and act on behalf of the company. If directors act contrary to the wishes of the members, or if the performance of the company brings into question their abilities as directors, they may be sanctioned or dismissed at a general meeting. In small companies, the directors will often be the sole shareholders, so such considerations will be irrelevant.

There are a number of advantages in operating a business as a limited company:

- shareholders have limited liability (financially they can lose only what they have put into or committed to the business);
- additional capital can be raised through share issues;
- banks may be inclined to lend larger amounts when the shareholders' stake (equity) is substantial;
- the business is able to grow and operate on a larger scale, thus achieving a higher volume of output at a lower cost;
- the company name is protected by law (another business cannot start up and lawfully trade under the same name).

These advantages must be offset against the possible drawbacks:

- formation of the company can be expensive (legal costs, registration fees etc.);
- decision-making may become more complex;
- employees of the business can often feel distant from its owners, the company shareholders;
- the records of the company, such as its annual accounts, are open to the public, enabling not only creditors but also competitors to examine its financial health;
- its activities are closely regulated by company legislation.

Differences between private limited companies and public limited companies

The most significant difference between the two types of company is the way in which shares can be bought and sold. A private company's shares are not quoted on the Stock Exchange, which means that they are unavailable on the open market. If an individual wishes to 'buy a share' in a private company then, effectively, he or she must be invited by the existing shareholders to do so.

In practice, many private limited companies are family concerns where the majority of shares (and thus the ultimate power of decision-making) stays within the family. Any increase in share issues outside that 'family' will dilute those powers and, ultimately, may result in a loss of control. In contrast, shares in public limited companies are available for purchase through the Stock Exchange and this can lead to some interesting battles for control of a business.

Some advantages of 'floating' the company or 'going public' are that it:

- increases the opportunities for raising additional finance;
- heightens awareness and increases the public profile of the business.

Some disadvantages of 'going public' are that:

- original shareholders may lose control of power and decision-making;
- only certain parts of the business may be attractive to investors, requiring parts of the business to be sold separately before the flotation;
- the likelihood of a takeover increases as share ownership becomes more widespread;
- decisions need to be justified and explained to a wider and much more public audience.

Activity

Form a group of four made up from fellow students studying with you on your GNVQ course. Assume that collectively you have decided to set up a small business. This may be any kind of business you choose. Further assume that each of you, either from personal savings or money you have borrowed, is to put £2,000 into a common fund to finance the setting up of the business. Which form of business organisation, partnership or limited company, would you choose to operate your business under and why?

Other types of organisation

Co-operatives

Co-operatives are few in number: in 1990 there were only around 2,000, compared to almost one million companies. The idea of a business co-operative is that people join together to:

- work;
- share in the profits or losses of the business;
- take joint responsibility for decisions.

The various forms of co-operatives operate mainly in the production, marketing and retailing sectors. Their common features are:

- the business is owned by its employees;
- each employee usually owns a single share which carries an entitlement of one vote;
- each employee receives an equal share in the profits of the business;
- each employee shares an equal liability for any losses which occur;
- there is either equal pay for all workers or limited pay differentials exist between workers.

Franchises

An increasingly popular form of business is the franchise. There are now thousands of franchises in the UK, operating mainly in the retail trade. Franchising involves one person (the franchisee) buying the right to operate a business (the franchise) from the owner of that business (the franchisor). The franchise allows the franchisee to:

- use an established business model and name (e.g. Wimpy);
- sell or distribute an established or recognised product (e.g. the British School of Motoring);
- take advantage of marketing and advertising which is organised centrally by the *franchiser* (e.g. The Body Shop or FastFrame).

Many successful business such as Swinton Insurance, Prontaprint and Kentucky Fried Chicken, including those quoted in the above examples operate in this way.

For a franchise to work the original business needs to be established and proven. The original owners of the business will have decided that they do not wish to expand by owning and operating a range of branches throughout the country themselves. Instead they sell franchises to other people. This allows the franchisees to run their own branches of the business in particular areas of the country. From a legal standpoint the franchise is a contract which binds franchisee and franchisor. Often the franchise agreement requires the franchisee to operate in a particular way maintaining the standard of the product, using the franchise brand and equipping the premises in a specified way. The franchisee may also have to buy the product direct from the franchisor. In return for the franchise fee, which may involve an initial payment and then an annual payment (or royalty) often based on a percentage of sales, the franchisor will pay for national advertising to establish and develop the brand name and for additional product research and development. There are many forms of contract possible in franchise arrangements. Some of the usual terms are:

- the franchisee pays a proportion of the set up cost of the franchise (the purchase of the shop site, its fixtures and fittings);
- the franchisee pays a proportion of the annual profits to the franchisor;
- the franchisee must provide a standard of product or service which is expected by the franchisor;
- the franchisor provides help and support on all aspects of business operations;
- the franchisor provides advertising and promotion on a local (and sometimes national) scale;
- the franchisor agrees not to open further franchises within a specified radius of an existing franchise.

The advantages of franchises to the franchisee are:

- franchisees own their own businesses;
- the franchisee will have a 'protected' environment in which to open a business;
- the business idea should have been well tried and tested and could in fact be a ready-made market;
- a franchise has a much lower risk of business failure than other types of business organisation;
- the franchisor will continue to give advice and practical help in developing the business;
- with national advertising the franchisee gains a much greater marketing exposure for the product often as a result of TV, radio and national newspaper advertising.

The advantages to the franchisor are:

- business expansion is achieved without increasing the number of direct employees;
- business risk is shared with the franchisee;
- franchisees are self-motivated and therefore more likely to succeed;
- access is gained to very wide markets through many outlets.

The disadvantages of franchising are:

- while the owners of the franchises are their own bosses they must operate their franchises in a manner specified by the franchisor in the franchise agreement. This could restrict the owner of the franchise who might see ways of developing the business which are not acceptable within the terms of the agreement;
- the cost of owning a franchise can be quite high because as well as the initial cost of purchasing the franchise there will normally be annual payments to the franchisor which will reduce the franchisee's final profits;
- if the franchisor's marketing efforts are poor, then the franchisee's payments towards such costs may be wasted;
- if the franchisees wish to sell the business before the end of the franchise term they may be restricted in this by the terms of the agreement or by the refusal of the franchisor to the sale of the franchise to a third party of whom they do not approve;

- if the franchisor fails nationally, and there have been several examples of this in recent years such as Fast Frame and Exchange Travel, then the franchisee may be left with a worthless franchise.

Roles and Responsibilities in Organisations

When a person is appointed to a job in an organisation they enter into a contractual relationship with their new employer. They are promising to provide their service, their time and labour, for the benefit of their employer. In return the employer is promising a salary or wage. This is known as the work/wage bargain. It is the basis upon which organisations acquire their human resources. The number of employees engaged, and the tasks required of them, are factors as variable as the different organisational activities carried out by the enterprises which take them on. In complex modern economics the knowledge and skills demanded of a workforce, not only across the nation as a whole but within particular employment sectors, is characterised by its diversity and refinement. We shall now be examining the nature of the work performed by staff in organisations. In order to make sense of different types of work which an enterprise demands of its workforce we need first to step back and look at the overall shape of organisations. This will show us how they are structured, and what kind of systems they use. Once we are aware of their structures and systems we can begin to appreciate the staffing arrangements which the organisation needs; whom it should employ and what general and specific tasks are required of the workforce.

The Major Structural Characteristics of Organisations

So far our classification of business organisations has merely demonstrated their range and diversity. We now need to explore them in greater depth, looking at the way they are structured. In doing so it will be useful to look at as broad a range of organisations as possible, so that comparisons can be made between them. In particular we need to examine the way in which the state is organised, although as we have already seen the state does not generally engage in commercial activities in the way that private sector organisations do.

Structures and systems

All organisations, large and small, carry out their activities using structures and systems. At first sight these expressions might appear to suggest the same idea, but they do not mean the same thing. A structure is the framework an organisation uses to enable it to carry out its decision making. A system describes the construction and interrelationships of a set of separate parts which combine together to form a complex unified whole. For example, suppose a business uses committees for the purpose of enabling certain kinds of decision making to take place. In such an arrangement we can describe its committees by reference to what they are called, who serves on them, what their terms of reference are, and where they fit within the overall decision making framework of the business. This committee structure however will be just one component in a more complex network of interrelated and interdependent parts that taken together make up the whole communication system of the organisation. We talk about the structure of a report meaning its organisation or shape. We talk about management information systems meaning the identification of major information requirements of an organisation, the obtaining and storing of relevant data, and the use of this data to inform and support management decision making.

An organisation structure which enables staff to meet the objectives of the enterprise is an effective one, although other factors will need to be considered in measuring the attainment of objectives, such as the cost involved, worker satisfaction and so on. These issues are considered in other elements.

Setting up an organisation

The structures which an enterprise uses to meet its objectives are likely to emerge when it is being set up. A standard sequence is likely to take the shape shown in the figure below:

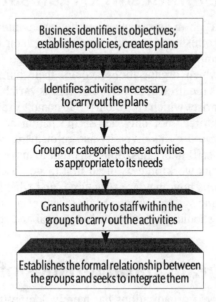

Steps in setting up an organisation

Formal and informal structures

Structures, like systems, are a fundamental characteristic of every kind of organisation. They show us the way in which the organisation is designed, and thus to a limited extent how it works as well. The structural framework of an organisation is like an anatomical diagram of the human body. All the principal physical features are revealed. Looking at structures tells us more about the real shape of the organisation we are studying. It can reveal why a particular organism works successfully. Equally it may assist us in diagnosing the cause of the difficulties it is having in functioning effectively. The formal structure of an organisation, the way in which it is regularly constituted, is determined by two groups of people;

(i)   those who originally set it up, and

(ii) those who at any given time are involved in managing it.

Some businesses operate with very durable structures which change very little over time. Others find that alterations to their structural design are essential to improve performance or to adapt to changing environments. Very small concerns may have little need for anything more than simple, rudimentary structures, but larger enterprises are normally only capable of functioning with well established and often sophisticated structures, and it is these that are most likely to require adaptation by managers as a response to change. One structural feature of all organisations, irrespective of their size, is the division of work within the labour force. Managers usually handle this by creating departments to carry out groups or sets of associated functions. The arrangement of the activities of an enterprise by function or task is known as 'departmentation'

All members of the workforce will belong to a particular department, some to more than one if they have cross-departmental roles. The most senior managers, such as the managing director of a registered company, may have non-departmental roles however, since their responsibilities extend to the whole organisation rather than sub-sets of it. Departmentation provides us with an example of how formal structures may need to adapt as a response to change. A business which suddenly expands as a result of a merger with another organisation is likely to find some restructuring of its departments inevitable, as a reflection of its greater size and perhaps the greater diversity of the economic activity. Maybe the business managed previously by dealing with administration matters on a department by department basis. It now finds however, that such an arrangement is unworkable. A new administration department is formed. Appropriate staff from other departments are transferred to it, and all the original departments are subsequently instructed that new administrative arrangements will apply to them. Similar situations may occur in reverse where an organisation is contracting rather than expanding, and the work of two departments is combined within one department in the interests of economy.

Departmentation is merely one illustration of a structural characteristic of an organisation. There are many others, and we shall consider them shortly. We need to bear in mind however, that organisations often house informal structures, which are not the result of anything designed by their managers, but are the product of the workforce. Being informal, these structures are not always easy to identify, nor is it possible to generalise about them except in a very loose way because they are irregular. At best we can say that informal structures emerge where groups of workers, usually working closely together as team members, develop their own ideas and attitudes towards their working environment, using the grapevine to pass messages around the organisation or parts of it. They may for example use this approach to arrange ad hoc meetings to discuss working conditions, or threatened redundancies. At a more subtle level, the informal network may be active in developing staff attitudes towards the boss or what people regard as being acceptable and unacceptable collective behaviour. In enterprises where the management and the workforce do not work in harmony these informal structures are likely to be particularly strong, and potentially harmful to the business. The characteristics of formal and informal structures are contained in the following figure:

Formal	Informal
Easily describable and definable – can be expressed in the form of organisation charts	Often difficult to identify; and will not be revealed in organisation charts.
Aim is to control and co-ordinate activities	Characterised by representing the norms, values and customs of the workforce
Formalisation tends to be more marked as organisation grows	May hinder the achievement of organisational objectives if informal structures pursue alternative conflicting objectives
Highly formalised structures can limit individualism and reduce organisational flexibility	
In large organisations handling complex administrative tasks, the formal structures will create bureaucratic organisations	

The characteristics of formal and informal structures

Bureaucratic structures

In the preceding figure reference is made to bureaucratic organisations. The term bureaucratic has come to be used in a derogatory way to describe officialdom. Bureaucrats are decision-makers who are distant and apparently unaccountable for their actions. Bureaucracy is associated with the institutions of the state and their staffs, the civil servants working in central government departments and the officers of the local authority in the Town Hall. It is also associated with the work of the European Community (the EC), whose senior officials in Brussels have been dubbed Eurocrats. But these observations tell us nothing about what a bureaucratic organisation is, nor indeed whether they are found only within the public sector.

During the early part of the twentieth century the sociologist Max Weber studied organisations and their structures. His work led him to certain conclusions regarding the nature of bureaucratic structures, ideas which make up what we now refer to as the classic bureaucratic model. Weber's general sociological analysis of organisational structures revealed three distinct types of structure, all of them based upon the way the organisation is managed.

(a) *the traditional model*
This recognises that ultimate authority within the enterprise rests with the head of the organisation;

(b) *the rational/legal model*
Such a structure relies upon a system which grants identifiable powers to particular staff. When these powers are exercised within their prescribed limits others in the organisation accept them;

(c) *the charismatic model*
Here the dominant role is held by a person with special qualities of leadership which are recognised and admired by others in the organisation.

In practice these models may overlap. Some of the great entrepreneurs, such as Henry Ford, have combined authority with charisma, to the considerable benefit of their businesses.

Weber's work in exploring bureaucratic structures led him to construct what he saw as an ideal type of bureaucracy which would operate as a rational model of administrative organisation. According to Weber the characteristics of the ideal model were:

(a) *specialisation*
a clearly established division of organisational tasks allocated to a number of positions within the organisation;

(b) *a hierarchical structure*
staff ordered into the hierarchy with officers responsible for the actions and decisions of their subordinates;

(c) *standardisation*
a system of standard procedural rules to facilitate uniformity in the performance of tasks;

(d) *impersonalisation*
duties carried out by staff in an impartial and emotionally detached way to ensure equal treatment of clients;

(e) *career structure*
and properly qualified staff – staff appointed on the basis of technical qualifications to perform tasks and promotion prospects based upon merit and/or service record.

According to Weber the presence of these characteristics would lead to organisational efficiency, but what he overlooked was the existence of the informal organisation beneath the surface of the formal one. The work of Elton Mayo and his associates in the USA during the 1920s and 1930s revealed that whatever the formal organisation within the workplace, a crucial element in organisational performance was the social interaction of workers. This led to the development of the human relations approach to management, which emphasises the need for managers to recognise and utilise the social needs of workers.

As we have already noted, organisations that fit within the bureaucratic model are generally those involved in employing large numbers of staff (i.e. they are labour intensive) engaged in a wide span of administrative activity. They enjoy a number of advantages, such as clearly established lines of authority and impartiality when they apply rules. This may be essential in state organisations responsible for providing social supports such as the payment of benefits. However they do suffer certain disadvantages. They do not provide for personal growth, their size can lead to poor internal communications, and they may be slow to adapt to the changing external environment, for instance by failing to respond to technological developments. In smaller organisations handling less complex activities the organisational structure will not need to be heavily formalised and the result is often a more adaptable organisation which is more enjoyable to work in. This is the view that 'small is beautiful'.

Specific structural arrangements

Having considered a number of general issues related to structures, we can now look at specific structural arrangements adopted by organisations. As we have seen, structure relates to the co-ordination and grouping of related activities as a means of achieving objectives. Obviously therefore the nature of the objectives an organisation is pursuing will have an impact on the design of its internal structures. A useful illustration is provided by local authorities. Through the introduction of legislation designed to increase competition for the work traditionally carried out by local authorities, the authorities have found their role changing. From being deliverers of services, they increasingly find themselves in what is described as an enabling role, that is overseeing delivery of services by other private sector providers. In areas such as environmental health, school meals and building work, authorities are required to operate competitive tendering arrangements, the aim being to carry out the work involved as cost effectively as possible. In many cases, authorities have voluntarily withdrawn from delivering such services themselves, whilst in other cases they have found themselves undercut by tenders from outside organisations. The effect of the drive towards competition in providing local public services on the structures of the enabling authorities has been the reorganisation of the departments involved, with changes in the levels of staffing and in job descriptions reflecting the reformulated objectives now being pursued. As indicated, the structures in this instance are a response to changes in the external environment of the organisations affected, namely the introduction of the *Local Government Act*, 1988. New structures may also result from activities generated internally, for example, where the organisations procedures for evaluating its own performance have revealed the need for revision.

Efficient organisations divide their activities into a logical sequence, and allocate specific parts of the sequence to be carried out by sub-sets of the organisation. Each of these sub-sets or divisions will require the authority and autonomy to perform their functions adequately. To take an extreme example it would be absurd for a senior executive of a multi-national company to spend time reading through all the outgoing mail produced by subordinates of the departments or divisions for which the executive is responsible. A senior and highly paid manager's talents need to be used more effectively elsewhere within the organisation, in corporate decision making. Similarly, if every time the phone rang in the social services department of a local authority its administrative staff were unable to answer the call before obtaining the approval of a senior member of staff, the difficulties in functioning would be considerable. The problem would be a structure lacking an appropriate level of autonomy to match the activity involved. Nevertheless too great a level of autonomy may also produce structural inadequacies, and lead to lack of proper communication between the component parts of the organisation. This is a criticism which has often been levelled at public sector organisations, which as a consequence of their size and their bureaucratic systems often become very rigid, and fell prey to the allegation that 'the left hand does not know what the right hand is doing'. This is another way of saying that there is a lack of co-ordination.

The setting up of a formal organisational structure should ensure that each individual is able to identify his or her position within the organisation. Each employee should be aware of their own responsibilities, to whom they are directly accountable and for whom they are responsible. A further advantage of a formal structure is that it may allow management to develop areas of specialism and expertise within the organisation. If you work in an organisation you will probably be allocated specific duties. For example, if you are in a clerical post scale 2 in the housing department of a local authority, your duties may be general clerical and administrative. You will be accountable to a Section Head, and ultimately to the Director of Housing. Eventually, as you are promoted, you may be given the responsibility of supervising more junior clerical posts.

Almost certainly there will also exist some form of informal structure within the organisation. This will be the result of personal friendships, work patterns and practical expediency. Thus you may make friends with the people who work in your section or others that you come into contact with in the course of your job. Such informal structures are usually to be encouraged by the organisation as they improve the quality of the working environment and make people enjoy their job more. Only when such an informal structure conflicts with the efficient operation of the organisation should it be discouraged. No doubt we are all aware of some people who spend more time discussing their planned nights out than actually getting their work done.

Most organisations have a pyramid structure in which authority and responsibility extend downwards in a hierarchical pattern. (This is shown in the next figure.) In such a structure, senior management will make the major executive and policy decisions. They have the overall responsibility for the success or failure of such policies and are given the authority to make such decisions. As we move down the organisational pyramid, status, responsibility and authority normally decrease. Junior staff will not

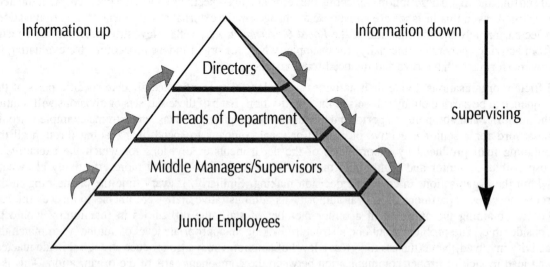

An organisational pyramid of a large business

normally be expected to make decisions upon which the future reputation of the organisation will hinge. For example, a clerk in the finance department will not be responsible for choosing the software system that will control the issue of invoices and final demands. In most organisations you will usually know when you are doing something which oversteps your authority. A senior employee is likely to inform you that you have acted out of line. In any case your job description should indicate the limits of your responsibility.

Organisation charts as a way of presenting structures

Organisation charts are an attempt to record the formal structure of the organisation and to show the main relationships, the downward flow of authority and responsibility, and the main lines of communication. Obviously it would be impossible to show on such a chart all the informal structures that can exist. Imagine being faced with the task of drawing lines to describe all the informal friendships in an organisation. Even if you managed to achieve it you would have to revise it constantly.

Organisation charts have the advantage of forcing senior management to define clearly organisational relationships. They also provide a useful introduction to the organisation for outsiders, and particularly for new starters. Additionally, they can form the starting point from which management can initiate change or evaluate the strengths and weaknesses of the organisation and are thus an aid to organisational design. However, they quickly become out of date as people join or leave the organisation, and existing staff have their job descriptions changed. They can also introduce a degree of rigidity into the organisation as people feel constrained by the limits of their job as defined by the organisational chart.

The simplicity or complexity of an organisation chart will be a reflection of the enterprise it is representing. A sole trader running a small shop with one full-time and four part-time staff will yield a straightforward chart, as in the next figure.

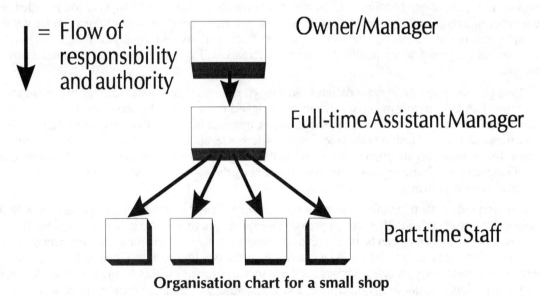

Organisation chart for a small shop

This chart only shows us who wields authority over whom. Even a diagram as simple as this however may need to be modified to reflect how authority is implemented in practice, if the evidence shows that the owner as well as the assistant manager controls the part-time staff.

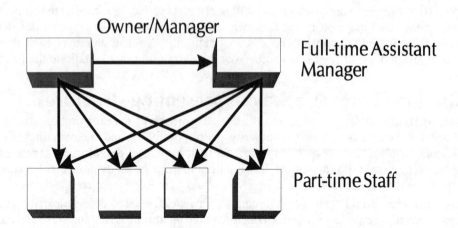

Owner/Manager

Full-time Assistant Manager

Part-time Staff

A modified organisation chart for a small shop

The modified diagram immediately alerts us to the potential for conflict here. Who is the real boss for the part-time staff? Has the assistant manager formal authority over the other staff or is the assistant manager acting in the name of the owner? In organisations as small as this however, relationships tend to be informal, rules are basic and there is little if any job specialisation. Often small organisations fit the job to suit the person. The reverse is generally the case in larger businesses where a person is appointed who fits the job description. As the organisation grows so the levels or tiers of authority increase. In organisations handling a large administrative load where closer supervision is called for, the number of tiers of authority will be greater than for a manufacturing business with a similar number of employees, (since the ratio of supervisors to shop floor workers will usually be a high one) and as the organisation grows so its modified organisation chart will reflect the greater complexity of its structure.

It follows that the shape of an organisation chart can tell us a great deal about the way the organisation is structured. A tall, narrow pyramid indicates many levels in the hierarchy and a small span of control (span of control refers to the number of subordinates a manager is responsible for controlling). A short, broad pyramid i.e. one with a wide base, indicates fewer levels in the hierarchy and a wide span of control. In a dynamic organisation which adapts to its changing environment, the boundaries of its shape will of course, alter. Some organisations however are largely static – their shape will remain constant. Our small shop is probably an example.

Organisation charts, then, enable us to view the component parts of the organisation and identify the relationships between them. They do not provide an explanation of why the structure exists but they do show us what it is, and they can be used to express almost any form of structural management by which an organisation conducts its activities. As we have seen in the two figures above, one particular structural characteristic which they can clearly reveal is the authority structure within an organisation. Authority structures are fundamental to any enterprise, and we now need to examine them more closely.

Authority structure

The term 'authority' when used to describe organisations has been variously defined. People with authority are those who have the capacity to command and thus have power over others. Henri Fayol, one of the pioneers in the study of management, saw it as "the right to give orders and the power to exact obedience." Power and authority are not however the same thing. A person with authority can delegate it to others. Delegation involves transferring authority, and in organisations this is a standard practice. We shall be considering it shortly. Power is essentially a description of a personality characteristic. You cannot invest power in a person – it is something they develop themselves. Perhaps rather confusingly we also talk about "powers', and powers are rather different. The term 'powers' is normally used to describe the constitutional capacity of a person. It covers those matters and activities which an individual has formally been given the capacity to carry out. Thus in a company the managing director will have formal authority regarding the business activities of the enterprise: the capacity to command. The extent of this authority can be discovered by looking at the constitution of the company, which will set out the specific powers which the managing director enjoys – borrowing money, entering into commercial agreements and so on. Whether the managing director has power in the sense of the way in which the authority is exercised will depend on the character and qualities of the individual office holder.

Authority carries with it responsibility and accountability. Responsibility is the obligation to perform the duties of office, and accountability involves a person with authority being answerable to a superior regarding the way in which duties – the responsibilities of office, have been performed. Our managing director is ultimately accountable to the shareholders of the company.

Other terms commonly encountered when considering authority structure are formal authority, functional authority and personal authority. Formal authority is simply a way of describing the mechanism by which the authority has been granted. Formal authority is acquired either directly, through the constitution of the organisation, or by means of a delegated power being granted. Thus a company secretary will obtain formal authority regarding that particular post through powers granted under the company's constitution (known technically as its articles of association), but may also from time to time be granted delegated powers from the board of directors to act in the name of the board.

Functional authority arises from specialised knowledge and skills held by an individual. Thus a senior research chemist working in a pharmaceuticals company is likely to enjoy a high level of functional authority within the organisation, even though that person is not a senior manager of it.

Delegation

Delegation involves the act of transferring powers held by a person or a group, to a subordinate or subordinates. The subordinate, or delegate, becomes responsible to the superior for doing whatever has been delegated. The superior remains responsible however for seeing that the job has been done, for delegating a task does not enable the superior to plead, when the task has not been carried out satisfactorily, that the fault lies with the subordinate alone. The act of the subordinate becomes the act of the superior when a delegated task is performed. The superiors' powers have been devolved. Diagrammatically the process can be represented as is seen in the figure on the following page.

It is not possible for a superior to delegate all his or her authority. Were this to happen, the subordinate would assume the role of the superior, and would no longer be accountable to the superior. There is clearly a risk involved in delegating, since the subordinate may lack the capacity to carry out the delegated responsibility. A superior is likely therefore to exercise some supervision over the subordinate, although supervision will need to be gently handled; the subordinate may feel inhibited or pressurised, and the superior may end up by finding that they have actually performed the task themselves.

The main reasons why organisations delegate are:

   (i)   to off-load parts of the workload of an individual or group through pressure of time, or lack of interest;

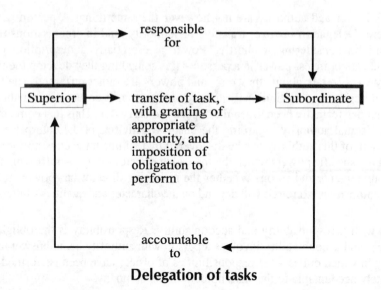

Delegation of tasks

  (ii) to employ the subordinates' specialist knowledge or skills in performing tasks more appropriate to them than to the superior;

  (iii) to give subordinates the experience of handling tasks they would not otherwise have the chance to. This is really an on the job training for the managers of the future.

In some organisations, particularly very formal ones, detailed arrangements exist for delegating. For example local authorities are allowed to delegate their functions under the *Local Government Act* 1972 to committees, sub-committees and officers, and to other local authorities as well. Under these arrangements delegation may pass down through many tiers of the organisation. A local authority is legally obliged to maintain a public register containing a list of the powers which it has delegated to its officers. The mechanism by which delegation is authorised within local authority is through the use of standing orders created by the authority. Standing orders represent the internal constitution of the authority – its internal rules. In much the same way registered companies usually make formal arrangements for delegating responsibilities. A standard internal constitutional management arrangement in such organisations is to permit the board of directors, the most senior managers of a company, to delegate all or any of their powers to a managing director. If the board wishes to exercise such capacity they would do so by means of a resolution passed at a board meeting.

Line structures

These are structures based upon who exercises authority over whom. In an organisation chart such a structure will normally appear with solid lines connecting staff vertically to illustrate direct line relationships. Senior staff in such an arrangement will often be referred to as line managers. An illustration is provided in the figure at the top of the next page.

Each person is directly responsible to the member of staff immediately above them. Such a diagram clearly illustrates the levels of authority which operate within the organisation. What it does not do however is to reflect the shape of the organisation horizontally. In practice our figure above could be expanded horizontally. The company involved will doubtless have a number of departments or divisions each with its own director, and each of these departments, specialist areas in themselves, will be divided up into sub-units, which will provide a greater level of specialisation still. In the figure, these sub-units are identified as sections within the particular department. Represented in this way, the majority of

A simple line structure

organisations, certainly larger ones, appear in the classic pyramid structure which we looked at earlier. At its apex, the most senior managers, at its base, the bulk of the workforce – in a manufacturing organisation the shop floor workers, in an administrative organisation, the junior clerical staff. Authority and status decrease the further down the pyramid one travels, and the greater the number of tiers or levels of authority, the more complex the lines of communication and chains of command. Organisations arranged on a line structure basis tend to be small ones, where managers are able to effectively control and direct business operations.

Departmentation Structure

The term departmentation has already been discussed. It is used to describe the various ways in which the work of an enterprise can be carried out by means of grouping its tasks or functions. Departmentation can be functional, geographical, by product/service, or by customer type.

Functional

This is by far the most common arrangement. It is based upon specialisation and involves the establishment of departments which are responsible for specific functions required by the organisation. The titles used to describe departments are likely to vary according to the nature of the organisation. Organisations involved in innovative activities will have a research and development department, organisations engaged in productive processes will have a production department, but service organisations will not since they are not producers. Buying and selling departments are terms likely to be used in wholesaler enterprises, and so on. The two figures below provide a simple comparison of the functional structures of a manufacturing organisation and a local authority.

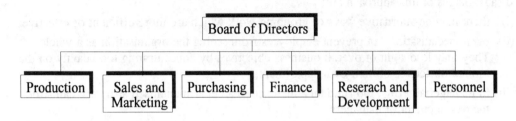

Departments of a manufacturing organisation

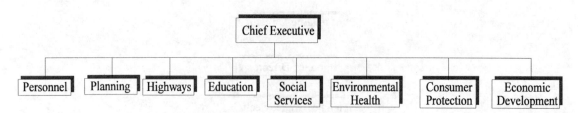

Departments of a Shire County

An organisation may operate with two apparently independent functional structures running in parallel with each other. In the case of a local authority its officers may be organised on the lines described in the figure above, whilst at the political level its councillors use a different functional structure to determine policy. An illustration is provided in the figure below.

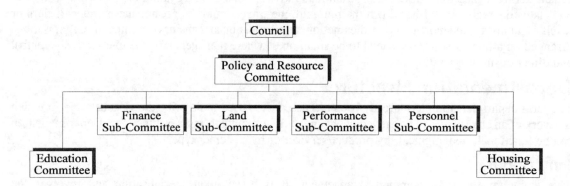

Committee structure of a Metropolitan Borough Council

The main benefits of functional groupings are:

(i)   they are easy for the workforce and the organisation's customers to understands

(ii) they are a logical and apparently rational way of organising, since they are based on specialisation, and should therefore be efficient i.e. the optimum way of using human resources.

The disadvantages of this approach are:

(i)   there may be alternative ways of grouping work which are more efficient or effective;

(ii) over specialisation can prevent employees from seeing the organisation as a whole. They may lose sight of overall business objectives by concentrating too heavily on the limited objectives of their own department;

(iii) in managerial terms, too rigid an adherence to a departmentalised structure can stifle the development of managers.

Geographical

Organisations may for a variety of reasons, find it useful to divide up their business operations on geographical lines. Where this occurs, it is likely that certain functions remain the responsibility of some centralised part of the organisation, for example where the head office of a manufacturing or service organisation retains overall control of activities such as staff recruitment and training. Other functions however, will be located elsewhere. This may be administratively convenient as well as more appropriate to customers' needs, for instance where an insurance company handles its business on a region by region basis, with offices located in each region manned by staff who have local knowledge, and which are physically more accessible to customers than a single main office. In the public sector, similar arrangements apply. The education department will usually have area offices located in the different administrative areas which the council has established to manage its education functions more efficiently. In both these examples the work of the individual offices or branches will be exactly the same.

Different types of organisations, particularly those involved in manufacturing, may find it useful to locate different functional aspects of their activities according to relevant geographical criteria. For example a car manufacturer may locate the manufacturing site according to consideration of land costs, the availability of skilled labour, central and local grants, the transport infrastructure and so on. The manufacturing site may not however be an ideal position from which to operate general distribution arrangements; space may be limited and the site generally geographically isolated. Similarly if the manufacturer has recently bought out a components company it may be easier to continue manufacturing components from the existing plant than to relocate it and its workforce at the car plant.

The benefits of geographical departmentalisation are reduction in operating costs, and the advantages of bringing the product closer to the customer and being able to make decisions locally. Disadvantages tend to focus upon the greater demands of co-ordinating and controlling operations in an organisation wide basis when the business is geographically spread. In particular, the communications systems of an organisation may be strained in such an arrangement.

By product/service

This form of departmentalisation is usually only found in large organisations, although it may be used in an organisation of any size. It involves organising individual productive units for each product or service the enterprise is involved in. There are a number of advantages in this kind of arrangement. It allows for specialisation of staff and equipment around the specific unit, can provide a better customer service, and can introduce a greater degree of responsibility for managers, for example by making product/service managers responsible for a range of functions (buying, selling, etc.). However as we have seen previously, some functions are likely to remain under central control, in particular, finance.

Customer

Where organisations have a range of customers it is possible to departmentalise around pre-determined customer categories. Examples of the kinds of categories which could be employed are public sector/private sector, wholesaler/retailer, business/private, or even small/large. Financial institutions such as banks go some way towards departmentalising in this fashion with, for example, a commercial loans department and a small business department. Whilst this approach carries with it clear advantages to the customer of specialisation and a tailored service, co-ordination between departments can be difficult.

Other structures based on activity

There are two other types of structure which are of relatively modern origin, which an organisation may use to conduct its operations. They are based upon the activities of the organisation and are systems oriented. These are the matrix and the clover leaf structure.

Matrix structure

Whilst most organisations operate on a pyramid structure, there are occasions where a business requires a structural arrangement which is more adaptable and flexible. The matrix structure may be used in such circumstances, either in substitution for the traditional pyramid arrangement, or in conjunction with it. Matrix structure is particularly suited to handling specific projects where innovation and creativity are required, and a multi-disciplinary team based approach is felt to be the best way to achieve this. Usually a matrix arrangement will be organised in the following way. A project manager or director will be appointed. The project manager will determine what the project team has to do to achieve its objectives, and what the composition of the project team should be. Authority may be granted to the project manager to second or withdraw staff from their normal duties to join the team, and the team members will work under the direction of the project manager for the duration of the project. Team members will accept the authority of the project manager and will thus be accountable to him or her.

The manager will create a team which continues the various skills necessary to carry out the project successfully. This will involve drawing on staff who are located in different functional areas of the organisation, for example in marketing and sales, or research and development, or production. Staff in these functional areas will make up the component parts of the project team, and within these groups there may be functional managers whose role is to determine not what, but how the project objectives are to be achieved. A simple illustration of a matrix structure is shown in the following figure.

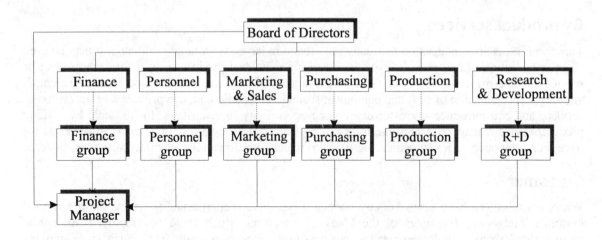

Matrix structure of an organisation

In the figure each functional department is responsible for providing the necessary support to its seconded staff for the needs of the project. Each group is accountable to the project manager, who is in turn ultimately accountable to the board.

The possible advantages and disadvantages of such a structure are contained in the next table.

Advantages	Disadvantages
Team chosen to match project needs	Re-arrangement of lines authority – conflict and confusion
Team members highly motivated	Complexity of organisational structures
More effective control over project	Staff training programmes harder to organise
Staff training programmes harder to organise	
Project objectives met more quickly	
More customer oriented	

Advantages and Disadvantages of a matrix structure

For a matrix structure to work it is essential that the authority enjoyed by the project manager, and the relationship between that person and the functional departments involved be clearly specified. The project manager may have staff in the project group who in line terms are more senior to him or her. Clearly the skills involved in handling project management are wide ranging. A project manager is someone who combines technical knowledge of the project specification with the ability to select appropriate staff and manage them for the duration of the project, handling meetings with the team, reporting to senior management, and negotiating with customers.

Clover leaf structure

Whereas the matrix structure involves a project management approach to business operations within the context of a conventional functional structure made up of departments, the clover leaf structure provides a more radical design involving a systems approach to the entire organisation. Essentially it replaces the pyramid shape with a clover leaf design in which the management of the organisation is shifted from the apex of the pyramid to the centre of the leaf, from which it acts as the focus of activity. The management participates in each of four major organisational systems, co-ordinating the work of each of these systems as well as determining organisational objectives and the politics required to carry them out. This form of structure can be seen in the following figure, together with the four main systems which make up the clover leaf.

Clover-leaf structure of an organisation

Activity

Bearing in mind the information you have read on organisational structures, try to arrange a meeting with a manager employed in a public or private sector organisation which is local to you. Explain in your letter or telephone call that you would like to spend no more than 20 minutes finding out about the structures of the organisation the manager works in, looking at issues of authority, delegation, and the functional (or other) departmentation structure that it operates. Produce an organisation pyramid to present your findings diagrammatically.

Specific Roles and Responsibilities in an Organisation

Having explored the kinds of structures usually found in organisations we can now apply this information to examine specific posts held by people in organisations, looking at their individual roles and responsibilities. It may be useful to summarise the most important terms applied to employees which are descriptive of their capacity.

- Authority – a person who has authority can command others and thus exercise power over them;
- Responsibility – this is the obligation to carry out the duties which are attached to the job one holds;
- Accountability – this involves being answerable to a superior for the way in which responsibilities have been discharged;
- Work role – this describes the package of rights, duties or responsibilities of the office the employee holds.

Defining the Job

When a person is appointed to a job there are certain assumptions we can realistically make:

(a) the employer has identified the tasks that the new employee is going to perform;

(b) that these tasks have been made known to the employee;

(c) that both the employer and the employee are satisfied the employee is capable of performing the job, or if not, what education and training is necessary to bring them up to the necessary level of knowledge and skill to be able to perform it.

If the organisation has a personnel department, it will have the task of defining and setting out what a particular job involves. In doing so it will be advised by other departments about specialist requirements. Good practice displayed in a personnel department is to carry out a job analysis, and from this an outline job description can be drawn up. This is likely to contain the following information:

- the title of the post;
- the main objectives of the post;
- the range of decision making involved in it;
- the responsibilities of the post holder – for staff/resources;
- the source(s) of supervision and guidance.

This information makes up a relatively simple statement of the job, which will be used as the basis upon which advertisements of the post are made. A copy of the job description will be sent to applicants for the post.

It is common nowadays for personnel departments to prepare a further document which seeks to describe the skills and attributes required of the post holder. This is referred to as a job specification. It will consider matters such as the practical and intellectual skills required, for instance the ability to problem solve, and will specify the personal attitudes demanded of the job, for instance drive and dynamism, as well as attributes, like flair or patience. A person specification may be designed by the personnel department to help it summarise the attributes which a post holder should possess ideally, and such a specification often indicates which attributes are essential and which are merely desirable. A job specification can be a useful tool in any subsequent appraisal of the post holder to determine how well they are measuring up to the job, whilst a job description is a valuable document in handling grievances about what tasks the job actually extends to.

Once the job description and job specification have been produced, and the appointment made on the basis of how they define the job, the new employee then begins to perform the job itself.

Job skills and knowledge

We have already commented on the diversity of roles and responsibilities which are associated with working in organisations. It is possible to broadly classify into categories the kinds of skills (and levels of knowledge) which are to be found within the workforce of most organisations. These categories are:

(a) *unskilled*
Workers who do not require training or previous experience to perform their jobs are normally found at the base of the organisational hierarchy. They are involved in repetitive manual tasks, which inevitably are usually boring and poorly paid. Increasingly such tasks are being taken over by machines;

(b) *motor or mechanical skills*
Jobs involving the use of equipment require motor (manipulative) skills. They range from tasks involving repetitive action such as feeding raw materials into a vat, through the use of keyboards used with personal computers, to the handling of laser equipment in human surgery, thus they may involve minimal skills or very high levels of manipulative ability used in conjunction with great knowledge and understanding of systems;

(c) *knowledge and intelligence*
Examples of jobs combining these capacities are professional areas such as law and accountancy, and the fields of research and design where creative abilities are essential.

(d) *managerial and administrative skills*
The terms management and administration are often used indiscriminately. The writer EFL Brech, in his book *Principles and Practice of Management*, defines administration as "That part of the management process concerned with the institution and carrying out procedures by which the programme is laid down and communicated, and the progress of activities is regulated and checked against targets and plans". He sees management as "a social process entailing responsibility for the effective and economical planning and regulation of the operations of an enterprise, in fulfilment of a given purpose or task";

(e) *decision making skills and initiative*
Decision making in organisations is the task essentially of managers, who use their judgement to determine actions to be taken, or not to be taken by the organisation they represent. This will invariably involve demonstrating initiative, and is associated with risk – deciding on the wrong strategy can seriously harm an organisation.

Activity

Which kinds of jobs in business organisations are esay to describe in terms of skills and knowledge, and which are likely to be more difficult to define in this way. Are there advantages to be gained for an organisation in using such descriptions for its workforce?

The jobs themselves

We shall conclude this part of the Unit by looking at examples of the different roles and responsibilities of post holders at different levels within the organisational hierarchy. We can do this in two ways – by considering the roles and responsibilities associated with specific posts in organisations, such as company secretary, and the roles and responsibilities of those in general spheres of the work environment, like managers. We shall use the various posts held in a company involved in manufacturing as our example.

The managing director

The managing director of a registered company is the most senior director on the board of directors. There is no legal requirement to make such an appointment, however for reasons we shall explain, it is usual for a company to make one of the directors the managing director. Table A, the set of model articles of association adopted by most companies, provides that such an appointment may be made constitutionally by a decision of the board. They may also choose to appoint one of their number to act as the chairman of the board. The chairman will often be the managing director. The task of the chairman will be to preside at every meeting of the board at which he or she is present i.e. chair the meeting.

A managing director may act in two capacities. Firstly, as a member of the board, he or she has all the powers and duties associated with directorship generally. Secondly the managing director may, constitutionally, have delegated to him or her powers that are otherwise exercisable by the whole board, in other words act as the representative of the board. Again Table A provides for this possibility. It says the directors may delegate "such of their powers as they consider desirable" to be exercised by the managing director, and this may be subject to any conditions they impose.

Since directors are the senior managers of registered companies the choice of who is appointed as managing director, in a sense 'ultimate' manager, will be based upon the collective judgement of the directors regarding the skills and qualities they believe such a person will require. These will certainly include business experience and acumen, strength of character, and of course the capacity to make the right decisions at the right time. In exercising the powers of the board, the managing director will be accountable to the board members, and in turn, the board as a whole is accountable to the company itself – the shareholders. The directors must answer to the shareholders for the way in which they have managed the business of the company: has it met its objectives, and if not why not? Shareholders dissatisfied with the performance of the directors may seek to remove them from management of its affairs. Company law requires an ordinary resolution (a simple majority of members voting in favour) at a general meeting of the company, to remove a director, and this can be for any reason. By taking such action the company may put itself in breach of a contract of employment the director has with it, and the director may claim for unfair dismissal, but so long as the majority of members no longer wish a director to act in such a capacity, company law enables them to exclude the director as a company manager.

Essentially the managing director is the link between policy formulation, and the execution of company policy by its managers. Such a person, as we have seen, represents the board of directors, and interprets policy, develops programmes to meet corporate objectives, and is responsible for a framework in which activities can be delegated whilst effective control of company affairs is maintained. In performing these duties the managing director will report back to the board, keeping members informed about those aspects of corporate activity of which they need to be aware.

The directors

All registered companies must have directors; a private company can have just one director, the minimum for a public company is two. As we have seen, they must account to the company members for the way in which they handle the business of the company. They may be full time or part time, and subject to the company articles, they do not have to hold shares in the company.

Directorship carries with it a dual role. It involves direction and management. Direction concentrates on the longer term affairs of the business, such as the development of manpower plans, and the acquisition of resources. It determines the course of action which the board is to take. Direction can be performed by both executive and non-executive directors. An executive director will be a full-time staff member, whose primary role is implementing policy. Non-executive directors are commonly involved with the company on a part time basis, brought in because of their experience and the ability to act objectively.

Management, carried out by executive directors, concerns the operations of the company on a daily basis and the detailed allocation of the company's resources. Implementation of decisions is usually immediate. This dichotomy between direction and management can create difficulties in handling the role of director, since the activities involved are very different in character. As a result some companies organise their boards into two parts, one, sometimes referred to as a management board which establishes objectives, devises policies, and carries out long term planning; the other which is responsible for interpreting the decisions of the management board and converting them into practicable tangible plans which can be carried out, and which it is responsible for executing. In this way, as long as the membership of the two boards is not shared by the same personnel (with the exception of the managing director who will normally serve on both) conflict of interest through duality of role can be avoided.

The powers of directors

In order to understand the significance of directors' powers we need to reflect on the way in which power is divided within a company. What this reveals is that there are two power bases in companies; the board of directors and the members in general meeting. There are certain things which can be lawfully done by a company in general meeting only, for example, alteration of the articles, and alteration to the objects clause. Moreover, it may be necessary under the Companies Act to secure the passing of a special resolution, requiring seventy five per cent support of the voting shareholders, in order to make certain decisions in general meeting; alteration of the articles and the objects clause are both examples.

Many other matters affecting companies are not required to be decided in general meeting, and can be dealt with by the board of directors as part of the ordinary day-to-day running of the business. It will be recalled that Table A gives directors the power to manage the business of the company and exercise all its powers, that is, carry out the activities expressly or implicitly contained in the objects clause, subject to any restrictions under the Act, the memorandum and articles. The members can also control the activities of the board through any directions issued to the board under the terms of any special resolution they pass. This power-sharing arrangement recognises that a balance must be struck between enabling the managers to manage effectively, whilst ensuring that ultimate control is vested in the proprietors of the organisation, the shareholders.

Despite the power-sharing structure which applies to registered companies, real power undoubtedly rests in the hands of the board, partly because of Table A which, as we have seen, grants the board wide management powers, but also because in companies with a large membership, the board members are in close and regular contact with each other. The shareholders are unlikely to maintain such contacts amongst themselves, thus reducing their effectiveness as decision-makers in general meeting. Indeed, in larger companies the management is so firmly placed in the hands of the directors, that the only occasion when members are likely to hear from them is when they receive notice of the Annual General Meeting. In such companies there is nothing artificial about the division of the power; it is an appropriate practical way of conducting business.

The duties of directors

In broad terms, the duties of a director are:

    (i)   fiduciary duties, arising as a result of the equitable view of directors as quasi-trustees;

    (ii) duties of care and skill, arising under the common law through the operation of the tort of negligence; and

    (iii) statutory duties, arising out of the provisions contained in the Companies Act 1985.

Fiduciary duties

The fiduciary duties owed by a director can be treated as coming under two headings; firstly the obligation to exercise powers in good faith and for the benefit of the company, and secondly, the obligation to avoid any conflict between their personal interests and those of the company, or as it is sometimes expressed, the duty not to make a secret profit.

Duties of care and skill

These are duties which arise from the obligation of a director not to act negligently in managing the company's affairs. The question is essentially that of identifying the standard of care and skill owed by the particular director towards his or her company. The leading case is that of *Re City Equitable Fire Insurance Co.* (1925). Here the company directors had delegated almost all responsibilities of management to the managing director. As a result, the directors failed to recognise a loss of over £1,200,000 from the company's funds, which was caused by the deliberate fraud of the managing director, described by the judge as, "a daring and unprincipled scoundrel". The loss was discovered in the course of the winding-up of the company, and the liquidator successfully sought to make all the other directors liable for negligence. Romer J. stated the following general propositions of law:

    (i)   a director need not show a greater degree of skill than may reasonably be expected of a person with his knowledge and experience;

    (ii) a director need not give continuous attention to the affairs of the company. He is not bound to attend all meetings of the board, although he ought to attend whenever he is reasonably able to do so;

    (iii) a director may delegate duties to other officials in the company and trust them to be performed properly so long as there is no reason to doubt or mistrust them.

The judge commented:

> *"It is indeed impossible to describe the duties of directors in general terms.... The position of a director of a company carrying on a small retail business is very different from that of a director of a railway company. The duties of a bank director may differ widely from those of an insurance director, and the duties of a director of an insurance company may differ from those of a director of another."*

It is clear, therefore, that the duties of care and skill owed to a company by its directors are of a variable kind. Much higher standards of expertise will be expected of directors who are employed in a professional capacity in executive posts, for example, finance and engineering directors, than of directors who neither have nor claim to have such professional expertise. Yet, even non-executive directors who have experience or qualifications in a field of relevance to the company's affairs may find that high objective standards appropriate to their specialist fields will be expected of them in law, despite their non-executive roles. This point emerged in the recent case of Dorchester Finance Co. Ltd. v. Stebbing 1989 where the company lost money as a result of the gross negligence of the actions of the company's one executive director. He failed to take out adequate securities on loans made by the company and the company subsequently found itself unable to recover the loans made. The two non-executive directors, who had little to do with the company, had signed cheques in blank at the request of the executive director. All three directors had considerable financial experience. The court held the two non-executive directors equally liable with the executive director in damages to the company.

Auditors

The auditing of company accounts is a process by which the company auditors carry out an annual investigation into the financial affairs of the company, so that they can confirm, primarily for the shareholder's benefit, that the company's books reflect the actual position of the company's finances.

Auditors are outside professionals who are engaged by companies.

All registered companies must appoint auditors, unless the company is a dormant one, that is a "small" company which has had no "significant accounting transaction" since the end of the previous financial year. Appointment is made at each general meeting at which accounts in respect of an accounting reference period are laid. It is thus the members who make the appointment.

It is clearly important that auditors be both independent from the company, and suitably qualified to perform their functions. Only a "registered auditor" can carry out company auditing work, and a registered auditor is someone who is regarded as qualified by the Chartered Institute of Accountants, the Chartered Association of Certified Accountants, or the Department of Trade and Industry as having the appropriate overseas or other professional qualifications. Education, training and other matters affecting the work of auditors have now been brought under general statutory control. Certain persons are not permitted to act as auditors:

  (a) an officer or servant of the company;

  (b) a person who is employed by or is the partner of an officer or servant of the company ("officer" includes any director or manager and the secretary);

  (c) officers and servants of the company's holding or subsidiary companies and their employees or partners;

  (d) a person who has a "connection" with the company (as defined in regulations).

The auditor's duties are to:

  (i) audit the company accounts; and

  (ii) report to the members of the company on the accounts.

The company secretary

All companies are legally obliged to appoint a company secretary. The company secretary's role is as chief administrative officer, although precisely what this role involves depends upon the size of the company. Lord Denning has referred to the company secretary as someone who "regularly makes representations on behalf of the company and enters into contracts on its behalf which come within the day to day running of the company's business", and is "entitled to sign contracts connected with the administrative side of the company's affairs".

As well as this administrative role as a representative and contract maker of the company, the secretary is also responsible for particular duties. These include:

(i)   keeping the statutory books of the company – the various registers such as the register of members as well as the general minute book of the company and the minute book of directors' meetings;

(ii) keeping secure the company seal and its papers (for example the memorandum and articles);

(iii) arranging company and directors 'meetings and keeping the minutes of such meetings; and

(iv) sending the various returns that by law must be delivered to the Registrar of Companies, for example, the annual financial return.

Like directors, company secretaries also owe a general fiduciary duty to the company.

Managers

We have seen that in a company its most senior managers are its directors. Executive directors often represent the different functional departments of the organisation. Below them in the organisation hierarchy are the middle and junior managers. Whatever the area of functional responsibility handled by a manager, it is the tier to which they have been appointed that will determine their roles and responsibilities. Here we select one example to examine, the personnel manager.

A personnel manager is concerned principally with maintaining the physical well being of the workforce so that it is able to perform to maximum efficiency. Functional responsibilities will usually cover the following areas:

(i)   employment matters, including recruitment, selection, promotions, transfers and dismissals;

(ii) education and training;

(iii) wages and salaries issues, such as pay policies, job analysis and evaluations;

(iv) industrial relations;

(v)   health and safety; and

(vi) staff welfare, for instance employment services and social facilities

A personnel manager who is not already a member of the board will be accountable to it, and will commonly be directly accountable to the managing director. Often such a manager will not have the power to take on or dismiss staff, or decide on rates of pay, without obtaining the prior approval of a relevant senior executive, such as the personnel director, or the managing director. The personnel manager will be the line manager with authority over specialised functions which fall within his or her area of responsibility, for example a training department.

The kinds of attributes required of a good personnel manager are a sound understanding of how people behave in a social and psychological sense, the ability to make accurate judgements about character, to be firm but fair, and be patient and impartial. Obviously as for any manager, an understanding of organisations is a very valuable attribute also.

Team members

In an organisation employees rarely work autonomously. Usually they work together as teams. Sometimes these teams will be formally created, for instance when particular staff are selected by a manager to carry out a specific project or task collectively. Often however, teams emerge spontaneously, through the coming together of like minded colleagues who share similar interests in sport, or laugh about the same things. A team is simply a group working collectively to achieve a common objective. The objective may be externally set by a superior, or internally generated by the group itself.

In an organisational context, when the objective of the group becomes accepted as the personal objective of each team member, then the team is well on the way towards efficient operation. But this coincidence of objectives still requires a structure, a set of terms of reference, by which the group is organised. There will usually need to be some form of internal authority for example, and a clear understanding of the part each team member is to play in the collective activity.

Organisations are made up of teams. Indeed it has been remarked elsewhere in this book that an organisation can itself be regarded as a group. It is not unusual to find job specifications stating that the ability to work as a member of a team is essential. It may of course be more difficult to establish how well a prospective employee is likely to perform as a team member if appointed. You may find it useful to reflect on your own experience, past and present, of organisations you know, considering them from the perspective of the team approach to working. Look at job advertisements to see how often the expression 'team' appears. Bear in mind that being an effective team member requires a variety of inter-personal skills. Such skills may be developed by training programmes offered by the employer, through team building activities. Perhaps you are aware of the more radical approaches to encouraging the team spirit taken by some organisations, who require their managers to attend activity centres and engage in strenuous physical and mental tasks to develop their team spirit.

Activity

Using local and/or national newspapers compile a file of material illustrating the way in which corporate advertisements for staff describe and define the work roles business organisations seek to fulfil. Try to obtain a range of material spanning the organisational hierarchy, from senior management posts through to posts at the bottom of the organisational pyramid.

Assignment *Owen Print Ltd.*

Owen Print Ltd. is a private limited company employing over 150 staff spread across six departments; Sales and Administration, Finance, General Office, Production, Technical and Despatch. The company is an old family business that has rapidly expanded its production over the past five years. It is operated from two sites in the market town of Hereford. The main site houses the production, technical and despatch departments. A new building, first used four years ago when expansion forced the company to increase its accommodation, houses the other three departments.

As a family business the company is run on rather old fashioned lines. It is autocratic. Of the four directors three are members of the family. The Chairman and Managing Director is Cecil Owen; his son Colin and daughter Madelaine are also directors, and Barry Grant, who is not a member of the family, is the remaining director. Cecil Owen still sees the company as it used to be many years ago; a small business in which everybody knew each other and he knew exactly what was going on everywhere within the company. He is still referred to by older employees as the 'gaffer', and if they have problems Cecil Owen is always willing to hear them. But he is not a man who likes labels for people, and most employees have no formal job descriptions. Nor does the company have any formally stated aims and objectives other than those contained in its Memorandum of Association.

Barry Grant, as well as being director, is also Company Secretary and in overall charge of the Sales and Administration Department, Finance and the General Office.

Recently Mr. Grant has become increasingly anxious about the lack of any clear organisations structure, and the difficulty of establishing precisely who does what in the company, and where power lies. He has identified that:

- new and existing staff are often unclear about their role within the company;
- no single individual has responsibility for personnel matters;
- the physical and organisational structure of the company is not conducive to effective communication;

Task

1. You are an employee of the company directly responsible to Barry Grant. You have been asked to produce an informal report for Mr. Grant that he can present to the next meeting of the Board of Directors. In the report you should take each of the points raised by Mr. Grant and indicate:

    - Why it appears that the problem exists?
    - Why it represents an unsatisfactory position for the companys? and
    - How the situation might best be overcome?

Development Task

1. Draw up a draft job description for a post as personnel manager in a small but expanding business like Owen Print. The description should take account of both the general responsibilities of a manager and the specific responsibilities associated with the personnel function.

Element 4.3 Job Applications and Interviews

Earlier in this Unit we noted that the recruitment of staff is an extremely important function for any organisation. In this element, therefore, we shall examine in some detail the procedures that an organisation should follow when seeking to recruit new staff and the legal and ethical obligations which are involved in the recruitment process. We shall also look at the process from the view-point of the person who is to be interviewed, the potential employee. This will be important to you because at some time in the future you will be apply for a job and knowing what to expect and how to act will improve your prospects of success.

Recruitment and Selection

All organisations should be efficient and effective in recruitment and selection of the personnel needed for the future of the organisation. Let us begin by considering what we mean by each term.

- *Recruitment* can be seen as the first step in filling a vacancy. It involves examining the job to be done, where the best candidates are likely to be found and how best to make contact and attract them.
- *Selection* is the next process where various means are employed to choose the most suitable candidate, in particular the selection interview, which should be prepared for both by the employer and the candidate!

Recruitment

In small organisations, recruitment is often the responsibility of the departmental manager. In larger organisations the responsibility will fall to the the personnel department to make all the necessary arrangements within organisational policies. For important posts some organisations will even use the services of recruitment and selection consultants.

The recruitment process

A systematic approach to recruitment involves the following stages:

- manpower planning;
- job analysis;
- job evaluation;
- attracting a field of candidates;
- interviewing;
- selection;

Manpower planning

The purpose of manpower planning is:

- to estimate the demand for each grade and skill of employee (or new job);
- to estimate the supply of labour available to the organisation;
- where there are differences between supply and demand to take steps to either reduce demand or increase supply.

We have already examined the process of manpower planning in some detail in Element 4.1.

Job analysis

There are three parts to job analysis:

- a job description
- a job specification
- a personnel specification

A job description

This is a statement of the tasks, duties, objectives and standards attached to the job.

Job descriptions are in fairly common usage, though their layout can vary. A typical layout is shown below.

BLUE PRINT GRAPHIC DESIGN

Department:	Design
Post:	Senior Designer
Grade	Grade V
Accountable to:	Chief Design Engineer
Responsibilities:	General design work for various projects/products
Main duties:	

to prepare accurate designs for ....
to liase with ....
to prepare variations on ....
to prepare estimated costing's for new designs to review....
to be responsible for the supervision of junior staff...

A job specification

This is the production of a detailed specification of the skills, knowledge and qualities needed to perform the job. Social and physical environmental matters maybe included.

A personnel specification

This is a rewording of the job specification in terms of the kind of person needed to perform the job.

These three components represent an 'ideal' and often you will find that the term *job description* is used loosely to describe all three components. Despite the usefulness of this comprehensive approach, such a process takes skill and time and in small organisations the needs of a job can be assessed from experience and without any elaborate analysis on paper or standard forms.

Job evaluation

Job evaluation is concerned with comparing one job with others and finding a suitable grade or salary for the job. Elaborate systems involving the allocation of points are quite widely used. Another method is the design of a grading scheme into which all jobs can be slotted. The Institute of Administrative Management (IAM) suggests the following grading scheme for office jobs:

- *Grade I* – routine, unskilled work requiring little or no training and carried out under close supervision;

- *Grade II* – supervisor work requiring basic mechanical skills or clerical work requiring some aptitude;
- *Grade III* – skilled work requiring a longer period of training/experience and some degree of responsibility/initiative;
- *Grade IV* – responsibility for a group or work requiring semi-professional training;
- *Grade V* – responsibility for a department or complex work requiring specialist or professional training;
- *Grade VI* – control of a wide range of people and activities requiring experience and specialist training/qualifications.

We need to exercise some care with these 'scientific' approaches to grading and payment. Whilst they provide a useful framework there are still large areas which involve subjective judgements to arrive at a decision. Take for example, Grade V of the IAM gradings. How should one define '*complex*' work? Similarly these schemes do not decide the salary or structure in terms of actual salaries nor the differences between grades. Also there is the frequent problem of the market; supply and demand factors which force employers to pay salaries which contradict the general job evaluation scheme.

Attracting a field of candidates

There are various practices and methods used to attract candidates. Many organisations advertise internally and/or externally depending upon the job on offer and on the policy of the organisation. Balancing the need to reward internally by promotion, with the need for new ideas and new approaches from outside appointments, is an area of management needing considerable care.

Internal advertising

There are various methods of internal advertising for jobs. The commonest are staff bulletins, notice boards, and sending copies of advertisements to each section/department.

External advertising

Various ways of advertising externally are:

- *The local and national press*. Advertising in national papers is expensive, but for senior jobs, where the widest possible field is required, the cost is justified by alerting a very wide market to the available post;
- *Specialist journals – trade and professional*. These two methods are frequently used because the press and journals have expert staff who assist advertisers with layout. They also have a known market of readers;
- *Recruitment agencies and consultants*. This method has increased in recent years, demonstrating the willingness of organisations to use the specialist services available from these agencies. They have lead to the use of the expression '*head hunting*' when an organisation is looking for a particularly important post to be filled;
- *Schools, colleges and universities*. This source of candidates can be tapped either by printed material or by visits to give talks and create a favourable image, or by specific recruitment visits. Increasingly the educational institutions tend to organise career conventions as a means by which potential candidates and employers can meet. Many employers have professionally designed and highly transportable displays which can be taken to any organised convention. Such displays are also used within the company for various image purposes such as visits to the work place by organised groups.

- *Local shops and personal contact.* Many small organisations will rely upon advertisements in local shops or simply word of mouth to fill vacancies. Many part-time jobs are also filled in this way.

- *Department of Employment* agencies. *The D of E assists employers to find suitable candidates through various schemes. A common method is the Job Centre where advertisements are on post cards in racks with further details and help available from officials.*

Selection

Interviewing

How an organisation decides to organise its selection procedures often depends on the number of applicants it has received. Suppose one hundred applications are received for one job, then the organisation has to go through the process of matching applications to the job to reduce the number to produce a short-list of those who will be interviewed. Short-lists vary but a typical short-list would include five or six applicants. If sorting applicants through this procedure of matching applicants to jobs still indicates fifty suitable candidates, then some other filtering and elimination process is required. All suitable candidates could be invited to a pre-selection interview or test situation in order to whittle down the candidates, who will then be further interviewed to determine who will be offered the job.

The other possibility is that the organisation faces a shortage of applicants. Suppose for a very senior post in your organisation, which had been nationally advertised, there was only one applicant. What kind of questions would you wish to ask regarding the cause of the poor demand? A frequent response would be to advertise again. Consider how many people may not see an advertisement for a post which appears perhaps only once. Inevitably questions about the job, the salary, the organisation, and the supply of certain skills will need to be considered when responses to advertisements are very low. However, let us suppose we have a short-list of six candidates for a job and we are proceeding to hold interviews. The process involves five phases:

Arranging the interview

The arrangements will include:

- agreeing the composition and size of the panel;
- agreeing a date for the selection interviews;
- seeking responses from referees;
- inviting short listed candidates to the interview and specifying date, time, place and any other details and asking if it is their intention to be present; and arranging a room and other facilities for the interview for example, refreshments.

The interview

Interviews are perceived differently by interviewers and interviewees. We will consider the skills required by the interviewee later in this section and concentrate on the role of the interviewer for the moment.

Many interviewers are not formally trained in effective interviewing, but are expected to have developed such skills as part of their career progression. The importance of the interviewer managing the interview efficiently cannot be overstated as the face-to-face interview is still the most commonly used method of selecting new recruits. If you adopt an inappropriate style as an interviewer then it could result in your organisation employing a candidate who is not the best suited for the post in question.

Candidates attending for interview will naturally be nervous and anxious, some will be highly stressed. As the interview is to some extent a 'false' situation, in that all the participants will be playing specific roles which may not be a true reflection of their typical behaviour, it is important for the interviewer to carefully organise the interview process so that an accurate assessment can be made of each candidate.

Interviewers should:

- be familiar with the job description/specification;
- study the application forms together with references;
- decide a strategy for the interview, for example, is it to be highly structured and formal with a list of specific questions or more informal and interactive between applicant and the panel? How will a decision be made, by a discussion to arrive at consensus or by a ballot?;
- if specific questions are to be asked, these will need to be typed, and may be given to the candidates a few minutes before the interview;
- candidates should be welcomed and the interview procedure explained;
- the panel should be introduced indicating who they are and their roles;
- questions should be clearly phrased so that they are unambiguous and easily understood, and designed to draw out the qualities of the candidate. If candidates struggle to answer a question, they should be allowed time to think of a response before probing more deeply.
- responses should be listened to carefully and any questions arising or any points to be later considered should be noted as unobtrusively as possible until the interview is finished, then any more detailed notes or observations can be made to help towards the decision on appointment;
- questions should aim to discover facts, experience, qualifications and so on. Questions can also discover attitudes, values, opinions on specific issues related to the job, the organisation or the industry. Equally they can be directed towards values and views related to life, the economy, social change or whatever;
- candidates should be invited to ask any questions about the job and the organisation;
- the interview should finish appropriately by thanking the candidate and explaining subsequent procedure. For example, it might be explained that a decision will be made that day and candidates should wait, or that a decision will be made in a few days and the notification will be made by telephone or letter.

After the interview

- communicate the decision to the successful and unsuccessful candidates, either face to face if they have waited, or in writing and/or by telephone otherwise;
- if face to face the successful candidate is normally invited back into the interview room to receive the offer and to arrange any further details including starting date;
- arrange any necessary medical clearance or other clearance necessary for the job (for example, verification of certain qualifications);
- prepare a contract of employment and initiate a personnel file in order to bring the new employee onto the payroll and onto other records.

Selection decisions

Although we have mentioned the actual selection within the previous sections, it is worth remembering that a decision has to be made to select the one candidate for the one job.

How is the selection made? Apart from liking the candidate or being guided by intuition, there are some more scientific approaches available which reflect the job description and personal specification referred to earlier.

The factors usually included in a plan to assess candidates are:

- physical attributes (appearance, speech etc.);
- educational attainment;
- special aptitudes;
- disposition (e.g. friendly);
- background and motivation.

Jobs and organisations vary so much that it is impossible to suggest that these factors are always used. What is important is that a systematic approach is better than an intuitive haphazard approach to the selection of staff.

Employment

Arrangements to commence employment are the final phase in the recruitment process. Yet in many ways it is the beginning of a new relationship and hence the importance of an induction process.

Having looked at the recruitment and selection procedures from the point of view of the company attempting to recruit, we shall now consider the applicant's role in the selection process.

Interview skills

Interview situations require the applicant to show highly developed personal skills, no matter whether it be an interview for a job or an appraisal interview with a colleague. In this section we will concentrate on the first of these, discussing how to improve the likelihood of being called for interview by writing an effective application form or curriculum vitae and then we shall consider how to handle the interview situation itself.

Making an application

We all at some stage in our careers have to make some form of application, whether it be for a new post, a training course, to join a club or society, or to enter college. Making an application requires careful thought as frequently there are no second chances if the first application does not result in being invited for interview. Applications can be made in two main ways:

- using a standard application form;
- or by sending a curriculum vitae.

Application forms

Before even starting to think about completing an application form, the applicant must appreciate that its purpose is to convince the recruiter that his/her application is the ideal one for the vacancy. There is usually only one opportunity to apply for a particular job. A successful applicant will have assessed the main requirements of the post and tailored the application to reflect these requirements.

We mentioned earlier that the recruiter will have prepared certain criteria which he envisages the eventual successful candidate to meet. Thus, before completing the application forms the candidate must 'read between the lines' of the advertised vacancy and draw a profile of the applicant that the recruiter is looking for. The next step is to determine whether you, as an applicant match the recruiter's desired profile. If you think that your profile does match that which the recruiter is looking for, then complete the application form. Should you meet most, but not all of the recruiter's criteria, however, then you should still apply as it is very unlikely that the 'ideal' candidate will exist.

Completing the application form

Once you have established that your profile is suitable for the vacancy then you must set about completing the application form, but before completing the application form, you should note certain guidelines:

- you should answer all questions in rough before writing on the actual application form. Give a great deal of thought to answering each question;
- check all your spellings and your grammar carefully for errors on the rough copy;
- always use black ink for writing - forms are photo-copied and black ink will print out best.

Application forms tend to be broken down into various sections reflecting the stages of the profile set by the recruiter. Each section of the application form will provide the recruiter with further insights into each applicant's profile. A number of sections are common to most application forms:

- *Personal details*. Name, address, telephone number, vacancy applied for, qualifications etc.
  This section might appear relatively straightforward to complete, but pay attention to make sure that you answer completely and legibly. This will be the first part of the form that the recruiter reads, so it is vital to make a favourable first impression. When detailing your qualifications, consider the nature of the vacancy. Can you use any projects that you have completed or options that you have studied at school or college to illustrate a special skill or competence that you have which the recruiter might look favourably upon?

- *Skills questions*. Can you speak languages, use a computer, drive etc.?
  Skills are important to recruiters and if you are competent in them, then emphasise this. Take care to indicate that the skills you possess will help you do the job better, rather having the organisation thinking that you are applying for the post simply because you want to use your particular skills.

- *Achievements*. Successes, accomplishments, assignments completed etc.
  The majority of people have achieved something in their lives and it is important to show this on the application form. To answer this question you need to list down all the achievements that you consider to have been important to your own personal development in your business, college, or social life. You could mention a great variety of achievements: work experiences, examination successes, leading groups in leisure time, being a member of a successful activity, overseas travel, or sporting achievements. In mentioning your achievements, however, show what you have gained from them and what new skills you have developed as a result. This will show that you have an interest in your own development. The space on the application form may dictate how many achievements you can mention and the detail that you can provide for the recruiter.

- *Proof questions*. Asking for evidence about work experience, training.
  There will be questions on the application form asking for details of previous work experience, training and education - 'proof questions' - requesting evidence that shows you have the experience and qualifications for the vacancy. Your answers to these questions should be factual, giving dates, the name of the organisation where you gained the experience, and the position you held, placing stress on the successes you have achieved.
  Part-time jobs can impress the recruiter, especially when you highlight the special responsibilities of the job, or you mention the skills that you developed.
  If you have had a certain job or activity which was very interesting or especially relevant

to the application, then you should elaborate further to explain its relevance. An example is given below:

EASTERN TOURS LTD., NORTHSEA, 1992- 93 (summer season)
Tour operator's representative on coach tours to Europe
'This post has been of great benefit as it involved working in foreign counties making sure that the tour clients gained maximum satisfaction from their holidays. All client and company difficulties that were encountered had to be overcome, often involving great use of tact, initiative and interpersonal skills.'

- *The crucial question.* There often tends to be an open-ended question(s) on application forms to which much importance is attached by the recruiter. Answers to these questions are frequently decisive:

  - *'Why have you applied for this post?';*

  - *'Why do you think you will succeed if you are appointed?';*

  - *'Explain how your background will assist you if you are offered a post with this organisation?';*

  - *'Successful managers are able leaders, effective problem solvers and competent decision takers. Can you provide any evidence that shows you possess these qualities?'*

To answer these questions competently you will have to have a clear understanding of:

- what the post applied for entails;

- the skills and competencies you can offer that match the recruiter's requirements;

- why you wish to be successful in obtaining the post.

Before answering this type of question, it is important that you know as much as possible about all these three areas. You should also ask yourself why this question is being asked, what is its purpose, and what will it tell the recruiter about me.

When answering this type of question, you need to show how your qualities and experience fit the needs of the organisation. If you concentrate on your needs and wants and what you expect from the position, then your application will probably be unsuccessful. You should whet the recruiter's appetite when reading the response to this question, and include points that you can elaborate on in the interview.

- *Referees.* You need to select your referees with care. They should be people who know you well and hold respected positions in the community. You have to obtain their consent before they are mentioned as referees. It will be useful if the referee knows why you are seeking the position and what qualities and strengths you have that makes you a suitable candidate.

- *Concluding comments.* Before finally committing the rough draft to the application form, you should ask yourself a few final questions:

  - have all the questions on the application form been answered ?;

  - have any time periods in your career been left unexplained?;

  - do the answers given actually address the questions asked?;

  - has your tone in answering the questions been positive and is the style of presentation appropriate?;

  - Will the recruiter gain a favourable impression of you as a result of reading the application form?

And before you post the form to the recruiter:

- are any additional items to be included with the application form e.g. examination certificates, photograph etc.?

If you bear in mind all of the above points then your chance of being invited for interview will be much improved. Some organisations, though, will not ask you for an application form, but will wish to see your curriculum vitae (C.V.).

The Curriculum Vitae

A C.V. is another means of communicating with the recruiter, and as with application forms, attention should be given to its design and submission. Normally a C.V. should not be used where the recruiter issues an application form. Use a C.V. when, for example, the advertised vacancy says:

> *'send full details to...'*

or simply asks for a C.V. If you are making a speculative application, however, a C.V. with a covering letter is essential.

The purpose of the C.V.

In Latin *curriculum vitae* means 'course of life' and as such should chart your progress in career, educational, and social terms. The purpose of a C.V. is to summarise personal details and experience. Whereas application forms are structured with questions and spaces for replies, a C.V. can be designed to personal taste. A C.V, therefore, should include information that will be of relevance to the recruiter. Thus, each C.V. that is produced has to be tailored for the specific requirements of each position to which it applies. A standard, 'mass-produced' C.V. is not the most effective means of presenting yourself for a specific job.

The style of your C.V.

An important point about the style of any C.V. is that it should be easy to read. In addition it should be concise, using brief, clear statements. Your C.V. will have a stronger impact if actual facts or figures are included, such as grades achieved in examinations, and successes that you have enjoyed at work, for example increasing sales turnover by 100% in 12 months. There is normally no need, however, for sentences to be used as a note-format will suffice.

You should use certain key verbs, such as:

> *achieved, contributed, created, developed, established, implemented,*
> *initiated, mediated, motivated, negotiated, organised, persuaded, planned, supported,*
> *tested, wrote.*

When applying for posts which demand creativity, use a creative approach in designing the C.V., for example writing it as if it were a press release that gives your details. Alternatively, you could provide an additional 'fact file' that includes further details and examples of your creative work. You will need to give this approach careful consideration and attention to detail. If you are sending a fact file it must encourage the selector to read it rather than file it in the waste paper bin.

The content of the C.V.

As indicated above, the content of your C.V. will depend upon the position you are applying for. A C.V. to impress an advertising agency will be of a different style and content to that intended to impress an accountant.

Your C.V. though, has to provide the recruiter with a picture of your accomplishments and experiences, as well as your potential capabilities. When you write your C.V. however, while you must use facts, adopt a style that allows the recruiter to make favourable assumptions about you.

Once you have decided on the style and content of your C.V. you need to follow a number of guidelines: You should produce an initial first draft and check the following points:

- the length of your C.V. should not normally exceed two A4 side - the C.V. is a summary, not a full-blown report. The recruiter will receive many C.V.s and needs to be able to read through them quickly, gaining an initial first impression of the applicant's suitability;
- the various sections of the C.V. should be well spaced out with ample margins all round. A tightly packed C.V. will be difficult to read and digest;
- your style of writing should be 'snappy' using verbs that suggest dynamism. If you use sentences, these should be short and to the point. Just include facts;
- the tone of your C.V. should be positive and optimistic creating a strong and favourable image.

Ask another person to read through your C.V. to confirm its appropriateness, and to make sure it creates the intended impact. The next stage is to:

- have the C.V. professionally typed on high quality paper;
- post the C.V. with a covering letter;
- keep a copy of the C.V. and read it before the interview.

As with application forms, your immediate objective in using a C.V. is to obtain an interview. The golden rule for achieving this is to relate any skills and accomplishments to the recruiter's needs. To support your C.V. and to encourage the recruiter to read it, you will also have to write a covering letter. On the next two pages we show examples of a typical covering letter and a C.V.

Covering letters

A covering letter must always accompany a C.V. Sometimes it is also wise to include one when sending an application form, especially when you have had limited previous correspondence with the organisation to which you are applying. The purpose of the covering letter is to introduce you to the recruiter and to encourage the latter to read your attached C.V. or application form. As such, you must give considerable thought and attention to writing the covering letter to ensure that it encourages the recruiter to read your C.V. It is a vital component of the selection process.

Writing a covering letter

Covering letters should be brief, not exceeding one A4 side of high quality paper. If you have neat hand writing then there is nothing wrong with a hand written covering letter, supported by a typed C.V. However, if your handwriting is illegible then you should have the covering letter typed. You should always follow proper letter writing conventions. However, you need to bear a number of additional guidelines in mind:

- always write a rough draft before producing the actual letter;
- you should explicitly state the post that you are applying for, along with any reference numbers quoted in the advertisement;
- indicate where you saw the advertised vacancy, or how you heard the details about it, or why you are making a speculative application;
- stress the factors relevant to the application such as your previous work experience, skills, knowledge, interests, aptitudes etc.;
- include any relevant information that is not given in your C.V., such as your motivation for applying;

POSITIONS OF RESPONSIBILITY

School: Head of House - organising the prefects and motivating the children.
Hockey Captain - arranging fixtures, planning a tour, liaising with teachers
University: Treasurer of the Nomadics Walking Society - collecting expedition funds, maintaining accounts, presenting the accounts AGM

WORK EXPERIENCE

Summer 1990 - NBC Advertising Agency, London - work responsibility for 5 accounts, liaising with the client and buying media space.
Summer 1991 - Procterlever Household Division - work placement, sales rep., servicing existing accounts and prospecting for new ones. Increased sales in the territory by 30% in 3 months

OTHER SKILLS/HOBBIES

Full driving licence, overseas expeditions, jazz music, Shakespeare

CURRICULUM VITAE

PERSONAL DETAILS

Name:	WILLIAMS, Anne, Alison
Date of Birth:	23rd January 1971
Nationality:	British
Home Address:	14, Woolcot Terrace, Northsea, NE45 9TH
Tel:	0909 767831
Term Address:	Flat G, College Halls of Residence, Wall Steet, Southwall, SO6 5RF

EDUCATION and QUALIFICATIONS

1982 - 1989 Trinity School, Northsea

1987 GCSE's: English Literature (A)
History (A)
Mathematics (A)
English Language (B)
Geography (B)
French (B)
Physics (C)

1989 `A` Levels: English Literature (A)
History (B)
Geography (C)

1989 - date Southwall University
BA (Hons) Business Studies
Sandwich degree

Marketing Management
Market Research
Quantitive Methods
Buyer Behaviour

Final Year Project: "The Effectiveness of Advertising Expenditure for Tour Operators"

Flat G College Halls of Residence,
Wall Street,
Southwall,
SO6 5RF.
02/12/93

Ms W J Wilkes
Personnel Director
Gamble UK LTD.
33, Western Road
Westcliffe
WE24 9UH

Dear Ms Wilkes,

Marketing Assistant, Post MA24

I read with interest the above career vacancy that was advertised in 'Marketing', 29 November, and would like to be considered for the post. Please find enclosed my Curriculum Vitae.

As you will see from my C.V., I am in my final year at University reading for a Business Studies degree, specialising in the Marketing Option. The work placements that are integral parts of the degree have enabled me to gain valuable experience of two important activities of the Marketing Department - advertising and selling. The successes I achieved on placement, plus my studies at university, have given me a clear understanding of Marketing and its relevance to business. These experiences have also shown me the importance of marketing people developing effective transferable personnel skills.

The positions of responsibility that I have held at school and university have further developed these skills. I work well with others, am capable of leading others and taking decisions. Being treasurer of the Nomadic Society has shown me the importance of administrative skills and communication skills.

The market your company operates in appeals to me because it is involved with marketing fast-moving-consumer-goods. The work experiences I have already enjoyed have been in this sector, and will enable me to make an effective and rapid contribution as a Marketing Assistant to the Detergent's Product Manager, using my planning and analytical skills.

I am free to travel to Westcliffe at any time during December or January. I look forward to hearing from you in the near future.

Yours sincerely,

Anne Williams (Miss)

- inform the recruiter of convenient interview dates and any dates when you will not be available for interview.

As we discussed at the beginning of this section, making applications is important. Normally, you will have only one opportunity available to be called for interview. If your application form is poorly completed, if your C.V. is ill-conceived and your covering letter unstimulating, then it is unlikely that you will be called for interview. If you do pay careful attention to succeeding at the pre-selection stage however, you could well be rewarded by being offered an interview.

Activity

Search through the recruitment section of your local newspapers and identify a job for which you are or will be potentially qualified. Draft your own curriculum vitae and a covering letter which you could send in support of a job application for the post.

Succeeding at the interview

When applying for a career vacancy there are a number of steps that have to be followed for the interview to be a success.

Preparing for the interview

To walk into an interview ill-prepared is foolish. You have to carry out research beforehand into a number of areas:

- *The recruiter's business* - what is the nature of the organisation, its markets and products, who are the consumers and competitors, what position does the recruiting organisation hold in the market place. This information can be found from company reports, press articles, and informal discussions with other employees of the firm;
- *The responsibilities involved in the job* - what will be expected of you, where will you fit into the organisation. It is very helpful to have had a discussion with the person for whom you will directly be working prior to the interview. By contacting this person before the interview you will be showing that you are keen to be selected for the vacancy.

You need to collect as much background material as possible. You will also have to review:

- why you have applied for the post, your motivations and ambitions, where the post fits into the logic of your career development;
- why you will find the job interesting;
- the skills you will be able to offer the employer;
- previous achievements that you have which will be relevant.

You should prepare questions to ask at the interview. The clothes that you are to wear for the interview will require preparation - do they need dry cleaning, should you wear a new pair of shoes, what about your hair style, what will be appropriate for the interview, do you have to conform to certain standards of appearance and dress or will a more individualistic style be appropriate? Your appearance and grooming are most important as they help to create that vital first impression that the interviewer will gain of you.

If possible find the location of the interview in advance, as well as how to get there. Allow sufficient time for the journey so that unforeseen problems and delays do not lead you to being late for the interview.

The night before the interview have a 'test-run' with a friend of the likely questions that you might be asked.

On arrival

You should plan to arrive before the interview is scheduled to start. This will allow you time to gather your thoughts and calm your nerves.

The interview

When you are invited into the interview room enter confidently and with a smile. Greet the interviewer, or the chairperson if it is a panel interview, with:

> *"Good morning/afternoon Mr./Mrs .... Pleased to meet you. My name is..."*

give a firm handshake, smile and make eye contact. When you are asked to sit down, sit up straight, making sure that you maintain eye contact with the interviewer.

The interviewer will then take control by outlining how the interview is to be organised. Then the questioning will commence. If your research and preparation have been thorough, then a number of the questions will come as no surprise, such as:

> *"Why are you applying to this organisation?"*
>
> *"Why did you choose that particular course to study?"*
>
> *"What other organisations have you applied to?"*
>
> *"Where do you see yourself in five years time?"*
>
> *"What do you know about....(a technical point)....?"*
>
> *"How would you define......(a technical term).....?"*
>
> *"What skills or qualities do you possess that make you a suitable candidate?"*
>
> *"What do you know about our business?"*
>
> *"Who do you see as our main competitors?"*
>
> *"What would you say are the main difficulties facing us?"*
>
> *"What has been your greatest achievement?"*
>
> *"What are your weaknesses?"*
>
> *"How do your friends perceive you?"*

When answering questions you need to remember a number of points:

- always look at the interviewer and other members of the panel;
- use effective verbal and non-verbal communication skills - don't fidget, avoid distracting mannerisms, control your facial expressions, use appropriate gestures, try to hide your nervousness by controlling your voice and speaking with varied tones and pitch, and different speeds of speech. Use pauses in speech to stress important points;
- always be positive and optimistic when you are replying to questions, look for opportunities to highlight your achievements, turn unsuccessful elements in your career to date into successes;
- never be derogatory, cynical, facetious, or sarcastic. Use humour to show the warmth of your character and personality;
- be honest, don't invent answers. If you cannot answer a question say so - this will earn more respect from the interviewer than a garbled invention;
- answer the question that is posed, not the one that you wish you had been asked. Recognise those questions requiring brief answers and those intended to produce a more in-depth response. Don't use one-word answers, always elaborate;

- if you do not understand a question, ask for it to be repeated.

One purpose of the interview is to allow you to communicate with the interviewer using your well-developed verbal and non-verbal communication skills. In addition, the interviewer will be seeking to establish your intellectual skills and so a problem may be set, or specific situations put before you to solve:

> *"Sales of our product have been declining, what would you do?"*
> *"How would you motivate other people who are working with you?"*
>
> *"The quality of the products produced fluctuates greatly, how can this be overcome?"*

These problems are not posed to test your in-depth knowledge of the given situation, but to establish whether you can think logically and solve problems in a structured way.

When the interviewer's questioning has finished you will be given the opportunity ask questions. Valid questions which you could ask are those relating to:

- the job, the organisation, its employees, products and processes;
- future career prospects;
- additional staff development and training which you might receive.

You should ask only three or four questions at most, after which the interviewer will conclude the session by thanking you for attending and informing you of the next stage in the selection process. End the interview on a positive note with a smile and a handshake - remember to smile even if you think the interview has not gone terribly well. Thank the interviewer for the opportunity to discuss your application in more detail, and then walk out of the room in a confident and purposeful manner. Your hard work does not end here as there are follow-up procedures to complete.

After the interview

You should make notes as soon after the interview as possible on the questions that were asked and the responses that you gave. This will be useful to you if you are offered a second interview, and will help you to think of more effective ways of answering such questions. Spend time on analysing where your weaknesses were shown and think about how you might improve them.

The first interview will probably be used by the recruiter as a means of drawing up a short list of candidates for the second, and final, interview - your last hurdle before they offer you the job.

The second interview

The purpose of the second interview is for the recruiting organisation to come to a final decision as to who the successful applicant will be. The first interview will have been a further screening process, rejecting those applicants thought to be incompatible with the organisation's needs. The second interview will establish from the short list of applicants which one has the skills, qualities, experience and potential to succeed in the vacant post.

In preparing for the second interview you should follow similar steps as you did for the first. The main difference between the two interviews will be the way they are organised. Second interviews are frequently spread over a two day period and include a variety of activities.

The night before

Second interviews for more senior posts frequently commence the 'night before' where the candidates are invited to dine with senior managers from the recruiting organisation. Recently recruited employees may also be present. It will probably be stated that the evening session is to be informal, but the senior managers and other employees will be observing your social behaviour which may be fed back to the interviewers (if they are not present). Thus, you will need to display personal skills of a high standard to ensure that another favourable first impression is created:

- you will have to display the appropriate etiquette - the hosts will be observing how you cope with such situations, and evaluating the image you will portray when you work for the organisation;

- you should be careful about your verbal and non-verbal behaviour so that the observers develop a favourable impression;

- you should prepare intelligent questions and topics for conversation beforehand as this will show an interest in the organisation and its work;

During the evening it may be possible to steer the conversation around to the proceedings of the next day. You do this sensitively in order to find out a bit more about how the day will be organised and the skills and competencies that the interviewers will be looking for.

The next day

The format of the interview day will vary according to the interviewing practice of the recruiting organisation, and as we have already stated you should, if possible, try and find the likely format beforehand. The organisation could provide a variety of activities for the candidates:

- interviews by different people, with different numbers of people on each panel, each with a different objective;

- written and scientific tests, such as psychometric tests, to determine the mental agility of the candidates, their aptitudes, and suitability for the work in question;

- 'in-tray' exercises, a type of situational analysis, where certain tasks or problems relevant to the vacancy have to be completed in a certain period of time;

- group exercises where a problem has to be solved by the candidates working as a team. This identifies those with leadership skills, those who can work effectively with others as well as each individual's intellectual skills;

- case studies which are completed individually, to establish the knowledge and understanding of the candidates, and their ability to analyse, synthesise, and evaluate a problem, before taking a decision;

- formal presentations which are either spontaneous, for example having to speak for three minutes on a particular unknown topic or on a topic chosen by you;

- group discussions to determine the ability of the candidates to develop persuasive arguments and to defend their views when questioned by others.

Clearly, you must obtain as much information beforehand about the type of tests you are likely to encounter and you should endeavour to practise the skills involved. You should prepare thoroughly before the second interview. You should plan a short presentation on a 'topic of your choice'. Try, however, to chose an interesting or slightly different topic that highlights a particular element of your character, your leadership skills for example. Plan such a presentation so that it appears well-structured and organised - the interviewers will be looking for this.

If you are involved in group discussions, ensure that you make a contribution, rather than sitting back and saying nothing. The interviewers will be looking for your ability to relate to others. Take care, though, to ensure that you do not dominate the discussion to the extent that you appear to be insensitive to the views of others. You should accept and acknowledge the views of others, and wherever possible develop them even further. If you can give an indication of your leadership potential then all well and good. This might involve the summarising of the arguments that have been made, and inviting comments from the less vociferous candidates.

If role-playing exercises are used you should firmly slip into the role to be adopted, but be careful not to over-exaggerate your behaviour. If the role-playing involves performing a situational task, such as completing work in the 'in-tray' then you need to prioritise the work in the 'in-tray' so that you complete the more pressing tasks first. Should you be asked to solve problems, then you need to identify the underlying causes of the problem before you take action to overcome them. At all times, you should fully justify the decisions that you reach.

Situational tasks are favoured by some interviewers because they enable a number of traits and skills to be identified, such as the candidates' abilities to solve problems and take decisions, as well as their ability to maintain relationships with others, or to show sensitivity to the feelings of others. When attending a second interview, you should try and anticipate a number of different situations that might be put before you, and think about possible solutions to these situations. You may need to consider some additional points:

- a second interview will be more related to the work involved with the post than was the case with the first interview. Therefore you might need to do some further research;

- interviewers for a technical post will be more interested in technical knowledge and competence than was the case with the first interview – you must emphasise such competencies if you have them;

- you need to keep a positive frame of mind at all times. You should try and project the appropriate image that the recruiter is looking for;

- the person for whom you will be working will probably be a major influence on the decision made at the second interview;

- recruiters will be looking for evidence that you will be committed to the employing organisation and will be able to follow a structured career path.

Legal and Ethical Obligations in Recruitment

The law relating to the recruitment of staff is both complex and diverse. There is a number of legal constraints on advertising and interviewing prospective employees, particularly in relation to equal opportunities. Also a distinction must be drawn between employees and contractors, fixed term and periodic contracts and full-time and part-time workers. There are legal formalities covering the creation of a contract of employment, the terms of which are not only expressly agreed by the employer and employee, but are also implied from some external source such as a collective agreement or the Industrial Tribunal.

It is through the process of collective bargaining that recognised Trade Unions and employers produce collective agreements in which terms of employment are often negotiated. Those terms may then be implied into individual contracts of employment and so become legally enforceable. Industrial Tribunals and Courts find it necessary to imply terms into contracts of employment in relation to mutual trust and confidence, good faith, health and safety etc. in order to more fully express the bargain that has been made and give it business effect.

A failure to comply with legal requirements in relation to the recruitment of staff could lead to legal action being brought by an aggrieved individual before a court or tribunal. In addition, by ensuring that recruitment criteria are clear and concise and the terms of employment are precise and clearly understood, with a well drafted job description, then it is less likely that legal problems will arise in the future, when the contractual terms may be subjected to change or it becomes necessary to bring the employment relationship to an end.

Formation of employment contracts

Despite the unique nature of a contract of service, common law principles of the law of contract are still applicable to its formation, construction and discharge. The general contractual rules governing offer and acceptance are relevant to determine when a contract of employment has been entered into. A job advertisement is a mere invitation to treat. This could lead to a written application followed by an interview at which the employer will assess the merits of the various candidates. An express contractual offer of the job is then made to the successful candidate on specific terms which may differ from the initial advertisement. A counter offer by the applicant would extinguish the original offer. Usually, at this stage of course, the parties to the contract have reached consensus, and the contract is concluded on the communication of the applicant's acceptance.

Quite often an offer of employment is made conditional, for instance "subject to the receipt of satisfactory written references" or the "passing of a medical examination".

> Recently the Court of Appeal in *Wishart v. National Association of Citizens Advice Bureaux Ltd.* 1990 considered a case where the plaintiff had been offered the post of information officer "subject to satisfactory references" and then when the employer discovered his past attendance record withdrew the job offer. The issue before the Court of Appeal was whether the employer's decision to treat the references as unsatisfactory could be viewed objectively and tested by the standard of the reasonable person in the position of the employer. In fact the court decided that unlike medical opinion as to the employee's fitness which could be tested objectively, there was no obligation in law on the employer other than to decide in good faith whether the references were satisfactory. "The natural reading of a communication, the purpose of which is to tell the prospective employee that part of the decision on *whether* he is firmly offered the post has yet to be made, is that the employer is reserving the right to make up his own mind when the references have been received and studied. "

Equal Opportunities

As a general principle, employers are free to pick and choose to whom they offer employment. A limitation on the freedom to employ is embodied within the *Disabled Persons (Employment) Act* 1958 which provides that an employer with twenty or more employees must in the absence of an exemption certificate, have a minimum of three percent of the workforce registered as disabled persons. Indeed in certain jobs, disabled persons must be given priority. Furthermore, rather than stigmatising an individual for life because of his past conduct, the *Rehabilitation of Offenders Act* 1974 allows past offenders who have criminal convictions to regard them as 'spent' in certain circumstances. This means that on a job application the past conviction need not be mentioned and the failure to disclose it is no ground for an employer to refuse to employ or dismiss a past offender. It is reasonable of course for an employer to expect full disclosure of information on a job application and this would most certainly include a prospective employee providing details of criminal convictions which were not spent. A failure to fully disclose details of previous employment or trade union activities however may not be regarded as fatal to the validity of the contract of employment.

> In *Fitzpatrick v. British Railways Board* 1991 the complainant obtained a job with British Railways Board and deliberately failed to provide full details of her previous employment and participation in trade union activities. When it became obvious to the employer that the complainant was, and had been a union activist, they dismissed her on the ground that she

had obtained the job by deceit. The complainant then claimed that her dismissal was unfair as it was on the ground of trade union activities contrary to s.58 of the *Employment Protection (Consolidation) Act* 1978. If the reason for a dismissal is trade union membership or activities then the requirement of two years continuous employment to qualify for protection does not apply. The Court of Appeal held that the true reason for the complainant's dismissal was her union activities in previous employment and the fear that these activities will be repeated in her present employment. As a consequence the dismissal fell within s.58 and was unfair.

Unfortunately you should appreciate that despite the superficial emphasis given to equal opportunities in business, industry and the professions, numerous studies have shown that discriminatory practices are still widespread in staff recruitment in the UK. Prospective employees are discriminated against for various reasons including racial origin, sex, sexuality, religion, age and disability. In an attempt to reduce and hopefully eradicate these practices, legislation has been passed in the UK to make sex and race discrimination unlawful in employment.

As yet there is no legislation covering age and sexuality while there is increasing pressure to make discrimination against the disabled unlawful. As a consequence of discriminatory recruitment practices we have a workforce in the UK divided by sex and race.

Members of racial and ethnic minority groups generally occupy a low position in the occupational structure, concentrated in unskilled manual jobs and unrepresented in skilled manual jobs, managerial and professional occupations. They are found mainly in low paying industries such as clothing and textiles, in service sector jobs and in hospitals, shops and catering. Furthermore male black workers earn considerably less than male white workers and suffer a much higher rate of unemployment. Female workers are similarly concentrated in low paid unskilled jobs in a relatively small number of occupations including mainly clerical and related jobs and industries such as cleaning, catering and manufacturing. Because of child care responsibilities many women take part-time or casual work, often unskilled with poor pay and conditions. Economic trends in the labour market indicate an increase in the use of wage payment systems which encourage overtime, shift work and bonus payments, which necessarily discriminate against women. In addition to UK legislation on discrimination there is also European Community law which can be directly applicable in British Courts and also incorporated into United Kingdom law by Statute and by Statutory Instruments.

The right not to be discriminated against on the grounds of sex, race or marital status is one of the few individual employment rights that has not been weakened but rather strengthened over recent years. This has been mainly due to the impact of Community law and judgments of the European Court of Justice particularly in relation to gender.

The tendency to stereotype sexes and races and also perceive jobs to have male or female characteristics means that discrimination in Britain is still widespread. Nevertheless there are still relatively few complaints brought and success rates are consistently low. Studies have shown that there are numerous reasons for this, ranging from ignorance as to legal rights, insufficient support for complainants, difficulties of proof, low levels of compensation, and fear of victimisation. On the positive side however, there have been some notable successes recently which have caused change in employment practices. Unlawful discrimination has been found in a number of important equal pay cases, in employment practices in relation to part-time workers, in unnecessary demands for British qualifications, in maximum age limits and in stringent language tests. There is no doubt that there is a change in attitude, for there is increasing evidence that employers in the public and also in the private sector of the economy are adopting equal opportunity employment practices. Equal opportunity is an important issue in industrial relations, and the law can act as an important stimulus to both employers and trade unions to ensure that organisations adopt employment practices designed to combat discrimination. Bear in mind also, that there is increasing pressure in Britain to extend the law to protect those in our society who are less favourably treated in employment because of their age, religion, sexuality or disability.

Sex and race discrimination

The *Race Relations Act* 1976 (RRA 76) and the *Sex Discrimination Act* 1975 (SDA 75) as amended, identify similar categories of unlawful acts in relation to discrimination, namely direct discrimination, indirect discrimination, and victimisation. It is convenient to set out these unlawful acts of discrimination in tabular form as a means of comparison.

Race Relations Act, 1976	Sex Discrimination Act, 1975
Direct Discrimination	
This occurs where one person: Treats another less favourably on racial grounds e.g. by segregating workers by race.	This occurs when one person: Treats another less favourably on the grounds of sex or marital status e.g. by providing women with different working conditions or selecting married women first for redundancy.
Indirect Discrimination	
This occurs where one person: Requires another to meet a condition which as a member of a racial group is less easily satisfied because: (a) the proportion of that group who can comply with it is smaller; and (b) the condition is to the complainant's detriment and is not justified. There would therefore be indirect discrimination if an employer required young job applicants to have been educated only in Britain.	This occurs where one person: Requires another to meet a condition which as a member of a particular sex or as a married person is less easily satisfied because: (a) the proportion of that sex or married persons who can comply with it is smaller; and (b) the condition is to the complainant's detriment and is not justified. There would therefore be indirect discrimination if an employer advertised for a clerk who is at least six feet tall.
Victimisation	
This occurs where one person: Treats another less favourably because the other has given evidence or information in connection with, brought proceedings under, or made allegations under the Act against the discriminator.	This occurs where one person: Treats another less favourably because the other has given evidence or information in connection with, brought proceedings under, or made allegations under the Act or the Equal Pay Act, 1970, against the discriminator.

The fact that both pieces of legislation were drafted in a largely similar fashion means that case-law involving the Sex Discrimination Act will also serve as an aid to the interpretation of the provision of The Race Relations Act. It is proposed therefore to consider the provisions of both Acts in unison.

The *Sex Discrimination Act* 1975 is concerned with discrimination on grounds of gender either by males against females, or vice versa, and on grounds of marital status by treating a married person less favourably than an unmarried person.

> In *Nemes v. Allen* 1977 an employer in an attempt to cope with a redundancy situation dismissed female workers when they married. This was held to be unlawful direct discrimination on the grounds of sex and marital status.

The *Race Relations Act* 1976 is more complex in relation to those it protects and is concerned with discrimination on racial grounds which, is based upon colour, race, nationality, or ethnic or national origin.

In *Race Relations Board v. Mecca* 1976 an individual telephoned to apply for a job but when the employer discovered the applicant was black, he put the telephone down. This was held to be unlawful direct discrimination as the applicant had been denied the opportunity to apply for a job on racial grounds.

While the definition of racial grounds is wide there is no reference to discrimination based on religion. It does seem however that some religions would normally be covered by the definition colour, race, nationality, or ethnic or national origins.

In *Seide v. Gillette Industries* 1980 the EAT held that the term "Jewish" can mean membership of a particular race or ethnic group as well as a religion. Also in *Mandla v. Dowell Lee* 1983 the House of Lords held that Sikhs were a racial group within the meaning of the Act.

Certainly to share a common language would not on its own be sufficient to establish a racial group.

In *The Commission for Racial Equality v. Dutton* 1989 the Court of Appeal was required to determine whether the display of a sign at a public house saying "sorry no travellers" unlawfully discriminated against gypsies on racial grounds contrary to the *Race Relations Act* 1976. The court held that gypsies could come within the definition of "racial group" as an identifiable group defined by reference to ethnic origins, having a long shared history, customs, and unique dialect. There remains a discernible minority who have not merged wholly in the population and have not lost their separateness and self awareness as being gypsies.

In *Crown Supplies PGA v. Dawkins* 1993 the Court of Appeal held that Rastafarianism is no more than a religious sect and not an ethnic group for the purposes of the Race Relations Act. As a consequence when a Rastafarian is refused employment because of the way in which he wears his hair that does not amount to discrimination under the 1976 Act.

In relation to employment, any discriminatory practice which comes within any of the three categories (direct, indirect or victimisation) is unlawful. It is therefore unlawful for a person in relation to employment by him to discriminate in the arrangements he makes for the purposes of deciding whom should be offered employment, the terms on which it is offered or by refusing to offer employment. Also where there is an existing employment relationship it is unlawful for an employer to discriminate in the way he gives access to opportunities for promotion, transfer, training or any other benefits, or refuses to afford such access. Furthermore, it is unlawful to discriminate by dismissing the complainant or subject him to any other detriment.

It should be noted however, that originally unlawful discrimination practices in employment did not apply to employment for the purposes of a private household or where the number of employees was less than five. In a number of cases in the 1980s the European Commission criticised the United Kingdom sex discrimination law as being out of step with the Equal Treatment Directive. The law did not cover internal work rules, rules governing independent professions, private households or undertakings where five or fewer were employed. Furthermore in *Marshall v. Southampton and South West Hampshire Area Health Authority (Teaching)* 1986 it was held that in public sector employment, the difference in retirement age of men and women also contravened the Directive.

The result of these criticisms was that the UK Parliament passed the *Sex Discrimination Act* 1986. The 1986 Act applies the discrimination law to undertakings with five or fewer employees, removes the private household exemption and extends the law to collective agreements, work rules and professional associations. The Equal Treatment Directive has had considerable impact on UK discrimination law and in *Johnston v. Chief Constable of the RUC* 1987 it was confirmed that the Directive was unconditional and sufficiently precise to be used by an individual against a member state or in a national court. An individual could not enforce the Directive against a private employer however.

The anti-discrimination legislation provides redress for those who "contract personally to execute any work or labour". In *Quinnen v. Hovells* 1984 the EAT confirmed that the legislation was not confined to employees therefore and would also protect the self employed provided they are supplying personal services. In *Daley v. Allied Suppliers Ltd.* 1983 an allegation of racial discrimination could not be entertained because it was felt that working as a YOP trainee created relationships which were neither ones of employment or personally executing work. Now however, trainees have been brought within the discrimination legislation by departmental order.

Complaints of unlawful discrimination are made to the Industrial Tribunal and the time limit for presenting a complaint is three months from the act or last act of discrimination. The Tribunal has power to permit a claim presented out of time if it is just and equitable in the circumstances. While time begins to run from the date of the last act complained of, the statutes also provide that "any act extending over a period shall be treated as done at the end of the period".

> In *Calder v. James Finlay Corporation* 1989 the employers operated a subsidised mortgage scheme which had an unwritten rule excluding women. An employee lodged a complaint of unlawful discrimination five months after she was refused a mortgage subsidy but within three months of leaving employment. The EAT held that as long as the complainant was an employee, and the scheme operated, it constituted discrimination against her in the way she was 'afforded access to the scheme'. The last 'act' of discrimination was when her employment terminated so that she was within the three month time limit for lodging a complaint.

> In *Forster v. South Glamorgan Health Authority* 1988 the failure to present the complaint within the time limits was found to be understandable as it was due to a change in the law. In such circumstances the EAT held that whether or not it is "suitable" to hear a complaint out of time is a "question of fact and degree for the tribunal to determine in each case".

A copy of a complaint of unlawful discrimination must be sent to ACAS (the Advisory Conciliation and Arbitration Service) who will pass it on to a conciliation officer. It is the duty of the conciliation officer to attempt to resolve the conflict between the parties, if requested by them to do so, or if he feels that he has a reasonable prospect of success. If there is no settlement and the tribunal finds that there has been discrimination it can declare the rights of the parties, award compensation up to the unfair discrimination limits, and recommend action to be taken by the guilty party to reduce the adverse affects of the discrimination. A failure to respond to a recommendation without good reason could lead to an award of increased compensation.

Finally you should appreciate that the Commission for Racial Equality and the Equal Opportunities Commission have a role to play in encouraging, advising and providing financial assistance to prospective litigants. Furthermore only the Commission may bring proceedings in respect of certain unlawful acts including discriminatory advertising, unlawful instruction to discriminate and unlawful inducements to discrimination.

Discrimination in recruitment

Direct discrimination occurs where one person treats another less favourably on the grounds of sex, race or marital status. In an allegation of direct discrimination in recruitment the formal burden of proof is on the complainant. The difficulty is of course that often direct evidence of discrimination is not available and consequently it is sufficient if the complainant can establish primary facts from which inferences of discrimination can be drawn. Evidence is necessary therefore to draw comparison with some person, actual or hypothetical who falls outside the relevant racial group or gender who was or would be treated differently by the employer.

A good example of this approach is provided by *Humphreys v. St. Georges School* 1978. Here a complainant woman teacher established the following primary facts. As an experienced teacher along with two less experienced and less well qualified male applicants, she had applied for two vacant posts within a school. These facts, along with the fact that both male applicants were appointed, were sufficient to raise a prima facie (on the face of it) case of sex discrimination. The Court of Appeal stressed that it is only in an "exceptional or frivolous case" that the complainant will fail to establish a prima facie case.

Once the primary facts indicate a prima facie case of discrimination therefore "the employer is called on to give an explanation and, failing a clear and specific explanation being given by the employer to the satisfaction of the industrial tribunal, an inference of unlawful discrimination from the primary facts will mean the complaint succeeds".

This approach of drawing inferences from primary facts has since been approved in *Noone v. North West Thames Regional Health Authority* 1988. Here the complainant, Dr. Noone, who was born and obtained her initial qualification in Sri Lanka, had unsuccessfully applied for the post of consultant microbiologist with the Health Authority despite superior qualifications, experience and publications than the successful candidate. Her complaint of unlawful discrimination on the grounds of race, was upheld by the industrial tribunal and she was awarded £5,000 for injury of feelings. The tribunal found that the interview procedure was "little more than a sham" and had been driven to the conclusion that the interviews had treated the applicant less favourably than they would have treated an indigenous applicant of the same experience. The health authority successfully appealed to the Employment Appeal Tribunal however who concluded that while the decision not to select Dr. Noone was unsatisfactory and unreasonable there was no evidence to justify a finding of discrimination on racial grounds. Recognising that there is rarely direct evidence of discrimination the Court of Appeal reversed the EAT's decision and found that there was sufficient material to entitle the Industrial Tribunal to drawn an inference of discrimination on racial grounds in this case. The court did feel however that the award of damages was on the high side and reduced it to £3,000.

Certainly there is no burden on an employer to disprove discrimination but once a prime facie case has been made out a Tribunal is entitled to turn to an employer for an explanation of the facts.

In *King v. The Great Britain–China Centre* 1991 the applicant who was Chinese and educated in Britain, failed to secure the post of deputy director of the China Centre despite her obvious qualifications for the job. She was not one of the eight candidates short-listed who were all white and no other ethnic Chinese person had ever been employed at the Centre. The Court of Appeal held that the Tribunal was entitled to conclude that it was legitimate for them to draw an inference of discrimination on racial grounds in the absence of a satisfactory explanation by the employer.

The Court of Appeal in the above case produced some helpful guidelines in determining a claim of unlawful race discrimination.

- It is for the applicant to make out a case of race discrimination on the balance of probabilities;

- Direct evidence of race discrimination is rare, it is rarely admitted and is based on an assumption that the applicant may not fit in rather than be ill-intentioned;

- Outcomes will often depend upon inferences drawn from primary facts and these can include evasive or equivocal replies to a questionnaire;

- If there are primary facts which point to a finding of a difference in race and the possibility of discrimination, in the absence of a satisfactory and adequate explanation by the employer it is legitimate for a Tribunal to infer that the discrimination was on racial grounds;
- At the conclusion of all the evidence the Tribunal should make findings as to the primary facts and draw such inferences as they consider proper. They should then reach a conclusion on the balance of probabilities bearing in mind both the difficulties which face a person who complains of unlawful discrimination and the fact that it is for the complainant to prove his or her case.

Direct discrimination extends not only to acts based on sex but also decisions made on gender-based criteria. The nature of the alleged discrimination is immaterial and Tribunals should focus simply on whether the act or decision satisfies the "but for" test. Would the complainant have received the same treatment but for his or her sex?

If the employer puts forward a number of reasons for his conduct, some valid and some discriminatory, then provided the discriminatory reason was an important factor, there is unlawful discrimination.

> In *Owen & Briggs v. James* 1982 a case involving race discrimination, the complainant was a young black girl who had applied for a job as a shorthand typist with a firm of solicitors. She was interviewed for the job but rejected. When the post was re-advertised some months later she re-applied, but when she arrived for her interview the employer refused to see her. The same day a young white girl was appointed to the post despite the fact that her short-hand speed (35 words per minute) was far inferior to the complainant's (80 words per minute). It was also established that one of the partners of the firm had said to the successful candidate "why take on a coloured girl when English girls were available". The applicant's unlawful direct discrimination on the grounds of race was upheld in the Industrial Tribunal and on appeal in the Employment Appeal Tribunal. On further appeal to the Court of Appeal by the employer, it was argued that there could be no unlawful discrimination unless the sole reason for the conduct was the racial factor. This argument was rejected, the court deciding that it is sufficient if race is an important factor in the employer's decision and accordingly the appeal was unsuccessful.

One major difficulty facing a complainant is that proving discrimination may be impossible without access to documents which the employer holds. Since they may be confidential the applicant cannot have access to them unless the Industrial Tribunal chairman believes that they are relevant.

> The Court of Appeal in *Nass v. SRC* 1979 held that an Industrial Tribunal should not order or permit the disclosure of a report or reference, given and received in confidence, except in rare cases where, after inspection of the document, the chairman decides that it is essential in the interests of justice that the confidence should be overridden.

The words 'on the grounds of' sex, race or marital status in the statutes would cover the situation where the reason for discrimination was a generalised assumption that men, women, married persons, or persons of a particular race, possess or lack certain characteristics.

> In *Skyrail Oceanic Ltd. v. Coleman* 1981 two rival firms employed a man and woman who were subsequently married and for reasons of confidentiality, the woman was dismissed. The Court of Appeal held by a majority that, as the reason for dismissing the woman rather than the man was based on a general assumption that the man in a marriage is the breadwinner, and this is an assumption based on sex, this amounted to unlawful discrimination.

A useful tool to attack the credibility of the employer's denial of discrimination is statistical evidence. This is particularly so when the management decisions on matters such as promotion or access to benefits are based upon subjective criteria such as 'excellence', 'potential' or 'efficiency'. In *Owen & Briggs v. James* 1982 if the firm of solicitors could have shown that they had other black employees, this could have gone a long way towards enabling the tribunal to reach a contrary decision.

> In *West Midlands Passenger Transport Executive v. Singh* 1988 the Court of Appeal ruled that statistical evidence of the employer's record of appointing ethnic minority applicants in the past, is material as to whether he has discriminated on racial grounds against a particular complainant. This enables a tribunal to scrutinise the employer's stated reason for rejecting the complainant and test it against comparative evidence of the employer's overall record.

The types of questions asked in interviews may be of relevance to determine whether there has been discrimination.

> In *Saunders v. Richmond on Thames LBC* 1978 the EAT confirmed that it is not in itself unlawful to ask a question of a woman which would not be asked of a man. Here in an interview for a job as a golf professional, the female applicant was asked whether there were other female golf professionals and whether she thought that men would respond as well to a woman golf professional as to a man. Her claim of unlawful discrimination when she was not appointed did not succeed. The existence of direct discrimination depended upon whether she was treated less favourably on the grounds of sex than a man. Here, while the questions demonstrated an out of date attitude, the industrial tribunal was entitled to find that they were not asked with the intention of discriminating.

It is also unlawful to show an intention to commit an act of discrimination in relation to employment. Therefore the publication of an advertisement which invites applicants for the post of salesman or barmaids would constitute unlawful discrimination.

Indirect discrimination in recruitment

Indirect discrimination, a more subtle form of discrimination than direct discrimination, is designed to cover overt yet not blatant acts of discrimination. It occurs where a person requires another to meet a requirement or condition which as a member of a particular sex, race or marital status is less easily satisfied. This is because the proportion of those of that type who can comply with the requirement or condition is smaller, and it is to the complainant's detriment and not justifiable. In an allegation of indirect discrimination it is necessary to show that the requirement of a condition is mandatory rather than one of a number of criteria which the employer would take into account.

> In *Meer v. London Borough of Tower Hamlets* 1988 the requirement was alleged to be job selection criteria, one of which was to have experience working in Tower Hamlets. The fact that this particular criteria was not mandatory meant that it could not constitute a requirement for the purposes of indirect discrimination.

Also for the purposes of showing that the proportion of the complainant's type who can comply with the condition is smaller there is no need to produce elaborate statistical evidence, but rather a common sense approach is to be encouraged. Nevertheless to succeed it is necessary to show that the proportion who can comply is considerably smaller.

> In *Price v. Civil Service Commission* 1978 the complainant alleged indirect discrimination on the grounds of sex because far fewer women than men could comply with the age limits of seventeen and a half to twenty eight to qualify as an eligible candidate for the executive officer grade. By comparing the proportion of qualified women with the proportion of qualified men, it is obvious that as a larger number of women of that age group will be likely to be having or bringing up children, then the proportion who can comply with the age require-

ment is less. The EAT held that as the proportion who can comply in practice is less and the requirement was not justifiable, there was unlawful indirect discrimination.

Even where indirect discrimination is established there are no damages payable if it is shown to be unintentional. Where the fundamental purpose of the claim is to secure compensation for the victim there is little point in presenting a complaint where there was no intention to discriminate. Where the requirement or condition to be satisfied applies unequally to one sex, for instance, not to get pregnant, it is still possible to allege successfully that such a requirement constitutes indirect discrimination.

The approach to be adopted by a tribunal in a complaint of indirect race discrimination was laid down in T*ower Hamlets LBC v. Qayyum* 1987. The tribunal should:

- identify the applicant's race, colour, nationality or ethnic origin;
- ascertain whether there is a racial group similar;
- see whether the requirement or condition is imposed generally;
- decide whether the proportion is considerably smaller than a comparable proportion of the indigenous group.

It is a question of fact in each case to determine the proportion of the complainant's group who can comply with the requirement or condition in practice. By deciding what proportion of the complainant's group can comply and comparing that figure with the proportion of qualified persons who can comply but fall outside the group, it is possible to decide whether it is considerably smaller.

> In *Fulton v. Strathclyde Regional Council* 1986 the employer decided that certain social work posts should be exclusively for full-time staff. Of the basic grade social workers the statistics showed that 90% of the women could comply with the full-time requirement and all of the men. It was held on a complaint of indirect discrimination that 90% is not "considerably smaller" than 100% and so the claim must fail.

The success of an indirect discrimination claim will turn on the choice of the pool for comparison.

> In *Pearse v. Bradford MC* 1988 one 'requirement' of eligibility to apply for a post as a senior lecturer in a college was that the applicant was presently a full-time employee of the local authority in the college. This 'requirement' was claimed to be indirectly discriminatory, the complainant alleging that the proportion of women who could comply with it, 21.8% of the academic staff, was considerably smaller than the proportion of men, 46.7% of the academic staff. The EAT held that the correct pool for comparison was not all of the full-time academic staff but rather those academic staff who had appropriate qualifications for the post. Consequently the statistical evidence put forward by the complainant was inappropriate and she had failed to show that the requirement of being employed full-time had a disproportionate impact on the qualified women. The argument that the pool for comparison must be extended to those eligible to apply, could not be accepted, for it would be irrational to ignore the fact that appropriate qualifications were a pre-requisite to apply for the post.

The definition of indirect discrimination also requires the complainant to have suffered a detriment and the requirement or condition must not be justifiable. The fact that the complainant has been adversely affected by the condition is sufficient to establish a detriment. It is open however for the defendant to show as a question of fact that in all the circumstances the requirement is justifiable.

> In *Singh v. Rowntree Mackintosh* 1979 the complainant objected to a 'no beard rule' operated by confectioners, which was alleged to be indirectly discriminatory against Sikhs. Here the EAT held that while the rule was discriminatory, it was a justifiable requirement on the grounds of hygiene, supported by medical advice, and therefore not unlawful. The burden of proof was on the employer to justify the requirement or condition and here the tribunal

recognised that in adopting standards the employer must be allowed that independence of judgement as to what he believes is a common expedient in the conduct of his business. Certainly the requirement must be more than convenient but need not be necessarily essential.

If a person produces reasons for doing something which would be acceptable to right thinking people as sound and tolerable reasons for so doing, then he has justified his conduct.

In *Hampson v. Department of Education and Science* 1989 Balcombe L J held that to determine whether a condition is justifiable or not, an objective standard is required in each case. 'Justifiable' "requires an objective balance to be struck between the discriminatory effect of the condition and the reasonable needs of the party who applies that condition".

> In *Cobb v. Secretary of State for Employment and Manpower Services Commission* 1989 on a complaint of unlawful indirect discrimination, the tribunal held that the eligibility criteria for admission to the Community Programme, which included receipt of the appropriate social security benefit, had a disproportionate impact on women in general and married women in particular. Nevertheless the EAT confirmed that the tribunal is entitled to find that such a criterion is justifiable in the circumstances without reliance on a mass of statistical or sociological evidence but rather by taking a broad and rational view of the circumstances. *"In a case of indirect discrimination it is for the respondent to satisfy the tribunal that the decisions which he took were objectively justified for economic, administrative or other reasons. It is for the tribunal to decide what facts it found proved and to carry out the balancing exercise involved, taking into account all the surrounding circumstances and giving due emphasis to the degree of discrimination caused against the object or aim to be achieved, - the principle of proportionality".*

Genuine occupational requirement

Both the *Sex Discrimination Act* 1975 and the *Race Relations Act* 1976 identify circumstances where discrimination in employment is lawful. They are referred to as instances of genuine occupational qualification (GOQ).

The categories of genuine occupation requirements under the Sex Discrimination Act are as follows.

- where the job requires a man or woman for physiological reasons other than physical strength, or in dramatic performances or other entertainment for reasons of authenticity, e.g. female stripper or male model;
- where there are considerations of decency or privacy because the job is likely to involve physical contact with men in circumstances where they might reasonably object to it being carried out by a woman, e.g. male toilet attendant;
- where there are statutory requirements, e.g. woman may not work underground in coal mines. Following the *Sex Discrimination Act* 1986 there are few statutory restrictions that survive;
- where the work location makes it impracticable to live elsewhere than the employer's premises and it is unreasonable to expect the employer to provide separate facilities for sleeping or sanitation, e.g. an oil rig;
- where the personal service is most effectively provided by a man or woman, e.g. a female social worker dealing with unmarried mothers;
- where the nature of the establishment within which the work is done requires the job to be held by a man because it is a hospital, prison or other establishment for males, requiring special care, and it is reasonable that the job should not be held by a woman;

- where the job needs to be held by a man because it is likely to involve the performance of duties outside the United Kingdom, in a country whose law and customs are such that the duties could not be effectively performed by a woman, e.g. Saudi Arabia;

- where the job is one of two to be held by a married couple.

The *Race Relations Act* 1976 also identifies circumstances where membership of a particular racial group is a genuine occupational requirement.

- drama and entertainment where the person of that racial group is required for reasons of authenticity, e.g. employing only a black actor to play the part of 'Martin Luther King';

- artist's or photographic models in order to achieve authenticity, e.g. a photograph depicting a national scene;

- bar or restaurant work where the setting requires an employee from a particular race, again for reasons of authenticity, e.g. Chinese Restaurant;

- the holder of the job provides persons of that racial group with personal services promoting their welfare and those services can most effectively be provided by a person of that racial group, e.g. a Bangladeshi social worker.

In *London Borough of Lambeth v. Commission for Racial Equality* 1990 the EAT held that this GOQ exception provides a defence only if the post advertised is for the provision of personal services, and the particular racial groups of the holder of the post and persons to whom the services are provided are sufficiently identified so as to establish that they are both of the same racial group. Here the fact that the local authority's advertisement related to posts which were of a managerial and administrative nature which involved very little contact with the public meant that they should not be confined to applicants of Afro-Caribbean or Asian origin. The intention of this exception under the 1976 Act *"envisaged circumstances where there was direct contact, mainly face to face or where there could be physical contact, and where language, cultural understanding and religious backgrounds were of material importance"*. Subsequently the Court of Appeal agreed with the EAT that the holders of the jobs advertised, being managerial positions, did not provide personal services promoting the welfare of persons of a particular racial group.

Positive action

In addition to these specific instances where the sex or race of an employee is regarded as a genuine occupational requirement there are provisions in the Sex Discrimination Act and the Race Relations Act which enable employers and others (trade unions, employer's organisations and professional bodies) to achieve a more balanced work force. Employers are authorised to take positive action to encourage females or members of a particular racial group to apply for positions in their organisations where they are under-represented in those jobs. The requirement for positive encouragement to do certain work under the Sex Discrimination Act is that during the previous twelve months there were no or comparatively few women doing that type of work. Under the Race Relations Act it must be shown that either no members of the racial group are doing the work in question at the organisation or that the proportion of that group who do that work is small among those employed, or among the population of the area from which recruitment normally takes place. Of course it is one thing positively to encourage applicants from under-represented groups by stating in a job advertisement that applications from ethnic minorities or women will be particularly welcomed. If it is shown however than an employer is attempting to limit recruitment exclusively to the members of a racial group, where there is no genuine occupational requirement, then this will be unlawful.

In *Hughes and Others v. L B Hackney* 1986 the defendant council advertised for gardeners stating that applicants from ethnic minority people would be warmly welcomed. Subsequently three white applicants for the jobs were told that the posts were only open to applicants who were ethnic minority members. The tribunal found that to limit job recruitment in this way was not authorised by the legislation, and in fact in this particular case neither was the criterion for encouraging applicants from a particular racial group satisfied. The defendant council had argued that the proportion of ethnic minorities doing work of this kind was small in comparison with the population of the recruitment area. This argument was rejected by the tribunal who found that the population area should not be restricted to Hackney for a substantial number of workers were recruited from outside the borough.

Enforcement and remedies

Discrimination law in employment may be enforced by individual complaint to an Industrial Tribunal. Also both the Commission for Racial Equality and the Equal Opportunities Commission have a role to play in the enforcement of the law and where certain unlawful acts are alleged, their role is an exclusive one. The process and time limits relating to the presentation of a complaint were considered earlier.

If despite the attempts at conciliation the complainant decides to go ahead, there is a special pre-tribunal procedure to assist in the effective presentation of the complaint and access to information.

The remedies available to a tribunal who felt that a complaint has been made out are:

- an order declaring the rights of the parties;
- an order requiring the respondent to pay the complainant damages subject to the upper limit for unlawful dismissal claims;
- a recommendation of action to be taken by the respondent to reduce the adverse effect of discrimination.

A failure by the respondent without reasonable justification to comply with a recommendation may lead to an award of increased compensation. In the case of indirect discrimination if the respondent proves that the requirement or condition was applied without any intention to discriminate then no compensation will be awarded.

In *Noone v. North West Thames Regional Health Authority* 1988 the Court of Appeal confirmed that awards for incidents of racial discrimination were subject to the same rules as awards for damages for personal injury in respect of any other breach of statutory duty. Here the complainant was 'devastated' by the discriminatory act and suffered a severe injury to feelings which should be acknowledged by the award of damages. Nevertheless bearing in mind that she suffered no actual loss, the award of £5,000 was too high and should be reduced to £3,000.

It now seems that following *Marshall v. Southampton and South West Hampshire Area Health Authority (No 2)* 1988 the maximum compensation under the Sex Discrimination Act does not provide an adequate remedy as required by Article 6 of the EC Equal Treatment Directive. The European Court of Justice held that an employee of the State is entitled to rely on Article 6 to challenge the employer's discriminatory retirement policy successfully and compensation payable is not restricted to the statute's limit under the Sex Discrimination Act. Here the complainant's total loss was assessed at £19,405, well in excess of the statutory limit. The award was made for being discriminated against on the grounds of sex contrary to the Equal Treatment Directive when the complainant was dismissed at the age of 62 on the grounds that she had passed the respondent's normal retirement age for women when men could go on working until 65.

In *British Gas Plc v. Shama* 1991 the Employment Appeal Tribunal confirmed that there are limits to the extent that Tribunals have power to make recommendations to reduce the adverse affects of unlawful discrimination. While the Tribunal had found that the complainant had been the victim of direct racial discrimination when she was not promoted, the Tribunal had no power to recommend that she should be promoted to the next suitable vacancy.

Enforcement of the legislation is also the role of the Commissions who having instituted a formal investigation and, being satisfied that unlawful discriminatory acts or practices have taken place, may issue a non-discrimination notice on any person. Such a notice will require the person on whom it is served not to commit the acts complained of and also comply with any required changes in conduct. The Commissions may seek an injunction to prevent repeated discrimination within five years of the non-discrimination notice becoming final.

Where an unlawful act is committed by an employee in the course of his employment, the principles of vicarious liability apply and the employer is also made liable for the act whether or not it is done with his approval. It is a defence for an employer to prove that he took such steps as were reasonably practicable to prevent the employees from doing that act or from doing, in the course of his employment, acts of that description. Such steps would certainly include full implementation of the Commission for Racial Equality Code of Practice on discrimination. Furthermore an employer is not liable unless the discriminatory act is done in the course of employment.

In *Irving & Irving v. Post Office* 1987 the complaint of race discrimination was based on the conduct of an employee of the post office who when sorting the mail had written a racially insulting comment on a letter addressed to his neighbours who were of Jamaican origin. The issue before the Court of Appeal was whether the employee was acting in the course of his employment so that the Post Office could be made vicariously liable for the discriminatory act. The employee's act of writing on the mail was clearly unauthorised so the question was whether the act was an unauthorised mode of doing an authorised act. Here the misconduct formed no part of the postman's duties and could not be regarded as an unauthorised way of performing his work. *"An employer is not to be held liable merely because the opportunity to commit the wrongful act had been created by the employee's employment, or because the act in question had been committed during the period of that particular employment."*

If it does little else, discrimination law should stimulate equality of opportunity and act as a framework within which to identify barriers facing women and ethnic minority workers at work. As was suggested earlier, there is a view that there should be similar laws to protect people who are discriminated against because of their disability, sexuality or age. Ethically, job applicants should be judged on the basis of their ability rather than their sex or the colour of their skin.

Legal Formalities and the Contract of Employment

Contrary to popular belief, apart from merchant seamen and apprentices, there is no legal requirement that a contract of employment be in writing. While there are problems associated with identifying the terms of an oral agreement, nevertheless given the fluid nature of a contract of employment there is no guarantee that a requirement to reduce the original contract to writing would solve all the problems of interpreting its content.

Under s.1 *Employment Protection (Consolidation) Act* 1978 (EPCA 78), there is a statutory requirement on employers to provide their employees within thirteen weeks of the commencement of employment with a written statement of the main terms of employment. The section applies to full-time employees (those engaged under an employment contract for sixteen hours or more a week) or part-time workers (engaged between eight and sixteen hours) after five years employment. Certain classes of employees are excluded from s.1 including registered dock workers, Crown employees, employees who work wholly or mainly outside Great Britain and part time workers. The objective of s.1 is to ensure that employees have written confirmation and a source to scrutinise at least the main terms of their employment contracts. Particulars which must be included in the statutory statement include:

- reference to the parties and the dates on which the period of continuous employment began (stating whether a previous period of employment is included as part of continuous employment);
- the scale of remuneration and the method of calculation;
- the intervals at which remuneration is paid (whether weekly or monthly or some other period);
- the terms and conditions relating to hours of work;
- the terms and conditions relating to holidays and holiday pay (sufficient to enable the employee's entitlement to accrued holiday pay on the termination of employment to be precisely calculated);
- the terms and conditions relating to sickness or injury and sickness pay;
- the terms and conditions relating to pension and pension scheme;
- the length of notice which the employee is obliged to give and entitled to receive;
- the title of the job which the employee is employed to do;
- in addition every statement given shall include a note containing a specification of any disciplinary rules or reference to an accessible document containing such rules;
- the name of the person to whom the employee can apply if he is dissatisfied with any disciplinary decision relating to him;
- the name of the person to whom the employer can apply to seek the redress of any grievance;
- whether a contracting out certificate under the provisions of the *Social Security Act* 1975 is in force in relation to the employment.

Following an amendment made by the *Employment Act* 1989 an employer is exempt from the requirement to include a note on disciplinary proceedings in the written statement if he has less than twenty employees on the date of commencement of employment. To satisfy the requirements of the Act it is not sufficient to be told or shown the particulars of employment. The employer must present the employee with a document containing the information or at least make such a document available for inspection. It should be stressed that a statutory statement is not the contract of employment but rather strong evidence of the terms of employment.

Contractual terms are often subject to change in which case an employer is obliged to notify the employee of changes in the statement, within one month of the change. An employer who fails to comply with obligations in relation to the statutory statement could be the subject of a complaint to the Industrial Tribunal. Those employers who do provide their employees with a written contract of employment which covers all the matters which must be referred to in the statutory statement do not have to supply their employees with a separate statutory statement. The writing should of course reflect what has been orally agreed by the contracting parties.

In *Discount Tobacco and Confectionery Ltd. v. Armitage* 1990 the complainant was a shop manageress with only a short period of continuous employment who enlisted the help of her trade union official to secure a written contract of employment from her employer. When finally such a contract was issued, and she felt that it contained discrepancies, the complainant attempted to raise them with her employer. The response of the employer was to dismiss her, giving the reason for dismissal as lack of suitability or capability. This led to a complaint of unfair dismissal, the complainant alleging that the true reason for dismissal was her trade union membership which was unfair under s.58 of the *Employment Protection (Consolidation) Act* 1978. If trade union membership or activities is the reason for dismissal there is no need to qualify with two years continuous employment for protection against unfair dismissal. Both the Industrial Tribunal and the Employment Appeal Tribunal thought that there was no genuine distinction between trade union membership and making use of the essential services of a union officer and as a consequence the dismissal in this case was unfair by virtue of s.58.

European employment legislation

Increasingly individual employment rights in the UK will be subject to change as a result of European Law. This is particularly so where there is seen to be obvious disparity between member states as to employment rights. One area where action has already been taken is the requirement that employers should provide their employees with sufficient information as to the essential aspects of their employment contracts so that employees are made aware of the main right and obligations in their employment relationships.

On the 14 October 1991 the EC Council of Ministers adopted a directive called 'An Employer's Obligation to Inform Employees of the Conditions of Employment Relationships'

This is the first directive affecting employees' rights at work other than in the field of health and safety under the Commission's Social Charter Action Programme. All member states are required to comply with its terms by 30 June 1993.

The information must be supplied within two months of employment rather than thirteen weeks, and to employees with a working week of at least eight hours rather than sixteen. The information includes the following:

- place of work;
- job title;
- category;
- brief description of the work;
- amount of paid leave;
- working hours;
- collective agreements.

This directive attempts to ensure that workers throughout the Community are made aware of what is required of them under an employment contract and also treats part-time employees, working a minimum of eight hours per week, the same as full-time workers as far as the right to information is concerned.

The extension of a right to information to a large category of part-time employees represents the view that part-time workers, the majority of whom are inevitably women, should be put in the same legal position as full-time employees.

Activity

Search through the recruitment section of your local newspapers and identify those employers who state they have an equal opportunity policy and how this is indicated in the advertisement. State any jobs for which a particular sex or role is a genuine occupational requirement.

The Contents of Employment Contracts

A contract of employment is, like any other contract, composed of terms which confer rights and impose obligations on the parties to it. Such terms may be expressly agreed by the parties, or incorporated into the contract from another source. The express terms of a contract can be identified by establishing what was orally agreed and reduced to writing at the time the contract was negotiated. In many contracts of employment however, terms of employment are negotiated on behalf of staff by trade unions through the process of collective bargaining with employers or employers associations. The product of collective bargaining is called a collective agreement and terms of employment within such an agreement are incorporated into individual contracts of employment. Furthermore the courts and tribunals have found it necessary to imply terms into a contract of employment to more fully express the presumed intention of the parties to the contract.

Express terms

These are the terms expressly agreed by the employer and employee, and may be in writing or may be purely oral. The statutory statement of the main terms and conditions of employment will normally provide sound evidence of the express terms. They will usually relate to matters such as wages, hours, holidays, sick pay, job description, restraints, etc. Of course, what has expressly been agreed by the parties may often require interpretation in the courts and Industrial Tribunals.

It is the ordinary courts that deal with disputes surrounding the interpretation of the terms of a contract of employment based on an action for breach of contract. The majority of employment disputes however relate to statutory employment rights such as unfair dismissal, redundancy and discrimination and they are heard by Industrial Tribunals and on appeal by the Employment Appeal Tribunal.

As a general rule, the express terms cannot be varied by either party without the other's consent unless an express term confers this right on one of the parties. Any attempt by the employer to impose an unreasonable variation of the contractual terms on the employee, such as the employee being requested to attend a place of work outside travelling distance from home, or to accept a reduced wage or lower status will constitute a breach of contract.

> In *Rigby v. Ferodo Ltd.* 1987, the employer attempted to impose a lower wage on the employees. On behalf of the employees, their trade union made it clear that the lower wage was unacceptable and while the employees continued to work they regarded the employer in repudiatory breach of the contract of employment. When an action was brought to recover the unpaid wages, the House of Lords held that the employees were entitled to the full original contractual wage for the whole period from the time the reduction was imposed.

A tribunal may also be called on to determine the rights of the parties by interpreting the exact wording of the express terms of a contract of employment.

> So in *McCaffrey v. A.E. Jeavons & Co. Ltd.* 1967, an employee expressly employed as a 'travelling man' in the building trade was held to be bound to move anywhere in the country.

It is a question of fact in each case whether a change of job will amount to a breach of the contract of employment. If the contract expressly provides that the nature of the employee's job may be changed, even a variation which would constitute a demotion may be within the contractual terms. In order for a change in an employee's job to constitute a consensual variation of the contract of employment, the courts must be satisfied that the employee gives a clear indication that he voluntarily accepts the new terms of his employment.

> In *Marriott v. Oxford District Co-op Soc. Ltd.* 1970, the Court of Appeal was required to determine whether there had been a consensual variation of the contractual terms in the

following case. A foreman supervisor was told by his employer that the position of foreman was no longer required and that his wages were to be reduced by £1 to reflect his loss of status. The employee continued to work under protest for three weeks before terminating his employment by notice, claiming redundancy. The Court of Appeal held, reversing the Divisional Court's decision, that there had been no free consent to the contractual variation and the change in terms amounted to a repudiation of the contract of employment.

In *Jones v. Associated Tunnelling Co. Ltd.* 1981, the EAT stressed that continuing to work is not necessarily an implied assent to a unilateral variation by the employer. This is particularly so where the variation has no immediate practical effect and it would be unreasonable to expect the employee to object to it. Problems surrounding contractual variation are often associated with the interpretation of the content of the contract of employment and usually arise during, or are the cause of, industrial action.

In *Royle v. Trafford BC* 1984, a school teacher's pay had been withheld for refusing to work in accordance with the instructions of the head teacher in pursuance of an industrial dispute. In an action for breach of contract it was held that by refusing to take on more pupils (by increasing the size of the class from 31 to 36) the teacher was indeed in breach of contract. However by allowing the teacher to render an imperfect performance of the contract the employer had affirmed the contract despite withholding salary. Accordingly the teacher was awarded his unpaid salary less 5/36ths for his breach of contract over the relevant period. The High Court held that the plaintiff would be entitled to be paid full salary only if he had properly and fully performed his duties under his contract of employment. Therefore the court was entitled to make a deduction representing the notional value of the services the plaintiff did not render.

To determine whether action by an employer could amount to a breach of the contract of employment it is possible to apply to the High Court for a declaration.

In *Cresswell v. Board of Inland Revenue* 1984, employees sought a declaration that their employer had broken the terms of their contracts of employment by introducing new technology and expecting them to adapt to it. The High Court declared however, that provided they received adequate training, employees were expected to adapt to new methods and new techniques. There is a general contractual duty on employees to adapt to changing working methods. There was also a right for the employer to withhold pay from those employees who refused to conform to the new methods.

Over recent years there seems to be a general acceptance that the contract of employment constitutes a wage/work bargain and failure to fulfil contractual obligations by one employee entitles the employer to make a corresponding deduction in wages.

In *Miles v. Wakefield DC* 1987, the House of Lords held that it is permissible for an employer to make deductions from salary where the employee, in this case a Registrar, was not performing the contract in full by refusing to conduct marriage ceremonies on a Saturday.

A similar deduction was endorsed by the court in *Sim v. Rotherham MBC* 1986, where teachers were refusing to cover for absent colleagues. The teachers contract was interpreted to cover the proper running of the school and consequently the refusal to provide cover constituted a breach of contract and the teachers were therefore only entitled to a reduced wage.

Finally the court in *Wiluszynski v. Tower Hamlets LBC* 1988, stressed that only an appropriate percentage should be deducted from wages to reflect the amount of work that the employee is refusing to do. The court also held that provided the employer made it clear that during industrial action any work done would be regarded as voluntary, then no wages were payable.

Implied terms

As we said previously, employment terms are incorporated into a contract of employment by the common law through the intervention of courts and tribunals. Also if a wage rise or reduction in working hours is negotiated in a collective agreement, that new terms will be implied into individual contracts of employment.

It is common practice in many spheres of employment for the employer to issue work rules by printing notices or handing out booklets. Such work rules often contain instructions as to time-keeping, meal breaks, disciplinary offences and grievance procedure, sickness and pension rights, and the employer's safety policy. Although there is still some doubt as to their legal significance, it seems at present such documents are unlikely to contain contractual terms.

> In *The Secretary of State for Employment v. Associated Society of Locomotive Engineers and Firemen* 1972, Ld. Denning stated that the rule book issued to railwaymen by their employer did not contain contractual terms but rather instructions to an employee on how he was to do his work.

At the present time, it is unlikely that a custom or practice will be incorporated into a contract of employment by implication. Certainly a custom would have to satisfy the tests of being certain, reasonable and notorious (notable) before it would be regarded as legally enforceable. This was the case in *Sagar v. Ridehalgh* 1931, where a custom that deductions could be made from the wages of a weaver for bad work was held to be legally binding.

Terms implied by the common law

In every contract of employment, certain terms are implied by the courts and tribunals through the operation of the common law. These terms are the source of many of the rights and duties of both the employer and employee, and are an integral part of the contract of employment. In addition to the well-established common law duties, there is an increased willingness by courts and tribunals to imply terms into individual contracts of employment, usually to accommodate the doctrine of constructive dismissal. Furthermore, numerous individual employment rights are attached to the contract of employment by statutory intervention. In some cases these arise after a period of continuous employment, for instance the right not to be unfairly dismissed. (See Element 4.1)

Statutory employment rights cover such matters as redundancy payments, equal opportunities and unfair dismissal. An employee's remedy for infringement of his or her rights is by way of complaint to an Industrial Tribunal.

Terms are implied into a contract of employment by the common law imposing duties on both the employer and employee. Duties are imposed on the employer maintain a relationship of trust and confidence to pay wages, to provide the opportunity for the employee to earn the expected wage, to indemnify, and to provide a safe system of work. Duties of the employee include duties to act in good faith, to account for money received, to respect trade secrets, and to obey lawful instructions.

Implied terms imposing duties on the employer

To pay wages

The common law implies a term into the contract of employment imposing a duty on the employer to pay a reasonable wage for the work done. In the majority of cases, of course, the parties to the contract of employment will have expressly agreed a rate of pay or referred to a rate of pay contained in a collective agreement. However, in the unlikely event that no wage is expressly agreed, in the case of a dispute the courts will value the service provided and imply a reasonable wage. In addition to the common law, there are a number of statutory provisions surrounding the payment of wages. Under the *EPCA* 1978, every employee is entitled to receive a written itemised statement of his pay, including deductions. This statement should include the gross amount, deductions and their purpose, the net amount, and if the net amount is paid in different ways, the amount and methods of payment.

To provide work, indemnify and provide a reference

Generally there is no duty on an employer to provide work for his employees as long as their contractual remuneration is paid. If, however, an employee's pay depends upon the performance of work (piece-work), then the employer is under an obligation to provide sufficient work to enable a reasonable wage to be earned. A further exception is where the employee's occupation is such that the opportunity to work is an essential part of the contract because of the possibility of loss of reputation, as for example in the case of an actor, entertainer or journalist.

Under the common law, an employee is entitled to be indemnified for loss or expense incurred in the course of employment. In most cases, of course, expenses are provided for expressly in the contract of employment.

There is, however, no legal duty to provide employees with a reference on the termination of their employment. If a reference is given, however, the tort of defamation will provide a remedy for an employee if the employer has maliciously included false statements which damage the employee's character. Also, an employer could be sued under the tort of deceit, or negligent mis-statement, by another employer who suffers loss as a result of employing someone following an unwarrantable good reference.

To provide a safe system of work

The present law relating to an employer's duties in relation to the safety of his work-force is embodied within the common law and statute. The common law duty arises under the tort of negligence and involves providing employees with a safe system of work. Statutory duties are imposed under various Acts, for example the *Factories Act* 1961 and the *Office Shops and Railway Premises Act* 1963 (the contents of which are being incorporated by regulation into the *Health and Safety at Work* Act *1974). Health and safety is dealt with in Element 4.1.*

To maintain trust and confidence

In *Courtaulds Northern Textiles Ltd. v. Andrew* 1979 the EAT stated that *"there is an implied term in a contract of employment that the employers will not, without reasonable and proper cause, conduct themselves in a manner calculated or likely to destroy or seriously damage the relationship of confidence and trust between the parties".* It has been held to be a breach of this term by an employer who failed to treat an allegation of sexual harassment with due seriousness and gravity, to unjustly criticise an employee, to abuse an employee publicly and to fail to treat an employee fairly in relation to a disciplinary matter.

To provide information

In *Scally v. Southern Health and Social Services Board* 1991 the House of Lords held that there is an implied term in a contract of employment imposing a duty on the employer to take reasonable steps to provide an employee with certain information. Here the information in question related to pension rights which had been negotiated on the employee's behalf but they had not been informed of the benefits they conferred.

Implied terms imposing duties on the employee

The duty of good faith

This duty is the most fundamental obligation of an employee and involves serving his employer faithfully. Faithful service involves working competently, respecting the employer's property, and not taking industrial action such as strikes, go-slows, working to rule etc., which would disrupt the employer's business.

> In *The Secretary of State for Employment v. ASLEF* 1972, the Court of Appeal held that wilful disruption of the employer's undertaking would amount to breach of this implied duty of good faith. Here the railwaymen were disrupting British Rail services by working to the letter of the British Rail rule book, but nevertheless were held to be in breach of contract.

The relationship of trust and confidence which is said to exist between employer and employee may also demand that an employee reports matters of interest to his employer.

> In *Sybros Corporation and Another v. Rochem Ltd. and others* 1983, the Court of Appeal held that, while there is no general duty to report a fellow employee's misconduct or breach of contract, an employee might be so placed in the hierarchy of an organisation as to have a duty to report either his 'superiors" or 'inferiors" misconduct.

To account for money received

There is an implied duty on an employee not to accept any bribes, commissions or fees in respect of his work other than from his employer.

> In *Boston Deep Sea Fishing & Ice Co. v. Ansell* 1888, an employee who received a secret commission from other companies for placing orders with them was treated as having been in breach of his duty and his dismissal was justified.

To respect trade secrets

An employee would be in breach of this duty by working for a competitor in his spare time.

> In *Hivac v. Park Royal Scientific Instruments Co.* 1946, an employee was restrained from working for a competitor engaged in work of a similar nature.

Certainly, there would be a flagrant breach of contract if an employee were to disclose trade secrets or other confidential information during the course of his employment. Even an ex-employee may be restrained.

> In *Printer & Finishers Ltd. v. Holloway* 1965, an ex-employee was restrained from showing secret documents to a competitor and disclosing confidential information he had obtained during his employment.

To obey reasonable orders

This duty could be included within the general obligation to render faithful service. To be reasonable an order must be lawful, for there is no duty to obey an unlawful order, for instance to falsify records. In determining the reasonableness of an order, all the circumstances must be considered and a close examination made of the contract of employment.

> In *UK Atomic Energy Authority v. Claydon* 1974, the defendant's contract of employment required him to work anywhere in the UK Accordingly, it was held to be a reasonable order to require him to transfer to another base within the UK
>
> Also, in *Pepper v. Webb* 1969, when a head gardener, asked to plant some flowers, replied "I couldn't care less about your bloody greenhouse or your sodding garden" and walked

away, the court held that the refusal to obey the instructions, rather than the language which accompanied the refusal, amounted to a breach of contract.

Finally in relation to implied terms, some mention should be made of the Court of Appeal decision in *Johnstone v. Bloomsbury Health Authority* 1991 where it was held by a majority that an employer's implied obligation to ensure the health and welfare of his employees could be broken even where the employer was exercising an express option in the contract to require the employee to work a large number of hours overtime. The court felt that if the employer is aware that by requiring a junior doctor to work long hours his health is suffering it would be a breach of contract to impose such long hours on him despite the fact that it was authorised by an express term of the contract.

Activity

Identify, a particular job for which you are or hope to be qualified to apply.

Make a list of the express terms you would expect to be included in the contract of employment relating to the job so that s.1 of the Employment Protection (Consolidation) Act 1978 is complied with.

Collective agreements and the contract of employment

In practice, the process of negotiating and varying terms and conditions of employment is not carried on by employees individually bargaining with their employers but by employers and trade unions engaging in collective bargaining on their behalf. The product of collective bargaining is called a collective agreement which will normally contain, along with a number of other matters, specific reference to individual terms and conditions of employment. Over seventy five percent of workers are still covered by collective agreements so that it is crucial to appreciate their legal standing and those parts of a collective agreement that are suitable for incorporation into individual contracts of employment. The legal status of collective agreements is referred to in the *Trade Union and Labour Relations (Consolidation) Act* 1992 which provides that such agreements are conclusively presumed not to be legally enforceable unless in writing and expressed to be so. As between the parties to a collective agreement therefore, (the trade union or unions and the employer or employer's association), collective agreements while in writing are not usually expressed to be legally enforceable and are consequently not legally binding. Those parts of the collective agreement that are incorporated into individual contracts of employment will become legally enforceable however between the employer and employee.

The process of incorporation

The usual method of incorporation is by the individual contract of employment making express reference to the collective agreement or agreements. Statements such as 'union conditions' or 'subject to a national agreement' either in the contract of employment or even the statutory statements of the main terms and conditions of employment would normally suffice for the purpose of incorporation. It should be stressed however, that the agreed terms of employment prevail over the statutory statement.

In *Robertson and Jackson v. British Gas Corporation* 1983 the Court of Appeal held that an express reference in the contract of employment to the effect that "incentive bonus conditions apply to the work carried on" made the payment of an incentive bonus a contractual obligation, the terms of which were to be found in the collective agreement which existed at the time of appointment. A conflicting reference in the statutory statement of particulars of employment to the effect that the bonus scheme could be unilaterally withdrawn by the employer had no significance.

The suggestion is, therefore, that collective agreements can only be varied by the parties to them rather than some unilateral act of the employer. Of course the employer is free to seek an individual's agreement that collectively agreed terms should no longer apply but to attempt to achieve that result unilaterally would result in a repudiatory breach of the contract of employment.

Part of the process of identifying the terms of a contract of employment must involve discovering those parts of a collective agreement which have been incorporated into individual contracts of employment. This is by no means an easy task, for it is a question of sorting out those parts of the agreement that deal with employer/trade union matters, for instance the machinery for collective bargaining, and those parts which have significance for individual employees, such as wage negotiations.

> In *British Leyland (UK) Ltd. v. McQuilken* 1978 a collectively agreed redundancy scheme was negotiated between the employer and a trade union to deal with a massive reorganisation which involved employees in retraining and possible transfer to other work locations. When the employer failed to implement the agreed scheme in relation to the complainant, he resigned due to uncertainty about his future. To succeed in a claim for unfair dismissal it was necessary for the complainant to show that he had been constructively dismissed. Constructive dismissal is established by proving that the employer has been guilty of a significant breach of the employment contract. One issue in the case therefore, was whether by failing to implement the scheme the employer had been guilty of such a breach. The EAT thought not. The redundancy scheme was a long term plan dealing with policy rather than individual employment rights and was not therefore capable of incorporation into individual contracts of employment.

Subject to the approval of the Secretary of State for Employment, a collective agreement can replace certain of the statutory rights, for example, to a redundancy payment or guaranteed payment. In cases where approval is granted the statutory right is substituted by the right under the collective agreement which becomes legally enforceable as a term of the individual contract of employment to which it relates.

Assignment *Staff Recruitment*

Tweedson Ltd. is a medium sized private company engaged primarily in the manufacture of office equipment. At the company's head office in Manchester there is a general office staffed by a number of clerical and typing staff, all of whom are female. Other than Mrs. Jones who manages the general office, the remaining managerial and junior managerial staff at head office are all male. The role of the typists is mainly to type letters to customers and suppliers, minutes of meetings, and memos and reports from managers. Most managers are unconcerned as to which typist completes their work but two or three insist on their work going to a particular typist and often say "please give this work to my typist". Over the years the typing pool became skilled at reading the poor handwriting of individual managers and often modified the format and structure of letters and reports to suit their individual whims. In early February Mrs. Jones was faced with a staff problem when an experienced clerk and two typists coincidentally served notice that they were leaving the company to start a family. After discussing the matter with the Managing Director, Mrs. Jones began the process of replacing the staff. She drew up an advertisement to place in the Thursday edition of one of the two main Manchester evening newspapers.

The advertisement read

Tweedson Ltd.,
12-14 Chandler Place,
Moorside,
Manchester M1Q 473, Tel 7320473

Three staff required   - Tweedson Ltd. require replacements for three female staff.
One to carry out clerical work and the other two for general office typing.
Hours of work 9 am to 5 pm. Monday to Friday with a 37 hour week.
Salaries to be agreed.

Fourteen applications were received, all from females. The applicants had a wide age range and half of them had sent C.V.s. As Mrs. Jones had little experience in selection interviewing, she sought the assistance of Ed Clark, the Production manager. Mr. Clark manages the production department with mainly semi-skilled operatives. Also, with a 10% staff turnover, he was often involved with selecting staff. He told Mrs. Jones not to worry about the interview, he would do most of the questioning. "It shouldn't take very long" he said, " "I can spot a good worker as they walk through the door". With the staff leaving, Mrs. Jones was kept very busy and gave little further thought to the interviews. Mr. Clark's secretary sent letters to all the applicants indicating that they should report to the head office at 9.30 am to be interviewed for the posts. The interview was planned to be in Mr. Clark's office. It had an imposing desk in front of a picture window. The two interviewers were to sit behind the desk, in front of the window. The interviewees were to sit at the other side of the desk facing them. At 9 am on the day of the interview, the interviewers had a discussion in Mr. Clark's office. "I will start the questioning." Mr. Clark said. "Let's make sure that we don't take on anybody who is likely to leave to have a family in the near future!" "You add any questions you feel like, just butt in, it keeps them on their toes." "If they have a family, I think I will ask them about who looks after the kids. It is really annoying having staff taking days off when their kids are sick." Also, noticing that one of the candidates had an Indian surname, Mr. Clark added "I don't see why we should take on a coloured girl when English girls are unemployed." Mrs. Jones said "Well let's give them ten minutes each, a few questions should sort them out. We don't need to do anything else, do we?"

Tasks

1. Identify the legal and managerial problems that could arise because onf the actions of the managers.
2. State what should have to be done to achieve a reasoned and rational approach to man-power planning, recruitment and selection in this scenario.
3. Draft statutory statements of the main terms of employment which by law should be provided to the successful candidates.
4. Collect at least twenty job advertisements from local and national newspapers and trade journals. Categorise the advertisements into groups such as excellent, good, fair and poor. Check for any common faults.

Unit 5

Employment in the Market Economy

This unit has been written to cover the following specifications of the General National Vocational Qualification Business Level 3

Unit 5   Employment in the Market Economy Level 3

Element 5.1:   Investigate employment in business sectors

Performance criteria:
1   changing features of employment are identified using a variety of information sources
2   employment trends in the UK and EC are identified and explained
3   employment trends within different business sectors are investigated and explained
4   economic relationships are analysed in relation to different business sectors
5   economic relationships used to investigate employment trends are explained

Element 5.2:   Analyse external influences relating to employment

Performance criteria:
1   external influences on business actions relating to employment are analysed and explained
2   current examples of business actions relating to employment practice are identified
3   actions taken by business are explained using economic relationships

Element 5.3:   Evaluate the workforce performance of business sectors

Performance criteria:
1   features of the workforce performance of different business sectors are identified
2   data relating to workforce performance of business is accessed from a variety of sources
3   economic relationships are used to analyse the workforce performance of business
4   workforce performance of two businesses is evaluated and recorded

(extract from General National Vocational Qualifications Mandatory Units for Business GNVQ3 offered by Business Education and Technology Council, City and Guilds and RSA Examinations Board - published by the National Council for Vocational Qualifications April 1993 - reproduced by kind permission of the National Council for Vocational Qualifications)

GNVQ3 Business - Unit Number U1016178

Element 5.1 Employment in Business Sectors

The Changing Features of Employment

In this section we shall examine some significant features which have altered the face of British employment over the last two decades. We shall see that the British workforce has changed from being predominantly male, full-time and employed in manufacturing industry. Today it is much more varied. The workforce is older. There has been a significant shift away from traditional manufacturing employment into jobs in the service sector. Many more people are employed on a part-time or temporary basis and there is a greater proportion of female workers.

Changes in the age structure of the workforce

A significant factor which has affected the makeup of the working population has been the change in the age structure of the population. There was a relatively high birth rate in the 1950s and 1960s and, by the 1990s this has led to a population bulge in the 30-40 year old age group. However the birth rate fell dramatically in the late 1970s and 1980s and this has meant that the number of 16 year olds coming on to the labour market in the early 1990s has fallen.

The UK now has an ageing population and consequently an ageing workforce. This means that over the next decade the percentage of the workforce which is under 25 will fall from 25% in the late 1980s to about 17% by the turn of the century. Equally important is the fact that by the year 2001 the percentage of the workforce over 45 years of age will have risen to over 33% of the active working population.

The numbers who are retired will also continue to increase as a percentage of the total population as people retire earlier and live longer. This will place increasing demands on those still working to support a growing dependent retired population. This fact has not escaped the government who realise that the total cost of old age pensions will grow as the number entitled to claim state pension increases and we are currently seeing attempts by the government to get people to make their own provision for retirement by taking out private pensions and not relying on the state. There are also proposals to increase the age at women can claim state pension from 60 to 65 in an effort to reduce the numbers claiming state pensions.

Changes in the nature of employment as a consequence of industrial restructuring

One feature of the British workforce over the last two decades is the change in the industries in which most people are employed. In Unit 1, *Business in the Economy*, we examined the major shift in the structure of the British economy, away from manufacturing towards industries such as retailing and finance, and its impact on employment cannot be too heavily stressed.

As we have already seen, one of the most noticeable changes in the restructuring of the British economy over the last thirty years has been the decline in manufacturing employment. Almost three million jobs have been lost in this sector since the 1970s. This process has been described as de-industrialisation, and while it is also apparent in many other developed nations in the world, it is in Britain that it is most pronounced. In fact, for long periods during the 1980s, it seemed that the British government was determined to allow the service sector of the economy to grow at the expense of manufacturing. While this service sector growth did happen, its benefits to employment may prove to be somewhat short-lived.

For as the 1990s unfold it is becoming increasingly apparent that the impact of technology may be felt greatest in these service industries. Many of the financial institutions, such as banks and insurance companies, are finding that they are now over-staffed as computers are found to be capable of doing much of the work of those recruited in the 1980s.

The decline of employment in manufacturing

The change in the industrial structure of the UK is obviously reflected in employment in each of the respective categories. In fact as industries such as agriculture and manufacturing have declined they have become less labour intensive and more capital intensive and so the numbers employed in these industries have fallen faster than the industries' share of GDP. The number of jobs lost in manufacturing throughout the 1980s has been quite staggering. In the late 1970s about 30% of the work force were employed in some aspect of manufacturing but by the end of the 1980s this figure had fallen to about 20% – a reduction of 50%.

Some economists would argue that this reduction in the workforce of British industry is in fact a good thing as productivity per worker in manufacturing has generally risen considerably throughout this period. British industry is said to be leaner and fitter and therefore more capable of competing with other more efficient economies. Nevertheless this reduction in manufacturing has meant increasing unemployment in many areas of Britain and particularly in the traditional industrial heartlands.

The rise of the service sector

The service industries now account for almost three quarters of all employment in this country with the numbers employed in Banking and Finance doubling over the last decade. However as we have already noted, the recession and changing technology has threatened the growth of such jobs and the dramatic growth of the 1980s will not be repeated in the 1990s. In fact it is anticipated that the numbers working in the Financial sector will decline.

Activity

From your library obtain a copy of 'Social Trends' which is a government publication published by HMSO. In this book find the section on Employment. In this section you will see that there are a number of different graphical presentations of changing trends in the labour market. Use you imagination to produce three other types of graphs or charts which will illustrate the changes which the data describes.

Employment Trends

The growth of the self-employed

One significant change in employment patterns which has been strongly encouraged by the government has been the growth in self-employment. The percentage of the workforce which is self-employed has risen from less than 8% at the end of the 70s to almost 14% by the end of the 80s. There are now almost 3.5 million people who are self-employed of whom about 60% are in the service industry. The economic philosophy behind this has been to encourage entrepreneurship and use small businesses as the motor to drive economic growth. This area has been particularly hard hit by the recession of the last few years with many small business which were established in the 1980s collapsing during this period.

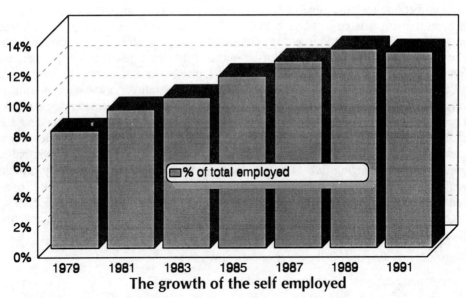

14%

12%

10%

8%

6% ▭% of total employed

4%

2%

0%
1979   1981   1983   1985   1987   1989   1991

The growth of the self employed

Traditionally in the UK when an organisation recruits someone to its workforce it does this by entering into a contract of employment. This is also called a contract of service. (We examine the nature of the contract of employment in some detail in Unit 4, *Human Resources*.)

There is a number of ways in which the terms of this contract can be established:

- in some cases the organisation may bargain individually with the prospective employee;
- the employer could bargain collectively with a trade union to agree the terms of the contract of employment for a number of workers;
- in other cases, the employer organisation may simply present the terms of the contract to the prospective employee in a standard form without giving the prospective employee any opportunity for negotiation.

The majority of the workers in the UK are employed as full-time workers and paid a weekly wage or monthly salary. Under such contracts the employment may be ended by either the employee or the employer exercising their respective right to resign or dismiss by serving the appropriate notice or statutory minimum notice period, if this is longer. Since 1971, however, full-time employees, who qualify with generally two years continuous employment with the same employer, have some degree of employment security conferred by Statute, in that they have right not to be unfairly dismissed. This means that if an employer wishes to end the contract of employment of a qualified worker, the employer may be called upon to provide a statutory reason for the dismissal if the employee complains of unfair dismissal to an industrial tribunal. The tribunal has jurisdiction to determine whether the dismissal is fair or unfair and if it finds that the dismissal is unfair it has the power to award the complainant redress in the form of reinstatement, re-engagement or compensation.

At present part-time workers can also qualify for the right not to be unfairly dismissed but only if they can show that they have been in continuous employment with the same employer for between eight and sixteen hours a week over a period of five years. Needless to say many part-time workers do not qualify under this condition and this lack of security of employment is a significant feature in employment trends in the UK, given the significant increase in the number of part-time and temporary workers.

We also need to mention the most flexible form of employment relationship, the contract for services, under which an individual is engaged as a self employed contractor. Certainly the requirements of employers will range from the need to engage full-time employees where a long standing relationship with their workers is envisaged, characterised by mutual trust and confidence between the parties, to the use of workers engaged to complete a particular task. It may be that the worker, such as the accountant or solicitor, provides a specialist skill which is required by the employer only on an intermittent basis. Alternatively the employer may only offer casual employment, because of economic necessity or need to expand or contract the size of the workforce in line with demand. The use of independent contractors (or self employed workers) is now a well established practice in a number of industries, for instance, the media, catering and construction. Of the million or so construction workers, well over half a million are self employed. The changing face of employment patterns in Britain is shown by official figures which reveal that while 62.3% of household income is earned from wages and salaries, over 10% is now derived from self-employment. This form of employment has many advantages for both sides. The employer 'gets the job done' and the contractor is normally well paid in return. There are, however, a number of criticisms of this system in that:

- it provides no support for the older or infirm worker;
- there is no security of employment for the employee; and
- it may lead to a general reduction in health and safety standards.

Because of the increasing use of self employed workers in business to carry out work and provide services both in the public and private sectors we need to examine the distinction between the employed and self employed. You should appreciate that there are a large number of legal and economic consequences stemming from the distinction between employed and self employed status. For this reason it is necessary to be able to identify the status of the employment relationship that a person has been entered into. The recent wide publicity given to the controversial nature of the employment status of the Director General of the BBC demonstrates the extent to which this is a matter of wide public interest.

Employment relationships

Employment legislation and the common law both recognise the distinction between employment under a contract of service and self employment under a contract for services. The distinction is a relatively straightforward one to make in the majority of cases. It is only in a small proportion of cases that difficulties arise, often where employers, or those they employ are seeking to achieve contractor status for economic advantage or in order to evade legal responsibilities. In the table on the following page there is a summary of the major legal and economic consequences of the employment classification.

By comparing the major characteristics of the two types of contract you can see that the status enjoyed by both the employed and the self-employed have advantages and disadvantages from the point of view both of employer and of worker. The major advantage of self-employed status is an economic one, both for the contractor, in terms of tax advantages and lower national insurance contributions, and for the employer, in terms of reduced costs of administration. This benefit, of course, must be weighed against the cost to the worker of less job security and that to the employer of less control. Certainly an employer who requires the performance of a specialist task either once, or only intermittently, would be advised to employ a contractor rather than engage a full-time employee. We should stress, however, that it is not possible to create a particular employment relationship simply by pinning a label upon it. Thus an employer could not rid himself of the numerous statutory duties he has in relation to his employees by simply reclassifying them as contractors. It is the substance of any employment relationship which will determine its status.

Distinguishing between employed and self-employed status

The task of distinguishing between a contract of service and a contract for services has been left to the courts. Over the years, various tests have been formulated to determine a worker's status. Originally, the courts would consider only the level of control an employer had over the worker. Therefore, if an employee could tell workers not only what to do, but also how and when to do it, then the workers were regarded as employees, employed under a contract of service. Today, the courts adopt a much wider approach and, while conceding that degree of control is an important factor, they also take into account all other circumstances in determining a worker's status.

> In *Ready Mixed Concrete Ltd., v. Ministry of Pensions* 1968, the court had to decide the status of a driver working for the plaintiff company. His written contract of employment (thirty pages long) stated that he was not an employee, but this, the court said, was not decisive. It was merely a factor to be taken into account. All aspects of his job were considered. For instance, he purchased the lorry from the company, he had to maintain it himself, his pay was calculated on the basis of concrete carried, and he could in some circumstances delegate the driving. These factors pointed to him being a contractor, while others pointed to his status as an employee. For instance he had to paint the lorry in the company colours, he had to use it exclusively on company business and he was required to obey reasonable orders. Here, the court held that the majority of the provisions were consistent with there being a contract for services. McKenna J. stated that there is a contract of service if an individual agrees to provide his own work, submits to his employer's control and the majority of the contractual provisions are consistent with it being a contract of service. Certainly the power of the employer to delegate work was regarded as indicative of there being a contract for services. This approach has since been referred to as the mixed or multiple test and is still applied today when attempting to determine the employment status of a worker.

The status of 'self-employed' cannot be achieved simply by an employer including an express provision in a contract, for the courts will look to the substance of an employment relationship to decide a worker's status.

> In *Ferguson v. John Dawson Ltd.* 1976, a builder's labourer agreed to work on what was known as 'the lump' and was described as a 'self-employed labour-only sub-contractor'. Having suffered injuries as a result of the employer's breach of a statutory duty, the labourer could only succeed in an action for damages if he could show that he was an 'employee' and therefore protected by the Statute. The court held that the 'lump' was no more than a device to attempt to gain tax advantages, and in reality, taking all the circumstances into account, the relationship was one of employer and employee and a contract of service existed.

The problem of determining employment status where there is uncertainty as to the true relationship arose again in *O'Kelly and Others v. Trusthouse Forte Plc* 1983. Here a banqueting department ran by the employer was staffed in part by full time employees, but in the main it was staffed by so-called 'casuals'. In addition, the casuals included among them certain 'regulars', who were given preference where there was work available, and were expected to work long hours. Consequently they had no other employment. The applicants, who were 'regulars' and Trade Union stewards, were told by their employers that their services were no longer required, and so they complained of unfair dismissal. In determining their employment status, the Industrial Tribunal acknowledged that its role was to 'consider all aspects of the relationship'. Applying the mixed or multiple test, the Tribunal isolated factors consistent with a contract of service and those which were inconsistent. Among the factors deemed

Legal and Economic Consequences of Employment Classification

Contract of Service *(Employed Persons)*	*Contract for Services* *(Self-employed Persons)*

Liability

An employer may be made vicariously liable for the wrongful acts of employees committed during the course of their employment.

As a general principle an employer may not be made liable for the wrongful acts of contractors he employs other than in exceptional cases.

Common Law Employment Terms

Numerous terms are implied into a contract of employment by the common law to regulate the relationship of employer and employee e.g. trust and confidence.

The common law is much less likely to intervene in the relationship of employer and contractor.

Health and Safety

A high standard of care is owed by an employer both under statute and the common law with regard to the health and safety of his employees.

While both the common law and statute recognise the existence of a duty of care by an employer in relation to the contractors he employs at common law it is of a lesser standard than the duty owed to employees.

Statutory Employment Rights

A large number of individual employment rights are conferred on employees by statute which generally arise after a period of service e.g. the right to unfair dismissal protection, redundancy payments, to belong to a trade union and take part in trade union activities, to protection in the event of the employer's insolvency, to guarantee payments, to security of employment after maternity leave, to statutory maternity pay, to a written statement of the main terms and conditions of employment and the right not to be discriminated against on the grounds of sex, race or marital status.

Contractors are effectively excluded from the mass of individual employment rights conferred by statute. One notable exception however is the legislation in relation to sex and race discrimination which protects the self-employed when they are providing personal services.

Income Tax

The income tax payable by an employee is deducted at source by the employer under the pay as you earn scheme i.e. PAYE (Schedule E).

The income tax of a self employed person is payable by the taxpayer and not his employer on a lump sum preceding year basis (Schedule D). Apart from the obvious advantage of retaining the tax until it falls due at the end of the year it is also felt that such a taxpayer has more favourable treatment of reasonable expenses when assessed for tax. Furthermore an independent sub-contractor may have to charge VAT on services.

Welfare Benefits

Under the Social Security Act 1975 both employer and employee must contribute to the payment of Class 1 National Insurance contributions assessed on an earnings related basis which entitles the employee to claim all the available welfare benefits e.g. unemployment benefit, statutory sick pay, industrial disablement benefit, state retirement pension.

Under the Social Security Act 1975 a self-employed person is individually responsible for the payment of lower Class 2 National Insurance contributions and has only limited rights to claim welfare benefits e.g. statutory sick pay.

inconsistent were the lack of a mutuality of obligation to provide work and offer services, and the custom and practice of the industry. These factors swayed the Tribunal to find that the applicants were not employees. The Employment Appeals Tribunal, however, allowed the applicants appeal, deciding that the question of status was one of law which the Tribunal had applied incorrectly. On further appeal to the Court of Appeal, however, it was held that the Tribunal had not misdirected itself in law and had come to a conclusion which a reasonable tribunal could have reached. Its original finding had to stand, and the applicants' action failed.

Unfortunately, the Tribunal's decision in *O'Kelly* 1983 does seem to ignore the economic reality of the 'regulars' employment, for failure to work when required had for them the drastic consequences of their removal from the company's regular casual list. A rational application of the 'business account' test would reveal that the employee had no capital equipment, no share in the profits, no multiple employment and there was no delegation of work and that substantial control stayed with the employer. Certainly it is difficult to reconcile *O'Kelly* with the decision of the Court of Appeal in *Ferguson* 1976, where clearly expressed intentions were overturned to find employment status for a worker who was badly injured.

More recently the Privy Council, which acts as a final appeal court for some commonwealth countries, was asked to rule the legal status of a worker in Hong Kong.

In *Lee v. 1.Chung and 2.Shun Shing Construction and Engineering Company Ltd.* 1990 the appellant, a mason, claimed compensation when he suffered injury during the course of his work on a construction site in Hong Kong. The accident happened when he was working for a building sub contractor who had been delegated work by the main contractor on the site. Both the District Court and the Court of Appeal of Hong Kong had rejected the claim on the basis that the right to compensation arose in respect of injury caused to a person who worked under a contract of service, and in the circumstances the appellant was employed as an independent contractor. On final appeal, the Privy Council held that as the relevant Ordinance in Hong Kong which dealt with the legal position had been modelled on English Workman's Compensation Acts, then the status of a worker should be determined by applying English common law standards. Confirming that no single test is decisive, the court felt that the standard to be applied was best stated by Cooke J. in *Market Investigations v. Ministry of Social Security* 1969 when he set out the fundamental test as being *"Is the person who has engaged himself to perform these services performing them as a person in business on his own account"*. Control is important but not the sole determining factor. *"Other matters which may be of importance are whether the worker provides his own equipment, whether he hires his own helpers, what degree of financial risk he takes, what degree of responsibility he has for investment and management and whether and how far he has an opportunity to profit from sound management in the performance of his task."* The decision will depend upon an evaluation of the facts...*"There will be many borderline cases in which similarly instructed minds may come to different conclusions"*. Such a decision should therefore be left to the trial court and changed only by an appellate court in exceptional cases where the trial court *"took a view of the facts which could not reasonably be entertained"*. In the present case, their Lordships were entitled to reverse the lower court's decision and find that the worker was in reality an employee. All the indicators pointed to the conclusion that the appellant was an employee. *"The picture that emerged from the facts was that of a skilled artisan earning his living by working for more than one employer as an employee, not as a small businessman venturing into business on his own account as a independent contractor, with all the attendant risks. The appellant ran no risk whatsoever save that of being unable to find employment which is a risk faced by all 'employees'"*.

The fact that there has been such litigation on the employed/self employed distinction suggests that in the borderline cases in particular, decisions are by no means clear cut. The courts are faced with the difficult task of maintaining a balance between the freedom of employers to offer employment on the terms that best suit their interest and the rights of workers, for the most part in an unequal bargaining position, to obtain the benefits of status as an employee.

Activity

List those features of an employment relationship which would indicate that an individual is employed under:

1.   *A contract of services and;*
2.   *A contract for services.*

Women as part of the workforce

One of the most significant changes in the British labour market over the last twenty five years has been the growth of female workers. In the late 1960s only about 40% of all adult females were in paid employment. This meant that approximately eight million women had paid jobs at that time. Today there are almost thirteen million women in paid employment, an increase of over 40% on the figure of two decades ago. Of course much of this increase has been the result of women taking lower paid or part-time employment and the position of women workers in terms of their employment status has not increased as dramatically as the numbers may suggest. By the year 2001 it is anticipated that women will make up 45% of the adult workforce.

Another significant factor is that the percentage of adult women who are now in employment or who are actively seeking employment is now over 50%. Thus the balance of the workforce between men and women has shifted dramatically over this period and increasingly the British economy is becoming dependent on women as a major element of the workforce. The number of men in employment over this period has remained relatively stable although there has been a decrease in the number of older men, particularly those over the age of 60, who are economically active. This has been the result of increasing early retirement and the fact that older men, if they lose their job, find it increasingly difficult to find another. The pattern of women's employment relates to their stage in life with many women working full-time before having children, spending their children's early years as part-time workers or out of employment but returning to full-time employment when their children start school.

There are a number of reasons why there has been such a marked increase in the number of women who are in employment or are seeking jobs. These include:

- a greater necessity for women to work. Two factors are important in this case:
  - the increase in single parent families has made it economically imperative for a single woman bringing up children to work to support both herself and her children;
  - in traditional family units, the notion that the man provides the family wage is often now unrealistic and will often mean that the woman's wage becomes a significant element of the family's income. It is increasingly common to find households in which either both adults are economically active or, because of the way the benefit system works, neither adult is working;
- a trend for women to have children at a later age and this has led to an increase in the number of younger women who stay in the employment market before having children;

- increased sexual equality for women. Gender discrimination is made unlawful under the Sex Discrimination Act 1975, 1986, the *Equal Pay Act* 1970 and also under EC law. We discuss this in more detail in Unit 4, *Human Resources*;

- the increase in the number of women in professional and managerial jobs who are more likely to continue working while their children are young or to return to their jobs once their children reach school age;

- the increase in the provision of child care with the growth of playgroups and nurseries;

- a change in social attitudes towards women working. It is now much more socially acceptable for women to return to work once they have had children. Between 1981 and 1992 the percentage of married women who were economically active (in other words those who were in paid employment or who are actively seeking employment) increased from 60% to 70%.

While these factors have contributed to the ability of women to return to work, the increase in the number of women looking for jobs has to be met by an increase in the demand for women's labour. This increased demand has been for the following reasons:

- as we have already discussed, a major change in the British economy over the last thirty years has been the decline of heavy industry. This has seen a decrease in the numbers employed in traditional industries such as mining, shipbuilding, iron and steel. Such industries mainly employed men. This decline has been balanced to some degree by the growth of the service industries and light manufacturing. These industries can employ either men or women but as women have traditionally been paid less than men and have often been more willing to work on a part-time basis such industries have a greater proportion of their workforce. In 1992 only 6% of men were in part-time employment while 45% of women had part-time jobs.

- employers have also tended to seek more part-time workers as this often gives the employer more flexibility to increase or decrease their production volume as part-timers are more likely to have their hours of work varied and have a weaker legal status should the employer wish to get rid of them. Women are often forced to seek part-time work or chose this type of employment because they have family ties. In fact in a recent survey, 90% of part-time women workers who were married said that they did not want a full-time job.

- as we shall discuss in the next section there has been a change in the age structure of the workforce which has meant that there are fewer young people coming onto the workforce. Employers are therefore turning to women to take on jobs which in the past have been filled by school leavers.

- if employers wish to attract more women back into the workforce they will have to become increasing flexible in the hours of work they offer and the facilities, such as child care and creches, which they provide. If this happens we may see an even greater increase in the number of women who are returning to work after having children.

It is interesting to note that female activity rates in employment varies according to ethnic origin. There are much higher female participant rates among white women, with almost 66% of the total of working age being either in employment or actively seeking employment. This is in comparison with less than 33% of women in the Pakistani and Bangladeshi ethnic groups.

When we compare female activity rates in the UK with those in the rest of Europe we find that British women are among the most economically active within the EC. In fact only in Denmark is there a higher female participation rate than there is in the UK. As we have already noted the UK has over 50% of its adult women who are economically active while countries such as Spain, Italy Greece and Ireland have only about one third of women who are economically active.

Activity

Identify three industries or occupations in which females make up the majority of the labour force. Explain the reasons for this gender imbalance considering economic, social and historical factors.

The growth of part-time employment

A significant trend of employment over the last decade has been the growth of reliance on part-time workers. In spring 1992 23% of all people in work (45% of women and 6% of men) worked part-time in their main job. While as a general rule self employed workers tend to work longer hours then employees, there are nevertheless over a half a million (9.5%) self employed part-timers in Britain.

Legally a full-time worker is anyone who works under a contract of employment for sixteen hours a week or more and as an employee such a person will enjoy the full range of statutory employment rights generally after two years continuous employment. A part-timer who is employed for between eight and sixteen hours a week will qualify for those rights after five years continuous employment. Working for less than eight hours a week, an individual is still protected by discrimination law and to comply with European Community law all part-time women will soon be entitled to 14 weeks maternity leave under the *Trade Union Reform and Employment Rights Act* 1993.

Employers across the full range of occupational categories offer part-time employment but there are particular concentrations of part-time workers in;

- sales and services (check out operators, cleaners, catering assistants, porters)
- teaching and health professionals (school teachers, lecturers, nurses, physiotherapists)
- personal services (cooks, bar staff, hairdressers, domestic staff)
- clerical and secretarial (clerks, typists, computer operators)

Clearly while a number of part-time workers would prefer the opportunity to enter full-time employment a significant proportion of part-time workers choose to work part-time because of the impracticably of full-time hours, given their other responsibilities. There is also evidence to suggest that some people actually prefer the life style afforded by part-time work and in addition to money, are motivated by the social contact and variety from home-life that part-time employment provides.

Temporary workers

There is a significant increase in recent years of the use of temporary workers rather than employing full-time staff. Temporary workers could be classified as either employees or self employed workers. They were originally used as replacements for staff taking maternity leave but increasingly employers are offering temporary employment as an alternative to full-time jobs. A temporary worker is much less likely to acquire employment rights based on continuity of employment so that the benefits are obvious to employers in industries which require a flexible workforce. Currently in the United States of America one in four workers has only temporary status.

Activity

On March 3 1994 the House of Lords delivered a judgment in the case of Regina v. Secretary of State for Employment ex parte E.O.C. Find a report of this landmark decision in the press and state how it has changed the legal position of part-time workers.

Changing contractual arrangements

It is inevitable that the success and in some cases the survival of any organisation in the public or private sector will depend on its ability to respond positively to legal, economic or social change. Change will usually have impact upon the organisation's workforce and in order to achieve a successful outcome in implementing the change process the management of an organisation should be aware of the legal position relating to changing contractual arrangements.

The legal position

As a result of a change process in any organisation, members of the workforce could be required to accept an increase or decrease in hours or pay, different contractual duties or responsibilities, a change in job location or different job functions or work practices. Later when we consider how the change process should be managed, the importance of seeking the consent of the workforce to change will be stressed and this applies equally when terms of employment are the subject of change. Such consent should be sought even where the workforce may be legally required to accept the change within their terms of employment. If express terms of employment authorise the employer to implement the change, then an employee is legally obliged to accept it provided the term is interpreted reasonably.

> In *McCaffery v. A.E. Jeavons Ltd.* 1967 an employee employed expressly as a 'travelling man' in the building trade was held to be bound to move anywhere in the country.

Even where there is a well drafted mobility clause in a contract of employment, for example, 'the bank may from time to time require an employee to be transferred temporarily or permanently to any place of business which the bank may have in the UK for which a relocation or other allowance may be payable at the discretion of the bank', an employer must act reasonably when relying upon it.

> In *United Bank Ltd. v. Akhtar* 1989 the employer was in repudiatory breach of an implied term of the contract of employment requiring reasonable notice when he sought to rely on the above clause to require a junior bank employee to move from the Leeds branch to Birmingham after giving only six days notice. As a consequence the employee who refused to move without more notice could regard himself as being constructively dismissed. Furthermore the employer's conduct in relation to the transfer could also be said to be in breach of the general implied contractual duty of trust and confidence.

From the above case you will see that courts and tribunals have a wide discretion to imply terms into contracts of employment to give effect to the parties' intentions by more fully expressing the contractual bargain.

> In *Jones v. Associated Tunnelling Co. Ltd.* 1981, the EAT held that, in the absence of express terms to the contrary, there is an implied term in a contract of employment that the employer has the right to transfer the employee to a different place of work within reasonable daily commuting distance of his home.

By implying a term into employment contracts that employees should be flexible and adaptable and react positively to change, an employer is authorised to implement quite sweeping changes in job functions provided staff are given sufficient training to enable them to cope with the different demands placed upon them.

In *Creswell v. Board of Inland Revenue* 1984, employees sought a legal declaration that their employers had broken the terms of their contract of employment by introducing new technology and expecting them to adapt to it. The High Court declared, however, that, provided they received adequate training, employees were expected to adapt to new methods and new techniques. There is a general contractual duty on employees to adapt to changing working methods. There was also a right for the employer to withhold pay for those employees who refused to conform to the new methods, for they are in breach of their contractual obligations.

The legal position is much more complex if the changing contractual arrangements are not expressly or impliedly authorised by the contract of employment. An obvious example would be the situation where an employer requires his staff to move from full-time to part-time work or accept a reduction in wages. Here the employer must seek the express or implied assent of his workforce or their trade union to the change and he cannot legally impose the change unilaterally.

Certainly by continuing to work under protest the employee is demonstrating his unwillingness to accept a contractual change and is entitled to a period of grace during which he can assess his legal position.

In *Marriott v. Oxford District Co-operative Society Ltd.* 1969 a foreman supervisor was told by his employer that the position of foreman was no longer required and that his wages were to be reduced by £1 per week to reflect his loss of status. The employee continued to work under protest for three weeks before terminating his contract of employment by notice and claiming a redundancy payment. The Court of Appeal held, reversing the Divisional Court's judgement, that as there was no implied assent to the contractual change, it amounted to a repudiation of the contract of employment. The employee's reaction of continuing to work for a short period under protest was understandable and in no way constituted implied assent to the contractual change.

One option for an employee who feels that his employer is unreasonably requiring him to do work which is not part of his contractual obligations is to seek an interlocutory (temporary) injunction to maintain the status quo at work.

In *Hughs v. London Borough of Southwark* 1988 a number of social workers applied to the High Court for an interlocutory injunction to stop their employers requiring them to staff community areas on a temporary basis and so terminate their normal hospital work. The High Court held that the employer's instruction was in breach of contract and the plaintiff social workers were entitled to an interlocutory injunction to restrain the breach. The Court of Appeal in *Powell v. The London Borough of Brent* 1987 had previously held that the court has power to grant an interlocutory injunction to restrain the breach of a contract of service provided that there was mutual confidence between the employer and employee. Here, despite the dispute, the employers retained confidence in the social workers.

If there is no agreement to a proposed change and the employer attempts to unilaterally impose a more onerous term on an employee, for example a wage cut, then the employee has a number of options. He could:

- accept the variation as a repudiatory breach of the contract, walk out and claim constructive dismissal;
- remain passive without protest and eventually be taken to have accepted the varied contract;
- continue to work under protest and sue for damages for breach of contract.

In *Rigby v. Ferodo Ltd.* 1988 the employee, in response to a unilateral wage cut, took the final option and sued for damages representing the unpaid wages. Both the High Court and the Court of Appeal agreed that there had been no mutual variation of the contract of employment so that the unreduced wage was payable and, further, that the damages should not be limited to the twelve week notice period under which the employee could have been dismissed. The House of Lords agreed and held that a repudiatory breach does not automatically terminate a contract of employment unless the breach is accepted by the employee as a repudiation. Damages were not limited therefore to the notice period of twelve weeks and the primary contractual obligation to pay the full wage survived.

More recently in *Alexander v. Standard Telephones and Cables Ltd.* (no 2) 1991 the High Court considered the legal position relating to contractual variation. Mr. Justice Hobhouse stated that "*Although an employer is not entitled unilaterally to vary a contract, it is always open to an employer, as a matter of contract, to say to his employee that after the expiry of the contractual notice period the employer will only continue the contract of employment on different terms. Such a notice is equivalent to giving notice to terminate the existing contract and offering a revised contract in continuation of and substitution for the existing contract. The period of notice has to be the notice that is required to terminate the existing contract. It is then up to the employee to decide whether he is willing to accept the revised terms*".

It seems therefore that provided the correct notice is given, then an employee is contractually bound to accept a change in terms of employment. This does not tell the full story however, for an employee with sufficient continuous employment (two years) has the right not be unfairly dismissed. By requiring such an employee to accept more onerous terms of employment an employer will be in repudiatory breach and if accepted by the employee this would constitute dismissal and potentially an unfair dismissal. In the present employment climate however, the potential redress for a successful complaint of unfair dismissal will hardly compensate for the loss of secure employment.(We examine this in more detail in Unit 4,*Human Resources.*)

Activity

An employer has decided that in the interests of efficiency it is necessary that staff will be required to work overtime when requested by management and that only the standard rate of pay rather than a higher rate will be payable. A letter detailing this change has been sent to all staff to take effect one month from the date of the letter.

Identify the legal options open to the staff effected.

Change and the working environment

A European Community draft directive which was given extensive publicity in 1992 related to Working Time. This directive was originally adopted by the European Commission in July 1990 as part of a package of measures concerned with the implementation of the social action programme. The theme of the directive is that physically demanding and socially disruptive working patterns are dangerous to the health, safety and welfare of the workforce.

The UK approach of leaving matters such as the length of the working week and annual leave to be decided by the parties to an employment contract provides, it is argued, insufficient protection to the weaker party, the employee. Legislating on such matters, as part of the Social Action Programme, has been the focus of profound disagreement between the UK government and the European Commission. The dominant feature of government thinking on employment has been a de-regulatory strategy, directly in conflict with the directive. The government view is that limiting working hours will also increase labour costs dramatically. In addition there remains a strong body of opinion in the UK government against the imposition of change by EC institutions in relation to such matters as working hours and also extended rights for part-time workers and a national minimum wage. The UK government disputes the assumption that health and safety concerns justify the imposition of the generalised regulation of the working time for all workers. The view of the Commission is that health and safety at work is an objective which should be achieved at the expense of purely economic considerations.

The revised directive 1/7/91 proposes:

- compulsory rest periods of twelve consecutive hours in each period of twenty four hours;
- one rest day every seven day period;
- a prohibition on overtime by night workers where the work involves special hazards or heavy physical or mental strain;
- regular health checks for night workers;
- maximum working hours;
- minimum periods of annual leave.

In June 1993 the Council of Ministers finalised the most controversial part of the directive, the maximum working week set at forty eight hours per week. The EC Council of Ministers approved the working time directive by eleven votes to nil with Britain abstaining. The view of the British government, expressed by David Hunt the Secretary of State for Employment, was that the directive would be a threat to jobs by having an adverse affect on Europe's international competitiveness. The British government has ten years to implement the directive and introduce a mandatory forty eight hour week but only three years to introduce law to protect workers who are asked to work longer hours and do not wish to do so. The British government still intends to challenge the validity of passing the directive as a health and safety measure. This is despite the fact that working hours have certainly been considered as a health and safety issue under the common law.

> In *Johnstone v. Bloomsbury Health Authority* 1991 the plaintiff, a senior house officer, was required to work forty hours by his contract with an additional average of forty eight hours per week on call. He alleged that some weeks he had been required to work for one hundred hours with inadequate sleep and as a consequence he suffered from stress, depression, diminished appetite, exhaustion and suicidal feelings. It was claimed that the employers were in breach of the legal duty to take reasonable care for the safety and well being of their employee by requiring him to work intolerable hours with deprivation of sleep. The majority of the Court of Appeal held that an employer's express contractual rights had to be exercised in the light of their duty to take care of the employee's safety and if the employer knew that they were exposing an employee to the risk of injury to health by requiring him to work such long hours, then they should not require him to work more hours than he safely could have done.

Although only a majority decision, the Court of Appeal by this judgement is recognising that the implied objective of health and safety in an employment contract may override a clear express contractual right in relation to the hours of work.

> In *George v. Plant Breeding International* 1991 a worker was dismissed because he refused to accept Sunday working for a three month period in a year. His work involved seed processing and the three month period covered harvesting time when the company was at its busiest. Working twelve hours a day seven days a week was claimed to be disruptive of family life despite the fact that the worker had fifteen years service with the company. The

employer relied on an express contractual term which provided that the employee was "required to work extra hours beyond those mentioned in your letter of appointment at the request of management when the workload made it necessary". The Industrial Tribunal held that this contractual power did not give the employer the right to demand seven day working for a three month period and it was unfair to dismiss the employee for refusing to obey the instruction to work. The Tribunal confirmed that unfair dismissal law is not based on contract and that even if an instruction is lawful it could still be unfair. The justification for the decision was that flexible working arrangements may be challenged on grounds of public policy. "Unless time is created for members of the family to meet and relate to one another, family life in Britain is likely to show fragmentation of family arrangements."

The above cases proved clear evidence that both the courts and tribunals recognise the relationship between working hours and the health, safety and welfare of the workforce.

Assignment *New Technology*

Monks plc is a large retail chain with its headquarters in Manchester. At the head office there is a Personnel department which employs over thirty clerical staff the majority of whom are members of the NUCS, The National Union of Clerical Staff.

Nine months ago the clerical staff in Personnel were required to attend a six week intensive in service training course to equip them with the skills necessary to operate a new computerised system of storing staff records installed at head office. On behalf of the clerical staff, the NUCS have attempted to negotiate a five per cent pay rise to reflect the willingness of the clerical staff to acquire new skills and use the new technology. The management of Monks have rejected the claim for a wage rise out of hand, and argued forcefully that all staff they employ are required to adapt to new working methods in the interests of efficiency.

The management also announces that when the new system is operating there will be a twenty per cent reduction in their clerical staff requirements in Personnel. In response and after consulting the members the NUCS inform the management of Monks that they are in dispute and instruct their members to boycott the new technology. For the last three months the gross wages of those staff boycotting the new system have been reduced by one third. Furthermore last week the management wrote to the staff in dispute stating that *"if they continued to boycott the new system their work would be regarded as purely voluntary and no wages would be paid. Failure to report for work will be regarded as an implied resignation".*

Task

You are employed as a regional officer by the NUCS and have been called to a meeting with local shop stewards at Monks to discuss the dispute and then address the union members at a union meeting. You will be required to give your opinion on the legal validity on the response of the management of Monks to the industrial action. For this purpose your task is to research the present law relating to industrial action and breach of contract and prepare some briefing notes which will assist you in the meetings with the stewards and the union members.

Element 5.2 The External Relationships Relating to Employment

Trade Unions

In Britain almost about 9.6 million workers are members of 275 independent trade unions and the activities of these unions affect many aspects of our lives. For example you were probably taught at school by members of the National Union of Teachers (NUT). Many functions in the public sector are carried out by members of the National Union of Public Employees (NUPE). If you have to go to hospital you may be cared for by nurses who are members of the Royal College of Nursing. We could list many more examples. Many other occupations have professional bodies which have some of the same characteristics and objectives as trade unions. These would include bodies such as the British Medical Association, of which most doctors are members, the Law Society, which is the professional body for solicitors and the Institute of Chartered Accountants, of which many accountants are members.

The law relating to trade unions covering matters such as their status, administration, elections, member rights and industrial relations has now been consolidated in the *Trade Union and Labour Relations (Consolidation) Act* 1992.

Activity

In your library find a copy of 'Social Trends' a government publication by HMSO. Find the section on participation. Identify the change in union members over recent years and present your analysis in a graphical form.

Independence

It is one of the roles of the Certification Officer, first appointed under the Employment Protection Act 1975, to maintain a list of trade unions which satisfy the statutory definition under s.1 of the Trade Union and Labour Relations (Consolidation) Act 1992 and also to determine whether a union can be certified as independent. The definition of trade union requires there to be an organisation, composed wholly or mainly of workers, having as its principal purpose the regulation of relations between workers and employers. An independent trade union must be one which is not under the control or domination of an employer or group of employers and not liable to interference.

The issue in *Squibb UK Staff Association v. Certification Officer* 1978 was whether the extensive facilities provided by the employer for the trade union (for example; paid time off for officials and free use of accommodation, stationery, telephone, photocopying and internal mailing) was indicative of the fact that the union was vulnerable to employer interference. The Certification Officer felt that the reliance on the employer's resources along with the fact that the membership was very narrow meant that the union was at the risk of interference and should not be certified as independent. The decision was subsequently upheld.

In a trade union which is certified as independent, its members and officials have a number of rights and privileges.

- Employees who are members of independent trade unions have the right to take time off work for trade union activities and employees who are officials have the right to take paid time off to carry out their duties;

- Employees who are members of independent trade unions have the right not to have discriminatory action taken against them short of dismissal;

- An employer must consult with representatives of independent trade unions prior to dismissing employees by reason of redundancy;

- For the purposes of collective bargaining, representatives of independent trade unions are entitled to be given certain information to assist in the negotiation process;

- An independent trade union can seek financial assistance from public funds for the purpose of holding various ballots and request an employer to permit the premises to be used for that purpose and an employer shall comply with the request so far as is reasonably practicable;

- A right to be consulted and given information is conferred on an independent trade union by the *Transfer of Undertakings (Protection of Employment) Regulations* 1981;

- A dismissal is automatically unfair if it is by reason of membership of an independent trade union or taking part in its activities and an employee is entitled to interim relief pending the determination of such a complaint.

The need for trade unions

Over the last decade its has been fashionable to challenge the need for trade unions. They are often portrayed by government and the media as a throwback to an earlier era when industrial disputes were rife and unnecessary. The right wing think tanks often suggest that unions are a cause of Britain's industrial problems in the second part of the twentieth century. So we need to pose the question "do we still need trade unions?"

If the market for jobs was completely unrestricted and no trade unions existed, employers would be free to buy the services of employees at the lowest possible cost to them, whilst employees would compete with each other to secure from an employer the highest possible price for their labour. In the middle ages, and even in to the nineteenth century, agricultural workers and farmers met on certain quarter days at just such labour markets, which were known as 'hirings', to do just that. The supply and demand for labour would determine the prevailing wage rate.

Such a system, however, tends to favour employers for they will often have a choice of workers to employ and the resources to decide not to employ workers if they feel that the workers are asking too high wages. On the other hand individual workers have little power. They are dependent on work to survive and so may be forced to accept wages and conditions which are very poor simply to put bread into their mouths and the mouths of their families.

Just as employers might band together to form a cartel that will secure the highest price for their products so, too, can employees band together in an attempt to secure for themselves the best possible price for their labour. Trade unions are the result of workers realising that, if they grouped together, then the price they could secure for their services would be higher than if they bargained individually, a process that has become known as collective bargaining. This collective strength of the trade union redresses the imbalance in power between employer and employee. Research shows that in industries which are heavily unionised, workers will usually have higher wages and better conditions than workers in industries which have weak trade unions or no union at all. Therefore there is still a role for trade unions and without them many workers would have much poorer working lives.

The objectives of trade unions

Trade unions have a number of objectives which they seek to achieve through collective actions. These include:

- *The highest possible wage for their members*. As we have just discussed the labour market involves a process of supply and demand to determine the wage rate. If workers can act collectively rather than individually they should be able to secure higher wages;

- *An improvement in the conditions of employment of members*. For example, by reducing the number of hours worked or the patterns of work that their members are expected to follow;

- *An improved working environment for their members*. The unions will seek this especially when the working conditions of their members or the environment in which they work threaten their health and safety. A recent example of this occurred when bank employees (working for the Midland Bank), journalists (on the Financial Times) and data processors (employed by British Telecom) suffered repetitive strain injuries (RSI) as a result of the work they did. Unions like the BIFU (the bank employees' union), NUJ (the National Union of Journalists and the National Communication Union all successfully fought for compensation for their members;

- *Protection for their members against unjust or illegal actions*. For instance most unions will provide legal help if they believe that one of their members has been unfairly dismissed. They will help to enforce equal opportunities if they see their members being discriminated against;

- *Full employment and job security for their members*. Trade unions will attempt to safeguard the jobs of their members. Clearly in times of recession employers may try to shed labour by introducing redundancies. Recognised independent trade unions have important rights in relation to dealing with a redundancy situation (see Unit 4);

- *Industrial democracy*. One of the significant causes for which the unions have struggled over many years has been to introduce industrial democracy. By this is meant that workers should have a greater say in how their organisations are managed and the policies which the organisation introduces. This can be achieved by greater consultation and by such measures as having workers as members of the Board of Directors;

- *A 'voice' for their members both in industry and with government*. The trade unions want to be able to represent their members' views and act as a pressure group in influencing government policy;

- The promotion of *training and 'upskilling' for their members*. Trade unions wish to see the skills of their members improved and they will try to achieve this either by encouraging employers to train and develop their staff or by providing education and training through the union itself;

- *To provide the advantages of collectivity*. 'Strength in numbers' and 'United we stand; divided, we fall' are traditional slogans of the trade union movement which exemplify the belief that workers should see themselves as part of a wider movement rather than simply as powerless individuals.

Although the priority in which these objectives are held varies from trade union to trade union, all would see that both trade unions and professional bodies have a common aim, namely, to improve the position of their members.

Activity

From a newspaper or television news report try to identify a story which describes a dispute involving a trade union. Which of the objectives from the list on the previous page is the union trying to achieve.

The structure of trade unions

Trade Unions still cover many areas of British industrial life. In fact there are about 250 recognised trade unions in the UK. It is possible to divide these unions into four categories:

- craft unions;
- industrial unions;
- 'white-collar' unions;
- general unions

Craft unions

These were the first trade unions to develop. There were often seen as the 'industrial aristocracy' and consisted of members who were qualified or 'time-served' in a particular skill or craft such as plumbing or electrical engineering. The craft unions now have members with same craft in many different industries. An example of a craft which has developed through amalgamation to include members with a variety of skills and crafts in many industries is the Electrical, Electronic, Telecommunication and Plumbing Union (EETPU).

Industrial unions

These unions are based on the workers in a particular industry. All levels of worker are included in the membership irrespective of the nature of their jobs. Industries such as mining and steel have traditionally had strong industrial unions. The National Union of Mineworkers (NUM) was once a very powerful union but has lost members as the size of the industry has been reduced and a similar fate has befallen the Iron and Steel Trades Federation (ISTF).

'White-collar' unions

One of the most significant changes in the trade union movement since the second world war has been the emergence of the 'white-collar' unions. These are so-called because they restrict membership to workers in managerial, administrative and professional jobs, traditionally an area which has had very limited unionisation. The largest of the 'white-collar' unions is the National and Local Government Officers' Association (NALGO) which has about three-quarters of a million members working predominantly in the public sector. Other professional unions include the National Union of Teachers

(NUT), the National Association of Teachers in Higher and Further Education (NATFHE), the Association of University Teachers (AUT) and the Royal College of Nursing.

General unions

Such unions do not limit their membership to a particular industry or type of worker. They were originally founded as a way of unionising the unskilled and semi-skilled workers who could not become members of the craft unions. The largest is the Transport and General Workers Union (TGWU) which is also the largest union in Britain with members doing all sorts of jobs in many industries. The General Municipal Boilermaker's and Allied Trades Union (GMB) is other general union which has over three-quarters of a million members.

The Trades Union Congress (TUC)

The majority of trade unionists in Britain belong to unions that are affiliated to the TUC. This is the body which collectively represents the trade union movement. Its aims are to express the common objectives of all its trade union members. Its objectives are as follows:

- *To represent the trade union movement in dealings with outside bodies.* One of the major roles of the TUC is to act as the voice of the trade union movement with the government. As a pressure group it seeks to influence government policies, particularly those relating to employment issues. Its power to influence government, however, has been considerably weakened over the last decade as the Thatcher and Major administrations have sought to marginalise the influence of the TUC;

- *To act as a regulator of inter-union conflicts.* The TUC has rules and regulations which govern the actions of its members on such issues as membership disputes where one union seeks to recruit members of other unions. Its ultimate sanction is to expel a union which acts in a way which it regards as not being in the best interests on the trade union movement as a whole;

- *To act as a focus for collective union action.* A major strength of the trade union movement is the ability of one trade union to seek the support of other unions when it is involved in an industrial dispute. So for example in the dispute between the miners and the government over pit closures in 1992 and 1993 the TUC was able to organise a show of support from other trade unionists;

- *To provide a range of services to its member trade unions.* The TUC is able to provide advice on legal and technical matters to its members in a way in which individual unions may not be able to. Therefore individual unions can draw on the expertise and experience of the TUC when facing common problems.

The annual meeting of the Trades Union Congress is seen as an important forum for formulating and agreeing joint union policies and the General Council of the TUC and the General Secretary are regarded as important spokespersons for the movement as a whole.

Activity

Find the address of the TUC headquarters in London and write to them asking for information on the trade union movement and the activities of the TUC.

The European Trade Union Confederation (ETUC)

The growth of the European Community has been seen by many as a major boost to the power and influence of multi-national and trans-European companies. They are more able to move factories as well as products from country to country to take advantage of the most favourable wage rates and sympathetic governments. Many trade unionists feared that this would lead to the big companies simply playing workers in one country off against workers in another. Workers would be faced with demands to accept lower wages or poorer working conditions with the threat that if they did not accept these their jobs would be simply transferred to another country.

The increasing isolation of the British trade union movement from the mainstream of political and economic decision-making during the 1980s under the Thatcher Government has forced its leadership to look outside the UK for support, especially towards the EC. As a result, the TUC is now more pro-European than the government. The turning point occurred in 1988 when Jacques Delors addressed the annual TUC conference. As Norman Willis, the then TUC general secretary put it, *"We realised that we must not just put up with the European Community, but make the best of it. And we got a response from the Community which was totally lacking from the government. We found a home in a Social Europe, not just on the rebound, but in a positive sense. Now I believe that we have a responsibility to show that European democracies can deliver the goods economically"*.

UK unions and their counterparts from continental Europe have joined together to form their own trans-European federation, the European Trade Union Confederation. Its role mirrors in Europe that of the TUC in the UK: to bring all unions together under one collective umbrella. Its aim is protect workers' rights throughout Europe by consolidating union power and strength throughout the Community. It is true to say that it has not been as successful as its founders would have hoped and we are still seeing the multi-nationals taking advantage of differential wage rates in different countries to move jobs. In fact Britain is seen as low wage economy and the British Government is actively seeking to persuade companies to move their operations from relatively high wage economies like Germany and France to Britain.

An important factor in strengthening the position of workers in Europe has come about with the acceptance of the *Social Chapter* as part of the Maastricht agreement. The *Social Chapter* has its origins in the *Charter of Fundamental Social Rights of Workers* (often referred to simply as the *Social Charter*) solemnly declared on December 8th 1989 by member states of the European Community with the sole dissent of the United Kingdom. While trades unions fully supported the social charter and the inclusion of the social chapter in the Maastricht Treaty the conservative government is vehemently opposed to it. Mrs Thatcher, when in office went so far as to say that it was "inspired by the values of Karl Marx and the class struggle".

The Social Chapter

One of the main purposes of the *Social Chapter* was to raise and standardise working conditions throughout the European Community and for this reason it was strongly supported by the UK trade union movement. A further aim was to ensure that the more affluent EC countries that provide superior working conditions do not become economically disadvantaged because of the costs they incur providing improved workplace conditions. The idea is to prevent '*social dumping*' which is the movement of investment to countries with lower standards.

We should stress that the *Social Charter* was not a treaty or an instrument of community law and so possesses no binding force. In fact many of the rights proclaimed in the Charter already fall within the legislative competence of the European Community, for example Rights to:

- freedom of movement;

- an equitable wage;
- improvement of living and working conditions;
- free collective bargaining;
- equal pay for men and women;
- paid holiday;
- social security for migrant workers;
- common vocational training.

The UK government's opposition to the *Social Chapter* of the Maastricht Treaty 1992 which continues on the path laid down in the 1989 *Social Charter*, is based upon the fact that it conflicts with its deregulatory approach to the labour market which the government sees as a key element in boosting competitiveness, creating jobs and attracting international investment. The Opposition Parties are generally in favour of the objectives contained within the Social Chapter including:

- the improvement of the working environment;
- the introduction of a minimum wage;
- increased protection during industrial action;
- increased rights for part-time workers;
- maximum working hours and minimum holidays;
- increased information and consultation of workers;
- increased equal opportunities;

In Unit 4, *Human Resources*, however you will see that if European employment policies are translated into directives by qualified majority voting then UK opposition cannot prevent measures such as maximum working hours and increased maternity rights becoming part of UK law.

Activity

Identify arguments to:

1. *reject the imposition of a minimum wage and a maximum number of working hours;*
2. *Support the imposition of a minimum wage and a maximum number of working hours.*

The decline in trade union membership

Trade union membership has declined quite dramatically during the 1980s and early 1990s. From its peak in 1979 when there were over 13 million trade union members and over 50% of the total workforce was unionised, numbers have declined until today there are less than 9 million people who are members and this now accounts for less than 40% of the country's workforce. This decline of over 30% is the most marked reduction in trade union numbers since the 1930s. The following table illustrates the decline:

Union	representing	1989	1988
TGWU	(transport and manufacturing workers)	1.27	1.32
GMB	(unskilled workers in most industries)	.82	.86
NALGO	(public service workers)	.75	.75
AEU	(engineering workers)	.74	.79
MSF	(car production, universities, NHS, banks)	.65	.65
NUPE	(local government, water workers)	.63	.64
USDAW	(shopworkers; distributive trades)	.38	.40
UCATT	(construction workers)	.25	.26
COHSE	(NHS)	.21	.22
UCW	(Post Office; British Telecom)	.20	.20

The decline in membership of the UK's ten biggest unions (figures in millions)

These are a number of causes:

- *The increase in unemployment.* Traditionally the greatest periods for union growth are at times when unemployment is low. Conversely when unemployment rises union membership falls. This is for two reasons. Firstly many workers leave their trade union when they become unemployed as they can no longer keep up their union membership fees or feel that they no longer have the need for a trade union. Secondly during periods of high unemployment the power of the trade unions decreases and some studies have shown that this makes it less attractive to workers to join a trade union;

- *The change in the structure of industry.* As we discussed in the first part of this element there has been a significant change in the nature of industry over the last decade. Many of the industries which have declined are in the primary or manufacturing sectors and these have traditionally been the most heavily unionised. The growth of jobs, which have to some extent replaced the employment in the declining sectors has come in the service industries which have much lower union participation rates, although 'white-collar' workers now make up the largest proportion of union members;

- *The increase in the number of women in the workforce.* As we have already seen there has been a significant increase in the number of females in the workforce. Women now account for more than 35% of the workforce. Much of the increase in female jobs, however, has been in part-time and temporary work and there is a greater tendency for part-time and temporary workers not to join unions;

- *The changing political attitude towards trade unions.* The attitude of both Labour and Conservative Governments to unions during the 1960s and 70s was remarkably consensual, treating the unions as necessary and important players in the industrial scene. Union leaders were regarded as being an integral part of the constitutional process and they were well represented on parliamentary and quasi-parliamentary committees. By 1979, things were different. Prime Minister Thatcher refused to have anything to do with the unions and she, her ministers and political colleagues did everything in their power, by passing legislation as well as more unorthodox means, to strip them of any influence and power. The Conservative government reinforced the spectre that many people already carried with them: that of union members fighting with police at the Orgreave Cokeworks during the prolonged miners' strike of 1984-5; of print workers and police clashing violently at the new headquarters of Rupert Murdoch's *News International* in Wapping in 1986. The gloom engendered by 'The Winter of Discontent' of 1979 has been periodically re-invoked by the Conservatives in the election campaigns of 1983, 1987 and 1992 to remind the British people of the dire consequences that can result when the balance of political power tilts towards the unions.

By 1992, union membership had declined for the thirteenth consecutive year, from 13.2 million in 1979 to under 9 million in 1992. In order to compensate for their rapidly dwindling membership, some unions which, traditionally, competed fiercely for members, have opted to merge into '*super unions*': the AEU with the EEPTU; the old railway workers and seamen's unions into the RMT and NUPE, NALGO and COHSE have merged together to form a single union, UNISON, which will account for half of the total membership of the TUC.

Another feature of declining trade union membership has been the trend among employers not to recognise the trade unions as representatives of the workers when entering into wage negotiation. The Government chose to ban trade union membership at the Government Communication Headquarters (GCHQ) in Cheltenham on the grounds of national security and other private sector employers have decided to follow the Government's example.

Other employers have insisted on single union agreements when establishing new plants. Many of the Japanese companies which opened factories in the UK in the 1980s and 90s have chosen this option and this has led to conflict between the trade unions. This policy has weakened the influence of the trade unions and in certain cases the 'single-union' agreement has included a 'no-strike' clause where the union effectively gives up one of its most potent weapons in return for the single agreement. An example of such an agreement was Nissan's deal with the Amalgamated Engineering Union in its plant in Sunderland; such deals where unions competed with each other to become sole representative were disparaged as 'beauty contests' by some.

In the early 1990s the unions have presented a far more positive image than of old. In an effort to shed their obsolete, strike-bound image they have concentrated upon pressurising employers into improving conditions in the workplace. It is a role they are well suited to as people begin to realise that the '*second industrial revolution*', with its pervasive use of computers and robots, spawns its own sets of new physical and psychological afflictions and re-invigorates older ones.

The loss of union power has caused a significant gap in representation both in the workplace as well as in other areas of life where people are either too unorganised or too low-paid to influence events and government. The TUC has traditionally represented not only its membership but also the social underclass which now lacks a watchdog which will bark on its behalf.

The unions, employers and government

We have already explained that a major role of any trade union is to represent its members in negotiations with employers and the Government. This is referred to as collective bargaining as individual workers do not negotiate themselves but are collectively represented by their trade union.

Unions, employers and Government meet at a number of levels:

- Local level. Minor disputes, workplace grievances, unfair dismissal and complaints and concerns expressed by individual union members are generally dealt with on this level;
- National level. This is the area where the most widely seen conflict between unions and employers occurs. Basic rates of pay, conditions of service and contracts are dealt with on this level by full-time, paid union officials and the representatives of the employers;
- National advisory level. Despite the attempts of successive governments to reduce the influence of the unions and remove their opportunities for expression, some still remain.

The National Advisory Council (NAC) includes representatives of the TUC, the Confederation of British Industry (CBI) and the Government. Its role is to establish guidelines within which collective bargaining can take place.

Collective Bargaining and Recognition

Collective bargaining is legally defined in the *Trade Union and Labour Relations (Consolidation) Act 1992* as negotiations related to or connected with one or more of the matters listed in the Act which could be the subject of a legitimate trade dispute.

- terms and conditions of employment (including physical conditions);
- engagement or non engagement, or termination or suspension of employment;
- allocation of work or duties of employment;
- matters of discipline;
- membership or non membership of a trade union;
- facilities for officials of trade unions;
- machinery for negotiation or consultation and other procedures.

Clearly then it is crucial to the status of a trade union that it is 'recognised' by an employer for collective bargaining purposes. Since 1980 however there is no longer a statutory recognition procedure so that today there is no legal machinery by which an employer is obliged to recognise a trade union for collective bargaining purposes. Nevertheless numerous employers see the benefits of collective bargaining and recognise trade unions for this purpose. There could be an express or implied recognition agreement between an employer and a trade union but absence of legal machinery means that an employer could de-recognise a trade union without any legal sanction. Recognition conflicts could result in industrial action by the trade union involving strikes, working to contract, overtime bans or go slows. Later in this section we shall examine how recent legislation has restricted the power of trade unions to take industrial action.

There are some statutory provisions which are designed to assist the parties, in particular a recognised trade union to engage in meaningful collective bargaining. A general duty is imposed on an employer in relation to a recognised independent trade union to declare or request information relating to his undertaking which is both:

- information without which the trade union representative would be to a material extent impeded in carrying on such collective bargaining and
- information which, in accordance with good industrial relations practice, he should disclose to them for the purposes of collective bargaining.

Guidance as to the type of information that should be disclosed to accord with good industrial practices is provided by the ACAS Code of Practices *Disclosure of Information to Trade Unions for Collective Bargaining Purposes*.

Having examined the role of the trade unions in this process we need to understand how employers are represented and the role of the government.

Employers' associations

In the same way that workers join together to form trade unions, employers in many industries have come together to form organisations and associations which represent their collective views. There are currently over 150 such employers' associations representing wide areas of industry. The largest of these is the Engineering Employers' Federation which represents the views of employers in that industry. Similar associations exist in most major industries. These bodies act as pressure groups by trying to influence Government policy on matters relating to their particular industry. They may also take part in collective bargaining on issues such as pay and conditions with the trade unions. In this way, many industries have common agreed standards of pay and conditions for workers throughout the industry. The law relating to employers' associations is contained in the *Trade Union and Labour Relations (Consolidation) Act 1992*.

The Confederation of British Industry

While the TUC represents the majority of trade unions, the Confederation of British Industry has as its members the majority of employers' associations as well as many individual companies. It is often seen as representing the collective views of British industry and will undertake surveys and other forms of research to find out how British industry is performing and the views of a wide range of companies on the state of the economy and on issues relating to government policy.

Activity

As we noted on the previous page there are currently over 150 employers' associations in Britain today. From the reference section in your local or college library try to identify ten. In particular try and find out which employers' association would represent major employers in your area.

The Role of Government in Employment

The Government clearly has a number of roles in the area of employment. These are:

- as a legislator;
- as a mediator;
- as an employer.

Past and present governments have introduced a wide range of legislation relating to employment dealing with:

- *Individual employment law* which includes the contract of employment, equal opportunities, health and safety, unfair dismissal etc. (See Unit 4)
- *Collective employment law* which includes industrial relations, trade unions, industrial action, collective bargaining etc.

Statute law is also supplemented by centuries of common law, in particular relating to the contract of employment. It is the role of the ordinary courts and industrial tribunals to declare the common law and interpret statutory provisions in the event of conflict. Trade unions have often argued that courts, while constitutionally independent of the government, have interpreted the law in such a way that trade unions and their members are disadvantaged.

Recent legislation to curb union power

The 1980s saw the introduction of several pieces of legislation that fitted in to the Conservative strategic plan to erode the significance of union power. While individual union members who participate in industrial action are normally in breach of contract and are given little protection under the law, trade unions have been given statutory immunity from legal action since the *Trades Disputes Act* 1906. It is this immunity from legal action that has been dramatically restricted by conservative legislation.

- 1980: *The Employment Act* outlawed secondary action and restricted the closed shop;
- 1982: *The Employment Act* made unions liable for the unlawful acts of their members;
- 1984: *The Trade Union Act* initiated secret ballots on trade disputes;
- 1988: *The Employment Act* gave union members the right not to strike and outlawed industrial action in support of the closed shop;
- 1990: *The Employment Act* made it unlawful to refuse employment on the grounds of union membership so outlawing the pre-entry closed shop.

This legislation, now contained in the *Trade Union and Labour Relations (Consolidation) Act* 1992, had led to a diminution in the power of trade unions to organise or encourage industrial action. The threat of legal action by employers, suppliers, customers and even their own members has made unions wary of using the strike weapon.

> The case of *Falconer v. NUR and ASLEF* 1986 provides an example of damages being awarded for liability arising from industrial action. The plaintiff was prevented from travelling from Sheffield to London because of a rail strike called by the defendant trade unions. As a consequence he incurred additional expense because he travelled a day early to keep business appointments. His claim was based on the fact that he purchased a ticket to travel on British Rail on any day within three months of its issue and the union strike action prevented British Rail from fulfilling its contractual obligations. Damages were claimed for the civil wrong of unlawful interference with contract by the indirect action of a third party. Usually when damages are claimed for a civil wrong arising from industrial action, a trade union would normally rely on statutory immunity. One requirement to establish such an immunity is that the union has complied strictly with the balloting requirement of the Trade Union Act 1984. Here the industrial action had been called without a ballot and so the immunity was lost. The county court Judge held that damages would be awarded to the plaintiff against the defendant unions.

Even where there is a genuine trade dispute and the union has complied strictly with the legal requirements in calling for industrial action, those members who choose not to strike are now protected from union disciplinary action. Also by making secondary action unlawful, the unions cannot put pressure on the employer during industrial action by calling for sympathetic action from fellow workers. There are also examples over the years of employers responding to strike action by simply dismissing all those workers engaged in industrial action. Timex workers employed in Dundee were dismissed in 1992 for taking strike action, and while they continue to picket their place of work, provided the employer does not re-employ any workers within three months of the dismissal their right to complain of unfair dismissal is lost.

The closed shop is a situation where a trade union insists that all workers in an organisation must belong to a trade union if they are to get or keep a job. This will give the trade union considerable power as it can justifiably say that it represents 100% of the organisation's workforce. The union is also in effect the monopoly supplier of labour to that organisation and as such it increases the union's power as it can use a total withdrawal of labour as a weapon in its bargaining for higher wages or better conditions. Management knows that if it disagrees with the union there will be a higher price to pay as the union can effectively stop output. Of course there are benefits to the employer from a closed shop. Once an agreement is reached between the employer and the union then it is easier to enforce as the company is dealing with one collective body. This has often meant that closed shops bring more organised and orderly industrial relations than is the case when the employer is dealing with a number of unions or a workforce that is only partially unionised.

The government, however, is opposed to closed shops on principle and recent legislation now allows individuals to choose whether or not they wish to be members of the trade union. They cannot now be dismissed if they decide not to join the union. The *Employment Act* 1988 removed a trade union's legal immunity if it takes action to maintain a *closed shop*. *The 1990* Employment Act *has effectively banned 'pre-entry' closed shops, where individuals had to be members of a trade union before they could be employed. The Act makes it unlawful to refuse a person employment on the grounds of trade union membership.*

One further aspect of recent legislation has been the attempt to increase internal union democracy. As we have already noted, unions are now required to hold a secret ballot before strike action is taken. One encouraging aspect of this legislation is that the ballot allows both the union and the employer to judge the strength of feeling of the workforce before actually going on strike. In fact many employers wait for the ballot result and if there is a substantial majority in favour of strike action they settle the dispute before the strike takes place. In some respects the process of balloting has made dispute settlement easier.

A further movement to increase the degree of internal union democracy is that the law now requires that all elections for union governing bodies must be held by postal ballot. This is seen as reducing the likelihood of vote rigging or pressure being placed on members if voting is limited to a show of hands at an open meeting.

The effectiveness of such anti-union legislation occurred at the same time as union power was being weakened in other ways, too.

- Public sympathy was diverted by the media portrayal of unions as being politically subversive;
- New approaches, such as 'human resource management', placed the emphasis on persuading an individual that it was in everyone's interest to co-operate and give corporate commitment;
- Regional and local pay bargaining partly replaced national, collective negotiations.

As we have already noted single-union and 'no strike' agreements became features of union/employer agreements which were designed to avoid conflict.

The effectiveness of anti-union legislation

If you accept that statistics, such as those below, reflect the effectiveness of the legislation passed to curb union power, then it is remarkable how effective the legislation passed during the 1980s has been. Its effectiveness has been enhanced since it has been enacted against a background of two economic recessions, two cycles of deep unemployment occurring against broad structural unemployment, and the widespread replacement of full-time jobs in the manufacturing sector by part-time jobs in the service sector. In the 1970s 12.9 million working days were lost, on average, in each year; in the 1980s, an average of 7.2 million days were lost; in 1991 fewer working days were lost to strikes than in any year since records were first kept and the first time the total fell below the one million mark since 1940. Of course there may be other reasons than government legislation for the reduction in the number of days lost through strikes. Past evidence shows that industrial disputes tend to decrease during periods of high unemployment and increase during periods of rising inflation. The reason for the first may be that workers are more conscious of losing their jobs – and being unable to find another when unemployment is high. There will also be a fall in union membership as employment rises. Conversely when inflation is rising workers need to maintain their wage levels to protect their standard of living and this might be achieved only by using strike action. In fact wage negotiations are the most common cause of strikes although it is often the case that industrial relations between employers and workers are poor for other reasons and the pay dispute is merely the final catalyst which leads to a strike.

To put strikes into their proper perspective, it is worth noting that four million days were lost in 1989, but 120 million days were lost as a result of absenteeism, sickness and injury.

1982	5.3
1983	3.8
1984	27.1
1985	6.4
1986	1.9
1987	3.5
1988	3.7
1989	4.1
1990	1.0
1991	0.8
1992	0.8

Number of working days lost through strikes (in millions)

Activity

Scan the national and local press to find an example of industrial action being carried on in response to an industrial dispute. Identify, the form of industrial action, the Union supporting it and the substance of the dispute.

Labour as a Factor of Production

We have already noted that for most organisations, it is the workforce which is their most important factor of production, for without the appropriate number of workers, holding the requisite skills and experience the business cannot operate efficiently. In this next section our central focus will be the organisation's labour force.

The demand for labour

An organisation's demand for labour, in common with its demand for other factors of production, is '*derived demand*'. This simply means that it is the demand for the products or services which the labour force helps to produce which is the determining factor in how large and what sort of workforce the organisation needs. For example a bricklayer is only in demand if there is a demand for new buildings. This, of course, may be something of an over-simplification, for many workers have skills and talents which could be used to produce a variety of products. The demand for typists is not related solely to the demand for one particular product. The typist is capable of moving from organisation to organisation or industry to industry as demand for different products change. The typist could have worked in an office at a engineering company which closed because of lack of demand for its products and then switched jobs to work in for a computer company whose sales were booming. However, we have have already been noted in Unit 1, *Business in the Economy,* the overall level of demand in the economy as a whole – aggregate demand – may also fluctuate according to the changes in combined demands of all consumers for all products. Therefore a decline in aggregate demand will be reflected in a fall in derived demand for labour and so will result in greater unemployment within the economy as a whole. Conversely a rise in aggregate demand will mean a general rise in the demand for labour and so unemployment will fall. This relationship is important for the government when it is seeking to control the level of unemployment within the economy. It is in the government's power to influence the level of aggregate demand for goods and services in order to increase or decrease the number of people employed. and as we noted in Unit 1, this is known as *aggregate demand management*. In this section let us concentrate not on demand in the economy as a whole but on demand for labour in specific organisations.

Any organisation will attempt to employ the most appropriate number of workers to efficiently meet the demand for its products. The two main factors which it should take into account when deciding how many people to employ are:

- *The level of output from each employee*;

- *The cost of employing each extra worker*. This takes into account the wages or salary they must be paid, plus any additional cost of hiring workers such as national insurance contributions, administrative overheads, training costs and so on.

The output of employees

It is often difficult to measure precisely the output of each worker. If the worker is performing a relatively straightforward repetitive manual task such as a machine operator then it may be simple enough to count the number of units produced in a day or week. It is much more difficult, however, to calculate the output of a person performing a variety of tasks or one task which may differ in length or complexity each time it is undertaken. So, for instance, in attempting to assess the output of an administrator or manager making decisions, it is not feasible to simply add together the number of decisions such as a person has made in a day. It is necessary to consider the complexity of the decisions and the time taken over them and the efficiency with which they are made. Often this is a matter of comparing one worker's performance against another's. In this way the organisation must make a more subjective assessment of an employee's output.

There are various of ways of trying to assess the work a person does. We could state it in actual tangible units produced, for instance a worker produced one hundred light fittings in one hour. Alternatively if this is not possible, we could express it in terms of work units, for example an administrator performed the equivalent of one hundred work units in a day.

Of course, all workers will not produce the same output doing the same job. Some will work harder, be more skilful, experienced, or have a greater understanding of the job done. Another factor which will influence the productivity of individual workers is the number of fellow workers employed by the organisation contributing to the same overall task. This process is known as the *division of labour* and basically it illustrates the fact that if one person is required to carry out an entire process alone then he or she must develop a certain level of expertise in each stage of the process. If the task is divided among several workers, each of whom concentrates on one aspect of the operation, then it is probable that individually they will acquire a higher degree of expertise in one particular aspect and thus a greater level of productivity than if they were each required to undertake the entire operation. Organisations find that as they employ more people their total output increases in a greater proportion than the increase in the workforce. The organisation benefits from *labour economics of scale* by developing expertise and employing specialists to undertake particular tasks.

Changes in the level of employment

The level of employment in an organisation will not remain static. Changes in certain factors will influence the number of workers who should be employed. If wage rates rose (due to pressure from within the organisation or to an increase in nationally negotiated pay levels) and productivity did not, then it may mean that fewer workers could be employed.

Shedding labour, however, is not the only option open to the organisation in these circumstances. One alternative is to increase the price at which the product is sold. Obviously this is only possible if the demand for the organisation's product is relatively inelastic and the price increase will not deter consumers. A further alternative which often accompanies an increase in wage rates is an agreed rise in worker productivity (a *'productivity deal'*). Here the workers agree to produce more in return for higher wages. This has the effect of raising their output without the organisation having to increase its price to consumers. So for example, a 20% increase in productivity would have the same effect as a 20% rise in price for it would mean that the organisation would not face the cost of possible redundancies. In many circumstances a rise in wages is accompanied by both an increase in productivity and an increase in price.

Changes in the price or availability of other factors of production

Labour is just one of the factors of production which a business must combine with others, such as machinery, to produce a finished product. How much labour it employs and how many machines it buys depends on the cost and availability of the each of the elements. For example in those parts of the world where population growth has led to a plentiful supply of cheap labour, such as India, most productive activity will be *labour intensive* and thus use little machinery. In the industrialised West, the reverse is true. Relatively few workers produce much more using sophisticated productive techniques. This type of production is described as being *capital intensive*. If wage rates in India rose sufficiently, the Indian businesses would substitute machines for workers. Of course this is only possible if the machines are capable of performing the tasks which are currently undertaken by people. History, however, has demonstrated that as people's ingenuity has grown and greater technological advances are made, increasingly jobs currently performed by men and women will be taken over by machines. A contemporary example has been the rapid development of micro-electronics. The demand for many administrative and clerical jobs and occupations such as bank cashiers and shop assistants will be reduced dramatically as cheaper and more sophisticated machines are introduced to replace human labour.

In this section we have considered how an organisation determines the number of workers it should employ and how factors such as:

- the level of demand for the organisation's final product;
- the productivity of its workers;
- the prevailing wage rate; and
- how the cost and availability of other factors of production which can be substituted for labour, affect the demand in the labour market.

Now let us examine how the interaction of the supply of labour with the demand for labour establishes the total number of people employed in the economy and the wage rate they are paid.

The supply of labour

In the previous section we considered how an organisation decides how many people to employ. Now we shall examine the broader perspective of the supply of labour to the economy as a whole, to specific industries and specific areas.

Supply of labour to the economy

As we discuss in Element 5.1 the number of people available and looking for work in the UK varies over time. Demographic factors such as the age and sex structure of the population influence the number of people seeking work. Out of the total population of about fifty six million the UK has a potential workforce of about twenty five million.

The size of the workforce is restricted by legislation as young people are not allowed to undertake full-time employment until they are over sixteen years of age. Also the government has set the retirement age at sixty five for men and sixty for women and although this does not mean that they cannot then work by law, it may affect their pension rights if they do. Other people such as married women or students may be physically capable of working but choose not to have a full-time job. These people, with the addition of those who are of working age but are permanently unfit for work, are classified as the *economically inactive*. Present trends are increasing this inactive element of the population. These trends are a combined result of delaying the entry of young people into the employment market by encouraging them to remain in further and higher education, and of increasing early retirement opportunities. They are to some extent a secondary source of workers, for if the wage rate rose sufficiently they may be attracted into giving up their studies, housework or retirement and taking on a job.

The amount of work a person chooses to do will vary according to individual preference. Some may opt for substantial periods of leisure. Others work for as many hours as possible. This choice is related to individual levels of income and expenditure and their chosen life styles.

It is normally assumed that as wage rates rise people will be willing to substitute work in place of leisure hours and so work longer. The extra incentive of higher rates for overtime working is used to induce people to give up leisure. If the wage rate paid is higher than the value put on the leisure time then people will substitute work for leisure. So, for many people, an increase in the wage rate will mean that the supply of their labour increases. This can be shown diagrammatically in the next figure.

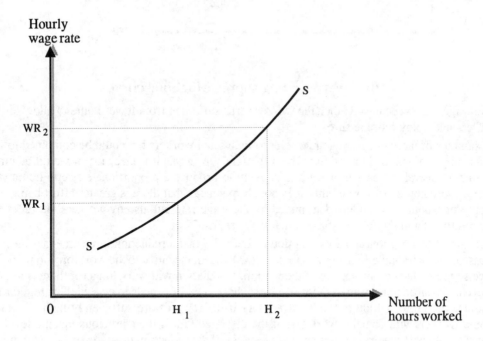

Supply of labour in relation to hourly wage rate

As the wage rate rises from WR_1 to WR_2, the number of hours worked also increases from H_1 to H_2. This example, however, disregards the fact that as a worker continues to work longer hours and have less leisure time, then the value of his or her remaining leisure time becomes greater. Therefore the worker may reach a stage when he or she will not give up any more leisure whatever the wage rate. In fact in certain circumstances as the wage rate rises, some people actually work less because they have reached a certain level of income sufficient to meet their needs and so they prefer to have increased leisure time. This results in a backward sloping supply cure for labour and can be shown graphically in the next figure.

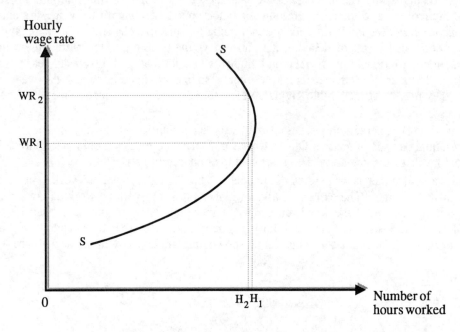

Backward sloping supply of labour curve

Once the wage rate exceeds WR_1 then the worker earns sufficient from fewer hours to allow him or her to work less and enjoy more leisure.

These examples of increases in wage rate refer to individual workers but could be combined to find the aggregate supply of labour in relation to the wage rate. From this it is clear that it would be unwise to assume that a general increase in wage rate is likely to produce a proportionate rise in hours worked, and even if more hours are worked this does not always mean that there is greater effort being exerted. The supply of labour is not solely determined by the wage rate but also by workers' attitudes to their jobs, commitment and the job satisfaction that they receive.

An extension of this misconceived assumption is the belief that a reduction in income tax rates (and so an increase in workers' take-home pay) will necessarily be an incentive to the workforce to work harder. Evidence suggests that certain sectors of the working population will work longer if there is a fall in the tax rate. This is particularly true of those workers whose spending tends to exceed their regular income and who are therefore willing to work extra hours if the rewards are sufficiently high. On the other hand some workers will actually work less if the tax rates fall as their previous income level, which they can still achieve by working shorter hours because of the reduction in tax, is sufficient to meet their needs. Changes in the tax rate, however, will not affect the working hours of the majority of people because they work a set number of hours fixed by their employer and cannot work longer even if the attraction of lower taxes was sufficiently strong.

Labour supply to specific industries

The supply of labour to a specific industry or occupation is determined by several factors. These include:

- the wage level offered by that industry, trade or profession;
- its comparability with other similar occupations;
- the amount of skill, or expertise required to do the job;
- the number of people in the workforce who have such skills;
- the length of training or academic qualifications required to do the job.

Obviously if an occupation requires little skill or formal training and happens to be very well paid, then it will attract a considerable number of people hoping to be employed. In such circumstances, however, the forces of supply and demand will dictate that with an excess supply of labour over demand (in other words more people wanting jobs than there are vacancies) the wage rate will fall. Therefore in our society those occupations which receive the highest pay should be those where demand for labour is high but few people are willing or able to do the job either because of its nature, the skills required, or the qualifications needed. This is true of professions such as surgeons, barristers and architects. Later in this unit, however, we shall see that in some industries or occupations the strength of the trade union or professional association is such that wages and salaries are kept high even though there are more qualified people seeking to work in that particular job than there are available vacancies.

Normally the wage or salary a person receives reflects the value which society or consumers place on his or her talents. For instance, the salary paid to computer experts has risen as more organisation install computers. A bi-lingual secretary can demand higher wages as more organisations become involved in international business. Many anomalies exist, however, where people carrying out valuable tasks are relatively lowly paid, for example nurses or care assistants. This is often because people enjoy doing the job and so are willing to do the job despite receiving low pay.

For most people, however, their choice to enter a profession or occupation is determined by a combination of monetary reward and job satisfaction. To attract workers into less satisfying jobs, the wage rates must be higher. An example perhaps would be jobs on the North Sea oil rigs mining industry where hard, dangerous and dirty working conditions must be compensated by high wages. Some jobs require considerable periods of training or apprenticeship during which earnings may be relatively low. An individual must decide to accept relatively low earnings initially on the basis of expected high future wages. For example, many professions such as medicine and accountancy require long periods of training at low rates of pay before becoming qualified and going on to earn a higher salary.

Locational factors affecting the supply of labour

The supply of labour is often restricted by regional factors. Some industries require a particular skill or expertise and this may have developed in one particular area. This effectively dictates the location of that industry. Workers are also often restricted to their local labour market, that is thay do not seek jobs in other regions because of their *geographical immobility of labour,* in other words their inability or unwillingness to move to a different region. The reasons for such immobility of labour could be the result of family ties, age (both school leavers and older workers tend to be less mobile), inability to finance a move to another area (for example house prices tend to be highest in areas with low unemployment – or a person who is a council tenant cannot arrange an exchange), or simply a lack of knowledge of job vacancies in other areas.

Many factors such as this affect an individual worker's geographical mobility and some employers encourage job mobility by providing financial assistance towards resettlement expenses.

A second similar factor is *industrial immobility of labour* and by this we mean a worker's ability to move from one occupation or industry to another. We often find that the more highly specialised a person's talents or skills are, the more difficult it is to find another job if he or she has to.

The determination of the wage rate

In a perfectly competitive market, wage levels would be established simply by the interaction of supply and demand.

The next figure illustrates the equilibrium of supply and demand for labour in a particular industry which establishes the wage rate. For £170 a week 100,000 people are willing to offer their services and at that wage rate employers are looking for 100,000 employees. If the wage rate were lower this would create a shortage of workers and vacancies would exceed the number of people looking for work and if it was higher wage there would be a surplus of labour and so unemployment for some.

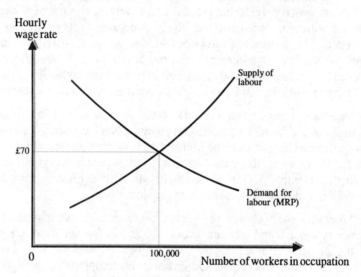

Determination of wage rates

This simple supply and demand relationship might exist if the labour market was perfectly competitive. There are, however, imperfections in both supply and demand and this will affect the wage level.

In most instances, the wage rate set for a job tends to be the same for all employees doing that particular job. Variations obviously occur with seniority or length of service but if we assume that all workers are on an equal grade doing the same job, it should be obvious that some workers would be willing to do the job for a lower wage rate than that which they are paid. A simple example will explain.

If, for a particular job, some people are willing to work for £150 a week because they cannot get other jobs at a higher rate and the next best paid jobs they can get pays £149 a week, then they would work for any wage above £149 (for example, £150). The £149 they receive is called their *transfer earnings*, that is the wage they could get by transferring to the next best paid job they could find. Any income above £150 is a profit to them as they would have been willing to work for £150. Other people are willing to work for £155 (their transfer earnings are £154), others for £160 (they could get £159 doing another job), This 'profit' above the person's transfer earnings is called *economic rent*. (The term rent is a little misleading. This is due to the fact that the same concept is used when assessing the rent of a piece of land.)

So the supply of labour in this case would look something like this.

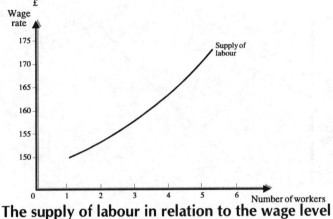

The supply of labour in relation to the wage level

If the demand curve were added the wage rate that would be offered could be found.

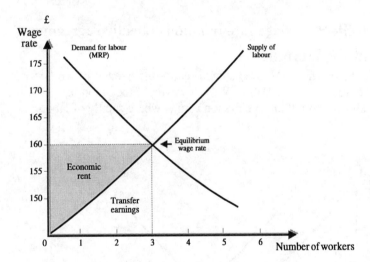

For the majority of employees the remuneration that they receive is the prime motive for working.

Trade union attempts to fix a wage rate

If the trade union and employer agree a wage rate through a process of collective bargaining, the result may be shown graphically in the figure on the following page using a supply and demand diagram for that particular labour market.

The agreed wage rate is shown at the point where the demand for labour intersects the supply. If the employer attempts to cut wages, the unions may impose sanctions which lead to a strike or work stoppage, thus effectively reducing the supply of labour to zero, and so below the agreed wage level the supply curve for labour becomes horizontal.

During periods of high unemployment, demand for labour is below potential supply, that is those looking for job.

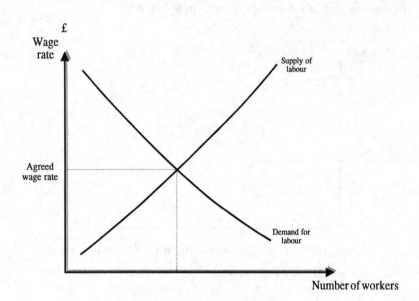

Effect on wage rate of union collective agreement

Fall in demand for labour

A fall in demand for labour from D_1 to D_2 should reduce the number of workers employed from N1 to N2 and so lower the wage rate from W_1 to W_2. However, if the union has fixed the wage rate at W1, then it may not be allowed to fall and a situation results where supply of labour exceeds demand.

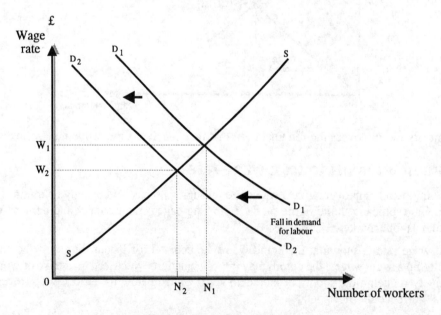

Fall in demand for labour

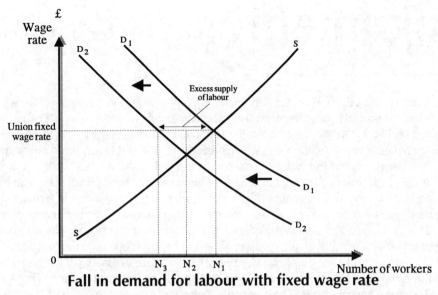

Fall in demand for labour with fixed wage rate

As you can see, if this situation prevailed and the wage rate was maintained, then the number of employees might fall from N_1 to N_3. Unions are obviously acutely aware of the need to protect the employment prospects of their members and may fight such redundancies.

Assignment *The Hotel Union*

The Hotel, Catering and Allied Workers Union (H.C.A.W.) is an independent Trade Union with a membership of approximately three hundred thousand. Its members are mainly classified as unskilled and semi-skilled ancillary staff working within the Hotel and Catering Industry, including cleaners, bar staff, reception staff and waiters/waitresses. While other trade unions do recruit membership from these occupations, in the majority of large hotel chains in England and Wales the H.C.A.W. is the recognised trade union for the purposes of collective bargaining. This is the case with Oliver Kingston PLC, a large hotelier operating in major cities throughout the north of England. In practice the terms and conditions of employment of ancillary hotel workers are determined by national collective agreements negotiated between the H.C.A.W. and the National Federation of Hotel Employers, on which Oliver Kingston PLC is represented. For a number of years Oliver Kingston PLC has operated the practice of employing ancillary staff as either 'full-time employees', 'regular casuals' or 'casuals'. The casual workers are regarded by the company as having self-employed status and are responsible for paying their own tax and National Insurance contributions. The distinction between 'regular casuals' and 'casuals' is that the 'regulars' are given the first opportunity to work when required, but if they refuse to work, which they are entitled to do at any time, then they become mere 'casuals'. Mrs. Ruby Marshall has worked as a regular casual in the banqueting suite of an Oliver Kingston hotel for the past five years as a waitress. She has worked on average 45 hours per week, 50 weeks per year, which is well in excess of the hours worked by full-time waiters. Having been accepted as a member of the H.C.A.W. Mrs. Marshall is informed by the management of Oliver Kingston that they no longer require her services and her contract is instantly terminated. When Mrs. Marshall made an oral representation to the management, asking why her contract was terminated, she was given a written statement which identified 'general incompetence' and 'sloppy work' as the reasons for dismissal.

Tasks

1. You are an officer of H.C.A.W. employed at the union's national headquarters. As part of a training exercise for the regional officials of the H.C.A.W. you are required to attend a seminar in which the role of the union is the topic for discussion. Specific items for discussion include:

   - the significance of the fact that the H.C.A.W. is registered as an independent trade union;

   - the meaning of the expression *recognised for the purpose of collective bargaining*.

   Prepare a set of notes which will enable you to participate in the discussion.

2. The National Executive of the Union is concerned about the large number of so called 'casual workers' employed in the hotel and catering industry. You have been asked to prepare an informal report in which you identify arguments which support the view that the employment status of 'regular casuals' at Oliver Kingston PLC is in reality the same as that of full-time employees.

3. You are required to write a letter to the local union officials at Oliver Kingston's hotel setting out your view of the legal position of Ruby Marshall in relation to her dismissal.

Element 5.3 Workforce Performance

In this element we shall examine how an organisation assesses the performance of its workforce and how it can motivate its staff through wages, benefits and other means. We shall see that different people work better when they are organised differently

Performance Appraisal

Performance appraisal is a human relations management activity to determine how effectively an employee is performing. It is part of the human resource monitoring system and can be related to several training and reward schemes to increase competence or productivity.

There are many terms organisations use to describe this activity including:

- performance evaluation;
- performance review;
- personnel rating;
- merit rating;
- staff assessment; and
- staff appraisal.

Guidance as to suitable systems are given by a number of organisations including the Advisory, Conciliation and Arbitration Service (ACAS).

Personal attributes

The way people perform in their jobs often depends on their own personal attributes and these may be difficult to define and measure. It is much easier to measure physical characteristics, such as height and weight, than it is to measure psychological attributes such as intelligence or personality. Nevertheless, many organisations have experimented with psychometric testing. For example, IQ (Intelligence Quotient) scores are used as a measure of a person's intelligence. Some tests can be applied at the stage of recruitment and selection. Relying solely on interviews can be unreliable as a real measure of a candidate's potential. Using the results from appropriate tests can aid decision making in selection processes. For example, Colour Perception tests can ensure that colour blind people are not recruited for paint matching or electrical wiring, as red/green colour blindness is not uncommon.

From the point of view of the personnel department, the following personal characteristics may be important:

- *Qualities or Abilities*. An individual will have a variety of qualities, abilities or attributes. Some will be easier to define and measure than others. We could include past education, training and experience. Individual skills in a general sense, such as writing ability or specific skills, such as typing speed may be useful to record. Also, particular groups of skills or competencies, may be important. For example, a license to drive a car or heavy goods vehicle, is a measure of competence in using a variety of skills. It may also meet a particular need of the organisation.
  One particular problem is determining the potential of an individual. Many people may have hidden qualities that can be turned into skills and competencies by training. It is

similar to photography where the latent image on the roll of film is only seen when the development process is complete. Tests have been devised to give indications of potential success. Formal examinations such as GCSE are used in this context. Nevertheless, they are by no means accurate predictors of success at work. Everyone knows of people who developed after they left school and became successful only in later life. However, it is also true that not everyone can be trained to be successful in every task. Not everyone could be an airline pilot, especially if they have vertigo or fear flying!

- *Preferences*. Given the opportunity, people will express their preferences for different tasks or ways of doing them. Often the differences in preferences are due in part to innate abilities and in part to socialisation. The nature/nurture debate will continue on this topic, as to which has the greater influence on people's outlook on life.
  In some organisations, people's individual preferences may be discussed and opportunities sought to allow choice. For example, employees may be consulted over shift working times. Also, when staff have shown a preference for a particular type of work, then they may be trained and moved to this work when the opportunity permits. Many organisations use this consultative approach to secure better staff morale and industrial relations.

- *Attitudes*. People's attitudes differ and can change throughout their lives. They can be influenced by socialisation outside and inside the workplace. Organisations wish their staff to have a positive attitude towards the organisation and their work within it. This is the case with successful organisations. However, if the organisation's objectives do not meet those of the staff, then differences in attitudes may appear and be in conflict. For example large organisations such as British Telecom have pursued a policy of staff reduction in the past few years. This has been as a direct result of adopting more productive technology. An opportunity to take early retirement or redundancy pay may suit some staff.
  However, enforcing redundancy, where no alternative employment exist, may cause strife. Examples of this have been seen in recent years where closure of coalmines, said to have been uneconomical, has taken place.
  Organisations will often strive to convince staff to adopt certain attitudes. This is done by a mixture of discussion, persuasion, training and regulations. Examples may found in the attitudes certain organisations wish all staff to adopt concerning Safety/Accident prevention or the priority given to high quality in all products and services.

- *Motivation*. The morale and motivation of the workforce as whole, must be as high as possible for increased effectiveness and efficiency. Motivating individuals and groups is discussed at length a little later in this element. However, the personnel department can take an overall view of the organisation. They have the opportunity to convince line managers to adopt policies and procedures, which will assist high morale and motivation. Motivation and morale can be measured by questionnaires or directly by comparing outputs between similar sections or types of work. The long term effects may only be measured in the survival or prosperity of the enterprise.

Activity

Undertake a little self assessment. Identify your own qualities and abilities, preferences and attitudes. Decide what really motivates you. Is it money, promotion, job satisfaction? Make a list of these in a way in which you could sell yourself at a job interview.

Formal and informal systems of appraisal

Most organisations would like to discover how to make better use of their staff and discover their strengths and weaknesses. The strengths could be used to better effect and training could be provided to remedy deficiencies. However, many organisations do not have formal appraisal methods and are not able, with any precision, to assess their human resource potential.

Some organisations dislike formal systems of appraisal because of the extra administrative costs involved, especially line manager's time. Moreover, individual managers may feel embarrassed in confronting a team member with a list of their deficiencies. Formal systems of staff assessment are also looked upon with some mistrust by certain unions and individuals. This is mainly due to the subjective nature of assessment. People must feel that they are being judged objectively and fairly and not downgraded because of unfair attitudes. However, even with the recognised faults of formal systems, they at least try to bring the appraisal system into the open . Employees can find out how they are judged and may be given the opportunity to remedy their deficiencies for their own and the organisation's benefit.

On the other hand, informal systems may be haphazard and the results unknown to the staff. It is possible that a member of staff believes that they are acting in a way that is valued highly by their manager. Whereas the truth may be that their manager is not fully satisfied with their job performance. Hints to this effect may have been misconstrued by the staff member. An opportunity, to exchange points of view, may never have been made. In some cases staff appraisal may be only a brief summary to a higher manager and a staff member may be summed up as "not bad"!

Purposes and uses of appraisal

The overall purpose of any appraisal system is to enhance the effectiveness and efficiency of the organisation by improving the human resource available. Taking this approach means there at least four practical uses of staff assessment:

- *Identifying staff strengths and weaknesses.* In analysing the education training and development of individuals, staff's strengths and weaknesses can be revealed. Then people's value to the organisation can be enhanced by training, further development or even secondment to other departments to broaden experience. Individuals may see the benefits of such a scheme to their advantage and receive satisfaction and increased confidence from the increase in their personal value;

- *Assessing potential rewards.* Performance appraisal can be used to determine salary increases. Every year staff's performance could be rated and the highest increases going those highest rated. This could act as a stimulus to improved job performance. Unfortunately, it could also undermine confidence in a system seen to be to everyone's benefit as noted above;

- *Identifying promotion potential*. The appraisal system could highlight potential talent which can be directed towards future promotions. This is of special significance to large organisations, where talented individuals can be seen as good prospects for promotion in other divisions of the organisation or even in other functions. For example, an experienced operative may join eventually the training section of the personnel department;

- *Helping the process of communication*. Communication between an individual and their manager takes place at regular intervals and can be planned to be at a mutually convenient time. In a busy organisation, most of the time will be devoted to producing goods and services and the ensuing problems. Using a formal system with scheduled appraisal meetings, both parties have an opportunity to communicate on a one-to-one basis. Sufficient time can be allotted for exchange of viewpoints. They will also be able to discuss their differences in private. This in itself may help to relieve minor stresses and strains that gather in working life.

Starting a successful appraisal scheme

There is a variety of appraisal schemes in existence and it is generally accepted that the most successful schemes have been developed on the basis of certain principles. These principles are:

- *Management committed to the scheme*. Top management are fully committed to the idea of formal appraisal systems. The draft policies and procedures may be developed by the personnel department for discussion and adoption as part of the organisation's strategy towards human resource management. It must be made clear and accepted that special training and sufficient appraisal time and resources must be made available for managers to carry out the work in an acceptable and uniform manner.

- *Time made available*. Time is made available for consultation with managers, employees and their union representatives, where appropriate. Agreement must be reached on the objectives of the scheme and a pilot scheme tried initially.

- *Simplify the scheme*. The scheme must be as simple as possible to avoid misunderstandings and overcomplicated paperwork. The recording systems should allow monitoring so higher management or the personnel department can ensure fair and even appraisal.

- *Agreed timetable*. A timetable is agreed for implementation of the scheme. This includes adequate consultation with all employees, training for all managers, development of the systems, a pilot scheme and the launch of the company wide scheme, and the regularity of assessment. A time for a review of the scheme will also boost confidence.

- *Training and guidance on how to implement the scheme*. Managers may have reservations about the scheme and low confidence in their ability to carry out appraisals. A well-developed scheme with appropriate training and training manuals will build confidence and commitment. The senior managers will also need guidance in monitoring the scheme to ensure equality in application.

Designing the appraisal system

Systems have been used based on a variety of techniques. Organisations will have to decide which are the most appropriate for their needs and can include the following:

- *Rating*. A technique known originally as '*merit rating*' has been developed to increase acceptability. Here a number of employee characteristics are rated on a scale ranging from 'outstanding' to 'unacceptable'. This is often a five point scale but a four point scale avoids people choosing the middle option and forces clearer decision making. Some of the characteristics chosen, such as productivity, may be measurable using agreed workstudy techniques.

However, these are rare except in jobs which are mainly simple and repetitive. The characteristics chosen must be able to be measured objectively. For example, quality of work (accuracy and presentation) is relatively easy to measure objectively. Other more subjective characteristics, such as the traits of dependability, drive, aptitude or attitude, may not be easily measured objectively.

They may give rise to complaints of prejudice or unfairness. Also, there is a tendency for inexperienced appraisers to rate mainly around the middle points. It is rare for anyone to be classed as outstanding or unacceptable. There is also the problem of the 'halo' effect. Here one outstanding piece of job performance, colours the judgement of the appraiser for all the other characteristics. The result is a higher than expected rating. The opposite is true for the 'horns' effect! Also, there is a tendency to rate without relating to the level of work. This means that relatively unskilled staff in jobs needing limited skills get a poor rating, while skilled workers in more skilled jobs receive an unjustifiably high rating.

- *Behaviourally Anchored Rating Scales (BARS)*. This method is a refinement of the previous rating method. The initial planning is time consuming as each job is considered separately. The aim is to relate the rating closer to the employee's actual job and to be more objective in the rating using the following format:

  - Meetings are held between the personnel department and the managers who are to carry out the rating. The job description of each member of staff is considered in turn. Key aspects of performance are then agreed and listed. For example a supervisor would be expected to "meet deadlines agreed on a day-to-day basis";

  - The meeting would then agree phrases which would provide guidance as to best, average and poorest performance. For example, with the supervisor meeting deadlines, the extremes of performance would be first noted. "Never late in meeting deadlines" would be an example of outstanding performance. Whereas "Usually late in meeting deadlines" would be an unacceptable performance. There may be phrases explaining three or four intermediate stages for rating purposes;

  - There will be five to ten sets of phrases relating to different parts of a person's job. Each will be rated on a similar scale of perhaps one (unacceptable rating) to five (outstanding performance). A high total depicts an overall high performance. Individual differences can be discussed for praise or action plans for improvement.

- The advantage of this method of rating is the attention given to behaviour relating to an individual's actual job. The rating system is anchored to what is actually expected of good work in that job. This is more practical than using abstract sets of behaviour, which make little difference to actual job results;

- *Comparison with objectives*. This is developed from the technique known as *'Management by Objectives'*. The manager will set agreed targets, goals or objectives for the employee and the appraisal will depend on how far they have been met. For example, an objective could be to reduce wastage or scrap levels in the employee's section from the present 7.2% to 5% by September next year. Other objectives could be based on quality, quantity and meeting deadlines or budgeted costs. The major advantage of this method is that those who rate the highest are those who can achieve the goals of the organisation. The employee may then feel job satisfaction in personal achievement and improve motivation. The major drawback to this system is in the complexity of organisations. A target not reached may be due to factors beyond the control of the person being rated. For example, an output of 5% higher than last year may be the target. However, if sales fall due to a depressed market, then extra production is unwise as it would lead to unsold stock. Nevertheless, such a system can still be used if the targets are monitored on a three monthly basis and new practical targets agreed. Some objectives are important but not easily measurable, such as long term morale of employees. It would be wrong to set short term easily measurable goals, if they would have long term undesirable consequences. Many organisations combine the rating system, with the comparison with objectives system, to gain the advantages of both;

- *Critical Incidents*. The appraiser records instances of good work and poor work by the employee. The appraisal meeting takes place as soon after each instance to give feedback to the employee. The employee can then learn from discussions of both positive and negative behaviour. The combined records can each year form the basis of the appraisal report. Employee's motivation and skill can improve from this learning process. The problem with this method lies in the time taken to identify instances, write them into a report and have a feedback or counselling meeting. Managers may feel that too much of their time is being taken up. It may also be true that employees feel 'spied upon' and are cautious in new approaches to tasks.
  In many organisations not all staff have jobs where initiative can easily be shown. Thus it may appear that some staff have an undue portion of the manager's time devoted to their work. A modification of this system would be for the manager to report on one or two critical incidents at the time of the appraisal interview;

- *Narrative Report*. Every year the appraising manager is expected to summarise the employees work in the form of a report. This allows a flexible approach and could combine any of the previously related techniques. The problem with this approach may lie in the literary skills of the appraiser. The report may also degenerate into a collection of time-worn phrases, such as "has worked well throughout the year". It is also open to bias with the selection of examples of work behaviour. Unless the manager is diligent in recording incidents of good and bad behaviour over the year, there will be a tendency for the most recent events to form a strong impression in the report. This may be the reason for staff hurriedly completing old projects just before the narrative report is due!

- *Appeals Procedure*. To ensure fairness, an appeals procedure must be determined. Any member of staff who feels that they have been unfairly treated must be able to follow a grievance procedure. In the case of the appraisal system, the first appeal may be to the appraiser's senior manager. Alternatively it may be a committee comprising senior managers, union representatives and members of the personnel department. With a good system it is unlikely that there would be many appeals. However, the presence of such a system denotes good faith.

Appraisal interviews

The employees should be able to see how they have been appraised and sign to this affect. Any appraisal information kept on computer records is open to inspection by the employee under the *Data Inspection Act* 1984. Employees should have advance knowledge of the format and time and place of the interview. The seating arrangements should be comfortable and the interview free from outside interruptions. Often it will last up to one hour to allow appraisal rating, discussions, advice and an agreed action plan for improvement and agreement on objectives.

Action following appraisal

- There must be action agreed between employee and the appraising manager as to the action plan following appraisal. This may include further training, promotion, delegation of new duties or secondment to a new department for broadening of experience or simply a commendation for good work done. Whatever the outcome, senior management must ensure that sufficient resources are available to put the action plan into practice. Otherwise, a potential improvement in the organisation's human resources will be wasted.

- Good administration will ensure that records are kept of appraisals and the action plans that follow. The personnel department will report at intervals to senior management on the strengths and weaknesses of the scheme and improvements that can be made.

- With a record of employees appraised success, it will be easier to forecast an individual's potential. Extra assistance could be provided by psychometric testing. Asking employees to carry out self-assessment would also be useful in making predictions of potential have a solid foundation.

Activity

Identify reasons for introducing a system of staff assessment and list the factors to take account of when starting a successful appraisal scheme.

Motivation

Motivating staff

Organisations need to make sure that their staff are trained to carry out their duties and responsibilities in a reliable way. However it may be insufficient for employees merely to carry out their assigned tasks. As the organisation grows it will seek new methods to improve effectiveness and efficiency. The employees must be able to cope with crises and challenges in a manner which creates improvements. They need to be active, creative and well motivated. To survive the challenge of competition, an organisation needs continual innovation and improvement. The ideas for change must come from the organisation's staff. Thus the important aim of achieving a well motivated workforce, likely to inspire change, should be incorporated into every personnel policy. The process of achieving well motivated staff is not a simple one. People are complex and individualistic. Unlike machines, they do not always 'think' or act in the same way. Thus the aim of this section is to consider the ways in which employees can be motivated and examine the factors, methods or processes which are of importance in achieving this.

A motivation model

Organisations hope both to achieve their goals and satisfy the needs of their employees at the same time. Thus the management seek to ensure that organisational goals are achieved by suitably rewarding good work done by those staff who are recognised as achievers. An ideal model may never be fully achieved in the real world. However, it could be used to analyse and test the 'needs and rewards system' of an organisation, to judge how effectively it operates. The model could be used by management to formulate questions which must be answered in a real situation. Answers could form the basis for new decisions, leading to corrective action. Examples of such questions that management should address are:

- do they know all the needs of staff and the rewards the staff expect?;
- have they ensured that the staff are aware of the tasks they have been set and the type of effort to apply in order to achieve task completion?;
- have they ensured that staff have the knowledge, skill and experience that is needed?;
- are they satisfied that staff have a full understanding of what goals must be achieved?;
- have they ensured that staff receive recognition for their efforts when these goals are achieved?;
- have they identified whether the rewards that staff receive are those which are expected by them?;
- are they satisfied that the rewards the staff receive are sufficient to motivate them to continue to give a sustained effort?;

Rewards

It is obvious that the needs of staff and the rewards that the organisation gives, are at the heart of the motivation process. The rewards that different organisations offer are many and varied. Some organisations have attempted to apply what is commonly known as the 'carrot and stick' approach! Put simply, a donkey is likely to move forward if tempted with a carrot on a stick in front of its nose. The alternative is to apply the stick to its other end, which may give a similar forward motion! Such treatment, suitably modified, could be used with people. Thus a boss may offer the 'carrot' of a weekly bonus, dependent upon higher targets being reached. The boss may also use the 'stick' by dropping veiled threats to the supervisors that, "if the quality drops, heads will roll"!

F.W. Taylor, who wrote a book called *Scientific Management* around the turn of the century, suggested that all a workforce wanted was a chance to earn more money. Nothing else was important. He devised financial incentives schemes where the increased output of workers produced large bonuses for themselves. The problem was to find a scheme which was 'fair' to both management and workers. Today many schemes are based upon measured work systems devised by work study practitioners. No one suggests that money is not important, but many question whether it is the only important reward that people seek from work.

People differ in the priority they give to the rewards they expect or receive from their work. Nevertheless there is evidence to suggest that for most people the following factors appear on an individual's list of priorities:

- money;
- performing useful and interesting work;
- using a full range of abilities and skills;
- avoiding being bored;
- meeting people;
- working with people;
- obtaining a sense of achievement;
- having achievement recognised;
- promotion;
- security;
- fringe benefits; and
- paid holidays.

The role of money as a motivator

It is not always clear what value money has as a motivator for any particular individual at work. For example charities and other organisations have voluntary workers who do not receive money for their services, but still give of their best. Even pools winners have been known to return to work because they miss the social environment or the work activity. On the other hand, there are those who take dangerous jobs or unpleasant tasks mainly because of the high pay such jobs carry. Thus money may have minimal effect, or a considerable one, depending on the individual.

Financial incentives as motivators

Financial incentive schemes which pay a money bonus for extra output have been used for many years. The most successful are based on a system that simply pays more money for more work. In other words, the striking of a bargain that balances pay with effort. Of course the *'rate'* that links money to effort should be objectively assessed, and recognised and accepted by both management and workforce. Previously it was the practice to adopt what were referred to as *'piece-work'* methods. These were based on rates of pay which were arbitrarily determined. The methods used were often the source of bitter argument. It was even suggested that some organisations actually produced less, due to the time wasted in industrial action caused by piece rate disputes. Nowadays work study measurements, undertaken by trained practitioners, are used to fix the rate of pay for a specific task. These have been found to be more accurate and acceptable to the workforce.

Many organisations have achieved up to 30% extra output from the same workforce, after incentive schemes have been applied. A bonus which is paid immediately allows the workers to see quickly the benefit of their greater endeavours. Otherwise the extra income is not as closely associated with the extra work done. Thus the incentive value of the bonus scheme diminishes.

A similar problem exists when the bonus is linked to the total output of the organisation, rather than directly to the individual's own efforts. For example clerical workers in British Coal could receive a bonus based upon the fluctuating output of face workers. The reason behind this is that the clerical work is a necessary service to achieve the output of coal. However, it is only indirectly linked to the physical productive process. To summarise, the three major factors that management should be aware of in introducing bonus schemes are:

- the need to pay bonuses as quickly as possible after they have been earned;
- the problem of attempting to tie the bonuses of those who are not involved in physical production to the output levels of the organisation as a whole.
- the perceived fairness of the scheme.

Activity

Try to identify four jobs in different industrial sectors which use financial incentives as a motivating factor for staff. Note that such schemes are described differently in different industries. They may be called piece-work or commission or some other title.

Workforce control

It is possible to view the effect of incentive schemes from a different perspective. Incentive schemes allow workers to partially determine their own output and so regulate their own pay. Such decisions were traditionally the province of management. Allowing some element of discretion in work methods or delegating decision making powers to staff may further increase the level of motivation. There is a possibility that bonus levels may fall if output cannot be sustained for a reason which is outside the control of the workforce. This is a fear that some workers guard against, by deliberately 'hiding' extra output and so not claiming the full bonus due each week. In this way they can add 'extra' output when it is needed. Consequently bonus levels will often show an unnaturally even level for considerable periods of time.

The workforce may also arrange between themselves an artificial 'ceiling' above which bonus levels are not allowed to rise. They will do this because they fear that unusually high bonus levels may attract unwanted attention from senior management. The workforce may even fear that the management may reduce their basic rate of pay and so they could end up working harder for smaller rewards. If, for any reason, the level of bonus drops, some individuals may view this as management's fault and believe that without the bonus the workforce is being exploited. This view may colour their attitude towards management and result in a lack of trust in future pay negotiations. In fact the bonus system may come to highlight the 'them and us' divide.

A further advantage of the change over to a bonus incentive system of working, is that such a change may highlight 'hidden' problems within the organisation. Often the increased level of output of the workforce may reveal inadequacies in other parts of the organisation's productive process. The purchasing, supply and storage of raw materials may appear to have been adequate in the past. Previously a hold-up in supplies to the factory floor may have been welcomed by the workforce as a unofficial break from the demands of production. With the introduction of the incentive scheme, any failings in the material supply system will be emphasised by the increased demands of the workforce for extra output. The supervisor may discover that both the higher management and the workforce are making demands to get supplies 'to the right place at the right time'.

Management and the management systems are expected to ensure that materials, methods, specifications and services are adequate. This will enable the production (direct) workers on bonus to carry out their tasks with the minimum of interruption.

Types of financial incentive schemes

Incentive schemes for direct workers

Production or direct workers are usually tied to schemes which provide an early 'feedback' on their progress by paying the bonus a week after it is earned. There are various types of bonus schemes that are used in organisations, all of which have benefits and disadvantages. The main types of scheme are:

- piece work;
- measured day work;
- high day rate scheme.

Piece work

The oldest type of scheme is the piece-work system, so called because a bonus is paid for each *'piece'* of work produced. Usually the price paid for each 'piece' of work is settled by *'negotiation'*. This may result in bitter arguments between management and workforce. The modern version is referred to as the 'straight proportional scheme'. This is determined by work study methods based on *'standard hours'* worked and is judged to be a fairer system than the old one. The bonus which is paid is directly proportional to output which has been objectively rated.

Measured day work

'Measured Day Work' has replaced earlier bonus schemes in many organisations. It has the advantage of maintaining a steady output and stable bonus, which is of benefit to both management and workforce. The bonus is paid on an agreed output of work which, with certain safeguards, the worker agrees to maintain. Such agreements are usually reached after employees have had some experience of this form of working.

High day rate scheme

Perhaps a greater trust in workers is shown by the '*high day rate*' scheme. Here the workforce is expected to produce levels of output which are predetermined by management. Often the pace of work is dictated by the speed of machinery or a conveyer with which the worker must keep pace. An attraction of such a scheme to the worker is that of a higher than average rate of pay which does not fluctuate. However, those who cannot maintain the output levels may be disciplined or removed.

Incentive schemes for indirect workers

Workers and management who are not directly involved in the manufacturing process often have their own incentive schemes. These include:

- a bonus share or share ownership scheme;
- merit rating.

A bonus share or share ownership scheme

A bonus share paid from profits, or a system by which shares in the organisation and subsequent dividends are made available to the workforce has proved popular in some organisations. Such schemes hope to gain a long term commitment to efficiency from employees but suffer the problem that participants cannot readily see the benefit of their own contributions.

Merit rating

Extra money paid for what is regarded as outstanding effort is called 'merit rating'. The payment of such awards is determined by management but the dubious objectivity of such payments may often cause disputes between management and trade unions. It may be thought that only the poorer paid sections of the workforce would be interested in such cash rewards but this is not necessarily so. In the National Health Service even top consultants and physicians are paid 'Merit Awards'. The amount that each consultant receives is partly based on the judgement of his performance by his peers. Thus the incentive is not only a monetary reward but also becomes a symbol of status within the profession. In fact whatever the level of remuneration employees receive, it is preferable that they believe that the amount of their pay is fair and relates to their worth as an employee. An employee's worth is not easily determined and will often fluctuate with market forces in the labour market. Thus at any given time an organisation may be keen to attract new employees and if necessary be willing to pay higher than normal salaries for the right people. Thus fairness, the worth of an employee to an organisation and changing market forces can all be important in setting the level of wages or salaries. Of course it can be argued that just as individuals have different characteristics, the wage incentives offered to individuals should be specifically tailored in the same way. Unfortunately an agreed scientific basis for this approach is difficult to implement.

Money as a motivator

Money and working conditions are seen as external or *'extrinsic rewards'*, and internal or *'intrinsic rewards'*, may be are those valued inwardly by an individual. Examples of these intrinsic rewards may be 'pride in workmanship' or 'satisfaction in a job well done'. Money is important to most people but other rewards from work may also be considered just as important. Try listing five rewards, in order of priority, that you would expect from your job. There may well be individual differences in the choice and priority of the rewards that people seek. However, experience has shown that certain factors are common to most people. These include:

- money;
- satisfaction in a job;
- security;
- the opportunity to meet other people;
- pride in good work;
- relief of boredom;
- paid holidays;
- the chance to display initiative;
- the opportunity for 'getting on' or promotion.

A person's level of remuneration is not always the sole source of job satisfaction: nor is it necessarily the major motivator. Nevertheless, dissatisfaction with pay is often the prime cause of employees leaving their present employer to seek better pay elsewhere.

Furthermore many staff who are dissatisfied with pay take collective industrial action. Consider a job where there is an annual pay rise in April. Every April, staff will be looking forward to the increase and may even have adjusted their standard of living in advance of the rise. When employees receive the rise on the due date they feel pleased, even elated. The short term result of the rise is likely to be an increase in motivation or an increased level of job satisfaction. However an important question is "how long does the beneficial effects of the increase last?" It may be less than a month. Clearly it would be unreasonable to expect a rise every month or so to regularly stimulate motivation. However, consider the likely outcome if the pay increase was not given when it was expected. In such circumstances a major emotional response will be a rapid increase in dissatisfaction. Thus while the annual increase in pay does not bring a prolonged increase in motivation to work, the rise is important to maintain the existing level of motivation.

Movement and motivation

If someone was bribed to carry out a task, it suggests that the individual had no internal or personal desire to complete the task. The task was a means to an end, to gain the bribe. Thus the bribe 'moved' the person to complete the task without any personal interest in the work. Is there a difference between 'moving' a person to complete a task and a person who is motivated or interested themselves in seeing the job done well? In which circumstances would staff give of their best efforts and ingenuity? We could argue that money bonuses, given as an incentive to work, are only giving 'movement'. A typical criticism of production output gained by financial incentives is that the standard of quality falls . This could suggest that the workforce is concerned less with the task and more with gaining the bonus. This may mean lowering of standards, 'fiddles and even unsafe 'short cuts'. Thus, it could be argued, that the workers completed tasks that the management wanted them to do. The workers now have little interest in the tasks themselves, which are seen as a means to an end, in this case, the bonus money.

Long term effects of financial incentive schemes

In our earlier examination of financial incentive schemes, we noted that they may have a short term effect in motivating people to work at a higher rate. However, in the long term, bonus schemes may prove to be less of an incentive to achieve greater productivity. Furthermore the high administration costs involved in timing the work, running the scheme, collecting the work sheets, calculating the bonus and settling the minor arguments and grievances, are a disadvantage. Examples of minor problems which could be experienced, include the difficulties involved in timing 'one-off' jobs, so that the bonus rates can be determined. Other factors are stoppages in work due to shortages of incoming materials and the consequent dissatisfaction this will cause when it prevents workers earning bonuses. The workforce may feel that such a problem is not their fault and that it would be unfair if they have to suffer financially. In such circumstances a new type of incentive scheme may be introduced, such as measured day work or high day rate, which will provide a more stable form of incentive.

In the long term, it is the attitude of the work force which may prove to be the most important determining factor in the choice of incentive scheme. For instance, a large proportion, say 40%, of a worker's pay may be dependent on bonus payments and overtime. Therefore, in times of worsening financial conditions, the worker may feel that this portion of his pay is insecure and depends on the whim of management. The same conditions may not exist for 'white collar' or monthly paid staff and so production workers regard the situation as being unfair. This could result in production workers adopting a 'them and us' approach and so proving to be less co-operative.

Individual bonus systems

Certain types of incentive scheme may even cause problems between the operatives themselves. Some types of bonus schemes are calculated and paid on the output of each individual worker. In effect, each 'works for his own bonus'. Piece work schemes, where a bonus is paid for each extra item of production, are typical of individual bonus systems. However, the rates set differ from job to job. Some are regarded by the workers as 'slack' or easy to achieve and others as 'tight' or difficult to achieve. This leads to arguments and disagreements between workers over who shall be given the 'best' jobs. The following quote from a worker involved in such a scheme illustrates the point.' "It was dog eat dog. If you wanted equipment for your next job you chained it to your bench to stop anyone else using it. Many of the older workers had secret methods, jigs and tools for completing jobs which they jealously guarded in their lockers." Such bonus schemes makes management spend much of their time in the administration of the scheme. In fact achieving the bonus can often come to be the worker's number one priority. Employees may lose sight of the organisation's objectives and specific customer needs may be ignored if they prove difficult to fit within the bonus system. Sometimes accurate forecasting of the time to complete a job, or an estimation of the cost, proves difficult if each new job means a drawn out wrangle over rates of pay.

Performance related pay

Most of the early financial incentive schemes were designed to increase the output of the hourly-paid workforce. This is still the case today with many organisations, from manufacturers to local authorities, using bonus schemes designed to increase the output and earning power of sections of the workforce. It may seem obvious that the lowest paid, with perhaps the least interesting of jobs, would be the most appropriate group to be offered financial incentives. However the top management in many organisations receive inducements to greater output. This can take the form of share options, where senior managers are able to purchase shares at attractively low prices. These shares are expected to increase in value as the company's fortunes improve. Other common examples include profit sharing schemes, where top manager's wages are linked to increasing business profit. Some companies encourage share ownership by all their employees. This can be achieved by free share issues based on length of service or seniority. Alternatively the employees may be offered shares at preferential rates. ICI have a long tradition of encouraging employees to become share-holders, and thus have a vested interest in the company's good fortunes.

Performance-related pay was introduced in 1986 for general managers in the NHS and in 1989 the scheme was broadened to include other members of senior management. This move is seen as a way of creating a more effective and modern style of management. The main aim of the scheme is to reward both short-term achievements and those who consistently meet agreed targets. It is suggested that if all general managers improve their performance then this will improve the level of service provided by the NHS for the public. The scheme has a basic pay rate above which are three higher pay bands where basic pay is increased by 7%, 14% and 20%. The managers are given measurable and agreed objectives against which their performance will be judged. The top performing managers who have met or exceeded all their objectives will join the enhanced pay scales. A manager judged only as 'satisfactory' will receive a modest increase on the basic scale. However, the manager performing less than expected will not gain any yearly salary increase, until there is an improvement in the performance. It is possible for that person's contract not to be renewed. A case of the carrot and the stick! The success of the scheme will depend on a number of factors. The most direct will be the ability to set the objectives that are truly needed for a successful health service. Also it needs a performance review system that can be seen to be fair, and not based on subjective measures which could lead to favouritism, rather than rewarding those who can achieve the desired results.

Extrinsic and intrinsic rewards

We can differentiate between the type of rewards that different people seek from their work. Reference has already been made to such rewards earlier in the Unit. They can be categorised as extrinsic (usually monetary rewards) and intrinsic (psychological rewards to the individual). Examples of an extrinsic reward could be a bonus incentive payment while an intrinsic reward could be the satisfaction felt from a job well done. Clearly it is not always possible to achieve both extrinsic and intrinsic rewards from every job. Furthermore individuals may vary as to the rewards that they believe are important.

Activity

Consider the following occupations

| teacher | steel worker | nurse |
| salesperson | social worker | car worker |

For each decide whether those involved in that occupation are primarily motivated by extrinsic or intrinsic rewards. Identify some other jobs which fall into each category.

Satisfying needs

An organisation should aim to reward its workers in ways which most fit their needs. In so doing they should achieve the greatest level of efficiency. Yet what the needs of any particular individual may be, or even what the general needs of all employees are, may not be clearly understood by management. One theorist, A. Maslow, believed that people's needs were ranked in ascending order, with the most basic needs at the bottom. The needs were then in an increasing order of complexity and importance.

He believed that an individual was motivated by the needs of each level but once that need was fulfilled, motivation would come only from higher levels of need. So for example an individual who is hungry, will be motivated by money to enable him or her to buy food but once he has sufficient money to satisfy his physical needs, he or she may require other motivators as shown in the figure.

Ascending Needs

Self fulfilment in using full potential in the job

Status, Recognition of achievement

Belonging, Joining or acceptance by others

Security or Safety needs.

Basic needs, water, food, etc.

Maslow's hierarchy of needs

Dissatisfiers and satisfiers

Other writers such as Herzberg, suggest that there is not a single set of factors affecting motivation but two distinct sets. These are referred to as:

- dissatisfiers ; and
- satisfiers.

Dissatisfiers or maintenance factors

These are factors which cause staff to feel dissatisfaction. Clearly however, the presence of such factors will not produce improvements in motivation of the staff. Take as an illustration the conditions of the work environment. If working conditions are overcrowded, badly ordered, noisy or poorly lit, then people may grumble and complain. This creates dissatisfaction and distracts from their work. If, however, the conditions are improved by a move to a better planned working environment then the cause of dissatisfaction is removed. It would be a mistake, however, to believe that the change provides a greater degree of motivation at work. It simply removes the dissatisfaction. As we explained earlier, money may be classified in the same way. The annual pay rise may prevent dissatisfaction but may provide little real incentive for increased motivation. Further examples could include an employee's good or bad relationships with management or colleagues. Also, a constant source of dissatisfaction may be stifling and petty policies, procedures and rules that are used in an attempt to order the pattern of behaviour within an organisation. An unfair distribution of fringe benefits may also result in dissatisfaction. It is worth noting that many of these dissatisfiers exist in the environment surrounding a person's job rather than in the job itself.

Satisfiers

If the source of dissatisfaction has been removed, then people become more amenable and so management may then be able to seek to improve motivation. As we noted, 'dissatisfiers' tend to be related to the working environment surrounding a job. On the other hand, 'satisfiers' normally fall within a person's job. Thus each person's job should be designed to incorporate factors which lead to positive job satisfaction. For example, a person may prefer to have greater discretion in making decisions about their work, rather than be forced to follow the directions of others. Employees may feel that they are capable of making such decisions and, as adults, are quite capable of taking responsibility for their own actions. Thus a salesman may be allowed to plan his own visits to customers rather than merely follow head office instructions. In this way, the job may be regarded by the employee as more satisfying and the salesman regards himself as being 'more of his own boss'. He may, for example, demonstrate his ability by choosing the most profitable customers to visit and so the result may be increased sales for the company.

Some of the factors which are classified as 'satisfiers' are:

- an increase in job interest;
- a higher level of achievement in the job;
- a greater recognition by superiors of achievement;
- an increase in authority and responsibility.

Therefore to increase the level of motivation it is necessary to incorporate 'satisfiers' into a person's job. To achieve this, some organisations will apply a technique known as 'Job Design'.

Job Design and redesign

Good working conditions and pay are important, but in themselves they cannot create interest in a boring job. People wish to be treated as 'thinking adults' and not just as 'organic machines' without ideas or emotions. Thus an improvement in the 'design' of jobs should mean that people are employed more effectively. Also, this could lead to higher productivity and better benefits and pay. However, if 'efficient' methods of production mean that the job has less variety, the worker is asked to perform fewer tasks and these require less skill, or there is a reduction in the freedom to make decisions, then the job design will have failed in its objective.

Decision making

Working people in their private lives make decisions and accept responsibilities. Therefore, we must ask why management often does not allow them to do so at work. Management's reluctance to allow the workforce to take decisions concerned with their work is often counter productive. It discourages initiative and fails to use the full potential of the organisation's workforce. Of course workers cannot be given a completely free rein, it is the management's responsibility to control and co-ordinate an organisation's operations. However, as long as the decisions which the workforce take do not conflict with overall policy, they should be allowed as much freedom as possible.

The consequences of poor job design

If jobs are not designed to meet people's needs, as well as the needs of the task and the organisation, then it is possible that:

- the potential of the workforce is not being fully used and therefore the organisation's most important and expensive resource is being wasted;
- the individual worker gains little satisfaction from the job. Consequently the person is less likely to take pride in his job and so may be less concerned about the quality of the output or the service given;
- worker's expectations are not realised and this may lead to frustration and resentment. As individuals develop they will normally expect to accept more responsibility for their actions and to rely more heavily on their own judgement. They may become

disenchanted with work if they are then expected to simply follow instructions and endlessly repeat the same simple operations.

Such resentment and frustration may lead to poor motivation, non co-operation, absenteeism, poor quality work, industrial unrest and a high turnover of staff.

Principles of job design

A well designed job will have certain characteristics and may follow many of principles listed below:

- the job will use as many as possible of the skills and abilities the individual possesses. This will involve both an individual's mental and physical skills;
- there should be aspects of the job in which the individual has both authority and responsibility allowing him to use discretion and make decisions;
- people enjoy working with others, thus opportunities should be available for group work;
- the job should not be so simple that workers feel that it is below their level of competence. It should be reasonably demanding and present a suitable level of challenge;
- people often feel powerless in a large organisation and regard their individual contribution as insignificant. Where possible the worker should recognise that he is making an identifiable contribution to the eventual product made or the service given;
- the job should not involve tasks which are merely an endless repetition of one another. To keep people's attention there must be a change in the pattern of work. Therefore there must be provision for variety in the range of tasks performed;
- people's values and beliefs are important. These provide the basis on which attitudes to work and the organisation are formed. The job must therefore be regarded as worthwhile and meaningful by the employee.

Activity

Consider the factors which constitute poor job design which we have listed on the previous page. Can you identify a job which has such characteristics? Similarly consider the principles of a well designed job as listed above. Which occupations might meet these criteria?

Methods of managing the work process

There are a number of methods of reorganising, redesigning or restructuring work process. The following represent some of the most popular and successful methods:

- job rotation;
- job enlargement ;
- group work and group technology;
- autonomous group working;
- job enrichment.

Job rotation

This is an attempt to alleviate the boredom of relatively simple and repetitive jobs. Workers are trained to be able to tackle a number of different jobs and they are moved from task to task to give them a variety of work. The rotation must not occur too often as work speeds have to be built up after each change. The best results may be obtained where the workforce decide themselves when to change jobs. There is a potential difficulty, in that a worker will not be on any one job long enough to build up satisfactory skills or working speed. Also, it is suggested that swapping one inherently boring job for another, does not bring a great deal of motivation. Some individuals do not like changing jobs on a regular basis and have a preference for certain types of work.

Job enlargement

Often a process or operation may be subdivided into a series of short, cyclical and repetitive tasks. An example is where one individual must check a small part of the information on a form, before it is passed to another person, to complete another part. It is almost a production line process, where each person does only a few seconds work on each item, before it is passed to the next worker in the chain. A further example could involve the assembly of a lawn mower from its component parts. At each stage individual employees receive their work on a conveyor. Each has a different task to do in a predetermined order. For example one worker could attach the cutting blades, then tighten the holding nut, before the part-assembled mower travels on. An alternative to this arrangement is to supply each employee with all the parts and allow them to complete the whole process. In this way more satisfaction is gained by a worker employing more skills and completing an easily identifiable part of the work output.

Critics suggest that in many cases this so called 'job enlargement' consists not of one short boring task, but just a collection of them! Many organisations have adopted an alternative approach to the problem of repetitive tasks. Instead of treating people like programmed human machines, they have replaced them with real machines which can run tirelessly under a variety of unpleasant work conditions. This has the added advantage that people are now required to set, modify, maintain and programme the machines, which places a greater demand on their ingenuity, skills and flexibility. For this type of flexibility, human beings are especially suited! However for relatively short production runs, where a wide variety of products is made, automated machinery would be too expensive, as it may stand idle when not needed for that particular operation.

Group working and group technology

Some organisations, such as the Volvo car company in Sweden, have moved from the production line method of manufacturing. Groups of workers complete a whole task, such as building an engine, and the company has experienced an increase in employee morale and motivation by implementing this method. This beneficial result comes from the increased productivity of team work. In a similar manner, some organisations have changed their production methods to take advantage of 'group technology'. Instead of many different departments each filled with a particular variety of machine, they have grouped together machines that can produce a specific product by an individual group of workers. For example, instead of turning, milling, drilling, polishing and plating departments, each containing their own specific type of machinery, groups of workers are each given the full range of machines they need to manufacture the complete product. The advantage of this approach is that it allows workers to identify with the organisation's product as a completed whole, rather than viewing their own part as a separate entity. It can also often speed up manufacture, because it removes the bottleneck of 'queuing' of work for each department.

Autonomous group working

Here an experienced group of workers is given more control over the order, planning and timing of their own operations. Instead of following instructions from a supervisor, they have discretion in decision making. They agree between themselves on the individual tasks. As an example, take a group of fork lift drivers in a brewery. When management decides that the group is sufficiently experienced, they could be given customer orders and allowed to decide between themselves how the transport is to be loaded. The role of the supervisor is then seen primarily as a communications link and a problem solver for the group. A similar experiment has been used successfully at Volvo for some years with the groups voting for their own informal leader, who acts as the link or co-ordinator for the group. This method of working does mean that the group have to be willing to accept the extra responsibility. Also, the supervisor has to relinquish considerable authority to the group. It may be more difficult for the management to adjust to their new roles rather than the workforce!

Job enrichment

Job Enrichment is the name given to the redesigning of jobs to include some of the 'satisfiers' or motivating factors as described by Herzberg. It is claimed that job enrichment provides the opportunity for the employee's psychological development. The employee's full potential is realised by allowing him to tackle more complex tasks. The new tasks are designed to 'stretch' people or give them greater challenges in their daily work. They will have an opportunity to utilise previously unused skills and expand their capabilities. Management must recognise that people vary in the degree to which they are attracted to take up these challenges. Certainly they must not be forced to accept their new role, otherwise they will resent the new tasks rather than be motivated by them. It is useful to present the changes in terms of opportunities, rather than demands. Also, training and support must be provided.

Job enrichment factors

The aim of job enrichment is to improve productivity and task efficiency while at the same time increasing worker satisfaction. This is done by :

- building greater scope for personal achievement into people's jobs ;
- recognising achievement;
- providing more responsible and challenging work; and
- creating opportunities to make decisions in their own sphere of work.

Measuring successful job enrichment

In implementing a job enrichment programme and measuring the validity of its resources it is important to distinguish between improvements which are the consequence of the programme and those which are the result of other factors. For example, an experiment was carried out to test methods of reducing high labour turnover in an organisation. Changes were made to company policy and procedures, pay levels, work supervision and working conditions. After several years it was noted that a lower percentage of people left the company each year and it was claimed that the new changes were successful. However unemployment rates had been steadily increasing over the same period and it was becoming increasingly difficult for employees to change jobs. The question which arose was whether the improvement in labour turnover was due to the changes made inside the organisation or to the external changes in the job market. Perhaps the only way to have answered this question was to have had a 'control' group of workers who had experienced no improvements or internal changes. Their behaviour could then have been compared with the workers taking part in the trials and the effect of the external influences determined. Trials and experiments in job enrichment have been carried out by Imperial Chemical Industries (ICI). A number of different job categories were chosen and attempts were made to ensure that any changes that were noted were brought about solely by the job enrichment factors and not by some other external effect.

The sales representative experiment

One of the successful trials carried out by ICI involved some of their salesmen. Initially these individuals, working outside the company premises, had a number of restrictions placed on their work. They were expected to visit their customers according to plans specified for them by their superiors and they had to make written reports on each call. If a customer complained of faulty material the salesmen were not allowed to take any action on their own initiative. They were given price lists for all products and were not permitted to vary the prices offered to the customers. After determining the initial sales levels (which had been falling) and deciding on a 'control' group, a number of changes were made:

- the representatives were allowed to decide when and what to write in reports about customers;
- where customers had a complaint regarding product performance, the representative had authority and could exercise his own judgement to make a small settlement;
- in cases of customers having faulty or unwanted products the salesman had the right to make a decision on whether to take back material or make a settlement;
- representatives were given the discretion to offer up to 10% discount if they felt this was the only way to make a sale.

The result at the end of the year was that the representatives involved in the trials had achieved a sales increase of over 18%, while those who formed the 'control' group actually experienced a decrease in sales.

Difficulties in adoption of job enrichment

The above example of successful job enrichment is only one example of the many which have been achieved. However, while it may be thought that such a successful technique would have become commonplace, an analysis of 125 industrial firms in the USA. showed that only five had attempted to formally introduce job enrichment programmes. Three major problems exist:

- the difficulty in measuring productivity benefits;
- the difficulty in redesigning existing jobs;
- the difficulty in that all employees may not react in the same way to the job enrichment changes.

Measuring productivity benefits

It is unlikely that management would be willing to introduce expensive and time consuming changes to job design if such changes did not result in improved productivity. Satisfying employees' needs must be linked to achieving organisational goals. We can easily assess the effects of change, with jobs which are directly related to production or sales (as in the previous example). Any alterations to the job can be related to the consequential changes in the output. Problems arise with jobs in which the improvements cannot be so easily and objectively measured over a short time. Suppose the changes result in improved employee attitudes towards the organisation. The benefits could not easily be measured in the short term. Also, the output of some jobs, especially those in the service or public sectors, is difficult to measure in a precise way. For example, suppose an office administrator has responsibility for analysing problems and producing reports for the guidance of management. If the administrator's motivation was improved it would be difficult to monitor the expected outcome. Would there be an expectation that reports would be produced more quickly, or with a greater degree of competence? The problem is that the reports may take longer to produce if the work is done in a more diligent fashion. Only a subjective appraisal of the scheme's success is possible. Thus the employee's superior may express the opinion that the reports are now an improvement over the standard previously attained. There is no doubt that this form of appraisal, because it is not based on hard fact, has less impact when it comes to persuading managers to change long established work systems.

Difficulty in redesigning existing jobs

Many organisations find that radical changes may be readily achieved, when introduced in a new factory or office or with a new workforce. In long established organisations, entrenched attitudes, customs and practices built up over a number of years, are not easily discarded. The resistance to change may be partly due to fear of the unknown, and to worries over potential loss of status. Furthermore it is not easy to change job structures, whilst trying to maintain output. Most successful organisations are busy, and reluctant to chance any possible breakdown in the supply of goods and services that could result from a major job designing exercise. Finally, available technology may restrict the manner in which jobs are performed making it difficult, if not impossible, for them to be redesigned.

Employees' reaction

Studies indicate that the majority of employees tend to react in a particular manner, but this does not mean that all act the same. Suppose a worker performed a repetitive and essentially boring task. He may become extremely skilled at this task and so be respected for being so adept. Consequently he receives a high wage. Such a worker may regard the job merely as a means of earning a good wage and so it is unlikely that this person will welcome any change. It may be also true that many workers do not wish, to increase their responsibilities. They may feel inadequately equipped to deal with the new challenges effectively. The demands of their private lives may deter them from accepting greater responsibilities.

Attitudes

Increasing motivation of the individual is not achieved by one simple method or some infallible technique. Much depends on identifying the motivating needs or factors of an individual and being able to satisfy these needs and at the same time achieve organisational goals. The attitudes of the workforce are critical. Management have to recognise the link between needs, goals and rewards. Workers have to believe that their efforts are worthwhile. Management attitudes are just as important, as any pressure for innovation or change must come from them. They must be willing to risk changes which involve some delegation of their authority over decision making to the workforce. They must also be able and willing to adopt a fresh approach to human relations rather than just pursue solutions to problems of output.

Assignment *The Bitter Pill*

Health Products Ltd. are a producer of pharmaceutical pills, powders and other medicines. Many of the products it makes use the latest technology and the production management work closely with research and development. Although they rarely admitted it, many of the production managers enjoyed the technical challenge of manufacturing the products. In fact many could be said to manage products and processes better than people. Every Monday the management team met to discuss the priorities and problems of the job. This Monday the least technological part of the process was under discussion for the first time. The problem lay in the packing section, which had just been taken over by a new manager, Ray East, and it was he who raised the particular problem. The products were packed using production-line techniques where operatives stood at 'stations' two metres apart. Here each operative had quantities of a few of the products which they placed into boxes that were slowly moving down the conveyor. Sometimes the order attached to the box required the products handled by a particular individual and sometimes not. The problems that Ray found on his appointment were recounted to the meeting. Absenteeism was the worst problem and it meant either high overtime bills or orders not being available to the customer at the promised time, or both. He said that discussions with the packers showed a lack of job interest or boredom which resulted in mistakes, accidents and suspected sabotage. One day the conveyor ground to a halt, with much cheering from the operatives who all sat down on the nearest box and all groaned when the repair was finished. The repair showed that the breakdown was caused by a bolt that had been dropped into the conveyor cogs. Sabotage was suspected but impossible to prove. Statistics showed that accidents and mistakes were on the increase. There was lack of team spirit and the operatives were unwilling to help each other when the occasion arose. The operatives were paid just the same as others doing the same type of job in the region. Ray proposed that the production line was scrapped and that the operatives worked in groups and sat at 'desks' which stocked all the company's products and then one packer could complete a whole order for a customer. Small groups may even deal with particular sets of customers which they may come to consider as 'theirs'. The 'desks' would be arranged so that they could see and talk to each other as they worked. The details were not worked out as Ray wanted to consult the packers first to seek their active participation in making the change. Some of the managers welcomed the idea but others were unconvinced. Their criticisms were: "Asking the workforce for their ideas will only complicate the issue, explain the plan and sell it to them", "They only work for the money, give them a bonus for better work", "We tried participation ten years ago and it did not work" and other disheartening statements.

Task

As Ray's assistant you have been asked to prepare an informal report to help him sell his idea for improving the effectiveness of the packing section at the next meeting of the management team. In the report you should:

- prepare arguments to answer the criticisms of Ray's proposals;
- stress the advantages of group working for the packers;
- suggest the likely consequences of adopting the proposal.

Also undertake a role play exercise of a meeting between Ray, his assistant and some of the packers where their active participation is sought for planning the proposed change.

Unit 6

Financial Transactions and Monitoring

This unit has been written to cover the following specifications of the General National Vocational Qualification Business Level 3

Unit 6   Financial Transactions and Monitoring Level 3

Element 6.1:   Explain financial transactions and supporting documents

Performance criteria:

1   purposes of financial transactions and documentation are explained
2   purchases documents are identified and their use explained
3   sales documents are identified and their use explained
4   payments documents are identified and their use explained
5   receipts documents are identified and their use explained
6   security checks for payments documents are identified and explained

Element 6.2:   Complete documents for financial transactions

Performance criteria:

1   purchases documents are clearly and accurately completed
2   sales documents are clearly and accurately completed
3   payments documents are clearly and accurately completed
4   receipts documents are clearly and accurately completed
5   reasons for the correct completion of documents are explained

Element 6.3:   Identify and explain data to monitor business performance

Performance criteria:

1   users of accounting information are identified
2   the reasons for monitoring a business are explained
3   key components of accounting information required to monitor a business are identified and explained
4   given set of accounting information is examined to judge the performance of the business
5   ratios are explained
6   financial information extracted from accounting information is explained
7   implications concerning the performance of the business are extracted from accounting information and explained

(extract from General National Vocational Qualifications Mandatory Units for Business GNVQ3 offered by Business Education and Technology Council, City and Guilds and RSA Examinations Board - published by the National Council for Vocational Qualifications April 1993 - reproduced by kind permission of the National Council for Vocational Qualifications)

GNVQ3 Business - Unit Number U1016179

Element 6.1 Financial Transactions
and 6.2 and Supporting Documents

In Unit 2 we examine organisational information systems and how information technology has revolutionised the way in which we use and control information. In this unit we will examine the way in which organisations establish systems to monitor and control their financial transactions and the type of documents they use to help in this process. The purpose of recording and documenting financial transactions

As we have already explained businesses operate through the buying and selling of goods and services. We sometimes describe this process as *businesses transacting* and each purchase and sale as an individual transaction. Keeping track of these transactions is a crucial function for any business. It is extremely easy to ignore the paper work and to concentrate on the more interesting aspects of running a business. Nevertheless any organisation needs to establish an efficient and effective means of control for the following reasons:

(i) *the recording of financial information*

The organisation needs to keep track of all its transactions because managers need to know how much is being spent on purchases or how much is being received through sales. It is all too easy to imagine that the business is selling more goods than it really is, or to ignore the number of faulty goods that are being returned by dissatisfied customers. Badly organised managers often lose control of the amount of money which is being spent by the administration department on copier paper or the manufacturing department on raw materials. If the daily transactions of the business are carefully monitored then managers are better able to control the current operation and anticipate its impact on the organisation's wealth.

(ii) *the provision of management information*

A business needs to monitor its performance so that the managers and owners of the business know what is going on. This will allow them to carry out the essential planning and control which is an important part of their managerial role. They should be able to budget more accurately for the future and change the way the business is operating if it is not meeting performance targets. Therefore its records need to be kept in such a way that they can be effectively analysed and interpreted. Managers need to be able to:

- establish and monitor the financial targets of the organisation;
- control income and expenditure within the organisation

(iii) *the 'stewardship' function*

One important aspect of recording and monitoring financial transactions is the need to monitor the performance of the managers and employees of the business. This is sometimes described as the 'stewardship' function. The business managers need to know how well employees are doing their job and owners and shareholders similarly want to know how well the managers are carrying out their roles. This is not simply to measure job performance but also to ensure that there is no fraud or 'fiddling' going on. Without accurate records which are checked and verified the opportunity to steal is too tempting to some people.

(iv) *the legal requirement to provide information to other parties*

All businesses need to produce accounts. If the business is operating as a limited company then these accounts will have to be audited by an independent firm of accountants. Even if the business is operating as a partnership or as a sole trader then accounts still have to prepared (although not audited) in a manner which will satisfy the tax inspector. We cannot over-stress the importance of keeping accurate accounts and documentation. Many small businesses still try to operate on a 'shoe-box approach'. By this we mean that all its documentation and sales and purchases records are simply thrown into a shoe-box (or some other similar container). Imagine the problems this causes for the accountant in trying to produce an accurate set of accounts which will satisfy the scrutiny of the tax inspector. The Inland Revenue and Customs and Excise have the right to inspect an organisation's records and documents either on a regular basis or as part of an investigation should the tax authorities believe that the accounts they have been presented with are inaccurate.

In this next section we shall examine some of the functions of organisations and the type of documentation needed to maintain accurate and effective control. We shall look at the following functions:

- Purchasing
- Sales
- Stock Control
- Payments
- Receipts
- Production control
- Wages and salaries

Purchasing

Purchasing goods and services is an extremely important function in any organisation. For many businesses the cost of their raw materials or components can often make up a major element of the overall cost of production. For example in many manufacturing organisations such costs will often account for more than 50% of their total expenditure. It is clearly essential then that the purchasing function of an organisation is carried out efficiently and at the lowest cost possible. You should recognise that a pound saved by the purchasing department of a business is a pound less of expenditure and therefore a pound more profit for the business. Compare this with an extra pound in sales. This does not necessarily bring an extra pound profit as the cost of the goods or services have to be subtracted before leaving any profit. The purchasing function of any organisation needs to make sure that:

- the organisation has the goods and services it needs for efficient production;
- the goods and services are available when organisation needs them;
- they are purchased at the right price;
- they are provided by reliable supplies;
- the goods and services are of the right quality.

The key to successful purchasing is to have the right suppliers. A company needs to have sufficient choice of supplier to allow it to taken advantage of competition and lower prices. If the organisation is too dependent on a single supplier it can find itself without supplies should its sole supplier be unable or unwilling to supply. This may be because the supplier has found that it can sell its goods more profitably elsewhere or because it goes out of business. However if the buying organisations uses too many suppliers it may not be able to monitor their individual performance or build up a sufficiently good business relationship – another key to good purchasing practice.

One of the lessons that British companies are having to learn from the Japanese is the process called 'Just in Time' (JIT) method. This involves establishing a number of trusted and reliable suppliers who can deliver the required quantity and quality of goods just when the company needs them. Holding large quantities of stock is expensive and cumbersome. The goods needed for production need to be coming into the organisation just as they are required. Hence the term 'Just in Time'. This method is designed to reduce excess supply, wastage and poor quality of supply. In return for good service the supplier should be given sufficient notice when the goods are required and be paid promptly. In this way both the purchaser and the supplier can do their jobs efficiently and make a profit.

One of the most important aspects of purchasing is to keep control of the process. This involves employing people who know what they are doing. It is a foolish organisation which would leave the purchasing of all major supplies to an inexperienced member of staff. Secondly you can control of the purchasing process through suitable documentation . This will keep a track of what the organisation is seeking to buy, who are the most suitable suppliers,

what has been ordered, when it has been received and when it has been paid for. In business there are hundreds of stories of organisations who have bought things they did not want, or who have ordered from suppliers who did not deliver and even paid for goods they did not order or which they never received. In this next part of the section we will describe the purchasing process and the documentation which should accompany it.

Activity

In this chapter we are going to examine the use of documents and forms, and while we use the documents of two fictitious companies to illustrate the process you will appreciate that one of the best ways to understand this is to complete the documents yourself. So as you work through this section prepare copies of each of the documents, but use your imagination and invent a buying company and a selling company and use the documents to follow a transaction between the two.

Purchasing documentation

There are usually a number of distinct stages in the purchase of any goods or services by an organisation and each of the stages requires appropriate documentation. To illustrate these stages we will use the example of Angela Heath, an accounts manager, with Blue Print Graphic Design. She wants to buy a new computer for her section and we will follow her progress through the purchasing and supply process.

Purchase requisition

If Angela has the authority to initiate such a purchase, she will issue a purchase requisition. This is a request to the Blue Print purchasing department asking for the piece of equipment she requires.

At this stage she may have a particular make of machine in mind which will meet her requirements. If this is the case she should specify it on the requisition form. Alternatively she may simply have a specific task in mind, in this case it is the ability to handle spreadsheets. This task can be accomplished by any of a range of machines, and so she may not specify a particular model but allow the purchasing department to choose the best purchasing option available.

She should also include on the purchase requisition form the date when the machine is needed as this will give some indication to the purchasing department of the urgency of the purchasing procedure. We show her purchase requisition here. Note that she will fill in her department (this will be used for budgetary purposes), her position (this will indicate to the purchasing department that she has the authority to generate the requisition) and

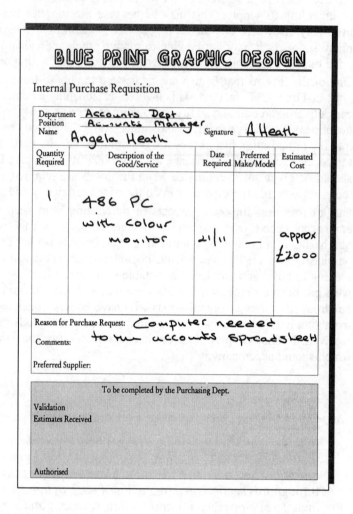

her name so that the purchasing department know who they are buying the machine for. In this case she is not specifying a particular make of machine or a particular supplier. She is leaving those choices to the expertise of the purchasing department. However she does give some indication of the amount she is willing to spend out of her department's budget.

Activity

As we suggested on the previous page draw up a purchase requisition for a company of your choosing. Complete the requisition giving similar information to that shown on the document above.

BLUE PRINT GRAPHIC DESIGN

Unit 7, The Technology Park,
Southwell,
London,
SE9 3HQ.
Tel. 081 555 8945
Fax. 081 554 3647

Microfile Computer Supplies,
1-4, The Parade,
New City,
Homeshire,
DH4 5AS

10/10/93

Our Ref. 1745/GR/93

Dear Sir,

Computer Equipment Enquiry

I would be grateful if you could supply me with a quotation for the following computer equipment. Could you please include in the quotation the price of a full parts and labour on-site maintenance agreement for 2 years from delivery date.

Bell Desktop PC   486DXc 33MHz   210MB Hard Disk

4MB RAM   17"Svga Monitor   3.5 inch DD   Mouse

Please note that we require the equipment to be delivered on or before the 20/11/93.

Thank you for your help in this matter.

Your sincerely

G. Rowell
Purchasing Manager

Directors: S. Storey BA (Art & Design), MBA, D.Watson, BA, MBIM
Registered in England No. 2379163

Letters of enquiry

When the purchasing department receives the requisition it will begin to make enquiries to find the most suitable supplier. Such enquiries can involve a number of different approaches such as:

- identifying potential suppliers through trade directories, trade journals or even the yellow pages;

- looking through suppliers' catalogues, price lists and advertisements;

- telephone enquiries to establish such details as price, specification and delivery;

- sending a formal letter of enquiry asking potential suppliers to give details of the goods and conditions they offer.

If the potential order involves substantial expenditure, and there are a large number of possible suppliers, the purchasing department may decide to advertise and ask for tenders or quotations.

In our example Blue Print's purchasing manager, Gary Rowell, has identified the type of machine he needs and has decided to contact a number of local computer dealers to compare prices and availability. He has written a letter of enquiry in which he asks for a quotation on a specific machine as well as asking for a price for a maintenance agreement and stating the date that Blue Print would require the machine to be delivered.

Activity

Imagine that you are Gary Rowell. Make a list of potential suppliers of the computer. Do not restrict yourself to your local area. Where else might you find suitable suppliers?

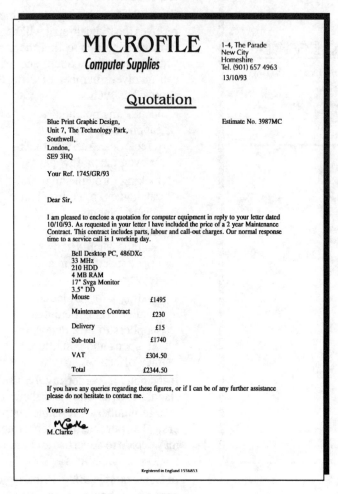

Quotations or tenders

Once potential suppliers become aware of the organisation's requirements they will normally submit a quotation or tender. This will normally constitute the supplier's legal offer to supply the goods or services and will include such details as:

- the specification of the goods;
- the price;
- payment terms;
- delivery dates;
- and other details such as the provision of guarantees or other terms and conditions of supply.

Quotation details

The quotation may also include the following:

- *trade discount*
  Many suppliers are willing to sell their products both to final consumers as well as intermediate organisations within 'the trade'. They will often charge final consumers the

full price for the product while allowing other trading organisations a 'trade discount'. The amount of such a discount will vary from supplier to supplier and from industry to industry and could be as little as 5% or as high as 50% depending on the nature of the market and the profit margin the supplier is working towards.

- *cash discount*
  As we shall see later in this section one of the major problems facing organisations is their cash flow. This can often mean that a supplier has to wait weeks or even months for payment for goods once they are supplied to the customer. The supplier will have paid to produce the goods and will have to carry the cost until the payment is made. In order to get cash into the business quickly the supplier may offer a 'cash discount'. This means that the price to the customer may be reduced by 2 – 10% if payment is made when the

goods are delivered. The supplier may also offer a 'prompt payment discount' if the invoice is settled within thirty days of delivery.

As you can see from our example, Gary had approached a local computer dealer, Microfile, and one of the sales executives, Margaret Clarke, has prepared a quotation offering to supply the computer to Blue Print.

Estimates

You should be careful to distinguish between a *quotation* or *tender* and an *estimate*. An estimate is often given by suppliers when they are uncertain of the precise nature of the goods or services they are being asked to supply. The customer may be asking for something which is not normally supplied or for which there is no fixed price. Estimates are often given in the building trade and will indicate the likely cost of labour and materials. If the customer then chooses to change the specification the estimate will be revised to take account of the alterations asked for and once these are finalised the customer can be given a 'firm price'. Estimates are less binding than a quotation and as such are less binding in law.

Placing the order

When the buyer has examined all the potential offers to supply the product , the most favourable will be selected and the buying organisation will issue a purchase order. This purchase order is the buyer' legal offer to the supplier.

The order should confirm the following details:

- a precise specification of the goods or services to be purchased. These specifications will often simply repeat the specifications outlined in the original enquiry or may be amended to match the specifications outlined in the supplier's quotation;
- the price and when it will be paid;
- the delivery date required;
- any other terms or conditions which the buyer wishes to include in the contract.

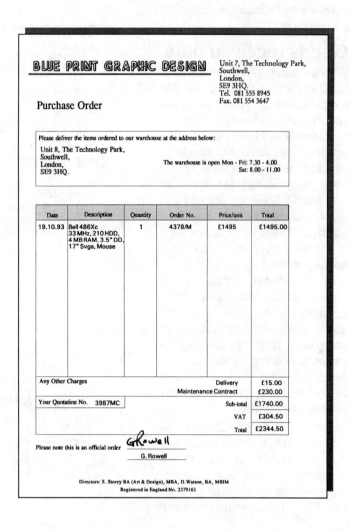

BLUE PRINT GRAPHIC DESIGN

Unit 7, The Technology Park,
Southwell,
London,
SE9 3HQ.
Tel. 081 555 8945
Fax. 081 554 3647

Purchase Order

Please deliver the items ordered to our warehouse at the address below:

Unit 8, The Technology Park,
Southwell,
London,
SE9 3HQ.

The warehouse is open Mon - Fri: 7.30 - 4.00
Sat: 8.00 - 11.00

Date	Description	Quantity	Order No.	Price/unit	Total
19.10.93	Bell 486Xc 33 MHz, 210 HDD, 4 MB RAM, 3.5" DD, 17" Svga, Mouse	1	4378/M	£1495	£1495.00

Any Other Charges		Delivery	£15.00
		Maintenance Contract	£230.00

Your Quotation No. 3987MC	Sub-total	£1740.00
	VAT	£304.50
	Total	£2344.50

Please note this is an official order   *GRowell*

G. Rowell

Directors: S. Storey BA (Art & Design), MBA, D. Watson, BA, MBIM
Registered in England No. 2379163

It should be signed by someone with sufficient authority to sanction the amount of money which is being spent. It is important that a copy of the order is forwarded by the purchasing department to the buying organisation's accounts department as 'accounts' will not pay the forthcoming invoice unless it can verify that an official order, which has an acceptable order number, has been placed.

Larger organisations will often have standard conditions of contract which they expect all suppliers to accept. In certain circumstances the supplier may have made its offer on its own standard terms. Conflict could arise if the purchaser's standard terms differ substantially from those offered by the supplier. This problem will normally be resolved through negotiation, but if there is still a dispute the law would determine the terms which would apply if a contract had been established.

In our example, Gary Rowell has raised a purchase order for the computer and has made it out to Microfile. In the order Gary has specified the precise machine the company wishes to buy. He has confirmed the price given in Mcrofile's quotation, noted their quotation number and has specified the delivery address. As this is an official purchase order it has Blue Print's order number on it and Gary has signed the order as the person with the authority to enter into a purchase agreement on behalf of his company.

Goods received note

Within the purchasing organisation it is important to have suitable mechanisms for recording and checking all goods which are delivered into the organisation. Once the goods are delivered they should be checked as soon as possible to make sure that they are the goods which have been ordered and that they have not been damaged in transit. When this has happened it is normal procedure to produce a goods received note. This is an internal document which records the acceptance of the goods into the organisation. A copy is held by the goods received department, copies are passed to the purchasing department and the accounts department. The goods can then be held in stock or passed immediately into the user department.

In our example Microfile have sent the computer with a carrier who has delivered it to Blue Print's warehouse. When our computer equipment arrived, Ron Guthrie, the Blue Print warehouseman,

BLUE PRINT GRAPHIC DESIGN

Goods Received Note

Red Copy Accounts
Green Copy Stores
White Copy Purchasing

Received by	R GUTHRIE		Signature	*R Guthrie*
Checked by	S WHITWORTH		Signature	*S Whitworth*
Carrier	TNT		Date Received	20/11/93

Quantity	Description of the Goods	Order No.	Supplier	Stores Location
1	Bell 486XL 33 MHz 210 HDD Monitor	4378M	Microfile	A72

Comments:

To be completed by the Accounts Dept.

Date Received _____
Authorisation for Payment _____
Amount of Payment _____
Cheque No. _____
Payment Sent _____

checked the goods to make sure they were not damaged and made out a Goods Received Note. In this case the Goods Received Note is a three part form. Ron keeps the green copy as his record of goods received into the stores. He sends the white copy to Gary Rowell in the purchasing to confirm that Microfile have supplied the goods and that they are in good condition. He also sends the red copy of the Goods Received Note to the Blue Print accounts department so that they will pay the invoice for the computer when they recieve it from Microfile.

Activity

Assume that when the computer was delivered to the Blue Print warehouse, Ron Guthrie had made a mistake and signed the Goods Received Note to say that the computer was not damaged when in fact it was. The mistake was only spotted when the computer was collected by the buying department. Write a letter from Blue Print to Microfile explaining the mistake. Be polite but firm.

Sales

In this section we need to consider the documentation used by the sales department of an organisation. As we have already seen purchase orders are issued by a buying organisation for the goods and services that it requires. The supplier may have already played a part in the process by supplying a quotation or tender and by negotiating on price and delivery. In many cases, however, the first that the sellers knows of the potential sale is when the organisation receives a purchase order from a buyer.

Orders received

Once an order is received into the supplier's organisation it needs to be recorded and processed. This will allow the supplier to allocate the goods from stock if they are available or to make the necessary arrangements to produce the goods or to buy them into stock from a third party supplier. If the order is not quickly and accurately recorded it could lead to delay and a possible loss of this or future sales.

Acknowledgement

Once an order has been received most suppliers will immediately acknowledge the order and this will allow the buyer to confirm that the terms have been formally agreed. It will also act as a check that an order has been received by the supplier.

Advice note

It is standard practice for a supplier to send an advice note when the goods are despatched. This acts as a warning to the buyer that the goods are in transit and also permits the buyer to prepare its goods received department for the imminent arrival of the goods.

Delivery or despatch note

The supplier usually provides a delivery or despatch note with the goods whether it is being delivered by the supplier's own transport or an outside carrier. This is an important check mechanism which details the goods which have been despatched from the supplier's premises. The carrier will then be clear about what goods are being carried and to whom they are to be delivered. The delivery or despatch note will not normally detail the price being paid for the goods as this should not be of concern to the carrier. If an outside carrier is delivering the goods the supplier may also provide a *consignment note* which details the weight of the delivery (e.g. 25 kilos), the number of parcels or packages being delivered, the precise delivery address, whether the carriage has been paid by the supplier or has to be paid by the receiver and whether or not the goods are sent at the purchaser's own risk.

A copy of the delivery note is normally signed by the receiving organisation and then retained by the carrier of the goods

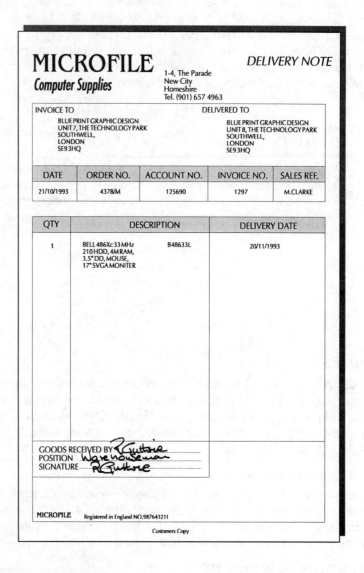

as proof that the goods have been delivered. Because of this it is important that the receiver checks that the goods are as specified on the delivery note. Any discrepancy should be notified immediately to the buying department and noted on the delivery note itself.

The delivery note shown was given by Microfile to the carrier who delivered the goods to Blue Print. At the warehouse, Ron Guthrie, having checked the goods, signed the delivery note, kept a copy himself and the carrier kept the original as proof that he had delivered the goods to the right person in good condition.

Sales Invoice

The supplier will now bill the buyer using a sales invoice. This is the demand for payment for the goods supplied. Once again it will detail:

- the goods or services supplied
- the quantity supplied
- the price agreed
- any discounts being offered
- the total cost payable by the purchaser to the supplier.

The buyer will check the invoice against the original order form and the goods received note and, if all three tally, payment will be authorised. If there is a discrepancy, the accounts department will usually ask the supplier to rectify the matter. If the buyer has been asked to pay too much the supplier will be required to issue a credit note which will allow the buyer either to reclaim the difference in the form of new goods or simply to pay the appropriate amount. If the buyer has been asked to pay too little then the supplier will issue a debit note to make up the difference.

The invoice is an important legal and financial document which must

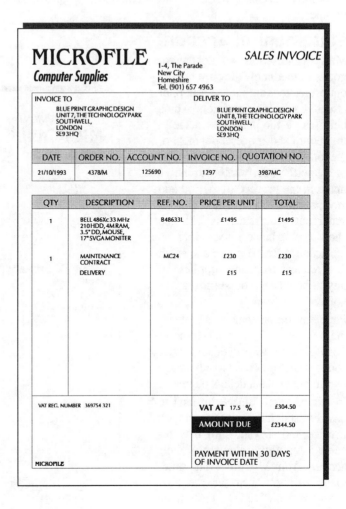

include certain information. For instance in the UK all businesses which are registered for VAT must show their VAT number on their invoice. The purchasing organisation must keep all invoices to prove that it has purchased and paid for its supplies as invoices are often checked by auditors and VAT inspectors.

As you can see Microfile has issued an invoice to Blue Print for the computer it has supplied. The invoice gives details of the goods which have been supplied and Blue Print's purchase order number so that that the Blue Print accounts department can easily reconcile the invoice with the original purchase order issued by Gary Rowell and the Goods Received Note, a copy of which they received from Ron Guthrie. The amount Microfile are charging for the computer is clearly shown with the VAT amount identified seperately for accounting purposes. The invoice is dated and it states that payment should be made within 30 days of the invoice date. Another item on the invoice to note is the account number. Blue Print have bought goods from Microfile in the past and have been assigned this number by Microfile to identify purchases made by Blue Print and to help Microfile's accounts department keep control of its sales.

Statement of account

Many organisations will not pay for goods immediately they are bought but prefer to wait until the supplier issues a monthly statement which itemises all the purchases made in the month and requests payment of the total sum still owing. The statement will specify all purchases made in the preceeding period and any payments made since the last statement was issued. It will also show the balance outstanding on the account. In effect the statement is a request from the supplier for payment of all outstanding invoices.

Payment on statement simplifies the number of financial transactions between the buyer and seller and is sometimes used to advantage by the buyer, as it delays payment.

In our example Blue Print tend to pay on statement rather than on invoice and so wait until they receive a monthly statement of their account from Microfile. The statement not only itemises the purchases which Blue Print have made during the preceeding month but also shows any payments they have made in this period. You will see that as well as buying the computer, Blue Print have also bought

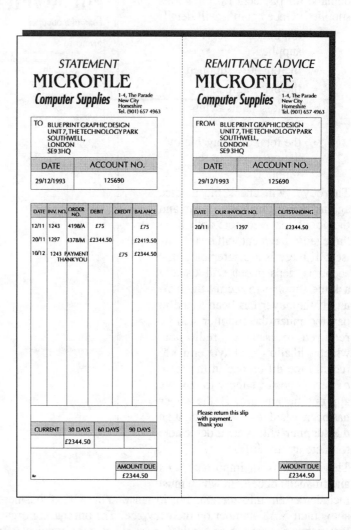

other goods to the value of £75 in the preceeding month. They have made one payment of £75 which covers the invoice for these goods. The balance which now remains is for £2344.50 which is the amount still owed by Blue Print to Microfile. The account number which we mentioned earlier is used to identify all Blue Print's purchases with Microfile. The statement has a remittance advice attached to it and when Blue Print's accounts department send their cheque to Microfile they enclose this slip to identify which account and invoice number the payment relates to.

Payments

Once a buying organisation has received the goods or services it ordered and checked that they match with those ordered it can proceed to pay the supplier. Before paying any invoice the buyer will make sure that the amount stated on the invoice, in other words what is being charged for the goods and services, tallies with the amount on the original purchase order. This is the responsibility of the buying organisation's accounts department and, as we explained earlier, is one reason why the accounts department needs to have copies of all original purchase orders. The accounts department therefore matches three documents:

- the original purchase order
- the goods received note
- the invoice

Pay Slip

If all three match the buying organisation should be confident that what it is paying for is what it ordered and what it received. It may also need authorisation for payment from the purchasing department in the form of a 'pay slip'. This is simply a document signed by an authorised person which instructs the accounts department to pay for the goods which the organisation has received.

Payment Methods

Payments can be made in a number of ways.

Petty Cash

If the goods or services purchased are of relatively low value and the supplier expects a payment in cash then it is normal to pay from petty cash. Even when these amounts are relatively small it is important to keep control of petty cash as even small amounts of money can prove a source of temptation for the light-fingered. Normally payments from petty cash involve the person handing over the cash in making out a petty cash voucher which is placed in the petty cash box. If the supplier has provided a receipt for the goods or services then this is often stapled to the back of the petty cash voucher. These can then be balanced on a regular basis, for instance once a week or once a month, to make sure that the petty cash is being used for appropriate purposes. The petty cash book will list the date on which the cash was spent, the amount spent and what it was spent on. It might also be important to distinguish those goods or services on which VAT has been paid as this can be reclaimed later.

Payment by Cheque

Most goods and services will be paid for by cheque. The cheque will have to be signed by someone in authority known as a 'cheque signatory'. Again it is necessary to record all cheque payments both in the purchase ledger and usually on the cheque book stub. To help the accountant match cheque payments to invoices it is common practice to record the name of the organisation to which the cheque is being made out, their invoice number and the buying organisation's order number. This will allow an auditor to follow through the purchase, supply and payment for each individual transaction if this is necessary.

Activity

On a cheque identify the following:
- *the payee;*
- *the drawer;*
- *the serial number of the cheque;*
- *the bank sort code;*
- *the customer account number.*

Other forms of Payment

If a organisation buys regularly from a supplier then it may establish a direct debit or standing order for payments. Both allow direct payments from the buying organisation's bank account into that of the supplier. The difference between the two is that standing orders are usually for set regular amounts, for instance £1,000 on the 21st of every month, while direct debits allow either the buying organisation or the supplier to change the amount each time the payment is made to match the different value of each individual order. The main advantage of this type of payment is that the amount of paper work is reduced and payment is made more quickly and directly. Of course it does remove the traditional excuse given by buyers trying to delay payment that "the cheque's in the post".

Receipts

Cheque Receipts

When a supplier receives payment for the goods or services it has supplied it should note the payment immediately. All cheques coming into an organisation are normally recorded in the cheque receipt book. This will show the date the cheque has been received, who has paid, the amount of the cheque and the invoice number against which the cheque has been paid. Unfortunately some buyers when paying their bills do not note the invoice number against which the payment is made or make out one cheque to cover a number of invoices. The cheques are still recorded but as 'unallocated' payments. It is then the responsibility of the accounts department to match up the payments against the invoices that it has sent to that buying organisation.

Cash Receipts

If the payment is made in cash it is usual for the seller to provide the buyer with a receipt as proof that the money has been paid. Again this should show the date, the goods for which payment has been made and the amount. The accounts department would then take the cash and pay it into the organisation's bank account.

Paying-in slip

To make sure that the amounts paid into the bank account can be matched to the invoices sent out it is usual to itemise all bankings on the back of a 'paying-in slip'. This is will show the name of the organisation paying the cheque, its bank reference code and the amount of the cheque.

Bank Statement reconciliation

Finally the supplier's financial controller needs to be able to match up all payments made into the bank with the bank statement the company will receive from its bank, usually at monthly intervals. This process is called bank reconciliation and involves matching the paying-in slips with the amounts shown in the bank statement to make sure that there have been no errors or omissions.

Activity

What is the difference between a direct debit and a standing order? If you do not know find out.

Stock Control

Most organisations need to carry stock. If the organisation is involved in manufacturing it must hold stocks of components and raw materials. A retail organisation must hold large stocks of goods to meet consumer needs and even an organisation in a service industry, such as a local authority housing office or an insurance company, must keep stocks of the stationery it uses. Holding too much stock unnecessarily adds to the costs of the organisation, while holding insufficient stock can result in production delays, loss of sales or other operational failures. The organisation needs, therefore, to keep appropriate stock records which not only monitor the movement of stock into and out of the organisation but also help to maintain minimum and maximum stock levels. This is usually achieved by the use of some form of stock record card, an example of which is shown on the following page.

The card shows the maximum and minimum stock levels which the organisation wishes to hold for that particular item. These levels are determined by the regularity of use of the item within the organisation and the speed with which stock can be replaced by suppliers.

In the example used, the organisation has found that it uses approximately 30 floppy disks a week and that it takes a maximum of 7 working days to get new supplies. Consequently it has decided never to hold less than 50 in stock, for if it did it might find itself out of disks before they could be replaced from the supplier. Furthermore the organisation has decided on a maximum stock level of 250. It does not wish to hold more as it will simply be tying up cash in unproductive stock. Yet it has found that if it buys 150 disks in bulk at one time from its supplier it is offered a substantial discount.

Movements into and out of the stock room are recorded on the card as they occur. Receipts are logged showing the date, the supplier and the invoice number. Issue of stock is shown with the appropriate requisition number and department or section which has received the goods. With each transaction the balance of stock is adjusted and it is the responsibility of the stock control clerk to re-order once stocks are running close to the minimum stock level. The amount ordered should keep the stock held below the maximum stock level. Information technology has, for many organisations, facilitated the control of stock. One high street retailer uses computers to check the price and availability of goods which people select from a catalogue in the store.

Production Control

If the organisation is involved in manufacturing, it will require some system to monitor and control production. Normally the activities of the production department are determined by the level of orders the organisation has received or anticipates receiving. Production can be initiated from three main sources: Individual orders placed by customers; demand anticipated by the marketing division; or low stock causing the stock controller to request additions.

If the organisation has a regular level of sales in a stable market then it is likely that production will be maintained at a steady level with no fluctuation in activity rates. However, some markets tend to be less stable and so the marketing department must work closely with production planning to adjust production to meet demand. It is the responsibility of the production planning section to co-ordinate production and to do this it must order sufficient materials either from the stores or from outside suppliers, through the purchasing department, to meet the production department's requirements. As some raw materials or components may need to be bought-in, the production planning department must anticipate the necessary lead time required to place such orders. 'Lead time' is the time taken between the initiation of the order and the delivery of the goods. Once the appropriate raw materials are assembled, the production department should ensure that production schedules are met. This requires the monitoring of progress

Wages and Salaries

Any employer must recognise that an efficient wages and salaries system (illustrated diagrammatically below) is essential to maintain the continued co-operation of the workforce. Employees must be paid the appropriate amount due and they must be paid on time. It is also the employer's responsibility to make the correct deductions' of Income Tax and National Insurance Contributions from employees' wages.

The wages process flow chart illustrates the individual stages involved in assessing and processing wages and salaries of employees in an organisation.

The first step is to determine the individual employee's gross pay. This may be fixed at the same level per pay period or depend on the amount of overtime the worker has completed in that period. Conversely, there may be a reduction in gross pay for time off work. Many employers use a time card or a clock card system which records the employees' attendance at work. Other employers leave it 'on trust' and accept the hours the employees claim. Once gross pay has been established the employer must calculate the tax and national insurance payments due and deduct them from gross pay. These are then forwarded to the Collector of Taxes who distributes them to the Inland Revenue and the Department of Social Security. Employers are required by law to keep detailed records of all employees who are paid over the statutory minimum for national insurance contributions. Such records will provide a basis for wages and salaries analysis and also allow the employer to produce a P60, which is a statement given to each employee at the end of a tax year showing the amount of wages, tax and national insurance paid in the year. If an employee leaves for any reason before the end of the financial year the employer must provide a P45, which details tax and national insurance payments for the financial year up to the date at which the employee left.

We have chosen salaries and wages as an example of personnel procedures. Naturally there are many more, for example: recruitment, selection and appointment procedures; grievance and disciplinary procedures; grading claims; etc.

Activity

Try to obtain a copy of a pay slip from a friend or relative. You will have to find someone who does not mind you knowing how much they earn. From the pay slip identify how much is the gross pay, the individual deductions and the net pay.

Control of the Flow of Documents

As we have already noted, organisations generate an immense number of documents. It is important that the flow of documents is controlled by appropriate systems so that the organisation does not become overwhelmed by paper. There are a number of techniques which can be used but here we will concentrate on the application of document flow charts.

Document flow charts identify the documents which are used and the departments which initiate them, take action because of them, or receive a copy for filing or future action. To illustrate a document flow chart we have traced the procedure a manufacturing company might use from the point at which it receives an inquiry from a customer, through production and despatch, until it receives final payment for the goods:

(a) customer sends a letter of inquiry (1) to the sales department;

(b) sales department replies with a quotation (2);

(c) customer places an order using an official order form (3);

(d) sales department raises a sales requisition (4) for the goods and passes the original to the production department. Copies are sent to the despatch and accounts departments which are filed awaiting further action;

(e) production department manufactures the goods and transfers them to the despatch department. Included with the goods is a goods to despatch note (5). Copies of this are sent to the accounts department and sales department for filing;

(f) despatch packages the goods and sends them to the customer with a delivery note (6). Copies of the delivery note are sent to the accounts department and sales department;

(g) accounts department checks the delivery note (6) with the sales requisition (4) and the goods to despatch note (5). If all three tally, an invoice (7) is sent to the customer with a copy to the sales department;

(h) once the customer has received the goods and is satisfied that they correspond to the order, payment will be sent (8) to cover the invoice (7). On receipt of the payment, the accounts department will verify it against the invoice and if it is satisfactory will process it through the customer's account.

Note the Sales Department receives copies of all the internal documentation. This is because it is the customer's link with the organisation and should some delay occur in processing the order, it may be asked by the customer to check the progress of the order.

Clearly it is possible to prepare flow charts for all the important procedures within an organisation. In identifying the flow of documents in this way management is able to identify potential delays and hold-ups in a process. If the procedure is not working as it should, it may be that some department is not receiving a copy of a document which it requires to play its part. Alternatively, from a flow chart it is possible to isolate unnecessary document flows. For instance, in our example there would be no need for the production department to receive a copy of the invoice which the accounts department sends to the customer. Thus unnecessary waste or duplication of documents can be eliminated.

Activity

Having followed Blue Print Graphic Design's purchase of a new computer from start to finish prepare a flow chart which shows each of the organisation's involved, each department which plays a part in these organisations in the process and the flow of documents between the departments and the organisations.

Assignment *Purchasing Made Easy*

"The trouble with trying to buy anything in this place is that the system is so complicated" said Harry Edwards, one day over coffee. "If I could only understand the purchasing procedures I'm sure I could run the office more smoothly". Harry is the Marketing Manager for Teeschem Ltd., a large chemical company based in Cleveland. He has recently been appointed to the company and has moved from a small business in which purchasing office supplies was simply a matter of asking the firm's accountant if there was money available in the budget and placing the order. In Teeschem, however, the company is such a large organisation that strict control has to be maintained over all aspects of the company's spending. Harry approached Jim Sunley, the Purchasing Manager of Teeschem and asked for some guidance. Jim, in his usual friendly way, tried to explain the system as simply as possible. "You raise a purchase requisition for the goods you require and pass it to us in the purchasing department. If you are not sure of the best supplier or the best price we will find these for you. We then place an order. Of course we keep you informed by sending you a copy of the order when it is placed. We also send a copy to the accounts department as they will have to pay the bill. When goods are received into the company, we are notified with a goods received note and again you will get a copy to say the goods have been received. If there is any problem with the goods when they are received this is noted both on the delivery note and on the goods received note. You can then arrange to have them brought up to your office. When the invoice comes in from the supplier, it is checked by the invoice verification section and if everything is OK then it will be paid by accounts. Is that clear enough?" Harry nodded but in a way that indicated that he had only vaguely grasped the system. Jim reflected on Harry's problem and decided to do something about it.

Tasks

1.   You are a clerical assistant in the purchasing department of Teeschem. Jim knows that you have a good understanding of the system. He has asked you to prepare a 'step by step guide to purchasing' which can be circulated throughout the organisation. Bearing in mind that this will be used by all grades of staff, prepare this guide using simple and concise language.

2.   Jim is concerned that the purchasing process is not over complicated. He wishes to be sure that there is not a duplication of documents 'floating around the organisation'. He has asked you to prepare a document flow chart similar to that shown earlier in the chapter but which is applicable to the purchasing process. Prepare this flow chart for Mr. Sunley.

Development Task

3.   Try to obtain copies of the documents used by any organisation in your area. Identify the common aspects and from them produce a standardised purchase order and invoice form.

Element 6.3 Monitoring Business Performance

In this element we will consider the way in which we can assess the performance of a business and in particular how we can measure its financial performance. We shall see that the business can be measured against targets which it sets itself but also against other businesses.

To manage an organisation effectively or to assess its performance it is necessary to interpret and analyse the information presented in financial statements. This involves three stages:

- identification of the relevant information;
- interpretation of that information;
- comparison of that information against some other measure of performance.

Business Objectives

Before we begin to look at the performance of a business we need to recognise that it can be measured only against its objectives. Different businesses have different objectives. These are dependent on the type of business it is. Later in the book we shall consider a range of objectives for different types of organisations and examine the way in which they can be set externally or internally.

A trading company seeking to maximise its profit will have very different objectives to a government department serving the community. A nationalised industry may be seeking to achieve the dual objectives of being commercially profitable, and providing as wide a service to its consumers as possible. In this part of the Element we will restrict our study to measures of performance in commercial organisations. In saying that, we will be stressing the need for a business to provide a satisfactory return on investment, to be profitable and to use efficiently the resources at its disposal. Of course all of these are to some extent inter-linked but it is only by examining each individually that it is possible to begin to appreciate where the strengths and weaknesses of a business lie and how these can be improved to make financial management more effective.

Activity

1a. *Identify as many different classes of users of accounting information as you can. You should be able to identify at least 10 different classes. One example to get you started is employees of a business.*

1b. *Identify particular aspects of accounting information which would be of special interest to each of the user groups identified.*

   For example: employees would be particularly interested in the cash solvency of the organisation for which they work (no cash - no pay). They would also be interested in the profits earned by the business and future forecasted sales figures to ensure continuity of employment.

2. *Make a list of the main reasons why a business should be monitored.*

The Use Of Performance Ratios

Often on the evening news bulletin you will hear an item which mentions the trading performance of a large company such as ICI or BP. The newsreader may say that it has earned profits of hundreds of millions of pounds. Is this a good, bad or indifferent performance for the company this year? It may sound impressive but what we do not know is how much is invested in the company in relation to its profit or whether it is so inefficient that its profits represent only a tiny percentage of its sales. To be able to judge such figures we use performance ratios. These are comparisons of one piece of financial information against another, expressed as a percentage, proportion or ratio. The following simple example may illustrate this.

You will understand that if you deposit £100 in a building society you may receive £8 interest at the end of the year. This can be expressed as a performance indicator on your savings in the following way:

$$\frac{\text{Interest paid}}{\text{Money deposited}} \quad = \quad \frac{£8}{£100} \quad \times \quad 100 \quad = \quad 8\%$$

Therefore we find that you are getting an 8% return on your savings. Is this a good return? The answer to such a question depends on the rate of return you could get if you invested your money elsewhere, and also on a number of other important considerations. With your money in the building society you know that it is safe and so you may be willing to accept a lower rate of return than you might receive on a more risky investment. A further consideration is perhaps that you were able to get 10% from the same building society last year before interest rates fell, and so you are less satisfied with the 8% now. These, and other factors will influence your feelings as to whether or not you are getting a good return, but in each case you are using a performance ratio indicator to make a judgement. Commercial organisations use similar ratios to measure their performance which we will now examine.

The financial statements of Broadwood Distributors plc. (BD plc.) will be used to illustrate the points made. Therefore you should refer to the Balance Sheet and the Profit and Loss Account of BD plc. which are given in Element 7.4 *Financial Statements* to examine and calculate the ratios as they are explained.

Activity

Which elements of information provided by accounts should be concentrated on when performing a monitoring operation? Explain why you have chosen those elements.

Return on Capital

We have already noted that the capital invested in a business can come from a number of sources. For sole traders and partnerships, the money usually comes from the owners themselves. This will be either from their own savings or from borrowing, normally from a bank. In a limited company, the capital consists of share capital provided by the shareholders plus reserves. In the case of a small private company there may be only a few shareholders, whilst in a large public company there may be hundreds or thousands of investors.

Wherever the initial capital comes from, all the persons providing it have similar objectives - they wish to see a return on the money which they have invested in the business. This is assessed by determining the return on capital employed.

Return on capital employed (ROCE)

This means that the profit made by the business is expressed as a percentage of the capital invested in it. It is not meant to measure the actual money received by an owner or part owner of a business as a percentage of the money invested in it, but rather to measure the amount earned by the business for the benefit of the owner or part owner.

In the case of a sole trader or a partnership this return will consist of the net profit of the business expressed as a percentage of the owner(s) capital as follows:

$$\text{For a Sole Trader:} \quad \frac{\text{Net Profit}}{\text{Owner's Capital}} \times 100 = \text{ROCE}$$

$$\text{For a Partnership:} \quad \frac{\text{Net Profit}}{\text{Partners' Capital}} \times 100 = \text{ROCE}$$

Note that since sole traders and partners are responsible for their own taxes based on their own share of the business profits, the profit figures are expressed before tax is considered.

In the case of a limited company the return on capital employed will depend to a large extent on the way in which a company raises its capital. For example, if a company raises £1m in ordinary shares, £0.25m in preference shares carrying a fixed dividend of 10%, £0.5m in 12% debenture stock, and has accumulated retained profits (reserves) of £0.75m, there are three alternative figures which can be used as capital employed. These are:

- total capital - £2.5m (£1m + £0.25m + £0.5m + £0.75m);
- shareholders' capital - £2m (£1m + £0.25m + £0.75m)
  (note that borrowed capital is now excluded);
- equity capital (ordinary shareholders' share of the business) - £1.75m (£1m + £0.75m)
  (note that preference share capital is now excluded).

It follows then that in order to effectively measure the return on capital it is necessary to use three alternative profit figures which will correspond with the above. These are respectively:

- net profit BEFORE charging debenture interest and BEFORE providing for preference share dividend;
- net profit AFTER charging debenture interest BUT BEFORE providing for preference share dividend;
- net profit AFTER charging debenture interest and AFTER providing for preference share dividend.

It is better to use pre-tax profits for comparison purposes because changes in tax regulations or rates from one year to the next, or different levels of tax allowances in other businesses may have a distorting effect on the after-tax figures, thus making comparisons difficult.

Continuing our example, if the business mentioned above made a net profit in a particular year of £440,000 (£0.44m), the return on capital employed using the criteria already discussed would be as follows:

(a) $\dfrac{£440,000 \text{ (net profit)} + £60,000 \text{ (debenture interest)}}{£2,500,000} \quad \dfrac{£500,000}{£2,500,000} \times 100 = 20\%$

(b) $\dfrac{£440,000 \text{ (net profit)}}{£2,000,000 \text{ (shareholders capital)}} \times 100 = 22\%$

(c) $\dfrac{£440,000 \text{ (net profit)} - £25,000 \text{ (preference Dividend)}}{£1,750,000 \text{ (equity capital)}} \quad \dfrac{£415,000}{£1,750,000} \times 100 = 23.7\%$

You will notice that the return on capital employed expressed as a percentage increases as part of the capital is omitted. This is because part of the overall total capital carries a fixed rate of return which is less than the total rate of return (12% and 10% respectively). Now let us look at the rates of return at different levels if the total rate of return is less than the fixed rates of return. Assume a net profit of £140,000 but with the other figures exactly as before, the rates of return on capital employed would be as follows:

(a) $\dfrac{£200,000}{£2,500,000} \times 100 = 8\%$

(b) $\dfrac{£140,000}{£2,000,000} \times 100 = 7\%$

(c) $\dfrac{£115,000}{£1,750,000} \times 100 = 6.57\%$

Obviously the reason for this is that the capital which carries a fixed rate of return has a higher percentage than that of the total capital.

For most purposes the return on equity capital (ordinary share capital plus reserves) is considered to be the best measurement to take, but care must be taken to deduct any preference dividend from the net profit before calculating the return. One final point to make is that wherever possible the ROCE should be based upon the average capital employed throughout the year. This will entail adding the opening capital to the closing capital and dividing the result by 2. If the information given precludes this then obviously any figure available for capital employed should be used. When discussing the accounting ratios of BD plc. for the year ended 31 August 1992 we will be using average figures wherever possible.

Return on capital employed for Broadwood Distributors plc.

In the case of BD plc. the figures which we used to measure the rate of return on capital employed are as follows:

Net profit before deduction of debenture interest   £1.48m (£1.35m + £0.13m)

Net profit for the year   £1.35m

Net profit for the year after providing for pref share dividend   £1.295m (£1.35m – £0.055m)

Total average shareholders' capital employed consists of £4.925m (opening share capital + reserves) + £6.130m (closing share capital + reserves) divided by 2 = £5.5275m

Since the debenture stock is constant at £1m, and preference share capital is constant at £0.5m between the beginning and the end of the year, the average for total capital employed becomes £6.5275m, and for equity capital employed £5.0275m.

The various returns on capital employed for BD plc. can now be readily calculated as follows:

Return on total capital employed:

$$\frac{£1.480m}{£6.5275m} \times 100 = 22.67\%$$

Return on shareholders' capital employed:

$$\frac{£1.350m}{£5.5275m} \times 1000 = 24.42\%$$

Return on equity capital employed:

$$\frac{£1.295m}{£5.0275m} \times 100 = 25.76\%$$

As mentioned earlier, perhaps the best one to use is the return on equity capital employed, since it is the ordinary shares which carry the greatest risk and it is the rate of return to equity shareholders which is subject to fluctuation depending upon the level of profits earned. The returns to debenture holders in this company are constant at 13%, and likewise the returns to preference shareholders are constant at 11%.

In the case of BD plc. the return on equity capital employed before tax is 25.76%, but whether this is a good return or not can only be determined by comparing it with similar returns for other companies, or with its own returns for earlier years. For the purpose of comparison with other companies the profit before tax should be used, but for the purpose of comparison with earlier years it may be desirable to use after tax profits as the measure of what is finally left for the ordinary shareholders after all other claims have been made on the profits (including tax).

The after tax return for BD plc. would therefore be:

$$\frac{£0.905m}{£5.0275m} \times 100 = 18\%$$

As stated earlier this is not what the shareholders are actually paid in cash, it is the percentage return on their capital invested which the company has earned for them. Paradoxically the more successful a company is, the returns on capital employed can fall, due to a large proportion of the profits earned being retained in the business (increasing the capital employed) without there being a corresponding increase in future profits.

Profit margins

Profit margins are calculated by expressing profit as a percentage of sales, and are used to compare:

- the results of one time period against another;
- the results of one business against another or;
- the results of a particular business against the standard for that type of business.

The profit so expressed can be either the gross profit, the net profit, or both.

The gross profit margin

The gross profit margin is the gross profit (sales less cost of sales) expressed as a percentage of sales. The formula for calculating it is gross profit over sales multiplied by 100. So for example if a greengrocer has sales of £80,000 which cost him £48,000 to purchase, his gross profit will be £32,000. Expressing this as a percentage of sales will show a gross profit margin of 40% by applying the formula:

$$\frac{£32,000}{£80,000} \times 100 = 40\%$$

This can then be used to compare the margin earned in the previous or earlier accounting periods. If there are any major deviations from earlier years they should be investigated. Causes of decreases in the gross profit margins are:

- loss of stock through deterioration or pilferage;
- increase in cost prices without a corresponding increase in selling prices. For example, if in the case of the greengrocer, the cost to him of fruit and vegetables rose by 10% in the

following year, but he kept his selling prices at the same level as before, and if he carried out the same amount of trade as previously, his sales would be £80,000, his cost of sales £52,800 (£48,000 + 10% (£4,800)), and therefore his gross profit £27,200. Expressing this as a percentage of sales would give a gross margin of 34%, which is quite a considerable fall;

- decrease in selling prices without a corresponding decrease in cost prices. Obviously this will have the same effect as (ii) above;

- failure to record cash sales to enable embezzlement of cash by an employee.

Increases in gross margins are obviously brought about by the reverse of the above events happening, but an additional contributory factor could be the over-valuation of closing stock, which has the effect of decreasing cost of sales and therefore increasing gross profits.

The gross margin can also be used to compare one business with another providing it carries on the same type of business. It would be pointless for the greengrocer to compare his gross margins with say a jeweller or an owner of a petrol filling station as they will have vastly different gross margins. Generally speaking as a rough guide, the more rapid the turnover, the lower the gross margin. Hence the petrol filling station owner may only get a gross margin of say 5% as against a jeweller's 60%. The former gets his profit from the rapid speed of turnover of petrol, whereas the latter will have to carry large volumes of stock of very slow turnover goods, so that when a sale is made a large margin is required to compensate for the slowness of the turnover.

Another use to which gross margins can be put is the establishment of selling prices of goods. If the gross margins for the last two or three accounting periods are known and are reasonably constant, a businessman can fix the price at which he needs to sell a product to achieve the necessary margins, by applying a correlating percentage to the cost price of the goods. Take the case of the greengrocer above: if he has established that the gross margin is 40%, and he knows that something has cost him say £600 to buy, he can calculate the selling price by adding 66.67% (2/3rds) to the cost price, which would be £400 to fix a selling price of £1,000. Expressing the £400 profit as a percentage of the selling price (£1,000) would now give 40% which is the required gross margin. The reason for this is that just as the gross profit can be expressed as a percentage of sales, it can also be expressed as a percentage of cost of sales. This is called the mark-up. There is a relationship between gross margin and mark-up which is based on the equation: Sales less Cost of Sales equals Gross Profit. If sales are expressed as 100, cost of sales as 75, and gross profit as 25, the 25 expressed as a percentage of 75 is 33.33%, which is the mark-up required on the cost of goods to give a gross profit of 25%. Look again at the greengrocer: Sales 100, Cost of Sales 60, Gross Profit 40. 40 as a percentage of 60 equals 66.67%.

Gross profit margin for Broadwood Distributors plc.

The gross profit margin for BD plc. in respect of the year ended 31 August 1992 is 25% and is calculated by dividing the gross profit of the business £9.1m by the sales revenue £36.4m and multiplying by 100. This is a slight improvement on the previous year's figure of 23.49% (£7.775m as a percentage of £33.1m).

Net profit to sales ratio

This is the net profit expressed as a percentage of sales after all expenses have been deducted from the gross profit, but before tax and dividends have been provided for. This can really only be used as a comparison with earlier years in respect of the same business, as different businesses will have different expenses patterns which are a major factor in the calculation of this ratio. For example, if two separate businesses both had gross margins of 30% and one of the businesses had a net profit to sales ratio of 7% as opposed to the other business's 5%, it simply means that the second business has more expenses in relation to sales than the first, which may be beyond the control of the management or owner. But it does render comparison of the two businesses in terms of net profit to sales pointless. However if the same set of circumstances applied to two separate years of the same business, it would show a comparative increase in expenses in relation to sales between the two years, which may enable management to take steps to rectify the situation. This may be achieved by establishing economies in the following years, or perhaps by increasing selling prices to an extent which would increase gross margins and re-establish net profit to sales ratio at the previous level.

The net profit to sales ratio for Broadwood Distributors plc.

The BD plc. Profit and Loss Account for the year ended 31 August 1992 shows that the company had a net profit before tax and dividends of £1.35m and a sales revenue of £36.4m. This produced a net profit to sales ratio of 3.71% (the corresponding figure for the previous year being 1.75%). This shows an improvement of almost 2% between 1990/91 and 1991/92; when this is compared to the increase of 1.5% in the gross margin (see above) we can see that there has been a saving in the expenses to sales ratio of approximately 0.5%.

It is worth noting at this point that it is possible to express any expense item in the Profit and Loss Account as a percentage of sales revenue. For example if we wished to find the percentage of sales revenue spent on advertising, we know that sales are £36.4m and the advertising expenditure is £130,000 the percentage would be 0.36% (1990/91 – 0.45%)

Thus in the current trading year every 36p spent on advertising generated £100 in sales. We could use similar calculations to show wages/sales ratio or motor running expenses/sales ratio or any other ratio we need to make to assess whether any element of cost is too excessive and requires monitoring.

Turnover of Capital

This ratio measures the use that has been made of the businesses capital in producing the level of sales. In other words has the capital employed which has financed the business assets been fully utilised in the period? It is normally expressed not as a percentage but as a turnover of capital. A very low turnover of capital would indicate that the organisation has not produced a great level of sales in comparison to the amount of capital it holds. This is often a charge which is levelled against some of the more capital intensive nationalised industries. It is calculated simply by comparing the sales revenue with the capital employed. So if an engineering company has a capital of £300,000 which is represented by plant and machinery and earns sales figures of £900,000 we can say that it has a turnover of capital of three times. Note that this is not given as a percentage but as a multiple of the capital employed.

$$\text{Turnover of capital} = \frac{\text{Sales revenue}}{\text{Capital employed}} = \frac{£900,000}{£300,000} = 3 \text{ times}$$

It is important to note that capital employed must include all capital employed except long term borrowed capital. So capital employed is equivalent to fixed assets plus current assets minus current liabilities and long term liabilities.

The relationship between the three ratios

We have just examined three important ratios:

- the return on capital employed;
- the net profit to sales ratio; and
- the turnover of capital.

They are all concerned with the profitability of the business and its rate of return on capital invested. In fact all three are inter-linked. The return on capital is determined by the relationship between the net profit to sales and the turnover of capital. Using the following example we can illustrate the relationship. Assume that a business has a profit of £100,000, sales of £1,600,000 and capital employed of £800,000.

$$\text{return on capital employed} = \text{profit margin} \times \text{turnover of capital}$$

$$\frac{\text{profit}}{\text{capital employed}} \times 100 = \frac{\text{profit}}{\text{sales revenue}} \times 100 = \frac{\text{sales revenue}}{\text{capital employed}}$$

$$\frac{£100,000}{£800,000} \times 100 = \frac{£100,000}{£1,600,000} \times 100 = \frac{£1,600,000}{£800,000}$$

$$12.5\% = 6.25\% \times 2$$

From the above example you can see the interdependence of the ratios. Clearly an increase or decrease of profit, capital employed or sales will influence the others. However it also means that we may find similar returns on capital employed in industries operating on very different profit margins. So, for example, food retailing which has a rapid turnover and very competitive prices may have a net profit to sales ratio of only 3% or 4%. However it has a high turnover of capital because of the high volume of trade so the low net profit to sales ratio of 3% - 4% may be compensated by a turnover of capital employed of five times which would give a return on capital employed of 15% - 20%. Alternatively a manufacturing industry might expect a net profit to sales ratio of about 8% - 10% but because of the relatively long time required to produce each individual product, may have a comparatively low capital turnover of 1.5 giving a return on capital employed of between 12% and 15%. As you can see, a potential investor will wish to carefully scrutinise all of these ratios before determining where to place his investment.

The position of Broadwood Distributors plc.

As we have noted earlier from its balance sheet and profit and loss account BD plc. has a net profit of £1.35m, sales revenue of £36.4m and capital employed of £5.5275m. Thus it has the following ratios:

$$= \frac{\text{profit}}{\text{sales revenue}} \times 100$$

$$\text{Return on Capital Employed} = \text{Net Profit to Sales Ratio} \times \text{Capital Turnover}$$

$$24.42\% = 3.71\% \times 6.58$$

Control of Working Capital and Liquidity

We have seen that a business must attempt to maintain its profitability if it is to provide a satisfactory return to those who have provided capital. However in order to survive it must also remain solvent and so it becomes necessary to keep a close watch on the short term liquidity position. By this we mean the ability to pay its immediate debts. A business can easily become insolvent and as a consequence be wound up. Its employees will expect to be paid and certain creditors such as landlords or suppliers of materials may be unwilling to give the business any degree of extended credit. So if the business cannot get credit either from its suppliers or from the bank then it may be unable to produce and so may be forced to close. Thus it is important that a business has some means of assessing its liquidity position and to do this it can use two ratios:

1. current ratio;
2. liquidity ratio (acid test).

Current ratio

The current ratio expresses the relationship between the current assets and the current liabilities of a business. Current liabilities are those liabilities which have to be paid within a short period of time. The funds available to meet them are contained within the current assets, first as cash in hand and at the bank (the most liquid of current assets), next as debtors (the next most liquid of current assets) on the grounds that debtors are the next in line to produce cash, and finally as stock (generally the least liquid of current assets). The latter will take longer to turn into cash because it has to be sold first, and then the money represented by the sale has to be collected from debtors. One possible exception to this is if the business is the type which has a large proportion of its sales made on a cash basis. If it is then obviously cash will be collected at the time the stock is sold.

Current ratios are always expressed in ratio format, that is as 'something' to 1, for example 5:1. The current ratio is expressed as:

Current Assets : Current Liabilities

The current liabilities should always be shown as the '1'. The ratio is calculated by dividing both sides of the equation by the current liabilities. So for example a business with current assets of £7,500 and current liabilities of £5,000 would have a current ratio of 7,500 : 5,000 or 1.5 : 1.

It is difficult to generalise about what is an acceptable current ratio but any business would be very wary of having a ratio which was less than 1 : 1 for this would mean that current liabilities exceeded current assets and it may not be able to pay its immediate debts. However it is almost as bad to have a current ratio which is too high, for this could mean that too much cash was being tied up in stocks, or that the debtors were taking too long to pay. Most businesses would therefore be satisfied with a current ratio of between 1.3 : 1 and 2.5 : 1.

The current ratio for Broadwood Distributors plc.

At 31 August 1992 BD plc. has current assets of £9.03m and current liabilities of £4.62m and so its current ratio is:

9.03 : 4.62 or 1.95 : 1

At 31 August 1991 (the previous year) the ratio was:

7.485: 3.78 or 1.98 : 1

So there has been very little change in the ratio between the two points in time, and the company looks to be reasonably solvent in that the current liabilities are covered by current assets 1.95 times.

Liquidity ratio

The liquidity ratio is expressed as liquid current assets (current assets excluding stock) to current liabilities, and as with the current ratio is expressed as 'something' to 1 with the current liabilities being expressed as the '1'. This ratio is often described as the quick assets ratio, or 'acid test' because it is a much more stringent test of a business's solvency, in that it leaves stock out of the equation on the grounds that it takes longer than any other current asset to convert into cash. In other words, it is concerned with how much ready money will be available when the creditors are queuing up at the door. This includes all available cash, short term investments such as government stock or shares which can be quickly cashed in, and debtors who can be pressed for payment. It is expressed as follows:

$$\text{Current Assets (less stock) : Current Liabilities}$$

or

$$\text{Debtors and Cash balances : Current Liabilities}$$

Some businesses can operate with a liquidity ratio of less than 1; in other words with current liabilities exceeding available liquid assets. This can happen if a business has a bank overdraft facility which is not at its limit and can be drawn on at short notice. It may also be possible to relieve a short term liquidity crisis by re-scheduling the debt and paying off short term loans with more long term credit.

In the case of BD plc. the current assets excluding stock are £4.85m (31/8/91 £3.865m), current liabilities are as used before in calculating the current ratio viz. £4.62m (31/8/91 £3.78m). The liquidity ratios are therefore:

At 31 August 1992	1.05 : 1
At 31 August 1991	1.02 : 1

In both cases the ratios indicate that the company is and was reasonably solvent in that its immediate liabilities are covered just about equally by quick assets.

When looking at liquidity ratios it is well to note that we are measuring the liquidity at a particular point in time (the date of the balance sheet from which the ratio is taken), but this gives us no idea of the time element involved in:

- converting stock and debtors into cash; and
- payments being made to the creditors of the company.

We can therefore use a further series of ratios which will give an indication of the time span involved in the cashflow. These are:

- stock turnover (cash in);
- debtors' turnover (cash in);
- creditors' turnover (cash out).

Stock turnover

This can be expressed in two ways which are inter-related:

1. the number of times the average stock is turned over in the trading period (usually one year);
2. the length of time it takes (in days) to turn over (or 'move') the average stock once.

To determine the stock turnover ratio we need to know the average stock figure, which can usually be determined by adding the opening stock to the closing stock and dividing the result by two; and also the cost of sales figure, which can be obtained from the Trading and Profit and Loss Account. The calculation for 1) above is:

$$\frac{\text{Cost of Sales}}{\text{Average Stock}} = \text{Number of times turned over}$$

and for (2) above is:

$$\frac{365}{\text{The answer} \quad 1)} = \text{Number of days to turn over average stock once}$$

An alternative way of calculating 2) above is:

$$\frac{\text{Average Stock}}{\text{Cost of Sales}} \qquad \times \qquad 365$$

For example if a business had had sales of £600,000, an opening stock of £40,000, purchases of £460,000, and a closing stock of £50,000 then the cost of sales would be £40,000 + £460,000 - £50,000 = £450,000. The stock turnover is therefore:

$$\frac{450,000}{45,000} \quad = \quad 10 \text{ times} \qquad \text{or} \qquad \frac{365}{10} \quad = \quad 36.5 \text{ days}$$

This means that the average stock is turned over (sold) 10 times in one year. This can then be expressed in days by dividing 365 by 10 to give 36.5 days. This means that in 36 or 37 days the money tied up in stocks will be released by the sale of that stock. It does not mean that there will be no stock left after 36 or 37 days, as any stock sold will be replaced by new purchases, which will form part of the next cycle. Neither does it mean that the actual cash represented by the stock will be available for the payment of creditors, because if the sales are made on credit terms, there will be a further delay before the cash is finally collected (see Debtors turnover).

As mentioned above an alternative way of calculating the time-span involved is to divide the average stock by the cost of sales figure and multiply the result by 365. This gives:

$$\frac{45,000}{450,000} \qquad \times \qquad 365 \quad = \quad 36.5 \text{ days}$$

An increase in the stock turnover figure will produce a reduction in the time-span. For example if stock was turned over 12 times in the following year this would give a time-span of 30.5 days (365 divided by 12). Clearly a decrease in the stock turnover figure would increase the time span.

An increase in the stock turnover from one year to the next would indicate either:

- increased sales with no corresponding increase in stockholding; or
- decreased stock holding with no corresponding decrease in sales.

For example if sales were increased to £640,000 with the same gross margin of 25% and the same average stock, the cost of sales would become £480,000. The stock turnover would now be:

$$\frac{480,000}{45,000} \qquad = \qquad 10.67 \text{ times}$$

If sales and gross profit remained constant at £600,000 and £150,000 respectively, but the average stock fell to £40,000, the stock turnover would increase to:

$$\frac{450,000}{40,000} \qquad = \qquad 11.25 \text{ times}$$

Stock turnover for Broadwood Distributors plc.

In the case of BD plc., the stock turnover can be calculated as follows:

$$\frac{£27.3m \, (\text{cost of sales})}{£3.9m \, (\text{Average stock})*} \qquad = \qquad 7 \text{ times} \qquad = \qquad 52 \text{ days}$$

$$*\frac{£3.62m \, (\text{opening stock}) + £4.18m \, (\text{closing stock})}{2}$$

The corresponding figures for the previous year were 7.5 times or 48/49 days. This means that in the current year there has been a slight decrease in the speed at which the average stock is turned over.

It should be made clear that the higher the stock turnover rate, the sooner profit is earned on the stock sold, and that therefore a business with a high stock turnover is able to operate on lower profit margins. In essence the profit is determined by the speed of turnover. Therefore businesses with a quick turnover such as petrol filling stations and fruit and vegetable businesses can still make acceptable profits with low profit margins. On the other hand a slower stock turnover rate means that higher margins must be earned when stock is finally sold, to compensate for the slower turnover. For example a jeweller's business, which must carry high stocks to attract customers, may have a low stock turnover rate but relies on higher profit margins.

You should also note that it is the cost price of stock which is used in the calculation of the stock turnover rate and not the price at which it is sold. This is because the selling price would include the profit margin and any other costs incurred in the sale whilst this ratio is concerned about how often the stock is replaced at cost price.

Debtors' turnover

This is very similar to the stock turnover in the method of its calculation in as much as it expresses the relationship between sales on credit and the debtors arising from those sales. As with the stock turnover figure it may be expressed either as the number of times the average debtors are turned over in a year, or as the number of days it will take to collect the average debt. Since the age of debts is important, it is preferable to express the debtors' turnover ratio in terms of days. The equation is therefore as follows:

$$\frac{\text{Average Debtors}}{\text{Credit Sales}} \quad \times \quad 365 \quad = \quad \text{Number of days}$$

Carrying on the example which we used for the stock turnover figures, if the debtors at the start of the year had been £90,000 and at the end of the year £110,000, the average for the year would be £100,000. If the whole of the sales of £600,000 had been on credit, the debtors' turnover ratio would be:

$$\frac{£100,000}{£600,000} \quad \times \quad 365 \quad = \quad 61 \text{ days}$$

This means that from the figures given it will take on average 61 days to collect the average debts once. However it must be stressed that this does not mean that nothing will be collected for 61 days, and then all outstanding debtors from 61 days ago suddenly pay up. What it does mean is that even though money comes in from debtors daily, it will be 61 days before all the debtors represented by a debtors figure will have finally cleared their debts. In the meanwhile, new debtors will continue to be created by the act of making further sales to them on credit terms.

When the stock turnover (36 days) is added to the debtors' turnover (61 days) we can see that on average it will take 97 days, or just over three months to convert stock into cash . However because of the profit element contained in sales, the cash when finally collected should be more than that which was originally paid out to purchase the stock.

The debtors turnover for BD plc. is as follows:

$$\frac{£4.35m}{£36.4m} \quad \times \quad 365 \quad = \quad 43.6 \text{ days}$$

In calculating the above ratio we have assumed that all sales made are on credit terms, and we have used the sum of opening and closing debtors divided by 2 in order to arrive at an average figure. We have also used gross debtors' figures before deducting the provision for doubtful debts (see note 4 to the balance sheet) as the basis of our calculation.

Now we can see that if we add the debtors collection period of 44 days to the stock turnover period of 52 days, we can say that it will be 96 days before the average cash tied up in stock (at 31/8/92 £4.18m) will be recovered, and that it will be 44 days before the current level of debtors will be converted back into liquid funds (cash). In other words, we have established a speed of cash flow in to the business, which we can compare with earlier years, and also with the speed of cash outflow.

In retail outlets such as supermarkets and department stores, etc. which mainly deal on a cash over the counter basis, the stock turnover rate will be more important than the debtors' turnover rate, because the credit sales will tend to be a very small proportion of the total sales. However even retail outlets can have substantial debtors, particularly if they accept credit cards such as Access or Barclaycard from customers, or as is the tendency nowadays, if they issue their own in house credit cards.

Although the debtors' turnover figure is a very useful ratio, it may be distorted by old or long standing debts being included as part of the debtors' figure, therefore an attempt should be made to analyse debts by age.

Analysis of debtors by age

The 'age' of a debt means the length of time that it has been outstanding. A business should prepare schedules at regular intervals which list and analyse outstanding debtors by age. Thus those debtors who have owed money to the business for the longest periods will be highlighted, and it is to those debtors that most attention should be paid. In other words, they are the ones to whom the strongest letters demanding payment are sent, and who may be referred to a business's solicitors so that legal action may be taken to seek payment. The schedules should also highlight those debtors who are particularly slow in paying, and the business may then decide that it will not trade with such customers in future without some improvement in their promptness of payment. Unfortunately it is often the larger companies who are most tardy in their payment of bills and for the small business these may be very important customers which it can ill afford to lose. Therefore it must bear the difficulties inherent in the slow payment of debts rather than offend a major customer.

There are organisations which are willing to help small businesses by factoring their debts for them. That is they (the factors) will buy the debts off a business for a commission, and will then collect the money from individual debtors, keeping it for themselves. The advantage to a small business of factoring debts is that the business is more or less guaranteed no bad debts, is guaranteed speedy and regular settlement of its debtors, does not have to spend valuable time in pressing slow payers for payment, and can therefore plan the future more effectively. It will however never receive the full amount due in respect of debtors, because of the factor's commission, but this is a small price to pay for the peace of mind brought about by not having to worry about cash flow.

Creditors' turnover ratio

In the examples above we have considered the length of time it takes a business to receive money from its debtors. However, it is important to recognise that there are two sides to the picture and it is more than likely that the business itself is taking time to pay its creditors. The length of time taken to pay creditors can be calculated in the same way as the debtors' turnover. The figures used in the calculation will be average creditors (the sum of the opening and of the closing creditors divided by 2) and credit purchases made during the year:

$$\frac{\text{Average Creditors}}{\text{Credit Purchases}} \quad \times \quad 365 \quad = \quad \text{Number of days}$$

For BD plc. the creditors' turnover rate is:

$$\frac{\text{£3.62m}}{\text{£27.86m}} \quad \times \quad 365 \quad = \quad 47.4 \text{ days}$$

At this point it is worth making a comparison between the stock and debtors' turnover figures and the creditors' turnover figure for BD plc. As we saw earlier the stock turnover for the business was 52 days. In other words, the average item of stock stays on BD plc.'s shelves for 52 days. Yet as we have seen, the creditors turnover ratio for 1988/89 is only 48 days. This means that the creditors are in effect being paid before the stock is sold to customers. This may place a strain on the company's cashflow as the outflow to creditors is quicker than the inflow from customers, particularly as the debtors' turnover rate is a further 44 days. Effectively what is happening is that creditors are being paid twice as quickly as cash is being received from sales (48 days as opposed to 96 days), and this could lead to liquidity problems arising in future. However it should be recognised that each sale should earn a profit for the company above the cost of the purchase, which means that when cash is finally collected, it will be more than was expended. This, coupled with the fact that cash is continually being collected from earlier sales, will keep the company buoyant for some time. Nevertheless steps should be taken to narrow the gap between the two turnover rates, perhaps by decreasing the stock levels or by chasing up debtors to get them to pay more promptly. What should be avoided is the necessity to increase the delay in settling creditors, as this could only result in the company gaining a reputation as a poor credit risk.

Cash Control

The final element of working capital is cash, or an overdraft facility which would enable a business to pay other creditors. For most businesses there is a limit either to the cash it has available or to the overdraft it is able to secure from a bank. With this in mind, it must therefore control its debtors, creditors and stock levels accordingly.

Circulation of working capital

As we have noted earlier, the current and liquidity ratios are good indicators of working capital stability with any positive ratio indicating the presence of some working capital. However, financial managers will also be concerned to examine how efficiently the working capital is being used. This is done by measuring the speed at which the working capital is circulated. The ratio for this is:

$$\frac{\text{Sales}}{\text{Average Working Capital in one year}} \quad = \quad \text{Number of times turned over}$$

Broadwood Distributors plc., average net current assets (or working capital) for 1991/992 was £4.0575m (£4.41m + £3.705m divided by 2) and sales for the year were £36.4m. Thus its circulation of working capital was:

$$\frac{£36.4m}{£4.0575m} \quad = \quad 8.97 \text{ times}$$

This shows that each £1 of working capital has generated sales of approximately £9.

Investment ratios

Having looked at the main accounting ratios used to measure the performance and the position of a business, it will now be of benefit to look at some ratios which are used by those investors who have no particular interest in running the business, but who spread their money around and look for the best returns they can get. This type of investor is looking for a good return in terms of income from, and also capital appreciation of, the investment.

Some of the ratios which may help to make the correct decisions about how and where to invest money are:

- earnings per share;
- earnings yield;
- price/earnings ratio;
- dividend per share and dividend yield;
- dividend cover.

Earnings per share

When the profit of a limited company is finally determined in respect of a particular financial year, there are certain claims (appropriations) made on that profit. The first of these is by the Inland Revenue in respect of Corporation Tax. There may also be preference shareholders who are entitled to a dividend at a pre-determined fixed rate. After tax and preference dividends are provided for, the remainder of the profit is available for the ordinary or 'equity' shareholders. This amount is divided by the number of ordinary shares issued to give the earnings per share ratio.

$$\frac{\text{Net profit after tax and preference dividends}}{\text{Number of ordinary shares}} = \text{Earnings per share (EPS)}$$

This figure shows an investor (shareholder) exactly how much the company has earned for him after all other claims have been met. Care must be taken when calculating this ratio since it is the number of shares which have been issued which is used. A company with an issued capital of £50,000 may have 50,000 shares of £1 each, 100,000 shares of 50p each or 500,000 shares of 10p each.

Note that the key phrase is 'earned for him', which means that during the year the company has accumulated a sum of money for its shareholders from its trading activities. It does not mean that this amount is actually paid to shareholders, because the company may wish to retain some profit for expansion or for some other purpose. The amount actually paid to the shareholders is described as the 'dividend' which is usually expressed as a percentage of the issued share capital; so a dividend of £8,000 on an issued share capital of £80,000 would be expressed as a dividend of 10%, or 10p per £1 share or 5p per 50p share.

The EPS for BD plc. for the year ended 31 August 1992 would therefore be as follows:

$$\frac{\text{£0.905m}}{5,000,000} = 18.1\text{p per share}$$

This can be compared with the corresponding figure for the previous year which was 9p per share (£360,000 divided by 4,000,000). By all accounts this represents a considerable improvement in performance especially as the ordinary share capital has been increased by 1,000,000 shares during the year.

Earnings yield

Rarely will the nominal value of a share be the same as the market value. The latter is the price at which the share will change hands on the market, and is determined by a number of factors such as the value of a company's net assets as represented by ordinary share capital plus reserves, its performance in terms of profitability, and other market forces. For instance if a company has an issued ordinary share capital of £50,000 and reserves of £50,000 it's net worth can be expressed as £100,000. If the nominal value of its ordinary shares is £1, each share could be worth £2 on the market, determined by the balance sheet value of the company.

A more accurate picture of the relationship between earnings and investment is obtained by expressing the earnings per share as a percentage of the market value of the share. This is calculated by using the following formula:

$$\frac{\text{Earnings per share}}{\text{Market value of share}} \times 100 = \text{Percentage yield}$$

For example if a company has an issued share capital of £100,000 in ordinary shares of 50p, and reserves of £50,000, it has a balance sheet value of £150,000 which (using the above criteria) gives a market value of 75p per share. If it earned an after tax profit of £30,000, the earnings per share would be:

$$\frac{£30,000}{200,000} = \text{15p per share}$$

The earnings yield would be:

$$\frac{15p}{75p} \times 100 = 20\%$$

This means that if you were thinking of investing in that particular company you would receive a return in terms of earnings (not dividends) of 20% on the cost of your investment (the amount you would have had to pay for it on the market). To determine whether this is a good or a bad investment, you would have to compare it with the earnings yield figures from other companies or the yields from this company in earlier years.

For BD plc. in order to work out the earnings yield we will have to assume a market price for the ordinary shares. Based on the level of reserves this could be £1.10 per share, so this is the market price which we will work on. The earnings yield now becomes:

$$\frac{18.1p}{110p} \times 100 = 16.45\%$$

Price/earnings ratio

This is the relationship between the market price of the share and its earnings, and is in fact the earnings yield ratio inverted, the formula being:

$$\frac{\text{Market value of the share}}{\text{Earnings per share}} = \text{Price/Earnings Ratio}$$

In the example used above the P/E ratio will be calculated as follows:

$$\frac{75p}{15p} = \text{5 times}$$

This means that on current figures it would take 5 years to recover in earnings the price that would have to be paid for the share. Obviously there is a relationship between the P/E ratio and the earnings yield. In effect the higher the P/E ratio, the lower the yield and therefore the less favourable the prospects for an investor.

Generally speaking the lower the P/E ratio the better it is to invest in that particular share. It may mean however that the share is undervalued by the market and since other factors, not necessarily highlighted by the above ratios, may influence the share's valuation, further enquiries should be made before making a decision to invest.

Other examples of the relationship between the P/E ratio and the Earnings yield are:

> P/E Ratio 10: Earnings Yield 10%
>
> P/E Ratio 8 : Earnings Yield 12.5%
>
> P/E Ratio 20 : Earnings Yield 5%

You will notice that as a check the P/E ratio multiplied by the earnings yield always equals 100.

The P/E ratio for BD plc. is 6.08 (110p divided by 18.1p).

Dividend per share and dividend yield

For most investors the dividend per share and subsequently the dividend yield are probably more important ratios than the earnings ones already discussed. This is because these particular ratios measure exactly what the shareholder receives in his pocket from the investment. Dividend per share is calculated by dividing the total ordinary share dividend paid and proposed for the year by the number of ordinary shares issued, and expressing the result as Xp per share. Alternatively the dividend may be expressed as a percentage of the issued ordinary share capital by using the formula:

$$\frac{\text{Dividends paid and proposed}}{\text{Ordinary share capital}} \quad \times \quad 100$$

Leading on from this as with the earnings ratios above, it is easy to calculate the dividend yield, which represents the actual return that an investor would receive in his pocket if he purchased the shares at the current market price. As with the earnings ratios, the calculation of dividend yield is: Dividend per share divided by the market price of the share, multiplied by 100, and expressed as a percentage.

For BD plc. the dividend per share is:

$$\frac{\text{£0.45m (Total ordinary dividend for the year)}}{\text{5,000,000 (Number of ordinary shares issued)}} = \quad 9p$$

This represents a dividend rate of 18% since the ordinary shares have a value of 50p each.

Using the same assumed market value for the share as previously (£1.10) the dividend yield for BD plc. is:

$$\frac{9p}{110p} \quad \times \quad 100 \quad = \quad 8.18\%$$

The above figures mean that for every share held by an investor in BD plc. he will receive 9p (or 18% of the nominal value of the share) in dividend, which represents a yield of 8.18% on the current market price of the share.

Dividend cover

Another important aspect of investment is capital growth, and anyone who is looking to invest in a company will wish to see how much of the company's profits after tax and preference dividend has been provided for, is retained by the company for expansion and growth. This can be done by calculating a dividend cover, which is effectively the number of times the dividend is covered by the profit available out of which the dividend is to be paid. For example if a company with an issued ordinary share capital of £500,000, earns a profit after tax of £100,000 out of which a dividend of 10% (£50,000) is paid, the dividend cover is 2 (£100,000 divided by £50,000). In other words the company is keeping half of the available profit for expansion and distributing half of it to the shareholders as dividend. If the dividend had been say 5% (£25,000) the cover would have been 4 (£100,000 divided by £25,000).

Dividend cover shows the relationship between earnings per share and dividend per share, which is perhaps best illustrated by referring to BD plc. In that company, the net profit after tax was £960,000 out of which a preference share dividend of £55,000 was paid, leaving £905,000 available for ordinary shareholders. Since they received a dividend of £450,000 the cover can be calculated as:

$$\frac{£905,000}{£450,000} \qquad = \qquad 2.01 \text{ times}$$

The earnings per share has already been established as 18.1p, and the dividend per share as 9p. Dividing EPS (18.1) by DPS (9) we get 2.01. Alternatively the dividend per share multiplied by the cover equals EPS. $9 \times 2.01 = 18.1$.

The same results can be obtained by using the yields as can be seen by the example of BD plc. which has an earnings yield of 16.45 % and a dividend yield of 8.18 %.

$$\frac{16.45}{8.18} \qquad = \qquad 2.01 \text{ times}$$

In the previous year the dividend cover was not nearly as good as the most recent year, being 360 divided by 280, which was 1.29 times.

Generally speaking the higher the dividend cover the better the retention (growth) policy, but, unless profits are very high, it will probably mean a smaller dividend per share with a correspondingly smaller yield. An investor looking for growth would probably be quite happy with that situation, but one looking for good short-term returns would not be.

Capital Gearing

No chapter on interpretation of Accounts would be complete without discussing capital gearing. We have already seen in the section on ROCE that capital can be raised from different sources. These are loans (debentures), preference shares, and ordinary shares plus reserves (equity). The first two carry fixed rates of interest and dividend, whilst the latter receive what is left, so if profits are not very high they will receive very little, but if on the other hand profits are quite high they stand to gain quite substantially. For this reason the ordinary share capital is classed as the risk taking capital.

Gearing shows the relationship between equity capital and fixed interest/dividend bearing capital and can be expressed as:

$$\frac{\text{Ordinary share capital} + \text{reserves}}{\text{Loan Capital} + \text{preference share captal}}$$

expressed in ratio format similar to the liquidity ratios discussed earlier,
or:

$$\frac{\text{Loan capital} + \text{preference share capital}}{\text{Total capital (Loan} + \text{preference} + \text{equity)}} \qquad \times \qquad 100$$

expressed as a percentage that the fixed interest/dividend bearing capital relates to the total capital.

A company is said to be highly geared when the fixed interest/dividend bearing capital is high in relation to the equity capital. So in the first equation shown above, if the ratio is low, it indicates a higher geared company than one with a higher ratio (1:2 is high geared; 3:1 is low geared). In the second equation the higher the percentage the higher the gearing. For the sake of uniformity and to avoid too much confusion some people prefer to express the first equation the other way around that is with the loan capital etc. as the numerator and the equity as the denominator, in which case the higher the ratio the higher the gearing. When looking at these ratios you should adopt a consistent approach, so as not to come to the wrong conclusions. We will use the percentage of total capital method to illustrate the effects of gearing on equity shareholders.

Suppose we have the following capital structures for three separate but similar companies:

	COMPANY A	COMPANY B	COMPANY C
	£'000	£'000	£'000
15 % Debentures	1,000	500	200
10 % Preference Shares	1,000	500	200
Ordinary shares	500	1,000	1,500
Reserves	500	1,000	1,100
Total Capital	3,000	3,000	3,000
Gearing (Percentage)	66.67	33.33	13.33
	High		Low

Suppose each of the three companies make a net profit of £300,000 after tax but before interest and dividends are paid. The distribution (share-out) of that profit would be as follows:

Debenture interest	150	75	30
Preference dividend	100	50	20
Balance remaining for ordinary shareholders (Equity)	50	175	250
Return to equity shareholders expressed as a percentage of capital invested	5%	8.75%	9.6%

Note that the return to equity shareholders is fairly small in all three companies, but that the lower the gearing, the better returns are made on investment in risk capital.

Using exactly the same capital structures as above, and with a net profit of £400,000 after tax, and before interest and dividends are paid since the debenture holders and preference shareholders will still want their fixed interest and dividend as above, the amount available for ordinary shareholders will be as follows:

In £000's	150	275	350
Return on equity	15%	13.75%	13.46 %

If the profits were £500,000 the respective figures would now be as follows:

Profit available £000's	250	375	450
Return on equity	25%	18.75%	17.3%

From the above examples, we can conclude that as profits get higher, in a highly geared company the returns to ordinary shareholders get progressively better, and at a faster rate than they do in a lower geared company. This means that a highly geared company offers more risk to the ordinary shareholders than a low geared one, simply because there is a higher prior claim on profits in the form of fixed interest and dividend bearing capital, which must be met before consideration can be given to the ordinary shareholders. Put another way, this means 'the greater the fluctuation in profits from one year to another, the greater the fluctuation in returns to ordinary shareholders in a highly geared company'. In lower geared companies the returns to ordinary shareholders are steadier, even in times of fluctuating profits. To sum up then, the rewards for ordinary shareholders can be very good in a highly geared company but they must be prepared to take small returns when profits are low.

In Broadwood Distributors plc. the gearing percentage at 31 August 1992 is 21 % (Debentures £1m; Preference shares £0.5m; Total capital £7.13m). This is quite low.

Finally it must be said that the use of accounting ratios must be tempered with common sense. It is all too easy to come to incorrect conclusions using accounting information, without balancing it against other business information which may be available. Accounting ratios are very useful tools for the measurement and comparison of profitability, solvency and investment potential of a business, but care must be taken not to jump to the wrong conclusions without looking at other sources of information.

Activity

1. *Given below and on the next page are the summarised profit and loss accounts for the year ended 30 June 1994 together with balance sheets as at that date of two companies, each of which run similar businesses.*

    a. *Identify and explain relevant ratios which will help you to assess and compare the performance of each company in terms of:*

       (i)   *profitability*

       (ii)   *solvency*

       (iii) *investment potential (or return on investment).*

    b. *Calculate, for each company, the ratios which you have identified in a) above.*

    c. *Write a report comparing the performance of the two companies, using the ratios calculated in b) above.*

Profit and Loss Accounts for the Year ended 30 June 1994

	Hutton plc		Dexter plc	
	£'000	£'000	£'000	£'000
Sales	4,500		7 500	
Less: Cost of Sales:				
Stock as at 1 July 1993	390		660	
Purchases	3,270		5,880	
	3,660		6,540	
Less: Stock as at 30 June 1994	510		540	
		3,150		6,000
Gross profit for the year		1,350		1,500
Other overhead expenditure		1,080		1,050
Net profit for the year before Tax		270		450
Less: Appropriations				
Provision for corporation tax	70		111	
Preference dividend paid	15		30	
Proposed dividend on ordinary shares	75		225	
		160		366
Retained Profit for the year		110		84

Balance Sheets as at 30 June 1994

	Hutton plc £'000	Hutton plc £'000	Dexter plc £'000	Dexter plc £'000
Fixed Assets	945		2,550	
Current Assets:				
Stock	510		540	
Debtors (1993 in brackets) (350)	600	(420)	732	
Bank Balance	-		57	
	1,110		1,329	
Creditors: Amounts falling due within one year	555	555	879	450
		£1,500		£3,000
Share capital and reserves:				
Ordinary shares of £1 each, fully paid		750		1,800
10 % preference shares of £1 each, fully paid		150		300
Retained profits		600		900
		£ 1,500		£3,000

Creditors: Amounts falling due within one year are made up as follows:

	Hutton plc £'000	Hutton plc £'000	Dexter plc £'000	Dexter plc £'000
Trade creditors (1993 in brackets)	(176)	390	(280)	558
Corporation tax due		75		96
Proposed dividend		75		225
Bank overdraft		15		-

The market values of the ordinary shares as at 30 June 1994 were Hutton plc. £1.75 and Dexter plc were £1.40

Activity

You have received the following information in respect of two separate companies, both of which are in the same line of business:

Capital structure as at 31 March 1992

	Chilton PLC. £'000	Dalton PLC. £'000
Ordinary shares of £1 each	2,500	-
Ordinary shares of 50 pence each	-	1,000
10 % Preference shares of £1 each	500	2,000
Revenue reserves	3,500	1,500
15 % Debenture stock	1,000	3,000
	7,500	7,500

NOTE: *There have been no issues or redemptions of shares or debentures since that date.*

Information relating to the year ended 31 March 1993:

	£'000	£'000
Net profit for the year before interest or dividends	800	800
Ordinary share dividend proposed	6p per share	7.5p per share

Information relating to the year ended 31 March 1994:

Both companies have experienced an upturn in activities during the year ended 31 March 1994. The draft final accounts of each of the companies show profits of 2,000,000 before interest and dividends.

The management of each company has decided that 50 per cent of the profit available for the ordinary shareholders for the year ended 31 March 1994 will be provided for them as dividend, the remaining 50 per cent being added to the revenue reserves.

Tasks:

1.   Calculate the gearing ratio as at 31 March 1992 for each of the companies, clearly indicating which company has the higher gearing.

2.   Prepare statements in tabular form showing how the profits for each of the years ended 31 March 1993 and 31 March 1994 are divided between the respective providers of capital of each company.

3.   a) Calculate the percentage return on **Equity Capital** for each of the two years ended 31 March 1993 and 31 March 1994 for each company.

     b) Explain the reasons for the fluctuations in the returns calculated in 3a) above between each year and between each company.

4.   Calculate the rate of ordinary dividend per share for the year ended 31 March 1994 for each company.

5.   Calculate the gearing ratio as at 31 March 1994 for each of the companies, and explain why these may have changed since 31 March 1992.

Ignore taxation.

Assignment *The Aspen Takeover*

Aspen Ale Plc is a large public company which was originally founded as a brewery but which is now engaged in a wide range of activities. At a recent board meeting it was resolved to further diversify into food retailing. In the board's view the safest and most prudent way to do this would be to acquire an existing business already operating in this field. Two relatively small companies have been identified, Foodline Ltd. and Handy Stores Ltd. as possible candidates for takeover. Both are suitable for acquisition by Aspen Ale and the final decision as to which of the companies to takeover rests on the issue of their respective financial positions. The final accounts of Foodline and Handy Stores are given below:

Balance Sheet as 31st July 1992

	Foodline Ltd.		Handy Stores Ltd.	
Fixed Assets	£'000	£'000	£'000	£'000
		345		270
Current Assets				
Stock	160		135	
Debtors	260		219	
Balance at Bank	45		–	
	465		354	
Creditors: Amounts due within One Year	180		306	
Current Assets less Current Liabilities		285		48
Total Assets less Current Liabilities		630		318
Creditors: Amounts due after more than one year (10% Debentures)		–		90
		630		228
Share Capital and Reserves				
Issued Share Capital*		300		150
Reserves		330		78
		630		228
Market Value of an Ordinary Share at the Balance Sheet Date		£1.80		40p

*The Shares issued by Foodline Ltd. are £1 shares and those issued by Handy Stores Ltd. are 25p shares.

Profit and Loss Accounts
for the Year Ending 31st July 1992

	Foodline Ltd.		Handy Stores Ltd.	
	£'000	£'000	£'000	£'000
Sales		1,080		1,290
Less: Cost of Sales				
Opening Stock	111		123	
Purchases	742		942	
	853		1065	
Less: Closing Stock	159		135	
	694		930	
Other Cost of Sales	116	810	102	1,032
Gross Profit		270		258
Selling and Distribution Costs	105		86	
Administration Expenses	90		103	
Interest on Debentures	–	195	9	198
Net Profit for the Year before Tax		75		60
Less Corporation Tax Provided		30		22
Net Profit for the Year after Tax		45		38
Less Dividend Proposed		15		18
Retained Profit for the Year		30		20

Task

1. You are employed as an assistant to the financial manager of Aspen Ale. You are required to advise on the possible takeover of Foodline Ltd. or Handy Stores Ltd. For this purpose produce a report in which you:

(a) use suitable accounting ratios to draw a comparison between the two companies in relation to their profitability, solvency and investment potential;

(b) make recommendations on the basis of your findings.

Development tasks

2. Undertake a role play exercise in which you present the financial report to the senior management of Aspen Ale plc.

3. Obtain the annual reports of a number of major public limited companies. Compare their performance using appropriate accounting ratios.

Unit 7

Financial
Resources

This unit has been written to cover the following specifications of the General National Vocational Qualification Business Level 3

Unit 7   Financial Resources Level 3

Element 7.1:   Identify sources of finance for a business plan

Performance criteria:

1   asset and working capital requirements for a given business plan are identified
2   financing requirements for asset and working capital are identified
3   finance methods appropriate to the requirements are identified
4   sources of finance appropriate to the finance methods are identified

Element 7.2:   Produce and explain a projected cash flow for a single product business

Performance criteria:

1   the purpose of a cash flow to a business seeking finance are explained
2   cash in-flow and cash out-flow headings are identified and explained
3   data is collected for each heading to support informed forecasts
4   feasible forecasts of cash in-flow and cash out-flow for twelve month periods are produced
5   monthly and cumulative net balances for twelve month periods are produced
6   the significance of timing of in-flow and out-flow forecasts is explained
7   the consequences of incorrect forecasting are explained

Element 7.3:   Calculate the cost of goods and service

Performance criteria:

1   direct and indirect costs of businesses are explained
2   a unit of the goods or service is correctly identified
3   number of units of the goods produced or service provided in a time period is calculated
4   direct costs of the goods or service for a time period are calculated
5   indirect costs of the organisation for a time period are calculated
6   allocation of indirect cost to unit production cost over the time period is calculated
7   total cost of a unit of the goods or service is calculated

Element 7.4:   Produce and explain profit and loss statements and balance sheets

Performance criteria:

1   purposes of profit and loss statements and balance sheets are explained
2   trading periods are correctly identified and explained
3   single column trial balance is extracted from given accounting records and correctly totalled to zero
4   each account on the trial balance is correctly identified as relating to trading profit and loss or balance sheet items
5   profit and loss account and balance sheet are correctly extended and the profit or loss for the period is entered in each column as the number required to produce a zero total
6   profit and loss balance sheets are restated in conventional form and explained

GNVQ3 Business - Unit Number U1016180

Element 7.1 Sources of Finance

In this Unit we will examine the financial resources of a business. In particular we will consider how a business can raise the finance that it requires and how it controls its finance. We shall also look at the financial statements of the business and examine how they are prepared and what they show about the business. We will begin by examining the sources of business finance.

The Need for Finance

Anticipating when the business will need finance, how much it will need and where is the most cost effective and beneficial source to get it from is a vital aspect of the foundation of any successful business.

Any business starting up will need finance for two main purposes:

- to buy fixed *assets* such as land, premises, machinery and vehicles;
- to provide *working capital*, for the day-to-day running of the business, such as the payment of wages and suppliers and the financing of any stock it must hold.

Once a business has been operating for a period of time, it will hope to grow; more finance is usually needed for this purpose to allow it to extend its operations, pay for marketing, hire more specialist staff and buy better equipment.

In broad terms, finance (or *capital*, as it is more properly called) can come from only two sources:

- from lenders (known as *borrowing* or *debt*). This will normally come from financial institutions such as banks, building societies or finance houses.
- from investors (known as *equity*). The investors in the business may be the owners themselves or the business may seek to raise equity finance from shareholders. who although outside the business buy a part (a *share*) of the business

In practice, a business will usually seek to strike a balance between the funds which it acquires from each of the two sources. Each source will have a cost and a risk factor attached to it;

- lenders will want *interest* on their loans and will require some degree of *security* to protect their loan should the business be unable to repay it;
- shareholders will want a *dividend* on their shares(in effect a share of the profit the business has made). In addition as part owners of the business they will have some degree of *control* over the way the business is run.

Therefore when seeking to raise finance for a business you must weigh up the pros and cons of each source of finance. Borrowing can be expensive and the lender could withdraw the loan if they felt the business was not prospering. On the other hand selling part of the business to shareholders means giving up not only part of the profit but also part of the control. The ability of the business to assess these costs and risks can make the difference between bankruptcy, survival and growth.

Before we examine the different sources of finance available to a business let us take an overview of the business' cash inflows and outflows. The diagram on the next page should help to explain this.

At the centre is the business itself and its need for cash. Cash comes into the business in three ways:

- as share capital (from the original owners and any new shareholders);
- as loans (from financial institutions,which can be short, medium or long term);
- as revenue from the sale of its goods and services (in other words as payments from debtors).

Cash then is used by the business as follows:
- to pay the wages of its employees;
- to buy the raw materials it needs;
- to pay other expenses such as rent, rates, heating, lighting, etc.;
- to pay interest on any loans it has borrowed;
- to buy fixed assets such as property or plant and machinery;
- to pay corporation tax on profits and value added tax on the sale of its goods and services
- as dividends as a share of the profit to the shareholders.

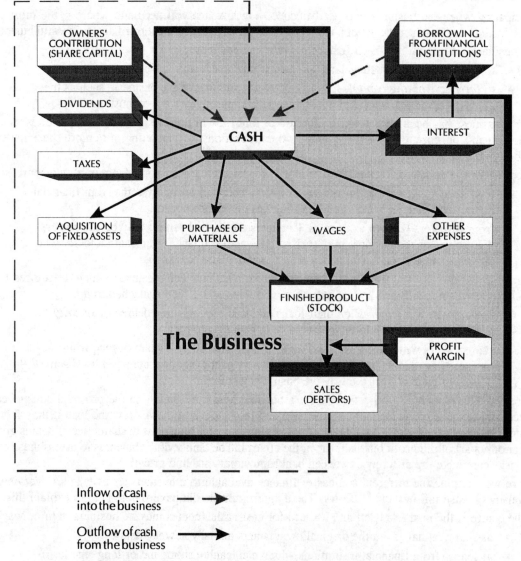

A business organisation's inflow and outflow of cash

Debt Finance

Borrowing as a means of raising finance

Any new business will find that it is difficult to raise finance from outside sources and anyone hoping to establish a new business may be forced to provide their own capital. A person starting in business as a sole trader, therefore, will normally provide at least part of the *start-up finance* and, similarly, a partnership will rely heavily on the partners to make a contribution to the initial capital required. However, many businesses will also need to borrow money from an outside source and this will depend upon a number of economic factors. Any prudent banker making a loan will want an acceptable *rate of return* (in the form of interest charged), some guarantee of *security* on the loan (also called collateral) and a reasonable prospect of financial success for the business. Therefore, anyone who seeks to borrow money from a bank should approach the matter in a business-like manner. If you want a loan to run a business, the first step is to approach the bank manager in the way that a business person would. This involves the preparation of a *business plan*.

Preparing a case for a business loan

When a business seeks finance from a bank, the bank manager will want to be convinced that the business is sound and there is a high probability that the loan will be repaid. If the business has been in operation for some time, then the bank will wish to see sets of accounts for previous years. These will need to have been prepared by an accountant, who will verify their accuracy. If the business is just beginning, and requires a start-up loan from the bank, there will be no accounts of previous years' trading. Thus, in order to allow the bank to judge the potential of a new business and the safety of its loan, the borrower needs to produce the following:

1. a business plan; and
2. a cashflow forecast and a projected profit and loss account.

A business plan

A *business plan* is what it appears to be, a plan of operation for a business in the short – and/or medium – term. If the business idea is viable and the plan is well prepared, it will help the case for the loan by impressing the bank that the business will be run by competent people. However, if the idea is not viable, then no amount of good presentation will help. A business plan should include some brief background introduction to the business, setting out the product or service it is intended to supply and an indication of the scale of operation. The plan should specify those who will be directly involved in running the business, either the partners or the directors, and indicate the relevant experience that they have. Clearly, if the person starting the business has a number of years of useful experience in that particular trade or industry, it is likely that he or she will be more sure of what they are doing than someone who is completely new to the business. This does not mean that a total lack of experience will be a complete bar to a business start-up loan, but it does mean that a borrower in such a situation will have to prove that some extensive groundwork on the business project has been done.

The next part of the plan should discuss the product or service to be supplied and evaluate the need for it in the area in which the business will operate. This means that existing competition will have to be assessed and a reasonable estimate made of market potential. Other problems to be considered include the availability of skilled labour, supplies of raw materials and suitable premises. The plan should indicate the proposed level of output over the coming period and the price which it should be possible to charge for the product or service. If the borrower has some experience of the problems involved in running a business, this will help to convince the bank of the potential success of the business idea. A good business plan will also weigh up the strengths and weaknesses of the proposal. You should always be honest with the bank manager: if the strengths and weaknesses have already been considered and the business idea is still considered to be viable, despite the possible drawbacks, then a bank manager should also be convinced. We shall discuss business plans and how they should be prepared in more detail in Unit 8, *Business Planning*.

A cashflow forecast and a projected profit and loss account

The *cashflow forecast* is an attempt to show the anticipated inflow and outflow of money from the business in the coming year. *Inflow* is the revenue from sales of the product or service. Unless the proposed business is in retailing, it is often common for a supplier to have to wait some considerable time for eventual payment after the goods have been delivered. Most business customers expect to be given some element of trade credit; others are simply slow payers. This is fine if it is you who owes the money, but it is potentially disastrous when it is your business that is waiting to be paid.

If you consider the costs of operation that make up the outflows, the business will have to pay wages and other bills on a much more prompt and regular basis than some other payments. It may be fine to leave the bill for the supply of raw materials to be paid until the end of the month, but try explaining to your workforce that they are not getting their wages for the next six weeks! Therefore, at different times throughout the trading year, the business will find that it has varying levels of cash shortage at those times when it must pay bills but is waiting to be paid itself. These circumstances need to be anticipated so that agreement can be made with the bank to provide sufficient funds at the times when they will be needed. In essence, this is all that a cashflow forecast is – a monthly statement of cash spent and cash received leaving a balance which may be in surplus, or in debit, which will need financing by the bank. It should be borne in mind that severe cashflow problems that are not resolved by appropriate borrowing can lead to a business collapsing. Creditors may soon lose patience with the business debtor who regularly pleads that the debt will be paid as soon as its outstanding accounts are settled. One of the most familiar excuses when a creditor rings asking for payment is that "the cheque is in the post" - a delaying tactic which rarely works. At worst if they are not paid quickly enough unsympathetic creditors may respond by bringing bankruptcy proceedings against the business.

Thus the cashflow forecast is not simply a means of impressing a bank manager sufficiently to be granted the loan. It is, in fact, a very useful (and often vital) management tool and should be compared carefully with what actually happens once the business is operating. If the actual cash balances regularly appear lower than those forecast, then it is time to consult the bank manager again to ensure that additional finance can be arranged. In the next element in this Unit, *Producing a cash flow*, we will go through the necessary steps in producing a cash flow.

The second financial statement required is a *projected profit and loss account*. This will simply show the total projected sales from the business in the coming year and place against it a total for the projected costs of operation. This will allow a projected net profit to be estimated by subtracting costs from revenue. We will consider the structure and interpretation of the profit and loss account in more detail in Element 7.4, *Financial Statements*.

Activity

Write or call into your local branch of one of the major high street banks such as Barclays or National Westminster. Explain that as part of your course you have to look at sources of business finance. Ask if they have any leaflets or booklet on setting up a small business. If they can't help try writing to their head office.

Short-term borrowing

Borrowing over fewer than three years is considered to be *short-term finance*. Mostly, such borrowing is needed to maintain a satisfactory cashflow and act as a buffer between paying suppliers and employees and receiving money from debtors. Occasionally, short-term finance is used to buy an asset which has a relatively short life, a car or van, for example.

Bank overdraft

This is generally the most common and cheapest way of raising short-term finance from outside the business. An overdraft occurs when a business has a negative sum in its current account with the bank. The bank will agree an overdraft limit and the business should avoid exceeding this. Many businesses will operate permanent overdraft facilities which will give them some flexibility in their cashflow management.

The advantage of an overdraft, or *overdraft facility* as it is often called, is that a business will only be required to pay interest owed on a daily basis on the amount. The bank manager may have granted an overdraft facility of £5,000, but on a particular day a business is only £2,000 overdrawn. Interest is due only on the £2,000 and not on the £5,000, which is the *potential* loan. The rate of interest you are asked to pay on your overdraft depends on three factors:

- *the current base rate of the bank*. This is the basic rate of interest rate the bank will charge and is determined by government policy ;
- your *credit standing* with your bank; and
- the amount of *security* you can offer.

Together these factors influence whether or not you will get the overdraft and the rate of interest you will be asked to pay. For instance if the bank's base rate is 10% then the bank may ask 2% more for all overdrafts plus an extra percentage according to the status of the borrower and the amount of security which the borrower is able to offer. Therefore a person regarded as being a poor credit risk with no security may be asked to pay 10% base rate plus 2% overdraft rate plus another 5% because of their credit standing and lack of security, 17% in all. While someone who is regarded as a good risk and is able to offer sufficient security will get an overdraft at say 13% – base rate plus 3%

Getting an overdraft is not always easy. The bank may ask questions about what the loan is for and may advise the borrower on how the business should be operated. The bank will set a time limit on the length of the overdraft and will normally keep to this unless an extension is negotiated. However, most banks are usually sympathetic to a customer who they know and will normally provide reasonable overdraft facilities.

Perhaps at this point we should offer a word of warning. It is very unwise to ask the bank for an overdraft and mislead them about its purpose. An overdraft is not a means of living on credit for life. As we have already noted the overdraft will have a fixed time limit and the bank will wish to see it repaid promptly. If you abuse your overdraft facilities the bank will not look kindly on any future requests and a bad credit rating can be difficult to live down. If the borrower does not have sufficient security to cover the overdraft the bank may require a guarantor to agree to cover the debt should the actual borrower default on repayment. This person may be a parent or a friend who has assets sufficient to cover the debt. But remember that if you can cannot repay the overdraft when it is due the guarantor will be forced to do so. Many young people have found their relationship with friends or family deteriorate when the latter have acted as guarantors and been forced to pay up in the end.

A business should avoid using an overdraft to finance capital spending, such as the purchase of new plant or machinery. This should be financed through other forms of debt. In fact, it is wisest to restrict the use of an overdraft to solving a business's cashflow problems in circumstances where money is owed to the business, but has not yet been received by it, though its debts now have to be paid.

Short-term loan

This is more specific than an overdraft. It is normally negotiated for a agreed sum in order to purchase a particular asset, such as a car, van or machinery . The loan is over a fixed period of time, for instance 1 - 3 years and monthly repayments will be agreed and interest charged on the full sum borrowed.

Short term loans have the advantage of imposing a discipline on the borrower to repay regularly and the loan may be spread over a number of years, but as we have said they are normally more expensive than overdrafts They are, however, a better way of borrowing than hire purchase to make large purchases, if your credit rating is good, for the interest will be considerably less.

As with all borrowing on a relatively large scale, it is unwise to take on a large loans if you will be unable to meet the commitments. Thus banks will want details of the present and future income and expenditure of the business and to reassure themselves that the loan is not going to over-stretch the finances of the business. In the same way as with an overdraft, you will have a much better chance of being given a business loan if you have a reasonably good banking history.

Activity

Go into your local branch of any of the major banks. On the wall there will be a board showing the current interest rates the bank offers to depositors and charge to lenders. Compare the different rates and try to identify the factors which determine what rate you would be paid as a depositor and what you would be charged as a lender.

Now compare the rates that the bank is offering with those charged by stores and credit companies.

Financing equipment

There are a number of ways that a business can pay for its equipment. These are

- buying the equipment outright;
- buying on hire purchase;
- leasing equipment;
- contract hire.

Buying the equipment outright

A business can buy equipment outright. This will mean that the equipment becomes an asset of the business immediately and will be entered on the company's balance sheet. Of course, this can be expensive and use up cash which could be put to other purposes such as working capital. Alternatively, the business could borrow to buy the equipment either through a business loan or an overdraft from a bank as we have just considered. Such loans will become a business liability and will form a matching entry on the company's balance sheet.

Hire purchase (or credit sale)

This form of credit is a very popular way of purchasing large items such as cars. However it can be a rather expensive way of borrowing. In fact there are two different types of legal agreement which you can enter into which many people often describe under the general term 'hire purchase'. These are:

- hire purchase; and
- credit sales.

Hire Purchase

This is not a simple purchase of a product. What actually happens is that a finance company buys the item, for instance a car, from the seller and then 'hires' them to the consumer, who agrees to make regular payments to the finance company until the full value of the goods plus interest is made. The goods remain the property of the finance company until the final payment is made. Because the consumer does not own the goods until the end of the agreement there are important legal implications relating to default on payments, resale of the goods or damage to the goods prior to the final payment.

In the case of default on payments the law states that if less than one third of what is owed has been paid before the payments fall into default the finance company has the right to repossess the goods without reference to the courts. If more than one third has been paid, the company must seek a court order to repossess and in such circumstances the court may review the agreement and order that lower repayments should be made over a longer period. Alternatively it may simply grant an order allowing the company to take back the goods. Of course the hire purchase company may not wish to take you to court as the value of repossessed goods will normally be low. It may therefore be willing to renegotiate the repayments and the time period for those who face financial problems.

As the consumer is not the legal owner until all payments have been made he cannot resell the goods until the agreement ends. This can be a problem for those who run into financial difficulties while they still have hire purchase commitments. Finally as the goods are still the property of the finance company until they are paid for, the hirer will often be required to keep them in a good condition until the ownership passes at the end of the repayments.

While the business does not legally own the equipment until the final payment is made, the asset can be shown on the company's balance sheet and the business can claim tax allowances from the time it takes original possession of the equipment although the amount still outstanding to the finance company will be shown as a liability on the balance sheet. While buying equipment on hire purchase means that the business will not have to pay out such a large sum in one go it does mean that the repayments include interest as well as capital and tax relief is available only on the interest part of the repayments.

Credit Sales

With a credit sale, ownership of the goods passes to the consumer immediately. However he or she will still have to repay the finance company the full amount for the goods plus interest by regular payments. There is an important legal difference between credit sales and hire purchase. In a credit sale if you default on payment the credit company may require the full amount immediately even if one third of the amount owed has already been paid. If the full amount is not forthcoming the goods can be reclaimed. As the purchaser is the legal owner, however, he or she can treat the goods as he or she wishes and resell them as long as the finance company is paid what it is owed.

We should make some general points about both hire purchase agreements and credit purchases. The first is that you will not be allowed to enter into either if you have a bad *credit rating*. This usually means that you have defaulted on some form of credit agreement in the past. Most of the large credit companies hold computer records of consumers' credit ratings and specialised agencies keep track of poor creditors. These records are available to all credit companies so it is no good being a bad payer with one company and then hoping that you can get credit easily with another.

Another major disadvantage of gaining credit in this way is that the interest rates are usually very high. The reason for this is simple. Finance companies find that many of their borrowers default. They have to repossess goods which have fallen in value or the court orders repayments over a very long time which is clearly to the lender's disadvantage. Some people simply disappear with the goods without completing payment. Therefore the finance companies must take account of substantial bad debts. To cover themselves they charge very high rates of interest to all borrowers so that those of us who do repay on time are penalised by those who default. Occasionally you may find some credit companies which offer special low interest or even 'interest free' deals on certain products. If you find these, they are usually well worth considering. But they tend to be somewhat out of the ordinary. Therefore generally if you want to buy a large item on credit, you have a bank account and your credit standing with the bank is good then borrow the money through a personal loan rather than through a hire purchase or credit sale agreement. It will work out much cheaper.

Activity

Using a copy of your local paper prepare a file of clippings showing the different credit deals on offer by new and used car dealers in your area. Note the different rates of interest on offer and the varying periods of repayment. Analyse the deals on offer and suggest which would be the most attractive.

Leasing

When a business leases equipment it never becomes the legal owner. The equipment continues to be the property of the leasing company which allows the business to use the equipment in return for a series of regular payments. While the business cannot treat the equipment as an asset on its balance sheet and so cannot claim a tax allowance, the leasing payments are regarded as a business expense and are included in the business' profit and loss account and so will reduce the profits which will mean that any tax liability is reduced.

There are a variety of different types of leases. These include:

- *closed-ended leases* which last for a particular period of time such as three or five years. At the end of the leasing period the business could extend the lease for a further period or the leasing company may sell the equipment to the business for a reduced price;

- *open-ended leases* do not have a specified life and the business can end the lease at any time once a minimum period has been completed.

- a final form of lease is the '*balloon-lease*'. In this form of lease the business will pay reduced repayments for the period of the lease and then pay a substantial final payment – the balloon payment – to complete the lease. With such leases the leasing company will often allow the business to arrange the sale of the equipment to some third party to generate the cash required to make the balloon payment.

Contract hire

This is a form of leasing often used to allow a business to operate a fleet of vehicles. The agreement does not normally relate to a specific vehicle or vehicles but requires the leasing company to supply a certain number of vehicles for the business to use. The contract will often include the maintenance of the vehicles. In this way the business will be confident that it always has the vehicles that it needs and does not need to worry about unforeseen running costs such as breakdowns or replacements.

Factoring

A further means of raising short-term finance open to businesses facing cash flow problems is factoring. This involves a business, which has debts owed to it, selling the right to this money to a *factor* (an organisation willing to provide immediate cash in return for the right to collect and keep the monies owed by the business's debtors).

The factors are often subsidiaries of clearing banks or major financial groups. Factors will usually pay the business less than the face value of the debts (usually 3 – 10% less) and so, if they can collect the debts in full, this percentage is their profit on the transaction. This illustrates how a debt is an *asset* owed by the business and, like any other type of asset, can be sold if a suitable buyer is available.

This method of short-term fund raising is particularly useful to smaller firms who wish to avoid the task of debt collection and who need an efficient cashflow in order to aid expansion.

Bill finance

One form of factoring, bill finance, involves a business selling a specific debt to a discount house or bank. The business receives the amount (less commission) straight away and the bank collects the full sum when it falls due from the debtors.

For example, suppose Business A sells a piece of equipment to Business B for £20,000. Business A, in order to ease its cashflow, sells this debt to a bank for £18,000. Business A gets £18,000 immediately; the bank eventually collects the full £20,000 debt from Business B, thereby making a £2,000 'profit' on the deal. Bill finance is cheaper than an overdraft and has clearly identifiable costs. It is often used in conjunction with an overdraft as a source of short-term funds.

Medium-term borrowing

Approximately 40% of all business loans are now taken for periods ranging from three to ten years. Most of these loans are *secured* against the assets of the business or are guaranteed by the owners of the business. A secured loan means that the lender accepts all or some of the assets of the business as security on the loan and could claim these assets and sell them should the business fail to repay the loan.

Borrowing money in this way has major advantages for a business. It allows the liability to be spread over a longer period and the repayments can be made on a regular monthly or quarterly basis. The period for which the loan is given is usually sufficient to allow the business to make profits from the investment in new plant or machinery for which the loan was first negotiated.

Such medium-term loans are especially useful for the purchase of assets which have a particular lifespan. So, for instance, if a machine lasts five years before it needs replacing, it is sensible to take out a five year loan to finance it and spread its cost over its lifetime.

A medium-term loan may also be used to refinance an overdraft. In this way, the cost of finance can be spread over a longer term, avoiding financial difficulties should an overdraft facility come to an end.

Normally, then, a medium-term loan is designed for a business which has established itself and has solved the initial start-up difficulties which most companies face.

Term loan

This is the main form of medium-term finance. It can be provided by the clearing banks as well as merchant banks. The conditions for such a loan vary quite widely and are usually open to some negotiation. The stronger the financial position and prospects of the borrower, the more favourable terms the business is likely to obtain from the lender. Among the elements which can be varied are the repayment pattern and the interest rate. The rate may be fixed or floating (that is, varying according to changes in the economy).

Long-term borrowing

Long-term loans are usually provided to allow a business to buy plant or machinery which will have a prolonged lifespan. *Long-term* is normally ten years or longer and, as well as being used to buy plant, it may also finance takeovers or other forms of expansion. If the business is sound, however, as it must be if it is to contemplate such long-term finance, it may be better advised to raise finance through a share issue, rather than take on such long-term debts. Banks may well be reluctant to make such long-term loans to a small business if they lack confidence about its long-term prospects for growth. Certainly, no long-term loan of this sort will be given by a bank without concrete guarantees and security. It is also likely that the bank will seek a higher rate of interest on such loans. You may argue that the business is wiser to seek shorter term and cheaper loans, but this ignores the advantages that the business gains from not having to repay its debts quickly. It is able to schedule its debts repayment in line with its revenue growth without having the problem of continually renegotiating its loan position.

Debentures

Companies often borrow money by means of issuing debentures. These may be *secured* or *unsecured*. The definition of a debenture is very wide and includes all forms of securities: in other words, undertakings to repay any money borrowed, which may or may not be secured by a charge on the company's assets. A *charge* simply means a legal right to take the asset. Debentures usually consist of trust deeds which will create a fixed charge over a specific piece of company property by mortgage, and/or a floating charge over the rest of the company assets. The difference between *fixed* and *floating* charges is that a company is not free to do what it wishes with assets which are subject to a fixed charge. In other words, it is not free to sell or mortgage them. However, a company is free to do what it likes with any of its assets covered by a floating charge.

The floating charge will normally be created over a class of assets, such as the company's trading stock. A floating charge is said to 'crystallise' and become a fixed charge should money become repayable under a condition in the debenture which is then not paid. This might happen, for instance, when repayment on part of the interest on the loan is due. The lender may subsequently take steps to enforce his security, because the interest due has not been paid by the borrower.

The principal rights of a debenture holder are outlined in the debenture deed and will include:

- the date of repayment of the loan and the rate of interest
- a statement of the assets of the company which are subject to fixed or floating charges
- the rights of the company to redeem the whole or any part of the monies owing
- the circumstances in which the loan becomes immediately repayable, such as if the company defaults in payment of interest
- the powers of the debenture holder to appoint a receiver and manager of the assets charged.

Sale and leaseback

Often seen as a 'last resort' by which to raise larger sums of money, this involves selling a fixed asset which is owned by the business (usually land or buildings) to a buyer. The asset is then leased back from the buyer by means of a rental agreement.

Commercial mortgages

Commercial mortgages are available to businesses which wish to buy land or buildings. Building societies do not lend to businesses, so the usual source of the mortgage is a bank. The period of the loan is usually between ten and thirty years. There are normally two major factors determining whether or not a business will be able to raise a mortgage:

- the value, age and type of the property on which the mortgage is being sought;
- the financial circumstances of the business borrowing the money.

The property

The building society or bank which is lending the money will have to ensure that the property which is its security on the mortgage has a value which is at least equal to the size of the loan. Therefore it will have the property valued by a surveyor who will look at its location, condition and assess a market value. Some banks and building societies are reluctant to advance money on certain types of property. So for instance it may be more difficult to find a lender for a mortgage on an office which is part of a converted old house. The mortgage offer may also only be a percentage of the value of the property depending on the age of the property, (for example only 60% may be offered on old property).

The borrower

The bank or building society will wish to be sure that the borrower will be able to repay the mortgage. Despite the fact that it holds the security of the deeds to the property it will not want to have to take possession as this will involve the difficulties of eviction and resale. Therefore the business will have to show that it has a relatively secure future and, even with other outgoings, there will be sufficient finance left to pay the mortgage.

Legal restrictions on borrowing by business

As far as a sole trader is concerned, there is no limitation on his or her borrowing powers but, of course, a sole trader remains personally liable to the full extent of his or her personal wealth for any debts entered into. In a partnership, every partner is the agent of the firm and its partners. Therefore, in a trading partnership, every partner has the power to borrow money for a purpose apparently connected with the partnership business. This rule has the effect of making every partner in a firm jointly liable, with all other partners, for all of the debts incurred by the firm while that person is a partner.

The law makes a distinction between the borrowing of non-corporate and corporate businesses. We will now examine each in turn.

Non-corporate bodies

If you are to consider the legal rights which a business lender, such as a bank, has when it lends money to a sole trader or a partnership, you will need to determine whether the loan is secured or unsecured. An unsecured loan means that the lender has no rights over the borrower's property in the event of the borrower defaulting on the repayments. The lender's only option is to bring a court action in an attempt to recover the debt. In the present economic climate, it is more usual for a lender, such as a bank, to demand the added protection of a secured loan. As we have already mentioned one of the most common forms of secured loan is a 'commercial mortgage', which uses freehold or leasehold land, or other business assets, as security.

Corporate bodies

Power to borrow money is usually conferred on the company directors in the Articles of Association. There is nothing to prevent a business limiting its own borrowing powers to a specific amount in its Memorandum of Association. It can do this, for instance, by including a limit on borrowing of not more than two-thirds of the value of its paid up capital. In effect, the company will be introducing a self-imposed loan limit. Power to borrow will also carry with it an implied power to offer company property as security for a loan. As a general rule, if a business borrows beyond its powers, then the loan and any security given for it is void on the grounds of *ultra vires,* which is the legal term given to an act which is beyond the powers of the company.

Loan gearing

In Element 6.3, *Monitoring Business Performance*, we consider a number of financial indicators which will allow judgements to be made as to the financial health and stability of a business. It is worth briefly mentioning one of them now. This is the concept of *loan gearing*, which is simply a measurement of the degree to which a business is financed by loans rather than by equity. When a business seeks a loan from a financial institution such as a bank, the lender will often require the business to put up a proportion of its financial needs itself from its internal funds to demonstrate the ability of the business to be self-financing. So for instance the bank may specify that for every pound the bank loans the business, the owners must match it, pound for pound. This is referred to as a 1:1 gearing ratio. Many banks will now accept a much higher ratio of loan to internal financing but this will depend on their belief in the business and their confidence in its future.

The Government's Loan Guarantee Scheme

We have already recognised that one of the difficulties any business will face when it seeks to raise money from a bank is that it may well have a lack of security. To try to help overcome such problems the government has introduced a loan guarantee scheme for small businesses. Under the scheme the government is willing to act as guarantor for 70% of a loan to small businesses up to a limit of £100,000. One major disadvantage to the small business borrower is the requirement to pay a premium on top of the interest rate to cover the costs of the guarantee. Of course this makes any loan more expensive but it is still a possibility for businesses which cannot provide sufficient security to cover the loan themselves.

The Business Expansion Scheme

A further government attempt to encourage the provision of funds for private business is the Business Expansion Scheme. This allows private investors to put their money into new and growing companies by giving substantial tax concessions to the investor, who is able to offset against personal income tax any investment in non-listed companies up to a value of £40,000. The investment must be held for a period of at least five years if it is to qualify for the tax relief. The idea is to encourage investment in small or medium sized businesses which will provide the investor with a more attractive return because of the tax advantages.

Other sources of finance from public funds

The number of sources of public money is not as proliferate as it used to be. Funds are still available for capital projects from sources such as the EC, but the government now prefers to offer businesses inducements to use various financial services. The 'Enterprise Initiative' provides grants towards projects such as market research, financial planning, design and export research. Such policies form part of the government's 'supply side' approach .

Activity

From your local reference library try to find out as much as you can about government schemes to provide financial support to businesses in your area. Prepare a brief report which identifies each source of funds and the criteria which must be met to qualify for the support.

Equity Finance

The issue of shares as a means of raising finance

If a business wishes to expand, it may be faced with the problem that the funds needed to finance its expansion cannot be met either internally, from business profits, or through borrowing from financial institutions. One of the other options open to it is to bring in new capital from outside sources. This means issuing shares and spreading the ownership of the business. Many small businesses may resent this reduction in their direct control. Broadening ownership, however, need not always lead to a reduction in control; it is often found that new investors are not interested in the day-to-day management of the business and only want a safe and profitable return on their investment. There are many professional investors who are looking for small businesses in which to invest funds and this can have a number of major commercial benefits.

The additional capital introduced into the business by the sale of its shares can give it a much sounder financial base and also open up other avenues for raising funds. The company's bankers will recognise that the new investors have endorsed the future potential of the business and so it may be easier to arrange overdrafts or other forms of short- and medium-term finance.

If the new share capital is sold to a professional investor, such as a merchant bank, then it is likely that the bank will want to appoint a representative to the board of the company. This may seem like an imposition on the management and policy-making functions of the business, but often such appointees have wide business experience; as they seek to protect their investment they will want the business to succeed and, to this end, will usually offer sound advice. It is unlikely that professional investors will want to share in the capital of small businesses or those which are just starting up, but, for a medium-sized business in need of funds to expand, it may prove to be a mutually profitable move. Small businesses will not be able to get professional investors to buy their shares, but must seek individuals who are willing to buy shares.

Before moving on to consider the mechanics of share issue and the restrictions involved in raising capital in this way, you need to consider some of the distinctions between the expressions used. Unfortunately, the use of the term '*capital*', when applied to companies, can have many different meanings, so in order to try and minimise confusion, we will begin this section by considering some of the more widely used expressions.

Authorised capital

This expression refers to *the value of shares that a company is authorised to issue* and is included in the capital clause of the Memorandum of Association of a company.

Issued capital

This is *the value of the company's capital which has actually been issued to the shareholders in the form of shares*.

Paid up capital

This is the amount of *capital which has actually been paid to the company on the shares issued*. It is possible to issue shares which are not paid for or which are partly paid. Under the European Communities Act, 1972, if a company makes a reference to share capital on its business stationery or order forms, it must refer to its paid up share capital – that is, the amount of capital the company has actually raised and received.

Unpaid capital

If shares which have been issued are not fully paid for, then the amount outstanding is referred to as unpaid capital. For example, if 10,000 shares are issued, each having a nominal value of £1, and only 50p has been paid up on them (in other words, paid to the company), then the issued share capital is £10,000, the paid up capital is £5,000 and the unpaid capital is £5,000. Shareholders may be required to pay up the unpaid amount on their shares by the company making a '*call*' on them to do so. This may happen if the business begins to face financial difficulties and cannot meet its debts.

Classes of shares

Most companies in the UK have one class of shares which is referred to as '*ordinary shares*' or as the '*equity share capital*' of the company. However, there is nothing to prevent a limited company from having more than one class of shares. If different classes of shares are issued, they will confer on their purchasers certain rights, relating to such matters as voting rights, payment of dividend (in other words, the sum distributed to shareholders out of any profit made) and the return of capital to shareholders should the company go into liquidation. The two main types of shares are preference shares and ordinary shares.

Preference shares

The main characteristic of a preference share is that it will grant its holder the right to a preferred fixed dividend. This simply means that the holder of a preference share is entitled to a fixed amount of dividend, for instance 6% on the value of his share, before the ordinary shareholders are paid any dividend. A preference share is, therefore, a safe investment with a fixed reward, no matter how small or how large is the company's profit. Some preference shares are *non-cumulative*, while others are *cumulative*. If the share is cumulative this means that, if in any year, the company's profits are not sufficient to declare a dividend, the shortfall must be made up out of profits of subsequent years. Often preference shares carry no voting rights.

Ordinary shares

Ordinary shares are often referred to as the 'equity share capital' of a company. These are the shares which involve risk, for having declared a dividend and paid the preference shareholders, the company will now pay a dividend to the holders of ordinary shares out of the remainder of the profit. It follows, therefore, that an ordinary shareholder in a well-managed company, which is making high profits, will receive a good return on his or her investment and the nominal value of those share will rise: so, for instance, a £1 ordinary share could rise in its market value to £1.50. Unfortunately, the opposite is also true and share values can fall as well as rise. If there is no profit, then there is no dividend and the shares may fall in value, so inevitably ordinary shares involve a certain risk. This risk is reflected in the amount of control that an ordinary shareholder has over the company's business, for while voting rights are not normally attached to preference shares, they are to ordinary shares. The ordinary shareholder can usually voice an opinion in the company's annual general meeting (AGM) and vote on major issues involving the running of the company. Ordinary shares also carry the right to a share of any surplus assets, once liabilities have been met, should the company be wound up. While preference shares normally carry no such right, their capital is usually repaid in preference to the capital of ordinary shareholders.

Raising share capital

You have already seen in Unit 4, *Human Resources*, that the basic classification of companies is between those which are *public* and those which are *private* companies. Under the Companies Act 1985, a public limited company is one which, by its Memorandum of Association, states that it is a public limited company and has a nominal share capital of a least £50,000, of which at least one-quarter is paid up capital. All other companies are private. Also, a private company has no right to invite public subscription for shares by issuing a prospectus. (A *prospectus* is an advertisement offering shares or debentures for sale to the general public.)

Such a legal restriction effectively limits the ability of a private company to raise large amounts of capital, for it must rely totally on those individuals who are aware of its existence and who might be willing to subscribe to its shares. A public company, however, is not limited in its membership size or the rights of its shareholders to freely transfer their shares. However, only certain public companies are quoted on the stock exchange, so shareholders in unquoted companies have greater difficulty in buying and selling shares. To raise initial capital, or increase its issued capital, a public company will issue a prospectus to invite the public to subscribe for shares or debentures. The prospectus must, however, contain certain information including:

- Particulars of all contracts entered into by the company in the last two years which are likely to influence prospective investors
- An auditor's report showing the company's assets and liabilities, profits, losses and dividends paid over the last five years
- If the proceeds of the share issue are to be used to acquire property, or a business, a statement giving particulars of the prospective vendors and the purchase price.

The role of the merchant banks

Merchant banks have a variety of roles within the financial sector, ranging from the lending of large sums to companies, to financing mergers and takeovers, to assisting in exporting and importing. One of their major roles is to arrange the flotation of new companies on the Stock Exchange. The steps listed above will usually be handled by a merchant bank, including the preparation of the prospectus. The prospectus is often published in the 'quality' newspapers and, of course, must be truthful. An investor who can show that he or she was induced to buy shares because of false statements of fact in the prospectus, may sue to reclaim any money paid, terminate the share issue, and possibly obtain damages from the persons responsible.

It is usual practice, when a company makes an invitation to the public for a share issue, to have the issue *underwritten*. In return for a commission, an underwriter, again usually a merchant bank, will agree to subscribe for any shares which the public does not take up. This can be a very lucrative business, if all of the shares are taken up by the general public. In this instance, the merchant bank will receive its commission without actually purchasing any shares. However, should the issue be undersubscribed, the merchant bank may find itself in the position of having to purchase a large number of shares of which it may subsequently have difficulty in disposing.

The Stock Exchange

The Stock Exchange is the market place for 'securities'. These can be '*equities*' which are shares in companies or '*gilt-edged securities*' often referred to as 'gilts' which are loans to the government. A stock exchange is an important institution in any capitalist society as it allows people to buy and sell shares in the ownership of businesses in a relatively simple and convenient way.

Other Equity Markets

During the 1980s the growth in the buying and selling of stocks and shares led to the establishment of two subsidiary markets. These were:

- the Unlisted Securities Market
- the 'Third Market'.

These markets were formed as a response to the argument that the stock market was too inflexible to cater for small but expanding companies which were seen as the driving force behind Britain's economic expansion. Because they were small, many of these companies could not gain a full 'listing' on the stock exchange. This meant that they were hampered in their growth as they could not raise sufficient capital because they were unable to sell shares which could then be traded easily.

The *Unlisted Securities Market* provided a regulated market for such small companies. Many electronics and oil companies launched themselves on the USM and the market grew rapidly in the mid 1980s.

The *Third Market* was founded in 1987 and was designed to allow even smaller and younger companies to trade their shares. The market floundered, however, almost as soon as it had been established and was closed at the end of 1990.

The stock market crash in 1987 and the recession, however, meant that shares on the USM and the Third Market were increasingly difficult to trade and many of these smaller companies, which in the boom of the mid-1980s had outperformed larger companies in terms of profit growth, were now hit by a fall in demand and by the effect of high interest rates. A change in stock market regulations in 1991 also seriously damaged the USM. When it had been foundered companies had to have been trading for five years before they could seek a 'full listing' on the main stock exchange, whereas a USM listing required that the company should have been trading for only three years. This was an obvious attraction to growing companies which wanted to raise capital quickly and so many chose a USM listing. Since 1991, however, the Stock Exchange has reduced its minimum trading requirement to three years and the USM to two years. Many companies now feel that they can wait the extra year and achieve full listing rather than joining the USM. By the middle of 1992 only 326 companies were listed on the USM and during the first half of 1992 only 4 new companies joined, a decline from its peak in 1988 when 103 new companies joined the market. At the time of writing it appears that the end of the USM is near.

Activity

Get a copy of one of the 'quality' newspapers such as the Guardian, Times, Independent or Telegraph. Each of the newspapers list the previous days share prices on the stock exchange. From this stock exchange listing identify ten companies whose products you buy and check to see if their share price is rising or falling. If the share price has changed dramatically try to find out why.

Retained Profits as a Means of Raising Capital

You have looked at the need which a business might have for finance and at the main avenues which it might explore in order to obtain funds: borrowing and the issue of shares. In all of this, it is easy to overlook the fact that retained profits are still the biggest source of finance for businesses in the UK.

Whatever profitable businesses decide to do, they must first pay Corporation Tax to the Inland Revenue before they pay out dividends to their shareholders or retain what profit is left for re-investment. The trend in recent years has been towards a reduction in the rate of Corporation Tax. This has left more profits available for businesses to pay out as dividends,or to re-invest in their company.

Assignment *Russell-Hoban Plastics' Financial Crisis*

Russell-Hoban Plastics' Ltd. is a small private company formed in 1968 and engaged in the manufacture and supply of high grade plastic engineering materials.

The company structure is as follows:

Capital

Authorised Capital	£100,000
Issued Capital	£60,000 (comprising 60,000 £1 ordinary shares carrying one vote per share)
Paid up capital	£45,000 (comprising of 75% of the value of each ordinary share issued)

Membership:

There are three directors of the company – Ben Russell, Jack Hoban (Managing Director) and Andy Russell (Ben's son). Ben and Jack are the company's founders and each holds 20,000 ordinary shares, while Andy holds 11,000 shares. All three directors are actively involved in managing the company business. The remaining 9,000 shares are divided equally between three other shareholders who are ex-employees of the company.

Present Financial Position – June 1993

The company's main assets are its industrial premises over which the company own the freehold and which have a present valuation of £60,000. These are currently mortgaged for £40,000 of which £15,000 is outstanding and is repayable over the remaining four years of the mortgage period.

The company's main liability is a five year loan of £40,000 which the company obtained two years ago from its bankers (Barclays) and has £28,500 (capital and interest) remaining to be repaid.

Although having a history of trading at a healthy profit and declaring high dividends and providing capital for re-investment until 1990, the company has declared a net loss over the last 2 years of £4,200 and £6,750, respectively. This has been the result of increased costs of production. In fact, the company's wage bill has almost doubled over the last three years. The company has been reluctant to pass on increased costs to their consumers through higher prices and has had only two small price rises of 5% and 3% over the last two years. Generally, sales in quality terms, have increased by 10% per annum. In an attempt to meet the rising demand for their products, the company decided in January 1991 to invest in new advanced machinery purchased from Orbit Ltd., a West German manufacturer. The cost of the machinery, £36,000, was met by using the company's total reserve capital. The directors decided to make a cash purchase in return for a substantial 30% discount. Since the introduction of this machinery, production has increased dramatically and sales are rising. Nevertheless, although these signs are good for the future, the directors have calculated that in the present year, 1993-94, the company will continue to make a loss (projected at £4,800).

The Financial Crisis

Jack Hoban has called a directors' meeting for 21st June 1993 to discuss what he describes in the notice of the meeting as the company's 'financial crisis'. Jack is concerned by the news from the company's two major clients that they are both in short term financial difficulties and require an extension of credit facilities on debts owed to Russell-Hoban Ltd. for plastics supplied by the company to them. The amounts owing are £2,600 and £4,700, respectively, and had been earmarked as sufficient to pay the June wage bill of £7,000. This could not otherwise be met from cash on hand which amounts to £1,500.

Jack who tends to over-react, has openly said that "this is the last straw" and feels that it is "time to call it a day and shut up shop". He is supported by all three minority shareholders (the ex-employees) who are unhappy at not receiving any return on their investment for the last two years and are aware of the projected loss for 1993-94. They feel that a dissolution of the company and a sale of its assets would provide the best opportunity for a return of their investment.

Ben and his son, Andy, are adamant that the company has a future and are determined that it should survive.

Tasks

From the information given answer the following questions:

1.   Which alternative combinations of voting shareholders exercise control for
     *   the carrying on of normal company business;
     *   the authorisation of the company's dissolution?

2.   Advise the company on possible sources of short term finance necessary to meet the June wage bill.

3.   Suggest factors which may have influenced the company's decision not to increase the selling price of its products in the last two years despite the increased costs of production.

4.   In the event of a stalemate between Jack and the minority shareholders on one side and Ben and Andy on the other at the 21st June meeting, advise as to possible alternative courses of action which could be taken.

5.   Bearing in mind alternative sources of finance, how could the company be put on a firm financial footing for the future?

Element 7.2 Cash flow forecasting

Cash flow forecasting

In the previous section we discussed the ways in which a business can raise finance and we noted that often you will need to go to a bank for a loan. The bank manager will not only want to see your business plan, which we examine in some detail in Unit 8, *Business Planning,* he or she will also want to see a cash flow forecast for your business.

The cash flow forecast is an attempt to show the anticipated in-flow and out-flow of cash from a business. It sets out, usually in monthly periods these two major financial aspects of the business:

- *In-flow of cash*. In-flow is the revenue from sales of the product or service or from other sources such as rent from property or dividends from shares.
- *Out-flow of cash*. If we consider the costs of operation that make up the out-flows, the business will have to pay wages and other bills on a much more prompt and regular basis than some other payments. It may be fine to leave the bill for the supply of raw materials to be paid until the end of the month but try explaining to the workforce that they are not getting their wages for the next six weeks!

Therefore at different times throughout the trading year the business may find that it will have varying levels of cash shortage when it must pay bills but is waiting to be paid itself. These circumstances need to be anticipated so that agreement can be made with the bank to provide sufficient funds at the times when they will be needed. In essence this is all that a cash flow forecast is - a monthly statement of cash spent and cash received leaving a balance which may be in surplus (which is fine) or maybe in debit (which will need financing by the bank).

Activity

There are sure to be times in your personal life when you will have cash flow difficulties. This may be because you are tempted to spend too much or because your income, whether it comes from your family, a grant or from earnings is not as much as you had hoped or does not come when you need it. As an exercise draw up your own personal cash flow forecast for the following month. If you can, prepare it on a spreadsheet. Then adjust it by including some 'what ifs'. In other words what would happen to your cash flow if, for instance, someone gave you £50 as a present. Alternatively what would you cash flow look like if you lost your purse or wallet or had some unexpected expenditure to make.

On the following page we show an example of a typical cash flow forecast for a small business. In this instance the business is a small book shop which has just been taken over by a new owner. It is situated in the centre of a historic town and while it has been run down in the past, the new owner has high hopes of reviving its fortunes. Let us examine the aspects of this cash flow in some detail.

On the top line you will see that it is divided into twelve monthly periods. As we have already said you can produce a cash flow forecast for any period you wish but it is normal when presenting a cash flow to a banker to provide figures for the next twelve or twenty four months.

Below each months of the are shown the projected monthly sales figures. As you can see the owner is only anticipating sales of £12,000 in January but expects it to increase steadily over the year as he establishes the bookshop's reputation. So his forecast of £4800 worth of sales per month by next autumn may not be too optimistic - if he knows what he is doing!

The second top line shows the owners own cash, £5,000, which he intends to introduce into the business in January of this year. He regards this as start-up capital and his bank are pleased that he did not want to borrow all the money he needed and was willing to risk some of his own assets in the business.

The third source of income is rent from the flat upstairs above the bookshop. You can see that there are four separate payments made during the year. The first of these is reduced because the tenant has just moved in and only owes rent for two weeks.

When we add all the three top lines together we are able to calculate the bookshop's total income in any one month. Check the figures and you will see that the bookshop anticipates to get £5300 in October. This is made up of sales income of £4800 and £500 rent income.

Those are the in-flows of cash and we now we should consider the necessary out-flows. The biggest single area of spending is on salaries and this would be the case in many organisations. The bookshop employs two part-time workers,who despite being hardworking are not very well paid. The owner anticipates taking on a new part-timer who may be able to help with the developments he plans and reflects this increase in the workforce by increasing the provision for salaries from April.

The remaining entries under the expenditure heading are generally seen in many businesses. For instance the bookshop is leased and the owner must pay a £1000 rent every three months. As you can see the bookshop owner already has a bank loan which he is repaying at a rate of £280 per month. This loan is to finance the purchase of car which is necessary in this line of business.

Now move to the bottom three lines. These monitor the monthly difference between income and outflow of cash and relate the sum to the bookshop's bank account. So in February the projection is that the bookshop will begin the month with an opening balance at the bank of £4710. However in that month it is anticipated out-goings will exceed in-comings (£3490 out-goings and only £1200 coming in through sale of books). Yet at this stage the bookshop still has money in the bank. It is only in late spring and early summer that the predicted picture starts to darken. In May the cost of employing the extra staff has to be met but the training time for a good bookshop assistant reduces the immediate benefit in terms of extra sales. It is for these summer and autumn months that the bookshop will need an overdraft and so has produced this cash flow. If the predictions are correct things will pickup towards the end of the year.

Many people now run cash flows using spreadsheets on computers. This allows them to be adjusted simply as figures change.

	Jan	Feb	Mar	Apr	May	Jun	Jul	Aug	Sep	Oct	Nov	Dec
Sales	1200	1200	1200	1200	1800	2400	3000	3600	4200	4800	4800	4800
Start-up capital	5000											
Rent income	100			500			500			500		
Total Income	6300	1200	1200	1700	1800	2400	3500	3600	4200	5300	4800	4800
Expenditure												
Salaries	900	900	900	1100	1100	1100	1100	1100	1100	1100	1100	1100
Books	500	500	500	500	500	500	600	600	600	600	600	600
Travelling	200	200	200	200	200	200	200	200	200	200	200	200
Audit				700								
Advertising	300	300	300	300	700	300	300	300	300	300	300	300
Bank interest				500								
Bank loan	280	280	280	280	280	280	280	280	280	280	280	280
Lease of property		1000			1000			1000			1000	
Heat and Light			300			300			300			300
Computer Leasing	150	150	150	150	150	150	150	150	150	150	150	150
Rates	110	110	110	110	110	110	110	110	110	110	110	110
Petty Cash	50	50	50	50	50	50	50	50	50	50	50	50
Total Expenditure	2490	3490	3290	3390	4090	2990	2790	3790	3090	2790	3790	3090
Movement	3810	-2290	-2090	-1690	-2290	-590	710	-190	1110	2510	1010	1710
Opening Balance	900	4710	2420	330	-1360	-3650	-4240	-3530	-3720	-2610	-100	910
Closing Balance	4710	2420	330	-1360	-3650	-4240	-3530	-3720	-2610	-100	910	2620

Assignment *You've been framed!*

It was Lesley Reece's birthday and as she picked up the birthday cards from the mat she was dismayed to find among them a letter from her bank manager.

Lesley ran her own small business as a picture framer which she operated from a small shop in the centre of a tourist town. As well as framing other people's pictures she also sold pictures complete with frames which she bought either from wholesalers or from an auction sale which she attended every three months.

The letter she had received that morning from the bank was unwelcome news. She had inadvertently overdrawn her current account. The letter, while polite, was firm. She had overdrawn by £211 without having an arranged overdraft. She would be charged interest on the overdrawn amount, a separate charge for going overdrawn and a charge for the letter. What annoyed Lesley most was that only a month earlier she had been almost £2,000 in credit with the bank.

She decided that she must organise her finances and then go and see the bank manager in order to arrange an overdraft for those times in the year when she was likely to be have cash flow difficulties.

She sat down with a pen and a piece of paper and began to note down her income and her expenditure. This is what she came up with.

Income:

> Sales in January February and March of approximately £2,200 per month. This increased by 20% in the months of April, May, June, July, August and September when the tourist trade was at its height then fell back to about £2,200 per month for October and November. Coming up to Christmas was always a good time as people wanted pictures framed as presents so she was confident that her sales income in that month would be around the £3,500 mark.

Expenditure:

> Her expenditure also varied throughout the year. She began by noting down her regular payments. The rent on the shop was £6,000 per year which she paid quarterly by standing order on the first of January, April, July and October. She also paid business rates and water rates. She paid both on monthly standing orders of £98 and £24 respectively. She also had a standing order to pay her electricity bill and at present this was £54 per month. The telephone charges were paid quarterly and never came to more than £100 per quarter. These were paid in February, May, August and November.

> Finally her materials cost both for the picture frames and for stock which she bought in usually came to 40% of the sales value in the month. Obviously these costs went up in the busy months and fell in quieter months.

> Lesley also took £750 per month out of the business as drawings for her to live on.

After completing her list she set to work to prepare a cash flow forecast which she could present to the bank when she went in to arrange her overdraft.

Task

1. Put yourself in Lesley's position and prepare her cash flow for the year.
2. Prepare a second cash flow but this time assume the worst and that sales fell 10% below Lesley's original estimation.

Element 7.3 The Cost of Goods and Services

There are a number of ways that an organisation can assess what price to charge for its product or service. A simplistic approach may be to add up all the costs of producing it and add on a sufficient amount to provide some level of profit. Yet the costs of production may not be the only consideration in setting price. A business must decide what the customer is willing to pay. It must evaluate the demand for its product or service . It might produce a demand curve or demand schedule.(We look at these approaches in Unit 1, *Business in the Economy*.) It could use some form of market research to plan its marketing strategy. (Such market research techniques are considered in the Unit 3, *Marketing*.)

However in this Element we will concentrate on the way in which the business will determine the costs of production and show how these costs will be influential in determining at least the minimum price that the organisation is willing set.

The Organisation's Costs

The costs of production which face an organisation depend on the level of output or provision it seeks to make. Costs will include payment for the factors or production that are required; its labour force, premises, machinery and other capital equipment. It is necessary to classify them according to how they can be varied to meet an organisation's needs. In order to do this we must look at the timescale of operation, for this is crucial in influencing how they can be varied and combined.

The timescale needed to produce anything may be divided into short run and long run. This is an imprecise and rather arbitrary distinction. The length of time that each of these periods encompasses will depend on the type of operation that the organisation is involved in.

(a) The short run

The very short run is the period in which we define all organisational costs as being unable to be varied. In other words all costs of production are fixed. This simply means that the labour force cannot be increased or reduced, the organisation cannot change its premises or acquire new capital or equipment. For some businesses, this may be as short as a week or a month. For instance labour employed for a period of less than two years may be dismissed with only the minimum period of notice required. However, for staff employed for a longer period who are entitled to redundancy payments, more extensive notice is needed to inform them of their imminent redundancy. This entails 90 days notice for redundancies of more than 100 employees, who are members of recognised independent trade union. Thus the freedom of the organisation to vary its workforce may be limited by statute, in this case the Employment Protection (Consolidation) Act, 1978.

Time is obviously needed to recruit new staff if the organisation is trying to expand its workforce. Of course, this short run is much longer for factors of production such as buildings for it will be unable to buy, build or rent new premises in a matter of weeks and the length of time needed to dispose of existing property will be dependent on the state of the property market. For example if demand is low in the property market it may be difficult to sell existing premises at an acceptable price. This may take months or even years. Therefore costs which are fixed cannot be changed if the business wishes to vary its level of output. For instance, in the short run, if a business experiences a rapid decline in demand, it may be incapable of selling off machinery, moving to smaller premises or making staff redundant.

(b) The long run

If we take a longer timescale an organisation moves from the short run to the long run. Time allows the organisation to vary some of its costs. They become variable. Clearly, as the timescale increases even more, the organisation is able to vary all its costs by hiring new staff, buying new equipment and finding more spacious accommodation. Of course, if it wishes, it could lower potential output by doing the opposite.

Fixed and variable costs

By considering the timescale we are able to make the distinction between those costs which are fixed and those which are variable.

(a) Fixed costs

Once an organisation has established a certain scale of production it will have to pay rent, rates, interest on any loans, administration costs and certain other costs regardless of its output. These are fixed costs. Even if it produced nothing in a particular week, it will have to pay these costs. We can show fixed costs remaining constant as output increases in the first of the figures below. If the organisation wishes to increase the 'scale' of its operations, for instance by buying a new factory this will mean that its fixed costs are 'stepped' up to a higher level. This increase is shown in the second of the figures below.

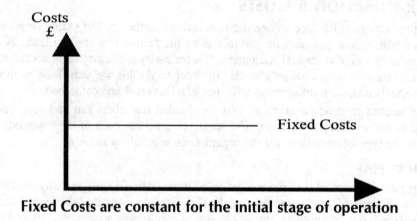

Fixed Costs are constant for the initial stage of operation

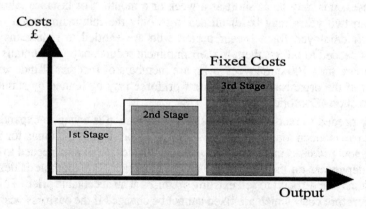

Fixed costs step up as output moves to higher stages

(b) Variable costs

There are some factors of production that an organisation need not contract to purchase before it is aware of the level of production it will require to meet demand. For example, it may not have to purchase raw materials or electricity to power its machines if it has no production in a slack period. It will not have to spend money on motor fuel if it has nothing to transport. Because these costs can be increased or decreased to match the level of production the business requires in a particular period they are referred to as variable costs. These are shown increasing proportionately with output in the next figure.

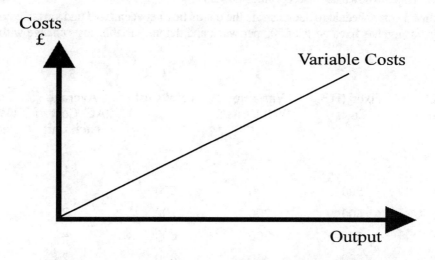

Variable costs increasing proportionately with output

(c) Semi-variable costs

Certain costs such as labour may not be easily classified in this way. They are said to be semi-variable. For instance the organisation may have to pay the basic wage of its workers for a week but if it wishes to expand output it can ask them to do overtime. This would clearly mean that the organisation would not be able to vary part of the wage bill (the basic wage for the workers which would be fixed) but could vary the amount of overtime it asked the staff to undertake (this element would be variable). Another example would be telephone costs. There is a quarterly rental for the telephone itself which is fixed and the calls are charged according to the number that are made. This element is variable.

A simple example will illustrate why it is necessary to make this distinction.

> Assume that a manufacturing organisation is producing small engineering components. Its fixed costs are the rent it pays for the factory, its rates, the repayment on the loan for its machines, and its administration costs. The last of these are sometimes called the organisation's overheads. These are its fixed costs . However it can vary the number of workers it employs and pay them on piece work, in other words they are paid a specific amount for each unit that they produce. It can also alter the amount of raw material it buys and the power it uses to work its machinery. These increase as the organisation makes more components. They are its variable costs. It is important to recognise that these variable costs do not always increase in direct proportion to the organisation's level of output. In some circumstances they will decrease proportionately as the organisation benefits from 'economies of scale', for instance it may benefit from

bulk buying and consequent cheaper prices as its output increases. Or it may be able to install more specialised and sophisticated machinery as its level of output increases and this may make it more efficient. However it may also face a situation where these variable costs increase proportionately as output rises. This may be due to the fact that it has employed all the most efficient workers and if it wished to produce more it must employ less skilled workers. It may have used up all the cheapest sources of raw materials and so it must search further afield, and at a higher cost, for additional supplies of its raw materials. The cost of each extra unit of production, the marginal cost, will rise. This is known as 'diseconomies of scale'.

Let us examine a cost schedule to demonstrate the distinction between fixed and variable costs. Assume that the organisation has fixed costs of 500 per week and that its variable costs change with the level of output.

1	2	3	4	5	6
Output in units	Fixed (FC) Costs	Variable (VC) Costs	Total Cost	Average (AC) Cost of each unit	Marginal (MC) Cost of each extra unit
£	£	£	£	£	£
0	500	0	500	–	–
100	500	200	700	7	2
200	500	300	800	4	1
300	500	350	850	2.8	0.5
400	500	450	950	2.4	1
500	500	600	1,100	2.2	1.5
600	500	800	1,300	2.17	2
700	500	1,050	1,550	2.21	2.5
800	500	1,350	1,850	2.3.	3
900	500	1,700	2,200	2.4	3.5
1,000	500	2,100	2,600	2.6	4

You can see from the above table that column 4 gives the total cost of production at various levels. Thus it costs 1,300 in total to produce 600 units. This total cost must rise as production increases. However you will note that fixed costs remain constant at all levels of production and it is variable costs which rise and so cause total costs to increase.

Total Cost (column 4) is made up of:

(a) Fixed Costs (column 2). As you can see, these do not vary with output. In this example it is 500 whatever the level of production in the range given. It includes rent, rates, debt repayment, etc. We have illustrated a short run situation for eventually if the organisation wishes to substantially increase its level of production it will have to find bigger premises, more machines and thus have to pay more in rent, rates, loan interest and repayments.

(b) Variable Costs (column 3). These increase as the level of organisation's output rises. In this case, it must pay its workforce more, buy extra raw materials and use more power.

The table also shows the average cost per unit (column 5). This is calculated by dividing total costs by the level of output. So for example:

$$AC = \frac{\text{Total Cost}}{\text{Quantity}} = \frac{1,100}{500 \text{ units}} = 2.20 \text{ per unit}$$

From the table you will note that AC decreases until 600 units are made and then rises. This is because at this point the extra variable cost (column 3) required to produce an extra 100 units also rises. In this case to 250 to produce the 100 units between 600 and 700.

Finally, we show Marginal cost (column 6) which is the extra cost of producing an additional unit. This is found by dividing the additional cost by the extra units made. For example to produce 100 units more than 400 incurs 150 extra total cost. This is then divided by the extra units.

$$MC + \frac{\text{Extra Cost}}{\text{Extra Output}} \frac{=150}{100 \text{ extra units}} = 150$$

Clearly, it is very difficult to evaluate marginal cost as precisely as this in most cases, but it is important to try. This is because marginal cost will indicate to the producer what each extra unit costs to produce and if he seeks to make a profit he must be able to sell that unit at a price which is greater than the marginal cost. You will see from the table that MC starts to rise after the production of 300 units. This is because the variable cost of producing the extra 100 units (300-400), that is 150, is greater than the cost of producing the previous 100 units (200-300), that is 100. These points can be illustrated graphically as follows.

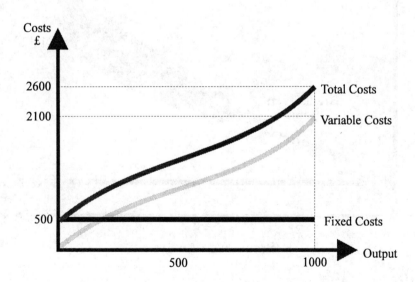

An organisation's Total Cost, Fixed Costs & Variable Costs

Break-even point analysis

As you can see from the above diagram we are able to combine all the cost figures onto one diagram. However this diagram can also be used to calculate the amount of loss or profit the organisation will make at any particular level of output and specifically the level of output which will allow it to 'break-even'. In other words to completely cover all its costs of production. This is found by adding a line to show the total sales revenue that the organisation would receive from selling the goods or services that it produces. Assume that the organisation was able to sell every unit that it produced at the same price, for example at 3 each. This would produce a total revenue line which will rise proportionately from the origin of the graph. Therefore if no units were sold the total sales revenue would be 0; if 100 were sold it would be 300 and so on. This total revenue line is now shown on the graph. As you can see the break even point is at 285 units for at that point total revenue equals total cost.

If the variable cost has been increasing proportionately there is a simple formula which will indicate the break-even point. This is

$$\text{Break-even point} = \frac{\text{Fixed Costs}}{\text{Selling Price per unit} - \text{Variable Cost per unit}}$$

If for example the variable cost per unit had been a constant 2, the fixed costs had been 500 and the selling price had been 3 then the organisation would have had to sell the following number of units to break even:

$$\text{BEP} = \frac{500}{3-2} = \frac{5}{1} = 500$$

Once the break-even point has been passed the organisation will be making profit. However if variable costs begin to rise then profits may fall and there may come a point when the business goes back to a loss making situation. This is illustrated in the next figure.

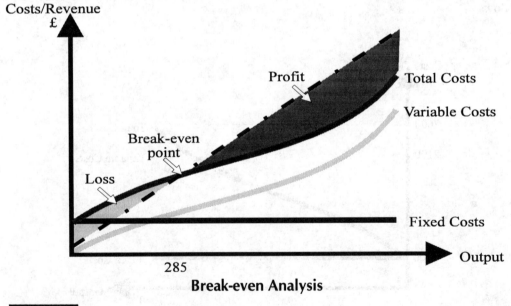

Break-even Analysis

Activity

As a simple exercise, calculate what the break-even point would be for a business which had fixed costs of £575, variable costs of £3 per unit and a sale price of £7 per unit.

Average and marginal costs

In the short run, the organisation's average cost curve is somewhat U-shaped and it is at the lowest point of the U that the organisation is at its optimum level of production, its most efficient size. If it produces more it will do so less efficiently and so average costs will rise. You can see from the diagram that MC cuts AC's lowest point. This is because if MC is less than AC then the additional cost (MC) of each unit will pull AC down. Once MC is greater than AC it will pull it up.

It is important to be clear on this point. The Marginal Cost is the extra cost of producing an additional unit. The Average Cost is the total cost of producing a certain amount of units divided by the quantity made.

You will understand that this example of the short run of an organisation has been deliberately simplified in order to illustrate the concepts of fixed and variable costs and to allow you to appreciate how the average and marginal costs of an organisation are calculated. In reality, most organisations will not be able to distinguish fixed and variable costs as easily as we have done in this example.

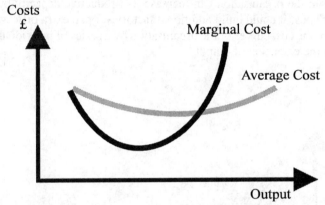

An organisation's short run Marginal and Average Costs

Clearly, many of an organisation's costs can be subdivided into fixed, variable and semi-variable costs. For example, part of the organisation's machinery may require substantial initial investment and so this would be regarded as fixed because to change it would necessitate massive redirection of capital. Other machinery may be relatively inexpensive and so easily discarded and other machines could be hired or leased for relatively short periods and so make that part of the productive capacity relatively variable. The same characteristics will be found in the labour force. Senior management may require long periods of notice and substantial redundancy payments. Other workers may be more easily hired or fired, such as contractors. Of course as we have already noted, labour laws relating to the rights of employees in respect of unfair dismissal and redundancy payments contained in the Employment Protection (Consolidation) Act 1978, as amended, mean that all labour costs are less readily variable. Temporary workers may be employed for relatively short periods to meet a particular expansion in demand for service but it is less simple to reduce the workforce for short periods.

If an organisation is involved in providing a variety of different products or services then it may be possible to move factors of production from one part of the organisation to another if demand is varying between them. For instance, in a local authority, a reduction in the level of provision of recreation may allow clerical staff to be transferred to the housing department where, for instance, the council is implementing the government's policy of selling council houses to tenants. However, from this analysis of short term costs it is clear that fixed costs which are determined by the organisation's scale of production are spread over the average cost of providing the product or service.

Long term costs

As we have already noted, it is impossible to set a specific time period as 'the long run'. This is dependent on the type of organisation, the product it provides and the factors of production it uses. However, we classify the long run or long term as the timescale required to be able to vary all the factors of production. In other words, sufficient time to acquire new machinery or equipment, new premises or more labour if the organisation is seeking to expand, or alternatively to shed these costs if it is contracting. In the long term, the organisation should be able to accurately asses the level of demand for the good/service it provides and so adjust the scale of the manufacture of the product or the provision of its service to achieve the optimum level of production. We have defined this as the point where average costs are at a minimum. However this does not mean that the organisation will always produce at the optimum level for this will be determined by the relationship between the costs of production and the extent of the demand. In the long run the organisation can increase its productive capacity by increasing the fixed factors of production. Thus, it could build additional factories, open extra offices, hire more premises. This will be reflected in the cost curves of the organisation by a series of individual short run cost curves reflecting each step in the extension of output.

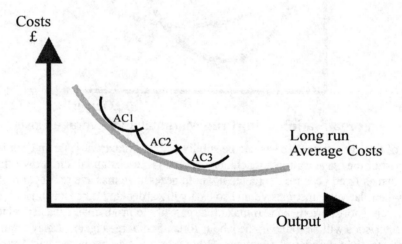

Long run average costs of an organisation

The average cost curves AC1, AC2, AC3, etc. represent the costs at different scales of production. They show how costs would change in a situation with fixed factors of production which could not easily be varied. For instance, if the organisation operated one factory only, the average costs would be shown by AC1. The second factory would have costs represented by AC2 and so on. The first few AC curves tend to move downward because the organisation is able to spread some of its fixed costs over production at a few factories. The organisation will still only employ one managing director even if it has 2 or 3 factories and so the cost of his salary is spread over a greater level of output and so average costs come down. The organisation can gain increasing economies of scale as it moves from one level of production to the next. It will be able to purchase in bulk, employ specialist staff, cut average distribution costs by purchasing its own fleet of lorries, and so on. These are only possible as it increases the level of its output by moving to a larger scale of production.

Eventually the organisation will reach its optimum level of long term production, that is it will have achieved the scale of production at which overall average costs are at their lowest. (In the diagram this is gained with scale of production 3). Following this, the organisation begins to suffer from diminishing returns to scale (or diseconomies of scale). This means that as output is raised average costs tend to rise. This can be the result of several different causes - the organisation may become too large to manage efficiently, sources of raw materials or labour may become more difficult to find and thus more expensive, labour unrest may develop due to the massive impersonal nature of the organisation and so increase costs as strikes or stoppages halt production. Whatever the causes, it is a characteristic of all organisations that eventually average costs will tend to increase as output rises. The scale of production at which this happens will depend upon the type of industry. Some industries such as the Chemical Industry may be able to continue to reduce average costs until a massive scale of production is achieved. These short run average costs curves are summated to give the long run average cost curve. It is the extent of the output that an organisation can achieve before average costs begin to rise, which will determine the structure of the industry. If one producer can continue to reduce average costs while meeting the total needs of the market it is possible that a monopoly will evolve. If it can only meet part of demand, this may result in imperfect competition or oligopoly. The costs of production of the organisation are therefore crucial in determining which part of the market it will supply or the extent of demand that it will meet.

Assignment *Dave Daybreak and the Sunsets*

This year the city of Westhampton celebrates its 900th anniversary. As part of the festivities, the City Council resolves that it should hold a series of concerts reflecting the City's musical heritage. The Director of Leisure Services is given the task of promoting these concerts; and, although the Council has allocated a substantial budget for these events, it is clear that some will make considerable losses while others should prove profitable. The concerts will include early church music, medieval music, chamber music and rock and roll. One of the events which it is hoped will be profitable is a show given by Day Daybreak and the Sunsets. Dave, an ageing rock star, is a "local boy made good" and should prove to be a crowd-puller. However, the Director is wary in case crowd trouble should break out and blemish the festival, so he insists that there must be a more than adequate number of bouncers to control fans. The event is to be held in one of the Council's public halls in the city centre. The hall is quite old and not particularly safe, and so stringent conditions have to be laid down.

Under these conditions there must be at least 30 bouncers if 3,000 or fewer tickets are sold, one extra bouncer for each 20 tickets sold between 3,000 and 4,000, and one extra bouncer for each 10 extra tickets sold over 4,000. Each bouncer is paid £20 per night. The capacity of the hall is 5,000. The price of tickets is set at £3 each. The cost of heating, lighting and administrative staff for the event is £1,500 and this must be paid regardless of the number of tickets sold. Dave Daybreak and the Sunsets charge £1,000 performing fee, and £650 must be spent on hiring a PA System for the evening. It is clear that, in order to sell tickets for the concert, it must be advertised, and this can be done in three ways: on posters at a cost of 20p each; in the local papers at £50 per advert; and on the local radio at £100 per spot. The Director estimates that to attract 3,000 customers it is necessary to spend £200 on posters and £500 on newspaper ads. If local radio is used, however, more tickets can be sold, as follows:

1st radio ad sells 1,000 more tickets;

2nd radio ad sells an extra 500 tickets;

3rd radio ad sells an extra 250 tickets;

4th radio ad sells an extra 50 tickets.

Task

1. As an officer in the Leisure Services Department of the Council, advise the Director on the following:
   - what are the fixed costs of the concert and what are the variable costs?
   - how many tickets must be sold to break-even?
   - how many tickets should be sold to make the maximum profit?
   - how much advertising should be carried out?

Explain your advice in words and in the form of a break-even chart.

2. Contact any organisation which promotes social activities such as dances or concerts. This may be your students union, youth club or your employer's social and entertainments committee. Analyse any social event which they have or intend to promote. Prepare a break-even analysis to demonstrate its profitability.

Element 7.4 Financial Statements

The Purpose of Financial Statements

In this Element we will examine financial statements and in particular we will consider the Profit and Loss Account, the Balance Sheet and the Cash Flow Statement of a business. We shall see that they provide:

- management information to those running the business; and
- financial information to others such as:
  - the shareholders;
  - lenders of capital; and
  - the Inland Revenue.

We will now examine these in some detail.

The recording of financial information

The function of accounting is to provide at the end of given periods of time (usually one year) a summary of what has happened during that period, together with a statement as to how a business stands at the end of the period in terms of the assets it possesses and the liabilities it has still to pay. The summary is called a Profit and Loss Account which is always made up for a period of time, for example, Profit and Loss Account for the year ended 31st December 1992. Sometimes the Profit and Loss Account is extended into a Trading and Profit and Loss Account in order to show more detailed information about the business. The statement which usually accompanies the Profit and Loss Account is called a Balance Sheet and is prepared as at a particular point in time, for example Balance Sheet as at 31st December 1992. We will examine Profit and Loss Accounts and Balance Sheets which are known as Financial Accounts later in this Unit.

In order to be able to draw up the Financial Accounts it is necessary to have some means of recording and analysing transactions undertaken by the business as they happen on a day to day basis. The means that we use is called book-keeping and is based on double-entry principles established over the years as a result of the dual nature of business transactions. A book-keeping system should be designed which will not only provide the information required at the end of the financial year, but which will also be capable of providing information at intervals throughout the year. This information will enable the business managers to make decisions about activities of the business, and allow them to take the necessary corrective action if things are going wrong.

Before we examine book-keeping in detail it is necessary to understand some of the accounting terms which we will regularly come across from now on; these are as follows:

Assets

Assets are items of value which are owned by the business, or amounts of money which are owed to the business (for instance from customers to whom goods have been sold, which have not yet been paid for). Assets are divided into two main categories, namely Fixed Assets and Current Assets.

Fixed Assets are those assets which are acquired for permanent use in the business usually for more than one financial year. They consist of items such as Land and Buildings, which can be either Freehold or Leasehold; Plant and Machinery; Motor Vehicles; Office Furniture and Equipment. The value that these items are shown at is cost, that is how much they cost to buy, less any amounts subsequently written off by way of depreciation.

Current Assets are those assets which a business holds for a short period, usually less than one year. They consist of stock, debtors and cash at the bank or cash in hand. We will be discussing these items in detail later.

Liabilities

Liabilities are amounts of money which are owed by the business to outside parties. They can be split into long-term and short-term (current) liabilities.

Long-term liabilities are those which are not due to be paid back until after a year. They consist mainly of loans made to the business by outside parties or sometimes by the owners themselves in addition to any other capital invested.

Current liabilities consist in the main of amounts due to suppliers of goods or services to the business, which have not yet been paid for (trade creditors), and sometimes bank overdrafts which are technically repayable on demand. In the case of a business which operates as a limited company another current liability will be tax due but not yet paid.

Capital

Capital is really another long-term liability and it is represented by the amount a business owes to its owner(s). The amount is made up of the original capital invested in the business by the owners, plus any profits made by the business (for the owner(s)), less any money already paid out to the owners (drawings, dividends) and any losses made by the business. It is often difficult for students in the early stages of an introduction to accountancy to see capital as a liability but it must be remembered that it is an amount of money owed by the business to its owner(s).

Revenue income

Revenue income is the term which we use to describe the income of a business which is derived from the normal trading activities of that business. Income is mainly derived from sales of the business's product or service but other income can be derived from rent receivable, interest on investments etc.

Revenue Expenditure

Revenue expenditure consists of the expenditure which is incurred by a business on a day to day basis in the process of earning income. The types of expenditure included in this category are purchase of the product in which the business deals, or the raw material from which it is made; wages of employees; rent, rates etc. in respect of property; insurance; advertising; heating and lighting; motor vehicle running costs; etc. Any expenditure incurred in acquiring fixed assets (for instance a new vehicle) is classified as Capital Expenditure. It is the revenue income and revenue expenditure of a business which forms the nucleus of the Profit and Loss Account.

Debit

In accounting the word debit is used as a noun which means an accounting entry on the left hand side of an account; or as a verb meaning we make an entry on the left hand side of an account; e.g.

Wages Account

	£		£
Cash	3,500		

This £3,500 is a debit entry (*noun*) or we have debited (*verb*) the account with £3,500.

Credit

This is the opposite of a debit and thus denotes an entry on the right hand side of an account, or the act of making an entry on the right hand side of an account.

Armed with the above terms we can now confidently look into the subject of book-keeping: let us just summarise the main accounting terms:

Assets - fixed, current	Liabilities - long-term, short-term
	Capital
Revenue Expenditure	Revenue Income
Debit	Credit

The Principles of Book-keeping

Every business organisation should keep books of account; indeed business organisations such as limited liability companies must, by law, keep proper books of account. Nowadays it is quite common to find even comparatively small businesses keeping the accounting records on computer based systems, but it must be stressed that even such a sophisticated method as that will be based on the basic principles of double entry book-keeping. It is these basic principles which we will now consider.

The basis of any system of book-keeping is a book which is called a Ledger. The ledger consists, as does any type of book, of a number of pages, but in a ledger each page is called an Account. Each account is divided into two halves by a vertical dividing line drawn down the middle, thus giving us a Debit (left hand) and a Credit (right hand) side. Each account is given a name or a title and a distinctive number for reference purposes. The name or title will depend on the type of business it is and what degree of analysis of information the managers or owners of the business require. Every business will have suppliers of goods; other businesses from which goods are purchased on credit terms. Thus a business will need to have an account for each of its suppliers. Every transaction between the business and a particular supplier will be entered in the account of that supplier. This means that at any time it will be possible to determine how much the business owes to that particular supplier. Just as a business needs to have an account for each supplier, so too it should have one for each customer to whom it sells goods on credit. The accounts of suppliers and customers are called Personal Accounts. All other accounts are called Impersonal Accounts and these are often further sub-divided into Real or Nominal accounts. However for our purposes Impersonal (or Nominal) will suffice.

Ledgers

So we now have two types of account – Personal and Impersonal (or Nominal). It is therefore customary to keep two ledgers – a Personal ledger and a Nominal Ledger. The personal ledger is often divided into two parts – one for the accounts of suppliers (Purchase or Creditors Ledger), and one for the accounts of customers (Sales or Debtors Ledger). Summing up we can now see that there are basically three types of ledger:

- Purchase Ledger (also known as Creditors Ledger);

- Sales Ledger (also known as Debtors Ledger);
- Nominal Ledger.

The headings of accounts in the nominal ledger will represent an analysis of the income and the expenditure of the business and also of the assets (other than debtors) and liabilities (other than creditors) of the business. Examples are:

- Sales Account – which records all the sales made by the business;
- Purchases Account – which records all the purchases of goods for re-sale, or the purchase of raw materials, made by the business;
- Wages Account – which records all the wages paid by the business to its employees;
- Heat & Light Account – which records all the expenditure incurred in heating and lighting the business premises;
- Capital Account – which records the amount of the owner's capital at any time;
- Property Account – which records the amount that has been paid by the business to acquire property.

Further examples of account headings are:

- rent;
- rates;
- telephone;
- postage;
- motor expenses;
- travelling expenses;
- insurance;
- advertising;
- interest payable or receivable;
- plant and machinery;
- motor vehicles;
- fixtures and fittings; and
- loans to the business.

We will see the significance of these headings later when we look at the final accounts of a business.

The following is a typical example (but not the only example) of a ledger account ruling:

| **Debit** | | | | | **Credit** | | | | |
Date	Details	Fo.	£	p.	Date	Details	Fo.	£	p.

An explanation of the columns, which are the same on both sides, is as follows:

- *Date*: All transactions occur on a date – as a transaction is recorded in an account, the date of it is entered in this column;

- *Details*: Brief details of the type of transaction it is are entered in this column;
- *Fo.*: This means folio and is merely a reference point to where the other side of the entry is made in respect of the transaction;
- *£.p.*: This is where the monetary amount of the transaction is entered.

Another type of ledger account, with which you may be familiar as it is similar to a typical bank statement, is one which can give a running balance as each entry is made. It is quite often this type of account which is kept on computerised systems. The ruling is as follows:

			Debit		Credit		Balance	
Date	Details	Fo.	£	p.	£	p.	£	p.

This type of account is very useful for personal accounts, as the balance due to or from the other business can be identified immediately after every transaction is entered. When demonstrating the use to which ledger accounts are put we will use a simplified form of the above which will be either like this -

Debit	Credit

This is known as a T account.

or like this -

Details	Debit	Credit	Balance

Cash books

The other major book kept by an organisation will be a Cash Book. A typical ruling of a cash book (one side only) is as follows:

Date	Details	Fo.	Cash		Bank	

You will notice that it is very similar to a ledger account, with the exception that there are two columns for the monetary amounts, the use of which will be explained shortly. For any demonstration of book-keeping entries a simplified form of cash book ruling will be used as follows:

Debit			**Credit**		
	Cash	**Bank**		**Cash**	**Bank**

The basic rules for making entries in the cash book and which ought to be learned are as follows:

1. all cash received physically by the business, whether in the form of notes and coins, cheques, money orders or postal orders should be entered in the cash book on the DEBIT side in the CASH column;

2.   any payments made in cash, such as employees wages or travelling expenses, should be entered in the cash book on the CREDIT side in the CASH column;

3. any payments made by cheque should be entered in the cash book on the CREDIT side in the BANK column. This is because cheque payments directly affect the balance of money in the bank;

4. when money is paid into the bank – this involves physically taking the cash and cheques previously received (as in point 1. above) to the bank and handing it over. There are two entries to make in the cash book. The first is to enter the amount of cash paid into the bank on the DEBIT side in the BANK column, whilst the second is to enter the same amount on the CREDIT side in the CASH column. As you can see this has the effect of being a payment out of cash and a payment into the bank;

5.   if a cheque is cashed – that is exchanged at the bank for cash, the transaction is again entered in the cash book in two places – on the CREDIT side in the BANK column (A payment out of the bank) and on the DEBIT side in the CASH column (a receipt of cash);

6.   direct transfers into or out of the bank should be entered in the cash book in the BANK column on the appropriate side – DEBIT for transfers in and CREDIT for transfers out. Direct transfers include standing orders, direct debits etc.

You will see from the above that the cash book is really two accounts – one which records cash in and out, the other records amounts paid into and out of the bank.

Keeping a two-column cash book in this way dispenses with the necessity of keeping a petty cash book, since the cash column serves as a record of cash received and paid. Some businesses however prefer to keep a petty cash book for recording small amounts of cash expenditure. The petty cash book is usually a multi-column book, particularly on the payments side, in order to facilitate analysis of petty cash expenditure – an example of a petty cash book ruling is shown below:

Receipts					**Payments**				
Date	Details	Fo.	Amount	Date	Details	Fo.	Total	Motor Expenses	Postage

There can be as many columns on the payments side as the business considers necessary. Some suggested headings are stationery, travelling expenses, office expenses etc. Petty cash is usually kept on what is described as the imprest system. In this system a weekly float is agreed of say £200 – a cheque is cashed for this amount and the money given to the petty cashier – the amount is entered on the receipts side of the petty cash book and on the payments side (bank column) of the cash book. Any petty cash payments are entered in the total column on the payments side of the petty cash book and also in the appropriate analysis column (e.g. stationery). At the end of the week the book is totalled and the total payments are deducted from the total receipts to give a balance of petty cash left in the float. This should be checked with the actual amount of cash held, any differences being investigated. A cheque should then be cashed equal to the payments made, thus making the float up to the original figure again. An example is shown below.

Receipts			**Payments**			
			Total	Petrol	Postage	Stationery
From cash book	200	Expense Voucher				
		No 1	40	20	10	10
		No 2	35	25	2	8
		No 3	50	30	15	5
		Total expenditure	125	75	27	23
		Balance c/d	75			
	200		200			
Balance b/d	75					
From cash book	125					

The totals of the individual columns will be entered on the DEBIT side of:

- the Motor Expenses Account;
- the Postage Account; and
- the Stationery Account.

This will complete the double entry with regard to the petty cash book.

Making entries

Now that we have looked at the types of books which a business should keep, let us look at the entries that are made in them.

The basic rule of Double Entry Book-keeping is quite simple – it is that every business transaction is entered twice in the books of account, once on the DEBIT side of an account and once on the CREDIT side of another account. The rule arises out of the fact that every transaction has a dual effect on the business. For example, if a business spends £100,000 on the purchase of some property, the bank balance will fall by £100,000 (or the overdraft will rise) and at the same time the business will acquire an asset (which it did not have before) with a monetary value of £100,000. This dual aspect of the transaction will be recorded in the books of account by entering the £100,000 in the Property Account on the DEBIT side and also in the cash book in the Bank column on the CREDIT side. The simple rule to follow is that ALL cash received, in whatever form, should be entered on the DEBIT side of the cash book and the CREDIT side of some other account. For example, if the cash received is in respect of capital invested in the business by its owner, the credit entry will be made in the Capital Account. Let us look at a few examples of business transactions and at the entries that each one will require in the books. Each transaction will be identified by a letter of the alphabet, the same letter being used to identify the entries in the ledger accounts.

Type of transaction

A. the introduction of £50,000 capital into the business by its owner, by a direct transfer to a business bank account.

B. the purchase of property for £30,000.

C. the purchase of a motor vehicle for £10,000.

D. the purchase of goods, which will be re-sold to customers, for £8,000.

All items B to D inclusive will be paid for by cheque.

E. the sale of goods to customers for cash for £6,000.

F. the payment of wages of £2,500 in cash to employees.

G. the purchase of goods for re-sale, on credit terms from G Hope and Sons Ltd. for £7,500.

H. the sale of goods on credit terms to B. Miller for £2,800.

I. the sale of goods on credit terms to J. Lewis Ltd. for £4,500.

J. the payment of £450 by cheque to the Electricity Board for power supplied for lighting and heating.

K. the receipt of a cheque for £1,500 from B. Miller as part payment for goods previously supplied to him.

L. the payment of £4,600 cash and cheques received earlier into the bank account.

The book-keeping entries are as follows:

Dr			The Cash Book		Cr.
	Cash	**Bank**		**Cash**	**Bank**
A.Capital		50,000	B.Property		30,000
E. Sales	6,000		C.Motor Vehicles		10,000
K.B.Miller	1,500		D.Purchase		8,000
L.Cash		4,600	F.Wages	2,500	
			J.Heat and Light		450
			L.Bank	4,600	
			Balance c/fwd	400	6,150
	7,500	54,600		7,500	54,600
Balance b/fwd	400	6,150			

Notice that transactions G,H and I are not entered in the cash book – this is because those particular transactions do not involve the exchange of cash. *only money coming in or going out is to be entered in the cash book*. Notice that the totals of the debit and credit side cash columns are equal, as are the totals of the debit and credit sides of the bank columns. This is only possible in this case by inserting what are called balancing figures of £400 and £6,150 respectively to make the credit sides add up to the same as the debit sides. These two figures represent the cash that is left on the business premises after all the above transactions are completed, and the amount of money which the business has in its bank current account. The double entry for the balances is completed by entering the same figures on the debit side of each column below the totals of the previous period. These figures now become the opening figures for the next period. Remember all these transactions happen on specific dates and will thus be entered in the books in chronological order.

Dr.	Capital Account		Cr.
	£		**£**
		A.Bank	50,000

This is the other side of transaction A and is entered on the credit side of the Capital Account. Only changes in the capital of the business will be entered in this account. By turning to this account, it is possible to ascertain how much capital a business has at any time. Note that the capital of the business is £50,000, but the amount of money it has is only £6,550 (see cash book above). It is very important to remember in Accounting that Capital is not to be confused with cash. Capital is the amount a business owes to its owner. Initially the capital is the same as the cash introduced, but since that date much of the cash has been replaced by other assets.

Dr.	Property Account		Cr.
	£		£
B.Bank	30,000		

Dr.	Motor Vehicle Account		Cr.
	£		£
C.Bank	10,000		

These two accounts show how much has been spent on the acquisition of property and motor vehicles. These accounts are Asset Accounts, and the entries represent the corresponding entries to those made in the cash book.

Notice the pattern developing:

One Transaction – Two Entries – One Debit: One Credit.

This never varies.

Dr.	Purchase Account		Cr.
	£		£
D.Bank	8,000		
G.G.Hope and Sons Ltd.	7,500		
	15,500		

Dr.	Sales Account		Cr.
	£		£
		E.Cash	6,000
		H.B.Miller	2,800
		I.J.Lewis Ltd.	4,500
			13,300

These accounts show the monetary value of purchases and sales of goods. Note that only the purchase of goods specifically for the intention of re-selling them should be entered in the Purchases account. Any other purchase such as stationery, petrol etc; should be entered in the relevant expense account; stationery, motor expenses, etc. Note also transaction G – although no cash changes hands at this point, it is still considered to be an expense incurred – the corresponding credit entry will be made in the personal account of G Hope and Sons Ltd. (see next page).

As with purchases, the Sales Account should only record sales of the product which the business is set up to sell and nothing else. Also note transactions H and I; these are both credit transactions in that they will be paid for later. Nevertheless the income from these sales is deemed to have arisen at the time when the sale is made.

It is a fundamental concept in Accounting that income is deemed to arise at the point of sale, and expenditure is deemed to have been incurred at the point of purchase, irrespective of when cash is received or paid; therefore expenditure does not necessarily equate with payments and income does not necessarily equate with receipts. Notice the totals of the Purchases and Sales Account – we will discuss the significance of these figures later, but for the moment it is sufficient to remember that they represent the total purchases and the total sales for the accounting period under review.

Dr.		Wages Account		Cr.
	£			£
F.Cash	2,500			

This account shows us the amount of money expended in the payment of wages.

Dr.		G.Hope & Sons Ltd. Account		Cr.
	£			£
		G.Purchases		7,500

This account indicates how much the business owes to G. Hope and Sons Ltd. – the amount is shown as a liability.

Dr.		B.Miller Account		Cr.
	£			£
H.Sales	2,800	K.Cash		1,500
		Balance c/fwd		1,300
	2,800			2,800
Balance b/fwd	1,300			

Dr.		J.Lewis Ltd. Account		Cr.
	£			£
I.Sales	4,500			

These two accounts are personal accounts and show how much each of the business's customers owes to the business. Note that B. Miller only owes £1,300 because although he bought goods to the value of £2,800, he has actually subsequently paid £1,500 to the business, leaving £1,300 still to pay.

Dr.	Heat & Light Account		Cr.
	£		£
J.Bank	450		

Trial balance

Having completed the double entry in respect of each of the transactions listed (A to L) and where necessary totalled or balanced each account, the next step is to see if any errors have been made. This is done by listing the balances remaining on each account under the heading of Debit or Credit, to see if the totals of the two sides agree (they ought to, if everything has been entered correctly). The list of balances is called a Trial Balance and is shown below, with a description as to what type of balance each one is. If the total of the debit balances fails to agree with the total of the credit balances this indicates that some form of error has been made in the recording of the transactions in the books and must be investigated. Final Accounts cannot be correctly prepared unless the books balance.

Trial Balance

	Debit	Credit	
	£	£	
Cash in hand (from cash book)	400		Asset
Cash at bank (from cash book)	6,150		Asset
Capital		50,000	Liability
Property	30,000		Asset
Motor Vehicle	10,000		Asset
Purchases	15,500		Revenue Expense
Sales		13,300	Revenue Income
Wages	2,500		Revenue Expense
G.Hope and Sons Ltd.		7,500	Liability
B. Miller	1,300		Asset
J.Lewis Ltd.	4,500		Asset
Heat and Light	450		Revenue Expense
	70,800	70,800	

Trading and Profit And Loss Account

After extracting the Trial Balance from the books, all the revenue items are transferred to an account called the Trading and Profit and Loss Account. This is to enable the business to ascertain whether it has made a profit or a loss on its activities over a period of time. In the above business it looks as if a loss has been incurred because the total revenue expenditure (15,500 + 2,500 + 450) is £18,450 whilst the total revenue income is only £13,300, which gives an apparent loss of £5,150. However we must bear in mind another fundamental accounting concept that is revenue income should be matched with revenue expenditure for the same period of time and for the same quantity of goods. It is pointless to compare the purchase of say 30 articles against the sale of 20; the 10 articles bought but not sold should be treated as unsold stock, valued accordingly, and eliminated from the expenditure side so that the sale of 20 articles can be compared with the purchase of 20. Similarly it is pointless to compare income for 6 months against expenditure for 4 months; the two are not comparable. This concept is called the Matching or Accruals concept.

Bearing this in mind, let us assume that goods to the value of £7,000 (at cost price) remained unsold at the end of the accounting period being measured. The £7,000 is entered in a new account entitled Stock on the debit side; this account now becomes an asset account. The credit entry is made in the Trading Account and has the effect of reducing the purchases figure by the value of stock.

Let us now look at the closing entries:

Closing entries

M. Transfer Purchases to the debit side of the Trading Account.

N. Transfer Sales to the credit side of the Trading Account.

P. Debit the Stock Account credit the Trading Account with the closing stock value.

R. The balance left on Trading Account is transferred to the Profit and Loss Account as Gross Profit or   Gross Loss.

S. Transfer other expenses to the debit side of the Profit and Loss Account.

T. Calculate net profit or loss and transfer the amount to the Capital Account. A profit increases the
     capital – more money is owed to the owner. A loss reduces the capital.

Let us look at the above entries in the Accounts.

Dr.		Purchase Account		Cr.
	£			**£**
D.Bank	8,000	M.Trading Account		15,500
G.G.Hope and Sons Ltd.	7,500			
	15,500			15,500

The Account is now closed

Dr.		Sales Account		Cr.
	£			**£**
N.Trading Account	13,300	E.Cash		6,000
		H.B.Miller		2,800
		I.J.Lewis Ltd.		4,500
	13,300			13,300

The Account is now closed

Dr.	Stock Account		Cr.
	£		£
P.Trading Account	7,000		

This figure of £7,000 (Debit Balance) is an asset.

Dr.	Wages Account		Cr.
	£		£
F.Cash	2,500	S.Profit and Loss A/C	2,500

Dr.	Heat & Light Account		Cr.
	£		£
J.Bank	450	S_2.Profit and Loss A/C	450

Dr.	Trading Account		Cr.
	£		£
M.Purchases	15,500	N.Sales	13,300
R.Profit and Loss A/C* (Gross Profit)	4,800	P.Stock	7,000
	20,300		20,300

* This is the figure which makes the Trading Account balance, and is described as Gross Profit.

Dr.		Profit and Loss Account		Cr.
	£			**£**
S.Wages	2,500	R.Trading Account (Gross Profit)		4,800
S2.Heat and Light	450			
T.Net Profit (to Capital Account)**	1,850			
	4,800			4,800

** This is the figure which makes the Profit and Loss Account balance and is described as the Net Profit. The net profit is transferred to the credit side of the capital account as follows:

Dr.		Capital Account		Cr.
	£			**£**
		A.Bank		50,000
		T.Profit and Loss A/c		1,850
				51,850

Notice how all the entries in the Trading Account and in the Profit and Loss Account obey the Double Entry principle – a debit entry is matched by a credit entry elsewhere in the books and vice versa.

It has become customary in recent years to merge the Trading Account and the Profit and Loss Account into one Account and to present it in vertical format as shown on the following page.

Trading and Profit and Loss Account for the Period Ended _ _ _ _ _

	£	**£**
Sales		13,300
Cost of Sales		
Purchases	15,500	
Less: Closing Stock	7,000	8,500
Gross profit		4,800
Expenditure		
Wages	2,500	
Heat and Light	450	2,950
Net Profit		1,850

Notice how the same information is disclosed as was in the debit/credit (horizontal) format. It must also be pointed out that opening stock is part of the cost of sales figure. In the example above, there was no opening stock, but there will be in the next accounting period. Such stock will be the closing stock of the present accounting period (£7,000). The normal format for the cost of sales figure will be (using assumed figures):

	£	£
Cost of Sales		
Opening stock	7,000	
Add: Purchases	20,000	
	27,000	
Less: Closing stock	9,000	18,000

Balance sheet

After the preparation of the Trading and Profit and Loss Account by the transfer thereto of all revenue income and expenditure account totals, the remaining accounts with balances left on them will be Asset or Liability accounts and will be listed as such in what is called a Balance Sheet. A Balance Sheet is an Accounting Statement which lists assets and liabilities expressed in monetary terms. Our example is shown on the next page.

Balance Sheet As At_ _ _ _ _

	£	£
<u>Fixed Assets</u>		
Property		30,000
Motor Vehicles		<u>10,000</u>
		40,000
<u>Current Assets</u>		
Stock	7,000	
Debtors (Miller £1,300, Lewis £4,500)	5,800	
Cash at Bank	6,150	
Cash in Hand	400	
	<u>19,350</u>	
<u>Current Liabilities</u>		
Creditors	<u>7,500</u>	<u>11,850</u>
		<u>51,850</u>
<u>Capital Account</u>		
Balance at commencement of period		50,000
Add: Net Profit for the period		<u>1,850</u>
		<u>51,850</u>

Applying double entry principles

Now that we have looked at the double entry system, let us draw up a list of typical transactions and see how they are dealt with in the books:

Type of Transaction	Account to be Debited	Account to be Credited
Introduction of capital to business	Cash book	Capital
Borrowing money from the business	Cash book	Loan
Purchase of fixed assets on credit	Fixed Asset	Named Supplier
Purchase of goods for resale for cash	Purchases	Cash book
Sales of goods for cash	Cash book	Sales
Purchase of goods for resale on credit from J. Jones and Co.	Purchases	J. Jones and Co.
Sale of goods on credit to R. Smith	R. Smith	Sales
Payment of employees' wages	Wages	Cash book
Cash payment for petrol	Motor Expenses	Cash book
Invoice received for electricity	Heat and Light	Electricity Board
Payment to J. Jones and Co	J. Jones and Co	Cash book
Discount received from J.Jones and Co	J. Jones and Co	Discount received
Receipt from R. Smith	Cash book	R. Smith
Discount allowed to R. Smith	Discount allowed	R. Smith
End of year transfers:		
Sales to Trading Account	Sales	Trading Account
Purchases to Trading Account	Trading Account	Purchases
Opening stock to Trading Account	Trading Account	Stock
Closing stock to Trading Account	Stock	Trading Account
Expenses:		
Wages to Profit and Loss Account	Profit and Loss	Wages
Heat and Light to Profit and Loss Account	Profit and Loss	Heat and Light
Net Profit to Capital	Profit and Loss	Capital

This list as shown is not meant to be fully comprehensive but it establishes the principles of double entry book-keeping as far as entries in the books are concerned. You should familiarise yourself with it. From what we have looked at so far it should now be clear to you that during the course of an accounting period (usually one year) each account tells part of the story of the business's activities; it is only when all the information is collated in the Trading and Profit and Loss Account and Balance Sheet, that the full picture can be seen.

The use of day books (or journals)

From what we have seen already it should be apparent that if a business has say 100 different suppliers of goods and 2,000 customers, then the chances are that in any month there could be up to 100 transactions in respect of purchases and up to 2,000 transactions in respect of sales. The first situation would result in one entry being made in each supplier's account but 100 entries being made in the Purchases Account, whilst the latter would result in one entry being made in 2,000 individual customer's accounts and 2,000 entries being made in the Sales Account. This would tend to overload the Purchases and Sales Accounts with lots of entries.

In order to avoid this happening, businesses often keep subsidiary books called Day Books or Journals in which day to day records of sales and purchases are entered. The Day Books are totalled at the end of a month and only the monthly total is debited to the Purchases Account or credited to the Sales Account. If the business deals in more than one product the Day Books may have analysis columns to show the sales or purchases of different products. An example of a Sales Day Book or Journal is shown below, with an indication of the accounts which are debited and credited. The Purchase Day Book operates on the same principle with the entries reversed i.e. individual suppliers accounts being credited whilst Purchases Account is debited.

Example of an Analysed Sales Day Book or Journal

Date	Customer	Fo.	Total	Freezers	Cookers	Washers
May 2	Asteroid Plc*		8,500	3,500	3,000	2,000
May 6	Rochborough Co-op*		25,000	12,000	5,000	8,000
May 16	M. Crossley and Sons*		3,000	2,000	1,000	
May 20	A.C. Electrics Ltd.*		9,500		4,500	5,000
May 25	Mercury Plc*		12,000	6,000	3,000	3,000
			58,000	23,500	16,500	18,000

* Each of the above items marked with an asterisk will be entered in the individual accounts of each customer on the debit side e.g. Asteroid PLC. will have a debit entry in the account of £8,500 whilst Rochborough Co-op will have a debit entry of £25,000 etc. At the end of the month EITHER the Sales Account will be credited with £58,000 or Freezer Sales Account will be credited with £23,500; Cooker Sales Account will be credited with £26,500; and Washer Sales Account will be credited with £18,000. Often businesses will only have one Sales Account; the analysis in the Sales Day Book or Journal being used for statistical purposes rather than accounts purposes.

One final book to mention is the Transfer (or General) Journal. This book is often used when making transfers from one ledger account to another, if the transaction does not appear in either of the Day Books or the Cash Book. It shows the name of the account to be debited and the name of the account to be credited with the amount involved and a brief description of why the entry is being made. An example of a General Journal entry is if say, the purchase of a motor vehicle for £8,000 had been incorrectly debited in the Purchases Account, whereas it should have been debited in the Motor Vehicles Account. The correction of that entry would look like this:

Date	Details	Fo.	Debit	Credit
June 13	Motor Vehicle A/c		8,000	
	To Purchase A/c			8,000
	Being the correction of an amount incorrectly debited to Purchase A/c			

In the above example Motor Vehicles Account will be debited with £8,000 and Purchases Account will be credited with £8,000. This has the effect of putting the £8,000 spent on vehicles into the correct account, and reducing the amount in the Purchases Account accordingly.

Other books which ought to be kept include, but not necessarily for every type of business:

- a *Wages Book* in which the wages of employees are calculated and entered before being entered in the books of account proper;

- a *Plant Register* in which details of individual machines or other assets are kept. The balances on these individual accounts should agree with the total entered in the respective Fixed Asset Account in the Nominal Ledger;

- a *Share Register* in which details of individual shareholders and their holdings are kept. Again the balances on the individual shareholders accounts should agree in total with the Share Capital Account in the Nominal Ledger;

It must be stressed that limited companies must, by law, keep a Share Register. Sometimes it is known as a Register of Members.

Book-keeping errors

No chapter on double entry book-keeping would be complete without mentioning the types of error that can be made. Some errors will cause the Trial Balance to have different debit and credit totals, others won't.

The types of error which affect the Trial Balance are as follows:

- *a one sided entry*. An amount is entered on one side of an account, but the corresponding entry is not made on the other side. The difference will be the amount of the transaction;

- *an entry made twice on one side in error*. For example, a sale on credit to a customer being credited correctly to the Sales Account, and also being credited incorrectly to the Customers Account. The difference will be twice the amount of the transaction;

- *a transposition of a figure*. An amount of say £5,960 is entered on the debit side of one account, but is entered on the credit side of another account as £9,560. The difference will be the difference between the two figures. Transposition error differences always divide by 9, but they are difficult to spot;

- *an addition error in an Account or in a Day Book*. This is self explanatory and should be obvious. If an account is incorrectly added, the balance will be incorrect.

Types of error which do not affect the Trial balance are very difficult to spot and include such errors as:

- *complete omission of a transaction;*

- *entering one side of a transaction in the wrong account.* (As seen above in the Transfer Journal correction). This type of error is more frequently found in entering personal accounts, e.g. an amount which should be debited to say A. Jones & Co Ltd. is debited to A Jones & Sons in error.

The latter type of error is often not discovered until A. Jones & Sons are asked for payment of the amount due, and write back saying that such an amount is not represented by the value of goods sent to them.

Understand and Interpret Financial Statements

Most business organisations fall into one of four categories:

- sole trader;
- partnership;
- limited liability company;
- local authorities.

In addition to the above, there are some non-profit making organisations, such as Clubs, Associations, Societies etc. set up for the benefit of members wishing to indulge in specific activities e.g. golf, cricket, squash etc.

In this part of the Unit the emphasis will be on the first four types of organisation. To begin with, it is important to appreciate the major differences between them.

Sole trader

A sole trader is a business owned and run by one person. It may be a retail shop such as a newsagent and tobacconist or a business which provides a service e.g. a plumber, electrician, hairdresser etc.

The owner has to provide the finance to set up and run the business, although quite frequently borrowing from outside sources may be necessary.

Each year the owner will prepare statements which will show:

- how much profit the business has earned (revenue income less revenue expenditure);
- the value of its fixed and current assets, how much is owed to outside parties, and how much is owed to the owner by way of capital.

The owner of this type of business is personally liable for all debts incurred by the business, and is also personally liable for any income tax due in respect of profits earned from the business.

Note: It is not the business which is taxed, it is the owner.

The owner of such a business is responsible to no other person than himself/herself.

He/she makes all the necessary decisions about further investment in fixed assets, expenditure, etc. and about how much of the profit to leave in the business and how much to take out.

Partnership

A partnership is a business which is financed and run by two or more persons. It may consist of a husband and wife, father and son, brothers, sisters, or merely business acquaintances. In a partnership, each of the partners should contribute some of the capital required by the business, and each of them will be entitled to a share of the profits.

The essence of any business partnership is agreement. It is therefore advantageous for a formal partnership agreement to be drafted. It is preferable that a partnership agreement should be in writing, but there is no law which specifically requires it. If partners agree verbally to vary any terms of a written agreement, it is perfectly valid for them to do so providing that they all agree freely with such variations. A partnership agreement (verbal or written) should cover the following:

- how much capital each of the partners is to contribute to the business;
- what proportion of the business profit each partner is to receive.
- whether any interest should be allowed on partners' capital or current accounts, and if so, at what rate;
- whether any interest should be charged on drawings or debit balances on current accounts;
- whether any partner should receive a salary for work done on behalf of the business.

If there is no written agreement and partners are not able to agree verbally on some issues then the provisions of the *Partnership Act* 1890 will apply. Briefly these are:

- profits or Losses are to be shared equally between the partners;
- no interest is to be allowed on capital account balances nor charged on drawings or debit balances on current accounts;
- no partner is to receive any salary;
- interest is to be paid at the rate of 5% on any loans made to the business by any partner in excess of the amount of capital required from him/her.

In any business partnership, each of the partners is entitled to enter into any contract on behalf of the business, but must also be prepared to be personally liable for the debts of the business, even though not specifically incurred by him/her. In the event of the business ceasing to operate, any final deficit on a partner's capital account has to be made good by that particular partner unless he/she is insolvent and cannot pay, in which case it has to be borne by the remaining partners.

Each partner will be personally liable for any income tax payable based on his/her share of the partnership profits.

> *Note: As with the sole trader, it is not the business which is taxed, it is the individual partners.*

Limited liability companies

Limited Liability Companies in the United Kingdom were developed as a business concept directly as a result of the late eighteenth and nineteenth century industrial revolution. Greater investment in business ventures was required to meet the demands of technological change. The idea grew that if many people could be persuaded to invest relatively small amounts of money in a viable business venture, it should be possible to raise more money than if very few people were to invest larger sums. In order to persuade people to invest in business ventures of this type, they had to be given some incentive and this took the form of limited personal liability.

It should be clearly understood what limited liability means. It means that the liability of an individual investing money in a business is limited to the amount that he/she has either already contributed to the business, or has agreed to contribute when first investing. It does not mean that an individual cannot lose money but it does restrict the amount of money that can be lost.

The creation of a limited company requires that there be at least two persons who are prepared to take a share of the company's capital, but often there are more than two. Indeed in some of the larger public companies there may be thousands of investors.

There are two main sources of finance which are available for limited companies: these are:

1.   the issue of shares to those interested in investing in the company as owners;

2.   borrowing, usually by means of an issue of Debenture Stock which does not grant ownership of the company to the lenders in any way.

Issue of Shares

The capital requirement of a company is divided into shares of a specific amount. Investors are invited to apply for as many shares as they require, and must enclose with their application a specified amount of money sufficient to cover the number of shares applied for. Shares are then allotted to applicants who must then pay a further specified sum required by the company on allotment. The amount due on allotment may be the total sum remaining due in respect of the shares or it may be part of it, with the balance due at some future time. It must be stressed that quite often an applicant for shares does not always receive the exact number of shares applied for, a situation brought about by excessive applications being made.

Looking at a specific example

Suppose a company requires £1,000,000 capital. Its requirement may be divided into one million shares of £1 each, two million shares of 50p each, four million shares of 25p each, or 200,000 shares of £5 each, or any other combination of shares and value considered necessary. Taking the first option as an example, 1,000,000 shares of £1 each may be offered for sale on the basis of 25p payable with application, 25p payable on allotment, and 50p payable at some future date. If someone applies for 5,000 shares then £1,250 will be enclosed with the application; £1,250 will be due on allotment; and £2,500 will be due at some time in the future. If the same person was only allotted say 3,000 shares, then only £250 would be due on allotment (£1,250 having been received with the application) and £1,500 due at the later date. The liability of the applicant would be limited to £5,000, or in the second circumstance £3,000. Any amount due at any point in time in respect of an issue of shares is described as Called up Share Capital, and any amount paid is described as Paid up Share Capital. These two should be equal to each other.

Shares in a limited company may be divided into two basic types, Ordinary Shares and Preference Shares. To appreciate the major difference between them you should understand the concept of profit distribution. The reward that shareholders get for their investment in a company is a share of the profit in the form of dividend. Preference shares carry a fixed rate of dividend (e.g. 8%, 10% etc.), which is payable before the dividend in respect of Ordinary Shares; whereas ordinary share dividend may fluctuate from year to year depending on the level of profits available.

Ordinary shares confer the right to vote at general meetings of the company, whereas preference shares under normal circumstances don't. The relationship between the two types of share and borrowings was discussed earlier in the context of capital gearing.

Borrowings

Limited companies may from time to time require more funds for additional investment in fixed assets or some other form of expansion. The company's management may decide to borrow the money rather than issue further shares which may either put an additional burden on existing shareholders or dilute the value of their holding. Such borrowing is likely to be by means of an issue of Debentures. Debentures are formal acknowledgements of debts due by a company in respect of loans made to it. They are loans and as such carry the right to interest at an agreed rate. The difference between debenture interest and share dividend is very important and should be clearly understood. Interest is an expense which must be paid and which reduces the profits of the company by being charged in the Profit and Loss Account, whereas dividend is a distribution (sharing out) of the profits.

Management

Because there are potentially thousands of shareholders in a limited company, it is not possible to allow them to make day to day decisions about company matters. The management of a company is therefore vested in a Board of Directors, elected by the shareholders (members). The Board is responsible for the efficient running of the company on behalf of the members. To make this possible the Board will appoint professional staff to carry out the routine daily activities of the business. All limited companies must have the annual accounts audited (checked) by an independent auditor, who acts on behalf of and reports to the members. Ordinary Shareholders are entitled to attend, and vote at the Annual General Meeting of a company.

Limited Companies are taxed as a corporate body on the profits earned, before any other distribution of profit can be made. Limited Company Taxation is done by means of assessing an amount due from the company by way of Corporation Tax.

Financial Statements

The first three types of organisation discussed above are very similar in that they are all businesses which are intended to provide profits for the benefit of the owners. Therefore each one should produce annual statements of account which show:

- how much profit or loss is made;
- assets owned by the business with the values ascribed to them, or amounts owing to the business by outside parties;
- amounts owing by the business to outside parties (liabilities);
- owners' capital.

These statements are common to all businesses. However Limited Companies must produce additional statements to show the movement of cash in and out, together with Reports of Directors and Auditors. Limited Companies fall into one of two categories. They are Private Limited Companies (Ltd.) and Public Limited Companies (Plc.). It is the latter which is used as the model for detailed explanations of the information contained in the financial statements.

Financial statements of limited liability companies must, by law, be prepared annually and must conform to certain standards of presentation specified by the *Companies Act* 1985. Each financial year a limited company must produce a set of accounts which are published and are available for public inspection. These accounts consist of:

- a Profit and Loss Account (including appropriate explanatory notes and additional information required by the Act);
- a Balance Sheet (also including appropriate explanatory notes and additional information required by the Act);
- a Cash Flow Statement;
- a Director's Report;
- an Auditor's Report.

In the demonstration model used, a Balance Sheet prepared in the standard format required by the *Companies Act* 1985 will be shown, but the Profit and Loss Account will be in the traditional format required by management; the reason for this is it is easier to see the make-up of the Profit and Loss Account when presented in the traditional format and to see how it relates to the book-keeping system. Later in the Unit we will see the Profit and Loss Account reproduced in the standard format.

In addition to the *Companies Act* 1985 laying down the required format for accounts, there are also Statements of Standard Accounting Practice (SSAP's) which have been drawn up by the Professional Accountancy bodies and which cover particular aspects of accounts and their presentation (such as stock valuation, depreciation, deferred tax etc.). SSAP's are being replaced by financial reporting standards (FRS), the first of which requires a cash flow statement to be published with the accounts of limited companies (FRS 1). Exemption from publishing a cash flow statement is granted to small companies and certain wholly owned subsidiaries.

An example of a set of financial accounts is shown on the following pages. It is for a public limited company Broadwood Distributors plc., which is engaged in the wholesale trade and it is this company which will be used to explain financial statements.

These accounts will be examined in detail beginning with the Profit and Loss Account.

The profit and loss account

The Profit and Loss Account is headed, and is always stated as being for a specific period of time (for example Year ended 31st August 1992). This means that the Account is a summary of the trading activities of the company, in terms of its income and expenditure for the period commencing on 1st September 1991 and ending on 31st August 1992. Notice that the account also shows figures relating to the previous year: this is to enable comparisons to be made between the current year and the previous year. We have see earlier how such comparisons can be made. The Profit and Loss Account is drawn up from information obtained from the company's book-keeping system.

Turnover (£36,400,000)

This is the amount of income derived from selling the product or products in which the company deals. It does not necessarily mean the amount of cash collected, because sales are often made on credit. Income is deemed to arise from sales at the time when the sale is made and not when the cash is received.

Cost of sales (£27,300,000)

This figure represents the net cost of buying the products which have been sold during the same period of time, and consists of three basic items:

Opening stock (£3,620,000)

This is the value of the stock which had not been sold by the end of the previous year, and is therefore part of the cost of goods sold in the current year.

Purchases (£27,860,000)

This is the cost of buying goods for resale during the current year. Purchases do not include the purchase of any items which are not for resale (such as stationery etc.). In some businesses, which are involved in manufacturing, purchases will refer to the purchase of the raw material used for the manufacture of the finished product which is to be sold. In the business which we are looking at purchases simply means the expenditure incurred on goods bought for resale.

Closing stock (£4,180,000)

This is the value of goods bought for resale which have not been sold, and they are thus still held in stock. The value of these goods at cost price is deducted from the purchase figure so that the cost of goods sold equates with the income derived from the sale of those goods. This closing stock will of course be the opening stock of the following year. It also appears on the Balance Sheet as an asset, as will be seen later.

To summarise, opening stock plus purchases minus closing stock equals cost of sales.

Broadwood Distributors plc.

Profit and Loss Account for the year ended 31st August 1992

1991		£'000	£'000
33,100	Turnover		36,400
	Cost of Sales:		
3,130	Stock as at 1st September 1991	3,620	
25,815	Purchases	27,860	
28,945		31,480	
3,620	Less: Stock as at 31st August 1992	4,180	27,300
25,325			
7,775	Gross Profit		9,100
	Add: Other Income		
100	Rents Received	137	
10	Investment Income	22	
690	Discount Received	836	995
8,575			10,095
	Less: Expenditure		
6,460	Wages & Salaries	7,110	
440	Directors' Remuneration	475	
75	Heating & Lighting	80	
40	Rates	50	
150	Advertising	130	
25	Carriage Outwards	25	
100	Motor Running Expenses	110	
12	Telephone	15	
16	Printing & Stationery	18	
22	Insurance	27	
18	Audit & Accountancy Fees	20	
2	Bank Charges	5	
130	Debenture Interest	130	
80	Bad Debts Written off	100	
-	Increase in Provision for Doubtful Debts	55	
320	Depreciation of Fixed Assets	290	
30	Repairs and Renewals	35	
75	Miscellaneous Expenditure	70	
7,995			8,745
580	Net Profit for the year before tax		1,350
165	Provision for Corporation Tax		390
415	Net Profit for the year after tax		960
	Less: Appropriations		
55	Preference Share Dividend Paid	55	
-	Interim Ordinary Share Dividend Paid	200	
280	Final Ordinary Share Dividend Proposed	250	505
335			
80	Retained Profit for the year		455
50	Transfer to General Reserve		400
30			55
45	Balance brought forward from previous year		75
75	Balance to be carried forward		130

Gross profit (£9,100,000)

This figure represents the difference between sales revenue and cost of sales; it is the profit earned on trading, before deduction of other expenses (overheads) essential to the running of the business. It effectively reflects the difference between the selling price and the cost price of the goods being traded.

Broadwood Distributors plc.

Balance Sheet as at 31st August 1992

	1992		1991	
	£'000	£'000	£'000	£'000
Fixed Assets:				
Tangible Fixed Assets (Note 1)		2,632		2,190
Intangible Fixed Assets (Note 2)		168		210
Investments at Cost		200		100
		3,000		2,500
Current Assets:				
Stock (Note 3)	4,180		3,620	
Debtors (Note 4)	4,655		3,610	
Prepayments	25		20	
Cash at Bank	140		210	
Cash in Hand	30		25	
	9,030		7,485	
Creditors: Amounts due within one year (Note 5)	4,620		3,780	
Current Assets Less Current Liabilities		4,410		3,705
Total Assets Less Current Liabilities		7,410		6,205
Creditors: Amounts due after more than one year (Note 6)		1,280		1,280
		6,130		4,925
Share Capital & Reserves (Note 7)				
Issued and Fully Paid Share Capital		3,000		2,500
Share Premium Account		250		–
Property Re-valuation Reserve		150		150
General Reserve		2,600		2,200
Profit and Loss Account		130		75
		6,130		4,925

Notes to the Balance Sheet

1. Tangible fixed assets are as follows:

	31st August 1992			31st August 1991		
	Cost or Valuation	Dep'n	NBV	Cost or Valuation	Dep'n	NBV
	£'000	£'000	£'000	£'000	£'000	£'000
Freehold Land & Buildings	1,750	–	1,750	1,200	–	1,200
Plant & Equipment	650	354	296	560	280	280
Motor Vehicles	990	540	450	940	390	550
Office Equipment	230	94	136	230	70	160
	3,620	988	2,632	2,930	740	2,190

No fixed assets were disposed of during the year ended 31st August 1992.

Freehold land and buildings had been re-valued in 1989 from £1,050,000 to £1,200,000.

2. Intangible fixed assets consist of Goodwill and Research and Development Expenditure of which
   £42,000 was written off during the year ended 31st August 1992.

3. Stock is valued at cost or net realisable value, whichever is the lower.

4. Debtors are made up as follows:

	31st August 1992	31st August 1991
	£'000	£'000
Gross Debtors	4,900	3,800
Less: Provision for Doubtful Debts	245	190
	4,655	3,610

5. Creditors: Amounts due within one year are made up as follows:

	31st August 1992	31st August 1991
	£'000	£'000
Trade Creditors	3,950	3,290
Accruals	45	40
Current Taxation	375	170
Proposed Dividend	250	280
	4620	3780

6. Creditors: Amounts due after more than one year are made up as follows:

	31st August 1992	31st August 1991
	£'000	£'000
13% Debenture stock	1,000	1,000
Provision for Deferred Tax	280	280
	1,280	1,280

7. The authorised capital is £5,000,000 divided into 8,000,000 Ordinary Shares of 50 pence each and
   1,000,000 11 per cent Preference Shares of £1 each. The Issued Share Capital is as follows:

	31st August 1992	31st August 1991
	£'000	£'000
Ordinary Shares of 50 pence each, fully paid	2,500	2,000
11% preference shares of £1 each, fully paid	500	500

There had been an issue of Ordinary Shares during the year ended 31st August 1992.

Other income (£995,000)

This figure represents income earned from activities other than sales. In this particular business it is made up of Rents Receivable (which arise as a result of the business having property surplus to its own requirements and renting such property out); Investment Income (which arises from investments purchased by the company); and Discount Received (which are cash discounts allowed to the company by suppliers, usually for prompt settlement of amounts due). It should be said here, that investments can mean anything from the purchase of shares in another company to deposits in interest earning bank or building society accounts.

Expenditure (£8,745,000)

This represents the total amount of expenditure, which is of a revenue nature, incurred by the company during the financial year. Most of it is self explanatory (by the description) i.e.. rates, heating and lighting, etc. but some of the expenditure shown needs to be further explained. This is highlighted below.

Wages and salaries (£7,110,000)

This is the total amount of expenditure incurred by the business in paying its employees during the year. This expenditure includes the company's contributions to pension schemes and to the State National Insurance Scheme. In order to record the amount spent in this area it is necessary for the company to keep a salaries and wages book, and also to install a system for recording the time worked by the employees. It is usual to find that salaries and wages records are computerised.

Directors remuneration (£475,000)

This is the total expenditure incurred by the company in remunerating its directors. Directors are persons who have been elected to run the business on behalf of the shareholders. For this they may be paid salaries (if they are working directors), commission etc. They may also be paid fees for attending board meetings, where decisions are made about the management of the company. Directors' Remuneration may also include benefits in kind which they may be given such as the use of a company car, rent free accommodation, contributions to a pension fund made by the company for their benefit, and so on.

Carriage outwards (£25,000)

This is the cost to the business of transporting goods to the customers, usually by outside contractors such as British Rail. It may also represent the cost of running it's own delivery service. Usually however the cost of running a delivery service will be shown as part of the wages and salaries (for drivers, etc.) and motor running expenses.

Motor running expenses (£110,000)

This represents the costs of running motor vehicles such as, delivery vehicles, salesmen's cars, directors' cars, etc. as opposed to the cost of buying them. Such running costs include petrol, oil, insurance, road fund tax, and maintenance, but not usually depreciation (see later).

Audit and accountancy fees (£20,000)

Every company which has the benefit of limited liability for its members must appoint an Auditor. It is the Auditor's responsibility to verify the accuracy of the accounts presented to the shareholders. He is appointed by the shareholders and is responsible to them. He reports on the stewardship function of the board of directors, and if there are any major discrepancies he must report on them in his report which is attached to the accounts (see later). An auditor receives a fee for the work which he does, which is negotiated with the company in advance. The auditor may also undertake some accountancy work such as preparation of Final Accounts, Tax Computations etc. for which he is remunerated separately.

Debenture interest (£130,000)

Debentures are loans made to the company. Unlike shares they do not grant rights of ownership in the company. In common with most loans, debentures carry interest at a fixed rate. In Broadwood Distributors plc. the debentures carry interest at 13 per cent per annum, and since there is £1m in debenture stock, the interest paid on this amount is £130,000.

Bad debts written off (£100,000)

Sometimes, quite inadvertently, a company may sell goods on credit to a customer who ends up not being able to pay for them. When this situation arises, if the company were to continue to show the customer as an asset (i.e. an amount due to the company), it would be overstating the value of its assets and thus overstating the value of the business. The debt of such a customer should therefore be written off as a loss, and this is what the above figure represents.

Increase in provision for doubtful debts (£55,000)

A provision is an amount set aside to meet a specific known future liability (the exact amount of which need not be known), or a specific known or anticipated reduction in value of an asset. A provision is created by making a debit entry in the Profit and Loss Account and a credit entry in the Provision Account. The same is done to increase a provision. If a provision is required against the value of an asset, it is usual to deduct the amount of the provision from the value of the asset shown in the Balance Sheet (see note 4 in notes to the Balance Sheet). A provision for doubtful debts should be considered necessary if the management of the company is of the opinion that there may be debtors of the business who are potentially bad debts. In the business we are looking at, there is a provision for doubtful debts of £190,000 at 31st August 1991. This has been increased by £55,000 in the year to 31st August 1992, and therefore at 31st August 1992, stands at £245,000. You should get into the habit of looking at the Profit and Loss Account and the Balance Sheet as linked statements. The increase in provision for doubtful debts is a useful example of how the two statements can be linked. The effect of making such a provision is to take the potential future loss into account in the current financial year. This is an application of the concept of prudence, which will be discussed later.

Depreciation of fixed assets (£290,000)

Fixed Assets consist of items such as Land and Buildings, Plant and Equipment, Motor Vehicles, Office Equipment, etc. They are acquired for use in the business over a number of years. The cost of acquiring them should therefore be spread over the number of years during which the assets are expected to be of use to the business in helping to generate revenue income. This spreading of the cost is achieved by creating a Provision for Depreciation Account and building it up by annual amounts being transferred from the Profit and Loss Account. In Broadwood Distributors Plc. the depreciation provided in the year amounted to £290,000. If you look at note 1 attached to the Balance Sheet, you will see an analysis of the fixed assets as at 31st August 1992 and as at 31st August 1991. The analysis is broken down into types of assets and also into the original cost of the assets (or re-valuation in the case of Land and Buildings), the Provision for Depreciation in respect of the assets, and the Net Book Value of the assets (NBV), which is the difference between cost and depreciation. You will see, by looking at the totals, that the company has spent £690,000 on the acquisition of new fixed assets between 31st August 1991 and 31st August 1992 (£3,620,000 minus £2,930,000). The provision for Depreciation has increased by £248,000 (£988,000 minus £740,000). This, together with the £42,000 written off goodwill and research and development expenditure makes up the amount of £290,000 debited in the Profit and Loss Account. Where depreciation is concerned you will always find one years charge in the Profit and Loss Account, and the total provision to date in the Balance Sheet. Again it is useful to recognise the link between the Profit and Loss Account and the Balance Sheet.

How is depreciation calculated?

Suppose an asset costs £10,000, is expected to be of use to the business for 5 years and will then be worth £1,000 in second-hand sales value. An easy method of calculating depreciation is to deduct the anticipated residual value (£1,000) from the cost (£10,000) and then to divide the remainder (£9,000) by the number of years anticipated usefulness (5). This gives an annual amount (£1,800) to be charged for depreciation. Each year the Profit and Loss Account will be debited with £1,800 and the Provision for Depreciation Account will be credited with the same amount, until after five years the Provision Account will stand at £9,000 which when deducted from the original cost of the asset (£10,000) will give a net book value of £1,000 (the estimated residual value). This method is known as the straight line method and consists of applying the same percentage (in this case 18 per cent) of original cost to each year.

An alternative way is to apply a higher percentage but to the previous year's net book value; thus the charge for depreciation will get smaller each year as the asset reduces in value. This method is known as the reducing balance method. A comparison of the two methods is shown on the following page:

	Straight Line Method	Reducing Balance Method
Rate to be applied	18 %	40 %
	£	£
Cost of Asset Year 1	10,000	10,000
Depreciation Year 1	1,800	(40%) 4,000
Net Book Value	8,200	6,000
Depreciation Year 2	1,800	(40%) 2,400
Net Book Value	6,400	3,800
Depreciation Year 3	1,800	(40%) 1,520
Net Book Value	4,600	2,280
Depreciation Year 4	1,800	(40%) 912
Net Book Value	2,800	1,368
Depreciation Year 5	1,800	(40%) 547
Net Book Value	1,000	821

You will see that the reducing balance method is not quite as accurate as the straight line method but it is easier to apply, and can continue to be applied even after the five years is over, whereas to continue to apply the straight line method at the same rate as before would reduce the asset to – £800 at the end of the 6th year. One final word on depreciation; it is, at best, an estimate. The only thing known is the cost of the asset; its life is estimated and so is its residual value. The net book values of assets shown in the Balance Sheet are not necessarily the actual value of the assets, since the true value is equivalent to what any other business would be prepared to pay for them. If you look at the example above, at the end of year 2 the value of the asset using one basis of depreciation is £6,400, whereas the value using the other basis is £3,800, yet they are both valid methods of calculating depreciation. Choosing a method of depreciation is thus essentially subjective.

Net profit for the year before tax (£1,350,000)

This represents Gross Profit (£9,100,000) plus other revenue income (£995,000) less total revenue expenditure (£8,745,000), and shows the net profit earned during the year on the trading activities of the business.

Provision for corporation tax (£390,000)

Every limited company is liable to pay Corporation Tax, based on profits earned. At the time of preparing the Accounts it is not usually known exactly what the tax liability will be. The company must therefore make a provision for the liability in the Accounts by estimating how much tax will need to be paid. This estimate may not necessarily be the final agreed figure, but that may take some time after the year end to determine. In the Accounts of Broadwood Distributors plc., £390,000 is provided for in the Profit and Loss Account but the liability shown in the Balance Sheet (Note 5) is £375,000. This means that £15,000 had been under provided in previous years. Corporation Tax is payable nine months after the date of the Balance Sheet (1st June in this case), or when it is finally agreed with the Inland Revenue, whichever comes later.

Net profit for the year after tax (£960,000)

This is self-explanatory, in that it is the net profit remaining after providing for corporation tax. This figure represents the net amount earned for the owners of the company (the shareholders).

Appropriations (£505,000)

Appropriations of profit are distributions. Shareholders receive dividends on their shares as a reward for investing in the company. Note that some of the dividend is paid and some is not yet paid (proposed). There are two types of shares in this company, namely Ordinary Shares and Preference Shares. In Broadwood Distributors plc. the Preference Shares carry a fixed dividend rate of 11 per cent and so the dividend in respect of these is £55,000 and can be paid; such dividend is usually paid half-yearly but not necessarily so. Ordinary Share Dividend (£450,000) is not paid at a fixed rate, and is not usually decided upon until it is finally known how much profit has been earned by the company. However if it is anticipated that the company will make a profit, it is quite common to pay an interim dividend part of the way through the year, which is what has happened in the case of Broadwood Distributors plc. The actual rate of dividend is £450,000 expressed as a percentage of £2,500,000 which is 18 per cent. Of this amount 8 per cent has already been paid as interim dividend, leaving 10 per cent yet to be paid as the final dividend. Note that the final dividend, being only proposed, is also shown as a liability in the balance sheet (Note 5).

Retained profit for the year (£455,000)

This amount represents the part of the profit earned which the company has kept back. It is still shown in the balance sheet as a liability, because even though it has not been paid to them, it belongs to the shareholders. The company has earned this profit for the benefit of its owners, therefore from the point of view of the company, it is a liability due to the owners.

Transfer to general reserve (£400,000)

All profits earned by a company and not distributed either as taxes or dividends, are classed as reserves. A transfer from the Profit and Loss Account (which is itself a reserve) to a general reserve is merely a book entry and is possibly a matter of convenience in order to avoid having unnecessarily large amounts in the Profit and Loss Account.

Balance brought forward from previous year (£75,000)

This is the amount that was left in the Profit and Loss Account, after all appropriations had been made, in respect of the previous year. When this is added to the amount left in the Profit and Loss Account in respect of the present year (£55,000), it gives the amount to be carried forward to the next year (£130,000), which also appears in the balance sheet under the general heading of reserves.

The balance sheet

The Balance Sheet is a list of assets and liabilities expressed in monetary terms. It is prepared at a specific time point, the last day of the company's financial year, and shows Total Assets less Total External Liabilities which should equal Total Capital Invested plus Undistributed Profits. Notice that for the balance sheet, the comparative figures (those for 31st August 1991) are shown alongside the current year's figures. This is done merely to demonstrate a possible alternative way of showing comparable figures. Let us now look at the balance sheet of Broadwood Distributors plc. in detail.

Tangible fixed assets (£2,632,000)

This figure represents the total net book value (cost, less depreciation) of all of the company's tangible fixed assets. We have already discussed the effect that depreciation has on the fixed asset value. One point that perhaps needs to be clarified is the analysis of the assets. Three of the headings are self-explanatory; Land and Buildings, Motor Vehicles and Office Equipment, but the other, Plant and Equipment probably needs further explanation. The term Plant and Equipment would usually refer to machinery used in the process of manufacture, however in the case of Broadwood Distributors plc., which is not a manufacturing company, it would refer to such items as lifting equipment, fork lift trucks, storage equipment, refrigeration equipment and so on. Office Equipment will include such items as desks, chairs, computers, word processors and filing cabinets. Motor Vehicles will consist of delivery vans, salesmen's cars etc.

Intangible fixed assets (£168,000)

Goodwill is an intangible asset, in that it has had to be paid for and yet there is nothing tangible to represent it. It exists because of the reputation of a business possibly acquired by Broadwood Distributors plc. in the past. In the case of limited companies, goodwill should only appear in the balance sheet if it has been paid for. However in a partnership it is customary to value goodwill when a change in the partnership occurs due to the retirement or the admission of a partner or to a change in the profit-sharing ratio. Often in partnership the goodwill is adjusted between the partners at the time of the change and thus never appears in the balance sheet. Goodwill should be written off as soon as possible.

Research and Development costs are another example of an intangible asset. These costs cover expenditure incurred on researching and developing new or better products, and they should be written off as soon as possible. However if the benefit to be gained by the development will not accrue until the future it is permissible to carry the expenditure incurred in the development forward as an intangible asset. It is unlikely that Broadwood Distributors plc. would incur such research and development expenditure on product development, since it is not a manufacturing company. Its research and development expenditure is more likely to be in respect of better storage or distribution facilities.

Investments (£200,000)

These will either be in respect of surplus cash from time to time invested in the shares of other companies or placed on deposit in banks or other financial institutions, or investments in companies which have become subsidiary companies of Broadwood Distributors plc. Investments will be shown at cost, less any amount deemed necessary to be written off. Investments should never be included in the balance sheet at Market Value but the latter should be mentioned in a note attached to the balance sheet, if significantly different from cost. This is to ensure that users of the accounts are made aware of possible gains or losses made in respect of investments.

Stock (£4,180,000)

This is the closing stock of goods, which the company has purchased but not sold. Stock should always be valued at cost or net realisable value (the value at which the stock could be sold), whichever is the lower. Stock should never be valued at selling price (unless selling price has for some reason fallen below cost price) since this would mean that the profit element contained in the purchase and sale of goods would be anticipated before being earned. This would go against the accounting concept of prudence.

Debtors (£4,655,000)

This figure represents the net amount due to the company as at 31st August 1992 (after deduction of any provision for doubtful debts) from customers who have bought goods from the company on credit terms. The reason that debtors are shown as an asset is that because they owe money to the company they have a value. The value is the amount they owe which is derived from sales made to them. At the point of sale, the income is deemed to have arisen, although the cash has not been collected. Income generates assets and therefore if the assets generated are not cash, then they must be something else, which in the case of sales on credit are debtors.

Prepayments (£25,000)

In every business certain expenses (e.g. Insurance, Rates, Motor Vehicle Road Fund Tax etc.) are payable in advance. For example rates are payable on or immediately after 1st April in any year. The rates so paid may be for the half year to 30th September or for the full year to the following 31st March. In either case, since the company's year end is 31st August, the portion paid for September 1992 or for the period September 1992 to March 1992 should not be entered in the Profit and Loss Account for the year ended 31st August 1992 as an expense, since it is not an expense for that year. Such portion is therefore deducted from the amount paid in respect of rates, thus reducing the expense item shown in the Profit and Loss Account. The same figure is shown in the balance sheet under the heading prepayments. Prepayments are very similar to debtors, in that at the date of the balance sheet, the person or organisation to whom the payment has been made in respect of a date in the future, technically owes that amount to the business and would be expected to repay it if for some reason the service paid for did not materialise.

Cash at bank (£140,000; Cash in hand £30,000)

These two items are self-explanatory, they simply represent the amount of cash held by the business at 31st August 1992 – some of it in a bank current account (£140,000), and some of it on the company premises (£30,000). The latter will be amounts collected from customers remaining unbanked.

Creditors: amounts due within one year (£4,620,000)

These are represented by amounts of money which Broadwood Distributors plc. will have to pay out of company funds within the following year. Now let us look at these amounts as broken down and analysed in note 5 to the balance sheet.

Trade creditors (£3,950,000)

This is the amount of money owed to other business organisations which have supplied goods on credit terms to Broadwood Distributors Plc. and for which payment has not been made.

Accruals (£45,000)

Accruals are amounts owing for goods or services supplied which have not been invoiced by the suppliers. An example is electricity. The Electricity Board invoice customers on a quarterly basis, so for example,if the electricity account is rendered for the quarter ending 30th September 1992, by the time the accounts are prepared for 31st August 1992 an estimate will need to be made for electricity consumed during July and August. This estimate will be converted into a monetary amount and added to the electricity expense (in the Profit Loss Account) and shown as an accrual (an amount due to be paid for goods or services supplied, but which has not been invoiced) in the balance sheet.

Current taxation (£375,000)

This has already been discussed above in respect of the provision for the year made in the Profit and Loss Account. However it is worth having a look at the way in which the tax account works. At 31st August 1991 (previous year) the company owed £170,000 in tax. This amount must have been underestimated by £15,000 because £390,000 was provided in the current year's Profit and Loss Account, but only £375,000 is showing as outstanding by 31st August 1992. Perhaps it would be a good idea to show this in the Corporation Tax Account as follows:

Corporation Tax Account

		£			£
1/6/92*	Cash Paid	185,000	1/9/91	Balance B/fwd	170,000
31/8/92	Balance C/fwd	375,000	31/8/92	Profit and Loss A/C	390,000
		560,000			560,000
			1/9/92	Balance B/fwd	375,000

*Corporation Tax is payable 9 months after the company's financial year end.

(d) Proposed dividend (£250,000)

This has already been discussed at some length under the heading Appropriations (above). The £250,000 represents the amount of dividend for the current year which has not yet been paid.

Creditors: amounts due after more than one year (£1,280,000)

These are longer-term liabilities in that they do not have to be paid within the next 12 months. They consist of:

13% Debenture Stock (£1,000,000)

13% Debenture Stock represents a loan made to the company by debenture holders. Often debentures are issued with some security as back-up for the debt. The security may be a specific asset (such as property) and is then described as a fixed charge on that specific asset. This means that the company could not dispose of that asset without the permission of the debenture holders. On the other hand the security could be in respect of a floating charge on the general assets of the company as from time to time exist. Obviously the company must be able to dispose of the assets comprising a floating charge, since they will include stock, debtors, etc. A fixed charge means that in the event of a company winding up (closing down and selling off all the assets), the proceeds of the sale of the asset comprising the fixed charge would be used to pay off the debenture holders first, any surplus being used to pay the general creditors. On winding up where a floating charge exists, the proceeds of disposal of all assets will first go to the debenture holders who carry such a charge but only after liquidation expenses and preferential creditors have been paid. There is no indication that the debentures issued by Broadwood Distributors plc. carry any form of security, which most probably accounts for the high interest rate (generally speaking the greater the risk, the greater the return expected). To sum up, the company has borrowed £1 million at 13 per cent per annum.

Provision for deferred tax £280,000

Companies are taxed on Net Profits. However there are certain adjustments to be made to net profit before the tax can be ascertained. For example companies are not allowed depreciation of fixed assets as a deduction from profits for tax purposes. Therefore profits must be adjusted by the depreciation before the tax liability can be determined. However the Inland Revenue allows companies to deduct capital allowances (which is the Inland Revenue's way of allowing depreciation) at rates determined by them. If these capital allowances come to more than the depreciation then the tax payable will be based on a figure smaller than the profit. In such a case an amount should be transferred to the Provision for Deferred Tax Account equivalent to the tax on the difference between taxable profit and net profit. This is illustrated in the following example:

A company makes a profit of £500,000 after charging depreciation of £200,000. It receives capital allowances of £300,000 and corporation tax is 30 per cent. Its adjusted profit for tax purposes is:

	£'000
Net Profit for the year	500
Add: Depreciation	200
	700
Less: Capital allowances	300
Adjusted profit	400
Tax to be provided £400,000 x 30%	120

But since the company actually made a profit of £500,000 a deferred tax provision of £30,000 should be made (500,000 – 400,000) × 30 per cent.

This deferred tax provision can be utilised in a future year when the company's depreciation exceeds the Inland Revenue's capital allowances, for instance if in ten years time the profit was £500,000 with depreciation of £200,000 and capital allowances of £100,000. Tax will be payable on £600,000 at 30 per cent (500 + 200 – 100) = £180,000. However only £150,000 (£500,000 × 30 per cent) will be taken from profit, the remainder (£30,000) being transferred back from the Provision for Deferred Tax Account. In the case of Broadwood Distributors plc. there has been no movement on the deferred tax account during the year ended 31st August 1992.

Share capital and reserves

The authorised capital (note 7 attached to the balance sheet) is the amount of capital that the company is authorised to issue. This authorisation is contained in the company's Memorandum of Association. An issue of capital cannot exceed the amount authorised. The difference between ordinary shares and preference shares has already been discussed.

Issued and fully paid share capital (£3,000,000)

This is the actual nominal value of the shares that have been issued and fully paid for. The amount is made up of 5,000,000 ordinary shares of 50p each (nominal value) and 500,000 1 per cent preference shares of £1 each (nominal value). The nominal value of a share will rarely change and must not be confused with the market value, which is the price it will sell for currently on the Stock Exchange. Market values should be never be used in balance sheets.

Share premium account (£250,000)

This is a capital reserve. It arose because the company issued a further 1,000,000 ordinary shares of 50p during the year ended 31st August 1992 but at a price of 75p per share. The extra 25p per share being classed as a premium. Shares may be issued at a premium if the company's balance sheet indicates (by the level of its reserves) that the existing shares are worth more than nominal value or if the current market price indicates the same. Any premium on an issue of shares is a capital reserve and cannot be distributed as dividend. Capital reserves arise out of capital transactions.

Property re-valuation reserve (£150,000)

This is also a capital reserve and arose out of the revaluation of freehold land and buildings per note: attached to the balance sheet. the book-keeping entry would have been to debit the property account (increasing the value of the property) and to make a credit entry in the Property Re-valuation Reserve Account with £150,000.

General reserve

This is retained profits which have been transferred from the Profit and Loss Account to a General Reserve Account. You will note that at 31st August 1991 the balance was £2,200,000, and that at 31st August 1992 the balance was £2,600,000. The additional £400,000 is represented by the transfer from the Profit and Loss Account (see above). When a company makes a profit it does so for the benefit of the shareholders (the owners). Some of the profit is paid out in taxes, some is paid out as dividends, and some is retained. It is the retained portion which constitutes the general reserve. This reserve is a revenue reserve, as it has arisen out of revenue transactions. It is therefore available for distribution as dividends if required by the company. For example if in a particular year a company does not earn enough profit to pay a dividend, then reserves of a revenue nature may be utilised to make a distribution. One common mistake often made by students in accounting is to confuse reserves with cash resources. Reserves are not cash. Reserves are liabilities: liabilities of the company to its owners. Cash is an asset. Therefore reserves can never be cash.

Profit and loss account (£130,000)

This balance is also a reserve in that it represents profits earned but not distributed. We have already discussed this in dealing with the Profit and Loss Account.

The layout of the balance sheet

One final point to make in respect of the balance sheet is to note the way in which it is laid out. First we have fixed assets, then current assets, from which current liabilities are deducted (those due within one year); the amount determined by deducting current liabilities from current assets is known as Working Capital or Net Current Assets. The Net Current Assets are added to the fixed assets to give Total Assets less Current Liabilities. Long term liabilities are deducted from Total Assets less Current Liabilities to give Total Net Assets and these are balanced out by Share Capital and Reserves. In the balance sheet of Broadwood Distributors Plc.the amounts concerned are:

Total Current Assets (in £'000)	9,030
Net Current Assets	4,410
Total Assets less Current Liabilities	7,410
Total Net Assets	6,130

Limited companies:standard format presentation of accounts

The *Companies Act* 1985 is the statute which controls the behaviour of limited companies, and one of the areas which it covers is concerned with the presentation of company accounts. The Act prescribes a standard form for the drawing up and presentation of the Profit and Loss Account and Balance Sheet. This is designed to produce some degree of uniformity in the presentation of accounting information to the public. It actually involves showing much less information in the main statements, such as the Balance Sheet and Profit and Loss Account, but necessitates the disclosure of much more information in the form of attached notes. The aim is to present accounts in a much simpler manner. Examples of the standard formats required by the Act are shown on the next three pages. You should attempt to acquire the published accounts of a Public Limited Company and study them. This will give you an idea of the type of information contained therein, and will be a valuable backup to the information contained in this Unit.

Profit And Loss Account

		£	£
1.	Turnover		XXX
2.	Cost of Sales		(XXX)
3.	Gross Profit or (Loss)		XXX
4.	Selling and Distribution costs	(XXX)	
5.	Administrative expenses	(XXX)	
			(XXX)
			XXX
6.	Other Operating Income		XXX
7.	Income from shares in Group Companies	XXX	
8.	Income from shares in Related Companies	XXX	
9.	Income from other fixed asset investments	XXX	
10.	Other interest receivable and similar income	XXX	
			XXX
			XXX
11.	Amounts written off investments	(XXX)	
12.	Interest payable and similar charges	(XXX)	
			(XXX)
	Profit or (Loss) on ordinary activities before taxation	XXX	
13.	Tax on Profit or Loss on ordinary activities		(XXX)
14.	Profit or (Loss) on ordinary activities after Taxation		XXX
15.	Extraordinary Income	XXX	
16.	Extraordinary Charges	(XXX)	
17.	Extraordinary Profit or (Loss)		XXX
			XXX
18.	Tax on extraordinary Profit or Loss	(XXX)	
19.	Other taxes not shown under the above items	(XXX)	
			(XXX)
20.	Profit or (Loss) for the financial year		XXX
21.	Dividends paid and proposed		(XXX)
	Retained Profit for the year		XXX
	Retained Profit brought forward		XXX
	Retained Profit to be carried forward		£XXX

Balance Sheet

			£	£
A.	Called up share capital not paid			XXX
B.	Fixed Assets			
	I. Intangible Assets	(Note 1)	XXX	
	II. Tangible Assets	(Note 2)	XXX	
	III.Investments	(Note 3)	<u>XXX</u>	
		(Total of B)		XXX
C.	Current Assets			
	I. Stocks	(Note 4)	XXX	
	II. Debtors	(Note 5)	XXX	
	III.Investments	(Note 6)	XXX	
	IV.Cash at bank and in hand		<u>XXX</u>	
		(Total of C)	XXX	
D.	Prepayments and accrued income		<u>XXX</u>	
		(Total of C + D)	XXX	
E.	Creditors: Amounts falling due within one year	(Note 7)	<u>(XXX)</u>	
F.	Net current assets (liabilities)	(Total of C + D - E)		<u>XXX</u>
G.	Total assets less current liabilities	(Total of A+B +/- F)		XXX
H.	Creditors: Amounts falling due after more than one year (Note 8)			<u>(XXX)</u>
	(Total of G-H)			XXX
I.	Provisions for liabilities and charges	(Note 9)	(XXX)	
J.	Accruals and deferred income		<u>(XXX)</u>	
		(Total of I + J)		<u>(XXX)</u>
		(Total of G - H - I - J)		<u>XXX</u>
K.	Capital and Reserves			
	I. Called up share capital			XXX
	II. Share Premium account			XXX
	III.Re-valuation reserve			XXX
	IV.Other reserves			XXX
	V.Profit and Loss Account			<u>XXX</u>
		(Total of K)		<u>XXX</u>

Notes Relating To The Balance Sheet

1. Intangible Assets

    1 Development costs

    2. Concessions, patents, licences, trade marks and similar rights and assets

    3. Goodwill

    4. Payments on account

2. Tangible Assets

    1. Land and buildings

    2. Plant and machinery

    3. Fixtures, fittings, tools and equipment

    4. Payments on account and assets in the course of construction

3. Investments

    1. Shares in group companies

    2. Loans to group companies

    3. Shares in related companies

    4. Loans to related companies

    5. Other investments other than loans

    6. Other loans

    7. Own Shares

4. Stock

    1. Raw materials and consumables

    2. Work in progress

    3. Finished goods and goods for resale

    4. Payments on account

5. Debtors

    1. Trade debtors

    2. Amounts owed by group companies

    3. Amounts owed by related companies

    4. Other debtors

    5. Called up share capital not paid

    6. Prepayments and accrued income

6. Investments

    1. Shares in group companies

    2. Own shares

3. Other investments

7. Creditors: Amounts falling due within one year

    1. Debenture loans

    2. Bank loans and overdrafts

    3. Payments received on account

    4. Trade creditors

    5. Bills of exchange payable

    6. Amounts owed to group companies

    7. Amounts owed to related companies

    8. Other creditors including taxation and social security

    9. Accruals and deferred income

8. Creditors: Amounts falling due after more than one year

    1. Debenture loans

    2 Bank loans and overdrafts

    3. Payments received on account

    4. Trade creditors

    5. Bills of exchange payable

    6. Amounts owed to group companies

    7. Amounts owed to related companies

    8. Other creditors including taxation and social security

    9. Accruals and deferred income

9. Provisions for liabilities and charges

    1. Pensions and

    2. Taxation including deferred taxation

    3. Other provisions

Commentary on standard statements

You will see from the above pro-forma statements that the detailed information in respect of expenditure contained in the Profit and Loss Account is found under four main headings:

- cost of sales;
- selling and distribution costs;
- administration expenses;
- interest payable and similar charges.

This will involve re-analysing the expenditure. For example in Broadwood Distributors plc. the allocation of wages and salaries to the appropriate headings will be determined by the functions carried out by different employees. Note that in the standard format the cost of sales includes more than just opening stock plus purchases minus closing stock. It will include an element of wages, some depreciation, some rates and so on. It should be stressed that the standard format does not require companies to fill in zeros; in other words, if a company does not have income or expenditure which fits into a particular category then that category need not be shown.

With regard to the Balance Sheet:

- if an item is prefixed with a capital letter or a Roman numeral, it must be shown on the face of the balance sheet;
- if an item is prefixed by an Arabic number (1, 2, 3, etc.) then it may be shown by way of notes attached to the balance sheet.

It must be stressed that the Companies Act 1985 lays down only the minimum information to be shown on the face of the balance sheet. Companies may show more if it is considered desirable. There are one or two areas where a degree of choice can be made. For example item A (to be shown on the face of the balance sheet) also appears under item C II 5 (which need not be shown on the face of the balance sheet). Other examples are item D (item C II 6) and item J (item E9 or H9). In drawing up the accounts of Broadwood Distributors plc. the balance sheet has already been produced in the standard format, but the Profit and Loss Account has not. The Profit and Loss Account may look like the example shown on the next page if it is re-stated in standard format. Do not attempt to reconcile figures in the original Profit and Loss with these new figures as it is merely an illustration of how the account may be presented. Note that the figures from Profit on Ordinary activities before tax, down to retained profit to be carried forward are basically the same as in the detailed Profit and Loss Account shown earlier.

Broadwood Distributors plc.
Profit and Loss Account for the Year Ended 31st August 1992

	£'000	£'000
Turnover		36,400
Cost of sales		30,300
Gross profit		6,100
Selling and distribution costs	3,420	
Administrative expenses	2,040	5,460
		640
Other operating income		973
Income from other fixed asset investments		22
		1,635
Interest payable and similar charges*		285
Profit on ordinary activities before taxation		1,350
Tax on profit on ordinary activities		390
Profit on ordinary activities after taxation		960
Dividends paid and proposed		505
Retained profit for the year		455
Retained profit brought forward		75
		530
Transfer to general reserve		400
Retained profit to be carried forward		130

*Includes Bad Debts and Increase in Provision for Doubtful Debts.

The notes to the financial statement
Certain items will always be found in the notes. These are:
- details of the accounting policies used in the preparation of the Financial Statements. These are the specific methods chosen by the company to apply the fundamental accounting concepts;
- detailed analysis of Balance Sheet items, e.g. the types of fixed assets owned by the company;
- detailed analysis of Profit and Loss Account items. For example the notes will show how the charge for corporation tax has been estimated, when it is payable and any corrections due as a result of adjustments to the previous year's provision;
- details of Post Balance Sheet events. Quite often events occur in the time between the date of the balance sheet and the point at which the Financial Statements are prepared.

Such events may have a bearing on the information contained in the balance sheet and should therefore be highlighted.

The Director's report

The Director's Report is a statement issued by the Directors of a company to the shareholders. It normally contains:

- a summary of the company's performance for the financial year just ended, and its expected performance in the coming year;
- details of the directors of the company and their shareholdings in it;
- a statement of the principal activities of the company;
- details of the proposed dividend.

The Auditor's report

The shareholders of a company are often not the people who run it. This task falls to the directors and it is their responsibility to prepare the accounts and present them to the members. The shareholders need to know if the accounts are an accurate reflection of the profit the company has made and of its financial position at the balance sheet date. To determine this, the shareholders appoint an independent qualified person to examine the accounts and to pass an opinion on them. The independent person is the auditor, who must be a qualified Accountant.

The Auditor's report is an expression of his opinion as to the 'truth and fairness' of the accounts and of the profit of the company. This opinion is based upon his examination of the accounts and upon various financial tests which he has carried out. Auditor's reports can be 'unqualified' where the auditor states that the accounts do show a true and fair view, or they may be 'qualified'. Where the auditor's report is qualified the auditor will explain those aspects of the accounts with which he is not satisfied and the effect that this has had upon them. Occasionally an auditor will issue a 'disclaimer of opinion'. This means that the result of his examinations have been inconclusive and he cannot form an opinion whether or not the accounts show a true and fair view. In all cases you should read the auditor's report before going on to interpret information contained in accounts.

Cashflow Statements

The Balance Sheet and the Profit and Loss Accounts of a business show respectively the position with regard to its assets and liabilities at the beginning and at the end of a financial year, and the amount of profit or loss made between those two points in time. However, the Profit and Loss Account shows revenue items only i.e. sales, purchases and other expenses such as wages, heating and lighting, motor running costs, etc. It does not show expenditure incurred for the acquisition of fixed assets nor does it show income from injections of capital or from loans. Since most business transactions are on credit terms it follows that income from sales during a period is not necessarily the same as the cash received because some customers will still owe money for goods sold to them. The same is true of purchases, other expenses and cash paid. The Balance Sheet shows the position at two dates only and it may not be evident where money has come from nor in which way it has been spent.

In order to clarify this all limited companies (except those specifically exempt) must produce a statement for the financial year which shows where cash has been generated and in which areas it has been used. This statement is called "The Cashflow Statement". It is prepared in accordance with the requirements of Financial Reporting Statement no. 1. Financial Reporting Statements (FRS) are replacing Statements of Standard Accounting Practice (SSAP) and this particular one (the first) replaces SSAP 10. The standard headings required in cashflow statements are:

- operating activities;

- returns on investments and servicing of finance;
- taxation;
- investing activities;
- financing

Operating Activities

This section shows the cash generated or otherwise from the trading operations of a business i.e. Sales less Cost of Sales less expenses, and will be adjusted by increases or decreases in stock, debtors, creditors and by items shown in the Profit and Loss Account which do not involve the movement of cash such as depreciation of fixed assets, etc. This section of the statement will not show cash receipts from investments nor cash outflow in respect of loan or debenture interest.

Returns on investments and servicing of finance

This section shows cash received from long-term investments held by a business, and payments made to providers of finance, such as loan or debenture interest and dividends to shareholders.

Taxation

This section shows cash payments made during a financial year in respect of taxation, including Advance Corporation Tax where applicable.

Investing activities

This section shows cash payments made to acquire tangible and intangible fixed assets and long-term investments. It also shows receipts from the disposal of these items where applicable.

Financing

This section shows cash inflows from share or debenture issues and cash outflows from repayment of shares or debentures. From the above it can be clearly seen that sources of cash are:

- Share capital contributed by the owners;
- Borrowed capital such as loans or debentures;
- Proceeds of disposal of fixed assets and long-term investments;
- Profit generated from trading activities before charging depreciation;
- Interest and dividends received in respect of long-term investments.

and cash outflows are in respect of:

- Purchase of fixed assets and long-term investments;
- Repayment of share capital, and loans or debentures;
- Payment of taxes;
- Payment of dividends to shareholders;
- Payment of interest on loans or debentures;
- Losses incurred on trading activities before charging depreciation.

One of the major uses of a cashflow statement is that it acts as a link between the balance sheet position at the beginning of a trading period, the profit and loss account, and the balance sheet position at the end of the period. To facilitate interpretation the cashflow statement identifies the major changes that have taken place in the company's position over the period in question. For example, a balance sheet may show that a company owns freehold land worth £200,000 at the start of an accounting period and £250,000 at its close. From the balance sheet it may be difficult to recognise that what has happened is that the company initially had two pieces of land worth £120,000 and £80,000 respectively. During the accounting period the land worth £80,000 had been sold and replaced with a different piece of land costing £130,000. The sale of the land and the acquisition of its replacement would be clearly shown in the cashflow statement. A Cashflow Statement in respect of Broadwood Distributors follows.

Broadwood Distributors plc.
Cashflow Statement for the Year Ended 31 August 1992

	£'000	£'000
Net cash inflow from operating activities		803
Returns on investments and servicing of finance:		
Interest received	22	
Interest paid	(130)	
Dividends paid	(535)	
Net cash inflow (outflow) from returns on investments and servicing of finance		(643)
Taxation:		
Corporation tax paid	(185)	
Tax paid		(185)
Investing activities:		
Payments to acquire tangible fixed assets	(690)	
Payments to acquire long-term investments	(100)	
Net cash inflow (outflow) from investing activities		(790)
Net cash inflow (outflow) before financing		(815)
Financing:		
Issue of ordinary share capital	750	
Net cash inflow (outflow) from financing		750
Increase (decrease) in cash and cash equivalents		(65)

Notes to the cashflow statement:

1.Reconciliation of operating profit to net cash inflow from operating activities:	£'000
Operating Profit	1,350
Interest payable	130
Interest receivable	(22)
Depreciation charges	290
Increase in stocks	(560)
Increase in debtors	(1,050)
Increase in creditors	665
Net cash inflow from operating profit	803

2. Analysis of changes in cash and cash equivalents during the year:	
Balance at 1 September 1991	235
Net cash outflow	(65)
Balance at 31 August 1992	170

3. Analysis of changes in financing during the year:	Share Capital	Share Premium
Balance at 1 September 1991	2,500	–
Cash inflow (outflow) from financing	500	250
Balance at 31 August 1992	3,000	250

Activity

The following list of balances taken from the ledger accounts of Whitwell Plc. as at 30 June 1994 have been handed to you:

	£'000		£'000
Ordinary shares of £1 each	10,000	Bad debts written off	200
8 % Preference shares of £1 each	2,000	Provision for doubtful debts	1,200
Share premium account	1,000	7 % Debenture stock	3,000
Profit and loss account	15,360	Debtors	30,000
Sales	155,000	Creditors	17,710
Purchases	125,600	Preference share dividend paid	160
Stock as at 1 July 1993	11,600	Freehold property at cost	8,500
Wages and salaries	14,400	Plant and machinery at cost	5,800
Business rates and insurance	1,640	Motor vehicles at cost	3,060
Advertising	1,700	Fixtures and fittings at cost	960
Telephone and postage	760	Provision for depreciation as at 1 July 1993:	
Motor expenses	2,100		
Heating and lighting	770	Plant and machinery	2,300
Miscellaneous expenses	1,030	Motor vehicles	1,300
Debenture Interest paid	210	Fixtures and fittings	360
Cash at Bank	740		

Additional information:

A physical stock check at the close of business on 30 June 1994 revealed that the company owned stock which was valued at £13,200,000.

Provision has to be made for accrued motor expenses of £150,000 and an audit fee of £600,000.

Business rates and insurance paid in advance as at 30 June 1994 was £260,000.

It is company policy to keep the provision for doubtful debts at 5 per cent of the outstanding debtors.

Company depreciation policy is to depreciate fixed assets using the reducing balance basis at the following rates:

Plant and machinery	*20 per cent per annum*
Motor vehicles	*25 per cent per annum*
Fixtures and fittings	*10 per cent per annum*

The directors of the company are proposing to pay a dividend on ordinary share capital of 12 pence per share.

Tasks:

1. Re-arrange the list of balances into a conventional trial balance.

2. Identify each item in the trial balance as either an asset, liability, income or expenditure and indicate whether they are trading and profit and loss account items or balance sheet items.

3. Using the trial balance as a basis, together with the additional notes, prepare the trading and profit and loss account of Whitwell Plc. for the year ended 30 June 1994 and the balance sheet as at that date.

4. Explain why trading and profit and loss accounts and balance sheets are prepared by business enterprises such as Whitwell Plc.

5. Explain why business accounts relate to specific periods of time (usually one year).

Assignment *Glenn's Mistakes*

Glenn Headley has been in business for three years, supplying wines and spirits etc. to the retail trade. For the first two years his business accounts had been prepared by a friend who is an accountant, but he has now left the area.

Glenn has made an attempt to prepare his own accounts for the current year, but he is upset by the fact that he seems to have made a loss, and also that he cannot get the balance sheet to balance.

He is now seeking your help and has sent you his version of the annual accounts of his business (see below), which he would like you to examine with a view to correcting any errors he may have made.

The Accounts which he has produced are as follows:

Glenn Headley
Trading and Profit and Loss Account as at 31 March 1993

	£	£
Sales		123,840
Less: Cost of sales:		
Stock as at 31 March 1993 at selling price	12,984	
Purchases during the year	83,360	
	96,344	
Less: Stock as at 1 April 1992 at selling price	11,784	
		84,560
Gross Profit		39,280
Less: Expenditure		
Wages and Salaries	22,320	
Personal Drawings	8,320	
Heating and Lighting	1,536	
Rates and Insurance	672	
Advertising	1,088	
Motor Expenses	2,296	
Telephone and Postage	445	
Discount Received from suppliers	1,664	
Purchase of New Van	8,960	
Depreciation for the year – Motor Van	968	
Equipment and Fittings	292	
Miscellaneous Expenses	728	
		49,289
Net Loss for the year	£	(10,009)

Glenn Headley
Balance Sheet for the Year Ended 31 March 1993

Fixed Assets:	£	£
Freehold Land and Buildings at cost		20,000
Motor Vehicle at cost	6,880	
Less: Depreciation up to 31 March 1992	3,010	
		3,870
Equipment and Fittings at cost	3,600	
Less Depreciation up to 31 March 1993	976	
		2,624
		26,494
Current Assets:		
Stock as at 31 March 1993 at cost price	8,656	
Debtors	15,262	
Bank Overdraft	1,412	
		25,330
Less: Current Liabilities		
Creditors	7,993	
		17,337
		£43,831
Capital Account		
Balance as at 1 April 1992		44,720
Add: Loss for the year	10,009	
Less: Drawings	8,320	
		1,689
		£46,409

Difference in balance unaccounted for = £2,578

In response to your questions Glenn has supplied you with the following information:

1. He adds 50% to the cost of goods purchased to arrive at his selling prices.

2. Vans have been depreciated in the past at the rate of 25% per year using the reducing balance method but he doesn't understand what that means. The first van was bought at the commencement of his business on 1 April 1990.

3. The equipment was bought at the same time, and is depreciated at the rate of 10% per year using the reducing balance method.

Tasks

1. Make a list of all the errors that Glenn Headley appears to have made in drawing up the Accounts.

2. Write short notes explaining to him what each error is, and indicate how he should correct them.

3. Prepare a corrected Trading and Profit and Loss Account for the year ended 31 March 1993.

4. Prepare a corrected Balance Sheet as at 31 March 1993.

Unit 8

Business Planning

This unit has been written to cover the following specifications of the General National Vocational Qualification Business Level 3

Unit 8   Business Planning Level 3

Element 8.1:   Prepare work and collect data for a business plan

Performance criteria:

1   objectives of business are identified and agreed
2   legal and insurance implications of the objectives are identified
3   feasibility of proposals is checked through discussion with others
4   resource requirements to design and produce the goods or service are identified and estimated
5   resource requirements to sell and market the goods or service are identified and estimated
6   time constraints on production, sales, marketing and administration are identified on a flow chart
7   potential support for the plan from external sources is identified

Element 8.2:   Produce and present a business plan

Performance criteria:

1   purposes of a business plan are explained
2   business objectives for a single product or service are identified and explained
3   marketing plan is identified
4   production plan is described
5   resource requirements and ability to meet the requirements are identified and explained
6   financial data and forecasts to support the plan are produced
7   monitoring and review procedures for plan are identified
8   business plan is presented to an audience

Element 8.3:   Produce a sales and marketing plan

Performance criteria:

1   purposes of a sales and marketing plan are explained
2   planning activities to market a product are described
3   marketing budget is estimated
4   timing of sales and marketing activities is scheduled
5   sales and marketing plan for a single product is produced

(extract from General National Vocational Qualifications Mandatory Units for Business GNVQ3 offered by Business Education and Technology Council, City and Guilds and RSA Examinations Board - published by the National Council for Vocational Qualifications April 1993 - reproduced by kind permission of the National Council for Vocational Qualifications)

GNVQ3 Business - Unit Number U1016181

Element 8.1 Planning a Business

Developing Business Opportunities

In this Unit we shall examine how you can put some of your skills and knowledge to practical use and devise a plan for a business which you could launch now, or later, or perhaps simply use as a practice for the real thing. How are you going to go about it? First we have to decide on a business opportunity and develop it. To develop any business opportunity you will need:

- a good idea (or ideas);
- sound and readily available finance;
- good quality people or employees with the right skills;
- a strategy or overall plan for the future;
- a structure or form of business organisation which is appropriate to the enterprise;
- managers who are skilled decision-makers and effective motivators.

Ideas

Any business needs a *good idea* to start. This idea does not necessarily have to be novel or unique. It might help if you come up with an idea that no one has had before – alternatively this might prove to be a disadvantage as trying to sell a product which nobody has heard of can sometimes be difficult. Being the first business with a good new idea does not always guarantee success. The first into the market may have to break down consumer resistance to a new product and overcome the teething problems of effective marketing and distribution. Companies coming into the market later can learn from the first company's mistakes and capitalise on the established market. In the UK, Sinclair were the first company to market home computers at a reasonable cost, yet it is other companies which have developed the market while Sinclair has fallen by the wayside.

Yet a good business idea does need to have something different. As some people in business say '*you need to spot a gap in the market*'. If you are trying to enter a market with a product or service which is identical to that on offer from many other companies you may struggle as consumers stay with their existing suppliers. Your product needs to have something which distinguishes it from the rest. This might mean a new design, additional features or merely that there are no other suppliers selling that product in a particular area.

How then do people come up with good business ideas? They usually come in two ways:

(i) *People have particular skills or knowledge that they have gained over time while working for others*. They then use some aspect of their skills and experience to develop their own business. Most new business ventures start in this way and have the greatest chance of success. For instance a salesman selling beds to department stores recognises that there is a gap in the market for headboards and so leaves his existing employer and sets up his own business making headboards and selling them to the same stores he has always visited. Another example might be a typist who works for a large company and realises that students need their dissertations typed. She has the skills to do this and so buys her own word processor and sets up in business as a secretarial service for students.

(ii) *A person identifies a market which has not been developed and even though they have no skills or experience they set about trying to gain the knowledge and business skills necessary to exploit the gap in the market.* This approach is more hazardous. The person may have misjudged the opportunity or may find that they cannot develop the business acumen necessary to run the business. But it can work. About twenty five years ago a young man thought there was a market for cheap records. He had no experience in record retailing but he thought he would give it a go. He began by selling discount LPs, first from the back of a van and then by mail order. He made some money and developed his business ideas. That young man's name was Richard Branson and today he is a successful multi-millionaire as the Chairman of the Virgin Group. Another successful business began when a young women recognised that there were other women like her who wanted cosmetics made from natural ingredients that were not tested on animals. She had some cosmetics made in this way and opened a shop selling them. Her name is Anita Roddick and from her initial idea has developed the chain of Body Shops.

As a business expands, it needs to refine and develop its original ideas and aims. If its ideas have proved successful in allowing the business to make profits, survive and grow, then perhaps other entrepreneurs will be drawn in to compete in the market. The successful, growing business will always be looking to its customers and potential customers: it will constantly be assessing changes in tastes and demand – ready to respond by refining its ideas accordingly. If a business stands still and relies on its original customer base, it runs a great risk of withering away. In larger businesses, the job of researching, generating and refining ideas generally falls to the marketing department. We will examine this vital role in Unit 3, *Marketing*, where we consider the role of business marketing.

Activity

Get together in groups of three or four people and brainstorm potential business ideas. Think about the two reasons for good ideas we have just mentioned. Have you or any of the group a potential skill which you could exploit, or can you see a 'gap' in the market.

Exploiting business opportunities

How might a group of people decide whether or not to exploit a business opportunity? Take, for example, a potential business with three partners. One of the partners thinks that there may be the possibility of moving into car and van rental. The business could buy several cars and transit vans and start to rent them out on a daily or weekly basis. They meet to consider the proposal. How should they go about making the decision whether or not to expand into the rental area. A simple process the partners might follow is:

1. Identify the opportunity;
2. Brainstorm possible pros and cons of the idea;
3. Refine ideas;
4. Collect financial information on the opportunity;
5. Assess the non-numerical factors;
6. Analyse the information using decision-making techniques;
7. Make the decision;

8. Implement the decision;
9. Review the decision.

Identify the opportunity

Identifying the opportunity is often not as easy as it appears. It might appear to be an obvious and natural business opportunity to one of the partners but does the opportunity really exist? For example, the opportunity may suggest itself because:

- one of the partners works part-time in a garage and has seen that there has been a number of enquiries from customers asking if the garage rents out cars;
- there are no other car rental firms in the immediate vicinity.

The first of these may suggest that there is a potential market for renting cars. But has the partner quantified the number of people who have made enquiries? Is it merely the occasional request or have there been many people wanting to rent cars and vans and has this demand been over a long period of time. The second factor may be easier to assess. How far away is the nearest car rental business and are people willing or unwilling to travel there to rent vehicles?

Embarking on a business venture when no real opportunity exists can be a very costly exercise and one that you should avoid. One way of ensuring that this does not happen is by allocating sufficient time for the opportunity to be accurately assessed. It is extremely foolhardy to pursue a business opportunity merely because someone has a 'gut feeling' that there is money to be made.

Brainstorm possible pros and cons of the idea

Getting the partners together for a brainstorming session can be a good way of initially assessing a business idea. Different people think in different ways and one of the group may come up with a good alternative or variation on the idea. Another person may be able to see some obvious drawback that the others have missed. This can involve *lateral* and *creative* thinking. Even when the opportunity seems obvious, one spark of imaginative thinking may be all that is required to make it feasible or alternatively to kill the idea.

Refine ideas

This stage involves refining the ideas generated by the brainstorming process. Brainstorming produces random ideas: they are raw and unsifted. You should not rush into a venture simply because it seemed a good idea at the time. Many 'good' ideas may prove to be unfeasible when you have had sufficient time to consider them carefully, systematically and quietly. The idea must be checked against three basic factors if it is to progress to the next stage of the process:

- *The objectives of the business:* does the new proposal fit in with the partners' business objectives. If it does, fine. If it does not, then should the objectives be changed or the idea dropped?
- *Internal constraints*: do the partners have sufficient available finance to pursue the idea and do they have the managerial and operational expertise to make it work?
- *External factors*, such as interest rates, the level of competition and the prices the business could charge will influence a decision. Other external factors will include the law relating to the hiring or vehicles and the need for insurance which must be examined if an informed decision is to be made.

Collect financial information on the opportunity

Once the business opportunity has been clearly identified and ideas on how to operate it have been sorted, sifted and measured against the objectives and constraints that might affect the business, then as much information about the opportunity needs to be collected. As the venture involves spending money and selling a service which should generate income, then a cash-flow should be drawn up. This is called *quantitative information* and needs to be as accurate as possible.

Assess the non-numerical factors

All business decisions will involve some non-numerical factors. These factors may include such things as:

- the effect of the decisions on the partners and employees of the business;
- the effect on competitors.

This is known as *qualitative information*. Do the partners want to bear the extra risk? However much effort is put into the collection of quantitative information, it is frequently such qualitative factors which ultimately determine the success or failure of the venture.

Analyse the information using decision-making techniques

There are many techniques which help business managers analyse the effect of alternative decisions. The business can use a computer spreadsheet to help in the decision making process. The owners can put various alternative costs and revenues into the spreadsheet to show them 'what if?' alternative situations arise.

Make the decision

At this stage, when the final decision to proceed is made, there is always a choice. At the most basic level it is: *to do something or to do nothing*. In certain circumstances, a range of options have been investigated and the problem lies in making a choice between them. In our example it might be between buying four cars to rent or perhaps concentrating only on renting vans. The final decision will rest on three main criteria:

- *Financial costs*: the money costs and benefits of a decision;
- *Opportunity costs*: this is the value of the best alternative opportunity which has to be forgone as a result of making a particular choice;
- *Human costs*: the effects of the decision on the partners and any workers they may have to employ.

Implement the decision

Implementing the decision means putting it into practice. This may involve buying the vehicles and setting up systems to monitor and control the process. It will clearly need to be marketed and this may involve advertising. Whatever the actual process requires it must be controlled. Control is a vital part of any decision-making process as it must:

- guide the project towards achieving its goal;
- set a target for measuring its success or failure;
- measure what actually happens against what was intended to happen.

By controlling the implementation, the managers will have the chance to correct their actions and this increases the likelihood of success.

Review the decision

The review of a decision is sometimes neglected, yet it is an important step in collecting feedback on the success of the decision. So after a period of time, say one month, three months or a year, the owners of the business need to sit down and assess whether their business venture has been a success. Have they met their sales targets and has the business proved as possible as they had hoped?. It is only through this process of review that they will gain sufficient information to judge the wisdom of their decision and to increase the chance of success for future ventures.

Finance

When you start a business, you require finance or *start up capital*. Usually, you will have to provide a significant proportion of this finance yourself. People intending to start their own business will use their life savings or re-mortgage their house; they may use redundancy payments from a previous job or a legacy from a relative. Whatever the source, these amounts form the basis of the finance of the business, but are seldom enough on their own. In addition, you will have to seek more finance in the form of a loan from a bank or other financial institution. Most lenders will require you to produce a business plan and cash-flow forecast before they put their loan at risk; we consider the alternative sources of finance in detail in Unit 7, *Financial Resources*, where we consider the business resources need to develop and expand a successful business idea and we look at how to produce a cash flow in Element 7.3, *Producing a Cash Flow*, and how to produce a business plan in the next Element, *Producing a Business Plan*.

As the business grows, then so will its need for cash if you wish to expand it. Money (or capital) is the crucial key to success in any business. As we explain in Unit 7, this capital can come from only two sources: from profits generated by the business (internal finance) or from loans or investment from outside (external finance). Each source brings its respective costs and risks and balancing these can result in a very skilful and tricky management decision.

People

In the early weeks and months of its existence, a business will usually employ few people: the owner will usually be one of them, perhaps along with some relatives or trusted friends. As the business expands, so there is a need to employ others. Both the quality and quantity of employees needed may increase and finding people who will share the values and objectives of the original business is critical. As the business first begins to expand, you may still carry out recruitment by word of mouth and it may be based on first-hand knowledge of potential employees. As growth continues, however, you may need to consult specialists in recruitment. We consider the way a business can recruit good staff and then manage them effectively in Element 4.3, *Job Applications and Interviews*.

The larger the business becomes the more managers it will have. Their role will be to manage the resources of the business efficiently and effectively. Resources include people, finance, property and equipment.

Legal constraints

You will need to appreciate the legal implications of running a business. There is a mass of civil and criminal law which applies to business activity which would not otherwise be applicable to an individual. In Unit 1, *The Business in the Economy*, we explore a number of areas of consumer protection law which apply to the supply of goods and services such as the *Consumer Credit Act* 1974, the *Consumer Protection Act* 1987, the *Trade Descriptions Act* 1968 and the *Unsolicited Goods and Services Act* 1971.

We consider the recruitment of staff in Unit 4, *Human Resources*, where we examine areas of employment law such as equal opportunities, contracts of employment, statutory employment rights and health and safety.

It is fundamental to the implementation of a business idea that if it is possible to foresee potential legal liability then if possible it is prudent to insure against the risk. In some cases the requirement to insure is mandatory so that under the Employers Liability (Compulsory Insurance) Act 1969 an employer must insure against the risk of injury to his employees.

All businesses require premises, whether office accommodation, factory premises or open land. If the freehold of land is acquired this will be very costly. Freehold is virtually absolute ownership and the full market value must be paid for it. Alternatively business premises may be acquired as leasehold and the organisation will be a business tenant in possession with a landlord under the terms of a business lease.

In a business lease the deed creating it will contain a number of covenants. A *covenant* is simply a contractual term contained in a deed. One such covenant will normally restrict business use, and this could come in a positive or negative form. It could restrict the tenant from carrying on a particular business or using the property for a particular purpose, for instance carrying on the business of a retail travel agent. Alternatively the covenant could prevent the tenant from carrying on a particular form of trade or any activity causing a nuisance or annoyance, such as a public house. Both the landlord and tenant have bound themselves personally by the covenants in the lease and will retain this contractual liability throughout its term. A covenant restricting business use will also be enforceable against a sub tenant or an assignee of the business lease, by the original landlord or even a new landlord who has purchased the freehold estate.

Restrictive covenants may also apply to a freeholder. Such restrictive covenants could originate from a transaction under which one landowner, Smith sold part of his land to a purchaser, Jones. In the deed conveying the land to Jones, Smith may for the benefit of land retained by him, have extracted a promise from Jones not to use the land for anything except residential purposes. Thus if Jones now attempts to break the covenant by setting up a business, Smith can seek an injunction to prevent him.

The freedom to use premises for business purposes is also subject to constraints imposed by the criminal and civil law. An occupier of land may be restrained by injunction from using his property in such a way as to cause a nuisance to his neighbours, adjoining occupiers or to the public as a whole.

> In *Halsey v. Esso Petroleum* 1961 the plaintiff was the owner of a house on a residential estate and the defendant owned and occupied an oil storage depot on the river bank nearby. On various occasions noxious acid smuts were emitted from metal chimney stacks at the depot which caused damage to the plaintiff's washing, and the paint work of his car. There was also a particularly pungent oily smell from the depot of a nauseating character but which was not a health risk. Further cause for complaint was the noise emitted from the boilers during nightshift which varied in intensity but at its peak reached sixty three decibels causing the plaintiff's windows and doors to vibrate. The noise was exacerbated by the arrival of heavy tankers at the depot, sometimes in convoy and as many as fifteen in one night. It was on the basis of these complaints that the plaintiff brought an action alleging nuisance and claiming damages and injunctions to restrain the activity. The Court held that:
>
> - the acid smuts emitted from the chimneys constituted the crime of public nuisance and as the plaintiff had suffered special damage in relation to his motor car he could recover damages for the tort of private nuisance;
> - injunctions and damages were awarded to restrain the unlawful activities to the extent that they constituted an actionable nuisance.

Some activities on land have also been made unlawful by statute and may constitute a statutory nuisance. From the 1st January 1991 a range of provisions formerly contained in the *Public Health Act* 1936 and the *Public Health (Recurring Nuisances) Act* 1969 cease to have effect and are replaced and extended by the *Environmental Health Act* 1990. Under the Act a list of circumstances may amount to a statutory nuisance including emissions of smoke, gas, fumes, dust, steam, smells or other effluvia and noise from premises which are prejudicial to health or a nuisance.

Structure

The structure of a business is primarily determined by the way it is legally formed. All business start-ups in the UK occur in the private sector of the economy. The private sector is that sector of the economy which is self-financing and receives no direct support from government. The three main forms of structure to consider are:

- sole trader;
- partnership;
- limited company.

We consider the implications of each of these forms in Element 4.2, *Job Roles and Organisational Structures*. Often a business will set up as a sole trader and, as it expands, it will change its structure to that of a limited company. When a business reaches a certain size it may decide to 'go public'; that is, it will open up its share ownership to any individual or institution which has the necessary money to buy.

Strategy

Business ideas need to be converted into a strategy – a long-term plan for the business. This business strategy involves setting goals and objectives which are achievable and which are understood not just by the managers of the business but by all those involved in its operation. It is far better to involve people in the running of the business in such a way that they are committed to attaining its overall goals. We have already mentioned Anita Roddick and her success with Body Shop. She has been astute enough to recognise that that those working in the retail outlets must believe in the product and recognise where the company wants to go.

A business strategy which is:

- properly thought through;
- is making the best use of its present resources; and
- is planning the development of its future resources

will go a long way to achieving success.

It is important that as many employees as possible share in the objectives of the business and work towards the achievement of a common goal. If the business does not achieve this then it will face conflict both from within the organisation and pressure from outside the organisation.

Organisation

In any small business, it is usually possible for decisions, discussions and instructions to be conducted directly between the owner(s) and the workforce. As the business becomes more complex, so the need to provide an organisational framework for efficient and effective operation and communication increases. For example, in a a small catering business, the same person that takes orders from customers over the phone may also plan the preparation of the food, do the cooking and deliver it. As the business grows, it may be that different people or departments have separate responsibility for such areas as:

- order processing;
- buying raw materials;
- producing the goods;
- delivering the goods;
- invoicing customers;
- paying bills and wages.

As you can imagine, the organisation required to co-ordinate this and satisfy the customer is considerable. If you've ever been let down by a shop, garage, or builder, then usually that will be because of poor organisation and communication in the business. Sometimes a business will choose to remain small to avoid getting involved in these challenges. The owners prefer to do all these things themselves and not to get involved in managing people. That is their choice. A business does not have to be big to be a success.

Decision-making in business

Most people in business make decisions every day. Some decisions are minor and relatively routine. A supervisor in a garage may have to make daily decisions about the sequence of work to be done there: Should customer A's car be serviced before customer B's car? In this instance, the decision taken will be based on the supervisor's own experience, intuition and information. The supervisor will know how long each job is likely to take, and when customers are calling back for their vehicles, and will often subconsciously process this information before communicating the decision to the mechanics.

Generally, the more complex and important the decision, the longer the time span it takes to make. The decision-making process that considered which route would be followed by the rail link between Central London and the Channel Tunnel spanned years. The decision was based on masses of financial and statistical information, as well as other factors, such as environmental and social costs and was shaped by the influence of pressure groups.

Effective decision-making is an important part of business success. If a business is to function smoothly and minimise the risk that results from any decision-making process, then decision-making must be approached in a logical and methodical manner.

Whether it is an individual acting in a personal capacity, or as a representative or employee of a business, some general observations can be made about the decision-making process. Decisions are likely to take longer to make (the time-span of decisions) when:

- costs associated with the decision are high;
- risk is great;
- many people are involved in the process;
- the information required is substantial;
- the problem to be solved is not urgent or immediate;
- many people will be affected;
- options are many;
- opponents are many and/or influential and/or vociferous.

Activity

Think about a major decision you have made. For instance it might have been the decision to come onto the course you are studying or where to go on holiday. Examine the process of decision making you went through. Did this involve the collection of information, assessment of alternatives, and a final choice based on clear criteria - or was it a snap decision made on the spur of the moment. Consider what lessons you could learn from this process which you could apply later if you had to make decisions in business.

Running a Business

The larger a business becomes, the more departments or specialist functions it develops. A sole trader running a small printing business is likely to have few employees. Each employee will, however, have several roles. The production assistant may take delivery of the inks and paper, set up the printing press, check the quality of the output, quote for new jobs, telephone customers and much more. The clerical assistant may receive and process orders, handle correspondence, invoice customers, pay bills, bank cheques, check bank statements, advertise in newspapers, calculate wages, and so on. The small size of the business doesn't justify one person being allocated to each separate task; jobs within the business are, as a result, varied, flexible, relatively unspecialised (and probably interesting!).

Contrast this with that which you might find in a large manufacturing business, such as British Aerospace. BAe will have many separate departments or functions including:marketing; accounting; production; personnel and purchasing.

Within each of these functions there will be sub-functions. For example, the production function may be subdivided into: manufacture; assembly; engineering; inspection; maintenance; research and development and production planning.

Even within these sub-branches, further division of responsibility will occur. Engineering may be split into: plant and equipment engineering; mechanical engineering; electrical engineering and process engineering.

Most businesses start off as sole traders, partnerships or private limited companies. In such organisations the aims and direction are usually clear-cut; conflict is rare since those responsible for decision-making and strategic planning are also the owners of the business. As it continues to grow, it might widen its ownership base by selling shares to 'incomers'. Now it will have to take account of a wider spectrum of views: it is here that conflict can arise. Shareholders who are 'incomers' may want dividends and short-term returns: conversely, the original founders want long-term, steady growth which will provide security and ensure better returns in the future.

In business, success can only be achieved by the setting, and communicating, of clear objectives. The overall strategy for the business will be set by the owner or Board of Directors (who represent the owners or shareholders in the company). It is vital that when objectives and targets are set that they are communicated to the entire workforce and thereby pervade the whole business. Failure to achieve this results in, at best, uncertainty and lack of direction and, at worst, conflict – leading to underperformance and failure to thrive. A business is held together by efficient and effective communication.

Virgin Group: from an idea to a multi-million pound business

We have already mentioned the Virgin Group and it founder, Richard Branson. Now let us use this company as an example of how an individual can recognise a business opportunity and develop it successfully despite the constraints and difficulties faced by any growing business.

In the beginning was an idea

This business idea began with Richard Branson in his schooldays, when he perceived a need that no one else noticed. On a very small amount of capital, Branson, at the age of seventeen, launched a national magazine called *Student*. Soon, Branson took on his second cousin, Simon Draper, to help him to run the business.

The idea began to develop

From the proceeds of this magazine Branson acquired enough capital to start up as a discount mail-order record retailer. This venture proved profitable and successful until a postal strike badly affected business, forcing him to open his first retail outlet, a record shop in Oxford Street, London. With the proceeds from these enterprises, he built a recording studio in Oxfordshire and the following year he launched the *Virgin* record label.

Good management and good luck

Up to this point, Virgin had been growing nicely, extending its base and providing itself with stability and a platform for growth. Keen business acumen and an element of luck led to Virgin signing up its first star: Mike Oldfield, whose album *Tubular Bells* became the soundtrack for the film, *The Exorcist*; it sold a huge amount of copies, thus providing the business with additional finance that gave Branson the option to expand, should he so wish.

Going for growth

He did: he expanded into nightclubs, signed more artists on the Virgin label and set up Virgin Vision to distribute videos and films. In addition, Vanson Developments was formed with the intention of exploiting opportunities in the property development market. The following year, 1984, Branson diversified his interests again, by setting up *Virgin Atlantic Airways* with its North American and Japanese routes, and buying the first of several acquisitions in hotel chains. Draper was underwhelmed by his decision, telling Branson that, *"this is the beginning of the end of our relationship"*. But Branson, as holder of a majority of Virgin shares, could afford to push through his plans in the face of his colleague's opposition, He did, and Simon Draper was given an attractive consolation prize: the right to run Virgin Music unimpeded.

At this point in their growth, many businesses act with an uncertain purpose: some nervously consolidate their financial and market positions and set out to accumulate cash in preparation for the next stage of expansion. Some, who have already accumulated spare cash, look around for attractive businesses to acquire through takeover or friendly merger, whilst a minority – usually the most ambitious – decide that they will have to find funds to feed their appetite for expansion. It was this last course of action upon which Branson and Virgin decided.

Changing the structure

Virgin, now a sizeable and successful company, considered two possible sources for finance. For any company, large or small, there are really only two places that they can look for extra cash: inside or outside. '*Inside*' means using the profits that the business has retained from previous profitable years. '*Outside*' means debt: borrowing money from commercial or merchant banks or finance houses; raising equity by selling shares in one's own company or, as it is usually known, 'going public'. And going public is what Branson chose to do. The main advantage Branson gained in doing that was time: in the short-term it is quicker to raise finance from the market. The second advantage Virgin gained was a heightened public image: a public flotation normally improves a company's profile, especially if public relations are as adeptly exploited in the way that Branson manages.

In order to raise additional finance to enable his planned growth, Branson 'went public' and floated shares on the London Stock Exchange; 35% of its equity was bought by 87,000 new shareholders – Branson had opened Virgin Group to 'outsiders'.

There are also disadvantages. The major drawback is that there is a loss of control, since ownership of the company is now much more widely spread. Then there is the increased potential for conflict, especially between the original founders of a business, its management and, perhaps, the new members of the board of directors who may want to see a different business strategy and management policies pursued. Some directors will have earned their places by being representatives of pension funds and insurance companies, investment trusts and banks – the so-called *institutional shareholders*.

As well as the dilution of power that arises because of the number of shares available on the open market, a public company is, of course, now fair game for predators. It is vulnerable to takeover since its shares can be purchased by anyone and even the largest majority shareholder, Branson himself, might be voted off the board: going public really does expose the company to the cold winds that can blow in the financial world and make it vulnerable to external factors.

These thoughts were not the ones most in evidence when Virgin shares first went on sale, in 1986, at an offer price of 140p. The shares failed to maintain their original valuation and declined to a low point of 85p. A major reason why Virgin shares 'failed' was because they did not prove attractive enough to the big investors, and to would-be institutional shareholders. And the reason why they were reluctant to buy in to Virgin was that they did not share Branson's faith in the long-term plans and prospects of the company.

It was not long before Branson realised his mistake. The new shareholders sought to exert considerable influence, if not direct pressure, on the direction in which Virgin was going.

Having to rethink

Not liking what he was experiencing, in 1988 Branson bought out the new shareholders and returned the company to private status in early 1989. Though Branson's ownership of Virgin does not extend to owning all of its shares, those who have a stake in it tend to be those whose attitudes and values coincide with his and who have confidence in Branson's strategy and leadership.

In 1988 Branson and his top managers, including his 'lieutenants', Ken Berry and Simon Draper, bought Virgin shares back at their original price of 140p. In doing so, Branson effectively stifled the potential threat to which he had, for the best of motives, exposed his company through that original decision to go public.

Was Virgin, then, capable of providing enough income on its own to sustain growth and fulfil Branson's desire to make it "the greatest entertainment business in the world"? A good question. And one worth asking at this point in an unfinished story, when Virgin Music – once the core business – has been sold to EMI for £560 million through a one-for-four rights issue. What might Branson's decision to sell mean? Has he chosen this option as a long-term tactic to raise finance to expand in a different direction? Has Branson done it deliberately to avoid having to return to the 'City' a second time in order to raise capital to finance expansion in some undisclosed direction – possibly an expansion of his airline business, which is cash-hungry and has heavy start-up costs?

The answer is, 'Probably, yes'. What has emerged is that Branson has changed his business strategy; his ambition to make Virgin 'the greatest entertainment business in the world' will not become reality. His new ambition – which is also the new business strategy – is summarised in the phrase, "to create a real quality airline that manages to survive on a world-wide basis!". Nine years after he launched Virgin Atlantic, Branson has gone halfway to his target of running eighteen planes to thirteen major cities over five continents.

Where Virgin is Now

At present Virgin has four major divisions: communications; travel; music and retail. Parts of these businesses have been sold off. Fujisankei, for example, holds 25% of the music business for which it paid $150 million and WH Smith owns half of Virgin's megastores. Virgin Music, which Branson built into the seventh largest record company in the world has been sold for a substantial sum to Thorn EMI, with Draper and Berry going with it as part of its sale price. Branson's energies are clearly turning to a new challenge: building an airline that can compete with the 'giants' of world aviation, like British Airways. Already he has faced the unpleasant side of the airline business as BA waged a 'dirty tricks' campaign to attract passengers from Virgin to BA by tapping into Virgin's reservations computer. BA have also been accused of spreading false information to the media suggesting that Branson was in financial difficulties in an attempt to undermine his business credibility. He has won his first legal battle and received considerable damages from BA.

The resources required for starting up and running an airline are enormous: a single factor, such as the Gulf crisis of 1990-91, can plunge a successful business into illiquidity very quickly. (Branson has already witnessed this: pre-tax profits of less than £800,000 were declared for Voyager Travel in 1991, compared to £8.5 million for the previous year.) But Branson's strategy is unambiguous: "The airline is more than a business, it is a crusade".

Where Virgin Might Be ...

Will Virgin's growth be organic, as it has been traditionally, or will Virgin Group become more predatory than it has been, building through acquisition? Having sold off Virgin Music, Branson currently sits on a formidable mini-mountain of cash. He seems to be turning his back on the business that metamorphosed the 'hippy entrepreneur' in to one of the country's best-known business people. At the same time, he is clearly intent upon elbowing himself in to a prominent place in the notoriously competitive airline business. Whether he succeeds or fails, there is no way presently of knowing. But what we can be certain of is that we cannot predict what the size and shape of Branson's business will be; at present we can only be sure that it will continue to grow for some time yet.

Adapt or die: a business opportunity from a potential disaster

The time is the late 1970s; the place is Ireland. Around a table sits a group of people obliged to find a solution to a very pressing problem. The background to their problem is simple: they have thousands of gallons of cream that no one wants. Increasingly health-conscious Irish consumers are reluctant to buy a product that they associate with fat, cholesterol and coronary heart disease. With the supply of cream steadily outstripping demand, the Irish Milk Marketing Board has a huge surplus of an unneeded product. From somewhere around that table, an idea slowly emerges ... what about blending the surplus cream with surplus Irish whiskey to make a new and distinctive liqueur? Attractively packaging the bottle whilst retaining the Irish character of the product? Giving the product a name that suggests that behind it there is a pedigree of quality and tradition? A name? Perhaps a family name? Ideas begin to emerge thick and fast as the marketing brainstorm takes on its own momentum.

A fictitious scene? Yes and no. The brainstormers that day certainly got up from that table with a new idea and a new product. They had found the answers they were looking for. What they had done was to come up with the five answers that any good marketer would want:

- whatever it is that we make, will consumers buy it?;
- whatever it is that we make, can we provide it in sufficient quantity?;
- whatever it is that we make, can we make it at the right price?;
- whatever it is that we make, can we make it cost effectively?;
- whatever it is that we make, can we make it at the right quality?;

There were three further questions to which they had to get answers:

- once they had designed their product, could they raise the money that would support its production and promotion?;
- could they get people of the right quality to develop, market and produce their product effectively?;
- could their organisation adapt so that the new product could be integrated into its product range?

The answer to all three questions turned out to be 'Yes'; the product that they 'invented' found its way on to supermarket shelves as *Bailey's Irish Cream*. It was followed in a short space of time by other competing products, such as Bewley's Irish Coffee.

The moral of the above tale is that an astute business person will always, given the slightest chance in the most adverse circumstances, convert a threat in to an opportunity.

Assignment *The Advisory Unit*

Hansborough suffers from a high level of unemployment, and the council is anxious to promote industrial and commercial activity in the area. At a full meeting of the Council two months ago it was resolved to set up a small advisory unit in premises in the city centre to provide information and assistance to people interested in establishing new businesses. You have been seconded to the unit from your post in the Administrative and Legal Department of the Council, for a period of six months. Including yourself, the unit has a staff of three.

During its first month of operation the unit has had to deal with a wide range of questions and has given assistance to a large number of individuals. To assist in the advisory process it has been decided to produce a 'Business Start up' booklet in which a number of the more obvious matters of concern could be included. It is thought that a question and answer format would be most appropriate for the booklet. You have been given the responsibility for the production of this booklet.

Tasks

1. Draft the questions and answers to be included in the booklet. Examples of matters you should cover include the meaning of the expression 'business', the various legal forms of business, the formalities involved in business formation and the difference between corporate and non-corporate bodies.

2. As a section of the booklet you should identify the sources of finance available to a new business and the problems involved in raising finance from such sources.

3. The final part of the booklet should explain the importance of a business plan and outline the contents of such a plan.

Development Tasks

4. Decide upon the information that you feel should be included on the front, back and inside covers of the booklet and draft the layout of the cover. Bear in mind that the cover must be A5 size.

5. City Printers, a local printing company has contracted with the council to produce the booklet. You are required to meet with Chris Beardsley, the company's graphic artist to decide on the booklet's final format. Prior to this meeting produce a set of notes which set out your ideas on the total layout of the booklet so that you can clearly communicate your thoughts to Mr. Beardsley.

Element 8.2 Producing a business plan

Producing a Business Plan

The purposes of a business plan

Any business activity involves an element of risk. It is important therefore that if you are going to run a business that you accurately assess this risk by predicting the potential problems which the business will face. This means that the business must prepare a realistic assessment of the revenue it will generate in the future and the costs it will incur. The business needs to prepare:

- a business plan; and
- a cash flow projection. (We examine how to prepare a cashflow projection in Unit 7, *Financial Resources*.)

By doing this you will be able to assess the viability of the business and how you should manage it in the future. Sensible business planning will also allow you to assess its financial requirements in the future and you can use it as part of a proposal to a bank when seeking to raise funds. When a business seeks finance from a bank, the bank manager will want to be convinced that the business is sound and that there is a good likelihood of the loan being repaid.

What are the characteristics of a business plan?

Your business plan should have the following characteristics:

- It should be *simple, clear* and *concise*. This is important because the person reading your business plan needs to understand as quickly and simply as possible what your business is trying to do. Remember that you will have thought about your business idea for some considerable time. In your mind it is obvious what the business is attempting to achieve. You do not need convincing of its worth. Yet the outsider who reads it for the first time does need convincing that it is a good idea. You will not have the opportunity to spend hours explaining every last detail to him or her;

- It should be *realistic* and *truthful*. All bank managers at some time in their careers will have been presented with business plans which are simply not feasible. An inexperienced entrepreneur who predicts that his or her business is going to compete on equal terms with Marks and Spencer or ICI within six months will be regarded as a time-wasting crank who has little or no business sense. What is worse is if the plan contains blatant lies. Robert Maxwell may have been able to persuade the banks that he was honest and trustworthy but you are no Robert Maxwell – at least we hope not! It is vital that you establish a relationship with your bank manager that is open, honest and based on mutual trust. A business based on lies, half truths or exaggerations has its foundations in sand;

- It should be *accurate* and, wherever possible, *supported with data and figures*. If you over-estimate or miscalculate the value of your potential sales or under-estimate the degree of competition or level of expenses then you will not be able to predict your need for cash. The bank manager who reads your business plan thinks in terms of money. He or she wants to know what you will earn, what you will spend and what profit you will make. Always under-estimate your likely earnings (sales rarely work out in practice as optimistically as they may appear initially on paper). Always assume the worst when it comes to your expenses (it is the unexpected drain on your finances which can catch you out). Be conservative in your prediction of profit (do not feel that your plan must show vast profits to be accepted – breaking even in the early days of a business is often enough). It is far better to be able to go to your bank manager at a later date and say that you will not need to draw on the total amount of finance you have been offered than to go and say that you had misjudged the level of your debts and please could you borrow more.

Activity

Role play an exercise where the teacher (or one member of you group) acts as a bank manager and one or more of the student group take the role of the person presenting a business plan in order to obtain a loan. Note the sort of questions which the bank manager will ask.

What a business plan should contain

Your business plan needs to have the following sections:

1. *A statement of your business objectives.* This should tell the reader what you intend to do. At this stage do not go into detail about markets, costings or personnel. These will all come later.

2. *An evaluation of the market.* Without a market for your product or service the business will not survive. It is an essential ingredient for business success. No matter how clever an idea you have or how innovative a product you can make if there is no one out there who wants to buy it then you will not be in business for long. This is where your market research skills come in. In Unit 3, *Marketing,* we discuss the need for accurate market research and suggested techniques you can use to find out if there is a market for your product. Show in your business plan that you have done your homework.

3. *An explanation of how you intend to produce your product or service.* Not only do you need to show that you can sell what you make, you also need to show that you can make it. This does not simply mean an explanation of the productive process but should also cover such aspects as: your product design; where you are going to operate or manufacture; the equipment, machinery or plant that you will use; and your sources of raw materials or other supplies. When Nissan sets up a factory it makes sure that all these factors have been considered and planned and while your business is not likely to be as big as Nissan's you can learn a lot from that company's degree of preparation.

4. *An analysis of the resources you will need.* Throughout this book we have stressed that you should recognise that the term 'resources' does not simply refer to money. While financial resources are important, it is perhaps the human resources of any business which are most crucial. If you are running the business you will need to outline your skills and experience and those of your partners or co-directors. But only the smallest

business does not require other workers. Will you need production workers or administrative staff? Will they be full-time or part-time, experienced or trainees? Your business plan needs to specify the types of skills you will need and whether you already have staff identified or whether you will have to recruit new staff. If you are going to recruit then you have to be confident that the sort of staff you will need are available on the labour market.

It is also necessary to show the extent of your business' need for finance. If you are asking a bank or other lender to risk its money then it is also important to demonstrate that you are willing to risk some of your own. In a business start-up this may not always be a large commitment on your part but if you have little capital to put into the business the lender may well want some form of security as a guarantee that, should the business fail, all the money loaned will not be lost. Many people starting in business have to use personal assets such as a house as security. When young people start in business they will sometimes get their parents or other relatives or friends to act as personal guarantors for any loans. However you should be careful when getting someone else to guarantee your debts in this way for if the lender does have to call on the guarantor then you could lose not only their money but also their friendship.

5. *An explanation of your product*
    In section two of your plan you should have already described the market which you intend to exploit. In this section you need to explain clearly what your product is and does. No doubt you are convinced that your product will be better, cheaper and more attractive to customers than anything else on the market. Now is your chance to explain why. Describe your product in some detail, how it will work and why it is any different from the products of your competitors. If you can explain technical details in layman's language this will help and if you show how it is better than other products by using figures and actual examples such as price comparisons this will strengthen your case.

Marketing Plan

The purpose of a marketing plan is to bring together the different aspects of marketing into a single coherent strategy. It needs to recognise that each individual various aspect of marketing cannot alone bring success but only when they are related and co-ordinated will they bring the sales that the business needs. (We discuss the preparation of a marketing plan in more detail in the next Element, *Preparing a Sales and Marketing Plan.*) Here we outline the main aspects of the marketing plan.

A organisation's marketing plan should have a number of distinct component parts.

1. *A quantifiable target or objective.* It is not sufficient to state that we wish to increase sales significantly or see turnover grow in the next year. The plan needs to state these targets in quantifiable terms. This can either be as an increase in turnover. For instance the company seeks to increase turnover by 25% in the next twelve months, or in quantity terms, for example, the organisation intends to sell twice as many computers in the next quarter than it did in the last. Many businesses will also state their marketing objectives in terms of the market share they seek to achieve. So for example the business may be aiming to have a 20% share of sales in a particular region within the next two years.

2. *A clear idea of its current and planned products.* One of the traditional sayings in marketing is 'know what you are selling'. This might seem obvious. The business must

surely be aware of the product it is making. Nevertheless what the product is may not be obvious to the general public. A clear product identity needs to be established. Perhaps the product has traditionally been regarded as having certain characteristics or a particular kind of market. Lucosade is a good example. In the past it was regarded as drink for people who were ill – you took it into hospital as a present for a sick aunt. Yet it has now been repositioned as a fitness drink and is heavily promoted for people taking part in sports. Perhaps the product can be improved or developed so that it reaches a wider market. New products could be introduced which extend and enhance the company's product range, either strengthening its position in traditional markets or moving it into new markets.

3. *The price of the product*. Again this may seem an obvious point in that the company should have set prices for its products which allow it to make a profit. But does the price of our product compete with those of our competitors? Do we need to lower the price, perhaps offer discounts or special offers in order to increase sales? Will we be able to change the price of our product in the future, for example once we have established a strong market loyalty?

4. *Market information needed*
   Clearly if the organisation is to develop a successful marketing strategy then it will need certain types of market information. The organisation may need to know the size of the market, what the consumers currently buy and what they would like to buy in the future. Once the organisation has determined the sort of information it needs then it must decide what is the best way of finding this information. In other words, what kinds of market research will it have to employ. Should it undertake surveys and other forms of primary research or is there sufficient information already available in other forms such as marketing reports or government statistics which it can use at a much lower cost?

5. *A sales plan*. The company should identify the geographical areas it seeks to sell in. It may be that the organisation is better concentrating on a regional market rather than trying to compete on a national scale. Factors which can influence this decision may include the distribution networks that it has and the cost of reaching a wider market. Many products are test marketed in a particular region to assess consumer reaction before being launched on the national or international market. The initial response from the test marketing can be used to refine and develop the product or to change the emphasis in its advertising and promotional material.
   The company may have to decide its channels of distribution. In other words, should it sell direct to the public either through its own outlets, through mail or teleordering or should it use retailers or other distributors who may be able to reach the consumer more easily but who will want their share of the final price?

6. *Advertising and promotion*. In this aspect of the plan the organisation needs to evaluate the alternative forms of advertising which are available to it. As we saw in Unit 3 there are many different forms of advertising and the organisation must decide which is the most appropriate both in terms of effectiveness and in terms of cost. A series of television adverts may be expensive but may have a much greater impact on sales than hundreds of billboards.
   The organisation also needs to pay considerable attention to the way in which the product is packaged and the point of sale material which will be used in retailers or

other outlets. This can often be crucial to the customer's perception of the product and its quality.

7. *The marketing team required to market and sell the product.* The product may be good and the advertising may be right but if the people who are selling the product do not know what they are doing or are unpleasant and unhelpful to the customer then the whole marketing plan can be a failure. In any promotion the sales staff must be aware of the product they are selling and recognise that it is the customer who ultimately counts. If the organisation is using telephone sales then they need people who understand the product. If you are trying to sell computers over the phone then a telesales person who does not know what a floppy disk or a keyboard is will be of little use to a customer who is deciding what to buy.

   Similarly if the company is selling through retail outlets then it will need a sales staff who are experienced in selling to that particular sort of retailer.

   Therefore the company has to decide whether it has staff who are sufficiently experienced to handle the sales of its products or whether it should hire new staff or train the existing workforce. Many organisations will organise training sessions for staff when a new product is introduced. This has the dual objective of teaching the staff how to sell the product and selling the idea of the new product to the staff themselves.

8. *The cost of implementing the plan.* Many of the previous aspects of the marketing plan cost money. Advertising, training and distribution may not come cheap. All of these costs need to be carefully calculated to make sure that the cost of marketing the product is not going to be so great that it outweighs the profit that the company is likely to make from it.

A Production Plan

An organisation needs a production plan to be able to match its production requirements. In other words the orders it has received or sales which are anticipated, with its productive resources. It will need to have the right people, machines and raw materials available when needed so that the business can operate as efficiently and profitably as possible. If the resources are not available when the company needs to produce products then customers must wait. They may become dissatisfied and take their custom elsewhere. Equally if the business has resources standing idle waiting for production to begin, this is clearly inefficient and wasteful.

The production plan needs to address a number of important questions.

- what goods have to be produced?;
- when are they required?;
- do certain orders take priority?;
- what resources are needed to produce the goods?;
- are these resources available within the organisation or do they need to be bought in?;
- if it is not possible to complete all the production within our own organisation should we contract out some of the work?;
- how long will it take to buy in any goods that are needed?;
- can we keep our available workforce, plant and machinery operating to capacity?

To tackle these questions the production plan should take a number of stages.

- *order sequencing*;

- *resource identification*;
- *production balancing*;
- *maximising continuous production*.

Order sequencing

The first part of production planning is order sequencing. This involves arranging the orders or predicted orders into the time schedule when they will be produced. It may be necessary to classify orders according to some measure of priority such as urgent, normal production timescale, not required immediately and so on.

Resource identification

The next stage in the production plan is to identify the parts or components needed to produce the order. This is particularly important if some parts have to be bought in from outside the organisation. The production control department should be aware of all resources they need and requisition them from the stores or order them through purchasing to make sure that they are available when needed. There are few more frustrating problems than having a production line held up because somebody forgot to order a component or because a supplier let you down on delivery.

Production balancing

Balancing the production is another key element in production planning. If the company produces more than one product it is important wherever possible to have some degree of flexibility in the use of labour and machinery. For instance if one product is in demand it may be necessary to transfer resources from other production areas which are less busy so that one area is not working under tremendous pressure (and perhaps incurring overtime costs) while other areas are comparatively slack.

Maximising continuous production

If possible the production process should be kept working continuously. The organisation can usually gain *economies of scale* if it can produce goods in multiple quantities rather than producing a short run of one product and then having to transfer to a short run of another. Therefore if possible, the production plan should batch together orders for the same or similar products.

Keeping the customer informed of progress is also an important aspect of good customer relations. The production controller should make sure that major customers are aware of the different stages that their order has reached and, should difficulties arise, the customer should be informed of any likely delay. While customers may not be happy with a delay in delivery they will be even less happy if they do not know that the delay is likely until the day scheduled for delivery.

Quality

'Quality' is now a familiar word to consumers. It has a straightforward definition: *the level of product or service which it takes to satisfy the customer.*

When a consumer considers buying a product, three main questions will be borne in mind:

- is the product suitable for the purpose i have in mind?;
- is the price right?;
- is it available for purchase?

It is most likely that the consumer will have products from several manufacturers to consider, and that each manufacturer will attempt to persuade the consumer to buy their product by the use of various promotional and marketing techniques; these were explained in some detail in Unit 3, *Marketing*.

Increasingly, though, consumers will discriminate between products according to their actual or perceived quality. Actual quality is that which can be clearly and definitely established; for example, the quality of upholstery inside a new car. Perceived quality is what the consumer believes to be the quality, either by the image which the product portrays or the reputation which it has built. For example, no-one questions the quality of the Jaguar motorcar; it is 'perceived' to be a quality product.

To illustrate the concept of quality, consider a couple contemplating the purchase of a new lawn mower. They visit their local garden centre, where they know there is a wide selection from which to choose. On arrival they find there are three different manufacturers who have products which meet their need, which is to mow a small lawn in a family garden. The price differential between all three models of lawnmower is only £5 and the product specifications of all three machines are similar.

On what basis might the couple make a decision? Promotional techniques, such as a free first service or discount coupons for other garden products, might influence the decision, but an increasingly important factor for the discerning consumer is the issue of quality. The couple might try to establish:

- the quality of the 'finish' on the lawn mower;
- whether the paint work, cabling and cutting blade on one mower is significantly better than on its competitors;
- the length of product guarantee: is a longer guarantee a statement of confidence in the product quality?;
- the efficiency and convenience of after sales service: are service depots close at hand?;
- the availability of spares;
- the clarity of instructions in the instruction booklet.

How does a producer achieve quality?

Once it recognises the importance of quality to its customers, a business must have a strategy for achieving the necessary quality from its production facility.

The ability of a business to produce 'quality' goods is dependent on two main factors:

- *Its suppliers*. They must deliver material and components of the right quality, otherwise the product will never be right;
- *Its workforce*. The importance of the quality concept must be recognised by them. Traditionally, managers have kept the issues of special training and knowledge of quality and customer satisfaction to themselves. Many managers fail to educate their workforces to understand quality and its impact on competitiveness. They have also failed to empower their workers to make suggestions and act to improve quality. Improving quality is a gradual process; constant improvement is needed. Workers must understand and own the objective of improved quality and be motivated to make it a reality.

Investment in training, consultative processes, new machines and techniques is vital for the maintenance of a highly skilled and motivated workforce which can generate the crucial, constant improvements in products that win customers.

Quality is about people and their attitudes rather than simply methods and systems of production. The responsibility for management of quality lies with all employees – managers and shop floor together.

Total Quality Management

Traditionally, the UK approach to quality control in industry has been based on the practice of post-production inspection. At the end of the manufacturing process the product was examined and measured to see whether it measured up (conformed) to a set specification.

The disadvantages of this approach are:

- it depends on outcome only;
- it is expensive;
- it wastes valuable material (talent and time);
- it wastes production time and effort in making scrapped or failed products.

Since the late 1970s the emphasis has begun to shift from systems of end-inspection to one where systematic and scrupulous inspection is integral to the process itself so that sub-standard products are eliminated. This approach depends on:

- a specification of the process;
- close monitoring of the process;
- continuous inspection of the product at all stages;
- every participant in the process being 'quality conscious' and accountable for quality at each stage of the process.

This approach is often referred to as '*total quality management*' and ensures that products meet stringent international standards. It is the approach favoured particularly by Japanese industries which seek quality assurance. Its advantages are:

- it is efficient;
- it makes the best use of resources;
- it provides reliable and early feedback loops to ensure consistent products;
- it leads eventually to increased customer satisfaction.

Deciding Where to Locate the Business

The choice of where to locate is one of the most important questions facing any business. For organisations which have been long established the choice may be whether or not the existing location is the most suitable for the business's needs. There will be considerations of cost and availability of suitable premises, an appropriate labour force, access to markets or accessibility of sources of raw materials or suppliers. If you are in the process of establishing a business you will have more freedom of choice in your locational decision. We now need to consider the factors which could influence you in where to locate.

Factors affecting organisational location

Regional location

A substantial proportion of all organisations in the UK may be described as 'foot-loose'. That is, they are capable of establishing in any region and are not tied to any specific area. Estimates suggest that about 70% of organisations in the UK's manufacturing industry fall into this category. This does not mean that they are necessarily dispersed or scattered all over the country. It simply means that they are capable of moving to those areas where economic conditions are most suitable. They are seeking a region which will provide a number of factors. These considerations would include:

- labour costs; and
- manufacturing costs.

The types of organisations which characterise foot-loose businesses could be those concerned with light engineering or assembly, capable of locating or relocating in almost all the industrial regions in the country.

Labour costs

In the UK wage rates differ substantially from region to region. The South East of England has wage rates often 50% higher than those in Northern Ireland, 25% higher than in Scotland and the North East and 15% higher than in the West Midlands. These are the results of traditional wage patterns and the level of unemployment and demand for labour in the respective areas.

Although in many industries there are nationally negotiated wage rates agreed between the unions and the employers which can lead to a levelling of pay in all regions, there is still a tendency for a wage drift, where employers in areas of full employment pay above nationally agreed wage levels in order to attract and hold workers, while in those regions with higher unemployment, employers are capable of only offering nationally agreed minimums. There is much greater likelihood that there will be a nationally agreed wage level in those industries which are highly unionised. Also employers who have workers throughout the country such as the civil service or the nationalised industries are more likely to have standardised wage levels.

Differential wage levels will tend to be attractive to those organisations seeking cheaper labour. However it should be emphasised that this may only be attractive to businesses which do not require labour with a particular skill, for this may be only available in a certain region.

Manufacturing or operating costs

The costs of production or operation may vary from area to area and so may act as an influence on the location of industry. The cost of capital tends to be relatively homogeneous throughout the country because of the comprehensive banking system which is operated nationwide. However smaller organisations may be more restricted in their sources of capital and tend to have to raise it from established connections. This can well act as a limiting factor on the mobility of industry and prevent it from moving to different areas.

The government has used the availability of capital as a means of inducing industrial mobility by offering cheaper means of finance to those businesses willing to move to development areas. Other important operational costs will be those incurred in the acquisition of offices, factories or other premises. In practice this may be one of the major considerations in influencing locational decision. Property prices and rent are often much higher in those areas with a high level of economic activity. This may act as a sufficient incentive to move industry out of city centre sites, or away from the South East of England. Also the central government and local authorities have made conscious efforts to attract industry to depressed regions by offering subsidies and grants such as rent-free properties or low rents for a period of years. The availability of suitable sites may also be a considerable attraction to foot-loose industry and the government has used a policy of 'sticks and carrots' in restricting industrial development in the South East while facilitating sites for new organisations in other regions. One attempt to attract industry to development areas has been to create *enterprise zones*. Notable features of these zones are the less rigid adherence to planning restrictions and rate relief. Town and Country Planning legislation restricts development in other areas, so making these enterprises zones more attractive. Property values will always reflect development potential.

These measures have been successful to some extent in attracting companies but unfortunately, there are instances of organisations who, having sited in the development areas, abandon them once the incentives have expired. Often there are examples of businesses taking advantage of free factories, capital allowances and so on and then moving on after these costs move back to their unsubsidised levels.

Organisations tied to a particular area

Earlier we noted that some organisations may be described as foot-loose in that they are capable of locating in a variety of areas. However, many organisations are tied to particular regions because of the need to be close to markets, suppliers of raw materials or components, or the availability of a pool of labour with a specific skill.

Accessibility of markets

It is often the nature of the product or service produced which restricts an organisation's choice of location. Most service organisations requiring personal contact with the public will obviously be sited conveniently for their customers. Banks, retailers, restaurants must be near to centres of population. This is because the service which they sell cannot easily be transported. In manufacturing industry too, it is the portability or ease of transport of the final product which can determine whether or not a manufacturer must site close to customers. If the product has high value in relation to its bulk then transport costs may add little to the final selling price and so the producer may site a considerable distance from customers. Other products may be costly to transport and so make it necessary to locate near to markets. In the past transport costs were much more important both nationally and internationally in determining the location of industry but as transport systems have developed, this has become much less of a constraint. However as the European market has developed, there has been a drift of industrial location to areas with access to European markets.

Supply of skilled labour

Certain businesses require a specific skill or talent in their labour force. If workers of this type are available throughout the country then this does not pose a constraint. But if an organisation requires workers with a particular talent and such people are found only in certain regions this will act as a pull to an organisation requiring such workers. For example a business hoping to establish as glass manufacturers may require experienced glass blowers and so choose to locate in St. Helens or Sunderland with their long-established tradition of glass making and pool of skilled labour. However it is not only the type of labour which may act as an attraction for an organisation to a particular region, it may also be the attitude of the workforce. For example, a tradition of shift working or female workers may prove attractive. The region's record on industrial relations may prove to be a deciding factor. An area which is regarded as 'strike prone' may be unattractive while those regions with a comparatively good industrial relations history may attract and hold industry.

In those regions which have faced the industrial decline of major employers such as Scotland, Wales and the North East, a large pool of redundant labour may develop. This may appear attractive to potential new employers but they may have to retrain their new labour force and the costs of retraining may offset the benefits achieved by relatively low wage levels.

The availability of the supply of raw materials

If an organisation requires large supplies of raw materials for its productive process, and if the raw materials used are bulky and costly to transport then it may be most suitable for it to locate close to suppliers. As noted in the comments on the access to a market, transport costs were much more of a determining factor in the past and particularly during and after the industrial revolution when the manufacturers of products such as steel tended to move close to their suppliers of coal, iron ore, etc. This trend is clearly not so prominent now as transport costs have reduced and movement of raw materials is easier. However manufacturers do tend to congregate in areas where suppliers of parts and components are situated. This infrastructure of suppliers and services related to their particular industry tends to keep down costs. Examples include the concentration of much of the motor industry in the West Midlands and another example is in the United States where many of the micro-electronics manufacturers have located in California's so-called 'Silicon Valley'. The advantages of concentration of an industry in a particular area are referred to as external economies of scale. These would include such gains as the development of a skilled labour force, the provision of education and training facilities by local colleges and training centres and the growth of mutually dependent systems of suppliers and subcontractors.

The decision by management on location

While it has been noted that the economic factors of labour, materials and market accessibility may play an important part in determining the most appropriate location for an organisation's operation, it is often the managers of the business who will have the final say. This decision may be influenced by the management's decision of where to live and work. One of the major factors quoted for many organisations' reluctance to move from the South East to the regions is the unattractive impression these areas have in the eyes of senior management. They prefer to live in the South East and work in London than move to the North East or Northern Ireland despite the obvious economic advantages to their organisation of moving. Despite the fact that this may be an irrational judgement it could nevertheless prove to be a crucial factor in locational decisions.

Activity

Imagine that you work for you local council. Prepare the copy for a brochure of not more than one side of A4 which 'sells' the advantages of your area to someone who is considering locating a business there.

Assignment *Planning for Gold*

This assignment is somewhat different from the rest in this book. In this assignment we are not going to give you a role, we are not even going to give you a problem. No! Instead we are going to give you a challenge - don't phone Anneka she has enough on her plate already. The challenge we are setting you to undertake either individually or in a group is to identify a business opportunity and to produce an outline business plan which will convince someone that your idea is a good one.

While we would like your idea to be feasible for you in your present situation to undertake that is not necessary. If you can come up an idea as good as Richard Branson's and prove that it is not just wistful thinking then that would be good.

Try to undertake this assignment in a sensible and logical manner. It involves identifying an opportunity, researching it, weighing up the pros and cons, before deciding it is worth following.

Gather information from as wide a variety as sources as possible but remember that gathering too much information is expensive in both time and money both to yourself and others so be sensible in your approach.

Preparing the plan will help to formalise your ideas and you should be prepared to present it to your tutor and your fellow students both verbally and in writing.

Good luck!

Element 8.3 Sales and Marketing Planning

The Philosophy of Marketing Planning

As with all elements of planning which take place within a business, marketing planning is aimed to provide various benefits, namely:

- a direction for the business;
- a scale upon which to measure the success of an organisation's operations; and
- energy which will assist the organisation in its drive towards success.

The marketing plan provides the business with the framework within which its future marketing activities will take place. As you will see throughout this element, the marketing plan will provide you with not only a general guide to the future but also specific a action plan for each area which falls within the marketing function. The underlying concept is to recognise the importance of the current situation in which a business finds itself, and to relate that to all its future activities. You should recognise that a written plan for all the important areas of activity is vital to the success of the organisation.

The planning process

In Unit 3, *Marketing*, we explain that the aim behind the whole marketing function is to enable the business to discover the needs and wants of a target market, and attempt to satisfy them, usually with the objective of making a profit. The planning role is designed to assist the marketer in the process of problem recognition and problem solving. The problem in this instance is usually the gap that exists between the organisation's current activities and those necessary to satisfy consumers' needs. The marketing planning process, in keeping with other planning functions, employs various stages:

- an evaluation of the current situation;
- the establishment of goals and objectives;
- the designing of strategies for the allocation of scarce resources;
- the specific tactical steps to achieve the goals;
- an evaluation of the success or failure of the plans.

Marketing planning cannot operate in isolation from other aspects of the organisation's planning process. In the previous Element, we considered the general area of business planning and it is important that you should realise that the marketing plan must not only be consistent in itself but must also be consistent with the overall plans for the business.

Marketing planning and strategic planning

All good plans start from the very top. A business must have an overall strategic plan if it is to operate in a coherent and consistent manner, and it is from this overall corporate strategy that all other plans must evolve. To derive a marketing plan in isolation from the overall plan would be like attempting to build the various parts of a car without an overall blue print. With the time to fit the pieces together, there would be no guarantee that they would come together to form a coherent whole. It is vital therefore to make sure that the overall business or strategic plan comes first.

Corporate culture is also important in the design of a marketing plan. In Unit 3, *Marketing*, we explain that marketing should be seen as a philosophy which pervades the whole organisation, and not simply as an additional functional area. The input of marketing into the design of the overall strategic plan should therefore be integral, and marketing should not be seen as operating in a vacuum. If this is the case, the design of the marketing plan itself should follow logically from the strategic plan.

Most successful large organisations already embrace the marketing philosophy, but it is just as important for smaller businesses. Within large organisations, formal mechanisms often exist to make sure that there is a degree of co-ordination between the various departments in adhering to common objectives. With smaller companies, written plans are just as important. Whilst the bank will usually require a formal written business plan if you are trying to raise money, a written marketing plan will also provide an element of stability and direction, which can be of particular importance during the inevitable times of crisis which are faced by most smaller companies.

The following sections will consider in detail the specific stages and contents of the marketing plan. Essentially, these fall into three parts:

- the situational analysis
- the strategy
- the action plans

Situational Analysis

The first step in any marketing plan is to establish the organisation's current situation. This is effectively a photograph of the current state of affairs, and should be as detailed as possible. It should cover all variables which are likely to have any impact upon the future marketing activities of the organisation, and as such it is important to remember the problems of 'marketing myopia', which is where an organisation's activities are too narrowly defined. It is easy to consider that a company operates only within a very narrow field, and as such will only be affected by a small number of variables. In the marketing planning process you need to make sure that this does not happen, and that you take as wide a view of the organisation and its environment as possible. The following sections provide a detailed checklist for any business involved in marketing planning. Much of the information required to successfully complete the situational analysis can be found by using the process discussed in Elements 3.1. and 3.2 earlier in the book, which considered the area of market research. You should read those Elements in conjunction with this section. The individual elements of the marketing plan are as follows:

- the company;
- the product/service;
- benefit/segment matrix;
- the price/contribution;
- promotion;
- sales force;
- distribution;
- competitive analysis;
- sources of information.

The Company

The introductory section of the marketing plan should include a single page description of the company, outlining its main features and areas of operation. It should include the mission of the company, and a list of all of those who will be involved in the marketing effort. The description should be brief but contain sufficient detail to place the marketing plan within the context of the overall operation of the organisation.

The product/service

Most businesses will offer more than one product or service. Even if the organisation is specialising in only one product or service, this section of the situational analysis is important. Each product or service should be listed, and then analysed in various ways. Define the specific benefits which are offered to the end user, as this often forms the basis for the *Unique Selling Proposition* (USP) which will be integral to the positioning of the product within the marketplace. It is also necessary at this stage to research consumer perceptions of the products and their benefits, as any discrepancy between what the *company* thinks the product offers and what the *consumer* thinks the product offers is an area of concern. You should identify the strengths and weakness of the products, to allow you to decide whether you need to change some of the variables, for instance by introducing a new design or new promotional campaign. Remember to consider the products as a range rather than in isolation, as many organisations offer their products in bundles. Product ranges should complement each other, and attempt to provide as wide a coverage of the market as possible.

Benefit/segment matrix

It may be useful at this point to construct a product/benefit matrix, which will define the benefit which a product can offer to different market segments. For example, look at a leisure centre. Various market segments will use the centre, but for differing reasons and at differing times. The matrix may look like this:

Segment	Squash	Gym	Swimming	Solarium
Business People	H	M	L	L
Families	L	H	H	M
Students	M	L	M	M
H = High Usage				
M = Medium Usage				
L = Low Usage				

This very simplified matrix will allow the operators of the leisure centre to target specific activities to specific target segments. It can also be combined with a study of the timing of this usage, which may suggest periods when certain facilities are not very well used. This would then provide the opportunity to attempt to increase usage at these slack times by repositioning the service, for example by providing off peak pricing for the squash courts or creche facilities to allow parents with children below school age to use facilities during the day.

The price/contribution

This section of the situational analysis will include the price of each product, the margin of contribution which each product makes (that is the price charged for the product minus its variable costs), and a consideration of any special promotional pricing offers which may be in existence, such as group discounts or bulk-buying reductions. Also consider the pricing of the competitors within the industry, as no organisation can operate in isolation. Always give due account to market price levels, irrespective of the level of competition.

The area of *contribution* is an important one. All products should be able to contribute towards the fixed costs of an organisation. Once these fixed costs are covered, the contribution becomes profit. The listing of the contribution for each product can be a daunting task, especially if the product range is wide. You could also argue that this is not the function of the marketer but of the financial department. This may be true in terms of the gathering of the information, but the use of the data is vital when drawing up any marketing strategies. As you will remember from Unit 1, *Business in the Economy*, price is a major factor in determining the level of demand. However, if you set a price which is too low to generate sufficient contribution to the organisation's costs, then a high level of demand is of little comfort to an organisation destined for liquidation.

When contributions have been defined, they can be used to influence a whole range of activities within the marketing field. For example, sales executives may be instructed to push a product with a lower list price but a higher contribution. The consumer may be convinced that the sales pitch is designed to provide the best for them in terms of value for money, when it is actually designed to secure the largest contribution towards the organisation's costs and profit levels.

Promotion

A full audit should be carried out of all promotional activity which takes place within the business. All activities should be listed, and examples gathered of things such as promotional literature or PR projects. If the promotional activity has been designed correctly, each project should have specific goals and objectives, and these should be included. An evaluation of the success of the campaigns in terms of their objectives should also be carried out. Again, this should be an ongoing process, and the information should be readily to hand. Without evaluation of variables such as the change in the levels of sales or the level of customer feedback or awareness, it is impossible to even attempt to identify the success or otherwise of such activities.

Whilst it is hoped that all promotional activity will produce a benefit, it will also bear an accompanying cost. This section should therefore also include an analysis of the costs and benefits of each project, as well as the technical success or failure. The problem of actually quantifying the benefits of specific activities has already been discussed earlier in the book. Promotional activity does not operate within a vacuum. It is only part of the overall marketing mix, and can be aided or hindered by factors which are both within and beyond the control of the organisation. It is therefore vital that the overall context of the activity be cited, to provide as full picture as possible. A classic example of a phenomenally expensive failure in terms of promotion was the launch some years ago of BP's shares onto the open market. Many millions of pounds were spent on advertising the privatisation of the company, and the benefits to shareholders of purchasing the shares at the offer price. However, days before the launch, stock prices throughout the world plummeted, and the launch was an unmitigated disaster, with the price being set far too high. Instead of the anticipated massive oversubscription, the underwriters of the issue were left to purchase the vast majority of shares. This was not a result of a poor promotional campaign, but of an external uncontrollable force impacting on the promotional effort.

Sales force

This section is separate to promotion, and may not be important for certain organisations which do not use this particular type of promotional technique. However, for many organisations, the sales force form a large part of their costs, and as such it is vital to gather as much information as possible upon their activity. A full list of all salespeople should be included as the starting point for this analysis. Usually, most salespeople will have quotas which they are required to achieve, and these should also be fully considered. The success rate against achieving these quotas is another aspect of this section. Once again, success in achieving quotas must be placed in a financial context. As such, a comparison with costs must be made. The actual time which a sales executive spends 'selling' is often very small when compared to travelling time, waiting time, administration and so on. Various studies have shown that an average sales person spends only between 15 and 20% of their employed (paid) time involved in what could be termed the actual 'selling process', that is in face to face negotiation with a customer. Whilst all of the other activities are obviously essential to the overall process, it is important to discover what actual return is being made on the sales achieved.

Distribution

The actual way in which the product or service is distributed is obviously vital to the success of the organisation. This section of the situational analysis should consider this area in as much detail as possible. Information on each stage in the distribution channel should be obtained and included. Relevant details would include the mark-up involved at each stage of distribution, the overall integration of the network or channel, and some assessment of the effectiveness of the distribution system. Once again, it should be stressed that this type of assessment should be an ongoing activity in any organisation. All organisations should be constantly seeking to improve their efficiency and effectiveness, and also to maintain the consistency of their overall marketing mix activity. For example, Glenfiddich, the famous Malt Whisky, was not distributed through the Co-operative retail outlets for a long time, as they were felt to be incompatible with the brand's image. However, as the 'Co-op' started to introduce hypermarkets in response to the general trend within retailing, Glenfiddich were forced to reconsider their position, and now sell very successfully through these outlets. This was part of an ongoing review of the distribution policies of the organisation.

Competitive analysis

As has been stressed throughout various sections of this book, no organisation operates in isolation. Generally, monopoly markets do not exist, and as such most businesses must take account of the activities of their competitors. In most markets, supply exceeds demand, and competitors are constantly trying to steal each other's market share. In any competitive situation, the more knowledge you have about your rivals, the better placed you will be to win. Football managers spend many hours analysing forthcoming opponents by watching them play, assessing video tapes and listening to information from scouts. They isolate various tactics which are employed, the key players for the opposition and so on. Business is exactly the same, and you should gather as much information as possible on your competitors.

The basic data which is required in this area includes a detailed list of the competition. In certain industries it may be difficult to actually define what the competition is, but this should be done on whatever criteria are most important, for example geographically, product range and so on. Details should be obtained on a rival's products and prices, on their means of distribution and their sales and promotional techniques. Estimates must be made of the market share of all competitors, and a comparative analysis should be carried out of the strengths and weaknesses of their products. It may be that the products appear the same, but they may offer substantially different benefits which are targeted in a different way at a different market segment. This will allow the business to assess the possibility of gaining a competitive advantage over an opponent.

Sources of Information

In Elements 3.1 and 3.2 we consider ways in which you can obtain information on competitors, but it is worthwhile addressing this issue again here. The best source of information on competitors are the competitors themselves. Buy their products and visit their premises. You can also get useful information from trade journals and the general press. Your customers provide vital information as well, and sales people can be used to tap into this particular source. You should always remember, however, that the ways in which you obtain information on your rivals should be ethical and legal. Industrial espionage no doubt does exist, but it is usually possible to glean sufficient information from the products and the employees of an opponent to tell you what you need to know without resorting to criminal means. On the same note, it is also worth pointing out the importance of confidentiality to an organisation's own employees. The search for information is a two way process, so all organisations should be seeking to protect whatever competitive position they hold. Anyone dealing with the outside world in any way should be trained to recognise over-inquisitive callers, and should be able to pass them on to the appropriate manager without giving away any confidential information. One frequently used method of obtaining such information is to use students carrying out projects. Unfortunately, this means that students may not always gain the information they are seeking, but it is worth remembering that this is not usually simply because the organisation cannot be bothered to deal with students, but more frequently because they are attempting to protect a hard earned competitive position.

The existing market

You will obviously need a detailed analysis of the state of the existing market. List all market segments and examine their size and relative importance. There are various ways in which a market may be segmented and these are discussed in Elements 3.1 and 3.2, but it is important to segment markets in as many ways as is necessary to gain an overall view of the total market. Try to identify the different levels of usage in each segment, in order to identify opportunities where you could increase sales. If you can, quantify the overall level of demand in the market as accurately as possible.

Whilst the situational analysis is meant to be a photograph of the current position of various factors, it is also important when looking at the market to consider all recent trends, and their effects. For example, the brewing industry over the last few years has seen a number of changes in the types of product consumed. For many years, 'beer' was the number one selling product, but this has gradually been displaced by lager. The growth in more expensive 'designer label' lagers, usually imported, is another trend that has massively influenced thinking within the industry. Also, there is currently a resurgence in the demand for 'real' or 'cask conditioned' beers, a further complication for the planners.

At this point you should also assess the position of the organisation's products within each market segment. This should come from two sides – the organisation itself and the consumer. Tools such as perception mapping are useful in this instance, where customers views are sought on a number of variables such as quality and reliability. The organisation's position and that of its major competitors is placed on a map to identify possible market gaps. Position, however, is not the only important variable. You should also assess market penetration or market share at this point in order to evaluate the relative success of each competing product. Each segment should then be combined to provide an overview of the organisation's standing within the market as a whole.

Activity

Take a product of your choice, preferably a consumer product which you purchase fairly regularly. For this product, you are asked to carry out an audit of the competition which exists within that market. You should carry out research to discover the total size of the market, and also who are the major players within that market. For each of these competitors, you should try to find out:

- *the price of the product;*
- *any specific details of the product which differentiate it from the competition;*
- *what promotion is undertaken for the product; and*

- *which outlets stock the product.*

When you have gathered the information, assume the position of one of the companies (not the market leader) and critically assess the strengths and weaknesses of your rivals in a way which would be useful for drawing up your own Marketing Strategy.

The external environment

The external environment consists of those variables which will impact upon the success of an organisation, but over which the organisation itself has no control. A PEST Analysis, which is discussed in Element 3.2, is the appropriate method of analysis in this instance, and would consist of a consideration of:

- Political/Legal Factors;
- Economic Factors;
- Social/Cultural Factors;
- Technological Factors.

This analysis should be as broad ranging as possible. It is often difficult at first to think about which external factors are likely to be important, but it is important to cast the analytical net as wide as possible. In terms of predicting the future, the external environment is inevitably more difficult to assess accurately than the internal environment of the organisation itself. The more information is obtained on the current situation, however, the more accurate any future predictions are likely to be.

Situational analysis summary

Your Situational Analysis should now be complete. The organisation should now be in a position to consider the main elements of the plan for the future, having accurately assessed the existing position. The main areas which have been considered within this analysis are:

- the customers and their needs/wants;
- the strengths and weaknesses of the organisation in meeting those needs;
- the position of competitors within that market.

The scene should now be set to draw up appropriate plans for the future.

Marketing information systems

On first reading of this section you must think that the actual drawing up of a situational analysis appears to be a daunting prospect. You need a vast amount of information to make sure that your plans for the future are based on as accurate information as possible. It is worth emphasising at this point, however, that the whole process of gathering information of this nature should be continuous. To do this all businesses need to establish an appropriate Marketing Information System (MIS) so that the situational analysis can be carried out fairly simply. The MIS should cover all of the elements of market research we mention in Elements 3.1 and 3.2 and this will help the planning process. The various steps involved in any MIS are as follows:

- identify information needs;
- identify potential sources of that information;
- establish a system for the gathering of the appropriate data;
- create summaries of the information;
- establish a system for using the information;
- evaluate the MIS.

The creation of an accurate and reliable MIS is vital to the success of the planning function. While it is often expensive in the short term to establish such a system, this is very much outweighed by the long term benefits.

Marketing Strategy

Once you have completed the situational analysis, you are now in the position to develop plans and strategies for the business's future marketing activities. Strategy is seen as the broad direction in which the business seeks to go. Many strategy theories are based on the theories of warfare, where industry is seen as a battlefield and competitors as bitter enemies. Whilst this is true to an extent, the bottom line for all marketing strategies is that they should constructive towards the consumers, rather than destructive towards the competitors. If the consumers' needs and wants are clearly identified, and the business satisfies those needs and wants in a better way than the competition, then the 'war' need never take place. Any marketing led organisation should always consider the consumer first, with the competition taking very much a secondary role.

The strategy statement

The broad strategy statement should not be too specific. It should serve as a guide to the marketing process, and should not at this stage identify the specific procedures required. It should reflect the policies and culture of the organisation, but should not contain detailed operational information. This detail should be contained in the specific plans, as opposed to the broad strategy statement itself.

A strategy statement should include various important aspects. These include:

- a time scale for the strategy;
- an action statement;
- a description of the product;
- details of the target market;
- details of the position to be adopted with that target market.

The strategy statement should always be supported and justified and the justification should come from all of the information contained in the Situational Analysis.

Objectives

All planning objectives should clearly identify the ideal situation which the business wants to achieve. The objectives are the specific statements that establish a target and allow the success (or failure) of the strategy to be evaluated. As such, they should always be quantifiable and contain a timescale, so that they can be measured.

Unique selling proposition

The Unique Selling Proposition (USP) of a product is a statement of the specific benefit which that product or service will provide to the consumer. The USP will form the basis for all future marketing activities, and as such, the message which it contains should be strong and clear. For example, the USP for Volvo cars is generally one of quality and safety. The vehicle is promoted as being very strong, but is priced so as to attract the quality end of the market. Superdrug, on the other hand, adopt a USP of Value for Money. They supply a 'no frills service' and compete in terms of the price of the products which they offer.

The market

Much of this section of the marketing plan is similar to that contained in the complementary section within the situational analysis. The major difference, however, is that the organisation is now attempting to predict the future trends, rather than to identify past or current positions. The market can be predicted under a number of different frameworks.

Total market

Attempts can and should be made to identify the likely size of the total market in which the business is competing. This will identify whether or not the overall market is likely to grow, remain static or to decline. An estimate should already have been made as to the current size of the total market and the organisation's own share of that market, and the prediction should be an extension of this, with a quantifiable target placed upon the share of the total market sought.

Competitive or segmented market

Within the overall market, it is likely that the organisation will be competing in more than one segment. Predictions must therefore be made as to the likely development of each segment, in order to clearly establish which are the potential growth areas. This will clearly influence the allocation of resources between different segments, as growth segments will be much more attractive but also much more competitive.

Internal

This framework is usually used in combination with the competitive or segmented market approach to identify the relative importance of each segment. For example, if a commercial radio station discovers from its situational analysis that only 20% of its listeners are aged 18 to 25, but that this is the likely growth area in terms of advertising expenditure, then it will need to reconsider its programming policies.

It is important to include as much detail as possible in predictions for market size. All appropriate calculations should be included, as the process should be an ongoing one. The more information included this year, the fewer problems will be faced in following years when the plans are assessed, evaluated and possibly amended.

Marketing mix strategies

Once you have estimated the overall market size and you have made decisions on the target for market share, you can draw up the specific strategies for the elements of the marketing mix. These are the variables which the marketer can control and each requires a general statement of direction. Each mix variable should have its own strategy for each market segment. All of the strategies will be based upon the Situational Analysis, the general Strategy Statement and the Unique Selling Proposition. By this stage, it should be fairly simple to derive the individual strategies, as they must be consistent with the above factors. As such, they are to an extent predetermined. The specific details of the plans, which are often described as the tactical elements, are then detailed with the Marketing Action Plans

Marketing Action Plans

Once you have completed the detailed Situational Analysis and the general Strategy statements, you can go on to write the specific Marketing Action Plans. Each element of the marketing mix requires a separate Action Plan, although we should again stress that they cannot be drawn up in isolation, as all mix elements interact. Any organisation which has reached this stage of the planning process, however, should find no difficulty in completing coherent and consistent plans for each element which complement rather than compete for scarce resources.

Elements of marketing action plans

Each Action Plan should contain certain key elements, and should be written in a consistent style to emphasise the overall message.

Title

It might seem fairly obvious but each Action Plan should have a title. The title serves the purpose of reinforcing the purpose and objectives of the plan, and emphasises its specific focus.

The person responsible

Plans are unlikely to succeed without allocating responsibilities to named individuals. Choosing the appropriate people is crucial to the successful implementation of any plan. They should be chosen because of their background, training, ability and so on. Their own futures will largely depend upon the success of the Action Plan, so they need not only the confidence of the organisation but also sufficient authority to carry out the requirements.

Objectives

Once again, it is essential that your objectives are clearly stated and quantifiable. These provide the goal to aim for, and the benchmark for the measurement of success. As with any objectives, they must be

- *Measurable*. This allows for evaluation. For example, the objective of a promotional Action Plan might be to increase Customer Awareness from 15% to 40%;
- *Timed*. All objectives must possess a timescale. Without deadlines, prioritising of tasks becomes infinitely more difficult, and the objectives are unlikely to be met. In the example above, the timescale set might be six months;
- *Realistic*. There is nothing more frustrating for anyone than to be set unrealistic objectives. All objectives must be attainable, otherwise they will simply be counter-productive. Any targets which are set too high will lead to frustration and dissatisfaction amongst the workforce, whilst those set too low are not efficiently and effectively exploiting the potential that exists, and as such the overall organisation will suffer.

Detailed plan of action

These are the specific, step-by-step instructions which will guide those involved in the implementation of the plan towards achieving its goals. It is vital that this section of the plan is designed with the employees in mind, and it should contain all the relevant detail which they will require.

Time frame

This is slightly different to the timescale set previously for the objectives. It relates specifically to the completion of the Action Plan. The objectives may take longer to achieve because of time lags in the effect of certain marketing mix variables.

Costs

Once again it is important to recognise what these activities cost. As they say in business 'remember the bottom-line'. The costs are the budget which has been allocated to the Action Plan, and are again based on projections. The cost will also serve as an evaluative tool to assess the success of the programme. On occasions, it may be that costs have to be ignored, for example if the business faces a particular threat from a rival. In this instance, the business needs to assess what the costs would be if the defensive action were not taken, and then compare this to the actual costs of the Action Plan itself.

Setting the marketing budget

The methods available for setting the overall marketing budget are basically the same as those outlined in Element 3.3 which looked at the budget for promotional activities. The overall budget will be the sum of the budgets for each of the individual Action Plans. It is worthwhile reconsidering the approaches which can be adopted very briefly:

- *Percentage of sales*. With this method, a percentage of the total sales of an organisation is allocated towards the promotional budget. This can be done either on a historical basis or on a projected basis;
- *Competitive parity*. This is a very reactive approach. Organisations simply assess or ascertain the levels of spending of their rivals, and allocate their own budgets as a reaction to this;
- *The investment approach*. With this technique, promotion is viewed as an investment for the future, and its future benefits are regarded as more important than any immediate or short term gains;
- *The objective and task method*. This is very much the approach favoured by academic marketers. Objectives are set, and the appropriate budget allocated in order to achieve them;
- *The affordable approach*. The most commonly adopted method is to simply decide how much an organisation can afford to 'spare' and to see what can be bought for this money;

We discuss the benefits and drawbacks of each method in Unit 3, *Marketing*, but we should emphasise that in practice most businesses employ a combination of two or more of these methods to arrive at the overall level of spending for marketing. Each budget is obviously based upon forecasted costs, and as such must be monitored to compare predicted and actual costs. If the actual costs turn out to be higher, this does not necessarily mean that the approach has failed as predicted benefits may have been underestimated as well as predicted costs. Should the actual costs turn out to be lower than expected, it may be a cause for celebration, or merely an indication that the Action Plans have not been carried out properly.

Evaluation of marketing plans

Remember that all plans must be evaluated. Successful businesses learn from everything that they do, whether they have worked or not. It is important to evaluate each individual action plan, as well as having some mechanism for determining the overall success of the marketing effort.

Activity

For this activity you are asked to assume that you work for the Marketing Department of a local brewery which produces draught beer for sale in the local region only. The company has decided that it needs to relaunch one of its older more established brands 'Monty', a bitter ale which is primarily targeted at the 25-40 year old male drinker. Your Department has been given a promotional budget of £250,000 to spend, and you have been asked to draw up a rough outline of the Promotional Strategy which you would employ. In order to do this, you will need to discover the prices of various promotional media which are available within the region, such as Local TV, radio, newspapers, posters and so on. When you have established these costs, draw up the guidelines for the campaign which will use the budget most efficiently. Remember that your objective is to relaunch the product, which has something of a 'tired' image, but that the budget is finite. The name cannot be changed on the orders of the Managing Director, but you have freedom to alter anything else, including packaging and design, provided it is within reason. Draft this outline for consideration by your Departmental manager.

Assignment *Clarkie's Kissograms*

Maxine Clarke decided that she wanted to be her own boss. After working for other people all of her life, she determined that she wanted to run her own company, and stand or fall by her own merits. She had saved up £1000 from her previous job as a cocktail waitress in a Working Men's Club, and resolved to set up 'Clarkie's Kissograms - the cheeky way to celebrate'. Having been the victim herself of a 'Tarzanogram' at her 21st Birthday, Maxine knew what fun these occasions could be. She also knew how much people were willing to pay for the service, and felt that it would make a viable business proposition. With a view to raising extra capital to purchase speciality costumes, mobile phones and other essential equipment, Maxine decided to approach her local bank. She realised that if she was to be taken seriously, she would have to be well prepared, and as such decided that one of the things she should do would be to prepare a marketing plan which would allow her to present a rational case for funding.

She had carried out some initial research into the market, and had discovered that there were only two other companies offering similar novelty services in the surrounding area. Each, she discovered, had approximately 40% of the market, with the remaining market share being divided by 'outsiders' and people who performed kissograms on an occasional as opposed to professional basis. She proposed initially to have a team of five people working alongside her - all part time performers or minders. She herself would manage the company and deal with all of the bookings and finance, as well as occasionally performing the odd Police Woman act. She was unsure about how exactly to break into the market, and to what degree, and approached you as an old friend to provide her with some free advice. She was unsure about the whole planning process, and was seeking guidance as to the best way to produce a convincing Marketing and Sales Plan which would ensure the funds from the bank to purchase the necessary equipment.

Task

Acting as Maxine Clarke's friend, take her through the major steps in the production of an appropriate plan. You should consider all variables which you believe are relevant, and attempt to apply marketing theory to this practical situation. There is obviously a lot of further information which you will require. Where this is not available, you are required to make appropriate assumptions, with an explanation as to why these assumptions are justified and reasonable. You should aim to produce a plan which would be acceptable to a financing institution as a supplement to the main Business Plan, and as such should aim to include all relevant costs, projected market demand and a timed Action Plan for all areas of the Marketing Mix. You should also make brief recommendations as to what extra research Maxine might usefully undertake in order to provide her plan with more credibility and to reduce the risk of her business venture failing.

Index